Peter van Beek (Ed.)

Principles and Practice of Constraint Programming - CP 2005

11th International Conference, CP 2005
Sitges, Spain, October 1-5, 2005
Proceedings

Volume Editor

Peter van Beek
University of Waterloo
Waterloo, Canada N2L 3G1
E-mail: vanbeek@uwaterloo.ca

Library of Congress Control Number: 2005933262

CR Subject Classification (1998): D.1, D.3.2-3, I.2.3-4, F.3.2, I.2.8, F.4.1, J.1

ISSN   0302-9743
ISBN-10   3-540-29238-1 Springer Berlin Heidelberg New York
ISBN-13   978-3-540-29238-8 Springer Berlin Heidelberg New York

This work is subject to copyright. All rights are reserved, whether the whole or part of the material is concerned, specifically the rights of translation, reprinting, re-use of illustrations, recitation, broadcasting, reproduction on microfilms or in any other way, and storage in data banks. Duplication of this publication or parts thereof is permitted only under the provisions of the German Copyright Law of September 9, 1965, in its current version, and permission for use must always be obtained from Springer. Violations are liable to prosecution under the German Copyright Law.

Springer is a part of Springer Science+Business Media

springeronline.com

© Springer-Verlag Berlin Heidelberg 2005
Printed in Germany

Typesetting: Camera-ready by author, data conversion by Scientific Publishing Services, Chennai, India
Printed on acid-free paper   SPIN: 11564751   06/3142   5 4 3 2 1 0

Lecture Notes in Computer Science

For information about Vols. 1–3646

please contact your bookseller or Springer

Vol. 3750: J. Duncan, G. Gerig (Eds.), Medical Image Computing and Computer-Assisted Intervention – MICCAI 2005, Part II. XL, 1018 pages. 2005.

Vol. 3749: J. Duncan, G. Gerig (Eds.), Medical Image Computing and Computer-Assisted Intervention – MICCAI 2005, Part I. XXXIX, 942 pages. 2005.

Vol. 3739: W. Fan, Z. Wu, J. Yang (Eds.), Advances in Web-Age Information Management. XXII, 930 pages. 2005.

Vol. 3738: V.R. Syrotiuk, E. Chávez (Eds.), Ad-Hoc, Mobile, and Wireless Networks. XI, 360 pages. 2005.

Vol. 3735: A. Hoffmann, H. Motoda, T. Scheffer (Eds.), Discovery Science. XVI, 400 pages. 2005. (Subseries LNAI).

Vol. 3734: S. Jain, H.U. Simon, E. Tomita (Eds.), Algorithmic Learning Theory. XII, 490 pages. 2005. (Subseries LNAI).

Vol. 3731: F. Wang (Ed.), Formal Techniques for Networked and Distributed Systems - FORTE 2005. XII, 558 pages. 2005.

Vol. 3728: V. Paliouras, J. Vounckx, D. Verkest (Eds.), Integrated Circuit and System Design. XV, 753 pages. 2005.

Vol. 3726: L.T. Yang, O.F. Rana, B. Di Martino, J. Dongarra (Eds.), High Performance Computing and Communcations. XXVI, 1116 pages. 2005.

Vol. 3725: D. Borrione, W. Paul (Eds.), Correct Hardware Design and Verification Methods. XII, 412 pages. 2005.

Vol. 3724: P. Fraigniaud (Ed.), Distributed Computing. XIV, 520 pages. 2005.

Vol. 3723: W. Zhao, S. Gong, X. Tang (Eds.), Analysis and Modelling of Faces and Gestures. XI, 423 pages. 2005.

Vol. 3722: D. Van Hung, M. Wirsing (Eds.), Theoretical Aspects of Computing – ICTAC 2005. XIV, 614 pages. 2005.

Vol. 3721: A. Jorge, L. Torgo, P. Brazdil, R. Camacho, J. Gama (Eds.), Knowledge Discovery in Databases: PKDD 2005. XXIII, 719 pages. 2005. (Subseries LNAI).

Vol. 3720: J. Gama, R. Camacho, P. Brazdil, A. Jorge, L. Torgo (Eds.), Machine Learning: ECML 2005. XXIII, 769 pages. 2005. (Subseries LNAI).

Vol. 3719: M. Hobbs, A.M. Goscinski, W. Zhou (Eds.), Algorithms and Architectures for Parallel Processing. XI, 448 pages. 2005.

Vol. 3718: V.G. Ganzha, E.W. Mayr, E.V. Vorozhtsov (Eds.), Computer Algebra in Scientific Computing. XII, 502 pages. 2005.

Vol. 3717: B. Gramlich (Ed.), Frontiers of Combining Systems. X, 321 pages. 2005. (Subseries LNAI).

Vol. 3715: E. Dawson, S. Vaudenay (Eds.), Progress in Cryptology – Mycrypt 2005. XI, 329 pages. 2005.

Vol. 3714: H. Obbink, K. Pohl (Eds.), Software Product Lines. XIII, 235 pages. 2005.

Vol. 3713: L. Briand, C. Williams (Eds.), Model Driven Engineering Languages and Systems. XV, 722 pages. 2005.

Vol. 3712: R. Reussner, J. Mayer, J.A. Stafford, S. Overhage, S. Becker, P.J. Schroeder (Eds.), Quality of Software Architectures and Software Quality. XIII, 289 pages. 2005.

Vol. 3711: F. Kishino, Y. Kitamura, H. Kato, N. Nagata (Eds.), Entertainment Computing - ICEC 2005. XXIV, 540 pages. 2005.

Vol. 3710: M. Barni, I. Cox, T. Kalker, H.J. Kim (Eds.), Digital Watermarking. XII, 485 pages. 2005.

Vol. 3709: P. van Beek (Ed.), Principles and Practice of Constraint Programming - CP 2005. XX, 887 pages. 2005.

Vol. 3708: J. Blanc-Talon, W. Philips, D. Popescu, P. Scheunders (Eds.), Advanced Concepts for Intelligent Vision Systems. XXII, 725 pages. 2005.

Vol. 3707: D.A. Peled, Y.-K. Tsay (Eds.), Automated Technology for Verification and Analysis. XII, 506 pages. 2005.

Vol. 3706: H. Fuks, S. Lukosch, A.C. Salgado (Eds.), Groupware: Design, Implementation, and Use. XII, 378 pages. 2005.

Vol. 3703: F. Fages, S. Soliman (Eds.), Principles and Practice of Semantic Web Reasoning. VIII, 163 pages. 2005.

Vol. 3702: B. Beckert (Ed.), Automated Reasoning with Analytic Tableaux and Related Methods. XIII, 343 pages. 2005. (Subseries LNAI).

Vol. 3701: M. Coppo, E. Lodi, G. M. Pinna (Eds.), Theoretical Computer Science. XI, 411 pages. 2005.

Vol. 3699: C.S. Calude, M.J. Dinneen, G. Păun, M. J. Pérez-Jiménez, G. Rozenberg (Eds.), Unconventional Computation. XI, 267 pages. 2005.

Vol. 3698: U. Furbach (Ed.), KI 2005: Advances in Artificial Intelligence. XIII, 409 pages. 2005. (Subseries LNAI).

Vol. 3697: W. Duch, J. Kacprzyk, E. Oja, S. Zadrożny (Eds.), Artificial Neural Networks: Formal Models and Their Applications – ICANN 2005, Part II. XXXII, 1045 pages. 2005.

Vol. 3696: W. Duch, J. Kacprzyk, E. Oja, S. Zadrożny (Eds.), Artificial Neural Networks: Biological Inspirations – ICANN 2005, Part I. XXXI, 703 pages. 2005.

Vol. 3695: M.R. Berthold, R. Glen, K. Diederichs, O. Kohlbacher, I. Fischer (Eds.), Computational Life Sciences. XI, 277 pages. 2005. (Subseries LNBI).

Vol. 3694: M. Malek, E. Nett, N. Suri (Eds.), Service Availability. VIII, 213 pages. 2005.

Vol. 3693: A.G. Cohn, D.M. Mark (Eds.), Spatial Information Theory. XII, 493 pages. 2005.

Vol. 3692: R. Casadio, G. Myers (Eds.), Algorithms in Bioinformatics. X, 436 pages. 2005. (Subseries LNBI).

Vol. 3691: A. Gagalowicz, W. Philips (Eds.), Computer Analysis of Images and Patterns. XIX, 865 pages. 2005.

Vol. 3690: M. Pěchouček, P. Petta, L.Z. Varga (Eds.), Multi-Agent Systems and Applications IV. XVII, 667 pages. 2005. (Subseries LNAI).

Vol. 3688: R. Winther, B.A. Gan, G. Dahll (Eds.), Computer Safety, Reliability, and Security. XI, 405 pages. 2005.

Vol. 3687: S. Singh, M. Singh, C. Apte, P. Perner (Eds.), Pattern Recognition and Image Analysis, Part II. XXV, 809 pages. 2005.

Vol. 3686: S. Singh, M. Singh, C. Apte, P. Perner (Eds.), Pattern Recognition and Data Mining, Part I. XXVI, 689 pages. 2005.

Vol. 3685: V. Gorodetsky, I. Kotenko, V. Skormin (Eds.), Computer Network Security. XIV, 480 pages. 2005.

Vol. 3684: R. Khosla, R.J. Howlett, L.C. Jain (Eds.), Knowledge-Based Intelligent Information and Engineering Systems, Part IV. LXXIX, 933 pages. 2005. (Subseries LNAI).

Vol. 3683: R. Khosla, R.J. Howlett, L.C. Jain (Eds.), Knowledge-Based Intelligent Information and Engineering Systems, Part III. LXXX, 1397 pages. 2005. (Subseries LNAI).

Vol. 3682: R. Khosla, R.J. Howlett, L.C. Jain (Eds.), Knowledge-Based Intelligent Information and Engineering Systems, Part II. LXXIX, 1371 pages. 2005. (Subseries LNAI).

Vol. 3681: R. Khosla, R.J. Howlett, L.C. Jain (Eds.), Knowledge-Based Intelligent Information and Engineering Systems, Part I. LXXX, 1319 pages. 2005. (Subseries LNAI).

Vol. 3679: S.d.C. di Vimercati, P. Syverson, D. Gollmann (Eds.), Computer Security – ESORICS 2005. XI, 509 pages. 2005.

Vol. 3678: A. McLysaght, D.H. Huson (Eds.), Comparative Genomics. VIII, 167 pages. 2005. (Subseries LNBI).

Vol. 3677: J. Dittmann, S. Katzenbeisser, A. Uhl (Eds.), Communications and Multimedia Security. XIII, 360 pages. 2005.

Vol. 3676: R. Glück, M. Lowry (Eds.), Generative Programming and Component Engineering. XI, 448 pages. 2005.

Vol. 3675: Y. Luo (Ed.), Cooperative Design, Visualization, and Engineering. XI, 264 pages. 2005.

Vol. 3674: W. Jonker, M. Petković (Eds.), Secure Data Management. X, 241 pages. 2005.

Vol. 3673: S. Bandini, S. Manzoni (Eds.), AI*IA 2005: Advances in Artificial Intelligence. XIV, 614 pages. 2005. (Subseries LNAI).

Vol. 3672: C. Hankin, I. Siveroni (Eds.), Static Analysis. X, 369 pages. 2005.

Vol. 3671: S. Bressan, S. Ceri, E. Hunt, Z.G. Ives, Z. Bellahsène, M. Rys, R. Unland (Eds.), Database and XML Technologies. X, 239 pages. 2005.

Vol. 3670: M. Bravetti, L. Kloul, G. Zavattaro (Eds.), Formal Techniques for Computer Systems and Business Processes. XIII, 349 pages. 2005.

Vol. 3669: G.S. Brodal, S. Leonardi (Eds.), Algorithms – ESA 2005. XVIII, 901 pages. 2005.

Vol. 3668: M. Gabbrielli, G. Gupta (Eds.), Logic Programming. XIV, 454 pages. 2005.

Vol. 3666: B.D. Martino, D. Kranzlmüller, J. Dongarra (Eds.), Recent Advances in Parallel Virtual Machine and Message Passing Interface. XVII, 546 pages. 2005.

Vol. 3665: K. S. Candan, A. Celentano (Eds.), Advances in Multimedia Information Systems. X, 221 pages. 2005.

Vol. 3664: C. Türker, M. Agosti, H.-J. Schek (Eds.), Peer-to-Peer, Grid, and Service-Orientation in Digital Library Architectures. X, 261 pages. 2005.

Vol. 3663: W.G. Kropatsch, R. Sablatnig, A. Hanbury (Eds.), Pattern Recognition. XIV, 512 pages. 2005.

Vol. 3662: C. Baral, G. Greco, N. Leone, G. Terracina (Eds.), Logic Programming and Nonmonotonic Reasoning. XIII, 454 pages. 2005. (Subseries LNAI).

Vol. 3661: T. Panayiotopoulos, J. Gratch, R. Aylett, D. Ballin, P. Olivier, T. Rist (Eds.), Intelligent Virtual Agents. XIII, 506 pages. 2005. (Subseries LNAI).

Vol. 3660: M. Beigl, S. Intille, J. Rekimoto, H. Tokuda (Eds.), UbiComp 2005: Ubiquitous Computing. XVII, 394 pages. 2005.

Vol. 3659: J.R. Rao, B. Sunar (Eds.), Cryptographic Hardware and Embedded Systems – CHES 2005. XIV, 458 pages. 2005.

Vol. 3658: V. Matoušek, P. Mautner, T. Pavelka (Eds.), Text, Speech and Dialogue. XV, 460 pages. 2005. (Subseries LNAI).

Vol. 3657: F.S. de Boer, M.M. Bonsangue, S. Graf, W.-P. de Roever (Eds.), Formal Methods for Components and Objects. VIII, 325 pages. 2005.

Vol. 3656: M. Kamel, A. Campilho (Eds.), Image Analysis and Recognition. XXIV, 1279 pages. 2005.

Vol. 3655: A. Aldini, R. Gorrieri, F. Martinelli (Eds.), Foundations of Security Analysis and Design III. VII, 273 pages. 2005.

Vol. 3654: S. Jajodia, D. Wijesekera (Eds.), Data and Applications Security XIX. X, 353 pages. 2005.

Vol. 3653: M. Abadi, L. de Alfaro (Eds.), CONCUR 2005 – Concurrency Theory. XIV, 578 pages. 2005.

Vol. 3652: A. Rauber, S. Christodoulakis, A M. Tjoa (Eds.), Research and Advanced Technology for Digital Libraries. XVIII, 545 pages. 2005.

Vol. 3651: R. Dale, K.-F. Wong, J. Su, O.Y. Kwong (Eds.), Natural Language Processing – IJCNLP 2005. XXI, 1031 pages. 2005. (Subseries LNAI).

Vol. 3650: J. Zhou, J. Lopez, R.H. Deng, F. Bao (Eds.), Information Security. XII, 516 pages. 2005.

Vol. 3649: W.M. P. van der Aalst, B. Benatallah, F. Casati, F. Curbera (Eds.), Business Process Management. XII, 472 pages. 2005.

Vol. 3648: J.C. Cunha, P.D. Medeiros (Eds.), Euro-Par 2005 Parallel Processing. XXXVI, 1299 pages. 2005.

Lecture Notes in Computer Science 3709

Commenced Publication in 1973
Founding and Former Series Editors:
Gerhard Goos, Juris Hartmanis, and Jan van Leeuwen

Editorial Board

David Hutchison
 Lancaster University, UK
Takeo Kanade
 Carnegie Mellon University, Pittsburgh, PA, USA
Josef Kittler
 University of Surrey, Guildford, UK
Jon M. Kleinberg
 Cornell University, Ithaca, NY, USA
Friedemann Mattern
 ETH Zurich, Switzerland
John C. Mitchell
 Stanford University, CA, USA
Moni Naor
 Weizmann Institute of Science, Rehovot, Israel
Oscar Nierstrasz
 University of Bern, Switzerland
C. Pandu Rangan
 Indian Institute of Technology, Madras, India
Bernhard Steffen
 University of Dortmund, Germany
Madhu Sudan
 Massachusetts Institute of Technology, MA, USA
Demetri Terzopoulos
 New York University, NY, USA
Doug Tygar
 University of California, Berkeley, CA, USA
Moshe Y. Vardi
 Rice University, Houston, TX, USA
Gerhard Weikum
 Max-Planck Institute of Computer Science, Saarbruecken, Germany

Preface

The 11th International Conference on the Principles and Practice of Constraint Programming (CP 2005) was held in Sitges (Barcelona), Spain, October 1–5, 2005. Information about the conference can be found on the web at http://www.iiia.csic.es/cp2005/. Information about past conferences in the series can be found at http://www.cs.ualberta.ca/~ai/cp/.

The CP conference series is the premier international conference on constraint programming and is held annually. The conference is concerned with all aspects of computing with constraints, including: algorithms, applications, environments, languages, models and systems.

This year, we received 164 submissions. All of the submitted papers received at least three reviews, and the papers and their reviews were then extensively discussed during an online Program Committee meeting. As a result, the Program Committee chose 48 (29.3%) papers to be published in full in the proceedings and a further 22 (13.4%) papers to be published as short papers. The full papers were presented at the conference in two parallel tracks and the short papers were presented as posters during a lively evening session. Two papers were selected by a subcommittee of the Program Committee—consisting of Chris Beck, Gilles Pesant, and myself—to receive best paper awards. The conference program also included excellent invited talks by Héctor Geffner, Ian Horrocks, Francesca Rossi, and Peter J. Stuckey. As a permanent record, the proceedings contain four-page extended abstracts of the invited talks.

CP 2005 continued the tradition of the CP doctoral program, in which PhD students presented their work, listened to tutorials on career and ethical issues, and discussed their work with senior researchers via a mentoring scheme. This year, the doctoral program received 53 submissions. The field of constraint programming is indeed alive and growing! Each of the PhD students who did not already have a paper in the main conference was given one page in the proceedings to describe their ongoing research. As well, CP 2005 once again held a systems demonstration session to highlight the state of the art in industrial and academic applications, or prototypes. As a permanent record of the session, the proceedings contain a one-page description of each demo.

On the first day of the conference, 13 workshops were held (listed on page IX), each with their own proceedings. Four excellent tutorials were presented during the conference: "SAT Solving and Its Relationship to CSPs" by Fahiem Bacchus; "Advances in Search, Inference and Hybrids for Solving Combinatorial Optimization Tasks" by Rina Dechter; "Programming with a Chinese Horse" by Thom Frühwirth; and "Complete Randomized Backtrack Search Methods: Connections Between Heavy-tails, Backdoors, and Restart Strategies" by Carla Gomes.

On behalf of the constraint programming community, I would like to publicly thank and acknowledge the hard work of the many people involved in putting this year's conference together. Thank you to Pedro Meseguer and Javier Larrosa, the conference chairs, for their many hours organizing, budgeting, planning, and coordinating that resulted in a most enjoyable conference for the rest of us. Thank you to Michela Milano and Zeynep Kiziltan, the doctoral program chairs, for smoothly and efficiently putting together the largest doctoral program so far. Thank you to Alan Frisch and Ian Miguel, the workshop/tutorial chairs, for their efforts in putting together excellent workshop and tutorial programs. Thank you to Felip Manya, publicity chair, for prompt and efficient handling of the publicity for the conference. Thank you to Chris Beck and Gilles Pesant for their help on the Best Paper Award Committee. Thank you to the Program Committee and the additional referees for their service to the community in writing reviews and extensively discussing and choosing which papers to accept at the conference. It was truly a pleasure to work with all of you. I would also like to add a personal thank you to the Executive Committee of the Association for Constraint Programming for inviting me to be program chair this year. It has been a rewarding experience.

Finally, a thank you to the institutions listed below (page IX) who helped sponsor the conference. Their generosity enabled the conference to bring in invited speakers and fund students, thus greatly contributing to the success of the conference.

September 2005   Peter van Beek

Organization

Conference Organization

Conference Chairs	Pedro Meseguer, IIIA-CSIC, Spain
	Javier Larrosa, UPC, Spain
Program Chair	Peter van Beek, University of Waterloo, Canada
Doctoral Program Chairs	Michela Milano, University of Bologna, Italy
	Zeynep Kiziltan, University of Bologna, Italy
Workshop/Tutorial Chairs	Alan Frisch, University of York, UK
	Ian Miguel, University of St Andrews, UK
Publicity Chair	Felip Manya, IIIA-CSIC, Spain

Program Committee

Pedro Barahona, U Lisbon, Portugal
Chris Beck, U of Toronto, Canada
Nicolas Beldiceanu, EMN, France
Frédéric Benhamou, U Nantes, France
Christian Bessiere, LIRMM, France
Mats Carlsson, SICS, Sweden
David Cohen, Royal Holloway, UK
Rina Dechter, UC Irvine, USA
Boi Faltings, EPFL, Switzerland
Alan Frisch, U of York, UK
Carmen Gervet, IC-Parc, UK
Carla Gomes, Cornell U, USA
Warwick Harvey, IC-Parc, UK
Martin Henz, NUS, Singapore
John Hooker, CMU, USA
Peter Jeavons, U of Oxford, UK
Peter Jonsson, Linköping U, Sweden
Zeynep Kiziltan, U of Bologna, Italy
François Laburthe, Bouygues, France
Javier Larrosa, UPC, Spain
Jimmy Lee, CUHK, Hong Kong, China
Kevin Leyton-Brown, UBC, Canada
Pedro Meseguer, IIIA-CSIC, Spain
Laurent Michel, U of Conn., USA
Ian Miguel, U of St Andrews, UK
Michela Milano, U of Bologna, Italy
Eric Monfroy, U Nantes, France
Barry O'Sullivan, 4C, Ireland
Gilles Pesant, Montréal, Canada
Jean-Charles Régin, ILOG, France
Francesca Rossi, U of Padova, Italy
Michel Rueher, U of Nice, France
Christian Schulte, KTH, Sweden
Meinolf Sellmann, Brown U, USA
Helmut Simonis, IC-Parc, UK
Barbara Smith, 4C, Ireland
Stephen F. Smith, CMU, USA
Peter Stuckey, U Melbourne, Australia
Pascal Van Hentenryck, Brown U, USA
Gérard Verfaillie, ONERA, France
Mark Wallace, Monash U, Australia
Toby Walsh, UNSW, Australia
Roland Yap, NUS, Singapore
Weixiong Zhang, Washington U, USA

Additional Referees

Stefan Andrei
Ola Angelsmark
Carlos Ansotegui
Francisco Azevedo
Ismel Brito
Fahiem Bacchus
James Bailey
Philippe Balbiani
Joe Bater
Belaid Benhamou
Bozhena Bidyuk
Simon Boivin
Lucas Bordeaux
Sebastian Brand
Pascal Brisset
Ken Brown
Andrei Bulatov
Marco Cadoli
Tom Carchrae
Carlos Castro
Martine Ceberio
Amedeo Cesta
Yixin Chen
Kenil Cheng
Jeff Choi
Lau Hoong Chuin
Hélène Collavizza
Jean-François Condotta
Martin Cooper
Jorge Cruz
Vilhelm Dahllöf
Victor Dalmau
David Daney
Simon de Givry
Romuald Debruyne
Iván Dotú
Thomas Drakengren
Greg Duck
Ulle Endriss
Andrew Eremin
Alex Ferguson
Pierre Flener
Spencer Fung

Marco Gavanelli
Cormac Gebruers
Michel Gendreau
Bernard Gendron
Ian Gent
Vibhav Gogate
Alexandre Goldsztejn
Frédéric Goualard
Laurent Granvilliers
Martin Green
Youssef Hamadi
James Harland
Emmanuel Hebrard
Mark Hennessy
Federico Heras
Brahim Hnich
Alan Holland
David Hsu
Tudor Hulubei
Christopher Jefferson
Christophe Jermann
Albert Xin Jiang
Ulrich Junker
Narendra Jussien
Olli Kamarainen
Kalev Kask
Tom Kelsey
Ludwig Krippahl
Vitaly Lagoon
Arnaud Lallouet
Frédéric Lardeux
Yahia Lebbah
Michel Lemaître
Paolo Liberatore
Gérard Ligozat
C. Likitvivatanavong
Andrea Lodi
Ines Lynce
Gregory M. Provan
S. Macho-Gonzalez
Radu Marinescu
Robert Mateescu
Pascal Mathis

Claude Michel
Pragnesh J. Modi
Bertrand Neveu
Peter Nightingale
Gustav Nordh
Brice Pajot
Justin Pearson
Thierry Petit
Karen Petrie
Nicola Policella
Steven Prestwich
Claude-Guy Quimper
Philippe Refalo
Maria Cristina Riff
Andrea Roli
Emma Rollon
Colva Roney-Dougal
Horst Samulowitz
Mati Sanchez
Abdul Sattar
Frédéric Saubion
Thomas Schiex
Joachim Schimpf
Philippe Serré
Zoltan Somogyi
Martin Sulzmann
Radoslaw Szymanek
Carme Torras
Guido Tack
Armagan Tarim
Gilles Trombettoni
Charlotte Truchet
Edward Tsang
Marc van Dongen
Willem-Jan van Hoeve
K. Brent Venable
Petr Vilim
Xuan-Ha Vu
Magnus Wahlström
Richard J. Wallace
Jean-Paul Watson
Grant Weddell
Nic Wilson

Zhao Xing
Roland Yap
Makoto Yokoo

Neil Yorke-Smith
Yuanlin Zhang
Xing Zhao

Neng-Fa Zhou
Terry Zimmerman

Executive Committee of the ACP

Krzysztof Apt, NUS, Singapore
Fahiem Bacchus, University of
  Toronto, Canada
Christian Bessiere, LIRMM, France
James Bowen, UCC, Ireland
Michela Milano, University of Bologna,
  Italy
Jean-François Puget, ILOG, France

Francesca Rossi, University of Padova,
  Italy
Peter van Beek, University of
  Waterloo, Canada
Mark Wallace, Monash University,
  Australia
Toby Walsh, UNSW, Australia

Workshops

Applications of Constraint Satisfaction and Programming to Computer Security
Constraint Propagation and Implementation
Preferences and Soft Constraints
Cooperative Solvers in Constraint Programming
Distributed and Speculative Constraint Processing
Constraint Programming Beyond Finite Integer Domains
Interval Analysis, Constraint Propagation, Applications
Constraint Solving Under Change and Uncertainty
Constraints and Design
Modelling and Reformulating CSPs
Local Search Techniques in Constraint Satisfaction
Quantification in Constraint Programming
Symmetry and Constraint Satisfaction Problems

Sponsoring Institutions

Association for Constraint Programming (ACP)
Catalan Ministry of Universities, Research and Information Society (DURSI)
CoLogNET
Cork Constraint Computation Centre (4C)
ILOG Inc.
Intelligent Information Systems Institute (IISI), Cornell University
MusicStrands Inc.
Spanish Association for Artificial Intelligence (AEPIA)
Spanish Ministry of Education and Science (MEC)
Spanish Council for Scientific Research (CSIC)
Springer, Publisher of the Constraints Journal

Swedish Institute of Computer Science (SICS)
Technical University of Catalonia (UPC)
University of Lleida (UdL)

Table of Contents

Invited Papers

Search and Inference in AI Planning
  Héctor Geffner 1

OWL: A Description Logic Based Ontology Language
  Ian Horrocks 5

Preference Reasoning
  Francesca Rossi 9

The G12 Project: Mapping Solver Independent Models to Efficient Solutions
  Peter J. Stuckey, Maria Garcia de la Banda, Michael Maher, Kim Marriott, John Slaney, Zoltan Somogyi, Mark Wallace, Toby Walsh 13

Best Papers

Symmetry Definitions for Constraint Satisfaction Problems
  David Cohen, Peter Jeavons, Christopher Jefferson, Karen E. Petrie, Barbara M. Smith 17

Dynamic Ordering for Asynchronous Backtracking on DisCSPs
  Roie Zivan, Amnon Meisels 32

Full Papers

Incremental Algorithms for Local Search from Existential Second-Order Logic
  Magnus Ågren, Pierre Flener, Justin Pearson 47

Inter-distance Constraint: An Extension of the All-Different Constraint for Scheduling Equal Length Jobs
  Konstantin Artiouchine, Philippe Baptiste 62

Mind the Gaps: A New Splitting Strategy for Consistency Techniques
  Heikel Batnini, Claude Michel, Michel Rueher 77

Graph Invariants as Necessary Conditions for Global Constraints
*Nicolas Beldiceanu, Mats Carlsson, Jean-Xavier Rampon,
Charlotte Truchet* 92

Allocation and Scheduling for MPSoCs via Decomposition and
No-Good Generation
Luca Benini, Davide Bertozzi, Alessio Guerri, Michela Milano 107

Sub-optimality Approximations
Russell Bent, Irit Katriel, Pascal Van Hentenryck 122

A Linear-Logic Semantics for Constraint Handling Rules
Hariolf Betz, Thom Frühwirth 137

Distributed Stable Matching Problems
Ismel Brito, Pedro Meseguer 152

Beyond Hypertree Width: Decomposition Methods Without
Decompositions
Hubie Chen, Víctor Dalmau 167

Ad-hoc Global Constraints for Life
Kenil C.K. Cheng, Roland H.C. Yap 182

Tractable Clones of Polynomials over Semigroups
Víctor Dalmau, Ricard Gavaldà, Pascal Tesson, Denis Thérien 196

CP(Graph): Introducing a Graph Computation Domain in Constraint
Programming
Gregoire Dooms, Yves Deville, Pierre Dupont 211

Interval Analysis in Scheduling
Jérôme Fortin, Paweł Zieliński, Didier Dubois, Hélène Fargier 226

Assumption-Based Pruning in Conditional CSP
Felix Geller, Michael Veksler 241

Conditional Symmetry Breaking
*Ian P. Gent, Tom Kelsey, Steve A. Linton, Iain McDonald,
Ian Miguel, Barbara M. Smith* 256

Symmetry and Consistency
Ian P. Gent, Tom Kelsey, Steve Linton, Colva Roney-Dougal 271

Solving the MOLR and Social Golfers Problems
Warwick Harvey, Thorsten Winterer 286

Advances in Polytime Isomorph Elimination for Configuration
Laurent Hénocque, Mathias Kleiner, Nicolas Prcovic 301

Planning and Scheduling to Minimize Tardiness
J.N. Hooker 314

Search Heuristics and Heavy-Tailed Behaviour
Tudor Hulubei, Barry O'Sullivan 328

2-Way vs. d-Way Branching for CSP
Joey Hwang, David G. Mitchell 343

Maintaining Longest Paths in Cyclic Graphs
Irit Katriel, Pascal Van Hentenryck 358

Applying Constraint Programming to Rigid Body Protein Docking
Ludwig Krippahl, Pedro Barahona 373

Maximum Constraint Satisfaction on Diamonds
Andrei Krokhin, Benoit Larose 388

Exploiting Unit Propagation to Compute Lower Bounds in Branch and Bound Max-SAT Solvers
Chu Min Li, Felip Manyà, Jordi Planes 403

Generalized Conflict Learning for Hybrid Discrete/Linear Optimization
Hui Li, Brian Williams 415

Parallel Local Search in Comet
Laurent Michel, Pascal Van Hentenryck 430

Generating Corrective Explanations for Interactive Constraint Satisfaction
Barry O'Callaghan, Barry O'Sullivan, Eugene C. Freuder 445

spREAD: A Balancing Constraint Based on Statistics
Gilles Pesant, Jean-Charles Régin 460

Automatic Detection of Variable and Value Symmetries
Jean-François Puget 475

Breaking All Value Symmetries in Surjection Problems
Jean-François Puget 490

AC-*: A Configurable, Generic and Adaptive Arc Consistency Algorithm
  Jean-Charles Régin 505

Maintaining Arc Consistency Algorithms During the Search Without
Additional Space Cost
  Jean-Charles Régin 520

Weak Composition for Qualitative Spatial and Temporal Reasoning
  Jochen Renz, Gérard Ligozat 534

Boosting Distributed Constraint Satisfaction
  Georg Ringwelski, Youssef Hamadi 549

Depth-First Mini-Bucket Elimination
  Emma Rollon, Javier Larrosa 563

Using SAT in QBF
  Horst Samulowitz, Fahiem Bacchus 578

Tree Decomposition with Function Filtering
  Martí Sánchez, Javier Larrosa, Pedro Meseguer 593

On Solving Soft Temporal Constraints Using SAT Techniques
  *Hossein M. Sheini, Bart Peintner, Karem A. Sakallah,
  Martha E. Pollack* 607

Eplex: Harnessing Mathematical Programming Solvers for Constraint
Logic Programming
  Kish Shen, Joachim Schimpf 622

Caching Search States in Permutation Problems
  Barbara M. Smith 637

Repair-Based Methods for Quantified CSPs
  Kostas Stergiou 652

Handling Implication and Universal Quantification Constraints in FLUX
  Michael Thielscher 667

Solving Simple Planning Problems withMore Inference and No Search
  Vincent Vidal, Héctor Geffner 682

Solving Large-Scale Nonlinear Programming Problems by Constraint
Partitioning
  Benjamin W. Wah, Yixin Chen 697

Factor Analytic Studies of CSP Heuristics
Richard J. Wallace 712

Short Papers

Lookahead Saturation with Restriction for SAT
Anbulagan, John Slaney 727

Evolving Variable-Ordering Heuristics for Constrained Optimisation
Stuart Bain, John Thornton, Abdul Sattar 732

Multi-point Constructive Search
J. Christopher Beck 737

Bounds of Graph Characteristics
Nicolas Beldiceanu, Thierry Petit, Guillaume Rochart 742

Acquiring Parameters of Implied Global Constraints
Christian Bessiere, Rémi Coletta, Thierry Petit 747

Integrating Benders Decomposition Within Constraint Programming
Hadrien Cambazard, Narendra Jussien 752

Using Boolean Constraint Propagation for Sub-clauses Deduction
*S. Darras, G. Dequen, L. Devendeville, B. Mazure, R. Ostrowski,
L. Saïs* 757

Extending Systematic Local Search for Job Shop Scheduling Problems
Bistra Dilkina, Lei Duan, William S. Havens 762

Interactive Reconfiguration in Power Supply Restoration
Tarik Hadzic, Henrik Reif Andersen 767

Neighbourhood Clause Weight Redistribution in Local Search for SAT
*Abdelraouf Ishtaiwi, John Thornton, Abdul Sattar,
Duc Nghia Pham* 772

Computing and Exploiting Tree-Decompositions for Solving Constraint Networks
Philippe Jégou, Samba Ndojh Ndiaye, Cyril Terrioux 777

Encoding Requests to Web Service Compositions as Constraints
Alexander Lazovik, Marco Aiello, Rosella Gennari 782

Test Instance Generation for MAX 2SAT
  Mistuo Motoki 787

Consistency for Quantified Constraint Satisfaction Problems
  Peter Nightingale 792

Alternate Modeling in Sport Scheduling
  Laurent Perron 797

Approximations in Distributed Optimization
  Adrian Petcu, Boi Faltings 802

Extremal CSPs
  Nicolas Prcovic 807

Beyond Finite Domains: The All Different and Global Cardinality Constraints
  Claude-Guy Quimper, Toby Walsh 812

Views and Iterators for Generic Constraint Implementations
  Christian Schulte, Guido Tack 817

Approximated Consistency for the Automatic Recording Problem
  Meinolf Sellmann 822

Towards an Optimal CNF Encoding of Boolean Cardinality Constraints
  Carsten Sinz 827

Approximate Constrained Subgraph Matching
  Stéphane Zampelli, Yves Deville, Pierre Dupont 832

Doctoral Papers

Distributed Constraints for Large-Scale Scheduling Problems
  Montserrat Abril, Miguel A. Salido, Federico Barber 837

Solving Over-Constrained Problems with SAT
  Josep Argelich, Felip Manyà 838

A Constraint Based Agent for TAC–SCM
  David A. Burke, Kenneth N. Brown 839

Solving the Car-Sequencing Problem as a Non-binary CSP
  Mihaela Butaru, Zineb Habbas 840

Dimensioning an Inbound Call Center Using Constraint Programming
  Cyril Canon, Jean-Charles Billaut, Jean-Louis Bouquard 841

Methods to Learn Abstract Scheduling Models
  Tom Carchrae, J. Christopher Beck, Eugene C. Freuder 842

Automated Search for Heuristic Functions
  Pavel Cejnar, Roman Barták 843

Constraint-Based Inference: A Bridge Between Constraint Processing
and Probability Inference
  Le Chang, Alan K. Mackworth 844

Scheduling Social Tournaments
  Iván Dotú, Álvaro del Val, Pascal Van Hentenryck 845

Domain Reduction for the Circuit Constraint
  Latife Genc Kaya, John Hooker 846

Using Constraint Programming for Solving Distance CSP with
Uncertainty
  Carlos Grandon, Bertrand Neveu 847

Improved Algorithm for Finding (a,b)-Super Solutions
  Emmanuel Hebrard, Toby Walsh 848

Local Consistency in Weighted CSPs and Inference in Max-SAT
  Federico Heras, Javier Larrosa 849

Modeling Constraint Programs with Software Technology Standards
  Matthias Hoche, Stefan Jähnichen 850

Solution Equivalent Subquadrangle Reformulations of Constraint
Satisfaction Problems
  Chris Houghton, David Cohen 851

Mechanism Design for Preference Aggregation over Coalitions
  Eric Hsu, Sheila McIlraith 852

LP as a Global Search Heuristic Across Different Constrainedness
Regions
  Lucian Leahu, Carla Gomes 853

Consistency for Partially Defined Constraints
  Andreï Legtchenko, Arnaud Lallouet 854

Subnet Generation Problem: A New Network Routing Problem
  Cheuk Fun Bede Leung, Barry Richards, Olli Kamarainen 855

Partial Redundant Modeling
  Tiziana Ligorio, Susan L. Epstein 856

AND/OR Branch-and-Bound for Solving Mixed Integer Linear
Programming Problems
  Radu Marinescu, Rina Dechter 857

Weak Symmetries in Problem Formulations
  Roland Martin, Karsten Weihe 858

Towards the Systematic Generation of Channelling Constraints
  B. Martínez-Hernández, A.M. Frisch 859

AND/OR Search Spaces and the Semantic Width of Constraint
Networks
  Robert Mateescu, Rina Dechter 860

Statistical Modelling of CSP Solving Algorithms Performance
  Carles Mateu, Ramon Béjar, Cèsar Fernández 861

Probabilistic Arc Consistency
  Deepak Mehta, M.R.C. van Dongen 862

GOOSE – A Generic Object-Oriented
Search Environment
  Henry Müller, Stefan Jähnichen 863

Randomization for Multi-agent Constraint Optimization
  Quang Huy Nguyen, Boi V. Faltings 864

Uncertainty in Soft Constraint Problems
  Maria Silvia Pini, Francesca Rossi 865

Speeding Up Constrained Path Solvers with a Reachability Propagator
  Luis Quesada, Peter Van Roy, Yves Deville 866

From Linear Relaxations to Global Constraint Propagation
  Claude-Guy Quimper, Alejandro López-Ortiz 867

Encoding HTN Planning as a Dynamic CSP
  Pavel Surynek, Roman Barták 868

Specialised Constraints for Stable Matching Problems
  Chris Unsworth, Patrick Prosser 869

Bounds-Consistent Local Search
  Stefania Verachi, Steven Prestwich 870

Robust Constraint Solving Using Multiple Heuristics
  Alfio Vidotto, Kenneth N. Brown, J. Christopher Beck 871

Scheduling with Uncertain Start Dates
  Christine Wei Wu, Kenneth N. Brown, J. Christopher Beck 872

The Role of Redundant Clauses in Solving Satisfiability Problems
  Honglei Zeng, Sheila McIlraith 873

Applying Decomposition Methods to Crossword Puzzle Problems
  Yaling Zheng, Berthe Y. Choueiry 874

Asymmetric Distributed Constraints Satisfaction Problems
  Roie Zivan, Amnon Meisels 875

Full Arc Consistency in WCSP and in Constraint Hierarchies with
Finite Domains
  Josef Zlomek, Roman Barták 876

System Demonstrations

CoJava: A Unified Language for Simulation and Optimization
  Alexander Brodsky, Hadon Nash 877

Programming with $\mathcal{TOY}(\mathcal{FD})$
  *Antonio J. Fernández, Teresa Hortalá-González,
  Fernando Sáenz-Pérez* 878

Computing *Super*-Schedules
  Emmanuel Hebrard, Paul Tyler, Toby Walsh 879

Proterv-II: An Integrated Production Planning and Scheduling System
  András Kovács, Péter Egri, Tamás Kis, József Váncza 880

The Comet Programming Language and System
  Laurent Michel, Pascal Van Hentenryck 881

Random Stimuli Generation for Functional Hardware Verification as a
CP Application
  Yehuda Naveh, Roy Emek 882

A BDD-Based Interactive Configurator for Modular Systems
  Erik R. van der Meer 883

Author Index 885

Search and Inference in AI Planning

Héctor Geffner

ICREA & Universitat Pompeu Fabra,
Paseo de Circunvalacion 8,
08003 Barcelona, Spain
hector.geffner@upf.edu

Abstract. While Planning has been a key area in Artificial Intelligence since its beginnings, significant changes have occurred in the last decade as a result of new ideas and a more established empirical methodology. In this invited talk, I will focus on Optimal Planning where these new ideas can be understood along two dimensions: branching and pruning. Both heuristic search planners, and SAT and CSP planners can be understood in this way, with the latter branching on variables and pruning by constraint propagation, and the former branching on actions and pruning by lower bound estimations. The two formulations, however, have a lot in common, and some key planners such as Graphplan can be understood in either way: as computing a lower bound function and searching backwards from the goal, or as performing a precise, bounded form of variable elimination, followed by backtracking. The main limitation of older, so-called Partial Ordered Causal Link (POCL) planners, is that they provide smart branching schemes, in particular for temporal planning, but weak pruning rules. Indeed, the computation and even the formulation of good lower bounds for POCL plans is far from trivial. However, the pruning that cannot be obtained by the use of good monolithic lower bounds, can often be achieved by simple propagation rules over a suitable constraint-based formulation. We show this to be the case for CPT, currently the best domain-independent temporal planner, and then explore briefly further branching and pruning variations in parallel and conformant planning.

1 Introduction

AI Planning studies languages, models, and algorithms for describing and solving problems that involve the selection of actions for achieving goals. Most work so far has been devoted to *classical planning* where actions are deterministic, and plans are sequences of actions mapping a fully known initial situation into a goal. Other variants considered, however, are *temporal planning*, where actions have durations and some can be executed concurrently, and *contingent* and *conformant planning*, where actions are not deterministic, and their effects may or may not be observable. In each case, the form and semantics of plans can be defined precisely [1], the key problem is *computational:* how to search for plans effectively given a compact description of the task (e.g., in Strips).

2 Branching and Pruning: Heuristic Search and SAT

The search for optimal plans, like the search for optimal solutions in many intractable combinatorial problems, can be understood in terms of *branching* and *pruning*. Both Heuristic Search and SAT (and CSP) approaches in planning can be understood in this way; the former branches on actions and prunes by extracting and using lower bounds [2], the latter, branches on variables and prunes by constraint propagation and consistency checking [3]. The two approaches for taming the search, however, are closely related, and indeed, current SAT approaches [4] work on the encoding extracted from the *planning graph* [5]: a structure that can be interpreted as representing both a *heuristic function* and a *precompiled* theory.

Simplifying a bit, the planning graph can be thought as a sequence of layers $P_0, A_0, P_1, \ldots A_1, \ldots$ such that each layer P_i contains facts and each layer A_i contains actions. If computed in a state s, the facts in the first layer P_0 are the ones that are true in s, while then, iteratively, the actions in layer A_i are the ones whose preconditions are in P_i, and the facts in layer P_{i+1} are the ones added by actions in A_i (for this construction, no-op actions are assumed for each fact p with pre and postcondition p; see [5]). This is actually the *relaxed planning graph* also called the *reachability graph*, a simplification of the graph computed by Graphplan that ignores the so-called *mutex* information.

It is easy to show in either case that the heuristic function $h(s) = i$ where i is the index of the first layer P_i that contains the goals is a *lower bound* on the number of actions that are needed for achieving the goals from s. A generalized formulation of this class of lower bounds is given in [2], where a family of admissible heuristic functions $h^m(s)$ for a fixed integer $m = 1, 2, \ldots$ are defined that recursively approximate the cost of achieving a set of atoms C by the cost of the achieving the most costly subset of size m in C. Relaxed reachability corresponds to h^m with $m = 1$, while mutex reachability corresponds to h^m with $m = 2$.

From a logical perspective, if $L_0, L_1, L_2, \ldots$, refer to the collections of fact variables at time 0, action variables at time 0, fact variables at time 1, and so on, it is easy to verify that all the clauses in *planning theories* involve variables in the same layer L_i, or variables in adjacent layers. The *stratified* nature of these theories suggests a stratified form of inference: starting with the set of clauses Γ_i in the first layer L_i for $i = 0$, iteratively compute the sets of consequences $\Gamma_{i+1} = C_{i+1}(\Gamma_i \cup T_{i,i+1})$ over the next layer L_{i+1}, for $i = 0, 1, \ldots$, using Γ_i and the clauses $T_{i,i+1}$ that involve variables in both layers. If $C_{i+1}(X)$ is defined as the set of *prime implicates* of size no greater than m in L_{i+1} that follow from X, then the derived clauses turn out to be in correspondence with the clauses obtained from the planning graph: $m = 1$ yields a correspondence with the relaxed planning graph, while $m = 2$ yields a correspondence with the planning graph with pairwise mutexes. This inference is polynomial in the context of planning theories, where it corresponds precisely to a form of *bounded form of variable elimination* [6], where variables are eliminated in *blocks* inducing constraints of size no greater than m; see [7] for details.

3 Branching and Pruning in POCL Planning

Partial Order Planners were common in AI during the 80's and early 90's but could not compete with Graphplan and successors in terms of performance [5]. The reason being that POP planners, and in particular Partial Order Causal Link (POCL) planners [8], provide a branching scheme particularly suited for temporal planning [9], but no comparable pruning mechanisms. This limitation has been addressed recently in [10], where an optimal temporal planner that combines a POCL branching scheme with strong pruning mechanisms has been formulated in terms of constraints. The key element that distinguishes this planner, called CPT, from previous constraint-based POCL planners is the ability to reason about *all actions in the domain* and not only *the actions in the current plan*. The latter planners do not infer anything about an action until it is included in the plan, and something similar occurs in the standard methods for solving Dynamic CSPs. Yet often a lot can be inferred about such actions even before any commitments are made; the lower bounds on the starting times of *all* actions as computed in the planning graph being one example. In order to perform these and other inferences, CPT represents and reasons with a set of variables associated with *all* the actions in the domain. By means of a suitable set of constraints, propagation rules, and preprocessing, CPT has been shown to be the top performing optimal temporal planner, approching the performance of the best SAT planners in the special case in which all actions have unit duration [10].

The inference capabilities of CPT are illustrated in [10] by means of a simple TOWER-n domain, where n blocks $b_1, \ldots, b_n$ that are initially on the table, need to be stacked in order with b_1 on top. This is trivial problem for people but not for an optimal *domain-independent* planner that fails to recognize the structure of the problem. Indeed, none of the optimal planners considered, including Graphplan, SAT, and Heuristic Search planners can solve instances larger than $n = 15$. CPT, on the other hand, solves these and larger instances, in a few seconds by *pure (polynomial) inference and no search*. Actually, in [11], it is shown that many of the standard benchmarks used in planning, including all instances of Blocks, Ferry, Logistics, Gripper, Miconic, Rovers and Satellite, are solved *backtrack free* by an extension of CPT that performs further but still polynomial inference in every node.

4 Further Variations on Branching and Pruning

Graphplan computes the planning graph once from the initial situation and then searches the planning graph backwards for a plan. In [12], an alternative branching scheme is considered based on forcing a selected action in or out of the plan at a given time. The planning graph is then recomputed in every node in a way compatible with the commitments made, and a node is pruned when its planning graph pushes the goal beyond planning horizon. It is then shown that this alternative branching scheme, that preserves the same lower bound mechanism as

Graphplan (the planning graph), does much better than Graphplan when many actions can be done in parallel. In [13], the same branching scheme is used for *conformant planning* where the plan must work for a number of possible initial states (the initial state is partially unknown). Then partial conformant plans are pruned when they become incompatible with the plan for some initial state. This is determined by *model-count* operations that are rendered efficient by a precompilation of the planning theory into a suitable logical form [14].

Clearly, branching and pruning go a long way in optimal problem solving, yet it is not *all* branching and pruning. Two other ideas that have been shown to be important as well in problem solving are *Learning* in both CSP/SAT [15] and State Models [16], and *Decomposition* [14,17], in particular in problems that are harder than SAT.

Acknowledgments. Many of the ideas in CPT as well as all the code are due to Vincent Vidal. My work is supported in part by Grant TIC2002-04470-C03-02, MCyT, Spain.

References

1. Geffner, H.: Perspectives on AI Planning. In: Proc. AAAI-02. 1013–1023
2. Haslum, P., Geffner, H.: Admissible heuristics for optimal planning. In: Proc. AIPS-00. 70–82
3. Kautz, H., Selman, B.: Pushing the envelope: Planning, propositional logic, and stochastic search. In: Proc. AAAI-96, 1194–1201
4. Kautz, H., Selman, B.: Unifying SAT-based and Graph-based planning. In Proc. IJCAI-99, (1999) 318–327
5. Blum, A., Furst, M.: Fast planning through planning graph analysis. In: Proceedings of IJCAI-95, Morgan Kaufmann (1995) 1636–1642
6. Dechter, R.: Bucket elimination: A unifying framework for reasoning. Artificial Intelligence **113** (1999) 41–85
7. Geffner, H.: Planning graphs and knowledge compilation. In: Proc. KR-04. 662–672
8. Weld, D.S.: An introduction to least commitment planning. AI Magazine **15** (1994)
9. Smith, D., Frank, J., Jonsson, A.: Bridging the gap between planning and scheduling. Knowledge Engineering Review **15** (2000) 61–94
10. Vidal, V., Geffner, H.: Branching and pruning: An optimal temporal POCL planner based on constraint programming. In: Proc. AAAI-04. (2004) 570–577
11. Vidal, V., Geffner, H.: Solving simple planning problems with more inference and no search. In: Proc. CP-05. (2005)
12. Hoffmann, J., Geffner, H.: Branching matters: Alternative branching in graphplan. In: Proc. ICAPS-2003. (2003) 22–31
13. Palacios, H., Bonet, B., Darwiche, A., Geffner, H.: Pruning conformant plans by counting models on compiled d-DNNF representations. In: Proc. ICAPS-05. (2005)
14. Darwiche, A.: Decomposable negation normal form. J. ACM **48** (2001) 608–647
15. Dechter, R.: Enhancement schemes for constraint processing: Backjumping, learning, and cutset decomposition. Artificial Intelligence **41** (1990) 273–312
16. Bonet, B., Geffner, H.: Learning in DFS: A unified approach to heuristic search in deterministic, non-deterministic, probabilistic, and game tree settings. (2005)
17. Dechter, R.: AND/OR Search spaces for Graphical models. TR (2004)

OWL: A Description Logic Based Ontology Language
(Extended Abstract)

Ian Horrocks

School of Computer Science, University of Manchester,
Oxford Road, Manchester M13 9PL, UK
horrocks@cs.man.ac.uk

Description Logics (DLs) are a family of class (concept) based knowledge representation formalisms. They are characterised by the use of various constructors to build complex concepts from simpler ones, an emphasis on the decidability of key reasoning tasks, and by the provision of sound, complete and (empirically) tractable reasoning services.

Although they have a range of applications (e.g., reasoning with database schemas and queries [1,2]), DLs are perhaps best known as the basis for ontology languages such as OIL, DAML+OIL and OWL [3]. The decision to base these languages on DLs was motivated by a requirement not only that key inference problems (such as class satisfiability and subsumption) be decidable, but that "practical" decision procedures and "efficient" implemented systems also be available.

That DLs were able to meet the above requirements was the result of extensive research within the DL community over the course of the preceding 20 years or more. This research mapped out a complex landscape of languages, exploring a range of different language constructors, studying the effects of various combinations of these constructors on decidability and worst case complexity, and devising

At the same time, work on implementation and optimisation techniques demonstrated that, in spite of the high worst case complexity of key inference problems (usually at least ExpTime), highly optimised DL systems were capable of providing practical reasoning support in the typical cases encountered in realistic applications [4]. With the added impetus provided by the OWL standardisation effort, DL systems are now being used to provide computational services for a rapidly expanding range of ontology tools and applications [5–9].

Ontology Languages and Description Logics

The OWL recommendation actually consists of three languages of increasing expressive power: OWL Lite, OWL DL and OWL Full. Like OWL's predecessor DAML+OIL, OWL Lite and OWL DL are basically very expressive description logics with an RDF syntax. OWL Full provides a more complete integration with RDF, but its formal properties are less well understood, and key inference problems would certainly be *much* harder to compute.[1] For these reasons, OWL Full will not be considered here.

More precisely, OWL DL is based on the $\mathcal{SHOIQ}$ DL [11]; it restricts the form of number restrictions to be unqualified (see [4]), and adds a simple form of Datatypes (often called concrete domains in DLs [12]). Following the usual DL naming conventions, the resulting logic is called $\mathcal{SHOIN}(\mathbf{D})$, with the different letters in the name standing for (sets of) constructors available in the language: $\mathcal{S}$ stands for the basic $\mathcal{ALC}$ DL extended with transitive roles [10], $\mathcal{H}$ stands for role hierarchies (equivalently, inclusion axioms between roles), $\mathcal{O}$ stands for nominals (classes whose extension is a single individual) [13], $\mathcal{N}$ stands for unqualified number restrictions and ($\mathbf{D}$) stands for datatypes) [14]. OWL Lite is equivalent to the slightly simpler $\mathcal{SHIF}(\mathbf{D})$ DL (i.e., $\mathcal{SHOIQ}$ without nominals, and with only functional number restrictions).

These equivalences allow OWL to exploit the considerable existing body of description logic research, e.g.:

– to define the semantics of the language and to understand its formal properties, in particular the decidability and complexity of key inference problems [15];
– as a source of sound and complete algorithms and optimised implementation techniques for deciding key inference problems [16,10,14];
– to use implemented DL systems in order to provide (partial) reasoning support [17,18,19].

Practical Reasoning Services. Most modern DL systems use *tableaux* algorithms to test concept satisfiability. Tableaux algorithms have many advantages: it is relatively easy to design provably sound, complete and terminating algorithms; the basic technique can be extended to deal with a wide range of class and role constructors; and, although many algorithms have a higher worst case complexity than that of the underlying problem, they are usually quite efficient at solving the relatively easy problems that are typical of realistic applications.

Even in realistic applications, however, problems can occur that are much too hard to be solved by naive implementations of theoretical algorithms. Modern DL systems, therefore, include a wide range of optimisation techniques, the use of which has been shown to improve typical case performance by several orders of magnitude; key techniques include lazy unfolding, absorption and dependency directed backtracking [16,20,19,21].

Research Challenges

The effective use of logic based ontology languages in applications will critically depend on the provision of efficient reasoning services to support both ontology

---

[1] Inference in OWL Full is clearly undecidable as OWL Full does not include restrictions on the use of transitive properties which are required in order to maintain decidability [10].

design and deployment. The increasing use of DL based ontologies in areas such as e-Science and the Semantic Web is, however, already stretching the capabilities of existing DL systems, and brings with it a range of challenges for future research.

These challenges include: improved scalability, not only with respect to the number and complexity of classes, but also with respect to the number of individuals that can be handled; providing reasoning support for more expressive ontology languages; and extending the range of reasoning services provided to include, e.g., explanation [22,23], and so-called "non-standard inferences" such as matching, approximation, and difference computations [24,25,26].

Finally, some applications will almost certainly call for ontology languages based on larger (probably undecidable) fragments of FOL [27], or on hybrid languages that integrate DL reasoning with other logical knowledge representation formalisms such as Datalog rules [28,29] or Answer Set Programming [30]. The development of such languages, and reasoning services to support them, extends the research challenge to the whole logic based knowledge representation community.

References

1. Calvanese, D., De Giacomo, G., Lenzerini, M., Nardi, D., Rosati, R.: Description logic framework for information integration. In: Proc. of the 6th Int. Conf. on Principles of Knowledge Representation and Reasoning (KR'98). (1998) 2–13
2. Calvanese, D., De Giacomo, G., Lenzerini, M.: On the decidability of query containment under constraints. In: Proc. of the 17th ACM SIGACT SIGMOD SIGART Symp. on Principles of Database Systems (PODS'98). (1998) 149–158
3. Horrocks, I., Patel-Schneider, P.F., van Harmelen, F.: From $\mathcal{SHIQ}$ and RDF to OWL: The making of a web ontology language. J. of Web Semantics 1 (2003) 7–26
4. Baader, F., Calvanese, D., McGuinness, D., Nardi, D., Patel-Schneider, P.F., eds.: The Description Logic Handbook: Theory, Implementation and Applications. Cambridge University Press (2003)
5. Knublauch, H., Fergerson, R., Noy, N., Musen, M.: The protégé OWL plugin: An open development environment for semantic web applications. In Proc. of the 2004 International Semantic Web Conference (ISWC 2004). (2004) 229–243
6. Liebig, T., Noppens, O.: Ontotrack: Combining browsing and editing with reasoning and explaining for OWL Lite ontologies. In Proc. of the 2004 International Semantic Web Conference (ISWC 2004). (2004) 229–243
7. Visser, U., Stuckenschmidt, H., Schuster, G., Vögele, T.: Ontologies for geographic information processing. Computers in Geosciences (to appear)
8. Oberle, D., Sabou, M., Richards, D.: An ontology for semantic middleware: extending daml-s beyond web-services. In: Proceedings of ODBASE 2003. (2003)
9. Wroe, C., Goble, C.A., Roberts, A., Greenwood, M.: A suite of DAML+OIL ontologies to describe bioinformatics web services and data. Int. J. of Cooperative Information Systems (2003) Special Issue on Bioinformatics.
10. Horrocks, I., Sattler, U., Tobies, S.: Practical reasoning for expressive description logics. In Proc. of the 6th Int. Conf. on Logic for Programming and Automated Reasoning (LPAR'99). (1999) 161–180

11. Horrocks, I., Sattler, U.: A tableaux decision procedure for $\mathcal{SHOIQ}$. In: Proc. of the 19th Int. Joint Conf. on Artificial Intelligence (IJCAI 2005). (2005) To appear.
12. Baader, F., Hanschke, P.: A schema for integrating concrete domains into concept languages. In: Proc. of the 12th Int. Joint Conf. on Artificial Intelligence (IJCAI'91). (1991) 452–457
13. Blackburn, P., Seligman, J.: Hybrid languages. J. of Logic, Language and Information **4** (1995) 251–272
14. Horrocks, I., Sattler, U.: Ontology reasoning in the $\mathcal{SHOQ}$(D) description logic. In: Proc. of the 17th Int. Joint Conf. on Artificial Intelligence (IJCAI 2001). (2001) 199–204
15. Donini, F.M., Lenzerini, M., Nardi, D., Nutt, W.: The complexity of concept languages. Information and Computation **134** (1997) 1–58
16. Baader, F., Franconi, E., Hollunder, B., Nebel, B., Profitlich, H.J.: An empirical analysis of optimization techniques for terminological representation systems or: Making KRIS get a move on. Applied Artificial Intelligence. Special Issue on Knowledge Base Management **4** (1994) 109–132
17. Horrocks, I.: The FaCT system. In Proc. of the 2nd Int. Conf. on Analytic Tableaux and Related Methods (TABLEAUX'98). (1998) 307–312
18. Patel-Schneider, P.F.: DLP system description. In: Proc. of the 1998 Description Logic Workshop (DL'98), CEUR Electronic Workshop Proceedings, http://ceur-ws.org/Vol-11/ (1998) 87–89
19. Haarslev, V., Möller, R.: RACER system description. In: Proc. of the Int. Joint Conf. on Automated Reasoning (IJCAR 2001). (2001) 701–705
20. Horrocks, I.: Using an expressive description logic: FaCT or fiction? In: Proc. of the 6th Int. Conf. on Principles of Knowledge Representation and Reasoning (KR'98). (1998) 636–647
21. Horrocks, I., Patel-Schneider, P.F.: Optimizing description logic subsumption. J. of Logic and Computation **9** (1999) 267–293
22. Borgida, A., Franconi, E., Horrocks, I.: Explaining $\mathcal{ALC}$ subsumption. In: Proc. of the 14th Eur. Conf. on Artificial Intelligence (ECAI 2000). (2000)
23. Schlobach, S., Cornet, R.: Explanation of terminological reason-ing: A preliminary report. In: Proc. of the 2003 Description Logic Workshop (DL 2003). (2003)
24. Baader, F., Küsters, R., Borgida, A., McGuinness, D.L.: Matching in description logics. J. of Logic and Computation **9** (1999) 411–447
25. Küsters, R.: Non-Standard Inferences in Description Logics. Volume 2100 of Lecture Notes in Artificial Intelligence. Springer Verlag (2001)
26. Brandt, S., Küsters, R., Turhan, A.Y.: Approximation and difference in description logics. In: Proc. of the 8th Int. Conf. on Principles of Knowledge Representation and Reasoning (KR 2002). (2002) 203–214
27. Horrocks, I., Patel-Schneider, P.F., Bechhofer, S., Tsarkov, D.: OWL rules: A proposal and prototype implementation. J. of Web Semantics **3** (2005) 23–40
28. Motik, B., Sattler, U., Studer, R.: Query answering for owl-dl with rules. J. of Web Semantics **3** (2005) 41–60
29. Rosati, R.: On the decidability and complexity of integrating ontologies and rules. J. of Web Semantics **3** (2005) 61–73
30. Eiter, T., Lukasiewicz, T., Schindlauer, R., Tompits, H.: Combining answer set programming with description logics for the semantic web. In: Proc. of the 9th Int. Conf. on Principles of Knowledge Representation and Reasoning (KR 2004), Morgan Kaufmann, Los Altos (2004) 141–151

Preference Reasoning

Francesca Rossi*

Department of Pure and Applied Mathematics, University of Padova, Italy
frossi@math.unipd.it

Abstract. Constraints and preferences are ubiquitous in real-life. Moreover, preferences can be of many kinds: qualitative, quantitative, conditional, positive or negative, to name a few. Our ultimate goal is to define and study formalisms that can model problems with both constraints and many kind of preferences, possibly defined by several agents, and to develop tools to solve such problems efficiently. In this paper we briefly report on recent work towards this goal.

Motivation and Main Goal. Preferences are ubiquitous in real life. In fact, most problems are over-constrained and would not be solvable if we insist that all their requirements are strictly met. Moreover, solvable problems have solutions with different desirability. Finally, many problems are more naturally described via preferences rather than hard statements. In some cases it could be more natural to express preferences in quantitative terms, while in other situations it could be better to use qualitative statements. Moreover, preferences can be unconditional or conditional. Furthermore, in many real life problems, constraints and preferences of various kinds may coexist.

Unfortunately, there is no single formalism which allows all the different kinds of preferences to be specified efficiently and reasoned with effectively. For example, soft constraints [1] are most suited for reasoning about constraints and quantitative preferences, while CP-nets [2] are most suited for representing qualitative and possibly conditional preferences. Our ultimate goal is to define and study formalisms that can model problems with both constraints and many kind of preferences, and to develop tools to solve such problems efficiently. Moreover, we also want to be able to deal with scenarios where preferences are expressed by several agents, and preference aggregation is therefore needed to find the optimal outcomes.

Preference Modelling Frameworks: Soft Constraints and CP-Nets. Soft constraints [1] model quantitative preferences by generalizing the traditional formalism of hard constraints. In a soft constraint, each assignment to the variables of a constraint is annotated with a level of its desirability, and the desirability of a complete assignment is computed by a combination operator applied to the local preference values. By choosing a specific combination operator and an ordered set of levels of desirability, we can select a specific class of soft constraints. Given a set of soft constraints, an ordering is induced over the assignments of the variables of the problem, which can be partial or total. Given two solutions, checking whether one is preferable to the other one is

---

* This is joint work with C. Domshlak, M. S. Pini, S. Prestwich, A. Sperduti, K. B. Venable, T. Walsh, and N. Yorke-Smith.

easy: we compute the desirability values of the two solutions and compare them in the preference order. However, finding an optimal solution for a soft constraint problem is a combinatorially difficult problem.

CP-nets [2] (Conditional Preference networks) are a graphical model for compactly representing conditional and qualitative preference relations. They exploit conditional preferential independence by structuring a user's possibly complex preference ordering with the ceteris paribus assumption. CP-nets are sets of conditional ceteris paribus preference statements (cp-statements). For instance, the statement "I prefer red wine to white wine if meat is served." asserts that, given two meals that differ only in the kind of wine served and both containing meat, the meal with a red wine is preferable to the meal with a white wine. Given a CP-net, an ordering is induced over the set of assignments of its features. In general, such an ordering is a preorder (that is, reflexive and transitive). Given an acyclic CP-net, finding an optimal assignment to its features can be done in linear time. However, for cyclic CP-nets, it becomes NP-hard. Comparing two outcomes is NP-hard as well, even when the CP-net is acyclic.

Summarizing, CP-nets and soft constraints have complementary advantages and drawbacks. CP-nets allow one to represent conditional and qualitative preferences, but dominance testing is expensive. On the other hand, soft constraints allow to represent both hard constraints and quantitative preferences, and have a cheap dominance testing.

Comparing the Expressive Power of Different Formalisms. It would be very useful to have a single formalism for representing preferences that have the good features of both soft constraints and CP-nets. To achieve this goal, we may start by comparing their expressive power.

We could say that a formalism B is at least as expressive than a formalism A if from a problem expressed using A it is possible to build in polynomial time a problem expressed using B such that the optimal solutions are the same. If we use this definition to compare CP-nets and soft constraints, we see that hard constraints are at least as expressive as CP-nets. In fact, given any CP-net, we can obtain in polynomial time a set of hard constraints whose solutions are the optimal outcomes of the CP-net. On the contrary, there are some hard constraint problems for which it is not possible to find in polynomial time a CP-net with the same set of optimals. If instead, not only we must maintain the set of optimals, but also the rest of the ordering over the solutions, then CP-nets and soft or hard constraints are incomparable.

However, it is possible to approximate a CP-net ordering via soft constraints, achieving tractability of dominance testing while sacrificing precision to some degree [4]. Different approximations can be characterized by how much of the original ordering they preserve, the time complexity of generating the approximation, and the time complexity of comparing outcomes in the approximation.

Constraints and Preferences Together. Many problems have both constraints and qualitative and/or quantitative preferences. Unfortunately, reasoning with them both is difficult as often the most preferred outcome is not feasible, and not all feasible outcomes are equally preferred. For example, consider a constrained CP-net, which is a CP-net plus a set of hard constraints. This structure allows to model both qualitative conditional preferences and hard constraints. Its optimal outcomes (called "feasible

Pareto optimals" in [3]) are all the outcomes which are feasible and not dominated in the CP-net by any other feasible outcome. It is possible to obtain all such optimal outcomes by just solving a set of hard constraints [7]. In well defined cases, this avoids expensive dominance testing. If we want to avoid dominance testing completely, we can do that at the price of obtaining a superset of the feasible Pareto optimals by hard constraint solving. The same constraint-based procedure can be used also when we add soft constraints to a CP-net.

Learning Preferences. It is usually hard for a user to describe the correct preferences for his real-life problem. This is especially true for soft constraints, which do not have an intuitive graphical representation. We have shown that the use of learning techniques can greatly help in this respect, allowing users to state preferences both on entire solutions and subsets of the variables [8].

Preferences and Uncertainty. Preferences are a way to describe some kind of uncertainty. However, there is also uncertainty which comes from lack of data, or from events which are under Nature's control. Fortunately, in the presence of both preferences and uncertainty in the context of temporal constraints, we can reason with the same complexity as if we just had preferences [11]. Many approaches to deal with uncertainty are based on possibility theory. The handling of the coexistence of preferences and uncertainty via possibility theory allows for a natural merging of the two notions and leads to several promising semantics for ordering the solutions according to both their preference and their robustness to uncertainty [6].

Preference Aggregation: Fairness and Non-manipulability. In many situations, we need to represent and reason about the simultaneous preferences of several agents. To aggregate the agents' preferences, which in general express a partial order over the possible outcomes, we can query each agent in turn and collect together the results. We can see this as each agent "voting" whether an outcome dominates another. We can thus obtain different semantics by collecting these votes together in different ways [9].

Having cast our preference aggregation semantics in terms of voting, it is appropriate to ask if classical results about voting theory apply. For example, what about Arrow's theorem [5], which states the impossibility of a fair voting system? Can we fairly combine together the preferences of the individual agents?

The definition of fairness considered by Arrow consists of the following desirable properties:

- Unanimity: if all agents agree that A is preferable to B, then the resulting order must agree as well.
- Independence to irrelevant alternatives: the ordering between A and B in the result depends only on the relation between A and B given by the agents.
- Monotonicity: whenever an agent moves up the position of one outcome in her ordering, then (all else being equal) such an outcome cannot move down in the result.
- Absence of a dictator: a dictator is an agent such that, no matter what the others say, will always dictate the resulting ordering among the outcomes.

Under certain conditions, it is impossible for a preference aggregation system over partially ordered preferences to be fair [10]. This is both disappointing and a little surprising. By moving from total orders to partial orders, we expect to enrich greatly our ability to combine preferences fairly. In fact, we can use incomparability to resolve conflict and thereby not contradict agents. Nevertheless, under the conditions identified, we still do not escape the reach of Arrow's theorem. Even if we are only interested in the most preferred outcomes of the aggregated preferences, it is still impossible to be fair.

Of course fairness is just one of the desirable properties for preference aggregations. Other interesting properties are related to the non-manipulability of a preference aggregation system: if an agent can vote tactically and reach its goal, then the system is manipulable. Results for totally ordered preferences show that non-manipulability implies the existence of a dictator. Unfortunately, this continues to hold also for partially ordered preferences.

Future Work. Much work has yet to be done to achieve the desired goal of a single formalism to model problems with both constraints and preferences of many kinds, and to solve them efficiently. For example, we are currently considering extensions of the soft constraint formalism to model both positive and negative preferences. Also, we are studying the relationship between optimal solutions in preference formalisms and Nash equilibria in game theory. Finally, we plan to study the notion of privacy in the context of multi-agent preference aggregation.

References

1. S. Bistarelli, U. Montanari, and F. Rossi. Semiring-based Constraint Solving and Optimization. Journal of the ACM, vol. 44, n. 2, pp. 201-236, 1997.
2. C. Boutilier, R. I. Brafman, C. Domshlak, H. H. Hoos, and D. Poole. CP-nets: A tool for representing and reasoning with conditional ceteris paribus preference statements. Journal of Artificial Intelligence Research, 21:135–191, 2004.
3. C. Boutilier, R. I. Brafman, C. Domshlak, H. H. Hoos, and D. Poole. Preference-based constraint optimization with CP-nets. Computational Intelligence, vol. 20, pp.137-157, 2004.
4. C. Domshlak, F. Rossi, K. B. Venable, and T. Walsh. Reasoning about soft constraints and conditional preferences: complexity results and approximation techniques. Proc. IJCAI-03, 215–220. Morgan Kaufmann, 2003.
5. J. S. Kelly. Arrow Impossibility Theorems. Academic Press, 1978.
6. M. S. Pini, F. Rossi, K. B. Venable. Possibility theory for reasoning about uncertain soft constraints. Proc. ECSQARU 2005, Barcelona, July 2005, Springer-Verlag LNAI 3571.
7. S. Prestwich, F. Rossi, K. B. Venable, T. Walsh. Constraint-based Preferential Optimization. Proc. AAAI 2005, Morgan Kaufmann, 2005.
8. F. Rossi and A. Sperduti. Acquiring both constraint and solution preferences in interactive constraint systems. Constraints, vol.9, n. 4, 2004, Kluwer.
9. F. Rossi, K. B. Venable, and T. Walsh. mCP Nets: Representing and Reasoning with Preferences of Multiple Agents. Proc. AAAI 2004, AAAI Press, 2004.
10. F. Rossi, M. S. Pini, K. B. Venable, and T. Walsh. Aggregating preferences cannot be fair. Proc. TARK X, Singapore, June 2005, ACM Digital Library.
11. F. Rossi, K. B. Venable, N. Yorke-Smith. Controllability of Soft Temporal Constraint Problems. Proc. CP 2004, Toronto, Springer LNCS 3258, 2004.

The G12 Project: Mapping Solver Independent Models to Efficient Solutions

Peter J. Stuckey[1], Maria Garcia de la Banda[2], Michael Maher[3],
Kim Marriott[2], John Slaney[4], Zoltan Somogyi[1], Mark Wallace[2],
and Toby Walsh[3]

[1] NICTA Victoria Laboratory,
Department of Computer Science and Software Engineering,
University of Melbourne, 3010 Australia
{pjs, zs}@cs.mu.oz.au
[2] School of Comp. Sci. & Soft. Eng., Monash University, Australia
{mbanda, marriott, mgw}@mail.csse.monash.edu.au
[3] NICTA Kensington Laboratory,
University of New South Wales, 2052, Australia
{michael.maher, toby.walsh}@nicta.com.au
[4] NICTA Canberra Laboratory,
Canberra ACT 2601, Australia
john.slaney@nicta.com.au

Abstract. The G12 project recently started by National ICT Australia (NICTA) is an ambitious project to develop a software platform for solving large scale industrial combinatorial optimisation problems. The core design involves three languages: Zinc, Cadmium and Mercury (Group 12 of the periodic table). Zinc is a declarative modelling language for expressing problems, independent of any solving methodology. Cadmium is a mapping language for mapping Zinc models to underlying solvers and/or search strategies, including hybrid approaches. Finally, existing Mercury will be extended as a language for building extensible and hybridizable solvers. The same Zinc model, used with different Cadmium mappings, will allow us to experiment with different complete, local, or hybrid search approaches for the same problem. This talk will explain the G12 global design, the final G12 objectives, and our progress so far.

1 Introduction

The G12 project aims to build a powerful and easy-to-use open source constraint programming platform for solving large scale industrial combinatorial optimization (LSCO) problems. The research project is split into four related threads: building richer modelling languages, building richer solving capabilities, a richer control language mapping the problem model to the underlying solving capabilities, and a richer problem-solving environment.

The underlying implementation platform will be the Mercury system. On top of Mercury the project will build a generic modelling language, called Zinc, and a mapping language, called Cadmium, which takes a Zinc model and generates a

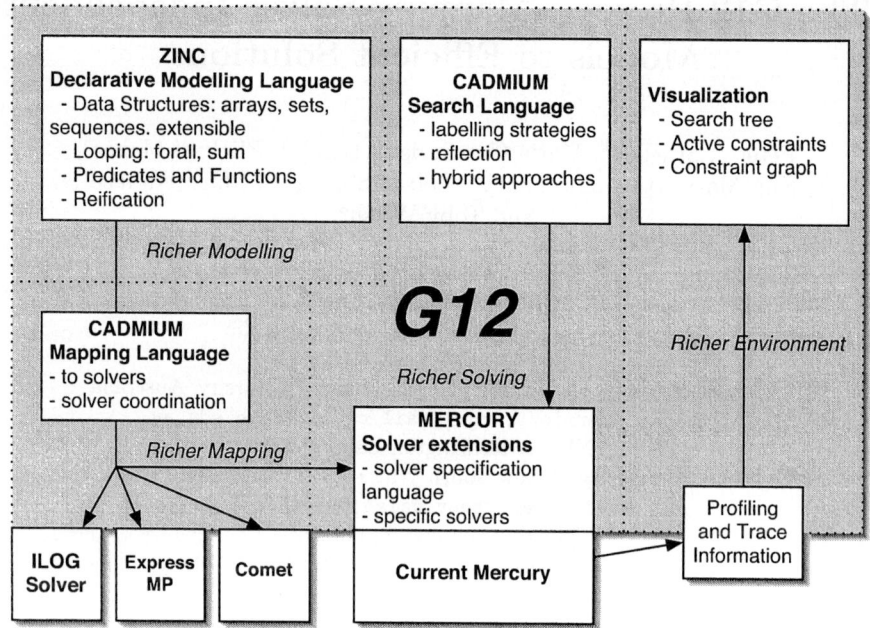

Mercury program. We also plan that Zinc and Cadmium will combine to output programs for different constraint solving systems such as ILOG Solver [6], Xpress MP [7] and Comet [2]. A diagram showing the four threads and how they interact with existing solvers and the current language Mercury is shown below.

2 Richer Modelling

The process of solving LSCO problems can be separated into creating the conceptual model, and an algorithm development process for mapping the conceptual model to a design model. This depends upon a language for writing conceptual models, and usually another language for writing design models.

In order to maintain clarity, flexibility, simplicity and correctness, we separate the conceptual modelling language Zinc from the mapping language Cadmium, which is both the design modelling language and the search language.

The best starting point for a universal conceptual modelling language is a purely declarative modelling language. Such a language allows the modeller to give a high-level specification of the constraint problem in terms natural to the problem itself. In order to do so it must include data structures that naturally arise in modelling such as arrays and sets, as well as be extensible in order to incorporate new problem specific structures such as jobs and tasks. We need natural constructs for specifying large constraints and large conjunctions of constraints. In order to encapsulate common problem structure we need to be able to specify predicates and functions in the modelling language for reuse.

The modeller needs to be able to specify requirements for robust, as well as optimal, solutions. *Robust* solutions are less sensitive to change in parameters, and reflect the reality that real solutions often need to be repaired when they are put into practice. It must be possible for the modelling language to specify the required type of robustness.

There are many challenges in the design of the Zinc language. For example, how can we make the language suitable for both an operations researcher experienced in using restricted mathematical modelling languages such as AMPL [1], as well as computer scientists used to the flexibility and power of programming languages. OPL [5] is the closest current language to how we envisage Zinc.

3 Richer Mapping

In order to make use of a conceptual model we must have some way of compiling it, that is mapping it to a design model. One advantage of separating of the conceptual modelling language from the design model is the ability to then rapidly experiment with different design models for the same conceptual model.

We wish to provide transparent and flexible ways of specifying how a conceptual model is mapped to a design model. Experience in developing solutions to industrial constraint problems has shown that we will often need to use two or more solving technologies to tackle a hard constraint problem. Various constraints will be treated by one solver, while other constraints will be treated by another. Some constraints may be treated by two or more solvers. When we are using multiple solvers we not only need to specify which constraints are sent to each solver, and how they are mapped to that solver, but how the solvers will interact. This must be supported by Cadmium.

G12 will not only need to provide a modelling interface to distinct solving methods from mixed integer programming (MIP), constraint programming (CP) and local search, but will also need to provide a modelling and mapping interface to methods for integrating these techniques. The design models for such an integrated scheme may involve combinations of algorithms from all three areas. The Cadmium language in which the design models are expressed must therefore subsume the expressive power of all the above languages. Much more is required however, since the interaction between local search and *branch-and-infer* search open a huge space of possible hybridisations.

4 Richer Solving

Constraint programming systems typically employ tree search to complement constraint propagation. Moreover the search is depth first and alternative search choices are only explored after backtracking to the relevant choice point. By contrast MIP search typically explores the search tree in a best-first fashion, which requires a multitude of *open* nodes to be recorded, ready for expansion at a later time. Recently systems like Mozart [4] have incorporated the open nodes approach in CP. With G12 we shall pursue the convergence of CP and MIP search by reducing the cost of jumping between open nodes, and maintaining flexibility between the many different tree search strategies.

However local search techniques are playing an increasingly important role in CP. The Comet CP system [2] supports a wide range of local search techniques, with constraint handlers adapted to the local search paradigm. The final addition to the arsenal of search methods offered by G12 will be population-based search methods, such as genetic algorithms. These methods explore a whole population of solutions concurrently, and then combine the results from the population to focus the search on promising areas of the search space.

To date no system has enabled the user to specify the problem in terms of an algorithm-independent conceptual model, and have the computer map this into, say, an ant colony optimisation algorithm. The challenge for Cadmium is to make this mapping straightforward and concise, yet precise and flexible.

Another important research direction for richer solving will be developing algorithms for returning more robust solutions, more diverse solutions, or finding similar solutions to previous solutions.

5 Richer Environment

The key to solving complex industrial application problems is rapid applications development, with close end-user involvement. To support rapid application development, a rich solution development environment is essential.

The first stage in developing an application is constructing a correct Zinc and Cadmium model. This is much easier for the application programmer if solutions are graphically realized in a way that they can readily understand. The second and more time consuming phase is performance debugging in which we study the behaviour of the algorithms at runtime and understand exactly what is going on. Interaction with a running algorithm is necessary to detect its weaknesses, and to understand and build on its strengths. To support close end-user involvement, the problem solving behaviour must be made meaningful and transparent to the end-user. This requires that the algorithm behaviour be mapped back onto the problem model, so that the user can understand the behaviour in terms of the original application.

6 Conclusion

The G12 project aims, using the separation of the conceptual model from the design model, to provide a software framework where many, perhaps all, optimizations approaches can be experimented with efficiently. By allowing this exploration we hope to get closer to the ultimate goal of simply specifying the problem and letting the G12 system determine the best way to solve it.

References

1. AMPL: www.ilog.com/products/ampl/
2. Comet: www.cs.brown.edu/people/pvh/comet1.html
3. Mercury: www.cs.mu.oz.au/mercury/
4. Mozart: www.mozart-oz.org
5. OPL Studio: www.ilog.com/products/oplstudio/
6. ILOG SOLVER: www.ilog.com/products/solver/
7. Xpress MP: www.dashoptimization.com

Symmetry Definitions for Constraint Satisfaction Problems

David Cohen[1], Peter Jeavons[2], Christopher Jefferson[3], Karen E. Petrie[4], and Barbara M. Smith[4]

[1] Department of Computer Science, Royal Holloway, University of London, UK
D.Cohen@rhul.ac.uk
[2] Computing Laboratory, University of Oxford, UK
peter.jeavons@comlab.ox.ac.uk
[3] Department of Computer Science, University of York, UK
christopher.jefferson@cs.york.ac.uk
[4] Cork Constraint Computation Centre, University College Cork, Ireland
{kpetrie, b.smith}@4c.ucc.ie

Abstract. We review the many different definitions of symmetry for constraint satisfaction problems (CSPs) that have appeared in the literature, and show that a symmetry can be defined in two fundamentally different ways: as an operation preserving the solutions of a CSP instance, or else as an operation preserving the constraints. We refer to these as *solution symmetries* and *constraint symmetries*. We define a constraint symmetry more precisely as an automorphism of a hypergraph associated with a CSP instance, the microstructure complement. We show that the solution symmetries of a CSP instance can also be obtained as the automorphisms of a related hypergraph, the *k-ary nogood hypergraph* and give examples to show that some instances have many more solution symmetries than constraint symmetries. Finally, we discuss the practical implications of these different notions of symmetry.

1 Introduction

The issue of *symmetry* is now widely recognised as of fundamental importance in constraint satisfaction problems (CSPs). It seems self-evident that in order to deal with symmetry we should first agree what we mean by symmetry. Surprisingly, this appears not to be true: researchers in this area have defined symmetry in fundamentally different ways, whilst often still identifying the same collection of symmetries in a given problem and dealing with them in the same way.

In this paper, we first survey the various symmetry definitions that have appeared in the literature. We show that the existing definitions reflect two distinct views of symmetry: that symmetry is a property of the solutions, i.e. that any mapping that preserves the solutions is a symmetry; or that symmetry preserves the constraints, and therefore as a consequence also preserves the solutions. We propose two new definitions of *solution symmetry* and *constraint symmetry* to capture these two distinct views, and show that they are indeed different: although any constraint symmetry is also a solution symmetry, there can be many solution symmetries that are not constraint symmetries. We discuss the relationship between the symmetry groups identified by these definitions and show that each is the automorphism group of a hypergraph, derived from either the solutions or the constraints of the CSP. We illustrate these ideas by discussing how they apply to a well-studied example problem, the n-queens problem. Finally, we discuss how these definitions of symmetry may be used in practice.

2 A Brief Survey of Symmetry Definitions

There have been many papers in recent years on symmetry in constraint satisfaction and related problems, not all of which give a clear definition of symmetry. In this section, we review the variety of definitions that have been used.

We first fix our terminology by defining a CSP instance as follows.

Definition 1. *A CSP instance is a triple $\langle V, D, C \rangle$ where:*

- *V is a set of variables;*
- *D is a universal domain, specifying the possible values for those variables;*
- *C is a set of constraints. Each constraint $c \in C$ is a pair $c = \langle \sigma, \rho \rangle$ where σ is a list of variables from V, called the constraint scope, and ρ is a $|\sigma|$-ary relation over D, called the constraint relation.*

An assignment of values to variables is a set $\{\langle v_1, a_1 \rangle, \langle v_2, a_2 \rangle, ..., \langle v_k, a_k \rangle\}$ where $\{v_1, v_2, ..., v_k\} \subseteq V$ and $a_i \in D$, for all i such that $1 \leq i \leq k$. Note that the constraint relation of a constraint c is intended to specify the assignments that are allowed by that constraint.

A solution to the CSP instance $\langle V, D, C \rangle$ is a mapping from V into D whose restriction to each constraint scope is a member of the corresponding constraint relation, i.e., is allowed by the constraint.

We will call a CSP k-ary if the maximum arity of any of its constraints is k.

There are two basic types of definition for symmetry in a CSP instance: those that define symmetry as a property of the set of solutions, and those that define symmetry as a property that can be identified in the statement of the problem, without solving it. We shall refer to these informally in this section as *solution symmetry* and *problem symmetry* or *constraint symmetry*. In Section 3 we will define them formally and use these definitions to show how the two types of symmetry are related.

An example of an early definition of *solution symmetry* is given by Brown, Finkelstein & Purdom [5], who define a symmetry as a permutation of the problem variables that leaves invariant the set of solutions. Backofen and Will [2] similarly define a symmetry as a bijective function on the set of solutions of a CSP: they allow a symmetry to be specified by its effect on the individual assignments of values to variables.

A number of papers have defined *problem symmetry* in propositional calculus. Aguirre [1] and Crawford, Ginsberg, Luks & Roy [6] each define symmetry similarly: if S is a set of clauses in CNF, then a permutation π of the variables in those clauses is a symmetry of S if $\pi(S) = S$. The expression $\pi(S)$ denotes the result of applying the permutation π to the clauses in S. If this permutation simply re-orders the literals in individual clauses, and reorders the clauses, then it leaves S effectively unchanged, and so in this case $\pi(S) = S$ and π is a symmetry. Benhamou and Sais [4] use a slightly more general definition, in which a symmetry is a permutation defined on the set of *literals* that preserves the set of clauses. For example, given two variables x and y, x may be mapped to $\neg y$.

In CSPs, some authors have similarly defined a symmetry as a mapping that leaves the constraints unchanged, but have often restricted the allowed mappings to those that affect only the variables or only the values. Note that a constraint may be specified *extensionally* by listing its allowed tuples, or *intensionally* by giving an expression such as $x < y$ from which the allowed tuples could be determined. Permuting the variables in a constraint will in general change it: for example, the constraint $x + y = z$ is not the same as the constraint $x + z = y$. Puget [15] defines the notion of a *symmetrical constraint*, that is, a constraint which is unaffected by the order of the variables. For example, the binary inequality constraint, $\neq$, is symmetrical. He defines a symmetry of a CSP as a permutation of the variables which maps the set of constraints into an equivalent set: any constraint is either unchanged by the permutation or is an instance of a symmetrical constraint and is mapped onto a constraint on the same set of variables.

A similar idea was introduced by Roy and Pachet [17]. They define the notion of *intensional permutability*: two variables are intensionally permutable if: they have the same domain; any constraint affecting either of them affects both; for any constraint affecting these two variables, interchanging them in the expression defining the constraint does not change it. (The constraint is assumed to be defined intensionally, hence the name.) For example, in a linear constraint, any two variables with the same coefficient are intensionally permutable (with respect to that constraint, and assuming that they have the same domain).

Both Puget [15] and Roy and Pachet [17] restrict their definitions of symmetries to mappings that permute the *variables* of the problem only. Meseguer and Torras [14] define symmetries that act on both the variables and the values of a CSP. They define a symmetry on a CSP with n variables as a collection of $n+1$ bijective mappings $\Theta = \{\theta, \theta_1, ..., \theta_n\}$. The mapping θ is a bijection on the set of variables $\{x_1, x_2, ..., x_n\}$; each θ_i is a bijection from $D(x_i)$ to $D(\theta(x_i))$ (where $D(x_i)$ is the domain D restricted to the acceptable values for x_i by unary constraints). These mappings will also transform each constraint. The set Θ is called a symmetry if it does not change the set of constraints C, as a whole.

Meseguer and Torras's definition allows both *variable* symmetries (that permute only the variables) and *value* symmetries (that permute only the values) as special cases, and hence is more general than many earlier definitions. However, it does not allow mappings in which variable-value pairs involving the same variable (say $\langle x_i, a_1 \rangle$ and $\langle x_i, a_2 \rangle$) can be mapped to variable-value pairs involving different variables (say $\langle x_j, a_j \rangle$ and $\langle x_k, a_k \rangle$, where $x_j \neq x_k$). For example, Meseguer and Torras consider the n-queens problem, in the commonly-used CSP formulation in which the variables correspond to the rows of the chessboard and the values to the columns. They show that the reflections in the horizontal and vertical axes and the rotation of the chessboard through 180° are symmetries of the corresponding CSP according to their definition, but the other four chessboard symmetries (reflection in the diagonals, rotation through 90° and 270°) are not. This example will be considered in more detail in Section 4 below.

Finally, we consider the notion of *interchangeability*, as defined by Freuder [9]. This is a form of solution symmetry: two values a, b for a variable v are *fully interchangeable* if every solution to the CSP containing the assignment $\langle v, a \rangle$ remains a solution when b is substituted for a, and vice versa. As Freuder notes, in general identifying fully interchangeable values requires finding all solutions to the CSP. He therefore defines local forms of interchangeability that can be identified by inspecting the problem. Neighbourhood interchangeability, for example, is a form of constraint symmetry: two values a, b for a variable v are said to be neighbourhood interchangeable if for every constraint c whose scope includes v, the set of assignments that satisfy c which contain the pair $\langle v, a \rangle$ still satisfy c when this is replaced by $\langle v, b \rangle$, and vice versa.

Benhamou [3] extends the ideas of interchangeability slightly and distinguishes between *semantic* and *syntactic* symmetry in CSPs, corresponding to our notions of solution symmetry and constraint symmetry, respectively. He defines two kinds of semantic symmetry: two values a_i and b_i for a CSP variable v_i are *symmetric for satisfiability* if the following property holds: there is a solution which assigns the value a_i to v_i if and only if there is a solution which assigns the value b_i to v_i. The values are *symmetric for all solutions* if: each solution containing the value a_i can be mapped to a solution containing the value b_i. (The latter property implies the former.) Identifying semantic symmetries requires solving the CSP to find all solutions, and examining them. The notion of *syntactic symmetry* in [3] is defined as follows. Let $P = \langle V, D, C \rangle$ be a binary CSP instance, whose constraint relations are all members of some set R. A permutation π of D is a syntactic symmetry if $\forall r_{ij} \in R$, we have $(d_i, d_j) \in r_{ij} \implies (\pi(d_i), \pi(d_j)) \in r_{ij}$. In other words, the permutation π does not change any constraint relation of P, considered as a set of tuples.

From this brief survey of existing symmetry definitions, it can be seen that they differ both in what aspect of the CSP they act on (only the values, only the variables, or variable-value pairs) and in what they preserve (the constraints or the set of solutions). It should be noted that it has become standard in the symmetry breaking methods that act during search (e.g. [2,7,8,11]), as opposed to adding constraints to the CSP, to describe symmetries by their action on variable-value pairs. Hence, almost all the definitions described in this section are more restrictive than these systems allow.

Under all the definitions, symmetries map solutions to solutions and non-solutions to non-solutions; the definitions disagree over whether this is a defining property, so that any bijective mapping of the right kind that preserves the solutions must be a symmetry, or whether it is simply a consequence of leaving the constraints unchanged. In the next section we will show that this distinction is critical: the choice we make can seriously affect the symmetries that we find.

3 Constraint Symmetries and Solution Symmetries

In this section we will introduce two definitions of symmetries for constraint satisfaction problems that are sufficiently general to encompass all the types of symmetry allowed by the definitions given in the last section.

Note that the essential feature that allows any bijective mapping on a set of objects to be called a symmetry is that it leaves some property of those objects unchanged. It follows from this that the identity mapping will always be a symmetry, and the inverse of any symmetry will also be a symmetry. Furthermore, given two symmetries we can combine them (by composing the mappings) to obtain another symmetry, and this combination operation is associative. Hence, the set of symmetries forms a *group*.

The particular group of symmetries that we obtain depends on exactly what property it is that we choose to be preserved. Our first definition uses the property of being a solution, and is equivalent to the definition used in [2].

Definition 2. *For any CSP instance* $P = \langle V, D, C \rangle$, *a* solution symmetry *of P is a permutation of the set* $V \times D$ *that preserves the set of solutions to P.*

In other words, a solution symmetry is a bijective mapping defined on the set of possible variable-value pairs of a CSP, that maps solutions to solutions. Note that this general definition allows variable and value symmetries as special cases.

To state our definition of *constraint symmetries* we first describe a mathematical structure associated with any CSP instance. For a binary CSP instance, the details of the constraints can be captured in a graph, the *microstructure* [9,12] of the instance.

Definition 3. *For any binary CSP instance* $P = \langle V, D, C \rangle$, *the* microstructure *of P is a graph with set of vertices* $V \times D$ *where each edge corresponds either to an assignment allowed by a specific constraint, or to an assignment allowed because there is no constraint between the associated variables.*

For our purposes, it is more convenient to deal with the complement of this graph. The *microstructure complement* has the same set of vertices as the microstructure, but with edges joining all pairs of vertices which are *disallowed* by some constraint, or else are incompatible assignments for the same variable. In other words, two vertices $\langle v_1, a_1 \rangle$ and $\langle v_2, a_2 \rangle$ in the microstructure complement are connected by an edge if and only if:

- the vertices v_1 and v_2 are in the scope of some constraint, but the assignment of a_1 to v_1 and a_2 to v_2 is disallowed by that constraint; or
- $v_1 = v_2$ and $a_1 \neq a_2$.

Recall that any set of vertices of a graph which does not contain an edge is called an *independent set*. An immediate consequence of the definition of the microstructure complement is that a solution to a CSP instance P is precisely an independent set of size $|V|$ in its microstructure complement.

The definition extends naturally to the non-binary case. Here the microstructure complement is a *hypergraph* whose set of vertices is again the set of all variable-value pairs. In this case, a set of vertices E is a hyperedge of the microstructure complement if it represents an assignment *disallowed* by a constraint, or else consists of a pair of incompatible assignments for the same variable. In other words, a set of vertices $\{\langle v_1, a_1\rangle, \langle v_2, a_2\rangle, \ldots, \langle v_k, a_k\rangle\}$ is a hyperedge if and only if:

- $\{v_1, v_2, \ldots, v_k\}$ is the set of variables in the scope of some constraint, but the constraint disallows the assignment $\{\langle v_1, a_1\rangle, \langle v_2, a_2\rangle, \ldots, \langle v_k, a_k\rangle\}$; or
- $k = 2$, $v_1 = v_2$ and $a_1 \neq a_2$.

Example 1. The system of linear equations $x + y + z = 0$; $w + y = 1$; $w + z = 0$ over the integers modulo 2 (that is, where $1 + 1 = 0$) can be modelled as a CSP instance $P = \langle V, D, C \rangle$, with $V = \{w, x, y, z\}$, $D = \{0, 1\}$ and $C = \{c_1, c_2, c_3\}$, where c_1, c_2, c_3 correspond to the three equations.

The microstructure complement of P is shown in Figure 1. It has eight vertices: $\langle w, 0\rangle, \langle w, 1\rangle, \langle x, 0\rangle, \langle x, 1\rangle, \langle y, 0\rangle, \langle y, 1\rangle, \langle z, 0\rangle, \langle z, 1\rangle$, and twelve hyperedges. The equation $x + y + z = 0$ disallows the assignment $\{\langle x, 0\rangle, \langle y, 0\rangle, \langle z, 1\rangle\}$ and three other assignments. Hence, the microstructure complement has four ternary hyperedges arising from this constraint, including $\{\langle x, 0\rangle, \langle y, 0\rangle, \langle z, 1\rangle\}$. Each binary constraint also gives two binary hyperedges. Finally, there are four binary hyperedges (one per variable) corresponding to pairs of different values for the same variable; for example, the hyperedge $\{\langle y, 0\rangle, \langle y, 1\rangle\}$.

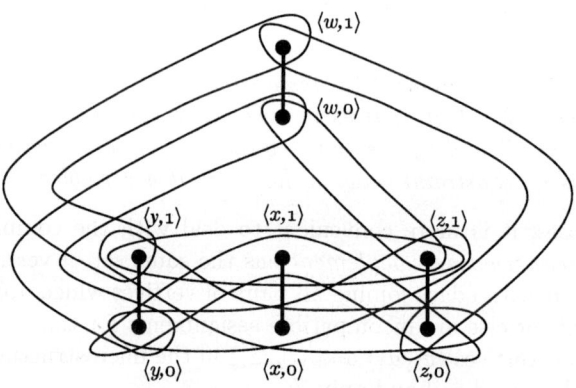

Fig. 1. The microstructure complement of the CSP instance P defined in Example 1

We are now in a position to define a constraint symmetry. Recall that an *automorphism* of a graph or hypergraph is a bijective mapping of the vertices that preserves the edges (and hence also preserves the non-edges).

Definition 4. *For any CSP instance $P = \langle V, D, C \rangle$, a constraint symmetry is an automorphism of the microstructure complement of P (or, equivalently, of the microstructure).*

The microstructure complement is related to the direct encoding of a CSP as a SAT instance [18]. The direct encoding has a variable for each variable-value pair in the original CSP; a clause for each pair of values for each variable, forbidding both values being assigned at the same time; and a clause for each tuple of variable-value pairs not allowed by a constraint (as well as other clauses ensuring that a value is chosen for every variable). A constraint symmetry as defined here is therefore equivalent to a permutation of the variables in the SAT encoding that does not change the set of clauses, and so is related to the definition of symmetry in SAT given by Crawford *et al.* [6].

Example 2. We consider the constraint symmetries of the CSP defined in Example 1, whose microstructure complement is shown in Figure 1. The automorphisms of this graph are the identity permutation together with the following permutations:

- $(\langle w, 0 \rangle \langle w, 1 \rangle) \ (\langle y, 0 \rangle \langle y, 1 \rangle) \ (\langle z, 0 \rangle \langle z, 1 \rangle)$;
- $(\langle w, 0 \rangle \langle w, 1 \rangle) \ (\langle y, 0 \rangle \langle z, 0 \rangle) \ (\langle y, 1 \rangle \langle z, 1 \rangle)$;
- $(\langle y, 0 \rangle \langle z, 1 \rangle) \ (\langle y, 1 \rangle \langle z, 0 \rangle)$;

(These permutations of the vertices are written in cycle form: for example, the first swaps the vertices $\langle w, 0 \rangle$ and $\langle w, 1 \rangle$ while simultaneously swapping $\langle y, 0 \rangle$ and $\langle y, 1 \rangle$ and swapping $\langle z, 0 \rangle$ and $\langle z, 1 \rangle$, but leaves $\langle x, 0 \rangle$ and $\langle x, 1 \rangle$ unchanged.) Hence, these four mappings are the constraint symmetry group of this CSP.

This example also shows that there can be more solution symmetries than constraint symmetries. The CSP has only two solutions: $\{\langle w, 0 \rangle, \langle x, 1 \rangle, \langle y, 1 \rangle, \langle z, 0 \rangle\}$ and $\{\langle w, 1 \rangle, \langle x, 1 \rangle, \langle y, 0 \rangle, \langle z, 1 \rangle\}$. The permutation $(\langle w, 0 \rangle \langle z, 0 \rangle \langle y, 1 \rangle)$, which maps $\langle w, 0 \rangle$ to $\langle z, 0 \rangle$, $\langle z, 0 \rangle$ to $\langle y, 1 \rangle$, $\langle y, 1 \rangle$ to $\langle w, 0 \rangle$ and leaves all other variable-value pairs unchanged, is a solution symmetry. This mapping preserves both solutions, but clearly is not a constraint symmetry.

Although Definition 2 and Definition 4 appear to be very different, we now show that there are some simple relationships between solution symmetries and constraint symmetries.

Theorem 1. *The group of constraint symmetries of a CSP instance P is a subgroup of the group of solution symmetries of P.*

Proof. Let P be a CSP instance and let π be any automorphism of the microstructure complement of P. We will show that π maps solutions to solutions, and hence is a solution symmetry of P.

Let s be any solution of P, and let W be the corresponding set of vertices in the microstructure complement of P. By the construction of the microstructure complement, W is an independent set of size $|V|$. Since π is an automorphism, we know that $\pi(W)$ is also an independent set of size $|V|$, and so is a solution. □

Next we show that the group of all solution symmetries of an instance P is also the automorphism group of a certain hypergraph. We first define a *nogood*.

Definition 5. *For any CSP instance P, a k-ary nogood is an assignment to k variables of P that cannot be extended to a solution of P.*

The k-nogood hypergraph of P is a hypergraph whose set of vertices is $V \times D$ and whose set of edges is the set of all m-ary nogoods for all $m \leq k$.

The k-nogood hypergraph of a CSP instance has the same vertices as the microstructure complement. For a k-ary CSP (one whose constraints have maximum arity k), the k-ary nogood hypergraph contains every hyperedge of the microstructure complement, and possibly some others. The additional hyperedges represent partial assignments of up to k variables that are allowed by the constraints, but do not appear in any solution because they cannot be extended to a full assignment satisfying all the constraints.

Example 3. Consider again the CSP instance P defined in Example 1, with solutions, $\{\langle w,0\rangle, \langle x,1\rangle, \langle y,1\rangle, \langle z,0\rangle\}$ and $\{\langle w,1\rangle, \langle x,1\rangle, \langle y,0\rangle, \langle z,1\rangle\}$.

This instance has a large number of 3-ary nogoods, and the 3-nogood hypergraph of P has a large number of hyperedges, in addition to those in the microstructure complement. These include the hyperedge $\{\langle x,0\rangle, \langle y,0\rangle, \langle z,0\rangle\}$, for example. This assignment is allowed by the 3-ary constraint on the variables x, y, z, but cannot be extended to a complete solution of P. Many of the additional hyperedges do not correspond to the scope of any constraint: for example, the hyperedge $\{\langle w,0\rangle, \langle x,1\rangle, \langle y,0\rangle\}$.

Theorem 2. *For any k-ary CSP instance P, the group of all solution symmetries of P is equal to the automorphism group of the k-nogood hypergraph of P.*

Proof. Let F be the k-nogood hypergraph of P and let π be any automorphism of F. We will show that π preserves solutions, and hence is a solution symmetry.

Let s be any solution of P, and let W be the corresponding set of vertices in F. By the construction of this hypergraph, W is an independent set of size $|V|$. Since π is an automorphism of F, we know that $\pi(W)$ is also an independent set of size $|V|$. Hence $\pi(W)$ is not disallowed by any of the constraints of P, and is a solution.

Conversely, let π be a solution symmetry of P. We will show that π maps every set of k or fewer vertices of F which is not a hyperedge to another non-hyperedge, and hence π is an automorphism of this hypergraph.

Let E be any set of k or fewer vertices in F which is not a hyperedge. Since every nogood of P of size k or less is a hyperedge of the k-nogood hypergraph, it follows that E can be extended to at least one solution of P.

Hence we may suppose that E is part of some solution s. Now, s is mapped to the solution $\pi(s)$ by the solution symmetry π. Every k-ary projection of this solution, including the image $\pi(E)$ of E, is a non-hyperedge in F, and so we are done. □

Theorem 2 shows that to obtain the solution symmetries of a CSP instance it is sufficient to consider the automorphisms of the hypergraph obtained by adding

Table 1. The number of additional binary nogoods derived from the sets of solutions to the n-queens problem, and the number of solution symmetries

n	Additional binary nogoods	Solution symmetries
3	8	$9! = 362{,}880$
4	32	$4! \times 4! \times 2 \times 8! = 46{,}448{,}640$
5	40	28,800
6	280	3,089,428,805,320,704,000,000
7	72	8
8	236	8
9	40	8
10	0	8

and adding these to the microstructure complement, will give an automorphism group that is nearer to the solution symmetry group, if not equal to it.

When finding all solutions, the aim in symmetry breaking is to find just one solution from each symmetry equivalence class; in the 5-queens problem, the solutions fall into two equivalence classes when using the constraint symmetries and only one when using the solution symmetries. Hence, if the aim is to find a set of nonisomorphic solutions, the appropriate symmetry group should be chosen in advance, since the choice can affect the number of solutions found.

This raises the question of how to identify the symmetries of a CSP, either the constraint symmetries or the solution symmetries; we discuss this next.

5 Identifying Symmetry in Practice

Symmetry in CSPs is usually identified, in practice, by applying human insight: the programmer sees that some transformation would transform a hypothetical solution into another hypothetical solution. The definition of constraint symmetry given earlier can be used to confirm that candidate transformations are genuine symmetries. It is not necessary to generate the entire microstructure complement for this purpose, but only to demonstrate that each candidate mapping will map edges to edges and non-edges to non-edges in this hypergraph.

Identifying symmetry in a CSP by inspection is prone to missing some of the symmetry. Using Definition 4 we can, in principle, be sure to identify all the constraint symmetries in a problem by generating the microstructure complement and finding its automorphism group. However, it will often be impracticable to generate the microstructure, especially for large CSPs with non-binary constraints. It may in that case be possible to represent the constraints more compactly while preserving the important details; for instance, Ramani and Markov [16] propose to represent constraints by parse trees and find the automorphisms of the resulting graph.

Many authors have defined symmetry in CSPs in a similar way to our definition of solution symmetry, but have effectively only identified constraint symmetries; we have shown that the solution symmetry group can be much larger than the constraint symmetry group. This suggests a novel, *incremental* approach to using symmetry during search, in which we maintain a set of currently known symmetries throughout the solution process. This set is initialised to the group of constraint symmetries. Each time a nogood of arity k or less is found during preprocessing, or during the search for solutions, it is added to our current view of the k-nogood hypergraph, together with all of its images under currently known symmetries. Adding these edges might increase the number of automorphisms of this graph, and hence increase the set of currently known symmetries. The bigger this group of symmetries gets, the more information we get from each additional nogood.

Methods such as those proposed here may find a potentially very large group of symmetries, but with possibly only a small number of generators. For instance, as shown earlier, the solution symmetry group of 5-queens has 28,800 elements but just three generators. Symmetry-breaking methods that combine dynamic symmetry breaking during search with computational group theory, e.g. [10], can exploit such symmetry groups effectively.

6 Conclusion

We have reviewed definitions of symmetry in CSPs and have proposed definitions of *constraint symmetry* and *solution symmetry* to encompass two types of definition that have been used. We have shown that there can be many more solution symmetries, i.e. permutations of the variable-value pairs that preserve the solutions, than constraint symmetries, i.e. permutations that preserve the constraints. In practice, researchers have identified constraint symmetries in CSPs rather than solution symmetries, regardless of their definition of symmetry, because of the difficulty of identifying solution symmetries that are not also constraint symmetries without examining the set of solutions. However, we have shown that for a k-ary CSP, the solution symmetries are the automorphisms of the k-ary nogood hypergraph; hence, finding new nogoods of arity up to k and adding them to the CSP can allow the constraint symmetry group to expand towards the solution symmetry group. Symmetry-breaking methods avoid exploring assignments that are symmetrically equivalent to assignments explored elsewhere; hence, working with a larger symmetry group allows more assignments to be pruned and can further reduce the search effort to solve the problem.

Acknowledgments

We thank the SBDS group, especially Warwick Harvey, Ian Gent and Steve Linton for helpful discussions on this topic; a review of symmetry definitions by Iain McDonald was also useful. We are grateful to Brendan McKay for his help in finding automorphism groups of graphs using NAUTY. We thank Marc van Dongen and Nic Wilson for helpful feedback. This material is based in part on works supported by the Science Foundation Ireland under Grant No. 00/PI.1/C075 and by the UK EPSRC under Grant No. GR/R29673; the authors were also supported by SymNet, the U.K. Symmetry and Search Network, funded by EPSRC.

References

1. A. Aguirre. How to Use Symmetries in Boolean Constraint Solving. In F. Benhamou and A. Colmerauer, editors, *Constraint Logic Programming: Selected Research*, pages 287–306. MIT Press, 1992.
2. R. Backofen and S. Will. Excluding Symmetries in Constraint-Based Search. In J. Jaffar, editor, *Principles and Practice of Constraint Programming - CP'99*, LNCS 1713, pages 73–87. Springer, 1999.
3. B. Benhamou. Study of symmetry in constraint satisfaction problems. In *Proceedings of the 2nd Workshop on Principles and Practice of Constraint Programming, PPCP'94*, pages 246–254, May 1994.
4. B. Benhamou and L. Sais. Theoretical study of symmetries in propositional calculus and applications. In D. Kapur, editor, *Automated Deduction - CADE-11*, LNAI 607, pages 281–294. Springer-Verlag, 1992.
5. C. A. Brown, L. Finkelstein, and P. W. Purdom. Backtrack Searching in the Presence of Symmetry. In T. Mora, editor, *Applied Algebra, Algebraic Algorithms and Error-Correcting Codes*, LNCS 357, pages 99–110. Springer-Verlag, 1988.
6. J. Crawford, M. Ginsberg, E. Luks, and A. Roy. Symmetry-Breaking Predicates for Search Problems. In *Proceedings KR'96*, pages 149–159, Nov. 1996.
7. T. Fahle, S. Schamberger, and M. Sellmann. Symmetry Breaking. In T. Walsh, editor, *Principles and Practice of Constraint Programming - CP 2001*, LNCS 2239, pages 225–239. Springer, 2001.
8. F. Focacci and M. Milano. Global Cut Framework for Removing Symmetries. In T. Walsh, editor, *Principles and Practice of Constraint Programming - CP 2001*, LNCS 2239, pages 77–92. Springer, 2001.
9. E. C. Freuder. Eliminating Interchangeable Values in Constraint Satisfaction Problems. In *Proceedings AAAI'91*, volume 1, pages 227–233, 1991.
10. I. P. Gent, W. Harvey, T. Kelsey, and S. Linton. Generic SBDD using Computational Group Theory. In F. Rossi, editor, *Principles and Practice of Constraint Programming - CP 2003*, LNCS 2833, pages 333–347. Springer, 2003.
11. I. P. Gent and B. M. Smith. Symmetry Breaking During Search in Constraint Programming. In W. Horn, editor, *Proceedings ECAI'2000*, pages 599–603, 2000.
12. P. Jégou. Decomposition of Domains Based on the Micro-Structure of Finite Constraint-Satisfaction Problems. In *Proceedings AAAI'93*, pages 731–736, 1993.
13. B. McKay. Practical Graph Isomorphism. *Congressus Numerantium*, 30:45-87, 1981. (The software tool NAUTY is available for download from http://cs.anu.edu.au/~bdm/nauty/)
14. P. Meseguer and C. Torras. Exploiting symmetries within constraint satisfaction search. *Artificial Intelligence*, 129:133–163, 2001.
15. J.-F. Puget. On the Satisfiability of Symmetrical Constrained Satisfaction Problems. In J. Komorowski and Z. W. Ras, editors, *Proceedings of ISMIS'93*, LNAI 689, pages 350–361. Springer-Verlag, 1993.
16. A. Ramani and I. L. Markov. Automatically Exploiting Symmetries in Constraint Programming. In B. Faltings, A. Petcu, F. Fages, and F. Rossi, editors, *CSCLP 2004*, LNCS 3419, pages 98–112. Springer, 2005.
17. P. Roy and F. Pachet. Using Symmetry of Global Constraints to Speed up the Resolution of Constraint Satisfaction Problems. In *Workshop on Non Binary Constraints, ECAI-98*, Aug. 1998.
18. T. Walsh. SAT v CSP. In R. Dechter, editor, *Proceedings CP'2000*, LNCS 1894, pages 441–456. Springer, 2000.

Dynamic Ordering for Asynchronous Backtracking on DisCSPs

Roie Zivan and Amnon Meisels*

Department of Computer Science,
Ben-Gurion University of the Negev,
Beer-Sheva, 84-105, Israel
{zivanr, am}@cs.bgu.ac.il

Abstract. An algorithm that performs asynchronous backtracking on distributed $CSPs$, with dynamic ordering of agents is proposed, ABT_DO. Agents propose reorderings of lower priority agents and send these proposals whenever they send assignment messages. Changes of ordering triggers a different computation of $Nogoods$. The dynamic ordered asynchronous backtracking algorithm uses polynomial space, similarly to standard ABT.

The ABT_DO algorithm with three different ordering heuristics is compared to standard ABT on randomly generated $DisCSPs$. A *Nogood-triggered* heuristic, inspired by dynamic backtracking, is found to outperform static order ABT by a large factor in run-time and improve the network load.

1 Introduction

Distributed constraint satisfaction problems (*DisCSPs*) are composed of agents, each holding its local constraints network, that are connected by constraints among variables of different agents. Agents assign values to variables, attempting to generate a locally consistent assignment that is also consistent with all constraints between agents (cf. [16,14]). To achieve this goal, agents check the value assignments to their variables for local consistency and exchange messages with other agents, to check consistency of their proposed assignments against constraints with variables owned by different agents [1].

Distributed CSPs are an elegant model for many every day combinatorial problems that are distributed by nature. Take for example a large hospital that is composed of many wards. Each ward constructs a weekly timetable assigning its nurses to shifts. The construction of a weekly timetable involves solving a constraint satisfaction problem for each ward. Some of the nurses in every ward are qualified to work in the *Emergency Room*. Hospital regulations require a certain number of qualified nurses (e.g. for Emergency Room) in each shift. This imposes constraints among the timetables of different wards and generates a complex Distributed CSP [14].

A search procedure for a consistent assignment of all agents in a distributed CSP ($DisCSP$), is a distributed algorithm. All agents cooperate in search for a globally consistent solution. The solution involves assignments of all agents to all their variables

---

* Supported by the Lynn and William Frankel center for Computer Sciences.

and exchange of information among all agents, to check the consistency of assignments with constraints among agents.

Asynchronous Backtracking (*ABT*) is one of the most efficient and robust algorithms for solving distributed constraints satisfaction problems. Asynchronous Backtracking was first presented by Yokoo [17,16] and was developed further and studied in [6,2,11,1]. Agents in the *ABT* algorithms perform assignments asynchronously against their current view of the system's state. The method performed by each agent is in general simple. Later versions of *ABT* use polynomial space memory and perform dynamic backtracking [2,1]. The versions of asynchronous backtracking presented in all of the above studies use a static priority order among all agents.

In centralized *CSPs*, dynamic variable ordering is known to be an effective heuristic for gaining efficiency [4]. Recent studies have shown that the same is true for algorithms which perform sequential (synchronous) assignments in Distributed *CSPs* [10,3]. These studies suggest heuristics of agent/variable ordering and empirically show large gains in efficiency over the same algorithms performing with static order. These results are the basic motivation for exploring the possibilities for dynamic reordering of asynchronous backtracking.

In [6] the authors present a distributed ordering algorithm, according to the properties of the constraints graph. Once the order is determined, the asynchronous backtracking algorithm uses this fixed order.

An asynchronous algorithm with dynamic ordering was proposed by [15], Asynchronous Weak Commitment (*AWC*). According to [16], *AWC* outperforms *ABT*. However, in order to be complete, *AWC* uses exponential space which makes it impractical for solving hard instances of even small *DisCSPs*.

An attempt to combine *ABT* with *AWC* was reported by [12]. In order to perform asynchronous finite reordering operations [12] suggest that the reordering operation will be performed by abstract agents. The results presented in [12] show minor improvements to static order *ABT*.

The present paper proposes a simple algorithm for dynamic ordering in asynchronous backtracking, *ABT_DO* that uses polynomial space, as standard *ABT*. In the proposed algorithm the agents of the *DisCSP* choose orders dynamically and asynchronously. Agents in *ABT_DO* perform according to the current, most updated order they hold. Each order is time-stamped according to agents assignment. The method of time-stamp for defining the most updated order is the same that is used in [10] for choosing the most updated partial assignment. A simple array of counters represents the priority of a proposed order, according to the global search tree. Each agent can change the order of all agents with lower priority. An agent can propose an order change each time it replaces its assignment.

Having established a correct algorithm for dynamic variable ordering in *ABT*, one needs to investigate ordering heuristics. Surprisingly, some of the heuristics which are very effective for sequential assignments distributed algorithms, do not improve the run-time of *ABT*. It turns out that an ordering heuristic, based on *Dynamic Backtracking* [5], is very successful (see Section 6).

Distributed *CSPs* are presented in Section 2. A description of the standard *ABT* algorithm is presented in Section 3. Asynchronous backtracking with dynamic ordering

(ABT_DO) is presented in Section 4. Section 5 introduces a correctness and completeness proof for ABT_DO. An extensive experimental evaluation, which compares ABT to ABT_DO with several ordering heuristics is in Section 6. The experiments were conducted on randomly generated $DisCSPs$.

2 Distributed Constraint Satisfaction

A distributed constraints network (or a distributed constraints satisfaction problem - *DisCSP*) is composed of a set of k agents $A_1, A_2, ..., A_k$. Each agent A_i contains a set of constrained variables $X_{i_1}, X_{i_2}, ..., X_{i_{n_i}}$. Constraints or **relations** R are subsets of the Cartesian product of the domains of the constrained variables. For a set of constrained variables $X_{i_k}, X_{j_l}, ..., X_{m_n}$, with domains of values for each variable $D_{i_k}, D_{j_l}, ..., D_{m_n}$, the constraint is defined as $R \subseteq D_{i_k} \times D_{j_l} \times ... \times D_{m_n}$. A **binary constraint** R_{ij} between any two variables X_j and X_i is a subset of the Cartesian product of their domains; $R_{ij} \subseteq D_j \times D_i$. In a distributed constraint satisfaction problem *DisCSP*, the agents are connected by constraints between variables that belong to different agents [17,14]. In addition, each agent has a set of constrained variables, i.e. a *local constraint network*.

An assignment (or a label) is a pair $< var, val >$, where var is a variable of some agent and val is a value from var's domain that is assigned to it. A *compound label* is a set of assignments of values to a set of variables. A **solution** P to a *DisCSP* is a compound label that includes all variables of all agents, that satisfies all the constraints. Agents check assignments of values against non-local constraints by communicating with other agents through sending and receiving messages.

The following assumptions are routinely made in studies of $DisCSPs$ and are assumed to hold in the present study [16,1].

1. All agents hold exactly one variable.
2. The amount of time that passes between the sending and the receiving of a message is finite.
3. Messages sent by agent A_i to agent A_j are received by A_j in the order they were sent.

3 Asynchronous Backtracking (ABT)

The *Asynchronous Backtracking* algorithm, was presented in several versions over the last decade and is described here in the form of the more recent papers [16,1]. In the ABT algorithm, agents hold an assignment for their variables at all times, which is consistent with their view of the state of the system (i.e. their *Agent_view*). When the agent cannot find an assignment which is consistent with its *Agent_view*, it changes its view by eliminating a conflicting assignment from its *Agent_view* data structure. It then sends back a *Nogood* which is based on its former inconsistent *Agent_view* and makes another attempt to assign its variable [16,1].

The code of the Asynchronous Backtracking algorithm (ABT) is presented in figure 1. ABT has a total order of priorities among agents. Agents hold a data structure called *Agent_view* which contains the most recent assignments received from agents

when received (**ok?**, (x_j, d_j)) **do**
1. add (x_j, d_j) to $agent\_view$;
2. **check_agent_view**;**end_do**;

when received (**nogood**, x_j, $nogood$) **do**
1. add nogood to nogood list;
2. **when** $nogood$ contains an agent x_k that is not a neighbor **do**
3.   request x_k to add x_i as a neighbor,
4.   and add (x_k, d_k) to $agent\_view$; **end_do**;
5. $old\_value \leftarrow current\_value$; **check_agent_view**;
6. **when** $old\_value = current\_value$ **do**
7.   send (**ok?**, $(x_i, current\_value)$) to x_j ; **end_ do**; **end_do**;

procedure **check_agent_view**
1. **when** $agent\_view$ and $current\_value$ are not consistent **do**
2.   **if** no value in D_i is consistent with $agent\_view$ **then backtrack**;
3.   **else** select $d \in D_i$ where $agent\_view$ and d are consistent;
4. $current\_value \leftarrow d$;
5.   send (**ok?**,(x_i, d)) to $low\_priority\_neighbors$; **end_if**;**end_do**;

procedure **backtrack**
1. $nogood \leftarrow resolve\_Nogoods$;
2. **if** $nogood$ is an empty set **do**
3.   broadcast to other agents that there is no solution;
4.   terminate this algorithm; **end_do**;
5. select (x_j, d_j) where x_j has the lowest priority in nogood;
6. send (**nogood**, x_i, $nogood$) to x_j;
7. remove (x_j, d_j) from $agent\_view$; **end_do**;
8. **check_agent_view**

Fig. 1. Standard ABT algorithm

with higher priority. The algorithm starts by each agent assigning its variable, and sending the assignment to neighboring agents with lower priority. When an agent receives a message containing an assignment (an **ok?** message [16]), it updates its $Agent\_view$ with the received assignment and if needed replaces its own assignment, to achieve consistency (first procedure in Figure 1). Agents that reassign their variable, inform their lower priority neighbors by sending them **ok?** messages (Procedure **check_agent_view**, lines 3-5). Agents that cannot find a consistent assignment, send the inconsistent tuple in their $Agent\_view$ in a backtrack message (a $Nogood$ message [16]) and remove from their $Agent\_view$ the assignment of the lowest priority agent in the inconsistent tuple. In the simplest form of the ABT algorithm, the complete $Agent\_view$ is sent as a $Nogood$ [16]. The $Nogood$ is sent to the lowest priority agent whose assignment is included in the $Nogood$. After the culprit assignment is removed from the $AgentView$ the agent makes another attempt to assign its variable by calling procedure **check_agent_view** (procedure **backtrack** in Figure 1).

Agents that receive a $Nogood$, check its relevance against the content of their $Agent\_view$. If the $Nogood$ is relevant the agent stores it, and tries to find a consistent assignment. If the agent receiving the $Nogood$ keeps its assignment, it informs the

$Nogood$ sender by resending it an **ok?** message with its assignment. An agent A_i which receives a $Nogood$ containing an assignment of agent A_j which is not included in its $Agent\_view$, adds the assignment of A_j to its $Agent\_view$ and sends a message to A_j asking it to add a link between them, i.e. inform A_i about all assignment changes it performs in the future (second procedure in Figure 1).

The performance of ABT can be improved immensely by requiring agents to read all messages they receive before performing computation [16,1]. This technique was found to improve the performance of *Asynchronous Backtracking* on the harder instances of randomly generated Distributed CSPs by a large factor [18,3].

Another improvement to the performance of ABT can be achieved by using the method for resolving inconsistent subsets of the $Agent\_view$, based on methods of dynamic backtrack. A version of ABT that uses this method was presented in [1]. In all the experiments in this paper, a version of ABT which includes both of the above improvements is used. Agents read all incoming messages that were received before performing computation and $Nogoods$ are resolved, using the dynamic backtracking method.

4   ABT with Dynamic Ordering

For simplicity of presentation we assume that agents send **order** messages to all lower priority agents. In the more realistic form of the algorithm, agents send **order** messages only to their lower priority *neighbors*. Both versions are proven correct in section 5.

Each agent in ABT_DO holds a $Current\_order$ which is an ordered list of pairs. Every pair includes the ID of one of the agents and a counter. Each agent can propose a new order for agents that have lower priority, each time it replaces its assignment. An agent A_i can propose an order according to the following rules:

1. Agents with higher priority than A_i and A_i itself, do not change priorities in the new order.
2. Agents with lower priority than A_i, in the current order, can change their priorities in the new order but not to a higher priority than A_i itself.

The counters attached to each agent ID in the $order$ list form a time-stamp. Initially, all time-stamp counters are zero and all agents start with the same $Current\_Order$. Each agent that proposes a new order changes the order of the pairs in its ordered list and updates the counters as follows:

1. The counters of agents with higher priority than A_i, according to the $Current\_order$, are not changed.
2. The counter of A_i is incremented by one.
3. The counters of agents with lower priority than A_i in the $Current\_order$ are set to zero.

Consider an example in which agent A_2 holds the following $Current\_order$: $(1,4)(2,3)(3,1)(4,0)(5,1)$. There are 5 agents $A_1...A_5$ and they are ordered according to their IDs from left to right. After replacing its assignment it changes the order to:

when received (ok?, (x_j, d_j) **do**:
1.   add (x_j, d_j) to $agent\_view$;
2.   remove inconsistent $nogoods$;
3.   **check_agent_view**;

when received (order, $received\_order$**) do**:
1.   **if** ($received\_order$ is more updated than $Current\_order$)
2. $Current\_order \leftarrow received\_order$;
3.   remove inconsistent nogoods;
4.   **check_agent_view**;

when received (nogood, x_j, $nogood$**) do**
1.   **if** ($nogood$ contains an agent x_k with lower priority than x_i)
2.   send (**nogood**, $(x_i, nogood)$) to x_k;
3.   send (**ok?**, $(x_i, current\_value)$ to x_j;
4.   **else**
5.   **if** ($nogood$ consistent with $\{Agent\_view \cup current\_assignment\}$)
6.   store $nogood$;
7.   **if** ($nogood$ contains an agent x_k that is not its neighbor)
8.   request x_k to add x_i as a neighbor;
9.   add (x_k, d_k) to $agent\_view$;
10.   **check_agent_view**;
11.   **else**
12.   send (**ok?**, $(x_i, current\_value)$) to x_j;

Fig. 2. The ABT_DO algorithm (first part)

$(1,4)(2,4)(4,0)(5,0)(3,0)$. In the new order, agent A_1 which had higher priority than A_2 in the previous order keeps its place and the value of its counter does not change. A_2 also keeps its place and the value of its counter is incremented by one. The rest of the agents, which have lower priority than A_2 in the previous order, change places as long as they are still located lower than A_2. The new order for these agents is A_4, A_5, A_3 and their counters are set to zero.

In ABT, agents send **ok?** messages to their neighbors whenever they perform an assignment. In ABT_DO, an agent can choose to change its $Current\_order$ after changing its assignment. If that is the case, beside sending **ok?** messages an agent sends **order** messages to all lower priority agents. The **order** message includes the agent's new $Current\_order$. An agent which receives an **order** message must determine if the received order is more updated than its own $Current\_order$. It decides by comparing the time-stamps lexicographically. Since orders are changed according to the above rules, every two orders must have a common prefix of the agents IDs since the agent that performs the change does not change its own position and the positions of higher priority agents. In the above example the common prefix includes agents A_1 and A_2. Since the agent proposing the new order increases its own counter, when two different orders are compared, at lease one of the time-stamp counters in the common prefix is different between the two orders. The more up-to-date order is the one for which the first different counter in the common prefix is larger. In the example above, any agent

procedure **check_agent_view**
1. **if**(*current_assignment* is not consistent with all
        higher priority assignments in *agent_view*)
2.   **if**(no value in D_i is consistent with all higher priority
            assignments in *agent_view*)
3.   **backtrack**;
4.   **else**
5.   select $d \in D_i$ where *agent_view* and d are consistent;
6.   *current_value* $\leftarrow d$;
7.   *Current_order* $\leftarrow$ **choose_new_order**
8.   send (**ok?**,(x_i, d)) to *neighbors*;
9.   send (**order**,*Current_order*) to *lower priority agents*;

procedure **backtrack**
1. *nogood* $\leftarrow$ **resolve_inconsistent_subset**;
2. **if** (*nogood* is empty)
3.   broadcast to other agents that there is no solution;
4.   **stop**;
5. select (x_j, d_j) where x_j has the lowest priority in nogood;
6. send (**nogood**, x_i, *nogood*) to x_j;
7. remove (x_j, d_j) from *agent_view*;
8. remove all *Nogoods* containing (x_j, d_j);
9. **check_agent_view**;

Fig. 3. The ABT_DO algorithm(second part)

which will receive the new order will know it is more updated than the previous order since the first pair is identical, but the counter of the second pair is larger.

When an agent A_i receives an order which is more up to date than its *Current_order*, it replaces its *Current_order* by the received order. The new order might change the location of the receiving agent with respect to other agents (in the new *Current_order*). In other words, one of the agents that had higher priority than A_i according to the old order, now has a lower priority than A_i or vise versa. Therefore, A_i rechecks the consistency of its current assignment and the validity of its stored *Nogoods* according to the new order. If the current assignment is inconsistent according to the new order, the agent makes a new attempt to assign its variable. In *ABT_DO* agents send **ok?** messages to all constraining agents (i.e. their neighbors in the constraints graph). Although agents might hold in their *Agent_views* assignments of agents with lower priorities, according to their *Current_order*, they eliminate values from their domain *only if they violate constraints with higher priority agents*.

A *Nogood* message is always checked according to the *Current_order* of the receiving agent. If the receiving agent is not the lowest priority agent in the *Nogood* according to its *Current_order*, it sends the *Nogood* to the lowest priority agent and sends an **ok?** message to the sender of the *Nogood*. This is a similar operation to that performed in standard *ABT* for any unaccepted *Nogood*.

Figures 2 and 3 present the code of asynchronous backtracking with dynamic ordering (*ABT_DO*).

When an **ok?** message is received (first procedure in Figure 2), the agent updates the *Agent_view* and removes inconsistent *Nogoods*. Then it calls **check_agent_view** to make sure its assignment is still consistent.

A new order received in an order message is accepted only if it is more up to date than the *Current_order* (second procedure of Figure 2). If so, the received order is stored and **check_agent_view** is called to make sure the current assignment is consistent with the higher priority assignments in the *Agent_view*.

When a *Nogood* is received (third procedure in Figure 2) the agent first checks if it is the lowest priority agent in the received *Nogood*, according to the *Current_order*. If not, it sends the *Nogood* to the lowest priority agent and an **ok?** message to the *Nogood* sender (lines 1-3). If the receiving agent is the lowest priority agent it performs the same operations as in the standard *ABT* algorithm (lines 4-12).

Procedure **backtrack** (Figure 3) is the same as in standard *ABT*. The *Nogood* is resolved and the result is sent to the lower priority agent in the *Nogood*, according to the *Current_order*.

Procedure **check_agent_view** (Figure 3) is very similar to standard *ABT* but the difference is important (lines 5-9). If the current assignment is not consistent and must be replaced and a new consistent assignment is found, the agent chooses a new order as its *Current_order* (line 7) and updates the corresponding time-stamp. Next, **ok?** messages are sent to all neighboring agents. The new order and its time-stamp counters are sent to all lower priority agents.

5 Correctness of *ABT_DO*

In order to prove the correctness of the *ABT_DO* algorithm we first establish two facts by proving the following lemmas:

Lemma 1. *The highest priority agent in the initial order remains the highest priority agent in all proposed orders.*

The proof for Lemma 1 is immediate from the two rules of reordering. Since no agent can propose a new order which changes the priority of higher priority agents and its own priority, no agent including the first can move the highest priority agent to a lower position. □

Lemma 2. *When the highest priority agent proposes a new order, it is more up to date than all previous orders.*

This proof is again immediate. In all previous orders the time-stamp counter of the first agent is smaller than the counter of the time-stamp counter of the first agent in the new proposed order. □

To prove correctness of a search algorithm for $DisCSPs$ one needs to prove that it is sound, complete and that it terminates. *ABT_DO*, like *ABT*, reports a solution when all agents are idle and no messages are sent. Its soundness follows from the soundness of *ABT* [1]. One point needs mentioning. Since no messages are traveling in the system in the idle state, all overriding messages have arrived at their destinations. This means that for every pair of constraining agents an agreement about their pairwise order has been achieved. One of each pair of constraining agents checks their constraint and no messages mean no violations, as in the proof for ABT [1].

To prove the completeness and termination of ABT_DO we use induction on the number of agents (i.e. number of variables) in the $DisCSP$. For a single agent $DisCSP$ the order is static therefore the completeness and termination of ABT implies the same for ABT_DO. Assume ABT_DO is complete and terminates for every $DisCSP$ with k agents where $k < n$. Consider a $DisCSP$ with n agents. According to Lemma 1 the agent with the highest priority in the initial order will not change its place. The highest priority agent assigns its variable for the first time and sends it along with its order proposal to other agents. The remaining $DisCSP$ has $n - 1$ agents and its initial order is that proposed by the first agent (all other orders are discarded according to Lemma 2). By the induction assumption the remaining $DisCSP$ is complete and terminates. If a solution to the induced $DisCSP$ is found, this means that the lower priority $n - 1$ agents are idle. So is the first (highest priority) agent since none of the others sends it any message. If a solution is not found, by the $n - 1$ lower priority agents, a single assignment $Nogood$ will be sent to the highest priority agent which will cause it to replace its assignment. The new assignment of the first agent and the new order proposed will induce a new $DisCSP$ of size $n-1$. The search on this new $DisCSP$ of size $n-1$ is also complete and terminates according to the induction assumption. The number of induced $DisCSPs$, created by the assignments of the highest priority agent is bound by the size of its domain. Therefore, the algorithm will terminate in a finite time.

The algorithm is complete since a solution to the $DisCSP$ must include one of the highest priority agent value assignments, which means that one of the induced $DisCSPs$ includes a solution iff the original $DisCSP$ includes a solution. This completes the correctness proof of ABT_DO □

If the network model, or privacy restraints, enable agents to communicate only with their neighbors in the constraints network, some small changes are needed in order to keep the algorithm correct. First, agents must be allowed to change only the order of lower priority *neighbors*. This means that the method **choose_new_order**, called in line 7 of procedure **check_agent_view**, changes the order by switching between the position of lower priority neighbors and leaving other lower priority agent at their current position. Second, whenever an updated order message is received, an agent informs its neighbors of its new $Current\_order$.

In order to prove that the above two changes do not affect the correctness of the algorithm we first establish the correctness of Lemmas 1 and 2 under these changes. Lemma 1 is not affected by the change since the rules for changing agents positions have become more strict, and still do not allow to change the position of higher priority agents. Lemma 2 holds because the time-stamp mechanism which promises its correctness has not changed. These Lemmas are the basis for the correctness of the induction which proves the algorithm is complete and terminates. However, we still need to prove the algorithm is sound. One of the assumptions that our soundness proof dependent on was that an idle state of the system would mean that every constrained couple of agents agrees on the order between them. This claim might not hold since the most up to date order is not sent to all agents. The following Lemma proves this claim is still true after the changes in the algorithm:

Lemma 3. *When the system reaches an idle state, every pair of constrained agents hold the same order.*

According to the changes described above, whenever one of the constrained agents receives an updated order message, it informs its neighbors. Therefore, all agents which have constraints with it will be notified and hold the updated order. If two agents are not informed with the most updated order, this would mean both of them are not lower priority neighbors of the reordering agent and as a result their current position in the order stays the same.

Lemma 3 implies that the algorithm is still sound according to our previous proof.□

6 Experimental Evaluation

The common approach in evaluating the performance of distributed algorithms is to compare two independent measures of performance - time, in the form of steps of computation [8,16], and communication load, in the form of the total number of messages sent [8].

Non concurrent steps of computation, are counted by a method similar to that of [7,9]. Every agent holds a counter of computation steps. Every message carries the value of the sending agent's counter. When an agent receives a message it updates its counter to the largest value between its own counter and the counter value carried by the message. By reporting the cost of the search as the largest counter held by some agent at the end of the search, a measure of non-concurrent search effort that is close to Lamports logical time is achieved [7]. If instead of steps of computation, the number of non concurrent constraints check is counted ($NCCC$s), then the local computational effort of agents in each step is measured [9].

Experiments were conducted on random networks of constraints of n variables, k values in each domain, a constraints density of p_1 and tightness p_2 (which are commonly used in experimental evaluations of CSP algorithms [13]). All three sets of experiments were conducted on networks with 20 agents ($n = 20$) each holding exactly one variable, 10 values for each variable ($k = 10$) and two values of constraints density $p_1 = 0.4$ and $p_1 = 0.7$. The tightness value p_2, is varied between 0.1 and 0.9, to cover all ranges of problem difficulty. For each pair of fixed density and tightness ($p1, p2$) 50 different random problems were solved by each algorithm and the results presented are an average of these 50 runs.

ABT_DO is compared to the run of standard ABT. For ordering variables in ABT_DO three different heuristics were used.

1. Random: each time an agent changes its assignment it randomly orders all agents with lower priorities in its $Current\_order$.
2. Domain-Size: This heuristic is inspired by the heuristics used for sequential assigning algorithms in [3]. Domain sizes are calculated based on the fact that each agent that performs an assignment sends its current domain size to all other agents. Every agent that replaces an assignment, orders the lower priority agents according to their domain size from the smallest to the largest.

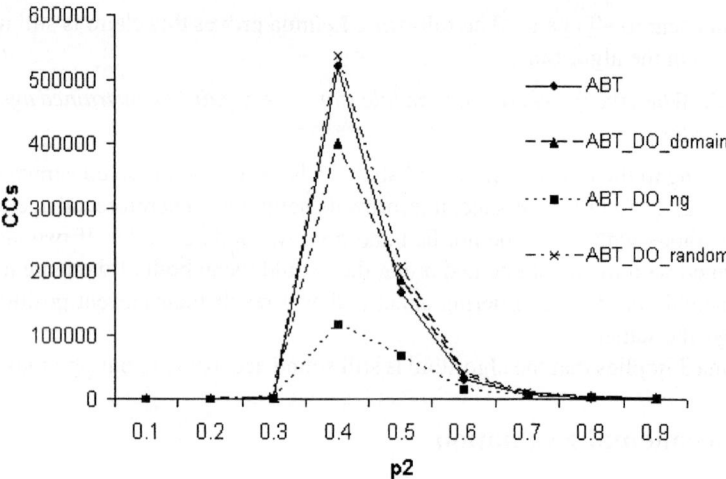

Fig. 4. Non concurrent constraints checks performed by ABT and ABT_DO using different order heuristics on low density DisCSPs ($p_1 = 0.4$)

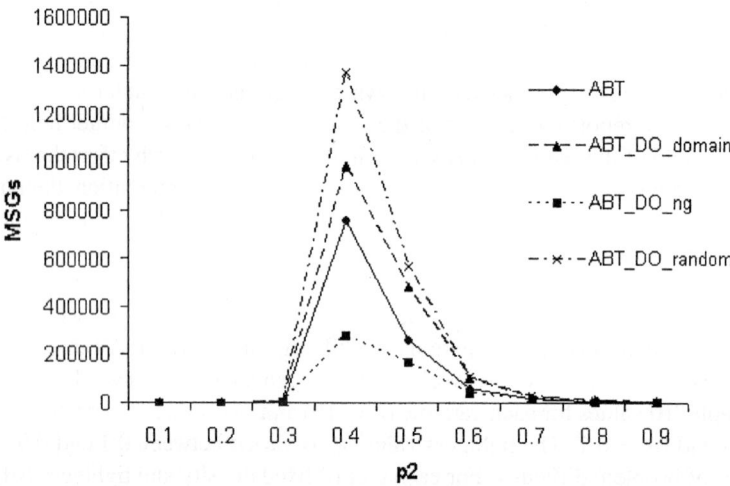

Fig. 5. Total number of messages sent by ABT and ABT_DO on low density DisCSPs ($p_1 = 0.4$)

3. Nogood-Triggered: Agents change the order of the lower priority agents only when they receive a $Nogood$ which eliminates their current assignment. In this case the agent moves the sender of the $Nogood$ to be in front of all other lower priority agents. This heuristic was first used for dynamic backtracking in centralized $CSPs$ [5].

Figure 4 presents the computational effort in number of non concurrent constraints checks to find a solution, performed by ABT and ABT_DO using the above three heuristics. The algorithms solve low density $DisCSPs$ with $p_1 = 0.4$. ABT_DO with

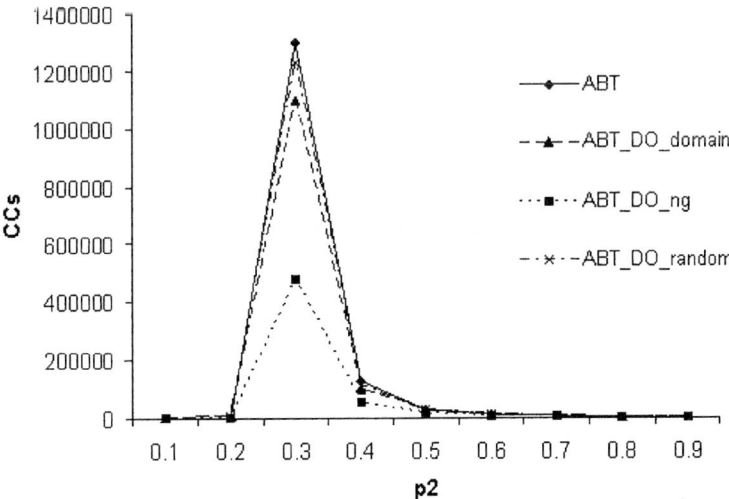

Fig. 6. Non concurrent constraints checks performed by ABT and ABT_DO using different order heuristics on high density DisCSPs ($p_1 = 0.7$)

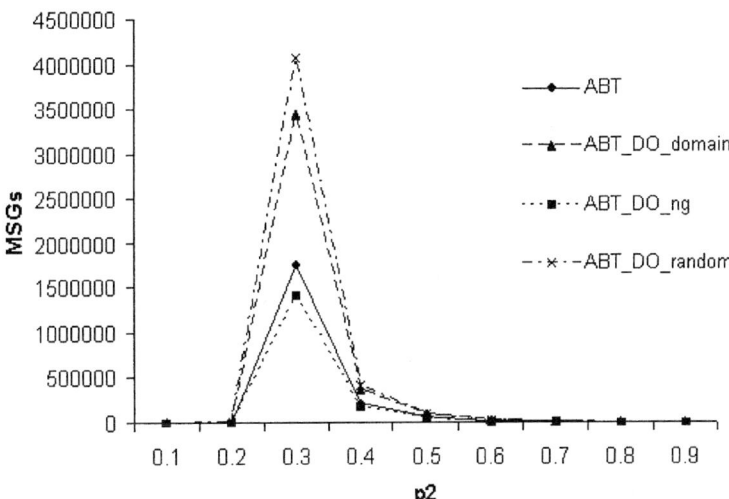

Fig. 7. Total number of messages sent by ABT and ABT_DO on high density DisCSPs ($p_1 = 0.7$)

random ordering does not improve the results of standard ABT. ABT_DO which uses domain sizes to order the lower priority agents performs slightly better than ABT. The largest improvement is gained by using the *Nogood-trigerred* heuristic. For the hardest $DisCSP$ instances, ABT_DO with the *Nogood-trigerred* heuristic improves the performance of standard ABT by a factor of 5.

Figure 5 presents the total number of messages sent by the algorithms for the same problems. While ABT_DO with random ordering heuristic shows similar run time results to standard ABT it sends almost twice as many messages. This can be expected since in ABT_DO agents send additional **order** messages and **ok?** messages to all their neighbors while in standard ABT, **ok?** messages are sent only to lower priority agents. ABT_DO with domain size ordering sends more messages than standard ABT but less than the random ordering version. The really interesting result is that ABT_DO with the *Nogood-triggered* heuristic sends *less* messages than ABT. Counting the additional **ok?** messages (sent to higher priority agents) and the **order** messages, it still sends fewer messages than standard ABT on the hardest $DisCSP$ instances.

Figures 6 and 7 present similar results in runtime, for high density *DisCSPs* with $p_1 = 0.7$. Clearly, the influence of good ordering heuristics on the performance of the algorithm is independent of network density. The results in total communication are closer than in the low density case.

7 Discussion

Dynamic ordering is a powerful heuristic used to improve the run-time of centralized CSP algorithms [4] and of distributed CSP algorithms with sequential assignments [3,10]. The results in the previous section, show that dynamic ordering must be combined with the right heuristic in order to improve the run-time and justify the overhead in message load of asynchronous backtracking. A random order heuristic does not improve the run-time of standard ABT and sends many more messages. Surprisingly, ordering the agents according to their domain size does not gain a large improvement as reported for sequential (synchronous) assignments algorithms by [3]. This can be explained by the fact that asynchronous backtracking prunes the $DisCSP$ search tree by storing *Nogoods* which prevent it from trying to extend inconsistent tuples. *Nogoods* are discarded in standard ABT whenever they become irrelevant [1]. In ABT_DO, this can happen when an agent holding a *Nogood* changes places with one of the other agents whose assignment appears in the *Nogood*. This generates the need for additional (redundant) messages reporting the same *Nogoods*.

On the other hand, the *Nogood* triggered heuristic, inspired by *Dynamic Backtracking* [5] was found to be very effective. In this heuristic, the above example of losing useful information cannot occur. *Nogoods* are resolved and created according to dynamic backtracking. They include all the conflicting assignments held by the *Nogood* sender. An agent that is moved to a higher priority position in the order, is moved lower than all the agents with conflicting assignments, therefore no *Nogoods* are discarded. The results show that this heuristic is very effective in both measures, run-time and network load. The improvement in network load is particularly striking in view of the additional ordering messages of ABT_DO.

8 Conclusions

Most of the studies of *Asynchronous Backtracking* used a static order of agents and variables [6,16,1,11]. An exponential space algorithm using dynamic ordering has shown improvement in run-time over ABT [16]. The only study that suggested dynamic ordering in ABT with polynomial space used a complex method including additional abstract agents [12]. The results presented in [12] show a minor improvement compared to standard, static order, ABT.

The present study proposes a simple way of performing dynamic ordering in ABT with polynomial space. The ordering is performed as in sequential assignment algorithms by each agent changing only the order of agents following it in the former order. A simple method of time-stamping [10] is used to determine the most updated proposed order.

When a heuristic order inspired by dynamic backtracking [5] is used to dynamically reorder agents, there is a significant improvement in run-time and network load over standard ABT.

References

1. C. Bessiere, A. Maestre, I. Brito, and P. Meseguer. Asynchronous backtracking without adding links: a new member in the abt family. *Artificial Intelligence*, 161:1-2:7–24, January 2005.
2. C. Bessiere, A. Maestre, and P. Messeguer. Distributed dynamic backtracking. In *Proc. Workshop on Distributed Constraint of IJCAI01*, 2001.
3. I. Brito and P. Meseguer. Synchronous,asnchronous and hybrid algorithms for discsp. In *Workshop on Distributed Constraints Reasoning(DCR-04) CP-2004*, Toronto, September 2004.
4. Rina Dechter. *Constraints Processing*. Morgan Kaufman, 2003.
5. M. L. Ginsberg. Dynamic backtracking. *J. of Artificial Intelligence Research*, 1:25–46, 1993.
6. Y. Hamadi. Distributed interleaved parallel and cooperative search in constraint satisfaction networks. In *Proc. IAT-01*, Singappore, 2001.
7. L. Lamport. Time, clocks, and the ordering of events in distributed system. *Communication of the ACM*, 2:95–114, April 1978.
8. N. A. Lynch. *Distributed Algorithms*. Morgan Kaufmann Series, 1997.
9. A. Meisels, I. Razgon, E. Kaplansky, and R. Zivan. Comparing performance of distributed constraints processing algorithms. In *Proc. AAMAS-2002 Workshop on Distributed Constraint Reasoning DCR*, pages 86–93, Bologna, July 2002.
10. T. Nguyen, D. Sam-Hroud, and B. Faltings. Dynamic distributed backjumping. In *Proc. 5th workshop on distributed constraints reasoning DCR-04*, Toronto, September 2004.
11. M. C. Silaghi and B. Faltings. Asynchronous aggregation and consistency in distributed constraint satisfaction. *Artificial Intelligence*, 161:1-2:25–54, January 2005.
12. M. C. Silaghi, D. Sam-Haroud, and B. Faltings. Hybridizing abt and awc into a polynomial space, complete protocol with reordering. Technical Report 01/#364, EPFL, May 2001.
13. B. M. Smith. Locating the phase transition in binary constraint satisfaction problems. *Artificial Intelligence*, 81:155 – 181, 1996.
14. G. Solotorevsky, E. Gudes, and A. Meisels. Modeling and solving distributed constraint satisfaction problems (dcsps). In *Constraint Processing-96*, pages 561–2, New Hampshire, October 1996.

15. M. Yokoo. Asynchronous weak-commitment search for solving distributed constraint satisfaction problems. In *Proc. 1st Intrnat. Conf. on Const. Progr.*, pages 88 – 102, Cassis, France, 1995.
16. M. Yokoo. Algorithms for distributed constraint satisfaction problems: A review. *Autonomous Agents & Multi-Agent Sys.*, 3:198–212, 2000.
17. M. Yokoo, E. H. Durfee, T. Ishida, and K. Kuwabara. Distributed constraint satisfaction problem: Formalization and algorithms. *IEEE Trans. on Data and Kn. Eng.*, 10:673–685, 1998.
18. R. Zivan and A. Meisels. Synchronous vs asynchronous search on discsps. In *Proc. 1st European Workshop on Multi Agent System, EUMAS*, Oxford, December 2003.

Incremental Algorithms for Local Search from Existential Second-Order Logic

Magnus Ågren, Pierre Flener, and Justin Pearson

Department of Information Technology,
Uppsala University, Box 337, SE – 751 05 Uppsala, Sweden
{agren, pierref, justin}@it.uu.se

Abstract. Local search is a powerful and well-established method for solving hard combinatorial problems. Yet, until recently, it has provided very little user support, leading to time-consuming and error-prone implementation tasks. We introduce a scheme that, from a high-level description of a constraint in existential second-order logic with counting, automatically synthesises incremental penalty calculation algorithms. The performance of the scheme is demonstrated by solving real-life instances of a financial portfolio design problem that seem unsolvable in reasonable time by complete search.

1 Introduction

Local search is a powerful and well-established method for solving hard combinatorial problems [1]. Yet, until recently, it has provided very little user support, leading to time-consuming and error-prone implementation tasks. The recent emergence of languages and systems for local search, sometimes based on novel abstractions, has alleviated the user of much of this burden [10,16,12,11].

However, if a problem cannot readily be modelled using the primitive constraints of such a local search system, then the *user* has to perform some of those time-consuming and error-prone tasks. These include the design of algorithms for the calculation of penalties of user-defined constraints. These algorithms are called very often in the innermost loop of local search and thus need to be implemented particularly efficiently: incrementality is crucial. Would it thus not be nice if also this task could be performed fully automatically and satisfactorily by a local search system? In this paper, we design a scheme for doing just that, based on an extension of the idea of combinators [15] to quantifiers. Our *key contributions* are as follows:

- We propose the usage of existential second-order logic with counting as a *high-level modelling language* for (user-defined) constraints. It accommodates set variables and captures at least the complexity class NP.
- We design a scheme for the *automated synthesis of incremental penalty calculation algorithms* from a description of a (user-defined) constraint in that language. We have developed an *implementation* of this scheme.

– We propose a *new benchmark problem* for local search, with applications in finance. Using our local search framework, we *exactly solve real-life instances* that seem unsolvable in reasonable time by complete search; the performance is competitive with a fast approximation method based on complete search.

The rest of this paper is organised as follows. In Section 2, we define the background for this work, namely constraint satisfaction problems over scalar and set variables as well as local search concepts. The core of this paper are Sections 3 to 6, where we introduce the used modelling language and show how incremental algorithms for calculating penalties can be automatically synthesised from a model therein. In Section 7, we demonstrate the performance of this approach by solving real-life instances of a financial portfolio design problem. Finally, we summarise our results, discuss related work, and outline future work in Section 8.

2 Preliminaries

As usual, a *constraint satisfaction problem (CSP)* is a triple $\langle V, D, C \rangle$, where V is a finite set of variables, D is a finite set of domains, each $D_v \in D$ containing the set of possible values for the corresponding variable $v \in V$, and C is a finite set of constraints, each $c \in C$ being defined on a subset of the variables in V and specifying their valid combinations of values.

Definition 1 (Set Variable and its Universe). *Let $P = \langle V, D, C \rangle$ be a CSP. A variable $S \in V$ is a set variable if its corresponding domain $D_S = 2^{\mathcal{U}_S}$, where $\mathcal{U}_S$ is a finite set of values of some type, called the* universe *of S.*

Without loss of generality, we assume that all the set variables have a common universe, denoted $\mathcal{U}$. We also assume that *all* the variables are set variables, and denote such a set-CSP by $\langle V, \mathcal{U}, C \rangle$. This is of course a limitation, since many models contain both set variables and scalar variables. Fortunately, interesting applications, such as the ones in this paper and in [2], can be modelled using only set variables.

A constraint program assigns values to the variables one by one, but local search maintains an (initially arbitrary) assignment of values to *all* the variables:

Definition 2 (Configuration). *Let $P = \langle V, \mathcal{U}, C \rangle$ be a set-CSP. A configuration for P (or V) is a total function $k : V \to 2^{\mathcal{U}}$.*

As usual, the notation $k \models \phi$ expresses that the open formula ϕ is satisfied under the configuration k.

Example 1. Consider a set-CSP $P = \langle \{S_1, S_2, S_3\}, \{d_1, d_2, d_3\}, \{c_1, c_2\} \rangle$. A configuration for P is given by $k(S_1) = \{d_3\}, k(S_2) = \{d_1, d_2\}, k(S_3) = \emptyset$, or equivalently as the set of mappings $\{S_1 \mapsto \{d_3\}, S_2 \mapsto \{d_1, d_2\}, S_3 \mapsto \emptyset\}$. Another configuration for P is given by $k' = \{S_1 \mapsto \emptyset, S_2 \mapsto \{d_1, d_2, d_3\}, S_3 \mapsto \emptyset\}$.

Local search iteratively makes a small change to the current configuration, upon examining the merits of many such changes. The configurations thus examined constitute the neighbourhood of the current configuration:

Definition 3 (Neighbourhood). *Let K be the set of all configurations for a (set-)CSP P and let $k \in K$. A neighbourhood function for P is a function $\mathcal{N} : K \to 2^K$. The neighbourhood of P with respect to k and $\mathcal{N}$ is the set $\mathcal{N}(k)$.*

Example 2. Reconsider P and k from Example 1. A neighbourhood of P with respect to k and some neighbourhood function for P is the set $\{k_1 = \{S_1 \mapsto \emptyset, S_2 \mapsto \{d_1, d_2, d_3\}, S_3 \mapsto \emptyset\}, k_2 = \{S_1 \mapsto \emptyset, S_2 \mapsto \{d_1, d_2\}, S_3 \mapsto \{d_3\}\}\}$. This neighbourhood function moves the value d_3 in S_1 to S_2 or S_3.

The penalty of a CSP is an estimate on how much its constraints are violated:

Definition 4 (Penalty). *Let $P = \langle V, D, C \rangle$ be a (set-)CSP and let K be the set of all configurations for P. A penalty function of a constraint $c \in C$ is a function $penalty(c) : K \to \mathbb{N}$ such that $penalty(c)(k) = 0$ if and only if c is satisfied under configuration k. The penalty of a constraint $c \in C$ with respect to a configuration $k \in K$ is $penalty(c)(k)$. The penalty of P with respect to a configuration $k \in K$ is the sum $\sum_{c \in C} penalty(c)(k)$.*

Example 3. Consider once again P from Example 1 and let c_1 and c_2 be the constraints $S_1 \subseteq S_2$ and $d_3 \in S_3$ respectively. Let the penalty functions of c_1 and c_2 be defined by $penalty(c_1)(k) = |k(S_1) \setminus k(S_2)|$ and $penalty(c_2)(k) = 0$ if $d_3 \in k(S_3)$ and 1 otherwise. Now, the penalties of P with respect to the configurations k_1 and k_2 from Example 2 are $penalty(c_1)(k_1) + penalty(c_2)(k_1) = 1$ and $penalty(c_1)(k_2) + penalty(c_2)(k_2) = 0$, respectively.

3 Second-Order Logic

We use *existential second-order logic* ($\exists$SOL) [8], extended with counting, for modelling the constraints of a set-CSP. $\exists$SOL is very expressive: it captures the complexity class NP [5]. Figure 1 shows the BNF grammar for the used language, which we will refer to as $\exists$SOL$^+$. Some of the production rules are highlighted and the reason for this is explained below. The language uses common mathematical and logical notations. Note that its set of relational operators is closed under negation. A formula in $\exists$SOL$^+$ is of the form $\exists S_1 \cdots \exists S_n \phi$, i.e., a sequence of existentially quantified set variables, ranging over the power set of an implicit common universe $\mathcal{U}$, and constrained by a logical formula ϕ. The usual precedence rules apply when parentheses are omitted, i.e., $\neg$ has highest precedence, $\wedge$ has higher precedence than $\vee$, etc.

Example 4. The constraint $S \subset T$ on the set variables S and T may be expressed in $\exists$SOL$^+$ by the formula:

$$\exists S \exists T ((\forall x(x \notin S \vee x \in T)) \wedge (\exists x(x \in T \wedge x \notin S))) \tag{1}$$

The constraint $|S \cap T| \leq m$ on the set variables S and T and the natural-number constant m may be expressed in $\exists$SOL$^+$ by the formula:

$$\exists S \exists T \exists I ((\forall x(x \in I \leftrightarrow x \in S \wedge x \in T)) \wedge |I| \leq m) \tag{2}$$

Note that we used an additional set variable I to represent the intersection $S \cap T$.

```
⟨Constraint⟩ ::= (∃ ⟨S⟩)⁺ ⟨Formula⟩

⟨Formula⟩  ::= (⟨Formula⟩)
             | (∀ | ∃)⟨x⟩ ⟨Formula⟩
             | ⟨Formula⟩ (∧ | ∨ | → | ↔ | ←) ⟨Formula⟩
             | ¬⟨Formula⟩
             | ⟨Literal⟩

⟨Literal⟩  ::= ⟨x⟩ (∈ | ∉) ⟨S⟩
             | ⟨x⟩ (< | ≤ | = | ≠ | ≥ | >) ⟨y⟩
             | |⟨S⟩| (< | ≤ | = | ≠ | ≥ | >) ⟨a⟩
```

Fig. 1. The BNF grammar for the language ∃SOL⁺ where terminal symbols are underlined. The non-terminal symbol ⟨S⟩ denotes an identifier for a bound set variable S such that $S \subseteq \mathcal{U}$, while ⟨x⟩ and ⟨y⟩ denote identifiers for bound variables x and y such that $x, y \in \mathcal{U}$, and ⟨a⟩ denotes a natural number constant. The core subset of ∃SOL⁺ corresponds to the language given by the non-highlighted production rules.

In Section 4 we will define the penalty of formulas in ∃SOL⁺. Before we do this, we define a core subset of this language that will be used in that definition. This is only due to the way we define the penalty and does not pose any limitations on the expressiveness of the language: Any formula in ∃SOL⁺ may be transformed into a formula in that core subset, in a way shown next.

The transformations are standard and are only described briefly. First, given a formula $\exists S_1 \cdots \exists S_n \phi$ in ∃SOL⁺, we remove its negations by pushing them downward, all the way to the literals of ϕ, which are replaced by their negated counterparts. Assuming that ϕ is the formula $\forall x(\neg(x \in S \land x \notin S'))$, it is transformed into $\forall x(x \notin S \lor x \in S')$. This is possible because the set of relational operators in ∃SOL⁺ is closed under negation. Second, equivalences are transformed into conjunctions of implications, which are in turn transformed into disjunctions. Assuming that ϕ is the formula $\forall x(x \in S_1 \leftrightarrow x \in S_2)$, it is transformed into $\forall x((x \notin S_1 \lor x \in S_2) \land (x \in S_1 \lor x \notin S_2))$.

By performing these transformations for ϕ (and recursively for the subformulas of ϕ) in any formula $\exists S_1 \cdots \exists S_n \phi$, we end up with the non-highlighted subset of the language in Figure 1, for which we will define the penalty.

Example 5. (1) is in the core subset of ∃SOL⁺. The core equivalent of (2) is:

$$\exists S \exists T \exists I ((\forall x((x \notin I \lor x \in S \land x \in T) \land (x \in I \lor x \notin S \lor x \notin T))) \land |I| \leq m) \quad (3)$$

From now on we assume that any formula said in ∃SOL⁺ is already in the core subset of ∃SOL⁺. The full language just offers convenient shorthand notations.

4 The Penalty of an ∃SOL⁺ Formula

In order to use (closed) formulas in ∃SOL⁺ as constraints in our local search framework, we must define the penalty function of such a formula according to Definition 4, which is done inductively below. It is important to stress that *this calculation is totally generic and automatable, as it is based only on the syntax of the formula and the semantics of the quantifiers, connectives, and relational operators of the* $\exists SOL^+$ *language, but not on the intended semantics of the formula.* A human might well give a different penalty function to that formula, and a way of calculating it that better exploits globality, but the scheme below requires no such user participation.

We need to express the penalty with respect to the values of any bound first-order variables. We will therefore pass around an (initially empty) environment Γ in the definition below, where Γ is a total function from the currently bound first-order variables into the common universe of values.

Definition 5 (Penalty of an $\exists SOL^+$ Formula). *Let $\mathcal{F}$ be a formula in $\exists SOL^+$ of the form $\exists S_1 \cdots \exists S_n \phi$, let k be a configuration for $\{S_1, \ldots, S_n\}$, and let Γ be an environment. The* penalty *of $\mathcal{F}$ with respect to k and Γ is given by a function penalty' defined by:*

(a) $penalty'(\Gamma)(\exists S_1 \cdots \exists S_n \phi)(k) = penalty'(\Gamma)(\phi)(k)$

(b) $penalty'(\Gamma)(\forall x \phi)(k) = \sum_{u \in \mathcal{U}} penalty'(\Gamma \cup \{x \mapsto u\})(\phi)(k)$

(c) $penalty'(\Gamma)(\exists x \phi)(k) = \min\{penalty'(\Gamma \cup \{x \mapsto u\})(\phi)(k) \mid u \in \mathcal{U}\}$

(d) $penalty'(\Gamma)(\phi \land \psi)(k) = penalty'(\Gamma)(\phi)(k) + penalty'(\Gamma)(\psi)(k)$

(e) $penalty'(\Gamma)(\phi \lor \psi)(k) = \min\{penalty'(\Gamma)(\phi)(k), penalty'(\Gamma)(\psi)(k)\}$

(f) $penalty'(\Gamma)(x \leq y)(k) = \begin{cases} 0, & \text{if } \Gamma(x) \leq \Gamma(y) \\ 1, & \text{otherwise} \end{cases}$

(g) $penalty'(\Gamma)(|S| \leq c)(k) = \begin{cases} 0, & \text{if } |k(S)| \leq c \\ |k(S)| - c, & \text{otherwise} \end{cases}$

(h) $penalty'(\Gamma)(x \in S)(k) = \begin{cases} 0, & \text{if } \Gamma(x) \in k(S) \\ 1, & \text{otherwise} \end{cases}$

(i) $penalty'(\Gamma)(x \notin S)(k) = \begin{cases} 0, & \text{if } \Gamma(x) \notin k(S) \\ 1, & \text{otherwise} \end{cases}$

Now, the penalty function *of $\mathcal{F}$ is the function $penalty(\mathcal{F}) = penalty'(\emptyset)(\mathcal{F})$.*

In the definition above, for (sub)formulas of the form $x \diamond y$ and $|S| \diamond c$, where $\diamond \in \{<, \leq, =, \neq, \geq, >\}$, we only show the cases where $\diamond \in \{\leq\}$; the other cases are defined similarly. (The same applies to the algorithms in Section 5.) The following proposition is a direct consequence of the definition above:

Proposition 1. *The penalty of a formula $\mathcal{F}$ with respect to a configuration k is 0 if and only if $\mathcal{F}$ is satisfied under k: $penalty(\exists S_1 \cdots \exists S_n \phi)(k) = 0 \Leftrightarrow k \models \phi$.*

In our experience, the calculated penalties of violated constraints are often meaningful, as shown in the following example.

Example 6. Let $\mathcal{U} = \{a, b\}$ and let k be the configuration for $\{S, T\}$ such that $k(S) = k(T) = \{a\}$. Let us calculate $penalty(\exists S \exists T \phi)(k)$, where $\exists S \exists T \phi$ is the formula (1) The initial call matches case (a) which gives the recursive call $penalty'(\emptyset)(\phi)(k)$. Since ϕ is of the form $\psi \wedge \psi'$ this call matches case (d), which is defined as the sum of the recursive calls on ψ and ψ'. For the first recursive call, ψ is the formula $\forall x(x \notin S \vee x \in T)$. Hence it will match case (b), which is defined as the sum of the recursive calls $penalty'(\{x \mapsto a\})(x \notin S \vee x \in T)(k)$ and $penalty'(\{x \mapsto b\})(x \notin S \vee x \in T)(k)$ (one for each of the values a and b in $\mathcal{U}$). Both of these match case (e) which, for the first one, gives the minimum of the recursive calls $penalty'(\{x \mapsto a\})(x \notin S)(k)$ and $penalty'(\{x \mapsto a\})(x \in T)(k)$. This value is $\min\{1,0\} = 0$ since $a \in T$. A similar reasoning for the second one gives the value $\min\{0,1\} = 0$ as well since $b \notin S$. Hence the recursive call on ψ gives $0 + 0 = 0$. This means that ψ is satisfied and should indeed contribute nothing to the overall penalty. A similar reasoning for the recursive call on ψ', which is $\exists x(x \in T \wedge x \notin S)$, gives $\min\{1,1\} = 1$. This means that ψ' is violated: the calculated contribution of 1 to the overall penalty means that no value of $\mathcal{U}$ belongs to T but not to S. Hence the returned overall penalty is $0 + 1 = 1$.

5 Incremental Penalty Maintenance Using Penalty Trees

In our local search framework, given a formula $\mathcal{F}$ in $\exists SOL^+$, we could use Definition 5 to calculate the penalty of $\mathcal{F}$ with respect to a configuration k, and then similarly for each configuration k' in a neighbourhood $\mathcal{N}(k)$ to be evaluated. However, a complete recalculation of the penalty with respect to Definition 5 is impractical, since $\mathcal{N}(k)$ is usually a very large set.

In local search it is crucial to use *incremental algorithms* when evaluating the penalty of a constraint with respect to a neighbour k' to a current configuration k. We will now present a scheme for incremental maintenance of the penalty of a formula in $\exists SOL^+$ with respect to Definition 5. This scheme is based on viewing a formula $\mathcal{F}$ in $\exists SOL^+$ as a syntax tree and observing that, given the penalty with respect to k, only the paths from the leaves that contain variables that are changed in k' compared to k to the root node need to be updated to obtain the penalty with respect to k'.

5.1 The Penalty Tree of a Formula

First, a syntax tree **T** of a formula $\mathcal{F}$ in $\exists SOL^+$ of the form $\exists S_1 \cdots \exists S_n \phi$ is constructed in the usual way. Literals in $\mathcal{F}$ of the form $x \in S$, $x \notin S$, $x \Diamond y$, and $|S| \Diamond k$ (where $\Diamond \in \{<, \leq, =, \neq, \geq, >\}$) are leaves in **T**. Subformulas in $\mathcal{F}$ of the form $\psi \square \psi'$ (where $\square \in \{\wedge, \vee\}$) are subtrees in **T** with $\square$ as parent node and the trees of ψ and ψ' as children. When possible, formulas of the form $\psi_1 \square \cdots \square \psi_m$ give rise to one parent node with m children. Subformulas in $\mathcal{F}$ of the form $\forall x \psi$ (resp. $\exists x \psi$) are subtrees in **T** with $\forall x$ (resp. $\exists x$) as parent node and the tree of ψ as only child. Finally, $\exists S_1 \cdots \exists S_n$ is the root node of **T** with the tree of ϕ as child. As an example of this, Figure 2 shows the syntax tree of formula (3). Note that it contains additional information, to be explained in Section 5.2.

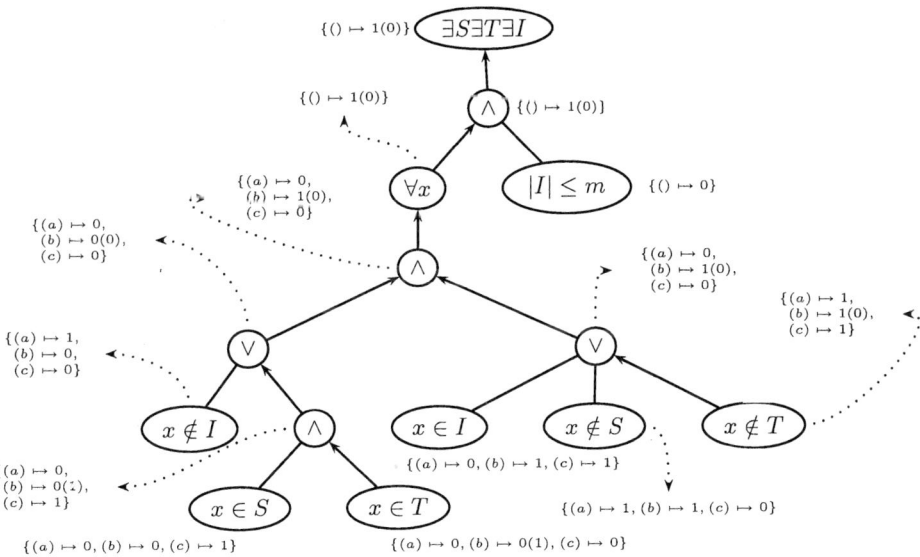

Fig. 2. Penalty tree of formula (3)

Assume that **T** is the syntax tree of a formula $\mathcal{F} = \exists S_1 \cdots \exists S_n \phi$. We will now extend **T** into a penalty tree in order to obtain incremental penalty maintenance of $\mathcal{F}$. Given an initial configuration k for $\{S_1, \ldots, S_n\}$, the penalty with respect to k of the subformula that the tree rooted at node **n** represents is stored in each node **n** of **T**. This implies that the penalty stored in the root node of **T** is equal to $penalty(\mathcal{F})(k)$. When a configuration k' in the neighbourhood of k is to be evaluated, the only paths in **T** that may have changed are those leading from leaves containing any of the set variables S_i that are affected by the change of k to k'. By starting at each of these leaves $l(S_i)$ and updating the penalty with respect to the change of S_i of each node on the path from l to the root node of **T**, we can incrementally calculate $penalty(\mathcal{F})(k')$ given k.

5.2 Initialising the Nodes with Penalties

For the descendants of nodes representing subformulas that introduce bound variables, we must store the penalty with respect to *every* possible mapping of those variables. For example, the child node **n** of a node for a subformula of the form $\forall x \phi$ will have a penalty stored for each $u \in \mathcal{U}$. Generally, the penalty stored at a node **n** is a mapping, denoted $p(\mathbf{n})$, from the possible tuples of values of the bound variables at **n** to $\mathbb{N}$. Assume, for example, that at **n** there are two bound variables x and y (introduced in that order) and that $\mathcal{U} = \{a, b\}$. Then the penalty stored at **n** after initialisation will be the mapping $\{(a, a) \mapsto p_1, (a, b) \mapsto p_2, (b, a) \mapsto p_3, (b, b) \mapsto p_4\}$ where $\{p_1, p_2, p_3, p_4\} \subset \mathbb{N}$. The first element of each tuple corresponds to x and the second one to y. If there are no bound variables at a particular node, then the penalty is a mapping $\{() \mapsto q\}$, i.e., the empty tuple mapped to some $q \in \mathbb{N}$.

Algorithm 1. Initialises the penalty mappings of a penalty tree

function $initialise(\mathbf{T}, \Gamma, \mathcal{U}, k)$
  match T **with**
    $\exists S_1 \cdots \exists S_n \phi \longrightarrow p(\mathbf{T}) \leftarrow \{tuple(\Gamma) \mapsto initialise(\phi, \Gamma, \mathcal{U}, k)\}$
    $|\ \forall x \phi \longrightarrow p(\mathbf{T}) \leftarrow p(\mathbf{T}) \cup \{tuple(\Gamma) \mapsto \sum_{u \in \mathcal{U}} initialise(\phi, \Gamma \cup \{x \mapsto u\}, \mathcal{U}, k)\}$
    $|\ \exists x \phi \longrightarrow$
      $p(\mathbf{T}) \leftarrow p(\mathbf{T}) \cup \{tuple(\Gamma) \mapsto \min\{initialise(\phi, \Gamma \cup \{x \mapsto u\}, \mathcal{U}, k) \mid u \in \mathcal{U}\}\}$
    $|\ \phi_1 \wedge \cdots \wedge \phi_m \longrightarrow p(\mathbf{T}) \leftarrow p(\mathbf{T}) \cup \{tuple(\Gamma) \mapsto \sum_{1 \leq i \leq m} initialise(\phi_i, \Gamma, \mathcal{U}, k)\}$
    $|\ \phi_1 \vee \cdots \vee \phi_m \longrightarrow$
      $p(\mathbf{T}) \leftarrow p(\mathbf{T}) \cup \{tuple(\Gamma) \mapsto \min\{initialise(\phi, \Gamma, \mathcal{U}, k) \mid \phi \in \{\phi_1, \ldots, \phi_m\}\}\}$
    $|\ x \leq y \longrightarrow p(\mathbf{T}) \leftarrow p(\mathbf{T}) \cup \left\{ tuple(\Gamma) \mapsto \begin{cases} 0, & \text{if } \Gamma(x) \leq \Gamma(y) \\ 1, & \text{otherwise} \end{cases} \right\}$
    $|\ |S| \leq m \longrightarrow p(\mathbf{T}) \leftarrow p(\mathbf{T}) \cup \left\{ tuple(\Gamma) \mapsto \begin{cases} 0, & \text{if } |k(S)| \leq m \\ |k(S)| - m, & \text{otherwise} \end{cases} \right\}$
    $|\ x \in S \longrightarrow p(\mathbf{T}) \leftarrow p(\mathbf{T}) \cup \left\{ tuple(\Gamma) \mapsto \begin{cases} 0, & \text{if } \Gamma(x) \in k(S) \\ 1, & \text{otherwise} \end{cases} \right\}$
    $|\ x \notin S \longrightarrow p(\mathbf{T}) \leftarrow p(\mathbf{T}) \cup \left\{ tuple(\Gamma) \mapsto \begin{cases} 0, & \text{if } \Gamma(x) \notin k(S) \\ 1, & \text{otherwise} \end{cases} \right\}$
  end match
  return $p(\mathbf{T})(tuple(\Gamma))$
function $tuple(\Gamma)$
  return $(\Gamma(x_1), \ldots, \Gamma(x_n))$ ▷ $\{x_1, \ldots, x_n\} = domain(\Gamma)$, introduced into Γ in that order.

Algorithm 1 shows the function $initialise(\mathbf{T}, \Gamma, \mathcal{U}, k)$ that initialises a penalty tree $\mathbf{T}$ of a formula with penalty mappings with respect to an (initially empty) environment Γ, a universe $\mathcal{U}$, and a configuration k. By abuse of notation, we let formulas in $\exists\text{SOL}^+$ denote their corresponding penalty trees, e.g., $\forall x \phi$ denotes the penalty tree with $\forall x$ as root node and the tree representing ϕ as only child, $\phi_1 \wedge \cdots \wedge \phi_m$ denotes the penalty tree with $\wedge$ as root node and the subtrees of all the ϕ_i as children, etc. Note that we use an auxiliary function $tuple$ that, given an environment Γ, returns the tuple of values with respect to Γ. We also assume that before $initialise$ is called for a penalty tree $\mathbf{T}$, the penalty mapping of each node in $\mathbf{T}$ is the empty set.

Example 7. Let $k = \{S \mapsto \{a, b\}, T \mapsto \{a, b, c\}, I \mapsto \{a\}\}$, let $\mathcal{U} = \{a, b, c\}$, and let $m = 1$. Figure 2 shows the penalty tree $\mathbf{T}$ with penalty mappings (dotted arrows connect nodes to their mappings) after $initialise(\mathbf{T}, \emptyset, \mathcal{U}, k)$ has been called for formula (3). As can be seen at the root node, the initial penalty is 1. Indeed, there is *one* value, namely b, that is in S and T but not in I.

5.3 Maintaining the Penalties

We will now present a way of incrementally updating the penalty mappings of a penalty tree. This is based on the observation that, given an initialised penalty tree $\mathbf{T}$, a current configuration k, and a configuration to evaluate k', only the paths leading from any leaf in $\mathbf{T}$ affected by changing k to k' to the root node of $\mathbf{T}$ need to be updated.

Algorithm 2 shows the function $submit(\mathbf{n}, \mathbf{n}', \mathcal{A}, k, k')$ that updates the penalty mappings of a penalty tree incrementally. It is a recursive function where informa-

Algorithm 2. Updates the penalty mappings of a penalty tree

function $submit(\mathbf{n}, \mathbf{n}', \mathcal{A}, k, k')$
    $update(\mathbf{n}, \mathbf{n}', \mathcal{A})$ ▷ First update **n** with respect to $\mathbf{n}'$.
    if All children affected by the change of k to k' are done **then**
        if n is not the root node **then**
            $submit(parent(\mathbf{n}), \mathbf{n}, \mathcal{A} \cup changed(\mathbf{n}), k, k')$
            $changed(\mathbf{n}) \leftarrow \emptyset$
        else ()   ▷ We are at the root. Done!
    else $changed(\mathbf{n}) \leftarrow changed(\mathbf{n}) \cup \mathcal{A}$ ▷ Not all children done. Save tuples and wait.
function $update(\mathbf{n}, \mathbf{n}', \mathcal{A})$
    $p'(\mathbf{n}) \leftarrow p(\mathbf{n})$ ▷ Save the old penalty mapping.
    for all $t \in \mathcal{A}|_{bounds(\mathbf{n})}$ **do**
        match n with
        $\exists S_1 \cdots \exists S_n \phi \longrightarrow p(\mathbf{n}) \leftarrow p(\mathbf{n}) \oplus \{() \mapsto p(\mathbf{n}')(())\}$
        | $\forall x \phi \longrightarrow$
            for all $t' \in \mathcal{A}|_{bounds(\mathbf{n}')}$ s.t. $t'|_{bounds(\mathbf{n})} = t$ **do**
                $p(\mathbf{n}) \leftarrow p(\mathbf{n}) \oplus \{t \mapsto p(\mathbf{n})(t) + p(\mathbf{n}')(t') - p'(\mathbf{n}')(t')\}$
        | $\exists x \phi \longrightarrow$
            for all $t' \in \mathcal{A}|_{bounds(\mathbf{n}')}$ s.t. $t'|_{bounds(\mathbf{n})} = t$ **do**
                Replace the value for t' in $min\_heap(\mathbf{n}, t)$ with $p(\mathbf{n}')(t')$
                $p(\mathbf{n}) \leftarrow p(\mathbf{n}) \oplus \{t \mapsto \min(min\_heap(\mathbf{n}, t))\}$
        | $\phi_1 \wedge \cdots \wedge \phi_m \longrightarrow p(\mathbf{n}) \leftarrow p(\mathbf{n}) \oplus \{t \mapsto p(\mathbf{n})(t) + p(\mathbf{n}')(t) - p'(\mathbf{n}')(t)\}$
        | $\phi_1 \vee \cdots \vee \phi_m \longrightarrow$ Replace the value for $\mathbf{n}'$ in $min\_heap(\mathbf{n}, t)$ with $p(\mathbf{n}')(t)$
            $p(\mathbf{n}) \leftarrow p(\mathbf{n}) \oplus \{t \mapsto \min(min\_heap(\mathbf{n}, t))\}$
        | $x \leq y \longrightarrow error$ ▷ Only leaves representing formulas on set variables apply!
        | $|S| \leq m \longrightarrow p(\mathbf{n}) \leftarrow p(\mathbf{n}) \oplus \left\{ t \mapsto \begin{cases} 0, & \text{if } |k'(S)| \leq m \\ |k'(S)| - m, & \text{otherwise} \end{cases} \right\}$
        | $x \in S \longrightarrow p(\mathbf{n}) \leftarrow p(\mathbf{n}) \oplus \left\{ t \mapsto \begin{cases} 0, & \text{if } t(x) \in k'(S) \\ 1, & \text{otherwise} \end{cases} \right\}$
        | $x \notin S \longrightarrow p(\mathbf{n}) \leftarrow p(\mathbf{n}) \oplus \left\{ t \mapsto \begin{cases} 0, & \text{if } t(x) \notin k'(S) \\ 1, & \text{otherwise} \end{cases} \right\}$
    end match

tion from the node $\mathbf{n}'$ (*void* when **n** is a leaf) is propagated to the node **n**. The additional arguments are $\mathcal{A}$ (a set of tuples of values that are affected by changing k to k' at **n**), k (the current configuration), and k' (the configuration to evaluate). It uses the auxiliary function $update(\mathbf{n}, \mathbf{n}', \mathcal{A})$ that performs the actual update of the penalty mappings of **n** with respect to (the change of the penalty mappings of) $\mathbf{n}'$.

The set $\mathcal{A}$ depends on the maximum number of bound variables in the penalty tree, the universe $\mathcal{U}$, and the configurations k and k'. Recall $\mathcal{U}$ and k of Example 7 and assume that $k' = \{S \mapsto \{a, b\}, T \mapsto \{a, c\}, I \mapsto \{a\}\}$ (b was removed from $k(T)$). In this case $\mathcal{A}$ would be the singleton set $\{(b)\}$ since this is the only tuple affected by the change of k to k'. However, if the maximum number of bound variables was two (instead of one as in Example 7), $\mathcal{A}$ would be the set $\{(b, a), (b, b), (b, c), (a, b), (c, b)\}$ since all of these tuples might be affected.

Some of the notation used in Algorithm 2 needs explanation: Given a set $\mathcal{A}$ of tuples, each of arity n, we use $\mathcal{A}|_m$ to denote the set of tuples in $\mathcal{A}$ projected on their first $m \leq n$ positions. For example, if $\mathcal{A} = \{(a, a), (a, b), (a, c), (b, a), (c, a)\}$, then $\mathcal{A}|_1 = \{(a), (b), (c)\}$. We use a similar notation for projecting a particular tuple: if $t = (a, b, c)$ then $t|_2$ denotes the tuple (a, b). We also use $t(x)$ to denote the value of the position of x in t. For example, if x was the second introduced bound variable, then $t(x) = b$ for $t = (a, b, c)$. We let $changed(\mathbf{n})$ denote the set of tuples that has affected **n**. We let $bounds(\mathbf{n})$ denote the number of bound variables at node **n** (which is equal to the number of nodes of the form $\forall x$ or $\exists x$ on the path from **n** to the root node). We use the operator $\oplus$ for replacing the current bindings of a mapping with new ones. For example, the result of $\{x \mapsto a, y \mapsto a, z \mapsto b\} \oplus \{x \mapsto b, y \mapsto b\}$ is $\{x \mapsto b, y \mapsto b, z \mapsto b\}$. Finally, we assume that nodes of the form $\exists x$ and $\vee$ have a data structure min_heap for maintaining the minimum value of each of its penalty mappings.

Now, given a change to a current configuration k, resulting in k', assume that $\{S_i\}$ is the set of affected set variables in a formula $\mathcal{F}$ with an initialised penalty tree **T**. The call $submit(\mathbf{n}, void, \mathcal{A}, k, k')$ must now be made for each leaf **n** of **T** that represents a subformula stated on S_i, where $\mathcal{A}$ is the set of affected tuples.

Example 8. Recall $k = \{S \mapsto \{a, b\}, T \mapsto \{a, b, c\}, I \mapsto \{a\}\}$ and $m = 1$ of Example 7, and keep the initialised tree **T** in Figure 2 in mind. Let $k' = \{S \mapsto \{a, b\}, T \mapsto \{a, c\}, I \mapsto \{a\}\}$, i.e., b was removed from $k(T)$. The function $submit$ will now be called twice, once for each leaf in **T** containing T.

Starting with the leaf $\mathbf{n}_{11}$ representing the formula $x \in T$, $submit$ is called with $submit(\mathbf{n}_{11}, void, \{(b)\}, k, k')$. This gives the call $update(\mathbf{n}_{11}, void, \{(b)\})$ which replaces the binding of (b) in $p(\mathbf{n}_{11})$ with $(b) \mapsto 1$ (since b is no longer in T). Since a leaf node has no children and $\mathbf{n}_{11}$ is not the root node, $submit(\mathbf{n}_{12}, \mathbf{n}_{11}, \{(b)\}, k, k')$ is called where $\mathbf{n}_{12} = parent(\mathbf{n}_{11})$. Since $\mathbf{n}_{12}$ is an $\wedge$-node, $update(\mathbf{n}_{12}, \mathbf{n}_{11}, \{b\})$ implies that the binding of (b) in $p(\mathbf{n}_{12})$ is updated with the difference $p(\mathbf{n}_{11}) - p'(\mathbf{n}_{11})$ (which is 1 in this case). Hence, the new value of $p(\mathbf{n}_{12})(b)$ is 1. Since there are no other affected children of $\mathbf{n}_{12}$ and $\mathbf{n}_{12}$ is not the root node, $submit(\mathbf{n}_{13}, \mathbf{n}_{12}, \{(b)\}, k, k')$ is called where $\mathbf{n}_{13} = parent(\mathbf{n}_{12})$. Since $\mathbf{n}_{13}$ is an $\vee$-node, $update(\mathbf{n}_{13}, \mathbf{n}_{12}, \{b\})$ gives that the binding of (b) in $p(\mathbf{n}_{13})$ is updated with the minimum of $p(\mathbf{n}_{12})(b)$ and the values of $p(\mathbf{n})(b)$ for any other child **n** of $\mathbf{n}_{13}$. Since the only other child of $\mathbf{n}_{13}$ gives a 0 for this value, $p(\mathbf{n}_{13})(b)$ remains 0. Now, call $submit(\mathbf{n}_3, \mathbf{n}_{13}, \{(b)\}, k, k')$ where $\mathbf{n}_3 = parent(\mathbf{n}_{13})$. The call $update(\mathbf{n}_3, \mathbf{n}_{13}, \{b\})$ gives that $p(\mathbf{n}_3)(b)$ is unchanged (since $p(\mathbf{n}_{13})(b)$ was unchanged). Now, not all possibly affected children of $\mathbf{n}_3$ are done since the leaf $\mathbf{n}_{21}$ representing the formula $x \notin T$ has not yet been propagated. By following a similar reasoning for the nodes $\mathbf{n}_{21}$ and $\mathbf{n}_{22} = parent(\mathbf{n}_{21})$ we will see that the value of $p(\mathbf{n}_{22})(b)$ changes from 1 to 0 (since b is now in T). When this is propagated to $\mathbf{n}_3$ by $submit(\mathbf{n}_3, \mathbf{n}_{22}, \{(b)\}, k, k')$, the value of $p(\mathbf{n}_3)(b)$ will also change from 1 to 0. A similar reasoning for $parent(\mathbf{n}_3)$, $parent(parent(\mathbf{n}_3))$ and the root node gives the same changes to their penalty mappings consisting of only $() \mapsto 1$. This will lead to an overall penalty decrease of 1 and hence, the penalty of formula (3) with respect to k' is 0, meaning that (3) is satisfied under k'. The values of the changed penalty mappings with respect to k' of **T** are shown in parentheses in Figure 2.

6 Neighbourhood Selection

When solving a problem with local search, it is often crucial to restrict the initial configuration and the neighbourhood function used so that not all the constraints need to be stated explicitly. It is sometimes hard by local search alone to satisfy a constraint that can easily be guaranteed by using a restricted initial configuration and neighbourhood function. For example, if a set must have a fixed cardinality, then, by defining an initial configuration that respects this and by using a neighbourhood function that keeps the cardinality constant (for example by swapping values in the set with values in its complement), an explicit cardinality constraint need not be stated. Neighbourhoods are often designed in such an ad-hoc fashion. With the framework of $\exists SOL^+$, it becomes possible to reason about neighbourhoods and invariants:

Definition 6. *Let formula ϕ model a CSP P, let K be the set of all configurations for P, and let formula ψ be such that $k \models \phi$ implies $k \models \psi$ for all configurations $k \in K$. A neighbourhood function $\mathcal{N} : K \to 2^K$ is invariant for ψ if $k \models \psi$ implies $k' \models \psi$ for all $k' \in \mathcal{N}(k)$.*

Intuitively, the formula ψ is implied by ϕ and all possible moves take a configuration satisfying ψ to another configuration satisfying ψ. The challenge then is to find a suitable neighbourhood function for a formula ϕ.

Sometimes (as we will see in Section 7), given formulas ϕ and ψ satisfying Definition 6, it is possible to find a formula δ such that ϕ is logically equivalent to $\delta \wedge \psi$. If the formula δ is smaller than ϕ, then the speed of the local search algorithm can be greatly increased since the incremental penalty maintenance is faster on smaller penalty trees.

7 Application: A Financial Portfolio Problem

After formulating a financial portfolio optimisation problem, we show how to exactly solve real-life instances thereof in our local search framework. This is impossible with the best-known complete search algorithm and competitive with a fast approximation method based on complete search.

7.1 Formulation

The synthetic-CDO-Squared portfolio optimisation problem in financial mathematics has practical applications in the credit derivatives market [7]. Abstracting the finance away and assuming (not unrealistically) interchangeability of all the involved credits, it can be formulated as follows.[1] Let $V = \{1, \ldots, v\}$ and let $B = \{1, \ldots, b\}$ be a set of credits. An *optimal portfolio* is a set of v subsets $B_i \subseteq B$, called *baskets*, each of size r (with $0 \leq r \leq b$), such that the maximum intersection size of any two distinct baskets is minimised.

There is a universe of about $250 \leq b \leq 500$ credits. A typical portfolio contains about $4 \leq v \leq 25$ baskets, each of size $r \approx 100$. Such real-life instances of the portfolio *optimisation* problem are hard, so we transform it into a CSP by also providing a targeted value, denoted λ (with $\lambda < r$), for the maximum of the

---
[1] We use the notation of the related balanced incomplete block design problem.

pairwise basket intersection sizes in a portfolio. Hence the following formulation of the problem:

$$\forall\, i \in V : |B_i| = r \qquad (4)$$

$$\forall\, i_1 \neq i_2 \in V : |B_{i_1} \cap B_{i_2}| \leq \lambda \qquad (5)$$

We parameterise the portfolio CSP by a 4-tuple $\langle v, b, r, \lambda \rangle$ of independent parameters. The following formula gives an optimal lower bound on λ [13]:[2]

$$\lambda \geq \frac{\lceil \frac{rv}{b} \rceil^2 (rv \bmod b) + \lfloor \frac{rv}{b} \rfloor^2 (b - rv \bmod b) - rv}{v(v-1)} \qquad (6)$$

7.2 Using Complete Search

One way of modelling a portfolio is in terms of its *incidence matrix*, which is a $v \times b$ matrix, such that the entry at the intersection of row i and column j is 1 if $j \in B_i$ and 0 otherwise. The constraints (4) and (5) are then modelled by requiring, respectively, that there are exactly r ones (that is a sum of r) for each row and a scalar product of at most λ for any pair of distinct rows. An optimal solution, under this model, to $\langle 10, 8, 3, \lambda \rangle$ is given in Table 1, with $\lambda = 2$.

Table 1. An optimal solution to $\langle 10, 8, 3, \lambda \rangle$, with $\lambda = 2$

	c	r	e	d	i	t	s	
basket 1	1	1	1	0	0	0	0	0
basket 2	1	1	0	1	0	0	0	0
basket 3	1	1	0	0	1	0	0	0
basket 4	1	1	0	0	0	1	0	0
basket 5	0	0	1	1	1	0	0	0
basket 6	0	0	1	1	0	1	0	0
basket 7	0	0	1	1	0	0	1	0
basket 8	0	0	0	0	1	1	0	1
basket 9	0	0	0	0	1	0	1	1
basket 10	0	0	0	0	0	1	1	1

The baskets are indistinguishable, and, as stated above, we assume that all the credits are indistinguishable. Hence any two rows or columns of the incidence matrix can be freely permuted. Breaking all the resulting $v! \cdot b!$ symmetries can in theory be performed, for instance by $v! \cdot b! - 1$ (anti-)lexicographical ordering constraints [4]. In practice, strictly anti-lexicographically ordering the rows (since baskets cannot be repeated in portfolios) as well as anti-lexicographically ordering the columns (since credits can appear in the same baskets) works quite fine for values of b up to about 36, due to the constraint (5), especially when

---

[2] It often improves the bound reported in [7] and negatively settles the open question therein whether the $\langle 10, 350, 100, 21 \rangle$ portfolio exists or not.

labelling in a row-wise fashion and trying the value 1 before the value 0. However, this is one order of magnitude below the typical value for b in a portfolio. In [7], we presented an approximate and often extremely fast method of solving real-life instances of this problem by complete search, even for values of λ quite close, if not identical, to the lower bound in (6). It is based on embedding (multiple copies of) independent sub-instances into the original instance. Their determination is itself a CSP, based on (6).

7.3 Using Local Search

It is easy to model the portfolio problem in $\exists \text{SOL}^1$ using additional set variables. The problem can be modelled by the following formula:

$$\exists B_1, \ldots, \exists B_v \exists_{i<j} I_{(i,j)} \ \phi_1 \wedge \phi_2 \wedge \phi_3 \tag{7}$$

where $\exists_{i<j} I_{(i,j)}$ is a shorthand for the sequence of quantifications $\exists I_{(1,2)}, \ldots, I_{(i,j)}, \ldots$ for all $i < j$.[3] The formula $\phi_1 = |B_1| = r \wedge \cdots \wedge |B_v| = r$ states that each set B_i is of size r. Using similar conventions, the formula $\phi_2 = \forall i < j \ \forall x (x \in I_{(i,j)} \leftrightarrow (x \in B_i \wedge x \in B_j))$ states that each set $I_{(i,j)}$ is the intersection of B_i and B_j. Finally, the formula $\phi_3 = \forall i < j |I_{(i,j)}| \leq \lambda$ states that the intersection size of any B_i and B_j should be less than or equal to λ.

The local search algorithm can be made more efficient by using the ideas in Section 6. First, we define a neighbourhood function that is invariant for the formula ϕ_1. Assuming that the initial configuration for (7) respects ϕ_1, the neighbourhood function that swaps any value in any B_i to any value in its complement is invariant for ϕ_1. We denote this neighbourhood function by *exchange*. We may even extend *exchange* such that it is invariant also for ϕ_2. In order to do this, we assume that the initial configuration for (7) respects $\phi_1 \wedge \phi_2$. Now, we extend *exchange* in the following way. Given a configuration k and a configuration k' in $exchange(k)$ where B_i is the only variable affected by the change of k to k', the variables $I_{(i,j)}$ such that there exists a subformula $x \in I_{(i,j)} \leftrightarrow (x \in B_i \wedge x \in B_j)$ or $x \in I_{(j,i)} \leftrightarrow (x \in B_j \wedge x \in B_i)$ are all updated (by adding or removing a value to $I_{(i,j)}$) so that those formulas still hold.

We use a similar algorithm to the one in [2] for solving the portfolio problem with local search, i.e., a Tabu-search algorithm with a restarting criterion if no overall improvement was reported after a certain number of iterations.

7.4 Results

The experiments were run on an Intel 2.4 GHz Linux machine with 512 MB memory. The local search framework was implemented in OCaml and the complete search algorithm was coded in SICStus Prolog.

The local search algorithm performs well on this problem. For example, the easy instance $\langle 10, 35, 11, 3 \rangle$ is solved in 0.2 seconds, the slightly harder instance

---

[3] This shorthand is a purely conservative extension of $\exists \text{SOL}^+$ and does not increase the expressiveness.

⟨10, 70, 22, 6⟩ in 0.6 seconds, and the real-life instance ⟨15, 350, 100, 24⟩ in 133.9 seconds. Bear in mind that these results were achieved (by our current prototype implementation) under the assumption that no built-in constraints existed, and thus that the incremental penalty maintenance algorithms were automatically generated as described in this paper.

For comparison, the complete search approach without embeddings needs 0.6 seconds for finding a first solution of ⟨10, 35, 11, 3⟩, 929.8 seconds for ⟨10, 70, 22, 6⟩, and does not terminate within several hours of CPU time for ⟨15, 350, 100, 24⟩.

Using the extended implementation [13] of the embedding method of [7] for the real-life instance ⟨15, 350, 100, 24⟩, two embeddings were constructed but both timed out after 100 seconds. Hence, local search approaches can outperform even this approximation method.

8 Conclusion

Summary. In the context of local search, we have introduced a scheme that, from a high-level problem model in existential second-order logic with counting ($\exists SOL^+$), automatically synthesises incremental penalty calculation algorithms. This bears significant benefits when ad hoc constraints are necessary for a particular problem, as no adaptation by the user of the modelling part of the local search system is then required. The performance of the scheme has been demonstrated by solving real-life instances of a financial portfolio design problem that seem unsolvable in reasonable time by complete search.

Related Work. The usage of existential second-order logic ($\exists SOL$) as a modelling language has also been advocated in [9]. The motivation there was rather that any automated reasoning about constraint models must *necessarily* first be studied on this simple core language before moving on to extensions thereof. Modern, declarative constraint modelling languages, such as NP-SPEC [3], OPL [14], and ESRA [6], are extensions of $\exists SOL$. In contrast, our motivation for $\exists SOL$ is that it is a *sufficient* language for our purpose, especially if extended (only) with counting.

The adaptation of the traditional combinators of constraint programming for local search was pioneered in [15]. The combinators there include logical connectives (such as $\wedge$ and $\vee$), cardinality operators (such as *exactly* and *atmost*), reification, and expressions over variables. We extend these ideas here to the logical quantifiers ($\forall$ and $\exists$). This is not just a matter of simply generalising the arities and penalty calculations of the $\wedge$ and $\vee$ connectives, respectively, but made necessary by our handling of set variables over which one would like to iterate, unlike the scalar variables of [11,15].

Future Work. We have made several simplifying assumptions in order to restrict this paper to its fundamental ideas. For instance, the handling of both scalar variables and set variables requires special care in the calculation of penalties, and has been left as future work. Also, many more shorthand notations than the ones used in this paper could be added for the user's convenience, such as quantification bounded over a set rather than the entire universe. Furthermore, it would be useful if appropriate neighbourhood functions that are invariant for some of the constraints could automatically be generated from an $\exists SOL^+$ model.

Conclusion. Our first computational results are encouraging and warrant further research into the automatic synthesis of local search algorithms.

Acknowledgements. This research was partially funded by Project C/1.246/ HQ/JC/04 of EuroControl. We thank Olof Sivertsson for his contributions to the experiments on the financial portfolio problem, as well as the referees for their useful comments.

References

1. E. Aarts and J. K. Lenstra, editors. *Local Search in Combinatorial Optimization*. John Wiley & Sons, 1997.
2. M. Ågren, P. Flener, and J. Pearson. Set variables and local search. In *Proc. of CP-AI-OR'05*, volume 3524 of *LNCS*, pages 19–33. Springer-Verlag, 2005.
3. M. Cadoli, L. Palopoli, A. Schaerf, and D. Vasile. NPSPEC: An executable specification language for solving all problems in NP. In *Proc. of PADL'99*, volume 1551 of *LNCS*, pages 16–30. Springer-Verlag, 1999.
4. J. M. Crawford, M. Ginsberg, E. Luks, and A. Roy. Symmetry-breaking predicates for search problems. In *Proc. of KR'96*, pages 148–159. Morgan Kaufmann, 1996.
5. R. Fagin. *Contributions to the Model Theory of Finite Structures*. PhD thesis, UC Berkeley, California, USA, 1973.
6. P. Flener, J. Pearson, and M. Ågren. Introducing ESRA, a relational language for modelling combinatorial problems. In *LOPSTR'03: Revised Selected Papers*, volume 3018 of *LNCS*, pages 214–232. Springer-Verlag, 2004.
7. P. Flener, J. Pearson, and L. G. Reyna. Financial portfolio optimisation. In *Proc. of CP'04*, volume 3258 of *LNCS*, pages 227–241. Springer-Verlag, 2004.
8. N. Immerman. *Descriptive Complexity*. Springer-Verlag, 1998.
9. T. Mancini. *Declarative constraint modelling and specification-level reasoning*. PhD thesis, Università degli Studi di Roma "La Sapienza", Italy, 2004.
10. L. Michel and P. Van Hentenryck. Localizer: A modeling language for local search. In *Proc. of CP'97*, volume 1330 of *LNCS*, pages 237–251. Springer-Verlag, 1997.
11. L. Michel and P. Van Hentenryck. A constraint-based architecture for local search. *ACM SIGPLAN Notices*, 37(11):101–110, 2002. Proc. of OOPSLA'02.
12. A. Nareyek. Using global constraints for local search. In *Constraint Programming and Large Scale Discrete Optimization*, volume 57 of *DIMACS: Series in Discrete Mathematics and Theoretical Computer Science*, pages 9–28. American Mathematical Society, 2001.
13. O. Sivertsson. Construction of synthetic CDO Squared. Master's thesis, Computing Science, Department of Information Technology, Uppsala University, Sweden, 2005.
14. P. Van Hentenryck. *The OPL Optimization Programming Language*. The MIT Press, 1999.
15. P. Van Hentenryck, L. Michel, and L. Liu. Constraint-based combinators for local search. In *Proc. of CP'04*, volume 3258 of *LNCS*, pages 47–61. Springer-Verlag, 2004.
16. J. P. Walser. *Integer Optimization by Local Search: A Domain-Independent Approach*, volume 1637 of *LNCS*. Springer-Verlag, 1999.

Inter-distance Constraint: An Extension of the All-Different Constraint for Scheduling Equal Length Jobs

Konstantin Artiouchine[1,2] and Philippe Baptiste[1]

[1] CNRS LIX, Ecole Polytechnique, 91128 Palaiseau, France
Konstantin.Artiouchine@polytechnique.org
[2] Thales TRT, Domaine de Corbeville, 91404 Orsay CEDEX, France
Philippe.Baptiste@polytechnique.fr

Abstract. We study a global constraint, the "inter-distance constraint" that ensures that the distance between any pair of variables is at least equal to a given value. When this value is 1, the inter-distance constraint reduces to the all-different constraint. We introduce an algorithm to propagate this constraint and we show that, when domains of the variables are intervals, our algorithm achieves arc-B-consistency. It provides tighter bounds than generic scheduling constraint propagation algorithms (like edge-finding) that could be used to capture this constraint. The worst case complexity of the algorithm is cubic but it behaves well in practice and it drastically reduces the search space. Experiments on special Job-Shop problems and on an industrial problem are reported.

Keywords: Global Constraint, Scheduling, Constraint Propagation.

1 Introduction

We introduce a global constraint, the "inter-distance constraint" that ensures that the distance between any pair (S_i, S_j) of variables in some set $\{S_1, ..., S_n\}$ is not smaller than a given value p, i.e., $\forall i, j, |S_i - S_j| \geq p$. To our knowledge, this constraint has been introduced for the first time by Régin [20]. When p is 1, the inter-distance constraint reduces to the well-known all-different constraint [19], [18], [13].

This study was motivated by an industrial application for Air Traffic Management in the Terminal RAdar Control Area of airports [2]. When aircraft reach the final descent in the "Terminal Radar Approach CONtrol" area (TRACON), a set of disjoint time windows in which the landing is possible, can be automatically assigned to each aircraft. The objective is then to determine landing times within these time windows which maximize the minimum time elapsed between consecutive landings. The decision variant of this problem, (i.e., when the minimum time elapsed between consecutive landings is fixed and when the question is to determine if there are feasible landing times or not), can be modeled with an inter-distance constraint. The inter-distance constraint is also useful to model scheduling situation in which all jobs that have to be processed on the same machine have the same processing time. This is often the case in manufacturing scheduling problems (see for instance the testbed proposed by Ilog www2.ilog.com/masclib described in [16]).

The objective of this paper is to present a global constraint propagation algorithm for the inter-distance constraint. As explained in Section 2, standard scheduling constraint propagation algorithms, like edge-finding or "Not-First/Not-Last", can be used to model this constraint. We also show that these more generic algorithms do not perform all possible deductions. An algorithm that determines whether the constraint is globally consistent or not is described in Section 3. We then introduce propagation rules (Section 4) and a polynomial time algorithm to propagate the inter-distance constraint (Section 5). We show that, when variables domains are intervals, our algorithm achieves the arc-B-consistency (*i.e.*, arc consistency restricted to the bounds of the domains of the variables [12]) of the global constraint and hence performs the best possible filtering. The worst case complexity of the algorithm is cubic but it behaves well in practice and it drastically reduces the search space. Experiments (Section 6) on special Job-Shop problems and on our industrial application are reported.

2 Inter-distance Constraint *vs.* Scheduling Constraints

Régin [20] relies on the sequencing constraint [21] to propagate the "inter-distance constraint". However, we believe it is somewhat easier to consider this constraint as a pure scheduling constraint. To each variable S_i, we associate a job i starting at time S_i and whose processing time is p. The disjunctive constraint directly ensures that activities are not processed simultaneously and hence, the distance between any pair of starting times is at least p. So both models are identical.

Over the last decade, several resource constraint propagation algorithms have been designed to address a variety of scheduling situations (see [3] for a review). We first describe two constraint propagation schemes known as "Edge-Finding" and "Not-First/Not-Last" that are widely used in the literature for disjunctive scheduling. Then we show that they can be improved when all processing times are equal.

2.1 Edge-Finding

The edge-finding algorithm [7], [8], [14] is one of the most well known OR algorithm integrated in CP. This global constraint propagation algorithm for disjunctive scheduling is a key ingredient for solving complex scheduling problems such as the Job-Shop Scheduling problem

The term "Edge-Finding" denotes both a "branching" and a "bounding" technique [1]. The branching technique consists of ordering jobs that require the same resource. At each node, a set of jobs Ω is selected and, for each job $i \in \Omega$, a new branch is created where i is constrained to execute first (or last) among the jobs in Ω. The bounding technique consists of deducing that some jobs from a given set Ω must, can, or cannot, execute first (or last) in Ω. Such deductions lead to new ordering relations ("edges" in the graph representing the possible orderings of jobs) and new time bounds, *i.e.*, strengthened earliest start times and latest end times of jobs.

In the following, r_Ω and d_Ω respectively denote the smallest of release dates and the largest deadline of the jobs in Ω. Moreover, p_Ω is the sum of the processing times of the jobs in Ω. Finally, let $i \gg \Omega$ mean that i executes after all the jobs in Ω and let S_i be the variable representing the starting time of the job i. The following rules capture the "essence" of the Edge-Finding bounding technique:

$$\forall \Omega, \forall i \notin \Omega, [d_\Omega - r_{\Omega \cup \{i\}} < p_\Omega + p_i] \Rightarrow [i \gg \Omega]$$
$$\forall \Omega, \forall i \notin \Omega, [i \gg \Omega] \Rightarrow [S_i \geq \max_{\emptyset \neq \Omega' \subseteq \Omega}(r_{\Omega'} + p_{\Omega'})]$$

An algorithm that performs all the time-bound adjustments in $O(n^2)$ is presented in [7]. Another variant of the Edge-Finding technique is presented in [8]. Its time complexity is $O(n \log n)$ but it requires much more complex data structures.

2.2 Not-First/Not-Last

The algorithms presented earlier focus on determining whether a job i must execute first (or last) in a set of jobs $\Omega \cup \{i\}$ requiring the same resource. A natural complement consists of determining whether i can execute first (or last) in $\Omega \cup \{i\}$. If not, i is "Not-First" and cannot start before at least one job in Ω is completed. This leads to the following rules [17]:

$$\forall \Omega, \forall i \notin \Omega, [d_\Omega - r_i < p_\Omega + p_i] \Rightarrow \neg(i \ll \Omega)$$
$$\forall \Omega, \forall i \notin \Omega, \neg(i \ll \Omega) \Rightarrow S_i \geq \min_{j \in \Omega} S_j + p_j$$

A quadratic algorithm is described in [4]. Alternative approaches can be found in [23], [9], [24].

2.3 Missed Deductions

It is well known that Edge-Finding and Not-First/Not-Last propagation rules do not ensure the consistency of the global disjunctive constraint (determining whether this constraint is consistent is NP-Complete in the strong sense). What happens when processing times are equal ? The following examples show that Edge-Finding and Not-First/Not-Last do not perform all possible deductions.

In the example described in Figure 1, 6 jobs with processing time 2 are to be scheduled on a single machine. The time window (release dates / deadlines) of a job is drawn as white rectangle. The job itself (black rectangle) has to be scheduled inside this window. There is no feasible schedule (the machine is occupied from 3 to 9 because of the last three jobs, hence 3 jobs have to be scheduled in two disjoint time windows of size 3; contradiction) but neither edge-finding nor Not-First/Not-Last rule detect this. In the example of Figure 2,

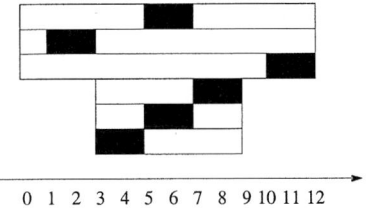

Fig. 1. Edge-Finding and Not-First/Not-Last do not detect all inconsistencies

3 jobs with processing time 5 have to be scheduled on a single machine. There is a feasible schedule but neither edge-finding nor Not-First/Not-Last deduce that the third job cannot start earlier than 10.

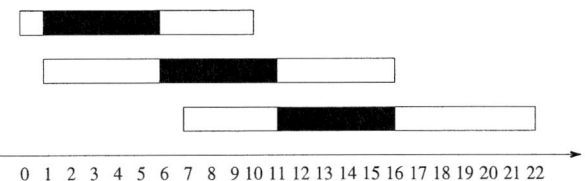

Fig. 2. Edge-Finding and Not-First/Not-Last do not achieve Arc-B-Consistency

3 Feasibility Test

From now on, we focus on the scheduling problem with identical processing times. Garey, Johnson, Simons and Tarjan [10] have introduced an $O(n \log n)$ algorithm to solve this problem. We describe a cubic version of this algorithm based on similar techniques as in [10]. We have however modified the presentation of the algorithm (and also the proofs) to be able to introduce the adjustments of release dates and deadlines described in Sections 4 and 5.

3.1 Why EDD Fails

EDD (Earliest DeaDline) is a dispatching rule that builds a schedule chronologically as follows: Whenever the machine is idle, select among the jobs that are released before or at the current time point the job with minimal deadline. Schedule the job and iterate. When preemption is allowed, the preemptive EDD rule computes a feasible schedule if one such exists [7] (this also holds in the general case with arbitrary processing times). It is well known that this is not the case in the non-preemptive case. We show in Figure 3 a 3 job instance with identical processing times for which EDD fails while there is a feasible schedule. When processing times are all equal, Garey, Johnson, Simons and Tarjan propose to modify the EDD rule to ensure that it builds a feasible schedule, if one exists. The modification consists in introducing a set of forbidden regions F in which no job can start on any feasible schedule.

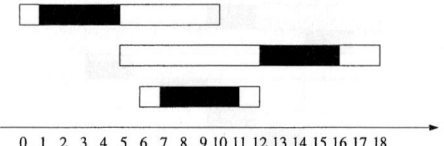

Fig. 3. EDD fails while there is a feasible schedule

Given a set of forbidden regions F, the modified EDD rule keeps the schedule idle when the current time point t belongs to F (see Algorithm 1). Throughout this algorithm, U denotes the set of yet unscheduled jobs. At each iteration one job of U is scheduled.

Algorithm 1. Modified EDD schedule

1: $U := \{1, ..., n\}$
2: $t := \min_{i \in U} r_i$
3: **while** $U \neq \emptyset$ **do**
4:    $t := \min(t, \min_{i \in U} r_i)$
5:    **if** $t \in F$ **then**
6:      $t := \min\{t' \geq t : t' \notin F\}$
7:    Let k be the job with smallest deadline s.t. $r_k \leq t$
8:    Start job k at time t, $U := U - \{k\}$, $t := t + p$

3.2 Computing Forbidden Regions

The crucial point is how to compute the set F of "forbidden regions". We first provide an *intuitive description* of this mechanism. F is built step by step, starting from $F = \emptyset$. Given a set of jobs X, compute an upper bound lst of the largest time point such that there is a feasible schedule of the jobs in X that is idle before lst and in which no job starts in F (lst stands for latest start time). If lst is smaller than $\min_{i \in X} r_i$ then there is no feasible schedule. If $lst - p < \min_{i \in X} r_i$ then no job can start after $lst - p$ and before $\min_{i \in X} r_i$ (if this were the case, the job would finish after lst. Thus, we would not have a feasible schedule). So no job starts in the interval $[lst - p + 1, \min_{i \in X} r_i - 1]$ and this interval is added to the set of forbidden regions F.

To give a formal description of this mechanism, we introduce the following notations:

Definition 1. *Given a time point t, an integer q and a set of forbidden regions F, $ect(F, t, q)$ and $lst(F, t, q)$ respectively denote the **earliest completion time** (resp. **latest start time**) of a schedule of q jobs, with no release date and no deadline, starting after or at (resp. completed before or at) t.*

Algorithms 2 and 3 compute respectively $ect(F, t, q)$ and $lst(F, t, q)$. The proof of correctness is easy to make by induction on q and is skipped.

Algorithm 2. Earliest Completion Time of q jobs starting after or at t

1: **for** $i = 1$ to q **do**
2:    **if** $t \in F$ **then**
3:      $t := \min\{t' \geq t : t' \notin F\}$
4:    $t := t + p$
5: $ect(F, t, q) = t$

Algorithm 3. Latest Start Time of q jobs to be completed before or at t

1: **for** $i = 1$ to q **do**
2:    $t := t - p$
3:    **if** $t \in F$ **then**
4:      $t := \max\{t' \leq t : t' \notin F\}$
5: $lst(F, t, q) = t$

We are now ready to explain Algorithm 4 that computes all forbidden regions. In the following, $\mathbf{\Delta(r,d)}$ **stands for the set of jobs** $\{i : \mathbf{r} \leq \mathbf{r_i}, \mathbf{d_i} \leq \mathbf{d}\}$ and $|\Delta(r,d)|$ is the cardinality of this set.

Algorithm 4. Forbidden Regions

1: $F := \emptyset$
2: **for all** release date r taken in non-increasing order **do**
3:    $lst := \infty$
4:    **for all** deadline d taken in non-increasing order **do**
5:      $lst := \min(lst, lst(F, d, |\Delta(r,d)|))$
6:      **if** $lst < r$ **then**
7:        There is no feasible schedule
8:      **else if** $r \leq lst < r + p$ **then**
9:        $F := F \cup [lst - p + 1, r - 1]$

Lemma 1. *If Algorithm 4 fails then there is no feasible schedule. Moreover, in any feasible schedule, jobs do not start in F.*

Proof. Assume that the lemma holds for all the regions that have been added by Algorithm 4 up to the current iteration (r, d). If $lst < r$ then in any feasible schedule, one job of $\Delta(r,d)$ starts before the minimal release date in this set; contradiction. Now assume that $r \leq lst < r + p$ (otherwise no forbidden region is added to F and our claim holds up to the next iteration). If there is a feasible schedule in which a job u starts at $t \in [lst - p + 1, r - 1]$ then no job of $\Delta(r,d)$ is scheduled before $t + p \geq lst + 1$ which contradicts the definition of lst. □

Lemma 2. *Given two time points $t_1 \leq t_2$, an integer q and a set of forbidden regions F, $ect(F, t_1, q) > t_2$ if and only if $lst(F, t_2, q) < t_1$.*

Proof. If $ect(F, t_1, q) \leq t_2$ then there is a schedule of q jobs that can be executed between t_1 and t_2. Hence a schedule of q jobs completed at t_2 with no starting times in F can start after or at t_2. Hence $lst(F, t_2, q) \geq t_1$. □

Lemma 3. *If Algorithm 4 does not fail, there is a feasible schedule.*

Proof. We claim that, given the set of forbidden regions F computed by Algorithm 4, a feasible schedule is built by Algorithm 1 when applied to the set of forbidden regions F. Let us assume this is not true and let k' denote the first job that is completed after its deadline by Algorithm 1. We iteratively build a set of jobs S'. Initially, $S' = \{k'\}$; we then add in S' all the jobs preceding k' until we either reach a time point $t \notin F$ at which all jobs released before t are scheduled or until we reach a job u with $d_u > d_{k'}$.

- If we have reached a time point $t \notin F$ at which all jobs released before t are scheduled. Let j' be the job in S' with minimal release date. So, at some step of the algorithm the interval $r_{j'}, d_{k'}$ was considered. All jobs of S' belong to this interval. When building the EDD schedule of this set, note that the forbidden regions that are encountered are those in the set F as built at iteration r. Indeed, forbidden regions added at a later iteration end before r so they do not interact with jobs considered at this step.
  Also note that time points at which the machine is idle are forbidden (these time points do not correspond to release dates because of the construction of S'). Hence the shape of the EDD schedule after $r_{j'}$ up to $d_{k'}$ is exactly the same as the one computed by the forward scheduling algorithm when applied to the same set of jobs with the forbidden list built while processing the release date r. Hence $ect(F, r_{j'}, |\Delta(r_{j'}, d_{k'})|) > d_{k'}$. So, according to Lemma 2, $lst(F, d_{k'}, |\Delta(r_{j'}, d_{k'})|) < r_{j'}$. Hence Algorithm 4 would declare the failure.
- If we have reached a job u with $d_u > d_{k'}$. Then All jobs i in S' are such that $d_i \leq d_{k'}$ and $r_i > r_u$ (otherwise EDD would have scheduled another job than u at time r_u). As before, let j' denote the job in S' with minimal release date. So S' is a subset of $\Delta(r_{j'}, d_{k'})$.
  Algorithm 1 fails, hence, $ect(F, r_u + p, |S'|) > d_{k'}$. So, according to Lemma 2, $lst(F, d_{k'}, |S'|) < r_u + p$. Since no failure has been triggered, we have also $r_u < r_{j'} \leq lst(F, d_{k'}, |S'|)$. Hence, r_u must belong to a forbidden region declared by Algorithm 4, but it is not the case. □

3.3 Runtime Analysis

It is easy to see that there are no more than n forbidden regions hence algorithms 2 and 3 can be implemented in quadratic time. This would lead to an overall $O(n^4)$ algorithm. We can improve this to cubic time as follows:

When a new forbidden region is created (Algorithm 4), its endpoint is smaller than or equal to the endpoints of the previously build forbidden regions. So, we can easily maintain – in constant time – the set of forbidden regions as a list of ordered disjoint intervals whenever a new interval is added. Finally, note that forbidden regions end right before a release date. Hence, it is easy to maintain the set F in such a way that we have no more than n forbidden regions throughout the algorithm.

Moreover, we can incrementally compute $\min\{t' \geq t : t' \notin F\}$ since t increases at each iteration. Moreover, inside the loop, all operations can be done in linear time except $\min\{t' \geq t : t' \notin F\}$. Hence the overall complexity of Algorithm 1 is $O(n^2 + |F|)$ since overall time needed for the computations of $\min_{i \in U} r_i$ is linear if all jobs are sorted in increasing order of release dates. Following the same remarks, both Algorithms 2 and 3 run in $O(q + |F|)$.

This directly ensures that Algorithm 4 runs in $O(n^3)$.

4 Propagation Rules

From now on, we assume that there is a feasible schedule. We denote by F the set of forbidden regions computed by Algorithm 4. The following lemmas characterize a set of time points at which jobs cannot start. Lemma 7 shows that all other time points are possible starting times.

Lemma 4 (Internal Adjustment). *Given two time points r, d, and an integer $0 \leq q \leq |\Delta(r,d)| - 1$, job i cannot start in*

$$I_{r,d,q} = [lst(F, d, |\Delta(r,d)| - q) + 1, ect(F, r, q+1) - 1].$$

Proof. Assume there is a feasible schedule in which a job i starts at time $t < ect(F, r, q+1)$, for some $q \in \{0, ..., |\Delta(r,d)| - 1\}$ (if $t \geq ect(F, r, q+1)$ then the job does not start in $I_{r,d,q}$). Given the definition of ect, at most q jobs are completed strictly before $ect(F, r, q+1)$. Hence $|\Delta(r,d)| - q$ jobs are completed after t. So $t \leq lst(F, d, |\Delta(r,d)| - q)$, i.e., job i does not start in the interval $[lst(F, d, |\Delta(r,d)| - q) + 1, ect(F, r, q+1) - 1]$. □

Note that in the above lemma, we could restrict to jobs $i \in \Delta(r,d)$ but it also works for jobs $i \notin \Delta(r,d)$.

Lemma 5 (External Adjustment). *Given two time points r, d and an integer $0 \leq q \leq |\Delta(r,d)|$, a job $i \notin \Delta(r,d)$ cannot start in*

$$E_{r,d,q} = [lst(F, d, |\Delta(r,d)| - q + 1) + 1, ect(F, r, q+1) - 1].$$

Proof. Assume there is a feasible schedule in which a job $i \notin \Delta(r,d)$ starts at time $t < ect(F, r, q+1)$, for some $q \in \{0, ..., |\Delta(r,d)| - 1\}$. Given the definition of ect, at most q jobs are completed strictly before $ect(F, r, q+1)$. Hence $|\Delta(r,d)| - q$ jobs of $\Delta(r,d)$ as well as job i are completed after t. So $t \leq lst(F, d, |\Delta(r,d)| - q + 1)$, i.e., job i does not start in the interval $[lst(F, d, |\Delta(r,d)| - q + 1) + 1, ect(F, r, q+1) - 1]$. □

In the following, we say that a time point $t \geq r_i$ is a *candidate starting time* for job i if it has not been discarded by internal and/or external adjustment (Lemmas 4, 5). Given a candidate starting time t for job i, we note I' the the instance obtained from I in which we have replaced r_i by t and d_i by $t + p$. So in I' the job i is fixed, and our objective is to prove that there is a feasible schedule for this instance. This claim is proven in Lemma 8 but we first need some technical lemmas.

Definition 2. *The **associated deadline** of a release date r is the largest deadline d such that $lst(F, d, |\Delta(r, d)|)$ is minimal.*

Lemma 6. *If Algorithm 4 declares a forbidden region $[lst' - p + 1, r - 1]$ for the instance I' that strictly extends the forbidden region $[lst - p + 1, r - 1]$ computed for the instance I then the associated deadline of r for the instance I' is greater than or equal to $t + p$.*

Proof. Let r be the largest release date of instance I' such that
- its associated deadline d is strictly lower than $t + p$
- $lst(F', d, |\Delta(r, d)|) < lst(F, d, |\Delta(r, d)|)$.

Note that if r does not exist then our lemma holds. When scheduling backward from d with the forbidden set F, at least one starting time must belong to F' but not to F otherwise $lst(F, d, |\Delta(r, d)|) = lst(F', d, |\Delta(r, d)|)$. Let then t be the largest starting time in this backward schedule that belongs to F' but not to F and let $r' > r$ be the release date that makes t forbidden in the new instance. As $r' > r$, we know that the associated deadline d' of r' is greater than or equal to $t + p$. When back-scheduling $|\Delta(r', d)|$ jobs from d using F', no starting time belongs to F' (recall that t is maximal). Hence, the corresponding latest start time is larger than $t + p$ (on the back-schedule) otherwise $t \in F$. So we have

$$lst(F', d', |\Delta(r', d')|) < lst(F', d, |\Delta(r', d)|).$$

Now note that $lst(F', d', |\Delta(r, d')|) = lst(F', lst(F', d', |\Delta(r', d')|), q)$ where q is exactly $|\{i : r \le r_i < r', d_i \le d\}|$, or similarly,

$$lst(F', d, |\Delta(r, d)|) = lst(F', lst(F', d, |\Delta(r', d)|), q).$$

As the function $h \to lst(F', h, q)$ is non decreasing, we have

$$lst(F', d', |\Delta(r, d')|) \le lst(F', d, |\Delta(r, d)|).$$

This contradicts the fact that d is the associated deadline of r. □

In the the proofs of the subsequent lemmas, we use the following notation: given a release date r and deadline d,

$$\Theta_i(r, d) = \begin{cases} 0, & \text{if } r \le r_i \le d_i \le d \\ 1, & \text{otherwise} \end{cases}$$

Lemma 7. *If t has not been discarded by the propagation, for any v, $lst(F, t, v) \notin F'$.*

Proof. Let v be the first integer value such that $lst(F, t, v) \in F'$. Let then $r > lst(F, t, v)$ be the release date that made the time point $lst(F, t, v)$ forbidden. According to Lemma 6, d, the associated deadline of r, is greater than or equal to $t + p$. So we have

$$lst(F, t, v) < r \le lst(F', d, |\Delta(r, d)| + \Theta_i(r, d)) < lst(F, t, v) + p$$

Now let q denote the largest integer such that $lst(F', d, q) \ge t$. Given this definition, we have

$$lst(F', d, |\Delta(r,d)| + \Theta_i(r,d)) \geq lst(F', t, |\Delta(r,d)| + \Theta_i(r,d) - q)$$

Because t has not been discarded by propagation, we immediately have

$$lst(F', t, |\Delta(r,d)| + \Theta_i(r,d) - q) \geq r$$

and thus we must have

$$|\Delta(r,d)| + \Theta_i(r,d) - q < v$$

and because of our hypothesis on v,

$$lst(F', t, |\Delta(r,d)| + \Theta_i(r,d) - q) = lst(F, t, |\Delta(r,d)| + \Theta_i(r,d) - q) < lst(F, t, v) + p$$

This contradicts the fact that the distance between two starting times in any back-schedule is at least p. □

The following lemma shows that we achieve Arc-B-Consistency on the global constraint.

Lemma 8 (Feasible Starting Times). *If t has not been discarded by the propagation, there is a feasible schedule in which i starts at t.*

Proof. If the instance I' is not feasible the Algorithm 4 fails at some iteration. Let then r and d be the corresponding release date and deadline. First assume that $d < t + p$ then, when applying the back-scheduling algorithm from d, we must have at least one starting time in F' and not in F (otherwise, we would have the same lst value). By the same reasoning as in Lemma 6 we could prove that there is also a deadline $d' \geq t + p$ such that the backward schedule fails.

So now assume that $d \geq t + p$. We have

$$lst(F', d, |\Delta(r,d)| + \Theta_i(r,d)) < r.$$

As we know that i starts exactly at t, we can decompose the backward scheduling (before t and after $t+p$). And we get a better bound on the latest possible start time, *i.e.*,

$$\max_q \{lst(F', t, q) : lst(F', d, |\Delta(r,d)| + \Theta_i(r,d) - q) \geq t\} < r.$$

The back-scheduling algorithm computes exactly the same schedules before t when applied either to F or to F'. Moreover, for any v, $lst(F, t, v) \notin F'$. So, the above equation leads to

$$\max_q \{lst(F, t, q) : lst(F, d, |\Delta(r,d)| + \Theta_i(r,d) - q) \geq t\} < r.$$

So propagation would have detected that t is not a possible starting time. □

5 A Constraint Propagation Algorithm

For any deadline d, all intervals $I_{r,d,q}$ and $E_{r,d,q}$ are completed at the same time $ect(F, r, q+1) - 1$. So we define $I_{r,q}$ as the maximum, over all d, of $I_{r,d,q}$. It is then easy to compute all intervals $I_{r,q}$ in cubic time. The situation is a bit more complex for intervals $E_{r,d,q}$ as we cannot merge all these intervals since external adjustments are only valid for jobs that are not in $\Delta(r,d)$. To solve this issue, we consider jobs in non-decreasing order of deadlines and we add, at each iteration, all intervals corresponding to external adjustments associated to this deadline. This is valid since these intervals are used (Algorithm 5) to adjust release dates of jobs with a greater deadline.

The algorithm runs in cubic time. Indeed, there are $O(n^2)$ values to precompute and each time, this can be done in linear time. Moreover, the union of two intervals can be done in constant time and finally, the adjustment $r_k = \min\{t \geq r_k, t \notin \cup_{r,q} I_{r,q} \cup E_{r,q}\}$ can be computed in quadratic time since there are $O(n^2)$ intervals to consider. To simplify the presentation of the algorithm, we do not explicitly define the data structure in which we store the intervals $I_{r,q}$ and $E_{r,q}$. In practice, we rely on a quadratic array indexed by jobs.

Algorithm 5. An $O(n^3)$ Constraint Propagation Algorithm

1: Precompute all $lst(F,d,i)$ and $ect(F,r,i)$ values
2: Initialize $I_{r,q}$ and $E_{r,q}$ to $\emptyset$
3: **for all** deadline d **do**
4:     **for all** release date r **do**
5:         **for all** $q \leq |\Delta(r,d)| - 1$ **do**
6:             $I_{r,q} = I_{r,q} \cup [lst(F,d,|\Delta(r,d)|-q)+1, ect(F,r,q+1)-1]$
7: **for all** job k taken in non-decreasing order of deadlines **do**
8:     $r_k = \min\{t \geq r_k, t \notin \cup_{r,q}(I_{r,q} \cup E_{r,q})\}$
9:     **for all** release date r **do**
10:        **for all** $q \leq |\Delta(r,d_k)|$ **do**
11:           $E_{r,q} = E_{r,q} \cup [lst(F,d_k,|\Delta(r,d_k)|-q+1)+1, ect(F,r,q+1)-1]$

A similar algorithm can be used to adjust deadlines.

6 Experiments

Our constraint propagation algorithm has been tested on two disjunctive scheduling problems. The first one is a special case of the Job-Shop scheduling problem in which all operations on the same machine have the same processing time. The second one is a combinatorial problem from Air-Traffic Management (ATM). In both case, we briefly describe the problem and the CP model but we do not describe the branching scheme nor the heuristics used. The objective of this section is only to evaluate the efficiency of the Inter-Distance Constraint Propagation Scheme.

6.1 Job-Shop Scheduling

The Job-Shop Scheduling Problem consists of n jobs that are to be executed using m machines. Each job consists of m operations to be processed in a specified order. Each operation requires a specified machine and each machine is required by a unique activity of each job. The Job-Shop is an optimization problem. The goal is to determine a solution with minimal makespan and prove the optimality of the solution. In this paper we study a variant of the problem in which processing times of operations that require the same machine are identical. Even with this restriction, the problem is strongly NP-hard ([11]).

We use a standard model for the Job-Shop (see [3]) where starting times of operations are integer constrained variables and the makespan is represented as an integer variable constrained to be greater than or equal to the end of any job. Arc-B-Consistency is applied on precedence constraints between operations. Machine constraints are enforced either with Edge-Finding (EF) or with the Inter-Distance Constraint (IDC). The branching scheme and the heuristics are those provided by default in ILOG SCHEDULER, the constraint based scheduling tool of ILOG.

As for the standard Job-Shop problem, randomly generated instances are very easy to solve with EF. Among 150 random instances with up to 15 jobs and 15 machines, 34 instances requiring a significant amount of time to be solved (more than 10 seconds on Dell Latitude D600 running XP) were selected. For each instance, the two variants (EF and IDC) have been run for up to 3600 seconds. EF is able to solve 23 instances while IDC can solve 29 instances. On the average, less than 27 seconds were required by IDC to solve the 6 instances that could not be solved within one hour by EF. Among the 23 instances solved by both variants, EF requires 588999 backtracks and 249 seconds while IDC requires 249655 backtracks and 232 seconds. In term of CPU, the relatively low improvement comes, we believe, from the fact that we compare the highly optimized Edge-Finding implementation of Ilog Scheduler with a straightforward implementation of IDC.

6.2 Runway Sequencing with Holding Patterns

We study a scheduling problem that occurs when aircraft reach the final descent in the "Terminal Radar Approach CONtrol" area (TRACON) of an airport with a single runway. When entering the TRACON, a set of disjoint time windows in which the landing is possible, can be automatically assigned to each aircraft. Roughly speaking, the distance between two consecutive windows corresponds to a waiting procedure known as a "Holding Pattern". The objective is then to determine landing times, within these time windows, which maximize the minimum time elapsed between consecutive landings. More formally, the decision variant of this problem can be described as follows.

THE RUNWAY SCHEDULING PROBLEM

Input integers $n, p, (s_1, \ldots, s_n), (r_1^1, d_1^1, \ldots, r_1^{s_1}, d_1^{s_1}), \ldots, (r_n^1, d_n^1, \ldots, r_n^{s_n}, d_n^{s_n})$.

Meaning each job i has processing time p and has to be fully scheduled (*i.e.*, started and completed) in one of the intervals $[r_{iu}, d_{iu}]$. We wish to find a schedule such that every job is scheduled non-preemptively, and no two jobs overlap.

Output a set of starting times $S_1, \ldots, S_n \in \mathbb{N}$ such that (1) $\forall i \in \{1, \ldots n\}$, $\exists j \in \{1, \ldots, s_i\}$ such that $S_i \in [r_{ij}, d_{ij} - p]$ and (2) $\forall i, k \in \{1, \ldots n\}$ with $k \neq i$, $|S_i - S_k| \geq p$.

This problem is NP-Complete in the strong sense [2]. We refer to [5], [6] and [2] for a complete description of the problem together with MIPs and Branch and Cut procedures to solve it.

We build a constraint based model as follows. For each aircraft i, we have a decision variable P_i that determines whether i is scheduled in its j-th time window $[r_{ij}, d_{ij}]$, ($P_i = j$) or not ($P_i \neq j$). We also associate a start time variable S_i for each job $i : P_i \geq j \iff r_j \leq S_i$ and $P_i \leq j \iff d_j \geq S_i + p$.

The fact that jobs do not overlap in time is modeled as an Inter-Distance constraint. To solve the problem, we look for an assignment of the P_i variables and at each node of the search tree we test whether the IDC constraint is consistent or not (Section 3). This directly ensures that, when all P_i variables are bound, we have a solution to the scheduling problem. Two variants have been tested. In the first one, the machine constraint is propagated with Edge Finding (EF) while in the second one we use the Inter-Distance Constraint (IDC) propagation algorithm.

Two sets of instances have been generated (instances can be downloaded at http://www.lix.polytechnique.fr/~baptiste/flight_scheduling_data.zip). The first set of instances corresponds to "mono-pattern" problems in which all aircraft have the same number of time windows, each of them having the same size and being equally spaced. The second set of instances corresponds to the general problem. Instances with up to 90 jobs have been randomly generated (see [2] for details). For this problem, all tests were made on top of ECLAIR©[15]. Within 1 minute of CPU time, 189 and 32 instances of the first and second set of instances could be solved with EF while with IDC, we can solve respectively 192 and 46 instances. Among instances solved by EF and IDC the number of backtracks is reduced of 60 % (first set) and 91% (second set) when using IDC. The CPU time is also decreased of 4 % and 73 %.

7 Conclusion

We have introduced a new global constraint, the "inter-distance constraint" that ensures that the distance between any pair of variables in some set is at least equal to a given value. We have introduced a constraint propagation algorithm that achieves arc-B-consistency on this constraint and we have shown that it allows to drastically reduce the search space on some combinatorial problems.

Our constraint propagation algorithm is more costly than the edge-finding algorithm (although it is much more powerful and achieves the best possible bounds). Its complexity can be reduced to $O(n^2 \log n)$ but the algorithm requires specific data structures that are not in the scope of this paper. An open question is whether the worst case complexity of the constraint propagation algorithm can be reduced to $O(n^2)$.

We also believe that a generalization of this constraint to the situation where m identical parallel machines are available could be interesting. Such a constraint would be immediately useful for car-sequencing problems where "a/b" constraints (no more than a cars with some special feature among b consecutive ones) can be expressed in scheduling terms: Schedule identical jobs with processing time b on a parallel identical machines (each time point in the scheduling model corresponds to a slot in the sequence of cars). The global consistency of the corresponding constraint can be achieved in polynomial time thanks to a beautiful algorithm of Simons [22]. However, no specific constraint propagation algorithm is known.

References

1. D. Applegate and W. Cook. A Computational Study of the Job-Shop Scheduling Problem. *ORSA Journal on Computing*, 3(2):149–156, 1991.
2. K. Artiouchine, Ph.Baptiste and C.Dürr. Runway Sequencing with Holding Patterns. *http://www.lix.polytechnique.fr/Labo/Konstantin.Artiouchine/ejor04.pdf*
3. Ph. Baptiste, C. Le Pape, and W. Nuijten. *Constraint-based Scheduling*. Kluwer Academic Publishers, 2001.
4. Ph. Baptiste and C. Le Pape. Edge-Finding Constraint Propagation Algorithms for Disjunctive and Cumulative Scheduling. *Proc. 15th Workshop of the UK Planning Special Interest Group*, 1996.
5. A. M. Bayen and C. J. Tomlin, Real-time discrete control law synthesis for hybrid systems using MILP: Application to congested airspace, Proceedings of the *American Control Conference*, 2003.
6. A. M. Bayen, C. J. Tomlin, Y. Ye, J. Zhang, MILP formulation and polynomial time algorithm for an aircraft scheduling problem, *cherokee.stanford.edu/~bayen/publications.html*.
7. J. Carlier and E. Pinson. A Practical Use of Jackson's Preemptive Schedule for Solving the Job-Shop Problem. *Annals of Operations Research*, 26:269–287, 1990.
8. J. Carlier and E. Pinson. Adjustment of Heads and Tails for the Job-Shop Problem. *European Journal of Operational Research*, 78:146–161, 1994.
9. U. Dorndorf, E. Pesch and T. Phan-Huy. Solving the Open Shop Scheduling Problem. *Journal of Scheduling*, 4, 157–174, 2001.
10. M.R. Garey, D.S. Johnson, B.B. Simons, and R.E. Tarjan. Scheduling unit-time tasks with arbitrary release times and deadlines. *SIAM Journal on Computing*, 10(2), 256–269, 1981.
11. J.K. Lenstra and A.H.G. Rinnooy Kan. Computational complexity of discrete optimization problems. *Ann. Discrete Math.*, 4:121-140, (1979).
12. O. Lhomme. Consistency Techniques for numeric CSPs. *Proceedings of the thirteenth International Joint Conference on Artificial Intelligence*, Chambéry, France, (1993).
13. A. Lopez-Ortiz, C.-G. Quimper, J. Tromp, and P. van Beek. A fast and simple algorithm for bounds consistency of the alldifferent constraint. Proceedings of the 18th *International Joint Conference on Artificial Intelligence*, Acapulco, Mexico, 2003.
14. P. D. Martin and D. B. Shmoys. A New Approach to Computing Optimal Schedules for the Job-Shop Scheduling Problem. *Proc. 5th Conference on Integer Programming and Combinatorial Optimization*, 1996.
15. N. Museux, L. Jeannin, P. Savéant, F. Le Huédé, F.-X. Josset and J. Mattioli. Claire/Eclair©: Un environnement de modélisation et de résolution pour des applications d'optimisations combinatoires embarquées, *Journées Francophones de Programmation en Logique et de programmation par Contraintes*, 2003.

16. W. Nuijten, T. Bousonville, F. Focacci, D. Godard and C. Le Pape. Towards an industrial Manufacturing Scheduling Problem and Test Bed, Proc. of the 9th *International Workshop on Project Management and Scheduling*, 2004.
17. E. Pinson. *Le problème de Job-Shop*. Thèse de l'Université Paris VI, 1988.
18. J.-F. Puget. A fast algorithm for the bound consistency of all-diff constraints. *Proc. 15th National Conference on Artificial Intelligence*, 1998.
19. J.-C. Régin. A filtering algorithm for constraints of difference in CSPs. *Proc. 12th National Conference on Artificial Intelligence*, 1994.
20. J.-C. Régin. The global minimum distance constraint. Technical report, ILOG, 1997.
21. J.-C. Régin and J.-F. Puget. A filtering algorithm for global sequencing constraints. Proceedings of the Third International Conference on Principles and Practice of Constraint Programming, 1997.
22. B. Simons. A fast algorithm for single processor scheduling. *19th Annual Symposium on the Foundations of Computer Science*, pages 246–252, October 1978.
23. Ph. Torres and P. Lopez. On Not-First/Not-Last conditions in disjunctive scheduling. *European Journal of Operational Research*, 127:332–343, 2000.
24. P. Vilím. $o(n \log n)$ filtering algorithms for unary resource constraint. In Jean-Charles Régin and Michel Rueher, editors, *Proceedings of CP-AI-OR*, volume 3011 of *LNCS*, pages 335–347. Springer, 2004.

Mind the Gaps: A New Splitting Strategy for Consistency Techniques

Heikel Batnini, Claude Michel, and Michel Rueher

Université de Nice Sophia-Antipolis,
COPRIN project I3S-CNRS/INRIA/CERTIS,
INRIA, 2004 Route des Lucioles,
BP 93, 06902 Sophia-Antipolis, France
Heikel.Batnini@sophia.inria.fr
{cpjm, rueher}@essi.fr

Abstract. Classical methods for solving numerical CSPs are based on a branch and prune algorithm, a dichotomic enumeration process interleaved with a consistency filtering algorithm. In many interval solvers, the pruning step is based on local consistencies or partial consistencies. The associated pruning algorithms compute numerous data required to identify gaps within some domains, *i.e.* inconsistent intervals strictly included in the domain. However, these gaps are only used to compute the smallest approximation of the box enclosing all the solutions. This paper introduces a search strategy, named MindTheGaps, that takes advantage of the gaps identified during the filtering process. Gaps are collected with a negligible overhead, and are used to select the splitting direction as well as to define relevant cutting points within the domain. Splitting the domain by removing such gaps definitely reduces the search space. It also helps to discard some redundant solutions and helps the search algorithm to isolate different solutions. First experimental results show that MindTheGaps significantly improves performances of the search process.

1 Introduction

Many application problems ranging from robotics to chemistry and geometry can be seen as numerical constraint satisfaction problems (NCSPs). A NCSP is defined by a set of variables and a set of nonlinear constraints on the variables. The domain of the variables are closed intervals of real values. Numerical CSPs can be used to express a large class of problems, particularly problems with imprecise data or partially defined parameters. The goal is to find sharp boxes that approximate the solutions. Correct approximations of the solutions can be obtained by interval-based solvers; most of them implement a search algorithm that combines enumeration techniques and local consistencies techniques.

Consistencies techniques over numerical CSPs are derived from finite domains CSPs techniques. The associated filtering algorithms remove from the interval domains some values for which at least one constraint does not hold (inconsistency). In practice, the pruning is limited to a contraction of the bounds of the intervals.

Classical techniques for solving numerical CSPs are based on a branch and prune algorithm. This algorithm interleaves domain pruning and domain splitting, until a given precision of the domains is reached. The splitting step selects a direction and splits the corresponding interval in several pieces. The standard splitting technique is bisection, which splits the selected domain in its middle.

Among the strategies for selecting the domain to split, the method considered as the most efficient on average is the Round Robin method (RR) : the domains of the variables are processed alternately. However, other domain selection strategies have been proposed. The Largest First (LF) strategy, also called geometric splitting [1], selects first the domain of maximal width. The Maximal Smear (MS) strategy has been introduced by [2] for interval Gauss-Seidel method : the selected domain maximizes the smear function[1] [3], informally speaking, the domain of the variable the projection of which has the strongest slope.

In most interval solvers, the pruning step is based on local consistencies (Hull-Consistency [4,5], Box-consistency [6,7,8]) or stronger consistencies (kB-consistencies [4,9], Bound-consistency [10]). The associated pruning algorithms often identify gaps within some domains, i.e., inconsistent intervals strictly included in the domain. These gaps are only used to compute the smallest approximation of the box enclosing all the solutions.

This paper introduces a search strategy, named MindTheGaps, that takes advantage of the gaps identified by local consistencies filtering algorithms. These gaps are collected with a negligible overhead, and are used to select the splitting direction as well as to define relevant cutting points within the domain. Splitting a domain by removing such a gap definitely reduces the search space. It also helps to discard some redundant solutions and helps the search algorithm to isolate different solutions. If no gap has been found, the branching step is achieved by a standard splitting process combined with classical selection strategies.

In general, chronological backtracking is used to handle the subproblems generated by the splitting step. However, more sophisticated strategies may also be used, as for instance a dynamic backtracking strategy [11]. Note that MindTheGaps is fully compatible with any backtracking technique.

A similar approach has been suggested by Hansen [12,2] for interval Newton method. The search algorithm exploits the gaps identified by Gauss-Seidel steps. This approach has been used by Ratz [1] for handling global optimization problems. Three different box-splitting strategies have been suggested :

- Use only the largest gap to split the box, and generate 2 subproblems [12].
- Use k gaps found in the same domain to split the box and generate $k+1$ subproblems [1].
- Use at most three gaps in three different domains, and combine the subdomains to generate up to 8 subproblems [2].

We generalize Hansen's approach for all classical consistency filtering algorithms : Hull-consistency, Box-consistency and kB-consistencies. We demonstrate that this approach works well for solving satisfaction problems, that is to say for finding all isolated solutions or solutions spaces.

---
[1] The smear function of x_k is : $s_k = \max_{1 \leq j \leq m} \{\max\{|\underline{J}_{i,j}|, |\overline{J}_{i,j}|\} w(\mathbf{x}_i)\}$, where $\mathbf{J}_{i,j} = [\underline{J}_{i,j}, \overline{J}_{i,j}]$ is the (i,j)-th entry of the interval extension of the Jacobian matrix of the system.

Hyvönen [13] used the gaps to enforce strong consistency. He proposed an algorithm to enforce union-consistency by combining sets of intervals, but this method is strongly limited by its exponential character. MindTheGaps uses the gaps to guide the solution space exploration, and can thus limit the number of generated gaps. To limit the cost of the management of unions of intervals, we avoid gap identification on trigonometric functions. More precisely, we restrict gap identification to power terms and divisions, which produce at most one gap.

The paper is organized as follows: section 2 briefly describes the notations used in the rest of the paper. Section 3 gives an overview of MindTheGaps. Section 4 describes the extensions of Hull-consistency, Box-consistency filtering algorithms that collect the gaps. Section 5 reports some experimental results on classical benchmarks. Finally, section 6 proposes different extensions of the method to handle stronger consistencies.

2 Notations

Let $\overline{\mathbb{R}}$ be the set of real numbers $\mathbb{R}$ extended to infinites values $\{-\infty, +\infty\}$ and let $\overline{\mathbb{F}} \subset \overline{\mathbb{R}}$ be the subset of reals corresponding to binary floating-point numbers in a given format. A closed interval $\mathbf{x} = [\underline{x}, \overline{x}]$ with $\underline{x}, \overline{x} \in \overline{\mathbb{F}}$ denotes the set of real values x such that $\underline{x} \leq x \leq \overline{x}$. Open intervals will be denoted by $(\underline{x}, \overline{x}) = \{x \in \overline{\mathbb{R}} \text{ s.t. } \underline{x} < x < \overline{x}\}$. $\mathbb{I}$ stands for the set of such intervals and $\cap_{\mathbb{I}}$ denotes the intersection operator over $\mathbb{I}$.

A union of intervals is denoted by $\mathbf{u} = \bigcup \mathbf{u}_{(j)}$, where the subintervals $\mathbf{u}_{(j)}$ are disjoint and sorted by increasing lower bound, i.e. $\overline{u}_{(j)} < \underline{u}_{(j+1)}$. The number of subintervals of $\mathbf{u}$ is denoted by $|\mathbf{u}|$. The lower bound (resp. upper bound) of $\mathbf{u}$ is denoted by $\underline{u}$ (resp. $\overline{u}$). $\mathbb{U}$ stands for the set of such unions of intervals and $\cap_{\mathbb{U}}$ denotes the intersection operator over $\mathbb{U}$, such that $\mathbf{u} \cap_{\mathbb{U}} \mathbf{v} = \{x \in \mathbb{R} : x \in \mathbf{u} \wedge x \in \mathbf{v}\}$.

Real variables are denoted by x, y and X, Y denote variable vectors whereas $\mathbf{X}, \mathbf{Y}$ denote interval vectors and $\mathbf{U}, \mathbf{V}$ denote vectors of union of intervals. We note $\mathbf{X} = \emptyset$ whenever one of the interval components of $\mathbf{X}$ is empty. The width of an interval $w(\mathbf{x})$ is the positive quantity $\overline{x} - \underline{x}$, while the midpoint $m(\mathbf{x})$ of the interval $\mathbf{x}$ is $(\overline{x} + \underline{x})/2$. $w(\mathbf{X})$ denotes the size of the largest interval component of $\mathbf{X}$.

This paper focus on numerical CSPs defined by $X = (x_1, \ldots, x_n)$, a vector of variables, $\mathbf{X} = (\mathbf{x}_1, \ldots, \mathbf{x}_n)$, a vector of associated domains, and $\mathbf{C} = \{c_1, \ldots, c_m\}$, a set of nonlinear constraints. The set of variables of the constraint c is denoted by $\mathbb{V}_c$.

3 MindTheGaps: General Framework

Classical techniques for solving numerical CSPs are based on a branch and prune algorithm (see figure 1(a)). This algorithm interleaves domain pruning and domain splitting until a given precision ω_{sol} of the domains is reached. Prune (line 4) is one of the standard filtering algorithm based on numerical constraint programming consistency techniques: Hull-consistency, Box-consistency or kB-consistencies. In the rest of the paper, Hull-consistency algorithm will be denoted by HCPrune and Box-consistency algorithm by BCPrune. Split (line 9) is a function that selects a splitting direction and splits the corresponding interval. The generated subproblems are added to the set Q. In

BranchAndPrune(in :$\mathbf{X}_0, \mathbf{C}, \omega_{sol}$ out : S)	MindTheGaps(in:$\mathbf{X}_0, \mathbf{C}, \omega_{sol}$ out: S)
%% $\mathbf{X}_0 = (\mathbf{x}_1, \ldots, \mathbf{x}_n)$	%% $\mathbf{X}_0 = (\mathbf{x}_1, \ldots, \mathbf{x}_n)$
1: $Q \leftarrow \{\mathbf{X}_0\}$; $S \leftarrow \emptyset$	1: $Q \leftarrow \{\mathbf{X}_0\}$; $S \leftarrow \emptyset$
2: **while** $Q \neq \emptyset$ **do**	2: **while** $Q \neq \emptyset$ **do**
3: Extract $\mathbf{X}$ from Q	3: Extract $\mathbf{X}$ from Q
4: $\mathbf{X} \leftarrow$ Prune$(\mathbf{C}, \mathbf{X})$	4: $\mathbf{X} \leftarrow$ Prune*$(\mathbf{C}, \mathbf{X}, \mathbf{U})$
5: **if** $\mathbf{X} \neq \emptyset$ **then**	5: **if** $\mathbf{X} \neq \emptyset$ **then**
6: **if** $w(\mathbf{X}) \leq \omega_{sol}$ **then**	6: **if** $w(\mathbf{X}) \leq \omega_{sol}$ **then**
7: $S \leftarrow S \cup \mathbf{X}$	7: $S \leftarrow S \cup \mathbf{X}$
8: **else**	8: **else if** $\exists k$ s.t. $|\mathbf{u}_k| > 1$ **then**
% Standard splitting process	% Gap Splitting
9: $Q \leftarrow Q \cup$ Split$(\mathbf{X})$	9: $Q \leftarrow Q \cup$ GapSplit$(\mathbf{U})$
10: **endif**	10: **else**
11: **endif**	% Standard splitting process
12: **endwhile**	11: $Q \leftarrow Q \cup$ Split$(\mathbf{X})$
13: **return** S	12: **endif**
	13: **endif**
	14: **endwhile**
	15: **return** S
(a) Standard BranchAndPrune algorithm	(b) MindTheGaps:Overview

Fig. 1. Overall scheme of MindTheGaps

general, bisection is used and the intervals are split in their middle. Different domain selection strategies may be used such as RR, LF or MS (as mentioned in section 1).

In contrast, MindTheGaps (see figure 1(b)) takes advantage of the gaps produced by consistency filtering algorithms. Function Prune* (line 4) collects the gaps generated during the filtering process. The identified gaps are stored in $\mathbf{U}$, which is a vector of union of intervals $(\mathbf{u}_1, \ldots, \mathbf{u}_n)$, such that : $\mathbf{u}_i = \bigcup \mathbf{u}_{i(j)}$, where $\mathbf{u}_{i(j)} = [\underline{u}_{i(j)}, \overline{u}_{i(j)}]$ denotes the j-th sub-domain of x_i. As long as $w(\mathbf{X})$ is larger than some ω_{sol}, MindTheGaps splits at first among a domain that contains at least one gap (line 9). Several heuristics for selecting the domain to split and for choosing the gaps to remove have been explored (see section 5). The splitting is actually done by the function GapSplit which removes one or more gaps from the selected domains, and stores the subproblems in the stack Q. MindTheGaps splits first the domains that contain gaps. If no gap has been found, the standard Split is used (line 11).

4 Local Consistencies and Gaps

Most constraint solvers (*e.g.* IlogSolver [14], Numerica [7], Realpaver [15]) are based on local consistencies (Hull-consistency [4,5], Box-consistency [7,6]). The corresponding filtering algorithms perform a pruning of the domains of the variables by removing values for which some constraints do not hold (inconsistency). This reduction is achieved by narrowing operators which are correct, monotone and contracting functions. The reductions are propagated using the standard interval narrowing algorithm, derived from AC3 [16] (see figure 2).

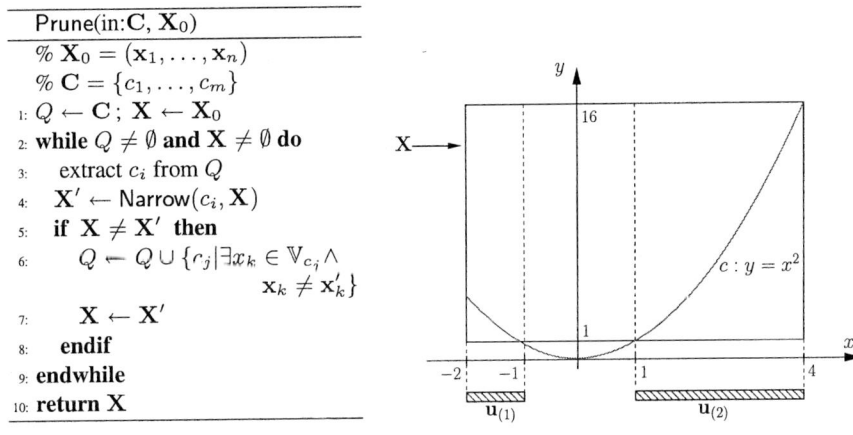

Fig. 2. Standard interval narrowing algorithm

Fig. 3. Approximation of a projection function by a union of intervals

Hull-consistency and Box-consistency are based on this standard interval narrowing algorithm, but they use a specific Narrow function. In this section, we describe extended Narrow functions that collects the gaps identified by the respective consistency. These extended versions, called Narrow*$(c_i, \mathbf{X}, \mathbf{U})$, store the gaps identified in a vector of unions of interval $\mathbf{U} = (\mathbf{u}_1, \ldots, \mathbf{u}_n)$. Then we define extended Hull-consistency and Box-consistency filtering algorithms that collect the identified gaps.

4.1 Interval Extensions and Projection Functions

An interval evaluation of a real-valued function f for a given range $\mathbf{X} = (\mathbf{x}_1, \ldots, \mathbf{x}_n)$ is an interval $\mathbf{y}$ such that : $\underline{y} \leq f(x_1, \ldots, x_n) \leq \overline{y}, \forall x_i \in \mathbf{x}_i, 1 \leq i \leq n$. In other words, $\mathbf{y}$ is an interval that contains the values of f, when the values of the unknowns are restricted to the box $\mathbf{X}$. The simplest way to compute $\mathbf{y}$ is to evaluate the *natural* interval extension of f, obtained by substituting all classical mathematical operators (resp. constants, variables) in f by their *basic* interval extension [17].

Example 1. Let $f(x,y) = 2x + xy - 1$ with $x \in [-1,1], y \in [1,2]$. The interval evaluation of f for the given ranges is $[2,2] \otimes [-1,1] \oplus [-1,1] \otimes [1,2] \ominus [1,1] = [-5,3]$.

The same principle can be applied to compute a union of intervals that contains the values of f using the *extended* interval extension of the basic mathematical operators [17,2,18,19].

Interval narrowing algorithms use projection functions [8] to prune the domains of the variables. Informally speaking, $\pi_c^{x_k}(\mathbf{X})$ denotes the projection over the variable x_k of the solutions of c when the values of the variables are restricted to the range $\mathbf{X}$. Note that $\pi_c^{x_k}(\mathbf{X})$ may be conservatively approximated either by the smallest enclosing interval denoted by $\Box_\mathbb{I}(\pi_c^{x_k}(\mathbf{X}))$, or by the smallest enclosing union of intervals denoted by $\Box_\mathbb{U}(\pi_c^{x_k}(\mathbf{X}))$ (see example 2).

Example 2. Consider the constraint $c : y = x^2$ where $x \in [-2, 4]$ and $y \in [1, 16]$ and let $\mathbf{X} = [-2, 4] \times [1, 16]$. Figure 3 shows that the interval approximation of $\pi_c^x(\mathbf{X})$ is $\Box_{\mathbb{I}}(\pi_c^x(\mathbf{X})) = [-2, 4]$, whereas the union approximation of $\pi_c^x(y)$ is $\Box_{\mathbb{U}}(\pi_c^x(\mathbf{X})) = [-2, -1] \cup [1, 4]$.

To limit the cost of the management of unions of intervals, we avoid gap identification on trigonometric functions. More precisely, gap identification is restricted to power terms and divisions whose projections produce at most one gap[2]. The influence of the syntactic form of the constraint over gap identification will be explored in section 5.

4.2 Hull-Consistency and Gaps

Hull-consistency states a local property on the bounds of the domains. A constraint c is Hull-consistent if for any variable x_i of c, there exist values in the domains of all the other variables which satisfy c when x_i is fixed to $\underline{x}_i$ or $\overline{x}_i$. A more formal definition of Hull-consistency can be found in [4].

The basic implementation of Hull-consistency, named 2B-consistency [4,20], decomposes the system of constraints into primitive constraints for which projection functions are easy to compute. The most powerful implementation of Hull-consistency is HC4 [5], based on the narrowing operator HC4revise. This implementation does not require any explicit decomposition of the constraints. All the projection functions are evaluated by traversing a tree-structured representation of the constraints from bottom to top and conversely. Forward propagation evaluates the expression associated to each nodes, using the domains or the values associated to its subtrees. Backward propagation traverses the tree in the opposite direction to reduce the domains of the variables using the projection functions associated to each operator.

We detail now HCNarrow, the narrowing operator used for computing Hull-consistency in HC4. That is to say, HCNarrow corresponds to function Narrow in the generic algorithm of figure 2. Basically, HCNarrow (figure 4(a)) prunes the domain vector $\mathbf{X}$ by applying a constraint narrowing operator on each variable x_k of $\mathbb{V}_c$. This narrowing operator reduces the bounds of the domain of x_k by computing the natural extension of the projection function $\pi_c^{x_k}$. The evaluation of $\pi_c^{x_k}$ by union of intervals is intersected with $\mathbf{x}_k$ (line 2), but the possible gaps are lost during the intersection operation. In fact, they are used only to compute a stronger pruning of $\mathbf{x}_k$. However, the gaps could be collected by replacing the interval intersection operation, $\cap_{\mathbb{I}}$, in HCNarrow (line 2) by the pending operation on union of intervals, $\cap_{\mathbb{U}}$. Actually, it is not necessary to compute the intersection of the union of intervals at each projection, which may be costly. The narrowing operators being contracting functions ($\Phi(\Omega) \subseteq \Omega$), the last projection provides the smallest union of intervals (w.r.t. set inclusion) that approximate $\pi_c^{x_k}$. For this reason, HCNarrow* (see picture 4(b)) maintains a set S of constraint/variable pairs for which gaps have been identified. The effective computation of the gaps is delayed to the end of the propagation step. More precisely, HCNarrow* checks whether the evaluation of the projection function $\pi_c^{x_k}$ produces a gap within the domain $\mathbf{x}_k$ (line 5-9). In this case, the (c, x) is added to set of pairs of constraint/variable S. Otherwise (c, x) is

---

[2] Note that several gaps may be produced by intersecting the projections of different constraints on the same domain.

HCNarrow(in:c, $\mathbf{X}$) : Interval vector
% $\mathbf{X} = (\mathbf{x}_1, \ldots, \mathbf{x}_n)$
1: **foreach** $x_k \in \mathbb{V}_c$ **do**
2: $\quad \mathbf{x}_k \leftarrow \Box_\mathbb{I}(\mathbf{x}_k \cap_\mathbb{U} \Box_\mathbb{U}(\pi_c^{x_k}(\mathbf{X})))$
$\quad$ % Possible gaps are lost
3: $\quad$ **if** $\mathbf{x}_k = \emptyset$ **then**
4: $\quad\quad$ **return** $\emptyset$
5: $\quad$ **endif**
6: **endfor**
7: **return** $\mathbf{X}$

(a) HCNarrow

HCNarrow*(in:c, $\mathbf{X}$, in-out: S) : Interval vector
% $\mathbf{X} = (\mathbf{x}_1, \ldots, \mathbf{x}_n)$
1: **foreach** $x_k \in \mathbb{V}_c$ **do**
2: $\quad \mathbf{u} \leftarrow \mathbf{x}_k \cap_\mathbb{U} \Box_\mathbb{U}(\pi_c^{x_k}(\mathbf{X}))$
3: $\quad$ **if** $\mathbf{u} = \emptyset$ **then return** $\emptyset$
4: $\quad$ **else** % Mind the gap
5: $\quad\quad$ **if** $|\mathbf{u}| > 1$ **then**
6: $\quad\quad\quad$ $S \leftarrow S \cup (c, x_k)$
7: $\quad\quad$ **else**
8: $\quad\quad\quad$ $S \leftarrow S \setminus (c, x_k)$
9: $\quad\quad$ **endif**
10: $\quad\quad$ $\mathbf{x}_k \leftarrow \Box_\mathbb{I}(\mathbf{u})$
11: $\quad$ **endif**
12: **endfor**
13: **return** $\mathbf{X}$

(b) HCNarrow*

Fig. 4. Hull-consistency narrowing function and its variant which collects the gaps

deleted from S to handle the case where a gap has been previously identified but pushed out of the domain during the propagation step.

Let HCPrune$^+$(C,$\mathbf{X}$,S) be the algorithm Prune (see figure 2), in which the call to the narrowing function have been replaced by HCNarrow*(c_i,$\mathbf{X}$,S). HCPrune$^+$ enforces hull-consistency over the box $\mathbf{X}$ and fills the set S with pairs of constraint/ variables for which gaps have been identified.

Then, for each pair (c, x_k) of S, HCPrune* retrieves the gaps by intersecting $\mathbf{u}_k$ with the evaluation by union of intervals of the projection $\pi_c^{x_k}$ (see figure 5).

4.3 Box-Consistency and Gaps

Box-consistency [6,7] is a coarser approximation of arc-consistency than Hull-consistency, but it achieves a stronger pruning in practice [8]. Moreover, Box-consistency tackles some dependency problems when variables have multiple occurrences in the same constraint. A constraint c is Box-consistent if for any variable x_i of $\mathbb{V}_c$, the bounds of $\mathbf{x}_i$ satisfy the unary constraint obtained by replacing each occurrence of a variable x_j other that x_i by the constant interval $\mathbf{x}_j$. A more formal definition of Box-consistency can be found in [6,7].

Box-consistency generates a set of univariate functions which can be tackled by numerical method such as Interval Newton [2]. The pruning consists in finding the leftmost and the rightmost quasi-zero[3] of these univariate functions. Let BCNarrow be the narrowing function used to compute Box-consistency. BCNarrow(c,$\mathbf{X}$) prunes the domain of each variables of c until c is Box-consistent. For each variable x_k of c, an interval univariate function $\mathbf{f}_{\mathbf{x}_k}$ is generated from c by replacing all the variables but x_k by their interval domain. Then, the pruning consists in finding the leftmost quasi-zero and the rightmost quasi-zero of $\mathbf{f}_{\mathbf{x}_k}$. This narrowing is achieved on the lower bound

---

[3] A quasi-zero of the interval function $\mathbf{f}$ is an interval vector $\mathbf{X}$ such that $0 \in \mathbf{f}(\mathbf{X})$.

HCPrune*(in:C, in-out: X, U)
% $\mathbf{X} = (\mathbf{x}_1, \ldots, \mathbf{x}_n)$
% $\mathbf{U} = (\mathbf{u}_1, \ldots, \mathbf{u}_n)$
1: $S \leftarrow \emptyset$
2: HCPrune$^+$(C,X,S)
3: if $\mathbf{X} \neq \emptyset$ then
% Collect the gaps
4:   foreach $(c, x_k) \in S$ do
5:     $\mathbf{u}_k \leftarrow \mathbf{u}_k \cap_\mathbb{U} \square_\mathbb{U}(\pi_c^{x_k}(\mathbf{X}))$
6:   endfor
7: endif

Fig. 5. HCPrune* enforces Hull-consistency and collects the gaps

BCNarrow(in:c, $\mathbf{X}$) : Interval vector
% $\mathbf{X} = (\mathbf{x}_1, \ldots, \mathbf{x}_n)$
1: foreach $x_k \in V_c$ do
2:   $\mathbf{x}_k \leftarrow$ LeftNarrow($\mathbf{f}_{\mathbf{x}_k}, \mathbf{f}'_{\mathbf{x}_k}, \mathbf{x}_k$)
3:   $\mathbf{x}_k \leftarrow$ RightNarrow($\mathbf{f}_{\mathbf{x}_k}, \mathbf{f}'_{\mathbf{x}_k}, \mathbf{x}_k$)
4:   if $\mathbf{x}_k = \emptyset$ then
5:     return $\emptyset$
6:   endif
7: endfor
8: return $\mathbf{X}$

Fig. 6. Box-consistency narrowing function

by LeftNarrow (see figure 7(a)) and on the upper bound RightNarrow (see [6] for a detailed description of these algorithms). These functions are based on MonoNewton, which prunes the domain of a variable x w.r.t. a constraint c using the classical univariate interval Newton algorithm. Whenever x is reduced less than a given ϵ, a splitting process is applied to ensure that $\underline{x}$ is a quasi-zero of $\mathbf{f}_\mathbf{x}$. LeftNarrow* (see figure 7(b)) collects the gaps identified by the Box-consistency narrowing operator.

The point is that the call of MonoNewton (line 3 of LeftNarrow) produces gaps in two different ways:

1. If the right bound of the current interval domain x is reduced by MonoNewton, the removed interval ($[\overline{x}', \overline{x}]$) does not satisfy c.
2. By the interval newton method, MonoNewton, itself.

To explain how MonoNewton may produce gaps, let us recall the definition of the interval Newton method:

$$\mathbf{x}^{(0)} = \mathbf{x}$$
$$\mathbf{x}^{(n+1)} = N(\mathbf{f}, \mathbf{f}', \mathbf{x}^{(n)}),$$
where $N(\mathbf{f}_\mathbf{x}, \mathbf{f}'_\mathbf{x}, \mathbf{x}^{(n)}) = \mathbf{x}^{(n)} \cap (m(\mathbf{x}^{(n)}) - \frac{\mathbf{f}_\mathbf{x}(m(\mathbf{x}^{(n)}))}{\mathbf{f}'_\mathbf{x}(\mathbf{x}^{(n)})})$

The function MonoNewton computes the fix-point of $N(\mathbf{f}_\mathbf{x}, \mathbf{f}'_\mathbf{x}, \mathbf{x})$ and returns the resulting interval. The evaluation of the division $\mathbf{f}(m(\mathbf{x}^{(n)}))/\mathbf{f}'(\mathbf{x}^{(n)})$ with extended interval arithmetic [2,17] may produce a gap as illustrated on example 3 below.

Example 3. Let $f(x, y) = x^2 - y$ with $x \in [-4, 4]$ and $y \in [1, 16]$. The interval functions $\mathbf{f}_\mathbf{x}$ and its derivative $\mathbf{f}'_\mathbf{x}$ are defined by $\mathbf{f}_\mathbf{x}(x) = x^2 - [1, 16]$ and $\mathbf{f}'_\mathbf{x}(x) = 2x$. Then,
$\mathbf{x}^{(0)} = [-4, 4]$
$\mathbf{x}^{(1)} = [-4, 4] \cap (0 \ominus ((0^2 \ominus [1, 16]) \oslash (2 \otimes [-4, 4])))$
$\phantom{\mathbf{x}^{(1)}} = [-4, 4] \cap ([1, 16] \oslash [-8, 8])$
$\phantom{\mathbf{x}^{(1)}} = [-4, -1/8] \cup [1/8, 4]$

Thus $N(\mathbf{f}_\mathbf{x}, \mathbf{f}'_\mathbf{x}, \mathbf{x})$ is not in general a single interval but may be a union of intervals. Let us denote by MonoNewton*, the function that returns this union of intervals. We

LeftNarrow(in:**f**,**f**′,**x**): Interval
1: $r \leftarrow \overline{x}$
2: **if** $0 \notin \mathbf{f}(\mathbf{x})$ **then return** $\emptyset$
3: $\mathbf{x} \leftarrow$ MonoNewton$(\mathbf{f}, \mathbf{f}', \mathbf{x})$
% 1. MonoNewton may produce a gap
% 2. A gap appears
%   when right bound is reduced
4: **if** $0 \in \mathbf{f}([\underline{x}, x^+])$ **then**
5:    **return** $[\underline{x}, r]$
6: **else**
7:    $l \leftarrow$ LeftNarrow$(\mathbf{f}, \mathbf{f}', [\underline{x}, m(\mathbf{x})])$
8:    **if** $l = \emptyset$ **then**
9:      $l \leftarrow$ LeftNarrow$(\mathbf{f}, \mathbf{f}', [m(\mathbf{x}), \overline{x}])$
10:   **endif**
11:   **return** $[\underline{l}, r]$
12: **endif**
13: **return x**

(a) LeftNarrow

LeftNarrow*(in:**f**,**f**′,**x**, in-out: $S, \mathbf{u}$): Interval
1: $r \leftarrow \overline{x}$
2: **if** $0 \notin \mathbf{f}(\mathbf{x})$ **then return** $\emptyset$
3: $\mathbf{u}' \leftarrow$ MonoNewton*$(\mathbf{f}, \mathbf{f}', \mathbf{x})$
% Mind the gap
4: $\mathbf{u} \leftarrow \mathbf{u} \cap_\mathbb{U} (\mathbf{u}' \cup [r, +\infty))$
5: $\mathbf{x} \leftarrow \Box_\mathbb{I}(\mathbf{u})$
6: **if** $0 \in \mathbf{f}([\underline{x}, x^+])$ **then**
7:    **return** $[\underline{x}, r]$
8: **else**
9:    $l \leftarrow$ LeftNarrow*$(\mathbf{f}, \mathbf{f}', [\underline{x}, m(\mathbf{x})], S)$
10:   **if** $l = \emptyset$ **then**
11:      $l \leftarrow$ LeftNarrow*$(\mathbf{f}, \mathbf{f}', [m(\mathbf{x}), \overline{x}], S)$
14:   **endif**
15:   **return** $[\underline{l}, r]$
16: **endif**
17: **return x**

(b) LeftNarrow*

Fig. 7. Box narrowing operators and its variant which collect the gaps

define the LeftNarrow* (see figure 7(b)), which extends the classical box narrowing operator to collect the gaps. MonoNewton* collects the gaps produced by the extended interval newton method (line 3). The gap produced by the right bound contraction is collected in line 4.

5 Experimental Results

This section reports experimental results of MindTheGaps on a variety of classical benchmarks : two classical benches of interval arithmetics (*i1, i4*), an application of robot kinematics (*kin1*), some applications of economic modeling (*eco7* up to *eco10*), some problem made of Euclidean distance equations (*ponts, ext-penta* and some particular instances) and a polynomial system from the Posso test suite (*caprasse*). More details on *i1, i4, kin1* and *ecoN* can be found in [7], *ponts* in [21], *ext-penta* in [22] and *caprasse* in [23].

5.1 Customizing MindTheGaps

This section introduces three categories of strategies for customizing MindTheGaps. These heuristics have been investigated to answer the three following questions :

1. Gap validation : Which gaps are not relevant and should not be considered ?
2. Domain selection : Among the domains for which gaps have been found, which ones are the more relevant to split ?
3. Gap splitting : Given one or more selected domains, how to perform the splitting ?

To answer these questions, the following strategies have been explored :

- *Gap validation strategies* : Suppose that a gap has been identified by the filtering algorithms in the domain $\mathbf{x} = [a, d]$, such that $\mathbf{u} = [a, b] \cup [c, d]$. Two different strategies have been explored to validate the gap (b, c), depending on its position within the domain or its relative size :
  - Hansen [2] Keep (b, c) if $\min\{d - b, c - a\} \geq 0.25w(\mathbf{x})$. This strategy eliminates gaps strictly included in one of the extremal quarters of the domain.
  - Large-Gaps : Keep (b, c) if $c - b \geq 0.1w(\mathbf{x})$. This strategy eliminates small gaps with respect to the width of the domain.

  Note that these two strategies can be combined. By default, all the gaps identified by the filtering algorithms are kept (AllGaps).
- *Domain selection strategies* : Different heuristics have been explored :
  - LW (Largest Width) / SW (Smallest Width) : the selected domain holds the largest (resp. smallest) gap found [2].
  - LRW (Largest Relative Width) / SRW (Smallest Relative Width) : the selected domain maximizes (resp. minimizes) the ratio between gap width and domain width.
  - LTW (Largest Total Width) / STW (Smallest Total Width) : The selected domain maximizes (resp. minimizes) gap width sum.
- *Gap splitting strategies* :As mentioned above, three different strategies for splitting have been explored :
  - B1G (Bisect One Gap) : use only one gap to split the selected domain, and generate 2 subproblems [12].
  - BkG (Bisect k Gaps) : use k gaps in the selected domain to split the box and generate $k + 1$ subproblems [1].
  - M3G (Multisect 3 Gaps) : use at most three gaps in three different domains, and combine the subdomains to generate up to 8 subproblems [2]. The three domains and the gaps are determined by the domain selection strategy.

5.2 Analysis of Experimental Results

The above mentioned different strategies have been experimented on various benchmarks. However, due to lack of space, the tables presented in this section are limited to the results obtained with RR, LW and B1G. The other strategies did provide very similar results for most benches, except for the one explicitly discussed in the rest of the section.

All the tests use Realpaver [15] version 0.3. The tests have been run on a Pentium IV at 2.6Ghz running Linux. MindTheGaps has been implemented on the top of Realpaver. The different strategies, as well as the gap gathering process, have been added to the default Realpaver algorithm[4]. Note however that the Box filtering algorithm has been modified in order to fit to the default algorithm which made use of a univariate Newton algorithm[5].

---

[4] Note that the multivariate Newton algorithm has also been extended to collect gaps [2].

[5] The Box implementation of Realpaver does not use a univariate Newton algorithm. It only relies on interval computation to exclude some subparts of the domain.

Table 1. Experimental results for HC4 on the left and HC4+Newton on the right. The results were obtained using RR, LW and B1G.

	Filtering: HC4							Filtering: HC4+Newton						
	RR		MindTheGaps(RR)			Ratio		RR		MindTheGaps(RR)			Ratio	
	t(s)	B	t(s)	B	H	t	B	t(s)	B	t(s)	B	H	t	B
eco7	57.07	754885	14.74	231595	1	-74%	-69%	61.99	468799	12.74	107817	11	-79%	-77%
eco8	133.51	1614495	112.77	1360061	1	-15%	-16%	56.77	353155	40.54	246927	49	-29%	-30%
ponts	34.19	174915	33.12	171251	1043	-3%	-2	25.61	32643	16.80	21025	946	-35%	-36%
ponts0	0.30	1395	0.29	1395	0	-	-	0.06	71	0.07	71	0	-	-
ponts1	5.19	26523	4.54	22475	274	-13%	-16%	5.78	7465	3.61	4563	254	-38%	-39%
ponts2	23.63	123585	22.93	120993	779	-3%	-2%	18.77	24009	12.33	15567	670	-35%	-35%
pentagon	0.60	6131	0.59	5891	52	-2%	-4%	0.26	1655	0.23	1415	52	-12%	-15%
ext-penta	-	-	-	-	-	-	-	474.92	1006031	437.37	890943	11723	-8%	-12%
ext-penta0	0.34	873	0.11	423	51	-68%	-52%	0.45	873	0.17	423	51	-62%	-52%
ext-penta1	0.32	263	0.05	255	17	-85%	-3%	0.39	263	0.10	255	17	-74%	-3%
ext-penta2	0.77	2825	0.25	2047	9	-68%	-28%	1.23	2825	0.60	2047	9	-51%	-28%
i1	29.60	515909	28.75	501677	82	-3%	-3%	49.46	340057	53.73	370449	38	8%	9%
i4	0.83	2047	0.77	2047	1023	-8%	-	1.19	2047	1.07	2047	1023	-10%	-
kin1	25.69	264685	19.99	203987	1	-22%	-23%	0.41	1447	0.30	1263	1	-27%	-13%
caprasse	0.79	6527	0.80	6527	0	1%	-	0.65	2567	0.65	2567	0	-	- %

In tables 1 – –4, t is the execution time in seconds ("-" signifies more than 1 hour), B is the total number of boxes generated by the splitting process and H is the number of splits in a gap. The column ratio introduces the reduction percent in terms of CPU time (t) and total number of branchings (B).

Table 1 displays the results for a search combined with a HC4 filtering and a search combined with a HC4 interleaved with a multivariate newton algorithm. In both cases, MindTheGaps improves significantly the execution time and reduces the number of splitting. For example, on *eco7*, the execution time is reduced by a factor of 3.8 or more, depending on the kind of consistency we use, and the number of splits is reduced by a factor of 3 up to 4. Even on problems where the number of splits is left unchanged, like on *i4*, the MindTheGaps strategy has still room to improve the execution time. This example underline the key role of the cutting direction in the search process.

Other strategies than choosing the variable with the biggest gap and splitting on this gap do not change significantly the results. However, when applied to a Box filtering or a Box filtering interleaved with a multivariate Newton (see table 3), the strategies which rely on selecting the gaps lying at the center of the domain (Hansen's strategy) or which reject the smallest gaps improve the search on some problems (see table 2). For example, it solves *eco8* in less than half an hour while other strategies require more than an hour. This success is largely due to the way Box filtering produces gaps. Box filtering attempts to reject some part of the variable domains lying at the bounds. As a result, it tends to produce more gaps and smaller gaps near the bounds of the domains. This behavior is exemplified on *ext-penta2*, where the number of gaps used by the search goes from 7037 gaps down to 9 gaps (see table 2). The same remarks can be done when the Box filtering is combined with a multivariate Newton though this last smooth the effect of these strategies. However, whatever the strategies, MindTheGaps still succeeds in improving the execution time over a classical round robin.

MindTheGaps offers others advantages than improving search performances. For example, on the well known *combustion* benchmark, MindTheGaps provides the four

Table 2. Experimental results for Box on the left and on the right, Box with Hansen's criterion for eliminating small gaps. The results were obtained using RR, LW and B1G.

	\multicolumn{8}{c}{Filtering: Box}							
	RR		MindTheGaps(RR)			Ratio		MindTheGaps(RR)+Hansen			Ratio	
	t(s)	B	t(s)	B	H	t	B	t(s)	B	H	t	B
eco7	995.12	595505	-	-	-	-	-	276.91	192699	104	-72%	-68%
eco8	-	-	-	-	-	-	-	1372.13	847373	177	-	-
ponts	659.70	173331	644.60	170721	968	-2%	-2%	676.36	172515	1015	3%	-1%
ponts0	5.60	1481	4.90	1203	6	-12%	-10%	5.61	1481	0	-	- %
ponts1	105.47	25943	103.67	23335	122	-2%	-10%	99.83	22911	255	-5%	-12%
ponts2	461.20	122865	440.99	118123	656	-5%	-4%	459.61	121017	538	-1%	-2%
pentagon	11.27	6283	11.02	6275	173	-3%	- %	10.99	6033	51	-3%	-4%
ext-penta	-	-	-	-	-	-	-	-	-	-	-	-
ext-penta0	5.80	873	2.20	1771	666	-62%	102.86%	1.84	423	51	-68%	-52%
ext-penta1	6.65	263	1.09	873	306	-84%	232%	0.81	255	17	-88%	-3%
ext-penta2	11.36	2825	12.05	17865	7037	6%	533%	2.12	2047	9	-82%	-28%
i1	353.70	484511	369.60	502035	7614	5%	4%	353.67	482565	39	-	-
i4	5.51	2047	6.07	2047	1023	10%	-	6.05	2047	1023	10%	-
kin1	235.74	132547	-	-	-	-	- %	217.18	120309	56	-8%	-10%
caprasse	10.55	2023	10.50	1991	48	- %	-2%	10.52	1991	48	- %	-2%

Table 3. Experimental results for Box+Newton on the left and on the right, Box+Newton with Hansen's criterion for eliminating small gaps. The results were obtained using RR, LW and B1G.

	\multicolumn{8}{c}{Filtering: Box+Newton}							
	RR		MindTheGaps(RR)			Ratio		MindTheGaps(RR)+Hansen			Ratio	
	t(s)	B	t(s)	B	H	t	B	t(s)	B	H	t	B
eco7	797.72	429263	207.32	109267	685	-74%	-75%	196.39	102487	145	-76%	-76
eco8	-	-	-	-	-	-	-	516.92	224513	371	-	-
ponts	163.31	31735	180.84	35475	1098	11%	12%	133.51	25829	1014	-19%	-19%
ponts0	0.47	71	0.47	71	0	-	-	0.47	71	0	-	- %
ponts1	33.78	7363	27.56	4981	261	-18%	-32%	27.39	4981	261	-19%	-32%
ponts2	117.27	23417	110.37	21881	646	-6%	-7%	96.50	18675	563	-18%	-21%
pentagon	3.76	1639	0.27	1399	62	-93%	-15%	3.45	1399	62	-9%	-15%
ext-penta	-	-	-	-	-	-	-	-	-	-	-	-
ext-penta0	6.43	873	1.58	707	133	-75%	-19%	2.02	423	51	-69%	-52%
ext-penta1	7.18	263	1.12	747	209	-84.40%	184%	0.92	303	41	-88%	15%
ext-penta2	12.55	2825	7.28	8721	3167	-42%	208.70%	2.57	2047	9	-80%	-28 %
i1	247.22	309681	244.86	302397	576	-1%	-3%	247.38	305797	52	-	-1%
i4	6.26	2047	6.84	2047	1023	9%	-	6.82	2047	1023	9%	-
kin1	2.78	791	1.87	641	72	-33%	-19%	1.86	629	66	-33%	-20%
caprasse	10.54	1495	10.52	1463	48	-	-2%	10.54	1463	48	-	-2%

solutions when a basic round robin found only two enclosures of the four solutions[6]. Here, MindTheGaps takes benefit of two gaps found by HC4 or a Box to isolate the four solutions.

5.3 Gaps and Constraint Evaluation

Factorization rules have been designed for univariate or multivariate polynomials [24]. These symbolic tools aim at reducing the negative effects of interval computations. In general, the evaluation of polynomial constraints in factorized form is tighter. Similarly,

---

[6] These results were obtained with the default precision of Realpaver (1.0e-8). When the precision is increased, then Realpaver find all the solutions with a basic search strategy.

Table 4. Experimental results for *ecoN* and its corresponding Horner form *ecoNH*

	\multicolumn{2}{c}{RR}	\multicolumn{3}{c}{Filtering: HC4+Newton MindTheGaps(RR)}	\multicolumn{2}{c}{Ratio}
	t(s)	B	t(s)	B	H	t	B
eco6	1.04	12087	0.56	6383	3	-46.15%	-47.19%
eco6H	0.69	9301	0.29	3729	1	-57.97%	-59.90%
eco7	61.99	468799	12.74	107817	11	-79.44%	-77.00%
eco7H	49.78	412957	8.42	82143	4	-83%	-80%
eco8	56.77	353155	40.43	246927	49	-28.78%	-30.07%
eco8H	30.93	216955	24.17	164733	4	-21.85%	-24.07%
eco9	636.75	2931479	641.75	2934801	1720	.78%	.11%
eco9H	301.20	1541855	233.67	1303655	103	-22.42%	-15.44%
eco10	7569.05	25751025	7381.65	24939453	17949	-2.47%	-3.15%
eco10H	554.72	2620443	475.00	2156345	808	-14.37%	-17.71%

it should provide tighter gaps within the domains. Moreover, it may provide gaps that might have not been identified using the developed form :

Example 4. Let $c : x^2 + x * y = 1/2$ and its factorized form $c' : x(x+y) = 1/2$, with $\mathbf{x} = \mathbf{y} = [-1,1]$. $\Box_\mathbb{U}(\pi_c^x(\mathbf{X})) = [-1,1]$ while $\Box_\mathbb{U}(\pi_{c'}^x(\mathbf{X})) = [-1, 0.25] \cup [0.25, 1]$.

We have performed some experimentations on *ecoN* to compare the developed form and the corresponding Horner form (see table 4). These experimentations clearly show that Horner form provides a significant improvement (factor 2 to 15) with respect to the classical form for standard bisection. The number of Gap splitting (H) performed by MindTheGaps is strongly reduced (for instance by a factor 16 for *eco9*). However, the impact of MindTheGaps both on computation time and number of branching is stronger.

6 Extension to Partial Consistencies

kB-consistencies are not strictly local consistencies. Informally speaking, these higher consistencies try to shrink the domain by proving that no solution exists in some part of the domain. To do so, they use a lower order consistency $((k-1)$B-consistency). The point is that they only reduce the bounds of the domains. kB-consistency has a recursive definition based on 2B-consistency which is equivalent to Hull-consistency. Bound-consistency [10] is similar to 3B-consistency but it is based on Box-consistency, rather than 2B-consistency. Thus, partial consistencies also allow to identify gaps within the domains. Whenever kB-consistency tries to refute some interval $\alpha \subset \mathbf{x}_i$, it applies a $(k-1)$B-consistency over $P_{\mathbf{x}_i \leftarrow \alpha}$. Suppose that α is not eliminated but reduced to α'. Then, gaps can be retrieved in three different ways :

1. $\alpha \setminus \alpha'$ is a gap for $\mathbf{x}_i$
2. The gaps found by $(k-1)$B-consistency within α' holds also for $\mathbf{x}_i$.
3. The gaps found during the filtering of $P_{\mathbf{x}_i \leftarrow \alpha}$ within the domains of the other variables are only valid if they have been found also during the filtering of $P_{\mathbf{x}_i \leftarrow \mathbf{x}_i \setminus \alpha}$

For example, let $\mathbf{C} = \{x^2 + y^2 = 1, y = -x^2 + 1\}$, with $\mathbf{x} = \mathbf{y} = [-10, 10]$. A 2B-consistency filtering reduces $\mathbf{x}$ to $[-0.99, 0.99]$ and $\mathbf{y}$ to $[0.1, 1]$. Then, consider that $\mathbf{y}$ is split in two parts $\mathbf{y}_1 = [0.55, 1]$ and $\mathbf{y}_2 = [0.1, 0.55]$:

- $X_1 = (x, y_1)$ is reduced by 2B-consistency to $([-0.54, 0.54], [0.8, 1])$. Thus, there is no solution for $y \in (0.55, 0.8)$ (pruned by 2B-consistency (case 1)). Moreover, a gap has been identified for variable x : $x_2 = [-0.54, -0.316] \cup [0.316, 0.54]$.
- $X_2 = (x, y_2)$ is not reduced by 2B-consistency, but a gap is identified for variable x : $x_1 = [-1, -0.84] \cup [0.84, 1]$.

Consequently, if $y \in y_1$ or $y \in y_2$, then the set of allowed values for variable x is $x_1 \cup x_2$, that is to say $[-1, -0.84] \cup [-0.54, -0.316] \cup [0.316, 0.54] \cup [0.84, 1]$ (case 3).

Note that, the bound reductions (case 1) have been used in [25] to improve kB-consistency complexity. The gaps produced in case 2 and 3 could be used in a similar way to improve kB-consistency efficiency. A very first implementation of MindThe-Gaps combined with 3B-consistency shows significant improvements.

7 Conclusion

We have introduced in this paper a new splitting strategy for search algorithm in nonlinear CSPs. This splitting strategy takes advantage of the gaps generated by consistency filtering algorithms. These gaps provide indications for selecting which domain to split and for selecting cutting points inside the domains. Splitting the domain by removing such gaps definitely reduces the search space. It also helps to discard some redundant solutions and helps the search algorithm to isolate different solutions. Experimental results show that in numerous problems, the performances of the search process are significantly improved in comparison with classical search algorithm.

References

1. Ratz, D.: Box-splitting strategies for the interval Gauss–Seidel step in a global optimization method. Computing **53** (1994) 337–354
2. Hansen, E.: Global optimization using interval analysis. Marcel Deckler (1992)
3. Kearfott, R.: Rigorous global search: continuous problems. Kluwer (1996)
4. Lhomme, O.: Consistency techniques for numerical csps. In: IJCAI-93. (1993) 232–238
5. Benhamou, F., Goualard, F., Granvilliers, L., Puget, J.: Revising hull and box consistency. In: International Conference on Logic Programming. (1999) 230–244
6. Benhamou, F., McAllister, D., Van Hentenryck, P.: CLP(intervals) revisited. In Bruynooghe, M., ed.: International Symposium of Logic Programming. MIT Press (1994) 124–138
7. Van Hentenryck, P., McAllister, D., Kapur, D.: Solving polynomial systems using a branch and prune approach. SIAM, Journal of Numerical Analysis **34(2)** (1997) 797–827
8. Collavizza, H., Delobel, F., Rueher, M.: Comparing partial consistencies. Journal of Reliable Computing **5** (1999) 213–228
9. Lebbah, Y.: Contribution à la résolution de contraintes par consistance forte. Thèse de doctorat, École des Mines de Nantes (1999)
10. Puget, J., Van Hentenryck, P.: A constraint satisfaction approach to a circuit design problem. Journal of Global Optimization **13** (1998) 75–93
11. Jussien, N., Lhomme, O.: Dynamic domain splitting for numeric CSPs. In: European Conference on Artificial Intelligence. (1998) 224–228
12. Hansen, E., Greenberg, R.: An interval newton method. Applied Mathematics and Computations **12** (1983) 89–98

13. Hyvönen, E.: Constraint reasoning based on interval arithmetic: the tolerance propagation approach. Artificial Intelligence **58** (1992) 71–112
14. ILOG: Solver Reference manual http://www.ilog.com/product/jsolver. (2002)
15. Granvilliers, L.: Realpaver: Solving non linear constraints by interval computations. User's manual (2003) http://www.sciences.univ-nantes.fr/info/perso/permanents/granvil/realpaver.
16. Macworth, A.: Consistency in networks of relations. Artificial Intelligence (1977) 99–118
17. Moore, R.: Interval analysis. Prentice-Hall (1977)
18. Kearfott, R.: A review of techniques in the verified solution of constrained global optimization problems. In Kearfott, R.B., Kreinovich, V, eds.: Applications of Interval Computations. Kluwer, Dordrecht, Netherlands (1996) 23–59
19. Jaulin, L., Kieffer, M., Didrit, O., Walter, E.: Applied Interval Analysis. Springer (2001)
20. Lhomme, O.: Contribution à la résolution de contraintes sur les réels par propagation d'intervalles. Thèse de doctorat, Université de Nice-Sophia Antipolis (1994)
21. Jermann, C., Trombettoni, G., Neveu, B., Rueher, M.: A constraint programming approach for solving rigid geometric systems. In: Proc. of CP'00, Singapore (2000) 233–248
22. Batnini, H., Rueher, M.: Décomposition sémantique pour la résolution de systèmes d'équations de distances. JEDAI **2** (2004) Édition spéciale JNPC 2003.
23. Traverso, C.: The posso test suite examples (2003) http://www.inria.fr/saga/POL/index.html.
24. Ceberio, M.: Contribution à l'étude des CSPs numériques sous et sur-contraints. Outils symboliques et contraintes flexibles continues. PhD thesis, Université de Nantes (2003)
25. Bordeaux, L., Monfroy, E., Benhamou, F.: Improved bounds on the complexity of kb-consistency. In Kaufmann, M., ed.: Proceeding of IJCAI'2001. (2001) 303–308

Graph Invariants as Necessary Conditions for Global Constraints

Nicolas Beldiceanu[1], Mats Carlsson[2], Jean-Xavier Rampon[3], and Charlotte Truchet[3]

[1] LINA FRE CNRS 2729, École des Mines de Nantes, 44307 Nantes Cedex 3, France
Nicolas.Beldiceanu@emn.fr
[2] SICS, P.O. Box 1263, SE-164 29 Kista, Sweden
Mats.Carlsson@sics.se
[3] LINA FRE CNRS 2729, 2 rue de la Houssinière, BP-92208, 44322 Nantes Cedex 3, France
{Jean-Xavier.Rampon, Charlotte.Truchet}@lina.univ-nantes.fr

Abstract. This article presents a database of about 200 graph invariants for deriving systematically necessary conditions from the graph properties based representation of global constraints. This scheme is based on invariants on the graph characteristics used in the description of a global constraint. A SICStus Prolog implementation based on arithmetic and logical constraints as well as on indexicals is available.

1 Introduction

Adding necessary conditions to a constraint program has been recognized in the early time of constraint programming [1] as a key point in order to enhance efficiency. However this was usually done manually after a careful analysis of the problem under consideration or by identifying typical constraint patterns [2]. Beldiceanu presented in [3] a systematic description of global constraints in terms of graph properties: among the 227 constraints of the catalog of global constraints [3], about 200 constraints are described as a conjunction of graph properties where each graph property has the form P op V, where P is a graph characteristic, op is a comparison operator in $\{\leq, \geq, =, \neq\}$, and V a variable that ranges over a finite set of integers (a *domain variable*). Within this context, this article presents a database of graph invariants: given a specification of a constraint C in terms of graph properties, we can automatically extract, from that database, graph invariants that mention the graph characteristics used in the specification of C, and post these invariants as necessary conditions for the feasibility of C.

Example 1. Consider the nvalue$(N, \{x_1, ..., x_m\})$ constraint [4], where $N, x_1, ..., x_m$ are domain variables. The nvalue constraint holds iff the number of distinct values assigned to the variables in $\mathcal{X} = \{x_1, ..., x_m\}$ is equal to N. It can been seen as enforcing the following graph property: the number of strongly connected components of the *intersection graph* $G(\mathcal{X}, E)$, where $E = \{x_i \in \mathcal{X}, x_j \in \mathcal{X} : x_i = x_j\}$, is equal to N. From Bessière et al. [5] we have the necessary condition $\mathbf{NSCC} \geq \left\lceil \frac{\mathbf{NVERTEX}^2}{\mathbf{NARC}} \right\rceil$ (see Turán [6]) relating the number of arcs **NARC**, the number of vertices **NVERTEX** and the number of strongly connected components **NSCC** of the *intersection graph*.

Using graph invariants is especially useful when a global constraint mentions more than one graph property in its description. In this context, these graph properties involve several graph characteristics that cannot vary independently.

Example 2. Consider again the nvalue constraint introduced in Example 1, and assume we want to put a restriction on the minimum and the maximum number of occurrences (respectively denoted by $\underline{occ}$ and by $\overline{occ}$) of each value that is effectively used. In terms of the intersection graph, this can be interpreted as putting a restriction on the number of vertices of its strongly connected components. Let **MIN_NSCC** and **MAX_NSCC** respectively denote the number of vertices of the smallest and the largest strongly connected components of the intersection graph. Our initial constraint on the minimum and maximum number of occurrences is now expressed by **MIN_NSCC** $\geq \underline{occ}$ and **MAX_NSCC** $\leq \overline{occ}$. We have recast our original balanced assignment problem to the search of a digraph on which we restrict its number of vertices **NVERTEX**[1], its number of strongly connected components **NSCC**, and the sizes **MIN_NSCC** and **MAX_NSCC** of its smallest and largest strongly connected components. By querying our database of invariants in order to extract those graph invariants that only mention the four graph characteristics **NVERTEX**, **NSCC**, **MIN_NSCC** and **MAX_NSCC** we get the following invariants **NVERTEX** $\leq \max(0, \mathbf{NSCC} - 1) \cdot \mathbf{MAX\_NSCC} + \mathbf{MIN\_NSCC}$ and **NVERTEX** $\geq \max(0, \mathbf{NSCC} - 1) \cdot \mathbf{MIN\_NSCC} + \mathbf{MAX\_NSCC}$, which are necessary conditions for the balanced assignment constraint.

Section 2 recalls the graph-based representation of global constraints. Section 3 introduces graph invariants, while Section 4 presents the database of graph invariants. The database and its 200 graph invariants and their corresponding proofs is available in Chapter 3 of [3]. Finally, Section 4 provides an evaluation of the approach on two constraints, which mention various graph characteristics.

2 Graph-Based Representation of Global Constraint

This section summarizes the representation of global constraints as graph properties in [3] and illustrates this framework on the group [7] and the change_continuity [3] constraints, which will be used throughout this paper. They both correspond to timetabling constraints which allow for expressing conditions on sliding sequences of consecutive working days of a given person.

The Graph-Based Representation. A global constraint C is represented as an initial digraph $G_i = (\mathcal{X}_i, E_i)$: to each vertex in $\mathcal{X}_i$ corresponds a variable involved in C, while to each arc e in E_i corresponds a binary constraint involving the variables at both extremities of e. To generate G_i from the parameters of C, the set of arc generators described in [3] is used. Figure 1 illustrates the most commonly used arc generators by depicting the initial digraph generated from a sequence of four vertices. When all variables of C are fixed, we remove from G_i all binary constraints that do not hold as well as isolated vertices, i.e., vertices that are not extremities of an arc. This final digraph is denoted by G_f. C is equivalent to a conjunction of graph properties which should be satisfied by G_f. Within the global constraint catalog [3], commonly used graph characteristics on the final digraph G_f are:

---
[1] In fact, **NVERTEX** is fixed to the number of variables of the nvalue constraint.

- **NARC** and **NVERTEX** denote the number of arcs and vertices,
- **NCC** and **NSCC** denote the number of connected and strongly connected components,
- **MIN_NCC** and **MAX_NCC** (resp. **MIN_NSCC** and **MAX_NSCC**) respectively denote the number of vertices of the smallest and the largest connected components (resp. the strongly connected components).

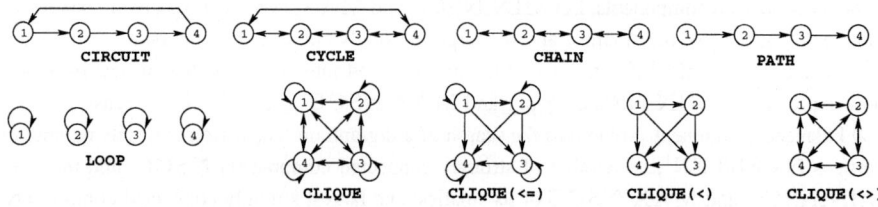

Fig. 1. Examples of arc generators (when considering **NARC**, double-arcs are counted twice)

Illustrative Examples of the Graph-Based Representation. We now define the group and the change_continuity constraints and present their links with the graph-based description. Since they respectively use 6 and 8 graph characteristics these constraints can potentially benefit from the use of graph invariants.

Example 3. The first six parameters of the group(NGROUP,MIN_SIZE,MAX_SIZE, MIN_DIST,MAX_DIST,NVAL,VARIABLES,VALUES) constraint are domain variables, while VARIABLES is a sequence of domain variables and VALUES a finite set of integers. Let n denote the number of variables of the sequence VARIABLES. Let $X_i, X_{i+1}, \ldots, X_j$ ($1 \leq i \leq j \leq n$) be consecutive variables of the sequence VARIABLES such that all the following conditions simultaneously apply: (1) All variables $X_i, \ldots, X_j$ take their value in the set of values VALUES, (2) $i = 1$ or X_{i-1} does not take a value in VALUES, (3) $j = n$ or X_{j+1} does not take a value in VALUES. We call such a set of variables a *group*. The constraint group is fulfilled if all the following conditions hold:

- There are exactly NGROUP groups of variables,
- MIN_SIZE and MAX_SIZE are the number of variables of the smallest and largest group,
- MIN_DIST and MAX_DIST are the minimum and maximum number of variables between two consecutive groups or between one border and one group,
- NVAL is the number of variables that take their value in the set of values VALUES.

group$(2, 2, 4, 1, 2, 6, \langle 0, 0, 1, 3, 0, 2, 2, 2, 3 \rangle, \{1, 2, 3\})$ holds since the sequence $\langle 0, 0, 1, 3, 0, 2, 2, 2, 3 \rangle$ contains 2 groups $\langle 1, 3 \rangle$ and $\langle 2, 2, 2, 3 \rangle$ of non-zero values of size 2 and 4, 2 groups $\langle 0, 0 \rangle$ and $\langle 0 \rangle$ of zeros, and 6 non-zero values. The graph-based description of the group constraint uses two graph constraints which respectively mention the graph properties **NCC** = NGROUP, **MIN_NCC** = MIN_SIZE, **MAX_NCC** = MAX_SIZE, **NVERTEX** = NVAL and **MIN_NCC** = MIN_DIST, **MAX_NCC** = MAX_DIST. The leftmost part of Figure 2 depicts the initial graph of well as the two final graphs associated to the two graph constraints of the example given for the group constraint.

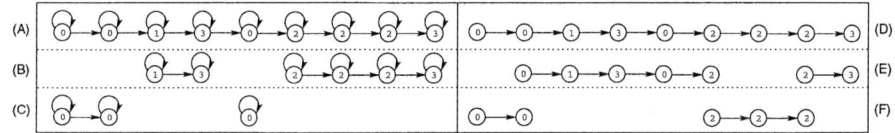

Fig. 2. Initial (A) and final graphs (B,C) of group$(2, 2, 4, 1, 2, 6, \langle 0, 0, 1, 3, 0, 2, 2, 2, 3 \rangle,$ $\{1, 2, 3\})$. Initial (D) and final graphs (E,F) of change_continuity$(2, 2, 2, 5, 2, 3, 5, 3,$ $\langle 0, 0, 1, 3, 0, 2, 2, 2, 3 \rangle, \neq)$.

Example 4. The first eight parameters of the change_continuity (NB_PERIOD_CHANGE, NB_PERIOD_CONTINUITY, MIN_SIZE_CHANGE, MAX_SIZE_CHANGE, MIN_SIZE_CONTINUITY, MAX_SIZE_CONTINUITY, NB_CHANGE, NB_CONTINUITY, VARIABLES, CTR) constraint are domain variables, while VARIABLES is a sequence of domain variables and CTR a binary constraint in $\{=, \neq, \leq, >, \geq, <\}$. A *change* (resp. *continuity*) is defined by the fact that constraint CTR holds (resp. does not hold) between two consecutive variables of the sequence VARIABLES. Let n denote the number of variables of the sequence VARIABLES, and let $X_i, X_{i+1}, \ldots, X_j (1 \leq i < j \leq n)$ be consecutive variables of the sequence VARIABLES. $X_i, X_{i+1}, \ldots, X_j$ corresponds to a *period of change* if X_k CTR X_{k+1} holds for all $k \in [i, j-1]$, and if $i = 1$ or X_{i-1} CTR X_i does not hold, and if $j = n - 1$ or X_j CTR X_{j+1} does not hold. A *period of continuity* is defined in a similar way by considering the negation of CTR. The constraint change_continuity holds if and only if:

- NB_PERIOD_CHANGE and NB_PERIOD_CONTINUITY are respectively equal to the number of periods of change and of continuity,
- MIN_SIZE_CHANGE and MAX_SIZE_CHANGE are respectively equal to the number of variables of the smallest and largest period of change,
- MIN_SIZE_CONTINUITY and MAX_SIZE_CONTINUITY are respectively equal to the number of variables of the smallest and largest period of continuity,
- NB_CHANGE and NB_CONTINUITY are respectively equal to the total number of changes and continuities.

change_continuity$(2, 2, 2, 5, 2, 3, 5, 3, \langle 0, 0, 1, 3, 0, 2, 2, 2, 3 \rangle, \neq)$ holds since the sequence $\langle 0, 0, 1, 3, 0, 2, 2, 2, 3 \rangle$ contains 2 periods of changes $\langle 0, 1, 3, 0, 2 \rangle$ and $\langle 2, 3 \rangle$ of minimum and maximum size 2 and 5, 2 periods of continuities $\langle 0, 0 \rangle$ and $\langle 2, 2, 2 \rangle$ of minimum and maximum size 2 and 3. Finally, the total number of changes and continuities are respectively equal to 5 and 3. The graph-based description of the change_continuity (NB_PERIOD_CHANGE, NB_PERIOD_CONTINUITY, MIN_SIZE_CHANGE, MAX_SIZE_CHANGE, MIN_SIZE_CONTINUITY, MAX_SIZE_CONTINUITY, NB_CHANGE, NB_CONTINUITY, VARIABLES, CTR) constraint uses two graph constraints which respectively mention the graph properties **NCC** = NB_PERIOD_CHANGE, **MIN_NCC** = MIN_SIZE_CHANGE, **MAX_NCC** = MAX_SIZE_CHANGE, **NARC** = NB_CHANGE and **NCC** = NB_PERIOD_CONTINUITY, **MIN_NCC** = MIN_SIZE_CONTINUITY, **MAX_NCC** = MAX_SIZE_CONTINUITY, **NARC** = NB_CONTINUITY. The rightmost part of Figure 2 depicts the initial graph of well as the two final graphs associated to the two graph constraints of the example given for the change_continuity constraint.

3 Graph Invariants

Within the scope of the graph-based description this section introduces implied constraints which are systematically linked to the description of a global constraint:

- We then describe the different contexts where graph invariants can be used.
- Finally, we show how to get sharper graph invariants by taking advantage of the structure of the global constraint under consideration.

Since no final digraph contains isolated vertices, the database of graph invariants considers digraphs for which each vertex has at least one arc.

Context for Using Graph Invariants. They can be used in the following contexts:

- Quite often, it happens that one wants the final digraph to satisfy more than one graph property. This was illustrated by the balanced assignment constraint (see Example 2) as well as by the group and change_continuity constraints. In this context, these graph properties involve several graph characteristics which cannot vary independently.
- Even if the description of a global constraint involves one single graph characteristic **C**, we can introduce the number of vertices, **NVERTEX**, and the number of arcs, **NARC**, of the final digraph. In this context, we can take advantage of graph invariants linking **C**, **NARC** and **NVERTEX**. This is in fact what was done for the nvalue constraint in Example 1.
- It also happens that we enforce two graph constraints $\mathcal{GC}_1$ and $\mathcal{GC}_2$, which have the same initial digraph $\mathcal{G}$. In this context we consider the following situations:
  - Each arc of $\mathcal{G}$ belongs to one of the final digraphs associated to $\mathcal{GC}_1$ or to $\mathcal{GC}_2$ (but not to both). An example of such global constraints is the change_continuity constraint depicted by Example 4.
  - Each vertex of $\mathcal{G}$ belongs to one of the final digraphs associated to $\mathcal{GC}_1$ or to $\mathcal{GC}_2$ (but not to both). An example of such global constraint is the group constraint depicted by Example 3.

  In these situations the graph properties associated to the two graph constraints are not independent. This will be illustrated by Example 12.

Graph Classes. By definition, a graph invariant has to hold for any final digraph. For instance, we have the graph invariant $\mathbf{NARC} \leq \mathbf{NVERTEX}^2$, which relates the number of arcs and the number of vertices of any digraph. This invariant is sharp since the equality is reached for a clique. However, by considering the structure of a final digraph, we can get sharper invariants. For instance, if our final digraph is a subset of an elementary path (e.g. we use the $PATH$ arc generator depicted by Figure 1) we have that $\mathbf{NARC} \leq \mathbf{NVERTEX} - 1$, which is a tighter bound of the maximum number of arcs since $\mathbf{NVERTEX} - 1 < \mathbf{NVERTEX}^2$. For this reason, we consider recurring graph classes that show up for different global constraints. For a given global constraint, a graph class specifies a general property which holds on all its final digraphs. In addition, we also consider graph constraints such that their final digraph is a subset of the digraph generated by the arc generators depicted by Figure 1.

Example 5. We provide typical examples of graph classes and, for each of them, we point to some global constraints that fit in that class:

- acyclic: graph constraint for which the final digraph doesn't have any circuit (e.g. change [7], change_continuity [3], common [3]).

- apartition: constraint defined by two graph constraints having the same initial digraph, where each arc of the initial digraph belongs to one of the final digraphs (but not to both) (e.g. change_continuity [3]).
- bipartite: graph constraint for which the final digraph is bipartite (e.g. alldifferent_on_intersection [3], common [3]).
- consecutive_loops_are_connected: denotes the fact that the graph constraints of a global constraint use only the $PATH$ and the $LOOP$ arc generators and that their final digraphs do not contain consecutive vertices which have a loop and which are not connected together by an arc (e.g. group [3]).
- equivalence: graph constraint for which the final digraph is reflexive, symmetric and transitive (e.g. balance [3], nvalue [5]).
- no_loop: graph constraint for which the final digraph doesn't have any loop (e.g. change_continuity [3], common [3]).
- one_succ: graph constraint for which all the vertices of the initial digraph belong to the final digraph and for which all vertices of the final digraph have exactly one successor (e.g. alldifferent [8], cycle [9], tree [10]).
- symmetric: graph constraint for which the final digraph is symmetric (e.g. connect_points [3]).
- vpartition: constraint defined by two graph constraints having the same initial digraph, where each vertex of the initial digraph belongs to one of the final digraphs (but not to both) (e.g. group [3]).

4 The Database of Graph Invariants

This section introduces the database of graph invariants we have built so far. It first provides a taxonomy of graph invariants and discusses their implementation. It then presents the organization of the database. Finally, it explains how to use the database in order to automatically extract the relevant invariants for a given global constraint.

Taxonomy of Graph Invariants. Within the database of graph invariants we currently have seven categories of graph invariants. These categories stem from the structure of the formulae associated to the invariants.

I1. Invariants involving *one single* graph characteristics C, restricting the initial set of possible values of C.

Example 6. When the final digraph does not contain any loops, we have that $2 \cdot \mathbf{NCC} \leq \mathbf{NVERTEX}_{INITIAL}$, where $\mathbf{NVERTEX}_{INITIAL}$ is the number of vertices of the initial digraph and where $\mathbf{NCC}$ is the number of connected components of the final digraph. This invariant restricts the initial domain of $\mathbf{NCC}$ to $\left[0, \lfloor \frac{\mathbf{NVERTEX}_{INITIAL}}{2} \rfloor \right]$.

I2. Invariants characterizing the *lower bound* (resp. *upper bound*) of a given graph characteristics C in terms of other graph characteristics $C_1, \ldots, C_n (n > 1, C_i \neq C)$. They are defined as an inequality of the form $C \geq f(C_1, \ldots, C_n)$ (resp. $C \leq f(C_1, \ldots, C_n)$), where $f(C_1, \ldots, C_n)$ is a formula involving the graph characteristics $C_1, \ldots, C_n$.

Example 7. As illustrated by Figure 3, the invariant $\mathbf{NARC} \geq \mathbf{NVERTEX} - \lfloor \frac{\mathbf{NSCC}-1}{2} \rfloor$ can be interpreted as the minimum number of arcs $\mathbf{NARC}$ of a digraph according to a fixed number of vertices $\mathbf{NVERTEX}$ and a fixed number of strongly connected components $\mathbf{NSCC}$.

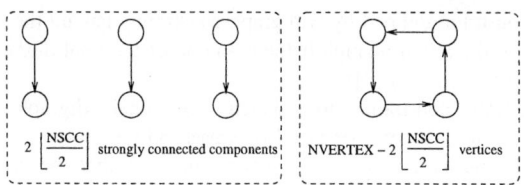

Fig. 3. A digraph which achieves the minimum number of arcs according to a fixed number of strongly connected components as well as to a fixed number of vertices (**NSCC** = 7, **NVERTEX** = 10, **NARC** = $10 - \lfloor \frac{7}{2} \rfloor = 7$)

I3. Invariants defining, for a given graph characteristics C, a *forbidden interval* of values of the form $[f_1(C_1, \ldots, C_n), f_2(C_{n+1}, \ldots, C_m)]$, where $f_1(C_1, \ldots, C_n)$ and $f_2(C_{n+1}, \ldots, C_m)$ are formulae involving graph characteristics distinct from C. These invariants usually come from a disjunction of the form $C \leq f_1(C_1, \ldots, C_n) - 1 \vee C \geq f_2(C_{n+1}, \ldots, C_m) + 1$.

Example 8. Consider the invariant **MIN_NCC** $\notin [\lfloor \frac{\mathbf{NVERTEX}}{2} \rfloor + 1, \mathbf{NVERTEX} - 1]$, which specifies that the number of vertices **MIN_NCC** of the smallest connected component of a digraph does not belong to an interval defined according to the number of vertices **NVERTEX**. This invariant stems from the following disjunction:

– On the one hand, if the digraph contains no more than one connected component, we have that **MIN_NCC** $\geq$ **NVERTEX**,
– On the other hand, if the digraph contains at least two connected components, we have that **MIN_NCC** + **MIN_NCC** $\leq$ **NVERTEX**.

I4. Invariants of the form $C \leq \max(f_1(C_1, \ldots, C_n), f_2(C_{n+1}, \ldots, C_m))$, where C is a graph characteristics and $f_1(C_1, \ldots, C_n)$ and $f_2(C_{n+1}, \ldots, C_m)$ are formulae involving graph characteristics distinct from C. These invariants usually come from a disjunction of two invariants $C \leq f_1(C_1, \ldots, C_n) \vee C \leq f_2(C_{n+1}, \ldots, C_m)$.

Example 9. Consider the invariant **MAX_NCC** $\leq$ max(**NVERTEX** − **MIN_NCC**, **MIN_NCC**), which restricts the maximum number of vertices **MAX_NCC** of the largest connected component according to the number of vertices in the smallest connected component and to the number of vertices **NVERTEX**. This invariant stems from the following disjunction:

– On the one hand, if the digraph contains no more than one connected component, we have that **MAX_NCC** $\leq$ **MIN_NCC**,
– On the other hand, if the digraph contains at least two connected components, we have that **NVERTEX** $\geq$ **MIN_NCC** + **MAX_NCC** (i.e. **MAX_NCC** $\leq$ **NVERTEX** − **MIN_NCC**).

I5. Invariants described by an implication between two conditions. These invariants have the form $Cond_1 \Rightarrow Cond_2$ where $Cond_1$ is a condition involving one or two graph characteristics, and where $Cond_2$ is either a condition involving one or two graph characteristics, either an invariant of type **I2** or **I3**.

Example 10. As an example, consider the invariant **MIN_NCC** $\neq$ **MAX_NCC** $\Rightarrow$ **NCC** ≥ 2, which depicts the fact that, if the number of vertices of the smallest connected component is not equal to the size of the largest connected component, the number of connected components is at least 2.

16. Invariants depicted by an equivalence between two given conditions where each condition involves one single graph characteristics.

Example 11. **MAX_NCC** $= 0 \Leftrightarrow$ **MIN_NCC** $= 0$ is an instance of such invariant.

17. Invariants involving graph characteristics coming from more than one graph constraint.

Each graph invariant has a precondition which defines its applicability. The precondition consists of an, possibly empty, conjunction of elementary conditions which characterize the graph class for which it can be applied. An elementary condition is either one of the keywords[2] acyclic, bipartite, no_loop, one_succ, symmetric, equivalence, apartition, vpartition, consecutive_loops_are_connected characterizing a specific graph class which was previously introduced, either an expression of the form arc_gen $=$ *arc generator*, where *arc generator* is an arc generator used for generating the arcs of the initial digraph.

Example 12. apartition $\wedge$ arc_gen $= PATH : |\mathbf{NCC}_1 - \mathbf{NCC}_2| \leq 1$ [3] is an invariant which can be applied when:

- As specified by apartition, a global constraint is defined by two graph constraints having the same initial digraph, where each arc of the initial digraph belongs to one of the final digraphs (but not to both),
- All the graph constraints of a global constraint use only the arc generator $PATH$.

This is in fact the situation of the change_continuity constraint introduced in Example 4: in this context, this invariant enforces the number of groups of changes NB_CHANGE and the number of groups of continuities NB_CONTINUITY to differ by at most 1.

Example 13. Consider the graph invariants **NARC** $\leq$ **NVERTEX**^{2} and arc_gen $= PATH :$ **NARC** $\leq$ **NVERTEX** $- 1$ of type **I3** which both relate the number of arcs and the number of vertices of a digraph. The first one has no precondition and therefore holds on any digraph, while the second one applies only on those digraphs that are a subset of an elementary path.

Implementing Graph Invariants. Most graph invariants are usually directly implemented as constraints which directly reduce the domains of the graph characteristics they involve. For this purpose we use:

- The arithmetic constraints of SICStus, which include constraints over non linear expressions [11–page 501],
- Propositional formulae over arithmetic constraints [11–page 461].

---

[2] Within the global constraint catalog, these keywords are explicitly given for each global constraint. However, note that these keywords could be automatically extracted from the graph-based description of a global constraint.

[3] $\mathbf{NCC}_1$ and $\mathbf{NCC}_2$ respectively denote the number of connected components of the final digraph of a first graph constraint and the number of connected components of the final digraph of a second graph constraint.

Finally, we also use indexicals [12,13] for implementing some graph invariants. An *indexical* is a reactive function rule of the form X in R, where X is a domain variable and R is a set valued range expression.

Indexicals are used for encoding invariants that define a forbidden interval of values for a given graph characteristics (e.g. category **I3**) and for explicitly implementing the propagation of some non-linear arithmetic constraints for which the existing constraint propagation is too weak. Invariants of category **I3** have the form $C \notin [f_1(C_1, \ldots, C_n), f_2(C_{n+1}, \ldots, C_m)]$, where $f_1(C_1, \ldots, C_n)$ and $f_2(C_{n+1}, \ldots, C_m)$ are formulae involving the graph characteristics $C_1, \ldots, C_m$ distinct from C. The idea is to evaluate the maximum value, U, of $f_1(C_1, \ldots, C_n)$ as well as the minimum value, L, of $f_2(C_{n+1}, \ldots, C_m)$ and to remove from C all values in $[U, L]$ when $U \leq L$. For this purpose we write range expressions for defining L and U.

Example 14. As an illustrative example of how to encode invariants defining a forbidden interval of values, consider the constraint $X \leq L \vee X \geq R$, which comes in handy for invariants such as $\mathbf{MIN\_NCC} \notin \left[\lfloor \frac{\mathbf{NVERTEX}}{2} \rfloor + 1, \mathbf{NVERTEX} - 1\right]$. This constraint can be encoded by three indexicals maintaining bounds consistency as follows:

```
not_strictly_between(X, L, U) +:
  X in (inf..max(L)) \/ (min(U)..sup),
  L in ((min(U)..max(X)) ? (inf    ..sup  )) \/ (min(X)..sup   ),
  U in ((min(X)..max(L)) ? (inf    ..sup  )) \/ (inf    ..max(X)).
```

Database Organization. As we previously saw, we have graph invariants that hold for any digraph as well as tighter graph invariants for specific graph classes. As a consequence, we partition the database into groups of graph invariants. A *group of graph invariants* corresponds to several invariants such that all invariants relate to the same subset of graph characteristics and are variations of the first invariant of the group taking into accounts the graph class. Thus, the first invariant of a group has no precondition, while all other invariants have a non-empty precondition that characterizes the graph class for which they hold.

Example 15. As a first example, consider the following group of invariants, which relate the number of arcs **NARC** to the number of vertices of the smallest and largest connected component (i.e. **MIN_NCC** and **MAX_NCC**) of a digraph:

- $\mathbf{MIN\_NCC} \neq \mathbf{MAX\_NCC} \Rightarrow \mathbf{NARC} \geq \mathbf{MIN\_NCC} + \mathbf{MAX\_NCC} - 2 + (\mathbf{MIN\_NCC} = 1)$[4],
- equivalence : $\mathbf{MIN\_NCC} \neq \mathbf{MAX\_NCC} \Rightarrow \mathbf{NARC} \geq \mathbf{MIN\_NCC}^2 + \mathbf{MAX\_NCC}^2$.

On the one hand, since the first invariant has no precondition, it can be applied to any digraph. On the other hand, the second invariant specifies a tighter condition (since $\mathbf{MIN\_NCC}^2 + \mathbf{MAX\_NCC}^2 \geq \mathbf{MIN\_NCC} + \mathbf{MAX\_NCC} - 2 + (\mathbf{MIN\_NCC} = 1)$) which only holds for a digraph that is reflexive, symmetric and transitive.

Example 16. As a second example, consider the following group of invariants, which relate the number of arcs **NARC** to the number of vertices **NVERTEX** according to the arc generator

---

[4] The expression ($\mathbf{MIN\_NCC} = 1$) is equal to 1 if $\mathbf{MIN\_NCC} = 1$ and 0 otherwise.

(see Figure 1) used for generating the initial digraph. Each invariant has the form $\mathbf{NARC} \leq \ldots$ since **NARC** stands for the number of arcs of a final graph which is a subgraph of a graph corresponding to a specific arc generator.

- $\mathbf{NARC} \leq \mathbf{NVERTEX}^2$,
- arc_gen = $CIRCUIT$: $\mathbf{NARC} \leq \mathbf{NVERTEX}$,
- arc_gen = $CHAIN$: $\mathbf{NARC} \leq 2 \cdot \mathbf{NVERTEX} - 2$,
- arc_gen = $CLIQUE(\leq)$: $\mathbf{NARC} \leq \frac{\mathbf{NVERTEX} \cdot (\mathbf{NVERTEX}+1)}{2}$,
- arc_gen = $CLIQUE(<)$: $\mathbf{NARC} \leq \frac{\mathbf{NVERTEX} \cdot (\mathbf{NVERTEX}-1)}{2}$,
- arc_gen = $CLIQUE(\neq)$: $\mathbf{NARC} \leq \mathbf{NVERTEX}^2 - \mathbf{NVERTEX}$,
- arc_gen = $CYCLE$: $\mathbf{NARC} \leq 2 \cdot \mathbf{NVERTEX}$,
- arc_gen = $PATH$: $\mathbf{NARC} \leq \mathbf{NVERTEX} - 1$.

The database currently contains 13, 50, 34, 12, 2 groups of invariants respectively mentioning 1, 2, 3, 4 and 5 graph characteristics. It also contains groups of invariants relating the graph characteristics of two digraphs. It contains 8, 6, 4, 10, 2 groups respectively mentioning 2, 3, 4, 5, 6 graph characteristics.

Extracting the Relevant Invariants. Once we have the graph invariants we can use them systematically by applying the following steps:

- For a given graph constraint we extract all the graph characteristics occurring in its description. This can be done automatically by scanning the corresponding graph properties. Let $\mathcal{GC}$ denote this subset of graph characteristics. For each graph characteristic gc of $\mathcal{GC}$ we check if we have a graph property of the form $gc = var$ where var is a domain variable. If this is the case we record the pair (gc, var); if not, we create a new domain variable var and also record the pair (gc, var).
- We then search for all groups of graph invariants involving a subset of the previous graph characteristics $\mathcal{GC}$. For each selected group we filter out those graph invariants for which the preconditions are not compatible with the graph class of the graph constraint under consideration. In each group we finally keep those invariants that have the maximum number of preconditions (i.e. the most specialized graph invariants).
- Finally we state all the previously collected graph invariants as implied constraints. This is achieved by using the variables associated to each graph characteristic.

Observe that, for a given global constraint, the number of invariants is always fixed (i.e. it does not change as the number of variables of the global constraint increases).

5 Experimental Results

This section illustrates the approach on the group as well as on the change_continuity global constraints, which were previously introduced. We have compared the following approaches:

- In a first approach each graph characteristic was handled independently. This was concretely done by constructing an automaton for each graph characteristic and by reformulating that automaton as a conjunction of constraints as described in [14][5].

---

[5] An alternative would have been to use the bounds on the graph characteristics introduced in [15] which can be seen as graph invariants involving one single graph property.

- The second approach reuses the first one but, in addition, also exploits the database of graph invariants in order to generate invariants which link the graph characteristics used in the description of group and of change_continuity.

We first detail the automata used for the group constraint. Since it is very similar to the group constraint, we then shortly discuss the implementation of the change_continuity constraint. Finally, we present the computational results obtained for the first and second approaches on the group as well as on the change_continuity constraints.

Implementing the group Constraint. Parts (A), (B), (C) and (D) of Figure 4 respectively depict the automata associated to the graph characteristics **NCC**, **MIN_NCC**, **MAX_NCC** and **NVERTEX** of the first graph constraint. Each automaton is applied to the sequence of variables corresponding to the VARIABLES parameter. A transition with a standard line depicts the fact that a variable takes its value within the set VALUES, while a thick line denotes the fact that a variable does not take its value within VALUES. Finally, a transition with a dashed line indicates the end of the sequence of variables. Since all the four automata use counters, we indicate how these counters are initialized in the initial state s, how a counter is unified to an argument of the group constraint in the final state t, and how they are possibly updated on a given transition. When there are several transitions between a given pair of states, we indicate with a dotted line or a standard line its type (see for instance the two transitions between s and s of the automaton depicted by part (C)).

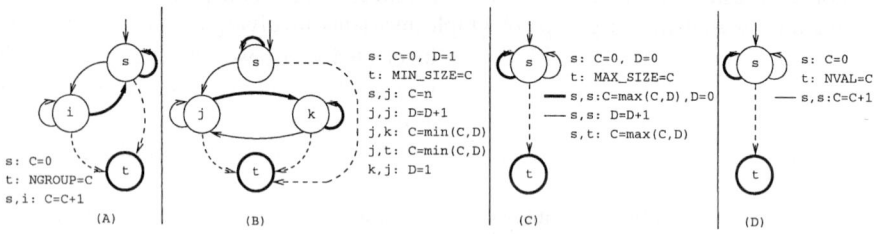

Fig. 4. Automata associated to the graph characteristics of the group constraint

The automata associated to **MIN_NCC** = MIN_DIST and to **MAX_NCC** = MAX_DIST are similar to the automata depicted by part (B) and (C), except that we change a thick line to a standard line and vice versa. The first approach for implementing the group constraint uses these six automata we just depicted. In the second approach we reuse the six automata and, in addition, extract a set of 51 graph invariants from the database of invariants.

Implementing the change_continuity Constraint. As for the group constraint, we came up with one automaton for each graph property. Parts (A), (B), (C) and (D) of Figure 5 respectively depict the automata associated to the graph characteristics **NCC**, **MIN_NCC**, **MAX_NCC** and **NARC** of the first graph constraint. Each automaton is applied to the sequence of pairs of consecutive variables of the VARIABLES parameter.

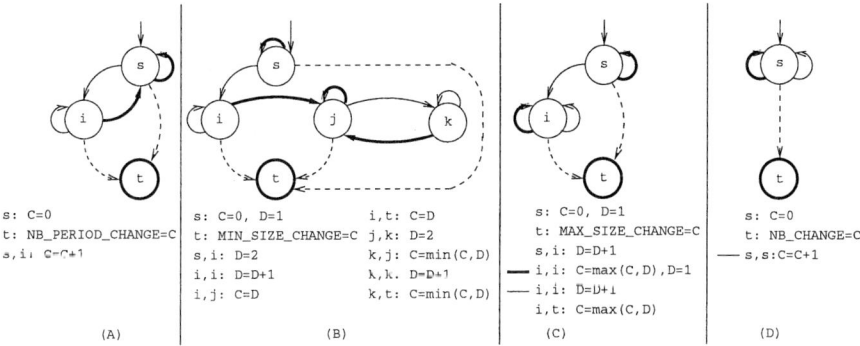

Fig. 5. Automata associated to the graph characteristics of the change_continuity constraint

A transition with a standard (resp. thick) line depicts the fact that VAR$_i$ CTR VAR$_{i+1}$ holds (resp. does not hold). Finally, a transition with a dashed line indicates the end of the sequence of pairs of variables. Since all four automata use counters, we indicate how these counters are initialized in the initial state s, how a counter is unified to an argument of the change_continuity constraint in the final state t, and how they are possibly updated on a given transition. Since the second graph constraint of change_continuity is similar to the first graph constraint we don't give the four corresponding automata.

The first approach for implementing the change_continuity constraint uses these eight automata. In the second approach we reuse the eight automata and, in addition, extract a set of 32 graph invariants from the database of invariants.

Performance. In order to evaluate the efficiency gained by adding graph invariants, we performed three experiments, generating random instances of the group and change_continuity constraints. VARIABLES was chosen as a sequence of N domain variables ranging over $[0, 1]$, VALUES as the singleton set $\{1\}$, and CTR as =. A constraint instance was generated by setting the initial domain of each domain variable to a randomly chosen interval.

In the first experiment, we computed the total domain size of the domain variables after posting, without invariants vs. with invariants, discarding infeasible instances, for $N = 8$. In the second experiment, we computed the time for posting the constraint instance and searching for all solutions, without invariants vs. with invariants, for $N = 8$. In the third experiment, we computed the time for posting the constraint instance and looking for the first solutions[6], without invariants vs. with invariants, for $N = 100$. Furthermore, with 10% probability, the variables in VARIABLES were fixed.

The results are presented in six scatter plots in Figure 6, one row per experiment. Each point represents a random instance, its X coordinate corresponding to excluding the invariants, and its Y coordinate corresponding to including them. The $X = Y$ line is shown in each graph. In the second and third rows, feasible and infeasible instances are denoted differently. Runtimes are in milliseconds.

---

[6] Each constraint instance was run with a 10 seconds time limit.

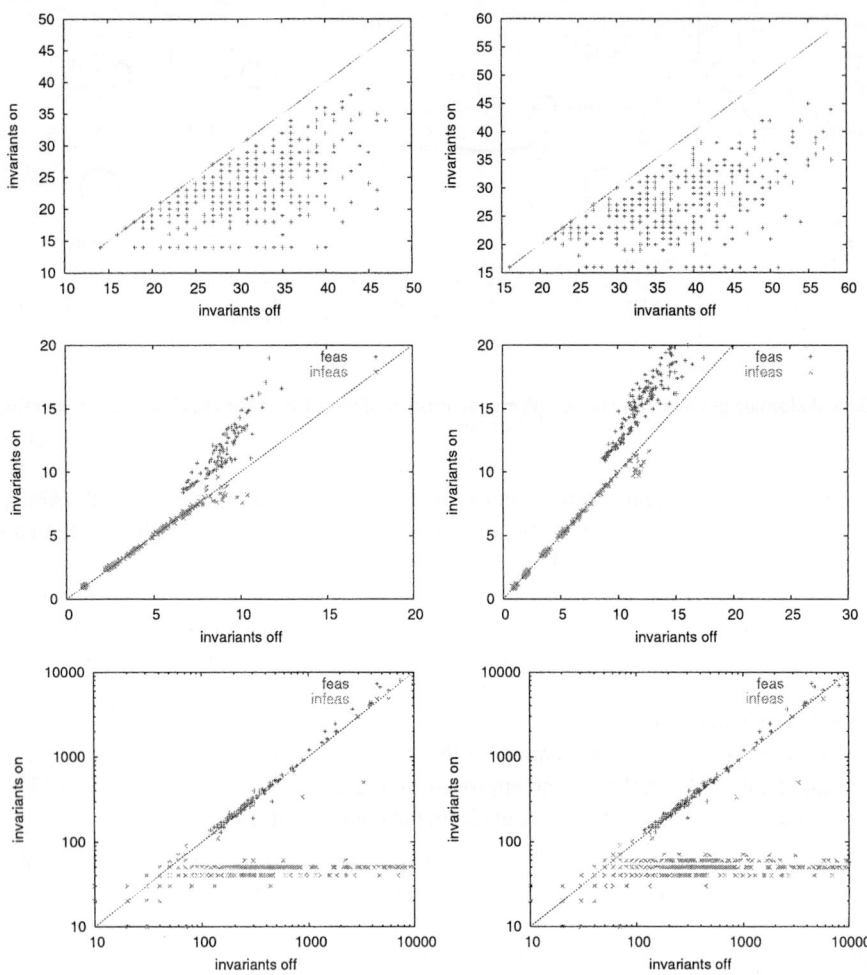

Fig. 6. Scatter plots of random instances. Top: comparing domain sizes. Middle: comparing runtime for finding all solutions. Bottom comparing runtime for finding first solution. Left: group. Right: change_continuity.

From these experiments, we observe that the invariants significantly improve the domain reduction including detecting infeasible instances, but that they do not pay off for the purpose of just finding all solutions of feasible instances. However, in a more realistic setting, the improved domain reduction may well lead to savings in search effort that outweigh the overhead of the invariants.

6 Conclusion

The database of graph invariants introduced in this article can be seen as a way to automatically generate necessary conditions for global constraints that can be described in terms of graph properties. In fact, it complements the computation of lower and upper bounds for the graph characteristics presented in [15]. The key advantages of the approach are:

- Instead of developing a specific code for a given global constraint, we come up with graph invariants that can be applied to all global constraints sharing a given graph property.
- The database of graph invariants can be enriched incrementally and systematic experiments can point out missing graph invariants.

Finally, as demonstrated by our experiments on the group and the change_continuity constraints, it also clearly shows that the graph-based representation and the automaton-based representation of global constraints are not competing approaches for representing the meaning of a global constraint. In fact, when for a given global constraint, both representations are available[7] we can, without developing any specific code, get a filtering algorithm that takes advantage of both representations.

References

1. M. Dincbas, H. Simonis, and P. Van Hentenryck. Solving the car-sequencing problem in constraint logic programming. In Y. Kodratoff, editor, *8th European Conference on Artificial Intelligence, ECAI-88*, pages 290–295, Munich, Germany, August 1988. Pitmann Publishing, London.
2. A. Frisch, I. Miguel, and T. Walsh. Extensions to proof planning for generating implied constraints. In *Proceedings of Calculemus*, 2001.
3. N. Beldiceanu, M. Carlsson, and J.-X. Rampon. Global constraint catalog. Technical Report T2005-06, Swedish Institute of Computer Science, 2005.
4. N. Beldiceanu. Pruning for the *minimum* constraint family and for the *number of distinct values* constraint family. In T. Walsh, editor, *Principles and Practice of Constraint Programming (CP'2001)*, volume 2239 of *LNCS*, pages 211–224. Springer-Verlag, 2001. Preprint available as SICS Tech Report T2000-10.
5. C. Bessière, E. Hebrard, B. Hnich, Z. Kızıltan, and T. Walsh. Filtering algorithms for the *nvalue* constraint. In Romand Barták and Michela Milano, editors, *International Conference on Integration of AI and OR Techniques in Constraint Programming for Combinatorial Optimization Problems (CP-AI-OR'05)*, volume 3524 of *LNCS*, pages 79–93, Prague, Czech Republic, May 2005. Springer Verlag.
6. P. Turán. On an extremal problem in graph theory. *Mat. Fiz. Lapok*, 48:436–452, 1941. In Hungarian.
7. COSYTEC. *CHIP Reference Manual*, release 5.1 edition, 1997.
8. J.-C. Régin. A filtering algorithm for constraints of difference in CSP. In *12th National Conference on Artificial Intelligence (AAAI-94)*, pages 362–367, 1994.
9. N. Beldiceanu and E. Contejean. Introducing global constraints in CHIP. *Mathl. Comput. Modelling*, 20(12):97–123, 1994.
10. N. Beldiceanu, P. Flener, and X. Lorca. The *tree* constraint. In Romand Barták and Michela Milano, editors, *International Conference on Integration of AI and OR Techniques in Constraint Programming for Combinatorial Optimization Problems (CP-AI-OR'05)*, volume 3524 of *LNCS*, pages 64–78, Prague, Czech Republic, May 2005. Springer Verlag.

---

[7] Out of the 227 constraints of the catalog of global constraints [3], more than 100 global constraints use both representations.

11. Mats Carlsson et al. *SICStus Prolog User's Manual*. Swedish Institute of Computer Science, 3.11.1 edition, February 2004. http://www.sics.se/sicstus/.
12. Pascal Van Hentenryck, Vijay Saraswat, and Yves Deville. Constraint processing in cc(FD). Manuscript, 1991.
13. Björn Carlson, Mats Carlsson, and Daniel Diaz. Entailment of finite domain constraints. In P. Van Hentenryck, editor, *ICLP'94, Int. Conf. on Logic Programming*, MIT Press Series in Logic Programming, S. Margherita Ligure, Italy, 1994. The MIT Press.
14. N. Beldiceanu, M. Carlsson, and T. Petit. Deriving filtering algorithms from constraint checkers. In M. Wallace, editor, *Principles and Practice of Constraint Programming (CP'2004)*, volume 3258 of *LNCS*, pages 107–122. Springer-Verlag, 2004.
15. N. Beldiceanu, T. Petit, and G. Rochart. Bounds of graph characteristics. In P. van Beek, editor, *Principles and Practice of Constraint Programming (CP'2005)*, LNCS. Springer-Verlag, 2005.

Allocation and Scheduling for MPSoCs via Decomposition and No-Good Generation

Luca Benini[1], Davide Bertozzi[2], Alessio Guerri[1], and Michela Milano[1]

[1] DEIS, University of Bologna,
V.le Risorgimento 2, 40136, Bologna, Italy
{lbenini, aguerri, mmilano}@deis.unibo.it
[2] Dipartimento di Ingegneria, University of Ferrara,
V. Saragat 1, 41100, Ferrara, Italy
dbertozzi@ing.unife.it

Abstract. This paper describes an efficient, complete approach for solving a complex allocation and scheduling problem for Multi-Processor System-on-Chip (MPSoC). Given a throughput constraint for a target application characterized as a task graph annotated with computation, communication and storage requirements, we compute an allocation and schedule which minimizes communication cost first, and then the makespan given the minimal communication cost. Our approach is based on problem decomposition where the allocation is solved through an Integer Programming solver, while the scheduling through a Constraint Programming solver. The two solvers are interleaved and their interaction regulated by no-good generation. Experimental results show speedups of orders of magnitude w.r.t. pure IP and CP solution strategies.

1 Introduction

This paper proposes a decomposition approach to the allocation and scheduling of a multi-task application on a multi-processor system-on-chip (MPSoCs) [1]. This is currently one of the most critical problems in electronic design automation for Very-Large Scale Integrated (VLSI) circuits. With the limits of chip integration reaching beyond one billion of elementary devices, current advanced integrated hardware platforms for high-end consumer application (e.g. multimedia-enabled phones) contain multiple processors and memories, as well as complex on-chip interconnects. The hardware resources in these MPSoCs need to be optimally allocated and scheduled under tight throughput constraints when executing a target software workload (e.g. a video decoder).

In a typical embedded system design scenario, the platform always runs the same application. Thus, extensive analysis and optimization can be performed at design time; in particular, allocation and scheduling can be pre-computed statically. The target application is pre-characterized and abstracted as a task graph. The task graph is annotated with computation (e.g., execution time), communication (e.g., number of bits to be communicated between tasks), storage (e.g., size of data and instruction memory required to execute the task) requirements. After solving the allocation and scheduling problem, the application can be loaded onto the target hardware platform, together with system software which orchestrates its execution according to the pre-computed solution.

The problem of allocating and scheduling tasks and memories to MPSoCs is NP-complete. We propose here an hybrid Constraint Programming (CP) and Integer Programming (IP) approach. The solution scheme is based on problem decomposition which interleaves (i) allocation of tasks to processors and required memory slot to storage devices and (ii) scheduling tasks in time. Since the two sub-problems are not independent, their interaction is regulated by no-good generation. Eventually the process converges, producing the optimal solution. The method is inherited by Operations Research and it is known with the name of *Benders Decomposition* [2]. This method partitions the problem variables in two sets x and y, assigns trial values to x by solving the master problem (containing only variables in x) to optimality, so as to define a sub-problem containing only the variables belonging to y. If the solution of the subproblem reveals that the trial values are not acceptable, a no-good is generated and new trial values are assigned according to the no-good. It is proved that this method converges, hopefully after few steps, by providing the optimal solution [2].

Benders Decomposition has been successfully applied in conjunction with Constraint Programming as we will extensively describe in section 6. For example, [3] and [4] face a similar problem using Benders Decomposition and found very promising results. Our main purpose in this paper is to show how a hybrid Constraint and Integer Programming approach can be used to solve a very complex optimization problem which has been traditionally approached with heuristic techniques or (for small instances) with complete Integer Programming approaches. We show that our method outperforms on one hand Integer Programming approaches which can be considered the state of the art complete approaches for this problem, and on the other hand Constraint Programming approaches that have been exploited much less frequently in this context.'

2 Problem Description

Advances in very large scale integration (VLSI) of digital electronic circuits have made it possible to develop multi-processor systems-on-chip (MPSoCs), which are finding widespread application in embedded systems (such as cellular phones, automotive control engines, etc.). Once deployed in field, these devices always run the same application, in a well-characterized context. It is therefore possible to spend a large amount of time for finding an optimal allocation and scheduling off-line and then deploy it on the field. For this reason, many researchers in digital design automation have explored complete approaches for allocating and scheduling pre-characterized workloads on MPSoCs [1], instead of using on-line, dynamic (sub-optimal) schedulers [5,6].

The multi-processor system we consider consists of a pre-defined number of distributed computation nodes, as depicted in Figure 1. All nodes are assumed to be homogeneous and made by a processing core and by a tightly coupled local memory. This latter is a low-access-cost *scratchpad memory*, which is commonly used both as hardware extension to support message passing and as a storage means for computation data and processor instructions which are frequently accessed. Data storage onto the scratchpad memory is directly managed by the application, and not automatically in hardware as it is the case for processor caches.

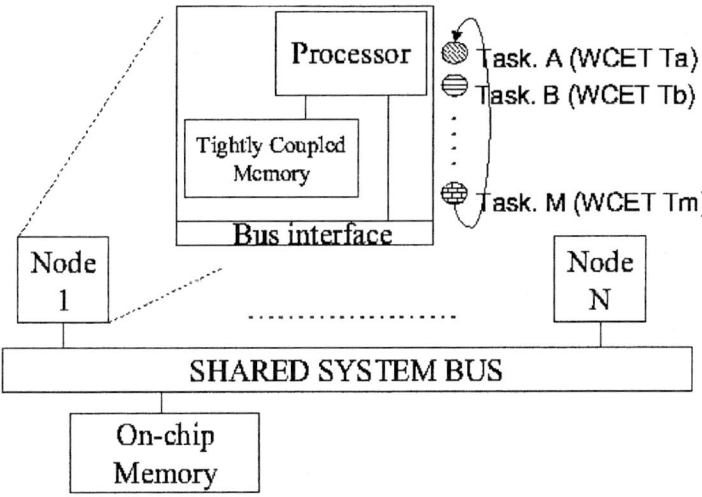

Fig. 1. Single chip multi-processor architecture

Unfortunately, the scratchpad memory is of limited size, therefore data in excess must be stored externally in a remote on-chip memory, accessible via the bus. The bus for state-of-the-art MPSoCs is a shared communication resource, and serialization of bus access requests of the processors (the bus masters) is carried out by a centralized arbitration mechanism. The bus is re-arbitrated on a transaction basis (e.g., after single read/write transfers, or bursts of accesses of pre-defined length), based on several policies (fixed priority, round-robin, latency-driven, etc.). Modelling bus allocation at such a fine granularity would make the problem overly complex, therefore a more abstract bus model was devised, thus also bridging the gap with our high-level task models, which express communication requirements of the tasks in terms of their required bus bandwidth for the duration of their execution. We will discuss this point in detail in section 4.

Whenever predictable performance is needed for applications, it is important to avoid high levels of congestion on the bus, since this makes completion time of bus transactions much less predictable. Moreover, under a low congestion regime, performance of state-of-the-art shared busses scales almost in the same way as that of advanced busses with topology and communication protocol enhancements. Finally, bus modelling is simpler under these working conditions (e.g., additive models). Communication cost is therefore critical for determining overall system performance, and will be minimized in our task allocation framework.

The target application to be executed on top of the hardware platform is input to our methodology, and for this purpose it must be represented as a task graph. This latter consists of a graph pointing out the parallel structure of the program. The application workload is therefore partitioned into computation sub-units denoted as tasks, which are the nodes of the graph. Graph edges connecting any two nodes indicate task dependencies. Computation, storage and communication requirements are annotated onto the graph. In detail, the worst case execution time (WCET) is specified for each node/task and plays a critical role whenever application real time constraints (expressed here in terms of minimum required throughput) are to be met. The sum of the WCETs of the tasks for one iteration of the time wheel must not exceed time period RT (i.e., the minimum task scheduling period ensuring that throughput constraints are met), which is the same for each processor since the minimum throughput is an application (not single processor) requirement.

Each node/task also has 3 kinds of associated memory requirements:

- **Program Data:** storage locations are required for computation data and for processor instructions. They can be allocated either on the local scratchpad memory or on the remote on-chip memory.
- **Internal State:** when needed, an internal state of the task can be stored either locally or remotely.
- **Communication Queues:** the task needs queues to transmit and receive messages to/from other tasks, eventually mapped on different processors. In the class of MPSoCs we are considering, such queues should be allocated only on local memories, in order to implement an efficient inter-processor communication mechanism.

Finally, communication requirements of each task are automatically determined once computation data and internal state are physically allocated to scratchpad or remote memory, and obviously depend on the size of such data.

The methodology proposed in this paper has been applied to a task graph extracted from a real video graphics application processing pixels of a digital image. Many real-life signal processing applications are subject to tight throughput constraints, therefore leverage a pipelined workload allocation policy. As a consequence, the input graph to our methodology consists of a pipeline of processing tasks, and can be easily extended to all pipelined applications.

3 Motivation for the Approach

The problem described in the previous section has a very interesting structure. As a whole, the problem is a scheduling problem with alternative resources. In fact, each task should be allocated to one of the processors (Node i in Figure 1). In addition, each memory slot required for processing the task should be allocated to a memory device. Clearly, tasks should be scheduled in time subject to real time constraints, precedence constraints, and capacity constraints on all unary and cumulative resources. However, from a different perspective, the problem decomposes into two problems:

- the allocation of tasks to processors and the memory slots required by each task to the proper memory device;
- a scheduling problem with static resource allocation.

The objective function of the overall problem is the minimization of communication cost. This function involves only variables of the first problem. In particular, we have a communication cost each time two communicating tasks are allocated on different processors, and each time a memory slot is allocated on a remote memory device. Once we have optimally allocated tasks to resources, we can minimize the schedule makespan.

The allocation problem is difficult to solve with Constraint Programming (CP). CP has a naive method for solving optimization problems: each time a solution is found, an additional constraint is added stating that each successive solution should be better than the best one found so far. If the objective function is strongly linked to decision variables, CP can be effective, otherwise it is hopeless to use CP to find the optimal solution. In case the objective function is related to a single variable, like for makespan in scheduling problems, CP works well. However, if the objective function is a sum of cost variables, CP is able to prune only few values, deep in the search tree since the connection between the objective function and the problem decision variables is weak. If the objective function relates to pairs of assignments the situation is even worse. This is the case of our application where the objective function relates alternative resources to couples of tasks. In fact, data transfer on the bus (and thus the objective function increase) occurs when two communicating tasks are allocated to different processors. Integer Programming (IP), instead, is extremely good to cope with these problems.

On the contrary, IP is weaker than CP in coping with time. Scheduling problems require to assign tasks to time slots, each slot being represented by an integer variable. The number of variables increases enormously if the granularity of the timeline is fine.

Therefore, the first problem could be solved with IP effectively, while for the second CP is the technique of choice. The question is now: how do these problems interact?

We solve them separately, the allocation problem first (called master problem), and the scheduling problem (called subproblem) later. The master is solved to optimality and its solution passed to the subproblem solver. If the solution is feasible, then the overall problem is solved to optimality. If, instead, the master solution cannot be completed by the subproblem solver, a no-good is generated and added to the model of the master problem, roughly stating that the solution passed should not be recomputed again (it becomes infeasible), and a new optimal solution is found for the master problem respecting the (set of) no-good(s) generated so far. Being the allocation problem solver an IP solver, the no-good has the form of a linear constraint.

Now let us note the following: the assignment problem allocates tasks to processors, and memory requirements to storage devices minimizing communication costs. However, since real time constraints are not taken into account by the allocation module, the solution obtained tends to pack all tasks into the minimal number of processors. In other words, the only constraint that prevents to allocate all tasks to a single processors is the limited capacity of the tightly coupled memory devices. However, these trivial assignments do not consider throughput constraints which make them most probably infeasible for the overall problem. To avoid the generation of these (trivial) assignments, we should add to the master problem model a relaxation of the subproblem. In particular, we should state in the master problem that the sum of the durations of tasks allocated to a single processor does not exceed the realtime requirement. In this case, the allocation is far more similar to the optimal one for the problem at hand. The use of a relaxation in the master problem is well known and widely used in practice and helps in producing better solutions.

A similar method is known in Operations Research as Benders Decomposition [2], where the overall problem can be decomposed in two parts connected by some variables. Indeed, in this method, the subproblem should be easy.

In [3], for example, Logic-Based Benders Decomposition is used to solve an allocation and scheduling problem where precedence constraints among tasks assigned to different resources are not considered; in this case we have a set of independent subproblems, for each facility. In our case, we can have precedence constraints between tasks allocated to different facilities and the subproblem is therefore an NP-complete problem, but CP is a very effective method to solve it.

4 Model Definition

As described in section 3, the problem we are facing can be split into the resource allocation master problem and the scheduling sub-problem.

4.1 Allocation Problem Model

We start from the task graph presented in section 2. Each task should be allocated to a processor. In addition it needs a given amount of memory to store data. Data can be allocated either in the local memory of the processor running the task or in the remote one except for communication queues that are always mapped locally. The allocation problem is the problem of allocating n tasks to m processors, such that the total amount of memory allocated to the tasks, for each processor, does not exceed the maximum available.

We assume the remote on-chip memory to be of unlimited size since it is able to meet the memory requirement of the application we are facing (small granularity program data). The problem objective function is the minimization of the amount of data transferred on the bus. We model the problem as an integer program and we consider four decision variables in the model:

- T_{ij}, taking value 1 if task i executes on processor j, 0 otherwise,
- Y_{ij}, taking value 1 if task i allocates the program data on the scratchpad memory of processor j, 0 otherwise,
- Z_{ij}, taking value 1 if task i allocates the internal state on the scratchpad memory of processor j, 0 otherwise,
- X_{ij}, taking value 1 if task i executes on processor j and task $i+1$ does not, 0 otherwise.

The constraints we introduced in the model are:

$$\sum_{j=1}^{m} T_{ij} = 1, \forall i \in 1 \ldots n \qquad (1)$$

$$X_{ij} = |(T_{ij} - T_{i+1j})|, \forall i \in 1 \ldots n, \forall j \in 1 \ldots m \qquad (2)$$

Constraints (1) state that each process can execute only on a processor, while constraints (2) state that X_{ij} can be equal to 1 iff $T_{ij} \neq T_{i+1j}$, that is, iff task i and task $i+1$ execute on different processors. Constraints (2) are not linear (X_{ij} is the exor of T_{ij} and T_{i+1j}), thus we cannot use them in a IP model. If we consider that the sum $Xij + T_{ij} + T_{i+1j}$ must always equal either to 0 or 2, constraints (2) can be rewritten as:

$$T_{ij} + T_{i+1j} + X_{ij} - 2K_{ij} = 0, \forall i, \forall j \qquad (3)$$

where K_{ij} are integer binary variables that enforce the sum $T_{ij} + T_{i+1j} + X_{ij}$ to be equal either to 0 or 2.

We add to the problem the constraints stating that $T_{ij} = 0 \Rightarrow Y_{ij} = 0, Z_{ij} = 0$ meaning that if a processor j is not assigned to a task i neither its program data nor the internal state can be stored in the local memory of processor j.

As explained in section 3, in order to prevent the master problem solver to produce trivially infeasible solutions, we need to add to the master problem model a relaxation of the subproblem. For this purpose, for each set of consecutive tasks whose execution times sum exceeds the real time requirement (RT), we impose constraints preventing the solver to allocate all the tasks in the group to the same processor.

To generate this constraints, we find out all groups of consecutive tasks sum of whose execution times (Dur_i) exceeds RT. Constraints are the following:

$$\sum_{i \in S} Dur_i > RT \Rightarrow \sum_{i \in S} T_{ij} \leq |S| - 1 \; \forall j \qquad (4)$$

The objective function is the minimization of the total amount of data transferred on the bus for each pipeline. This amount consists of three contributions: when a task allocates its program data in the remote memory, it reads these data throughout the execution time; when a task allocates the internal state in the remote memory, it reads these data at the beginning of its execution and updates them at the end; if two consecutive tasks execute on different processors, their communication messages must be transferred through the bus from the communication queue of one processor to the other. Using the decision variables described above, we have a contribution respectively when: $T_{ij} = 1, Y_{ij} = 0$; $T_{ij} = 1, Z_{ij} = 0$; $X_{ij} = 1$. Therefore, the objective function is to minimize:

$$\sum_{i=1}^{n} \sum_{j=1}^{m} (mem_i(T_{ij} - Y_{ij}) + 2 \times state_i(T_{ij} - Z_{ij}) + (data_i X_{ij})/2) \qquad (5)$$

where mem_i, $state_i$ and $data_i$ are coefficients representing the amount of data used by task i to store respectively the program data, the internal state and the communication queue.

4.2 Scheduling Problem Model

Once tasks have been allocated to the processors, we need to schedule process execution. Since we are considering a pipeline of tasks, we need to analyze the system behavior at working rate, that is when all processes are running or ready to run. To do that, we need to consider several instantiations of the same process; to achieve a working rate configuration, the number of repetitions of each task must be at least equal to the number of tasks n; in fact, after n iterations, the pipeline is at working rate. So, to solve the scheduling problem, we must consider at least n^2 tasks (n iterations for each process), see Figure 2.

In the scheduling problem model, for each task $Task_{ij}$ we considered an activity A_{ij}, $(i = [0 \ldots n-1], j = [0 \ldots n-1])$, representing the computation of the task. A_{ij} is the j-th iteration of the i-th process. Once the allocation problem is solved, we statically know if a task needs to use the bus to communicate with another task, or to read/write computation data and internal state in the remote memory. In particular, each activity A_{ij} must read the communication queue from the activity A_{i-1j}, or from the pipeline input if $i = 0$. To schedule these phases, we consider the activities In_{ij}. If a process requires an internal state, the state must be read before the execution and written after the execution: we therefore consider the activities RS_{ij} and WS_{ij} for each task i requiring an internal state. The duration of these activities depends on whether the data are stored in the local or the remote memory (data transfer through the bus needs more time than the transfer of the same amount of data using the local memory) but, after the allocation, these durations can be statically calculated. These activity are introduced in the model using variables $Start\_A_{ij}$, $Start\_In_{ij}$, $Start\_RS_{ij}$ and $Start\_WS_{ij}$, representing the starting time of the corresponding activity. We also use the values Dur_A_{ij}, Dur_In_{ij}, Dur_RS_{ij} and Dur_WS_{ij} to represent the execution times of the corresponding activities.

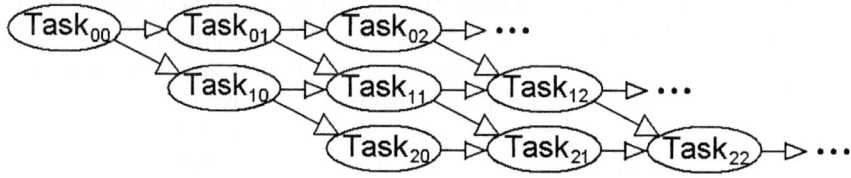

Fig. 2. Precedence constraints among the activities

Figure 2 depicts the precedence constraints among the tasks. Each task $Task_{ij}$ represents the activity A_{ij} possibly preceded by the internal state reading activity RS_{ij}, and input data reading activity In_{ij}, and possibly followed by the internal state writing activity WS_{ij}.

The precedence constraints among the activities introduced in the model are:

$$A_{i,j-1} \prec In_{ij}, \ \forall\, i, j \tag{6}$$
$$In_{ij} \prec A_{ij}, \ \forall\, i, j \tag{7}$$
$$A_{i-1,j} \prec In_{ij}, \ \forall\, i, j \tag{8}$$
$$RS_{ij} \preceq A_{ij}, \ \forall\, i, j \tag{9}$$
$$A_{ij} \preceq WS_{ij}, \ \forall\, i, j \tag{10}$$
$$In_{i+1,j-1} \prec A_{ij}, \ \forall\, i, j \tag{11}$$
$$A_{i,j-1} \prec A_{ij}, \ \forall\, i, j \tag{12}$$

where the symbol $\prec$ means that the activity on the left should precede the activity on the right, and the symbol $\preceq$ means that the activity on the right must start as soon as the execution of the activity on the left ends: i.e., $In_{ij} \prec A_{ij}$ means $Start\_In_{ij} + Dur\_In_{ij} \leq Start\_A_{ij}$, and $RS_{ij} \preceq A_{ij}$ means $Start\_RS_{ij} + Dur\_RS_{ij} = Start\_A_{ij}$.

Constraints (6) state that each task iteration can start reading the communication queue only after the end of its previous iteration. Constraints (7) state that each task can start only when it has read the communication queue, while constraints (8) state that each ask can read the data in the communication queue only when the previous task has generated them. Constraints (9) and (10) state that each task must read the internal state just before the execution and write it just after. Constraints (11) state that each task can execute only if the previous iteration of the following task has read the input data; in other words, it can start only when the memory allocated to the process for storing the communication queue has been freed. Constraints (12) state that the iterations of each task must execute in order.

Furthermore, we introduced the real time requirement constraints (13), whose relaxation is used in the allocation problem model. Each task must execute at most each time period RT.

$$Start(A_{ij}) - Start(A_{i,j-1}) \leq RT , \; \forall \, i,j \qquad (13)$$

Each processor is modelled as a unary resource, that is a resource with capacity one. As far as the bus is concerned, as explained in section 2, we make a simplification: a real bus is a unary resource but, if we model a bus as a unary resource, we should describe the problem at a finer grain with respect to the one we use, i.e., we have to model task execution using the clock cycle as unit of time. The resulting scheduling model would contain a huge number of variables. We therefore consider the bus as an additive resource, in the sense that more activities can share the bus resource using only a fraction of the total bandwidth available.

Figure 3 depicts this assumption. The leftmost figure represents the bus allocation in a real processor, where the bus is assigned to different tasks at different times. Each task, when owning the bus, uses its total bandwidth. The rightmost figure, instead, represents how we model the bus. The bus arbitration mechanism will then transform the bus allocation into the interleaving of fine granularity bus transactions on the real platform.

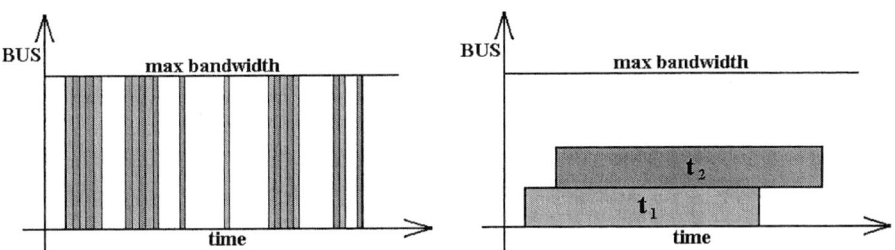

Fig. 3. Bus allocation in a real processor (left) and in our model (right)

In particular, to define the communication requirements of each task (the amount of computation data stored in the remote memory) we consider the amount of data they have to communicate and we spread it over its WCET. In this way we consume only a fraction of the overall bus bandwidth for the duration of the task. In the 2 graphs in figure 3 light grey and dark grey areas are equal.

When an allocation is provided, the minimal makespan schedule is computed if it exists. On the contrary, if no feasible schedule exists, we have to generate a no-good and pass it to the allocation module. The no-good should prevent the allocation to be the same of the previous iteration. Since the allocation module is an Integer Programming solver, the no-good should have the form of a linear constraint. In particular, we select all the resources that provoke a failure, e.g., either resources whose capacity is violated, or resources that lead to a violation of real time constraints. We call them *conflicting resources*, CR. Then, we impose that for each resource in $R \in CR$ the set of tasks ST_R allocated to R should not be reassigned to the same resource in the next iteration. For example if a conflicting resource R is a processor and ST_R the set of tasks previously allocated to it, the resulting no-good is:

$$\sum_{i \in ST_R} T_{iR} \leq |ST_R| - 1$$

In the same way, we have constraints for preventing failures in storage device.

These are the simplest kind of no-goods that can be added to the master problem since they state that the current solution must not be computed again. Even if they can be improved, as shown in [7], we will show in the next section that they are very effective.

5 Experimental Results

To validate the strength of our approach, we now compare the results obtained using this model (**Hybrid** in the following) with results obtained using only a CP or IP model to solve the overall problem. Actually, since the first experiments showed that both CP and IP approaches are not able to find a solution, except for the easiest instances, within 15 minutes, we simplified these models removing some variables and constraints. In CP, we fixed the activities execution time not considering the execution time variability due to remote memory accesses, therefore we do not consider the In_{ij}, RS_{ij} and WS_{ij} activities, including them statically in the activities A_{ij}. In IP, we do not consider all the variables and constraints involving the bus: we do not model the bus resource and we therefore suppose that each activity can access data whenever it is necessary.

We generated a large variety of problems, varying both the number of tasks and processors. All the results presented are the mean over a set of 10 problems for each task or processor number. All problems considered have a solution. Experiments were performed on a 2GHz Pentium 4 with 512 Mb RAM. We used ILOG CPLEX 8.1 and ILOG Solver 5.3 as solving tools.

In figures 4 and 5 we compare the algorithms search time for problems with a different number of tasks and processors respectively. Times are expressed in seconds and the y-axis has a logarithmic scale.

Although CP and IP deal with a simpler problem model, we can see that these algorithms are not comparable with Hybrid, except when the number of tasks and processors is low; this is due to the fact that the problem instance is very easy to be solved, and Hybrid loses time creating and solving two models, the allocation and the scheduling. As soon as the number of tasks and/or processors grows, IP and CP performances worsen and their search times become orders of magnitude higher w.r.t. Hybrid. Furthermore,

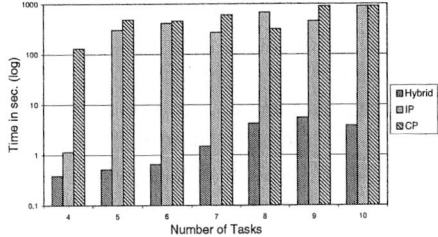
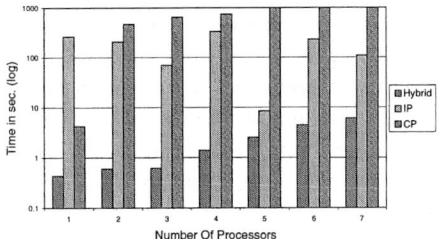

Fig. 4. Comparison between algorithms search times for different task number

Fig. 5. Comparison between algorithms search times for different processor number

we considered in the figures only instances where the algorithms are able to find the optimal solution within 15 minutes, and, for problems with 6 tasks or 3 processors and more, IP and CP can find the solution only in the 50% or less of the cases. On the contrary, we can see that Hybrid search time scales up linearly (in the logarithmic scale) for all the case.

We also measured the number of times the solver iterates between the master and the sub-problem. We found that, due to the limited size of the local memories and to the relaxation of the sub-problem added to the master, the solver iterates 1 or 2 times. Removing the relaxation, it iterates up to 15 times. This result gives evidence that, in a Benders decomposition based approach, it is very important to introduce a relaxation of the sub-problem in the master, and that the relaxation we use is very effective.

6 Related Work

The synthesis of distributed system architectures has been extensively studied in the past. The mapping and scheduling problems on multi-processor systems have been traditionally modelled as integer linear programming problems. An early example is represented by the SOS system, which used mixed integer linear programming (MILP) model [8]. SOS considers processor nodes with local memory, connected through direct point-to-point channels. The algorithm does not consider real-time constraints. Partitioning under timing constraints has been addressed in [9]. A MILP model that allows to determine a mapping optimizing a trade-off function between execution time, processor and communication cost is reported in [10].

Extensions of the IP formulation have also been used to account for memory allocation requirements, besides communication and computation ones. A hardware/software co-synthesis algorithm of distributed real-time systems that optimizes the memory hierarchy (caches) along with the rest of the architecture is reported in [11]. An integer linear programming model is used in [12] to obtain an optimal distributed shared memory architecture minimizing the global cost to access shared data in the application, and the memory cost.

The above techniques lead to static allocations and schedules that are well suited for applications whose behaviour can be accurately predicted at design time, with minimum run-time fluctuations. This is the case of signal processing and multimedia applications. Pipelining is one common workload allocation policy for increasing throughput of such applications, and this explains why research efforts have been devoted to extending mapping and scheduling techniques to pipelined task graphs. An overview of these techniques is presented in [13]. IP formulations as well as heuristic algorithms have been traditionally employed. In [14] a retiming heuristic is used to implement pipelined scheduling, that optimizes the initiation interval, the number of pipeline stages and memory requirements of a particular design alternative. Pipelined execution of a set of periodic activities is also addressed in [15], for the case where tasks have deadlines larger than their periods. Palazzari et al. [16], focus on scheduling to sustain the throughput of a given periodic task set and to serve aperiodic requests associated with hard real-time constraints. Mapping of tasks to processors, pipelining of system specification and scheduling of each pipeline stage have been addressed in [17], aiming at satisfying throughput constraints at minimal hardware cost.

In general, even though IP is used as a convenient modelling formalism, there is consensus on the fact that pure IP formulations are suitable only for small problem instances (task graphs with a reduced number of nodes) because of their high computational cost. For this reason, heuristic approaches are widely used. A comparative study of well-known heuristic search techniques (genetic algorithms, simulated annealing and tabu search) is reported in [18]. Eles et al. [19] compare the use of simulated annealing and tabu search for partitioning a graph into hardware and software parts while trying to reduce communication and synchronization between parts. More scalable versions of these algorithms for large real-time systems are introduced in [20]. Many heuristic scheduling algorithms are variants and extensions of list scheduling [21].

Heuristic approaches provide no guarantees about the quality of the final solution. On the other hand, complete approaches which compute the optimum solution (possibly, with a high computational cost), can be attractive for statically scheduled systems, where the solution is computed once and applied throughout the entire lifetime of the system.

Constraint Programming (CP) is an alternative approach to Integer Programming (IP) for solving combinatorial optimization problems. The work in [22] is based on Constraint Logic Programming to represent system synthesis problem, and leverages a set of finite domain variables and constraints imposed on these variables. Optimal solutions can be obtained for small problems, while large problems require use of heuristics. The proposed framework is able to create pipelined implementations in order to increase the design throughput. In [23] the embedded system is represented by a set of finite domain constraints defining different requirements on process timing, system resources and interprocess communication. The assignment of processes to processors and interprocess communications to buses as well as their scheduling are then defined as an optimization problem tackled by means of constraint solving techniques.

Both CP and IP techniques can claim individual successes but practical experience indicates that neither approach dominates the other in terms of computational performance. The development of a hybrid CP-IP solver that captures the best features of both would appear to offer scope for improved overall performance [24]. However, the issue of communication between different modelling paradigms arises. One method is inherited from the Operations Research and is known as Benders Decomposition [2]:

it is proved to converge producing the optimal solution. Benders Decomposition (BD) technique has been extensively used to solve a large variety of problems.

In [25] BD is applied to a numeric algorithm in order to solve the problem of verifying logic circuits: results show that, for some kind of circuits, the technique is an order of magnitude faster w.r.t. other state of the art algorithms. In [26], BD is embedded in the CP environment ECLiPSe and is shown that it can be useful in practice. There are a number of papers using Benders Decomposition in a CP setting. In [27] BD is applied to an allocation and scheduling problem; the master problem (allocation) is based on CP and the sub problem (scheduling) is solved using a real-time scheduler with fixed task priority. In [28] the branch and check framework is proposed using Benders Decomposition. This technique is applied to the problem of scheduling orders on dissimilar parallel machines, where a set of tasks, linked by precedence constraints, must be performed on a set of parallel machines minimizing the total cost of the process. The machines are dissimilar, so the same task can be executed on a different machine with a different cost and processing time. In [4], BD is applied to minimum cost planning and scheduling problems in a scenario similar to the one described in this paper, considering also release and due date constraints. Here costs depend only on the assignment of tasks to machines, differently from our problem, where contributes to the objective function depend on pairs of assignments. In [3] and [7], Logic-Based BD (a variant of BD introduced in [29], where the sub-problem should not necessarily be an IP problem) is used for Planning and Scheduling problems. Here different objective functions are considered: total cost minimization, makespan, tardiness, and number of late jobs. Precedence constraints among tasks assigned to different resources are not considered[1]: after the allocation phase, the scheduling can be done solving a separate scheduling problem for each facility. Our work addresses therefore an harder problem, being the schedules on different facilities all interconnected.

Although a lot of work has been done applying BD to allocation and scheduling problems, we believe that our approach is not directly comparable with them, mainly because we take in consideration a real application where data must be exchanged between tasks and each task must read/write data (and thus must use the bus resource) during its execution.

7 Conclusion and Future Works

In this paper, we have faced a challenging problem arising in the field of multi-processor systems-on-chip (MPSoCs). The structure of the problem suggests a decomposition approach based on the interaction of two problem solvers: one allocating tasks to alternative resources and memory requirement to storage devices; the second scheduling tasks subject to temporal and resource constraints. The first problem solver exploits mathematical programming techniques, while the second is based on CP. The interaction between these problem solvers is regulated by no-good generation.

We provide experimental evidence that our approach outperforms the one considering the problem as a whole and using a single technique (CP or IP) separately. The work in progress is aimed at generalizing the problem for introducing message queues

---

[1] In [7] the author considers precedence constraints among tasks allocated to the same facility.

on the shared memories so as to decouple the computation and communication through non blocking synchronization.

Currently, we are investigating the executability of the solutions found using a MPSoCs platform simulator. We are also extending our tool to an allocation and scheduling problem in a platform where processors can scale their voltage. An optimal solution must therefore not only allocate tasks to processors and memory slot to storage devices, but also associate a voltage and a clock frequency to each task execution, minimizing the total power consumption.

Acknowledgments

This work has been partially supported by ARTIST2 Network of Excellence on Embedded Systems Design (IST-004527).

References

1. Wolf, W.: The future of multiprocessor systems-on-chips. In: In Procs. of the 41st Design and Automation Conference - DAC 2004, San Diego, CA, USA, ACM (2004) 681–685
2. Benders, J.F.: Partitioning procedures for solving mixed-variables programming problems. Numerische Mathematik **4** (1962) 238–252
3. Hooker, J.N.: A hybrid method for planning and scheduling. In: Procs. of the 10th Intern. Conference on Principles and Practice of Constraint Programming - CP 2004, Toronto, Canada, Springer (2004) 305–316
4. Grossmann, I.E., Jain, V.: Algorithms for hybrid milp/cp models for a class of optimization problems. INFORMS Journal on Computing **13** (2001) 258–276
5. Culler, D.A., Singh, J.P.: Parallel Computer Architecture: A Hardware/Software Approach. Morgan Kaufmann (1999)
6. Compton, K., Hauck, S.: Reconfigurable computing: A survey of systems and software. ACM Computing Surveys **34** (1999) 171–210
7. Hooker, J.N.: Planning and scheduling by logic-based benders decomposition. Technical report (2004) http://web.tepper.cmu.edu/jnh/planning.pdf.
8. Prakash, S., Parker, A.: Sos: Synthesis of application-specific heterogeneous multiprocessor systems. Journal of Parallel and Distributed Computing **16** (1992) 338–351
9. Lee, C., Potkonjak, M., Wolf, W.: System-level synthesis of application-specific systems using A* search and generalized force-directed heuristics, San Diego, California (1996) 2–7
10. Bender, A.: Milp based task mapping for heterogeneous multiprocessor systems. In: EURO-DAC '96/EURO-VHDL '96: Procs. of the conference on European design automation, Geneva, Switzerland, IEEE (1996) 190–197
11. Li, Y., Wolf, W.H.: Hardware/software co-synthesis with memory hierarchies. **18** (1999) 1405–1417
12. Meftali, S., Gharsalli, F., Jerraya, A.A., Rousseau, F.: An optimal memory allocation for application-specific multiprocessor system-on-chip. In: Proceedings of the 14th international symposium on Systems synthesis - ISSS '01, ACM Press (2001) 19–24
13. De Micheli, G.: Synthesis and optimization of digital circuits. McGraw Hill (1994)
14. Chatha, K.S., Vemuri, R.: Hardware-software partitioning and pipelined scheduling of transformative applications. **10** (2002) 193–208

15. Fohler, G., Ramamritham, K.: Static scheduling of pipelined periodic tasks in distributed real-time systems. In: Procs. of the 9th EUROMICRO Workshop on Real-Time Systems - EUROMICRO-RTS '97, Toledo, Spain, IEEE (1997) 128–135
16. Palazzari, P., Baldini, L., Coli, M.: Synthesis of pipelined systems for the contemporaneous execution of periodic and aperiodic tasks with hard real-time constraints. In: 18th International Parallel and Distributed Processing Symposium - IPDPS'04. (2004) 121–128
17. Bakshi, S., Gajski, D.D.: A scheduling and pipelining algorithm for hardware/software systems. In: Proceedings of the 10th international symposium on System synthesis - ISSS '97, Washington, DC, USA, IEEE Computer Society (1997) 113–118
18. Axelsson, J.: Architecture synthesis and partitioning of real-time synthesis: a comparison of 3 heuristic search strategies. In: Procs. of the 5th Intern. Workshop on Hardware/Software Codesign (CODES/CASHE97), Braunschweig, Germany, IEEE (1997) 161–166
19. Eles, P., Peng, Z., Kuchcinski, K., Doboli, A.: System level hardware/software partitioning based on simulated annealing and tabu search. Design Automation for Embedded Systems **2** (1997) 5–32
20. Kodase, S., Wang, S., Gu, Z., Shin, K.: Improving scalability of task allocation and scheduling in large distributed real-time systems using shared buffers. In: Procs. of the 9th IEEE Real-Time and Embedded Technology and Applications Symposium (RTAS 2003), Toronto, Canada, IEEE (2003) 181–188
21. Eles, P., Peng, Z., Kuchcinski, K., Doboli, A., Pop, P.: Scheduling of conditional process graphs for the synthesis of embedded systems, Paris, France (1998) 132–139
22. Kuchcinski, K., Szymanek, R.: A constructive algorithm for memory-aware task assignment and scheduling. In: Procs of the Ninth International Symposium on Hardware/Software Codesign - CODES 2001, Copenhagen, Denmark, ACM Press (2001) 147–152
23. Kuchcinski, K.: Embedded system synthesis by timing constraint solving. IEEE Transactions on CAD **13** (1994) 537–551
24. Milano, M.: Constraint and Integer Programming: toward a unified methodolody. Kluwer Academic Publisher (2004)
25. Hooker, J.N., Yan, H.: Logic circuit verification by benders decomposition. In: Principles and Practice of Constraint Programming: The Newport Papers, Cambridge, MA, MIT Press (1995) 267–288
26. Eremin, A., Wallace, M.: Hybrid benders decomposition algorithms in constraint logic programming. In: Procs. of the 7th Intern. Conference on Principles and Practice of Constraint Programming - CP 2001, Paphos, Cyprus, Springer (2001) 1–15
27. Cambazard, H., Déplanche, A.M., Hladik, P.E., Jussien, N., Trinquet, Y.: Decomposition and learning for a hard real time task allocation problem. In: Procs. of the 10th Intern. Conference on Principles and Practice of Constraint Programming - CP 2004, Toronto, Canada, Springer (2004) 153–167
28. Thorsteinsson, E.S.: A hybrid framework integrating mixed integer programming and constraint programming, Paphos, Cyprus (2001) 16–30
29. Hooker, J.N., Ottosson, G.: Logic-based benders decomposition. Mathematical Programming **96** (2003) 33–60

Sub-optimality Approximations

Russell Bent[1], Irit Katriel[2], and Pascal Van Hentenryck[1]

[1] Brown University, Box 1910 Providence, RI 02912, USA
[2] BRICS, University of Aarhus, Åbogade 34, Århus, Denmark

Abstract. The sub-optimality approximation problem considers an optimization problem $\mathcal{O}$, its optimal solution σ^*, and a variable x with domain $\{d_1, \ldots, d_m\}$ and returns approximations to $\mathcal{O}[x \leftarrow d_1], \ldots, \mathcal{O}[x \leftarrow d_m]$, where $\mathcal{O}[x \leftarrow d_1]$ denotes the problem $\mathcal{O}$ with x assigned to d_i. The sub-optimality approximation problem is at the core of online stochastic optimization algorithms and it can also be used for solution repair and approximate filtering of optimization constraints. This paper formalizes the problem and presents sub-optimality approximation algorithms for metric TSPs, packet scheduling, and metric k-medians that run faster than the optimal or approximation algorithms. It also presents results on the hardness/easiness of sub-optimality approximations.

1 Introduction

In an increasing dynamic, interconnected, and real-time world, optimization technology faces new challenges and opportunities. Indeed, on many applications, it is no longer sufficient to produce optimal, or near-optimal, solutions offline. Optimization software should adapt dynamically to uncertainties, update existing solutions to accommodate new requests and events, and produce high-quality decisions under severe time constraints.

This paper introduces the sub-optimality approximation problem, which is at the core of many online and dynamic applications. Given an optimization problem $\mathcal{O}$ and an optimal solution σ^* to $\mathcal{O}$, the sub-optimality approximation problem consists of approximating the problems $\mathcal{O}[x \leftarrow d_1], \ldots, \mathcal{O}[x \leftarrow d_m]$, where x is a decision variable, $\{d_1, \ldots, d_m\}$ are its possible values, and $O[x \leftarrow d]$ denotes the problem $\mathcal{O}$ where x is assigned to d. The key property of the sub-optimality approximation problem is the availability of the optimal solution σ^*. Since each problem $\mathcal{O}[x \leftarrow d_i]$ is closely related to $\mathcal{O}$, the optimal solution is, in general, of tremendous help for the sub-optimality approximations. However, to be useful, a sub-optimality approximation algorithm should be faster than traditional approximation algorithms. This performance requirement is formalized by the concept of amortized sub-optimality algorithm that finds approximations to $\mathcal{O}[x \leftarrow d_1], \ldots, \mathcal{O}[x \leftarrow d_m]$ in the time it takes to solve $\mathcal{O}$ optimally or approximately. The sub-optimality approximation problem is a critical component of the regret algorithm for online stochastic optimization [3,6]. It can also be used for solution repair, for evaluating the robustness of solutions, and for approximate filtering of optimization constraints to name a few of its applications.

This paper makes three contributions. First, it identifies and formalizes the sub-optimality approximation problem and demonstrates its relevance for a number of applications. Second, it presents amortized sub-optimality approximation algorithms for three problems: the metric TSP, packet scheduling in networks, and the k-median problem. The proof techniques are interesting in the sense they reason about the optimal solutions to both $\mathcal{O}$ and $\mathcal{O}[x \leftarrow d]$. Third, it presents results on the hardness and easiness of sub-optimality approximations, showing that some "hard" problems become "easy", while others remain "hard".

This paper is organized as follows. Sections 2 and 3 formalize the problem and discuss its applications. Section 4, 5, and 6 present sub-optimality approximations for the metric TSP, the packet scheduling, and the metric k-median problem. Section 7 presents the hardness results.

2 Amortized Sub-optimality Approximation Algorithms

This section formalizes sub-optimality approximation problems and algorithms. The formalization uses the definition of CSPs from [15], where the set of constraints is abstracted by a Boolean function which holds if all the constraints are satisfied (since we are not interested in the constraint structure). Solutions are also represented as functions (assignments) from variables to their sets of values.

Definition 1. *A CSP is a triplet $\langle V, D, C \rangle$, where V denotes the set of variables, D denotes the set of possible values for these variables, and $C : (V \to D) \to Bool$ is a constraint which specifies which assignments of values to the variables are solutions. A solution to a CSP $\mathcal{P} = \langle V, D, C \rangle$ is a function $\sigma : V \to D$ such that $C(\sigma) = true$. The set of solutions to a CSP $\mathcal{P}$ is denoted by $Sol(\mathcal{P})$.*

Constraint Optimization Problems (COPs) are CSPs with an objective function.

Definition 2. *A COP is a pair $\langle \mathcal{P}, f \rangle$, where $\mathcal{P} = \langle V, D, C \rangle$ is a CSP and $f : V \to \mathcal{N}$ is an objective function. A solution to a COP $\mathcal{O} = \langle \mathcal{P}, f \rangle$ is a solution to $\mathcal{P}$. An optimal solution to $\mathcal{O}$ is a solution of $\mathcal{O}$ that minimizes f. The sets of solutions and optimal solutions to a COP $\mathcal{O}$ are denoted by $Sol(\mathcal{O})$ and $OptSol(\mathcal{O})$ respectively.*

Given a CSP $\mathcal{P} = \langle V, D, C \rangle$, $var(\mathcal{P})$ denotes the variables V and $dom(\mathcal{P})$ the domain D. Similar notations are used for COPs, the variables and values of a COP being those of its underlying CSP. Sub-optimality approximation problems consider sets of related CSPs where one variable is assigned different values. Given a CSP $\mathcal{P} = \langle V, D, C \rangle$, $\mathcal{P}[x \leftarrow d]$ ($x \in V$ & $d \in D$) denotes the CSP $\mathcal{P}$ where variable x is assigned the value d, i.e., the CSP $\langle V, D, C \wedge x = d \rangle$. Similarly, given a COP $\mathcal{O} = \langle \mathcal{P}, f \rangle$, $\mathcal{O}[x \leftarrow d]$ ($x \in V$ & $d \in D$) denotes the COP $\mathcal{O}$ where variable x is assigned the value d, i.e., the COP $\langle \mathcal{O}[x \leftarrow d], f \rangle$.

We are ready to specify the sub-optimality approximation problem. Informally, given an optimal solution σ^* to a COP $\mathcal{O}$, the sub-optimality approximation problem consists of finding constant factor approximations to the COPs $\mathcal{O}[x \leftarrow d_i]$ for all values $d_1, \ldots, d_m$ of variable x.

Definition 3 (The Sub-optimality Approximation Problem). *A sub-optimality approximation problem receives as input a COP $\mathcal{O} = \langle \mathcal{P}, f \rangle$ with $dom(\mathcal{P}) = \{d_1, \ldots, d_m\}$, an optimal solution $\sigma^* \in OptSol(\mathcal{O})$, and a variable x in $var(\mathcal{P})$. Its output is a set of solutions*

$$\tilde{\sigma}_i \in Sol(\mathcal{P}[x \leftarrow d_i]) \quad (1 \leq i \leq m)$$

satisfying $f(\tilde{\sigma}_i) \leq \beta f(\sigma_i^*)$ for some constant β, where $\sigma_i^* \in OptSol(\mathcal{O}[x \leftarrow d_i])$.

The fundamental property in the sub-optimality approximation problem is the fact that the input contains an optimal solution to $\mathcal{O}$. This solution should of course be used by the sub-optimality approximation algorithm in order to solve the COPs $\mathcal{O}[x \leftarrow d_i]$ efficiently. Observe that the definition can easily be generalized to accommodate stronger or weaker approximation requirements.

To capture performance requirements of great benefit in practical applications, we introduce the concept of amortized sub-optimality approximation algorithms. The intuition here is that a sub-optimality algorithm is amortized if it approximates the solutions of $\mathcal{O}[x \leftarrow d_1], \ldots, \mathcal{O}[x \leftarrow d_m]$ in the time it takes to solve $\mathcal{O}$ optimally. It is strongly amortized if it approximates such solutions for all variables in the same time.

Definition 4 (Amortized Sub-optimality Approximation). *Consider a class $\mathcal{C}$ of COPs, let $\mathcal{A}$ be an algorithm for solving $\mathcal{C}$ in time $O(g)$, and let $\tilde{\mathcal{A}}$ be a sub-optimality approximation algorithm for class $\mathcal{C}$ that runs in time $O(\tilde{g})$. Let $|dom(\mathcal{O})| = m$ and let $|var(\mathcal{O})| = n$. Algorithm $\tilde{\mathcal{A}}$ is amortized wrt $\mathcal{A}$ on class $\mathcal{C}$ if, for each COP $\mathcal{O} \in \mathcal{C}$ with $|dom(\mathcal{O})| = m$, we have that $m\,\tilde{g}$ is $O(g)$.. It is strongly amortized wrt $\mathcal{A}$ on class $\mathcal{C}$ if $nm\,\tilde{g}$ is $O(g)$.*

These definitions can be generalized to the important case where the COP is solved through an approximation algorithm with performance guarantees. This is especially significant in online optimization under strict time constraints where optimal solutions can rarely be obtained within the time limits.

Definition 5 (The Sub-optimality (α,β)-Approximation Problem). *A sub-optimality (α, β)-approximation problem receives as input a COP $\mathcal{O} = \langle \mathcal{P}, f \rangle$ with $dom(\mathcal{P}) = \{d_1, \ldots, d_m\}$, an approximation $\tilde{\sigma}$ satisfying $f(\tilde{\sigma}) \leq \alpha f(\sigma^*)$ for $\sigma^* \in OptSol(\mathcal{O})$, and x in $var(\mathcal{P})$. Its output is the solutions $\tilde{\sigma}_i \in Sol(\mathcal{P}[x \leftarrow d_i])$ $(1 \leq i \leq m)$ satisfying $f(\tilde{\sigma}_i) \leq \beta f(\sigma_i^*)$ and $\sigma_i^* \in OptSol(\mathcal{O}[x \leftarrow d_i])$.*

The concept of amortized sub-optimality (α, β)-approximation is similar to Definition 4, although its requirements are typically much stricter. However, as shown later, the same sub-optimality approximation may apply to both problems.

3 Applications

This section reviews a number of applications that benefit from sub-optimality approximation algorithms to demonstrate its relevance and applicability. The section does not aim to be comprehensive but to give some indication of where sub-optimality approaximations may be beneficial.

Online Stochastic Optimization. Our primary motivation for sub-optimality optimization came from online stochastic optimization. Online optimization problems (e.g., [11]) is a class of applications where the data is revealed online during the execution of the decision-making process. In many of these applications [8,3,4], a distribution of the data, or an approximation thereof, is available to the algorithm for sampling. Alternatively, the data distribution can be learned during the algorithm execution [6]. A natural framework for online stochastic optimization was defined in [5,3,2] and only its most basic version is considered here for simplicity. The key idea behind the framework is to consider a time interval H and to allow a single request to be served at each time $t \in H$. The selected request (if any) is selected from the set of available requests R at time t. Each request r has a weight $w(r)$ that specifies how valuable it is. Which requests may be served is problem-specific and left unspecified in the framework. The framework simply assumes that the underlying algorithms have access to two black-boxes: an optimization algorithm that can find an optimal solution for a set of requests and a distribution that can be sampled to obtain scenarios reflecting the future (to some degree). The goal of the online algorithms is to a choose requests online to maximize the weighted sum of the serviced requests. More formally, the algorithms are all instantiations of the online schema:

ONLINEOPTIMIZATION(H)
1   $R \leftarrow \emptyset$;
2   $w \leftarrow 0$;
3   for $t \in H$
4   do $R \leftarrow$ AVAILABLEREQUESTS(R, t) $\cup$ NEWREQUESTS(t);
5           $r \leftarrow$ CHOOSEREQUEST(R, t);
6   SERVEREQUEST(r, t);
7           $w \leftarrow w + w(r)$;
8           $R \leftarrow R \setminus \{r\}$;

but they differ in how they implement function CHOOSEREQUEST. The online optimization schema considers the set of available requests (i.e. those requests that may be served at time t without violating any constraints) and new requests at each time step. It chooses a request r which is then served and removed from the set of available requests. Function AVAILABLEREQUEST(R, t) returns the set of requests available for service at time t and function SERVEREQUEST(r, t) simply serves r at time t (i.e., $\sigma(t) \leftarrow r$). To implement function CHOOSEREQUEST, the algorithms have at their disposal two black-boxes:

1. A function OPTIMALSOLUTION(R, t, Δ) that, given a set R of requests, a time t, and a number Δ, returns an optimal solution for R over $[t, t + \Delta]$;
2. A function GETSAMPLE($[t_s, t_e]$) that returns a set of requests over the interval $[t_s, t_e]$ by sampling the arrival distribution.

Typically, the goal is to choose a request at time t that maximizes expectation. The exact computation of the expected value of servicing a request is often too computationally demanding and one of the traditional approaches approximates expectation by evaluating each decision with respect to samples from the distribution (Algorithm E) [8]. A simple implementation is as follows:

CHOOSEREQUEST-E(R, t)
1   for $r \in R$
2   do $f(r) \leftarrow 0$;
3   for $i \leftarrow 1 \ldots \mathcal{O}/|R|$
4   do $S \leftarrow R \cup$ GETSAMPLE($[t+1, t+\Delta]$);
5   for $r \in R$
6   do $f(r) \leftarrow f(r) + (w(r) + W(\text{OPTIMALSOLUTION}(S \setminus \{r\}, t+1)))$;
7   return $argmax(r \in R)\ f(r)$;

Lines 1-2 initialize the evaluation function $f(r)$ for each request r. The algorithm then generates a number of samples for future requests (line 3). For each such sample, it computes the set R of all available and sampled requests at time t (line 4). The algorithm then considers each available request r successively (line 5), it implicitly schedules r at time t, and applies the optimal offline algorithm using $S \setminus \{r\}$ and the time horizon. The evaluation of request r is updated in line 6 by incrementing it with its weight and the score of the corresponding optimal offline solution. All samples are evaluated for all available requests and the algorithm then returns the request $r \in R$ with the highest evaluation. Observe Line 3 of Algorithm E which distributes the available offline optimizations across all available requests. The expectation algorithm is typically too computationally demanding for an online setting as each evaluation of a request on a sample requires an optimization. A recent advance is the regret algorithm (R), where each sample is solved optimally once and sub-optimality approximations are used to evaluate the remaining requests [3]:

CHOOSEREQUEST-R(R, t)
1   for $r \in R$
2   do $f(r) \leftarrow 0$;
3   for $i \leftarrow 1 \ldots \mathcal{O}$
4   do $S \leftarrow R \cup$ GETSAMPLE($[t+1, t+\Delta]$);
5           $\sigma^* \leftarrow$ OPTIMALSOLUTION(S, t);
6           $f(\sigma^*(t)) \leftarrow f(\sigma^*(t)) + W(\sigma)$;
7   for $r \in R \setminus \{\sigma^*(t)\}$
8   do $f(r) \leftarrow f(r) + W(\text{SUBOPTIMALITYAPPROXIMATION}(\sigma^*, r, S, t))$;
9   return $argmax(r \in R)\ f(r)$;

Algorithm R (lines 7-8) computes an approximation of the best solution of s serving r at time t, i.e., $W(\text{SUBOPTIMALITYAPPROXIMATION}(\sigma^*, r, S, t))$. Hence, the value of scheduling each available request is approximated on every sample at time t for the cost of a single offline optimization (asymptotically). Observe that the regret algorithm solves the sub-optimality problem where variable $\sigma(t)$ is assigned the values $R \setminus \{\sigma(r)\}$ and that the optimal solution σ^*, or an approximation thereof, is naturally available since the sample is solved in line 5.

By solving the sub-optimality problem, algorithm R enjoys essentially the same theoretical performance guarantees as algorithm E at a fraction of the cost [7].

Solution Repair. Solution repair is another important application for sub-optimality approximations. For example, a catastrophic hub failure in a network may require a nearby hub to be opened quickly. Such applications are often modeled as dynamic facility location problems where one must quickly approximate the optimal solution to the problem in which a facility is forced to be closed or to be opened. Once again, the optimal solution, or an approximation thereof, is naturally available, and one is interested in solving the sub-optimality approximation problem for specific hubs. Solution repair is closely related to the issue of robustness. Sub-optimality approximations provide a computational method to evaluate the robustness of different optimal, or locally optimal, solutions. Solutions with small sub-optimality gaps may be preferred, since they entail smaller quality loss when some variables cannot be assigned some values. Again, optimal or approximated solutions are naturally available in these applications.

Partial or Approximate Filtering. Sub-Optimality approximations are also useful for partial or approximate filterings of optimization constraints (e.g., [12]). An optimization constraint captures a combinatorial substructure arising in many applications and can be specified as an optimization problem $\mathcal{O} = \langle \mathcal{P}, f \rangle$. During the search, an optimization constraint uses bounds on f to detect infeasibility and prunes the domains of the variables. Consider a minimization constraint $\mathcal{O} = \langle \mathcal{P}, f \rangle$ and assume that U is an upper bound on f. Typically, the minimization constraint searches for an optimal solution o^* to $\mathcal{O}$ to detect feasibility, i.e., $f(o^*) \leq U$. Once feasibility is established, the constraint filters the domains of the variables to remove all values that cannot appear in any solution not greater than U. Here sub-optimality approximation can be used to detect quickly values that can, or cannot, be filtered. Assume that the sub-optimality algorithm is a ρ-approximation and consider a variable x with domain D. The sub-optimality approximation problem provides a solution $\tilde{o}_d$ to $\mathcal{O}[x \leftarrow d]$ satisfying $f(\tilde{o}_d) \leq \rho f(o_d)$, where o_d is an optimal solution to $\mathcal{O}[x \leftarrow d]$. Hence, the value d cannot be filtered whenever $f(\tilde{o}_d) \leq U$ and must be filtered whenever $f(\tilde{o}_d) > \rho U$. Once again, observe that the optimal solution o^* is naturally available.

4 The Travelling Salesman Problem

The traveling salesman problem (TSP) is probably the most studied combinatorial optimization problem. It is also an important component in a wide variety of online applications, such as courier services.

The Sub-optimality Approximation Problem. The sub-optimality approximation problem consists of approximating the cost of assigning different successors to a vertex i. In other words, the variable under consideration is the successor of vertex i and the domains are all other vertices.

The Sub-optimality Approximation Algorithm. A simple relocation provides a sub-optimality approximation algorithm to bound the effect of traveling to customer j after i: remove j from the optimal solution and reinsert it after i. This amortized algorithm is a constant factor approximation for the Euclidean TSP.

Theorem 1. **[Amortized Sub-optimality for the Metric TSP]** *The metric TSP has a strongly amortized sub-optimality (α,β)-approximation algorithm.*

Proof. Let σ^* be the optimal solution to a TSP and let σ_{ij} be the optimal solution when j must follow i. The optimal solution σ^* consists of a tour with length $C(\sigma) = c_{i,i+} + C_{i+,j-} + c_{j-,j} + c_{j,j+} + C_{j+,i}$, where $C_{i,j}$ (resp. $c_{i,j}$) denotes the cost of the path (resp. arc) between i and j in σ^*. The approximation solution consists of a tour with length $C(\tilde{\sigma}_{x_{ij}}) = c_{i,j} + c_{j,i+} + C_{i+,j-} + c_{j-,j+} + C_{j+,i}$. By the triangle inequality,

$$\begin{aligned}
C(\tilde{\sigma}_{ij}) &= c_{i,j} + c_{j,i+} + C_{i+,j-} + c_{j-,j+} + C_{j+,i} \\
&\leq c_{i,j} + c_{j,i+} + C_{i+,j-} + c_{j-,j} + c_{j,j+} + C_{j+,i} \\
&\leq c_{i,i+} + C_{i+,j-} + c_{j-,j} + c_{i+,j} + C_{i+,j-} + c_{j-,j} + c_{j,j+} + C_{j+,i} \\
&\leq c_{i,i+} + C_{i+,j-} + c_{j-,j} + C_{i+,j-} + c_{j-,j} + C_{i+,j-} + c_{j-,j} + c_{j,j+} + C_{j+,i} \\
&\leq c_{i,i+} + 3C_{i+,j-} + 3c_{j-,j} + c_{j,j+} + C_{j+,i} \\
&\leq 3\, C(\sigma) \leq 3\, C(\sigma_{ij}) \text{ by optimality of } \sigma.
\end{aligned}$$

Now assume that $\tilde{\sigma}$ is an α-approximation of σ^*. We have that $C(\tilde{\sigma}_{ij}) \leq 3\, C(\tilde{\sigma})$ by the above proof and hence $C(\tilde{\sigma}_{ij}) \leq 3\,\alpha\, C(\tilde{\sigma}) \leq 3\,\alpha\, C(\tilde{\sigma}_{ij})$. Each such approximation takes $O(1)$ time. The algorithm is strongly amortized wrt all approximation algorithms (which are $\Omega(|E|)$, where E is the set of arcs). □

5 Packet Scheduling

The Optimization Problem. This section considers a simple scheduling problem used to model a variety of applications, including the packet scheduling problem from [8]. The problem is given as inputs a set R of tasks/requests for service and a time horizon $H = [\underline{H}, \overline{H}]$ during which requests must be scheduled. Each request r is characterized by a weight $w(r)$ and an arrival time $a(r)$, requires a single time unit to be processed, and must be scheduled in its time window $[a(r), a(r)+d]$. In other words, the request is lost if it is not served within its time window. In addition, no two requests can be scheduled at the same time. The goal is to find a schedule of maximal weight, i.e., a schedule which maximizes the sum of the weights of all scheduled requests. This is equivalent to minimizing weighted loss. More formally, assume for simplicity and without loss of generality, that there is a request scheduled at each time step. Under this assumption, a schedule is a function $\sigma : H \to R$ which assigns a request to each time in the schedule horizon. A schedule σ is feasible if it satisfies the constraints

$$\begin{aligned}
&\forall\, t_1, t_2 \in H : t_1 \neq t_2 \to \sigma(t_1) \neq \sigma(t_2) \\
&\forall\, t \in H : a(\sigma(t)) \leq t \leq a(\sigma(t)) + d.
\end{aligned}$$

The weight of a schedule σ, denoted by $W(\sigma)$, is given by $W(\sigma) = \sum_{t \in H} w(\sigma(t))$. and the goal is to find a feasible schedule σ maximizing $W(\sigma)$. This offline problem can be solved in quadratic time $O(|R||H|)$ [8].

The Sub-optimality Approximation Problem. The sub-optimality approximation problem for packet scheduling is motivated by online stochastic optimization, where future packets are known in advance and are revealed online as the algorithm makes decision. As discussed in Section 3, it is highly beneficial in online optimization to use stochastic information and to evaluate many scenarios at a time t in order to select a good packet to schedule. However, due to severe time constraints, only a few optimizations can be executed and the regret algorithm uses the sub-optimality approximation algorithm to estimate the value of scheduling all packets on all scenarios for the cost of one optimization. As a consequence, the sub-optimality approximation problem is given a set of request R and an optimal solution σ^* for scheduling these requests in the time horizon $[t, \overline{H}]$. For each request $r \in R$ available at time t, it must approximate the optimal schedule σ_r that schedules request r at time t, i.e., $\sigma_r(t) = r$. The results also generalize to arbitrary times in H.

The packet scheduling problem is an interesting case study because its offline algorithm takes quadratic time and hence an amortized sub-optimality approximation must approximate $|R|$ schedules within the same time bounds.

The Amortized Sub-optimality Approximation. The sub-optimality approximation consists of swapping a constant number of requests in the optimal schedule σ^* at a time t and performs a case analysis on the properties of the request r.

If a request r is not scheduled (i.e., $r \notin \sigma^*$), the key idea is to try rescheduling the request $\sigma^*(t)$ instead of the request of smallest weight in the schedule σ^*. The value of the sub-optimality approximation becomes

$$W(\sigma^*) - \min(s \in [t, a(\sigma^*(t)) + d])\, w(\sigma^*(s)) - w(r),$$

since the replaced request is removed from σ^* and r is added to the schedule. In the worst case, the replaced request is $\sigma^*(t)$ and the approximation is $W(\sigma^*) - (w(\sigma^*(t)) - w(r))$.

If request r is scheduled at time t_r, the sub-optimality approximation first tries to swap r and $\sigma^*(t)$ in which case the approximation is $W(\sigma^*)$. If this is not possible, the approximation tries rescheduling $\sigma^*(t)$ instead of the request of smallest weight in σ^*. If $\sigma^*(t)$ cannot be rescheduled, the approximation simply selects the best possible unscheduled request which may be scheduled at t_r and the approximation is

$$W(\sigma^*) - (w(\sigma^*(t)) - \max(u \in U_r)\, w(u))$$

where $U_r = \{r \mid a(r) \leq t_r \leq a(r) + d \land r \notin \sigma^*\}$. If $\sigma^*(t)$ is rescheduled at time s, then the approximation concludes by selecting the best possible unscheduled request which may be scheduled at t_r and the approximation is

$$W(\sigma^*) - (w(\sigma^*(s)) - \max(u \in U_{r,s})\, w(u))$$

where $U_{r,s} = \{r \mid a(r) \leq t_r \leq a(r) + d \land (r \notin \sigma^* \lor r = \sigma^*(s))\}$. Each sub-optimality approximation takes $O(d)$ time and is performed at most $|R|$ times (typically much less than $|R|$ since only one request of the same class must be evaluated). Thus all the approximations take $O(d|R|)$ time, which is $O(|R||H|)$ and is negligible in practice for this application. Theorem 2 shows that this amortized algorithm produces a 2-approximation.

Theorem 2. *Packet scheduling has an amortized suboptimality approximation.*

Proof. Let $r \in R$ be a request that can be scheduled at time t and σ^* be an optimal solution. let σ_r be an optimal solution when r is scheduled at time t (i.e., $\sigma_r(t) = r$) and let $\tilde{\sigma}_r$ be the solution obtained by the sub-optimality approximation. This theorem shows that $\frac{w(\sigma_r)}{w(\tilde{\sigma}_r)} \leq 2$. Most of the proof consists of showing that, for each lost request x, where x is typically $\sigma^*(t)$, there is another request in σ^* whose weight is at least $w(x)$ yielding a 2-approximation since $w(\sigma_r) \leq w(\sigma^*)$.

First observe that the result holds when $w(x) \leq w(r)$ since, in the worst case, the sub-optimality approximation only loses request x. So attention is restricted to $w(x) \geq w(r)$. If $x \in \tilde{\sigma}_r$, i.e., if the sub-optimality approximation swaps x with another request y (case 1), the result also holds since $w(y) \leq w(x)$. If $x \notin \tilde{\sigma}_r$ and x can be scheduled at a time other than t, it means that there exists a request y at each of these times satisfying $w(y) \geq w(x)$ and the result holds. It thus remains to consider the case where x can only be scheduled at time t and is thus lost in σ_r. If $r \notin \sigma^*$, the sub-optimality approximation is optimal, since otherwise r would be in the optimal schedule at a time other than t. Otherwise, it is necessary to reason about a collection of requests. Indeed,

$$w(\sigma^*) = w(x) + w(r) + w(S),$$

where $S = \{p \in \sigma^* \mid p \neq x \ \& \ p \neq y\}$. It is also known that $w(\tilde{\sigma}_r) \geq w(r) + w(S)$ since, in the worst case, the approximation loses request x. Finally, $w(\sigma_r) = w(r) + w(Z)$ where Z are the requests scheduled after time t. Since σ^* is optimal, we have $w(Z) \leq w(r) + w(S)$ and the result follows. □

Experimental Results. Figure 1 (taken from [3]) shows the significance of the sub-optimality approximation problem for online stochastic optimization. The plot depicts the performance of various algorithms as a function of the number of optimizations available for each decision. It considers two oblivious algorithms: greedy (G) which always schedules the available packet of highest weight, local optimization (LO) which uses the result of the optimization on the known requests to select the packet to schedule at time t. It also considers two stochastic algorithms: expectation (E) which runs the optimization algorithm when each available request is scheduled at time t in each scenario, and the regret algorithm (R) which solves each scenario once and uses the sub-optimality approximation to evaluate each available request. The figure also displays the optimal, a posteriori, solution, i.e., the solution that would be obtained if all requests had been known in advance. As can be seen from this plot, the regret algorithm provides great benefits over all the other algorithms. In particular, it significantly outperforms E when few optimizations are available for decision making.

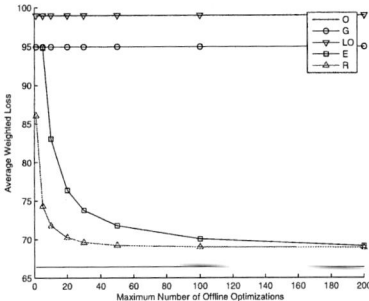

Fig. 1. Regret on Packet Scheduling

6 The k-Median Problem

The Optimization Problem. This section studies k-median problems and presents an amortized sub-optimality approximation performing a single local move. A k-median problem receives, as inputs, a set F of facilities, a set of customers S, a function $c_{a,b}$ specifying the connection costs between a and b $(a, b \in F \cup S)$, and an integer k. The goal is to find a subset A $(A \subseteq F)$ of cardinality k to minimize the objective function

$$W_A(S) = \sum_{s \in S} \min_{a \in A} c_{s,a}.$$

The Sub-optimality Approximation Problem. The computational complexity in the k-median problem consists of choosing which k facilities to open. Once the facilities are open, it suffices to assign the customers to the cheapest facility. As a consequence, the decision are whether to open or close a warehouse and the sub-optimality approximation problem consists of approximating the optimal solution whenever a facility is forced to be open or forced to be closed. This section considers metric k-median problems, i.e., k-median problems where the costs are taken from a metric space. The k-median problem has applications in networking where servers or specialized routers may be modeled as facilities. When a server fails (closing a facility), it is important to choose a replacing router quickly. Similarly, in order to contain failure propagation, it may be important to start a server (opening a facility) at some node. The amortized sub-optimality algorithm presented here handles these two cases very quickly. The Internet is typically not a metric space. However, recent research [10] has shown that it can conveniently be embedded in a metric space.

The Sub-optimality Approximation Algorithm. The sub-optimality approximation algorithm consists of performing the best swap of the considered facility. In other words, when a facility x must be closed (resp. open), the algorithm opens (resp. closes) the warehouse y that increases the cost the least. We now show that this local move is a constant approximation by showing a constant approximation for some swaps.

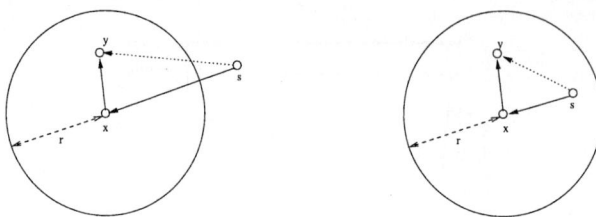

Fig. 2. Closing a Facility: Facility y is Inside the Circle

Proposition 1. [Closing] *Let A be an optimal solution to a metric k-median problem and B be an optimal solution when facility x is closed. There exists a facility $y \neq x$ such that $\tilde{B} = A \setminus \{x\} \cup \{y\}$ is a 5-approximation of B.*

Proof. Denote by S_x the set of customers assigned to x in A. Define a circle C centered at x of radius r and define *Inner* as the set of customers in S_x lying inside C, *Outer* as the set of customers in S_x lying outside C and *Other* the remaining customers $S \setminus S_x$. Moreover, choose r such $|Inner| = |Outer|$. We analyze the cost of the solution $\tilde{B}$ that opens the facility y nearest to x and assigns all customers in S_x to y.

First consider the case where y lies in C (see Figure 2). For each customer $s \in Outer$, we have by the triangular inequality

$$c_{s,y} \leq c_{s,x} + c_{x,y} \leq c_{s,x} + r \leq 2c_{s,x}$$

and it follows that $W_{\tilde{B}}(Outer) \leq 2W_A(Outer)$. For each customer $s \in Inner$, we have by the triangular inequality

$$c_{s,y} \leq c_{s,x} + c_{x,y} \leq c_{s,x} + r.$$

Since $r \times |Outer| \leq W_A(Outer)$ and $|Inner| = |Outer|$ it follows that $W_{\tilde{B}}(Inner) \leq W_A(Inner) + W_A(Outer)$. Hence

$$W_{\tilde{B}}(S) = W_{\tilde{B}}(Other) + W_{\tilde{B}}(Inner) + W_{\tilde{B}}(Outer)$$
$$\leq W_A(Other) + W_A(Inner) + 3W_A(Outer) \leq 3W_A(S) \leq 3W_B(S).$$

Consider now the case in which y is outside C and assume that y at a distance $r+d$ of x (Figure 3). Consider a customer $s \in Inner$. By the triangular inequality, $c_{s,y} \leq c_{s,x} + (r+d)$ and thus

$$W_{\tilde{B}}(Inner) \leq W_A(Inner) + (r+d) \times |Inner|$$

Since $r \times |Outer| \leq W_A(Outer)$ and $|Inner| = |Outer|$, it follows that $r \times |Inner| \leq W_A(Outer)$. By definition of y, each *Inner* customer must pay at least d to get to a facility in the optimal solution in which x is closed. Hence $d \times |Inner| \leq W_B(Inner)$ and $W_{\tilde{B}}(Inner) \leq W_A(Inner) + W_A(Outer) + W_B(Inner)$. Consider now a customer $s \in Outer$. By the triangular inequality, $c_{s,y} \leq c_{s,x} + (r+d)$ giving

$$W_{\tilde{B}}(Outer) \leq W_A(Outer) + (r+d) \times |Outer|.$$

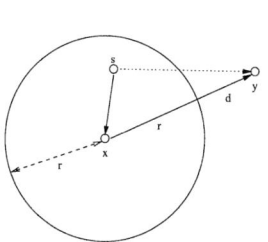
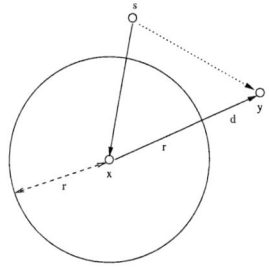

Fig. 3. Closing a Facility: Facility y is Outside the Circle

Once again, $r \times |Outer| \leq W_A(Outer)$ and $d \times |Outer| \leq W_B(Inner)$, since $|Inner| = |Outer|$. It follows that

$$W_{\tilde{B}}(Outer) \leq W_A(Outer) + W_A(Outer) + W_B(Inner).$$

Hence $W_{\tilde{B}}(S) \leq W_A(Other) + 3W_A(Outer) + 2W_B(Inner) + W_A(Inner)$ and

$$W_{\tilde{B}}(S) \leq 3W_A(S) + 2W_B(S) \tag{1}$$

and, by optimality of A, it follows that $W_{\tilde{B}}(S) \leq 5W_B(S)$. □

We now consider the case where a facility x is forced to be open. The following proposition indicates that swapping x in the optimal solution provides a constant approximation. The proof adapts some of the proof techniques from online k-median algorithms (Fact 1 in [9]).

Proposition 2. [Opening] *Let A be an optimal solution to a metric k-median problem and let B be the optimal solution where facility x must be open. There exists a facility $y \neq x$ such that $\tilde{B} = A \setminus \{y\} \cup \{x\}$ satisfies $W_{\tilde{B}}(S) \leq 3W_B(S)$.*

Proof. Let $B = B' \cup \{x\}$. Define A' as the set of facilities obtained by considering each facility w in B' and selecting its nearest facility in A and define $\tilde{B}$ as $A' \cup \{x\}$. The proof shows that $W_{\tilde{B}}(S) \leq 3W_B(S)$. Since $|B'| = k-1$, $|A'| \leq k-1$ and $\tilde{B}$ can be viewed as swapping x with one of the non-selected facility y of A and the results follows.

To bound the cost of $\tilde{B}$, partition S into S_x and S_o, where S_x are all the customers allocated to facility x in B. The bound on $\tilde{B}$ is obtained by assigning all the customers in S_x are assigned to x. Consider now a customer $s \in S_o$ and let a be its closest facility in A, b is closest facility in B, and let b' be the facility in A' nearest to b. The bound on $\tilde{B}$ is obtained by assigning s to b', giving the inequality (see Figure 4)

$$\begin{aligned} c_{s,b'} &\leq c_{s,b} + c_{b,b'} & \text{by the triangular inequality} \\ &\leq c_{s,b} + c_{b,a} & \text{since } c_{b,b'} \leq c_{b,a} \\ &\leq c_{s,b} + c_{b,s} + c_{s,a} & \text{by the triangular inequality} \\ &\leq 2c_{s,b} + c_{s,a} \end{aligned}$$

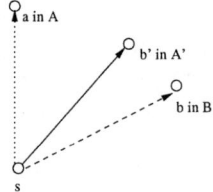

Fig. 4. Opening a Facility: Customer s is Assigned to b'

Summing on all vertices in S_o, we obtain $W_{\tilde{B}}(S_o) \leq 2W_B(S_o) + W_A(S_o)$. By the allocation of S_x, we obtain

$$W_{\tilde{B}}(S) \leq 2W_B(S) + W_A(S) \qquad (2)$$

and, by optimality of A, it follows that $W_{\tilde{B}}(S) \leq 3W_B(S)$. □

Theorem 3. Amortized Sub-optimality for the Metric k-Medians. *The metric k-median problem has an amortized sub-optimality approximation algorithm that runs in time $O(|S|\log|F|)$.*

Proof. Propositions 1 and 2 show that a single swap to open or close the considered facility x produces a 5-approximation of the optimal solution in the worst case. The best swap to open or close x is thus a constant approximation and it can be computed in $O(|S|\log|F|)$ using the data structures of [14]. □

The result continues to hold even when only an α-approximation of the k-median is available to the sub-optimality approximation algorithm. Indeed, the propositions only rely on the optimality of A in the last steps of their proofs (after Equations 1 and 2) and the same proof technique as in Theorem 1 can be used. Such α-approximations can be obtained by local search for instance [1]. The algorithm is amortized since it consists of a single swap and it is strongly amortized if one assumes that a local search performs at least $|F|$ swaps.

Theorem 4. Amortized Sub-optimality for the Metric k-Medians. *The metric k-median problem has an amortized sub-optimality (α, β)-approximation algorithm that runs in time $O(|S|\log|F|)$.*

The k-median is closely related to (uncapacitated and capacitated) facility location problems. The results described here apply directly to uncapacitated facility location with uniform fixed costs. It would be interesting to study whether they also apply when the costs are not uniform.

7 Hardness/Easiness of Sub-optimality Approximations

In general, the availability of an optimal solution σ^* is a significant advantage for sub-optimality approximation algorithms. In fact, some difficult problems become trivial when σ^* is available. Consider, for instance, the graph-coloring problem which consists of finding the chromatic number of a graph. No constant factor approximation for graph coloring likely exists (unless $P = NP$) [13], yet the suboptimality problem can be solved exactly in polynomial time.

Lemma 1. *The sub-optimality problem can be solved exactly in polynomial time for graph coloring.*

Proof. Let O be a graph-coloring problem with optimal solution σ^* and let c_x be the color of x in σ^*. The suboptimality problem $O[x \leftarrow c]$ can be solved optimally by swapping the colors c_x and c in σ^*. □

Some polynomial algorithms also enjoy simple sub-optimality approximation algorithms. Consider the problem of finding the shortest path from a source to a sink and the sub-optimality problem that consists of studying the choice of various successors to the source. This problem arises in online stochastic planning and can be solved (optimally) by two shortest paths: one from the source to the sink and one from the sink to the source (reverting all arcs).

One may thus think that suboptimality approximations are inherently simpler than the original problems. This is not case unfortunately: there are problems for which suboptimality approximation is as hard as the problem itself. One such problem is maximum satisfiability (MAX-SAT): given a CNF formula ϕ, find a truth assignment that satisfies the maximum number of clauses.

Lemma 2. *Suboptimality of MAX-SAT is as hard as MAX-SAT.*

Proof. Assume that there exists a polynomial-time (exact or approximate) suboptimality algorithm $\mathcal{A}$ for MAX-SAT. We can construct an algorithm $\mathcal{A}'$ that solves MAX-SAT (exactly or approximately) as follows. Given a CNF folmula $\phi = (C_1 \wedge \ldots \wedge C_k)$ where each C_i is a clause, $\mathcal{A}'$ constructs a formula $\phi = (C'_1 \wedge \ldots \wedge C'_k)$, where $C'_i = (C_i \vee x)$ $(1 \leq i \leq k)$ and x is a brand new variable. Obviously, any truth assignment in which x is *true* is an optimal solution. $\mathcal{A}'$ now calls $\mathcal{A}$ on the formula ϕ', variable x, and any such optimal assignment. Since $\mathcal{A}'$ returns the optimal solution for the case in which x is assigned *false*, $\mathcal{A}'$ returns an optimal solution for the original formula ϕ. □

The above proof uses the following scheme: It transforms the input by a small change into an instance for which computing an optimal solution is trivial. Then, the modified input with its optimum is given to a suboptimality algorithm, which faces the original problem. The method can also be applied to minimization problems. For example, an instance of minimum hitting set can be transformed by selecting an item e which does not appear in any set, and adding it to each of the sets. Now, the set $\{e\}$ is an optimal solution. A suboptimality algorithm can then be asked to compute (or approximate) the optimum when e is forbidden from belonging to the hitting set. Clearly, the solution solves (or approximates) the original minimum hitting set instance.

8 Conclusion

This paper introduced the sub-optimality approximation problem and the concept of amortized sub-optimality approximation algorithms, and discussed its applications to online stochastic optimization, solution repair, and approximate filtering of optimization constraints. The paper also presented amortized sub-optimality (α, β)-approximations for metric TSP, packet scheduling, and metric k-median problems, as well as some hardness (and easiness) results on the sub-optimality approximation problems. There are many avenues of further research. Paramount among them is the need to understand the nature of problems that admit (amortized) sub-optimality approximations.

Acknowledgments. Special thanks to Claire Kenyon and Neal Young for suggesting the proof of Proposition 2.

References

1. Arya, V. and Garg, N. and Khandekar, R. and Pandit, V. Local search heuristics for k-median and facility location problems. In *Proceedings of the 33rd ACM Symposium on the Theory of Computing (STOC 2001)*, 2001.
2. R. Bent and P. Van Hentenryck. Online Stochastic and Robust Optimization. In *ASIAN'04*, Chiang Mai University, Thailand, December 2004.
3. R. Bent and P. Van Hentenryck. Regrets Only. Online Stochastic Optimization under Time Constraints. In *AAAI'04*, San Jose, CA, July 2004.
4. R. Bent and P. Van Hentenryck. Scenario Based Planning for Partially Dynamic Vehicle Routing Problems with Stochastic Customers. *O.R.*, 52(6), 2004.
5. R. Bent and P. Van Hentenryck. The Value of Consensus in Online Stochastic Scheduling. In *ICAPS 2004*, Whistler, British Columbia, Canada, 2004.
6. R. Bent and P. Van Hentenryck. Online Stochastic Optimization without Distributions . In *ICAPS 2005*, Monterey, CA, 2005.
7. R. Bent and P. Van Hentenryck and Eli Ufval. Online Stochastic Optimization Under Time Constraints. Working Paper, 2005.
8. H. Chang, R. Givan, and E. Chong. On-line Scheduling Via Sampling. *Artificial Intelligence Planning and Scheduling (AIPS'00)*, pages 62–71, 2000.
9. Chrobak, M. and Kenyon, C. and Young, N. . The reverse greedy algorithm for the metric k-median problem. In *The Eleventh International Computing and Combinatorics Conference (Cocoon 2005)*, Kunming, Yunnan, 2005.
10. F. Dabek, R. Cox, F. Kaashoek, and R. Morris. Vivaldi: A Decentralized Network Coordinate System. In *SIGCOMM 2004*, August 2004.
11. A. Fiat and G. Woeginger. *Online Algorithms: The State of the Art.* 1998.
12. F. Focacci, A. Lodi, and M. Milano. Optimization-Oriented Global Constraints. *Constraints*, 7(3-4):351–365, 2002.
13. C. Lund and M. Yannakakis. On the Hardness of Approximating Minimization Problems. In *STOC-93*, New York, NY, 1993.
14. L. Michel and P. Van Hentenryck. A Simple Tabu Search for Warehouse Location. *European Journal of Operational Research*, 157(3):576–591, 2004.
15. P. Van Hentenryck, P. Flener, J. Pearson, and M. Ågren. Tractable symmetry breaking for csps with interchangeable values. *IJCAI'03*.

A Linear-Logic Semantics for Constraint Handling Rules

Hariolf Betz and Thom Frühwirth

Faculty of Computer Science, University of Ulm, Germany

Abstract. One of the attractive features of the Constraint Handling Rules (CHR) programming language is its declarative semantics where rules are read as formulae in first-order predicate logic. However, the more CHR is used as a general-purpose programming language, the more the limitations of that kind of declarative semantics in modelling change become apparent. We propose an alternative declarative semantics based on (intuitionistic) linear logic, establishing strong theorems on both soundness and completeness of the new declarative semantics w.r.t. operational semantics.

1 Introduction

Constraint Handling Rules (CHR) is a concurrent committed-choice constraint logic programming language, which was developed in the 1990s as an enhancement to the constraint programming paradigm. Its aim was to add flexibility and customizability to constraint programming by allowing for user-defined constraint-handlers. This is achieved by implementation of the eponymic *constraint handling rules*, which define the rewriting and transformation of conjunctions of atomic formulae.

However, over time CHR has proven useful for many tasks outside its original field of application in constraint reasoning and computational logic, be it agent programming, multi-set rewriting or production rules.

Owing to the tradition of logic and constraint logic programming, CHR features – besides a well-defined operational semantics, of course – a *declarative semantics*, i.e. a direct translation of a CHR program into a first-order logical formula. In the case of constraint handlers, this is a useful tool, since it strongly facilitates proofs of a program's faithful handling of constraints.

The classical-logic declarative semantics, however, poses a problem, when applied to non-traditional uses of CHR, i.e. CHR programs that use CHR as a general-purpose concurrent programming language. Many implemented algorithms do not have a first-order classical logical reading, especially when these algorithms are deliberately non-confluent[1]. This may lead to logical readings which are inconsistent with the intended meaning. This problem has recently been demonstrated in [9] and constitutes the motivation for our development of an alternative declarative semantics.

---
[1] Meaning that different rule applications may lead to different final results.

Example 1. For an example of an inconsistent classical reading, consider the following coin-throw simulator.

$$\text{throw(Coin)} \Leftrightarrow \text{Coin} = \text{head} \ (r1)$$
$$\text{throw(Coin)} \Leftrightarrow \text{Coin} = \text{tail} \ (r2)$$

The program handles the constraint *throw(Coin)* by committing to one of the rules, thereby equating either *head* or *tail* with the variable *Coin*. (This requires a fair selection strategy.)

Its classical declarative semantics is:

$$(throw(Coin) \leftrightarrow Coin = head) \land (throw(Coin) \leftrightarrow Coin = tail)$$

From this we would conclude $(Coin = head) \leftrightarrow (Coin = tail)$ and therefore $head = tail$. In natural language: Both sides of our coin are equal.

Obviously, this statement is not consistent with the intuitive idea of a coin throw. What our program describes is an algorithm, respectively a course of action. The logical reading misinterprets it as a description of stable facts. This shows the basic incompatibility between the classical declarative semantics and non-traditional CHR programs. (Non-traditional in the sense that it is not only a constraint handler.) First-order logic can in general not handle updates, change, dynamics without resorting to auxiliary constructions like adding time-stamps to predicates.

With the linear-logic declarative semantics as we will propose in Sect. 4 we get the following logical reading:

$$!\,(throw(Coin) \multimap (Coin = head)\&(Coin = tail))$$

Informally speaking, the above expression of linear logic says that we can replace *throw(Coin)* with either $(Coin = head)$ or $(Coin = tail)$ but not both, i.e. a committed choice takes place.

Ever since its introduction in 1987, linear logic has inspired uses as a means to logically formalize computational structures and dynamics. Several programming languages have been designed from scratch for the purpose of making linear logic executable. E.g. the programming language Linear Objects (LO) [3] extends Horn logic by an "additive" conjunction (as occurs in linear logic) to model structured processes. A more formal approach is taken with Lygon [11]. Lygon is based on a systematic proof-theoretic analysis of linear logic, which results in a large segment of linear logic to be covered.

As we will see, there are remarkable similarities between linear logic and the operational semantics of Constraint Handling Rules, which make a linear-logic declarative semantics of CHR a promising approach. Furthermore, intuitionistic logic can be embedded into (intuitionistic) linear logic, which will be an indispensable feature in our semantics. Our approach is somewhat similar to the ones taken in [7] and [5] in that we will define a linear-logic semantics for an existing programming paradigm.

This paper is structured as follows: Section 2 will give a short introduction to the segment of *intuitionistic linear logic*. In Sect. 3, *constraint handling rules* will be presented with a particular focus on declarative semantics. It will become clear what the limitations to the classical declarative semantics are, which we hope to overcome by using linear logic. Section 4 will introduce our linear-logic semantics for CHR, explain its benefits and present strong theorems concerning soundness and completeness of the linear-logic declarative semantics w.r.t. operational semantics. In Sect. 5 we will give an example for the application of our proposed semantics. A conclusion will be given in Sect. 6.

2 Intuitionistic Linear Logic

Intuitionistic linear logic (**ILL**) is a subset of linear logic [6,10,12,14] which is constituted by the symbols $\otimes$, &, $\oplus$, $\multimap$ and ! as well as the constants 1, $\top$ and 0. In the following a short explanation of its symbols will be given.

2.1 Connectives

Let us take a look at an easy example first:

$$A \multimap B$$

The above formula is an example for linear implication. It is pronounced *"consuming A yields B"*. Since the idea of "consuming" logical truth (in the classical sense) somewhat stresses the imagination, linear logic is generally considered as dealing with resources rather than with propositions.

The meaning represented by the symbol $\otimes$ (*"times"*) is reasonably close to the intuitive grasp we usually have of the classical conjunction $\wedge$. Which is, that both formulas connected hold at the same time. Consequently, the expression $A \otimes B$ is pronounced *"both A and B"*.

Note that an implication of the form $A \multimap B$ allows us to consume-produce exactly once, in the process of which the implication *itself* is used up. E.g. in classical first-order logic the following holds:

$$A \wedge (A \to B) \vdash B \wedge (A \to B)$$

On the contrary, the following is *not* true:

$$A \otimes (A \multimap B) \vdash B \otimes (A \multimap B)$$

The following conclusion is correct:

$$A \otimes (A \multimap B) \vdash B$$

The connective & (*"with"*) represents an option of (internal) choice. The formula $A \& B$ is pronounced *"choose from either A or B"* and allows us to infer either A or B (but not both, which would be $A \otimes B$).

Similar to the *with* conjunction, the connective ⊕ *"plus"* also denotes an alternative. However, the choice is external, i.e. if the formula $A \oplus B$ holds, then *either* A or B will hold (but not both!), although it is not stated which one. The formula $A \oplus B$ is consequently pronounced *"either A or B"*.

We mentioned before that linear logic is considered as discussing resources rather than stable facts. Nevertheless, it is extremely useful if not indispensable to have an option for stable truth (in the classical sense) to interact with variable truth (i.e. resources). This is provided for by the ! (*"bang"*) symbol.

In linear logic, the *bang* marks either a stable truth or an abounding resource that – within the boundaries of the model – cannot get used up (which essentially boils down to the same thing). A typical application for the bang is in implications that can be applied an unlimited number of times. It is thus correct to conclude the following:

$$A \otimes !(A \multimap B) \vdash B \otimes !(A \multimap B)$$

There are three ways to *actualize* a banged resource's potential, namely *weakening*, *contraction* and *dereliction* [10].

Dereliction designates the possibility to use a banged resource just like an un-banged instance.

$$\vdash !A \multimap A \ (dereliction)$$

Contraction denotes the fact, that we may duplicate any banged resource, time and again, to potential infinity.

$$\vdash !A \multimap !A \otimes !A \ (contraction)$$

Weakening is the property of a banged resource that – just like a classical proposition – it needs not be used at all and may just be omitted.

$$\vdash !A \multimap 1 \ (weakening)$$

Furthermore, the following equivalence holds:

$$!(A \& B) \dashv \vdash (!A \otimes !B)$$

2.2 Constants and Quantification

We will furthermore consider two constants: 0 (*zero*) and ⊤ (*top*). The constant ⊤ represents the goal in favor of which every resource can be consumed. As for an intuition, we may think of it as a trash can.

As for the 0: In classical logic, there is the principle *"ex falso, quod libet*, i.e. from a proposition that equals *false*, we can deduce any other proposition. This aspect of falsity is represented by 0, which by definition yields every resource. In this sense, 0 represents *impossibility*.

Just like classical logic, linear predicate logic offers the quantifiers ∀ and ∃. Since we cannot directly convey the classical concept of *truth* to linear logic, we will use the term *provability* instead. The proposition $\exists x Q(x)$ is provable if there is a term t for which $[t/x]Q(x)$ is provable. The proposition $\forall xQ(x)$ is provable, if $[a/x]Q(x)$ is provable for a new parameter a about which we can make no assumption. For convenience, we can define x to range over a domain $\mathbb{D}$.

The following equations hold:

$$\forall xQ(x) \equiv \bigwithout_{x \in \mathbb{D}} Q(x)$$

$$\exists xQ(x) \equiv \bigoplus_{x \in \mathbb{D}} Q(x)$$

2.3 Girard Translation

Among the key features of intuitionistic linear logic is the possibility to faithfully translate (classical) intuitionistic logic into intuitionistic linear logic while preserving the full power of the former. Fig. 1 presents one of several possible translations, called *Girard Translation* [10], in the notation of [12].

$$
\begin{aligned}
(A \wedge B)^+ &::= A^+ \& B^+ \\
(A \to B)^+ &::= (!A^+) \multimap B^+ \\
(A \vee B)^+ &::= (!A^+) \oplus (!B^+) \\
(\top)^+ &::= \top \\
(\bot)^+ &::= 0 \\
(\neg A)^+ &::= !A^+ \multimap 0 \\
(\forall x.A)^+ &::= \forall x.(A^+) \\
(\exists x.A)^+ &::= \exists x.!(A^+)
\end{aligned}
$$

Fig. 1. Translation $^+$ from intuitionistic logic into linear logic

3 CHR

CHR is a concurrent committed-choice constraint programming language, developed in the 1990s for the implementation of constraint solvers. It is traditionally used as an extension to other programming languages – especially constraint logic programming languages – but has been used increasingly as a general-purpose programming language in the recent past. In this section we will give an overview of its syntax and operational semantics as well as its classical declarative semantics [1,8,2].

3.1 CHR Syntax

Constraints are predicates of first-order logic. In CHR, there are two notably different types of constraints, which we will refer to as *built-in constraints* and *CHR constraints*. CHR constraints, will be handled by a CHR program whereas built-in constraint are predefined in the CHR implementation.

Definition 1. *An* atomic built-in constraint *is an expression of the form* $c(t_1, ..., t_n)$, *where c is an n-ary constraint symbol and $t_1,...,t_n$ are terms. A built-in constraint is either an atomic built-in constraint or a conjunction of built-in constraints.*

A CHR constraint *is a non-empty multiset, the elements of which have the form* $e(t_1,...,t_n)$, *where e is an n-ary constraint symbol and $t_1,...,t_n$ are terms. A CHR constraint is called* atomic *if it has exactly one element.*

Note that the syntactic equality constraint $=$ as well as the propositions *true* and *false* are built-in by definition.

Definition 2. *A* goal *is either* $\{\top\}$ *(top)*, $\{\bot\}$ *(bottom), an expression of the form* $\{C\}$ *– where C is an atomic built-in constraint –, a CHR constraint or a multi-set union of goals.*

Apart from definitions, we leave away the curly brackets from both CHR constraints and goals.

A CHR program consists of a set of rules, determining the transformation of constraints. These rules are the *constraint handling rules*, i.e. the CHR, of which we distinguish two types: **Simplify** and **Propagate**. A **Simplify** rule determines the replacement of a CHR constraint, usually a subset of a larger goal, with a multiset of simpler constraints whereas a **Propagate** rule augments an existing goal by one or several elements (which hopefully leads to further simplification later on).

Definition 3. *A* simplification rule *is of the form* $H \Leftrightarrow G|B$. *A* propagation rule *is of the form* $H \Rightarrow G|B$, *where the* head *H is a CHR constraint, the* guard *G is a built-in constraint and the* body *B is a goal.*

A CHR program *is a finite set of rules.*

3.2 CHR Operational Semantics

Note that the operational semantics defined here is not necessarily identical to the behavior of an actual implementation.

Definition 4. *A* state *is a pair* $\langle G; C \rangle$, *where G is a goal and C is a built-in constraint.*

Of the two components, only the goal store G is directly accessible by CHR, i.e. only elements stored here will be transformed by constraint handling rules. The built-in constraint store C is not directly accessible, i.e. CHR can add (built-in) constraints to the store, but cannot manipulate or remove its elements.

Definition 5. *The* constraint theory *CT is a non-empty, consistent first-order theory over the built-in constraints, including syntactic equality $=$, as well as the propostions* true *and* false.

The constraint theory CT is implicitly realized by the predefined constraint handlers.

At runtime, a CHR program is provided with an initial state and will be executed until either no more rules are applicable or a contradiction occurs in the constraint store (which will result in the constraint store equaling *false*).

Definition 6. *An* initial state *is of the form* $\langle G; true \rangle$. *A* failed final state *is of the form* $\langle G; false \rangle$. *A state is called a* successful final state *if it is of the form* $\langle E; C \rangle$ *with no transition applicable.*

Initial states are distinguished from states that appear in a derivation, since declarative semantics will assign a different logical reading to either type of state.

Definition 7. *A* derived state *is a state S_a which appears in a derivation from an initial state S_0. The variables $\bar{x}_a$ that appear in S_a but not in S_0 are called* local variables *of S_a.*

The transition rules in Fig. 2 describe the transition relation. Note that we omit the **Solve** transition here since it is irrelevant to our cause.

Simplify
If $(F \Leftrightarrow D|H)$ is a fresh variant of a rule in P with variables $\bar{x}$
and $CT \models \forall (C \rightarrow \exists \bar{x}(F = E \wedge D))$
then $\langle E \cup G; C \rangle \mapsto \langle H \cup G; (F = E) \wedge D \wedge C \rangle$

Propagate
If $(F \Rightarrow D|H)$ is a fresh variant of a rule in P with variables $\bar{x}$
and $CT \models \forall (C \rightarrow \exists \bar{x}(F = E \wedge D))$
then $\langle E \cup G; C \rangle \mapsto \langle E \cup H \cup G; (F = E) \wedge D \wedge C \rangle$

Fig. 2. CHR transition rules

The sequence $\bar{x}$ represents the variables in $(F \Leftrightarrow D|H)$. We require always a fresh variant of a rule $(F \Leftrightarrow D|H)$, i.e. that all variables are given unique new names. The CHR rule's head F must be matched (pairwise) with CHR constraints E from the goal store. The constraints in C and D as well as = are built-in constraints and thus are handled according to the constraint theory CT. On application of the rule, the constraint store is augmented by the matching $(F = E)$ as well as the guard D.

3.3 The (Classical) Declarative Semantics of CHR

Figure 3 defines the first-order-logic declarative semantics of CHR. In the transformations of CHR rules, $\bar{y}$ represents the variables that *only* appear in the body G of the rule. While these variables are existentially quantified, all other variables become universally quantified.

3.4 Soundness and Completeness

The first-order-logic semantics given in Fig. 3 maps every CHR program P to a set of logical formulae P' which form a mathematical theory. The following theorems will show that the operational and this declarative semantics are strongly related.

Built-in constraints:	C'	$::=$	C
CHR constraints:	$\{e(t_1,...,t_n)\}'$	$::=$	$e(t_1,...,t_n)$
	$(E \cup F)'$	$::=$	$E' \wedge F'$
Goals:	$\{\top\}'$	$::=$	$\top$
	$\{\bot\}'$	$::=$	$\bot$
	$\{c(t_1,...,t_n)\}'$	$::=$	$c(t_1,...,t_n)$
	$(G \cup H)'$	$::=$	$G' \wedge H'$
Initial states:	$\langle G; true \rangle'$	$::=$	G'
Derived states:	$\langle G; C \rangle'$	$::=$	$\exists \bar{x}_a (G' \wedge C')$
Simplify rules:	$(E \Leftrightarrow C \mid G)'$	$::=$	$\forall (C \to (E \leftrightarrow \exists \bar{y} G))$
Propagate rules:	$(E \Rightarrow C \mid G)'$	$::=$	$\forall (C \to (E \to \exists \bar{y} G))$
Programs:	$(R_1 ... R_m)'$	$::=$	$R_1' \wedge ... \wedge R_m'$

Fig. 3. Classical-logic declarative semantics P' of a program P

Definition 8. *A* computable constraint *of a state S_0 is the logical reading S_a' of a derived state of S_0. An* answer (constraint) *of a state S_0 is the logical reading S_n' of a final state of a derivation from S_0.*

The following theorems are proved in [2]:

Theorem 1. (Soundness). *Let P be a CHR program and S_0 be an initial state. If S_0 has a derivation with answer constraint S_n', then $P' \cup CT \models \forall (S_0' \leftrightarrow S_n')$.*

Theorem 2. (Completeness). *Let P be a CHR program and S_0 be an initial state with at least one finite derivation. If $P' \cup CT \models \forall (S_0' \leftrightarrow S_n')$, then S_0 has a derivation with answer constraint S_ν' such that $P' \cup CT \models \forall (S_\nu' \leftrightarrow S_n')$.*

4 A Linear-Logic Semantics for CHR

CHR is a powerful and flexible tool for writing not only constraint handlers but also general-purpose concurrent programs. As far as constraint handlers are concerned, there is a useful and consistent declarative semantics. However, when used as a general-purpose programming language and program rules go beyond a mere representation of a mathematical theory, programs tend to produce inconsistent logical readings as has been examined e.g. in [2].

In this section we will discuss the limitations of the classical declarative semantics. Then we will propose a declarative semantics for CHR which is based on intuitionistic linear logic and we will show it can provide a consistent logical reading for non-traditional CHR programs. We will also state two theorems proving the soundness and completeness of our approach.

4.1 Limitations of the Classical Declarative Semantics

In Sect. 1 we already gave an example for a CHR program with an inconsistent logical reading with respect to the classical declarative semantics. Below another such program is given to further illustrate the matter.

Example 2. The program given below applies the Sieve of Eratosthenes to an interval of cardinal numbers in order to "sieve out the prime numbers from that interval.

```
candidate(N) ⇔ N>1 | M is N-1, prime(N), candidate(M)   (r1)
candidate(1) ⇔ true                                      (r2)
prime(M), prime(N) ⇔ M mod N =:= 0 | prime(N)            (r3)
```

The program implements two constraints: candidate and prime. The candidate constraint is to create the set of numbers on which to work, represented as individual constraints. The actual sieving is perfomed by the prime constraint. The program is executed with the goal candidate(N) in the initial state, where N is the upper limit of the interval on which to work.

Consider the declarative semantics of the constraint *prime*:

$$\forall (M \bmod N = 0 \rightarrow (prime(M) \land prime(N) \leftrightarrow prime(N)))$$

What this logical expression actually says is that "a number is prime, if it is a multiple of another prime number (sic!). The problem is that the prime constraint does not consist of only static information. Its input is an initial range of cardinal numbers representing candidates for primes. Only upon completion of the calculation they do represent the actual primes. Predicate logic has no straightforward means to express this dynamics.

4.2 An Intuitionistic Linear-Logic Semantics

The obvious similarity between linear implication and CHR constraint substitution as well as the possible representation of multiplicities and embedding of intuitionistic logic make linear logic a likely candidate for providing a suitable declarative semantics.

In this section we introduce an intuitionistic linear logic (cf. Sect. 2.3) semantics of CHR. Figure 4 shows the proposed semantics. It adheres to some extent to the classical declarative semantics. The main differences are the interpretation of CHR constraints as linear resources (and that of built-in constraints as embedded intuitionistic propositions), as well as the distinctly different logical reading of CHR rules as expressing linear implementation rather than logical equivalence.

We assume that built-in constraints are propositions of intuitionistic logic, translated according to Girard Translation as introduced in Sect. 2.3. States are handled much the same as in classical declarative semantics: The logical reading of an initial state is again the logical reading of the goal. The logical reading of a derived state S_a is again a conjunction, now a $\otimes$ conjunction, of its components' readings with its local variables existentially quantified.

A **Simplify** rule $(E \Leftrightarrow C \mid G)$ maps to $!\forall ((!C^L) \multimap (E^L \multimap E^L \otimes \exists \bar{y} G^L))$, where $\bar{y}$ represents the variables that *only* appear in the body G of the rule. As before, the fulfillment of the guard is a premise. Instead of equivalence between head and body, however, it implies now that consuming the head produces the

Built-in constraints:	$c(t_1,...,t_n)^L$	$::=$	$!c(t_1,...,t_n)$
	$(C \wedge D)^L$	$::=$	$C \otimes D$
CHR constraints:	$\{e(t_1,...,t_n)\}^L$	$::=$	$e(t_1,...,t_n)$
	$(E \cup F)^L$	$::=$	$E^L \otimes F^L$
Goals:	$\{\top\}^L$	$::=$	$\top$
	$\{\bot\}^L$	$::=$	0
	$\{c(t_1,...,t_n)\}^L$	$::=$	$c(t_1,...,t_n)$
	$(G \cup H)^L$	$::=$	$G^L \otimes H^L$
Initial states:	$S_0^L = \langle G; true \rangle^L$	$::=$	G^L
Derived states:	$S_a^L = \langle G; C \rangle^L$	$::=$	$\exists \bar{x}_a(G^L \otimes C^L)$
Simplify rules:	$(E \Leftrightarrow C \mid G)^L$	$::=$	$!\forall((!C^L) \multimap (E^L \multimap \exists \bar{y} G^L))$
Propagate rules:	$(E \Rightarrow C \mid G)^L$	$::=$	$!\forall((!C^L) \multimap (E^L \multimap E^L \otimes \exists \bar{y} G^L))$
Programs:	$(R_1...R_m)^L$	$::=$	$R_1^L \otimes ... \otimes R_m^L$

Fig. 4. Linear-logic declarative semantics P^L of a program P

body. Note that the formula is banged, since it is to be used not only once, of course. A **Propagate** rule follows the same pattern. The only difference is that here, consuming the head produces the head *and* the body.

Example 3. We will take another look at Example 2 and see how its declarative semantics benefits from the linear-logic approach. This is what the **ILL** reading looks like (for the constraint "prime).

$$!\forall((M \bmod N =:= 0) \multimap (prime(M) \otimes prime(N) \multimap prime(N)))$$

As we can see, this reading is no longer inconsistent with the mathematical understanding of prime numbers. It is indeed rather a suitable **ILL** representation of the program's workings.

Example 4. The improvement regarding the coin-throw example mentioned in Sect. 1 is quite alike. The **ILL** reading for that program is:

$$throw(Coin) \multimap Coin = head$$
$$throw(Coin) \multimap Coin = tail$$

This is logically equivalent to the following:

$$!(throw(Coin) \multimap (Coin = head)\&(Coin = tail))$$

The above reads as: *Of course, consuming* Throw(Coin) *produces: Choose from* (Coin = head) *and* (Coin = tail). Thus, our logical reading implies internal, committed choice.

4.3 Soundness and Completeness

Concerning soundness, our approach is analogous to that one used in the classical framework, (cf. Sect. 3.4) relying basically on Lemma 1 which proves that all computable constraints of a state S_0 are linearly implied by the initial state's logical reading.

The constraint theory CT, which we require to be of intuitionistic logic, is translated according to the *Girard Translation* (cf. Sect. 2.3).

Lemma 1. *Let P be a program, P^L its linear-logic reading, S_0 be a state. If S_n is a computable constraint of S_0 then:*

$$P^L, !CT^+ \models \forall (S_0^L \multimap S_n^L)$$

From this lemma, Theorem 3 follows directly.

Theorem 3. (Soundness). *Let P be a CHR program and S_0 be an initial state. If S_0 has a derivation with answer S_n^L, then $P^L, !CT^+ \models \forall (S_0^L \multimap S_n^L)$.*

We also have a surprisingly strong completeness theorem.

Theorem 4. (Completeness). *If S_0 and S_n are states, such that $P^L, !CT^+ \vdash S_0^L \multimap S_n^L$ then S_0 has a derivable constraint S_ν such that $!CT^+ \vdash S_\nu^L \multimap S_n^L$.*

The complete proofs for both theorems can be found in [4]. Whereas the proofs for Lemma 1 and Theorem 3 parallel the respective proofs in the classical-logic case, the proof for Theorem 4 follows a unique approach, which is sketched below.

Proof Sketch. The proof of Theorem 4 consists of three parts [4].

The **first part** establishes a series of lemmas in order to transform the expression $P^L, !CT^+ \vdash S_0^L \multimap S_n^L$ into an equivalent form that is easier to work with. This transformation involves bringing the formula S_0^L to the precondition side, stripping the expression of bang symbols and finally removing quantifiers. The most difficult task is the removal of the bang symbols. We consider a cut-free proof of the original expression. We can show by structural induction that for at least one bang-free version of that expression a (cut-free) proof must exist.

At the end of the first part, we have transformed our expression $P^L, !CT^+ \vdash S_0^L \multimap S_n^L$ into the equivalent form $\overline{P^L, !CT^+}, S_0^L \vdash S_n^L$, where the horizontal bar marks the removal of all bangs and quantifiers [2]. Since there are no more bangs, all rules in $\overline{P^L}$ and $\overline{!CT^+}$ appear in certain multiplicities, according to how often each rule is applied.

In the **second part** we force the transformed expression to act similar to a CHR program, i.e. we prove by structural induction that there must be at least one implication in either $\overline{P^L}$ or $\overline{!CT^+}$ of the form $(A \multimap B)$ where A is a conjunction of atoms that is contained in S_0^L, so the implication can be applied to S_0^L. Assuming that $(A \multimap B)$ is in $\overline{P^L}$, this models the application of a CHR rule on the constraint store. Otherwise it corresponds to a rule of the constraint theory CT. By repeated application of the above reasoning we can force the application of all implications in $\overline{P^L}$.

---

[2] As $!(A \& B) \dashv\vdash (!A \otimes !B)$, the expression $\overline{!CT^+}$ is *not* equivalent to CT^+.

Having shown this, we are already quite close to our goal. We can now safely say that the logical transition from $\overline{P^L}, !CT^+, S_0^L$ to $\overline{S_n^L}$ can be cut into smaller steps, *similar* to the steps of a CHR program. Actually, the only difference is in the built-in constraints: a CHR computation neither allows the consumption of a built-in constraint nor the inference of a built-in constraint that is *unnecessary* in that it does not lead to another CHR rule to become applicable.

This final problem is dealt with in the **third part** where we prove that our logically derived expression S_n^L is so close to an actually derivable constraint S_ν^L that the former can be inferred from the latter by applying the constraint theory CT only, i.e. $!CT^+ \vdash S_\nu^L \multimap S_n^L$. This is done by a methodically simple, yet formally tedious induction over the transition steps identified in the second part of the proof.

5 Example: Union-Find in CHR

As CHR is increasingly being used as a general-purpose concurrent constraint programming language, focus has shifted to the question whether it can be used to implement classic algorithms in an efficient and elegant way. This has successfully been done for Tarjan's union-find algorithm in [9]. However, in that paper it has also been shown that this algorithm has a destructive update which cannot adequately be modeled in classical logic. We will show here how the linear-logic declarative semantics can provide a solution.

5.1 The Union-Find Algorithm in CHR

The original union-find algorithm was introduced by Tarjan in [13]. It serves to maintain collections of disjoint sets where each set is represented by an unambiguous representative element. The structure has to support the three operations:

- make(X): create a new set with the single element X.
- find(X): return the representative of the set in which X is contained
- union(X,Y): join the two sets that contain X and Y, respectively (possibly destroying the old sets and changing the representative).

In the basic algorithm discussed here the sets are represented by rooted trees, where the roots are the respective representative elements. Trees are represented by the constraints A ~> B and root(A). The three operations are implemented as follows.

- make(X): generate a new tree with the only node X.
- find(X): follow the path from node X to the root by repeatedly going to the parent. Return the root as representative.
- union(X,Y): find the representatives of X and Y and link them by making one root point to the other root.

The following CHR program implements the Union-Find Algorithm [9].

```
make(A) ⇔ root(A)                                    (make)
union(A,B) ⇔ find(A,X), find(B,Y), link(X,Y)         (union)

A ~> B, find(A,X) ⇔ A ~> B, find(B,X)                (findNode)
root(A), find(A,X) ⇔ root(A), X=A                    (findRoot)

link(A,A) ⇔ true                                     (linkEq)
link(A,B), root(A), root(B) ⇔ B ~> A, root(A)        (link)
```

5.2 Declarative Semantics

Concerning logical correctness we will limit ourselves to the link rule because it is here where the problem arises. The classical declarative reading for this rule reads as follows:

$$link(A,B) \wedge root(A) \wedge root(B) \Leftrightarrow B \rightsquigarrow A \wedge root(A)$$

The reading as given above establishes a supposed logical equivalence where the node B is a root and a non-root at the same time ($root(B)$ and $B \rightsquigarrow A$ hold), but actually a destructive update from a root to a non-root takes place. The problem is in principle the same as was presented in Sect. 4: Classical logic is able to deal with static truth only and has no capabilities to represent dynamic processes without resorting to explicit representation of time. In contrast, the linear-logic reading of the respective constraint reads as follows:

$$!(link(A,B) \otimes root(A) \otimes root(B)) \multimap (B \rightsquigarrow A) \otimes root(A))$$

The above can be read as: *Of course, consuming all of* link(A,B), root(A) *and* root(B) *yields both* $B \rightsquigarrow A$ *and* root(A). Or less formally: On the condition that both *root(A)* and *root(B)* hold, *link(A,B)* triggers the change of *root(A)* to $B \rightsquigarrow A$. This reading directly expresses the dynamic update process which is taking place.

This example shows how our linear-logic semantics can provide logical readings for non-traditional CHR programs in cases where there is no consistent reading with respect to the classical semantics. Thus, the process of proving logical correctness for CHR programs is considerably simplified.

6 Conclusion

We have developed a linear-logic semantics for CHR as an alternative to the classical declarative semantics. The new declarative semantics is based on the segment of intuitive linear logic.

We have shown that this declarative semantics indeed overcomes the limitations of the classical declarative semantics, which originally motivated this work. The new semantics features surprisingly strong theorems on both soundness and completeness, thus simplifying the process of proving logical correctness of CHR programs. Details can be found in [4]. How well this can be done in practice, and what insights it offers, remains a topic for future work.

Since this is the first paper relating CHR to linear logic, there are numerous options for further work in this field. An obvious follow-up project would be a thorough comparison of CHR to related works such as the LCC class of linear concurrent constraint programming languages [7], for which a linear-logic semantics exists as well.

In the program presented in Sect. 5, a large part of the program actually does have a consistent classical reading. In a case like this it might be more convenient to apply our linear-logic semantics only on those parts of the program where the classical semantics produces inconsistent results, in order to get to a more intuitive logical reading. To this end, it is necessary to more closely inspect the relationship between classical and linear-logic readings. Classical program parts could be identified by a modified confluence analysis, since confluence implies consistency of the classical-logic reading of a program [2].

Our linear-logic semantics for CHR may also shed light on executable subsets of linear logic and the related recent separation logic. An interesting approach would be to develop a CHR constraint handler for a larger segment of linear logic than that which is actually used in the declarative semantics. This would be an approach closer to the ones taken in [11] and [3].

References

1. Slim Abdennadher, Thom Frühwirth: *Essentials of constraint programming*. Springer, 2003.
2. Slim Abdennadher, Thom Frühwirth, Holger Meuss: *Confluence and semantics of constraint simplification rules*. Constraints 4(2):133-165 (1999).
3. Jean-Marc Andreoli, Remo Pareschi: *LO and Behold! Concurrent Structured Processes*. ACM SIGPLAN Notices, Proceedings OOPSLA/ECOOP '90, 25(10):44-56, October 1990.
4. Hariolf Betz, *A Linear Logic Semantics for CHR*, Master Thesis, University of Ulm, October 2004, www.informatik.uni-ulm.de/pm/mitarbeiter/fruehwirth/other/betzdipl.ps.gz
5. Marco Bozzano, Giorgio Delzanno, Maurizio Martelli: *A Linear Logic Specification of Chimera*. DYNAMICS '97, a satellite workshop of ILPS'97, Proceedings, 1997.
6. Vincent Danos, Roberto Di Cosmo: *Initiation to Linear Logic*. Course notes, June 1992.
7. François Fages, Paul Ruet, Sylvain Soliman: *Linear Concurrent Constraint Programming: Operational and Phase Semantics*. Information and Computation, 165(1):14-41, 2001.
8. Thom Frühwirth: *Theory and practice of constraint handling rules*. Journal of Logic Programming, 37(1-3):95-138, 1998.
9. Tom Schrijvers, Thom Frühwirth: *Optimal Union-Find in Constraint Handling Rules - Programming Pearl*. Theory and Practice of Logic Programming (TPLP), to appear 2005.
10. Jean-Yves Girard: *Linear Logic: Its syntax and semantics*. Theoretical Computer Science, 50:1-102, 1987.

11. James Harland, David Pym, Michael Winikoff: *Programming in Lygon: an overview.* Algebraic Methodology and Software Technology (AMAST 96), 5th International Conference, Proceedings, 391-405, 1996.
12. Frank Pfenning: *Linear Logic.* Material for the homonymous course at Carnegie Mellon University. Draft of 2002.
13. Robert E. Tarjan, Jan van Leeuwen. *Worst-case analysis of set union algorithms.* Journal of the ACM, 31(2):245-281, 1984.
14. Philip Wadler: *A taste of linear logic.* Invited talk, Mathematical Foundations of Computing Science, Springer LNCS 711, 1993.

Distributed Stable Matching Problems*

Ismel Brito and Pedro Meseguer

Institut d'Investigació en Intel.ligència Artificial,
Consejo Superior de Investigaciones Científicas,
Campus UAB, 08193 Bellaterra, Spain
{ismel, pedro}@iiia.csic.es

Abstract. We consider the Stable Marriage Problem and the Stable Roommates Problem, two well-known types of the general class of Stable Matching Problems. They are combinatorial problems which can be solved by centralized algorithms in polynomial time. This requires to make public lists of preferences which agents would like to keep private. With this aim, we define the distributed version of these problems, and we provide a constraint-based approach that solves them keeping privacy. We give empirical results on the proposed approach.

1 Introduction

We consider the Stable Marriage Problem and one generalization of it, the Stable Roommates Problem, two well-known types of the general class of Stable Matching Problems. They are classical combinatorial problems, also of interest for Economics and Operations Research. The Stable Marriage Problem consists of finding a stable matching between n men and n women, each having his/her own preferences on every member of the other sex. A matching is not stable if there exist a man m and a woman w not matched with each other, such that each of them strictly prefers the other to his/her partner in the matching. Any instance of this problem has a solution, and it can be computed by the centralized Gale-Shapley algorithm in polynomial time. The Stable Roommates Problem consists of finding a stable matching between n persons (n even), each having his/her own preferences on every other person. Not every instance of this problem is solvable. The solution (or the absence of it) can be found by a centralized algorithm in polynomial time.

These problems, by their own nature, appear to be naturally distributed. Each person may desire to act independently. For obvious reasons, each person would like to keep private his/her own preferences. However, in the classical case each person has to follow a rigid role, making public his/her preferences to achieve a global solution. These problems are very suitable to be treated by distributed techniques, trying to provide more autonomy to each person, and to keep preferences private. This paper is a contribution to this aim.

---

* Supported by the Spanish REPLI project TIC-2002-04470-C03-03.

The structure of the paper is as follows. We summarize basic concepts of Stable Marriage and Gale-Shapley algorithm, together with a constraint formulation for this problem from [4] (Section 2). Then, we define the Distributed Stable Marriage problem and provide means to solve it trying to enforce privacy. Thus, we present a distributed version of the Gale-Shapley algorithm, and a distributed constraint formulation under the TCK and PKC models (Section 3). We show how the problem can be solved using the Distributed Forward Checking algorithm with the PKC model, keeping private values and constraints. We define the Distributed Stable Roommates Problem, which differently from the Distributed Stable Marriage Problem, it cannot be solved by the distributed version of Gale-Shapley algorithm maintaining private preference lists (Section 4). However, a similar constraint formulation allows us to solve it keeping privacy. Experimental results show that, when applicable, the distributed Gale-Shapley algorithm is more efficient than the distributed constraint formulation (Section 5), something also observed in the centralized case. However, the distributed constraint formulation is generic and can solve both problems.

2 The Stable Marriage Problem

The Stable Marriage Problem (SM) was first studied by Gale and Shapley [2]. A SM instance consists of two finite equal-sized sets of players, called men and women. Each man m_i ($1 \leq i \leq n$, n is the number of men) ranks women in strict order forming his preference list. Similarly, each woman w_j ($1 \leq j \leq n$) ranks men in strict order forming her preference list. An example of SM appears in Figure 1. A matching M is just a complete one-to-one mapping between the two sexes. The goal is to find a *stable matching* M. A matching M is stable if there is no pair (m, w) of man m and a woman w satisfying the following conditions:

C1. m and w are not married in M,
C2. m prefers w to his current partner in M,
C3. w prefers m to her current partner in M.

If this pair (m, w) exists, M is unstable and the pair (m,w) is called a *blocking pair*. For the example of Figure 1, the matching $M = \{(m_1,w_1),(m_2, w_2), (m_3, w_3)\}$ is not stable because the pair (m_1, w_2) blocks M. For that problem, there is only one stable matching: $M1 = \{(m_1,w_2), (m_2,w_1), (m_3,w_3)\}$. Gale and Shapley showed that each SM instance admits at least one stable matching [2].

$m_1 : w_2\ w_3\ w_1$ $w_1 : m_1\ m_2\ m_3$
$m_2 : w_1\ w_2\ w_3$ $w_2 : m_1\ m_3\ m_2$
$m_3 : w_2\ w_1\ w_3$ $w_3 : m_2\ m_1\ m_3$

Fig. 1. A SM instance with three men and three women. Preference lists are in decreasing order, the most-preferred partner is on the left.

A relaxed version of SM occurs when some persons may declare one or more members of the opposite sex to be unacceptable, so they do not appear in the corresponding preference lists. This relaxed version is called the Stable Marriage Problem with Incomplete Lists (SMI). In SMI instances, the goal is also to find a stable matching. Like in the case of SM, SMI admits at least one stable matching. However, some specific features of stable matchings for SMI have to be remarked. First, condition C1 of the definition of *blocking pair* given above have to be changed as follows:

> C1'. m and w are not married in M, and m belongs to w's preference list, and w belongs to the m's preference list.

Second, it can not be assured that all the persons can find a partner. So a stable matching of a SMI instance needs not to be complete. However, all the stable matchings involve the same men and women [3].

2.1 The Gale-Shapley Algorithm

Gale and Shapley showed that at least one stable matching exists for every SM (or SMI) instance. They obtained a $O(n^2)$ solving algorithm, called the Gale-Shapley algorithm [2]. An extended version is the Extended Gale-Shapley algorithm (EGS). It avoids some extra steps by deleting from the preference lists certain pairs that cannot belong to a stable matching [6]. A man-oriented version of EGS [1] appears in Figure 2.

EGS involves a sequence of proposals from men to women. It starts by setting all persons free (line 1). EGS iterates until all the men are engaged or, for SMI instances, there are some free men because they have an empty preference list (line 2). Each man always proposes marriage to his most-preferred woman (line 3). When a woman w receives a proposal from a man m, she accepts it if m is on her preference list. Otherwise, m deletes w from his preference list (line 5) and then a new proposal is started (line 6). When m is on w's preference list and w is already engaged to p she discards the previous proposal with p and p is set free (line 8-9). Afterwards, m and w are engaged to each other (line 11). Woman w deletes from her preference list each man p that is less preferred than m (line 13). Conversely, man p deletes w from his preference list (line 14). Finally, if there is a free man with non-empty preference list a new proposal is started. Otherwise, men are engaged or have empty preference lists and the algorithm terminates.

During EGS execution, some people are deleted from preference lists. The reduced preference lists that result of applying man-oriented Gale-Shapley algorithm are called *man-oriented Gale-Shapley lists* or *MGS-lists*. On termination, each man is engaged to the first woman in his (reduced) list, and each woman

---

[1] For privacy requirements, that will be discussed deeper in this work, we prefer not assuming for SMI instances, like in [6], that if man m is not acceptable for a woman w, woman w is not acceptable for man m. For avoiding that, we have added Lines 4-7 to the original EGS.

```
1.   assign each person to be free;
2.   while some man m is free and m has a nonempty list loop
3.       w := first woman on m's list; {m proposes to w}
4.       if m is not on w's preference list then
5.           delete w from m's preference list;
6.           goto line 3
7.       end if
8.       if some man p is engaged to w then
9.           assign p to be free;
10.      end if
11.      assign m and w to be engaged to each other;
12.      for each successor p of m on w's list loop
13.          delete p from w's list;
14.          delete w from p's list;
15.      end loop;
16.  end loop;
```

Fig. 2. The man-oriented Gale-Shapley algorithm for SM and SMI

to the last man in hers. These engaged pairs constitute a stable matching, and it is called *man-optimal* (or *woman-pessimal*) stable matching since there is no other stable matching where a man can achieve a better partner (according to his ranking). Similarly, exchanging the role of men and women in EGS (which means that women propose), we obtain the *woman-oriented Gale-Shapley lists* or *WGS-lists*. On termination, each woman is engaged to the first man in her (reduced) list, and each man to the last woman in his. These engaged pairs constitute a stable matching, and it is called *woman-optimal* (or *man-pessimal*) stable matching.

The intersection of *MGS-lists* and *WGS-lists* is known as the Gale-Shapley lists (*GS-lists*). These lists have important properties (see Theorem 1.2.5 in [6]):

- all the stable matchings are contained in the *GS-lists*,
- in the *man-optimal* (*woman-optimal*), each man is partnered by the first (last) woman on his *GS-list*, and each woman by the last (first) man on hers.

Figure 3 shows the *GS-lists* for the example given in Figure 1. For this instance, the reduced lists of all persons have only one possible partner which means that only one solution exits. In that case, the *man-optimal* matching and *woman-optimal* matching are the same.

$$m_1 : w_2 \quad w_1 : m_2$$
$$m_2 : w_1 \quad w_2 : m_1$$
$$m_3 : w_3 \quad w_3 : m_3$$

Fig. 3. GS-Lists for the SM instance of Figure 1

2.2 Constraint Formulation

A constraint satisfaction problem (CSP) is defined by a triple $(\mathcal{X}, \mathcal{D}, \mathcal{C})$, where $\mathcal{X} = \{x_1, \ldots, x_n\}$ is a set of n variables, $\mathcal{D} = \{D(x_1), \ldots, D(x_n)\}$ is the set of their respective finite domains, and $\mathcal{C}$ is a set of constraints specifying the acceptable value combinations for variables. A solution to a CSP is a complete assignment that satisfies all constraints in $\mathcal{C}$. When constraints involve two variables they are called binary constraints.

The SM problem can be modeled as a binary CSP. In [4] authors propose a constraint encoding for SM problems, that we summarize next. Each person is representing by a variable: variables x_1, x_2, ..., x_n represent the men (m_1, m_2, ..., m_n) and variables y_1, y_2, ..., y_n represent the women (w_1, w_2 ..., w_n). $PL(q)$ is the set of people that belong to q's preference list. Domains are as follows:

$$D(x_i) = \{j : w_j \in PL(m_i)\} \quad \forall i, \ 1 \le i \le n$$
$$D(y_j) = \{i : m_i \in PL(w_j)\} \quad \forall j, \ 1 \le j \le n$$

In the CSP, when variable x_i takes value j, it means that man m_i marries woman w_j. Let be $d_i^m = |D(x_i)|$ and $d_j^w = |D(y_j)|$. Constraints are defined between men and women. Given any pair i and j ($1 \le i, j \le n$), the stable marriage constraint x_i/y_j involving x_i and y_j is representing by a $d_i^m \times d_j^w$ conflict matrix C_{ij}. For any pair k, l ($k \in D(x_i)$ and $l \in D(y_j)$), the element $C_{ij}[k, l]$ has one of the following four values:

- $C_{ij}[k, l] = $ **A**llows, when $k = j$ and $l = i$. It allows $x_i = j$ ($y_j = i$). At most one element in C_{ij} is A.
- $C_{ij}[k, l] = $ **I**llegal. This constraint assures the monogamy of the matching, only one man can be married with a woman and vice versa. Entry $C_{ij}[k, l]$ is set to I when either $k = j$ and $l \ne i$ or $k \ne j$ and $l = i$.
- $C_{ij}[k, l] = $ **B**locking pair, when m_i prefers w_j to w_k and w_j prefers m_i to m_l. Since $x_i = j$ blocks pairs $x_i = k$ and $y_j = l$.
- $C_{ij}[k, l] = $ **S**upport, for all the other entries that are not A, I or B.

Figure 4 shows the constraint matrix for man m_3 and woman w_1 of the example given in Figure 1. In the constraint matrix, the domains of x_3 and y_1 are listed in decreasing ordering of the preferences. From that example, we can see that assignment $x_3 = w_1$ does not block any other pairs which involve variable x_3 or variable y_1.

To encode SMI instances, it is needed to add a dummy man m_{n+1} and a dummy woman w_{n+1} to the problem. Man and woman variables remain the

	m_1	m_2	m_3		m_1	m_2	m_3
w_2	S	S	I	w_2	1	1	0
w_1	I	I	A	w_1	0	0	1
w_3	S	S	I	w_3	1	1	0

Fig. 4. C_{31} for example of Figure 1. Left: in terms of A,I,B,S. Right: in terms of 0/1.

same but their domains are enlarged with the value $n+1$, that is always the least preferred one. Whether a person p is not an accepted partner for a person q, of opposite sex, all entries in column or row assigning p to q on C_{pq} are I. The rest of the constraint table is filled with S.

Constraint tables in terms of A, I, B, S are transformed in terms of 1/0 (permitted/forbidden) pairs, using the natural conversion A, S → 1, I, B → 0.

In [4], it is shown that encoding a SMI instance I as a CSP instance J produces all stable matchings of I as solutions of J. It is easy to show that J has no more solutions. Special emphasis is put on the fact that achieving arc consistency on J produces a reduced domains which are exactly the GS lists obtained by the EGS algorithm.

3 The Distributed Stable Marriage Problem

The Distributed Stable Marriage problem ($DisSM$) is defined as in the classical (centralized) case by n men $\{m_1,\ldots,m_n\}$ and n women $\{w_1,\ldots,w_n\}$, each having a preference list where all members of the opposite sex are ranked, plus a set of r agents $\{a_1,\ldots,a_r\}$. The n men and n women are distributed among the agents, such that each agent owns some persons and every person is owned by a single agent. An agent can access and modify all the information of the owned persons, but it cannot access the information of persons owned by other agents. To simplify description, we will assume that each agent owns exactly one person (so there are $2n$ agents). As in the classical case, a solution is a stable matching (a matching between the men and women such that no blocking pair exists). A complete stable matching always exists.

Analogously to the classical case, we define the Distributed Stable Marriage with Incomplete lists problem ($DisSMI$) as a generalization of $DisSM$ that occurs when preference lists do not contain all persons of the opposite sex (some options are considered unacceptable). A solution is a stable matching, and it always exists, although it is not guaranteed to be a complete one (some men/women may remain unmatched).

This problem, by its own nature, appears to be naturally distributed. First, each person may desire to act as an independent agent. Second, for obvious reasons each person would like to keep private his/her preference list ranking the opposite sex options. However, in the classical case each person has to follow a rigid role, making public his/her preferences to achieve a global solution. Therefore, this problem is very suitable to be treated by distributed techniques, trying to provide more autonomy to each person, and to keep private the information contained in the preference lists.

3.1 The Distributed Gale-Shapley Algorithm

The EGS algorithm that solves the classical SMI can be easily adapted to deal with the distributed case. We call this new version the Distributed Extended Gale-Shapley ($DisEGS$) algorithm. As in the classical case, the $DisEGS$ algorithm has two phases, the man-oriented and the woman-oriented, which are

procedure Man()
$m \leftarrow free$;
$end \leftarrow false$;
while $\neg end$ **do**
  if $m = free$ and $list(m) \neq \emptyset$ **then**
    $w \leftarrow first(list(m))$;
    sendMsg(propose,m,w);
    $m \leftarrow w$;
  $msg \leftarrow$ getMsg();
  switch $msg.type$
    accept : do nothing;
    delete : $list(m) \leftarrow list(m) - msg.sender$;
          if $msg.sender = w$ **then** $m \leftarrow free$;
    stop : $end \leftarrow true$;

procedure Woman()
$w \leftarrow free$;
$end \leftarrow false$;
while $\neg end$ **do**
  $msg \leftarrow$ getMsg();
  switch $msg.type$
    propose: $m \leftarrow msg.sender$;
          if $m \notin list(w)$ **then**
            sendMsg(delete,w,m);
          else
            sendMsg(accept,w,m);
            $w \leftarrow m$;
            for each p after m in $list(w)$ **do**
              sendMsg(delete,w,p);
              $list(w) \leftarrow list(w) - p$;
    stop : $end \leftarrow true$;

Fig. 5. The man-oriented version of the $DisEGS$ algorithm

executed one after the other. Each phase produces reduced preference lists for each person. The intersection of these lists produces a GS list per person. As in the classical case, the matching obtained after executing the man-oriented phase is a stable matching (*man-optimal*).

The man-oriented version of the $DisEGS$ algorithm appears in Figure 5 (the woman-oriented is analogous, switching the roles man/woman). It is composed of two procedures, Man and Woman, which are executed on each man and woman, respectively. Execution is asynchronous. The following messages are exchanged (where m is the man that executes Man and w the woman that executes Woman),

- propose: m sends this message to w to propose engagement;
- accept: w sends this message to m after receiving a propose message to notify acceptance;

- delete: w sends this message to m to notify that w is not available for m; this occurs either (i) proposing m an engagement to w but w has a better partner or (ii) w accepted an engagement with other man more preferred than m;
- stop: this is an special message to notify that execution must end; it is sent by an special agent after detecting quiescence.

Procedure Man, after initialization, performs the following loop. If m is free and his list is not empty, he proposes to be engaged to w, the first woman in his list. Then, m waits for a message. If the message is accept and it comes from w, then m confirms the engagement (nothing is done in the algorithm). If the message is delete, then m deletes the sender from his list, and if the sender is w then m becomes free. The loop ends when receiving a stop message.

Procedure Woman is executed on woman w. After initialization, there is a message receiving loop. In the received message comes from a man m proposing engagement, w rejects the proposition if m is not in her list. Otherwise, w accepts. Then, any man p that appears after m in w list is asked to delete w from his list, while w removes p from hers. This includes a previous engagement m', that will be the last in her list. The loop ends when receiving a stop message.

Algorithm $DisEGS$ is a distributed version of EGS, where each person can access his/her own information only. For this reason there are two different procedures, one for men and one for women. In addition, actions performed by EGS on persons different from the current one are replaced by message sending. Thus, when m assigns woman w is replaced by sendMsg(propose,m,w); when w deletes herself from the list of p is replaced by sendMsg(delete,w,p). Since procedures exchange messages, operations of message reception are included accordingly.

$DisEGS$ algorithm guarantees privacy in preferences and in the final assignment: each person knows the assigned person, and no person knows more than that. In this sense, it is a kind of ideal algorithm because it assures privacy in values and constraints.

3.2 Distributed Constraint Formulation

In [1] we presented an approach to privacy that differentiates between values and constraints. Briefly, privacy on values implies that agents are not aware of other agent values during the solving process and in the final solution. This was achieved using the Distributed Forward Checking algorithm ($DisFC$), an ABT-based algorithm (see more details about ABT algorithm in [9]) that, after the assignment of an agent variable, instead of sending to lower priority agents the value just assigned, it sends the domain subset that is compatible with the assigned value. In addition, it replaces actual values by sequence numbers in backtracking messages. In this way, the assignment of an agent is kept private at any time.

Regarding privacy on constraints, two models were considered. The Totally Known Constraints (TKC) model assumes that when two agents i,j share a constraint C_{ij}, both know the constraint scope and one of them knows completely

```
              i                           i
        1 ... 1 0 1 ... 1          1/0 ... 1/0 0 1/0 ... 1/0
             ...                            ...
        1 ... 1 0 1 ... 1          1/0 ... 1/0 0 1/0 ... 1/0
     j  0 ... 0 1 0 ... 0       j    0 ...  0  1  0  ...  0
        1 ... 1 0 0 ... 0          1/0 ... 1/0 0 1/0 ... 1/0
             ...                            ...
        1 ... 1 0 0 ... 0          1/0 ... 1/0 0 1/0 ... 1/0
```

Fig. 6. Constraint C_{ij}. Left: rows and columns ordered by decreasing preferences of x_i and y_j, respectively. Right: rows and columns ordered lexicographically.

the relational part of the constraint (the agent in charge of constraint evaluation). The Partially Known Constraints (PKC) model assumes that when two agents i, j share a constraint C_{ij}, none of them knows completely the constraint. On the contrary, each agent knows the part of the constraint that it is able to build, based on its own information. We say that agent i knows $C_{i(j)}$, and j knows $C_{(i)j}$. This implies that the identification of the other agent is neutral. In the following, we apply these two models to the $DisSM$ problem using the constraint formulation of Section 2.2 from [4].

Totally Known Constraints. Solving a $DisSMI$ problem is direct under the TKC model. For each pair x_i, y_j, representing a man and a woman, there is a constraint C_{ij} that appears in Figure 6. We assume, without loss of generality, that agents owning men have higher priority than agents owning women. Using $DisFC$, constraint C_{ij} has to be known by the agent of variable x_i. Conversely, using ABT, constraint C_{ij} has to be known by the agent owning y_j. If an agent knows C_{ij}, it can deduce the preferences of the other agent.

Using ABT, there is no privacy of values. Using $DisFC$, there is privacy of values, since values are never made public to other agents. This model does not allow privacy of constraints.

Partially Known Constraints. A $DisSMI$ instance can be formulated in the PKC model as follows. The partially known constraint $C_{i(j)}$ is built from x_i, knowing its preference list but ignoring the preference list of y_j. Analogously, $C_{(i)j}$ is built knowing the preference list of y_j but ignoring the preference list of x_i. Assuming lexicographical ordering in rows and columns, they look like shown in Figure 7. Where 1/? means that the value can be either 1 (permitted) or ? (undecided). Undecided values appear in $C_{i(j)}$ (conversely $C_{(i)j}$) because x_i (y_j) does not know the preference list of y_j (x_i). As example, the partially known constraints corresponding to the constraint of Figure 4 appear in Figure 8.

One interesting property of these constraints is that in $C_{i(j)}$ (conversely $C_{(i)j}$) all columns (rows) are equal, except the column (row) corresponding to x_i (y_j).

Proposition 1. *In $C_{i(j)}$ (conversely $C_{(i)j}$) all columns (rows) are equal, except the column (row) corresponding to x_i (y_j).*

$$C_{i(j)} = \begin{matrix} & i \\ j & \begin{pmatrix} 1/? & \ldots & 1/? & 0 & 1/? & \ldots & 1/? \\ & & & \vdots & & & \\ 1/? & \ldots & 1/? & 0 & 1/? & \ldots & 1/? \\ 0 & \ldots & 0 & 1 & 0 & \ldots & 0 \\ 1/? & \ldots & 1/? & 0 & 1/? & \ldots & 1/? \\ & & & \vdots & & & \\ 1/? & \ldots & 1/? & 0 & 1/? & \ldots & 1/? \end{pmatrix} \end{matrix} \quad C_{(i)j} = \begin{matrix} & i \\ j & \begin{pmatrix} 1/? & \ldots & 1/? & 0 & 1/? & \ldots & 1/? \\ & & & \vdots & & & \\ 1/? & \ldots & 1/? & 0 & 1/? & \ldots & 1/? \\ 0 & \ldots & 0 & 1 & 0 & \ldots & 0 \\ 1/? & \ldots & 1/? & 0 & 1/? & \ldots & 1/? \\ & & & \vdots & & & \\ 1/? & \ldots & 1/? & 0 & 1/? & \ldots & 1/? \end{pmatrix} \end{matrix}$$

Fig. 7. Form of the partially known constraint tables

$$C_{3(1)} = \begin{array}{c|ccc} & m_1 & m_2 & m_3 \\ w_1 & 0 & 0 & 1 \\ w_2 & 1 & 1 & 0 \\ w_3 & ? & ? & 0 \end{array} \quad C_{(3)1} = \begin{array}{c|ccc} & m_1 & m_2 & m_3 \\ w_1 & 0 & 0 & 1 \\ w_2 & 1 & 1 & 0 \\ w_3 & 1 & 1 & 0 \end{array}$$

Fig. 8. Partially known constraints of constraint of Figure 4

Proof. We have to prove that $C_{i(j)}[k, l] = C_{i(j)}[k, l'], l \neq i, l' \neq i, l \neq l'$. Effectively, if x_i prefers woman k to woman j, both values $C_{i(j)}[k, l]$ and $C_{i(j)}[k, l']$ are 1, corresponding to S (supported, see Section 2.2). If x_i prefers woman j to woman k, both values $C_{i(j)}[k, l]$ and $C_{i(j)}[k, l']$ are ? (undecided). Their exact value could be 1 or 0, depending on the preferences of y_j, information which is not available when constructing $C_{i(j)}$. Therefore, both are undecided in $C_{i(j)}$. An analogous argument holds for $C_{(i)j}$ rows. □

It is interesting to observe the relation between $C_{i(j)}, C_{(i)j}$ and C_{ij}. It is easy to check that $C_{ij} = C_{i(j)} \diamond C_{(i)j}$, where $\diamond$ operates component to component with the following rules,

$$1 \diamond 1 = 1 \quad 1 \diamond 0 = error \quad 0 \diamond 0 = 0$$
$$? \diamond 1 = 1 \quad ? \diamond 0 = 0 \quad ? \diamond ? = 0$$

Rules including ? are quite intuitive (if a position in the constraint is decided (permitted/forbidden) in one constraint and undecided in the other, the result is the decided value). The last rule $? \diamond ? = 0$ is proved next.

Proposition 2. *If entry $[k, l]$ is undecided in both partially known constraints for variable x_i and variable y_j ($C_{i(j)}[k, l] =?$ and $C_{(i)j}[k, l] =?$), then entry $[k, l]$ is 0 in the complete constraint table ($C_{ij}[k, l] = 0$).*

Proof. From the construction of partially known constraints, all undecided entries in $C_{i(j)}$ are related to values which are less preferred than j. If $C_{i(j)}[k, l] = ?$, we can infer that x_i prefers j to k. Conversely, if $C_{(i)j}[k, l] =?$, we infer that y_j prefer i to l. Therefore, since x_i prefers j to k and y_j prefers i to l, the pair (i, j) is blocking pair to the pair (k, l) so $C_{ij}[k, l] = 0$. □

With these properties, we can specialize the $DisFC$ algorithm to solve $DisSMI$ instances, using phase I only. This specialized algorithm works as follows. Each agent instantiates its variable and sends to lower priority agents the domains compatible with its assignment. For $DisSMI$, after assignment each man agent sends to each woman agent the domain that she can take. A woman agent receives messages from every man agent, and assigns a value permitted by these n received domains. If no value is available, the woman agent performs backtracking. The process iterates until finding a solution. Since $DisFC$ is a complete algorithm, and the constraint encoding of SMI is correct (a SMI solution corresponds one-to-one with solutions of the constraint encoding), a solution will be found.

In the previous argument, something must be scrutinized in more detail. After assignment, what kind of compatible domain can a man agent send? If agent i assigns value k to x_i, it sends to j the row of $C_{i(j)}$ corresponding to value k. This row may contain 1's (permitted values for y_j), 0's (forbidden values for y_j), and ? (undecided values for y_j). If the compatible domain has 1 or 0 values only, there is no problem and the y_j domain can be easily computed. But what happens when the domain contains ? (undecided) values? In this case, agent j can disambiguate the domain as follows. When agent j receives a compatible domain with ? (undecided) values, it performs the $\diamond$ operation with a row of $C_{(i)j}$ different from i. Since all rows in $C_{(i)j}$ are equal, except row corresponding to value i (see Proposition 1), all will give the same result. Performing the $\diamond$ operation j will compute the corresponding row in the complete constraint C_{ij}, although j does not know to which value this row corresponds (in other words, j does not know the value assigned to x_i). After the $\diamond$ operation the resulting received domain will contain no ? (undecided) values, and the receiving agent can operate normally with it.

4 The Stable Roommates Problem

The stable roommates problem (SR) is a generalization of the SM in which each person in a set of even cardinality ranks *all* the other in order of preference. Like in SM, a matching is *unstable* if it contains a *blocking pair*. A pair (p_i, p_j) is a blocking pair in M if p_i prefers p_j to his/her current partner in M and p_j prefers p_i to his/her current partner in M (conditions *C1* - *C3* in section 2). If this pair exists, it is said that p_i and p_j block M and M is *unstable*. The major difference with SM is that there exist SR instances that admit no stable matching. It is easy to prove it building a counterexample (see section 4.1 in [6]). Therefore, for SR the goal is to determine whether a given SR instance is solvable, and if so, find an stable matching.

In [6] (section 4.2), Gustfield and Irving presented an $O(n^2)$ algorithm to solve SR instances. This algorithm consists of two phases. The first phase is an extended version of the Gale-Shapley algorithm where every person sends and receives matching proposals from the rest of people. During this phase, certain matching pairs that are not part of any stable matching are deleted. At the end of this phase, we can assure that the problem is unsolvable if there is an empty preference list. If not, it may happen that all preference lists are already reduced to a single entry. In that case, this is the only stable matching for this instance. Otherwise, at the end of this phase some lists have more than one entry. In that case, the algorithm enters into the second phase because, unlike of the corresponding situation in SM after applying EGS, if we match every person to his/her more preferred person in his/her reduced preference lists it does not constitute a matching, stable or otherwise.

The second phase of the algorithm iterates reducing further the preference lists until all lists contain just one entry, in which case it constitutes a stable matching or until any preference list becomes empty, in which case no stable matching exists. This phase consists of two parts. Firstly, the algorithm builds a special sequence of matching pairs from the reduced preference lists. This sequence is called *rotation* and has the following form:

$$\{(x_0, y_0), (x_1, y_1), ..., (x_{r-1}, y_{r-1})\},$$

such that y_i is the most preferred partner for x_i and y_{i+1} is the second most preferred partner for x_i for all i, $0 \leq i \leq r-1$, where $i+1$ is taken as module r. Secondly, the algorithm deletes from reduced preference lists the rotation obtained in the first part of this phase (see section 4.2 of [6] for more details).

Like for SMI, we can consider instances of the SR where some persons can have unacceptable partners (called stable roommates problem with incomplete list or SRI). In this context, the goal is to find (if exists any) the longer stable matching which not necessarily involves all people. A matching M is stable if there is not a pair of persons p_i and p_j not matched in M, and each one prefers the other to his/her current partner in M. It is assumed that every person prefers more to be matched than to be free. It is straightforward to modify the above described algorithm to solve SRI instances.

4.1 Distributed Constraint Formulation

Similar to $DisSM$, a Distributed Stable Roommates Problem ($DisSR$) is defined by a number n of persons $\{p_1, p_2, ..., p_n\}$ plus a set of r agents. Each person ranks all the other in his/her preference list. Likewise, a distributed stable roommates problem with incomplete list ($DisSRI$) is defined by n persons and r agents. In that setting, people can have incomplete preference lists. For both problems, no person knows the others' preferences. Like in the centralized versions, the goal is to find (if exists any) a complete stable matching for $DisSR$ and the longer stable matching for $DisSRI$.

The main motivation of this work is to solve stable matching problems without making public preference lists. The simplest way to solve a $DisSRI$ we can think of ($DisSRI$ is a generalization of $DisSR$) is using a distributed version of the algorithm that appears in the previous section. However, from the description of that algorithm, we can observe that, when the algorithm builds a rotation in the first part of the second phase, some information of preference lists is revealed. In this sense, a distributed version of the centralized solving algorithm such that privacy is maintained, does not seem feasible in this case.

Considering constraints, the formulation introduced in Section 2.2 is fully applicable to encode SRI instances. The distributed version, presented in Section 3.2, is also applicable to $DisSRI$ instances, with the following remarks. In each setting, there are $n*(n-1)$ binary constraints. Constraint tables will have the form given in Figure 6 for SRI and the form given in Section 3.2 for $DisSRI$. However, we have to take into account that no person can match with himself/herself. To avoid that, we add unary constraints: $x_i \neq p_i$, for all i, $1 \leq i \leq n$. In that case, constraint tables are like the ones of $DisSMI$, Proposition 1 remains true, and we can use the specialized $DisFC$ algorithm with PKC model, as described in section 3.2, to solve $DisSRI$.

5 Experimental Results

We give empirical results on the $DisFC$ algorithm with PKC model on $DisSMI$ and $DisSRI$ random instances. For $DisSMI$, we also provide results on the $DisEGS$. In our experiments, we use four different classes of instances. Each class is defined by a pair $\langle n, p_1 \rangle$, which means the problem has n men and n women on $DisSMI$ (or just n persons on $DisSRI$) and the probability of incompleteness of the preference list is p_1. Class $< n, 0.0 >$ groups instances where all the n persons have complete preference lists. If $p_1 = 1.0$, preferences lists are empty. We study 4 different classes with $n = 10$ for $DisSMI$ and $n = 20$ for $DisSRI$, with $p_1 = 0.0, 0.2, 0.5$ and 0.8. For each problem and for each class, 100 instances were generated following the random instance generation presented in [5] considering p_2, the probability of ties, equal to 0.0.

For $DisSMI$, algorithms are modeled using $2n$ agents, each one representing a man or a woman. For $DisSRI$, $DisFC$ is modeled using just n agents, each representing a person. In $DisEGS$, each agent only knows its preference list. In $DisFC$, each agent only knows its partial constraint tables. In both, agents exchange different kind of messages to find a stable matching. When $DisEGS$ finishes the stable matching found is the *men-optimal* one. $DisFC$, like others asynchronous backtracking algorithms, requires a total ordering among agents. For $DisSMI$, men agents have higher priority than women agents. For $DisSRI$, person agents are lexicographically ordered.

Algorithmic performance is evaluated by communication and computation effort. Communication effort is measured by the total number of exchanged messages (msg). Since both algorithms are asynchronous, computation cost is measured by the number of concurrent constraint checks (ccc) (for $DisEGS$, an agent performs a constraint check when it checks if one person is more preferred than other), as defined in [7], following Lamport's logic clocks [8].

Table 1 details the experimental results of $DisEGS$ on $DisSMI$. Besides msg and ccc, we provide the total number of messages for each kind of message and the total number of checks. Regarding the communication effort, except for instances with $p_1 = 0.8$, the larger number of exchanged messages are for deleting persons from preference lists. When $p_1 = 0.2$, women agents receive more proposals than women agents for $p_1 = 0.0$. In general, the number of proposals,

Table 1. Results of $DisEGS$ for solving $DisSMI$ instances with 10 men, 10 women

p_1	propose	accept	delete	msg	checks	ccc
0.0	27.8	22.8	65.6	98.4	133.6	52.7
0.2	28.1	22.8	53.0	86.4	107.9	43.0
0.5	26.3	21.9	32.7	63.4	67.3	27.7
0.8	20.9	18.5	12.1	35.4	28.0	10.6

Table 2. Results of $DisFC$ for solving $DisSMI$ instances with 10 men, 10 women

p_1	info	back	link	msg	checks	ccc
0.0	39,686	5,987	72	45,745	4,833,478	3,153,363
0.2	31,636	5,272	62	36,970	3,941,676	2,580,822
0.5	4,324	840	48	5,212	355,436	223,469
0.8	222	47	27	296	10,022	5,651

Table 3. Results of $DisFC$ for solving $DisSRI$ instances with 20 persons

p_1	info	back	link	msg	checks	ccc
0.0	123,051	22,557	0	145,608	25,233,407	15,125,633
0.2	57,769	10,881	89	68,739	7,698,775	4,467,714
0.5	3,237	684	57	3,978	226,422	117,921
0.8	54	12	13	79	3,744	1,060

proposal acceptances and the total number of messages tend to decrease when p_1 increases. Considering the computation effort of $DisEGS$, the larger values of p_1 (shorter lists), the easier instances. In general, the communication and computation costs of $DisEGS$ are the largest with complete lists.

Table 2 resumes the experimental results of $DisFC$ on $DisSMI$. We observe the same trend as in $DisEGS$ results: instances with complete lists are the most difficult to solve (both in terms of msg and ccc) and they become easier to solve as lists become shorter. According to the reported results, $DisFC$ is much worse than $DisEGS$. This could be expected, since $DisEGS$ is a specialized algorithm for this particular problem, takes advantage of the problem features. $DisFC$ is a generic algorithm that is applicable to any CSP. When applied to this problem, a tractable CSP, it gets worse results than the specialized approach. Nevertheless, the distributed constraint formulation is generic and applicable to further generalizations of this problem, like $DisSRI$.

In Table 3 we resume the experimental results of $DisFC$ on $DisSRI$. For that problem, not all the instances are solvable. Only 89, 75, 85 and 97 (out of 100) instances are solvable for $p1 = 0.0, 0.2, 0.5$ and 0.8, respectively. As was expected, regarding msg and ccc, we observe the same trend as in the previous two tables. Instances are harder to solve when the number of preferred persons is higher. Contrasting results from Table 2 and Table 3 we see that $DisSRI$ instances, where persons have few unaccepted partners ($p_1 = 0.0, 0.2$), are harder than the corresponding $DisSMI$ instances. When preference lists are shorter ($p_1 = 0.5$ and 0.8), $DisSRI$ instances are easier than the corresponding $DisSMI$ instances.

6 Conclusions

We presented a distributed formulation for the Stable Marriage problem and the Stable Roommates problem. These problems appear to be naturally distributed and there is a clear motivation to keep their preference lists private during the solving process. For Stable Marriage, a distributed version of the centralized algorithm can efficiently solve the problem, keeping the required privacy. However, this is not possible for Stable Roommates. Using the constraint formulation of [4], we have provided a simple way to solve this problem using the Distributed Forward Checking algorithm with the Partially Known Constraint model, keeping the required privacy. We provide experimental results of this approach. The generic constraint formulation opens new directions for distributed encodings of harder versions of these problems.

References

1. Brito, I. and Meseguer, P. Distributed Forward Checking. *Proc. CP-2003*, 801–806, 2003.
2. Gale D. and Shapley L.S. College admissions and the stability of the marriage. *American Mathematical Monthly*. 69:9–15, 1962.
3. Gale D. and Sotomayor M. Some remarks on the stable matching problem. *Discrete Applied Mathematics*. 11:223–232, 1985.
4. Gent, I. P. and Irving, R. W. and Manlove, D. F. and Prosser, P. and Smith, B. M. A constraint programming approach to the stable marriage problem. *Proc. CP-2001*, 225-239, 2001.
5. Gent,I. and Prosser,P. An Empirical Study of the Stable Marriage Problem with Ties and Incomplete Lists. *Proc. ECAI-2002*, 141–145, 2002.
6. Gusfield D. and Irving R. W. *The Stable Marriage Problem: Structure and Algorithms*. The MIT Press, 1989.
7. Meisels A., Kaplansky E., Razgon I., Zivan R. Comparing Performance of Distributed Constraint Processing Algorithms. *AAMAS-02 Workshop on Distributed Constraint Reasoning*, 86–93, 2002.
8. Lamport L. Time, Clock, and the Ordering of Events in a Distributed System. *Communications of the ACM*, **21(7)**, 558–565, 1978.
9. Yokoo M., Durfee E., Ishida T., Kuwabara K. The Distributed Constraint Satisfaction Problem: Formalization and Algorithms. IEEE Trans. Knowledge and Data Engineering **10** (1998) 673–685.

Beyond Hypertree Width: Decomposition Methods Without Decompositions

Hubie Chen and Víctor Dalmau

Departament de Tecnologia,
Universitat Pompeu Fabra,
Barcelona, Spain
{hubie.chen, victor.dalmau}@upf.edu

Abstract. The general intractability of the constraint satisfaction problem has motivated the study of restrictions on this problem that permit polynomial-time solvability. One major line of work has focused on structural restrictions, which arise from restricting the interaction among constraint scopes. In this paper, we engage in a mathematical investigation of generalized hypertree width, a structural measure that has up to recently eluded study. We obtain a number of computational results, including a simple proof of the tractability of CSP instances having bounded generalized hypertree width.

1 Introduction

The *constraint satisfaction problem* (CSP) is widely acknowledged as a convenient framework for modelling search problems. Instances of the CSP arise in a variety of domains, including artificial intelligence, database theory, algebra, propositional logic, and graph theory. An instance of the CSP consists of a set of constraints on a set of variables; the question is to determine if there is an assignment to the variables satisfying all of the constraints. Alternatively, the CSP can be cast as the fundamental algebraic problem of deciding, given two relational structures **A** and **B**, whether or not there is a homomorphism from **A** to **B**. In this formalization, each relation of **A** contains the tuples of variables that are constrained together, which are often called the *constraint scopes*, and the corresponding relation of **B** contains the allowable tuples of values that the variable tuples may take.

It is well-known that the CSP, in its general formulation, is NP-complete; this general intractability has motivated a large and rich body of research aimed at identifying and understanding restricted cases of the CSP that are polynomial-time tractable. The restrictions that have been studied can, by and large, be placed into one of two categories, which–due to the homomorphism formulation of the CSP–have become known as *left-hand side* restrictions and *right-hand side* restrictions. From a high level view, left-hand side restrictions, also known as *structural restrictions*, arise from prespecifying a class of relational structures $\mathcal{A}$ from which the left-hand side structure **A** must come, while right-hand side restrictions arise from prespecifying a class of relational structures $\mathcal{B}$ from which the right-hand side structure **B** must come. As this paper is concerned principally with structural restrictions, we will not say more about right-hand side restrictions than that their systematic study has origins in a classic theorem of Schaefer [21], and that recent years have seen some exciting results on them (for instance [4,5]).

The structural restrictions studied in the literature can all be phrased as restrictions on the hypergraph $H(\mathbf{A})$ naturally arising from the left-hand side relational structure **A**, namely, the hypergraph $H(\mathbf{A})$ with an edge $\{a_1, \ldots, a_k\}$ for each tuple $(a_1, \ldots, a_k)$ of **A**. Let us briefly review some of the relevant results that have been obtained on structural tractability. The tractability of left-hand side relational structures having *bounded treewidth* was shown in the constraint satisfaction literature by Dechter and Pearl [9] and Freuder [10].[1] Later, Dalmau et al. [8] building on ideas of Kolaitis and Vardi [19,20] gave a consistency-style algorithm for deciding the bounded treewidth CSP. For our present purposes, it is worth highlighting that although the notion of bounded treewidth is defined in terms of *tree decompositions*, which can be computed efficiently (under bounded treewidth), the algorithm given by Dalmau et al. [8] does *not* compute any form of tree decomposition. Dalmau et al. also identified a natural expansion of structures having bounded treewidth that is tractable–namely, the structures *homomorphically equivalent* to those having bounded treewidth. The optimality of this latter result, in the case of bounded arity, was demonstrated by Grohe [15], who proved–roughly speaking–that if the tuples of $\mathcal{A}$ are of bounded arity and $\mathcal{A}$ gives rise to a tractable case of the CSP, then it must fall into the natural expansion identified by Dalmau et al. [8].

A number of papers, including [17,16,13,14,11,7], have studied restrictions that can be applied to relational structures of unbounded arity. (Note that any class of relational structures of unbounded arity cannot have bounded treewidth.) In a survey [13], Gottlob et al. show that the restriction of bounded hypertree width [11] is the most powerful structural restriction for the CSP in that every other structural restriction studied in the literature is subsumed by it. Since this work [11,13], whether or not there is a more general structural restriction than bounded hypertree width that ensures tractability, has been a tantalizing open question.

In this paper, we study *generalized hypertree width*, a structural measure for hypergraphs defined in [12] that is a natural variation of hypertree width; we call this measure *coverwidth*. Coverwidth is *trivially* upper-bounded by hypertree width, and so any class of hypergraphs having bounded hypertree width has bounded coverwidth. We define a combinatorial pebble game that can be played on any CSP instance, and demonstrate that this game is intimately linked to coverwidth (Theorem 13). Overall, the investigation we perform takes significant inspiration from methods, concepts, and ideas developed by Kolaitis, Vardi, and coauthors [19,20,8,2] that link together CSP consistency algorithms, the existential k-pebble games of Kolaitis and Vardi [18], and bounded treewidth.

---

[1] One way to define what we mean by treewidth here is the treewidth of the graph obtained from $H(\mathbf{A})$ by drawing an edge between any two vertices that are in the same hyperedge.

Using the pebble game perspective, we are able to derive a number of computational results. One is that the structural restriction of *bounded coverwidth* implies polynomial-time tractability; this result generalizes the tractability of bounded hypertree width. It has been independently shown by Adler et al. that the hypertree width of a hypergraph is linearly related to the coverwidth [1]. This result can be used in conjunction with the tractability of bounded hypertree width to derive the tractability of bounded coverwidth. However, we believe our proof of bounded coverwidth tractability to be simpler than the known proof of bounded hypertree width tractability [11], even though our proof is of a more general result.

To describe our results in greater detail, it will be useful to identify two computational problems that every form of structural restriction gives rise to: a *promise* problem, and a *no-promise* problem. In both problems, the goal is to identify all CSP instances obeying the structural restriction as either satisfiable or unsatisfiable. In the promise problem, the input is a CSP instance that is *guaranteed* to obey the structural restriction, whereas in the no-promise problem, the input is an *arbitrary* CSP instance, and an algorithm may, on an instance not obeying the structural restriction, decline to identify the instance as satisfiable or unsatisfiable. Of course, CSPs arising in practice do *not* come with guarantees that they obey structural restrictions, and hence an algorithm solving the no-promise problem is clearly the more desirable. Notice that, for any structural restriction having a polynomial-time solvable promise problem, if it is possible to solve the *identification problem* of deciding whether or not an instance obeys the restriction, in polynomial time, then the no-promise problem is also polynomial-time solvable. For bounded hypertree width, both the identification problem and the no-promise problem are polynomial-time solvable. In fact, the survey by Gottlob et al. [13] only considers structural restrictions for which the identification problem is polynomial-time solvable, and thus only considers structural restrictions for which the no-promise problem is polynomial-time solvable.

One of our main theorems (Theorem 20) is that the promise problem for bounded coverwidth is polynomial-time tractable, via a general consistency-like algorithm. In particular, we show that, on an instance having bounded coverwidth, our algorithm detects an inconsistency if and only if the instance is unsatisfiable. Our algorithm, like the consistency algorithm of Dalmau et al. [8] for bounded treewidth, can be applied to *any* CSP instance to obtain a more constrained instance; our algorithm does *not* need nor compute any form of decomposition, even though the notion of coverwidth is defined in terms of decompositions!

We then give a simple algorithm for the no-promise problem for bounded coverwidth (Theorem 21) that employs the consistency-like algorithm for the promise problem. The algorithm's behavior is reminiscent of self-reducibility arguments in computational complexity theory, and on an instance of bounded coverwidth, the algorithm is guaranteed to either report a satisfying assignment or that the instance is unsatisfiable. We believe that this result suggests an expansion of the view of structural tractability advanced in the Gottlob et al. survey [13], since we are able to give a polynomial-time algorithm for the bounded coverwidth no-promise problem without explicitly showing that there is a polynomial-time algorithm for the bounded coverwidth identification problem.

Returning to the promise problem, we then show that the tractability of structures with bounded coverwidth can be generalized to yield the tractability of structures *homomorphically equivalent* to those having bounded coverwidth (Theorem 22). This expansion of bounded coverwidth tractability is analogous to the expansion of bounded treewidth tractability carried out in [8].

We emphasize that *none* of the algorithms in this paper need or compute any type of decomposition, even though all of the structural restrictions that they address are defined in terms of decompositions.

In the full version of this paper, we use the developed theory as well as ideas in [6] to define a tractable class of quantified constraint satisfaction problems based on coverwidth.

Definitions. In this paper, we formalize the CSP as a relational homomorphism problem. We review the relevant definitions that will be used. A *relational signature* is a finite set of relation symbols, each of which has an associated arity. A *relational structure* **A** (over signature σ) consists of a universe A and a relation $R^{\mathbf{A}}$ over A for each relation symbol R (of σ), such that the arity of $R^{\mathbf{A}}$ matches the arity associated to R. We refer to the elements of the universe of a relational structure **A** as **A**-elements. When **A** is a relational structure over σ and R is any relation symbol of σ, the elements of $R^{\mathbf{A}}$ are called **A**-tuples. Throughout this paper, we assume that all relational structures under discussion have a finite universe. We use boldface letters $\mathbf{A}, \mathbf{B}, \ldots$ to denote relational structures.

A *homomorphism* from a relational structure **A** to another relational structure **B** is a mapping h from the universe of **A** to the universe of **B** such that for every relation symbol R and every tuple $(a_1, \ldots, a_k) \in R^{\mathbf{A}}$, it holds that $(h(a_1), \ldots, h(a_k)) \in R^{\mathbf{B}}$. (Here, k denotes the arity of R.) The *constraint satisfaction problem (CSP)* is to decide, given an ordered pair $\mathbf{A}, \mathbf{B}$ of relational structures, whether or not there is a homomorphism from the first structure, **A**, to the second, **B**. A homomorphism from **A** to **B** in an instance $\mathbf{A}, \mathbf{B}$ of the CSP is also called a *satisfying assignment*, and when a satisfying assignment exists, we will say that the instance is *satisfiable*.

2 Coverwidth

This section defines the structural measure of hypergraph complexity that we call *coverwidth*. As we have mentioned, coverwidth is equal to generalized hypertree width, which was defined in [12]. We begin by defining the notion of *hypergraph*.

Definition 1. *A* hypergraph *is an ordered pair* (V, E) *consisting of a* vertex set V *and a* hyperedge set E. *The elements of E are called* hyperedges; *each hyperedge is a subset of V.*

Basic to the measure of coverwidth is the notion of a tree decomposition.

Definition 2. *A* tree decomposition *of a hypergraph (V, E) is a pair $(T = (I, F), \{X_i\}_{i \in I})$ where*

- *$T = (I, F)$ is a tree, and*
- *each X_i (with $i \in I$) is called a* bag *and is a subset of V,*

such that the following conditions hold:

1. *$V = \cup_{i \in I} X_i$.*
2. *For all hyperedges $e \in E$, there exists $i \in I$ with $e \subseteq X_i$.*
3. *For all $v \in V$, the vertices $T_v = \{i \in I : v \in X_i\}$ form a connected subtree of T.*

Tree decompositions are generally applied to graphs, and in the context of graphs, the measure of *treewidth* has been heavily studied. The *treewidth* of a graph G is the minimum of the quantity $\max_{i \in I} |X_i| - 1$ over all tree decompositions of G. In other words, a tree decomposition is measured based on its largest bag, and the treewidth is then defined based on the "lowest cost" tree decomposition.

The measure of coverwidth is also based on the notion of tree decomposition. In coverwidth, a tree decomposition is also measured based on its "largest" bag; however, the measure applied to a bag is the number of hyperedges needed to cover it, called here the *weight*.

Definition 3. *A k-union over a hypergraph H (with $k \geq 0$) is a union $e_1 \cup \ldots \cup e_k$ of k edges $e_1, \ldots, e_k$ of H.*

The empty set is considered to be the unique 0-union over a hypergraph.

Definition 4. *Let $H = (V, E)$ be a hypergraph. The* weight *of a subset $X \subseteq V$ is the smallest integer $k \geq 0$ such that $X \cap (\cup_{e \in E} e)$ is contained in a k-union over H.*

We measure a tree decomposition according to its heaviest bag, and define the *coverwidth* of a hypergraph according to the lightest-weight tree decomposition.

Definition 5. *The* weight *of a tree decomposition of H is the maximum weight over all of its bags.*

Definition 6. *The* coverwidth *of a hypergraph H is the minimum weight over all tree decompositions of H.*

It is straightforward to verify that the coverwidth of a hypergraph is equal to the generalized hypertree width of a hypergraph [12]. Since the generalized hypertree width of a hypergraph is always less than or equal to its hypertree width, coverwidth is at least as strong as hypertree width in that results on bounded coverwidth imply results on bounded hypertree width.

There is another formulation of tree decompositions that is often wieldy, see for instance [3].

Definition 7. *A* scheme *of a hypergraph $H = (V, E)$ is a graph (V, F) such that*

- *(V, F) has a perfect elimination ordering, that is, an ordering $v_1, \ldots, v_n$ of its vertices such that for all $i < j < k$, if (v_i, v_k) and (v_j, v_k) are edges in F, then (v_i, v_j) is also an edge in F, and*
- *the vertices of every hyperedge of E induce a clique in (V, F).*

It is well known that the property of having a perfect elimination ordering is equivalent to being chordal. The following proposition is also well-known.

Proposition 8. *Let H be a hypergraph. For every tree decomposition of H, there exists a scheme such that each clique of the scheme is contained in a bag of the tree decomposition. Likewise, for every scheme of H, there exists a tree decomposition such that each bag of the tree decomposition is contained in a clique of the scheme.*

Let us define the *weight* of a scheme (of a hypergraph H) to be the maximum weight (with respect to H) over all of its cliques. The following proposition is immediate from Proposition 8 and the definition of coverwidth, and can be taken as an alternative definition of coverwidth.

Proposition 9. *The coverwidth of a hypergraph H is equal to the minimum weight over all schemes of H.*

We now define the hypergraph associated to a relational structure. Roughly speaking, this hypergraph is obtained by "forgetting" the ordering of the **A**-tuples.

Definition 10. *Let **A** be a relational structure. The hypergraph associated to **A** is denoted by $H(\mathbf{A})$; the vertex set of $H(\mathbf{A})$ is the universe of **A**, and for each **A**-tuple $(a_1, \ldots, a_k)$, there is an edge $\{a_1, \ldots, a_k\}$ in $H(\mathbf{A})$.*

We will often implicitly pass from a relational structure to its associated hypergraph, that is, we simply write **A** in place of $H(\mathbf{A})$. In particular, we will speak of k-unions over a relational structure **A**.

3   Existential k-Cover Games

We now define a class of pebble games for studying the measure of coverwidth. These games are parameterized by an integer $k \geq 1$, and are called existential k-cover games. They are based on the existential k-pebble games defined by Kolaitis and Vardi and used to study constraint satisfaction [18,20]. The pebble game that we use is defined as follows. The game is played between two players, the *Spoiler* and the *Duplicator*, on a pair of relational structures **A**, **B** that are defined over the same signature. Game play proceeds in rounds, and in each round one of the following occurs:

1. The Spoiler places a pebble on an **A**-element a. In this case, the Duplicator must respond by placing a corresponding pebble, denoted by $h(a)$, on a **B**-element.
2. The Spoiler removes a pebble from an **A**-element a. In this case, the corresponding pebble $h(a)$ on **B** is removed.

When game play begins, there are no pebbles on any **A**-elements, nor on any **B**-elements, and so the first round is of the first type. Both of the players have an unlimited supply of pebbles. However, when placing a new pebble, the Spoiler must obey the restriction that the weight of the elements on which the Spoiler has pebbles must be bounded by k. (Here, by "weight" we are using Definition 4.) We assume that the Spoiler never places two pebbles on the same **A**-element, so that h is a partial function (as opposed to a relation). The Duplicator wins the game if he can always ensure that h is a *projective homomorphism* from **A** to **B**; otherwise, the Spoiler wins. A *projective homomorphism* (from **A** to **B**) is a partial function h from the universe of **A** to the universe of **B** such that for any relation symbol R and any tuple $(a_1, \ldots, a_k) \in R^{\mathbf{A}}$ of **A**, there exists a tuple $(b_1, \ldots, b^k) \in R^{\mathbf{B}}$ where $h(a_i) = b_i$ for all a_i on which h is defined.

We now formalize the notion of a *winning strategy* for the Duplicator in the existential k-cover game. Note that when h is a partial function, we use $\mathrm{dom}(h)$ to denote the domain of h.

Definition 11. *A winning strategy for the Duplicator in the existential k-cover game on relational structures* **A**, **B** *is a non-empty set H of projective homomorphisms (from **A** to **B**) having the following two properties.*

1. *(the "forth" property) For every $h \in H$ and **A**-element $a \notin \mathrm{dom}(h)$, if $\mathrm{dom}(h) \cup \{a\}$ has weight $\leq k$, then there exists a projective homomorphism $h' \in H$ extending h with $\mathrm{dom}(h') = \mathrm{dom}(h) \cup \{a\}$.*
2. *The set H is closed under subfunctions, that is, if $h \in H$ and h extends h', then $h' \in H$.*

As we mentioned, the definition of this game is based on the *existential k-pebble game* introduced by Kolaitis and Vardi [18,20]. In the *existential k-pebble game*, the number of pebbles that the Spoiler may use is bounded by k, and the Duplicator need only must ensure that h is a *partial homomorphism*. A close relationship between this game and bounded treewidth has been identified [2].

Theorem 12. *[2] Let **A** and **B** be relational structures. For all $k \geq 2$, the following are equivalent.*

- *There is a winning strategy for the Duplicator in the existential k-pebble game on **A**, **B**.*
- *For all relational structures **T** of treewidth $< k$, if there is a homomorphism from **T** to **A**, then there is a homomorphism from **T** to **B**.*

We have the following analog of Theorem 12.

Theorem 13. *Let* **A** *and* **B** *be relational structures. For all $k \geq 1$, the following are equivalent.*

- *There is a winning strategy for the Duplicator in the k-cover game on* **A**, **B**.
- *For all relational structures* **T** *of coverwidth $\leq k$, if there is a homomorphism from* **T** *to* **A**, *then there is a homomorphism from* **T** *to* **B**.

Proof. ($\Rightarrow$) Let H be a winning strategy for the Duplicator in the k-cover game on **A** and **B**, let **T** be any structure of coverwidth $\leq k$, let f be any homomorphism from **T** to **A**, let $G = (T, F)$ be a scheme for **T** of weight $\leq k$, and let $v_1, \ldots, v_n$ be a perfect elimination ordering of G.

We shall construct a sequence of partial mappings $g_0, \ldots, g_n$ from T to B such that for each i:

1. $\mathrm{dom}(g_i) = \{v_1, \ldots, v_i\}$, and
2. for every clique $L \subseteq \{v_1, \ldots, v_i\}$ in G, there exists a projective homomorphism $h \in H$ with domain $f(L)$ in the winning strategy of the Duplicator, such that for every $v \in L$, $h(f(v)) = g_i(v)$.

We define g_0 to be the partial function with empty domain. For every $i \geq 0$, the partial mapping g_{i+1} is obtained by extending g_i in the following way. As $v_1, \ldots, v_n$ is a perfect elimination ordering, the set

$$L = \{v_{i+1}\} \cup \{v_j : j < i+1, (v_j, v_{i+1}) \in F\}$$

is a clique of G. Define L' as $L \setminus \{v_{i+1}\}$. By the induction hypothesis, there exists $h \in H$ such that for every $v \in L'$, $h(f(v)) = g_i(v)$. Let us consider two cases.

If $f(v_{i+1}) = f(v_j)$ for some $v_j \in L'$ then we set $g_{i+1}(v_{i+1})$ to be $g_i(v_j)$. Note that in this case property (2) is satisfied, as every clique in G containing v_{i+1} is contained in L and h serves as a certificate. (For any clique not containing v_{i+1}, we use the induction hypothesis.)

Otherwise, that is, if $f(v_{i+1}) \neq f(v_j)$ for all $v_j \in L'$, we do the following. First, since the weight of L is bounded above by k and f defines an homomorphism from **T** to **A** then the weight of $f(L)$ is also bounded by k. Observe that $f(L) = \mathrm{dom}(h) \cup \{f(v_{i+1})\}$. By the forth property of winning strategy there exists an extension $h' \in H$ of h that is defined over v_{i+1}. We set $g_{i+1}(v_{i+1})$ to be $h'(f(v_{i+1}))$. Note that h' certifies that property (2) is satisfied for very clique containing v_{i+1}; again, any clique not containing v_{i+1} is covered by the induction hypothesis.

Finally, let us prove that g_n indeed defines an homomorphism from **T** to **B**. Let R be any relation symbol and let $(t_1, \ldots, t_l)$ be any relation in $R^\mathbf{T}$. We want to show that $(g_n(t_1), \ldots, g_n(t_l))$ belongs to $R^\mathbf{B}$. Since G is an scheme for **T**, $\{t_1, \ldots, t_l\}$ constitutes a clique of G. By property (2) there exists $h \in H$ such that $h(f(t_i)) = g(t_i)$ for all i. Observing that as f is an homomorphism from **T** to **A**, we can have that $(f(t_1), \ldots, f(t_l))$ belongs to $R^\mathbf{A}$. Finally, as h is a projective homomorphism from **A** to **B**, the tuple $(h(f(t_1)), \ldots, h(f(t_l)))$ must be in **B**.

($\Leftarrow$) We shall construct a winning strategy H for the Duplicator. We need a few definitons. Fix a sequence $a_1,\ldots,a_m$ of elements of A. A *valid tuple* for $a_1,\ldots,a_m$ is any tuple $(\mathbf{T},G,v_1,\ldots,v_m,f)$ where $\mathbf{T}$ is a relational structure, G is an scheme of weight k for $\mathbf{T}$, $\{v_1,\ldots,v_m\}$ is a clique of G, and f is an homomorphism from $\mathbf{T},v_1,\ldots,v_m$ to $\mathbf{A},a_1,\ldots,a_m$. (By a homomorphism from $\mathbf{T},v_1,\ldots,v_m$ to $\mathbf{A},a_1,\ldots,a_m$, we mean a homomorphism from $\mathbf{T}$ to $\mathbf{A}$ that maps v_i to a_i for all i.) By $S(\mathbf{T},G,v_1,\ldots,v_m,f)$ we denote the set of all mappings h with domain $\{a_1,\ldots,a_m\}$ such that there is an homomorphism from $\mathbf{T},v_1,\ldots,v_m$ to $\mathbf{B},h(a_1),\ldots,h(a_m)$. We are now in a situation to define H. H contains for every subset $a_1,\ldots,a_m$ of weight at most k, every partial mapping h that is contained in all $S(\mathbf{T},G,v_1,\ldots,v_m,f)$ where $(\mathbf{T},G,v_1,\ldots,v_m,f)$ is a valid tuple for $a_1,\ldots,a_m$.

Let us show that H is indeed a winning strategy. First, observe that H is nonempty, as it contains the partial function with empty domain. Second, let us show that H contains only projective homomorphisms. Indeed, let h be any mapping in H with domain $a_1,\ldots,a_m$, let R be any relation symbol and let $(c_1,\ldots,c_l)$ be any tuple in $R^\mathbf{A}$. Let us define $\mathbf{T}$ to be the substructure (not necessarily induced) of $\mathbf{A}$ with universe $\{a_1,\ldots,a_k,c_1,\ldots,c_l\}$ containing only the tuple $(c_1,\ldots,c_l)$ in $R^\mathbf{T}$. It is easy to verify that the graph $G = (\{a_1,\ldots,a_k,c_1,\ldots,c_l\},F)$ where $F = \{(a_i,a_j): i \neq j\} \cup \{(c_i,c_j): i \neq j\}$ is an scheme of $\mathbf{T}$ of weight $\leq k$. Consequently, $(\mathbf{T},G,a_1,\ldots,a_m,id)$ is a valid tuple for $a_1,\ldots,a_m$ and therefore there exists an homomorphism g from $\mathbf{T}$ to $\mathbf{B}$, and hence satisfying $(g(c_1),\ldots,g(c_l)) \in R^\mathbf{B}$, such that $g(a_i) = h(a_i)$ for all $i = 1,\ldots k$.

To show that H is closed under subfunctions is rather easy. Indeed, let h' be any mapping in H with domain $a_1\ldots,a_m$. We shall see that the restriction h of h' to $\{a_1,\ldots,a_{m-1}\}$ is also in H. Let $(\mathbf{T},G,v_1,\ldots,v_{m-1},f)$ be any valid tuple for $a_1,\ldots,a_{k-1}$. We construct a valid tuple $(\mathbf{T}',G',v_1,\ldots,v_m,f')$ for $a_1,\ldots,a_m$ in the following way: v_m is a new (not in the universe of $\mathbf{T}$) element, $\mathbf{T}'$ is the structure obtained from $\mathbf{T}$ by adding v_m to the universe of $\mathbf{T}$ and keeping the same relations, f' is the extension of f in which v_m is map to a_m, and G' is the scheme of $\mathbf{T}$ obtained by adding to G an edge (v_j,v_m) for every $j=1,\ldots,m-1$. Since $(\mathbf{T}',G',v_1,\ldots,v_m,f')$ is a valid tuple for $a_1,\ldots,a_m$ and $h' \in H$, there exists an homomorphism g' from $\mathbf{T}',v_1,\ldots,v_m$ to $\mathbf{B},h'(a_1),\ldots,h'(a_m)$. Observe then that the restriction g of g' to $\{a_1,\ldots,a_{m-1}\}$ defines then an homomorphism from $\mathbf{T},v_1,\ldots,v_{m-1}$ to $\mathbf{B},h(a_1),\ldots,h(m_1)$.

Finally, we shall show that H has the forth property. The proof relies in the following easy properties of the valid tuples. Let $a_1,\ldots,a_m$ be elements of A and let $(\mathbf{T}_1,G_1,v_1,\ldots,v_m,f_1)$ and let $(\mathbf{T}_2,G_2,v_1,\ldots,v_m,f_2)$ be valid tuples for $a_1,\ldots,a_m$ such that $T_1 \cap T_2 = \{v_1,\ldots,v_m\}$, let $\mathbf{T}$ be $\mathbf{T}_1 \cup \mathbf{T}_2$ (that is, the structure $\mathbf{T}$ whose universe is the union of the universes of $\mathbf{T}_1$ and $\mathbf{T}_2$, and in which $R^\mathbf{T} = R^{\mathbf{T}_1} \cup R^{\mathbf{T}_2}$ for all relation symbols R), $G = G_1 \cup G_2$ and let f be the mapping from the universe T of $\mathbf{T}$ to B that sets a to $f_1(a)$ if $a \in T_1$ and to $f_2(a)$ if $a \in T_2$ (observe that f_1 and f_2 coincide over $\{v_1,\ldots,v_m\}$). Then $(\mathbf{T},G,v_1,\ldots,v_m,f)$ is a valid tuple for $a_1,\ldots,a_m$. We call $(\mathbf{T},G,v_1,\ldots,v_m,f)$, the *union* of $(\mathbf{T}_1, G_1, v_1, \ldots, v_m, f_1)$ and $(\mathbf{T}_2, G_2, v_1, \ldots, v_m, f_2)$. Furthermore, $S(\mathbf{T}, G, v_1, \ldots, v_m, f) \subseteq S(\mathbf{T}_1, G_1, v_1, \ldots, v_m, f_1) \cap S(\mathbf{T}_2, G_2, v_1, \ldots, v_m, f_2)$ (in fact, this is an equality, although we do not need the equality in our proof).

Let h be any mapping in H, let $\{a_1, \ldots, a_{m-1}\}$ be its domain, and let a_m be any element in the universe of $\mathbf{A}$ such that $\{a_1, \ldots, a_m\}$ has weight $\leq k$. Let us assume, towards a contradiction, that there is not extension h' of h in $\mathcal{H}$. Then there exists a *finite* collection $\{(\mathbf{T}_i, G_i, v_1, \ldots, v_m, f_i) : i \in I\}$ of valid tuples for $a_1, \ldots, a_m$ such that the intersection $\bigcap_{i \in I} S(\mathbf{T}_i, G_i, v_1, \ldots, v_m, f_i)$ does not contain any extension of h. We can rename the elements of the universes so that for every different $i, j \in I$ we have that $T_i \cap T_j = \{v_1, \ldots, v_m\}$.

Let $(\mathbf{T}, G, v_1, \ldots, v_m, f)$ be the union of $(\mathbf{T}_i, G_i, v_1, \ldots, v_m, f_i)$, $i \in I$, which is a valid tuple for $a_1, \ldots, a_m$. Since

$$S(\mathbf{T}, G, v_1, \ldots, v_m, f) \subseteq \bigcap_{i \in I} S(\mathbf{T}_i, G_i, v_1, \ldots, v_m, f_i)$$

we can conclude that $S(\mathbf{T}, G, v_1, \ldots, v_m, f)$ does not contain any extension of h. To finish the proof, it is only necessary to observe that $(\mathbf{T}, G, v_1, \ldots, v_{m-1}, f)$ is a valid tuple for $a_1, \ldots, a_{m-1}$ and since $S(\mathbf{T}, G, v_1, \ldots, v_m, f)$ does not contain any extension of h, $S(\mathbf{T}, G, v_1, \ldots, v_{m-1}, f)$ cannot contain h, in contradiction with $h \in H$. □

Theorem 13 can be easily applied to show that in an instance $\mathbf{A}, \mathbf{B}$ of the CSP, if the left-hand side structure has coverwidth bounded by k, then deciding if there is a homomorphism from $\mathbf{A}$ to $\mathbf{B}$ is equivalent to deciding the existence of a Duplicator winning strategy in the existential k-cover game.

Theorem 14. *Let $\mathbf{A}$ be a relational structure having coverwidth $\leq k$, and let $\mathbf{B}$ be an arbitrary relational structure. There is a winning strategy for the Duplicator in the k-cover game on $\mathbf{A}, \mathbf{B}$ if and only if there is a homomorphism from $\mathbf{A}$ to $\mathbf{B}$.*

We will use this theorem in the next section to develop tractability results. Although we use Theorem 13 to derive this theorem, we would like to emphasize that the full power of Theorem 13 is not needed to derive it, as pointed out in the proof.

Proof. If there is a homomorphism from $\mathbf{A}$ to $\mathbf{B}$, the Duplicator can win by always setting pebbles according the homomorphism. The other direction is immediate from Theorem 13 (note that we only need the forward implication and $\mathbf{T} = \mathbf{A}$). □

4 The Algorithmic Viewpoint

The previous section introduced the *existential k-cover game*. We showed that deciding a CSP instance of bounded coverwidth is equivalent to deciding if the Duplicator has a winning strategy in the existential k-cover game. In this section,

we show that the latter property–the existence of a Duplicator winning strategy–
can be decided algorithmically in polynomial time. To this end, it will be helpful
to introduce the notion of a *compact winning strategy*.

Definition 15. *A* compact winning strategy *for the Duplicator in the existential
k-cover game on relational structures* $\mathbf{A}, \mathbf{B}$ *is a non-empty set H of projective
homomorphisms (from $\mathbf{A}$ to $\mathbf{B}$) having the following properties.*

1. *For all $h \in H$, $\mathsf{dom}(h)$ is a k-union (over $\mathbf{A}$).*
2. *For every $h \in H$ and for every k-union U (over $\mathbf{A}$), there exists $h' \in H$ with
   $\mathsf{dom}(h') = U$ such that for every $v \in \mathsf{dom}(h) \cap \mathsf{dom}(h')$, $h(v) = h'(v)$.*

Proposition 16. *In the existential k-cover game on a pair of relational structures $\mathbf{A}, \mathbf{B}$, the Duplicator has a winning strategy if and only if the Duplicator
has a compact winning strategy.*

Proof. Suppose that the Duplicator has a winning strategy H. Let C be the set
containing all functions $h \in H$ such that $\mathsf{dom}(h)$ is a k-union. We claim that C
is a compact winning strategy. Clearly C satisfies the first property of a compact
winning strategy, so we show that it satisfies the second property. Suppose $h \in C$
and let U be a k-union. By the subfunction property of a winning strategy, the
restriction r of h to $\mathsf{dom}(h) \cap U$ is in H. By repeated application of the forth
property, there is an extension e of r that is in H and has domain U, which
serves as the desired h'.

Now suppose that the Duplicator has a compact winning strategy C. Let H
be the closure of C under subfunctions. We claim that H is a winning strategy.
It suffices to show that H has the forth property. Let $h \in H$ and suppose that
a is an $\mathbf{A}$-element where $\mathsf{dom}(h) \cup \{a\}$ has weight $\leq k$. Let U be a k-union
such that $\mathsf{dom}(h) \cup \{a\} \subseteq U$. By definition of H, there is a function $e \in C$
extending h. Apply the second property of a compact winning strategy to e and
U to obtain an $e' \in C$ with domain U such that for every $v \in \mathsf{dom}(e) \cap \mathsf{dom}(e')$,
$e(v) = e'(v)$. Notice that $\mathsf{dom}(h) \subseteq \mathsf{dom}(e) \cap \mathsf{dom}(e')$. Thus, the restriction of e'
to $\mathsf{dom}(h) \cup \{a\}$ is in H and extends h. □

We have just shown that deciding if there is a winning strategy, in an instance
of the existential k-cover game, is equivalent to deciding if there is a compact
winning strategy. We now use this equivalence to give a polynomial-time algorithm for deciding if there is a winning strategy.

Theorem 17. *For all $k \geq 1$, there exists a polynomial-time algorithm that,
given a pair of relational structures $\mathbf{A}, \mathbf{B}$, decides whether or not there is a
winning strategy for the Duplicator in the existential k-cover game on $\mathbf{A}, \mathbf{B}$.*

Proof. By Proposition 16, it suffices to give a polynomial-time algorithm that
decides if there is a compact winning strategy. It is straightforward to develop
such an algorithm based on the definition of compact winning strategy. Let H be
the set of all functions h such that $\mathsf{dom}(h)$ is a k-union (over $\mathbf{A}$) and such that
h is a projective homomorphism from $\mathbf{A}$ to $\mathbf{B}$. Iteratively perform the following

until no changes can be made to H: for every function $h \in H$ and every k-union U, check to see if there is $h' \in H$ such that the second property (of compact winning strategy) is satisfied; if not, remove h from H. Throughout the algorithm, we have maintained the invariant that any compact winning strategy must be a subset of H. Hence, if when the algorithm terminates H is empty, then there is no compact winning strategy. And if H is non-empty when the algorithm terminates, H is clearly a compact winning strategy.

The number of k-unions (over $\mathbf{A}$) is polynomial in the number of tuples in $\mathbf{A}$. Also, for each k-union U, the number of projective homomorphisms h with $\mathrm{dom}(h) = U$ from $\mathbf{A}$ to $\mathbf{B}$ is polynomial in the number of tuples in $\mathbf{B}$. Hence, the size of the original set H is polynomial in the original instance. Since in each iteration an element is removed from H, the algorithm terminates in polynomial time. □

The algorithm we have just described in the proof of Theorem 17 may appear to be quite specialized. However, we now show that essentially that algorithm can be viewed as a *general* inference procedure for CSP instances in the vein of existing consistency algorithms. In particular, we give a general algorithm called *projective k-consistency* for CSP instances that, given a CSP instance, performs inference and outputs a more constrained CSP instance having exactly the same satisfying assignments as the original. On a CSP instance $\mathbf{A}, \mathbf{B}$, the algorithm might detect an *inconsistency*, by which we mean that it detects that there is no homomorphism from $\mathbf{A}$ to $\mathbf{B}$. If it does not, then it is guaranteed that there is a winning strategy for the Duplicator.

Definition 18. *The* projective k-consistency algorithm *takes as input a CSP instance $\mathbf{A}, \mathbf{B}$, and consists of the following steps.*

- *Create a new CSP instance $\mathbf{A}', \mathbf{B}'$ as follows. Let the universe of $\mathbf{A}'$ be the universe of $\mathbf{A}$, and the universe of $\mathbf{B}'$ be the universe of $\mathbf{B}$. Let the signature of $\mathbf{A}'$ and $\mathbf{B}'$ contain a relation symbol R_U for each k-union U over $\mathbf{A}$. For each k-union U, the relation $R_U^{\mathbf{A}'}$ is defined as $(u_1, \ldots, u_m)$, where $u_1, \ldots, u_m$ are exactly the elements of U in some order; and $R_U^{\mathbf{B}'}$ is defined as the set of all tuples $(b_1, \ldots, b_m)$ such that the mapping taking $u_i \to b_i$ is a projective homomorphism from $\mathbf{A}$ to $\mathbf{B}$.*
- *Iteratively perform the following until no changes can be made: remove any $\mathbf{B}'$-tuple $(b_1, \ldots, b_m)$ that is not a projective homomorphism.*
  We say that a $\mathbf{B}'$-tuple $(b_1, \ldots, b_m) \in R_U^{\mathbf{B}'}$ is a projective homomorphism if, letting $(u_1, \ldots, u_m)$ denote the unique element of $R_U^{\mathbf{A}'}$, the function taking $u_i \to b_i$ is a projective homomorphism from $\mathbf{A}'$ to $\mathbf{B}'$.
- *Report an inconsistency if there are no $\mathbf{B}'$-tuples remaining.*

Theorem 19. *For each $k \geq 1$, the projective k-consistency algorithm, given as input a CSP instance $\mathbf{A}, \mathbf{B}$:*

- *runs in polynomial time,*
- *outputs a CSP instance $\mathbf{A}', \mathbf{B}'$ that has the same satisfying assignments as $\mathbf{A}, \mathbf{B}$, and*

– reports an inconsistency if and only if the Duplicator does not have a winning strategy in the existential k-cover game on $\mathbf{A}, \mathbf{B}$.

Proof. The first property is straightforward to verify. For the second property, observe that, each time a tuple is removed from $\mathbf{B}'$, the set of satisfying assignments is preserved. For the third property, observe that, associating $\mathbf{B}'$-tuples to functions as in Definition 18, the behavior of the projective k-consistency algorithm is identical to the behavior of the algorithm in the proof of Proposition 16. □

By using the results presented in this section thus far, it is easy to show that CSP instances of bounded coverwidth are tractable. Define the coverwidth of a CSP instance $\mathbf{A}, \mathbf{B}$ to be the coverwidth of $\mathbf{A}$. Let CSP[coverwidth $\leq k$] be the restriction of the CSP to all instances of coverwidth less than or equal to k.

Theorem 20. *For all $k \geq 1$, the problem CSP[coverwidth $\leq k$] is decidable in polynomial time by the projective k-consistency algorithm. In particular, on an instance of CSP[coverwidth $\leq k$], the projective k-consistency algorithm reports an inconsistency if and only if the instance is not satisfiable.*

Proof. Immediate from Theorem 14 and the third property of Theorem 19. □

Note that we can derive the tractability of CSP instances having bounded hypertree width immediately from Theorem 20.

Now, given a CSP instance that is promised to have bounded coverwidth, we can use projective k-consistency to decide the instance (Theorem 20). This tractability result can in fact be pushed further: we can show that there is a generic polynomial-time that, given an *arbitrary* CSP instance, is *guaranteed* to decide instances of bounded coverwidth. Moreover, whenever an instance is decided to be a "yes" instance by the algorithm, a satisfying assignment is constructed.

Theorem 21. *For all $k \geq 1$, there exists a polynomial-time algorithm that, given any CSP instance $\mathbf{A}, \mathbf{B}$,*

1. *outputs a satisfying assignment for $\mathbf{A}, \mathbf{B}$,*
2. *correctly reports that $\mathbf{A}, \mathbf{B}$ is unsatisfiable, or*
3. *reports "I don't know".*

The algorithm always performs (1) or (2) on an instance of CSP[coverwidth $\leq k$].

Proof. The algorithm is a simple extension of the projective k-consistency algorithm. First, the algorithm applies the projective k-consistency algorithm; if an inconsistency is detected, then the algorithm terminates and reports that $\mathbf{A}, \mathbf{B}$ is unsatisfiable. Otherwise, it initializes V to be the universe A of $\mathbf{A}$, and does the following:

– If V is empty, terminate and identify the mapping taking each $a \in A$ to the $\mathbf{B}$-element in $R_a^\mathbf{B}$, as a satisfying assignment.
– Pick any variable $v \in V$.

- Expand the signature of $\mathbf{A}, \mathbf{B}$ to include another symbol R_v with $R_v^{\mathbf{A}} = \{(v)\}$.
- Try to find a $\mathbf{B}$-element b such that when $R_v^{\mathbf{B}}$ is set to $\{(b)\}$, no inconsistency is detected by the projective k-consistency algorithm on the expanded instance.
  - If there is no such $\mathbf{B}$-element, terminate and report "I don't know".
  - Otherwise, set $R_v^{\mathbf{B}}$ to such a $\mathbf{B}$-element, remove v from V, and repeat from the first step using the expanded instance.

If the procedure terminates from V being empty in the first step, the mapping that is output is straightforwardly verified to be a satisfying assignment.

Suppose that the algorithm is given an instance of CSP[coverwidth $\leq k$]. If it is unsatisfiable, then the algorithm reports that the instance is unsatisfiable by Theorem 20. So suppose that the instance is satisfiable. We claim that each iteration preserves the satisfiability of the instance. Let $\mathbf{A}, \mathbf{B}$ denote the CSP instance at the beginning of an arbitrary iteration of the algorithm. If no inconsistency is detected after adding a new relation symbol R_v with $R_v^{\mathbf{A}} = \{(v)\}$ and $R_v^{\mathbf{B}} = \{(b)\}$, there must be a satisfying assignment mapping v to b by Theorem 20. Note that adding unary relation symbols to a CSP instance does not change the coverwidth of the instance. □

We now expand the tractability result of Theorem 20, and show the tractability of CSP instances that are *homomorphically equivalent* to instances of bounded coverwidth. Formally, let us say that $\mathbf{A}$ and $\mathbf{A}'$ are homomorphically equivalent if there is a homomorphism from $\mathbf{A}$ to $\mathbf{A}'$ as well as a homomorphism from $\mathbf{A}'$ to $\mathbf{A}$. Let CSP[$\mathcal{H}$(coverwidth $\leq k$)] denote the restriction of the CSP to instances $\mathbf{A}, \mathbf{B}$ where $\mathbf{A}$ is homomorphically equivalent to a relational structure of coverwidth less than or equal to k.

Theorem 22. *For all $k \geq 1$, the problem* CSP[$\mathcal{H}$(coverwidth $\leq k$)] *is decidable in polynomial time by the projective k-consistency algorithm. In particular, on an instance of* CSP[$\mathcal{H}$(coverwidth $\leq k$)], *the projective k-consistency algorithm reports an inconsistency if and only if the instance is not satisfiable.*

References

1. Isolde Adler, Georg Gottlob, and Martin Grohe. Hypertree-width and related hypergraph invariants. In preparation.
2. A. Atserias, Ph. G. Kolaitis, and M. Y. Vardi. Constraint propagation as a proof system. In *CP 2004*, 2004.
3. Hans L. Bodlaender. Discovering treewidth. In *SOFSEM 2005*, 2005.
4. Andrei Bulatov. A dichotomy theorem for constraints on a three-element set. In *Proceedings of 43rd IEEE Symposium on Foundations of Computer Science*, pages 649–658, 2002.
5. Andrei Bulatov. Tractable conservative constraint satisfaction problems. In *Proceedings of 18th IEEE Symposium on Logic in Computer Science (LICS '03)*, pages 321–330, 2003. Extended version appears as Oxford University technical report PRG-RR-03-01.

6. Hubie Chen and Victor Dalmau. From pebble games to tractability: An ambidextrous consistency algorithm for quantified constraint satisfaction. Manuscript, 2005.
7. D. Cohen, P. Jeavons, and M. Gyssens. A unified theory of structural tractability for constraint satisfaction and spread cut decomposition. To appear in IJCAI 2005, 2005.
8. Victor Dalmau, Phokion G. Kolaitis, and Moshe Y. Vardi. Constraint satisfaction, bounded treewidth, and finite-variable logics. In *Constraint Programming '02*, LNCS, 2002.
9. Rina Dechter and Judea Pearl. Tree clustering for constraint networks. *Artificial Intelligence*, pages 353–366, 1989.
10. Eugene Freuder. Complexity of k-tree structured constraint satisfaction problems. In *AAAI-90*, 1990.
11. G. Gottlob, L. Leone, and F. Scarcello. Hypertree decomposition and tractable queries. *Journal of Computer and System Sciences*, 64(3):579–627, 2002.
12. G. Gottlob, L. Leone, and F. Scarcello. Robbers, marshals, and guards: game theoretic and logical characterizations of hypertree width. *Journal of Computer and System Sciences*, 66:775–808, 2003.
13. Georg Gottlob, Nicola Leone, and Francesco Scarcello. A comparison of structural csp decomposition methods. *Artif. Intell.*, 124(2):243–282, 2000.
14. Georg Gottlob, Nicola Leone, and Francesco Scarcello. The complexity of acyclic conjunctive queries. *Journal of the ACM*, 43(3):431–498, 2001.
15. Martin Grohe. The complexity of homomorphism and constraint satisfaction problems seen from the other side. In *FOCS 2003*, pages 552–561, 2003.
16. M. Gyssens, P.G. Jeavons, and D.A. Cohen. Decomposing constraint satisfaction problems using database techniques. *Artificial Intelligence*, 66(1):57–89, 1994.
17. M. Gysssens and J. Paradaens. A decomposition methodology for cyclic databases. In *Advances in Database Theory*, volume 2, pages 85–122. Plenum Press, New York, NY, 1984.
18. Ph.G. Kolaitis and M.Y. Vardi. On the expressive power of Datalog: tools and a case study. *Journal of Computer and System Sciences*, 51(1):110–134, 1995.
19. Ph.G. Kolaitis and M.Y. Vardi. Conjunctive-query containment and constraint satisfaction. *Journal of Computer and System Sciences*, 61:302–332, 2000.
20. Ph.G. Kolaitis and M.Y. Vardi. A game-theoretic approach to constraint satisfaction. In *Proceedings 17th National (US) Conference on Artificial Intellignece, AAAI'00*, pages 175–181, 2000.
21. Thomas J. Schaefer. The complexity of satisfiability problems. In *Proceedings of the ACM Symposium on Theory of Computing (STOC)*, pages 216–226, 1978.

Ad-hoc Global Constraints for Life

Kenil C.K. Cheng and Roland H.C. Yap

National University of Singapore,
3 Science Drive 2, Singapore
{chengchi, ryap}@comp.nus.edu.sg

Abstract. Still-life is a challenging problem for CP techniques. We show how to use the global `case` constraint to construct ad-hoc constraints which can provide stronger propagation than existing CP models. We also demonstrate how to use BDDs to construct good representations for the `case` constraint which is critical for efficiency. Our results seem comparable to hybrid CP/IP models even though we are only using propagation albeit on ad-hoc global constraints. This is rather promising since it shows the potential of ad-hoc global constraints to do better than IP global constraints.

1 Introduction

The game of *Life* was invented by John Horton Conway in the late 60s and subsequently popularized by Martin Gardner [1]. A particularly difficult problem in the game of Life is the still-life problem which is to find a maximum density stable pattern. It has been used by many authors to explore issues in problem formulation, symmetry and hybrid approaches using techniques from Constraint Programming (CP) as well as Integer Programming (IP).

In this paper, our objective is two fold. Firstly, still-life is difficult because the constraints in it are loose and we want to investigate how to get better constraint propagation and search techniques for still-life. Secondly, and more importantly, we use still-life as a difficult representative problem in which to apply global constraints. The reason why we want to study global constraints for still-life is that it is a good vehicle for investigating ad-hoc global constraints since there are not special purpose global constraints with specialized algorithms such as `all_different` or `cumulative` which are designed for this problem.

We show how to create ad-hoc global constraints which can be used to get better propagation for the still-life problem. One challenge with using ad-hoc global constraints is the effectiveness of the algorithms and representations when the arity is high and this also leads to the difficulty of dealing with a large extensional constraint definition. The ad-hoc global constraints which we use in still life are all of high arity ranging from 3×3 to $3 \times n$ where n is the board size and the size of the extensional constraint definition is already 7.6E7 for $n = 10$. We demonstrate effective methods of using BDDs to construct ad-hoc `case` constraints.

One might expect that the constraint solver would be bogged down with solving the high arity ad-hoc constraints. We demonstrate using our methodology that one can construct effective global case constraints. While these constraints are more expensive to solve, they are sufficiently efficient and can give stronger propagation than the non-ad-hoc constraints such as arithmetic. While our objective is not to get the best results for still-life, the best results are with using bucket elimination [2], we are able to significantly improve on pure CP propagation based techniques and competitive with CP/IP hybrids.

2 Still Life Problem

The game of Life is played on an infinite (checker) board in which each square is called a *cell*. Each cell has eight neighbors. A cell is *alive* if there is a checker on it. Otherwise it is *dead*. The state of a board at time t determines its state at time $t + 1$ based on the following three rules:

- If a cell has exactly 2 living neighbors at time t, its state remains unchanged at time $t + 1$.
- If a cell has exactly 3 living neighbors at time t, then it is alive at time $t + 1$. This is the "birth" condition.
- If a cell has less than 2 or more than 3 living neighbors at time t, it is dead at time $t + 1$. These are the "death by isolation" and "death by over-crowding" conditions respectively.

It is natural from the problem definition to think of a cell and its eight neighbors as forming a "unit". Smith [3] calls such 3×3 square of cells a *super-cell*. We expand this view and introduce three more super-units: a *super-row* is a $3 \times n$ rectangle; a *super-column* is a $n \times 3$ rectangle; and a *super-block* is a 4×4 square of the board. Super-cells and other super-units will be the basis for constructing various models.

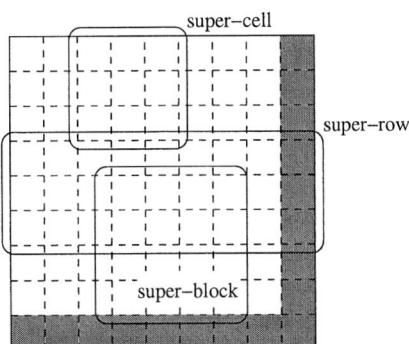

Fig. 1. A 8×8 board made to 9×9 by padding dead cells (shaded). A super-cell is any 3×3 square of cells. A super-row is a $3 \times n$ (here $n = 9$) rectangle of cells. A super-block is a 4×4 square of cells.

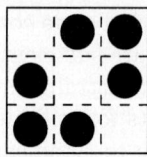

Fig. 2. A 3x3 still-life pattern

Figure 1 gives the graphical representation of an 8×8 board, and various super-units. Since a super-column is a transposed super-row, we focus our discussion on super-row only. In the remainder of the paper, we can assume without loss of generality that n is a multiple of 3 since it is always possible to enlarge the board by padding dead cells to size $n' \times n'$ where n' is a multiple of 3.

A *still-life* pattern of a board is one that remains unchanged over time. The *density* of a region is the number of living cells within that region. The *Still Life* problem in an $n \times n$ square of a board (all the rest of the board is dead) is to determine a still-life pattern with the maximum density. Figure 2 shows a 3×3 still-life pattern.

2.1 The Basic Model

Still-life in a $n \times n$ region can be modeled in a straightforward fashion as a CSP. Each cell at the i-th row and the j-th column is associated with a 0–1 variable $x_{i,j}$ which is 1 if the cell is alive and is 0 otherwise. Throughout this paper, we will abuse notation slightly when referring to a variable to mean either the variable or the object it represents. Let $N_{i,j} = \{x_{i+d,j+e} \mid d, e \in \{-1, 0, 1\} \wedge d^2 + e^2 \neq 0\}$ be the neighbors of $x_{i,j}$. The birth and death conditions can be formulated as

$$SC_{i,j} \equiv (x_{i,j} = 1 \rightarrow 2 \leq \sum_{u \in N_{i,j}} u \leq 3) \wedge (x_{i,j} = 0 \rightarrow \sum_{u \in N_{i,j}} u \neq 3).$$

We call $SC_{i,j}$ a *super-cell (SC) constraint*. The arity of $SC_{i,j}$ is 9. Extra constraints are added on every three adjacent cells along the border to forbid all of them from being alive, otherwise a cell outside the border would become alive. The objective is to maximize the density

$$f = \sum_{1 \leq i,j \leq n} x_{i,j}.$$

We call this model which employs only super-cell constraints (in arithmetic form) $\mathcal{M}_0$.

3 New Improved Still Life Models

As reported by Bosch et. al. [4], the super-cell constraints are too weak for constraint propagation to be effective, which results in late detection of local inconsistency and a huge search tree. They propose a hybrid CP approach combining CP with IP. They show that the use of IP to provide global constraints can significantly reduce the search space with a large improvement in overall search times. Smith [3] shows a dual encoding on the super-cells implemented using the table constraint in ILOG Solver. This paper is inspired by these two approaches and we use both super-cells and ad-hoc constraints.

One possible way to improve the efficiency of constraint propagation is to combine several constraints into a single larger constraint. The idea here is to see if the combination can be used to get more propagation. In the remainder of the paper, we show how to model still-life using increasingly complex ad-hoc constraints as follows:

- In model $\mathcal{M}_r$, a chain of super-cell constraints along a super-row are replaced by a single super-row constraint.
- In the model $\mathcal{M}_{r+d}$, a super-row density constraint is used in which the density of a super-row is "pushed" into the constraint itself.
- In the model $\mathcal{M}_{r+d+b}$, we join also the border constraints with the super-row density constraint.

Finally, there is a more general improvement that replaces four super-cell constraints with a single super-block constraint.

3.1 Model $\mathcal{M}_r$: Super-Rows and Super-Columns

The idea here is to investigate whether a super-cell constraint can be extended further. A natural extension is to consider a row or column of super-cells. A *super-row* (respectively *super-column*) is a horizontal $3 \times n$ rectangle (respectively $n \times 3$ rectangle for a super-column).

Model, $\mathcal{M}_r$, consists of the following constraints:

- A disjoint set of super-row SR_i constraints which partition the board into $3 \times n$ rectangles. Super-column constraints similarly partition the board in the vertical direction.
- A set of border constraints. These are as in model $\mathcal{M}_0$.
- A set of overlapping super-cell constraints that link up two adjacent super-rows. Similarly, these super-cell constraints also link up adjacent super-columns.

The constraints are illustrated in Figure 3. The super-cell constraints are needed since a super-row or super-cell doesn't consider cells outside its boundary.

Modeling and Representing the Super-Row Constraint. The question then with model $\mathcal{M}_r$ is how to represent the super-row constraint which is an ad-hoc constraint. There are three different frameworks to represent an ad-hoc constraint. The most straightforward one is to store the tuples (solutions) defining the ad-hoc in an extensional form [5,6], e.g. an array or table. The table constraint in ILOG Solver provides this way of defining ad-hoc constraints. The main drawback is that the size of the table is determined by the number

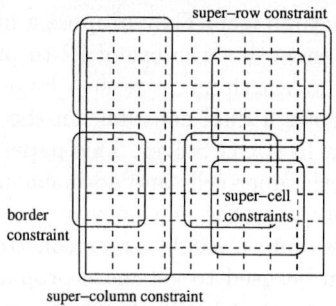

Fig. 3. Graphical representation of $\mathcal{M}_r$

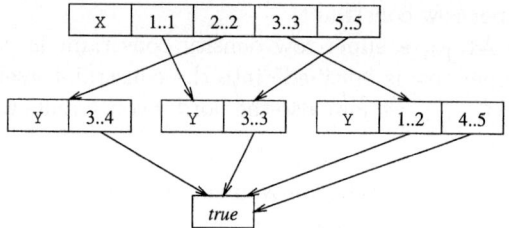

Fig. 4. A DAG representation of C_{adhoc}

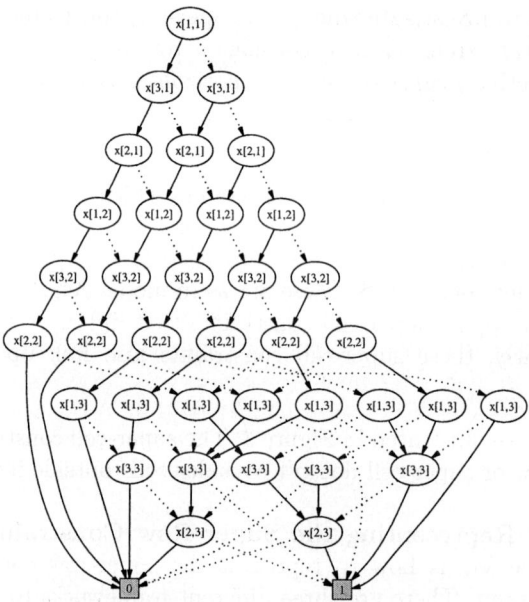

Fig. 5. The BDD representation of the super-cell constraint $SC_{2,2}$

of solutions, which can grow exponentially with constraint arity. This restricts their use to tight constraint with moderate arity. Unfortunately in the case of super-row constraints, the arity is high and the number of solution is large, e.g. a 3×7 super-row has 145365 tuples.

The second framework is to identify or extract some arithmetic or symbolic relations from the solution set (e.g. [7,8]). While the representation is usually more compact, these approaches often require expensive pre-processing and the propagation on such high-level could be weak. Since a super-row constraint aims for strong propagation, we cannot use this approach.

The last framework is to represent the solution set in some compact data structure and build a tailor-made propagation algorithm on top of it (e.g. [9]). The ad-hoc non-binary case/4 constraint provided by SICStus Prolog [10] belongs to this category. We are going to show why it is ideal for a super-row constraint.

User can specify the level of consistency the case constraint enforces, such as generalized arc consistency (GAC). To use the case constraint, the solutions of the ad-hoc constraint should be represented as a directed acyclic graph (DAG) which is recursively defined as follows. A case DAG whose root is of the form node$(G, x, [r_1 - G_1, \ldots, r_m - G_m])$ defines the constraint

$$\langle G \rangle \equiv \bigvee_{k=1}^{m} (x \in r_k \wedge \langle G_k \rangle)$$

where each G_k is a case DAG. For instance, Figure 4 depicts the DAG representation of C_{adhoc} with solutions $\{(x, 1), (y, 3)\}$, $\{(x, 2), (y, 3)\}$, $\{(x, 2), (y, 4)\}$, $\{(x, 3), (y, 1)\}$, $\{(x, 3), (y, 2)\}$, $\{(x, 3), (y, 4)\}$, $\{(x, 3), (y, 5)\}$, and $\{(x, 5), (y, 3)\}$.

Obviously the efficiency of case is related to the compactness of the DAG used.[1] For instance, if there are two case DAGs representing the same constraint, we should use the smaller DAG in the case. The problem of finding a compact case DAG is non-trivial, and SICStus Prolog assumes that the user comes up with a DAG for the case. Our approach is to make use of the fact that each $x_{i,j}$ in still-life is Boolean which allows us to construct a binary decision diagram (BDD) of the ad-hoc constraint. This can then be converted to a case DAG. In our experiments, we use the BDD package BuDDy 2.4 to manipulate BDDs.[2]

Binary decision diagram (BDD) [11] is a state of the art representation for propositional logic formulas which is heavily used in CAD. We can view a BDD as a special form of a case DAG: a BDD node rooted at node$(G, x, [(0..0) - G_0, (1..1) - G_1])$ defines the constraint

$$\langle G \rangle \equiv (x = 0 \wedge \langle G_0 \rangle) \vee (x = 1 \wedge \langle G_1 \rangle)$$

where G_0 and G_1 are BDDs. In BDD terms G_0 is the *0-successor* and G_1 is the *1-successor* of x. A BDD has two terminals, namely the *0-terminal* which

---

[1] We do not have any knowledge about the implementation; it is not described in the SICStus documentation.
[2] http://sourceforge.net/projects/buddy

means *false* and the *1-terminal* which means *true*. Figure 5 shows the BDD constructed for the super-cell constraint $SC_{2,2}$. Each node x[i,j] represents a cell variable $x_{i,j}$. The solid and the dotted out-going arrows of a node point to its 1 and 0-successors respectively. The two terminals of a BDD are drawn as two gray boxes.

While a BDD may give a compact representation for many Boolean functions, it can of course be exponentially large in the worst case. In practice, the BDD size is often sensitive to the underlying variable ordering. As an example, suppose we want to construct a single BDD for $SC_{2,2} \wedge SC_{2,3}$. Under the lexicographical ordering, the BDD (Figure 6(c)) has 180 nodes. Under a different spiral-like

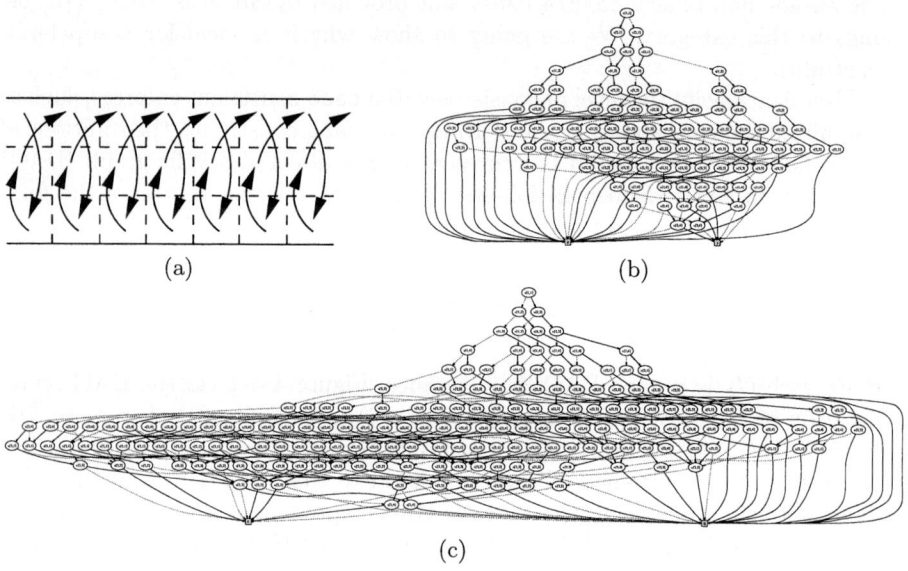

Fig. 6. (a) The BDD variable ordering for super-row constraint. (b) The BDD that represents a 3 × 4 super-row under the variable ordering in (a) has 95 nodes. (c) The same BDD under lexicographical variable ordering has 180 nodes.

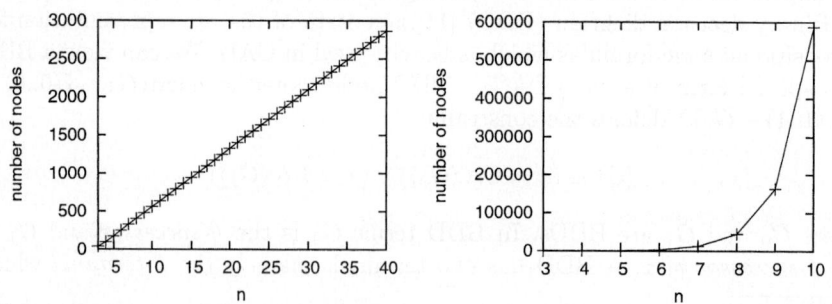

Fig. 7. Sizes of the BDD for SR_i under a "good" (left) and a "bad" (right) variable ordering

ordering (depicted in Figure 6(a)), namely, $x_{1,1}, x_{3,1}, x_{2,1}, x_{1,2}, x_{3,2}, \ldots, x_{2,4}$, the BDD has only 95 nodes. Figure 7 show the sizes of the BDD for the *super-row (SR) constraint*

$$SR_i \equiv \bigwedge_{i=2}^{n-1} SC_i$$

which is a conjunction of $n-2$ super-cell constraints. We observe that under a "good" (spiral-like) ordering, the size of the BDD grows linearly with n. Under a "bad" (lexicographical) ordering, however, the BDD blows up exponentially. For instance, at $n=10$ there are $\approx 7.6E7$ solutions and the good BDD ordering has 559 nodes while the bad has 1221965 nodes. At $n=40$, the good BDD only needs 2944 nodes to encode $\approx 1.9E28$ solutions. In all instances in Figure 7 under the good ordering, the BDD construction time takes within two seconds, thus the ad-hoc constraint construction time is not significant.

3.2 Results for Models $\mathcal{M}_0$ and $\mathcal{M}_r$

Similar to [3,12], search is done on a set of disjoint super-cells which partition the board. The super-cell is treated as a single auxiliary variable $y_{i,j}$ which represents its associated sub-cells using the following constraint:

$$y_{i,j} = x_{i-1,j-1} + 2x_{i-1,j} + 4x_{i-1,j+1} + 8x_{i,j-1} + 16x_{i,j} + 32x_{i,j+1} + 64x_{i+1,j-1} + 128x_{i+1,j} + 256x_{i+1,j+1}.$$

However, unlike in [3], the initial domains of the auxiliary variables are calculated from the constraint given and hence consist of the whole range of integers from 0 to 511.

We use a search strategy with variables being instantiated lexicographically and using domain splitting (i.e. $y_{i,j} \leq d \vee y_{i,j} > d$ where d is the mid-point of the domain). The upper region of the domain is explored first. We found this search strategy to be better than smallest domain.

Table 1 summarizes the experimental results for 3 models. The columns n and *opt* give the maximum density of the still-life pattern in a $n \times n$ region. Our experimental platform is SICStus Prolog 3.12.1. Experiments were run on a PC running Windows XP, with a P4 3.2GHz CPU and 2 GB physical memory. We give the number of backtracks (*bt*), execution time (*time* in seconds) and memory used (*mem* in MB in SICStus) for still-life on each model. A time limit of 3600 seconds is used. Model $\mathcal{M}_r(lex)$ is the $\mathcal{M}_r$ model with the case constraint on the "bad" variable ordering.

As we have observed that the super-row constraints are not tight, model $\mathcal{M}_r$ only gives slightly more propagation than $\mathcal{M}_0$ as expected. Here, the overhead of the global constraint outweighs the search pruning and $\mathcal{M}_r$ exceeds the time limit for $n=10$. The results on $\mathcal{M}_r(lex)$ show the importance of having a good representation for the ad-hoc constraint: while $\mathcal{M}_r$ used only 3.6 MB for $n=9$, $\mathcal{M}_r(lex)$ needed 182.1 MB. Note that $\mathcal{M}_r$ and $\mathcal{M}_r(lex)$ are equivalent models, hence give the same propagation, and they differ only in the representation of the SR_i constraints. For $n=10$ with $\mathcal{M}_r(lex)$, SICStus Prolog aborted with an out of memory error. Table 2 summarizes the experimental results from other papers: CP/IP [4] which uses a hybrid of CP super-cell constraints and IP; the dual encoding [3]; and super-cell variables [12]. We caution that comparison of time is not meaningful because of different systems are used, both the software and hardware differ. The column *cho* gives the number of choice-points and *bt* the number of backtracks. The super-cell variables is similar to $\mathcal{M}_0$ but it appears that our search heuristic is better for larger n.

We have not presented any results using symmetries. We found that the simple use of constraints to remove reflection symmetries did not give much pruning ([4] also found the same for their CP model). More sophisticated symmetry breaking techniques [12] could be used but we did not have a SBDS implementation in SICStus Prolog available to use. In any case, symmetry breaking is orthogonal to our goals in this paper.

Table 1. Experimental results on $\mathcal{M}_0$, $\mathcal{M}_r$ and $\mathcal{M}_r(lex)$

n	opt	$\mathcal{M}_0$			$\mathcal{M}_r$			$\mathcal{M}_r(lex)$		
		bt	time	mem	bt	time	mem	bt	time	mem
6	18	2568	0.3	2.2	2539	0.4	3.5	2539	0.4	6.6
7	28	3512	0.5	2.7	3438	0.6	3.5	3438	0.9	15.3
8	36	54623	7.8	2.7	53126	9.4	3.6	53126	23.1	40.4
9	43	2450406	314.4	3.5	2420472	408.7	3.6	2420472	1700.6	182.1
10	54	25236397	3587.5	3.5		> 3600.0				mem out

Table 2. Experimental results on CP/IP and dual encoding

n	opt	CP/IP [4]		Dual encoding [3]		Super-cell variables [12]	
		cho	time	bt	time	bt	time
6	18	-	-	181	2.2	1689	6.4
7	28	-	-	3510	16.2	10939	48.3
8	36	2310	3	53262	264.0	238513	1418.8
9	43	46345	85	2091386	10300.0	-	-
10	54	98082	291	-	-	-	-
11	64	268520	655	-	-	-	-
12	76	11772869	49166	-	-	-	-
13	90	10996298	50871	-	-	-	-

3.3 Model $\mathcal{M}_{r+d}$: Super-Rows with Density

The use of super-row constraints fails to improve the propagation efficiency because the underlying super-cells are themselves sufficiently loose that joining them doesn't prune the search space by much.

Since the super-row constraint is still loose, it suffers from the problem that unless a large part of a row is instantiated, one would not get much interaction between a super-row constraint and the maximum density. Summing the cells in a super-row will get little propagation since most of the cells can be 0 or 1.

Hence, our next step is to modify the super-row constraint to include the density of the super-row itself:

$$SRD_i \equiv (f_i = \sum_{d \in \{-1,0,1\}} \sum_{j=1}^{n} x_{i+d,j}) \wedge SR_i$$

We call this a *super-row density (SRD) constraint*. (Note we do not include the border constraints.) Its scope includes the variable f_i which gives the density of this super-row, and the variables in SR_i. In other words, it has $3n+1$ variables.

Generating the Super-Row Density Constraint. Since each super-cell has at most 6 living cells and for solving still-life, it is reasonable to assume to a super-row has at least 1 living cell, we know $1 \leq f_i \leq 2n$ (a super-row has at most $n/3$ super-cells). The case DAG for a ad-hoc SRD_i constraint can be constructed as follows. We first create $2n$ BDDs, each represents the constraint

$$C_k \equiv (k = \sum_{d \in \{-1,0,1\}} \sum_{j=1}^{n} x_{i+d,j}) \wedge SR_i$$

and link them with an extra node($SRD_i, f_i, [(1..1) - C_1, \ldots, (2n..2n) - C_{2n}]$). Note that the BDDs for any two constraints may overlap, i.e. they may share the same sub-BDDs. This is an important by product of using BDDs.

To fully utilize the densities of the super-rows, we add an extra constraint $f = \sum f_i$ which links the densities to the overall density of the board. Similarly, we use SRD_j for super-columns and add another constraint $f = \sum e_j$ where e_j is the density of the j-th super-column. We call this model $\mathcal{M}_{r+d}$.

3.4 Model $\mathcal{M}_{r+d+b}$: Specializing for the Border

In $\mathcal{M}_r$ or $\mathcal{M}_{r+d}$, the super-row (density) constraints involve only super-cell constraints. In the next model $\mathcal{M}_{r+d+b}$, we obtain an even stronger super-row constraint by joining also the border constraints:

$$SRDB_i \equiv SRD_i \wedge \bigwedge_{j \in \{1,n\}} (SC_{i,j} \wedge x_{i-1,j} + x_{i,j} + x_{i+1,j} \leq 3)$$

for $3 \leq i \leq n-2$ and

$$SRDB_2 \equiv SRD_2 \wedge \bigwedge_{j \in \{1,n\}} SC_{2,j} \wedge \bigwedge_{j=1}^{n}(SC_{1,j} \wedge x_{1,j-1} + x_{1,j} + x_{1,j+1} \leq 3)$$

$$SRDB_{n-1} \equiv SRD_{n-1} \wedge \bigwedge_{j \in \{1,n\}} SC_{n-1,j} \wedge \bigwedge_{j=1}^{n}(SC_{n,j} \wedge x_{n,j-1} + x_{1,j} + x_{n,j+1} \leq 3)$$

They are called *super-row density border (SRDB) constraints*.

3.5 Model $\mathcal{M}_{r+d+b} + SB$: Adding Super-Blocks

Finally, we can replace the four super-cells in a super-block by a single *super-block constraint*

$$SB_{i,j} \equiv \bigwedge_{d \in \{0,1\}} \bigwedge_{e \in \{0,1\}} SC_{i+d, j+e}.$$

The BDD for a super-block constraint has 647 nodes. A model $\mathcal{M}$ which uses super-block constraints are denoted as $\mathcal{M}+SB$. Recall in Figure 3 that super-cell constraints are needed to connect the super-row and super-column constraints among all models. Hence, we can replace these super-cell constraints with super-block constraints for any models as illustrated in Figure 8.

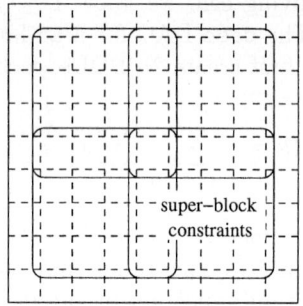

Fig. 8. Arrangement of four super-block constraints in a 9×9 board (super-row and super-column constraints not shown; border constraints are needed for $\mathcal{M}_r$ and $\mathcal{M}_{r+d}$)

4 Experimental Results

In this section, we present the experimental results on $\mathcal{M}_{r+d}$, $\mathcal{M}_{r+d+b}$ and $\mathcal{M}_{r+d+b} + SB$. We first show in Figure 9 the sizes and the time to generate the `case` DAGs for the SR, SRD and SRDB constraints for n from 6 to 20. We include two types of SRDB constraints, namely $SRDB_2$ which is the super-row on the board edge and $SRDB_i$ which is the super-row inside. While the size of the SR constraint is small, both SRD and SRDB have a slow exponential growth. This is because the join of the border and the density function perturbs the "perfect" structure of the underlying SR constraint. However, this problem is not serious because n is still small and in SICStus Prolog, we can share the same DAG between different ad-hoc constraints, Thus, for any fixed n, we only need to generate one `case` DAG for all SR (SRD or SRDB) constraints to share.

Table 3 lists the experimental results. First, all three models perform much better than $\mathcal{M}_0$ and $\mathcal{M}_r$. For example, while $n = 10$ is difficult for $\mathcal{M}_0$ and $\mathcal{M}_r$, it becomes quite easy for the new models. This justifies the integration of the density function and the super-row constraint. However, the density function alone is not enough as we see $\mathcal{M}_{r+d}$ could not solve $n = 11$ within the time limit. Both $\mathcal{M}_{r+d+b}$ and $\mathcal{M}_{r+d+b}+SB$ could solve $n = 11$. We only attempted $n = 12$

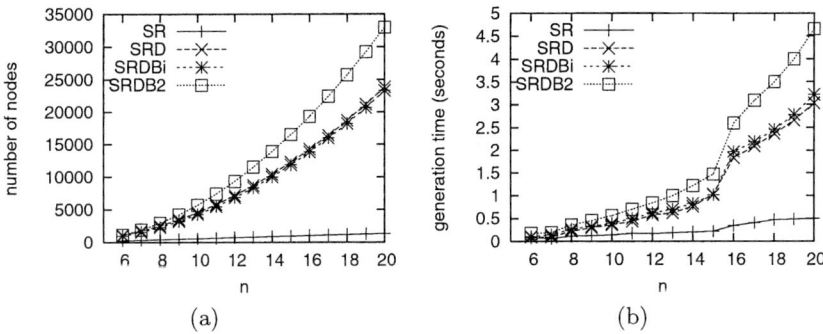

Fig. 9. (a) Number of nodes in the case constraints and (b) generation time of the BDDs for SR, SRD, SRD_i and SRD_2

Table 3. Experimental results on $\mathcal{M}_{r+d}$, $\mathcal{M}_{r+d+b}$ and $\mathcal{M}_{r+d+b} + SB$

n	opt	$\mathcal{M}_{r+d}$			$\mathcal{M}_{r+d+b}$			$\mathcal{M}_{r+d+b} + SB$		
		bt	time	mem	bt	time	mem	bt	time	mem
6	18	881	0.2	5.8	51	0.0	5.6	50	0.0	5.6
7	28	737	0.3	6.1	40	0.0	5.9	36	0.0	5.9
8	36	1881	1.0	6.5	175	0.1	6.1	172	0.1	6.2
9	43	370340	133.0	6.8	4507	2.1	7.0	4224	2.0	6.9
10	54	3304788	1551.5	7.6	75558	45.9	7.2	60010	38.9	10.7
11	64		> 3600.0		1195619	1034.3	7.4	1134526	1013.5	10.9
12	76		-		34235923	28635.8	14.1	33164165	28388.0	12.3

with $\mathcal{M}_{r+d+b}$ and $\mathcal{M}_{r+d+b} + SB$. Both found the maximum density within 8 hours. We also found the improvement by super-block constraints is not very significant.

When the search space is too large, one might try a limited discrepancy search (LDS) [13] to find a (nearly) optimal solution. Informally, w.r.t. our labeling strategy, restricting the discrepancy to k means, on the path leading to the maximum density, there are at most k choice-points in which a low branch (i.e. $y_{i,j} \leq d$) was taken. The assumption behind LDS is that a good variable ordering heuristic made only a few mistakes to find a solution. Intuitively this implies LDS would give a more accurate (or close to optimal) solution if the constraints inside a CSP model are tight. Note that a fairly tight lower bound on the maximum density can be obtained by using the symmetrical version of the still-life problem. Here, we simply want to investigate the differences between the models and effect of propagation on the maximum density.

Table 4 presents the nearest maximal density LDS can find using a discrepancy of 2 for our models. The column *opt* (from [2]) gives the maximal density for different n. Where LDS(2) gives the optimum, it been emphasized in bold. We see that the $\mathcal{M}_0, \mathcal{M}_r, \mathcal{M}_{r+d}$ and $\mathcal{M}_{r+d} + SB$ give the same results and where a dash indicates that LDS failed and was unable to find a solution within a discrepancy of 2. While we do not expect that LDS(2) can give good bounds

Table 4. Experimental results on LDS = 2

n	opt [2]	$\mathcal{M}_0, \mathcal{M}_r, \mathcal{M}_{r+d}, \mathcal{M}_{r+d}+SB$	$\mathcal{M}_{r+d+b}$	$\mathcal{M}_{r+d+b}+SB$
6	18	18	18	18
7	28	27	28	28
8	36	36	36	36
9	43	40	42	42
10	54	47	54	54
11	64	64	64	64
12	76	48	75	75
13	90	77	85	85
14	104	100	100	100
15	119	-	109	109
16	136	-	129	129
17	152	144	144	144
18	171	-	153	153
19	190	-	177	180
20	210	196	196	196

for still-life, it is interesting to note that the models with stronger constraints can find the lower bound more often than those with weaker constraints.

5 Discussion

We show that by using ad-hoc constraints, it is possible to get much more propagation for still-life. The number of backtracks is significantly better than the CP models in [3,4,12]. When comparing with the hybrid CP/IP model[3], the $\mathcal{M}_{r+d+b}+SB$ seems to be comparable (sometimes more pruning and sometimes less). While it is difficult to compare our ad-hoc global constraints with IP, we conjecture that from the results it seems to capture some of the same pruning power. In their CP/IP model, they had to remove some of the IP constraints in order to get results. This must have been because solving the additional IP constraints must have drastically increased the solver time. With the ad-hoc global constraints, as n increases, possibly similar solver effects should creep in that the cost of maintaining global constraints grows faster than the benefit. However, in the results, while the `case` constraint solving costs do increase, it seems to be reasonable.

The best results for still-life are with bucket elimination [2]. This is because of the structure of the life constraints which are quite localized, as such, one can expect that pure CP propagation and search cannot be as good. Bucket elimination however trades time for space and has a growing exponential space requirement. In still-life, it turns out that bucket elimination can still solve larger

---

[3] [4] uses the number of choice-points. Their backtracks should be at least as much as the number of choice-points.

problems than with a pure CP model though this paper narrows the gap. We believe that ideas from this paper are compatible with bucket elimination and this is scope for further work. We have also not investigated the use of more powerful symmetry removal such as SBDS, this is partly because of lack of support for SBDS in SICStus Prolog. Similarly, it might be interesting to investigate a hybrid ad-hoc constraints and IP model. Again because SICStus Prolog is the only CP system available with the case constraint and does not have an integration with an IP solver, we cannot test this. We emphasize that exploiting symmetries and IP models are not a restriction of this paper but one imposed by availability of the case constraint.

Finally, this paper is an instructive demonstration of how to use the case constraint effectively. The case constraint is difficult to use precisely because it is unclear how to build the DAGs. We show an approach using BDDs which work well for problems with 0–1 domains.

References

1. Gardner, M.: The fantastic combinations of John Conway's new solitaire game. Scientific American **223** (1970) 120–123
2. Larrosa, J., Morancho, E., Niso, D.: On the practical applicability of bucket elimination: Still-life as a case study. Journal of Artificial Intelligence Research **23** (2005) 21–440
3. Smith, B.M.: A dual graph translation of a problem in 'life'. In: Principles and Practice of Constraint Programming (CP). (2002) 402–414
4. Bosch, R., Trick, M.: Constraint programming and hybrid formulations for three life designs. In: Intl. Workshop on Integration of AI and OR Techniques in Constraint Programming for Combinatorial Optimization Problems (CP-AI-OR). (2002) 77–91
5. Bessière, C., Règin, J.C.: Arch consistency for general constraint networks: Preliminary results. In: Intl. Joint Conf. on Artificial Intelligence (IJCAI). (1997) 398–404
6. Barták, R.: Filtering algorithms for tabular constraints. In: Colloqium on Implementation of Constraint and Logic Programming Systems (CICLOPS). (2001) 168–182
7. Dao, T., Lallouet, A., Legtchenko, A., Martin, L.: Indexical-based solver learning. In: Principles and Practice of Constraint Programming (CP). (2002) 541–555
8. Cheng, C.K., Lee, J.H.M., Stuckey, P.J.: Box constraint collections for adhoc constraints. In: Principles and Practice of Constraint Programming (CP). (2003) 214–228
9. Beldiceanu, N.: Global constraints as graph properties on structured networks of elementary constraints of the same type. TR T2000-01, SICS (2000)
10. SICStus Prolog 3.12.1 manual. (2005)
11. Bryant, R.E.: Graph-based algorithms for Boolean function manipulation. IEEE Trans. on Comp. **35** (1986) 667–691
12. Petrie, K.E., Smith, B.M., Yorke-Smith, N.: Dynamic symmetry breaking in constraint programming and linear programming hybrids. In: European Starting AI Researcher Symp. (2004)
13. Harvey, W.D., Ginsberg, M.L.: Limited discrepancy search. In: Intl. Joint Conf. on Artificial Intelligence (IJCAI). (1995)

Tractable Clones of Polynomials over Semigroups

Víctor Dalmau[1,*], Ricard Gavaldà[2,**], Pascal Tesson[3,***],
and Denis Thérien[4,†]

[1] Departament de Tecnologia, Universitat Pompeu Fabra
victor.dalmau@upf.edu
[2] Department of Software (LSI), Universitat Politècnica de Catalunya
gavalda@lsi.upc.edu
[3] Département d'Informatique et de Génie Logiciel, Université Laval
pascal.tesson@ift.ulaval.ca
[4] School of Computer Science, McGill University
denis@cs.mcgill.ca

Abstract. We contribute to the algebraic study of the complexity of constraint satisfaction problems. We give a new sufficient condition on a set of relations Γ over a domain S for the tractability of CSP(Γ): if S is a block-group (a particular class of semigroups) of exponent ω and Γ is a set of relations over S preserved by the operation defined by the polynomial $f(x, y, z) = xy^{\omega-1}z$ over S, then CSP(Γ) is tractable. This theorem strictly improves on results of Feder and Vardi and Bulatov et al. and we demonstrate it by reproving an upper bound of Klíma et al.

We also investigate systematically the tractability of CSP(Γ) when Γ is a set of relations closed under operations that are all expressible as polynomials over a finite semigroup S. In particular, if S is a nilpotent group, we show that CSP(Γ) is tractable iff one of these polynomials defines a Malt'sev operation, and conjecture that this holds for all groups.

1 Introduction

Constraint satisfaction problems (CSPs) provide a natural way to study in a unified framework a number of combinatorial problems arising in various areas of computer science. An instance of CSP consists of a list of variables, a domain,

---

[*] Research partially supported by the MCyT under grants TIC 2002-04470-C03 and TIC 2002-04019-C03, the EU PASCAL Network of Excellence, IST-2002-506778, and the MODNET Marie Curie Research Training Network, MRTN-CT-2004-512234.
[**] Research partially supported by the EU PASCAL Network of Excellence, IST-2002-506778. Partly done while visiting McGill University, supported in part by the AIRE and ACI programs of the DURSI of the Generalitat de Catalunya.
[***] Research supported by NSERC and the Alexander von Humboldt Foundation.
[†] Research supported in part by NSERC, FQRNT and the von Humboldt Foundation.

and a set of constraints relating the variables and we ask whether the variables can be assigned domain values such that all constraints are satisfied.

In general, the CSP problem is NP-complete and one thus tries to identify tractable (i.e., polynomial-time solvable) restrictions of it. In particular, much attention has been paid to the case where the relations available to construct constraints lie in a fixed finite set Γ of relations over a finite domain. The CSP *dichotomy conjecture* states that for any such Γ the problem CSP(Γ) is always either tractable or NP-complete [10]. An algebraic approach has been particularly successful in making progress on this question [12,11]: it was shown that the tractability of CSP(Γ) depends on the algebraic properties of the set of operations under which all relations of Γ are closed. This has lead to the identification of broad classes of sets of relations (called "islands of tractability") for which CSP(Γ) is known to have polynomial-time algorithms [2,7,8,10,5] and has validated the dichotomy conjecture for domains of size two [16] and three [1].

A number of islands of tractability identified thus far have a common structure: they can be recast as constraint languages Γ invariant under a certain polynomial over a semigroup. To illustrate this, consider the tractable cases in the boolean domain, which were completely identified by Schaefer [16]. Of the six tractable families (0-valid, 1-valid, horn, dual horn, bijunctive and affine [16]), only the class of bijunctive problems cannot be accounted for in this framework. For example, the class of horn problems corresponds to the sets of boolean relations invariant under the polynomial $x \cdot y$, where $\cdot$ is the logical AND.

Additionally, some of the broadest conditions for tractability can also be expressed in terms of invariance under a polynomial over a semigroup. Indeed, Feder and Vardi [10] have shown that if a set Γ of relations over a finite group G is *coset-generating* (i.e. every R in Γ is a coset of a power of the group), then CSP(Γ) is tractable. Equivalently, Γ is coset-generating iff it is closed under the ternary operation $t(x, y, z) = xy^{-1}z$ where multiplication is taken in the group[1]. Another island of tractability uncovered by Bulatov, Jeavons, and Volkov [5] states that CSP(Γ) is tractable if Γ is closed under the multiplication of a particular type of semigroup called a block-group. This result generalizes a previous result of Jeavons, Cohen, and Gyssens [12] where multiplication is taken in a semilattice. In light of these results, we consider more systematically classes Γ of relations whose closure properties can, as above, be expressed using polynomials over a semigroup. Our long term objective is to classify all corresponding problems CSP(Γ) as either tractable or NP-complete.

By focusing on polynomials over semigroups (instead of considering general arbitrary operations) we can still cover a number of natural cases and, additionally, are able to potentially use the large corpus of known results in semigroup theory. This connection can help us tackle one of the most difficult questions in the study of tractable CSP's: that of combining different sources of tractability. Indeed, despite the large spectrum of results in the field, the algorithmic principles behind all known tractable cases are quite limited: every tractable

---

[1] In fact, [10] introduce the notion of *coset-generating operations* but it is more convenient for our discussion to use the relational counterpart of their definition.

case of CSP is solvable by either (1) enforcing some sort of local consistency, (2) efficiently encoding (potentially) large relations, or (3) combining the first two methods. Most of the recently identified tractable families fall into this third category, and one can expect that much of the future progress in the study of the complexity of CSPs is likely to come from a better understanding of the interaction between the different sources of tractability. Semigroup theory has developed many tools that allow one to view complex semigroups as "combinations" of simpler ones, which in the constraint satisfaction world might correspond to combining different sources of tractability.

In Section 3, we give a new sufficient condition for the tractability of CSP(Γ). We show that if S is a block-group of exponent ω and Γ is a set of relations over S that are preserved by the ternary operation $f(x,y,z) = xy^{\omega-1}z$ then CSP(Γ) is tractable. Our algorithm combines in a novel way the methods used in the results of [10,5] just cited and can be applied to reprove an upper bound of [13] which could not be inferred from the previously known islands of tractability.

In Section 4, we consider necessary conditions for the tractability of CSP(Γ) when Γ's closure operations are expressed as polynomials over a semigroup S. Results are given in terms of clones, or sets of such operations – definitions are given in Section 2. For technical reasons, we restrict ourselves to idempotent clones, which are known to still determine the complexity of CSP(Γ). We show:

– If S is a commutative semigroup the sufficient condition given by the previous theorem is also necessary: if $\mathcal{C}$ is a nontrivial idempotent clone of polynomials over S, then $\mathcal{C}$ is tractable iff it contains the operation $xy^{\omega-1}z$.
– If S is a nilpotent group and $\mathcal{C}$ is a nontrivial clone of polynomials over S then $\mathcal{C}$ is tractable iff it contains a Malt'sev operation. This is a type of operations of which $xy^{\omega-1}z$ is a prime example and that is known to imply tractability [2,3]. We conjecture that this in fact holds for any finite group.

2 Preliminaries and Background

2.1 Finite Semigroups

A *semigroup* is a set S with a binary associative operation that we denote multiplicatively as $\cdot_S$ or $\cdot$ when no ambiguity exists. An element $s \in S$ is said to be *idempotent* if it is its own square, i.e. $s^2 = s$. In this paper we are solely concerned with finite semigroups, and in that case there exists a minimal integer ω such that for all $s \in S$ the element s^ω is idempotent. We call ω the *exponent* of the semigroup. If S is a group then s^ω is the identity element of the group since it is the only idempotent element.

A class of finite semigroups **V** is a *pseudo-variety* if it is closed under finite direct products and formation of subsemigroups and homomorphic images. Some of the pseudo-varieties that we will use are:

– **SL**, the pseudo-variety of finite *semilattices*, i.e. of commutative semigroups in which every element is idempotent;

- **Ab**, the pseudo-variety of finite Abelian groups;
- **BG**, the pseudo-variety of *block-groups*, or semigroups that satisfy the identity $(x^\omega y^\omega)^\omega = (y^\omega x^\omega)^\omega$.

Our main theorem concerns block-groups, an important class in the theory of finite semigroups that admits a number of interesting characterizations [15]. We state some of their relevant properties. Most useful to us will be the following: the finite semigroup S is *not* a block-group iff it contains two distinct idempotents e, f such that $ef = e$ and $fe = f$ or such that $ef = f$ and $fe = e$. It can easily be deduced that semilattices and groups are special cases of block-groups, but not all block-groups are in the pseudo-variety generated by semilattices and groups.

Let $E_S : \{s^\omega : s \in S\}$ be the set of idempotents of S. If $S \in \mathbf{BG}$, the subsemigroup of S generated by E_S satisfies $(xy)^\omega = (yx)^\omega$. This can be used to show that if two sequences $e_1, \ldots, e_n$ and $f_1, \ldots, f_m$ of idempotents of S satisfy $\{e_1, \ldots, e_n\} = \{f_1, \ldots, f_m\}$ (as sets), then $(e_1 \ldots e_n)^\omega = (f_1 \ldots f_m)^\omega$.

For any semigroup S and any idempotent $e \in S$, the set of elements s such that $es = se = s$ forms a subgroup G_e with identity element e. For all $s \in G_e$ we have $s^\omega = e$ and thus $s^{\omega+1} = s$. We will say that $s \in S$ is a *subgroup element* if it lies in some G_e. We will say that a semigroup is a *union of groups* if all its elements are subgroup elements.

2.2 CSPs and Universal Algebra

Let D be a finite domain and Γ be a finite set of relations over D. In the sequel, D and Γ will always denote respectively a finite domain and a finite set of relations over that domain. The constraint satisfaction problem over Γ, denoted CSP(Γ) is the following decision problem. The input consists of a list of variables $x_1, \ldots, x_n$ and constraints that are pairs (S_i, R_i) where R_i is a k_i-ary relation in Γ and S_i, the scope of the constraint, is an ordered list of k_i variables. We ask whether the variables can be assigned values in D such that every constraint is satisfied. It is conjectured that for any Γ the problem CSP(Γ) is either tractable or NP-complete [10]. Over the last ten years, a lot of ground was covered towards establishing this conjecture using an algebraic approach pioneered by [12] that considers the closure properties of Γ, as we next explain formally.

An *operation* f on D is simply a function $f : D^t \to D$. We naturally extend f so that it takes as inputs t k-tuples $\overline{a_1}, \ldots, \overline{a_t}$ of values in D by defining

$$f(\overline{a_1}, \ldots, \overline{a_t}) = (f(a_{11}, \ldots, a_{t1}), \ldots, f(a_{1k}, \ldots, a_{tk})).$$

We say that a k-ary relation R over D is *closed under* f if for any t k-tuples of R, say $\overline{a_1}, \ldots, \overline{a_t}$ we also have $f(\overline{a_1}, \ldots, \overline{a_t}) \in R$.

By extension we say that Γ is closed under f if every relation of Γ is closed under f, and denote as Pol(Γ) the set of all such finitary operations f (the notation is due to the fact that every such f is called a *polymorphism* of Γ). The fundamental link to the complexity of CSPs is the following theorem.

Theorem 1 ([11]). *If Γ_1, Γ_2 are sets of relations over D such that* Pol(Γ_1) $\subseteq$ Pol(Γ_2) *then* CSP(Γ_2) *is polynomial-time reducible to* CSP(Γ_1).

The following is a crucial property of all the sets of the form $\text{Pol}(\Gamma)$.

Lemma 2 ([12]). *For any set of relations Γ over D: (1) $\text{Pol}(\Gamma)$ contains all the projection functions $\pi_{i,n}(x_1,\ldots,x_n) = x_i$. (2) If g is a k-ary operation in $\text{Pol}(\Gamma)$ and $f_1,\ldots,f_k$ are t-ary operations in $\text{Pol}(\Gamma)$, then their composition*

$$g(f_1,\ldots,f_k)(x_1,\ldots,x_t) = g(f_1(x_1,\ldots,x_t),\ldots,f_k(x_1,\ldots,x_t))$$

is also in $\text{Pol}(\Gamma)$.

Note that from (1) and (2) it follows that $\text{Pol}(\Gamma)$ is also closed under identification of variables, since this can be obtained by composition with projections. In universal algebra lingo, a set of operations containing all the projections and closed under composition is called a *clone*. For a set of operations F, we denote by $\langle F \rangle$ the clone generated by F, i.e. the smallest clone containing F.

Using the connection between $\text{CSP}(\Gamma)$ and $\text{Pol}(\Gamma)$ given by Theorem 1, we say that a clone $\mathcal{C}$ is *tractable* if $\text{CSP}(\Gamma)$ is tractable for every Γ such that $\mathcal{C} \subseteq \text{Pol}(\Gamma)$. On the other hand, we say that $\mathcal{C}$ is NP-complete if there exists a set of relations Γ such that $\mathcal{C} \subseteq \text{Pol}(\Gamma)$ and $\text{CSP}(\Gamma)$ is NP-complete.

We can thus view the task of resolving the CSP dichotomy conjecture as that of proving that any clone is either tractable or NP-complete. An important simplification is known [6]: in order to obtain such a classification it suffices in fact to consider clones in which every operation f is *idempotent*, i.e. satisfies $f(x,\ldots,x) = x$. We call these the *idempotent clones*.

The first half of this task is to identify tractable clones and many such islands of tractability have already been identified in this way. For example, a ternary operation $M(x,y,z)$ is said to be *Malt'sev* if it satisfies $M(x,x,y) = y$ and $M(x,y,y) = x$: Bulatov showed that any clone containing a Malt'sev operation is tractable [2,3]. This very general result covers an important special case first identified as tractable by [10]: Suppose that the domain D is a finite group and that any k-ary relation of Γ is a coset of a subgroup of D^k. We then say that Γ is *coset generating*, and it can be verified from the definition of a coset that Γ is closed under the operation $M(x,y,z) = x \cdot y^{-1} \cdot z$ (where multiplication and inverse are those of the group D). This operation is Malt'sev since $M(x,x,y) = xx^{-1}y = y$ and $M(x,y,y) = xy^{-1}y = x$ as required.

Bulatov et al. [5] considered the tractability of clones generated by a semigroup, i.e. generated by the binary operation $x \cdot_S y$ for some semigroup S. They showed that the clone $\langle \cdot_S \rangle$ is tractable if S is a block-group and NP-complete otherwise. This result extends another well-known result stating that any Γ closed under the multiplication in a semilattice is tractable [12]. In both cases, it is shown that such CSPs are solved by an arc-consistency algorithm [5,8,12].

For the remainder of this paper, we focus on clones whose operations can all be described by expressions over a finite semigroup S. Formally, a *polynomial* P over the semigroup S is simply a finite sequence $P = x_{i_1} \cdots x_{i_m}$ of (possibly repeating) variables. A polynomial containing k distinct variables naturally defines a k-ary function, but in order to express the projections with such polynomials we allow for unused variables and e.g. represent the projection $\pi_{i,n}(x_1,\ldots,x_n)$

by the polynomial x_i. We say that a clone is a *clone of polynomials* if every operation in the clone can be represented in this way. Note that the composition of polynomials is again a polynomial so that the clone generated by a set of polynomials is indeed a clone of polynomials.

3 A Polynomial that Guarantees Tractability

Our main goal in this section is to prove the following sufficient condition for the tractability of a clone.

Theorem 3. *If S is a block-group and C is a clone containing the polynomial $xy^{\omega-1}z$ then C is tractable.*

Note that when S is a group, this condition is equivalent to saying that every Γ such that $C \subseteq \text{Pol}(\Gamma)$ is coset-generating. Also if C is generated by $\cdot_S$ for some block-group S then in particular it must contain the polynomial $xy^{\omega-1}z$, which can be obtained from xy by composition. Hence this result generalizes the results of [10,5] mentioned before.

Proof (Theorem 3). Let $\mathcal{P}$ be an instance of CSP(Γ), with $C \subseteq \text{Pol}(\Gamma)$. If $\mathcal{P}$ has any solution then it has one in which every variable x_i has a value a_i that is a subgroup element. Indeed, by the closure properties of Γ, if $\bar{a}$ is a solution, then $\overline{aa}^{\omega-1}\bar{a} = \bar{a}^{\omega+1}$ also is and every component of the latter is a subgroup element.

We will give a polynomial-time algorithm to solve $\mathcal{P}$, which works in two stages. In the first stage, we assign to every variable x_i some subgroup G_{e_i} such that if $\mathcal{P}$ is satisfiable then it is satisfiable by an assignment that sets each x_i to a value in G_{e_i}. We will do this by using an arc-consistency procedure (see e.g. [5,8,12]). In the second stage we reduce the CSP(Γ) problem to an instance of CSP(Λ), where Λ is a coset-generating set of relations over the direct product of the subgroups G_e, and then solve this CSP with the algorithm of [10].

We begin by enforcing arc-consistency for $\mathcal{P}$: to every variable x_i, we associate a set of possible values $V_i \subseteq S$. We find the largest V_i such that for any constraint of $\mathcal{P}$, say $(\{x_{i_1}, \ldots, x_{i_r}\}, R)$ and for any value $a_{i_j} \in V_{i_j}$ there exist $a_{i_k} \in V_{i_k}$ s.t. $(a_{i_1}, \ldots, a_{i_r}) \in R$. It is well known that this can be done in polynomial time by initializing each V_i to S and gradually removing values that violate the requirement above. Also, if any V_i becomes empty then $\mathcal{P}$ has no solution.

If $V_1, \ldots, V_n$ are the sets produced by the arc-consistency algorithm, we define e_i to be the idempotent $(\prod_{a \in V_i} a^\omega)^\omega$. Recall that since S is a block group, the value of a product of the form $(s_1^\omega \ldots s_t^\omega)^\omega$ depends solely on the set $\{s_1, \ldots, s_t\}$ and our definition of e_i is thus sound.

Lemma 4. *If $\mathcal{P}$ has a solution then it has one in which each variable x_i is assigned a value a_i that lies in the subgroup G_{e_i} where the $e_i = (\prod_{a \in V_i} a^\omega)^\omega$ are the idempotents obtained through the arc-consistency algorithm.*

Proof. Let $\bar{b} \in S^n$ be any solution to $\mathcal{P}$ and $\bar{e} = (e_1, \ldots, e_n)$. We claim that $\bar{a} = \bar{e}\bar{b}\bar{e}$ is then a solution of $\mathcal{P}$ satisfying $a_i \in G_{e_i}$ for all i.

Since Γ is closed under the operation $xy^{\omega-1}z$, it is also closed under $x^\omega z$ (by identifying x and y) and under $x^\omega y^\omega z$ (by substituting $y^\omega z$ for z in the previous polynomial). By iterating this procedure, we get that for any m, Γ is closed under the polynomial $H(x_1, \ldots, x_{m+1}) = (x_1^\omega \ldots x_m^\omega)^\omega x_{m+1}$ and, similarly, under the polynomial $F(x_1, \ldots, x_m) = (x_1^\omega \ldots x_m^\omega)^\omega x_{m+1}(x_1^\omega \ldots x_m^\omega)^\omega$.

Consider any constraint of $\mathcal{P}$, e.g. $(\{x_{i_1}, \ldots, x_{i_k}\}, R)$. By assumption, we have $\bar{c} = (b_{i_1}, \ldots, b_{i_k}) \in R$. For a k-tuple $\bar{t}$, let us denote for the moment as $\bar{t}[j]$ the jth component of $\bar{t}$. Since we have enforced arc-consistency, we know that for each $1 \le j \le k$ and any value $s \in V_{i_j}$ there exists some k-tuple $\bar{t} \in R$ with $\bar{t}[j] = s$. If $\{\bar{t}_1, \ldots, \bar{t}_m\}$ are the k-tuples of R obtained by finding such witnesses for each j and each $s \in V_{i_j}$ we get $V_{i_j} = \{\bar{t}_r[j] : r = 1 \ldots m\}$. We can thus deduce that $e_{i_j} = (\prod_{r=1 \ldots m} \bar{t}_r[j])^\omega$ for each j. By the closure properties of Γ we also know that $F(\bar{t}_1, \ldots, \bar{t}_m, \bar{c})$ is in R. Since we have

$$F(\bar{t}_1, \ldots, \bar{t}_m, \bar{c})[j] = (\bar{t}_1[j]^\omega \ldots \bar{t}_n[j]^\omega)^\omega \bar{c}[j] (\bar{t}_1[j]^\omega \ldots \bar{t}_n[j]^\omega)^\omega = e_{i_j} b_{i_j} e_{i_j},$$

we get that $\bar{e}\,\bar{b}\,\bar{e}$ is indeed a solution to $\mathcal{P}$. Moreover, since each e_i is idempotent, we have $e_i a_i = e_i e_i b_i e_i = e_i b_i e_i = a_i$ and similarly $a_i e_i = a_i$. Thus, $a_i \in G_{e_i}$, as claimed. □

Thus, in polynomial time, we can associate to each variable x_i a subgroup G_{e_i} such that if $\text{CSP}(\Gamma)$ has any solution then it has one where x_i is assigned a value in G_{e_i}. Let G be the direct product $\prod G_e$ where the product is taken over the idempotents e of S. For each idempotent $e \in S$, the group G has an obvious subgroup isomorphic to G_e and we will identify any element lying in one of these subgroups G_e of G with the corresponding element in the subgroup G_e of S. For any k-ary relation $R \in \Gamma$ and any k-idempotents $e_{i_1}, \ldots, e_{i_k}$ (not necessarily distinct) we define the relation $R_{e_{i_1}, \ldots, e_{i_k}} \subseteq G^k$ as consisting of tuples $(a_1, \ldots, a_k)$ such that[2]

1. a_j lies in the subgroup G_{e_j} of G;
2. $(a_1, \ldots, a_k) \in R$ when we view the a_j's as elements of S.

The crucial observation is that each $R_{e_{i_1}, \ldots, e_{i_k}}$ is coset-generating, i.e. closed under the operation $xy^{\omega-1}z$ over the group G. Indeed, if $\bar{a}, \bar{b}, \bar{c}$ are k-tuples of $R_{e_{i_1}, \ldots, e_{i_k}}$ then certainly the jth component of $\bar{a}\bar{b}^{\omega-1}\bar{c}$ also lies in the subgroup G_{e_j}. Furthermore, $\bar{a}\bar{b}^{\omega-1}\bar{c} \in R_{e_{i_1}, \ldots, e_{i_k}}$ since R is closed under $xy^{\omega-1}z$.

Let $\Lambda = \{R_{e_{i_1}, \ldots, e_{i_k}} : R \in \Gamma; e_{i_j} \in S \text{ idempotent}\}$ be the set of all such relations over G. Given an instance of $\text{CSP}(\Gamma)$ where every variable has been restricted to lie in some particular subgroup we can naturally construct an instance of $\text{CSP}(\Lambda)$ that will be satisfiable iff the instance of $\text{CSP}(\Gamma)$ can be satisfied. Since Λ is coset-generating, we can solve $\text{CSP}(\Lambda)$ in polynomial time. □

As we mentioned earlier, the island of tractability uncovered by this theorem subsumes the tractability results for coset-generating relations of [10] and for

---

[2] Alternatively, we could view this relation as multi-sorted in the sense of [4].

clones generated by a block-group [5]. We give an application of this theorem to a problem studied in [13]: for a finite semigroup S, let EQN^*_S denote the problem of determining whether a system of equations over S has a solution. Note that by introducing dummy variables we can assume that a system of equations over S consists only of equations of the form $xy = z$ or $x = y$ where x, y, z are variables or constants. We can thus think of the problem EQN^*_S as $\text{CSP}(\Gamma_S)$ where Γ_S is the set of relations definable by such an equation over S.

Theorem 5 ([13]). *Let EQN^*_S be the problem of testing whether a system of equations over the semigroup S has a solution. If S is in* **SL** $\vee$ **Ab** *(the pseudo-variety generated by* **SL** *and* **Ab***) then EQN^*_S lies in P.*

Proof. Any semigroup in **SL** $\vee$ **Ab** is commutative and satisfies $x^{\omega+1} = x$ since both semilattices and Abelian groups have these properties. Consider an equation over S of the form $x_1 x_2 = x_3$. If (a_1, a_2, a_3), (b_1, b_2, b_3), and (c_1, c_2, c_3) are solutions of this equation then we have by commutativity

$$a_1 b_1^{\omega-1} c_1 a_2 b_2^{\omega-1} c_2 = a_1 a_2 (b_1 b_2)^{\omega-1} c_1 c_2 = a_3 b_3^{\omega-1} c_3.$$

Similarly, if we consider an equation in which a constant appears, e.g. $sx_1 = x_2$ then since $s = s^{\omega+1}$ we get $sa_1 b_1^{\omega-1} c_1 = sa_1 (sb_1)^{\omega-1} sc_1 = a_2 b_2^{\omega-1} c_2$.

Thus Γ_S is closed under the polynomial $xy^{\omega-1}z$ over the block-group S and EQN^*_S is tractable by Theorem 3. □

One cannot directly infer the tractability of EQN^*_S for $S \in$ **SL** $\vee$ **Ab** by simply using the tractability of Malt'sev operations or the tractability of clones generated by a block group so the result of Theorem 3 seems required in this case. It is worth noting that if S is a finite monoid then EQN^*_S is NP-complete when S is not in **SL** $\vee$ **Ab** [13]. An alternative proof of this latter fact was given in [14] using an elegant universal algebra argument.

4 Tractable Clones of Polynomials

We have just shown that for a clone of polynomials over a block-group S to be tractable, a sufficient condition is that it contains the operation $xy^{\omega-1}z$. In this section, we consider necessary conditions for tractability. Our goal is to eventually be able to classify all clones of polynomials over any S as either tractable or NP-complete. The following theorem shows that the question is only of real interest if S is a block-group.

Theorem 6. *If S is not a block-group, any clone of polynomials over S is NP-complete.*

We omit the proof, which can be obtained by suitably adapting the argument of Corollary 3.2 in [5].

We also provide a condition on clones of polynomials that guarantees NP-completeness over any semigroup. We need an extra semigroup-theoretic notion:

the *subgroup exponent* η of the semigroup S is the least common multiple of the exponents of the subgroups in S. When S is a union of groups, we have $\eta = \omega$ but in general we can only say that η is a divisor of ω. We say that an operation (polynomial) $x_{i_1}^{n_1} \cdots x_{i_r}^{n_r}$ is a *d-factor* if $d > 1$, d is a divisor of η (possibly η itself), and $|\{1 \leq i \leq r : d|n_i\}| = r - 1$, that is, if every n_i but one is divisible by d. We say that the clone $\mathcal{C}$ is a d-factor if every operation in $\mathcal{C}$ is a d-factor.

Theorem 7. *If $\mathcal{C}$ is a d-factor for some d then $\mathcal{C}$ is NP-complete.*

Proof. We have that $\eta = da$ for some $1 \leq a < \omega$. Since η is the least common multiple of the exponents of all subgroup elements of S, there exists some subgroup element $s \in S$ with exponent η' (i.e. $s^{\eta'}$ is idempotent) such that $lcm(\eta', a) = ka$ for some $k > 1$. Notice that k must divide d. Notice also that for every $1 \leq l < k$, η' does not divide la. Consequently s^a has exponent k.

Consider the subgroup A of S generated by s^a, that is $A = \{s^a, s^{2a}, \ldots, s^{ka}\}$. Clearly $|A| \geq 2$. Let $f(x_1, \ldots, x_q) = x_{i_1}^{n_1} \cdots x_{i_r}^{n_r}$ be any operation in $\mathcal{C}$. First, note that A forms a subuniverse for f: if $a_1, \ldots, a_q \in A$, $f(a_1, \ldots, a_q)$ is in A too. Furthermore, the polynomial $x_{i_1}^{n_1} \cdots x_{i_r}^{n_r}$ is a d-factor so there exists some $1 \leq j \leq r$ such that d divides n_i for every $1 \leq i \leq r$ with $i \neq j$. If again $a_1, \ldots, a_q \in A$, each a_i is $a_i = s^{l_i a}$ for some l_i. So we have $a_{t_i}^{n_i} = s^{l_{t_i} a n_i} = s^{m_i \eta}$, for some m_i, and then $f(a_1, \ldots, a_q) = s^{m\eta + l_{t_j} a n_j}$ for some $m \geq 0$, a value that depends only on x_j. Therefore, if g is the restriction g of f to A, we have $g(x_1, \ldots, x_q) = s^{m\eta} x_{t_j}^{n_j}$. It is easy to see that $s^{m\eta} x^{n_j}$ is one-to-one over A. Let $s^{k_1 a}$ and $s^{k_2 a}$ be two different elements in A and let $s^{m\eta + k_1 a n_j}$, $s^{m\eta + k_2 a n_j}$ be their corresponding images. In order to be identical, ka has to divide $(k_1 - k_2)a n_j$, or equivalently k has to divide $(k_1 - k_2) n_j$. First notice that since $s^{k_1 a}$ and $s^{k_2 a}$ are different, k cannot divide $k_1 - k_2$. Furthermore, we shall show that $gcd(k, n_j) = 1$. Let p be any common divisor to k and n_j. Since p divides k, it also divides d and then it also divides n_i for every i such that $1 \leq i \neq j \leq r$. If p also divides n_j then it must divide $\eta + 1$, in contradiction with the fact that p divides η.

Summarizing we have shown that there exists a set, namely A, of cardinality at least 2, that is a subuniverse of every operation in $\mathcal{C}$. Furthermore, for every operation $f(x_1, \ldots, x_r)$ in $\mathcal{C}$, the restriction $f_{|A}(x_1, \ldots, x_r)$ of f to A is equivalent to $g(x_j)$ for some one-to-one function $g : A \to A$. It is well known that this implies that $\mathcal{C}$ is NP-complete. □

In the next two subsections we will see that in the cases of commutative semigroups and nilpotent groups, an idempotent clone of polynomials is tractable iff it is not a d-factor.

4.1 The Commutative Case

As we mentioned in Section 2, in order to understand the tractability of clones, it suffices to consider idempotent ones. We concentrate on idempotent clones from now on; this allows us to consider only unions of groups.

Lemma 8. *Let S be a semigroup and $\mathcal{C}$ a nontrivial, idempotent clone over S. Then S is a union of groups and for every polynomial $x_{i_1}^{\alpha_1} \ldots x_{i_m}^{\alpha_m}$ in $\mathcal{C}$, $\sum \alpha_j$ is congruent with 1 modulo ω.*

Proof. Take any operation in $\mathcal{C}$ other than a projection, and suppose it is defined by the polynomial $x_{i_1}^{\alpha_1} \ldots x_{i_m}^{\alpha_m}$. This operation is idempotent if $\mathcal{C}$ is, so the semigroup S must satisfy $s^{\sum \alpha_j} = s$ for all s. Consequently, S must be a union of groups. Furthermore $\sum \alpha_j$ is congruent with 1 modulo ω for otherwise we contradict the minimality of the exponent ω. $\square$

So in the proofs of the rest of the section we will implicitly assume that S is a union of groups and that the polynomials in $\mathcal{C}$ satisfy the condition above.

Theorem 9. *Let S be a commutative semigroup and let $\mathcal{C}$ be a nontrivial idempotent clone of polynomials over S. If $\mathcal{C}$ is not a d-factor for any d, then it contains $xy^{\omega-1}z$.*

Proof. By Lemma 8 S is a union of groups, and is commutative, so we can assume that for every polynomial $x_1^{n_1} \ldots, x_r^{n_r}$ all x_i's are different. Furthermore, since $x^{\omega+1} = x$, every two polynomials $x_1^{n_1} \cdots x_r^{n_r}$ and $x_1^{n_1'} \cdots x_r^{n_r'}$ such that for every $1 \leq i \leq r$, $n_i \equiv n_i'$ mod ω, denote the same operation. We sometimes allow negative indices n_i in an expression, meaning by that any positive integer of the form $n_i + n\omega$. Note also that since we are dealing with unions of groups, the subgroup exponent of S is simply its exponent ω.

We need the following auxiliary lemma.

Lemma 10. *Let $x_1^{n_1} \cdots x_r^{n_r}$ be any operation in $\mathcal{C}$, let $1 \leq i \neq j \leq r$, let $a = \gcd(n_i n_j, \omega)$, and let $r \geq 1$. Then $x^{ra} y^{\omega - 2ra + 1} z^{ra}$ belongs to $\mathcal{C}$.*

Proof. First notice that we can identify and rename variables in the expression $x_1^{n_1} \cdots x_r^{n_r}$ to obtain in $\mathcal{C}$ the expression

$$y^{n_1} \cdots y^{n_{i-1}} x^{n_i} y^{n_{i+1}} \cdots y^{n_{j-1}} z^{n_j} y^{n_{j+1}} \cdots y^{n_r},$$

which is equivalent to $x^{n_i} y^{\omega - n_i - n_j + 1} z^{n_j}$. By a further replacement, the expression $(y^{n_i} y^{\omega - n_i - n_j + 1} x^{n_j})^{n_i} y^{\omega - n_i - n_j + 1} (z^{n_i} y^{\omega - n_i - n_j + 1} y^{n_j})^{n_j}$ also belongs to $\mathcal{C}$. Setting $c = n_i n_j$, this can be rewritten as as $x^c y^{\omega - 2c + 1} z^c$. Now we will show that for every $m \geq 1$ the expression

$$x_1^{c^m} \cdots x_{2^m-1}^{c^m} y^{\omega - 2^m c^m + 1} z_1^{c^m} \cdots z_{2^m-1}^{c^m}$$

belongs to $\mathcal{C}$. We will show it by induction on m. The case $m = 1$ has already been proven. Let us assume that the statement holds for m. Then by identification and composition we construct the expression

$$(x_1^{c^m} \cdots x_{2^m-1}^{c^m} \quad y^{\omega - 2^m c^m + 1} x_{2^m-1+1}^{c^m} \cdots x_{2^m}^{c^m})^c y^{\omega - 2c + 1}$$
$$\cdot (z_1^{c^m} \cdots z_{2^m-1}^{c^m} y^{\omega - 2^m c^m + 1} z_{2^m-1+1}^{c^m} \cdots z_{2^m}^{c^m})^c$$
$$= x_1^{c^{m+1}} \cdots x_{2^m}^{c^{m+1}} y^{\omega - 2^{m+1} c^{m+1} + 1} z_1^{c^{m+1}} \cdots z_{2^m}^{c^{m+1}}.$$

We are now almost done. There exists some $l \geq 1$ such that $c^{2l} \equiv c^l \mod \omega$. Since $\gcd(c^l, \omega) = \gcd(c, \omega) = a$ we have that for every $r \geq 1$, there exists some integers α, β such that $\alpha c^l + \beta \omega = ra$. We can also assume that $\alpha \geq 0$. Fix some n such that $2^{nl-1} \geq \alpha$. By setting $m = nl$ we can infer that the expression

$$x_1^{c^{nl}} \cdots x_{2^{nl}-1}^{c^{nl}} y^{\omega - 2^{nl} c^{nl} + 1} z_1^{c^{nl}} \cdots z_{2^{nl}-1}^{c^{nl}}$$

belongs to $\mathcal{C}$, and consequently that the expression

$$\overbrace{x^{c^{nl}} \cdots x^{c^{nl}}}^{\alpha} y^{c^{nl}} \cdots y^{c^{nl}} y^{\omega - 2^{nl} c^{nl} + 1} y^{c^{nl}} \cdots y^{c^{nl}} \overbrace{z^{c^{nl}} \cdots z^{c^{nl}}}^{\alpha},$$

obtained by identification and renaming of variables also belongs to $\mathcal{C}$. This becomes $x^b y^{\omega - 2b + 1} z^b$ if we set $b = \alpha c^{nl}$. Finally notice that

$$\alpha c^{nl} \equiv \alpha c^l \equiv ra \mod \omega. \qquad \square$$

We now continue the proof of Theorem 9. Assume that $\mathcal{C}$ is not a d-factor for every divisor $d > 1$ of ω. We will show that $xy^{\omega-1}z$ is in $\mathcal{C}$. Let $p_1, \ldots, p_k$ be the set of prime divisors of ω strictly larger than 1. We shall show by induction that for every $1 \leq l \leq k$, there exists some a such that $\gcd(a, p_1 \times \cdots \times p_l) = 1$ and such that $x^a y^{\omega - 2a + 1} z^a$ belongs to $\mathcal{C}$ (*). Notice that the statement follows from $l = k$ and Lemma 10 since in this case $\gcd(a, \omega) = \gcd(a \times a, \omega) = 1$. The case $l = 1$ is easy. Since $\mathcal{C}$ is nontrivial it contains an operation $x_1^{n_1} \ldots x_r^{n_r}$ and some $i \neq j$ such that p_1 does not divide n_i and does not divide n_j. Consequently p_1 does not divide $a = \gcd(\omega, n_i \times n_j)$. By Lemma 10, $x^a y^{\omega - 2a + 1} z^a$ belongs to $\mathcal{C}$. Assume now that statement (*) holds for $l < k$. We shall show that it also holds for $l+1$. By induction hypothesis there exists some a with $\gcd(a, p_1 \times \cdots \times p_l) = 1$ such that $x^a y^{\omega - 2a + 1} z^a$ belongs to $\mathcal{C}$. Also, by a reasoning analogous to the case $l = 1$ we can infer that since $\mathcal{C}$ is not a p_{l+1}-factor we have that there exists some b not divisible by p_{l+1} such that $x^b y^{\omega - 2b + 1} z^b$. We can also assume that $p_1 \times \cdots \times p_l$ divides b.

Let us consider two cases: if p_{l+1} does not divide a then we are done since we have that $\gcd(a, p_1 \times \cdots \times p_{l+1}) = 1$. Otherwise, we proceed as follows. Notice that the operation $x^a (x^b y^{\omega - 2b + 1} z^b)^{\omega - 2a + 1} z^a$ belongs to $\mathcal{C}$ since it is obtained by composition and identification of variables. Notice also that if we set $c = a + b(\omega - 2a + 1)$ the previous expression is equivalent to $x^c y^{\omega - 2c + 1} z^c$. It is easy to see that none of $p_1, \ldots, p_{l+1}$ divides c and consequently $\gcd(c, p_1 \times \cdots \times p_{l+1}) = 1$. To see this, note that for every $1 \leq l' \leq l$, we have that $p_{l'}$ divides b (and consequently $b(\omega - 2a + 1)$) but not a. Consequently $p_{l'}$ cannot divide its sum. Similarly since p_{l+1} divides a, it cannot divide $\omega - 2a + 1$ (since otherwise it would divide $\omega + 1$ in contradiction with the fact that it divides ω). Thus, p_{l+1} does not divide $b(\omega - 2a + 1)$, so it cannot divide c. $\qquad \square$

We obtain the following corollary from Theorems 7 and 9, plus the fact that the operation $xy^{\omega-1}z$ implies tractability.

Corollary 11. *Let S be a commutative semigroup and $\mathcal{C}$ a nontrivial, idempotent clone of polynomials over S. Then the following are equivalent:*

- $\mathcal{C}$ is tractable.
- $\mathcal{C}$ is not a d-factor, for any d.
- $\mathcal{C}$ contains $xy^{\omega-1}z$.

If S is a semilattice, one can obtain a stronger result whose proof we omit.

Theorem 12. *Every non-trivial clone of polynomials over a semilattice S is tractable.*

4.2 The Group Case

We now turn our attention to tractable clones of polynomials over groups. First, we do not think that Corollary 11 can be extended to groups. We believe in particular that the "near subgroup" operation of Feder [9] can in some cases be represented as a polynomial over a group. In any case, the closure function that defines near-subgroup problems is a Malt'sev operation and we conjecture:

Conjecture 13. Let $\mathcal{C}$ be an idempotent clone of polynomials over a group. Then $\mathcal{C}$ is tractable iff it contains a Malt'sev operation.

By Theorem 11, the conjecture is true for Abelian groups because, as noted in Section 2 the operation $xy^{\omega-1}z$ over a finite group is Malt'sev. Next we will show that our conjecture holds for nilpotent groups which, in many ways, form one of the simplest class of non-Abelian groups. A group is said to be *nilpotent* if it is a direct product of p-groups. An alternative description will be more useful for our purposes: Let G be a group. For every $g, h \in G$, the commutator $[g, h]$ of g and h is the element $g^{-1}h^{-1}gh$. Note that $gh = hg[g,h]$, so if g and h commute $[g, h]$ is the identity. An element of G is *central* if it commutes with every element in G; the set of central elements of G is an Abelian subgroup.

For two subgroups G_1 and G_2 of G, $[G_1, G_2]$ is the subgroup generated by all commutators $[g, h]$ with $g \in G_1$ and $h \in G_2$. Define the lower central series of G by $G_0 = G$, and $G_{i+1} = [G_i, G]$. Elements in G_i are called *commutators of weight $i+1$* of G. We say that G is *nilpotent class k* if G_k is trivial; note that if G_k is trivial all elements in G_{k-1} are central in G. A group is *nilpotent* if it is nilpotent class k for some k.

We define commutator polynomials analogously. For two polynomials p_1, p_2, $[p_1, p_2]$ is the polynomial $p_1^{\omega-1}p_2^{\omega-1}p_1p_2$. The only commutator polynomial of weight 1 is the empty polynomial. A commutator polynomial of weight 2 is $[x, y]$ for two variables x, y. A commutator polynomial of weight k is $[p, x]$, where x is a variable and p a commutator polynomial of weight $k-1$. Commutator polynomials of weight $k+1$ or more are the identity in a nilpotent class k group.

Theorem 14. *If $\mathcal{C}$ is an idempotent clone of polynomials over a nilpotent group and not a d-factor for any d, then $\mathcal{C}$ contains a Malt'sev operation.*

Proof. Any polynomial p defining an operation over G also defines an operation over any subgroup H of G since the value of p lies in H when all variables are themselves set to values in H. We will say that a polynomial (or a clone) is interpreted over a subgroup H to mean that the variables of the polynomial take values in H. Note that if $\mathcal{C}$ is not a d-factor interpreted over G it is not a d-factor interpreted over H. Suppose H is an Abelian subgroup and suppose we can show that $\mathcal{C}$ interpreted over H contains the polynomial x^2y. One cannot conclude that $\mathcal{C}$ interpreted over G contains the polynomial x^2y itself for it may be that it contains, say, xyx that, interpreted over the Abelian subgroup H is indeed the same as x^2y.

Fix a nilpotent group G of class r. It is more convenient for the proof to redefine the indices of the central series of G as follows: $G_r = G$ and $G_{k-1} = [G_k, G]$, so that G_1 contains only central elements of G and G_k is nilpotent of class k. By repeatedly using the relation $xy = yx[x,y]$ and the fact that commutators of weight k or more vanish in a nilpotent group of class k, it can be shown that any polynomial p in n variables over such a group can be rewritten in the following normal form:

$$p = \prod_{i=1}^{n} x_i^{\alpha_i} \prod_{i,j \leq n} [x_i, x_j]^{\alpha_{ij}} \cdots \prod_{i_1,\ldots,i_k \leq n} [\ldots[[x_{i_1}, x_{i_2}], x_{i_3}], \ldots, x_{i_k}]^{\alpha_{i_1 \cdots i_k}}.$$

In other words, p can be rewritten as a product of distinct commutator polynomials raised to some power, where the "lightest" commutators appear first. Note that if we interpret p over a nilpotent subgroup H of class $k < r$, it is equivalent to the polynomial obtained by deleting all occurrences of commutator polynomials of weight larger than k, since they are the identity over H.

We prove the following for all k, by induction: There is a sequence Q of commutator polynomials of weight at most k over the variables x, y, z such that the operation $xy^{-1}zQ$ is Malt'sev over G and belongs to $\mathcal{C}$ when interpreted over G_k. The theorem follows from this statement for $k = r$.

For $k = 1$, Q is the empty sequence. Since $\mathcal{C}$ interpreted over G_1 is not a d-factor, and G_1 is Abelian, $\mathcal{C}$ interpreted over G_1 contains $xy^{-1}z$ by Corollary 11.

Inductively, let Q be a sequence of commutator polynomials of weight at most $k-1$ such that $xy^{-1}zQ$ is Malt'sev over G and contained in $\mathcal{C}$ when interpreted over G_{k-1}. Then, $\mathcal{C}$ interpreted over G_k contains a polynomial of the form

$$P(x, y, z) = xy^{-1}zQ \cdot \odot_i C_i^{\alpha_i}$$

for some set of exponents α_i, where $\odot_i$ denotes concatenation over all commutator polynomials C_i of weight k on the variables x, y, z.

Let R be obtained by identifying x and y in P. If $\{D_j\}$ is the set of commutator polynomials of weight k in x and z, this identification maps each C_i to some D_j. Every commutator D_j is central in G_k, so we can group all its occurrences, and since $xy^{-1}zQ$ is Malt'sev,

$$R(x, z) = P(x, x, z) = z \cdot \odot_i D_i^{\beta_i}$$

for appropriate exponents β_i. Similarly, let S be obtained by identifying z and y in P, so we have, for appropriate exponents γ_i,

$$S(x, z) = P(x, z, z) = x \cdot \odot_i D_i^{\gamma_i}.$$

Now we move to the domain G_k and remain there until further notice. Let $R^{(2)}$ be obtained by replacing z with $R(x,z)$ in R, that is,

$$R^{(2)}(x,z) = R(x, R(x,z)) = R(x,z) \cdot \odot_i (D_i(x, R(x,z)))^{\beta_i}$$
$$= z \cdot \odot_i (D_i(x,z))^{\beta_i} \cdot \odot_i (D_i(x, R(x,z)))^{\beta_i}$$

Now observe that if c is central, then we have $[u, vc] = u^{-1}(vc)^{-1}u(vc) = u^{-1}v^{-1}uv = [u,v]$ for any u, v. Every D_j has weight k, so it is central in G_k. Thus $D_i(x, R(x,z)) = D_i(x,z)$ over G_k and

$$R^{(2)}(x,z) = z \cdot \odot_i (D_i(x,z))^{2\beta_i}.$$

Iterating this process $\omega - 1$ times, we deduce that the polynomial

$$R^{(\omega-1)}(x,z) = z \cdot \odot_i (D_i(x,z))^{(\omega-1)\beta_i}$$

is in $\mathcal{C}$ when interpreted over G_k. Similarly, let $S^{(2)}$ be obtained by replacing x with S in S. By the same argument as before, we see that the polynomial

$$S^{(\omega-1)}(x,z) = x \cdot \odot_i (D_i(x,z))^{(\omega-1)\gamma_i}$$

is in $\mathcal{C}$ when interpreted over G_k.

Now, build T by replacing x with $R^{(\omega-1)}(z,y)$ and z with $S^{(\omega-1)}(y,x)$ in P. Observe that the two previous replacements have no effect on Q and D_i other than permuting x and z, since any commutator of weight k placed in an argument of a commutator polynomial of weight larger than 1 can simply be deleted. Using again that the D_i are central in G_k we have

$$T(x,y,z) = zy^{-1}xQ(z,y,x) \cdot \odot_i D_i^{(\omega-1)\beta_i}(z,y) \cdot \odot_i D_i^{(\omega-1)\gamma_i}(y,x) \cdot \odot_i C_i^{\alpha_i}(z,y,x).$$

While still in G_k, reorder the D_i and C_i in the following way: Let $\phi(i)$ be such that $C_i(x,x,z)$ is $D_{\phi(i)}(x,z)$, and similarly let $\varphi(i)$ be such that $C_i(x,z,z)$ is $D_{\varphi(i)}(x,z)$. By the definition of β_i, γ_i, ϕ, and φ, there are just the right number of each of the D_i in T so that T can be equivalently written in G_k as

$$T(x,y,z) = zy^{-1}xQ(z,y,x) \cdot \odot_i (C_i(z,y,x)(D_{\phi(i)}(y,x))^{\omega-1}(D_{\varphi(i)}(z,y))^{\omega-1})^{\alpha_i}$$

So this polynomial $T(x,y,z)$ belongs to $\mathcal{C}$ when interpreted over G_k, although it need not be in $\mathcal{C}$ when interpreted in G. Still, it is easy to see that T is Malt'sev in all G: When $x = y$, all the commutators on x and y vanish so we have

$$T(x,x,z) = zx^{-1}xQ(z,x,x) \cdot \odot_i (C_i(z,x,x) \cdot (D_{\varphi(i)}(z,x))^{\omega-1})^{\alpha_i}$$
$$= z \cdot \odot_i (D_{\varphi(i)}(z,x) \cdot (D_{\varphi(i)}(z,x))^{\omega-1})^{\alpha_i} = z,$$

and when $y = z$, all the commutators on z and y vanish and

$$T(x,z,z) = zz^{-1}xQ(z,z,x) \cdot \odot_i (C_i(z,z,x) \cdot (D_{\phi(i)}(z,x))^{\omega-1})^{\alpha_i}$$
$$= x \cdot \odot_i (D_{\phi(i)}(z,x) \cdot (D_{\phi(i)}(z,x))^{\omega-1})^{\alpha_i} = x.$$

This concludes the induction step and the proof of the theorem. □

From Theorems 7 and 14 and the tractability of Malt'sev operations, we get:

Corollary 15. *Let G be a nilpotent group and $\mathcal{C}$ a nontrivial, idempotent clone of polynomials over G. Then the following are equivalent:*

- *$\mathcal{C}$ is tractable.*
- *$\mathcal{C}$ is not a d-factor, for any d.*
- *$\mathcal{C}$ contains a Malt'sev operation.*

It is tempting to conjecture in light of Corollaries 11 and 15 that if S is a block-group then an idempotent clone of polynomials over S is tractable iff it is not a d-factor. It would also be interesting to identify the largest class of finite groups for which the presence of $xy^{-1}z$ is necessary and sufficient for tractability.

References

1. A. Bulatov. A dichotomy theorem for constraints on a three-element set. In *Proc. of 43rd Foundations of Comp. Sci. (FOCS'02)*, pages 649–658, 2002.
2. A. Bulatov. Malt'sev constrains are tractable. *Electronic Colloquium on Computational Complexity (ECCC)*, 2002.
3. A. Bulatov and V. Dalmau. A simple algorithm for Malt'sev constraints. Submitted, 2005.
4. A. Bulatov and P. Jeavons. An algebraic approach to multi-sorted constraints. In *Principles and Practice of Constraint Programming (CP'03)*, pages 183–193, 2003.
5. A. Bulatov, P. Jeavons, and M. Volkov. Finite semigroups imposing tractable constraints. In G. Gomez, P. Silva, and J-E.Pin, editors, *Semigroups, Algorithms, Automata and Languages*, pages 313–329. WSP, 2002.
6. A. Bulatov, A. Krokhin, and P. Jeavons. Constraint satisfaction problems and finite algebras. In *Proc. 27th Int. Col. on Automata, Languages and Programming (ICALP'00)*, pages 272–282, 2000.
7. V. Dalmau. A new tractable class of constraint satisfaction problems. In *6th Int. Symp on Artificial Intelligence and Mathematics*, 2000.
8. V. Dalmau and J. Pearson. Closure functions and width 1 problems. In *Principles and Practice of Constraint Programming—CP'99*, pages 159–173, 1999.
9. T. Feder. Constraint satisfaction on finite groups with near subgroups. *Electronic Colloquium on Computational Complexity (ECCC)*, 2005.
10. T. Feder and M. Y. Vardi. The computational structure of monotone monadic SNP and constraint satisfaction: A study through datalog and group theory. *SIAM J. on Computing*, 28(1):57–104, 1998.
11. P. Jeavons. On the algebraic structure of combinatorial problems. *Theoretical Computer Science*, 200(1-2):185–204, 1998.
12. P. Jeavons, D. Cohen, and M. Gyssens. Closure properties of constraints. *J. ACM*, 44(4):527–548, 1997.
13. O. Klíma, P. Tesson, and D. Thérien. Dichotomies in the complexity of solving systems of equations over finite semigroups. *Theory of Computing Systems*, 2005.
14. B. Larose and L. Zádori. Taylor terms, constraint satisfaction and the complexity of polynomial equations over finite algebras. Submitted for publication, 2004.
15. J.-É. Pin. $PG = BG$, a success story. In J. Fountain, editor, *NATO Advanced Study Institute Semigroups, Formal Languages and Groups*, pages 33–47. Kluwer Academic Publishers, 1995.
16. T. J. Schaefer. The complexity of satisfiability problems. In *Proc. 10th ACM STOC*, pages 216–226, 1978.

CP(Graph): Introducing a Graph Computation Domain in Constraint Programming

Gregoire Dooms, Yves Deville, and Pierre Dupont

Department of Computing Science and Engineering,
Université catholique de Louvain,
B-1348 Louvain-la-Neuve - Belgium
{dooms, yde, pdupont}@info.ucl.ac.be*

Abstract. In an increasing number of domains such as bioinformatics, combinatorial graph problems arise. We propose a novel way to solve these problems, mainly those that can be translated to constrained subgraph finding. Our approach extends constraint programming by introducing CP(Graph), a new computation domain focused on graphs including a new type of variable: graph domain variables as well as constraints over these variables and their propagators. These constraints are subdivided into kernel constraints and additional constraints formulated as networks of kernel constraints. For some of these constraints a dedicated global constraint and its associated propagator are sketched. CP(Graph) is integrated with finite domain and finite sets computation domains, allowing the combining of constraints of these domains with graph constraints.

A prototype of CP(Graph) built over finite domains and finite sets in Oz is presented. And we show that a problem of biochemical network analysis can be very simply described and solved within CP(Graph).

1 Introduction

Combinatorial graph problems are present in many domains such as communication networks, route planning, circuitry, and recently bioinformatics. The motivation for this work lies in graph problems of biochemical network analysis. Biochemical networks model the components of the cells (molecules, genes, reactions, etc...) and their interactions. They can be modeled as directed labeled graphs. Their analysis consists in assessing the properties of these graphs. Various problems have been solved to better understand the structure of the biochemical networks [1]. Some of these problems can be modeled as constrained path finding or constrained subgraph extraction problems.

The analyses performed on biochemical networks are varied and evolve at a rapid pace. A declarative framework based on constrained programming could enable a quick expression and resolution of these problems. It would allow the bioinformaticians to spend less time on implementing dedicated algorithms, keeping the focus on designing new queries and analyzing the results.

This paper introduces a graph computation domain, called CP(Graph), in constraint programming. A new type of domain variables, graph domain variables, and constraints

---

* This research is supported by the Walloon Region, project BioMaze (WIST 315432). Thanks also to the EC/FP6 Evergrow project for their computing support.

on these variables are proposed. CP(Graph) can then be used to express and solve combinatorial graph problems modeled as constrained subgraph extraction problems.

Related Work. CP(Graph) is built over the finite set computation domain [2]. It also shares its lattice structure. The usage of sets in a language able to express and solve hard combinatorial problems dates back to 1978 with ALICE in the seminal work of Laurière [3]. The usage of graphs as structures of symbolic constraint objects was proposed in 1993 by Gervet [4]. In that work, a graph domain is modeled as an endomorphic relation domain. In 2002, Lepape et al. defined path variables [5] which were used to solve constrained path finding problems in a network design context.

Graphs play an important role in constraint programming for the specification, design and implementation of global constraints [6], but graphs are there mainly used for representing and exploiting a network of elementary constraints. A global path constraint has been proposed in [7,8] and a global tree constraint in [9]. A path constraint is included in CP(Graph) and its implementation is based on these related works. Finally, the theoretical framework is related to the work on edge set quantification in monadic second order logic of graphs [10] as our kernel constraint language on graphs also allows quantification on nodes and arcs. This work is also an extension of our preliminary work [11].

The first section presents the variables and constants used in CP(Graph) then the constraints linking graph domain variables to the other variables. The constraints of CP(Graph) can be separated into two classes: the kernel constraints (Section2.3) and the others. The kernel constraints form the minimal set of constraints necessary to express the other constraints as networks of kernel constraints. We show how to incrementally build graph constraints by combining kernel constraints for a specific class of problems: constrained subgraph extraction (Section 2.4).

The combination of kernel constraints is a rapid way of implementing other graph constraints. However, it is possible to achieve a better filtering by designing a so-called global constraint (Section 4). In order to characterize and compare the filtering of the propagators of the constraints in CP(Graph), we introduce *mixed consistency* in Section 3. It consists of bound consistency on sets and graph domain variables coupled with arc consistency on finite domain variables.

Finally, in Section 6, the practicality of CP(Graph) is assessed by expressing a CP(Graph) problem for a biochemical network analysis problem and by analyzing the evolution of computation time and memory usage with problems of increasing size.

Contributions. the main contributions of this work are the following:

– graph domain variables, and constraints on these variables are the major contribution of this work. We show how to use them to express other constraints on graphs and to solve constrained subgraph extraction problems. We generalize the mode of usage of the reachability and path constraints by allowing end-nodes to be domain variables.
– Definition of a graph computation domain in CP.
– Specification of a minimal set of constraints on graphs.
– Suitability assessment for expressing and solving the class of constrained subgraph extraction problems.
– Practical assessment of the suitability of CP(Graph) for constrained subgraph extraction problems.

2 The CP(Graph) Framework

This section presents the basics of the CP(Graph) computation domain. Graph domain variables and domains are described along with their integration with finite sets and finite domains. Then, primitive constraints called kernel constraints are presented. Finally, more complex constraints are built using the kernel constraints. The construction of the their propagator and the analysis of their consistency is presented in section 3.

2.1 Constants and Variables

A graph $g = (sn, sa)$ is a set of nodes sn, and a set of arcs $sa \subseteq sn \times sn$. We are first considering directed graphs. An extension to undirected graphs is handled in a later section.

CP(Graph) introduces graph domain variables (gd-variables for short) in constraint programming. However, CP(Graph) deals with many types of constants and variables related to graphs. They are presented in Table 1. This table presents the notations used in this paper for constants and domain variables of each type. It also shows one particular aspect of graphs: the inherent constraint stating a arc can only be present if both end nodes are present too. Nodes and Arcs in CP(Graph) can be labeled with integer weights through the use of weight functions. Such functions are seen as constants in CP(Graph), there is no domain variable for weight functions. CP(Graph) can handle graphs with multiple weights per node or arc by using multiple weight functions.

Table 1. The different variables and constants of CP(Graph) along with their notations. Note only the graph has an inherent constraint. $\mathcal{N}$ and $\mathcal{A}$ are the universal sets of nodes and arcs.

Type	Representation	Constraint	Constants	Variables
Integer	$0, 1, 2, ...$		$i_0, i_1, ...$	$I_0, I_1, ...$
Node	$0, 1, 2, ...$		$n_0, n_1, ...$	$N_0, N_1, ...$
Arc	$(0,1), (2,4), ...$		$a_0, a_1, ...$	$A_0, A_1, ...$
Finite set	$\{0,1,2\}, \{3,5\} ...$		$s_0, s_1, ...$	$S_0, S_1, ...$
Finite set of nodes	$\{0,1,2\}, \{3,5\} ...$		$sn_0, sn_1, ...$	$SN_0, SN_1, ...$
Finite set of arcs	$\{(0,3), (1,2)\}, ...$		$sa_0, sa_1, ...$	$SA_0, SA_1, ...$
Graph	(SN, SA) SN a set of nodes SA a set of arcs	$SA \subseteq SN \times SN$	$g_0, g_1, ...$	$G_0, G_1, ...$
Weight functions	$\mathcal{N} \cup \mathcal{A} \to \mathbb{N}$		$w_0, w_1, ...$	–

Similarly to sets, there exists a partial ordering among graphs, defined by graph inclusion: given $g_1 = (sn_1, sa_1)$ and $g_2 = (sn_2, sa2)$, $g1 \subseteq g2$ iff $sn_1 \subseteq sn_2$ and $sa_1 \subseteq sa_2$. We define graph domains as the lattice of graphs included between two bounds: the greatest lower bound and the least upper bound of the lattice.

The domain of each gd-variable is defined according to a least upper bound graph and a greatest lower bound graph. The least upper bound graph defines the set of possible nodes and arcs in the graph variable, while the greatest lower bound defines the set of nodes and arcs which are known to be part of the graph variable (see Figure 1). If G is

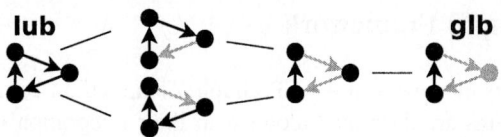

Fig. 1. Illustration of a small graph domain with its least upper bound (lub) and greatest lower bound (glb). Greyed nodes and arcs are displayed for convenience but are not part of the respective graphs.

a gd-variable, we will denote $dom(G) = [g_L, g_U]$ with $g_L = glb(G)$ and $g_U = lub(G)$. If S is a finite set variable, we denote $dom(S) = [s_L, s_U]$, with $s_L = glb(S)$ and $s_U = lub(S)$.

The presence of arc variables and set of arc variables along with the nodes and set of nodes is motivated first by the works on expressiveness of monadic second order logic on graphs [10]. That work shows that a logic where it is possible to existentially quantify sets of nodes can be strictly less expressive than one where it is possible to existentially quantify sets of nodes and sets of arcs. Another incentive, in the constraint community, was the comparison of the models used in [7,8] and [12] for a path constraint. Successor finite domain variables were used in [12] while [7,8] use arc boolean variables. Yet the path propagator in [8] reasons about mandatory nodes. It is clear that providing only arc variables is impractical as a graph cannot be constrained to contain isolated nodes and constraints about nodes must be stated as disjunctions of arcs. Hence, offering node and arc variables enables to express more CSPs and properties about graph variables.

2.2 Classical Finite Set Constraints

CP(Graph) is integrated with the finite domain and finite set computation domains. Classical constraints from these domains can be combined with graph constraints to express a CSP in CP(Graph). We present the minimal standard set of constraints on finite domain and finite sets assumed to be present in the system.

The set constraints used in this paper are set inclusion ($S_1 \subseteq S_2$), set intersection ($S_1 \cap S_2 = S_3$), set difference ($S_1 \setminus S_2 = S_3$), set cardinality ($\#S = I$), set membership ($I \in S$ and $I \notin S$), set inequality ($S_1 \neq S_2$) and the set weight constraint ($Weight(S, w, I)$) which holds if I is the sum of the weights of the elements of S according to the weight description w. We also suppose it is possible to post a constraint for each value in a set variable S: $\forall i \in S : C(i)$. This can be done in two ways. Either by posting $\#s_U$ constraints of the form $i \in S \Rightarrow C(i)$ or by waiting until i is known to be in S to post the constraint $C(i) : \sigma \models i \in S \to C(i)$ While the former filters more, the latter uses less memory.

In addition to the boolean constraints like implication, negation, conjunction and disjunction, we use the constraint of sum (linear combination of finite domain variables using constant factors) in CP(Graph).

2.3 Kernel Graph Constraints

The kernel graph constraints constitute the minimal set of constraints needed to express the other graph constraints of CP(Graph). These constraints relating graph variables with arc and node variables provide the suitable expressiveness of monadic second order logic [10].

The kernel graph constraints are *ArcNode*, *Nodes* and *Arcs*.

$Arcs(G, SA)$ SA is the set of arcs of G.

$Nodes(G, SN)$ SN is the set of nodes of G.

$ArcNode(A, N_1, N_2)$ The arc variable A is an arc from node N_1 to node N_2. This relation does not take a graph variable into account as every arc and node has a unique identifier in the system. If A is determined, this constraint is a simple accessor to the tail and head of the arc A and respectively if both nodes are determined.

All CMS-definable sets of graphs [13] can be defined as constraints in CP(Graph) by using these kernel constraints (CMS stands for countable monadic second order logic). This can be shown by translating the building blocks of CMS logic of graphs into CP(Graph). Monadic means that only 1-ary relation (i.e. sets) can be quantified. CP(Graph) allows quantification over sets of nodes and arcs. Countable stands for a predicate telling the size of a set. It is handled by the set cardinality constraint. The **edg** binary relation on nodes and the incidence (**inc**) ternary relation on an arc and two nodes are expressed by $\textbf{inc}_g(a, n_1, n_2) \equiv ArcNode(a, n_1, n_2) \wedge n_1 \in Nodes(g) \wedge n_2 \in Nodes(g) \wedge a \in Arcs(g)$ and $\textbf{edg}_g(n_1, n_2) \equiv \exists a : ArcNode(a, n_1, n_2) \wedge \textbf{inc}_g(a, n_1, n_2)$ where a is determined by n_1 and n_2. We do not know a common graph property which cannot be expressed using CP(Graph).

2.4 Building Graph Constraints over Kernel Constraints

While the kernel constraints enable to express the target problems of CP(Graph), defining higher level constraints eases the formulation of these problems. Such constraints can be built as combinations of kernel constraints. Such networks of constraints may not propagate as much as a dedicated global propagator for the constraint but are useful as a reference implementation or as a quickly implemented prototype. We focus here on constraints suitable for constrained subgraph extraction problems.

To alleviate the notation, we use a functional style for some constraints by removing the last argument of a constraint and considering that the resulting expression denotes the value of that omitted argument (e.g. $Nodes(G)$ denotes SN in $Nodes(G, SN)$). We also write $(n_1, n_2) \in Arcs(G)$ instead of $a \in Arcs(G) \wedge ArcNode(a, n_1, n_2)$.

The $SubGraph(G_1, G_2)$ constraint can be translated to

$$SubGraph(G_1, G_2) \equiv Nodes(G_1) \subseteq Nodes(G_2), Arcs(G_1) \subseteq Arcs(G_2)$$

To cope with linear optimization problems we introduce the *Weight* constraint for graphs:

$Weight(G, w, I)$ holds if I is the total weight associated to the graph variable G according to the weight function w.

$$Weight(G, w, I) \equiv I = Weight(Nodes(G), w_n) + Weight(Arcs(G), w_a)$$

Where w_a is the restriction of the weight function to the arcs domain, and respectively, w_n for nodes. CP(Graph) allows to express and solve constrained subgraph optimization problems and some examples are given in the next section. A constrained shortest path problem is also presented in the experiments section.

$InNeighbors(G, N, SN)$ holds if SN is the set of all nodes of G from which an inward arc incident to N is present in G. If N is not in G then SN is empty. It can be expressed as the following network of constraints.

$$InNeighbors(G, N, SN) \equiv SN \subseteq Nodes(G) \land (\#SN > 0 \Leftrightarrow N \in Nodes(G)) \land$$
$$\forall n \in Nodes(g_U) : n \in SN \Leftrightarrow (n, N) \in Arcs(G)$$

The last constraint must be posted for all possible member of SN and for all possible in-neighbor of N. In this expression it is posted on a superset of these sets: $Nodes(g_U)$.

Similar expressions exist for inward arcs and the "out" versions of these constraints. $OutDegree$ and $InDegree$ are the cardinality of these sets.

$Reachable(G, N, SN)$ states SN is the set of nodes reachable from N in G. Again, G, N and SN are domain variables. This constraint is presented in [14] in the case of N determined. First we need to define the $QuasiPath(G, SN, N, n_2)$ constraints stating the graph induced by SN in G is a path from N to n_2 with possibly additional mutually disjoint cycles also disjoint from the path [10]. This is expressed by forcing every node in SN to have an inward and outward degree of 1 in the induced subgraph (except for the source N and sink n_2).

$$QuasiPath(G, SN, N_1, N_2) \equiv N_1 \in SN \land N_2 \in SN \land$$
$$\forall n \in SN : O = OutNeighbors(G, n) \cap SN \land \#O \leq 1 \land (n \neq N_2) \Rightarrow \#O = 1 \land$$
$$\forall n \in SN : I = InNeighbors(G, n) \cap SN \land \#I \leq 1 \land (n \neq N_1) \Rightarrow \#I = 1$$

Then $Reachables(G, N, SN)$ is expressed by:

$$\forall n \in SN : \exists SN' \subseteq Nodes(G) : QuasiPath(G, SN', N, n)$$

The directed acyclic graph constraint $DAG(G)$ states a graph cannot contain cycles. $DAG(G)$ can be translated using this property: the set of in-neighbors of each node must be disjoint from the set of nodes it can reach.

$$DAG(G) \equiv \forall n \in Nodes(G) : InNeighbors(G, n) \cap Reachable(G, n) = \emptyset$$

The path constraint can be expressed in a similar way:

$Path(G, N_1, N_2)$ holds if G is a path from node N_1 to node N_2, all of which are domain variables.

$$Path(G) \equiv QuasiPath(G, Nodes(G), N_1, N_2) \land \#Nodes(G) = \#Arcs(G) + 1$$

The $InducedSubGraph(G_1, G_2)$ constraint is used in next section to express a k-cut problem.

$InducedSubGraph(G_1, G_2)$ holds if G_1 is an induced subgraph of the graph G_2 i.e. the greatest subgraph of G_2 containing the nodes of G_1.

$$InducedSubGraph(G_1, G_2) \equiv SN = Nodes(G_2) \setminus Nodes(G_1) \land$$
$$\forall (n1, n2) \in Arcs(G_2) : (n_1 \in SN \lor n_2 \in SN) \text{ XOR } (n1, n2) \in Arcs(G_1)$$

2.5 Combining Graph Constraints to Solve Problems

Numerous NP(Hard) graph problems can be stated in CP(Graph). The graph constraints presented in other works [6,7,8] can be implemented in the CP(Graph) framework and used to solve these problems. CP(Graph) is particularly suited for problems of subgraph extraction. We list a few example problems to show the expressiveness and conciseness of CP(Graph). In these expressions, $SubGraph(G, g)$ is used to declare a new graph domain variable G with initial upper bound g. The $Cycle(G)$ constraint holds if G is a closed directed path.

– Finding the TSP in graph g with weights w: minimize $Weight(G, w)$ s.t.

$$SubGraph(G, g) \land Cycle(G) \land Nodes(G) = Nodes(g)$$

– Finding the shortest weight constrained (maximum weight k) path of g with weights w, length function w_l, start node n_1, end node n_2: minimize $Weight(G, w_l)$ s.t.

$$SubGraph(G, g) \land Path(G, n_1, n_2) \land Weight(G, w) \leq k$$

– Finding the minimum vertex k-cut of g with source nodes $\{n_1, \ldots, n_s\}$, target node n_t and the weight function w :minimize $Weight(Nodes(g) \setminus Nodes(G), w)$ s.t.

$$InducedSubGraph(g, G) \land \forall i \in [1, n] : n_t \notin Reachable(G, n_i)$$

– Prize Collecting Steiner Tree Problem: g is the initial graph, the arc weights and node prices are w_a and w_n: minimize $Weight(G, w_a) + Weight(SN, w_n)$ s.t.

$$SubGraph(G, g) \land Tree(G) \land SN = Nodes(g) \setminus Nodes(G)$$

– Graph partitioning problem: equicut of a graph g of even order: minimize $\#(Arcs(g) \setminus (Arcs(G_1) \cup Arcs(G_2)))$ subject to:

$$SubGraph(G_1, g) \land SubGraph(G_2, g) \land Nodes(G_1) \cup Nodes(G_2) =$$
$$Nodes(g) \land \#Nodes(G_1) = \#Nodes(G_2) = \frac{1}{2}\#Nodes(g)$$

Section 6 will present the expression of a constrained shortest path finding problem: finding the shortest simple path in a graph given a set of nodes which must be present in the path and a set of pairs of mutually exclusive nodes.

3 Consistency in CP(Graph)

This section covers the propagation rules of the constraints in the kernel CP(Graph) language. We first define mixed consistency for constraints combining graph, finite set and finite domain variables. The constraints of the kernel are mixed consistent and mixed consistency will be applied to other constraints in a later section.

3.1 Mixed Consistency

Given a constraint $C(X)$ over the variables $X = X_1, \ldots, X_n$ with domains $\mathcal{D} = D_1 \times \ldots \times D_n$, we first define the set of solutions of the constraint C on the domain $\mathcal{D}$ of its variables.

$$Sol(C, \mathcal{D}) = \{\mathbf{x} \in \mathcal{D} \mid C(\mathbf{x})\}$$

We denote $Sol(C, \mathcal{D})[X_i]$, the projection of this set on the ith component of its tuples. We also note FD for finite domain variables, FS for finite set variables and GD for graph domain variables.

Definition 1. *For a graph domain variable or a finite set variable X_i with domain $D_i = [x_{iL}, x_{iU}]$, we say C is* bound consistent *on X_i with respect to $\mathcal{D}$ iff*

$$x_{iL} = glb\left(Sol(C, \mathcal{D})[X_i]\right), \quad x_{iU} = lub\left(Sol(C, \mathcal{D})[X_i]\right)$$

Definition 2. *For a finite domain variable X_i with domain $D_i = \{a_0, a_1, \ldots, a_n\}$, we say C is* arc consistent *on X_i with respect to $\mathcal{D}$ iff*

$$D_i = Sol(C, \mathcal{D})[X_i]$$

Definition 3. C *is* mixed consistent *with respect to $\mathcal{D}$ iff for all $1 \leq i \leq n$ if X_i is a GD or FS variable, C is bound consistent on X_i with respect to $\mathcal{D}$, if X_i is a FD variable, C is arc consistent on X_i with respect to $\mathcal{D}$.*

3.2 Propagation Rules of the Kernel Constraints

This section covers the consistency and propagation rules of the kernel constraints of CP(Graph). All of the rules have the domains of the variables implicitly defined by $dom(G) = [g_L, g_U]$, with $g_L = (gsn_L, gsa_L)$ and $g_U = (gsn_U, gsa_U)$, $dom(SA) = [sa_L, sa_U]$ and $dom(SN) = [sn_L, sn_U]$.

We consider an $O(1)$ complexity for the inclusion or exclusion of a value in/out of a finite domain or finite set bound and similarly for an arc of a graph domain variable. As we consider the internal constraint of graphs ($gsa_X \subseteq gsn_X \times gsn_X$ where X stands for both U and L), the removal of a node of G can trigger up to d arc removals where d is the maximal degree of g_U. We also consider a propagator knows for which variable and value it is run in case of an update event.

The Arcs Constraint. The $Arcs(G, SA)$ constraint propagation rule is unique. Its application leads to bound consistent domains. The new bounds of the variables G and SA are denoted with a prime. Obviously, only the set of arcs of the bounds of G are updated.

$$sa'_L = gsa'_L = sa_L \cup gsa_L$$
$$sa'_U = gsa'_U = sa_U \cap gsa_U$$

The complexity of this rule is $O(1)$ per update as it just suffices to forward update events from one variable to the other.

The Nodes Constraint. The propagation rule of the $Nodes(G, SN)$ constraint is similar to the $Arcs$ propagation rule:

$$sn'_L = gsn'_L = sn_L \cup gsn_L$$
$$sn'_U = gsn'_U = sn_U \cap gsn_U$$

This rule also achieves bound consistency and its complexity is $O(d)$ per update where d is the maximal degree of g_U. That is $O(|sa_U| + |sn_U|)$ over a branch of the search tree as each node and arc can only be removed once.

The ArcNode Constraint. The $ArcNode(A, N_1, N_2)$ constraint links an arc variable to two node variables. The update of the domains is straightforward:

$$dom'(A) = dom(A) \cap (dom(N_1) \times dom(N_2))$$
$$dom'(N_1) = \{n_1 \in dom(N_1) | \exists n_2 \in dom(N_2), (n_1, n_2) \in dom(A)\}$$
$$dom'(N_2) = \{n_2 \in dom(N_2) | \exists n_1 \in dom(N_1), (n_1, n_2) \in dom(A)\}$$

Once a fixed-point is reached, the domains are arc-consistent. The complexity is similar as the previous one. The removal of a node from a node domain leads to at most d removals of arcs. Here the graph under consideration is the union of the initial least upper bounds of the graph variables in the CSP.

4 Global Constraints

In Section 2.4, we showed how graph constraints can be built by combining kernel constraints. It however appears that dedicated propagators can be more efficient than a combination of propagators of kernel constraints. This amounts to write a so called global constraint, where global refers to operational globality when more pruning is achieved or algorithmic globality when the same level of pruning is achieved [15].

We here focus on the $Path$ and $Reachable$ constraints and sketch global propagators for these constraints. However, other existing global constraints enforcing graph properties or relations between graphs can be integrated with CP(Graph).

4.1 The Reachable Constraint

$Reachable(G, N, SN)$ holds if SN is the set of nodes reachable from N in G. This constraint encodes the transitive closure of the adjacency relation of the graph. It is expressible using kernel constraints but it requires to post a lot of constraints (see section 2.4). If more pruning is to be done (detection of cutnodes, bridges, etc...), then even more propagators have to be posted. On the other hand, an imperative algorithm can handle these problems easily. Computation of connected components, strongly connected components, bridges, etc... can be done with variants of depth first search in linear time. Incremental algorithms have also been designed to handle dynamic graphs [16]. Hence a global propagator is much more efficient for such constraints.

In CP(Graph), N is a node variable. Constraint propagators have been defined for a determined source node $N = n$ [14,11]. It is however simple to adapt these propagators to an unknown source. A simple schema is to execute these propagators for each of the values of the domain of the source node and perform their filtering for the values on which they all agree. For instance, if for each value in the domain of N, the node n of G is found to be mandatory, then it is indeed mandatory for any value of N. If one of these propagators would do a pruning which is inconsistent with the current domains, then it means the according value of N can be removed from its domain. By applying this generic reasoning to the existing propagators it is possible adapt them.

4.2 The Path Constraint

We introduce the constraint $Path(G, N_1, N_2, w, I)$, the global version of $(Path(G, N_1, N_2) \wedge Weight(G, w, I))$. It holds if G is a path from N_1 to N_2 whose total weight is I according to the weight function w. With such a constraint, it is possible to do cost based filtering. Note that all parameters of this constraint can be variables except the weight function w which must be a constant. In this section, we show how to adapt the work of [7] on cost-based filtering to this constraint in CP(Graph).

The most general mode of usage of the $Path$ constraint is the case with four unbound variables. However it can be directly reduced to a problem with two unbound variables G' and $I : Path(G', n_s, n_e, w', I)$ by introducing a virtual source n_s and sink n_e. These virtual nodes are assigned a null weight in w'. We do not introduce an additional graph domain variable G' to do this filtering. We just pretend to temporarily update the data structure of the least upper bound of G, g_U (the updated g_U is noted g'_U) to add these nodes, arcs and weights. The problem of filtering in this structure is equivalent to the filtering in the following problem:

$Path(G', n_s, n_e, w', I)$
$Nodes(G') = Nodes(G) \cup \{n_s, n_e\}$
$Arcs(G') = Arcs(G) \cup \{(n_s, n) | n \in dom(N_1)\} \cup \{(n, n_e) | n \in dom(N_2)\}$
$w'(x) = \begin{cases} w(x) & \text{if } x \in G, \\ 0 & \text{if } x \in G'/G. \end{cases}$

The domains of N_1 and N_2 are easily filtered: all filtering made on the arcs incident to n_s and n_e is reflected on the domains of N_1 and N_2.

$dom(N_1) := OutNeighbors(g'_U, n_s), \quad dom(N_2) := InNeighbors(g'_U, n_e)$

By introducing these virtual nodes, we can also move all the weights to the arcs (average of the end-nodes weights) while preserving the total weights of all the paths from n_s to n_e. It allows to apply an algorithm for the cost-based filtering of the domain of G using the lub of the domain of I. This consists in a shorter path constraint presented for arc-weighted graphs in [7]. A lower bound of I is also obtained as a side product of this algorithm. The complexity of this filtering is $O(|gsa|.|gsn|log|gsn|)$ over a branch of the search tree.

Using the lub of I to filter the domain of G is possible by applying the longest path propagator for directed acyclic graphs of [17] on the component graph (the graph where the strongly-connected components of the original graph are condensed to a single node).

5 Undirected Graphs

CP(Graph) also supports undirected graphs through an undirected view of a directed graph variable. Undirected graphs are handled like directed graphs by the framework, only the constraints differ. Some constraints have an undirected semantic while others have a directed graph semantic. Some graph properties like being a single connected component are indeed defined for undirected graphs. As a undirected graph is a special case of directed graph, properties defined for directed graphs can be applied as constraints on undirected graphs. On the other hand, a constraint with an undirected graph semantic can be applied to a directed graph as it just operates on the undirected view of the graph (regardless of the orientation of the arc). This view is handled by an additional constraint handling the unordered couples of nodes for the undirected arcs:

$UndirArcNode(A, N_1, N_2)$ A is an undirected arc between node N_1 and N_2. This relation holds iff $ArcNode(A, N_1, N_2)$ or $ArcNode(A, N_2, N_1)$ holds.

6 Experiments

This section describes the prototype of CP(Graph) and the constrained path finding experiments we did to show its practicality. Then, it discusses the results of the experiments.

6.1 Prototype of CP(Graph) Implemented in Oz/Mozart

We implemented a prototype of CP(Graph) over the Oz/Mozart[18] constraint programming framework. In this prototype, graph domain variables are implemented using set variables. One set is used for the nodes of the graph and one for the arcs of the graph. This prototypes allows to state constraint satisfaction problems as well as optimization problems. The constraint propagators are implemented as combinations of kernel constraints or as dedicated global propagators. We implemented the kernel constraints, a reachability propagator and the path propagator of [8] using the Oz language. The other constraints are implemented by combining these constraints with finite set constraints. As Mozart does not support finite sets of couples of integers, we use an integer encoding of arcs. $ArcNode$ provides an accessor for the end nodes of an arc and for the arc number of a couple of nodes through the use of hash tables.

6.2 Biochemical Network Analyses

We used CP(Graph) to model and solve a problem for biochemical network analysis. Biochemical network analysis consists in assessing the properties of the biochemical networks. These networks are composed of all the genes, molecules, reactions and controls (e.g. catalysis of a reaction) and their interactions, which may occur in one or several organisms. They can be modeled by a labeled simple digraph [1,11].

We focus here on metabolic networks, that is biochemical networks describing reactions and their substrates and products. A pathway is a specific subgraph of a metabolic network which has a known function in the metabolism. Such pathways were identified experimentally and described in the molecular biology literature.

One type of analysis of biochemical networks consists in trying to computationally find pathways in the metabolic network. An application of this type of analysis lies in the explanation of DNA chip experiments: in a given context, the cell will activate a subset of its possible reactions. A DNA chip enables to list the activated reactions. Given such a set of reactions actually used by the cell, biologists would like to know which pathways were at work in the cell. Our approach is to first develop a CSP able to recover known pathways and then use it to discover new pathways as a result of a DNA chip experiment.

Constrained Shortest Path Finding. As about half of the known pathways are simple paths [19], one type of experiment consists in trying to find these pathways by using constrained path finding in a directed graph (knowing a few nodes of the path). In [20], several computational path finding experiments were described. The best experiment consisted in doing point-to-point shortest path finding in a network where each node has a weight proportional to its degree.

Our experiment consists in redoing the former experiment with an additional constraint of inclusion of some intermediate reactions and mutual exclusion for certain pairs of reactions. These pairs are reverse reactions (the reaction from substrates to products and the one from products to substrates). Most of the time, these reactions are observed in a single direction in each species. Hence we wish to exclude paths containing both in our experiment. These two addtional constraints could not be easily integrated in the previous dedicated algorithm [20]. In CP(Graph) it just consists in posting a few additional constraints. If $n_1, ..., n_m$ are the included reactions and $(r_{i1}, r_{i2}), 0 < i \leq t$ the mutually exclusive nodes, the program looks like: miminize $Weight(G, w)$ s.t.

$$SubGraph(G, g) \wedge Path(G, n_1, n_m) \wedge \forall 0 < i \leq m : n_i \in Nodes(G) \wedge$$
$$\forall i \in [0, t] : (r_{i1} \notin Nodes(G) \vee r_{i2} \notin Nodes(G))$$

In our experimental setting we first extract a subgraph of the original metabolic bipartite digraph by incrementally growing a fringe starting by the included nodes. Then, given a subset of the reactions of a reference pathway, we try to find the shortest constrained path in that subgraph. The first process of extraction of a subgraph of interest is done for efficiency reasons as the original graph is too big to be handled by the CSP (it contains around 16.000 nodes). The results are presented in Table 2, it shows the increase of running time, memory usage and size of the search tree with respect to the size of the graph for the extraction of three illustrative linear pathways shown in [20]. All reactions are mandatory in the first experiment. The results of another experiment where one reaction out of two successive reactions in the given pathway is included in the set of mandatory nodes, is presented in Table 3. The running time increases greatly with the size of the graphs. The program can however be stated in a few lines and first results obtained the same day the experiment is designed. The limitation on the input graph size does not guarantee to get the optimal shortest path in the original graph. This should however not be a major problem as biologists are most of the time interested in a particular portion of the metabolic graph. The rapidity of expression and resolution of such a NP(Hard) [7] problem reduces this size limitation.

Future work focuses on the limitation of running time explosion with graph size which can be obsverved in the results tables. Current results are better than those ob-

Table 2. Comparison of the running time [s], number of nodes in the search tree and memory usage [kb], for the 3 pathways and for increasing original graph sizes. m is the number of node inclusion constraints and t the number of mutual exclusion constraints.

Glycolysis (m=8)					Heme (m=8)					Lysine (m=9)				
Size	t	Time	Nodes	Mem	Size	t	Time	Nodes	Mem	Size	t	Time	Nodes	Mem
50	12	0.2	20	2097	50	22	0.2	32	2097	50	18	0.2	38	2097
100	28	2.5	224	2097	100	36	0.3	22	2097	100	40	4.7	652	2097
150	48	41.7	1848	4194	150	62	1.0	28	2097	150	56	264.3	12524	15204
200	80	55.0	1172	5242	200	88	398.8	7988	18874	200	70	-	-	-
250	84	127.6	4496	8912	250	118	173.3	2126	9961	250	96	-	-	-
300	118	2174.4	16982	60817	300	146	1520.2	21756	72876	300	96	-	-	-

Table 3. Same experiment as in Table2, but with one reaction node included every two ($m = 5$ instead of 8 or 9).

Glycolysis (m=5)					Heme (m=5)					Lysine (m=5)				
Size	t	Time	Nodes	Mem	Size	t	Time	Nodes	Mem	Size	t	Time	Nodes	Mem
50	12	0.2	22	2097	50	22	0.3	44	2097	50	18	0.1	16	2097
100	28	2.5	230	2097	100	36	0.9	78	2097	100	40	13.3	1292	3145
150	48	79.3	5538	6815	150	62	7.3	144	3145	150	56	260.4	8642	14155
200	80	39.9	1198	5767	200	88	57.3	950	5242	200	70	4330.5	74550	192937
250	84	323.6	5428	14680	250	118	36.0	350	8388	250	96	-	-	-
300	118	10470.8	94988	296747	300	146	-	-	-	300	96	-	-	-

tained with our other implementations of graph variables [21,11]. We wish to design more efficient heuristics for labelling (a first-fail strategy from [12] has been used). Cost-based filtering will be implemented and used in order to limit the size of the graph according to an upper bound of the cost of the path. A second aspect of our future work consists in finding which constraints are needed to recover known pathways as it was shown in [20] that non-constrained shortest paths are not able to recover all of them.

7 Conclusion

This paper introduces the CP(Graph) computation domain with graph domain variables in order to state and solve subgraph extraction problems. CP(Graph) provides finites domains and finite sets of nodes and arcs along with the graph domain variables as this is more expressive than nodes or arcs alone.

The kernel constraints, a minimal set of constraints in order to build other graph constraints and problems, are introduced with their achieved consistency and complexity. Graph constraints are built using the kernel constraints and we sketch a global propagator for some of them. CP(Graph) provides a framework for the integration of existing and new global constraint on graphs. We describe a path constraint based on [7,8], with domain variables for the source and sink. Finally we showed that CP(Graph) can be used to simply express and solve a problem in biochemical network analysis requiring up to now a dedicated and sophisticated algorithm.

In the proposed CP(Graph) prototype, graph domain variables are represented by a finite set of nodes and a finite set of arcs. A dedicated data-structure for graph domain variables will be designed and compared to the current set implementation. It will most probably consist in a graph data-structure for both bounds of the graph domain variable. The integration of CP(Graph) in an existing constraint solver will then be pursued by integrating graph variables as native variables of the system. We are working on a Gecode [22] implementation.

The application of CP(Graph) to bioinformatics problems will be pursued. This should result in the need for more memory effective graph domain variables and better branching strategies as big graphs (*e.g.* 16000 nodes, 45000 arcs) are under consideration in this field. CP(Graph) will also be compared to other implementations of combinatorial graph problems using constraint programming.

CP(Graph) allows to state problems about multiple graphs. An important problem among those is the graph isomorphism problem. We are adapting the global constraints of (mono/iso)-morphism and subgraph (mono/iso)-isomorphism of two graph domain variables from the techniques developed in [23].

References

1. Deville, Y., Gilbert, D., van Helden, J., Wodak, S.: An overview of data models for the analysis of biochemical networks. Briefings in Bioinformatics **4(3)** (2003) 246–259
2. Gervet, C.: Interval propagation to reason about sets: Definition and implementation of a practical language. CONSTRAINTS Journal **1(3)** (1997) 191–244
3. Laurière, J.: A Language and a Program for Stating and Solving Combinatorial Problems. Artificial Intelligence **10** (1978) 29–127
4. Gervet, C.: New structures of symbolic constraint objects: sets and graphs. In: Third Workshop on Constraint Logic Programming (WCLP'93), Marseille (1993)
5. Lepape, C., Perron, L., Regin, J.C., Shaw, P.: A robust and parallel solving of a network design problem. In: Proceedings of the 8th International Conference on Principles and Practice of Constraint Programming. Volume LNCS 2470. (2002) 633–648
6. Beldiceanu, N.: Global constraints as graph properties on structured network of elementary constraints of the same type. Technical Report T2000/01, SICS (2000)
7. Sellmann, M.: Cost-based filtering for shorter path constraints. In: Proceedings of the 9th International Conference on Principles and Practise of Constraint Programming (CP). Volume LNCS 2833., Springer-Verlag (2003) 694–708
8. Cambazard, H., Bourreau, E.: Conception d'une contrainte globale de chemin. In: 10e Journ. nat. sur la résolution pratique de problèmes NP-complets (JNPC'04). (2004) 107–121
9. Beldiceanu, N., Flener, P., Lorca, X.: The tree constraint. In Bartak, R., Milano, M., eds.: Proceedings of CP-AI-OR'05. Volume LNCS 3524., Springer-Verlag (2005)
10. Courcelle, B.: On the expression of graph properties in some fragments of monadic second-order logic. In: Descriptive complexity and finite models, Providence, AMS (1997) 38–62
11. Grégoire Dooms, Yves Deville, Pierre Dupont: A mozart implementation of cp(bionet). In Van Roy, P., ed.: Multiparadigm Programming in Mozart/Oz. Number LNCS 3389, Springer-Verlag (2004) 237–250
12. Pesant, G., Gendreau, M., Potvin, J., Rousseau, J.: An exact constraint logic programming algorithm for the travelling salesman with time windows. Transp. Science **32** (1996) 12–29
13. Courcelle, B.: The monadic second-order logic of graphs. i. recognizable sets of finite graphs. Inf. Comput. **85** (1990) 12–75

14. Quesada, L., Roy, P.V., Deville, Y.: The reachability propagator. Research Report 2005-07, (UCL/INGI)
15. Bessière, C., Van Hentenryck, P.: To be or not to be ... a global constraint. In: Proceedings of the 9th International Conference on Principles and Practise of Constraint Programming (CP). Volume LNCS 2833., Springer-Verlag (2003) 789–794
16. Holm, J., de Lichtenberg, K., Thorup, M.: Poly-logarithmic deterministic fully-dynamic algorithms for connectivity, minimum spanning tree, 2-edge, and biconnectivity. Journal ACM **48(4)** (2001) 723–760
17. Michel, L., Van Hentenryck, P.: Maintaining longest paths incrementally. In: Proceedings of the International Conference on Constraint Programming (CP-2003), (Springer-Verlag)
18. Mozart Consortium: The mozart programming system version 1.2.5 (December 2002) http://www.mozart-oz.org/.
19. Lemer, C., Antezana, E., Couche, F., Fays, F., Santolaria, X., Janky, R., Deville, Y., Richelle, J., Wodak, S.J.: The aMAZE lightbench: a web interface to a relational database of cellular processes. Nucleic Acids Research **32** (2004) D443–D448
20. Croes, D.: Recherche de chemins dans le réseau métabolique et mesure de la distance métabolique entre enzymes. PhD thesis, ULB, Brussels (2005) (in preparation).
21. Dooms, G., Deville, Y., Dupont, P.: Recherche de chemins contraints dans les réseaux biochimiques. In Mesnard, F., ed.: Programmation en logique avec contraintes, actes des JFPLC 2004, Hermes Science (June 2004) 109–128
22. Gecode: Generic Constraint Development (2005) http://www.gecode.org/.
23. Zampelli, S., Deville, Y., Dupont, P.: Approximate constrained subgraph matching. In: Proceedings of the 11th International Conference on Principles and Practise of Constraint Programming (CP), Springer-Verlag (2005)

Interval Analysis in Scheduling

Jérôme Fortin[1], Paweł Zieliński[2], Didier Dubois[1], and Hélène Fargier[1]

[1] IRIT/UPS 118 route de Narbonne, 31062, Toulouse, cedex 4, France
{fortin, dubois, fargier}@irit.fr
[2] Institute of Mathematics and Computer Science, Wrocław University of Technology,
Wybrzeże Wyspiańskiego 27, 50-370 Wrocław, Poland
pziel@im.pwr.wroc.pl

Abstract. This paper reconsiders the most basic scheduling problem, that of minimizing the makespan of a partially ordered set of activities, in the context of incomplete knowledge. While this problem is very easy in the deterministic case, its counterpart when durations are interval-valued is much trickier, as standard results and algorithms no longer apply. After positioning this paper in the scope of temporal networks under uncertainty, we provide a complete solution to the problem of finding the latest starting times and floats of activities, and of locating surely critical ones, as they are often isolated. The minimal float problem is NP-hard while the maximal float problem is polynomial. New complexity results and efficient algorithms are provided for the interval-valued makespan minimization problem.

1 Introduction and Motivation

Temporal Constraint Networks (TCN) represent relations between dates of events and also allow to express constraints on the possible durations of activities from intervals of values [1]. To ensure a solution to the assignment problem, it is sufficient to check the well-known consistency properties of the network.

TCN have been extended to take into account uncertainty of durations of some tasks in realistic applications. A distinction is made between so-called contingent constraints (for example, when the duration of a task cannot be known before the execution of the task) and controllable ones (for example a time interval to be chosen between starting times of two tasks). The resulting network (called Simple Temporal Network with Uncertainty or STPU) becomes a decision-making problem under uncertainty, and notions of consistency must be refined so as to ensure controllability, that is, ensured consistency despite uncertainty [2–5]. As far as we know, the TCN community has extensively worked on the controllability of a network, but the question of optimizing the total duration of set of tasks described by a STPU has not been studied. Nevertheless, not all solutions to an STPU are equally valuable, and solutions minimizing the makespan are of obvious practical interest.

Given a set of tasks and a set of precedence constraints between them, the most elementary scheduling problem is to find the time window for the starting time of each task in order to ensure a minimal overall duration or makespan. When all task durations are precise, the well-known PERT/CPM (Critical Path Method) algorithm provides such time-windows for all tasks in polynomial time (see [6]). In particular, a subset of tasks is found to be critical (their starting time-windows reduce to a singleton), and they form a set of critical paths. When the durations of tasks are ill-known and modeled by intervals, this problem can be viewed as a special kind of STPU where all tasks are modeled by contingent constraints, and controllable constraints only describe precedence between tasks. Of course, the resulting network is always controllable if the graph of precedence constraints is acyclic. However, the problem of minimizing the makespan in the interval-valued setting is much more difficult. It seems to have received attention only recently [7]. This concern actually derives from the literature on fuzzy PERT, a topic existing since the early eighties (see [8] for a survey). Especially Buckley [9] was the first to propose a rigorous formulation for this problem. Recent results show that in the presence of uncertainty, the usual backward recursion algorithm for finding latest starting times of tasks is no longer applicable and the usual critical path analysis totally fails [10]. Yet, in the scope of selecting solutions to STPU which minimize the makespan, it is a basic problem to be solved in a first step.

Instead of being critical or not, tasks now form three groups: those that are for sure critical despite uncertainty (necessarily critical tasks), those that are for sure not critical, and tasks whose criticality is unknown, called possibly critical tasks (see [11]). Necessarily critical paths may fail to exist while necessarily critical tasks may be isolated. Finding the 3-partition of tasks in an interval-valued network turns out to be a NP-hard problem. Preliminary complexity results have recently appeared in [7], but some problems like the complexity of proving the necessary criticality of a task remained open. This paper provides a full picture of the complexity of the makespan minimization problem under the representation of interval-based uncertainty, and a set of efficient algorithms for determining the criticality of tasks, the optimal intervals containing their least ending times and their floats. It is shown that the only NP-hard problem is the one of finding the greatest lower bound of the float, which is closely related to asserting the possible criticality of a task. All other problems turn out to be polynomial. The fact that the two problems of asserting if an arc is necessarily critical or possibly critical do not have the same complexity is rather unexpected.

2 Preliminaries

An activity network is classically defined as a set of activities (or tasks) with given duration times, related to each other by means of precedence constraints. When there are no resource constraints, it can be represented by a directed, connected and acyclic graph. Of major concern, is to minimize the ending time of the last task, also called the makespan of the network. For each task, three quantities have practical importance for the management of the activity network: The *earliest starting time* est_{ij} of an activity (i, j) is the date before which the activity cannot be started without violation of a precedence constraint. The *latest starting time* lst_{ij} of an activity (i,j) is the date after which the activity cannot be started without delaying the end of the project. The *float* f_{ij} of an activity (i,j) is the difference between the latest starting time lst_{ij} and the earliest starting time est_{ij}. An activity is *critical* if and only if its float is equal to zero. Under the assumption of minimal makespan, critical tasks must be started and completed at prescribed time-points.

3   The Interval-Valued Scheduling Problem

A directed, connected and acyclic graph $G = <V, A>$, represents an activity network. We use the activity-on-arc convention. V is the set of nodes (events), $|V| = n$, and A is the set of arcs (activities), $|A| = m$.

The set $V = \{1, 2, \ldots, n\}$ is labeled in such a way that $i < j$ for each activity $(i,j) \in A$. Activity durations d_{ij} (weights of the arcs) $(i,j) \in A$ are only known to belong to time intervals $D_{ij} = [d_{ij}^-, d_{ij}^+]$, $d_{ij}^- \geq 0$. Two nodes 1 and n are distinguished as the initial and final node, respectively.

We introduce some additional notations.

- A configuration is a precise instantiation of the duration of all tasks $(i,j) \in A$. Ω denotes a configuration, while $d_{ij}(\Omega) \in D_{ij}$ denotes the duration of activity (i,j) in configuration Ω.
  Let $B \subseteq A$ be a subset of activities. The configuration Ω_B^+ such that
  $$d_{ij}(\Omega_B^+) = \begin{cases} d_{ij}^+ & \text{if } (i,j) \in B \\ d_{ij}^- & \text{otherwise} \end{cases}$$
  is called an *extreme configuration induced by B*.
- $\mathfrak{C}$ is the set of possible configurations of activity durations, $\mathfrak{C} = \times_{(i,j) \in A} D_{ij}$.
- $P(u,v)$ is the set of all paths $p(u,v)$ in G from node u to node v, we denote by P the set of all paths p in G from node 1 to node n.
- $l_p(\Omega)$ denotes the length of a path $p \in P(u,v)$ in Ω, $l_p(\Omega) = \sum_{(i,j) \in p} d_{ij}(\Omega)$.
- $Succ(i)$ (resp. $Pred(i)$) refers to the set of nodes that immediately follow (resp. precede) node $i \in V$.
- $SUCC(i,j)$ (resp. $PRED(i,j)$) denotes the set of all arcs that come after (resp. before) $(i,j) \in A$, and $SUCC(j)$ (resp. $PRED(j)$) stands for the set of all nodes that come after (resp. before) $j \in V$.
- $G(i,j)$ is the subgraph of G composed of nodes succeeding i and preceding j.
- $G(d_{ij} = d)$ is the graph where duration of task (i,j) is replaced by d.

Computing earliest starting dates is not a difficult issue [12]. Here we solve four problems, originally stated in [11,13].

The first one is that of determining the widest intervals LST_{kl} (bounds) of possible values of the latest starting times lst_{kl} of a given activity $(k,l) \in A$, i.e. the interval $LST_{kl} = [lst_{kl}^-, lst_{kl}^+]$ defined by $lst_{kl}^- = \min_{\Omega \in \mathfrak{C}} lst_{kl}(\Omega)$ and $lst_{kl}^+ = \max_{\Omega \in \mathfrak{C}} lst_{kl}(\Omega)$. $lst_{kl}(\Omega)$ is the float of activity (k,l) in configuration Ω. The problem of computing the greatest lower (resp. least upper) bound of the latest starting times is denoted GLBLST (resp. LUBLST). The second problem is that of determining the widest intervals F_{kl} of possible values of floats (total floats) f_{kl} of a given activity $(k,l) \in A$, i.e. the interval $F_{kl} = [f_{kl}^-, f_{kl}^+]$ bounded by $f_{kl}^- = \min_{\Omega \in \mathfrak{C}} f_{kl}(\Omega)$ and $f_{kl}^+ = \max_{\Omega \in \mathfrak{C}} f_{kl}(\Omega)$. $f_{kl}(\Omega)$ is the float of activity (k,l) in configuration Ω. The problem of computing the greatest lower (resp. least upper) bound of the floats is denoted GLBF (resp. LUBF). In both problems minimization and maximization are taken over all possible configurations $\mathfrak{C}$.

The next two problems are closely related to the ones defined previously. That is the problem of deciding the *possible criticality* of an activity and the problem of deciding the *necessary criticality* of an activity. An activity $(k,l) \in A$ is *possibly critical* in G if and only if there exists a configuration $\Omega \in \mathfrak{C}$ such that (k,l) is critical in G in Ω. An activity $(k,l) \in A$ is *necessarily critical* in G if and only if for every configuration $\Omega \in \mathfrak{C}$, (k,l) is critical in G.

There are obvious connections between the notions of criticality and the bounds on the float of an activity.

Proposition 1. *An activity $(k,l) \in A$ is possibly (resp. necessarily) critical in G if and only if $f_{kl}^- = 0$ (resp. $f_{kl}^+ = 0$).*

The solutions to problems GLBLST, LUBLST, LUBF and GLBF come down to finding an extreme configuration [11] where such bounds are attained. As there are 2^n extreme configurations, it explains the potentially exponential nature of the problem. GLBLST, LUBLST and GLBF have recently been solved in [7,14], and only GLBF is NP-hard. In this paper, we recall the solutions of these three problems, and present the solution to the last one LUBF, thus providing a full picture of the makespan minimization problem under incomplete information.

4 Computational Methods for Evaluating Criticality

This section presents a new method which can decide if a given task (k,l) is necessarily critical. First, under the assumption that the durations of the predecessors of task (k,l) are precisely known, we recall algorithms that respectively assert if (k,l) is possibly and necessarily critical. They constitute the basis for computing the LUB and GLB of the latest starting dates in polynomial time in [14]. We extend these results and give a general algorithm which asserts if (k,l) is necessarily critical in a network G in polynomial time without any consideration of the durations of tasks preceding (k,l). This result will lead in the next section to a polynomial algorithm which computes the LUB of the float of an activity.

Let us recall characteristic conditions of the non-necessary criticality of tasks.

Lemma 1 ([8]). *An activity $(k,l) \in A$ is not necessarily critical in G if and only if there exists a path $p \in P$ such that $(k,l) \notin p$, p is critical in configuration Ω_p^+ and no critical path in Ω_p^+ includes (k,l).*

Observation 1. *An activity $(k,l) \in A$ is not necessarily critical in G if and only if (k,l) is not critical in an extreme configuration in which the duration of (k,l) is at its lower bound and all activities from set $A \backslash SUCC(k,l) \backslash PRED(k,l) \backslash \{(k,l)\}$ have durations at their upper bounds.*

Now under the assumption that activities preceding (k,l) have precise durations, we can set the durations of tasks succeeding (k,l) at precise values while maintaining the status of (k,l) in terms of necessary criticality. It yields a configuration where (k,l) is critical if and only if it is necessarily critical in the interval-valued network. These durations are given by Propositions 2 and 3.

Proposition 2. *Let $(k,l) \in A$ be a distinguished activity, and (i,j) be an activity such that $(i,j) \in SUCC(k,l)$. Assume that every activity $(u,v) \in PRED(i,j)$ has precise duration. If (k,l) is critical in $G(1,i)$, then the following conditions are equivalent:*
(i) (k,l) is necessarily critical in G,
(ii) (k,l) is necessarily critical in $G(d_{ij} = d_{ij}^-)$.

Proof. (i) $\Longrightarrow$ (ii) Obvious.
(i) $\Longleftarrow$ (ii) We use a proof by contraposition. We need to prove that if (k,l) is critical in $G(1,i)$ and (k,l) is not necessarily critical in G, then (k,l) is not necessarily critical in $G(d_{ij} = d_{ij}^-)$. By assumption, (k,l) is not necessarily critical in G. From Lemma 1, it follows that there exists a path $p \in P$ such that $(k,l) \notin p$, p is critical in configuration Ω_p^+ and no critical path in Ω_p^+ includes (k,l). Since (k,l) is critical in $G(1,i)$, $(i,j) \notin p$ in Ω_p^+. Observe that $d_{ij}(\Omega_p^+) = d_{ij}^-$. From this and the fact that (k,l) is not critical in Ω_p^+, we conclude that (k,l) is not necessarily critical in $G(d_{ij} = d_{ij}^-)$. □

Proposition 3. *Let $(k,l) \in A$ be a distinguished activity, and (i,j) be an activity such that $(i,j) \in SUCC(k,l)$. Assume that every activity $(u,v) \in PRED(i,j)$ has precise duration. If (k,l) is not critical in $G(1,i)$, then the following conditions are equivalent:*
(i) (k,l) is necessarily critical in G,
(ii) (k,l) is necessarily critical in $G(d_{ij} = d_{ij}^+)$.

Proof. (i) $\Longrightarrow$ (ii) Straightforward.
(i) $\Longleftarrow$ (ii) To prove that (k,l) is necessarily critical in G, we only need to show that (k,l) is necessarily critical in $G(d_{ij} = d_{ij}^-)$. By assumption, (k,l) is necessarily critical in $G(d_{ij} = d_{ij}^+)$. From this, it follows that for every configuration in which the duration of (i,j) is at its upper bound, there exists a critical path traversing (k,l). Moreover, this path does not use (i,j), since (k,l) is not critical in $G(1,i)$. Thus (k,l) remains non critical, irrelevent of the duration of (i,j). Hence, (k,l) is critical for each configuration in which the duration of (i,j) is at its lower bound and consequently (k,l) is necessarily critical in $G(d_{ij} = d_{ij}^-)$. The necessary criticality of (k,l) in $G(d_{ij} = d_{ij}^-)$ and in $G(d_{ij} = d_{ij}^+)$ implies the necessary criticality of (k,l) in G. □

Propositions 2 and 3, together with Observation 1, lead us to Algorithm 1 for asserting the necessary criticality of a given activity (k,l) in a network in which all activities that precede (k,l) have precise durations. Testing if (k,l) is critical in $G(1,i)$ can be done in constant time because we already know if (k,l) is critical in $G(1,j)$ for all $j \in Pred(i)$, and so Algorithm 1 runs in $O(m)$.

We now present an algorithm for evaluating the necessary criticality of a fixed activity $(k,l) \in A$ in network G with interval durations, without any restriction. The key to the algorithm lies in Propositions 4 and 5 that enable a network with interval durations to be replaced by another network with precise durations for

Algorithm 1.

Input: A network G, activity (k,l), interval durations D_{uv}, $(u,v) \in A$ and for every task in $PRED(k,l)$ the duration is precisely given.
Output: true if (k,l) is necessarily critical in G; and false otherwise.
foreach $(u,v) \notin SUCC(k,l)$ do $d_{uv} \leftarrow d^+_{uv}$; $d_{kl} \leftarrow d^-_{kl}$
for $i \leftarrow l$ to $n-1$ such that $i \in SUCC(l) \cup \{l\}$ do
  | if (k,l) is critical in $G(1,i)$ then foreach $j \in Succ(i)$ do $d_{ij} \leftarrow d^-_{ij}$
  | else foreach $j \in Succ(i)$ do $d_{ij} \leftarrow d^+_{ij}$
If (k,l) is critical in $G(1,n)$ then return true
else return false

---

activities preceding a fixed (k,l), in such a way that (k,l) is necessarily critical in the former if and only if it is necessarily critical in the latter.

Proposition 4. *Let $(k,l) \in A$ be a distinguished activity, and (i,j) be an activity such that $(i,j) \in PRED(k,l)$. If (k,l) is necessarily critical in $G(j,n)$, then the following conditions are equivalent:*
(i) (k,l) is necessarily critical in G,
(ii) (k,l) is necessarily critical in $G(d_{ij} = d^-_{ij})$.

Proof. The proof goes in the similar manner to the one of Proposition 2. □

Proposition 5. *Let $(k,l) \in A$ be a distinguished activity, and (i,j) be an activity such that $(i,j) \in PRED(k,l)$. If (k,l) is not necessarily critical in $G(j,n)$, then the following conditions are equivalent:*
(i) (k,l) is necessarily critical in G,
(ii) (k,l) is necessarily critical in $G(d_{ij} = d^+_{ij})$.

Proof. (i) $\implies$ (ii) The proof is immediate.
(i) $\impliedby$ (ii) We need to show that if (k,l) is not necessarily critical in $G(j,n)$ and (k,l) is necessarily critical in $G(d_{ij} = d^+_{ij})$, then (k,l) is necessarily critical in G. To prove this, assume on the contrary that (k,l) is not necessarily critical in G. From Lemma 1, it follows that there exists a path $p \in P$ such that $(k,l) \not\in p$, p is critical in configuration Ω^+_p and no critical path in Ω^+_p includes (k,l) or equivalently (k,l) is not critical in Ω^+_p. We will show that for each such configuration, where (k,l) is not critical, the other assumptions lead to construct a critical path that traverses (k,l), which results in a contradiction. By assumption, (k,l) is not necessarily critical in $G(j,n)$. Then there exists a path $\hat{p} \in P(j,n)$ such that $(k,l) \not\in \hat{p}$, $\hat{p}$ is critical in configuration $\Omega^+_{\hat{p}}$ and no critical path of $G(j,n)$ traverses (k,l) in $\Omega^+_{\hat{p}}$ (see Lemma 1).

Consider the extreme configuration induced by $p \cup \hat{p} \cup \{(i,j)\}$ and denote it by Ω^*. Note that (k,l) is critical in Ω^*, since (k,l) is necessarily critical in $G(d_{ij} = d^+_{ij})$. Thus there exists a critical path $p^* \in P$ using (k,l) in Ω^*. We define r to be the common node of $p^*(1,k)$ and p such that $r = \max\{v \mid v \in V, v \in p^*(1,k), v \in p\}$ and define $\hat{r}$ to be the common node of $p^*(1,k)$ and $\hat{p}$ such that $\hat{r} = \max\{v \mid v \in V, v \in p^*(1,k), v \in \hat{p}\}$.

We claim that if node $\hat{r}$ exists, then $\hat{r} = r$ or node $\hat{r}$ lies on p^* before node r. Suppose, contrary to our claim, that $\hat{r}$ lies on p^* after r (see Figure 1a). Then subpath $p^*(\hat{r},n)$, $p^*(\hat{r},n) = p^*(\hat{r},k) \cup p^*(k,n)$, is at least as long as subpath $\hat{p}(\hat{r},n)$ in configuration Ω^*. Notice that $p^*(\hat{r},k)$ is one of longest paths from $\hat{r}$ to k in Ω^*. We may now

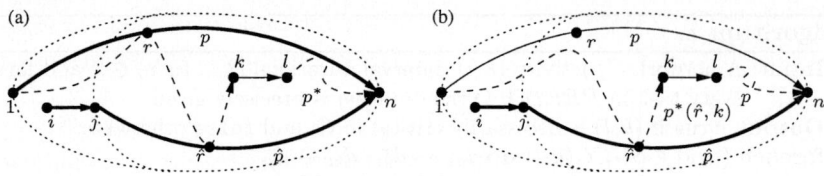

Fig. 1. (a) Configuration $\Omega^* - \hat{r}$ on p^* after r (b) Configuration Ω' (activities with the maximal durations are in bold)

decrease some activity durations to their lower bounds in configuration Ω^* in the following way (see Figure 1b) $\forall (u,v) \in A$, $d_{uv}(\Omega') = \begin{cases} d_{uv}^+ & \text{if } (u,v) \in \hat{p} \\ d_{uv}^+ & \text{if } (u,v) = (i,j) \\ d_{uv}^- & \text{otherwise} \end{cases}$. Duration $d_{ij}(\Omega') = d_{ij}^+$, and, by assumption, (k,l) is necessarily critical in $G(d_{ij} = d_{ij}^+)$. Consequently (k,l) is critical in this new configuration Ω'. Hence, there exists a critical path $p' \in P$ traversing (k,l). Since node $\hat{r}$ lies on p^* after node r, $l_{p^*(\hat{r},k)}(\Omega^*) = l_{p^*(\hat{r},k)}(\Omega')$. Therefore path $p^*(\hat{r},k) \cup p'(k,n)$ is at least as long as subpath $\hat{p}(\hat{r},n)$ in configuration Ω'. Decreasing $d_{ij}(\Omega')$ to its lower bound gives configuration $\Omega_{\hat{p}}^+$. Observe that the lengths of paths $p^*(\hat{r},k) \cup p'(k,n)$ and $\hat{p}(\hat{r},n)$ remain unchanged. Hence, there exists the path in $G(j,n)$ composed of two subpaths $\hat{p}(j,\hat{r})$ and $p^*(\hat{r},k) \cup p'(k,n)$ that is at least as long as $\hat{p}$, which is impossible because we have assumed that no critical path goes through (k,l) in $G(j,n)$ in configuration $\Omega_{\hat{p}}^+$. We can now return to the

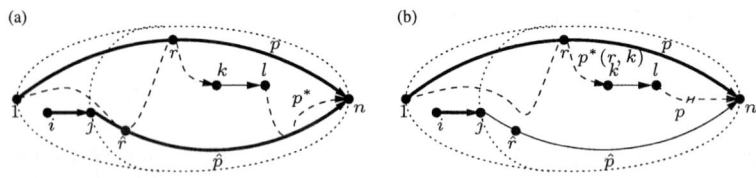

Fig. 2. (a) Configuration $\Omega^* - \hat{r}$ on p^* before r (b) Configuration Ω''

main proof. Consider configuration Ω^*. The previous claim shows that if node $\hat{r}$ exists, then $\hat{r} = r$ or node $\hat{r}$ lies on p^* before node r (see Figure 2a). In the case when $\hat{r}$ does not exist, the proof proceeds in the same manner. From the above and the criticality of p^* in Ω^*, it follows that subpath $p^*(r,n)$, $p^*(r,n) = p^*(r,k) \cup p^*(k,n)$, is at least as long as subpath $p(r,n)$ in this configuration. Notice that $p^*(r,k)$ is one of longest paths from r to k in Ω^*. Decreasing some of durations in Ω^* to their lower bounds, we obtain configuration Ω'' in the following form (see Figure 2b) $\forall (u,v) \in A$, $d_{uv}(\Omega'') = \begin{cases} d_{uv}^+ & \text{if } (u,v) \in p \\ d_{uv}^+ & \text{if } (u,v) = (i,j) \\ d_{uv}^- & \text{otherwise} \end{cases}$. Duration $d_{ij}(\Omega'') = d_{ij}^+$, by assumption, (k,l) is necessarily critical in $G(d_{ij} = d_{ij}^+)$, which implies the criticality of (k,l)

in this new configuration Ω''. Hence, there exists a critical path $p'' \in P$ using (k,l). By the claim, $l_{p^*(r,k)}(\Omega^*) = l_{p^*(r,k)}(\Omega'')$. It follows that path $p^*(r,k) \cup p''(k,n)$ is at least as long as subpath $p(r,n)$ in configuration Ω''. If $(i,j) \notin p$, we may decrease duration $d_{ij}(\Omega'')$ to its lower bound. Again by the claim, the lengths of subpaths $p^*(r,k) \cup p''(k,n)$ and $p(r,n)$ remain unchanged in this new configuration and so $p^*(r,k) \cup p''(k,n)$ is still at least as long as $p(r,n)$. It is easily seen that this new configuration is equal to Ω_p^+. If $(i,j) \in p$, configurations Ω_p'' and Ω_p^+ are equal. Consequently, path $p(1,r) \cup p^*(r,k) \cup p''(k,n)$ is at least as long as p and moreover $p(1,r) \cup p^*(r,k) \cup p''(k,n)$ uses (k,l). This contradicts our assumption that no critical path in Ω_p^+ includes (k,l). □

We are now in a position to give an algorithm (Algorithm 2) for asserting necessary criticality of a fixed activity in a general network. At each step of the algorithm, tasks between j and k have precise durations (so Algorithm 1 can be invoked), and Algorithm 2 assigns precise durations to tasks preceding j, while preserving the criticality of task (k,l). Since Algorithm 1 runs in $O(m)$, Algorithm 2 requires $O(mn)$ time.

Algorithm 2.

  Input: A network $G = <V, A>$, activity (k,l), interval durations D_{uv}, $(u,v) \in A$.
  Output: true if (k,l) is necessarily critical in G; and false otherwise.
  for $j \leftarrow k$ downto 2 such that $j \in PRED(k) \cup \{k\}$ **do**
    NC $\leftarrow$ Algorithm 1 with $G(j,n)$ and durations D_{uv}
    if NC =true **then foreach** $i \in Pred(j)$ **do** $d_{ij} \leftarrow d_{ij}^-$
    else foreach $i \in Pred(j)$ **do** $d_{ij} \leftarrow d_{ij}^+$
  NC $\leftarrow$ Algorithm 1 with $G(1,n),(k,l)$ and updated durations
  if NC =true **then return** true
    else return false

Remark: Lemma 1, Propositions 2 and 3 have counterparts for asserting possible criticality. So the reasoning which leads to the first algorithm can be applied for possible criticality [14]. This leads to an algorithm similar to Algorithm 1 swapping durations d_{uv}^- and d_{uv}^+, for asserting the possible criticality of tasks whose predecessors have deterministic durations. Unfortunately, Propositions 4 and 5 can not be adapted to the study of possible criticality, and asserting if a task is possibly critical in the general case is provably NP-Complete [7]. So, while the results of this section are instrumental for solving problem LUBF, the same approach cannot be applied to compute the GLB of the floats.

5 Computational Methods for the Latest Starting Times

5.1 Computing the Greatest Lower Bound on the Latest Starting Times

There already exists an algorithm that computes the GLB of latest starting times [14] in polynomial time whose basis is recalled below. This section presents a new polynomial method (more efficient than the already known one as shown in Section 7) derived from a path enumeration algorithm [8].

The Incremental Approach. Let us recall the following simple but important result that allows to reduce the set of configurations $\mathfrak{C}$ for the GLBLST problem.

Proposition 6 ([11]). *The greatest lower bound on the latest starting times lst_{kl}^- of activity (k,l) in G is attained on an extreme configuration in which the duration of (k,l) is at its upper bound and all activities that do not belong to set $SUCC(k,l)$ have durations at their lower bounds.*

The idea of the algorithm for computing lst_{kl}^- is based on Lemma 2. It consists in finding the minimal nonnegative real number f_{kl}^* that added to the upper bound of the duration interval of a specified (k,l) makes it possibly critical.

Lemma 2 ([14]). *Let f_{kl}^* be the minimal nonnegative real such that (k,l) is possibly critical with a duration $d_{kl}^+ + f_{kl}^*$. Then $lst_{kl}^- = est_{kl}^- + f_{kl}^*$.*

The sketch of the algorithm is simple: we begin to set the durations of tasks preceding (k,l) to their minimal value then we run the algorithm asserting the possible criticality of (k,l). If (k,l) is possibly critical then its minimal latest starting date equals the minimal earliest starting date. Otherwise for each task $(i,j) \in PRED(k,l)$ for which (k,l) is possibly critical in $G(j,n)$ and not in $G(i,n)$ we compute the minimal duration to add to (k,l) to make this task possibly critical in $G(i,n)$ (this value is easy to compute). Then we add the smallest computed value to the duration of (k,l) and reiterate the test of possible criticality of (k,l) in G. Contrary to the next one, this algorithm computes the latest starting date of only one task.

The Path Enumeration Approach. First let us state a result which describes the form of configurations where the GLB of the latest starting date of a task (k,l) in a network G is attained, given in [8]. Let $P_{kl}(u,v)$ be the set of all paths from node u to node v going through task (k,l).

Proposition 7. *Let $(k,l) \in A$ be a task of G. There exists a path $p_{kl} \in P_{kl}(k,n)$ such that the extreme configuration $\Omega_{p_{kl}}^+$ minimizes $lst_{kl}(.)$.*

Note that path p_{kl} is one of the longest paths from k to n including l in configuration $\Omega_{p_{kl}}^+$. We can recursively construct the path $p_{kl} \in P_{kl}(k,n)$ of Proposition 7 corresponding to the optimal configuration. Suppose that for each node $u \in Succ(l)$, we know a path $p_{lu} \in P_{lu}(l,n)$ for which the configuration $\Omega_{p_{lu}}^+$ minimizes the latest starting date of (l,u). Then we can construct an optimal path p_{kl} from paths p_{lu} for $u \in Succ(l)$.

Proposition 8. *Let (k,l) be a task of G, and $\forall u \in Succ(l)$, let $p_{lu} \in P_{lu}(l,n)$ be a path such that $lst_{lu}^- = lst_{lu}(\Omega_{p_{lu}}^+)$. Then $lst_{kl}^- = \min_{u \in succ(l)} lst_{kl}(\Omega_{\{(k,l)\} \cup p_{lu}}^+)$.*

From Proposition 8, we can deduce a polynomial algorithm to compute the GLB of the latest starting dates of all tasks: we recursively find a path p_{kl} for which the configuration $\Omega^+_{p_{kl}}$ minimizes $lst_{kl}(.)$ from the paths p_{lu} for $u \in Succ(l)$, starting from the nodes in $Pred(n)$. Algorithm 3 runs in $O(m(n + m))$ for the computation of all the GLBs of the latest starting dates. Note that it is similar to the backwards recursion technique used in the classical CPM method.

Algorithm 3.

Input: A network G, interval durations D_{uv}, $(u,v) \in A$.
Output: The GLB of latest starting dates of all the tasks in network.
foreach $(k,l) \in A$ **do** $lst^-_{kl} \leftarrow +\infty$
$V \leftarrow V \cup \{n+1\}; A \leftarrow A \cup \{(n, n+1)\}$
$D_{nn+1} \leftarrow 0; p_{nn+1} \leftarrow (n, n+1)$
foreach (k,l) such that $k \leftarrow n-1$ **downto** 0 **do**
$\quad$ **foreach** $u \in Succ(l)$ **do**
$\quad\quad$ $p' \leftarrow (k,l) \cup p_{lu}$
$\quad\quad$ Compute $lst_{kl}(\Omega^+_{p'})$ by the classical CPM
$\quad\quad$ **if** $lst_{kl}(\Omega^+_{p'}) < lst^-_{kl}$ **then** $lst^-_{kl} \leftarrow lst_{kl}(\Omega^+_{p'}); p_{kl} \leftarrow p'$

5.2 Computing the Least Upper Bound on the Latest Starting Times

Only a counterpart to the incremental method is known for computing the GLB on the latest starting times of an activity. There exists an exponential path enumeration algorithm [8], but it has not (yet) been adapted to compute the LUB of the latest starting dates in polynomial time (contrary to the GLB). Again a result of Dubois et al. [11], allows to reduce the set of configurations $\mathfrak{C}$.

Proposition 9 ([11]). *The least upper bound on the latest starting times lst^-_{kl} of activity (k,l) in G is attained on an extreme configuration in which the duration of (k,l) is at its lower bound and all activities that do not belong to set $SUCC(k,l)$ have durations at their upper bounds.*

The main idea of the algorithm for determining lst^+_{kl} of a given activity $(k,l) \in A$ is based on Lemma 3. It consists in determining the minimal nonnegative real number f^*_{kl} that added to the lower bound of the duration interval of a specified activity (k,l) makes it necessarily critical.

Lemma 3 ([14]). *Let f^*_{kl} be the minimal nonnegative real number such that (k,l) is necessarily critical with a duration $d^-_{kl} + f^*_{kl}$. Then $lst^+_{kl} = est^+_{kl} + f^*_{kl}$.*

6 Computational Methods for Floats

6.1 Computing the Least Upper Bound on Floats

To compute the LUB of the floats of an activity (k,l), we first set the durations of the tasks neither preceding nor succeeding (k,l) according to the following Lemma 4. The maximal float of (k,l) after this partial instantiation is the same as in the original network G.

Lemma 4 ([11]). *The least upper bound on float f_{kl}^+ of activity (k,l) in G is attained on an extreme configuration in which the duration of (k,l) is at its lower bound and all activities from set $A \setminus SUCC(k,l) \setminus PRED(k,l) \setminus \{(k,l)\}$ have durations at their upper bounds.*

Algorithm 2 is a polynomial algorithm which can already assert if the task (k,l) is necessarily critical. To compute the LUB of the floats, we are going to increase step by step the duration of (k,l) from $d_{kl} = d_{kl}^-$ until (k,l) becomes necessarily critical. Lemmas 5 and 7 give the hint to find the increment of d_{kl} at each step of the algorithm. According to Proposition 10, this incremental technique eventually yields f_{kl}^+.

Lemma 5. *Let activities $(i,j) \in PRED(k,l)$ have precise durations in G. Then (k,l) is necessarily critical in G if and only if there exists a path $p \in P(1,k)$ such that for every node $j \in p$, (k,l) is necessarily critical in $G(j,n)$.*

Proof. ($\Longrightarrow$) Let us denote by p a longest path from 1 to k. Note that activities $(i,j) \in PRED(k,l)$ have precise durations. From the necessary criticality of (k,l) in G, it follows that path p is part of a longest path from 1 to n and this path uses (k,l) for each configuration. Thus for every node $j \in p$, the subpath $p(j,n)$ is critical path in $G(j,n)$. Since this is true for each configuration, (k,l) is necessarily critical in $G(j,n)$.
($\Longleftarrow$) Just take $j=1$. $G(1,n) = G$ and so (k,l) is necessarily critical in G. □

If we assume that activities $(i,j) \in PRED(k,l)$ have precise durations, then there is a connection between the least upper bound on latest starting times lst_{kl}^+ and the least upper bound on floats f_{kl}^+ of activity (k,l).

Lemma 6 ([14]). *Let activities $(i,j) \in PRED(k,l)$ have precise durations in G. Then $f_{kl}^+ = lst_{kl}^+ - est_{kl}^+$.*

Accordingly, under the assumption that activities $(i,j) \in PRED(k,l)$ have precise durations, the least upper bound on floats f_{kl}^+ can be computed by means of algorithms for determining lst_{kl}^+ presented in Section 5. At each iteration of the while loop of Algorithm 4, (k,l) becomes necessarily critical in at least one new subnetwork $G(j,n)$. Thus the loop is executed at most n times, and so Algorithm 4 takes $O(n^3 m)$ time.

Lemma 7. *Let $\Delta = \min_j \{f_{kl}^+(j,n) \mid (k,l) \text{ is not necessarily critical in } G(j,n)\}$ where $f_{kl}^+(j,n)$ is the least upper bound on float of (k,l) in $G(j,n)$, $j \in PRED(k)$. Then for all $\epsilon < \Delta$, activity (k,l) is not necessarily critical in $G(j,n)$, $j \in PRED(k)$, with duration $d_{kl} = d_{kl}^- + \epsilon$. Moreover there exists $j^* \in PRED(k)$ such that (k,l) is not necessarily critical in $G(j^*,n)$ with duration $d_{kl} = d_{kl}^-$, and (k,l) becomes necessarily critical in $G(j^*,n)$ with duration $d_{kl} = d_{kl}^- + \Delta$.*

Proof. Consider a node j such that (k,l) is not necessarily critical in $G(j,n)$. By Observation 1, one can assume that activity (k,l) has the duration of the form $d_{kl} = d_{kl}^-$.
Let Ω be an extreme configuration where the float of (k,l) attains its maximal value $f_{kl}^+(j,n) > 0$ in $G(j,n)$, and $\epsilon < \Delta \leq f_{kl}^+(j,n)$ ($d_{kl}(\Omega) = d_{kl}^-$). p' denotes the

Interval Analysis in Scheduling   237

longest path in $G(j,n)$ in Ω, while p'' stands for the longest path in $G(j,n)$ in Ω using (k,l). Therefore, $f_{kl}^+(j,n) = l_{p'}(\Omega) - l_{p''}(\Omega) > \epsilon$.

Now let us define the configuration Ω' such that $d_{uv}(\Omega') = \begin{cases} d_{kl}^- + \epsilon & \text{if } (u,v) = (k,l) \\ d_{uv}(\Omega) & \text{otherwise,} \end{cases}$

p' remains a longest path in Ω' with same length, and p'' is still a longest path traversing (k,l) with length $l_{p''}(\Omega') = l_{p''}(\Omega) + \epsilon$. Since the float of (k,l) in Ω' is $l_{p'}(\Omega') - l_{p''}(\Omega') > 0$, (k,l) is not necessarily critical in $G(j,n)$, $j \in PRED(k)$, with duration $d_{kl} = d_{kl}^- + \epsilon$.

Consider a node j^* such that (k,l) is not necessarily critical in $G(j^*,n)$, and set $\Delta = f_{kl}^+(j^*,n)$. Then for all configurations, the difference between the longest path in $G(j^*,n)$ and the longest path using (k,l) is less or equal than Δ. If we increase the duration of (k,l) to $d_{kl}^- + \Delta$, a longest path, in this new configuration, will traverse (k,l) and thus (k,l) will be necessarily critical in $G(j^*,n)$ with duration $d_{kl} = d_{kl}^- + \Delta$. □

At the end of the incremental process, the least upper bound of the float of (k,l) is attained:

Proposition 10. *Let f_{kl}^* be the minimal nonnegative real number such that (k,l) is necessarily critical in $G(d_{kl} = d_{kl}^- + f_{kl}^*)$. Then $f_{kl}^+ = f_{kl}^*$.*

Proof. Consider any configuration Ω. Let p' be a longest path in Ω and p'' be a longest path including (k,l) in Ω. Note that $f_{kl}(\Omega) = l_{p'}(\Omega) - l_{p''}(\Omega)$. Let us now modify configuration Ω and denote it by Ω^x. Configuration Ω^x is defined as follows:

$$\forall (u,v) \in A, \ d_{uv}(\Omega^x) = \begin{cases} d_{uv}(\Omega) + x & \text{if } (u,v) = (k,l) \\ d_{uv}(\Omega) & \text{otherwise,} \end{cases}$$

where x is a nonnegative real number. It is clear that $l_{p''}(\Omega^x) = l_{p''}(\Omega) + x$ and p'' remains a longest path including (k,l) in new configuration Ω^x. Consider the following two cases.

Case: $x < f_{kl}(\Omega)$. Then $l_{p''}(\Omega^x) \leq l_{p'}(\Omega)$, and so p' is still a critical path in Ω^x and has the same length as in Ω. This gives $f_{kl}(\Omega^x) = f_{kl}(\Omega) - x$.

Case: $x \geq f_{kl}(\Omega)$. Then p'' becomes a critical path and so $f_{kl}(\Omega^x) = 0$. Thus, for all Ω and x equation $f_{kl}(\Omega^x) = \max(f_{kl}(\Omega) - x, 0)$ holds. In particular, for $x = f_{kl}^*$ and configuration $\Omega = \Omega^*$ such that Ω^* maximizes the float of task (k,l) in G. From the definition of f_{kl}^* we get $f_{kl}(\Omega^{f_{kl}^*}) = 0$, hence $f_{kl}(\Omega^*) - f_{kl}^* \leq 0$, and finally $f_{kl}^+ \leq f_{kl}^*$.

Suppose that $f_{kl}^+ < f_{kl}^*$. Set $y = (f_{kl}^* + f_{kl}^+)/2$. Then, for every Ω, $f_{kl}(\Omega^y) = \max(f_{kl}(\Omega) - y, 0) = 0$. Note that y is a nonnegative real number, smaller than f_{kl}^*,

---

Algorithm 4.

Input: A network G, activity (k,l), interval durations D_{uv}, $(u,v) \in A$.
Output: The least upper bound on floats f_{kl}^+.
NC $\leftarrow$ Algorithm 2 /*Set task durations preceding (k,l) according Prop. 4,5 */
$f_{kl}^+ \leftarrow 0; d_{kl} \leftarrow d_{kl}^-$
while NC =false **do**
$\quad \Delta \leftarrow \min\{f_{kl}^+(j,n) \mid j \in PRED(k), f_{kl}^+(j,n) \neq 0\}$
$\quad$ /*$f_{kl}^+(j,n) = lst_{kl}^+ - est_{kl}^+$(Lemma 6)   */
$\quad f_{kl}^+ \leftarrow f_{kl}^+ + \Delta; d_{kl} \leftarrow d_{kl} + \Delta$
$\quad$ NC $\leftarrow$ Algorithm 2 /*Update precise durations of tasks preceding (k,l) */
return f_{kl}^+

such that (k,l) is necessarily critical in $G(d_{kl} = d_{kl}^- + y)$, which contradicts the definition of f_{kl}^*. Hence, we conclude that $f_{kl}^+ = f_{kl}^*$. □

6.2 Computing the Greatest Lower Bound on Floats

Computing GLB on floats is NP-Hard in the general case. The reader should refer to [8,14] for some special tractable cases. However, an efficient algorithm has been proposed in [8]. The idea is to compute a PERT/CPM on each configuration Ω_p^+ such that p is a path of G from 1 to n. The number of tested configurations is of course potentially exponential, but in practice the algorithm runs very fast on realistic problems.

7 Complexity and Experimental Results

First, we summarize in Table 1 order of the complexity of the different problems of the PERT/CPM on intervals. Moreover, in Table 1, we give the order of

Table 1. The complexity of the interval problems and the running times of the best known algorithms

Earliest starting date (all tasks)	GLB	P	$O(n+m)$	[12]
	LUB	P	$O(n+m)$	[12]
Latest starting date (one task)	GLB	P	$O(mn)$	[14]
	LUB	P	$O(mn)$	[14]
Latest starting date (all tasks)	LUB	P	$O(m(m+n))$	Algorithm 3
Float (all tasks)	GLB	NP-Hard	$O((n+m)|P|)$	[8]
Float (one task)	LUB	P	$O(n^3 m)$	Algorithm 4

magnitude of the the running times of the best known algorithms, which compute the quantities of interest. In particular, the path algorithm which computes the GLB and LUB of floats and latest starting dates requires $O((n+m)|P|)$ time, where $|P|$ is the number of paths of network G. This time depends of the topology of the network. Note that, some algorithms need only one execution to compute a given quantity (for example, the latest starting date) for all tasks of a network. Other ones need to be executed for each task.

We now present some computational results in order to evaluate the performance of all these algorithms on a scheduling problems library of 600 networks of 120 tasks. Those instances of problems were generated by the ProGen, program for activity network generation [15], which can be downloaded from the PSPLIB web site (http://129.187.106.231/psplib/). We added a range of 20% to task durations to obtain intervals. Table 2 presents the minimal, maximal and average execution times (in second) of five algorithms on those 600 problems. All the algorithms were written in C language and ran on a PC computer equipped

Table 2. The minimal, maximal and average execution times (in second) of five algorithms on 600 problems

	Min	Max	Average	
Path algorithm LUBLST, GLBLST, LUBF, GLBF	0.02	0.45	0.12	[8]
Polynomial path algorithm LUBLST		0.01	0.03	0.017	Algorithm 3
GLBLST		0.01	0.05	0.023	[14]
LUBLST		0.02	0.12	0.056	[14]
LUBF		0.57	8.2	3.12	Algorithm 4

with 1GHz CPU. As seen from the experimental results, the path algorithm (potentially exponential) is very efficient in practice for simultaneous computing the latest starting dates and the floats. This comes from the fact that the number of paths in networks is not so huge (between 408 and 6559 different paths). Of course, one can construct more complex networks, but such networks would be not relevant to realistic scheduling problems. On the other hand, the polynomial algorithm that computes the LUB of the floats is not efficient in practice for realistic scheduling problems. However, its performance should be better for larger instances.

8 Conclusion

This paper has proposed a complete solution to the criticality analysis of a network of activities when durations of tasks are ill-known. It is shown that moving from precise to imprecise durations radically changes the nature and complexity of the problem, ruining the traditional critical path method. Part of the problem, pertaining to the GLB of the float, becomes NP-hard, the other questions remaining polynomial, although not straightforwardly so. These complexity results shed light on reasons why the more familiar stochastic counterparts to this basic scheduling problem are so difficult to handle, part of the difficulty being already present in the interval analysis. The proposed algorithms can be of obvious relevance to practical predictive project scheduling problems where durations of tasks are not known in advance. Clearly, due to the basic nature of the addressed problem, several lines of research can be envisaged for future research. For instance one may assume that part of the tasks durations are controllable and additional constraints relating durations and starting or ending times may be available. Then one obtains a makespan minimization problem in the more general setting of STPU's. Another interesting question is to relate the above results to robust scheduling when several scenarios are available. In the latter case scenarios embody dependencies between task durations while our approach makes no dependence assumptions. Robust scheduling becomes more and more difficult as the number of scenarios increases. In this case our approach may provide a good approximation if duration intervals are derived from a large number of scenarios. Alternatively robust and interval scheduling can be hybridized considering a small set of imprecise (interval-valued) scenarios derived from the large scenario set by means of a clustering method.

References

1. Dechter, R., Meiri, I., Pearl, J.: Temporal constraint networks. Artif. Intell. **49** (1991) 61–95
2. Morris, P., Muscettola, N., Vidal, T.: Dynamic control of plans with temporal uncertainty. In: IJCAI. (2001) 494–502
3. Vidal, T., Fargier, H.: Handling contingency in temporal constraint networks: from consistency to controllabilities. JETAI **11** (1999) 23–45
4. Morris, P.H., Muscettola, N.: Managing temporal uncertainty through waypoint controllability. In: IJCAI. (1999) 1253–1258
5. Khatib, L., Morris, P., Morris, R., Rossi, F.: Temporal constraint reasoning with preferences. In: IJCAI. (2001) 322–327
6. Kelley, J., Walker, M.: Critical path planning and scheduling. In: Proc. of the Eastern Joint Comp. Conf. (1959) 160–172
7. Chanas, S., Zieliński, P.: The computational complexity of the criticality problems in a network with interval activity times. Eur. J. Oper. Res. **136** (2002) 541–550
8. Dubois, D., Fargier, H., Fortin, J.: Computational methods for determining the latest starting times and floats of tasks in interval-valued activity networks. J. Intell. Manuf. (2005) To appear.
9. Buckley, J.: Fuzzy PERT. In: Applications of fuzzy set methodologies in industrial engineering. Elsevier (1989) 103–114
10. Dubois, D., Fargier, H., Fortemps, P.: Fuzzy scheduling: modeling flexible constraints vs. coping with incomplete knowledge. Eur. J. Oper. Res. **147** (2003) 231–252
11. Dubois, D., Fargier, H., Galvagnon, V.: On latest starting times and floats in activity networks with ill-known durations. Eur. J. Oper. Res. **147** (2003) 266–280
12. Chanas, S., Kamburowski, J.: The use of fuzzy variables in pert. Fuzzy Set Syst. **5** (1981) 1–19
13. Chanas, S., Dubois, D., Zieliński, P.: On the sure criticality of tasks in activity networks with imprecise durations. IEEE T. Syst. Man Cy. B **34** (2002) 393–407
14. Zieliński, P.: On computing the latest starting times and floats of activities in a network with imprecise durations. Fuzzy Set Syst. **150** (2005) 53–76
15. Kolisch, R., Sprecher, A.: Psplib - a project scheduling library. Eur. J. Oper. Res. **96** (1996) 205–216

Assumption-Based Pruning in Conditional CSP

Felix Geller and Michael Veksler

IBM Research Laboratory, Haifa, Israel
{felix, veksler}@il.ibm.com

Abstract. A conditional constraint satisfaction problem (CCSP) is a variant of the standard constraint satisfaction problem (CSP). CCSPs model problems where some of the variables and constraints may be conditionally inactive such that they do not participate in a solution. Recently, algorithms were introduced that use MAC at their core to solve CCSP. We extend MAC with a simple assumption-based reasoning. The resulting algorithm, Activity MAC (AMAC), is able to achieve significantly better pruning than existing methods. AMAC is shown to be more than two orders of magnitude more efficient than CondMAC on certain problem classes. Our algorithm is most naturally expressed using a variant of the CCSP representation that we refer to as Activity CSP (ACSP). ACSP introduces activity variables which explicitly control the presence of other variables in the solution. Common aspects of CCSP, such as activity clustering and disjunction, are easily captured by ACSP and contribute to improved pruning by AMAC.

1 Introduction

Standard constraint satisfaction problems (CSP) are being used to represent and solve complex combinatorial problems in many areas. Over the years, several specialized CSP variants were introduced to accommodate specific classes of problems.

1.1 Conditional CSP and Historical Overview

Conditional CSP (CCSP [1], CondCSP [2] or originally DCSP [3]) is a specialization in which it is possible to conditionally disable parts of the problem. This structural conditionality of CCSP is useful in several problem areas, such as configuration [3] and hardware test generation [4].

CCSP adds to CSP the notion of variable activity and inactivity. Only active variables are assigned values, while inactive variables are ignored.

Over the years, several CCSP solving techniques have been proposed. The original work of Mittal and Falkenhainer [3] offers three solution methods. The most comprehensive algorithm is a kind of backtrack-search algorithm. It uses an Assumption Based Truth Maintenance System (ATMS) [5] to perform simple deductions, cache constraint checks, and generate nogoods (i.e. learn conflicts). As any classic backtrack-search algorithm, it assigns values to variables, and backtracks once they lead to failure. The second algorithm uses backtrack-search with a limited forward-checking for activity constraints (resembling the backtrack-search used in [6]). The third algorithm reformulates CCSP to CSP, where inactive variables are assigned a special value referred to as *null*. None of the three algorithms use constraint propagation to prune the search space.

In contrast, Gelle and Faltings [2] preprocess the CCSP and then use mixed-CSP techniques combined with MAC [7]. Sabin, Freuder and Wallace [1] introduced CondMAC, a variant of MAC that takes variable activity into account. CondMAC considers only those variables that are active; variables with an activity status which is not determined yet are ignored. CondMAC consults activity constraints to find which variables should be active. Both works [2,1] suggest that algorithms based on MAC are about two orders of magnitude faster than either pure backtrack-search or *null* reformulated CCSP.

1.2 Disjunction and Clustering of Activity

Two widespread phenomena in configuration problems are disjunction and clustering of activity. Mittal and Falkenhainer [3] mentioned the necessity of *"disjunction over required* [activity of] *variables"* for expression some types of domain knowledge. However, they did not implement it due to performance issues with such constraints. Soininen, Gelle and Niemelä [6] also observed that CCSP (DCSP) models are too weak to represent some configuration tasks. One of their observations is that *" It is, e.g., difficult to encode, as an activity constraint that ... either a condenser or a cooler should be included"* (where *cooler* and *condenser* are variables). In this case, a valid configuration must have either a cooler or condenser; so it is not valid to have them both deactivated. They conclude that *disjunctive activity constraints* [3] would help. It is interesting to note that most Conditional CSP papers use configuration examples for which *disjunctive activity constraints* would be natural, most notably the car configuration problem [3].

Another important phenomenon is *clustering of activity*. Clustering occurs when several variables have identical activity status in all solutions. We refer to the set of variables with identical activity conditions as an *activity cluster*. We believe that clustering is quite common in CCSPs due to the inherent modularity of the problems, where variables within the same component have the same activity rules.

1.3 The Activity MAC Algorithm

This paper introduces a novel Activity MAC (AMAC) algorithm to solve CCSPs. Unlike CondMAC [1] AMAC tries to propagate constraints regardless of variable activity. This early constraint propagation allows significantly better domain pruning than CondMAC.

To enable early constraint propagation, AMAC concurrently checks several assumptions about activity of CCSP elements. The algorithm allows deduction-like information flow between different activity assumptions. This assumption-based reasoning allows AMAC to propagate constraints over the conditionality barrier, which eliminates a substantial number of backtracks at a reasonable cost.

In order to simplify the AMAC algorithm, we present a slightly modified variant of the CCSP representation. To avoid confusion with standard CCSPs, we refer to it as Activity CSP (ACSP). This representation has a new class of variables named *activity variables*. As the name suggests, activity variables control the activity of other variables. The domain of an activity variable is $\{true, false\}$ such that when it is assigned with *true* the controlled variables are all active. CCSP's activity constraints are no longer needed because regular constraints can operate directly on activity variables.

We show that ACSP and CCSP representations are computationally equivalent. Yet, ACSPs can represent important aspects of Conditional CSPs more naturally, such as *activity clustering* and *activity disjunction*. AMAC can easily use these aspects to achieve better pruning and improve performance. This paper does not deal with the nontrivial task of extracting *activity clustering* and *activity disjunction* from CCSPs. It is possible that one would prefer to model problems directly as ACSPs rather than CCSPs, because ACSPs eliminate the cost of extraction.

1.4 Minimality in CCSP and ACSP

The original work by Mittal and Falkenhainer [3] imposes a subset minimality rule over the activity of variables. According to this rule, a complete assignment is a valid solution only if removal of any of the assigned variables will violate at least one constraint. Subset minimality was discovered to be either too strong and impractical or irrelevant in some domains. According to Soininen, Gelle and Niemelä [6] some cases of configuration problems are not interested in plain subset minimality, and they propose a different minimality rule. This led us to believe that it would be useful to separate optimization goals (e.g., subset minimality) from core representation and algorithms. It should be simple and efficient to add goals such as minimality onto the basic algorithms.

In our work, we add minimality on top of the basic ACSP solver through variable and value ordering. ACSPs with added minimality have the minimality semantics of CCSPs. The separation of the ACSP structure and minimality goals makes it possible to define different goals. Possible goals range from optimization of an arbitrary cost function through minimal activity subset, to minimal assignment subset (as in the original [3]).

1.5 Benchmarks

Another interesting observation we made was that popular benchmarks of random CCSPs [2] take neither activity clustering nor activity disjunction into account. As a result, these benchmarks will generate problems with these properties with a negligible probability. We introduce a modified benchmark that generates problems with clustering and disjunction. On this benchmark, AMAC shows a significant performance improvement over CondMAC.

The rest of our paper is organized as follows, In Section 2 we discuss the benefits of early constraint propagation, in Section 3 we introduce Activity CSP, in Section 4 we describe the workings of Activity MAC, in Section 5 we present our experimental results, and we summarize with the conclusions in Section 6.

2 Early Constraint Propagation

None of the published solution techniques for Conditional CSP exploit constraint propagation to the full extent. Namely, constraint checking is invoked only after the constraint variables become active. In a sense, this limits the information flow during the solution process only from already active variables to variables whose activity is still undecided. However, as the example in Figure 1 shows, there are benefits in activating conditional constraints ahead of time. The early constraint propagation allows:

- Information flow in 'reverse' direction, from potentially active variables to definitely active ones:
  In the example the domain of x is initially $\{0,\ldots,100\}$. If active, y can affect x through constraint $x = y$ and produce domain $\{0,\ldots,4\}$ for x. Similarly, z being active implies domain $\{5,\ldots,9\}$ for x. Since either y or z has to eventually be active because of the activity disjunction, we can conclude that x's domain is at most $\{0,\ldots,9\}$. Note, this deduction is due to constraint propagation without any assignments or backtrack steps.
- Early activity conflict detection:
  We detect contradiction between the assignments $v_y^a = \text{true}$ and $v_z^a = \text{true}$ using the following argument: if we assume $v_y^a = \text{true}$, we obtain $D(x) = \{0,\ldots,4\}$. Similarly, $v_z^a = \text{true}$ implies $D(x) = \{5,\ldots,9\}$. Since the two domains are disjoint, we learn that $v_1^a \wedge v_2^a = \text{false}$. The detection of inconsistency between potential activity assignments lets us avoid backtrack steps.

We provide this sort of enhanced pruning in our solution method.

3 Activity CSP

The increased pruning is most easily gained when clustering and disjunction activity aspects of CCSP are stated explicitly. Hence, we introduce Activity

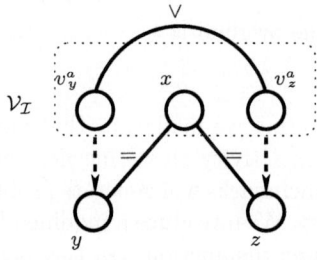

Fig. 1. A conditional CSP problem: $\mathcal{V} = \{x, y, z, v_y^a, v_z^a\}, \mathcal{V_I} = \{x, v_y^a, v_z^a\}, D(x) = \{0,\ldots,100\}, D(y) = \{0,\ldots,4\}, D(z) = \{5,\ldots,9\}, D(v_y^a) = D(v_z^a) = \{\text{true, false}\}, \mathcal{C_C} = \{x = y, x = z, v_y^a \vee v_z^a\}, \mathcal{C_A} = \{v_y^a = \text{true} \xrightarrow{incl} y, v_y^a = \text{false} \xrightarrow{excl} y, v_z^a = \text{true} \xrightarrow{incl} z, v_z^a = \text{false} \xrightarrow{excl} z\}$

CSP, a variant of CCSP, that allows us to capture the notion of clustering and express our solution algorithm in the natural way.

Before presenting the Activity CSP model, we recall the definition of the CCSP model [3].

3.1 CCSP

In the standard CCSP model, a problem is defined as tuple $\langle \mathcal{V}, \mathcal{V}_\mathcal{I}, \mathcal{D}, \mathcal{C}_\mathcal{C}, \mathcal{C}_\mathcal{A}\rangle$, where $\mathcal{V}$ are the variables, $\mathcal{D}$ are the domains, $\mathcal{V}_\mathcal{I} \subseteq \mathcal{V}$ is subset of initially *active* variables (that have to participate in all solutions). There are two types of constraints:

- $\mathcal{C}_\mathcal{C}$ - compatibility constraints, which specify valid combinations of the variables values.
- $\mathcal{C}_\mathcal{A}$ - activity constraints, which specify the conditions under which variables (in $\mathcal{V} \setminus \mathcal{V}_\mathcal{I}$) become active. Activity constraints are further subdivided into inclusion and exclusion constraints. An inclusion constraint $C \xrightarrow{incl} v$ states that if C holds, the variable is active (required in a solution). Alternatively, $C \xrightarrow{excl} v$ states that if C holds, the variable is not active (excluded from a solution). C is a regular compatibility constraint.

Solution Sol is assignment of values to $\mathcal{V}_{Sol} \subseteq \mathcal{V}$, s.t. $\mathcal{V}_\mathcal{I} \subseteq \mathcal{V}_{Sol}$, which satisfies *relevant* constraints. A compatibility constraint is relevant if all its variables are active. An activity constraint $C \xrightarrow{incl} v$ ($C \xrightarrow{excl} v$) is relevant, if C is relevant. An activity constraint $C \xrightarrow{incl} v$ ($C \xrightarrow{excl} v$) is satisfied if either C doesn't hold or v is active (inactive). A solution Sol is *minimal* if no assignment that is a proper subset of Sol is a solution.

3.2 ACSP

In ACSP, a problem is defined by $\langle \mathcal{V}, \mathcal{V}_\mathcal{I}, \mathcal{V}_\mathcal{A}, \mathcal{D}, \mathcal{C}, \mathcal{A}\rangle$, where $\mathcal{V}, \mathcal{V}_\mathcal{I}$ and $\mathcal{D}$ are the same as in CCSP, while there are two differences:

- $\mathcal{V}_\mathcal{A}$ are explicit *activity* variables with a Boolean domain. The activity variables participate in every solution: $\mathcal{V}_\mathcal{A} \subseteq \mathcal{V}_\mathcal{I}$. $\mathcal{A}$ is a mapping from $\mathcal{V} \setminus \mathcal{V}_\mathcal{I}$ to $\mathcal{V}_\mathcal{A}$. For each variable v, $\mathcal{A}(v)$ specifies its activation condition: v is active iff $\mathcal{A}(v)$ is *true*.
- We do not distinguish between compatibility and activity constraints: any constraint may refer to an activity variable.

The clustering effect is achieved when several variables share the same activation condition.

Solution Sol is an assignment of values to $\mathcal{V}_{Sol} \subseteq \mathcal{V}$, s.t.

1. Every active variable is assigned a value:

    $$\mathcal{V}_\mathcal{I} \subseteq \mathcal{V}_{Sol} \text{ and } \forall v \in \mathcal{V} \setminus \mathcal{V}_\mathcal{I}: \ v \in \mathcal{V}_{Sol} \text{ iff } Sol(\mathcal{A}(v)) = true$$

2. All *relevant* constraints are satisfied.

Solution *Sol* is (locally) minimal, if no solution can be obtained from *Sol* by changing the value of some activity variables from *true* to *false* (and shrinking $\mathcal{V}_{Sol}$ correspondingly). More formally, for any assignment $S \subset Sol$ with $\mathcal{V}_S$ being the set of the assigned variables, that

1. agrees with *Sol* on the values of variables in $(\mathcal{V} \setminus \mathcal{V}_\mathcal{A}) \cap \mathcal{V}_S$:
   $\forall v \in (\mathcal{V} \setminus \mathcal{V}_\mathcal{A}) \cap \mathcal{V}_S \ S(v) = Sol(v)$ and
2. assigns less *true* values to activity variables:
   $\{v : v \in \mathcal{V}_\mathcal{A}, S(v) = true\} \subset \{v : v \in \mathcal{V}_\mathcal{A}, Sol(v) = true\}$,

such S can't be a solution.

To express the example problem as ACSP, we declare v_y^a, v_z^a as explicit activity variables: $\mathcal{V}_\mathcal{A} = \{v_y^a, v_z^a\}$ and replace the activity constraints with activation conditions: $\mathcal{A}(y) = v_y^a, \mathcal{A}(z) = v_z^a$.

3.3 Model Equivalence

We don't lose in expressive power or representation efficiency when we switch from CCSP to ACSP. Moreover, the two models are equivalent:

- From CCSP to ACSP: With each variable $v \in \mathcal{V} \setminus \mathcal{V}_\mathcal{I}$, we associate an activity variable v^a, set $\mathcal{A}(v) = v^a$, and replace each activity constraint $C \xrightarrow{incl} v$ ($C \xrightarrow{excl} v$) with compatibility constraint $C' : C \to v^a = true$ ($C' : C \to v^a = false$)
- From ACSP to CCSP: We replace activation condition $\mathcal{A}(v) = v^a$ with pair of activity constraints: $v^a = true \xrightarrow{incl} v$ and $v^a = false \xrightarrow{excl} v$.

Throughout the rest of the paper we use only the ACSP representation.

4 Implementing Early Constraint Propagation

The underlying idea in the early constraint propagation is that we invoke constraints based on assumptions that some activity variables are *true*. In Section 4.1 we develop a framework that enables assumption-based reasoning about variable activity. Then we combine the assumption-based reasoning mechanism with a standard constraint propagation in section 4.2

4.1 Assumption-Based Reasoning

Activity Set. An activity set of a constraint C is the set of activity conditions of its variables, and is denoted AS(C). We call any constraint C with AS(C) $\neq \emptyset$ a *conditional* constraint. We say that an activity set is *violated* if at least one of its variables is assigned *false*. Activity set is said to be *true* if all its variables are assigned *true*.

Shadows. The notion of the variable shadow is central to our solution approach. For a variable $v \in \mathcal{V} \setminus \mathcal{V}_I$ and an activity set AS, shadow $v[AS]$ is a copy of variable v. The domain of the shadow consists of values that the variable may get if the activity set were *true*. For each conditional constraint C, and its variable v, we let the constraint operate on the shadow $v[AS(C)]$ instead of the original variable v. Initially, $D(v[AS]) = D(v)$. Over the course of the algorithm execution, the shadow's domain becomes more restricted than the variable's domain, as long as the activity set is not violated: $D(v[AS]) \leftarrow D(v[AS]) \cap D(v)$. The shadow 'sees' the changes in the variable's domain, and in addition, it is subject to the conditional constraint. If the activity set becomes true, the shadow's domain is kept identical to the variable's domain. If the activity set becomes falsified, the shadow variable is ignored for the rest of the solution process.

We demonstrate constraint parameter substitution on our example problem: Constraint $C_1(x,y)$ $x = y$ has the activity set $AS(C_1) = \{v_y^a\}$. We switch constraint C_1 to shadows $x[\{v_y^a\}]$, $y[\{v_y^a\}]$. Note that $y[\{v_y^a\}]$ coincides with the variable y, because the shadow's activity set is exactly the variable's activation condition. Constraint $C_2(x,z)$ $x = z$ has the activity set $AS(C_2) = \{v_z^a\}$. We substitute constraint parameters with $x[\{v_z^a\}]$, z.

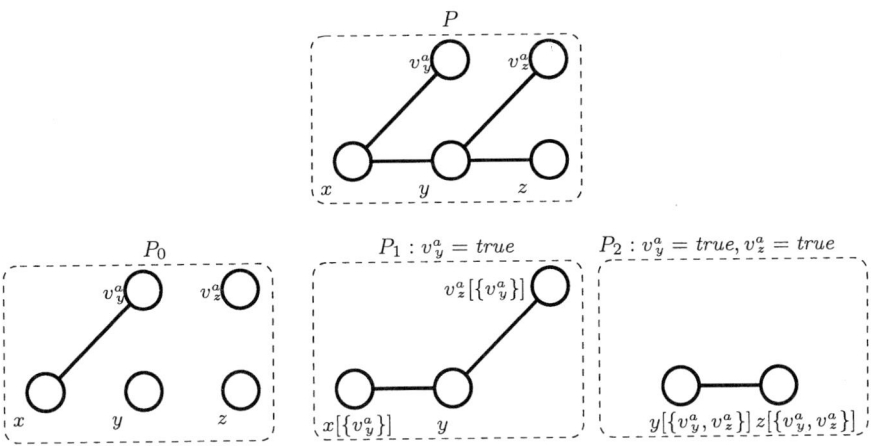

Fig. 2. Assumption-based decomposition of an ACSP: The original problem P contains five variables x, y, z, v_y^a, v_z^a. $\mathcal{V}_I = \{x, v_y^a, v_z^a\}$, $\mathcal{A}(y) = v_y^a$, $\mathcal{A}(z) = v_z^a$. Edges denote binary constraints. The constraints' activity sets dictate partition into three subproblems: P_0 (which is unconditional), P_1 and P_2.

Assumption-Based Decomposition. For each constraint, we make the assumption that its activity set is *true*. Creating and using shadow variables, for the activity set, effectively puts the constraint in a 'sandbox' in which it is run. Several conditional constraints may share the activity set and, possibly, shadows. This fact allows us to obtain assumption-based decomposition of ACSP problem:

we partition the problem constraints into groups according to their activity sets. Together with corresponding shadows, each group of constraints represents a conventional CSP problem that includes all the variables and constraints whose activity follows from the assumptions. An example of assumption-based decomposition is given in Figure 2. There is at most one shadow variable for each parameter of a conditional constraint.

The sub-problems corresponding to various activity sets can be handled independently. Upon reaching a failure in a sub-problem, we infer that the activity set is violated.

In our example, activations of C_1 and C_2, having different activity sets, are unrelated, even though initially (prior to parameter substitution) the constraints shared a variable. Reaching consistency over C_1, we get $D(x[\{v^a_y\}]) = \{0, \ldots, 4\}$ and the activation of C_2 results in $D(x[\{v^a_z\}]) = \{5, \ldots, 9\}$. Because the original problem's constraints are distributed over several sub-problems, we have to coordinate solving of the sub-problems and enable information exchange between them during the solution process. Propagating domain updates between shadows of the same variable provides the necessary communication link.

The assumption-based decomposition is performed on the conceptual level. It is intended to demonstrate that the conditional CSP may be transformed into a set of conventional CSPs. The resulting problems can be solved then using standard methods coupled with the shadow synchronization mechanism. The actual implementation does not create an explicit decomposition.

Shadow Synchronization Rules. Let's assume we have two shadows of the same variable v: $v[AS_1], v[AS_2]$. At some point in the solution process domain of $v[AS_1]$ is modified, and we want to *synchronize* shadow $v[AS_2]$ with $v[AS_1]$. We can assume that none of the variables in $AS_1 \cup AS_2$ is *false* (otherwise, at least one of the shadows is not active in the current partial assignment.) We consider the following cases:

1. If the assumption AS_1 is weaker than AS_2, the changes of $v[AS_1]$ should be reflected in $v[AS_2]$ More precisely, if, given the current partial assignment, all the variables in $AS_1 \setminus AS_2$ are *true*, then

$$D(v[AS_2]) \leftarrow D(v[AS_2]) \cap D(v[AS_1])$$

   If an empty domain results, we conclude that $\bigwedge_{v^a \in AS_2} v^a = \textit{false}$.
2. Even if the assumptions are incomparable (none is included in another), we still can benefit from comparing shadow domains. Specifically, the fact

$$D(v[AS_1]) \cap D(v[AS_2]) = \emptyset$$

implies, that the domains contradict each other and both shadows cannot exist in a solution at the same time. Therefore, we infer that $\bigwedge_{v^a \in AS_1 \cup AS_2} v^a = \textit{false}$.

In our example, computing $D(x[\{v^a_y\}]) \cap D(x[\{v^a_z\}]) = \emptyset$, leads the algorithm to conclusion that at least one of the variables v^a_y, v^a_z has to be *false*.

Essentially, the synchronization rules capture the semantics of the constraint $(\bigwedge_{v^a \in AS_1 \cup AS_2} v^a) \rightarrow (v[AS_1] = v[AS_2])$.

Propagating Constraints over Activity Variables. We consider constraints that refer only to activity variables apart from other constraints. Taking into account the constraints' semantics allows further improvement of pruning. Specifically, we focus on two types of constraints:

1. **Activity Disjunction** ($\bigvee$): $v_1^a \vee v_2^a \vee \ldots \vee v_k^a$
2. **Activity Implication** ($\rightarrow$): $v_1^a \rightarrow v_2^a$,

where v_i^a are activity variables.

Activity Disjunction. Until now we observed how the information flows from more 'certain' shadows to less 'certain' shadows. The propagation of information in the reverse direction is also possible. Suppose we have a disjunction constraint over activity variables: $v_1^a \vee v_2^a \vee \ldots \vee v_k^a$. The constraint imposes the following relationship between variable v and its shadows $v[\{v_1^a\}], v[\{v_2^a\}], \ldots, v[\{v_k^a\}]$: $D(v)$ can be no larger than $\bigcup_{i=1}^{i=k} D(v[\{v_i^a\}])$. In our example the algorithm infers that $D(x)$ can be no larger than $D(x[\{v_y^a\}]) \cup D(x[\{v_z^a\}]) = \{0, \ldots, 9\}$ and is reduced w.r.t. the initial $D(x)$.

Activity Implication. An implication between activity variables induces equivalence between activity sets. We can take advantage of this equivalence to merge shadows under equivalent activity sets into single shadow, and thus reduce the overall number of variables.

4.2 Activity MAC

We integrate the above ideas into a standard propagation-based algorithm (AC-3, see [7].) We call our modified propagation method Activity MAC. This section discusses AMAC implementation details. We consider in turn the preprocessing stage, the search and constraint propagation component, and the treatment of activity disjunctions and implications. For brevity we omit most of the code and concentrate on three important functions: ReachArcConsistency, SynchronizeShadows, ComputeUnionConstraints - see Algorithm 1. Finally, we describe an optimization for the case when there are no activity disjunctions.

Preprocessing Stage. The preprocessing stage computes the constraints' activity sets, builds shadows and replaces the constraint parameters with shadows. New constraints and new variables besides shadows are also created. The new constraints are referred to as *internal* constraints, as opposed to the user constraints that are part of the input problem. One kind of internal constraints are *inference* constraints which serve for manipulation of conclusions of the form $\bigwedge_{v^a \in AS} v^a = false$. We associate an internal Boolean variable v_{AS} with an activity set AS for which $|AS| \geq 2$ and introduce a constraint $\bigwedge_{v^a \in AS} v^a = v_{AS}$. For any two activity sets AS_1, AS_2, s.t. $AS_1 \subseteq AS_2$, we add a redundant constraint $v_{AS_2} \rightarrow v_{AS_1}$. Another type of internal constraints, Union Constraints, is discussed later.

Search and Constraint Propagation. After the preprocessing stage, AMAC calls the recursive Solve procedure. The recursive Solve procedure implements a standard enumeration algorithm combined with arc consistency, with the following exceptions:

- Only original problem variables, whose existence is not ruled out, are considered for instantiation.
- We can produce a *minimal* solution, if during the variable selection step we always prefer variables whose activity is decided, and when choosing a value for an activity variable, we try *false* before *true*

Our version of ReachArcConsistency incorporates several changes as compared to the standard ReachArcConsistency:

- The constraint queue Q is a priority queue: internal constraints have precedence over user constraints. User constraints are sorted according to activity set size (unconditional constraints first.) Q is initialized to contain all the constraints (including the internal ones) prior to the first call to ReachArcConsistency. On each subsequent invocation, Q holds all the constraints incident to an instantiated variable.
- Handling constraint projection failure (lines 1.10 – 1.12): whenever projection of constraint C with $AS(C) \neq \emptyset$ fails (discovers an empty set), instead of immediately returning FAILURE, we set $v_{AS(C)}$ to *false* and propagate this update further.
- Shadow synchronization (lines 1.19 – 1.22): once a constraint parameter's domain is modified, the update is propagated to the shadows of the same variable.

Propagating Activity Disjunctions and Implications

Activity Disjunction. Let's assume we have a constraint $v_1^a \vee v_2^a \vee \ldots \vee v_k^a$. We define UnionConstraint$(x_0, x_1, \ldots x_k)$ as $x_0 = x_1 \vee \ldots \vee x_0 = x_k$. The UnionConstraint$(x_0, x_1, \ldots x_k)$ propagation is performed by the following operation: $D(x_0) \leftarrow D(x_0) \cap \bigcup_{i=1}^{i=k} D(x_i)$. Assume that for some variable v there are k shadows : $v[AS_1], v[AS_2], \ldots, v[AS_k]$, such that:

$$\forall i, 1 \leq i \leq k : v_i^a \in AS_i \text{ and } \forall j, j \neq i, v_i^a \notin AS_j \tag{1}$$

We define AS'_0 to be the intersection of AS_i, $1 \leq i \leq k$. We define k activity sets AS'_i: $\forall i, 1 \leq i \leq k : AS'_i = AS'_0 \cup \{v_i^a\}$. For any $0 \leq i \leq k$, we create shadow $v[AS'_i]$ if it doesn't already exist.

The constraint $v_1^a \vee v_2^a \vee \ldots \vee v_k^a$ implies the constraint UnionConstraint$(v[AS'_0], v[AS'_1], \ldots, v[AS'_k])$. Union constraints are created in the function ComputeUnionConstraints which is executed during the preprocessing stage. Note, for a given variable v, the shadow set Shadows(v) changes during the iteration over disjunction constraints. This means we may need to consider the same disjunction constraint several times. In general, we repeatedly iterate over disjunction constraints until a fixed point.

Activity Implication. An implication constraint induces the equivalence relation between activity sets. Suppose, we are given an implication constraint $v_1^a \rightarrow v_2^a$

and we have activity sets AS_1 and AS_2, such that, $v_1^a \in AS_1, v_2^a \notin AS_1, AS_2 = AS_1 \cup \{v_2^a\}$, then they are equivalent from the point of view of our algorithm: $(\bigwedge_{v^a \in AS_1} v^a) \leftrightarrow (\bigwedge_{v^a \in AS_1 \cup \{v_2^a\}} v^a)$. Thus, we can identify shadow $v[AS_1]$ with $v[AS_1 \cup \{v_2^a\}]$.

Under given implication constraints, for an activity set AS we define *minimal equivalent set* AS_{min} as a set, such that:

1. AS_{min} is equivalent to AS.
2. For any proper subset of AS_{min}, AS', $AS' \subset AS_{min}$, AS' is **not** equivalent to AS.

The minimal equivalent set of an activity set AS is unique. The canonic representation allows for fast equivalence tests. Whenever the algorithm computes an activity set, the set is replaced by its canonic equivalent.

Timely Activation of the Conditional Constraints. If the problem does not contain activity disjunction constraints, the only benefit we gain from the conditional constraint propagation is the early detection of conflicts. A conflict implies that for some activity set AS $\bigwedge_{v^a \in AS} v^a = false$. In order to 'blame' the failure on specific variable, we defer constraint activation until its activation set has at most one free (unassigned) variable.

4.3 Discussion

Preprocessing. Gelle et al. [2] use preprocessing to reduce a CCSP problem to set of conventional CSPs, which are then sequentially solved. Interestingly enough, Sabin et al. [1] propose an idea of interleaving solving several CSPs that result from CCSP reformulation. This quite accurately describes one important aspect of our approach: namely, parallel solving of sub-problems resulting from the assumption-based decomposition.

Comparison with ATMS. The idea of conditioning data on assumptions has been introduced by de Kleer in his seminal paper on Assumption-based Truth Maintenance System [5]. ATMS is a general technique for solving search problems. Roughly speaking, ATMS consists of two components: the solver and the Boolean inference engine. The solution space is explored in parallel, and the solver maintains several contexts corresponding to different assumptions while the inference engine checks for assumption consistency. This resembles our notion of shadows and activity sets and their manipulation through the inference constraints.

ATMS has been applied subsequently to solving CSPs ([8], [9]), where the CSP is encoded using assumptions asserting that a certain, not necessarily Boolean, variable is assigned some value. (Note that in [3] ATMS is mainly used for nogoods recording.) However, for problems with large variable domains, the ATMS technique may be prohibitively expensive. In contrast, in AMAC, the assumptions are of very limited form; they refer only to activity variables and are known in advance. Overall, manipulation of assumptions in AMAC incurs a reasonable polynomial cost.

Algorithm 1. Activity MAC

```
1: function REACHARCCONSISTENCY( )
2:     // Q - is priority constraint queue.
3:     While Q ≠ ∅ do
4:         Select constraint C ∈ Q, s.t. AS(C) is not violated.
5:         Propagate constraint C
6:         If constraint failed then
7:             // some of the variables in Vars(C) have empty domains
8:             If AS(C) = ∅ then
9:                 return FAILURE
10:            else
11:                $v_{AS(C)} \leftarrow false$
12:                ModifiedVars ← $\{v_{AS(C)}\}$
13:        else
14:            // Propagate changes in C's variables to their shadows
15:            ModifiedVars ← {v|v ∈ Vars(C), D(v) modified by C propagation}.
16:            For all v ∈ ModifiedVars do
17:                // v is a shadow of some variable w
18:                // s.t. v = w[AS] for some activity set AS
19:                For all u ∈ Shadows(w), s.t. u = w[AS'], AS ≠ AS' do
20:                    // Propagate update from v to u
21:                    SynchronizeShadows(w, AS, AS')
22:                    Update ModifiedVars (if either u, $v_{AS'}$ or $v_{AS \cup AS'}$ has been modified)
23:            // Update Q
24:            For all v ∈ ModifiedVars do
25:                Q ← Q ∪ IncidentConstraints(v)
26:        Q ← Q \ {C}
27:    return SUCCESS
28: procedure SYNCHRONIZESHADOWS(v, AS, AS')
29:    // Propagate changes in v[AS] to v[AS']
30:    If AS \ AS' = ∅ or all variables in AS \ AS' are true then
31:        D(v[AS']) ← D(v[AS']) ∩ D(v[AS])
32:        If D(v[AS']) = ∅ then
33:            $v_{AS'} \leftarrow false$
34:    else
35:        If D(v[AS']) ∩ D(v[AS]) = ∅ then
36:            $v_{AS \cup AS'} \leftarrow false$
37: function COMPUTEUNIONCONSTRAINTS( )
38:    UnionConstraints ← ∅
39:    NewConstraints ← ∅
40:    For all v ∈ Vars(P) do
41:        repeat
42:            UnionConstraints ← UnionConstraints ∪ NewConstraints
43:            NewConstraints ← ∅
44:            For all C ∈ ActivityDisjunctionConstraints(P) do
45:                // C = $v_1^a \lor v_2^a \lor \ldots \lor v_k^a$
46:                If
                       exist distinct shadows $v_1, v_2, \ldots, v_k \in$ Shadows(v), s.t.
                       $\forall i, 1 \leq i \leq k : v_i = v[AS_i]$ for some $AS_i$ and
                       $v_i^a \in AS_i$, but $\forall j, j \neq i, v_i^a \notin AS_j$
                   then
47:                    $AS_0' \leftarrow \bigcap_{i=1}^{i=k} AS_i$
48:                    $\forall i, 1 \leq i \leq k : AS_i' \leftarrow AS_0' \cup \{v_i^a\}$
49:                    For all 0 ≤ i ≤ k do
50:                        Create $v[AS_i']$ (if it doesn't exist)
51:                    // Create UnionConstraint
52:                    $C' \leftarrow$ UnionConstraint($v[ES_0'], v[ES_1'], \ldots, v[ES_k']$)
53:                    If $C' \notin$ UnionConstraints then
54:                        NewConstraints ← NewConstraints ∪ {C'}
55:        until NewConstraints = ∅
56:    return UnionConstraints
```

5 Experimental Results

Our experiments show that AMAC is considerably faster than CondMAC on hard problems. It seems that most of the benefit comes from AMAC's better handling of clustering.

5.1 The Solvers

We used the Generation Core [4] CSP solver to perform our experiments. The solver implements AC-3 [7] with random selection of both variables and values. The solver tries to minimize the effects of the heavy tailed phenomena [10], when few bad initial selections cause massive backtracks. As a countermeasure the solver performs restarts after consecutive $1, 2, 4, \ldots, 256$ seconds and then gives up after another 512 seconds (1023 total). We implemented both CondMAC [1] and AMAC solving methods. We believe that the merits of more sophisticated algorithms, like MAC-DBT (Dynamic Backtracking [11]), are orthogonal to the gains AMAC has over CondMAC.

5.2 Benchmarking Technique and Definitions

Unlike in other CSP domains, there are no publicly known CCSP benchmark problems. The only published benchmarks are random CCSP generators. We use a random CCSP generator similar to the one used in [1,2] with several modifications. Because we want to give meaningful results for the CCSP community, we define our tests in terms of CCSP.

For simplicity, we test only binary constraints. We define the density of compatibility $d_c = \#constraints \cdot 2/(|\mathcal{V}|^2 - \mathcal{V})$. If $d_c = 1$, there is a constraint between every pair of regular variables. We define satisfiability of compatibility s_c as the ratio of number of valid tuples to the product of domain sizes. If $s_c = 1$, every constraint permits all possible value pairs, such that the CSP is trivially satisfiable. For activity constraints of the type $v_i \in A_i \xrightarrow{incl} v_j$, satisfiability of activation $s_a = |A_i|/|D_i|$. In these benchmarks there is exactly one activity constraint for each $v_i \in \mathcal{V} \setminus \mathcal{V_I}$. And density of activity is defined $d_a = |\mathcal{V} \setminus \mathcal{V_I}| / |\mathcal{V}|$.

We define N_c as the number of variables per conditional cluster. $N_c = 1$ means that all conditional variables (variables in $\mathcal{V} \setminus \mathcal{V_I}$) have independent activity constraints. On the other extreme, $N_c = |\mathcal{V} \setminus \mathcal{V_I}|$ means that all conditional variables have exactly the same activity constraints. We define $N_\vee$ as the total number of binary disjunctions between conditional clusters. A binary disjunction between v_1 and v_2 is a constraint that insures that at least one of v_1 or v_2 are active. This is similar to $true \xrightarrow{incl} 1\{v_1, v_2\}2$ in the language of [6].

5.3 Comparison with Other CCSP Benchmarks

Let's consider the benchmarks presented in [1]. The benchmark has $N = 10$ variables, $|D_i| = 10$ values in each domain, $1 - 3$ conditional variables, $d_a \in \{0.1, 0.2, 0.3\}$, fixed $d_c = s_c = 0.2$ and $s_a \in [0.1, 0.9]$. The times for both CondMAC and AMAC were below 2 milliseconds. This is almost four orders of magnitude faster than previously reported results. We can only speculate why our

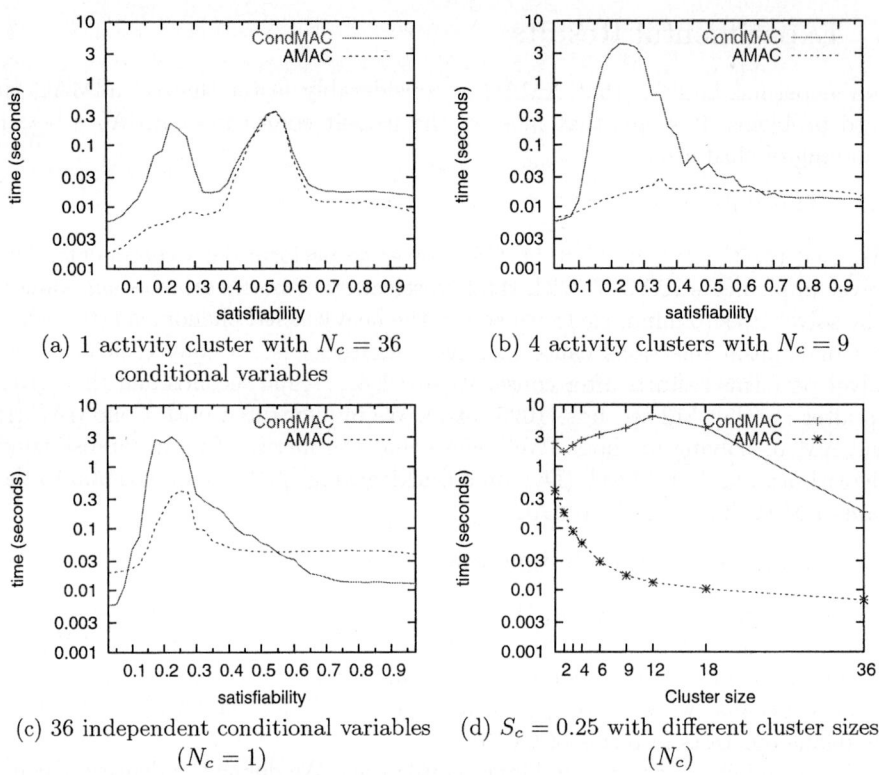

Fig. 3. Clustering: Density of compatibility is $d_c = 0.15$. Satisfiability of activity $s_a = 0.75$. Different values of $s_c \in [0.025, 0.975]$ are displayed.

implementation of CondMAC is so much faster. The only major algorithmic difference is that we use AC-3 while [1] uses AC-4. Differences in random problem generators may also contribute to the big difference. Other contributing factors could be newer hardware and software engineering differences. Both manual and automatic inspection of the results assured the correctness of our results.

5.4 AMAC vs. CondMAC

In all our tests, we averaged 5000 runs per sample. All our results are for the classic subset minimality [3] optimization goal.

For our clustering benchmarks we chose the following characteristics: $N = |\mathcal{V}| = 48$, $\mathcal{V}_\mathcal{I} = 12$, $s_a = 0.75$. Note that our 36 conditional variables decompose into a reasonable amount of 9 possible N_c values. In Figure 3 we tested $s_c \in [0.025, 0.975]$ using 0.025 intervals. Figure 3(d) shows us that AMAC is more than two orders of magnitude faster than CondMAC for nontrivial clustering.

As expected, AMAC is slower than CondMAC for trivial problems (up to 3 times, Figure 3(d)). In these cases, CondMAC finds a solution/failure without backtracking, while AMAC needlessly explores assumptions.

For disjunction, the difference between AMAC and CondMAC is more than five orders of magnitude. This gap makes it impossible to get comprehensible results. For example with $s_a = 0.3$, $s_c = 0.2$, $d_c = 0.15$, $|\mathcal{V}_\mathcal{I}| = 12$, $|\mathcal{V}| = 48$, $|D_i| = 12$ and two clusters of $N_c = 18$. All CondMAC instances finished within a time limit of 2046 seconds, while the average of AMAC was 2/100 of a second.

6 Conclusions

We have shown that combining assumption-based reasoning with constraint propagation can significantly enhance pruning for Conditional CSP. The increased pruning is supported by problem characteristics like activity clustering and presence of activity disjunction constraints. These problem's aspects are naturally captured by Activity CSP, a variant of CCSP.

A possible extension to the ACSP model can be to attach activation conditions to activity variables, such that an activity variable may depend on another activity variable. This enhancement may enable modeling of problems with hierarchical/nested structure.

Another possible extension may support negative activation conditions, this may permit simpler modeling of mutually exclusive alternatives.

Acknowledgments

The authors wish to thank Mati Joshua for his substantial contribution. We also wish to thank Eyal Bin, Yehuda Naveh and Gil Shurek for in depth discussions and comments throughout the writing of this paper.

References

1. Sabin, M., Freuder, E.C., Wallace, R.J.: Greater efficiency for conditional constraint satisfaction. In Rossi, F., ed.: CP. Volume 2833 of Lecture Notes in Computer Science., Springer (2003) 649–663
2. Gelle, E., Faltings, B.: Solving mixed and conditional constraint satisfaction problems. Constraints 8 (2003) 107–141
3. Mittal, S., Falkenhainer, B.: Dynamic constraint satisfaction problems. In: Proc. of AAAI-90, Boston, MA (1990) 25–32
4. Bin, E., Emek, R., Shurek, G., Ziv, A.: Using a constraint satisfaction formulation and solution techniques for random test program generation. IBM Systems Journal 41 (2002) 386–402
5. de Kleer, J.: An assumption-based tms. Artif. Intell. 28 (1986) 127–162
6. Soininen, T., Gelle, E., Niemelä, I.: A fixpoint definition of dynamic constraint satisfaction. In Jaffar, J., ed.: CP. Volume 1713 of Lecture Notes in Computer Science., Springer (1999) 419–433
7. Mackworth, A.K.: Consistency in networks of relations. Artificial Intelligence 8 (1977) 99–118
8. de Kleer, J.: A comparison of atms and csp techniques. In: IJCAI. (1989) 290–296
9. McAllester, D.A.: Truth maintenance. In: AAAI. (1990) 1109–1116
10. Gomes, C.P., Selman, B., Crato, N., Kautz, H.A.: Heavy-tailed phenomena in satisfiability and constraint satisfaction problems. Journal of Automated Reasoning 24 (2000) 67–100
11. Jussien, N., Debruyne, R., Boizumault, P.: Maintaining arc-consistency within dynamic backtracking. In: Principles and Practice of Constraint Programming. (2000) 249–261

Conditional Symmetry Breaking*

Ian P. Gent[1], Tom Kelsey[1], Steve A. Linton[1], Iain McDonald[1], Ian Miguel[1], and Barbara M. Smith[2]

[1] School of Computer Science, University of St Andrews, St Andrews, Fife, UK
[2] Cork Constraint Computation Centre, University College Cork, Cork, Ireland
{ipg, tom, sal, iain, ianm}@dcs.st-and.ac.uk, bms@4c.ucc.ie

Abstract. We introduce the study of *Conditional* symmetry breaking in constraint programming. This arises in a sub-problem of a constraint satisfaction problem, where the sub-problem satisfies some *condition* under which additional symetries hold. Conditional symmetry can cause redundancy in a systematic search for solutions. Breaking this symmetry is an important part of solving a constraint satisfaction problem effectively. We demonstrate experimentally that three methods, well-known for breaking unconditional symmetries, can be applied to conditional symmetries. These are: adding conditional symmetry-breaking constraints, reformulating the problem to remove the symmetry, and augmenting the search process to break the conditional symmetry dynamically through the use of a variant of Symmetry Breaking by Dominance Detection (SBDD).

1 Introduction

Constraint programming has been used successfully to tackle a wide variety of combinatorial problems. To apply constraint programming to a particular domain, the problem must be *modelled* as a constraint program. Typically, many alternative models exist for a given problem, some of which are more effective than others. Constructing an effective constraint model is a difficult task.

An important aspect of modelling is dealing with *symmetry*. Symmetry in a model can result in a great deal of wasted effort when the model is solved via systematic search. To avoid this, the symmetry must be broken effectively. Most research on symmetry in constraint models considers only the symmetry present in a model before search begins. As we will discuss, symmetries can often form during search. We call this *conditional* symmetry, since its formation depends on the choices made during search. To avoid redundant search, it is important to break this symmetry also.

This paper discusses three ways to deal with conditional symmetry. First, we can add constraints to a model to detect and break the symmetry as it arises.

---

* We thank Alan Frisch and Chris Jefferson. Ian Gent is supported by a Royal Society of Edinburgh SEELLD/RSE Support Research Fellowship. Ian Miguel is supported by a UK Royal Academy of Engineering/EPSRC Research Fellowship. This material is based in part on works supported by the Science Foundation Ireland under Grant No. 00/PI.1/C075.

Second, we can reformulate our model so that the new model does not have the conditional symmetry. Finally, we discuss how conditional symmetry can be broken during search.

2 Background

The finite domain *constraint satisfaction problem* (CSP) consists of a triple $\langle X, D, C \rangle$, where X is a set of variables, D is a set of domains, and C is a set of constraints. Each $x_i \in X$ is associated with a finite domain $D_i \in D$ of potential values. A variable is *assigned* a value from its domain. A constraint $c \in C$, constraining variables $x_i, \ldots, x_j$, specifies a subset of the Cartesian product $D_i \times \ldots \times D_j$ indicating mutually compatible variable assignments. A *constrained optimisation problem* is a CSP with some objective function, which is to be optimised.

A *partial assignment* is an assignment to one or more elements of X. A solution is a partial assignment that includes all elements of X. This paper focuses on the use of systematic search through the space of partial assignments to find such solutions. A sub-CSP, P', of a CSP P is obtained from P by adding one or more constraints to P. Note that assigning a value v to a variable x is equivalent to adding the constraint $x = v$.

A *symmetry* in a CSP is a bijection mapping solutions to solutions and non-solutions to non-solutions. A *conditional symmetry* of a CSP P holds only in a sub-problem P' of P. The conditions of the symmetry are the constraints necessary to generate P' from P. Conditional symmetry is a generalisation of unconditional symmetry, since unconditional symmetry can be seen as a conditional symmetry with an empty set of conditions. We focus herein on conditions in the form of partial assignments.

3 Conditional Symmetry-Breaking Constraints

A straightforward method of breaking conditional symmetries is to add constraints to the model of the form: *condition* → *symmetry-breaking constraint* where *condition* is a conjunction of constraints, for instance a partial assignment such as $x = 1 \wedge y = 2$, that must be satisfied for the symmetry to form. As in unconditional symmetry breaking [2], the symmetry-breaking constraint itself usually takes the form of an ordering constraint on the conditionally symmetric objects. We report case studies of breaking conditional symmetry in this way.

3.1 Graceful Graphs

The first case study is of conditional symmetry in finding all graceful labellings [6] in a class of graphs. A labelling f of the vertices of a graph with e edges is *graceful* if f assigns each vertex a unique label from $\{0, 1, ..., e\}$ and when each edge xy is labelled with $|f(x) - f(y)|$, the edge labels are all different. (Hence, the edge labels are a permutation of 1, 2, ..., e.) Finding a graceful labelling of a given graph, or proving that one does not exist, can easily be expressed as a constraint satisfaction problem. The CSP has a variable for each vertex, $x_1, x_2, ..., x_n$ each with domain $\{0, 1, ..., e\}$ and a variable for each edge, $d_1, d_2, ..., d_e$, each with domain $\{1, 2, ..., e\}$. The constraints of the problem are that: if edge k joins vertices i and j then $d_k = |x_i - x_j|$; $x_1, x_2, ..., x_n$ are all different; and $d_1, d_2, ..., d_e$ are all different (and form a permutation).

The graph shown in Figure 1 is an instance of a class of graphs listed in Gallian's survey [6] as $C_n^{(t)}$: they consist of t copies of a cycle with n nodes, with a common vertex. For $n = 3$, these graphs are graceful when $t \equiv 0$ or 1 (mod 4). The nodes are numbered to show the numbering of the variables in the CSP model, i.e. node 0 is the centre node, represented by the variable x_0.

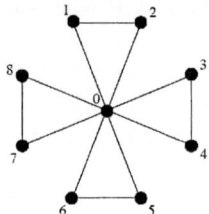

Fig. 1. The windmill graph $C_3^{(4)}$

The symmetries of the CSP are (i) swapping the labels of the nodes other than the centre node in any triangle, e.g. swapping the labels of nodes 1 and 2; (ii) permuting the triangles, e.g. swapping the labels of nodes 1 and 2 with those of nodes 3 and 4; (iii) changing every node label x_i for its complement $e - x_i$.

It is easy to show that the centre node cannot have a label > 1 and $< e - 1$, where e is the number of edges. Since there must be an edge connnecting two nodes labelled 0 and e, if the centre node's label is not 0 or e, then two other nodes in a triangle, e.g. nodes 1 and 2, must be labelled 0 and e. But then, unless the centre node is labelled 1 or $e - 1$ there is no way to get an edge labelled $e - 1$, given that the largest node label is e. The labels 0, 1, $e - 1$ and e are possible for the centre node, however, if there is a graceful labelling.

Suppose we have a graceful labelling of a graph in this class, with the centre node labelled 0. In any triangle, where the other two nodes are labelled a and b, with $a < b$, we can replace a with $b - a$ to get another solution. The edge labels in the triangle are permuted as shown in Figure 2. Any graceful labelling of $C_3^{(t)}$ with centre node labelled 0 has 2^t equivalent labellings by changing or not changing the labels within each of the t triangles in this way. The effect of an instance of this conditional symmetry, on nodes 0, 1, 2, say, depends on whether node 0 is labelled 0 and which of nodes 1 and 2 has the smaller label; hence, we need to know the assignments to these three variables. A graceful labelling with the centre node labelled 1 can be transformed into an equivalent labelling similarly: a triangle labelled 1, a, b, with $a < b$ can be relabelled 1, $b - a + 1$,

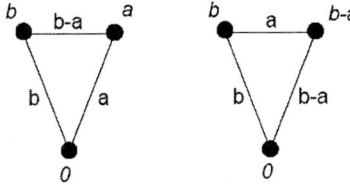

Fig. 2. Relabelling a triangle in a graceful labelling with centre node labelled 0

b. Again, this is conditional on the three assignments. There are equivalents for the other possible labels for the centre node, $e-1$ and e.

In a labelling with the centre node labelled 1, there must be a triangle labelled 1, 0, e, since there has to be an edge whose endpoints are labelled 0 and e. The remaining nodes have labels in the range 3, .., $e-1$. (Since we already have an edge labelled 1, we cannot have a node labelled 2, since it has to be connected to the centre node.)

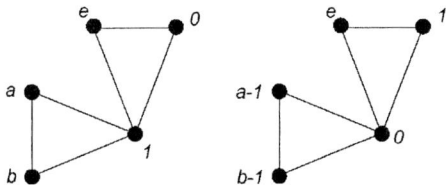

Fig. 3. Transforming a labelling with centre node labelled 1

Figure 3 (left) shows the 1, 0, e triangle and another representative triangle. We can transform the labels of all the nodes as shown in the right-hand figure. If the original labelling is graceful, so is the transformed labelling. Hence, any labelling with centre node labelled 1 is equivalent to one with centre node labelled 0. Note that the reverse is not true: if the centre node is 0, there need not be a triangle labelled 0, 1, e.

Hence, there are two conditional symmetries. One has precondition $x_0 = 1$ and its effect is to transform the node labels $0, 1, 2, 3, ..., e-1, e$ into $1, 0, 2, 2, ..., e-2, e$ respectively. (The effect on a node label of 2 is irrelevant, because it cannot occur.) The other has preconditions $x_0 = 0$ and $x_1 = 1, x_2 = e$ or $x_3 = 1, x_4 = e$ or ... The effect of the symmetry is again easily expressed as a permutation of the values: $0, 1, 2, 3, ...e-2, e-1, e$ become $1, 0, 3, 4, ...e-1, e-1, e$. Similarly, if the centre node is labelled $e-1$, we can transform any resulting graceful labelling into one with the centre node labelled e.

Ignoring the conditional symmetries for now, the symmetries of the CSP can easily be eliminated by adding constraints to the model.

- In each triangle, we can switch the labels of the nodes that are not the central node. Constraints to eliminate this are: $x_{2i-1} < x_{2i}, i = 1, 2, ..., t$

- We can permute the triangles. Given the previous constraints, we can add the following to eliminate this: $x_{2i-1} < x_{2i+1}, i = 1, 2, ..., t-1$
- To eliminate the complement symmetry, we can post: $x_0 < e/2$.

The conditional symmetries can also be eliminated easily. First, the conditional symmetry in the labellings where the central node is 0 requires knowing which of the two other nodes in each triangle has the smaller label. Because of the constraints just added, it is the first one. In terms of Figure 3, we choose the labelling 0, a, b for the triangle and want this to be lexicographically smaller than 0, $b-a$, b. We can add a conditional constraint: if $x_0 = 0$, then $2x_{2i-1} < x_{2i}$, for $i = 1, 2, ..., t$. We have shown that the labellings with the central node labelled 1 are equivalent to some of the labellings with node 0 labelled 0. Further, 0 and 1 are the only possible labels for the central node, given the constraint to eliminate the complement symmetry. Hence, we can simply add $x_0 = 0$ to eliminate this conditional symmetry. This simplifies the conditional constraints given earlier: since we know that $x_0 = 0$, we can drop the condition and just have $2x_{2i-1} < x_{2i}$, for $i = 1, 2, ..., t$. Hence, in this example, all the symmetries, including the conditional symmetries, can be eliminated by simple constraints.

Using the symmetry-breaking constraints to eliminate just the graph and complement symmetries, the graph in Figure 1 has 144 graceful labellings. Eliminating the conditional symmetries reduces these to 8. The resulting reduction in search would be greater still for larger graphs in the same class, $C_3^{(t)}$. This case study demonstrates that eliminating conditional symmetry can sometimes be done with little overhead and reduce the search effort enormously.

3.2 The Patience/Solitaire Game 'Black Hole'

We now show the value of conditional symmetries in a case study of the game 'Black Hole'. Different approaches to solving this game are described in [7]. It was invented by David Parlett with these rules:

"*Layout* Put the Ace of spades in the middle of the board as the base or 'black hole'. Deal all the other cards face up in seventeen fans [i.e. piles] of three, orbiting the black hole.

"*Object* To build the whole pack into a single suit based on the black hole.

"*Play* The exposed card of each fan is available for building. Build in ascending or descending sequence regardless of suit, going up or down ad lib and changing direction as often as necessary. Ranking is continuous between Ace and King." [11]

The table below shows an instance of the game: the 18 columns represent the A♠ in the black hole and the 17 piles of 3 cards each.

	4◇	7♡	7♠	3◇	5♠	T♣	6♠	J♣	J♠	9◇	7◇	2♣	3♡	7♣	3♠	6◇	9♣
	9♠	9♡	J♡	4♠	K◇	Q◇	T♠	T◇	A♣	Q♠	K♠	Q♡	5♡	K♣	8♡	J◇	2◇
A♠	8♠	5◇	2♡	5♣	T♡	3♣	8♣	A♡	2♠	K♡	Q♣	4♡	6♣	6♡	A◇	4♣	8◇

and a solution to this game is:

A♠-2♣-3♠-4◇-5♠-6♠-7♠-8♡-9♠-8♠-9♣-T♠-J♠-Q♡-J♡-T♣-J♣-Q◇-
-K◇-A♣-2♠-3♡-2◇-3♣-4♡-5♡-6♣-7♡-8♣-7♣-6◇-7◇-8◇-9♡-T♡
-9◇-T◇-J◇-Q♠-K♠-A♡-K♡-Q♣-K♣-A◇-2♡-3◇-4♠-5♣-6♡-5◇-4♣

We can see conditional symmetry in Black Hole from the example. The first two piles both have 9s in the middle. If, at some point in the game, both 4◇ and 7♡ have been played, the two 9s are interchangeable *provided that* we don't need to play 9♠ before 9♡ to allow access to 8♠, or 9♡ before 9♠ to access 5◇. That is, the 9s are interchangeable if they are both played after both of their predecessors and before either of their successors. In these circumstances, we can choose the order of the two 9s and not backtrack on this choice.

We can represent a solution to the game as a sequence of the 52 cards in the pack, starting with A♠, the sequence representing the order in which the cards will be played into the Black Hole. The game can be modelled as a permutation problem: if the cards are numbered 0 (the A♠) to 51, the sequence of cards can be represented as a permutation of these numbers. There are two sets of dual variables: x_i represents the ith position in the sequence, and its value represents a card; y_j represents a card and its value is the position in the sequence where that card occurs. We have the usual channelling constraints: $x_i = j$ iff $y_j = i$, $0 \leq i, j \leq 51$. We set $x_0 = 0$.

The constraints that a card cannot be played before a card above it has been played are represented by $<$ constraints on the y_j variables. The constraints that each card must be followed by a card whose value is one higher or one lower are represented by constraints between x_i and x_{i+1} for $0 \leq i < 51$.

The variables $x_0, x_1, ..., x_{51}$ are the search variables: the variables $y_0, y_1, ..., y_{51}$ get assigned by the channelling constraints. The x_i variables are assigned in lexicographic order, i.e. the sequence of cards is built up consecutively from start to finish. The value ordering chooses cards. The top or middle layers are chosen before cards of the same rank lower down in the initial piles, and ties are broken by choosing cards in increasing rank order and an arbitrary suit order (♠, ♡, ◇, ♣). This fits with the problem, in that it makes sense to clear off the top layer of cards as quickly as possible. This simple model using only binary constraints models the problem successfully, but in practice search is prohibitive. We need other techniques to make search practical.

We now deal with conditional symmetry. Recall that in the example 9♠ and 9♡ are interchangeable if both have been played after the cards above them, 4◇ and 7♡, and before the cards immediately below them, 8♠ and 5◇. To break this conditional symmetry, we can add the constraint: if 4◇ $<$ 9♡ and 9♠ $<$ 5◇ then 9♠ $<$ 9♡. This constraint forces 9♠ to be played before 9♡ when they are interchangeable. Based on the initial layout, all constraints of this form can be added, pairwise, before search. The constraints are simplified if the preferred card of the pair is at the top of its pile or the other card is at the bottom of its pile, or both. The conditional symmetry-breaking constraints are designed to respect the value ordering; the same order of cards of each rank is preferred by both. Hence, the solution found is the same as the solution that would be found without the constraints. The constraints simply prevent the search from exploring subtrees that contain no solution. Hence, the number of backtracks with the constraints is guaranteed to be no more than without them. Furthermore, they appear to add little overhead in terms of runtime; they cannot become active until their condition becomes false on backtracking, and they then become simple precedence constraints that are cheap to propagate.

Our CP model was implemented in ILOG Solver 6. We used a benchmark set of 2,500 games, of which 2,189 are winnable [7]. With the conditional symmetry-breaking constraints, the CP model was highly effective at solving these instances. The longest run-time was 1,454sec. (on a 1.7GHz Pentium M PC, running Windows 2000). The distribution was very skewed; 97.5% of instances were solved in 20.8 sec. or less. All the instances were solved in a total of less than 11,000 sec. We also solved the first 150 instances of the 2,500 without conditional symmetry breaking, using a cut-off of 1,500 sec. (i.e. more than long enough to solve any of the instances with symmetry breaking). 20 instances timed out, and the total time to solve the 150 instances was over 37,000 sec. Some instances could still be solved with very little search; even so, the median backtracks increased from 81.5 to 3,618. Overall, it is not practicable to use the CP model to solve random instances of Black Hole without conditional symmetry breaking.

3.3 Steel Mill Slab Design

Our next case study is the steel mill slab design problem [5] (problem 38 at www.csplib.org). Steel is produced by casting molten iron into slabs. A finite number, σ, of *slab sizes* is available. An order has two properties, a *colour* corresponding to the route required through the steel mill and a *weight*. The problem is to pack the d input orders onto slabs so that the total slab capacity is minimised. There are two types of constraint: *Capacity constraints* specify that the total weight of orders assigned to a slab cannot exceed the slab capacity. *Colour constraints* specify that each slab can contain at most p of k total colours (p is usually 2). These constraints arise because it is expensive to cut the slabs up to send them to different parts of the mill.

We use a matrix model to represent this problem. Assuming the largest order is smaller than the largest slab, at most d slabs are required. Hence, a one-dimensional matrix of size d, $slab_M$, can be used to represent the size of each slab, a size of zero indicating that this particular slab is unused. A $d \times d$ 0-1 matrix, $order_M$, is used to represent the assignment of orders to slabs; $order_M[i,j] = 1$ if the ith order is assigned to the jth slab. Constraints on the rows ensure that the slab capacity is not exceeded:

$$\forall j \in \{1..d\} : \sum_{i \in \{1..d\}} weight(i) \times order_M[i,j] \leq slab_M[j]$$

where $weight(i)$ is a function mapping the ith order to its weight. Constraints on the columns ensure that each order is assigned to one and only one slab:

$$\forall i \in 1..d : \sum_{j \in \{1..d\}} order_M[i,j] = 1$$

A second 0-1 matrix, $colour_M$ with dimensions $k \times d$, relates slabs and colours. A '1' entry in the ith column and jth row indicates that the ith colour is present on the jth slab. Constraints link $order_M$ and $colour_M$:

$$\forall i \in \{1..d\} \forall j \in \{1..d\} : order_M[i,j] = 1 \rightarrow colour_M[colour(i),j] = 1$$

where $colour(i)$ is a function mapping the ith order to its colour. Constraints on the rows of $colour_M$ ensure that each slab is given no more than p colours.

$$\forall j \in \{1..d\} : \sum_{i \in \{1..k\}} colour_M[i,j] \leq p$$

In this initial formulation, there is a symmetry involving $slab_M$ and the rows of $order_M$: a solution can be transformed into a solution by permuting the values assigned to each element of $slab_M$ and permuting the corresponding rows of $order_M$. This symmetry can be broken by forming d $slabAndOrderRow$ vectors, where the first element of $slabAndOrderRow[i]$ is $slab_M[i]$ and the remaining elements are the ith row of $order_M$, and lexicographically ordering as follows:

$$slabAndOrderRow[1] \geq_{\text{lex}} slabAndOrderRow[2] \geq_{\text{lex}} \ldots slabAndOrderRow[d]$$

Furthermore, $order_M$ has partial column symmetry. If two orders have equal weight and colour, the associated columns can be exchanged. This symmetry can be broken by combining symmetric orders into a single column, whose sum is constrained to be equal to the number of orders it represents.

There is a further symmetry conditional on the way that orders are assigned to slabs. Consider 3 'red' orders, order a of weight 6 and two instances of order b, with weight 3 (the last two are represented by a single column), and the following partial assignments to $order_M$:

$$\begin{pmatrix} & a & b & \ldots \\ slab_1 & 1 & 0 & \ldots \\ slab_2 & 0 & 2 & \ldots \\ \ldots & \ldots & \ldots & \ldots \end{pmatrix} \quad \begin{pmatrix} & a & b & \ldots \\ slab_1 & 0 & 2 & \ldots \\ slab_2 & 1 & 0 & \ldots \\ \ldots & \ldots & \ldots & \ldots \end{pmatrix}$$

These assignments are symmetrical. Note that the symmetry is conditional on both instances of b being assigned to the same slab, effectively creating a single 'super' order symmetrical to a. This is the simplest case of *compound order symmetry*, where individual orders combine to become symmetrical to single larger orders or other compounds.

To break compound order symmetry, we must know when and where the symmetry forms. For simplicity, we discuss only compound orders composed from multiple instances of the same order; the encoding can be extended straightforwardly to compounds formed from orders of different sizes. Consider an instance with 6 red orders of size 1. The assignment of these orders to slabs is represented by a single column of $order_M$, whose sum is constrained to be six. Up to two red compound orders of size three can form from the six red orders. Figure 4 (Top) presents example cases for which we must cater. In each example all the orders

$$a)\begin{pmatrix}1\\1\\1\\1\\1\\1\end{pmatrix} b)\begin{pmatrix}3\\3\\0\\0\\0\\0\end{pmatrix} c)\begin{pmatrix}0\\0\\6\\0\\0\\0\end{pmatrix} d)\begin{pmatrix}1\\1\\3\\0\\0\\0\end{pmatrix} e)\begin{pmatrix}1\\3\\1\\0\\0\\0\end{pmatrix} f)\begin{pmatrix}3\\1\\2\\0\\0\\0\end{pmatrix}$$

$$a)\begin{pmatrix}1\\2\\3\\4\\5\\6\end{pmatrix} b)\begin{pmatrix}3\\6\\6\\6\\6\\6\end{pmatrix} c)\begin{pmatrix}0\\0\\6\\6\\6\\6\end{pmatrix} d)\begin{pmatrix}1\\2\\3\\6\\6\\6\end{pmatrix} e)\begin{pmatrix}1\\4\\5\\6\\6\\6\end{pmatrix} f)\begin{pmatrix}3\\4\\6\\6\\6\\6\end{pmatrix}$$

Fig. 4. Top: Conditional formation of two compound orders. Bottom: Assignments to $subsum_M$ variables corresponding to order variable assignments in the Top part.

have been assigned to a slab, but in some cases one (Fig.4d, Fig.4e, Fig.4f) or both (Fig.4a) compounds have not formed.

It is useful to consider a first compound (formed from the first three orders, counting down the column) and a second compound (formed from the second three). A key observation is that, counting from the top of each column, a compound can form only when enough orders have been assigned (three orders for the first compound, six for the second). To exploit this observation, for each column on which compound orders may appear, we introduce a column of variables, $subsum_M$, which record the cumulative sum of assigned orders read down the column. Figure 4 (Bottom) presents the $subsum_M$ variables for our examples.

Given the $subsum_M$ variables, we introduce a *position* variable for each compound, whose domain is the set of possible slab indices, constrained as follows:

$$subsum_M[position - 1] < compoundSize \times instanceNo$$
$$subsum_M[position] \geq compoundSize \times instanceNo$$

where *compoundSize* gives the number of orders necessary to form the compound, and *instanceNo* denotes which of the compounds of *compoundSize* on this column that *position* is associated with. This pair of constraints ensure that *position* indicates a unique slab when the corresponding column of $order_M$ is assigned.

The remaining question, given some partial assignment, is whether the compound order associated with *position* has formed on the slab indicated by *position*. This is recorded in a 0/1 variable, *switch*, paired with each *position* variable and constrained as follows:

$$switch = (order_M[column][position] \geq compoundSize)$$

where *column* is the column of $order_M$ on which the compound may form.

Consider n symmetrical compound orders. We order these compounds ascending by the column on which they appear, breaking ties by ordering the 'first', 'second', ..., 'nth' compounds in a column, as defined in the previous section, ascending. We denote the *switch* and *position* variables of the ith compound under this ordering as $switch_i$ and $position_i$. The conditional symmetry can be broken straightforwardly as follows:

$$\forall i < j \in \{1, \ldots, n\} : (switch_i = 1 \land switch_j = 1) \rightarrow position_i \leq position_j$$

These ordering constraints are compatible with the *slabAndOrderRow* symmetry-breaking constraints given above. If the compound orders were ordered in the reverse direction, solutions might be pruned incorrectly. Given a set of symmetrical objects, it is normally only necessary to order adjacent elements in the set [4]. Here, since we cannot be certain that any particular conditional symmetry will form, we post the transitive closure of the ordering constraints.

The formation of compound order symmetry depends on the order instance data. Hence, we constructed 12 instances where compound order symmetries were highly likely to form. We used only one colour for all orders, and chose the size and number of the smaller orders so that several small orders are equivalent in size to one of the larger orders.

Table 1. Steel Mill Slab Design: Experimental Results. Times to 3 significant figures. A dash indicates optimal solution not found within 1 hour. Hardware: PIII 750MHz, 128Mb. Software: Ilog Solver 5.3 (Windows version).

Prob	$slab_M$ Symm. Breaking		$slab\&OrderRow$ Symm. Breaking		$slab_M$ + Comp. Order Symm. Breaking		$slab\&OrderRow$+Comp. Order Symm. Breaking	
	Choices	Time(s)	Choices	Time(s)	Choices	Time(s)	Choices	Time(s)
1	18,014,515	1120	79,720	5.64	-	-	68,717	36.4
2	6,985,007	439	15739	1.45	-	-	13,464	6.79
3	7,721	0.741	1,798	0.26	6,461	3.48	1,472	0.971
4	155,438	8.86	60,481	4.10	49,234	31.0	30,534	16.2
5	146,076	7.48	56,590	3.45	46,599	23.4	27,921	12.4
6	117,240	6.01	49,098	2.82	39,411	17.7	24,112	9.70
7	147,148	7.1	60,035	3.34	70,881	36.3	37,672	18.0
8	171,781	8.02	77,187	4.13	80,557	37.1	45,293	19.3
9	206,138	9.52	92,526	4.87	97,072	44.9	53,666	23.0
10	348,716	16.6	140,741	7.55	178,753	94.8	84,046	41.5
11	313,840	15.7	130,524	7.21	164,615	98.5	79,621	44.4
12	266,584	13.9	110,007	6.19	138,300	82.5	68,087	37.8

We ran four experiments on our test suite, summarised in the four columns of Table 1. Performance with no symmetry breaking at all was very poor, so column 1 gives results with a non-increasing ordering on $slab_M$ only (a simplification of *slabAndOrderRow* symmetry breaking). Column 2 presents the results of using full *slabAndOrderRow* symmetry breaking. Columns 3 and 4 respectively give the results of combining $slab_M$ and *slabAndOrderRow* symmetry breaking with compound order conditional symmetry breaking. The results show that the overhead of compound order symmetry breaking is significant. Although it clearly reduces search — in the instances tested a reduction of as much as 50% is gained — the time taken is increased overall

Given our results, the challenge is to make the encoding of detection of conditional symmetry of this type sufficiently lightweight that it can be used without increasing the overall search effort.

4 Breaking Conditional Symmetry by Reformulation

Modelling has a substantial effect on how efficiently a problem can be solved. An appropriate reformulation of a model can turn an insoluble problem into a soluble one in practical terms. Modelling and reformulation are equally important for symmetry breaking. Different models of the same problem can have different symmetries; one formulation can have symmetries which are easier to deal with than another. Thus, reformulation of a problem can be critical in dealing with symmetries. Unfortunately, there is no general technique for suggesting reformulations for breaking symmetry. If anything, conditional symmetry intensifies the difficulties, but here we present a successful example. The all-interval series problem (problem 7 in CSPLib) is to find a permutation of the n integers from 0 to $n-1$ so that the differences between adjacent numbers are also a permutation of the numbers from 1 to $n-1$.

We can model this using n integer variables $x_0, x_1, ..., x_{n-1}$ where x_i represents the number in position i in the permutation. There is an allDifferent constraint on the x variables. Following Choi and Lee [1], we use auxiliary variables $d_i = |x_i - x_{i+1}|$ for $0 \le i \le n-2$ to represent the differences between adjacent numbers; these variables are required to be all different. We use lexicographic variable ordering.

There are 4 obvious symmetries in the problem: the identity, reversing the series, negating each element by subtracting it from $n-1$, and doing both. There is also a conditional symmetry: we can cycle a solution to the problem about a pivot to generate another solution. The location of this pivot is dependent on the assignments made and so these symmetries are conditional. As an example, here are two solutions for $n = 11$. Differences are written underneath the numbers:

```
0 10 1 9 2 8 3 7 4 6 5         3 7 4 6 5 0 10 1 9 2 8
 10 9 8 7 6 5 4 3 2 1           4 3 2 1 5 10 9 8 7 6
```

The difference between the first number (0) on the left and last number (5) is 5. This means we can split the sequence between the 8 and 3, losing the difference 5. We can join the rest of the sequence on to the start, because the 5 − 0 will now replace 8 − 3. This yields exactly the solution shown on the right. In this case the pivot is between the values 8 and 3. The difference between first and last terms must always duplicate a difference in the sequence, so this operation can be applied to any solution.

We now give a reformulation which eliminates all symmetry including conditional symmetry, with a 50-fold runtime improvement on the best previous work. Consider a cycle formed by n nodes, with the n differences between consecutive nodes satisfying the constraint that every difference from 1 to $n-1$ appears at least once, and one difference appears exactly twice. From any solution to this we can form two all-interval series, by breaking the cycle at either one of the repeated differences. The reformulation introduces new symmetry because we can rotate the cycle, but it is broken by setting the first element to 0. Next, we note that 0 and $n-1$ must be adjacent, and since we can reverse any sequence, we insist that the second element is $n-1$. Finally, the difference $n-2$ can only appear by putting $n-2$ before 0 in the cycle, or by putting 1 after $n-1$. But after negation, reversal, and cycling, the two cases are the same. So we can insist that the sequence starts $0, n-1, 1$. This gives the reformulated problem:

Definition 1 (Reformulation of All-interval series problem). *Given $n \geq 3$, find a vector $(s_0, ..., s_{n-1})$, such that:*

1. *s is a permutation of $\{0, 1, ..., n-1\}$; and*
2. *the interval vector $(|s_1 - s_0|, |s_2 - s_1|, ... |s_{n-1} - s_{n-2}|, |s_{n-1} - s_0|)$ contains every integer in $\{1, 2, ..., n-1\}$ with exactly one integer repeated; and*
3. *$s_0 = 0$, $s_1 = n - 1$, $s_2 = 1$.*

Elsewhere [10] we show that: (i) for $n > 4$, there are exactly 8 times as many solutions to the original all-interval series problem as to the reformulated one, and (ii) the repeated difference is even iff n is congruent to 0 or 1 $mod 4$. To code this formulation, we simply replaced the allDifferent constraint by a constraint to ensure that every difference occurs at least once: since there are n differences, one must automatically appear twice. Finally we added the constraint on the parity of the repeated difference, which reduced run-time by about a third.

Table 2. Run times for reformulated version of the all-interval series problem. Where meaningful, the column for speedup indicates the factor by which these run times improve those of SBDS using the unconditional symmetries in [10] on the same machine. Our code is actually Solver 4.4 code compiled and run under Solver 5.2.

n	Solutions	Fails	Choice Points	Cpu (sec)	Speedup	Fails/Solution
3	1	0	0	0.01	-	0
4	1	0	0	< 0.01	-	0
5	1	0	0	< 0.01	-	0
6	3	1	3	< 0.01	-	0.33
7	4	1	4	< 0.01	-	0.25
8	5	9	13	< 0.01	-	1.80
9	15	14	28	0.01	9	0.93
10	37	69	105	0.02	13	1.97
11	81	278	358	0.02	61	3.43
12	166	858	1,023	0.06	116	5.17
13	400	3,758	4,157	0.28	121	9.40
14	1,239	19,531	20,769	1.78	103	15.76
15	3,199	91,695	94,893	8.85	-	28.66
16	6,990	389,142	396,131	36.94	-	55.67
17	17,899	2,093,203	2,111,101	215.61	-	116.95
18	63,837	13,447,654	13,511,490	1,508.26	-	212.15
19	181,412	79,270,906	79,452,317	9,778.94	-	436.97
20	437,168	435,374,856	435,812,023	53,431.50	-	995.90

Table 2 shows results using the reformulated encoding. Where we have meaningful comparisons, from about $n = 11$ to 14, this formulation is around 100 times faster than SBDS on unconditional symmetries. This is roughly a 50-fold speedup on Puget and Régin's results [12]. It is clear that this formulation is the best way known to count solutions to the all-interval series problem. Table 2 shows that the number of fails per solution roughly doubles for each increment in n. Thus, while sometimes regarded as the easiest problem in CSPLib, the all-interval series still seems to involve considerable combinatorial search.

There is little we can say in general about reformulating to break conditional symmetry except that it can lead to dramatic performance improvements, but seems to require considerable insight on a case-by-case basis. General techniques for reformulation would be highly desirable, but remain in the future.

5 A Generic Method of Breaking Conditional Symmetries

It is preferable for breaking conditional symmetries – as it is for unconditional symmetries – to have a generic method where the symmetries and conditions can be described easily and broken efficiently. To achieve this, we look to previous methods of breaking symmetries and examine how they could be modified to cope with conditional symmetries.

Gent, McDonald and Smith [10] give two implementations of SBDS modified to work for conditional symmetries. These implementations provide proof of concept only as both have serious problems. Both methods reduce the efficiency of constraint solving. The first requires a different symmetry function for each *possible* conditional symmetry, and naturally there will always be many more than the unconditional symmetries. The second removes this problem, but the implementation is grounded heavily in the specific CSP. Thus no general purpose method proposed to date for conditional symmetries can be regarded as satisfactory. In this section we describe the main disadvantage of using SBDS-like approaches when dealing with conditional symmetry. We also explain how we have modified SBDD [3] to effectively deal with generic conditional symmetries.

5.1 The Problem with Using SBDS to Break Conditional Symmetry

SBDS adds constraints to the local subtree. These constraints are discarded upon backtracking from the root node of the subtree. This means that we must have an SBDS constraint for each *possibly* applicable symmetry. This is a particularly high overhead where, as in the example of all-interval series, there are many more conditional symmetries than unconditional ones. An alternative is to check at a node whether or not a condition holds, and only to add the SBDS constraints in that local subtree where the condition is known to hold. Unfortunately, this approach fails. We might backtrack from this point and therefore discard the SBDS constraint, going back up the tree to a node where the condition is no longer true. Since the condition is not true, no conditional symmetry will be posted. Unfortunately, the condition could become true again on further reassignment of variables. Thus, this approach is untenable because it will miss duplicate solutions.

In contrast to SBDS, it seems that SBDD should adapt naturally to the conditional case. This is because the check is performed at a node about to be explored. At this point, we can calculate which conditional symmetries are known to hold. We can then calculate the resulting group, and check this against previously visited nodes. Unlike SBDS, when we backtrack from a node, we do not need to know what conditional symmetry holds in some future node. We can maintain the database of nodes visited in the same way as conventional SBDD: that is, we need merely to record the nodes at the roots of fully explored search trees. At a search node of depth d there are at most d such roots to store, which helps to make SBDD so efficient in general.

Unfortunately, the above analysis assumes that the correct algebraic structure (unconditional symmetries combined with conditional symmetries) is a group. This is not the case in general. Suppose that the unconditional symmetries form a group G, and that a conditional symmetry has group H, with both groups acting on the set of possible variable to value assignments of the CSP. If we naïvely compose all symmetries from both groups, then we may lose solutions: if the unconditional symmetry modifies the condition so that it does not hold, it is no longer sound to apply the conditional symmetry.

We now describe a sound method for breaking both conditional and unconditional symmetries dynamically using GAP–SBDD [9]. At each node in the search tree we discover each conditional symmetry that holds, and generate a symmetry group H_i for each one. We first check for dominance in G. If dominated we backtrack. If not we pick H_1 and check for dominance. Again, if dominated we backtrack, if not we pick H_2 and repeat until the H_i are exhausted.

This method is sound, since we never compose conditional and unconditional symmetries, although it introduces the computational overhead of generating groups and ensuring that the state of search maintained for each group generated. The method is incomplete in general for the same reason; it may be the case that composing symmetries results in the detection of dominance which correctly prunes the search tree. Our conditional–SBDD is the first satisfactory dynamic technique devised, and is fully generic: it can be applied to any CSP with known conditional and unconditional symmetries.

Table 3. Conditional–SBDD: Experimental Results. Times to 3 significant figures. Software: GAP v4.4 & ECLIPSE v5.7. BT denotes backtracks; MD denotes maximum depth attained during search.

	Conditional–SBDD						SBDD				
t	GAP cpu	ECL cpu	Σ-cpu	BT	MD	sols	GAP cpu	ECL cpu	Σ-cpu	BT	MD sols
4	10.44	1.50	11.94	199	16	8	3.47	2.66	6.13	782	23 128
5	340.54	24.58	365.12	1823	23	21	53.21	42.44	95.65	11,255	36 672
6	8,336.74	374.73	8,711.47	18,630	31	0	907.31	954.45	1861.76	186,015	50 0

As an example we report on a prototype implementation of conditional–SBDD applied to the graceful graphs $C_3^{(t)}$ described in Section 3.1. As there, we set the central node to be 0, but no longer add constraints to break the conditional symmetries on triangles. E.g. if one node in a triangle is 12, then the numbers i and $12 - i$ are equivalent on the other node of the triangle. The results are given in Table 3. We see that conditional–SBDD results in many fewer backtracks and much less search depth, at the cost of increased GAP cpu-time taken to identify and search through the H_i. Breaking no conditional symmetries results in several isomorphic solutions being returned. Conditional–SBDD is both sound and complete for these examples – exactly one member of each class of solutions is returned.

6 Conclusions and Future Work

We have introduced the study of *conditional* symmetry breaking in constraint programming. We demonstrate with concrete implementations and case studies that three methods – each well-known for breaking unconditional symmetries – can be applied to conditional symmetries. These are adding conditional symmetry-breaking constraints, reformulating the problem to remove the symmetry, and augmenting the search process to break the conditional symmetry dynamically through the use of a new variant of SBDD. We can conclude that the study of conditional symmetry is as rich and fertile for new developments as unconditional symmetry breaking, It is arguably even more important in practice, since many problems contain symmetries that arise during search.

References

1. C. Choi and J.H. Lee, *On the pruning behavior of minimal combined models for CSPs.*, Proceedings of the Workshop on Reformulating Constraint Satisfaction Problems 2002.
2. J. Crawford, M. L. Ginsberg, E. Luks, A. Roy. Symmetry-breaking Predicates for Search Problems. *Proc. of the 5th KRR*, pp. 148–159, 1996.
3. T. Fahle, S. Schamberger, M. Sellmann. Symmetry breaking. In: Proc. CP 2001. (2001) 93–107
4. A. M. Frisch, B. Hnich, Z. Kiziltan, I. Miguel, T. Walsh. Global Constraints for Lexicographic Orderings. *Proc. CP 02*, pp. 93–108, 2002.
5. A. M. Frisch, I. Miguel, T. Walsh. Symmetry and Implied Constraints in the Steel Mill Slab Design Problem. *Proc. Formul '01*, pp. 8–15, 2001.
6. J. A. Gallian. Graph Labeling. *The Electronic Journal of Combinatorics*, Dynamic Surveys (DS6), www.combinatorics.org/Surveys,2003.
7. I.P. Gent, C.A. Jefferson, I. Lynce, I. Miguel, P. Nightingale, B.M. Smith, A. Tarim, Search in the Patience Game Black Hole CP Pod Research Report 10, 2005
8. I. P. Gent, W. Harvey, T. W. Kelsey. Groups and Constraints: Symmetry Breaking During Search *Proc. 8th CP 02*, pp. 415-430, 2002.
9. I. P. Gent, W. Harvey, T. W. Kelsey, S. A. Linton. Generic SBDD Using Computational Group Theory. *Proc. CP 03*, pp. 333-347, 2003.
10. I. P. Gent, I. McDonald, B. M. Smith. Conditional Symmetry in the All-Interval Series Problem. *Proc. SymCon 03*, 2003.
11. David Parlett. *The Penguin Book of Patience*. Penguin, 1980.
12. J.-F. Puget and J.-C. Régin, *Solving the all-interval problem*, Available from http://www.csplib.org.

Symmetry and Consistency

Ian P. Gent, Tom Kelsey, Steve Linton, and Colva Roney-Dougal

School of Computer Science, University of St Andrews, St Andrews,
Fife, KY16 9SX, UK
{ipg, tom, sal, colva}@dcs.st-and.ac.uk

Abstract. We introduce a novel and exciting research area: symmetrising levels of consistency to produce stronger forms of consistency and more efficient mechanisms for establishing them. We propose new levels of consistency for Constraint Satisfaction Problems (CSPs) incorporating the symmetry group of a CSP. We first define $Sym(i,j)$-consistency, show that even $Sym(1,0)$-consistency can prune usefully, and study some consequences of maintaining $Sym(i, 0)$-consistency. We then present pseudocode for SymPath consistency, and a symmetrised version of singleton consistency, before presenting experimental evidence of these algorithms' practical effectiveness. With this contribution we establish the study of symmetry-based levels of consistency of CSPs.

1 Introduction

Symmetries arise in many Constraint Satisfaction Problems (CSPs). A rapidly growing literature looks at avoiding redundant search (and duplicate solutions) through a variety of techniques, such as enforcing a lexicographic ordering by enforcing lexicographic constraints [1], adding constraints dynamically during search [2], backtracking from the current node when it can be shown to be equivalent to a previous nogood [3] or constructing trees in which the symmetry has been eliminated [4].

Constraint solving is a balance between search and inference. There are various levels of consistency that can be maintained while searching for a solution, and many algorithms for enforcing levels of consistency. One can pick a level of consistency such as arc consistency (AC), a particular approach such as AC-3, and still find a variety of algorithms using interesting variants of that technique [5–7].

This work is foundational in establishing how symmetry and inference can be incorporated to the benefit of search in CSPs. At the heart of the thinking behind this research is the simple fact that any time we learn something about a CSP, the same is true of its symmetric equivalents. We suggest ways in which this insight can be used, specifically a number of new levels of consistency. These levels of consistency do one of two things: they either exploit the group structure to establish a higher level of consistency than corresponding notions without symmetry; or they establish the same level of consistency but the algorithm to establish consistency can exploit the group structure to potentially run faster. This paper considers both possibilities. The only precursor we are aware of is an exploitation of symmetry in a variant of AC2001 [8].

In Section 2 we introduce the fundamental definitions of CSPs, symmetries and consistency. In Section 3 we define a new, symmetric, kind of consistency called $Sym(i, j)$-

consistency, and go on to study various specialisations of it such as $\mathrm{Sym}(i,0)$-consistency. In Section 4 we present pseudocode for enforcing a symmetrised version of path consistency, then in Section 5 we present pseudocode for enforcing symmetrised singleton consistency. Both of these algorithms generalise the optimal known algorithms for their unsymmetrised versions. In Section 6 we present experimental evidence of the practical effectiveness of our new algorithms, before concluding with a discussion some of the possible directions for this exciting new research area.

2 Background and Definitions

Definition 1. *A CSP P is a triple* $(\Delta, \mathcal{D}, \mathcal{C})$, *where* Δ *is a finite indexed set of variables* $x_1, x_2, \ldots, x_n$, *each of which has finite domain of possible values* $D_i := \mathrm{Dom}(x_i) \subseteq \Lambda$. *The set* $\mathcal{D} = \{D_i : 1 \leq i \leq n\}$, *and the set* $\mathcal{C}$ *is a finite set of constraints on the variables in* Δ. *A* solution *to a CSP is an instantiation of all of the variables in* Δ *such that all of the constraints in* $\mathcal{C}$ *are satisfied.*

Statements of the form $(var = val)$ are *literals*: we denote the set of all literals of the CSP by $\chi(\Delta, \mathcal{D})$, or simply χ when the meaning is clear. We will write the literal $(x_i = a)$ as (x_i, a), or occasionally (i, a).

Definition 2. *A set of literals is a* partial assignment *if each variable occurs at most once in it, and a* full assignment *if each variable occurs exactly once.*

Let C be constraint and $\mathcal{I}$ a partial assignment, then by $\mathrm{Var}(C)$ we denote the *scope* of C, namely the variables over which the constraint C is defined, and by $\mathrm{Var}(\mathcal{I})$ we denote the variables in $\mathcal{I}$. We say that $\mathcal{I}$ *satisfies* C if $\mathcal{I}$ contains assignments to all variables in $\mathrm{Var}(C)$, and the restriction of $\mathcal{I}$ to $\mathrm{Var}(C)$ is a permitted tuple of C. The partial assignment $\mathcal{I}$ *violates* C if it contains assignments to all variables in the scope of C, but the restriction of $\mathcal{I}$ to $\mathrm{Var}(C)$ is a forbidden tuple of C. A partial assignment $\mathcal{I}$ is *consistent* if it satisfies all of the constraints that have no uninstantiated variables.

A permutation f of a set X is a bijection $f : X \to X$. We will denote the image of a point $x \in X$ under the map f by xf. This notation (which comes from group theory) means that if we apply a permutation f to $x \in X$ and then a permutation g to the result we can simply write xfg, rather than the more cumbersome $g(f(x))$. Given any permutation f on a set X we will abuse notation and allow f to act on (ordered or unordered) subsets of X, via $\{x_1, \ldots, x_n\}f := \{x_1 f, \ldots, x_n f\}$. Since f is an injection the size of the image set is the same as the size of the original set.

Definition 3. *Given a CSP* $P = (\Delta, \mathcal{D}, \mathcal{C})$, *a* symmetry *of P is a permutation of* $\chi(\Delta, \mathcal{D})$ *such that a full assignment* $\mathcal{A}$ *is a solution if and only if* $\mathcal{A}f$ *is a solution.*

It is well known that the collection of all symmetries of a CSP forms a *group*, that is, the composition of any two symmetries is itself a symmetry, and the inverse of a symmetry is a symmetry. To see this we note that if f and g are symmetries of a CSP P, then for any solution $\mathcal{S} \subseteq \chi(\Delta, \mathcal{D})$ the set $\mathcal{S}fg = (\mathcal{S}f)g$ is a solution. To see that the inverse of a symmetry is a symmetry, note that if $\mathcal{S}$ is a solution, and $\mathcal{S}f^{-1}$ is not a solution, then f is not a symmetry, since $(\mathcal{S}f^{-1})f = \mathcal{S}$. Any group G has a distinguished element called the *identity*, denoted 1_G or simply 1, with the property that acting with 1_G fixes everything.

Let G be a group of permutations of a set Ω, and let $a \in \Omega$. The *orbit*, a^G, of a under G is the set of all elements of Ω to which a may be mapped by permutations in G. Formally, $a^G := \{ag : g \in G\}$. The *stabiliser* of a in G is $G_a := \{g \in G : ag = a\}$, the set of all permutations in G that map a to itself. Let $A := \{a_1, \ldots, a_m\} \subseteq \Omega$. Then the *pointwise stabiliser* of A is $G_{(A)} := \{g \in G : a_i g = a_i \text{ for } 1 \leq i \leq m\}$, namely the set of all permutations in G that map each point in A to itself. The *setwise stabiliser* of A is $G_{\{A\}} := \{g \in G : \text{ for all } i \text{ there exists } j \text{ with } a_i g = a_j\}$. That is, the setwise stabiliser is the set of all permutations in G that map the set A to itself. It is an elementary fact that for any $a \in \Omega$ the point stabiliser G_a is a subgroup of G (a subset of G that is itself a group under the same operation as in G), and also that any setwise or pointwise stabiliser is a subgroup of G.

Our definition of symmetry is very general. In particular, if $\mathcal{A}$ is a consistent partial assignment, then, provided that $\mathcal{A}$ is not a subset of a solution, it is possible that there exists a symmetry g such that $\mathcal{A}g$ violates a constraint. For example, let P be a CSP with variables x, y, z, each with domain $[1, 2]$, and constraint set $\{x = y, y = z\}$. Then the symmetries of P allow us to freely interchange $(x, i), (y, i)$ and (z, i), for any fixed $i \in [1, 2]$, as this will preserve both of the solutions. Thus in particular there is a symmetry f which maps $(y, 2) \mapsto (z, 2)$, $(z, 2) \mapsto (y, 2)$, and fixes all other literals. However, the partial assignment $\{(x, 1), (z, 2)\}$ is mapped by f to the partial assignment $\{(x, 1), (y, 2)\}$, and this latter partial assignment violates a constraint.

Symmetries need not even map partial assignments to partial assignments, and this is perfectly acceptable. In the 8-queens puzzle, there is a symmetry which rotates the square by 90 degrees. Suppose we use the standard model, with one variable for the placement of the queen in each row. The partial assignment $\{(Q_1, 3), (Q_2, 3)\}$ maps to $\{(Q_3, 8), (Q_3, 7)\}$, which involves two values for Q_3 and therefore is not a partial assignment. However, the initial assignment violates the constraint that there is only one queen in each column. This observation generalises: if a symmetry f maps a partial assignment $\mathcal{A}$ to a set of literals $\mathcal{A}f$ that is not a partial assignment, then $\mathcal{A}$ is not a subset of any solution. To see this, suppose that $\mathcal{A} \subset \mathcal{S}$ for some solution $\mathcal{S}$, and note that by definition of f we have $\mathcal{A}f \subset \mathcal{S}f$. Conversely, the inverse of f will map a collection of literals that a not a partial assigment to one that is, in that f^{-1} maps $\mathcal{A}f$ to $\mathcal{A}$. This is one reason why we define symmetries as acting on literals and then induce up to sets of literals, rather than defining them originally as acting on partial assignments.

Definition 4. *Given a CSP $P = (\Delta, \mathcal{D}, \mathcal{C})$, a symmetry f of P is strict if for all sets $\mathcal{A} \subseteq \chi(\Delta, \mathcal{D})$ of literals, $\mathcal{A}$ is a consistent partial assignment if and only if $\mathcal{A}f$ is a consistent partial assignment.*

A symmetry is *not* strict if it can map a partial assignment violating some constraint to a partial assignment not violating any constraints, or *vice versa*.

Definition 5. *Let $L = (\Delta, \mathcal{D}, \mathcal{C})$ be a CSP with symmetry group G. A value symmetry of L is a symmetry $g \in G$ such that if $(x_i, a)g = (x_j, b)$ then $x_i = x_j$. Denote the elements of $D_i \in \mathcal{D}$ by a_{ij}. A variable symmetry of L is a symmetry $g \in G$ such that if $(x_i, a_{ij})g = (x_k, b_{kl})$ then $j = l$. In the case where the variables have common domains then we denote the elements of Λ as a_k, and the condition for a symmetry to be a variable symmetry can be simplified to: if $(x_i, a_k)g = (x_j, a_l)$ then $a_k = a_l$. That is, the symmetry fixes the values in each literal.*

We distinguish value and variable symmetries, as these have particularly nice algorithmic properties. If all elements of G are *pure* value symmetries (value symmetries such that if $(x_i, a)g = (x_i, b)$ then for all j we have $(x_j, a)g = (x_j, b)$) then we can consider G to consist of permutations of Λ. Similarly, if G contains only pure variable symmetries then we can consider it to consist of permutations of Δ. See [4,9] for more details. Note that we cannot in general write $(x_i, a)g$ as $(x_i g, ag)$ as the variable in $(x_i, a)g$ may depend on the choice of value a. The 8-queens example before Definition 4 gives a symmetry which demonstrates this.

We finish this section with some definitions of consistency. A CSP P is *k-consistent* if given a consistent partial assignment on any $k-1$ variables, along with a k-th variable, one can find a value for the k-th variable such that the resulting partial assignment of size k is consistent. A CSP that is k-consistent need not be $(k-1)$-consistent: see [10].

We now recall the more general form of consistency called (i,j)-*consistency* [11].

Definition 6. *Suppose that in a CSP P, given any consistent partial assignment on i variables, and given any other j variables, it is possible to find values for the additional j variables such that resulting partial assignment of size $i + j$ is consistent. Then P is (i, j)-consistent.*

Thus in this notation k-consistency is $(k-1, 1)$-consistency, and arc consistency is $(1, 1)$-consistency. We enforce (i, j)-consistency by posting constraints of arity i that expressly forbid each i-tuple that cannot be extended.

We denote a binary constraint between x_i and x_j by c_{ij}. A CSP $P = (\Delta, \mathcal{D}, \mathcal{C})$ is *path consistent* if and only if for any $c_{ij} \in \mathcal{C}$, any tuple $(a, b) \in c_{ij}$ and any variable $x_k \in \Delta \setminus \{x_i, x_j\}$, there exists a value $v \in D_k$ such that $\{(x_i, a), (x_j, b), (x_k, v)\}$ is a consistent partial assignment. For CSPs with no ternary constraints, path consistency is the same as $(2, 1)$-consistency; however in the presence of ternary constraints path consistency and 3-consistency differ.

3 Consistency and Symmetry

In this section we extend (i, j)-consistency to use additional information from the symmetry group of a CSP. We will then examine when this coincides with existing levels of consistency. The following proposition is one of the main motivations for our work.

Proposition 1. *If the partial assignment $\{(x_i, a_i) : i \in I\}$ can be extended to a solution of a CSP, then for all symmetries g the assignment $\{(x_i, a_i)g : i \in I\}$ violates no constraints.*

Proof. Suppose not, that is, suppose that $\{(x_i, a_i) : i \in I \cup J\}$ is a solution, but that for some symmetry g the assignment $\{(x_i, a_i)g : i \in I\}$ violates a constraint C. Then $\{(x_i, a_i)g : i \in I \cup J\}$ is a full assignment which is not a solution, contradicting the definition of a symmetry.

Thus if one discovers that $\{(x_i, a_i) : i \in I\}$ violates a constraint then none of its images under G can be part of a solution, hence they can all be forbidden without compromising soundness.

Lemma 1. *For any $X \subset \Delta$, the assignment $\mathcal{A} := \{(x_i, a_i) : x_i \in X\}$ can be consistently extended by $\mathcal{B} := \{(x_j, a_j) : x_j \in Y \subset \Delta\}$ if and only if for all strict symmetries g the assignment $\mathcal{A}g$ can be consistently extended by $\mathcal{B}g$.*

Recall the definition of orbit at the end of Section 2. One consequence of the above lemma is to say that a support $\mathcal{J}$ exists for a literal (x_i, a) if and only if there exist images of the support which are support for each literal in the orbit of (x_i, a) under the group of strict symmetries. That is, when symmetries are strict we may reuse symmetric support. Conversely, if a may be pruned from D_i, similar domain deletions occur for each element of $(x_i, a)^G$, even when G contains nonstrict symmetries.

Definition 7. *A CSP P with symmetry group G is* Sym(i, j)-*consistent if for each consistent partial assignment $\mathcal{I}$ of size i, for each symmetry $g \in G$ and each set of j variables that do not lie in the* Var$(\mathcal{I}g)$, *it is possible to find values for those j variables such that the $i + j$ values taken together (the image of the initial i and the new j) satisfy all constraints on those $i + j$ variables.*

Note that since all symmetry groups contain the identity permutation this definition encompasses that of standard (i, j)-consistency given in Definition 6. Thus, Sym(i, j) consistency is at least as strong as (i, j)-consistency.

As an initial example, we illustrate the fact that even Sym$(1,0)$-consistency is an interesting concept. Consider a simple graph 3-colouring problem on 4 nodes A, B, C, and D, containing all possible edges except between A and D. As a graph colouring problem, we add a not-equals constraint between all pairs of variables except A and D. Initially, each node has domain $[1, 2, 3]$, so the group G of symmetries of the CSP contains a symmetry f which simultaneously interchanges (B, i) with (C, i) for $i \in [1, 2, 3]$. There are also three symmetries $g_1, g_2, g_3 \in G$, such that g_i swaps (A, i) with (D, i) and leaves all other literals fixed. Of course, the overall symmetry group of this CSP contains all combinations of these four symmetries. Suppose now that our first choice during search is to set $(A, 1)$. We make the problem arc consistent, giving domains $A = [1]$, $B = [2, 3]$, $C = [2, 3]$, and $D = [1, 2, 3]$. However, because of the symmetries that interchange A and D, the problem is not Sym$(1,0)$ consistent. The new symmetry group is the stabiliser in G of the positive decision $(A, 1)$. Thus it still contains f, g_2 and g_3. We can establish Sym$(1,0)$-consistency by removing 2 and 3 from the domain of D (as g_2 maps $(D, 2)$ to $(A, 2)$, which has been deleted and g_3 maps $(D, 3)$ to $(A, 3)$). We can see that this is a correct deduction: since A=1, then B and C have to share the values 2, 3, and since D is connected to both, only the value 1 is available for D. Thus we see Sym$(1,0)$ making useful deductions in this simple example. We will explore more deeply the concept of Sym$(i, 0)$-consistency below.

We establish when Sym(i, j)-consistency is stronger than that of (i, j)-consistency.

Lemma 2. *If the symmetry group of a CSP contains only strict symmetries,* Sym(i, j)-*consistency is the same as (i, j)-consistency for all i, j.*

Proof. Let P be a CSP whose symmetry group G contains only strict symmetries, and suppose that P is (i, j)-consistent. We show that P is Sym(i, j)-consistent. Let $\mathcal{I}$ be a consistent partial assignment of size i, and let $g \in G$. Then since g is a strict symmetry, $\mathcal{I}g$ is a consistent partial assignment of size i. Thus for any j further variables there exists an extension of $\mathcal{I}g$ to a consistent partial assignment of size $i + j$, by (i, j)-consistency. Thus P is Sym(i, j)-consistent. The converse is clear, considering the identity element of the symmetry group of the CSP.

Even though the levels of consistency are not different when symmetries are strict, one may use symmetries to speed up the inference process. Suppose we have three variables x_1, x_2, x_3, with $\mathrm{Dom}(x_1) = \mathrm{Dom}(x_2) = [2, 3, 4]$ and $\mathrm{Dom}(x_3) = [3]$. Suppose our constraints are $x_1 = x_2$ and $x_2 \leq x_3$, so that our symmetry group interchanges x_1 and x_2, and fixes x_3. Then in enforcing (1,1)-consistency we first prune 4 from the domain of x_2 and then on a second iteration prune it from the domain of x_1, whereas when enforcing Sym(1, 1)-consistency we perform both domain deletions at once, as we know that there is a symmetry swapping x_1 and x_2.

Suppose that P is a CSP whose symmetry group G is not strict. In particular, suppose that $g \in G$ maps a consistent partial assignment $\mathcal{I}$ of size i to a collection of literals $\mathcal{I}g$ which violates at least one constraint, or has two values for the same variable. It is still possible that P is (i, j)-consistent for some j. However, P is not Sym(i, j)-consistent for any j, as for any choice of j additional variables there is no way of extending $\mathcal{I}g$ to a consistent partial assignment of size $i + j$. Thus Sym(i, j)-consistency is stronger than (i, j)-consistency.

We now consider a yet stronger type of symmetric consistency, called *total* Sym(i, j)-*consistency*. It differs from Sym(i, j)-consistency in its requirements on support: for Sym(i, j)-consistency we require that for each image of a partial assignment and each choice of j additional variables there exists a support. Now we reverse some quantifiers and require that there is a support $\mathcal{J}$ for our initial partial assignment $\mathcal{I}$ such that for all symmetries in G, the image of the support is a support of the image of $\mathcal{I}$.

Definition 8. *A CSP P is total* Sym(i, j)-*consistent if given any consistent partial assignment $\mathcal{I}$ of size i, and a further j-tuple of variables, there exists a j-tuple $\mathcal{J}$ of assignments to those variables such that for all $g \in G$ the assignment $\mathcal{I}g \cup \mathcal{J}g$ is consistent.*

Note that if $\mathcal{I} \cup \mathcal{J}$ is contained in a solution then by definition $\mathcal{I}g \cup \mathcal{J}g$ will be consistent for all g. Thus enforcing total Sym(i, j)-consistency will not jeopardise completeness. Total Sym(i, j)-consistency is potentially expensive to maintain: to find support for a consistent i-tuple of assignments may involve testing many possible j-tuples and symmetries g. However, as we will see in Section 4, if the symmetry group G consists only of pure variable symmetries then total Sym(i, j) consistency can be no more expensive than its non-total variant, whilst enforcing a stronger level of consistency.

We finish this section with a discussion of the special case of Sym(i, j)-consistency where $j = 0$. A CSP is Sym$(i, 0)$-consistent if whenever $\mathcal{I}$ is a consistent partial assignment of size i, the image $\mathcal{I}g$ of $\mathcal{I}$ under any symmetry $g \in G$ is also a consistent partial assignment. Since the symmetry group G partitions the set of all i-sets of literals into orbits, each orbit is either entirely consistent or all i-tuples in the orbit are expressly prohibited. The reason for our interest is the following key theorem.

Theorem 1. *A CSP is both* Sym$(i, 0)$-*consistent and* (i, j)-*consistent if and only if it is* Sym(i, j)-*consistent.*

Proof. Let P be a CSP that is both Sym$(i, 0)$-consistent and (i, j)-consistent. Let $\mathcal{I}$ be any consistent partial assignment of size i. Then since P is Sym$(i, 0)$-consistent, the image $\mathcal{I}g$ is consistent, for any g in the symmetry group of P. Since P is (i, j)-consistent, given the assignment $\mathcal{I}g$ and any set $\mathcal{J}$ of j further variables, we can find a set of values for the variables in $\mathcal{J}$ such that the assignment of all $i+j$ variables is consistent. Thus P is Sym(i,j)-consistent.

Conversely, let P be a CSP that is Sym(i,j)-consistent. Then it is clearly both (i,j)-consistent (consider the identity permutation) and Sym$(i,0)$-consistent, for given a consistent partial assignment $\mathcal{I}$ of size i, and any g in the symmetry group G of L, the partial assignment $\mathcal{I}g$ can be extended to a consistent partial assignment of size $i+j$, for any choice of j further variables, so must itself be consistent.

Standard (nonsymmetric) $(i,0)$-consistency is vacuous, as there is nothing to test. Sym$(i,0)$-consistency is the same as total Sym$(i,0)$-consistency, as there are no additional assignments to make.

One of the most useful levels of Sym$(i,0)$-consistency is Sym$(1,0)$, which is an intriguing strengthening of forward checking: if a domain value (x_i, a) is deleted at any point, the orbit $(x_i, a)^G$ is computed and all of its images are deleted too, even though they may currently appear to be consistent, as we know that they cannot occur in any solution. Let G be generated by s permutations (a finite group is *generated* by a set of permutations if the group consists of all possible products of the permutations in the set with one another). The cost of computing an orbit $\mathcal{O}$ of G is $O(s|\mathcal{O}|)$ [12]. Since for most practical applications the symmetry group of a CSP can be generated by a very small number of generators (typically 2), the cost of enforcing Sym$(1,0)$-consistency will generally be a small constant multiple of the number of domain deletions that it finds. Thus this is an extremely cheap and effective technique.

Before presenting an algorithm to enforce Sym$(2,1)$-consistency on binary CSPs, we briefly discuss which groups of symmetries should be used at which point in search, and the cost of computing these symmetry groups. At the root, it is clear that the group of symmetries is the full symmetry group G of the CSP (or as much of G as the constraint programmer has been able to identify). At later stages in search, an appropriate choice of symmetries to break is the setwise stabiliser in G of the positive decisions made so far. Computing this setwise stabiliser can be moderately expensive, but the use of setwise stabilisers has been shown in [13] to be an effective technique to reduce search space, so if we wish to use these groups for inference purposes they are available "for free". If the symmetry group of the CSP consists only of value symmetries then at a node $\mathcal{N}$ it suffices to take the pointwise stabiliser of the values seen so far, as in the current partial assignment the setwise stabiliser is equal to the pointwise stabiliser. Let $d := |\Lambda|$. Then, as is shown in [4], after an initial cost of $O(d^5)$ for setup, the running time is $\tilde{O}(d^2)$ at each node, where $\tilde{O}$ is the "soft-O" notation which means that we ignore logarithmic factors. Once again, if one were using a GE-tree based approach during search, these groups would already be computed by the search process, and hence could be used during inference at no extra cost.

4 An Algorithm to Enforce SymPC

Here we present a version of PC2001/3.1 [14] which has been adapted to use symmetry. Recall the definition of path consistency from Section 2. Our algorithm reduces precisely to PC2001/3.1 when no symmetries are specified, and hence has the best known time complexity in the worst case.

For this section, variables $x_i \in \Delta$ are denoted i, and literals (x_i, a) are denoted (i, a). To enforce path consistency it is necessary to assume that there is a constraint between any pair of variables in Δ. If there exist an unconstrained pair of variables, we add the universal relation between them, which permits them to take any pair of values. The relation between variables i and j is denoted c_{ij}.

SYMPC2001/3.1(P)
1   SYMINITIALISE(P);
2   **while** $Q \neq \emptyset$ **do**
3   Select and delete any $((i,a), j)$ from Q;
4   SYMREVISEPATH$((i,a), j, Q)$;

SYMINITIALISE(P)
1   **for all** $(i,a), (j,b) \in \chi$ and all $k \in \Delta$ **do**
2   Last$((i,a), (j,b), k)$:= false;
3   **for all** $i, j, k \in \Delta$ with $i \neq j \neq k \neq i$ **do**
4   **for all** $a \in D_i, b \in D_j$ **do**
5   **if** $(a,b) \in c_{ij}$ and Last$((i,a), (j,b), k)$ = false **then**
6   **if** there is no $v \in D_k$ s.t. $(a,v) \in c_{ij} \wedge (v,b) \in c_{kj}$ **then**
7   **for all** $g \in G$ **do**
8                       $(i', a') := (i,a)g; (j', b') := (j,b)g$;
9   remove (a', b') from $c_{i'j'}$ and (b', a') from $c_{j'i'}$;
10                      $Q := Q \cup \{((i', a'), j'), ((j', b'), i')\}$;
11   **else**
12   Let $v \in D_k$ be the first value satisfying $(a,v) \in c_{ik} \wedge (v,b) \in c_{kj}$
13   Last$((i,a), (j,b), k) := (v, \text{true})$;
14   **for all** $g \in G, g \neq 1$ **do**
15   **if** $(i,a)g, (j,b)g, (k,v)g$ is consistent and
                            Last$((i,a)g, (j,b)g, \text{Var}((k,v)g))$ is false **then**
16                          $(k', v') := (k,v)g$;
17   **if** G contains only pure variable symmetries **then**
18   Last$((i,a)g, (j,b)g, k') := (v', \text{true})$;
19   **else**
20   Last$((i,a)g, (j,b)g, k') := (v', \text{false})$;

The path consistency algorithm, which we have named SYMPC2001/3.1, is in two parts: initialisation and propagation. The initialisation function is SYMINITIAL- IZE, which seeks a first support for each ordered pair of literals $((i, a), (j, b))$ and each third variable k. In line 6, if we cannot find support for a pair $((i, a), (j, b))$, then (a, b) is removed from c_{ij}, and we also remove all of its images from the corresponding constraints. For the sake of clarity, we have written line 7 (and later line 14) to loop through all group elements, in fact we will loop only over the distinct images of (i, a) and (j, b). For each removal we enqueue in line 10 an image of $((i, a), j)$ and $((j, b), i)$ onto Q. If support can be found, then in line 13 we store this support in Last$((i, a), (j, b), k)$, along with a boolean value true to indicate that the support was found directly. If we find support for $((i, a), (j, b), k)$ then in lines 14 to 19 we reuse all of its images, but if G contains any symmetries other than pure variable symmetries we set a boolean to false to indicate that the value v' that we are storing as support may not be the minimal possible support in $D_{k'}$. If G consists only of pure variable symmetries then v' is in fact minimal since $(k, v)g = (k', v)$, so the boolean value is set to true.

The second function is SYMREVISEPATH, which takes as input an element $((i,a),j)$ from Q, and checks every variable $k \in \Delta \setminus \{i,j\}$ to see if any tuple in c_{ik} is affected by the modification of c_{ij}. There are two possibilities for the search for support. If this is the first time that c_{ij} has been examined with respect to k, and the previous support was the image under G of some other support and hence might not be minimal in D_k, then in line 6 SYMREVISEPATH tries to find a support from scratch. Otherwise, the boolean in Last$((i,a),(j,b),k)$ is true and SYMREVISEPATH starts its search in line 7 from the previous bookmarked value. If support cannot be found then in lines 10 to 14 we not only remove (a,b) from c_{ij} but also all of its images from the corresponding constraints. If support can be found then we store it.

SYMREVISEPATH$((i,a),j,Q)$
1 **for all** k with $i \neq k \neq j$ **do**
2   **for all** $b \in D_k$ s.t. $(a,b) \in C_{ik}$ **do**
3      $(v,x) :=$ Last$((i,a),(k,b),j)$;
4   **while** $v \neq NIL \wedge ((a,v) \notin c_{ij} \vee (v,b) \notin c_{jk})$ **do**
5   **if** $x =$ false **then**
6          $v := \min\{D_j\}; x :=$ true;
7   **else**
8          $v := succ(v, D_j)$;
9   **if** $v = NIL$ **then**
10   **for all** $g \in G$ **do**
11         $(i',a') := (i,a)g; (k',b') := (k,b)g$;
12   Remove (a',b') from $c_{i'k'}$ and (b',a') from $c_{k'i'}$;
13         $Q := Q \cup \{((i',a'),k'),((k',b'),i')\}$;
14   **elif** G consists only of pure variable symmetries **then**
15   **for all** $g \in G$ do
16         $(v',x) :=$ Last$((i,a)g,(k,b)g,\text{Var}((j,v)g))$;
17   **if** $v' < v$ **then**
18   Last$((i,a)g,(k,b)g,\text{Var}((j,v)g)) := (v, \text{true})$;
19   **else**
20   Last$((i,a),(k,b),j) := (v', \text{true})$;
21   **else**
22   Last$((i,a),(k,b),j) := (v,\text{true})$;

If G consists only of pure variable symmetries, then the algorithm has been modified to enforce total symmetric path consistency. This is because of the following observation: suppose that we are considering the pair of assignments $((i,a),(j,b))$ and the variable k, and suppose that we have found v to be the smallest element of D_k such that $(i,a),(j,b),(k,v)$ is consistent. Then since no element of G affects the values in any literal, for any $g \in G$ no element of $D_{\text{Var}((k,c)g)}$ that comes before v can be used as support when enforcing total SymPC. To see this note that if $c < v$ then $((i,a)g,(j,b)g,(k,c)g)g^{-1}$ is inconsistent. Therefore in line 18 of the initialisation function we reuse the image of a support without needing to mark it as reused, and in lines 15 to 20 of SYMREVISEPATH we ensure that the supports agree for a whole orbit of ordered pairs of literals.

5 Symmetrised Singleton Consistencies

A type of consistency which has been attracting much attention recently is that of *singleton* consistency. Like the notion of symmetrised consistency, it is different from other consistency techniques because of its meta character: it is not a standalone technique such as AC or PC, but improves the pruning techniques of all of them.

Let $P = (\Delta, \mathcal{D}, \mathcal{C})$ be a CSP, and let $x_i \in \Delta$ and $a \in D_i$. By $P|_{(x_i,a)}$ we denote the CSP obtained from P by setting $(x_i = a)$ and deleting all other values from the domain of x_i: we call this the CSP *induced* from P with respect to (x_i, a). Singleton consistency extends any consistency level X by requiring that for all $x_i \in \Delta$ and all $a \in D_i$, the problem $P|_{(x_i,a)}$ is X-consistent. For instance, a CSP $P = (\Delta, \mathcal{D}, \mathcal{C})$ is singleton arc consistent (SAC) if for all $x_i \in \Delta$ and all $a \in D_i$, the CSP $P|_{(x_i,a)}$ is arc consistent.

One advantage of singleton consistency is that enforcing it does not change the constraints of a problem – no matter what level of consistency X we choose, singleton X consistency will result in domain deletions.

Singleton consistency is a good candidate for symmetrisation: the basic notion to be applied is that whenever we discover a domain deletion, we can delete an entire orbit of literals without needing to recheck the X-consistency of each of the corresponding induced CSPs. Thus, as in Section 3, at a cost $O(s|(x_i, a)^G|)$, where G is generated by s permutations and (x_i, a) is a literal to be deleted, we can avoid $O(|(x_i, a)^G|)$ calls to enforce X-consistency on an entire induced CSP. If some symmetries are nonstrict then we may be able to delete literals that would not be deleted by singleton X-consistency alone, thus symmetrised singleton X-consistency is more pruningful than its unsymmetrised variant.

A second potential gain, which we can make at the cost of compromising completeness, is to only test the X-consistency of $P|_{(x_i,a)}$ when (x_i, a) is the orbit representative for $(x_i, a)^G$. If all symmetries of the problem are strict then this approach is clearly complete as well as sound. In the pseudocode below we do *not* take this approach, as in our experiments in Section 6 we wished to preserve completeness, however it would only require a minor adjustment to the algorithm.

Definition 9. *Let $P := (\Delta, \mathcal{D}, \mathcal{C})$ be a CSP with symmetry group G and let X be a level of consistency. Then P is* symmetrised singleton X-consistent *(written SymSingletonX-consistent) if for all $x_i \in \Delta$, for all $a \in D_i$ and for all $g \in G$, $P|_{(x_i,a)g}$ is X-consistent. We say that P is X+SymSingletonX-consistent if P is both X consistent and SymSingletonX consistent.*

It is clear that, provided enforcing X-consistency is sound, so is enforcing symmetrised singleton X-consistency.

There are many different algorithms for enforcing singleton consistency. Most of these are for enforcing SAC, where Dubruyne and Bessière initially proposed an algorithm that is similar in style to AC1 [15]. This was upgraded in the style of AC4 by Barták and Erben [16], and then further improved to give 'SAC-Opt' by Bessiére and Dubruyne, which has optimal time complexity [17]. It is this latter, optimal algorithm which we symmetrise: we present an algorithm X+SYMSINGLETONX, which enforces

X-consistency and symmetrised singleton X-consistency for any level X of consistency. We have chosen to present code which enforces X-consistency on P because in our experiments the level X of consistency which we will test is the default level of consistency in ECL^{i}PS^e[18], which is enforced automatically. If the level X of consistency is arc consistency, and the group of symmetries is trivial, then our algorithm reduces to SAC-Opt, and hence is time optimal in the worst case.

In X+SYMSINGLETONX we denote $D_i := \text{Dom}(x_i)$, as normal, and χ denotes the set of all literals (x_i, a) of P; by χ_{ia} we denote the set of all literals of the induced problem P_{ia}.

```
X+SYMSINGLETONX(P)
1  PROPAGX(P, ∅);
2  for all (i, a) ∈ χ do              /* initiation phase*/
3      P_ia := P;
4      if not PROPAGX(P_ia, {(i, b) : b ∈ D_i \ {a}}) then    /* set i = a in subproblem */
5          if PROPAGX(P, (i, a)^G) then
6              for all (j, b) ∈ (i, a)^G do
7                  for all P_kc such that (j, b) ∈ χ_kc do
8                      Q_kc := Q_kc ∪ {(j, b)};
9                      PendingList:= PendingList ∪{(k, c)};
10         else return false;
11 while PendingList ≠ ∅ do           /* propagation phase */
12     pop (i, a) from PendingList;
13     if PROPAGX(P_ia, Q_ia) then Q_ia := ∅;
14     else
15         if not PROPAGX(P, (i, a)^G) then
16             return false;
17         for all (j, b) ∈ (i, a)^G do
18             for all P_kc such that (j, b) ∈ χ_kc do
19                 Q_kc := Q_kc ∪ {(j, b)};
20                 PendingList:= PendingList ∪{(k, c)};
21 return true;
```

The function takes as input a CSP P, and runs in two phases - initialisation and propagation. In line 3 we initialise P_{ia}, where $(i, a) \in \chi$, to be a copy of P. If X is a level of consistency that only results in domain deletions (rather than the posting of non-unary constraints) then in P_{ia} we record only the domains and data structures of P, rather than all of the constraints, as we re-use the constraints in P. In line 4 we call the algorithm PROPAGX, which takes as input a CSP and a set of domain deletions (in this case i can no longer take any value in $D_i \setminus \{a\}$), and propagates the effect of these deletions under consistency level X. Any algorithm to enforce X can be used at this point. We assume that PROPAGX returns false if and only if propagating deletions in P_{ia} results in an empty domain, and returns true otherwise. We also assume that PROPAGX will modify P_{ia} to make it X-consistent, either by pruning values, or by posting additional constraints, or both. If a wipeout occurs in line 4 then we know that every image of (i, a) under G is not part of any solution to P, so in line 5 we compute all images of (i, a), delete them from our set χ of literals (and hence also from the corresponding domains), and then check that P can still be made X-consistent after these domain deletions. If it can be, then for each deleted literal (j,b), and each already created restricted problem P_{kc} with (j,b) in its set χ_{kc} of literals, in line 8 we add (j,b) to the list of future domain deletions to be made in P_{kc}, and in line 9 we add (k,c) to the list PendingList of subproblems to be processed. If P cannot be made X-consistent after deleting $(i,a)^G$ then P is unsatisfiable and in line 10 we return false.

Once the initialisation phase has finished, we know that PendingList contains all values (i,a) for which some symmetrised singleton X inconsistent value removals (contained in Q_{ia}) have not yet been propagated in P_{ia}. The loop in line 11 propagates each of these removals, along with any others which are forced by this propagation. In line 13, if we can successfully delete all of these values then we clear the Q_{ia} entry and move on. When propagation fails, this means that (i,a) is symmetrised singleton X inconsistent, and that the same will hold for all of its images under G. Therefore in line 15 we delete all images of (i,a) from P, and check whether the resulting CSP can still be made X-consistent. If it cannot, then P has no solutions. If it can, then in lines 17-20 we update our list of subproblems which require further propagation of domain deletions.

6 Experiments

To test our SYMPC2001/3.1 algorithm we used a collection of graph colouring problems. We define an infinite family of graphs based around triangles, as follows. Level 0 consists of a single triangle, as in the figure below. To make level 1 from level 0 we add a triangle to each vertex of the original triangle, giving a graph with 9 vertices, shown below. To make level 2 from level one we add a triangle to each vertex of valency 2 in the level 1 graph. This process can clearly be carried on indefinitely, adding a triangle to each vertex of valency 2 on level i to produce level $i+1$.

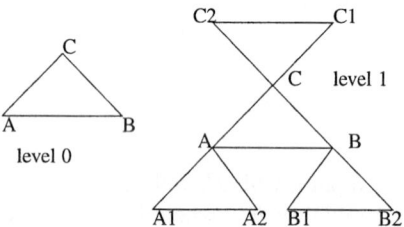

These graphs have a large symmetry group. We can freely permute the three vertices of the central triangle, giving an automorphism group of size six. For graphs of level at least 1, after determining the images of the central three vertices, we can still swap vertices A1 and A1, or vertices B1 and B2, or vertices C1 and C2, or any combination of these swaps. Thus there are a total of $2^3 \times 6 = 48$ symmetries of the level 1 graph. When going from level i to level $i+1$ we have an additional $3 \times 2^{i-1}$ triangles, each of which can be independently flipped over, giving an extra $2^{3 \times 2^{i-1}}$ symmetries. Thus the symmetry group of the graph at level i contains $6 \times \prod_{j=1}^{i} 2^{3 \times 2^{j-1}}$ symmetries. Specifically, the level 1 graph has 48 symmetries, the level 2 graph 3072, level 3 about 12.3 million and level 4 about 2×10^{14}. These act as pure variable symmetries on the colouring problem.

Table 1. Results for SYMPC2001/3.1 with the first family of problem

level	Full Syms		Graph Syms		No Syms	
	checks	time	checks	time	checks	time
1	212	19	245	5	7627	49
2	186201	1160	177544	994	165303	1128
3	2604343	19802	2427594	16794	3427582	23963
4	26803564	424553	24559120	386408	37290536	714441

Table 2. Results for SYMPC2001/3.1 with the second family of problem

level	Full Syms		Graph Syms		No Syms	
	checks	time	checks	time	checks	time
1	12791	114	12930	105	19345	157
2	253719	5480	250597	1672	369540	2135
3	2972582	33732	2851446	30186	4248742	40004
4	28355217	495557	26803731	479862	40130411	712005

Table 3. Results SYMPC2001/3.1 with the third family of problem

level	Full Syms		Graph Syms		No Syms	
	checks	time	checks	time	checks	time
1	4668	80	5093	65	14064	90
2	72559	2146	74970	1893	218736	2576
3	768740	53292	776944	53952	2315472	30090
4	7013763	638446	7035185	574108	21096720	763494

Given this basic setup, we can now assign domains to each node to produce problems which will respond differently to path consistency. We have three main families of problems. In the first, the vertices of valency 2 have domains $[1, 2]$ and all other vertices have domains $[1, 2, 3, 4]$. This problem is unsatisfiable, a fact which will be discovered by path consistency and SymPC. We use the full group of automorphisms of the graph, as well as the pure value symmetry which interchanges 1 and 2 and the pure value symmetry which interchanges 3 and 4. In fact, since the problem is unsatisfiable, we could have used any symmetries whatsoever, as there are no solutions to preserve. However, it is reasonable to assume that the constraint programmer would not know in advance that the problem was unsatisfiable, and hence would only use the obvious graph and colour symmetries. Our results are summarised in Table 1.

For our second family of experiments, with results given in Table 2, we give vertex A domain $[1, 2, 3, 4, 5]$, vertices of valency 2 domain $[1, 2]$, and all other vertices domain $[1, 2, 3, 4]$. Here we lose a factor of three in the number of graph automorphisms, as we can no longer rotate the central triangle. The value symmetries remain unchanged from problem 1. Path consistency and SymPC will deduce that only the value 5 for A is consistent, but the problem overall is satisfiable.

For our third family of experiments, with results described in Table 3, we give all vertices domain $[1, 2, 3]$, so that neither PC nor SymPC make any deductions at all.

The vertex numbering follows in turn the pre-order traversal of the binary trees rooted at each of the vertices of the central triangle. All times are in milliseconds, on a

Pentium M 2.1GHz. The implementation differed from the pseudocode in the following ways. In the loops at lines 7 and 14 of SymInitialize we use the orbit algorithm mentioned above to find all distinct images of $(i', a'), (j', b')$ (resp. $(i', a'), (j', b'), (k', v')$) without actually looping over all of G. We do the same at lines 10 and 15 of SymRevisePath. This is essential for handling larger groups. If the last allowed pair is removed from a constraint, then we terminate the calculation, reporting the problem unsatisfiable. We take advantage of the fact that the given symmetries of this problem are, in fact, strict symmetries to avoid the consistency check in line 15 of SymInitialize.

We have also succesfully implemented our X+SYMSINGLETONX algorithm. The generality of the algorithm meant that by implementing in the ECLIPSE constraint logic programming system [18], the base level of consistency X was that established by ECLIPSE. We do not know the internal details of the system, so we do not know what X is, but nevertheless, our algorithm is general enough to implement X+SYMSINGLETONX. For group-theoretic calculations, we used the GAP-ECLIPSE interface [19,20]. We use GAP to obtain orbits of singleton assignments. To evaluate our implementation, we compared X+SYMSINGLETONX against X+SINGLETONX. For the latter, the algorithm we presented above specialised to the trivial group formed the comparison.

As a test, we used constraint problems based on the same triangle graph schema used above, with different constraints on triangles. For example, suppose each variable has domain 1...4, and we constrain the sum of each triangle. If the outermost triangles have to sum to either 3 or 12 (and not any value inbetween), ECLIPSE performs no propagation – presumably because it is using bounds consistency. Setting a variable in a triangle and propagating in ECLIPSE results in failure if it is set to 2 or 3. Singleton consistency therefore removes those values, leaving domains as $\{1, 4\}$. We performed a test in which the outermost triangles were restricted to sum to $\{3, 12\}$, while all inner triangles had to sum to a value in $\{3, 4, 12\}$. The result is that the domains of variables in outer triangles become $\{1, 4\}$ and other variables become $\{1, 2, 4\}$ since the value 3 is impossible. We obtain the same deductions with both symmetric and asymmetric versions of singleton consistency, and the computation times were comparable. An interesting feature is that the high power of singleton consistency means that, in practice, the initialisation phase does all the work, and we did not see propagation happening after that. Under any sensible X, trying every possible singleton is so powerful that it is hard to construct examples where any domain deletions remain after initialisation.

7 Conclusions and Future Work

We have introduced a new research area: symmetrising levels of consistency to produce stronger forms of consistency and more efficient mechanisms for establishing them.

Many forms of consistency can be adapted to take advantage of symmetries of a CSP. We have focussed on two particular levels of consistency, and given algorithms and implementations of symmetrised versions of them. In the case of path consistency, experiments showed that we could improve runtime performance, despite having to maintain data structures representing groups of size, for example 10^14. We have shown that if the CSP has nonstrict symmetries then these new levels of consistency do not coincide with any previously defined levels of consistency. We have discussed how, even in the case of strict symmetries, it is possible to take advantage of symmetry to improve the performance of consistency algorithms. For high levels of consistency the cost of the added group theoretic machinery is negligible compared to the cost of maintaining consistency, although there is a need for optimisations to avoid repeating work.

Acknowledgements

We thank our reviewers for their helpful comments. Our research is supported by a Royal Society of Edinburgh SEELLD Support fellowship, and by EPSRC grant numbers GR/R29666 & GR/S30580. Special thanks go to Iain McDonald.

References

1. P. Flener, A. M. Frisch, B. Hnich, Z. Kızıltan, I. Miguel, J. Pearson, & T. Walsh. Breaking row and column symmetries in matrix models. *Proc. CP 2002*, pages 462–476. Springer, 2002.
2. R. Backofen and S. Will. Excluding symmetries in constraint-based search. *Proc. CP-99*, pages 73–87. Springer, 1999.
3. C.A. Brown, L. Finkelstein, and P.W. Purdom Jr. Backtrack searching in the presence of symmetry. *Nordic Journal of Computing*, 3(3):203–219, 1996.
4. C.M. Roney-Dougal, I.P. Gent, T. Kelsey, and S.A. Linton. Tractable symmetry breaking using restricted search trees. *Proc. ECAI'04*, 2004.
5. A. K. Mackworth. Consistency in networks of relations. *Artificial Intelligence*, 8:99–118, 1977.
6. C. Bessière and J-C. Régin. Refining the basic constraint propagation algorithm. *Proc. IJCAI'01*, 2001.
7. Y. Zhang and R.H.C. Yap. Making AC-3 an optimal algorithm. *Proc. IJCAI'01*, 2001.
8. I.P. Gent and I. McDonald. Symmetry and propagation: Refining an AC algorithm. *Proc. SymCon03*, 2003.
9. T.Kelsey, S.A.Linton, and C.M.Roney-Dougal. New developments in symmetry breaking in search using computational group theory. In *Proc. AISC'04*, 2004.
10. E.C. Freuder. A sufficient condition for backtrack-free search. *Journal of the ACM*, 29(1):24–32, 1982.
11. E.C. Freuder. A sufficient condition for backtrack-bounded search. *Journal of the ACM*, 37(4):755–761, 1985.
12. A. Seress. *Permutation group algorithms*. Number 152 in Cambridge tracts in mathematics. Cambridge University Press, 2002.
13. J.-F. Puget. Symmetry breaking using stabilizers. In *Proc. CP-03*, 2003.
14. C. Bessière, J-C. Régin, R.H.C. Yap, and Y. Zhang. An optimal coarse-grained arc consistency algorithm. *Artificial Intelligence*, 165:165–185, 2005.
15. R. Debruyne and C. Bessière. Some practicable filtering techniques for the constraint satisfaction problem. *Proc. IJCAI'97*, pages 412–417, 1997.
16. R. Barták and R. Erben. A new algorithm for singleton arc consistency. *Proc. FLAIRS 2004*, 2004.
17. C. Bessière and R. Debruyne. Optimal and suboptimal singleton arc consistency algorithms. *Proc. IJCAI'05*, 2005.
18. M. G. Wallace, S. Novello, and J. Schimpf. ECLiPSe : A platform for constraint logic programming. *ICL Systems Journal*, 12(1):159–200, May 1997.
19. I.P. Gent, W. Harvey, and T. Kelsey. Groups and constraints: Symmetry breaking during search. *Proc. CP 2002*, pages 415–430. Springer, 2002.
20. I.P. Gent, W. Harvey, T. Kelsey, and S.A. Linton. Generic SBDD using computational group theory. *Proc. CP 2003*, pages 333–347. Springer, 2003.

Solving the MOLR and Social Golfers Problems

Warwick Harvey and Thorsten Winterer

IC-Parc, Imperial College London

Abstract. We present a range of techniques for tackling the problem of finding sets of Mutually Orthogonal Latin Rectangles (MOLR). In particular, we use a construction that allows us to search for solutions of a particular form with much reduced effort, and a seeding heuristic for the MOLR problem that allows a local search approach to find much better solutions than would be possible otherwise. Finally, we use the MOLR solutions found to construct solutions to the social golfer problem that improve the best known number of rounds for 43 instances, by as many as 10 rounds.

1 Introduction

In [4], Dotú and Van Hentenryck used a constructive seeding heuristic to significantly improve the quality of the results they found using local search for the social golfer problem. As they noted, for certain instances their heuristic corresponds to constructing a complete set of Mutually Orthogonal Latin Squares (MOLS), and results in an optimal solution to the social golfers problem for those instances without any search required. There is a well-known construction [2–II.2.20] for complete sets of MOLS that works for more instances than Dotú and Van Hentenryck's heuristic, again yielding optimal solutions for the corresponding instances of the social golfers problem.

There are other methods that can be used to construct solutions to the social golfer problem using sets of MOLS, due to Sharma and Das [18] and mathtalk-ga [13]. These approaches also work when given a set of Mutually Orthogonal Latin Rectangles (MOLR), allowing solutions to the social golfer problem to be constructed for many cases where a set of MOLS of sufficient size is not known to exist.

Sets of MOLR are also useful for constructing solutions to other problems, for example perfect hash families [20] and low-density parity check codes [3]. However, it seems that little work has been done on this problem. Franklin [6] gives a set of 3 MOLR of order 9×10, while Wanless [22] improves this to a set of 4. Mullen and Shiue [15] give a simple construction that generates some useful sets of MOLR, mostly when the number of rows is small.

In this paper we present constructions and solutions that significantly extend and improve on the currently known results for the MOLR problem, and then use these to construct improved solutions for 43 instances of the social golfer problem.

In Section 2 we present background material on the MOLS, MOLR and social golfer problems and their constructions. In Section 3 we present a new direct construction for certain MOLR instances, and another construction that allows us to find MOLR solutions by solving a much simpler problem. The local search algorithms we applied to the MOLR and reduced problems are described in Section 4, while the results obtained from all the methods used are presented in Section 5.

2 Background

2.1 Latin Squares and Latin Rectangles

A *Latin Square* of order n is an $n \times n$ array where each entry in the array is taken from the set $\{0 \ldots n-1\}$ and for each row and column the elements of that row/column are all different. A *Latin Rectangle* of order $m \times n$ ($m \leq n$) is the obvious generalisation of a latin square to a non-square array: an $m \times n$ array where each entry in the array is taken from the set $\{0 \ldots n-1\}$ and for each row and column the elements of that row/column are all different. Clearly, a latin rectangle of order $n \times n$ is just a latin square of order n.

For a latin square or rectangle L, we denote the element in row i and column j by $L(i,j)$ ($i \in \{0 \ldots m-1\}, j \in \{0 \ldots n-1\}$). A square or rectangle L is then latin if it satisfies the constraints:

$$L(i,j) \in \{0 \ldots n-1\} \quad \forall i \in \{0 \ldots m-1\}, \forall j \in \{0 \ldots n-1\} \quad (1)$$

$$\text{alldifferent}(L(i,j) | j \in \{0 \ldots n-1\}) \quad \forall i \in \{0 \ldots m-1\} \quad (2)$$

$$\text{alldifferent}(L(i,j) | i \in \{0 \ldots m-1\}) \quad \forall j \in \{0 \ldots n-1\} \quad (3)$$

A set of *Mutually Orthogonal Latin Squares* (MOLS) is a set of latin squares such that for any pair of squares L_α and L_β from the set, the ordered pairs $(L_\alpha(i,j), L_\beta(i,j))$ must be distinct for all i and j:

$$\text{alldifferent}((L_\alpha(i,j), L_\beta(i,j)) | i \in \{0 \ldots m-1\}, j \in \{0 \ldots n-1\})$$
$$\forall \alpha, \beta \in \{1 \ldots r\}, \alpha \neq \beta \quad (4)$$

A set of *Mutually Orthogonal Latin Rectangles* (MOLR) is the straightforward generalisation of MOLS from latin squares to latin rectangles: $(L_\alpha(i,j), L_\beta(i,j))$ must be distinct for all i and j for any pair of distinct rectangles L_α and L_β from the set. Clearly, a set of MOLR of order $n \times n$ is just a set of MOLS of order n.

Let $N(n)$ be the maximum number of squares possible in a set of MOLS of order n; let $N(m,n)$ be the maximum number of rectangles possible in a set of MOLR of order $m \times n$. Clearly, $N(n) \leq N(m,n)$ for any $m \leq n$ since a set of MOLS of order n can be turned into a set of MOLR of order $m \times n$ by removing a suitable number of rows from the bottom of each square. We also have that $N(m,n) \leq n-1$ for any m such that $1 < m \leq n$. A set of MOLS or MOLR containing $n-1$ elements is said to be *complete*.

For $n = p^e$ for some prime p, there is a well-known construction [2–II.2.20] that yields a complete set of MOLS. Let $GF(n)$ be the finite field of order n. For each $\alpha \in GF(n) \setminus \{0\}$, let $L_\alpha(i,j) = \alpha i + j$, where $i, j \in GF(n)$ and the algebra is performed in $GF(n)$. The set $\{L_\alpha | \alpha \in GF(n) \setminus \{0\}\}$ is then a set of $n-1$ MOLS of order n.

Note that the existence of a complete set of MOLS for these values of n means that the $m \times n$ MOLR existence problem is solved as well: we have $N(n) = N(m,n) = n-1$. For other (non prime power) values of n — other than 6 [1] — the MOLS (and hence MOLR) problem is still open; the best known lower bound on $N(n)$ is generally much smaller than n (see [2–Table II.2.72]). For these n it is usually the case that $N(m,n) > N(n)$ if $m < n$, but prior to the current work, little was known about the value of $N(m,n)$ for these cases, even for small values of n.

---

[1] $N(6) = 1$; constructing two MOLS of order 6 is Euler's 36 Officers Problem, a famous problem with no solution.

0	1	2	3	4	5
6	7	8	9	10	11
12	13	14	15	16	17

Fig. 1. Sharma and Das's construction: the first round

2.2 The Social Golfer Problem

The *Social Golfer Problem* [9–Problem 10] involves trying to schedule w rounds of golf, where in each round the $g \times s$ players are arranged into g groups of size s such that no pair of players appear in a group together more than once. This problem has received significant attention from the constraint programming community recently, for example [1,4,5,12,16,17,19]. It is well-known that certain instances of the social golfer problem (when $w(s-1) = gs-1$) correspond to instances of the *Resolvable Balanced Incomplete Block Design* problem. Similarly, it is known that when $g = s$, the w-round social golfer problem corresponds to the problem of finding $w-2$ MOLS of order g. This correspondence was exploited in [4], where the authors used a heuristic construction to seed their local search; when $g = s$ was prime, their construction corresponded to the standard construction for a complete set of MOLS, and thus yielded an optimal solution to the golf problem without any search required. Clearly by exploiting the full power of the MOLS construction, one can also obtain optimal search-free solutions for the cases where $g = s$ is a prime power.

Sharma and Das's Construction. There are two other constructions of which we are aware that allow solutions to the social golfer problem to be constructed from a set of MOLS (in practice, MOLR). The first is that of Sharma and Das [18]. This construction uses a set of r MOLR of order $m \times n$ to construct a solution to the social golfer problem with $g = n$ and $s = m$: if s does not divide g a solution with $w = r+1$ rounds is obtained; if s does divide g an extra round may be obtained.

Write the golfers out in an $s \times g$ array G, as shown in Figure 1. One round of the golf schedule is obtained from taking each column as a group.

$$\{G(i,j) | i \in \{0 \ldots s-1\}\} \ \forall j \in \{0 \ldots g-1\}$$

The next r rounds are obtained using r MOLR of order $s \times g$. Each latin rectangle L_α yields a round, with each value appearing in L_α corresponding to a group in the round: a group contains those players in G that have the same corresponding value in L_α.

$$\{G(i,j) | L_\alpha(i,j) = k, i \in \{0 \ldots s-1\}, j \in \{0 \ldots g-1\}\} \ \forall k \in \{0 \ldots g-1\}$$

This is illustrated in Figure 2, where L_α has been superimposed on G; for example, group 0 corresponds to players 0, 7 and 16. Finally, if s divides g then a further round can be obtained by dividing each row up into groups, as illustrated in Figure 3. □

In the case where s divides g and $g \geq s^2$, Sharma and Das's construction can be extended. In this case, rather than just one extra round involving groups lying entirely

$$0^0 \ 1^1 \ 2^2 \ 3^3 \ 4^4 \ 5^5$$
$$6^1 \ 7^0 \ 8^3 \ 9^2 \ 10^5 \ 11^4$$
$$12^2 \ 13^3 \ 14^4 \ 15^5 \ 16^0 \ 17^1$$

Fig. 2. Sharma and Das's construction: another round

within a row of G, one can actually schedule a w'-round mini-tournament amongst the players in the row, where w' is the best known number of rounds for the golf problem with g/s groups of size s. Doing this simultaneously for all the rows means that a schedule for $r+1+w'$ rounds can be achieved.

mathtalk-ga's Construction. The other construction is due to mathtalk-ga [13]. This uses a set of r MOLS of order n to construct a solution with $g = w = n$ and $s = r+1$; again, if s divides g an extra round is possible.

As with Sharma and Das's construction, write the golfers out in an $s \times g$ array G. Each latin square is associated with a row of G after the first. The rows of the latin squares correspond to the rounds of the golf schedule and the columns to the groups of the rounds. Each entry in a latin square thus indicates which element of the latin square's corresponding row of G appears in a given group of a given round. The jth player in the first row of G always appears in group j in each round. The groups for round i are thus:

$$\{G(0,j)\} \cup \{G(\alpha, L_\alpha(i,j)) | \alpha \in \{1\ldots r\}\} \ \forall j \in \{0\ldots g-1\}$$

Since each group contains one player from each row of G, if s divides g an extra round is possible by dividing the rows into groups, as with Sharma and Das's construction. □

This construction can be adapted to work with MOLR instead of MOLS. If the best known set of MOLS is of insufficient size for the desired golf group size, a larger set of MOLR may be used instead, at the expense of a reduced number of rounds. In general, a set of r MOLR of order $m \times n$ allows the construction of a golf solution with $g = n$, $s \leq r+1$ and $w = m$ (if s does not divide g) or $w = m+1$ (if it does).

As before, more rounds can be achieved if s divides g and $g \geq s^2$, by scheduling parallel mini-tournaments of g/s groups of s amongst the players in the rows of G. Using known MOLS results, this immediately yields solutions for previously unsolved instances (g-s-w) 12-3-16, 18-3-26 (closing this instance) and 20-4-25.

0	1	2	3	4	5
6	7	8	9	10	11
12	13	14	15	16	17

Fig. 3. Sharma and Das's construction: an extra round

3 MOLR Constructions

3.1 Constructing MOLR Solutions Directly

In this section we present a generalisation of the classic construction for a complete set of MOLS of order $n = p^e$ that allows us to generate (incomplete) sets of MOLR for other values of n. Specifically, our construction allows us to generate $p^e - 1$ MOLR of order $p^e \times n'$ for $n' = \prod_{i=1}^{e} q_i$ where $q_i = p$ or $q_i \geq 2p - 1$ for $i \in \{1 \ldots e\}$.

As noted above, for the MOLS construction we have $L_\alpha(i,j) = \alpha i + j$, where $\alpha, i, j \in GF(p^e)$ and $\alpha \neq 0$ and the algebra is performed in $GF(p^e)$. Essentially, the elements in column 0 of each square are generated by the product αi, with the rest of the columns being generated by adding the column index. We leverage this for other values of n by taking the columns generated for $n = p^e$ and extending them to rectangles of size $p^e \times n'$ by performing the addition of the column index in a different group, carefully selected to preserve the orthogonality of the resulting rectangles. The key property is:

$$\text{alldifferent}(-L_\alpha(i_2,0) + L_\alpha(i_1,0)|\alpha \in \{1 \ldots r\}) \quad \forall i_1, i_2 \in \{0 \ldots m-1\}, i_1 \neq i_2 \quad (5)$$

where $r = p^e - 1$ is the number of rectangles and $m = p^e$ is the number of rows in each rectangle. This property holds when the evaluation is done in $GF(p^e)$ (or the MOLS construction would not work), and must hold in our chosen group of order n'.

One of the standard interpretations of $GF(p^e)$ is as polynomials of degree at most $e-1$ with coefficients being elements of the integers modulo p. Multiplication, addition, etc. are then done as for polynomials, with polynomials of degree e or more being reduced modulo an irreducible polynomial of degree e. Now consider the polynomials of degree at most $e-1$ where the coefficients of x^{i-1} are elements of the integers modulo q_i. These polynomials form a group G of order $n' = \prod_{i=1}^{e} q_i$ where the group operation is addition. For our construction, we take the '0' columns constructed by the MOLS construction, interpret them using the polynomial interpretation above, and map the coefficients so that $a \pmod{p}$ is mapped to $a \pmod{q_i}$ for $a \in \{0 \ldots p-1\}$. Each of the n' columns required to form the rectangles of the desired size are then constructed by adding different elements of G using the group operation of G.

These rectangles are mutually orthogonal if either $q_i = p$ or $q_i \geq 2p - 1$ for all q_i. It suffices to show that

$$-b + a \neq -d + c \pmod{p} \Rightarrow -b + a \neq -d + c \pmod{q_i}$$
$$\forall a, b, c, d \in \{0 \ldots p-1\} \quad (6)$$

as this means that the constraint (5) is maintained when we switch to generating the columns in the group G rather than in $GF(p^e)$. If $q_i = p$ then (6) is clearly satisfied. Suppose $q_i \geq 2p - 1$, and consider $-b + a$ and $-d + c$ using normal integer arithmetic. These differences must fall in the range $\{-p+1 \ldots p-1\}$. Each of these differences is mapped to a different equivalence class modulo q_i if $q_i \geq 2p - 1$, and hence (6) holds.

Using the above construction yields, for example:

$$\text{3 MOLR of order } 4 \times 6 \quad (p = 2, n' = 2 \cdot 3)$$
$$\text{4 MOLR of order } 5 \times 10 \quad (p = 5, n' = 10)$$

7 MOLR of order 8×12 $(p = 2, n' = 2 \cdot 2 \cdot 3)$
6 MOLR of order 7×14 $(p = 7, n' = 14)$
8 MOLR of order 9×15 $(p = 3, n' = 3 \cdot 5)$
8 MOLR of order 9×18 $(p = 3, n' = 3 \cdot 6)$
7 MOLR of order 8×20 $(p = 2, n' = 2 \cdot 2 \cdot 5)$

Moreover, if one relaxes the condition to also allow $q_i \in \{p+1\ldots 2p-2\}$, then one can obtain near-solutions to the MOLR problem. These solutions can be used to seed the local search (á là [4]), often giving a starting point with fewer violations than had been achieved using local search alone, and allowing previously unsolved instances to be solved. Note also that sometimes a near-solution constructed in this way can be turned into a solution of a slightly smaller instance simply by dropping one or more rectangles and/or rows; a proper investigation of this is beyond the scope of this paper.

3.2 Constructing MOLR Solutions by Solving a Reduced Problem

Many MOLR constructions follow the same basic pattern:

$$L_\alpha(i, j) = \alpha i + j$$

For the MOLS construction the computation is done in GF(n); for Mullen and Shiue's construction [15] it is done in Z_n (the integers modulo n); for our construction the product is computed in GF(p^e) and the addition in a group of order n. The basic premise is the same: the entry in column j of a row is computed by adding j to the entry in column 0, and the entries in column 0 of each rectangle are constructed or selected in such a way that the resulting rectangles are latin and mutually orthogonal.

This leads to a more general way to construct MOLR: if one wishes to find r MOLR of order $m \times n$, search for a set of r "0" columns of height m such that each of these columns can be extended to a full latin rectangle by adding j to form column j of the rectangle, and such that the resulting rectangles are mutually orthogonal. We refer to this reduced problem as the *column problem*.

Note that the addition in the construction can be performed in any group of order n. This choice must be reflected in the constraints of the column problem — in the rest of this section all arithmetic and algebra is assumed to be performed in the selected (possibly non-commutative) group. Note that the choice of group affects which instances can be solved in this way; for example, a solution for 4 MOLR of order 5×6 can be constructed if one uses the integers modulo 6, but not if one uses the other group of order 6.

There are two constraints for the column problem. The first is (5), the second is:

$$\text{alldifferent}(L_\alpha(i,0) | i \in \{0\ldots m-1\}) \quad \forall \alpha \in \{1\ldots r\} \tag{7}$$

The rectangles are then constructed as follows:

$$L_\alpha(i, j) = L_\alpha(i, 0) + j \quad \forall \alpha \in \{1\ldots r\}, \forall i \in \{0\ldots m-1\}, \forall j \in \{0\ldots n-1\} \tag{8}$$

Note that (8) implies that the entries in a row are distinct:

$$\text{alldifferent}(L_\alpha(i, j) | j \in \{0\ldots n-1\}), \forall \alpha \in \{1\ldots r\}, \forall i \in \{0\ldots m-1\}$$

and (7) with (8) implies that the entries in a column are distinct:

$$\text{alldifferent}(L_\alpha(i,j) | i \in \{0\ldots m-1\}), \forall \alpha \in \{1\ldots r\}, \forall j \in \{0\ldots n-1\}$$

That is, the rectangles are latin.

It remains to show that the rectangles are orthogonal. Consider two cells in L_α at positions (i_1, j_1) and (i_2, j_2) that have the same value:

$$L_\alpha(i_1, j_1) = L_\alpha(i_2, j_2)$$
$$\text{i.e.} \quad L_\alpha(i_1, 0) + j_1 = L_\alpha(i_2, 0) + j_2$$
$$\text{i.e.} \quad -L_\alpha(i_2, 0) + L_\alpha(i_1, 0) = j_2 - j_1 \tag{9}$$

Then for any other rectangle L_β, orthogonality requires that the values in the same positions must be different; that is, we need to show that:

$$L_\beta(i_1, j_1) \neq L_\beta(i_2, j_2)$$

From (5) we know that:

$$-L_\beta(i_2, 0) + L_\beta(i_1, 0) \neq -L_\alpha(i_2, 0) + L_\alpha(i_1, 0)$$
$$\text{i.e.} \quad -L_\beta(i_2, 0) + L_\beta(i_1, 0) \neq j_2 - j_1 \quad \text{(by (9))}$$
$$\text{i.e.} \quad L_\beta(i_1, 0) + j_1 \neq L_\beta(i_2, 0) + j_2$$
$$\text{i.e.} \quad L_\beta(i_1, j_1) \neq L_\beta(i_2, j_2)$$

as required.

Thus solving the column problem allows us to construct a solution to the corresponding MOLR problem. Of course, it only allows us to find MOLR solutions of this particular form; there may be solvable MOLR instances for which there are no solutions of this form. For example, it is known that there are 2 MOLS of order 10, yet a complete search of the corresponding column problem found no solutions (when using either of the two distinct groups of order 10 for the arithmetic).

4 Local Search for MOLR

In this section we present the local search approach we used to tackle the MOLR problem.

4.1 MOLR Model

The evaluation function used by local search algorithms for satisfaction problems is usually based on the number of violated constraints. In order to minimise the number of constraints that have to be checked for violation, we chose a model for the MOLR problem that observes as many constraints as possible implicitly.

For r MOLR of order $m \times n$, our model contains $r+1$ rectangles. The rectangles L_1 through L_r are initialised such that each row contains a permutation of $\{0\ldots n-1\}$, fulfilling constraint (2). If we restrict the move operator to exchange values only within a row, constraint (2) will always be observed during the search.

Rectangle L_0 is a control rectangle, which is initialised as

$$L_0(i,j) = j \quad \forall i \in \{0\ldots m-1\}, \forall j \in \{0\ldots n-1\}$$

The control rectangle ensures that any assignment σ observing constraint (4) for all pairs of rectangles (L_0, L_α), $1 \le \alpha \le r$ will also observe constraint (3), since

$$(L_0(i,j), L_\alpha(i,j))_\sigma = (j, L_\alpha(i,j))_\sigma$$

and in any solution that observes constraint (4)

$$i_1 \ne i_2 \Leftrightarrow (j, L_\alpha(i_1,j))_\sigma \ne (j, L_\alpha(i_2,j))_\sigma \Leftrightarrow L_\alpha(i_1,j)_\sigma \ne L_u(i_2,j)_\sigma$$

Using this model and restricting the search moves to exchange values only within a row, any value assignment σ that does not violate constraint (4) will also observe the two other constraints. Therefore, we can use the evaluation function

$$f(\sigma) = \sum_{\alpha=0}^{r-1} \sum_{\beta=\alpha+1}^{r} \sum_{x=0}^{n-1} \sum_{y=0}^{n-1} max(0, \#(\sigma, \alpha, \beta, x, y))$$

with $\#(\sigma, \alpha, \beta, x, y) = |\{(i,j) | (L_\alpha(i,j), L_\beta(i,j))_\sigma = (x,y)\}| - 1$

the sum of violations of constraint (4) for all pairs of rectangles. An assignment σ is a solution for an MOLR instance iff $f(\sigma) = 0$.

4.2 Neighbourhood

Since we only allow the exchange of values within a row, we generally use only one type of move operator, swapping the values of two cells within a row:

$$\mu(\alpha, i, j_1, j_2) = [L_\alpha(i,j_1) \leftrightarrow L_\alpha(i,j_2)]$$

For each search step, the algorithm chooses the move that reduces the number of violations most. Should there be more than one move with the same benefit, a move will be randomly chosen from that list. Since a swap between two cells can only improve the violation count if at least one of the cells is currently in violation, we can restrict the neighbourhood to such moves. The neighbourhood can then be defined as:

$$S = \{\mu(\alpha, i, j_1, j_2) | \exists \beta \in \{0\ldots r\} : \beta \ne \alpha \wedge$$
$$(\#(\sigma, \alpha, \beta, L_\alpha(i,j_1), L_\beta(i,j_1)) > 1 \vee \#(\sigma, \alpha, \beta, L_\alpha(i,j_2), L_\beta(i,j_2)) > 1)\}$$

However, if there is no move that will improve the evaluation of the assignment, the algorithm will choose with probability p_1 a move that least increases the violation count; with probability p_2, it will swap two randomly chosen values within a randomly chosen row; and with probability p_3, it will right-shift a randomly chosen row by a random amount.

The right-shift move (shifting row i of L_α by w positions) can be defined as:

$$\bar{\mu}(\alpha, i, w) = [L_\alpha(i, (j+w) \bmod n) \leftarrow L_\alpha(i,j), \forall j \in \{0\ldots n-1\}]$$

Right-shifting a complete row makes a larger step away from the local minimum, and often allows the algorithm to escape from the area of that minimum. In our experiments, we set $p_1 = 0.4$, $p_2 = 0.35$, and $p_3 = 0.25$. These values were chosen since they gave good results in our initial tests.

4.3 Tabu Search Algorithm

Our local search algorithm is based on a tabu search with restart. For each possible move $\mu(\alpha, i, j_1, j_2)$ or $\bar{\mu}(\alpha, i, w)$, the tabu table $\mathcal{T}$ contains the step number $t(\alpha, i, j_1, j_2)$ or $t(\alpha, i, w)$, respectively, until which this move is tabu. Moves that are currently tabu are filtered from the neighbourhood. The tabu is based on the location of the swapped cells, or the row and the shift, not on the particular values that are swapped: when the values of two cells are swapped, a swap between these two cells becomes tabu for a certain number of steps, even if the values in these cells change in the meantime.

When a move $\mu(\alpha, i, j_1, j_2)$ is performed at step h, the tabu table entry $t(\alpha, i, j_2, j_1)$ is set to $h+d$, where d is the current tabu tenure. For a right-shift move $\bar{\mu}(\alpha, i, w)$, the entry $t(\alpha, i, (n-w) \bmod n)$ is set accordingly.

The tabu tenure ranges dynamically between *maxTabu* and *minTabu* steps. On every non-improving step, the tenure is increased by one, up to *maxTabu*. On every improving step, the value is decreased by one, down to *minTabu*. In our experiments, *maxTabu* was set to 10, and *minTabu* to 2. These values were taken from [14].

In order to escape the area of a local minimum without a complete restart, we added a perturbation component that alters parts of the current assignment. When the algorithm fails to improve on the current best assignment for *maxStable* steps, the current assignment is perturbed by right-shifting a random row from each rectangle (except the control rectangle) by a random amount. In our experiments, *maxStable* was set to 150, since initial tests showed that the search rarely progressed further for higher values.

The perturbation makes a major step away from the current assignment, often allowing the algorithm to reach a different part of the search space, so that it can escape the area of local minimum where it got stuck. For each iteration of the search, the algorithm can make *maxPert* such perturbations, with *maxPert* set to 2 in our experiments.

If after *maxPert* perturbations the *stableIter* counter again reaches the value *maxStable*, the algorithm restarts the search with a new initial assignment. In total *maxIter* iterations of the search run are performed, with *maxIter* set to 10 in our experiments. (A relatively small value of *maxIter* was chosen in order to keep the amount of CPU time required for our experiments manageable.)

4.4 Seeding the Search

Initially, we used random permutations of $\{0 \ldots n-1\}$ to initialise the rows of the rectangles. However, this gave unsatisfactory results, with the search often starting with a very high violation count. The search usually became repeatedly stuck in local minima, failing to reach a solution despite the perturbation moves that allowed the search to escape the area of a local minimum.

Therefore, we also used constructive heuristics to improve the seeding, similar to Dotú and Van Hentenryck [4]. Our first seeding heuristic uses the MOLR construction described Section 3.1. We select parameters for the heuristic with the same value of n and where possible at least as many rectangles and rows as the final MOLR instance we desire, filling in any missing rows with random permutations of $\{0 \ldots n-1\}$.

Our second seeding heuristic uses the column problem construction described in Section 3.2. In this case we take a near-solution to the corresponding column problem (also found with local search) and use it to construct a near-solution to the MOLR problem, which is then used as the seed.

The performance of the different seeding heuristics is discussed in Section 5.

4.5 Local Search for the Column Problem

We model the column problem corresponding to r MOLR of order $m \times n$ using an array C of dimension $m \times r$, with elements taking values from $\{0 \ldots n-1\}$. Note that $C(i, \alpha)$ actually corresponds to $L_\alpha(i, 0)$ from the MOLR problem. We also associate with each column α the set of numbers $\mathcal{U}_\alpha \subset \{0 \ldots n-1\}$ that are unused in that column.

We initialise each column such that each cell in that column contains a different value, thus fulfilling the alldifferent constraint (7). If we allow only exchanges of values between cells within a column, or between a cell and the set of unused values for that column, constraint (7) will always be observed. Therefore, the evaluation function uses only the number of violations of constraint (5):

$$f_c(\sigma) = \sum_{i_1=0}^{m-2} \sum_{i_2=i_1+1}^{m-1} \sum_{x=0}^{n-1} \max(0, \#(\sigma, i_1, i_2, x))$$

with $\#(\sigma, i_1, i_2, x) = |\{\alpha \in \{1 \ldots r\} | (-C(i_2, \alpha) + C(i_1, \alpha))_\sigma = x\}| - 1$

where the arithmetic is done in the chosen group of order n.

The search uses two types of moves: swapping the values of two cells in a column, and swapping the value of a cell with a value from the set of unused values in its column:

$$\mu_c(\alpha, i_1, i_2) = [C(i_1, \alpha) \leftrightarrow C(i_2, \alpha)]$$
$$\text{and} \quad \mu'_c(\alpha, i, e) = [C(i, \alpha) \leftrightarrow e \in \mathcal{U}_\alpha]$$

Again, the neighbourhood is restricted to moves involving cells in violation. Formally, it is defined as:

$$S = S_s \cup S_e$$

where

$$S_s = \{\mu_c(\alpha, i_1, i_2) | \exists i \in \{0 \ldots m-1\} \, : \, (i \neq i_1 \wedge \#(\sigma, i_1, i, -C(i, \alpha) + C(i_1, \alpha)) > 1)$$
$$\vee \, (i \neq i_2 \wedge \#(\sigma, i_2, i, -C(i, \alpha) + C(i_2, \alpha)) > 1)\}$$

$$\text{and} \quad S_e = \{\mu'_c(\alpha, i_1, e) | \exists i_2 \in \{0 \ldots m-1\} : i_2 \neq i_1 \wedge$$
$$\#(\sigma, i_1, i_2, -C(i_2, \alpha) + C(i_1, \alpha)) > 1 \wedge e \in \mathcal{U}_\alpha\}$$

Should there be no move that will improve the evaluation, the algorithm will, as for the MOLR problem, choose with probability p_1 a move that least increases the violation count; with probability p_2, it will swap two randomly chosen values within a randomly chosen column; and with probability p_3, it will down-shift a randomly chosen column by a random amount.

The tabu search algorithm is the same as for the MOLR problem. In our experiments, we also set the parameters to the same values, with two exceptions. The first difference is that *maxPert* is set to zero; i.e. every time the stable iteration counter reaches the value *maxStable*, the search restarts with a random initialisation. Secondly, *maxIter* is set to 20, since the column problem model is much smaller than the corresponding MOLR model and the search progresses faster.

5 Results

We explored several approaches to solving the MOLR problem, eventually trying instances up to $n = 20$:

1. **Constructive backtracking search with symmetry breaking on the full MOLR problem.** This was implemented in ECL^{i}PS^e [21] using the SBDD symmetry library described in [8]. While this was able to completely solve (and enumerate) instances with $n = 6$, non-trivial instances with $n \geq 10$ seem beyond the reach of this kind of approach at this time.
2. **Local search on the full MOLR problem**, as discussed in Section 4. This was also implemented in ECL^{i}PS^e, and was able to solve some previously open instances, but it was not particularly effective and was later surpassed by other approaches.
3. **Construction**, as discussed in Section 3.1. This was implemented in GAP [7], with an ECL^{i}PS^e wrapper to allow integration with the other approaches. This approach generally provided a reasonably good solution of the form $m - 1$ MOLR of order $m \times n$ for each value of n. These solutions were later surpassed by other techniques, but of course it is a fast way to obtain some MOLR for problem instances that are too large to tackle with search.
4. **Local search on the full MOLR problem, seeded with a constructed near-solution**, as discussed in Section 4.4. This was much more effective than starting with a random seed; typically the seed for an instance had fewer violations than the best assignment found without the seed, and enabled a number of new instances to be solved. A number of these (notably for $n = 12$ and $n = 15$) have not been matched by any other technique.

    In section Section 3.1, we presented a construction that allowed us to generate $p^e - 1$ MOLR of order $p^e \times n$. In our experiments, we found that a good seeding heuristic for finding r MOLR of order $m \times n$ is to set p to the prime number nearest to $max(r,m)$ and leave n un-factorised, so that $e = 1$. Only for some instances where a factorisation of n exists such that r, m and p^e are close together did such a seed yield a better result (indicated by 4' in Table 1) — usually factorising n was worse.
5. **Constructive backtracking search on the column problem.** The most effective variant we tried was to simply assign variables random values from their domain, giving up if no solution was found after 60 seconds of CPU time. We tried two static variable ordering heuristics: rectangle-by-rectangle (good for instances with few rectangles) and row-by-row (good for instances with few rows). We also tried using groups other than the integers modulo n for the arithmetic, which sometimes yielded superior results (indicated by a 5' in Table 1). Solutions, when found, were generally found in just a few seconds. This was one of the most effective of the methods we tried for finding MOLR solutions; there were very few instances solved by other methods that were not solved by this one.

6. **Local search on the column problem**, as discussed in Section 4.5. This was the other very effective method, able to find a number of solutions not found by the constructive backtracking approach, but also failing to find some solutions that were found by that approach. As with the constructive approach above, we tried using different groups for the arithmetic, and sometimes this yielded better results (indicated by a $6'$ in Table 1). Solutions, when found, were generally found in just a few seconds; with our parameter settings even the largest instances ran for no more than a few minutes if no solution was found. One of the reasons for trying this approach is that even when it could not find a solution, any near-solutions it found could be used as seeds for local search on the full problem.

7. **Local search on the full MOLR problem, seeded with a near-solution from the column problem.** This approach turned out to be something of a disappointment, failing to find solutions (only near-solutions) for any instances we tried that were not solved by local search on the column problem. It is possible that a near-solution to the column problem is a poor heuristic choice for seeding the full problem.

A summary of the best results for $n \leq 20$ is given in Table 1. *LB* is the best known lower bound; *Method* indicates which of the above methods was able to solve that instance. We have included previously known results, from the extensively-studied MOLS problem [2–II.2] and from [22]. We have omitted those values of n for which a complete set of MOLS is known, since all such instances are solved by that set of MOLS. We have also omitted results for $m = 2$ since there is a trivial construction for a complete set of MOLR in this case. Finally we have omitted listing the methods for those entries that are dominated by another entry (i.e. the latter has more rectangles and/or more rows), except where it is useful to show how close our techniques are to matching the MOLS results of [2–II.2].

An expanded set of results including solutions can be found on the web [10].

We suspect that our failure to match most of the MOLS results is at least in part due to the fact that our most successful techniques can only find solutions of a certain form, and for some instances there are no solutions of this form. For example, a complete search of the column problem found no solution for 2 MOLS of order 10, even though a solution to the full problem exists. While we are very pleased with the results that we have obtained, for the most part we do not know how far from optimal they are. Complete search is currently out of the question for all but the smallest instances, and even for the well-studied MOLS problem very few good upper bounds are known. We do, however, expect that our results can be significantly improved upon, particularly for larger instances.

As shown in Section 2.2, MOLR solutions can be used to construct solutions to the social golfer problem. Using the new results in Table 1 we were able to construct solutions to the 43 instances listed in Table 2. The *gain* indicates the number of extra rounds achieved over the previously best known result from any source (RBIBD, MOLS, constructions, constraint programming, etc.). Solutions to much larger instances of the social golfer problem remain within easy reach using the techniques we have presented here; we merely had to stop somewhere. A full table of results for the social golfer problem from all sources can be found on the web [11].

Table 1. Summary of MOLR results: lower bounds for $N(m,n)$

	\multicolumn{2}{c	}{6}	\multicolumn{2}{c	}{10}	\multicolumn{2}{c	}{12}	\multicolumn{2}{c	}{14}	\multicolumn{2}{c	}{15}	\multicolumn{2}{c	}{18}	\multicolumn{2}{c	}{20}
m	LB	Method	LB	Method	LB	Method	LB	Method	LB	Method	LB	Method	LB	Method
3	4		8		11		12		14		16		19	
4	4		8		11		12	5',6	14	5	16	4,5	19	5'
5	4	1,2,4,5,6	8	5	11		11	5',6'	11	5,6	14	5,6	16	5,6'
6	1	(trivial)	6		11	5'	10	5'	10		13	5'	15	6'
7			6	5,6	8		8	4,5,6	10		12	5'	13	6
8			4		8	4'	7	5,6	10		10	4,5,6	11	5,6
9			4	[22],5	7	4'	6	4,5,6	10		9	6'	10	4,5
10			2	[2]	5		5		10		8	6'	9	5,6
11					5		5	4	10	4	7	5'	8	4,5',6
12					5	[2],5'	4	5	4	5,6	6	5	7	5
13							3	5	4		5	5,6	6	
14							3	[2]	4		4		6	5'
15									4	[2]	4		5	5,6
16											4	5'	4	
17											3	5,6	4	5,6'
18											3	[2]	4	
19													4	
20													4	[2]

Table 2. New solutions for the social golfer problem (g-s-w)

Instance	Gain	Instance	Gain	Instance	Gain	Instance	Gain	Instance	Gain
10-6-7	+1	14-5-12	+5	15-6-11	+6	18-5-16	+7	20-6-16	+10
10-7-7	+2	14-6-11	+4	15-7-11	+6	18-6-15	+6	20-7-14	+9
10-8-5	+1	14-7-10	+2	15-9-11	+6	18-7-13	+4	20-8-12	+7
10-9-5	+1	14-8-8	+4	15-10-11	+6	18-8-11	+2	20-9-11	+6
		14-9-7	+3	15-11-11	+6	18-9-11	+1	20-10-11	+5
12-7-9	+3	14-10-6	+2			18-10-9	+5	20-11-9	+4
12-8-9	+3	14-11-6	+2			18-11-8	+4	20-12-8	+3
12-9-8	+2	14-12-5	+1			18-12-7	+3	20-13-7	+2
						18-13-7	+3	20-14-7	+2
						18-14-6	+2	20-15-6	+1
						18-15-5	+1	20-16-6	+1
						18-16-5	+1		

6 Conclusions and Future Work

We have shown that by solving a reduced problem, one can construct good solutions to the MOLR problem, which can be used to construct solutions to various other problems of interest. In particular, we have shown how generalisations of MOLS-based constructions can use these solutions to yield improved solutions to 43 instances of the social golfer problem.

We have also confirmed Dotú and Van Hentenryck's result [4] that seeding a local search algorithm with heuristically-constructed solutions with low violation counts can dramatically improve results on this kind of combinatorial problem, where the local search landscape contains many local minima and it is in general hard to progress towards a global optimum. However, we have found that this is not always a benefit: the wrong kind of construction can yield a seed which has a good initial violation count, but starts the search in a local minimum from which it is almost impossible to escape.

The MOLR and social golfer problems are still both far from solved. It would be interesting to see how far our MOLR results can be improved, and what other techniques can be used to construct new solutions to the social golfer problem. One thing we plan to investigate further is seeding a local search for the social golfer problem with a constructed assignment based on a near-solution of the MOLR problem. Early experiments with this approach have yielded a solution to the previously unsolved 14-8-9 instance. We also plan to continue to investigate construction techniques for the MOLR and social golfer problems.

Acknowledgments

We would like to thank Jonathan Lever for his local search code for the social golfers problem that we adapted for the MOLR and column problems, and Ian Wanless for pointing out useful references and for providing encouragement to work on the MOLR problem. We would also like to thank Pascal Van Hentenryck and mathtalk-ga for interesting discussions on constructions for the social golfer problem. Finally, we would like to thank the anonymous reviewers for their feedback and suggestions.

References

1. Nicolas Barnier and Pascal Brisset. Solving the Kirkman's Schoolgirl Problem in a few seconds. In P. Van Hentenryck, editor, *CP 2002: Proc. of the 8th Int. Conf. on Principles and Practice of Constraint Programming*, LNCS 2470, pages 477–491. Springer-Verlag, 2002.
2. C.H. Colbourn and J.H. Dinitz, editors. *The CRC Handbook of Combinatorial Designs*. CRC Press, Rockville, Maryland, USA, 1996.
3. Ivan B. Djordjevic and Bane Vasic. LDPC codes for long haul optical communications based on high-girth designs. *Journal of Optical Communications*, 24(3):94–96, 2003.
4. Iván Dotú and Pascal Van Hentenryck. Scheduling social golfers locally. In Roman Barták and Michela Milano, editors, *CP-AI-OR 2005: Proceedings of the 2nd International Conference on Integration of AI and OR Techniques in Constraint Programming for Combinatorial Optimization Problems*, LNCS 3524, pages 155–167, 2005.
5. Torsten Fahle, Stefan Schamberger, and Meinolf Sellmann. Symmetry breaking. In Toby Walsh, editor, *CP 2001: Proceedings of the 7th International Conference on Principles and Practice of Constraint Programming*, LNCS 2239, pages 93–107, 2001.
6. M.F. Franklin. Triples of almost orthogonal 10×10 latin squares useful in experimental design. *Ars Combinatoria*, 17:141–146, 1984.
7. The GAP Group. *GAP – Groups, Algorithms, and Programming, Version 4.3*, 2002. (http://www.gap-system.org).

8. Ian P. Gent, Warwick Harvey, Tom Kelsey, and Steve Linton. Generic SBDD using computational group theory. In Francesca Rossi, editor, *CP 2003: Proceedings of the 9th International Conference on Principles and Practice of Constraint Programming*, LNCS 2833, pages 333–347. Springer-Verlag, 2003.
9. Ian P. Gent, Toby Walsh, and Bart Selman. CSPLib: a problem library for constraints. http://csplib.org/.
10. Warwick Harvey. Warwick's results page for the MOLR problem. http://www.icparc.ic.ac.uk/~wh/molr.
11. Warwick Harvey. Warwick's results page for the social golfer problem. http://www.icparc.ic.ac.uk/~wh/golf.
12. Warwick Harvey. Symmetry breaking and the social golfer problem. In Pierre Flener and Justin Pearson, editors, *Proc. SymCon-01: Symmetry in Constraints*, pages 9–16, 2001.
13. mathtalk-ga. Answer to "Unique combinations of 4 numbers between 1 to N". *Google Answers*, 2005. http://answers.google.com/answers/threadview?id=274891.
14. Laurent Michel and Pascal Van Hentenryck. A simple tabu search for warehouse location. *European Journal of Operations Research*, 157(3):576–591, 2004.
15. Gary L. Mullen and Jau-Shyong Shiue. A simple construction for orthogonal latin rectangles. *Journal of Combinatorial Mathematics and Combinatorial Computing*, 9:161–166, 1991.
16. Steven Prestwich. Randomised backtracking for linear pseudo-boolean constraint problems. In Narendra Jussien and François Laburthe, editors, *Proc. of the Fourth International Workshop on Integration of AI and OR Techniques in Constraint Programming for Combinatorial Optimisation Problems (CP-AI-OR'02)*, pages 7–19, Le Croisic, France, March, 25–27 2002.
17. Jean-François Puget. Symmetry breaking revisited. In Pascal Van Hentenryck, editor, *CP 2002: Proceedings of the Eighth International Conference on Principles and Practice of Constraint Programming*, LNCS 2470, pages 446–461. Springer-Verlag, 2002.
18. V. K. Sharma and M. N. Das. On resolvable incomplete block designs. *Austral. J. Statist.*, 27(3):298–302, 1985.
19. Barbara M. Smith. Reducing symmetry in a combinatorial design problem. In *CPAIOR'01: Proc. of the Third International Workshop on Integration of AI and OR Techniques in Constraint Programming for Combinatorial Optimization Problems*, pages 351–359, April 2001.
20. D. R. Stinson, R. Wei, and L. Zhu. New constructions for perfect hash families and related structures using combinatorial designs and codes. *Journal of Combinatorial Designs*, 8(3):189–200, 2000.
21. Mark G. Wallace, Stefano Novello, and Joachim Schimpf. ECLiPSe : A platform for constraint logic programming. *ICL Systems Journal*, 12(1):159–200, May 1997.
22. Ian M. Wanless. Answers to questions by Dénes on latin power sets. *Europ. J. Combinatorics*, 22:1009–1020, 2001.

Advances in Polytime Isomorph Elimination for Configuration

Laurent Hénocque, Mathias Kleiner, and Nicolas Prcovic

LSIS - Universités d'Aix-Marseille II et III,
Faculté de St-Jérôme - Avenue Escadrille Normandie-Niemen - 13013 Marseille
{laurent.henocque, mathias.kleiner, nicolas.prcovic}@lsis.org

Abstract. An inherent and often very underestimated difficulty in solving configuration problems is the existence of many structural isomorphisms. This issue of considerable importance attracted little research interest despite its applicability to almost all configuration problems. We define two search procedures allowing the removal of large portions of the search space that provably solely contain non canonical solutions. The tests performed on each node are time polynomial. Experimental results are reported on a simple generic configuration example.

1 Introduction

Configuring consists in simulating the constrained realization of a complex product from a catalog of component parts, using known relations between types, and instantiating object attributes. The industrial need for configuration applications is ancient [1], and has triggered the development of many configuration programs and formalisms [2–8].

The main objective of this research is to reduce the undue combinatorial effort incurred by isomorphisms during configuration search. We focus on the dynamic nature of configuration, which consists in generating the structure of possible solutions.

This difficulty is one among the most important to tackle in configuration, if one expects to solve problems having highly variable solutions. Solvers cannot currently handle the search space of these problems because of the exponential number of isomorphs that they generate for each canonical solution structure[1]. We propose a general search procedure eliminating a great number of such isomorphisms in configuration problems. More precisely, we first present a complete, non redundant procedure restricted to the generation of typed tree structures which also efficiently eliminates any non-canonical structure. Starting from this procedure, we generalize it to another able to generate all type of structures (DAGs), in a complete and non redundant way, while still avoiding the generation of an important number of isomorphic structures. This work is based upon the results obtained in [9] and [10], which demonstrated necessary existence conditions for such procedures but did not explicit any of them, leaving the crucial point of how defining them unmentioned.

---

[1] Industrial problems currently solved with configurators only involve models of limited size.

Plan of the Article

Section 2 describes the formalism used throughout the paper, the notion of *structural sub-problems* and the problem of generating them. We also briefly recall why representing the structure of a configuration problem as a graph is more efficient than defining it as a CSP. Section 3 presents a complete procedure for generating canonical structural problems when they have a tree structure. Section 4 presents a way to extend the procedure so that it applies to any configuration problem. Section 5 describes how to exploit the symmetries of covering tree structures so as to reject more isomorphisms. Section 6 provides experimental results on the benefits of using such an approach. Section 7 concludes.

2 Configuration Problems, Structural Sub-problems and Isomorphism

A configuration problem describes a generic product, in the form of declarative statements (rules or axioms) about product well-formedness. Valid configuration model instances (called *configurations*) involve objects and their relationships, notably *types* (unary relations involved in taxonomies) and binary relations. Some binary relations are *composition* relations having stronger functional semantics (an object is a component of at most one composite).

Here is a very simple example of a configuration problem which will allow us to illustrate notions throughout this paper. The problem is to configure a network of computers (C) and printers (P) (as illustrated in Figure 1). The network involves up to three computers, each of which being connected to at most two printers[2]. Conversely, each printer must be connected to at least one and at most three computers. Besides this, we have two global constraints: there is only one network, and there are only two printers available. In a real problem, computers and printers could have specific attributes that would be instantiated while obeying other constraints. This can be left aside as we solely focus on structural constraints.

Solutions to configuration problems involve interconnected objects, as illustrated in Figure 1, which makes explicit the existence of structural isomorphisms.

We isolate configuration sub-problems called *structural problems*, that are built from the binary relations, the related types and the structural constraints alone, and study their isomorphisms. For simplicity, we abstract from any configuration formalism, and consider a totally ordered set O of objects (we normally use $O = \{1, 2, \ldots\}$), a totally ordered set T_C of type symbols (unary relations) and a totally ordered set R_C of binary relation symbols.

For any binary injective relation R, we will use either $(x, y) \in R$ or $y = R(x)$.

Definition 1 (syntax). *A structural problem, is a tuple* (t, T_C, R_C, C), *where* $t \in T_C$ *is the root configuration type, and C is a set of structural constraints applied to the elements of T_C and R_C.*

---

[2] This is the Figure data, our experiments involve more computers and printers.

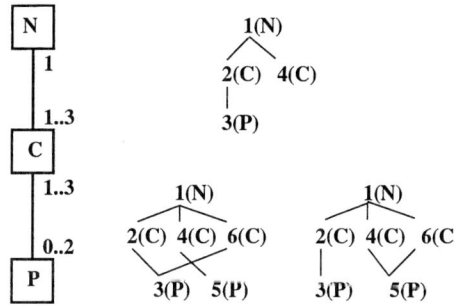

Fig. 1. A network connection problem. On the left, the model for the components types (network, computers and printers) and their relations. On the right, 3 examples of possible structures. The two structures at the bottom are isomorphic and therefore represent equivalent solutions.

In the network problem of Figure 1, we have t=N, T_C ={N, C, P}, R_C = { (N,C), (C,P) } and C is the set of structural constraints which enforce the minimum and maximum number of objects that can be connected for each binary relation.

Definition 2 (semantics). *An* instance *of a structural problem* (t, T_C, R_C, C) *is an interpretation I of t and of the elements of T_C and R_C, over the set O of objects. If an interpretation satisfies the constraints in C, it is a* solution *of the structural problem.*

We use the term *structure* or *configuration* to denote a structural problem solution.

A configuration can be represented using a vertex-colored DAG (directed acyclic graph) G=(t,X,E,L) with $X \subset O$, $E \subset O \times O$ and $L \subset O \times T_C$. The symbol t is the root type, X the vertex set, E the edge set and L is the function which associates each vertex to a type.

As an example, the upper solution of Figure 1 can be represented by the quadruple (N, {1,2,3,4}, {(1,2), (2,3), (1,4)}, {(1,N), (2, C), (3,P), (4, C)}).

For those who are not familiar with configuration problems, we recall now why it is more efficient to solve the structural problem by defining it as the construction of a graph rather than using the CSP formalism. Indeed, with CSPs, we would have to consider the maximal number C of PC's and P of printers to define the CSP variables. One possible model is to assign a variable to each PC and each printer (C+P variables). The domain of a variable assigned to a PC (resp. a printer) would contain all parts of the set {1, ... P} (resp. {1, ... C}) and therefore would be of size 2^P (resp. 2^C). The search space would then be of size $(2^P)^C \times (2^C)^P = 4^{C.P}$. This is the option chosen in [8] with the ports concept implemented using set variables. Another possibility is to define a variable $e_{i,j}$ that represents the choice of connecting the machine i with the printer j. Those P × C variables are boolean. The search space is of size $2^{P.C}$. There is however a drawback in using standard CSPs: generally, a solution contains fewer objects than the maximum number you had to define at start. Unused objects yield unwanted combinatorics and filtering. This is why extensions to the CSP formalism have been proposed [3,5] that allow to add variables during the resolution. The construction of a vertex-colored DAG that we consider in this paper captures this in an abstract way.

Definition 3 (Isomorphic configurations). *Two configurations G=(t, X, E, L) and G'=(t', X', E', L') are isomorphic iff t=t', L=L' and there exists a one-to-one mapping σ between X and X' such that $\forall$ x,y $\in$ X, (x,y) $\in$ E $\Leftrightarrow$ ($\sigma(x)$, $\sigma(y)$) $\in$ E' and $\forall$ (x,l) $\in$ L, ($\sigma(x)$,l) $\in$ L'.*

For instance the two solutions at the bottom of Figure 1 are isomorphic since σ =((1,1), (2,4), (3,5), (4,2), (5,3), (6,6)) is a one-to-one mapping satisfying the definition criterias.

Testing whether two graphs are isomorphic is an NP problem until today unclassified as either NP-complete or polynomial. The corresponding *graph isomorphism complete* class holds all the problems having similar complexity[3]. For several categories of graphs, like trees of course but also graphs having a bounded vertex degree, this isomorphism test is polynomial [11]. The graph iso problem is known as weakly exponential, and there exists practically efficient algorithms for solving it, the most efficient one being Nauty[12]. This being said, we must emphasize the fact that Nauty cannot be used in our situation. The reason is that we must maintain the property that all canonical structures can be obtained from at least one smaller solution itself being canonical. Using Nauty from within an arbitrary graph enumeration procedure yields a generate and test algorithm: the portions of the search space that can be explored by adding to a non canonical structure must still be generated, in case they would contain canonical representatives which cannot be obtained differently. This situation will be explained in more detail in a forthcoming section.

An *isomorphism class* represents a set of isomorphic graphs. All the graphs from a given isomorphism class are equivalent, therefore a graph generation procedure should ideally generate only one *canonical* representative per class. This is of crucial importance since the size of an isomorphism class containing graphs with n vertices can be up to $n!$ (the number of permutations on the vertex set that actually create a different graph). Isomorphism classes are huge in size in most cases because, counter-intuitively, the less symmetrical a graph is, the more isomorphic graphs it has. This means that when current configurators (which do not avoid isomorphisms or in a very restricted way) generate a solution, partial or complete, they also generate an often exponential number of isomorphic solutions.

Most graph generating procedures rely upon the central operation of adding an edge to an existing graph (*unit extension*). Starting from a graph, the unit extensions that are valid wrt. the model constraints yield a new set of graphs. We consider two distinct situations for inserting an edge in a graph: an *internal edge* connects two existing vertices, whereas an *extraneous edge* connects an existing vertex to a newly created one. Having an efficient canonicity test is of little help for generating canonical graphs. Testing graphs for canonicity can be used to reject redundant solutions, but in so doing one has to explore the entire search space. Ideally we should be able to directly reject graphs for which we know that all extended supergraphs are not canonical. To achieve this, the canonicity criterion must be defined in such a way that *any canonical graph has at least a canonical subgraph resulting from the removal of one of its edges*. We call this the *canonical retractability property*. This condition is necessary (but not sufficient, see below) to allow for backtracking as soon as a non-canonical graph is detected during

---

[3] For instance, the vertex-colored DAG isomorphism problem.

the search. Indeed if there exists a canonical graph not obtainable via extension of a canonical subgraph, the extension of a non-canonical graph will be needed to reach it. Such a canonicity criterion is not trivial to find, and most known canonicity tests, Nauty inclusive, do not respect it. There exist isomorphism-free graph generation procedures that impose conditions on the canonicity test, as for instance the *orderly algorithms* from [13] which however do not propose an efficient canonicity test. To the best of our knowledge, such an efficient test has not yet been found in the general case (if ever one exists). Specialized and efficient procedures for generating canonical graphs exist for trees, for cubic graphs [14] and more generally, for graphs having hereditary properties[4] [15]. Configuration problems unfortunately do not comply with these restrictions, which led us to develop specific procedures. In order to achieve this, we have based our research upon existing work around configuration problems.

2.1 Related Work in CSP and Configuration

There exists a large body of work on symetry elimination methods for CSPs (eg, [16,17] [18,19,20]). Unfortunately, transposing those techniques to graph generation is far from obvious. The common principle for symmetry breaking in CSP is to avoid generating two isomorphic partial solutions: either by adding additional constraints to the problem, or by checking during resolution whether an isomorphic partial solution has already been generated. Our approach would be close to the first method as our canonicity criteria is defined beforehand according to the particular context of graph generation. However, if we were to transpose the graph generation problem to the CSP formalism we would have to deal with a dynamic CSP containing particular constraints (the structual constraints), and this would make the comparison with symmetry breaking methods in CSP very difficult. This work is connected to graph isomorphism detection techniques rather than CSP symmetry breaking methods.

Several approaches were experimented to tackle configuration isomorphisms, mostly by reasoning at a single level. One possibility is to prevent redundant connections of interchangeable objects during search. Also experimented is the substitution of connecting actual objects by counting them according to their target types [8]. A pseudo-linear time canonicity test that complies with the canonical retractability property is given in [9] when the configuration problem only involves composition relations (in which case all structural solutions are trees). This result was generalized to generic configuration problems in [10], by describing a weak canonicity criterion compatible with canonical retractability, in the case of DAGS. However, not all configuration generation procedures are compatible with this canonicity criterion. This important aspect was left unmentioned in our previous papers in order to simplify our point by restricting ourselves to explaining the main ideas. Now, we go into the details of this practical aspect.

2.2 State Graph of a Configuration Problem

Let us consider the *state graph* $G_P = (X_P, E_P)$ of a configuration problem. The state set X_P contains all structures (vertex-colored DAGs) corresponding to the structural

---

[4] A graph property is hereditary if all its subgraphs respect it.

model, and E_P are all the pairs (g, h) such that g, h $\in X_P$ and h is the result of a unit extension from g. (G_P is itself a DAG for which the root is the state (t, $\{1\}, \emptyset, \{(1,t)\})$). A structure generation procedure must be complete and non-redundant, i.e able to generate all structures of X_P only once while exploring G_P. The search can be represented with a covering tree T_P of G_P. Let us consider now the state graph G'_P, which is the subgraph of G_P containing only canonical structures. The canonical retractability property ensures that G'_P is connected and therefore the existence of at least one complete search procedure able to backtrack on non-canonical graphs. However, this does not imply that all search procedures will meet the requirements if the intersection T'_P between T_P and G'_P is not a connected graph, backtracking on non-canonical structures will yield an incomplete procedure. As a consequence, T'_P must be a covering tree of G_P. We will now present procedures respecting these criteria.

3 Isomorph-Free Tree Structure Generation

We present a generation procedure for canonical configurations that can be used when the structural model only contains composition relations. A *composition* relation between type T_1 (called *composite*) and another type T_2 is a binary relation specifying that any T_2 instance can connect to at most one T_1. As an example, the relation between N and C in Figure 1 is of the composition kind, although this is not the case for the relation between C and P. In the composition case, solutions to the configuration problem can only be trees.

---

procedure **generate**(T, F)
    if canonical(T) **then** output T; **return**; **endif**
    // generate the set E = $\{(x_1,y_1), ..., (x_{|E|},y_{|E|})\}$ of acceptable unit extensions
    E = extensions(T, F)
    for $i := 1$ **to** $|E|$ **do**
        generate(T $\cup \{(x_i,y_i)\}$, F $\cup \{(x_1,$L$(y_1)),...,(x_{i-1},$L$(y_{i-1}))\})$

Fig. 2. The procedure **generate**. To generate all trees, the initial call is generate((t, $\{1\}$, $\emptyset$, $\{(1,t)\}$),$\{\}$).

The procedure listed in Figure 2 is complete, non-redundant and generates exclusively canonical structures. The function extensions(T, F) returns the sequence E of unit extensions for T that are compatible with the structural model and not forbidden by F. Then, set E contains extraneous edges e_i linking two vertices of the object set O: one vertex was already in the tree T whereas the other extremity has been created. All unit extensions that must be discarded are stored in parameter F. This avoids generating the same tree multiple times. Such a redundancy would happen if starting from T, we first produced T_1 by adding e_1 and T_2 by adding e_2, then later adding e_2 to T_1 and e_1 to T_2, resulting in producing the same tree twice. In order to avoid this, we split the search into extensions of T $\cup \{e_1\}$, and extensions of T $\cup \{e_2\}$ with e_1 removed from possible extensions. In more precise terms, not only e_1=(x, y): for all z, we forbid to add edge (x, z) if L(y)=L(z). Even if those two trees are different, they are isomorphic since swapping y and z yields the other. All such pairs (x, L(y)) are members of F, which forbids adding an edge connecting an object x to a new object of type L(y). In the general case, starting from a given tree there exist $|E|$ possible extensions. We hence split the search into $|E|$ parts by calling

$$generate(T \cup \{(x_i, y_i)\}, F \cup \{(x_1, L(y_1)), \ldots (x_{i-1}, L(y_{i-1}))\})$$

The edge sequence in E could be arbitrary if we didn't need to remove non canonical trees. However, as seen at the end of section 2, it has to be chosen according to the canonicity criterion to ensure completeness. We hence sort trees according to the total order $\preccurlyeq$ from [9], and define as canonical a tree being the $\preccurlyeq$-minimal in its isomorphism class. [9] proves that this canonicity criterion has the canonical retractability property. To ensure completeness, the edges of E must be sorted as follows: edge e_i is before e_j in E iff $T \cup \{e_i\} \preccurlyeq T \cup \{e_j\}$.

Proposition 1. *The procedure* generate *is complete.*

Proof. (sketch) We first inductively show that the edges are added by connecting new vertices to the rightmost branch of a tree, starting from the deepest vertex, and going

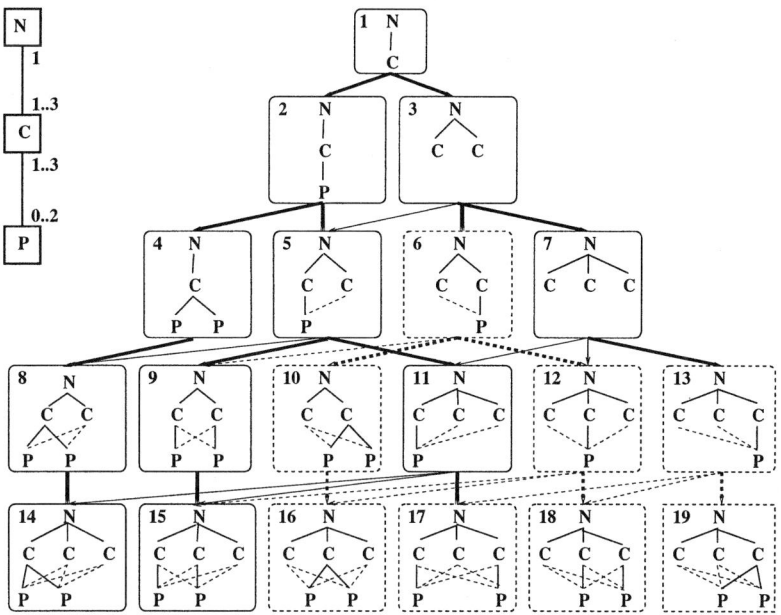

Fig. 3. A portion of the state graph for the network configuration problem. Nodes are labeled with their type alone. Trees framed in dotted lines are not canonical. Dotted lines joining nodes inside frames denote possible complementing internal edges. All edges of the state graph denote unit extensions. Edges between non canonical trees are dotted. Bold edges are explored by procedure without canonicity check. Only continuous and bold edges are transitions explored by the procedure generate.

up to the root vertex. This is true of the tree made of a single vertex (the start of a configuration). If the property holds for any tree T having n vertices, it means that the vertex y connected to an x in the right branch of the previous tree to form T now is the extremity of this branch. By inserting x, we lost the capacity to perform unit extensions to vertices located below x (by completing the set F). The sole remaining possibilities are parent nodes to x, as well as x and y, hence all the vertices in the right branch of T.

Now, from Proposition 6 in [21], we know that removing a node from the right branch preserves canonicity. As a consequence, since from any tree T, the procedure generate produces all T extensions such that the removal of their rightmost branch would yield T, it produces all the canonical trees that can be obtained by unit extension from T. The procedure is hence complete.

In our network example, if we restricted printers to be connected to at most one computer, it would become a composition relation. Then, the structural solutions of our problem would necessarily be trees. Figure 3 helps view the search tree that would result from this. The procedure would backtrack on non canonical trees 6, 13 and 17. As a consequence, the non canonical trees 10, 12, 16, 18 and 19 would not be generated either.

4 Isomorph Aware DAG Generation

We now present an instance of a procedure generating only what we will call *weakly canonical DAGs*, defined as DAGs for which the minimal covering tree for the order $\preccurlyeq$ is canonical. As the permutation that would make its covering tree canonical is the same that would make the DAG weakly canonical, this avoids generating all non weakly canonical DAGs[5].

The leading idea is to first generate a canonical tree, called the *structure tree*, then perform unit extensions that solely create internal edges. As presented before, we can generate all canonical trees very efficiently. From such canonical trees, we generate all the DAGs sharing it as a structure tree, by adding internal edges.

Figure 4 illustrates this idea. We start from a structural model containing general binary relations, from which we extract a sub-model having only composition relations[6]. The trees solution of this sub-model can be completed to produce solution DAGs of the original problem.

This procedure must however be implemented carefully to prevent from generating the same DAG multiple times. First, the possible extensions of a tree are ordered accordingly with some order $<$. Edges are always added according with $<$ and an edge e cannot be added anymore if there exists an edge e' already added and e $<$ e'. As for trees, it is obvious that this discards a certain amount of redundancies. Let a be the set of possible internal edges on a tree T, the number of DAGs that can be generated from T will be $2^{|a|}$ instead of $|a|^{|a|}$. This however does not suffice to remove all DAG redundancies. To achieve this, and for each newly generated DAG, we search for the

---

[5] The tractable generation of only one DAG per isomorphism class is an open problem.
[6] This sub-model is a covering tree of the original model!

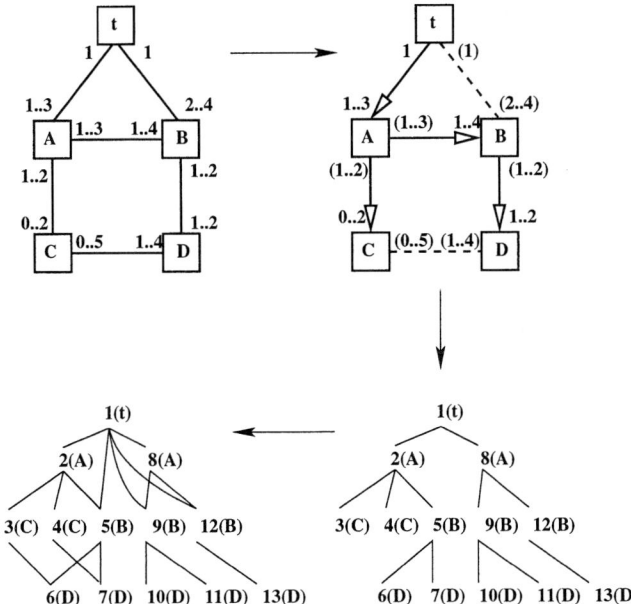

Fig. 4. Generating DAGs from trees. To the upper left, a structural model. To the upper right, a composition covering tree of the model. To the bottom right, a possible solution of the relaxed model. To the bottom left, a corresponding real solution after tree completion.

existence of a covering tree being ($\preceq$) less than the current structure tree, but not necessarily canonical. If such a covering tree exists, it means that the current DAG can be discarded whether the found covering tree is canonical or not[7]. Our procedure for finding such covering trees has the complexity of depth-first search in the worst case: $O(n)$.

Alternative Structure Tree Search Algorithm

At each newly created DAG (generated from tree T), we build the canonical covering tree T' by doing a depth-first search on the DAG. If at one point, the selected edge differs from T, the DAG is rejected as it means the current working tree T is not the canonical one anymore. For instance, in the tree number 15 in Figure 3, the internal edge connecting the first C to the second P must not be inserted, since the smallest ($\preceq$) covering tree becomes the tree number 14.

Proposition 2. *Our procedure* generate *with a call to* completion *(see fig. 5) at each canonical tree generates only once each weakly canonical DAG.*

---

[7] There exists a canonical tree that is isomorphic to it, and thus the current DAG (or an isomorphic one) is already obtained by completion when this canonical tree is generated (and our tree generation procedure ensures that it has been or will be generated during the search).

```
procedure completion(G, F)
    output G
    // generate the set E=(e₁, ...e_{|E|}) of acceptable unit extensions not in F
    E = internal-extensions(G, F)
    for i := 1 to |E| do
        completion(G ∪ {eᵢ}, F ∪ {e₁, ...eᵢ₋₁})
```

Fig. 5. The procedure **completion**

Proof. (sketch) The procedure `completion` never generates the same DAG twice from a given canonical tree and never a DAG that would result from the completion of another tree.

5 Exploiting Symmetries

The procedure `completion(G)` can be further improved to eliminate some isomorphic DAGS resulting from unit extensions. The intuition is as follows: if the internal edges e_1 and e_2 that can complete G lead to two isomorphic graphs G1 and G2, then we forbid the unit extension e_2.

For example, adding the edge (4,3) to the DAG on the bottom right of Figure 1 produces a DAG isomorphic to the one obtained by adding edge (6,3). We might want to avoid one of the two extensions.

One expensive approach is to consider each pair of graphs completed with an edge from the set E of valid extensions, and test whether they are isomorphic or not (using Nauty for instance). In case they are, we delete from E one of these edges. The major drawback of this method is that there are potentially $O(n^2)$ unit extensions for a graph with n nodes, that is $O(n^2)$ that can be canonicaly labelled (thanks to Nauty for instance), thus leading to $O(n^4)$ pairs of canonical graphs to be compared (or $O(n^2 \log n)$ comparisons if we sort the graphs). In addition, even if Nauty has a polynomial behavior on most graphs, it still has an exponential complexity in the worst case which disqualifies its use for large configuration problems.

We henceforth use an incomplete method for removing such isomorphisms, by using the automorphism group (ie, the set of symmetries) of the current DAG: the covering trees of the DAGS are canonical, hence all their subtrees are $\preccurlyeq$ sorted. Henceforth, at any level in the tree, there may exist nodes equal wrt. $\preccurlyeq$. They are interchangeable, and are immediate neighbors, and all their sub-trees are pairwise interchangeable.

Although node interchangeability is costly to detect in the general case of unrestricted graphs, it is fast and obvious in the case of canonical trees. Testing whether two sub-trees having the same parent are interchangeable simply consists in testing if they are identical, an operation of time linear complexity. As a consequence, marking which node pairs are interchangeable in a tree is an operation in $O(n^3)$ that can be done at once before the completion of a structure tree.

To account for the fact that interchangeability is lost by nodes newly connected by an internal unit extension, we introduce a Boolean marker. The connected nodes must be marked, as well as the whole list of their parents up to the root of the tree. The marking is illustrated in Figure 6 by small circles around the nodes. A search procedure can reject all DAGs in which a newly inserted internal edge results in marking a node not being the leftmost in its equivalence class of interchangeability.

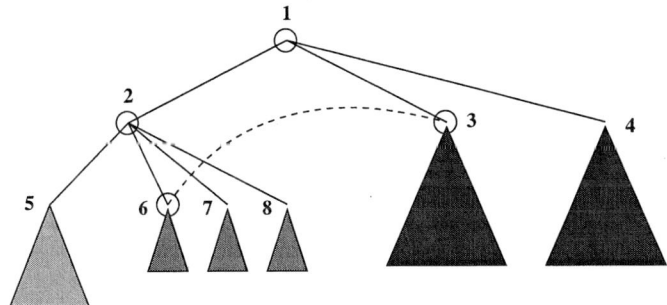

Fig. 6. Adding an internal edge and marking

In the canonical tree represented by Figure 6, the trees rooted in nodes 6, 7 and 8 are identical, and so are the trees rooted in nodes 3 and 4. If the choice of interconnecting nodes from this two groups must be made, the search procedure can select only nodes within the trees 3 and 6. No node appearing within the sub-trees rooted in 4, 7 and 8 can be connected by a newly inserted internal edge. Once a connection between 3 and 6 is established for instance, node 3 loses its interchangeability with 4, and 6 loses its interchangeability with 7 and 8.

6 Experimental Results

Our experiments were conducted for the computer-printer planning problem illustrated in Figure 1, on a 1.7 Ghz PC with 512M RAM, under Linux. We have chosen this simple problem because it is generic: it involves a cardinality constrained relation between two types, which occurs very frequently in configuration problems. It must not be seen as a real application example, but rather as a way to reveal the interest and efficiency of such a procedure for eliminating isomorphisms. Indeed, the results on real problems involving many relations would benefit from the gain on each relation. For each choice of numbers of printers and computers, we have generated all DAGs using two algorithm variants: *Covering Tree* or *ct* (generation of canonical trees, each being completed to DAGs using an ordered set of possible extensions and backtrack on DAGs that have a covering T-tree less than the current) and *full* (*ct* + backtrack on equivalent internal edges for interchangeability). We compare the number of graphs generated by both algorithms with the number of graphs that are a solution of the problem. There are as many of them as the number of bipartite graphs (canonical or not) joining a set of c vertices to p vertices: $2^{c \cdot p}$.

From Table 1 we see that the number of DAGs is significantly decreased when using the *ct* algorithm, due to the large number of avoided isomorphic DAGs. The *full* algorithm provides a good cut in the number of isomorphic DAGs, and overall computation time is also noticeably decreased.

Table 1. Results for the (C) PC - (P) printers problem. (times in seconds, "/" = time > 60 seconds).

C	P	all graphs	structure trees	ct graphs	ct time	full graphs	full time
1	3	8	4	4	0	4	0
2	3	64	16	32	0	30	0
3	3	512	46	273	0	262	0
4	3	4096	109	2234	0.01	2078	0.02
5	3	32768	219	17099	0.12	13095	0.1
6	3	262144	393	130404	1.01	69757	0.64
7	3	$2.1\ 10^6$	649	993197	8.34	329495	3.43
8	3	$1.6\ 10^7$	1006	/	/	$1.45\ 10^6$	17.23

Existing configurators are restricted to problems of limited size. Using these strategies lets us address larger problems, while avoiding the generation of useless solutions. Our computer/printer test problem should not be seen as artificial: any binary relation in an object model implies that a certain number of structures contain bipartite sub-graphs. The canonicity test for such graphs is graph iso complete, and current configurators would generate the graphs corresponding to the *all graphs* column of Table 1. These early results show that we can generate significantly fewer DAGs when the model involves only one binary relation. Should there be more than this (this is the common situation), the overall gain factor would benefit from individual gains, and in the particular case of a tree structural model it would be the product of the gains on each relation.

Insertion in a General Configuration Search

A configuration problem statement normally involves classes, relations, and constrained attributes. Generating the configuration structure is hence a fragment of the whole problem. Our approach is interesting in several respects in this general case. On the one hand, once a structure has been generated, the problem amounts to a standard CSP, hence amenable to usual techniques (including incomplete search methods). Also, as shown before, the automorphism group of the structure built is easily exploited. Further search may benefit from this in the process of instantiating attributes as well.

7 Conclusion

This work greatly extends the possibilities of dealing with configuration isomorphisms, until today limited either to the detection of the interchangeability of all yet unused individuals of each type or to the use of non configurable object counters. The generation procedures for tree-shape and vertex colored DAG structures that we have presented addresses the structural isomorphism problem of configurations and allows for important gains for any configuration problem, even of small size. Not all the non canonical structures are discarded in the general case of DAG structures. Polytime methods for eliminating more isomorphisms probably exist.

References

1. McDermott, J.P.: R1: A rule-based configurer of computer systems. Artificial Intelligence **19** (1982) 39–88
2. Barker, V., O'Connor, D., Bachant, J., Soloway, E.: Expert systems for configuration at digital: Xcon and beyond. Communications of the ACM **32** (1989) 298–318
3. Mittal, S., Falkenhainer, B.: Dynamic constraint satisfaction problems. In: Proc. of AAAI-90, Boston, MA (1990) 25–32
4. Amilhastre, J., Fargier, H., Marquis, P.: Consistency restoration and explanations in dynamic csps–application to configuration. Artificial Intelligence **135** (2002) 199–234
5. Sabin, D., Freuder, E.C.: Composite constraint satisfaction. In: Artificial Intelligence and Manufacturing Research Planning Workshop. (1996) 153–161
6. Soininen, T., Niemela, I., Tiihonen, J., Sulonen, R.: Representing configuration knowledge with weight constraint rules. In: Proc. of the AAAI Spring Symp. on Answer Set Programming: Towards Efficient and Scalable Knowledge. (2001) 195–201
7. Stumptner, M.: An overview of knowledge-based configuration. AI Communications **10(2)** (1997) 111–125
8. Mailharro, D.: A classification and constraint-based framework for configuration. AI in Engineering, Design and Manufacturing, (12) (1998) 383–397
9. Grandcolas, S., Henocque, L., Prcovic, N.: A canonicity test for configuration. In: Proceedings of CP'2003. (2003)
10. Henocque, L., Prcovic, N.: Practically handling configuration automorphisms. In: proceedings of the 16th IEEE International Conference on Tools for Artificial Intelligence, Boca Raton, Florida (2004)
11. Luks, E.M.: Isomorphism of graphs of bounded valence can be tested in polynomial time. J. Comput. System Sci. **25** (1982) 42–49
12. McKay, B.D.: Practical graph isomorphism. Congressus Numerantium **30** (1981) 45–87
13. Read, R.C.: Every one a winner or how to avoid isomorphism search when cataloguing combinatorial configurations. Annals of Discrete Mathematics **2** (1978) 107–120
14. Brinkmann, G.: Fast generation of cubic graphs. J. Graph Theory **23** (1996) 139–149
15. McKay, B.D.: Isomorph-free exhaustive generation. J. Algorithms **26** (1998) 306–324
16. Pascal Van Hentenrick, P. Flener, J.P., Agren, M.: Tractable symmetry breaking for csps with interchangeable values. In: proceedings of IJCAI 03. (2003) 277–282
17. Meseguer, P., Torras, C.: Exploiting symmetries within constraint satisfaction search. Artificial Intelligence **29(1-2)** (2001) 133–163
18. Backofen, R., Will, S.: Excluding symmetries in constraint-based search. In: Principles and Practice of Constraint Programming. (1999) 73–87
19. Gent, I., Smith, B.: Symmetry breaking during search in constraint programming. In: proceedings of ECAI. (2000)
20. Puget, J.F.: Symmetry breaking revisited. In: proceedings of CP'02. (2000)
21. Grandcolas, S., Henocque, L., Prcovic, N.: Pruning isomorphic structural sub-problems in configuration. Technical report, LSIS (2003) Available from the CoRR archive at http://arXiv.org/abs/cs/0306135.

Planning and Scheduling to Minimize Tardiness

J.N. Hooker

Carnegie Mellon University
john@hooker.tepper.cmu.edu

Abstract. We combine mixed integer linear programming (MILP) and constraint programming (CP) to minimize tardiness in planning and scheduling. Tasks are allocated to facilities using MILP and scheduled using CP, and the two are linked via logic-based Benders decomposition. We consider two objectives: minimizing the number of late tasks, and minimizing total tardiness. Our main theoretical contribution is a relaxation of the cumulative scheduling subproblem, which is critical to performance. We obtain substantial computational speedups relative to the state of the art in both MILP and CP. We also obtain much better solutions for problems that cannot be solved to optimality.

We address a planning and scheduling problem that occurs frequently in manufacturing and supply chain contexts. Tasks must be assigned to facilities and scheduled on each facility subject to release dates and due dates. Tasks assigned to a given facility may run in parallel if desired, subject to a resource constraint (cumulative scheduling). We consider two objectives: minimizing the number of late tasks, and minimizing total tardiness.

The problem can be formulated entirely as a constraint programming (CP) problem or a mixed integer/linear programming (MILP) problem. However, these models are hard to solve. By linking CP and MILP in a hybrid method, we obtain significant speedups relative to the state of the art in both MILP and CP. The linkage is achieved by logic-based Benders decomposition. The facility assignment problem becomes the master problem and is solved by MILP, while the scheduling problem becomes the subproblem (slave problem) and is solved by CP.

The primary theoretical contribution of this paper is a linear relaxation of the cumulative scheduling subproblem. We find that including such a relaxation in the master problem is essential to the success of the Benders method.

We solve problem instances in which tasks have the same release date and different due dates, although the the method is valid for different release dates as well. We obtain substantial speedups on nearly all instances relative to MILP (as represented by CPLEX), which in turn is generally faster than CP (as represented by the ILOG Scheduler). On larger instances, the hybrid method generally achieves speedups of two or three orders of magnitude when minimizing the number of late tasks, and it solves significantly more problems to optimality. There is a lesser but still significant speedup when minimizing total tardiness, and even when the hybrid method cannot obtain provably optimal solutions, it obtains much better solutions than provided by MILP in the same time period.

1 Previous Work

Logic-based Benders decomposition, which generalizes the classical Benders decomposition method [1,3], was introduced in [8] for purposes of logic circuit verification. The idea was later formally developed in [4] and applied to 0-1 programming in [7].

The application of logic-based Benders to planning and scheduling was proposed in [4]. Jain and Grossmann [10] successfully applied such a method to minimum-cost planning and scheduling problems in which the subproblems are disjunctive scheduling problems, where tasks must run one at a time, rather than cumulative scheduling problems. The Benders cuts are particularly simple in this case because the subproblem is a feasibility problem rather than an optimization problem. Thorsteinsson [11] improved on these results using a "branch-and-check" method suggested in [4].

It is less obvious how to define Benders cuts when the subproblem is an optimization problem. We showed in [5,6] how to derive effective Benders cuts for at least one such case, minimum makespan problems. The cuts are valid for cumulative as well as disjunctive scheduling, provided all tasks have the same release date. Computational tests showed the hybrid method to be 100 to 1000 times faster than MILP or CP when all tasks have the same deadline.

In this paper we address minimum tardiness problems, in which the subproblem is again an optimization problem. We obtain effective cuts by repeatedly solving the subproblem with slightly different task assignments. The idea is related to finding "minimal conflict sets" of tasks, or small sets of tasks that create infeasibility when assigned to a particular facility. Cambazard et al. [2] applied such an approach to real-time scheduling of computing resources. Here we develop cuts for an optimization rather than a feasibility subproblem.

As observed in [5,11], the success of hybrid methods in planning and scheduling relies on including a relaxation of the scheduling subproblem in the master problem. We find that deriving a useful relaxation requires deeper analysis when minimizing total tardiness than when minimizing cost or makespan. A relaxation of the cumulative scheduling problem is presented in [9], but it is expressed in terms of the start time variables, rather than the assignment variables as required for the Benders master problem. We derive here a very different relaxation in terms of 0-1 assignment variables, which is suitable for the MILP master problem.

2 The Problem

The planning and scheduling problem may be defined as follows. Each task $j \in \{1,\ldots,n\}$ is to be assigned to a facility $i \in \{1,\ldots m\}$, where it consumes processing time p_{ij} and resources at the rate c_{ij}. Each task j has release time r_j and due date d_j. The tasks assigned to facility i must be given start times s_j in such a way that the total rate of resource consumption on facility i is never more than C_i at any given time. If x_j is the facility assigned to task j, the problem may be written

$$\text{minimize } g(x,s)$$
$$\text{subject to } r_j \leq s_j, \text{ all } j \quad (a)$$
$$\sum_{j \in J_{it}(x)} c_{ij} \leq C_i, \text{ all } i,t \quad (b) \tag{1}$$

where x_j, s_j are the variables and $J_{it}(x) = \{j \mid x_j = i, s_j \leq t \leq s_j + p_{ij}\}$ is the set of tasks underway at time t in facility i.

Precedence constraints may be imposed on tasks that are assigned to the same machine. Thus one may require that tasks j and k be scheduled on the same facility, and that task j precede k, by writing the constraints $x_j = x_k$ and $s_j + p_{x_j j} \leq s_k$.

We investigate two objective functions:

- *number of late tasks*, given by $g(x,s) = \sum_j \delta(s_j + p_{x_j j} - d_j)$, where $\delta(\alpha)$ is 1 if $\alpha > 0$ and 0 otherwise.
- *total tardiness*, given by $g(x,s) = \sum_j (s_j + p_{x_j j} - d_j)^+$, where α^+ is α if $\alpha > 0$ and 0 otherwise.

3 Constraint Programming Formulation

A CP formulation of the problem can be written

$$\text{minimize } g(x,s)$$
$$\text{subject to } r_j \leq s_j, \text{ all } j \tag{2}$$
$$\text{cumulative}((s_j | x_j = i), (p_{ij} | x_j = i), (c_{ij} | x_j = i), C_i), \text{ all } i$$

where $(s_j | x_j = i)$ denotes the tuple of start times for tasks assigned to facility i. When minimizing the number of late tasks, $g(x,s) = \sum_j L_j$ where L_j is binary, and the constraint $(s_j + p_{x_j j} > d_j) \Rightarrow (L_j = 1)$ is added for each j. When minimizing total tardiness, $g(x,s) = \sum_j T_j$, and the constraints $T_j \geq s_j + p_{x_j j} - d_j$ and $T_j \geq 0$ are added for each j.

For purposes of computational testing we formulated (2) using the modeling language of OPL Studio. We used the assignAlternatives and setTimes search options specify a branching method that results in substantially better performance than the default method.

4 Mixed Integer Programming Formulation

The most straightforward MILP formulation discretizes time and enforces the resource capacity constraint at each discrete time. Let the 0-1 variable $x_{ijt} = 1$ if task j starts at discrete time t on facility i. The formulation for minimizing the number of late tasks is

$$\min \quad \sum_j L_j$$

$$\text{subject to} \quad NL_j \geq \sum_i (t + p_{ij})x_{ijt} - d_j, \quad \text{all } j,t \quad (a)$$

$$\sum_{it} x_{ijt} = 1, \quad \text{all } j \quad (b) \quad \quad (3)$$

$$\sum_j \sum_{t' \subset T_{ijt}} c_{ij}x_{ijt'} \leq C_i, \quad \text{all } i,t \quad (c)$$

$$x_{ijt} = 0, \quad \text{all } j,t \text{ with } t < r_j \text{ or } t > N - p_{ij} \quad (d)$$

where each x_{ijt} and each L_j is a 0-1 variable. Also N is the number of discrete times (starting with $t = 0$), and $T_{ijt} = \{t' \mid t - p_{ij} < t' \leq t\}$ is the set of discrete times at which a task j in progress on facility i at time t might start processing. Constraint (b) ensures that each task starts once on one facility, (c) enforces the resource limit, and (d) the time windows. The minimum tardiness problem replaces the objective function with $\sum_j T_j$ and constraint (a) with

$$T_j \geq \sum_i (t + p_{ij})x_{ijt} - d_j, \quad T_j \geq 0, \quad \text{all } j,t$$

We also investigated a smaller discrete event model suggested by [12], which uses continuous time. However, it proved much harder to solve than (3).

5 Hybrid Method for Minimizing Late Tasks

The Benders approach formulates a *master problem* that assigns tasks to facilities and a *subproblem* that schedules the tasks assigned to each facility. We write the master problem using an MILP model that minimizes the number of late tasks. In iteration h of the Benders algorithm, the master problem is

$$\text{minimize} \quad L$$

$$\text{subject to} \quad \sum_i x_{ij} = 1, \quad \text{all } j \quad (a)$$

$$\text{Benders cuts generated in iterations } 1, \ldots, h-1 \quad (b) \quad (4)$$

$$\text{relaxation of subproblem} \quad (c)$$

Here the binary variable x_{ij} is 1 when task j is assigned to facility i. The Benders cuts and relaxation will be described shortly.

Once an assignment $\bar{x}_{ij}$ of tasks to facilities is determined by solving the master problem, a cumulative scheduling subproblem is solved by CP. The subproblem decouples into a separate scheduling problem on each facility i:

$$\text{minimize} \sum_{j \in J_{hi}} L_j$$

$$\text{subject to } (s_j + p_{ij} > d_j) \Rightarrow (L_j = 1), \text{ all } j \in J_{hi} \qquad (5)$$
$$r_j \leq s_j, \text{ all } j \in J_{hi}$$
$$\text{cumulative}((s_j | j \in J_{hi}), (p_{ij} | j \in J_{hi}), (c_{ij} | j \in J_{hi}))$$

where J_{hi} is the set of tasks for which $\bar{x}_{ij} = 1$ (i.e., the tasks assigned to facility i in the master problem solution). If L_{hi}^* is the optimal value of (5), then $\sum_i L_{hi}^*$ is the minimum number of late tasks across all facilities.

At this point we know that whenever the tasks in J_{hi} (perhaps among others) are assigned to facility i, the number of late tasks on facility i is at least L_{hi}^*. This allows us to write a valid lower bound $\underline{L}_{hi}$ on the number of late tasks in facility i for any assignment of tasks to machines. Since $x_{ij} = 0$ when task j is not assigned to facility i, we have

$$\underline{L}_{hi} \geq L_{hi}^* - L_{hi}^* \sum_{j \in J_{hi}} (1 - x_{ij}), \text{ all } i \qquad (6)$$

$$\underline{L}_{hi} \geq 0, \text{ all } i$$

By summing over all facilities, we have a lower bound on the total number L of late tasks:

$$L \geq \sum_i \underline{L}_{hi} \qquad (7)$$

The inequality (7), together with (6), provides a *Benders cut* for iteration h. The cut says that the number of late tasks will be at least the number obtained in the subproblem unless a different assignment of tasks to facilities is used.

In iteration h, the Benders cuts (b) in the master problem (4) consist of inequalities (6)–(7) obtained in iterations $1, \ldots, h-1$. The algorithm terminates when the optimal value of the master problem equals the optimal value of the subproblem in the previous iteration. At any point in the algorithm, a feasible solution of the subproblem is a feasible solution of the original problem, and the optimal value of the master problem is a lower bound on the optimal value of the original problem.

Unfortunately the Benders cuts (6)–(7) are weak and do not perform well in practice. The cuts can be strengthened by identifying, for each facility i, a smaller set J_{hi} of tasks that result in the same number of late tasks. One way to do this is to track which tasks actually play a role in the determining the minimum number of late tasks, as suggested in [6]. However, since this information is not available from commercial CP solvers, the information must be obtained indirectly by repeatedly solving subproblems with different assignments of tasks to facilities.

The following approach was found to yield effective cuts with a modest amount of computation. Let $L_i(J)$ be the minimum number of late tasks on facility i when the tasks in J are assigned to facility i. First identify a set $J_{hi}^0 \subseteq J_{hi}$ of tasks that, when assigned to facility i, result in a minimum of L_{hi}^* late tasks; that is, a set J_{hi}^0 such that $L_i(J_{hi}^0) = L_{hi}^*$. This is done via the simple

Let $J_{hi}^0 = J_{hi}$.
For all $j \in J_{hi}$: if $L_i(J_{hi}^0 \setminus \{j\}) = L_{hi}^*$ then let $J_{hi}^0 = J_{hi}^0 \setminus \{j\}$.
Let $J_{hi}^1 = J_{hi}^0$.
For all $j \in J_{hi}^0$: if $L_i(J_{hi}^1 \setminus \{j\}) = L_{hi}^* - 1$ then let $J_{hi}^1 = J_{hi}^1 \setminus \{j\}$.

Fig. 1. Algorithm for generating Benders cuts when minimizing the number of late tasks

greedy algorithm in Fig. 1. Then identify a set $J_{hi}^1 \subseteq J_{hi}^0$ of tasks such that $L_i(J_{hi}^1) = L_{hi}^* - 1$, again using the algorithm of Fig. 1. The inequalities (6) can now be replaced by the generally stronger inequalities

$$\underline{L}_{hi} \geq L_{hi}^* - L_{hi}^* \sum_{j \in J_{hi}^0} (1 - x_{ij}), \text{ all } i$$

$$\underline{L}_{hi} \geq L_{hi}^* - 1 - L_{hi}^* \sum_{j \in J_{hi}^1} (1 - x_{ij}), \text{ all } i \quad (8)$$

$$\underline{L}_{hi} \geq 0, \text{ all } i$$

These cuts remain valid for any set of additional constraints that may be added to the subproblems.

It is straightforward to relax the subproblem when minimizing the number of late tasks. (It will be harder when minimizing total tardiness.) Let $J(t_1, t_2)$ be the set of tasks whose time windows are contained in $[t_1, t_2]$. Thus $J(t_1, t_2) = \{j \mid [r_j, d_j] \subseteq [t_1, t_2]\}$. When executed on facility i, these tasks span a time interval of at least

$$M = \frac{1}{C_i} \sum_{j \in J(t_1, t_2)} c_{ij} p_{ij} \quad (9)$$

If $M > t_2 - t_1$ then at least one task is late, and in fact the number of late tasks on facility i is at least

$$\frac{M - (t_2 - t_1)}{\max_{j \in J(t_1, t_2)} \{p_{ij}\}} \quad (10)$$

rounded up to the nearest integer.

Define $\bar{r}_1, \ldots, \bar{r}_{n_r}$ to be the distinct values among the release times $r_1, \ldots, r_n$ in increasing order, and similarly for $\bar{d}_1, \ldots, \bar{d}_{n_d}$. Then from (9) and (10) we have the following relaxation:

$$L \geq \sum_i L_i$$

$$L_i \geq \frac{\frac{1}{C_i} \sum_{\ell \in J(\bar{r}_j, \bar{d}_k)} c_{i\ell} p_{i\ell} x_{i\ell} - (\bar{d}_k - \bar{r}_j)}{\max_{\ell \in J(\bar{r}_j, \bar{d}_j)} \{p_{i\ell}\}}, \quad j = 1, \ldots, n_r, \ k = 1, \ldots, n_d, \text{ all } i$$

which becomes (c) in the master problem (4).

6 Hybrid Method for Minimizing Total Tardiness

In iteration h of the Benders method, the master problem for minimizing total tardiness is

$$\begin{aligned}
\text{minimize} \quad & T \\
\text{subject to} \quad & \sum_i x_{ij} = 1, \text{ all } j & (a) \\
& \text{Benders cuts for iterations } 1,\ldots,h-1 & (b) \\
& \text{relaxation of subproblem} & (c)
\end{aligned} \quad (11)$$

The subproblem again decouples into a cumulative scheduling problem for each facility i:

$$\begin{aligned}
\text{minimize} \quad & \sum_{j \in J_i} T_j \\
\text{subject to} \quad & T_j \geq s_j + p_{ij} - d_j, \text{ all } j \in J_i \\
& r_j \leq s_j, \text{ all } j \in J_i \\
& \text{cumulative}((s_j | j \in J_i), (p_{ij} | j \in J_i), (c_{ij} | j \in J_i))
\end{aligned} \quad (12)$$

We found the following scheme to generate effective Benders cuts. As before let J_{hi} be a set of tasks assigned to facility i in iteration h, and let T_{hi}^* be the resulting minimum tardiness on facility i. Let $T_i(J)$ be the minimum tardiness on facility i that results when the tasks in J are assigned to facility i, so that $T_i(J_{hi}) = T_{hi}^*$. Let Z_{hi} be the set of tasks in J_{hi} that can be removed, one at a time, without reducing the minimum tardiness. That is,

$$Z_{hi} = \{j \in J_{hi} \mid T_{hi}(J_{hi} \setminus \{j\}) = T_{hi}^*\}$$

Finally, let T_{hi}^0 be the minimum tardiness that results from removing the tasks in Z_{hi} all at once, so that $T_{hi}^0 = T_i(J_{hi} \setminus Z_{hi})$. Thus any or all tasks in Z_{hi} can be removed from facility i without reducing the minimum tardiness below T_{hi}^0. This yields the following Benders cuts in iteration h:

$$\begin{aligned}
T \geq T_{hi}^0 - T_{hi}^0 \sum_{j \in J_{hi} \setminus Z_{hi}} (1 - x_{ij}), \text{ all } i \\
T \geq T_{hi}^* - T_{hi}^* \sum_{j \in J_{hi}} (1 - x_{ij}), \text{ all } i
\end{aligned} \quad (13)$$

The second cut is redundant and can be eliminated for a given h, i when $T_{hi}^0 = T_{hi}^*$. This in fact substantially reduces the size of master problem, since computational testing suggests that $T_{hi}^0 = T_{hi}^*$ very often.

These cuts are again valid for any set of additional constraints that may be added to the subproblem.

7 Relaxation for Minimizing Total Tardiness

Our relaxation of the minimum tardiness scheduling subproblem has two parts. The first and simpler part is similar to the relaxation obtained for minimizing the number of late tasks. It is based on the following lemma. Recall that $J(t_1, t_2)$ is the set of jobs with time windows between t_1 and t_2.

Lemma 1. *Consider a minimum total tardiness problem in which tasks $j = 1, \ldots, n$ with time windows $[r_j, d_j]$ are scheduled on a single facility i, where $\min_j \{r_j\} = 0$. The total tardiness incurred by any feasible solution is bounded below by*

$$\left(\frac{1}{C_i} \sum_{j \in J(0, d_k)} p_{ij} c_{ij} - d_k \right)^+$$

for each $k = 1, \ldots, n$.

Proof. For any k, the last scheduled task in the set $J(0, d_k)$ can finish no earlier than time $t = \frac{1}{C_i} \sum_{j \in J(0, d_k)} p_{ij} c_{ij}$. Since the last task has due date no later than d_k, its tardiness is no less than $(t - d_k)^+$. Thus total tardiness is no less than $(t - d_k)^+$.

This gives rise to a relaxation consisting of

$$T \geq \frac{1}{C_i} \sum_{j \in J(0, d_k)} p_{ij} c_{ij} x_{ij} - d_k, \quad \text{all } i, k \qquad (14)$$

and $T \geq 0$.

The second part of the relaxation can be developed on basis of the following lemma. For each facility i let π_i be a permutation of $\{1, \ldots, n\}$ such that $p_{i\pi_i(1)} c_{i\pi_i(1)} \leq \cdots \leq p_{i\pi_i(n)} c_{i\pi_i(n)}$.

Lemma 2. *Consider a minimum tardiness problem in which tasks $1, \ldots, n$ with time windows $[r_j, d_j]$ are scheduled on a single facility i. Assume $\min_j \{r_j\} = 0$ and index the tasks so that $d_1 \leq \cdots \leq d_n$. Then the total tardiness T of any feasible solution is bounded below by $\underline{T} = \sum_{k=1}^{n} \underline{T}_k$, where*

$$\underline{T}_k = \left(\frac{1}{C_i} \sum_{j=1}^{k} p_{i\pi_i(j)} c_{i\pi_i(j)} - d_k \right)^+, \quad k = 1, \ldots, n$$

Proof. Consider any feasible solution of the one-facility minimum tardiness problem, in which tasks $1, \ldots, n$ are respectively scheduled at times $t_1, \ldots, t_n$. Thus

$$T = \sum_{k=1}^{n} (t_k + p_{ik} - d_k)^+ \qquad (15)$$

Let $\sigma_0(1), \ldots, \sigma_0(n)$ be the order in which tasks are scheduled in this solution, so that $t_{\sigma_0(1)} \leq \cdots \leq t_{\sigma_0(n)}$. For an arbitrary permutation σ of $\{1, \ldots, n\}$ let

$$\underline{T}_k(\sigma) = \left(\frac{1}{C_i}\sum_{j=1}^{k} p_{i\pi_i(j)}c_{i\pi_i(j)} - d_{\sigma(k)}\right)^+ \tag{16}$$

and $\underline{T}(\sigma) = \sum_{k=1}^{n} \underline{T}_k(\sigma)$.

We show first that $T \geq \underline{T}(\sigma_0)$. Since σ_0 is a permutation we can write (15) as

$$T = \sum_{k=1}^{n} \left(t_{\sigma_0(k)} + p_{i\sigma_0(k)} - d_{\sigma_0(k)}\right)^+$$

We observe that

$$t_{\sigma_0(k)} + p_{i\sigma_0(k)} \geq \frac{1}{C_i}\sum_{j=1}^{k} p_{i\sigma_0(j)}c_{i\sigma_0(j)} \geq \frac{1}{C_i}\sum_{j=1}^{k} p_{i\pi_i(j)}c_{i\pi_i(j)}$$

where the first inequality is based on the areas required by tasks, and the second inequality is due to the definition of π_i. From this and (16) it follows that $T \geq \underline{T}(\sigma_0)$.

Now suppose a bubble sort is performed on the integers $\sigma_0(1), \ldots, \sigma_0(n)$ so as to put them in increasing order, and let $\sigma_0, \ldots, \sigma_P$ be the resulting series of permutations. Thus $(\sigma_P(1), \ldots, \sigma_P(n)) = (1, \ldots, n)$, and σ_{p+1} is obtained from σ_p by swapping two adjacent terms $\sigma_p(k)$ and $\sigma_p(k+1)$, where $\sigma_p(k) > \sigma_p(k+1)$. This means σ_p and σ_{p+1} are the same except that $\sigma_{p+1}(k) = \sigma_p(k+1)$ and $\sigma_{p+1}(k+1) = \sigma_p(k)$. Since $T^* \geq \underline{T}(\sigma_0)$ and $\underline{T}(\sigma_P) = \underline{T}$, to prove the theorem it suffices to show $\underline{T}(\sigma_0) \geq \cdots \geq \underline{T}(\sigma_P)$.

Thus we consider any two adjacent permutations σ_p, σ_{p+1} and show that $\underline{T}(\sigma_p) \geq \underline{T}(\sigma_{p+1})$. We observe that

$$\begin{aligned}\underline{T}(\sigma_p) &= \sum_{j=1}^{k-1}\underline{T}_j(\sigma_p) + \underline{T}_k(\sigma_p) + \underline{T}_{k+1}(\sigma_p) + \sum_{j=k+2}^{n}\underline{T}_j(\sigma_p) \\ \underline{T}(\sigma_{p+1}) &= \sum_{j=1}^{k-1}\underline{T}_j(\sigma_p) + \underline{T}_k(\sigma_{p+1}) + \underline{T}_{k+1}(\sigma_{p+1}) + \sum_{j=k+2}^{n}\underline{T}_j(\sigma_p)\end{aligned} \tag{17}$$

Using (16), we note that $\underline{T}_k(\sigma_p) = (a-B)^+$, $\underline{T}_{k+1}(\sigma_p) = (A-b)^+$, $\underline{T}_k(\sigma_{p+1}) = (a-b)^+$, and $\underline{T}_{k+1}(\sigma_{p+1}) = (A-B)^+$ if we set

$$a = \frac{1}{C_i}\sum_{j=1}^{k} p_{i\pi_i(j)}c_{i\pi_i(j)}, \quad A = \frac{1}{C_i}\sum_{j=1}^{k+1} p_{i\pi_i(j)}c_{i\pi_i(j)}$$

$$b = d_{\sigma_p(k+1)}, \quad B = d_{\sigma_p(k)}$$

Note that $a \leq A$. Also, $b \leq B$ since $\sigma_p(k) > \sigma_p(k+1)$ and $d_1 \leq \cdots \leq d_n$. From (17) we have

$$\underline{T}(\sigma_p) - \underline{T}(\sigma_{p+1}) = (a-B)^+ + (A-b)^+ - (a-b)^+ - (A-B)^+$$

9 Computational Results

Table 3 illustrates the importance of relaxations in the hybrid approach, particularly when minimizing total tardiness. Lemmas 1 and 2 are clearly critical to the success of the hybrid method, especially when there are more than 16 tasks or so.

We solved randomly generated problems with MILP (using CPLEX), CP (using the ILOG Scheduler), and the logic-based Benders method. All three methods were implemented with OPL Studio, using the OPL script language.

Table 2. Computational results for minimum tardiness problems on three facilities. Computation is terminated after two hours (7200 seconds).

Tasks	Time (sec)			Hybrid/ MILP speedup	Best solution value found[1]		Benders lower bound[2]	Instance
	CP	MILP	Hybrid		MILP	Benders		
10	13	4.7	2.6	1.8	**10**	**10**		2
	1.1	6.4	1.6	4.0	**10**	**10**		1
	1.4	6.4	1.6	4.0	**16**	**16**		4
	4.6	32	4.1	7.8	**17**	**17**		5
	8.1	33	22	1.5	**24**	**24**		3
12	4.7	0.7	0.2	3.5	**0**	**0**		5
	14	0.6	0.1	6.0	**0**	**0**		1
	25	0.7	0.2	3.5	**1**	**1**		3
	19	15	2.4	6.3	**9**	**9**		4
	317	25	12	2.1	**15**	**15**		2
14	838	7.0	6.1	1.2	**1**	**1**		2
	7159	34	3.7	9.2	**2**	**2**		3
	1783	45	19	2.4	**15**	**15**		5
	> 7200	73	40	1.8	**19**	**19**		1
	> 7200	> 7200	3296	>2.2	26	**26**		4
16	> 7200	19	1.4	14	**0**	**0**		2
	> 7200	46	2.1	22	**0**	**0**		5
	> 7200	52	4.2	12	**4**	**4**		4
	> 7200	1105	156	7.1	**20**	**20**		3
	> 7200	3424	765	4.5	**31**	**31**		1
18		187	2.8	67	**0**	**0**		5
		15	5.3	2.8	**3**	**3**		4
		46	49	0.9	**5**	**5**		3
		256	47	5.5	**11**	**11**		1
		> 7200	1203	>6.0	14	**11**		2
20		105	18	5.8	**0**	**0**		1
		4141	23	180	**1**	**1**		5
		39	29	1.3	**4**	**4**		2
		1442	332	4.3	**8**	**8**		3
		> 7200	> 7200		75	37	9	4
22		6.3	19	0.3	**0**	**0**		4
		584	37	16	**2**	**2**		1
		> 7200	> 7200		120	40	7	3
		> 7200	> 7200		162	46	11	5
		> 7200	> 7200		375	141[3]	34	2
24		10	324	0.03	**0**	**0**		3
		> 7200	94	>77	20	**0**		5
		> 7200	110	>65	57	**0**		4
		> 7200	> 7200		20	5	3	2
		> 7200	> 7200		25	7	1	1

[1] Values in boldface are proved optimal.
[2] When omitted, the lower bound is equal to the optimal value shown in the previous column.
[3] Best known solution is 128, obtained using a slightly weaker relaxation.

Table 3. Effect of relaxations on performance of the hybrid method. Computation time in seconds is shown.

Tasks	Minimizing late tasks:		Minimizing tardiness:		Instance
	with relaxation	without relaxation	with relaxation	without relaxation	
16	0.5	2.6	1.4	4.4	2
	0.4	1.5	2.1	6.5	5
	0.2	1.3	4.2	30	4
	2.7	4.2	156	199	3
	24	18	765	763	1
18	0.1	1.1	2.8	10	5
	0.2	0.7	5.3	17	4
	3.4	3.3	47	120	1
	1.4	15	49	354	3
	8.5	11	1203	5102	2
20	0.4	88	18	151	1
	2.3	9.7	23	1898	5
	5.0	63	29	55	2
	11	19	332	764	3
	166	226	>7200	>7200	4

Table 1 shows computational results for minimizing the number of late tasks on three facilities using CP, MILP and the hybrid method. Since problem difficulty tends to increase with the minimum number of late tasks, the instances are ordered accordingly for each problem size. The problem instance identifier k appears in the last column. The instances are named ddnj3mk, where n is the number of tasks and k the instance identifier. The instances are available at the web site web.tepper.cmu.edu/jnh/planning.htm.

On all but two problem instances the hybrid method is faster than MILP, which in turn is generally faster than CP. The advantage of the hybrid method becomes greater as the instances grow in size. The speedup is generally two or three orders of magnitude for instances with 16 or more tasks. The average speedup factor relative to MILP is 295 for these instances. This is almost certainly a substantial underestimate for the instances averaged, since the MILP solver was cut off after two hours. (The average omits instances in which the hybrid method was also cut off.) In addition MILP failed to solve 10 instances, while the hybrid method failed to solve only one instance.

Table 2 shows computational results for minimizing total tardiness. Again the hybrid method is almost always faster than MILP, which is faster than CP. The advantage of the hybrid approach is not as great as in the previous table, but the speedup factor is still significant on instances with 16 or more tasks. The average speedup factor on these instances is 25, which is again an underestimate for these instances. (The average omits instances for which the hybrid method was also cut off.)

The hybrid method failed to solve 6 of the 40 instances to optimality, only a modest improvement over the 10 that were intractable for MILP. However, when the hybrid method failed to find provably optimal solutions, it obtained much better feasible solutions than obtained by MILP in the same two-hour period. In most cases these solutions were found very early in the solution process. Table 2 also shows the lower bounds obtained from the master problem, which in these instances are not very tight.

10 Conclusions

We find that integrating CP and MILP through a Benders scheme can substantially improve on the state of the art in planning and scheduling to minimize tardiness. The hybrid method is often two or three orders of magnitude faster than CP or MILP when minimizing the number of late tasks, and it solves significantly more problems. It is significantly faster when minimizing total tardiness, and when it fails to solve the problem to optimality, it nonetheless finds a much better feasible solution in the same time period.

The problems become hard for all the methods examined when there are more than a few late tasks in the optimal solution. However, in such cases it is probably best to relax some of the time windows so as to reflect scheduling priorities, perhaps by postponing due dates for less critical tasks. This makes the problem easier to solve and yields a more meaningful compromise solution in practice.

References

1. Benders, J. F., Partitioning procedures for solving mixed-variables programming problems, *Numerische Mathematik* **4** (1962) 238–252.
2. Cambazard, H., P.-E. Hladik, A.-M. Déplanche, N. Jussien, and Y. Trinquet, Decomposition and learning for a hard real time task allocation algorithm, in M. Wallace, ed., *Principles and Practice of Constraint Programming (CP 2004)*, Lecture Notes in Computer Science **3258**, Springer (2004).
3. Geoffrion, A. M., Generalized Benders decomposition, *Journal of Optimization Theory and Applications* **10** (1972) 237–260.
4. Hooker, J. N., *Logic-based Methods for Optimization: Combining Optimization and Constraint Satisfaction*, John Wiley & Sons (2000).
5. Hooker, J. N., A hybrid method for planning and scheduling, in M. Wallace, ed., *Principles and Practice of Constraint Programming (CP 2004)*, LNCS **3258**, 305–316.
6. Hooker, J. N., A hybrid method for planning and scheduling, *Constraints*, to appear.
7. Hooker, J. N. and G. Ottosson, Logic-based Benders decomposition, *Mathematical Programming* **96** (2003) 33–60.
8. Hooker, J. N., and Hong Yan, Logic circuit verification by Benders decomposition, in V. Saraswat and P. Van Hentenryck, eds., *Principles and Practice of Constraint Programming: The Newport Papers*, MIT Press (Cambridge, MA, 1995) 267–288.
9. Hooker, J. N., and Hong Yan, A relaxation for the cumulative constraint, in P. Van Hentenryck, ed., *Principles and Practice of Constraint Programming (CP2002)*, Lecture Notes in Computer Science **2470** (2002) 686–690.
10. Jain, V., and I. E. Grossmann, Algorithms for hybrid MILP/CP models for a class of optimization problems, *INFORMS Journal on Computing* **13** (2001) 258–276.
11. Thorsteinsson, E. S., Branch-and-Check: A hybrid framework integrating mixed integer programming and constraint logic programming, *Lecture Notes in Computer Science* **2239** (2001) 16–30.
12. Türkay, M., and I. E. Grossmann, Logic-based MINLP algorithms for the optimal synthesis of process networks, *Computers and Chemical Engineering* **20** (1996) 959–978.

Search Heuristics and Heavy-Tailed Behaviour

Tudor Hulubei and Barry O'Sullivan

Cork Constraint Computation Centre,
Department of Computer Science, University College Cork, Ireland
tudor@hulubei.net, b.osullivan@cs.ucc.ie

Abstract. The heavy-tailed phenomenon that characterises the runtime distributions of backtrack search procedures has received considerable attention over the past few years. Some have conjectured that heavy-tailed behaviour is largely due to the characteristics of the algorithm used. Others have conjectured that problem structure is a significant contributor. In this paper we attempt to explore the former hypothesis, namely we study how variable and value ordering heuristics impact the heavy-tailedness of runtime distributions of backtrack search procedures. We demonstrate that heavy-tailed behaviour can be eliminated from particular classes of random problems by carefully selecting the search heuristics, even when using chronological backtrack search. We also show that combinations of good search heuristics can eliminate heavy tails from Quasigroups with Holes of order 10, and give some insights into why this is the case. These results motivate a more detailed analysis of the effects that variable and value ordering can have on heavy-tailedness. We show how combinations of variable and value ordering heuristics can result in a runtime distribution being *inherently heavy-tailed*. Specifically, we show that even if we were to use an Oracle to refute insoluble subtrees optimally, for some combinations of heuristics we would still observe heavy-tailed behaviour. Finally, we study the distributions of refutation sizes found using different combinations of heuristics and gain some further insights into what characteristics tend to give rise to heavy-tailed behaviour.

1 Introduction

The Italian-born Swiss economist Vilfredo Pareto first introduced the theory of non-standard probability distributions in 1897 in the context of income distribution. These distributions have been used to model real-world phenomena, from weather forecasting to stock market analysis. More recently, they have been used to model the cost of combinatorial search methods. Exceptionally hard instances have been observed amongst certain classes of constraint satisfaction problems, such as graph colouring [12], SAT [7], random problems [2, 8, 20, 21], and quasigroup completion problems [10]. In studying this phenomenon, researchers have used a wide range of systematic search algorithms such as chronological backtracking, forward-checking, Davis-Putnam and MAC. It is widely believed that the more sophisticated the search algorithm, the less likely it is that the exceptionally hard problem instances will be observed.

Instances that are exceptionally hard occur in the under-constrained area and are often harder than those in the critically constrained region [21]. For a proper understanding of search behaviour one must study the runtime distributions [8] associated with either repeatedly solving a single instance with a randomised algorithm, or with solving a large ensemble of instances of some class of problems. Some runtime distributions exhibit an extremely large variance which can be described by heavy-tailed distributions whose tails have power-law decay. Gomes et al. [9] provided an overview of the heavy-tailed behaviour previously observed near the phase transition in NP-complete problems and introduced a rapid randomised restarts strategy aimed at avoiding the long tails. More recently, Gomes et al. [8] studied the transition between heavy-tailed and non-heavy-tailed behaviour in runtime distributions for random problems and have characterised when the phenomenon occurs and when it does not.

The motivation behind the work we present in this paper comes from a number of interesting observations we made while reproducing the random problem experiments presented by Gomes et al., particularly while studying the heavy tail behaviour in the context of MAC [19]. We observed that once we enhanced MAC with any of the well-known standard variable ordering heuristics, such as min-domain [11], max-degree, min-dom/ddeg[1] [3], brelaz [5] and min-dom/wdeg [4, 17], heavy tails cannot be observed even for problems with 100 variables, for any density and tightness setting. Moreover, for the random problems used by Gomes et al. in their experiments with chronological backtrack search, we no longer observed heavy tails when we used min-dom/wdeg.

Some have conjectured that heavy-tailed behaviour is largely due to the characteristics of the algorithm used to solve the problems, in particular that the search algorithm makes a mistake that results in a significant amount of work being required to recover from it. In this paper we attempt to explore this hypothesis in detail. We show how variable and value ordering heuristics impact the heavy-tailed phenomenon one observes in the runtime distributions of backtrack search procedures. Our analysis focuses on the MAC algorithm while solving a large ensemble of satisfiable instances of the Quasigroups with Holes (QWH) problem, encoded as a binary CSP. We combine different variable and value ordering heuristics with MAC to obtain a suite of algorithms that we can study. Our approach is based on analysing the refutations of insoluble (sub)trees encountered by MAC as it finds the first solution [13].

In this paper we present the following observations and results:

1. We observe that heavy-tailed behaviour associated with the runtime distribution of MAC on QWH of order 10 (QWH-10) can be eliminated by carefully selecting the search heuristics.
2. We perform a more detailed analysis of the effects that variable and value orderings have on heavy-tailedness. We show how combinations of variable and value ordering heuristics can result in a problem being *inherently heavy-tailed*. Specifically, we show that even if we were able use an Oracle to refute insoluble subtrees optimally, for some combinations of heuristics we would still observe heavy-tailed behaviour.
3. Finally, we study the distribution of refutations found using different combinations of heuristics and gain some further insights into what characteristics tend to give rise to heavy-tailed behaviour. Such a detailed analysis is the first of its kind to be reported in the literature.

---
[1] In this paper we abbreviate dynamic-degree as 'ddeg' and weighted-degree as 'wdeg'.

2 Motivation and Summary

Two important questions one can attempt to address when studying heavy-tailed behaviour are *when* does the phenomenon occur, and *why*. Gomes et al. [8] have characterised *when* the phenomenon occurs, in this paper we focus on studying the reasons *why*.

Our work is motivated by the observation that even when using chronological backtracking, for certain classes of problems heavy tails can be eliminated by using carefully chosen search heuristics. Runtime distributions are sometimes characterised by long tails, or *heavy tails*, and are generally modelled using the expression $1 - F(x) = P\{X > x\} \sim Cx^{-\alpha}, x > 0$, where $F(x)$ is the cumulative distribution function (CDF) of a probability distribution function $f(x)$ (PDF), and C and α are constants

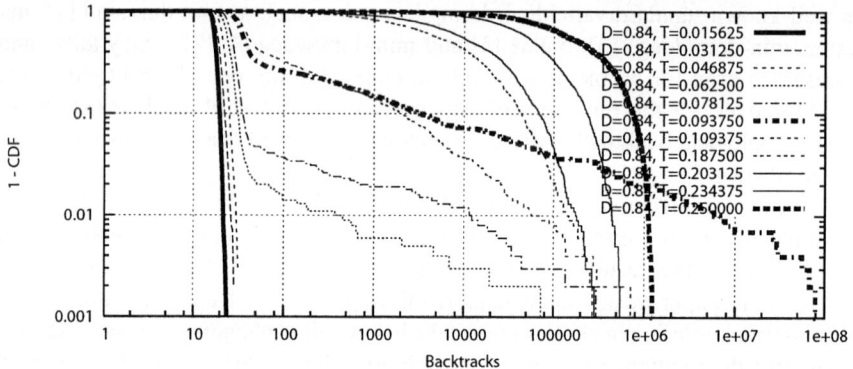

(a) random variable and value orderings

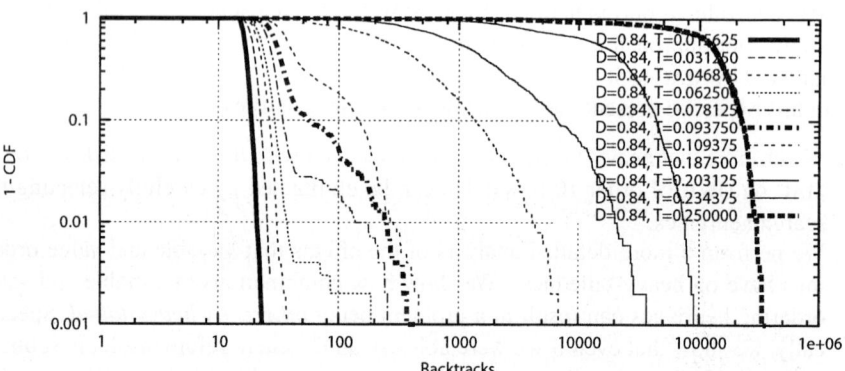

(b) min-dom/wdeg variable and random value orderings. Since chronological backtracking does no propagation, in this case min-dom/wdeg is effectively max-wdeg.

Fig. 1. The effect of the variable ordering on the cumulative distribution function of backtracks in random problems using chronological backtracking. Problems instances are from a Model B generator: 17 variables, 8 values, density 0.84, various tightness settings.

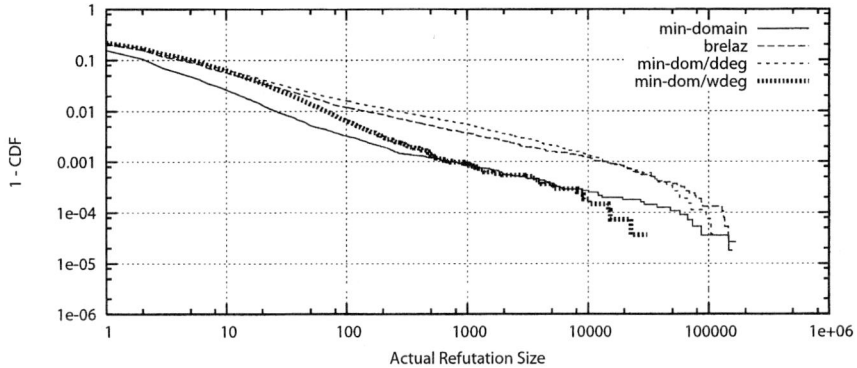

(a) random value ordering heuristic and various variable orderings

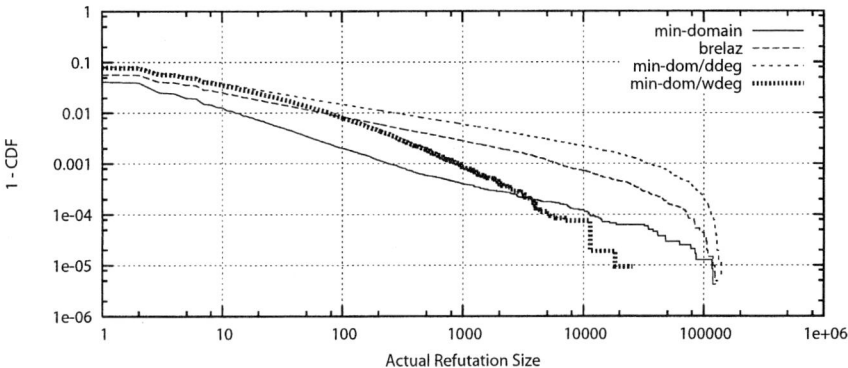

(b) min-conflicts value ordering heuristic and various variable orderings

Fig. 2. Cumulative distribution function of the actual refutation size for MAC solving QWH-10 with different variable and value ordering heuristics. Note that when using a min-conflicts value ordering and a min-dom/wdeg variable ordering we no longer observe heavy tails (Figure 2(b)).

with $\alpha \in (0, 2)$ and $C > 0$. A near-straight line in a log-log plot for $1 - F(x)$, with a slope equal to $-\alpha$, is a clear sign of heavy-tailed behaviour. For example, in Figure 1(a) we present results similar to those presented by Gomes et al. [8]. In this figure we use a chronological backtrack search procedure that uses both random variable and value orderings, solving problems with different levels of constrainedness (Model B; instances with 17 variables, 8 values, density 0.84, and tightness between 0.015 and 0.25, the point where the phase transition occurs). This figure shows that heavy-tailed behaviour can be observed in problems that are in the easy region, far from the phase transition, but are not necessarily trivial. However, as we approach the phase transition such behaviour disappears as instances become uniformly difficult.

In Figure 1(b), we present results for the same problems, but with the variable ordering changed to min-dom/wdeg [4, 17]. Note that this change is sufficient to eliminate heavy tails from these problems since no straight line can be observed for any tightness. Clearly, the change in variable ordering had a dramatic impact on the runtime distribution.

A common intuitive understanding of the extreme variability of the runtime of backtracking is that the search procedure sometimes must refute a very large inconsistent subtree, causing considerable "thrashing". In our efforts to gain an understanding of this intuition, we consider how search ordering affects the runtime distribution of MAC, rather than chronological backtracking, as it is one of the most commonly used algorithms in constraint satisfaction. We study its runtime distributions over many instances of QWH-10 for several configurations of the algorithm. By changing the variable and value ordering heuristics used, we vary MAC's "quality", essentially creating different algorithms that we can use for our investigation. As mentioned earlier, we used the following well-known *variable ordering heuristics*: min-domain [11], max-degree, min-dom/ddeg [3], brelaz [5] and min-dom/wdeg [4, 17]. As *value ordering heuristics*, we used max-conflicts, random and min-conflicts.

In Figure 2 we present MAC's runtime distributions when solving instances of QWH-10 with different variable and value ordering heuristics[2]. When using a random value ordering heuristic, as presented in Figure 2(a), we observe heavy-tailed behaviour for every variable ordering heuristic studied. However, when we replace the value ordering with min-conflicts, as presented in Figure 2(b), we no longer observe heavy tails when using the min-dom/wdeg variable ordering. Instead, for this configuration, we can see that the runtime distribution has become non-heavy-tailed, characterised by a curve in the log-log plot. Clearly, ordering heuristics also make a significant difference on this problem's runtime distribution.

As we will show later in this paper, there are a number of factors at play that explain the effects that ordering heuristics have on heavy-tailed behaviour.

3 Definitions and Problems

Definition 1 (Binary Constraint Satisfaction Problem). *We define a binary* CSP *as a 3-tuple* $P \triangleq \langle V, D, C \rangle$ *where V is a finite set of n variables $V \triangleq \{V_1, \ldots, V_n\}$, D is a set of finite domains $D \triangleq \{D(V_1), \ldots, D(V_n)\}$ such that $D(V_i)$ is the finite set of possible values for V_i, and C is a finite set of constraints such that each $C_{ij} \in C$ is a subset of $D(V_i) \times D(V_j)$ specifying the combinations of values allowed between V_i and V_j, where $i < j$. We say that P is arc-consistent (AC) if $\forall v_k \in D(V_i)$ and $\forall j$ such that $C_{ij} \in C$, $\exists v_l \in D(V_j)$ with $(v_k, v_l) \in C_{ij}$. An assignment $A_{ik} \triangleq \langle V_i = v_k \rangle$ represents a reduction of $D(V_i)$ to $\{v_k\} \subseteq D(V_i)$. A solution to P is a set of distinct assignments $\mathcal{S} \triangleq \{A_{l_1 k_1}, \ldots, A_{l_n k_n} | (v_{k_i}, v_{k_j}) \in C_{ij}\}$.*

Definition 2 (Search Algorithm). *A search algorithm $\Theta \triangleq \langle \Lambda, \Delta, \prec_V, \prec_v \rangle$ is a combination of a branching method Λ, a consistency enforcement method Δ, a variable ordering $\prec_V$ and a value ordering $\prec_v$, both of which can be either static or dynamic.*

---

[2] In Figure 2, and in the remainder of the paper, we measure search effort in terms of "refutation sizes", as this allows us to compare against search effort measured in terms of "optimal refutation sizes". Refutations are introduced in Section 3.

Definition 3 (Search Tree). *A search tree $\mathcal{T}$ for a problem P is a set of nodes and arcs. Each node corresponds to a set of assignments, $\mathcal{N} \triangleq \{A_{l_1 k_1}, \ldots, A_{l_{p-1} k_{p-1}}, A_{l_p k_p}\}$, totally ordered by a dynamic variable ordering heuristic $\prec_V$. The root of the search tree is a special node $\mathcal{R} \triangleq \emptyset$. Two nodes $\mathcal{N}_1$ and $\mathcal{N}_2$ are connected by an arc if $\exists A_{ij}$ such that $\mathcal{N}_2 = \mathcal{N}_1 \cup A_{ij}$, in which case we say that $\mathcal{N}_1$ is the parent of $\mathcal{N}_2$, and $\mathcal{N}_2$ is the child of $\mathcal{N}_1$. For every node $\mathcal{N}$, its children are totally ordered by a dynamic value ordering heuristic $\prec_v$.*

Search trees are defined in the context of a specific search algorithm. For a particular CSP instance P, and search algorithm Θ, a one-to-one mapping exists between the nodes in the search tree $\mathcal{T}$ and the assignments made by Θ.

3.1 Mistake Points and Refutations

To study the effects that variable and value ordering heuristics have on heavy-tailedness, we focus on the refutations of the mistakes made by each algorithm studied.

Definition 4 (Mistake Point). *For a soluble problem P, a mistake point $\mathcal{M}$ is a node identified by a set of assignments $\mathcal{M} \triangleq \{A_{l_1 k_1}, \ldots, A_{l_{p-1} k_{p-1}}, A_{l_p k_p}\}$, totally ordered by $\prec_V$, for which $\mathcal{M} \setminus \{A_{l_p k_p}\}$ can be extended to a solution, but $\mathcal{M}$ cannot. Since an insoluble problem does not admit any solutions, we define the mistake point associated with an insoluble problem as the root of its search tree.*

Informally, a mistake point corresponds to an assignment that, given past assignments, cannot lead to a solution even though, in the case of a soluble problem, a solution exists. Whenever the value ordering heuristic makes such a mistake, the role of the variable ordering heuristic is to guide the search out of that insoluble search tree as quickly as possible. However, it is important to realise that the actual set of mistake points encountered during search is also dependent upon the variable ordering used.

For a soluble problem P, let $P_{\mathcal{M}} \triangleq \{V_{\mathcal{M}}, D_{\mathcal{M}}, C_{\mathcal{M}}\}$ be the insoluble (sub)problem corresponding to $\mathcal{M}$, where $V_{\mathcal{M}} \triangleq V \setminus \{V_{l_1}, \ldots, V_{l_p}\}$, $C_{\mathcal{M}} \triangleq \{C_{ij} | V_i, V_j \in V_{\mathcal{M}}, C_{ij} \in C\}$, and $D_{\mathcal{M}}$ is the set of current domains after arc-consistency has been restored to reflect the domain reductions due to $\mathcal{M}$. If P is insoluble, as a notational convenience, we define $\mathcal{M} \triangleq \emptyset$ and $P_{\mathcal{M}}$ as the arc-consistent version of P. For brevity, we will refer to the *insoluble (sub)tree* rooted at a mistake point and its corresponding *insoluble (sub)problem* interchangeably.

Definition 5 (Refutations). *Given a search algorithm Θ, a **refutation** for a given insoluble (sub)problem $P_{\mathcal{M}}$, rooted at mistake point $\mathcal{M}$, is simply the corresponding search tree $\mathcal{T}_{\mathcal{M}}$. We will refer to $|\mathcal{T}_{\mathcal{M}}|$, the number of nodes in $\mathcal{T}_{\mathcal{M}}$, as the size of the refutation.*

We study the refutations found using a version of MAC that uses AC-3 [18] for consistency enforcement and selects values randomly. Also, our version of MAC employs k-way branching [22], rather than binary branching, so that selecting a variable V_i creates $|D(V_i)|$ branches in the search tree. Our goal is to determine how close to optimality are the refutations obtained when well known variable ordering heuristics, with randomly broken ties, are substituted for $\prec_V$. For each heuristic $\prec_V$, we first collect the mistake points it generates when using MAC (note that each variable ordering heuristic will generate a different set of mistake points). When we analyse MAC in conjunction with a certain $\prec_V$ on a mistake point $\mathcal{M}$, we will refer to the refutation for the (sub)problem $P_\mathcal{M}$ as the *actual refutation*. We will contrast the actual refutation with the *optimal refutation* for $P_\mathcal{M}$, obtained by replacing $\prec_V$ with a new variable ordering heuristic $\overline{\prec_V}$ s.t. $|\mathcal{T}_\mathcal{M}|$ is minimised.

Sometimes, when the optimal refutation is hard to find, we compute the *quasi-optimal refutation*, defined as the smallest refutation whose height does not exceed that of the actual refutation. By selecting variables based on a depth-first traversal of the tree of minimum size, $\overline{\prec_V}$ causes MAC to generate the smallest possible search tree proving insolubility for $P_\mathcal{M}$. Our experiments show that it is very rare that the quasi-optimal refutation is larger than the optimal (see Table 1). By accepting quasi-optimality, we can use the height of the actual refutation as an upper bound on the height of the optimal one, dramatically speeding-up the search for better refutations.

When searching for the quasi-optimal refutation it is oftentimes useful to compute a lower bound on its size. Firstly, this can improve the performance of the search since the search can be stopped when (and if) the smallest refutation found so far reaches that lower bound. Secondly, the lower bound can be plotted alongside with the quasi-optimal refutation size to visually reduce the factor of uncertainty introduced by quasi-optimality. Optimal refutations may, in theory, be smaller than quasi-optimal refutations, but they cannot be smaller than the lower bound.

Definition 6 (Refutation Size Lower Bound). *An n-level lower bound for a refutation corresponding to a mistake point is the minimum number of nodes that an n-level look-ahead determines any refutation for that particular (sub)tree must have.*

A lower bound can be computed using the look-ahead method described in [13]. Such a lower bound is quite conservative, as there is absolutely no guarantee that an optimal refutation of that size exists, although that is often the case with QWH-10. We briefly review the look-ahead methodology here.

Whenever a variable V_i is selected at a certain level all the values in its domain have to be tried, and they all have to fail for the current (sub)problem to be proved insoluble. Consequently, we know that by selecting V_i, the size of the current partial refutation will increase by at least a number of nodes equal to $|D(V_i)|$. We call this a 1-level look-ahead.

By temporarily assigning to V_i, in turn, every value v in its domain, and by attempting to restore arc-consistency after every such assignment, we can associate with each v a minimum contribution to the size of the refutation. If the assignment makes the subproblem arc-inconsistent, v's contribution will be 1, given by the node corresponding to the assignment itself. However, if arc-consistency can be restored after the assignment, at least one more variable will have to be considered before the current subproblem can be proved insoluble. Therefore, v will carry a minimum contribution equal to the smallest domain size amongst all the remaining unassigned variables. We call this a 2-level look-ahead.

In general, V_i's selection would increase the size of the current partial refutation by at least the sum of the minimum contributions of all the values in its domain.

Clearly, the further we look ahead, the less conservative the lower bound. However, look-ahead levels greater than 2 tend to be very time consuming and, therefore, the amount of look-ahead to use must be experimentally determined for each problem class being studied. We have concluded that for the class of quasigroup problems used in this paper, a look-ahead level of 3 was the most appropriate when computing the lower bound, and a look-ahead level of 1 was the most appropriate for the upper bound.

3.2 Problem Domain

As mentioned before, our experiments were focused around quasigroup completion problems. We briefly introduce them here.

Definition 7 (Quasigroup Completion Problems). *A quasigroup is a set Q with a binary operation $\star : Q \times Q \to Q$, such that for all a and b in Q there exist unique elements in Q such that $a \star x = b$ and $y \star a = b$. The cardinality of the set, $n = |Q|$, is called the order of the quasigroup.*

A quasigroup can be viewed as an $n \times n$ multiplication table defining a Latin square, which must be filled with unique integers on each row and column. The Quasigroup Completion Problem (QCP) is the problem of completing a partially filled Latin square. Quasigroup with Holes (QWH) are satisfiable instances obtained by starting with a complete Latin square and unassigning a number of cells according to the Markov chain Monte Carlo approach proposed by Jacobson and Matthews in [14]. QWH problem instances are considerably harder when the distribution of the holes is balanced, i.e, when the number of unassigned cells is approximately the same across the different rows and columns [1, 14, 15].

Originally just mathematical curiosities, Latin squares have found practical applications in many scientific and engineering fields such as statistics, scheduling, drug tests design, and cryptography. Quasigroup problems have a small-world topology [23] and are known to be NP-complete [6]. QWH problems pre-assign a percentage of the cells in the table, introducing perturbations into the structure of the constraint network and bringing problems closer to real-world instances.

4 Finding Optimal Refutations

We introduced in [13] an algorithm for obtaining optimal refutations for binary CSPs. In this paper we significantly improved that algorithm's efficiency so that it can tackle larger problems. All the optimisations described here are general in nature, i.e. they can be applied to any class of problems, but proved particularly useful in dealing with QWH-10 problems due to their relatively shallow refutations. We observed that for the problems under consideration, while most actual refutations have heights up to 30, early experiments showed that most optimal refutations have heights below 5. The nature of the search for optimal refutations is such that the branching factor is significantly larger than that of a normal search tree, and we estimate that searching for an optimal refutation of height 6 for an instance of a QWH-10 problem could take several months to complete on a Pentium M CPU. Consequently, limiting the height of the refutations considered can dramatically improve efficiency.

An important design decision in the optimal refutation search algorithm was to use an iterative-deepening strategy [16]. The algorithm starts off by searching for refutations of height 1, then for refutations of height 2, and so on, until it reaches a height equal to either the number of variables in the (sub)problem, or the size of the smallest refutation found up until that point. The motivation behind using an iterative-deepening strategy is based on the expectation that small refutations are likely to have smaller heights than larger refutations, an expectation that has been validated by our experiments. The successive expansions of the search horizon can increase the likelihood of finding earlier refutations that are better than the actual, thus lowering the current refutation size upper bound and significantly speeding up the search in the rest of the tree.

Our improved algorithm uses the refutation size lower bound to limit the height in the iterative-deepening loop. Consider an example where we use m levels of look-ahead and obtained a lower bound of l nodes. The number of nodes in excess of m that would be part of any refutation of height m is $e = l - m$. If the best refutation found up until this point is of size r, then we can immediately conclude that since *any* refutation of height $d \geq m$ would contain at least e additional nodes, searching for refutations of heights greater than $r - e$ cannot produce a smaller refutation. Moreover, updating the lower bound as we search deeper into the tree allows us to stop the search as soon as it discovers a refutation whose size equals the lower bound (this seems to occur quite frequently). Finally, once the algorithm completes the search for refutations of size $r-e$, we know that the best refutation found is *optimal*.

The number of uninstantiated variables involved in each refutation is indirectly a factor affecting the height limit in the iterative-deepening loop. We have modified MAC so that, before selecting a new variable, it automatically marks as *instantiated* every variable whose domain has been reduced to a single value as a result of restoring arc-consistency. This reduces the height of the search tree, avoids unnecessary backtracking over singletons, and makes sure that such variables do not take part in any refutation. Mistake trees thus involve a smaller number of variables and are easier to deal with.

Despite of all these optimisations, our data-set contains a small number of instances (23 out of over 1,000,000) for which the search for the optimal refutation timed out after 2 hours for at least one mistake point, and in some of these cases no *improved* refutation was found. For some of these instances we succeeded in finding improved refutations by using a rapid random restarts strategy [9]. For others, we employed a certain level of *optimism*, i.e. we tried at each level a limited number of variables, in effect searching only what appeared to be the most promising area of the search space. The shorter-than-actual refutations that we found using these two methods are not known to be optimal or quasi-optimal, yet they are significantly smaller than their corresponding actual refutations, and by finding them we avoided incorrectly elongating the tails of the plots.

5 Experiments

Our experiments[3] were performed on satisfiable QWH-10 problem instances (100 variables) with 90% random balanced holes[4], encoded as binary CSPs. We aimed to study

---
[3] Code freely available with source at http://hulubei.net/tudor/csp.
[4] Generated using code based on Carla Gomes' *lsencode* quasigroup generator.

the relationship between actual and optimal refutations, as well as the way they evolve as better and better search algorithms are used to solve a large set of instances.

Our empirical study included 4 variable ordering heuristics: brelaz, min-domain, min-dom/ddeg and min-domain/wdeg, and 3 value ordering heuristics: random, min-conflicts[5] and its anti-heuristic, max-conflicts. We always broke ties randomly. QWH-10 instances are too difficult to solve using random variable orderings or variable ordering anti-heuristics, which is why these heuristics could not be included.

Using a Beowulf cluster of 32 CPUs over a period of 6 weeks we accumulated experimental data on all the 12 variations of MAC, totaling over 1,000,000 instances. Our intention was to avoid running an artificially randomised algorithm multiple times on the same instance. We computed actual refutations, lower bounds, and attempted to compute optimal refutations, reporting the cumulative size of each for every instance. While in the vast majority of cases we did find the optimal refutations, we encountered some instances for which we could only find improved refutations (i.e. refutations for which we were not able to guarantee quasi-optimality), and some for which the search timed out without finding any improved refutation. Table 1 gives the actual percentages.

Table 1. Optimality (%optimal / %quasi-optimal / %improved / %timed out)

	max-conflicts	random	min-conflicts
min-domain	99.37 / 0.19 / 0.40 / 0.03	99.44 / 0.25 / 0.31 / 0.00	97.96 / 0.74 / 1.28 / 0.02
min-dom/ddeg	95.41 / 4.01 / 0.58 / 0.01	98.27 / 0.42 / 1.30 / 0.01	86.67 / 3.37 / 9.84 / 0.11
brelaz	99.24 / 0.19 / 0.53 / 0.03	98.69 / 0.33 / 0.97 / 0.01	87.22 / 3.10 / 9.47 / 0.22
min-dom/wdeg	99.26 / 0.38 / 0.36 / 0.00	97.97 / 0.81 / 1.22 / 0.01	86.64 / 3.70 / 9.33 / 0.33

Figure 3 includes results for each of our 12 experiments and shows the effects of the various heuristics on the shape of the refutation size cumulative distribution function. The plots are organised roughly in increasing order of efficiency from left to right and from top to bottom. It is important to point out that the shorter refutation and lower bound plots are specific to each search algorithm, simply because different algorithms make mistakes in different places. The lower bound is plotted to give an absolute minimum on the size of the refutations even for those instances where we could not find the optimal or quasi-optimal refutations (see Table 1).

We notice from the first column of Figure 3 that a search algorithm employing a poor value ordering heuristic (max-conflicts) always exhibits heavy tails, irrespective of which one of the 4 variable ordering heuristics we use. Moreover, heavy tails still exist, albeit with a different slope, even if, once a mistake has been made, the search algorithms were to use an Oracle that could provide the shortest refutation for that mistake. In other words, in such cases the runtime distribution of an algorithm would be *guaranteed to exhibit heavy-tailed behaviour*.

We increase the quality of the value ordering heuristic by switching from max-conflicts to a random ordering and observe that while the actual refutations remain

---
[5] This heuristic selects the value that is inconsistent with the smallest number of other values in the domains of neighbouring variables.

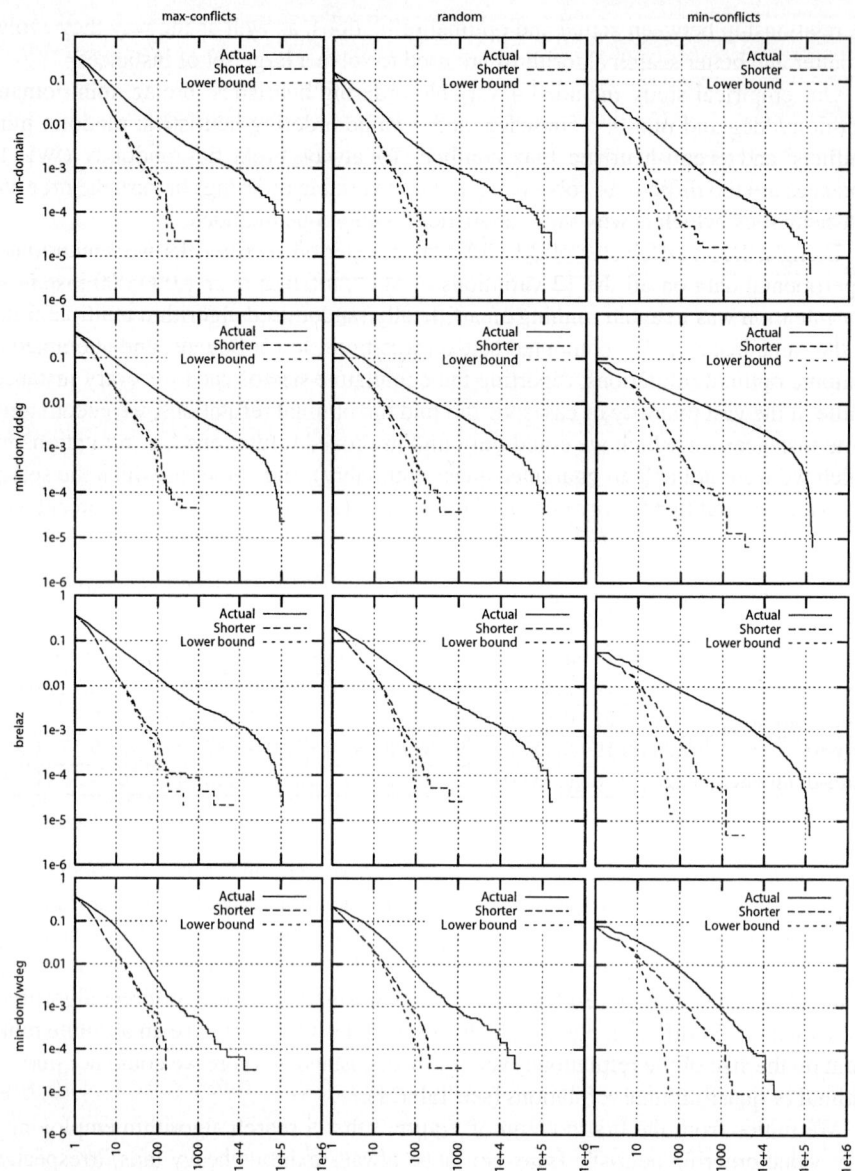

Fig. 3. Cumulative distribution function of the refutation size for QWH-10 problems with 90% holes. We vary the value ordering across columns and variable ordering across rows. Shorter refutations are either optimal, quasi-optimal, or simply the shortest improved refutations we could find that were smaller than the corresponding actual refutations.

heavy-tailed, as we improve the quality of the variable ordering, the *shorter* refutations and the lower bounds start becoming less and less heavy-tailed. For the lack of a better term, we call such plots *borderline heavy-tailed*. This phenomenon becomes even more

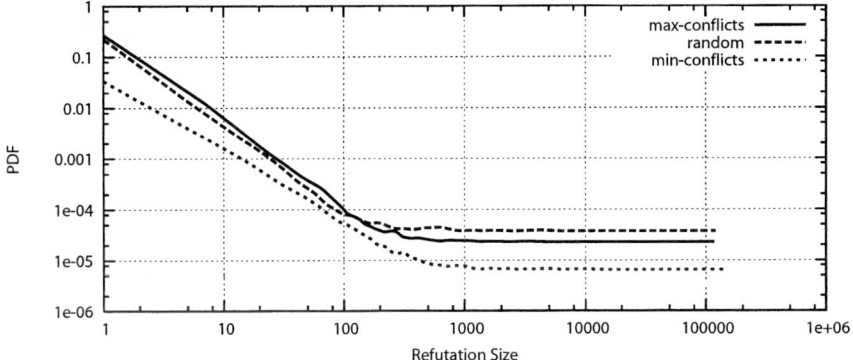

(a) Variable ordering: min-dom/ddeg (very similar results for min-domain and brelaz)

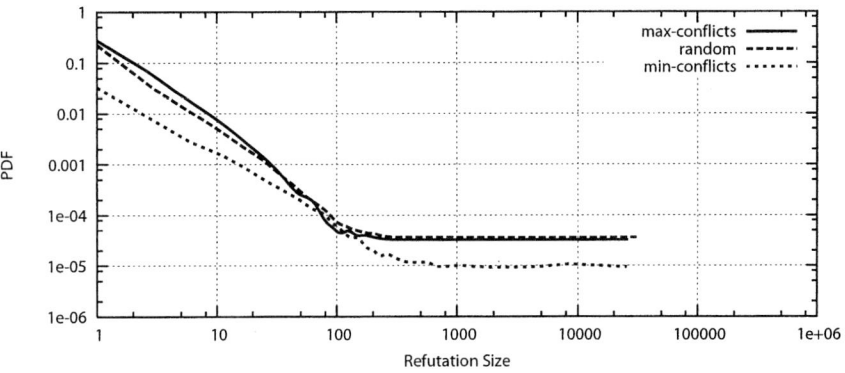

(b) Variable ordering: min-dom/wdeg

Fig. 4. Probability distribution function for the actual refutation sizes obtained with various search algorithms, grouped by variable ordering

pronounced as we move over to min-conflicts. In that case, all lower bounds become non-heavy-tailed, and with the exception of min-domain, shorter refutations become borderline heavy-tailed. Finally, the best combination of heuristics, min-conflicts + min-dom/wdeg, succeeds at eliminating heavy tails even from the actual refutations, while at the same time keeping the actual refutations much closer to their corresponding optimal than any of the other 11 variations of MAC[6].

We observe in Figure 4 several factors contributing to the behaviour of our best performing algorithm. Firstly, for QWH-10, algorithms using the min-domain, min-dom/ddeg, and brelaz variable orderings encounter similarly large maximum refutations *regardless* of the value ordering used. Secondly, any algorithm using min-dom/wdeg encounters a maximum refutation size that is a factor of 5 smaller than the maximum

---

[6] Table 1 shows that for this combination of heuristics we found the lowest percentage of optimal refutations, so the true runtime distribution can only be even more obviously non-heavy-tailed.

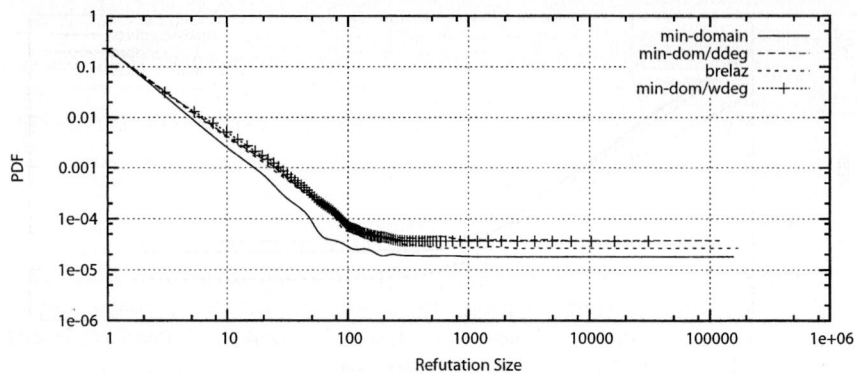

(a) Value ordering: random (very similar results for max-conflicts)

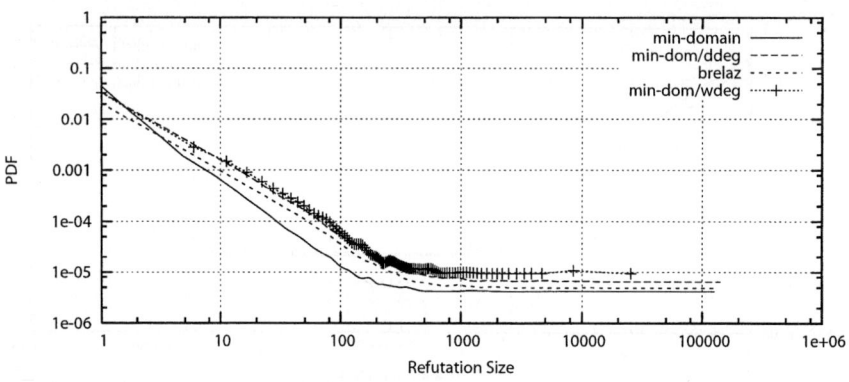

(b) Value ordering: min-conflicts

Fig. 5. Probability distribution function for the actual refutation sizes obtained with various search algorithms, grouped by value ordering

encountered by algorithms using the other variable ordering heuristics. Thirdly, improving the value ordering heuristic from max-conflicts or random to min-conflicts results in a decrease in the probability of each non-trivial[7] refutation size occurring.

However, it is interesting to see in Figure 5 that any algorithm using min-dom/wdeg, while not encountering extremely large refutations, tends to have a higher probability of encountering all other sized non-trivial refutations, i.e. over the range of refutation sizes it encounters, it does worse than any other variable ordering for all value orderings.

Therefore, to summarise, the combination of the factors outlined above seems to eliminate heavy tails from the QWH-10 problems we have studied, despite the fact that neither min-conflicts nor min-dom/wdeg alone seems to be capable of doing that. This is a somewhat more complex scenario that one might have initially envisaged.

---

[7] Obviously, this implies an increase in the probability of the occurence of trivial mistakes, i.e. those that can be refuted by propagation alone.

Finally, the inherent heavy-tailedness that we observe suggests that while recovering from failure is important (which is typically the focus of research on variable orderings), we should also focus considerable attention on the interrelationship between variable selection and value selection in order to mitigate heavy-tailed runtime distributions by failing less.

6 Conclusions

Much progress has been made on understanding problem hardness, typical-case complexity and the behaviour of backtrack search. The heavy-tailed phenomenon that characterises the runtime distributions of backtrack search procedures has received considerable attention. We have shown that a good choice of variable and value orderings can have a dramatic impact on the runtime distribution. A good combination can eliminate heavy-tailed behaviour from certain classes of problems, while a poor choice not only ensures that such behaviour is observed, but also that the nature of the insoluble subtrees encountered guarantees that this is the case.

We believe our work provides motivation for more focused research on the interplay between variable and value selection during search. We also believe that there are many directions that one can follow with respect to the utility of empirically studying optimal refutations of insoluble subtrees in relation to runtime distributions. We intend to explore these opportunities in more detail as part of our future work.

Acknowledgments

This material is based on work supported by Science Foundation Ireland under Grant 00/PI.1/C075. We would like to thank Mark Hennessy, Barbara Smith and Tom Carchrae for their comments and suggestions, and to John Morrison and the Boole Centre for Research in Informatics for providing access to their Beowulf cluster.

References

[1] D. Achlioptas, C.P. Gomes, H.A. Kautz, and B. Selman. Generating satisfiable problem instances. In *Proceedings of AAAI-2000*, pages 256–261, 2000.
[2] C. Bessière, C. Fernández, C.P. Gomes, and M. Valls. Pareto-like distributions in random binary csp. In *Proceedings of ACIA-2003*, 2004.
[3] C. Bessière and J-C. Regin. MAC and combined heuristics: two reasons to forsake FC (and CBJ?) on hard problems. In *Proceedings of CP-1996*, LNCS 1118, pages 61–75, 1996.
[4] F. Boussemart, F. Hemery, C. Lecoutre, and L. Sais. Boosting systematic search by weighting constraints. In *Proceedings of ECAI-2004*, pages 146–150, 2004.
[5] D. Brélaz. New methods to color the vertices of a graph. *Communications of the ACM*, 22(4):251–256, 1979.
[6] C. Colbourn. Embedding partial steiner triple systems is NP-complete. *Combinatorial Theory*, A(35):100–105, 1983.
[7] I.P. Gent and T. Walsh. Easy problems are sometimes hard. *Artificial Intelligence*, 70:335–345, 1994.

[8] C.P. Gomes, C. Fernández, B. Selman, and C. Bessière. Statistical regimes across constrainedness regions. In *Proceedings of CP-2004*, LNCS 3258, pages 32–46, 2004.
[9] C.P. Gomes, B. Selman, and N. Crato. Heavy-tailed distributions in combinatorial search. In *Proceedings of CP-1997*, pages 121–135, 1997.
[10] C.P. Gomes, B. Selman, N. Crato, and H. Kautz. Heavy-tailed phenomena in satisfiability and constraint satisfaction problems. *Automated Reasoning*, 24(1/2):67–100, 2000.
[11] R.M. Haralick and G.L. Elliott. Increasing tree search efficiency for constraint satisfaction problems. *Artificial Intelligence*, 14(3):263–313, 1980.
[12] T. Hogg and C.P. Williams. The hardest constraint problems: A double phase transition. *Artificial Intelligence*, 69:359–377, 1994.
[13] T. Hulubei and B. O'Sullivan. Optimal refutations for constraint satisfaction problems. In *Proceedings of IJCAI-2005*, 2005.
[14] M.T. Jacobson and P. Matthews. Generating uniformly distributed random latin squares. *Combinatorial Design*, 4:405–437, 1996.
[15] H.A. Kautz, Y. Ruan, D. Achlioptas, C.P. Gomes, B. Selman, and M.E. Stickel. Balance and filtering in structured satisfiable problems. In *Proceedings of IJCAI-2001*, pages 351–358, 2001.
[16] R.E. Korf. Depth-first iterative-deepening: an optimal admissible tree search. *Artificial Intelligence*, 27(1):97–109, 1985.
[17] C. Lecoutre, F. Boussemart, and F. Hemery. Backjump-based techniques versus conflict-directed heuristics. In *Proceedings of ICTAI-2004*, pages 549–557, 2004.
[18] A.K. Mackworth. Consistency in networks of relations. *Artificial Intelligence*, 8(1):99–118, 1977.
[19] D. Sabin and E.C. Freuder. Contradicting conventional wisdom in constraint satisfaction. In *Proceedings of ECAI-1994*, pages 125–129, 1994.
[20] B.M. Smith. In search of exceptionally difficult constraint satisfaction problems. In *Constraint Processing, Selected Papers*, LNCS 923, pages 139–156, 1995.
[21] B.M. Smith and S. Grant. Sparse constraint graphs and exceptionally hard problems. In *Proceedings of IJCAI-1995*, pages 646–651, 1995.
[22] B.M. Smith and P. Sturdy. An empirical investigation of value ordering for finding all solutions. In *Workshop on Modelling and Solving Problems with Constraints*, 2004.
[23] T. Walsh. Search in a small world. In *Proceedings of IJCAI-1999*, pages 1172–1177, 1999.

2-Way *vs.* *d*-Way Branching for CSP

Joey Hwang and David G. Mitchell

School of Computing Science, Simon Fraser University,
Burnaby, V5A 1S6, Canada
{jhwang, mitchell}@cs.sfu.ca

Abstract. Most CSP algorithms are based on refinements and extensions of backtracking, and employ one of two simple "branching schemes": 2-way branching or d-way branching, for domain size d. The schemes are not equivalent, but little is known about their relative power. Here we compare them in terms of how efficiently they can refute an unsatisfiable instance with optimal branching choices, by studying two variants of the resolution proof system, denoted *C-RES* and *NG-RES*, which model the reasoning of CSP algorithms. The tree-like restrictions, *tree-C-RES* and *tree-NG-RES*, exactly capture the power of backtracking with 2-way branching and d-way branching, respectively. We give a family instances which require exponential sized search trees for backtracking with d-way branching, but have size $O(d^2 n)$ search trees for backtracking with 2-way branching. We also give a natural branching strategy with which backtracking with 2-way branching finds refutations of these instances in time $O(d^2 n^2)$. The unrestricted variants of *C-RES* and *NG-RES* can simulate the reasoning of algorithms which incorporate learning and k-consistency enforcement. We show exponential separations between *C-RES* and *NG-RES*, as well as between the tree-like and unrestricted versions of each system. All separations given are nearly optimal.

1 Introduction

Most complete algorithms for solving finite-domain constraint satisfaction problems (CSPs) are based on backtracking, usually refined with various propagation schemes and sometimes extended with no-good learning. These algorithms are based on one of two "branching schemes". Most CSP papers study algorithms using d-way branching, in which an instance $\mathcal{I}$ is solved as follows. Select a variable x with domain $D(x) = \{1, 2, \ldots, d\}$. For each $a \in D(x)$, we restrict $\mathcal{I}$ by setting $x = a$, and recursively try to solve the restricted instance. $\mathcal{I}$ has no solution if and only if none of the d restricted versions do. In 2-way branching, we select variable x and a value $a \in D(x)$, and make two recursive calls. The first is with the restriction $x = a$; the second with the value a removed from the domain of x. $\mathcal{I}$ has no solution if neither recursive call finds a solution.

It is easy to check that any strategy for d-way branching can be simulated by a 2-way branching strategy with no significant loss of efficiency. But does the converse hold, or is d-way branching strictly more powerful than 2-way branching? Many practitioners believe that 2-way branching is more powerful, and several commercial solvers support use of this scheme, but little is known about how much more power might be available. It was shown in [11] that 2-way branching with learning is strictly more powerful than d-way branching with learning. In particular, a family of instances MPH_n was given, having the following property: Any d-way branching algorithm, even with optimal variable ordering and optimal learning strategy, cannot solve MPH_n in less than $n^{\Omega(\log n)}$ time, but there is a 2-way branching algorithm, with fairly simple branching and learning strategies, that solves MPH_n in time $O(n^3)$. This leaves open the question of the relative power of the branching schemes without learning, and also the question of whether a true exponential separation can be obtained in the case with learning.

Here, we answer the first question by giving instances which require exponential size search trees for backtracking with d-way branching, but are solved in polynomial time by backtracking with 2-way branching. We take a significant step toward answering the second, by giving instances establish an exponential separation between two proof systems which can simulate the algorithms of interest. However, it is an open question whether the classes of algorithms in question are as powerful as the proof systems. The analogous question in the context of SAT is whether or not conflict-directed clause learning is as powerful as unrestricted resolution, and is also open [2]. We also do not give an efficient strategy for finding the short 2-way branching proofs, although we believe there is one. Figure 1 summarizes our results on the proof systems.

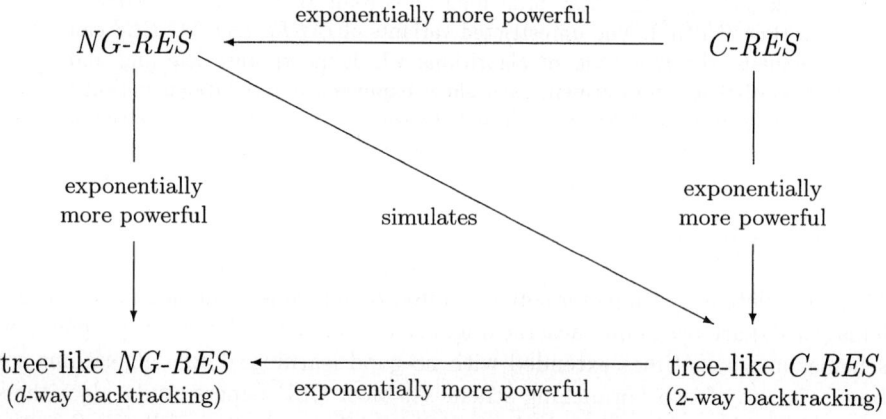

Fig. 1. Relative Efficiency of *NG-RES*, *C-RES* and their tree-like variants

A few experimental empirical studies on 2-way and d-way branching strategies have been reported. Park [12] showed that in most cases, with "standard" variable and value ordering heuristics, 2-way branching ends up simulating d-way branching. To see why, consider pure 2-way backtracking with branching based on "smallest domain first". Once a variable x is branched on, the following branches will also be on x. This simple reasoning does not directly generalize to more interesting cases, but does give some intuition. Smith and Sturdy [13] investigated the effect of changing the value ordering in 2-way branching, comparing performance to d-way branching. Their finding was that 2-way branching, even with the worst value ordering, is not worse than d-way branching. These studies, combined with our results, suggest that designers of heuristics should consider the properties needed to take advantage of the extra power available with 2-way branching.

Formally, we study only unsatisfiable instances, because an optimal strategy will solve satisfiable instances trivially. However, it would be wrong to think the results say nothing about satisfiable instances. Any polytime branching strategy will make bad choices, after which unsatisfiability of a restricted instance must be proven. Indeed, a reasonable backtracking algorithm can take a non-trivial amount of time only in this way.

2 Preliminaries

Constraint Satisfaction Problems. A CSP instance $\mathcal{I}$ is a triple $\langle X, \mathcal{D}, \Gamma \rangle$ where X is a finite set of variables, $\mathcal{D}(x)$ is the domain of a variable $x \in X$, and Γ is a set of nogoods. A *literal* is an expression of the form $x = a$, where $x \in X$ and $a \in D(x)$, and a *nogood* is a set of literals with distinct variables. We write nogoods as $\eta(x_1 = a_1, x_2 = a_2, \cdots, x_t = a_t)$. A (partial) assignment α for $\mathcal{I}$ is a (partial) function from variables to domain values. Assignment α *satisfies* a nogood N iff for some literal $(x = a) \in N$, $\alpha(x)$ is defined and $\alpha(x) \neq a$. A (total) assignment α satisfies $\mathcal{I}$ if there is no nogood $N \in \Gamma$ such that for each $(x = a) \in N$, $\alpha(x) = a$. We denote the set of variables occurring in a nogood N, set of nogoods Γ, or instance $\mathcal{I}$, by $vars(N)$, $vars(\Gamma)$ and $vars(\mathcal{I})$, respectively. We usually assume that all variables of an instance have the same domain, which is the set $[d] = \{1, \ldots d\}$.

Our choice to describe the constraints as a set of nogoods, rather than the usual scope–relation pairs, is purely for convenience. The size of this set as an encoding of a constraint is not relevant to our results, and we could as well assume that the encoding of each constraint is of zero size, with nogoods generated explicitly only as needed.

Propositional Resolution (*RES*). The resolution rule allows us to derive the clause $A \vee B$ from two clauses $x \vee A$ and $\overline{x} \vee B$. We will usually write clauses parenthesized and with $\vee$'s omitted, for example writing $(a\ b\ c)$ rather than $a \vee b \vee c$. A *resolution derivation* of clause C from CNF formula ϕ is a sequence of clauses $C_1, C_2, \cdots, C_m$ in which each C_i is either a clause of ϕ or is derived by the resolution rule from some C_j and C_k with $j, k < i$, and $C_m = C$. A resolution derivation of the empty clause from ϕ is called a *resolution refutation* of ϕ. A CNF formula ϕ is unsatisfiable iff it has a resolution refutation.

Nogood Resolution (*NG-RES*). If the domain of variable x is $\{1, 2, \cdots, d\}$, the *nogood resolution rule* allows one to infer a nogood from a set of nogoods by *resolving on x*:

$$\frac{\eta(x=1,\ N_1)}{\eta(x=2,\ N_2)}$$
$$\vdots$$
$$\frac{\eta(x=d,\ N_d)}{\eta(N_1, N_2, \ldots N_d)}\ x \in \{1, \ldots, d\}$$

A *nogood resolution derivation* of a nogood N from a CSP instance Γ is a sequence of nogoods $N_1, N_2, \cdots, N_m$ in which each nogood N_i is either in Γ or is derived from a set of previous nogoods in the sequence by the nogood resolution rule, and $N_m = N$. A *nogood resolution refutation* of $\mathcal{I}$ is a nogood resolution derivation of the empty nogood, $\square$, from Γ. NG-RES is a sound and complete refutation system, first proposed in [1].

Constraint Resolution (*C-RES*). Let $\mathcal{I} = \langle \mathcal{D}, \Gamma \rangle$ be a CSP instance. We encode $\mathcal{I}$ as a CNF formula, CNF($\mathcal{I}$), as follows. For each variable $x \in vars(\mathcal{I})$ and each value $a \in \mathcal{D}(x)$, we introduce a propositional variable $x\!:\!a$ asserting that x takes value a when $x\!:\!a$ is true. We have a set of *domain clauses*, ensuring that every variable in $\mathcal{I}$ is given a value, and a set of *unique value clauses* ensuring no variable takes multiple values. For each nogood $N \in \Gamma$, CNF($\mathcal{I}$) has a *constraint clause* which rules assignment forbidden by N. The CNF encoding of $\mathcal{I}$ is:

$$\text{CNF}(\mathcal{I}) = domainCls \cup uniqueValueCls \cup constraintCls$$

where $\quad domainCls = \{(x\!:\!a_1\ \cdots\ x\!:\!a_d) : x \in vars(\mathcal{I}), \mathcal{D}(x) = \{a_1, \cdots, a_d\}\}$
$uniqueValueCls = \{(\overline{x\!:\!a}\ \overline{x\!:\!c}) : x \in vars(\mathcal{I}), a, c \in \mathcal{D}(x), a \neq c\}$
$constraintCls = \{(\overline{x_1\!:\!a_1}\ \cdots\ \overline{x_k\!:\!a_k}) : \eta(x_1 = a_1, \cdots, x_k = a_k) \in \Gamma\}.$

There is a one-to-one correspondence between solutions of $\mathcal{I}$ and satisfying truth assignments for CNF($\mathcal{I}$). A *constraint resolution* (*C-RES*) refutation of a CSP instance $\mathcal{I}$ is a RES refutation of CNF($\mathcal{I}$), and clearly $\mathcal{I}$ is unsatisfiable iff it has a C-RES refutation.

Derivations, Graphs and Tree-Like Proofs. For T one of the refutation systems defined above, and π a derivation in T (T-derivation), we define the *graph of* π to be the directed acyclic graph (DAG) G_π in which vertices are nogoods (or clauses, as appropriate) of π and there is an edge from vertex v to vertex u if v is a premise for deriving u in π. Derivation π is *tree-like* if every vertex in G_π has out-degree 0 or 1, or equivalently, every derived nogood or clause is used at most once as a premise to derive another. We denote the restriction of T to tree-like derivations by *tree-T*. For example, a *tree-C-RES* refutation of $\mathcal{I}$ is a tree-like resolution refutation of CNF($\mathcal{I}$).

Proof Complexity. Let T be one of the proof systems defined above, and π be a T-derivation. The *size* of π, $|\pi|$, is the number of clauses or nogoods in π, as appropriate to T. The *width* of a clause or nogood C, $w(C)$, is the number of literals appearing in C and the width of a derivation π, $w(\pi)$, is the width of the widest clause or nogood in π. The T-complexity of formula or CSP instance ϕ, denoted $T(\phi)$, is the size of its smallest T-refutation. $tree\text{-}T(\phi)$ is the size of the smallest tree-like refutation.

We say that a proof system A *p-simulates* a proof system B if there is a function that maps any B refutation of a CSP instance $\mathcal{I}$ to some A refutation of $\mathcal{I}$ with at most polynomial blowup in size. We say that A *efficiently simulates* B if the degree of the polynomial in the p-simulation is small. There is an *exponential separation* of system B from system A if there is an infinite set of instances $\{\mathcal{I}_1, \mathcal{I}_2, \cdots\}$ such that the smallest B refutation of $\mathcal{I}_n$ is of size exponential in n, but the smallest A refutation of $\mathcal{I}_n$ is of size polynomial in n. If A efficiently simulates B and there is an exponential separation of B from A, then A is exponentially more powerful than B. For example, it is known that unrestricted resolution is exponentially more powerful than tree-like resolution [4, 3].

Refutations and Algorithms. It is straightforward to show that the size of minimal refutations in *tree-RES*, *tree-NG-RES*, and *tree-C-RES* are the same as the size of minimal search trees for backtracking for SAT (DPLL), CSP backtracking with d-way branching, and CSP backtracking with 2-way branching, respectively. This remains true when techniques such as unit propagation, forward checking, and conflict-directed backjumping are employed [1, 10, 11].

3 Results

3.1 Separating Instances for *tree-NG-RES*

Our first result is an exponential separation between *tree-NG-RES* and *NG-RES*. This involves exhibiting instances which require large *tree-NG-RES* refutations, but have short *NG-RES* refutations. The same instances we use for this also have short *tree-C-RES* refutations, and thus also provide the exponential separation between *tree-NG-RES* and *tree-C-RES*. The instances are based on directed acyclic graphs, generalizing the implication graph formulas used in [3] to provide a near-optimal separation of *RES* and *tree-RES*.

Definition 1 (Implication Graph Contradictions ($IMP_{G,S,T,d}$)). *Call a DAG in which every vertex has in-degree 2 or 0 a circuit. Let $G = (V, E)$ be a circuit with vertices $\{v_1, \ldots, v_n\}$, $d \geq 3$ be an integer, S the set of sources of G, and T the sets targets (sinks) of G. We associate to each vertex $v_i \in V$ a variable x_i. The implication graph contradiction of G, $IMP_{G,S,T,d}$, is the CSP instance with variables $x_1, \cdots, x_n$, having domain $[d]$, and the following nogoods:*

Source axioms: $\eta(x_i = 1)$ *for every $v_i \in S$*
Target axioms: $\eta(x_i = a)$ *for every $v_i \in T$, and for all $a \in [d] \setminus \{1\}$*
Pebbling axioms: $\eta(x_i = a, x_j = b, x_k = 1)$ *for every v_k with predecessors v_i and v_j, and for all $a, b \in [d] \setminus \{1\}$*

$IMP_{G,S,T,d}$ expresses the following contradiction: Each vertex of G is labeled with a number in $[d]$. Sources are not labeled 1, and if neither predecessor of an internal vertex v is labeled 1 then v is not labeled 1, but targets are labeled 1.

Theorem 1. *There exists an infinite family of n-vertex circuits G, with sources S and targets T, such that for any integer $d \geq 3$, tree-NG-RES($IMP_{G,S,T,d}$) = $(d-1)^{\Omega(n/\log n)}$.*

The proof is given in Section 4.

Theorem 2. *For any n-vertex circuit G, with sources S and targets T, and any integer $d \geq 3$, NG-RES($IMP_{G,S,T,d}$) = $O(d^2n)$.*

The following algorithm constructs such refutations.

Efficient 2-Way Branching for $IMP_{G_n,S,T,d}$. We may use the following 2-way branching strategy: Pick a variable x_i and a value a such that either setting $x_i = a$ or $x_i \neq a$ produces an instance which is found to be unsatisfiable by enforcing arc-consistency, and branch first to the "good" side. (We can replace arc consistency by other choices here, such as one-variable look-ahead plus forward checking.) If no such a combination exists, use any other scheme desired. We assume that singleton domains are always eliminated, including at startup. After startup every variable associated with a source node in G will have domain $\{2, \cdots, d\}$, and every variable x_t associated with a target node v_t would have been forced to take value 1, so the pebbling axioms for v_t with predecessors v_j and v_k in effect have become $\eta(x_j = a, x_k = b), a, b \in \{2, \cdots d\}$.

At any branching point, the chosen variable must be some x_i associated with a vertex v_i where both the variables x_j and x_k associated with predecessors of v_i have domain $\{2, \cdots, d\}$. Moreover, a_i will be 1. Setting $x_i = 1$ "falsifies" the literal ($x_1 = 1$), so the pebbling axioms for v_i effectively become $\eta(x_j = a, x_k = b), a, b, \in \{2, \cdots, d\}$. These are inconsistent, which can easily be established with a search tree of size d^2. For the branch with $x_i \neq 1$, the pebbling axioms for v_i are satisfied and 1 is removed from the domain of x_i. Observe that there will always be a variable satisfying the criteria of our branching scheme, and the algorithm will effectively work its way from sources to a target, at each vertex efficiently removing 1 from the domain of a variable, and obtaining a trivial contradiction at the target. (The algorithm proceeds exactly as we would to pebble the graph). The total time required is certainly $O(d^2n^2)$. The instances can be solved in about the same time by using repeated singleton arc consistency.

Separation of *tree-NG-RES* from *tree-C-RES*. The implication graph contradictions $IMP_{G,S,T,d}$ have polynomial sized *tree-C-RES* refutations. Hence, they also separate *tree-NG-RES* from *tree-C-RES*.

Proposition 1. *For any circuit G with n vertices, tree-C-RES($IMP_{G,S,T,d}$) = $O(d^2n)$.*

The refutations can be extracted from the algorithm above.

3.2 Separation of *tree-C-RES* from *C-RES*

Theorem 3. *There is an infinite family of instances $\{\mathcal{I}_n\}$ such that C-RES$(\mathcal{I}_n) = O(n)$, and tree-C-RES$(\mathcal{I}_n) = 2^{\Omega(n/\log n)}$.*

Proof. A family of CNF formulas $\{\phi_n\}$ such that $|\phi_n| = O(n)$, $RES(\phi_n) = O(n)$ and $tree\text{-}RES(\phi_n) = 2^{\Omega(n/\log n)}$ is given in [3]. Let $\mathcal{I}_n = \langle \{0,1\}, \Gamma_n \rangle$ be the transformation of ϕ_n to CSP, as follows. The variables of $\mathcal{I}\_n$ are just the variables in ϕ_n. For each clause C in ϕ_n, there is a nogood $\eta(\alpha)$ in Γ_n if and only if α is a minimal size truth assignment that makes C false. It is not hard to show that, if $\mathcal{I}$ is the transformation of ϕ as just described, then $RES(\phi) \leq C\text{-}RES(\mathcal{I}) \leq 3 \cdot RES(\phi)$, and $tree\text{-}RES(\phi) \leq tree\text{-}C\text{-}RES(\mathcal{I}) \leq 3 \cdot tree\text{-}RES(\phi)$ [10, 8]. The result follows.

3.3 Separation of *NG-RES* from *C-RES*

The family of CSP instances MGT'_n that separates *NG-RES* from *C-RES* is based on the unsatisfiable CNF formula GT_n introduced by [9]. For each $n \in \mathbb{N}$, GT_n encodes the negation of the fact that every loop-less transitive directed graph with n vertices and with no 2-cycles must have a source. The contradictory statement can be stated as a CNF formula containing the following clauses:

(1) $\overline{x_{j,j}}$ $j \in [n]$
(2) $x_{i,j} \wedge x_{j,k} \to x_{i,k}$ $i,j,k \in [n]$, $i \neq j \neq k$
(3) $x_{i,j} \to \overline{x_{j,i}}$ $i,j \in [n]$, $i \neq j$
(4) $\bigvee_{i \in [n]} x_{i,j}$ $j \in [n]$

where $x_{i,j}$ takes value 1 if and only if there is an edge from i to j. The first three sets of clauses ensure that the graph is loop-less, transitive, and free of 2-cycles, respectively. The clauses in (4) assure that for each vertex j, there exists some vertex i such that there is an edge from i to j, i.e., there is no source. There are $O(n^3)$-size *RES* refutations of GT_n[14].

Bonet and Galesi [5] gave a modified version of GT_n, called MGT_n. For each $j \in [n]$, they introduce $n+1$ new variables $y_{0,j}, \ldots, y_{n,j}$ and replace the set of clauses (4) by:

$$(4*) \quad \overline{y_{0,j}} \wedge \bigwedge_{i \in [n]} (y_{i-1,j} \vee x_{i,j} \vee \overline{y_{i,j}}) \wedge y_{n,j} \qquad j \in [n]$$

The total number of variables is still $O(n^2)$ but MGT_n has constant width clauses. It is easy to see that we can derive the clauses in (4) from those in (4*) by resolving on the y variables and this takes $O(n^2)$ steps. Then, by applying the $O(n^3)$-size refutation of GT_n, we obtain an $O(n^3)$-size *RES* refutation of MGT_n.

Our instances, MGT'_n, have the same set of variables as MGT_n but the domain for each variable is $D = \{1, 2, 3, 4\}$. If α is an assignment for MGT'_n, then

$$\alpha(x_{i,j}) = \begin{cases} 1 \text{ or } 2 & \text{means there exists an edge from } i \text{ to } j \\ 3 \text{ or } 4 & \text{means there is no edge from } i \text{ to } j. \end{cases}$$

So, every total assignment for the variables in MGT'_n corresponds to a directed graph with n vertices. To encode the contradictory statement, MGT'_n consists of the following nogoods:

(1') $\eta(x_{j,j} = 1), \eta(x_{j,j} = 2)$ $j \in [n]$
(2') $\eta(x_{i,j} = a,\ x_{j,k} = b,\ x_{i,k} = c)$ $i, j, k \in [n],\ i \neq j \neq k,$
    $a, b \in \{1, 2\},\ c \in \{3, 4\}$
(3') $\eta(x_{i,j} = a,\ x_{j,i} = b)$ $i, j \in [n],\ i \neq j,\ a, b \in \{1, 2\}$
(4') for each $i \in [n]$,
    $\eta(y_{0,j} = 1),\ \eta(y_{0,j} = 2)$
    $\eta(y_{i-1,j} = c,\ x_{i,j} = a,\ y_{i,j} = b)$ $j \in [n],\ a, b \in \{1, 2\},\ c \in \{3, 4\}$
    $\eta(y_{n,j} = 3),\ \eta(y_{n,j} = 4)$

Theorem 4. *Any NG-RES refutation of MGT'_n must have size $2^{\Omega(n)}$.*

The proof of this is given in Section 5.

Theorem 5. *C-RES(MGT'_n) $= O(n^3)$.*

Proof. Derive the clauses $(\overline{x_{i,j}:a}\ \overline{x_{j,k}:b}\ x_{i,k}:1\ x_{i,k}:2)$, $i, j, k \in [n]$, $i \neq j \neq k$, $a, b \in \{1, 2\}$, using the CNF encoding of (2') and the domain clauses of the x variables. Define

$$A(i, j, k) \stackrel{\text{def}}{=} \bigwedge_{a,b \in \{1,2\}} (\overline{x_{i,j}:a}\ \overline{x_{j,k}:b}\ x_{i,k}:1\ x_{i,k}:2).$$

Now, derive the clauses

$$P_m(j) \stackrel{\text{def}}{=} \bigvee_{\substack{i \in [m] \\ i \neq j}} X(i, j)$$

where

$$X(i, j) \stackrel{\text{def}}{=} (x_{i,j}:1\ x_{i,j}:2)$$

by resolving clauses in the CNF encoding of (4') together with the domain clauses of the y and x variables, and unit clauses from (1'). Define $B(m, j)$ as

$$B(m, j) \stackrel{\text{def}}{=} \bigwedge_{a,b \in \{1,2\}} (\overline{x_{m,j}:a}\ \overline{x_{j,m}:b})$$

which is just the clauses in the CNF encoding of (3'). Now, for each $m < n$ and $j \leq m$, we can derive $P_m(j)$ from $P_{m+1}(j), A(i, m+1, j)$, and $B(m+1, j)$. Once we get $P_2(1)$ and $P_2(2)$, the empty clause can be derived in six steps. The C-RES derivation of $P_m(j)$ is of size $O(n)$. Therefore, we need $O(n^3)$ steps in total to derive the empty clause.

3.4 Separation Upper Bounds

Having provided some exponential separations between systems, it seems natural to ask how big the separations can be. For example, if we know that the smallest *NG-RES* refutation of a CSP instance $\mathcal{I}$ is of size S, then what is the upper limit for the size of the smallest *tree-NG-RES* refutation of $\mathcal{I}$ in terms of S? Here, for each of the separations we have provided, we give an upper bound on the best possible separation which might be obtained. These are only slightly larger than the lower bounds we give, so those results are nearly optimal.

Theorem 6. *For any n-variable CSP instance $\mathcal{I}$ with domain size $d \geq 2$,*

1. *tree-NG-RES*$(\mathcal{I}) = d^{O(\frac{d^2 S \log \log S}{\log S})}$, *where $S = $ NG-RES$(\mathcal{I})$;*
2. *tree-C-RES*$(\mathcal{I}) = 2^{O(S \log \log S / \log S)}$, *where $S = $ C-RES$(\mathcal{I})$,*
3. *tree-NG-RES*$(\mathcal{I}) = d^{O(nd^3 S \log \log S / \log S)}$, *where $S = $ tree-C-RES$(\mathcal{I})$.*
4. *NG-RES*$(\mathcal{I}) = 2^{O(S \log \log S / \log S)}$, *where $S = $ C-RES$(\mathcal{I})$,*

Proof. In [3] it is shown that for any unsatisfiable CNF formula ϕ, if $S = RES(\phi)$, then *tree-RES*$(\phi) = 2^{O(S \log \log S / \log S)}$, from which 2 follows easily. 1 can be proven by adapting the technique from [3] to *NG-RES*. 3 is obtained by using 1 and a direct simulation of *tree-C-RES* by *NG-RES*. 4 follows from 2 and the fact that *NG-RES* efficiently simulates *tree-C-RES*.

4 Lower Bounds for *tree-NG-RES*$(IMP_{G,S,T,d})$

This section comprises the proof of Theorem 1. The *tree-NG-RES* complexity of $IMP_{G,S,T,d}$ depends on the pebbling number of G. Roughly speaking, if G has large pebbling number, *tree-NG-RES* refutations of $IMP_{G,S,T,d}$ must be long.

Definition 2. *The pebbling number of T on a DAG $G = (V, E)$ from S, denoted $P_G(S, T)$, where $S, T \subseteq V$, is the minimal number of pebbles needed to pebble some vertex in T by following the rules below.*

1. *A pebble can be placed on a vertex in S.*
2. *A pebble can be removed from any vertex.*
3. *If a vertex is not in S, then it can only be pebbled if all its immediate predecessors have a pebble on them.*

Lemma 1 ([3]). *Let $G = (V, E)$ be a DAG. For any $v \in V$ and any sets $S, T \subseteq V$, $P_G(S, T) \leq \max\{P_G(S, T \cup \{v\}), P_G(S \cup \{v\}, T) + 1\}$.*

Proof. To pebble T from S, we can first pebble $T \cup \{v\}$ from S with $P_G(S, T \cup \{v\})$ pebbles. If some vertex in T is pebbled, then we are done. Otherwise, only v is pebbled. Leave the pebble on v and try to pebble T from $S \cup \{v\}$. This requires $P_G(S \cup \{v\}, T) + 1$ pebbles.

Note that for a DAG G with n vertices, $P_G(S,T) = O(n)$ since we can always use n pebbles and thus do not need to remove pebbles from vertices. What we are interested is a lower bound on the number of pebbles needed. A family of DAGs G_n with n vertices, each of in-degree 2 or 0, for which $P_{G_n}(S,T) = \Omega(n/\log n)$ where S and T are the sets of sources and targets in G_n, was given in [7].

The implication graph instance based on G_n is hard for *tree-NG-RES*. In particular, every *tree-NG-RES* refutation of $IMP_{G_n,S,T,d}$ must be of size $(d-1)^{\Omega(n/\log n)}$. We show this using a modified version of the game from [3], as follows. Let $\mathcal{I} = \langle [d], \Gamma \rangle$ be an unsatisfiable CSP instance. The game involves two players: Prover and Delayer. In each round, Prover picks a variable from $vars(\Gamma)$. Then, Delayer can choose 1 or *. If 1 is chosen, the variable is set to 1. Otherwise, Prover can pick a value from $\{2, \cdots, d\}$ and assign it to the variable. Delayer scores one point if he chooses *. The game ends when the current assignment falsifies at least one of the nogoods in Γ.

Here is a rough idea of the proof. We first show that any *tree-NG-RES* refutation of $IMP_{G,S,T,d}$ is of size at least exponential in the number of points Delayer can score. Then, we prove that there is a good strategy for Delayer to win at least $\Omega(P_G(S,T))$ points. So, every *tree-NG-RES* refutation of $IMP_{G,S,T,d}$ must be of size exponential to $\Omega(P_G(S,T))$. We call the above Delayer's strategy *superstrategy*.

Lemma 2. *For $\mathcal{I}$ an unsatisfiable CSP instance with domain size d, if $\mathcal{I}$ has a tree-NG-RES refutation of size S, then Prover has a strategy where Delayer can win at most $\lceil \log_{d-1} S \rceil$ points.*

Proof. Suppose $\mathcal{I}$ has a *tree-NG-RES* refutation π of size S. We will give a strategy which allows Prover to bound the number of points Delayer can win and show that as long as Prover follows the strategy, the following invariant will be maintained after each round: If p is the current points Delayer has scored, then there is a nogood N in π such that N is falsified by the current partial assignment and the sub-tree rooted at N in G_π is of size at most $S/(d-1)^p$.

At the beginning, Delayer has no points and the only nogood that is falsified is the empty nogood. So, the invariant holds. Consider the i-th round. Let p_{i-1} be the number of points Delayer has scored after the previous round and N_{i-1} be the nogood satisfying the invariant at the previous round. If N_{i-1} is a leaf in G_π, then N_{i-1} is a nogood in Γ that is falsified by the current partial assignment and hence the game ends. Otherwise, Prover picks the variable x which is resolved on to derive N_{i-1} from nogoods $N_1, N_2, \cdots, N_d$ in π. W.L.O.G., suppose $(x = 1) \in N_1, (x = 2) \in N_2$, and so on. If Delayer assigns 1 to x, then N_1 is falsified and it becomes the new nogood for the invariant. In this case, Delayer does not score any points and the sub-tree rooted at N_1 is obviously smaller than the one rooted at N_{i-1}. Thus, the invariant holds. If the Delayer chooses *, then Prover assigns x the value $j \in \{2, \cdots, d\}$ which will falsify the nogood N_j, among $N_2, \cdots, N_d$, with the smallest sub-tree. The sub-tree rooted at N_j is of size at most $1/(d-1)^{p_{i-1}+1}$, and the number of points Delayer has scored after this round is $p_{i-1} + 1$. Therefore, the invariant is maintained.

When the game halts, the size of the sub-tree is 1. If Delayer scores p points at the end of the game, then $1 \leq S/(d-1)^p$. This implies $p \leq \log_{d-1} S \leq \lceil \log_{d-1} S \rceil$. So, if Prover follows the above strategy, Delayer wins at most $\lceil \log_{d-1} S \rceil$ points.

Corollary 1. *For unsatisfiable CSP instance $\mathcal{I}$ with domain size d, if Delayer has a strategy which always scores r, then tree-NG-RES($\mathcal{I}$) $\geq (d-1)^{r-1}$.*

Proof. Suppose the Delayer has a strategy which always scores r points on $\mathcal{I}$. Toward a contradiction, suppose tree-NG-RES($\mathcal{I}$) $< (d-1)^{r-1}$. Then, by Lemma 2, the Prover has a strategy where the Delayer can win at most $\lceil \log_{d-1}(d-1)^{r-1} \rceil = r - 1 < r$ points. This contradicts that the Delayer can always scores r points.

The superstrategy for Delayer is simple. Before each game, Delayer sets $S' = S$ and $T' = T$. Then, in each round, if Prover asks about variable $x_i, i \in [n]$, Delayer responds as follows:

1. If $v_i \in T'$, assign 1 to the variable.
2. If $v_i \in S'$, respond $*$.
3. If $v_i \notin S' \cup T'$ and $P_G(S', T' \cup \{i\}) = P_G(S', T')$, assign the variable 1 and add v_i to T'.
4. If $v_i \notin S' \cup T'$ and $P_G(S', T' \cup \{i\}) < P_G(S', T')$, respond $*$ and add v_i to S'.

We will prove that $P_G(S', T')$ can decrease by at most the number of points Delayer scores and it is at most 3 at the end of the game. This implies the superstrategy guarantees Delayer to earn at least $P_G(S, T) - 3$ points.

Lemma 3. *After each round, if Delayer has scored p points, then $P_G(S', T') \geq P_G(S, T) - p$.*

Proof. Let S'_i and T'_i be the sets S' and T' respectively in Delayers superstrategy after round i. Let p_i be the number of points Delayer has scored after round i. We show that the invariant $P_G(S'_i, T'_i) \geq P_G(S, T) - p_i$ will be maintained after each round. At the beginning, $p_0 = 0, S'_0 = S$ and $T'_0 = T$. So, $P_G(S'_0, T'_0) = P_G(S, T) - 0$ and the invariant holds. Now consider round i. For case 1, 2, and 3, $P_G(S'_{i-1}, T'_{i-1}) = P_G(S'_i, T'_i)$ and $p_i \geq p_{i-1}$. So, $P_G(S'_i, T'_i) = P_G(S'_{i-1}, T'_{i-1}) \geq P_G(S, T) - p_{i-1} \geq P_G(S, T) - p_i$. For case 4, $P_G(S'_{i-1}, T'_{i-1} \cup \{v\}) < P_G(S'_{i-1}, T'_{i-1})$, $p_i = p_{i-1}+1$, $S'_i = S'_{i-1} \cup \{v\}$, and $T'_i = T'_{i-1}$. By Lemma 1, we have $P_G(S'_{i-1} \cup \{v\}, T'_{i-1}) \geq P_G(S'_{i-1}, T'_{i-1}) - 1$. Hence, $P_G(S'_i, T'_i) = P_G(S'_{i-1} \cup \{v\}, T'_{i-1}) \geq P_G(S'_{i-1}, T'_{i-1}) - 1 \geq P_G(S, T) - p_{i-1} - 1 = P_G(S, T) - p_i$. Therefore, the invariant is maintained after each round.

Lemma 4. *At the end of the game, $P_G(S', T') \leq 3$.*

Proof. When the game ends, some nogood N must be falsified since $IMP_{G,S,T,d}$ is unsatisfiable. N cannot be a Source axiom for some source v_i because $v_i \in S \subseteq S'$ and thus it can only be assigned values from $\{2, \cdots, d\}$ through case 2. This assignment does not violate the Source axiom. Similarly, N cannot be a Target axiom either. Hence, N must be a Pebbling axiom for some vertex v_k with predecessors v_i and v_j. To falsify N, x_k must be set to 1 and both x_i and x_j must be set to some values from $\{2, \cdots, d\}$. So, $v_k \in T'$ (via case 1 or case 3) and $v_i, v_j \in S'$ (via case 2 or case 4). Therefore, to pebble T' from S', we can first pebble v_i and v_j, then v_k. This only requires three pebbles.

Corollary 2. *Following the superstrategy described, Delayer can score at least $P_G(S,T) - 3$ points at the end of the game.*

Proof. This is an immediate consequence of Lemmas 3 and 4.

Lemma 5. *tree-NG-RES$(IMP_{G,S,T,d}) = (d-1)^{\Omega(P_G(S,T))}$.*

Proof. Corollary 2 shows that Delayer has a superstrategy to score at least $P_G(S,T) - 3$ points on $IMP_{G,S,T,d}$. So, by Corollary 1, tree-NG-RES$(IMP_{G,S,T,d}) \geq (d-1)^{P_G(S,T)-4}$. Hence, tree-NG-RES$(IMP_{G,S,T,d}) = (d-1)^{\Omega(P_G(S,T))}$.

Proof. **(Theorem 1)** Let $d \geq 3$ be an integer. Let $\{G_n\}$ be an infinite family of circuits such that $|V(G_n)| = n$ and $P_{G_n}(S,T) = \Omega(n/\log n)$ where S and T are the sets of sources and targets in G_n [7]. By Lemma 5, we have tree-NG-RES$(IMP_{G_n,S,T,d}) = (d-1)^{\Omega(P_G(S,T))} = (d-1)^{\Omega(n/\log n)}$.

5 Lower Bounds for $NG\text{-}RES(MGT'_n)$

This section comprises a proof of Theorem 4, which states that any $NG\text{-}RES$ refutation of MGT'_n must have size $2^{\Omega(n)}$. The proof approach is inspired by [6]. We show that if there is a short $NG\text{-}RES$ refutation of MGT'_n, then we can construct a narrow RES refutation of MGT_n, which contradicts the following property of MGT_n.

Theorem 7 ([5]). *Any RES refutation of MGT_n has width $\Omega(n)$.*

Definition 3. *A restriction for a CSP instance $\mathcal{I} = \langle \mathcal{D}, \Gamma \rangle$ forbids some variables to take some domain values. A restriction ρ is written as a set of variables with the forbidden values. For example, the restriction $\rho = \{x \neq 2, x \neq 3, y \neq 1\}$ disallows x to take 2 and 3, and y to take 1.*

Let $\rho = \{x_1 \neq a_1, x_2 \neq a_2, \cdots, x_k \neq a_k\}$ be a restriction. Define $N\lceil_\rho$ as the result of applying ρ to a nogood N where
$$N\lceil_\rho \stackrel{def}{=} (\cdots (N\lceil_{x_a \neq a_1})\lceil_{x_2 \neq a_2}) \cdots \lceil_{x_k \neq a_k}),$$
and for x a variable, $a \in \mathcal{D}(x)$,
$$N\lceil_{x \neq a} \stackrel{def}{=} \begin{cases} 1 & \text{if } (x = a) \in N \\ N & \text{otherwise.} \end{cases}$$

We define $\mathcal{I}\lceil_\rho \stackrel{def}{=} \langle \mathcal{D}\lceil_\rho, \Gamma\lceil_\rho \rangle$, where
$$\Gamma\lceil_\rho = \{N : N \in \Gamma \text{ and } N\lceil_\rho \neq 1\}$$
$$\text{vars}(\mathcal{I}\lceil_\rho) = \text{vars}(\mathcal{I})$$
$$\mathcal{D}\lceil_\rho(x) = \mathcal{D}(x) \setminus \{a : (x \neq a) \in \rho\} \qquad \text{for all } x \in \text{vars}(\mathcal{I}\lceil_\rho).$$

For $\pi = (N_1, \cdots, N_S)$ an NG-RES derivation, define $\pi\lceil_\rho$ to be $(N_1\lceil_\rho, \cdots, N_S\lceil_\rho)$, but with any $N_i\lceil_\rho$ that is identical to 1 removed. Note that $\pi\lceil_\rho$ is actually a subsequence of π.

Lemma 6. *If π is an NG-RES refutation of a CSP instance $\mathcal{I}$ and ρ is a restriction, then there is an NG-RES refutation of $\mathcal{I}\lceil_\rho$ of width at most $w(\pi\lceil_\rho)$.*

Proof. Let $\mathcal{I} = \langle \mathcal{D}, \Gamma \rangle$ be a CSP instance and $\rho = \{x \neq a\}$ be a unit restriction. Let π be an NG-RES refutation of $\mathcal{I}$. Transform $\pi\lceil_\rho$ inductively to an NG-RES refutation π' as follows. Consider a nogood N_i in $\pi\lceil_\rho$. $(x=a)$ must not appear in N_i since $N_i\lceil_{x\neq a} \neq 1$. If $N_i \in \Gamma$, then $N_i \in \Gamma\lceil_\rho$. (Note that $\pi\lceil_\rho$ is a subsequence of π.) Otherwise, N_i must be derived, in π, by resolving some previous nogoods $N_{i_1}, \cdots, N_{i_d}$ on some variable v. If $v \neq x$, then $(x = a)$ does not appear in any of $N_{i_1}, \cdots, N_{i_d}$ because $(x=a) \notin N_i$. So, $N_{i_1}, \cdots, N_{i_d}$ must be in $\pi\lceil_\rho$ and they can be resolved to derive N_i in $\pi\lceil_\rho$. If $v = x$, then there is a nogood $N_{i_a} \in \{N_{i_1}, \cdots, N_{i_d}\}$ such that $N_{i_a} = \eta(x = a, N_a)$ and thus $N_{i_a}\lceil_\rho$ is not in $\pi\lceil_\rho$ since $N_{i_a}\lceil_\rho = 1$. But, all the nogoods in $\{N_{i_1}, \cdots, N_{i_d}\} \setminus \{N_{i_a}\}$ are in $\pi\lceil_\rho$. So, we can resolve them on x, over the new domain of x, to get a sub-nogood of N_i, which is sufficient to produce the desired refutation. The general case for non-unit restriction follows easily.

Lemma 7. *If there is an NG-RES refutation of MGT'_n of size at most S, then there is a RES refutation of MGT_n of width at most w, for any $w > \log S$.*

Proof. Let π be an NG-RES refutation of MGT'_n of size at most S. Let $w > \log S$. Define that a nogood is wide if its width is greater than w. Define a random restriction ρ as follows. For each variable $v_{i,j}$, $v \in \{x, y\}$, ρ randomly picks a value a from $\{1,2\}$ and a value c from $\{3,4\}$, and restricts that $v_{i,j} \neq a$ and $v_{i,j} \neq c$. So, for every variable, a domain value is prohibited by ρ with probability $1/2$. We say that a restriction is bad if not all wide nogoods in π are set to 1 by ρ. A wide nogood would be set to 1 by ρ if there is some literal, $(x = a)$, in it such that $(x \neq a) \in \rho$. The probability that this is not the case is at most $1/2^w$. Since there is at most S nogoods in π, the probability that ρ is bad is at most $S/2^w$ which is less than 1 as we have $w > \log S$. Therefore, there must exist at least one good restriction which would set all wide nogoods in π to 1.

Apply a good restriction ρ to π. By Lemma 6, there is an NG-RES refutation π' of $MGT'_n\lceil_\rho$ of width at most w. After we apply ρ to MGT'_n, some initial nogoods disappear. For example, for each j, two of the nogoods in (1') are set to 1 by ρ and thus not included in $MGT'_n\lceil_\rho$. Moreover, the domain size of each variable becomes 2.

Therefore, the CNF encoding of $MGT'_n\lceil_\rho$ consists of the following clauses:

(1'') $(\overline{x_{j,j}:a_{j,j}})$ $\qquad j \in [n]$

(2'') $(\overline{x_{i,j}:a_{i,j}}\ \overline{x_{j,k}:a_{j,k}}\ \overline{x_{i,k}:c_{i,k}})$ $\qquad i,j,k \in [n], i \neq j \neq k$

(3'') $(\overline{x_{i,j}:a_{i,j}}\ \overline{x_{j,i}:a_{j,i}})$ $\qquad i,j \in [n], i \neq j$

(4'') $(y_{0,j}:b_{0,j})$

$\bigwedge_{i \in [n]} (\ \overline{y_{i-1,j}:c_{i-1,j}}\ \overline{x_{i,j}:a_{i,j}}\ \overline{y_{i,j}:b_{i,j}}\ )$ $\qquad j \in [n]$

$(y_{n,j}:d_{n,j})$

Domain clauses: $(x_{i,j}\!:\!a_{i,j} \quad x_{i,j}\!:\!c_{i,j})$
$(y_{i,j}\!:\!b_{i,j} \quad y_{i,j}\!:\!d_{i,j})$

where each of $a_{i,j}$'s and $b_{i,j}$'s is equal to either 1 or 2 and each of $c_{i,j}$'s and $d_{i,j}$'s is equal to either 3 or 4.

Rename the variables $\overline{x_{i,j}\!:\!a_{i,j}}$, $\overline{x_{i,j}\!:\!c_{i,j}}$, $\overline{y_{i,j}\!:\!b_{i,j}}$, and $\overline{y_{i,j}\!:\!d_{i,j}}$ as $\overline{x_{i,j}}$, $x_{i,j}$, $\overline{y_{i,j}}$, and $y_{i,j}$, respectively. Now the constraint clauses of $\text{CNF}(MGT'_n\lceil_\rho)$ are exactly the clauses in MGT_n and the NG-RES derivation steps

$$\frac{\eta(x_{i,j}=a_{i,j},\ N_1) \quad \eta(x_{i,j}=c_{i,j},\ N_2)}{\eta(N_1,N_2)} \ x_{i,j} \in \{a_{i,j}, c_{i,j}\} \quad \text{and} \quad \frac{\eta(y_{i,j}=b_{i,j},\ N_1) \quad \eta(y_{i,j}=d_{i,j},\ N_2)}{\eta(N_1,N_2)} \ y_{i,j} \in \{b_{i,j}, d_{i,j}\}$$

in π' can be transformed into the following RES derivation steps

$$\frac{(\overline{x_{i,j}}\ X_1) \quad (x_{i,j}\ X_2)}{(X_1\ X_2)} \quad \text{and} \quad \frac{(\overline{y_{i,j}}\ X_1) \quad (y_{i,j}\ X_2)}{(X_1\ X_2)}.$$

The resulting RES refutation has the same width as π'. Hence, there is a RES refutation of MGT_n of width at most w.

Proof. **(of Theorem 4)** Let π be an NG-RES refutation of MGT'_n. Let S be the size of π. Pick $w = \log S + \epsilon$, $\epsilon > 0$. It follows from Lemma 7 that MGT_n has a RES refutation π' of width at most $\log S + \epsilon$. We know that any RES refutation of MGT_n must have width $\Omega(n)$ (Theorem 7). Therefore, $\log S + \epsilon \geq \Omega(n)$, and thus $S \geq 2^{\Omega(n)}$. Hence, any NG-RES refutation of MGT'_n must be of size $2^{\Omega(n)}$.

6 Conclusion and Future Work

We have shown that 2-way branching is much more powerful than d-way branching, for backtracking. It remains to establish an efficient strategy for 2-way branching with learning for the instances separating NG-RES from C-RES, to establish the analogous fact for the case with learning. The question of whether nogood learning algorithms are as powerful as these proof systems is an important open problem.

The algorithm suggested for efficiently solving the instances which separate *tree-NG-RES* and *tree-C-RES* are simple enough that they certainly will be faster, at least for large enough instances, than any d-way branching algorithm. However, developing good heuristics which take advantage of the extra power of 2-way branching in practical algorithms is an important remaining task.

References

[1] Andrew B. Baker. *Intelligent Backtracking on Constraint Satisfaction Problems: Experimental and Theoretical Results*. PhD thesis, University of Oregon, 1995.

[2] Paul Beame, Henry Kautz, and Ashish Sabharwal. Towards understanding and harnessing the potential of clause learning. *Journal of Artificial Intelligence Research*, 22:319–351, 2004.

[3] Eli Ben-Sasson, Russell Impagliazzo, and Avi Wigderson. Near-optimal separation of treelike and general resolution. Technical Report TR01-005, Electronic Colloquium on Computational Complexity (ECCC), 2000.
[4] M. L. Bonet, J. L. Esteban, N. Galesi, and J. Johansen. Exponential separations between restricted resolution and cutting planes proof systems. In *Proc. of the 39th Annual IEEE Symposium on Foundations of Computer Science (FOCS'98)*, pages 638–647. IEEE Press, 1998.
[5] M. L. Bonet and N. Galesi. A study of proof search algorithms for resolution and polynomial calculus. In *Proc. 40th Symposium on Foundations of Computer Science*, pages 422–432, 1999.
[6] J. Buresh-Oppenheim, D. Mitchell, and T. Pitassi. Linear and negative resolution are weaker than resolution. Technical Report TR01-074, Electronic Colloquium on Computational Complexity (ECCC), 2001.
[7] J.R. Celoni, W.J. Paul, and R.E. Tarjan. Space bounds for a game on graphs. *Mathematical Systems Theory*, 10:239–251, 1977.
[8] Cho Yee Joey Hwang. A theoretical comparison of resolution proof systems for csp algorithms. Master's thesis, Simon Fraser University, 2004.
[9] B. Krishnamurthy. Short proofs for tricky formulas. *Acta Informatica*, 22:253–274, 1985.
[10] David G. Mitchell. *The Resolution Complexity of Constraint Satisfaction*. PhD thesis, University of Toronto, 2002.
[11] David G. Mitchell. Resolution and constraint satisfaction. In *Lecture Notes in Computer Science, LNCS 2833*, pages 555–569. Springer, 2003.
[12] V. Park. An empirical study of different branching strategies for constraint satisfaction problems. Master's thesis, University of Waterloo, 2004.
[13] B. M. Smith and P. Sturdy. An empirical investigation of value ordering for finding all solutions. Presented at the ECAI 2004 workshop on Modelling and Solving Problems with Constraints.
[14] G. Stalmarck. Short resolution proofs for a sequence of tricky formulas. *Acta Informatica*, 33:277–280, 1996.

Maintaining Longest Paths in Cyclic Graphs

Irit Katriel[1] and Pascal Van Hentenryck[2]

[1] Max-Plank-Institut für Informatik, Saarbrücken, Germany
[2] Brown University, Box 1910, Providence, RI 02912

Abstract. This paper reconsiders the problem of maintaining longest paths in directed graphs, which is at the core of many scheduling applications. It presents bounded incremental algorithms for arc insertion and deletion running in time $O(\|\delta\| + |\delta| \log |\delta|)$ on Cyclic<0 graphs (i.e., graphs whose cycles have strictly negative lengths), where $|\delta|$ and $\|\delta\|$ are measures of the change in the input and output. For Cyclic≤0 graphs, maintaining longest paths is unbounded under reasonable computational models; when only arc insertions are allowed, it is shown that the problem can be solved in $O(\|\delta\| + |\delta| \log |\delta|)$ time even in the presence of zero-length cycles. The algorithms directly apply to shortest paths (by negating the lengths), leading to simpler algorithms than previously known and reducing the worst-case complexity of an operation from $\tilde{O}(n\,m)$ to $O(n+m)$ for Cyclic>0 graphs with n vertices and m arcs.

1 Introduction

Maintaining longest paths under arc insertion and deletion in cyclic graphs with arbitrary arc lengths is an important aspect of many combinatorial optimization applications. It arises in many scheduling algorithms, including heuristic procedures [16], local search for jobshop scheduling [4,12], and iterative flattening in cumulative scheduling [2,11], constraint-based scheduling with precedence graphs [9] (where only insertions must be considered, since deletions are typically performed by backtracking), and temporal constraint networks [3]. In addition, the maintenance of longest paths under arc insertion and deletion is naturally transformed into incremental shortest paths (by negating the lengths), further enlarging the class of applications.

Earlier work has considered the incremental maintenance of longest paths in directed acyclic graphs (DAGs) [10], with subsequent improvements for the case of arbitrary, i.e., both positive and negative, arc lengths [7]. Arbitrary lengths are important in real-world scheduling applications, which often contain complex distance constraints. The insertion and deletion algorithms run in time $O(\|\delta\| + |\delta| \log |\delta|)$ and $O(\|\delta\|)$ respectively, where $|\delta|$ and $\|\delta\|$ are measures of the changes in the input and output (precise definitions appear in Section 2). However, some significant scheduling applications (e.g., in the steel industry) also contain cyclic graphs, which arise, for instance, when an activity must not start too long after some of its predecessors. Consider a sequence of activities $v_1 \to \ldots \to v_n$ linked by precedence constraints and assume that activity v_n must start at most $d_1 +$

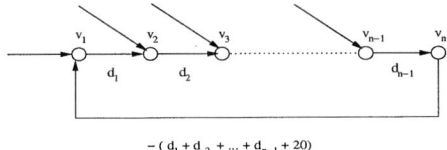

Fig. 1. A Cyclic Graph from a Scheduling Problem

$\ldots + d_{n-1} + 20$ minutes after the starting time of v_1. This constraint generates an arc $v_n \to v_1$ with length $-(d_1 + \ldots d_{n-1} + 20)$, producing a cycle of negative length as shown in Figure 1. Therefore, it is particularly important to design incremental longest paths algorithms for cyclic graphs with arbitrary lengths. We consider only graphs whose cycles have nonpositive lengths, as otherwise longest paths are not well-defined.

The main technical contribution of this paper is to propose bounded incremental algorithms for maintaining longest paths in cyclic graphs where all cycles have strictly negative lengths (Cyclic<0 graphs). Both the insertion and deletion algorithms run in $O(\|\delta\| + |\delta| \log |\delta|)$ time. When cycles of length zero are allowed, the problem becomes unbounded under reasonable computational models. However, when only arc insertions are allowed, it can be solved by the same algorithm in time $O(\|\delta\| + |\delta| \log |\delta|)$. The algorithms enjoy some very interesting properties. First, the insertion algorithm designed for DAGs also works in the presence of cycles, although a new and slightly more complex proof of correctness is necessary. Second, the deletion algorithm is novel (the original one strongly relies on the acyclic property) and propagates the changes like in the insertion algorithm. Third, unlike earlier bounded algorithms for shortest paths [14], which resemble their offline counterparts, our algorithms for longest paths have no natural offline counterpart and are organized around incremental concepts. Fourth, the time complexity of the incremental algorithms remains $O(\|\delta\| + |\delta| \log |\delta|)$ when moving from DAGs to cyclic graphs, although the best known upper bound for the offline problem moves from $O(|A| + |V|)$ to $O(|A||V|)$, where A is the set of arcs and V is the set of vertices; in the presence of cycles nothing faster than the Bellman-Ford algorithm is known. Finally, from a constraint satisfaction standpoint, the key insight underlying the algorithms is to find an appropriate order for applying the traditional propagation rules for precedence constraints so that each vertex is updated at most once. The algorithms can also be generalized to multiple insertions from the same vertex, using techniques presented in [10,8].

The results also have a significant corollary: the algorithms directly apply to shortest paths (by negating arc lengths) for which they provide bounded incremental algorithms for Cyclic>0 graphs with arbitrary arc lengths and for arc insertions in Cyclic$\geq$0 graphs. The resulting algorithms are significantly simpler than those proposed in [14] and reduce the worst-case complexity of an operation from from $O(nm)$ to $\tilde{O}(n+m)$ for Cyclic>0 graphs with n vertices and m arcs, since they do not use the Bellman-Ford algorithm. As a result, they apply directly to the incremental pruning of simple temporal networks [3].

The rest of this paper is organized as follows. Section 2 reviews the bounded incremental computational model and Section 3 gives the specifications of the algorithms. Sections 4, 5, and 6 are the core of the paper: they discuss Cyclic<0 and Cyclic≤0 graphs, and the applications to shortest paths.

2 Bounded Incremental Computation

Informally, incremental algorithms can be modelled as updating the output of a function subject to changes to its input. Let f be a function, x be an input, and ϵ be a change in x. An incremental algorithm receives x, $f(x)$, and ϵ as inputs and transforms $f(x)$ into $f(x + \epsilon)$, where $x + \epsilon$ denotes the result of applying change ϵ on input x. For instance, x may be a directed graph with a source, f may compute the length of the longest path from the source to each of the vertices, and ϵ may be the insertion of an arc $a \to b$ or the removal of such an arc. In general, it is useful in incremental algorithms to maintain auxiliary information in order to compute $f(x+\epsilon)$. Provided that the auxiliary information is polynomially related in size to the output, the problem can then be viewed as computing an enhanced function f' incrementally. Hence we can safely ignore this issue without loss of generality and work directly with f'.

Various models for analyzing incremental algorithms have been proposed and they include online algorithms, amortized analysis [15], and *bounded incremental computation* (BIC) [14]. Many such models analyze the complexity of incremental algorithms in terms of the input size (e.g., $x+\epsilon$). *The BIC model, on the contrary, studies the behavior of incremental algorithms in terms of the changes in the input and output.* As a consequence, the BIC model has a finer granularity and can differentiate algorithms that other models cannot.

Since this paper assumes the BIC model, let us describe its main concepts more precisely. Let $\Delta(f, x, \epsilon)$ denote the change between $f(x)$ and $f(x + \epsilon)$ and let $\delta(f, x, \epsilon)$ denote $\epsilon + \Delta(f, x, \epsilon)$. For instance, in an incremental longest path algorithm, $\Delta(f, x, \epsilon)$ may represent the pairs (vertex,length) which have changed (i.e., the affected pairs) when ϵ (e.g., an arc insertion) is performed. Since, in general, the function f and the change ϵ are clear from the context, we use Δ and δ for simplicity. The BIC model analyzes the performance of an algorithm in terms of $|\delta|$ and its generalization $\|\delta\|$ which typically includes some (unaffected) data that any reasonable algorithm would need to examine. For instance, in longest path algorithms, $\|\delta\|$ denotes the sum of the number of affected vertices and the number of arcs which are adjacent to affected vertices: It is reasonable to assume that any algorithm would necessarily have to examine every vertex which is adjacent to an affected vertex. For graphs with bounded degrees (e.g., jobshop scheduling), $\|\delta\| = O(|\delta|)$ so this issue is moot.

An incremental algorithm is *bounded* if, for all input x and any allowed change ϵ, its running time depends only on $|\delta|$ and $\|\delta\|$, not on the size of the input $x+\epsilon$. It is *unbounded* otherwise. Many incremental problems are unbounded (e.g., graph reachability under the local persistent model [14]) and hence the existence of a bounded algorithm is a strong guarantee for incremental performance.

3 Specifications

Given a graph $G = (V, A)$, with a source $s \in V$, the predecessors $pred(G, v)$ of a vertex v are given by $\{u | u \to v \in A\}$ and the successors $succ(G, v)$ by $\{u | v \to u \in A\}$. For every arc $u \to v \in A$, $d(u, v)$ denotes the length of the arc $u \to v$ and $lp(G, v)$ the length of a longest path from s to v. The projection of a graph $G = (V, A)$ wrt its longest paths is the graph $G_{|l} = (V, A')$ where

$$A' = \{x \to y \in A \mid lp(G, x) + d(x, y) = lp(G, y)\},$$

i.e., the subgraph consisting of all arcs belonging to longest paths. This projection plays a fundamental role in deletion algorithms and is maintained (at no asymptotic cost) by the algorithms. The incremental algorithms also maintain the length $l(v)$ of a longest path from s to v for each vertex.

Definition 1 (Specification of insertArc). *Let $G = (V, A)$ be a graph, $x \to y \notin A$, and $G' = (V, A \cup \{x \to y\})$. Procedure insertArc$(G, x \to y)$ must satisfy*

Pre: $\forall v \in V : l(v) = lp(G, v) \land G_l = G_{|l}$.
Post: $\forall v \in V : l(v) = lp(G', v) \land G_l = G'_{|l}$.

Definition 2 (Specification of deleteArc). *Let $G = (V, A)$ be a graph, $x \to y \in A$, and $G' = (V, A \setminus \{x \to y\})$. Procedure deleteArc$(G, x \to y)$ must satisfy*

Pre: $\forall v \in V : l(v) = lp(G, v) \land G_l = G_{|l}$.
Post: $\forall v \in V : l(v) = lp(G', v) \land G_l = G'_{|l}$.

As mentioned earlier, the set of vertices that are affected by an insertion or deletion is fundamental in bounded algorithms.

Definition 3 (Affected Vertices). *Let $G = (V, A)$, $x \to y \notin A$, and $G' = (V, A \cup \{x \to y\})$. The set of affected vertices by the insertion of $x \to y$ into G is defined as $\mathit{Aff}_I(G, x \to y) = \{v \in V \mid lp(G', v) > lp(G, v)\}$. Let $G = (V, A)$, $x \to y \in A$, and $G' = (V, A \setminus \{x \to y\})$. The set of vertices affected by the deletion of $x \to y$ from G is defined as $\mathit{Aff}_D(G, x \to y) = \{v \in V \mid lp(G', v) < lp(G, v)\}$.*

The variation of a vertex measures by how much the length of its longest path changes due to a modification of the graph.

Definition 4 (Variation of a Vertex). *Let $G = (V, A)$ be a graph and $G' = (V, A')$ be the graph obtained after inserting or deleting an arc. The variation of a vertex $v \in V$ from G to G', is defined as $\Delta(v, G, G') = lp(G', v) - lp(G, v)$.*

In the following, we abuse notation and use $\Delta(v)$ instead of $\Delta(v, G, G')$ when G and G' are clear from the context.

Convention 1. *When a vertex is not reachable from the source, the above concepts are not well-defined. To simplify the exposition, we assume that the lengths of longest paths are all in a range $[0, H)$. This is natural in scheduling applications where the lengths represent times from the start of the project and H is the scheduling horizon. With this assumption, we can add an arc of length $-H$ from the source to each vertex $v \in V \setminus \{s\}$. Then, all vertices with a negative length are unreachable. We will remove this assumption in Section 6.*

4 Cyclic<0 Graphs

Interestingly, the insertion algorithm for acyclic graphs [7] directly applies to Cyclic<0 graphs; only the correctness proof and the deletion algorithm change.

4.1 Insertion

By definition, bounded incremental algorithms can only consider affected vertices (and their neighbors). The insertion algorithms in [7,10] consider each affected vertex only once and compute the new longest paths while discovering the set of affected vertices. The critical issue is to determine an order of processing the vertices which guarantees correctness. Offline algorithms typically use a topological ordering of the acyclic graph, but such an ordering cannot be used in incremental algorithms since it evolves over time. When the lengths are strictly positive, the lengths of the longest paths in the current graph conveniently provide a topological ordering [10]. When the lengths are unrestricted however, even the lengths of longest paths are no longer a topological ordering. It is thus necessary to find another ordering of the vertices which considers the affected vertices exactly once and guarantees correctness.

The key observation behind the algorithm with unrestricted lengths [7] is the fact that the variations of the affected vertices are monotonically non-increasing along the longest paths. More precisely, if $\langle v_1, \ldots, v_k \rangle$ is a longest path in G', the variations of the vertices satisfy $\Delta(v_1) \geq \Delta(v_2) \geq \ldots \geq \Delta(v_k)$. Figure 2 shows the impact of adding the dashed arc to the DAG. The affected vertices are inside the ellipse and the changes to the $l(v)$ values are shown. Observe that the changes decrease monotonically along longest paths in G'. Indeed, the variation of a vertex is never larger than the maximum variation of its predecessors. As a consequence, the algorithm considers the affected vertices in non-increasing order of their variations. Let v be the vertex whose variation is maximal among all unprocessed vertices. Even if v is not the smallest topologically, the paths to v through its unprocessed predecessors can be ignored, because the variation propagated along them is not larger than the variation of v. Of course, the algorithm does not "know" the variations initially but discovers them, together with the affected vertices, as it proceeds. More precisely, the algorithm maintains a lower approximation $\alpha(v)$ to the variation of vertex v and is organized around a priority queue which contains the affected vertices to be processed. The priority queue is ordered by the approximations of the variations and must be implemented using a Fibonacci heap [6] (or another priority queue that enables to

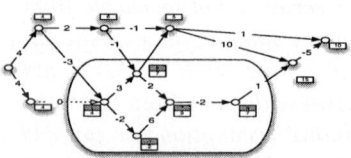

Fig. 2. The impact of inserting the dashed arc to the DAG

procedure insertArc$(G, x \to y)$
1. $Q = \{\}$;
2. $G = G \cup \{x \to y\}$;
3. $\alpha(y) = l(x) + d(x,y) - l(y)$;
4. $M = \{y\}$;
5. **if** $\alpha(y) > 0$ **then**
6. $insert(Q, \langle \alpha(y), y \rangle)$;
7. **while** $Q \neq \emptyset$ **do**
8. $u = extractMax(Q)$;
9. $l(u) = l(u) + \alpha(u)$;
10. $M = M \cup \{u\}$;
11. **forall** $w \in succ(G, u)$ **do**
12. $\alpha_w = l(u) + d(u, w) - l(w)$;
13.   **if** $\alpha_w > 0 \wedge (w \notin Q \vee \alpha_w > \alpha(w))$ **then**
14. $\alpha(w) := \alpha_w$;
15. $updatePriority(Q, \langle \alpha(w), w \rangle)$;
16. **forall** $u \in M$ **do**
17. $G_l = G_l \setminus \{p \to u \mid p \to u \in G_l\}$; $G_l = G_l \setminus \{u \to s \mid u \to s \in G_l\}$;
18. $G_l = G_l \cup \{p \to u \mid p \in pred(G, u) \wedge l(p) + d(p, u) = l(u)\}$;
19. $G_l = G_l \cup \{u \to s \mid s \in succ(G, u) \wedge l(u) + d(u, s) = l(s)\}$;

Fig. 3. An Incremental Algorithm for Arc Insertion

update a key in constant time), since the approximation of a vertex might be refined several times after it is inserted into the queue.

The Algorithm. Figure 3 depicts the algorithm. It receives $G = (V, A)$, the function l for G, an arc $x \to y$ to be inserted in A and the length $d(x, y)$ of this arc. It updates the function l for the graph $G' = (V, A \cup \{x \to y\})$. Initially, it pushes y into the queue Q with priority equal to $\alpha(y) = \Delta(y) = l(x)+d(x,y)-l(y)$ and inserts y into the set of affected vertices M. The core of the algorithm is lines 8-15 which are iterated until the queue is empty. Each iteration extracts a vertex u with maximal priority from the queue and updates its longest path $l(u)$. At that stage, we will prove that $\alpha(u) = \Delta(u)$ and hence $l(u)$ has reached its final value. Lines 11-15 consider the successors of u and update their priorities if necessary. A priority is updated if the variation propagated along the arc $u \to w$ is greater than the current priority. The variations of vertices from M cannot be updated at this point, since their lengths have reached the final values. The algorithm terminates with a linear scan of the affected vertices to update $G_{|l}$ by removing arcs incident on affected vertices and adding back the arcs that are incident and tight.

The Correctness Proof. The correctness proofs in [7,8] fail for Cyclic<0 graphs because they both assume the existence of a topological order in G. When G contains cycles, this assumption collapses. The key insight, captured in Figure 4, is that $G_{|l}$ is a DAG, providing an appropriate ordering for the proof. The figure shows that $G_{|l}$, which varies over time, may contain different arcs of a cycle but not all of them.

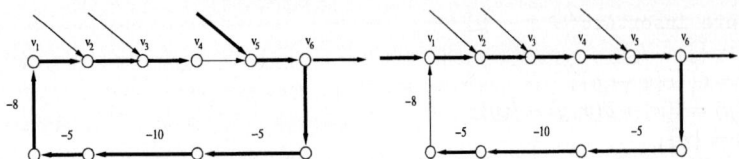

Fig. 4. Part of a Cyclic Graph and its Projection Before and After the Insertion of the Arc Incident to v_1: Arcs on the Longest Paths are in Bold

Proposition 1. *Let $G(V, A)$ be a Cyclic<0 graph with a source s. Then $G_{|l}$, the projection of G wrt to its longest paths, is a DAG.*

Proof. Assume that $G_{|l}$ contains a cycle of ℓ arcs and let $u_0, u_2, \ldots, u_{\ell-1} = u_0$ be its vertices and $(u_i, u_{(i+1)\bmod \ell})$ be its arcs. By the definition of $G_{|l}$, we have that for all $1 \leq i \leq \ell$ and $j = (i+1)\bmod \ell$, $lp(u_i) + d(u_i, u_j) = lp(u_j)$ or, equivalently, $d(u_i, u_j) = lp(u_j) - lp(u_i)$. The length of the cycle is then $\sum_{i=1}^{\ell} d(u_i, u_j) = \sum_{i=1}^{\ell} lp(u_j) - lp(u_i)$, which is equal to 0 because the right-hand side telescopes. This contradicts our assumption that G is Cyclic<0. □

The slack of an arc links the longest path lengths of its two endpoints.

Definition 5 (Slack of an Arc). *Let $G(V, A)$ and $x \to y \in A$. The slack of arc $x \to y$, denoted by $sl(G, x, y)$, is defined as*

$$sl(G, x, y) = lp(G, y) - (lp(G, x) + d(x, y)).$$

Once again, we abuse notation and omit G when it is clear from the context.

Proposition 2. *Let $G(V, A)$, $x \to y \notin A$, $G'(V, A \cup \{x \to y\})$ and $v \in Aff_I(G, x \to y)$ ($v \neq y$). We have $\Delta(v) = \max_{p \in pred(G, v)} (\Delta(p) - sl(p, v))$.*

Proof. By definition of longest paths, we have

$$lp(G', v) = \max_{p \in pred(G', v)} (lp(G', p) + d(p, v))$$

$$lp(G, v) + \Delta(v) = \max_{p \in pred(G, v)} (lp(G, p) + \Delta(p) + d(p, v))$$

$$\Delta(v) = \max_{p \in pred(G, v)} (\Delta(p) - (lp(G, v) - lp(G, p)) + d(p, v)))$$

$$\Delta(v) = \max_{p \in pred(G, v)} (\Delta(p) - sl(p, v)). \quad \square$$

We now show that the variations decrease monotonically along longest paths, giving an appropriate order to process the vertices.

Proposition 3 (Monotonicity). *Let $G(V, A)$, $x \to y \notin A$, $G'(V, A \cup \{x \to y\})$, and $v \to w$ be an arc on a longest path in G'. Then $\Delta(v) \geq \Delta(w)$.*

Proof. Since $v \to w$ is on a longest path in G', we have $lp(G', w) = lp(G', v) + d(v, w)$. Since $lp(G, w) \geq lp(G, v) + d(v, w)$, it follows that

$$\Delta(w) = lp(G', w) - lp(G, w) \leq lp(G', v) - lp(G, v) = \Delta(v). \quad \square$$

We also show that, after the insertion of an arc (x,y), for each affected vertex v, there is a longest path from s to v that goes through y. The predicate $path(G,v,w)$ holds if there exists a path from v to w in G.

Proposition 4. *Let $G(V,A)$, $x \to y \notin A$, $G'(V, A \cup \{x \to y\})$, and $v \in \mathit{Aff}_I(G, x \to y)$. Then, $path(G'_{|l}, y, v)$ holds.*

Proof. By Proposition 1, $G'_{|l}$ is a DAG. Let v by topologically minimal in $G'_{|l}$ such that the lemma does not hold. By definition of Aff_I, $\Delta(v) > 0$. By Proposition 3, for any predecessor u of v in $G'_{|l}$, $\Delta(u) \geq \Delta(v)$. Hence, by definition of Aff_I, $u \in \mathit{Aff}_I$. Since v was a topologically minimal vertex that violates the lemma, we can assume that there is a path p in $G'_{|l}$ from y to u. But the arc (u,v) is in $G'_{|l}$, so the path $p \cup (u,v)$ is a path in $G'_{|l}$ from y to v, a contradiction. □

We are now ready to prove the correctness of Procedure `insertArc`.

Theorem 1. *Procedure `insertArc` is correct for Cyclic<0 graphs.*

Proof. The proof relies on the observation that the algorithm partitions the affected vertices into three sets P, Q and R

$$P = \{v \in \mathit{Aff}_I \mid l(v) = lp(G', v)\}; \tag{1}$$
$$Q = \{v \in \mathit{Aff}_I \mid (v = y \vee \exists v' \in P : v' \to v) \,\&\, v \notin P\}; \tag{2}$$
$$R = \{v \in \mathit{Aff}_I \mid \exists v' \in Q : path(G'_{|l}, v', v) \,\&\, v \notin P \cup Q\} \tag{3}$$

as well as the following invariants in line 8 of the algorithm:

$$\mathit{Aff}_I = P \cup Q \cup R \tag{4}$$
$$\forall w \in Q \setminus \{y\} : \alpha(w) = \max_{v \in pred(G,w) \cap P} \Delta(v) - sl(v,w) \tag{5}$$
$$\alpha(y) = lp(G,x) + d(x,y) - lp(G,y) \tag{6}$$

Initially, $P = \emptyset, Q = \{y\}$ and all the other affected vertices are in R, thereby establishing Invariant 4. Invariants 5 and 6 trivially hold, since there can be no cycle of positive length.

Assume that the invariants hold at iteration i and let us show that they also hold at the beginning of iteration $i+1$. We first show that $\alpha(u) = \Delta(u)$ to satisfy the definition of P. It is obvious for the first iteration which extracts y. For subsequent iterations, by Proposition 2, $\Delta(u) = \max_{p \in pred(G,u)} \Delta(p) - sl(p,u)$ and, by Invariant 5, $\alpha(u) = \max_{p \in pred(G,u) \cap P} \Delta(p) - sl(p,u)$. Since $\alpha(u) = \max_{q \in Q} \alpha(q)$, it suffices to show that

$$\forall v \in Q \cup R : \Delta(v) \leq \max_{q \in Q} \alpha(q) \tag{7}$$

since it implies

$$\alpha(u) \geq \max_{p \in pred(G,u) \cap (Q \cup R)} \Delta(p) \geq \max_{p \in pred(G,u) \cap (Q \cup R)} \Delta(p) - sl(p,u)$$

and the result follows by the definitions of P, Q, and R. To show (7) consider the vertex $q^* \in Q \cup R$ such that

$$\Delta(q^*) = \max_{q \in Q \cup R} \Delta(q) \qquad (8)$$

and such that q^* is topologically smallest in $G'_{|l}$ among the vertices satisfying 8. Such a vertex q^* exists because $G'_{|l}$ is a DAG (Proposition 1) and there is a path in $G'_{|l}$ from y to all affected vertices (Proposition 4).

Since, by definition of R, the longest paths to a vertex $r \in R$ go through vertices in Q, it follows, by Proposition 3, that $q^* \in Q$. If q^* has a predecessor w in $Q \cup R$, it follows that $\Delta(w) < \Delta(q*)$, since q^* is topologically minimal and $\Delta(q^*)$ is maximal. It follows that the arc $w \to q^*$ cannot belong to a longest path to q^*, since this would contradict Proposition 3. As a consequence, the predecessors of q^* on any longest path must be in P. We have that

$$lp(G', q^*) = \max_{p \in pred(G', q^*) \cap P} lp(G', p) + d(p, q^*)$$

$$lp(G, q^*) + \Delta(q^*) = \max_{p \in pred(G, q^*) \cap P} lp(G, p) + \Delta(p) + d(p, q^*)$$

$$\Delta(q^*) = \max_{p \in pred(G, q^*) \cap P} \Delta(p) - (lp(G, q^*) - (lp(G, p) + d(p, q^*)))$$

$$\Delta(q^*) = \max_{p \in pred(G, q^*) \cap P} \Delta(p) - sl(p, q^*) = \alpha(q^*) \le \max_{q \in Q} \alpha(q).$$

It remains to show that Invariant 5 is preserved by lines 11-15. Consider a vertex w such that $u \to w$. The value $\alpha(w)$ becomes

$$\max(\alpha(w), l(u) - l(w) + d(u, w))$$
$$\max(\alpha(w), lp(G', u) - lp(G, w) + d(u, w))$$
$$\max(\alpha(w), \Delta(u) - (lp(G, w) - (lp(G, u) + d(u, w))))$$
$$\max(\alpha(w), \Delta(u) - sl(u, w)) = \max_{p \in pred(G, w) \cap P} \Delta(p) - sl(p, u).$$

The definitions of Q and R are also preserved by these instructions. Finally, the algorithm terminates, since the size of $Q \cup R$ strictly decreases at each iteration. Indeed, a vertex in P cannot be inserted in the queue more than once, since $l(u)$ reaches its final value in line 9 and, in line 12, $\alpha_w \le 0$ for all $w \in P$. □

Complexity. A vertex is inserted at most once into the queue and each arc outgoing from a vertex in Aff_I is examined once. Hence the algorithm performs a total of $|\delta|$ insertions, $|\delta|$ extractions, and at most $\|\delta\|$ *updatePriority* operations. The total running time, using a Fibonacci heap [6], is $O(\|\delta\| + |\delta| \log |\delta|)$.

4.2 Arc Deletion

We now turn to arc deletion. The algorithm from [10] is not efficient on cyclic graphs because it uses, as a subroutine, an offline longest-paths algorithm. For DAGs it is efficient, because longest paths can be computed offline in linear

```
function computeAffected($G_l, x \to y$)
1.    $Q = \{y\};\ M = \emptyset$;
2.    while $Q \neq \emptyset$ do
3.       $u = dequeue(Q);\ M = M \cup \{u\}$;
4.       forall $v \in succ(G_l, u)$ do
5.          $G_l = G_l \setminus \{u \to v\}$;
6.          if $pred(G_l, v) = \emptyset$ then $insert(Q, v)$;
7.    return $M$;
```

Fig. 5. Function computeAffected

time. As in [10], the deletion algorithm first computes the set of affected vertices by using $G_{|l}$. Then, it recomputes the longest paths to the affected vertices by processing them in decreasing order of the variations. Once again, the key insight is that the variations are monotonically decreasing in $G'_{|l}$.

Computing Affected Vertices. Figure 5 shows how to compute the affected vertices. The algorithm is taken from [10] and uses the projected graph G_l which is maintained by the algorithms. It is specified as follows.

Definition 6 (Specification of computeAffected**).** *Let $G = (V, A)$ be an arbitrary graph, $x \to y \in A$, $G' = (V, A \setminus \{x \to y\})$, and $lp(G', y) < lp(G, y)$. Procedure* computeAffected$(G, x \to y)$ *satisfies the specification:*

Pre: $G_l = G_{|l}$. **Post:** $G_l = G'_{|l} \setminus \{v \to w \mid v \in Aff_D\}$; *Returns Aff_D.*

Theorem 2. *Procedure* computeAffected *is correct.*

Proof. Similar to the proof in [10] since G_l is a DAG by Proposition 1. □

The Deletion Algorithm. Figure 6 depicts the arc-deletion algorithm. If y is affected (i.e., if it has no predecessor left in $G_{|l}$), the algorithm computes the affected vertices (line 5). Then it inserts all affected vertices into the queue (line 9) using, as priorities, lower approximations to their variations computed by ignoring their affected predecessors (line 8). The core of the algorithm are lines 10-17 which process the affected vertices by decreasing order of their variations. The vertex u with the largest approximation $\alpha(u)$ is selected in line 11 and its new longest path is computed in line 12. We will prove that $\alpha(u) = \Delta(u)$ in line 8. Lines 13-15 update the approximation and priority $\alpha(w)$ of each successor w of u if necessary. Lines 18-22 recompute $G'_{|l}$ by considering the predecessors and successors of each affected vertex. Note that the variation $\Delta(v)$ and its approximation $\alpha(v)$ of an affected vertex v are negative and thus a large variation corresponds to a small change. Also, a vertex is never reinserted into the queue, since its approximation is final when it is extracted from the queue.

The Correctness Proof. The proof also relies on the monotonicity of the variations along the longest paths of G', which may be counterintuitive at first. Its proof is identical to the proof of Proposition 3.

```
procedure deleteArc(G, x → y)
1.    G = G \ {x → y};
2.    if x → y ∈ G_l then
3.        G_l = G_l \ {x → y};
4.        if pred(G_l, y) = ∅ then
5.            Aff_D = computeAffected(G, x → y);
6.            Q = {};
7.            forall v ∈ Aff_D do
8.                α(v) = max{l(u) + d(u,v) | u ∈ pred(G,v) \ Aff_D} − lp(G,v);
9.                insert(Q, ⟨α(v), v⟩);
10.           while Q ≠ ∅ do
11.               u = extractMax(Q);
12.               l(u) = l(u) + α(u);
13.               forall w ∈ succ(G,u) ∩ Q do
14.                   α_w = l(u) + d(u,w) − l(w);
15.                   if (α_w > α(w)) then
16.                       α(w) := α_w;
17.                       updatePriority(Q, ⟨α(w), w⟩);
18.           forall u ∈ Aff_D do
19.               G_l = G_l \ {p → u | p → u ∈ G_l};  G_l = G_l \ {u → s | u → s ∈ G_l};
20.               G_l = G_l ∪ {p → u | p ∈ pred(G,u) ∧ l(p) + d(p,u) = l(u)};
21.               G_l = G_l ∪ {u → s | s ∈ succ(G,u) ∧ l(u) + d(u,s) = l(s)};
```

Fig. 6. The Arc-Deletion Algorithm for Cyclic<0 Graphs

Proposition 5 (Deletion Monotonicity). *Let $G(V, A)$, $x → y ∈ A$, $G'(V, A \setminus \{x → y\})$, and $v → w$ be an arc on a longest path in G'. We have $\Delta(v) \geq \Delta(w)$.*

Theorem 3. *Procedure deleteArc is correct.*

Proof. The proof relies on the following invariants

$$\forall v \in V \setminus Q : l(v) = lp(G', v) \tag{9}$$

$$\forall q \in Q : \alpha(q) = \max_{p \in pred(G',q) \setminus Q} l(p) + d(p,q) - l(q) \tag{10}$$

in line 10 of the algorithm. The invariants hold initially since, by Theorem 2, Q contains all the affected vertices. The rest of the proof shows that the invariants hold at iteration $i+1$ whenever they hold at iteration i. We first show that

$$\forall v \in Q : \Delta(v) \leq \max_{q \in Q} \alpha(q). \tag{11}$$

Indeed, consider the vertex $q^* \in Q$ such that

$$\Delta(q^*) = \max_{q \in Q} \Delta(q) \tag{12}$$

and such that q^* is topologically smallest in $G'_{|l}$ among the vertices satisfying (12). Such a vertex q^* exists because $G'_{|l}$ is a DAG (Proposition 1). If q^* has a predecessor w in Q, $\Delta(w) < \Delta(q*)$, since q^* is topologically minimal and $\Delta(q^*)$

is maximal. It follows that the arc $w \to q^*$ cannot belong to a longest path to q^* in G', since this would contradict Proposition 5. As a consequence, the predecessors of q^* on any longest path in G' are all in P. It follows that

$$lp(G, q^*) + \Delta(q^*) = \max_{p \in pred(G', q^*) \backslash Q} lp(G', p) + d(p, q^*)$$

$$\Delta(q^*) = \max_{p \in pred(G', q^*) \backslash Q} lp(G', p) + d(p, q^*) - lp(G, q^*)$$

$$\Delta(q^*) = \max_{p \subset pred(G', q^*) \backslash Q} l(p) + d(p, q^*) - l(q^*) = \alpha(q^*) \le \max_{q \in Q} \alpha(q).$$

We now show that $\alpha(u) = \Delta(u)$ in line 11, which restores Invariant 9 after line 12. First observe that Invariant 10 implies that

$$\forall q \in Q : \Delta(q) \ge \alpha(q). \tag{13}$$

Now consider vertex u. If none of its predecessors in G'_l are in Q, the result follows since, by Invariant 9,

$$lp(G', u) = \max_{p \in pred(G', u) \backslash Q} lp(G', p) + d(p, u) = \max_{p \in pred(G', u) \backslash Q} l(p) + d(p, u)$$

and thus $\alpha(u) = \Delta(u)$ by definition of $\alpha(u)$ and $\Delta(u)$. If $q \to u \in G'$ for some $q \in pred(G', u) \cap Q$, the result follows from $\Delta(q) \ge \Delta(u) \ge \alpha(u) \ge \max_{q \in Q} \alpha(q) \ge \Delta(q)$ by Proposition 5, (13), the definition of u, and (11).

Lines 13-17 restore Invariant 10. These instructions update (if necessary) the priorities $\alpha(q)$ for each vertex q in Q since u is no longer in the queue. Finally, $|Q|$ decreases at each iteration, ensuring termination. The result then follows from Invariant 9 and the fact that the queue is empty upon termination. □

Complexity. The proof shows that a vertex is inserted at most once into the queue and each arc outgoing from a vertex in Aff_D is examined once. Hence the algorithm performs a total of $|\delta|$ insertions, $|\delta|$ extractions, and at most $\|\delta\|$ updatePriority operations. The total running time, using a Fibonacci heap [6] is $O(\|\delta\| + |\delta| \log |\delta|)$, since the complexity of computeAffected is $O(\|\delta\|)$.

5 Cyclic≤ 0 Graphs

We now consider Cyclic≤ 0 graphs, which are particularly challenging for deletions due to the presence of zero-length cycles. The difficulty in deletions is illustrated in Figure 7. The figure shows a cycle of length zero, but there are two arcs justifying the longest path to the cycle vertices. Every time such an arc is deleted, the algorithm must make sure that there exists another supporting arc. However, observe that there are no affected vertices until the last supporting arc is deleted. In fact, the problem of maintaining longest paths in Cyclic≤ 0 graphs is unbounded under the locally-persistent and sparse-aliasing computational models [1,13]. The proof is a direct consequence of the unboundedness of reachability or shortest paths in Cyclic≥ 0 graphs. Note that the algorithms for

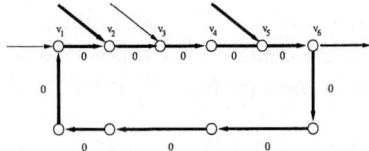

Fig. 7. The Difficulty in Deletion

Cyclic<0 graphs are locally persistent (since they only store information which is local to a vertex such as its approximation) and sparse-aliasing (since they only require constant space at each vertex).

Theorem 4. *The problem of maintaining longest paths in* Cyclic≤ 0 *graphs is unbounded under locally-persistent and sparse-aliasing computational models.*

Although there are no bounded algorithms for maintaining longest paths in cyclic graphs under arc insertions and deletions, it is interesting to study whether there is a bounded algorithm for insertions only, since this is directly relevant for constraint propagation in constraint programming. The proof of Theorem 1 fails for Cyclic≤ 0 graphs, since G'_l is not necessarily a DAG due to cycles of length 0. However, interestingly, the insertion algorithm is still correct for Cyclic≤ 0 graphs. The proof of Theorem 1 can be generalized by choosing q^* with respect to a subgraph of G'_l. The idea is to keep only the "shortest" longest paths in G'_l, i.e., those paths using as few arcs as possible. More precisely, denote by $sp(G,v)$ the shortest path from s to v in a graph G with a source s, where each arc has a distance of 1. The projection of a graph $G = (V, A)$ with respect to these shortest paths, is defined as $G_{|s} = (V, \{x \to y \in A \mid sp(G,x) + 1 = sp(G,y)\})$. and is a DAG. The proof is similar to that of Proposition 1.

Proposition 6. *Let $G(V, A)$ be a* Cyclic>0 *graph with a source s. Then $G_{|s}$, the projection of G wrt its shortest paths, is a DAG.*

Consider the graph $G_{|l|s}$, i.e., the projection of $G_{|l}$ that only keeps "shortest" longest paths. $G_{|l|s}$ is a DAG satisfying $\forall v \in G : lp(G_{|l|s}, v) = lp(G_{|l}, v)$ because $G_{|l|s}$ is a subgraph of $G_{|l}$ and *all* paths from the source to v in $G_{|l}$ have the same length. The vertex q^* in the proof can be chosen to be topologically minimal in $G_{|l|s}$, proving the correctness of the insertion algorithm for Cyclic≤ 0 graphs.

Theorem 5. *Procedure* `insertArc` *is correct for* Cyclic≤ 0 *graphs.*

6 Applications to Shortest Paths

The problem of maintaining shortest paths in cyclic graphs with arbitrary lengths was studied in the BIC model by Ramalingam and Reps (R&R) [14] who proposed bounded algorithms for graphs with no zero-length cycles. Their algorithms use an adaptation of Dijkstra's algorithm for shortest paths which does not work with negative arcs. As a result, they use the reduction of Edmonds and Karp [5] to transform, in each insertion and deletion, arbitrary lengths into nonnegative lengths by using a function f satisfying $f(a) + d(a,b) - f(b) \geq 0$. Their insertion and deletion algorithms run in $O(|\delta|\,\|\delta\|)$ and $O(\|\delta\| + |\delta|\log|\delta|)$ time respectively. The difficulty in their insertion algorithm arises when they insert an arc $u \to v$ to an unreachable vertex v, since there is no such function f. As a consequence, they need to use a a three-stage approach which finds the set U of vertices that were not reachable before, uses Bellman-Ford's algorithm on U to compute the shortest distances to v, and finally propagates the changes with the function f that can be defined after step 2.

Since shortest paths can be transformed into longest paths by negating the lengths, our algorithms also apply to shortest paths. They are simpler, manipulate arbitrary lengths directly, do not need the reduction of Edmonds and Karp, and reduce the running time to $O(\|\delta\| + |\delta|\log|\delta|)$. The ability to manipulate negative lengths allows the algorithms to avoid the three-step approach for insertions, since they keep (negative) distances to unreachable vertices at no cost (these distances are computed automatically during the deletion algorithm on the affected vertices and never updated until a vertex becomes reachable again). Interestingly and unlike the above shortest-path algorithms, our algorithms are not dynamic counterparts to existing offline algorithms: they use variations as their central concept which makes little sense in an offline setting. There is a technicality that must be mentioned however. Our algorithms are bounded for the problem extended with convention 1 but, without the convention, they are not bounded when arcs are inserted or deleted between two unreachable vertices, since the shortest paths in the original graph do not change and we are only allowed constant time. Such pathological operations are inherently batch however and are treated as such by R&R's algorithms. In contrast, our algorithms are truly incremental and their treatment in those cases speeds up the insertion that makes these vertices reachable again. In particular, this guarantees a worst case complexity of $O(n \log n + m)$ for each operation (where $n = |V|$ and $m = |A|$) instead of the $O(nm)$ for R&R's algorithms. Note that all the δ sets are the same with or without the convention except for the pathological operations. Moreover, by postponing these operations, our algorithms become bounded in an amortized sense for these cases although, in practice, it is of little or no benefit.

Finally, in full generality, the algorithm should manipulate pairs $\langle r(v), l_r(v) \rangle$ to encode Convention 1 when there is no a priori range on the lengths. The value $r(v)$ is a Boolean denoting whether vertex v is reachable from the source. When $r(v)$ holds, $l_r(v)$ simply represents the longest path $lp(G, v)$. Otherwise, $l_r(v)$ can be thought as representing the value $H + lp(G_r, v)$, where G_r is the graph G where an arc $s \to v$ with length $-H$ is added between the source and every unreachable vertex v and where H is simply one plus the difference between the largest and the smallest values $lp(G, v)$ for all reachable vertices v. The propagation of the $l(v)$ values, as well as the definition of variations, can be generalized appropriately to work with these pairs.

Acknowledgments. Special thanks to Andrei Missine and the three reviewers for their thorough debugging of the paper.

References

1. B. Alpern, R. Hoover, B. Rosen, P. Sweeney, and K. Zadeck. Incremental Evaluation of Computational Circuits. In *SODA-90*, 1990.
2. A. Cesta, A. Oddi, and S. Smith. Iterative Flattening: A Scalable Method for Solving Multi-Capacity Scheduling Problems. In *AAAI-00*, July 2000.
3. R. Dechter and J. Meiri, I.and Pearl. Temporal Constraint networks. *Artificial Intelligence*, 49:61–95, 1991.
4. M. Dell'Amico and M. Trubian. Applying Tabu Search to the Job-Shop Scheduling Problem. *Annals of Operations Research*, 41:231–252, 1993.
5. J. Edmonds and R.M. Karp. Theoretical Improvements in Algorithmic Efficiency for Network Flow Problems. *JACM*, 34:596–615, 1972.
6. M. L. Fredman and R. E. Tarjan. Fibonacci heaps and their uses in improved network optimization algorithms. *J. Assoc. Comput. Mach.*, 34:596–615, 1987.
7. I. Katriel. Dynamic Heaviest Paths in DAGs with Arbitrary Edge Weights. In *CP-AI-OR'04*, Nice, France, 2004.
8. I. Katriel, L. Michel, and P. Van Hentenryck. Maintaining Longest Paths Incrementally. *Constraints*, 10(2), 2005.
9. P. Laborie. Algorithms for Propagating Resource Constraints in AI Planning and Scheduling: Existing Approaches and New Results. *Artificial Intelligence*, 143(2):151–188, 2003.
10. L. Michel and P. Van Hentenryck. Maintaining Longest Path Incrementally. In *CP'03*, pages 540–554, Cork, Ireland, 2003.
11. L. Michel and P. Van Hentenryck. Iterative Relaxations for Iterative Flattening in Cumulative Scheduling. In *ICAPS'04*, Whistler, British Columbia, 2004.
12. E. Nowicki and C. Smutnicki. A Fast Taboo Search Algorithm for the Job Shop Problem. *Management Science*, 42(6):797–813, 1996.
13. G. Ramalingam. Bounded Incremental Computation. PhD thesis, University of Wisconsin-Madison, 1993.
14. G. Ramalingam and T. Reps. On the Computational Complexity of Dynamic Graph Problems. *Theoretical Computer Science*, 158:233–277, 1996.
15. R.E. Tarjan. Amortized Computational Complexity. *SIAM Journal of Algebraic Discrete Methods*, 6:306–318, 1985.
16. F. Werner and A. Winkler. *Insertion Techniques for the Heuristic Solution of the Job Shop Problem*. Technical report, T.U. Otto von Guericke, Magdebourg, 1992.

Applying Constraint Programming to Rigid Body Protein Docking

Ludwig Krippahl and Pedro Barahona

Dep. de Informática, Universidade Nova de Lisboa, 2825 Monte de Caparica, Portugal
{ludi, pb}@di.fct.unl.pt

Abstract. In this paper we show how Constraint Programming (CP) techniques can improve the efficiency and applicability of grid-based algorithms for optimising surface contact between complex solids. We use BiGGER [1] (Bimolecular complex Generation with Global Evaluation and Ranking) to illustrate the method as applied to modelling protein interactions, an important effort in current bioinformatics. BiGGER prunes the search space by maintaining bounds consistency on interval constraints that model the requirement for the shapes to be in contact but not overlapping, and by using a branch and bound approach to search the models with the best fit. This CP approach gives BiGGER some efficiency advantages over popular protein docking methods that use Fourier transforms to match protein structures. We also present an efficient algorithm to actively impose a broad range of constraints or combinations of constraints on distances between points of the two structures to dock, which allows the use of experimental data to increase the effectiveness and speed of modelling protein interactions and which cannot be done as efficiently in Fourier transform methods. This shows that constraint programming provides a different approach to protein docking (and fitting of shapes in general) that increases the scope of application while improving efficiency.

1 Introduction

The general problem we address in this paper is to fit two solids of arbitrary shape so as to maximize the surface of contact. This problem is important in bioinformatics for modelling protein interactions, also known as protein docking. Protein interactions play a crucial role in all biological systems, and knowing the structure of a protein complex is an essential step in understanding the interaction mechanism. In this paper we will focus on the particular case of protein docking, currently the area of greater application of these algorithms, but the results are general and applicable to calculating configurations of maximal contact for solids of arbitrary shape.

The most important aspects of this paper are the efficiency gained by using constraint propagation techniques, which puts our method on the same level of efficiency as other current approaches, and the propagation of distance constraints between sets of points in the two structures. The latter is of especial importance because the algorithm we present allows the pruning of the search space using partially ambiguous or uncertain data, and is thus applicable to a wide range of real-world situations.

Modelling software provides useful tools to help researchers elucidate protein interaction mechanisms, and two decades since the pioneering work of Katzir and others [2] have seen significant developments in algorithms to generate models and scoring functions to select the most likely candidates. The diversity of current approaches is evident in the CAPRI (Critical Assessment of PRediction of Interactions) experiment [3].

A common trend is to model interactions using only knowledge derived from the structure and physicochemical properties of the proteins involved. Some algorithms have been developed [1, 4, 5] or adapted [6] to use data on the interaction mechanisms, but this approach is still the exception rather than the norm. BiGGER is one of these exceptions [1, 4], and it has been developed from inception to help the researcher bring into the modelling process as much data as available. Previous results show that BiGGER can be a powerful modelling tool when used in this manner, even when the experimental data are only applied after the search stage to score the models produced [1, 4, 7, 8, 9, 10, 11].

Of all protein docking approaches, the most popular is to generate a three-dimensional matrix encoding the shape of each solid, and then match the two matrices by calculating a correlation matrix. This approach was first reported by Katchalski-Katzir [2], and relied on Fast Fourier Transform method (FFT) to generate the correlation matrix. Some current implementations of this algorithm to protein interaction modelling are MolFit [2], ZDOCK [12], FTDock [6], DOT [13], and GRAMM [14].

Our implementation, BiGGER, uses a search in real (geometrical) space instead of Fourier transforms to fit two solids of arbitrary shape. BiGGER and Chemera, the graphical interface, form a tool to study protein-protein interaction that is publicly available and can be downloaded from http://www.cqfb.fct.unl.pt/bioin/chemera/

In this paper we show that an algorithm that actively enforces the constraints inherent to the docking problem virtually eliminates the time advantage of the FFT approach, is in practice often significantly faster, and results in a hundred-fold reduction in memory requirements. Furthermore, this approach can be naturally adapted to additionally constrained searches using experimental data that are not efficiently accommodated with the FFT techniques.

The paper is organised as follows. In section 2 we elaborate on the docking problem and the grid method for fitting together two arbitrary shapes. Section 3 explains the BiGGER search algorithm and how constraints are enforced to improve efficiency. Section 4 shows the performance results, and the conclusions follow in section 5.

2 The Docking Problem

At the core of this approach to matching of irregular structures are the grid and the measure of surface contact. The grid is a very straightforward representation using a regular cubic lattice of cells, where each cell can be either an empty cell, a surface cell, or a core cell. The surface cells define the surface of the structure, and the overlap of surface cells measures the surface of contact. Figure 1 illustrates these

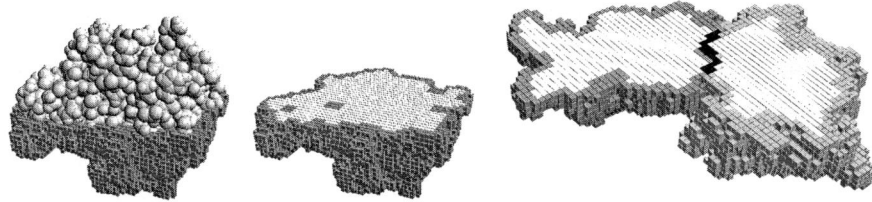

Fig. 1. The image on the left shows a protein structure overlaid on a cutaway of the respective grid, with grey spheres representing the atoms of the protein. The centre figure shows only the grid, cut to show the surface in grey and the core region in white. The rightmost image shows the contact between two grids as a black line of grid cells at the interface.

concepts, showing on the first two panels a cutaway diagram of the grid representing a protein structure, and on the third panel a cutaway diagram of two grids in contact, showing the contact region corresponding to a set of overlapping surface cells.

This approach is especially useful for molecular modelling because intermolecular contacts are not crisp like they appear to be at a macroscopic scale, but rather diffuse and a function of electrostatic repulsions between the atoms. The grid can model this feature quite naturally by adjusting the thickness of the surface region and its placement relative to the structure to be modelled. Closer inspection of the first panel on Figure 1 reveals that the surface cells lie outside the Van der Waals surfaces of the atoms (white spheres on the first panel). When these surface cells overlap with those of another grid, the placement of the grids corresponds to a small separation of the Van der Waals surfaces on the protein complex, which is more realistic than actual contact. The placement of the surface region can be modified according to the nature of the objects and contacts that are being modelled, from rigid macroscopic objects to diffuse electron clouds in atoms, so this is a general approach that can cover a wide range of applications.

The core cells mark the forbidden overlaps; overlapping core cells indicate that parts of the two structures are occupying the same space and this configuration is disallowed. Overlap between core and surface cells can be ignored because in our model the surface region corresponds to a layer external to the structure, as explained above.

2.1 Protein Docking and the Fast Fourier Transform Approach

Given these definitions of allowed configurations and of how to measure surface contact, one can search all configurations by moving one grid relative to the other and examining the overlapping cells of the two grids. This translation search must be repeated for each orientation of one partner relative to the other, in order to search the rotation space as well. Typically, the rotational space is sampled in steps of 15° around each of the three orthogonal axes of rotation, for a total of approximately six thousand orientations.

For each relative orientation, the naïve algorithm examines N^3 different configurations, where N is the width of the grid, and for each configuration $O(N^3)$ cells, for a time complexity of $O(N^6)$. Currently the most used algorithm in protein docking is the grid method using Fast Fourier Transform (FFT), in which the grids are three-dimensional matrices, and the surface overlap is measured by the correlation matrix calculated from the two matrices representing the two proteins. The FFT algorithm allows the correlation matrix to be calculated quickly as a matrix multiplication of the Fourier transforms of the two matrices to correlate. This computation has a time complexity of $O(N^3 Log(N))$, which clearly outperforms the $O(N^6)$) time complexity of the translational search of the naïve search described above, thus justifying the popularity of the FFT approach. Again, as in all grid-based docking approaches, one grid must be generated for each orientation of one of the partners relative to the other, and whether in BiGGER, the FFT approach, or in the naïve approach, this translational search must be repeated for every orientation, typically thousands of times.

Because of the efficiency of FFT, protein docking using grid algorithms with a real (geometrical) space search (instead of using Fourier transforms) were not competitive. However we discuss below how constraint programming techniques improve such search, overcome this basic disadvantage, and even give some advantages in computation time, memory requirements and, especially, in the efficient use of information about the interaction, as shown by the results obtained with BiGGER.

2.2 Using Data on Contacts and Distances

In some cases there is information about distances between points in the structures, information that can be used to restrict the search region. If this information is a conjunction of distance limits, then it is trivial to restrict the search to the volumes allowed by all the distances. However, real applications may be more complex.

For modelling protein interactions, it is often the case that one can obtain data on important residues or atoms from such techniques as site directed mutagenesis or NMR titrations, or even from theoretical considerations, but it is rare to be absolutely certain of these data. The most common situation is to have a set of likely distance constraints of which not all necessarily hold. Typically, we would like to impose a constraint of the form:

At least K atoms of set A must be within R of at least one atom of set B (1)

where set A is on one protein and set B on the other, and R a distance value. This constraint results in combinatorial problem with a large number of disjunctions, since the distances need only hold for at least one of any combination of K elements of A. The FFT approach is especially unsuited for taking advantage of this type of information, since one cannot use this technique to find the correlation only of parts of all possible configurations of the two grids. With FFT the only way to use constraints is after the search, in a passive generate and test approach, validating or rejecting candidate configurations after the search. Validating each configuration according to constraint (1) is simple, and any docking algorithm can do this. BiGGER itself has been used in this way with considerable success. Chemera, the application that accompanies BiGGER in our distribution of this software package, allows the user to score the models produced by BiGGER according to inter-atomic distances. Some examples of this approach using BiGGER are in electron transfer complexes [7, 8, 9] or in modelling complexes using NMR and site-directed mutagenesis data [10, 11].

But the best way to use this information is as active constraints, pruning the search space to improve computation time, and in Section 3.4 we show that the combination of grid representations and real (geometrical) space search is particularly suited to enforcing this global constraint due to the structure of the nested loops for the search in the X, Y, and Z directions.

Though we discuss this geometry constraints problem as it presents itself in protein docking, this is a general problem. These distance values may be from uncertain NMR data, but they may also be from alternative positions for mooring lines, a lower limit for the number of bolts to secure two parts, or any other case where there are more alternatives to distance limits between points in the two structures than those limits that must be enforced.

3 Method

The basic method of searching through the translation space for the configurations with the largest surface contact is simple and straightforward. This section focuses on the modifications that make this method much more efficient than the $O(N^6)$ time complexity of the basic approach. Two constraints contribute to this efficiency, when adequately enforced: a) restricting the search to positions where surface regions overlap, and b) eliminating positions where core regions overlap. In addition, restricting the search to those regions where it is possible to have a greater surface contact than that of the worst solution to be kept can improve efficiency in some cases, but this last constraint is not useful in general, and is only discussed briefly.

Finally, we show how the additional constraint (1) discussed above, can be efficiently implemented in this algorithm and further decrease computation time when the relevant information is available.

3.1 Restricting the Search to Surface Overlapping Regions

A significant proportion of all possible configurations for the two grids results in no surface overlap. Much can be gained by restricting the search to those configurations where surface cells of one grid overlap surface cells of the other. This is achieved by encoding the grids in a convenient way: instead of individual cells, grids are composed of lists of intervals specifying the segments of similar cells along the X coordinate. These lists are arranged in a two-dimensional array on the Y-Z plane.

Figure 2 illustrates this encoding process for two lines, along the horizontal axis, on an X-Y plane where Z = j. The line on the top contains only surface cells, and is encoded as two surface segments, from X coordinates 3 through 7 and 12 through 18. This line in the grid is thus encoded as a list of two intervals S_{ij} = [(3;7), (12;18)] where i is the Y coordinate. The other line in this example contains both surface and core cells, and is encoded as two lists: a list of surface cells S_{kj} = [(2;3), (7;9), (20;21)] and a list of core cells C_{kj} = [(4;6), (10;20)].

This encoding not only reduces the memory requirements for storing the grids, but also leads naturally to searching along the X axis by comparing segments instead of by running through all the possible displacements along this coordinate. Given two

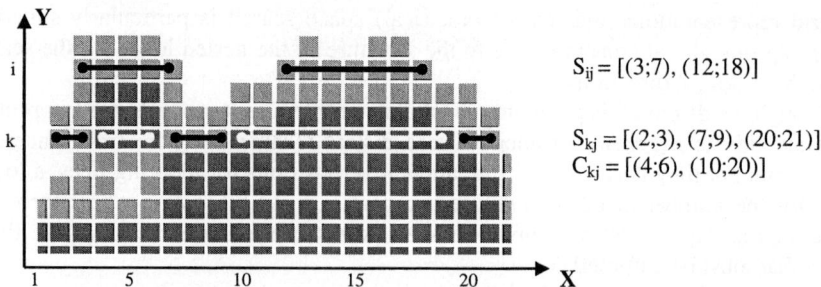

Fig. 2. This figure illustrates the encoding of the grid as segments, with each segment containing only the X coordinates of the start and end points of a row of consecutive grid cells of the same type. Surface grids are represented in light grey and surface segments in black, core grids in dark grey and core segments in white.

surface segments, one from each structure and aligned in the same Y and Z coordinates, we can calculate the displacements where overlap will occur simply from the X coordinates of the extremities of the segments.

Representing by variable x the displacement of one structure relative to the other along the X direction, this approach of comparing segments efficiently enforces the constraint requiring surface overlaps by reducing the domain of the variable, to only those values where the constraint is verified, as we explain in the next section.

3.2 Eliminating Regions of Core Overlap

Another important constraint in this problem is that the core regions of the grids cannot overlap, for that indicates the structures are occupying the same space instead of being in contact. By identifying the configurations where such overlaps occur, it is possible to eliminate from consideration those surface segments on each structure that cannot overlap surface segments on the other structure without violating the core overlap constraint. Some surface segments can thus be discarded from each search along the X axis. Figure 3 illustrates this procedure.

One structure, labelled A, is shown in the centre of the image. The other structure, labelled B, will be moved along the horizontal direction to scan all possible configurations but, from the overlap of core segments, a set of positions along the horizontal direction can be eliminated. Structure B is shown in position 1 to the right of A and in position 39 to the left of A, but, in this case, it cannot occupy positions in the centre. The domain of variable x (introduced in the previous section to represent the displacement of one structure relative to the other along the X direction) can be pruned from the values 5 to 30. This is a contiguous interval in this example, but the domain of x can be an arbitrary set of intervals in the general case. This domain reduction due to the core overlap constraint propagates to the surface overlap, since some surface segments of A and B will not overlap in valid configurations. Some of these are shown in Figure 3 by the group of arrows to the left of structure A (Discarded Segments, Figure 3). For the last double arrow, for example, the surface cells of structures A and B would only overlap for $x=7$, a value pruned from the

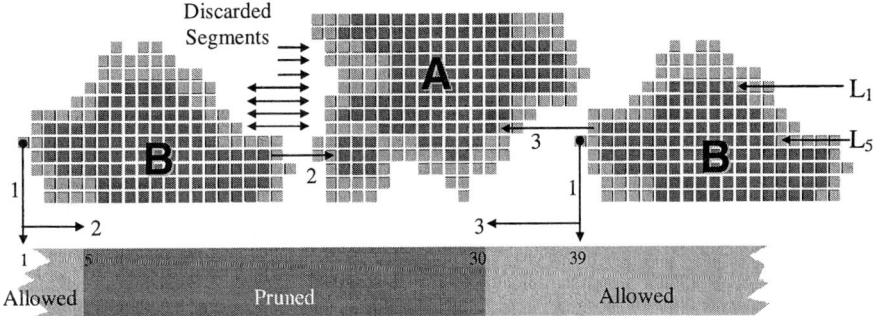

Fig. 3. Grid B is translated along the horizontal direction relative to grid A. The vertical arrows marked 1 indicate the position of B on the lower horizontal bar, which shows the allowed and forbidden values for the position of B. The arrows marked 2 and 3 show the allowed displacement of B. The group of horizontal arrows indicates segments to be discarded.

domain of x. In contrast, in the line below such overlap occurs for x = 3, a value kept in the domain. The top three arrows point to surface segments on structure A which can be ignored in this case. The top three surface segments on structure B cannot be ignored because they may overlap with the surface segments of A on the other side, once B is moved to the right of A, but the following four arrows indicate that both the segments to the left of A and those to the right of B can be ignored. Thus the core overlap constraint allows us to reduce the number of surface segments to consider when counting surface overlaps.

Figure 4 outlines the algorithm for the translational search. Three variables, z, y, and x, and their respective domains, D_z, D_y, and D_x, represent the translation of B with respect to A. The domains are initialised to include all translations that may result in contacts by a bounds consistency check: if MaxA/MaxB and MinA/MinB are the maximum/minimum coordinate values along the Z axis for the surface grid cells of the two structures, D_z is initialised to [(MinA-MaxB; MaxB-MinA)] (line 1). The same procedure applies to D_y and D_x (lines 3 and 5), but only considering the parts of the structure that can overlap (D_y depends on the value of z, D_x depends on the values of z and y). We shall see in the next sections that these domains can be further pruned by other constraints on the minimum overlap score (section 3.3) and distances between points in the two structures (Section 3.4), so D_z, D_y, and D_x are not necessarily single intervals but sets of intervals. This pruning (Sections 3.3 and 3.4) occurs at the initialisation of the domains (lines 1, 3, and 5).

For each z and y translation value, D_x is initialized (line 5), and the list CoreSets (line 6) is generated, containing the matching sets of core grid segments for the two structures. Grid segment sets are matching when they are aligned by the z, y translation of the B structure, so each entry on this list corresponds to a location in the Z,Y plane and contains the core segments of both structures that are aligned at that location by translating the B structure by the z, y values. Figure 3 shows two such sets, marked L_1 and L_5, which would be respectively the first and fifth entries of the list of matching core grid segments. L_1 contains one core grid segment from A and one from B, L_5 contains two core grid segments from A and one from B.

```
1. D_z ← Z_Translations
2. for each z ∈ D_z do
3.    D_y ← Y_Translations(z)
4.    for each y ∈ D_y do
5.       D_x ← X_Translations(z,y)
6.       CoreSets ← Matching_Core_Segs(z,y,D_y)
7.       D_x ← RemoveCoreOverlaps(D_y)
8.       SurfSets ← Matching_Surf_Segs(z,y,X)
9.       CountContacts(XT,SurfacePairs)
```

Fig. 4. Outline of the BiGGER translation search algorithm. The translation search must be repeated for each relative orientation of the two partners.

The BiGGER algorithm then (line 7) imposes bounds consistency on these sets of core grids segments, comparing the bounds of each segment in one structure with the bounds of all matching segments in the other structure for this z, y displacement. If MaxA, MaxB, MinA, and MinB are respectively the upper and lower bounds in the x coordinate for a pair of matching core segments, the algorithm removes the interval (MinA-MaxB; MaxA-MinB) from D_x. Maintaining such bounds consistency requires $O(k^2)$ operations, where k is the number of intervals defined by the core grid segments for each line and for each structure.

In line 8 the list of matching surface segments is generated, in a similar manner. Note that both the matching core and the surface segments lists take into account D_x, including only those segments that could overlap given this domain (again, by imposing bounds consistency on the intervals). Also, the list of matching surface segments uses D_x already pruned by ruling out the forbidden overlaps (line 7). Finally, the overlap of surface cells is determined for each allowed translation value in D_x. This requires testing the bounds of the matching surface segments in a way similar to imposing bounds consistency, which is of $O(k^2)$ for each line, and then counting the contacts along X, which is of $O(N)$.

The algorithm performs $O(N^2)$ steps by looping through the D_z and D_y (lines 2 and 4), and in each of these steps it loops through the Z,Y plane twice to find the matching core and surface segments (lines 6 and 8) and compare the segment bounds. So each step in the z, y loop is $O(N^2k^2)$, where k is the number of segments per line (the counting step in line 9 is $O(N)$ and can be ignored). Except for fractal structures, k is a small constant. For convex shapes, for example, k is always two or less, and even for complex shapes like proteins k is seldom larger than two. Thus the time complexity of the search algorithm when imposing bounds constraints on the overlap of surface and core grid cells is $O(N^4)$, a substantial improvement with respect to the naïve $O(N^6)$ algorithm, and much closer to the $O(N^3Log(N))$ of the FFT method. Furthermore, as we show in the Results section, the comparisons done in the BiGGER algorithm are much faster and this constant factor makes BiGGER more efficient for values of N up to several hundred. Finally, the space complexity of BiGGER is $O(N^2)$, significantly better and with a lower constant factor than the FFT space complexity of $O(N^3)$.

3.3 Restricting the Lower Bounds on Surface Contact

Branch and Bound is a common technique that Constraint Programming often uses in optimisation problems, to restrict the domains of the variables to where it is still possible to obtain a better value for the function to optimise. In this case, we wish to optimise the overlap of surface cells, and restrict the search to those regions where this overlap can be higher than that of the lowest ranking model to be kept.

This constraint is applied to the Z and Y coordinate search loops, by counting the total surface cells for each grid as a function of the Z coordinate (that is, the sum over each X, Y plane) and as a function of each Y, Z pair (that is, the sum of each line in the X axis). When determining the domain of the Z translation (line 1, Figure 4), the Z_Translations function considers the list of total surface cells for each surface along the Z axis. For each Z translation value these two lists will align in a different way, as the one structure is displaced in the Z direction relative to the other. The minimum of each pair of aligned values gives the maximum possible surface overlap for that X,Y plane at this Z translation, and the sum of these minima gives the maximum possible surface overlap for this Z translation. Since there are $O(N)$ possible Z translations to test and, for each, $O(N)$ values to compare and add, this step requires $O(N^2)$ operations.

The same applies to restricting the Y domain in function Y_Translations (line 3, Figure 4), but taking into account the current value of variable z. This is also an $O(N^2)$ operation identical to the pruning of the Z domain, but must be repeated for each value of the z translation variable, adding a total time complexity of $O(N^3)$ to the algorithm. Since the BiGGER algorithm has a time complexity of $O(N^4)$, these operations do not result in a significant efficiency loss.

By setting a minimum value for the surface contact count, or by setting a fixed number of best models to retain, this constraint allows the algorithm to prune the search space so as to consider only regions where it is possible to find matches good enough to include in the set of models to retain. In general, this pruning results in a modest efficiency gain. In the experiments reported on this paper the largest effect was a 30% decrease in computation time for a grid size of approximately 100, but with decreasing returns as higher grid sizes lead to thinner surface regions and shift the balance between the total surface counts and the size of the grid, so for larger values (N>230) the cost of enforcing this constraint can outweigh the benefits.

However, this can benefit some applications like soft docking [1], where the surface and core grids are manipulated to model flexibility in the structures to dock, or if the minimum acceptable surface contact is high.

3.4 Constraining the Search Space

Conceptually, the real-space (geometrical) search of BiGGER can be seen as three nested cycles spanning the Z, Y, and X coordinates (Figure 4), from the outer to the inner cycle. This allows us to decompose the enforcement of constraint (1) by projecting it in the three directions:

At least K atoms of set A must be within R_ω of at least one atom of set B (2) where R_ω replaces the Euclidean distance R and represents the modulus of coordinate differences on one axis Z, Y or X. R_ω has the same value of R; the different notation is to remind us that this is not a Euclidean distance value, but its projection on one coordinate axis. This makes the constraint slightly less stringent, by considering the distance to be a cube of side 2R instead of a sphere of diameter 2R, but this can be easily corrected by testing each candidate configuration to see if it also respects Euclidean distance (we have successfully adopted a similar approach when applying constraint programming to determine the 3D structure of proteins from NMR data: rather than representing the region within distance R of some point by a sphere of diameter 2R, we conservatively adopted a cube with side 2R to simplify constraint propagation [15]).

The propagation algorithm, is the same for each axis, and consists of two steps. The first step is to determine the neighbourhood of radius R of atoms in group B, projected on the coordinate axis being considered. The next step is to generate a list of segments representing the displacements for which at least K atoms of group A are inside the segments defining the neighbourhood R of the atoms in group B.

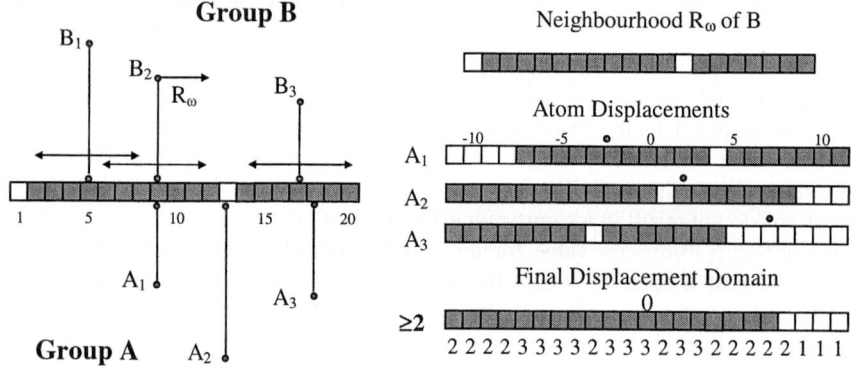

Fig. 5. Generating the displacement domain in one dimension. The left panel shows the generation of the neighbourhood of radius R of group B. The panel on the right shows the allowed displacements for each atom, and the final displacement domain for a K value of 2.

The calculation of the neighbourhood of B in some coordinate (either X, Y or Z) is illustrated in Figure 5. The positions of atoms B_1, B_2 and B_3 in this coordinate are respectively 5, 9 and 17. Their neighbourhoods within a distance 3 are (2;8), (6;12) and (14;20). Merging the two first intervals, the neighbourhood 3 of the atom set B is thus (2;12) and (14;20).

To calculate the displacement values that place an atom of group A inside the neighbourhood of group B we only have to shift the segments defining the neighbourhood of B by the coordinate value of the atom. For example, atom A_1, with coordinate 9, lies inside the neighbourhood 3 of B if its displacement lies in the range (-7;3) or (5;11). Similarly, atoms A_2 and A_3, with coordinate values 13 and 18, respectively may be displaced by (-11;-1) or (1;7) and (-16;-6) or (-4;2).

Once we have the displacement segments for all atoms, we must generate the segments describing the region at least K atoms are in the neighbourhood of B, which is a simple counting procedure (hence, the constraint (2) need not be limited to specifying a lower bound for the distances to respect. The value of K can also be an upper bound, or a specific value, or even any number of values).

In this case, there are at least two atoms of set A within neighbourhood 3 of atom set B if the displacement lies in ranges (-11;3) and (5;7). In ranges (-7;-6) and (-4;-1) all 3 A atoms are in the neighbourhood 3 of B. The algorithm is outlined in Figure 6.

```
1. DomainB ← Empty_Domain
2. for each b ∈ AtomsB do
3.    DomainB ← DomainB ∪ Domain(b,Dist)
4. D ← Zeroes
5. for each a ∈ AtomsA do
6.    D ← D + Shift_Domain(DomainB,AtomsA(a).Coord)
7. for each i ∈ D do
8.    Translation(i)← D(i) > Min_Contacts
```

Fig. 6. Propagation of one distance constraint in one dimension, where Dist is the distance value and Min_Contacts the minimum number of atoms in set B to be in contact with set A

The propagation of a constraint of the type (2) produces a translation domain (*Translation*, in the algorithm outlined in Figure 6). The intersection of all translation domains for all constraints of this type for one coordinate axis generates a translation domain that is used to initialise domains D_x, D_y and D_z in the translation search (Figure 4). Thus the propagation of constraint (2) prunes the domain of the allowed displacements in all 3 axes, in a nested sequence. First the domain along the Z axis is determined and pruned adequately; then, for each remaining value of the displacement along Z, the domain of the displacements along Y is pruned; finally, for each remaining (Z, Y) pair, the constraint is enforced on the displacement along X.

The time complexity of enforcing constraint (2) in one axis is O(a+b+N), where a is the number of atoms in group A and b the number of atoms in group B, and N is the grid size. Since this must be done for the translation dimensions the overall complexity contribution is $O(N^3)$, which does not change the $O(N^4)$ complexity of the geometric search algorithm. Nevertheless, pruning the search space makes the search faster, as demonstrated by the experimental results presented in the next section.

4 Results

To determine the performance of BiGGER relative to the FFT approach, we compared the search time with that reported with ZDock for the immunoglobulin complex between IgG1 Idiotypic Fab and Igg2A anti-idiotypic Fab [12]. For this complex the authors reported a run time of 19 CPU hours on an SGI Origin 2000 with 32 R10000 processors, for a search through 6,389 orientations. The performance of each R10000 processor in the SGI Origin workstation is roughly a third (SSBENCH floating point benchmark) to a fourth (SPECfp95 and SPECfp2000) of the performance of a Pentium 4 2.8GHz CPU for floating point operations, so this allows us to make an approximate comparison between the two algorithms.

To compare the algorithms we ran BiGGER on the same protein complex as reported in [12] (PDB structure codes 1AIF and 1IAI) at different resolutions to generate different grid sizes (the resolution is the size of the grid cell). The reason for using the same structure is that running time for BiGGER depends slightly on the shape and relative sizes of the docking partners, so in our comparisons with ZDock changes occur in only one variable, the size of the grid.

Chart **A** on Figure 7 shows the plot of the average for 10 orientations for BiGGER for each grid size (black dots) compared to the estimated time for ZDock on a similar platform, represented by the staircase plot. The FFT algorithm requires the grid to be decomposed into shorter sequences, so N must be factorable into powers of small prime numbers for FFT to be usable; ideally, N should be a power of 2. This results in a staircase-like performance plot, using the values of N for which FFT is most efficient. To simplify the plot, we represented the computation time for ZDock on the relevant N values where N is a power of two (64, 128, 256, 512). In protein docking it is unlikely that values outside this range are necessary.

Chart **B** (Figure 7) shows the experimental results using only the propagation of the surface overlap constraint (section 3.1) or both surface and core overlap constraints (sections 3.1 and 3.2). The experimental results are compared with the naïve $O(N^6)$ complexity of comparing all the grids in all configurations, and the $O(N^4)$ complexity estimated for BiGGER as the grid size tends to infinity.

The real-space (geometrical) search in BiGGER seems to be at least as efficient in computation time as the FFT approach, and significantly more efficient in those cases where the size of the structures is just enough to force the grid size in the FFT to a larger increment of N. This conclusion is valid for the practical range of grid sizes used in protein docking, though with a time complexity of $O(N^4)$, which is slightly worse than the $O(N^3 Log(N))$ of FFT, BiGGER eventually becomes slower than FFT as grid size increases.

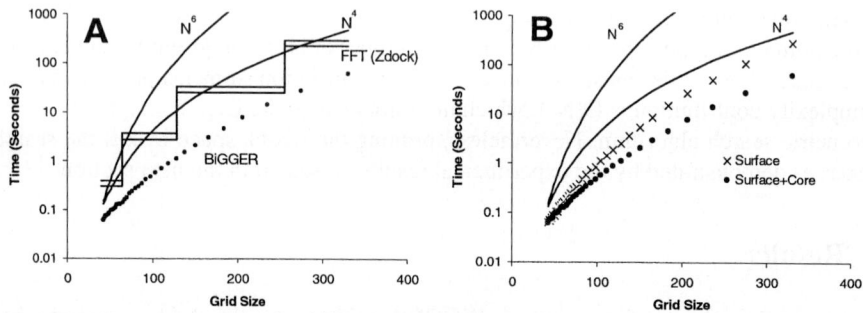

Fig. 7. Plots of search time as a function of the grid size. Chart A compares BiGGER (dots) to the estimated time for a FFT implementation (ZDock) on the same hardware. Chart B compares BiGGER with only the surface overlap constraint (Section 3.1) and both the surface and core overlap constraints (section 3.1 and 3.2). Both charts also show the theoretical values for $O(N^6)$ and $O(N^4)$ complexities assuming a constant scaling factor such that both correspond to the estimated factor for the ZDock implementation of the FFT method at N=40.

However, the space complexity of BiGGER is $O(N^2)$, except for fractal shapes, whereas the memory requirements for the FFT approach are $O(N^3)$, and the necessity of using floating point matrices makes it very demanding in this regard. With a 256 grid size and double precision, FFT docking requires 130Mb per grid. Since 3 grids are necessary, one for each protein and one for the correlation matrix, this amounts to approximately 500Mb, or 8Gb for N=512. The grid representation in BiGGER requires only a few megabytes, and the total memory usage of the program is approximately 10Mb of RAM at running time (15Mb for the largest example in the chart with N=330, 5Mb for the smallest with N=42). Space complexity may be as relevant as time complexity because the geometric search is trivial to parallelize, since each orientation in the rotation space can be explored independently.

The other advantage of our approach is the possibility of reducing the search space according to information about the interaction of the two proteins. Previous publications showed the advantages of using such information to score the models generated [4, 10, 11], without using this information to narrow the search, so here we address only the performance gains in restricting the search space with the algorithm described in section 3.4, using as example the CAPRI [1] targets 2 and 4 through 7, corresponding to our submitted predictions for CAPRI rounds 1 and 2 [4].

For the largest protein on each pair of proteins to dock we selected five alpha-Carbon atoms: three from the three interface residues that we had used to test the models obtained with an unconstrained search in [4], plus two from two decoy residues picked at random away from the interface region. The constraint imposed on the search was that at least 3 of the alpha-Carbon atoms of these five residues on the largest protein must be within 10Å of at least one atom of the smallest protein, which restricts the search the region of the three correct residues and away from the region with the two decoys. Even this modest information has a significant effect on the quality of the prediction of the protein complex, as shown in [4]. Here we focus exclusively on the performance issues of using the constraints to prune the search space, as a proper discussion of the evaluation of protein complex models would be outside the scope of this paper.

Table 1. Shows the residues selected as correct interface residues and decoys for each CAPRI target, and the time of the constrained and unconstrained searches in minutes

ID	Complex	Correct Residues	Decoys	Constr.	Unconst.
2	VP6-FAB	P171,A244,M300	D62,G43	210	720
4	Amilase-Amy10	S243,S245,G249	N364,D375	40	160
5	Amilase-Amy07	S270,G271,G285	R30,N220	90	180
6	Amilase-Amy09	N53,S145,V349	S471,T219	30	150
7	Exotoxin A1-TC AR	N20,N54,Y84	N178,G108	80	180

Table 1 shows the residues selected as correct interface residues and decoys for each protein, and the time for the constrained search as a fraction of the time for the unconstrained search. The total time for the constrained search (through 6,389 orientations) ranged from three and a half hours for ID 2 to 30 minutes for ID 6 (approximate results on a P4 at 2.8 GHz running Windows XP ™)

The time gains depend on how much the search space is pruned by the constraint, so it will depend on the shape and size of the structures as well as the number and placement of the distance constraints and the stringency of the cardinality constraint over the distances to enforce. Still, these results suggest a significant reduction in computation time (two to five times) even when constraining only a few points on only one of the partners. With more stringent constraints, such as requiring that one specific point on one structure be close to one of a few points in the other, the constrained search time can be less than 5% of the unconstrained search time (for example, 23 minutes instead of 12 hours in the case of complex ID 2).

5 Conclusion

By taking advantage of Constraint Programming techniques, BiGGER is faster than the FFT correlation method for matching three-dimensional shapes for N up to approximately 500. With larger grids, the $O(N^4)$ time complexity of BiGGER eliminates the advantage of simpler and faster operations, making it slower than the FFT algorithm with its $O(N^3 Log(N))$ time complexity. However, at large grid sizes the $O(N^3)$ space complexity of FFT is a severe disadvantage compared to the $O(N^2)$ space complexity of BiGGER. Although we cannot state categorically that, on performance alone, our approach is superior to the FFT method, this shows that our algorithm is at a similar performance level as the currently most popular approach for modelling protein-protein complexes.

The main advantage of BiGGER is in being suited for the efficient implementation of a wide range of constraints on distances between parts of the structures to fit, which is often important in protein docking, and potentially important in other problems of finding optimal surface matches between complex shapes subject to geometrical constraints.

For the problem of protein docking, in which we are most interested, the algorithm has been applied successfully to model the interaction between a Pseudoazurin and a Nitrite Reductase [16] and is currently being applied to modelling two other protein interactions (Fibrinogen-MMP2 and FNR-Ferredoxin) with promising results.

Acknowledgements. We thank Nuno Palma and José Moura for their role in the development of BiGGER and Chemera, and we thank the financial support of the Fundação para a Ciencia e Tecnologia (BD 19628/99; BPD 12328/03).

References

1. Palma PN, Krippahl L, Wampler JE, Moura, JJG. 2000. BiGGER: A new (soft) docking algorithm for predicting protein interactions. Proteins: Structure, Function, and Genetics 39:372-84.
2. Katchalski-Katzir E, Shariv I, Eisenstein M, Friesem AA, Aflalo C, Vakser IA. 1992 Molecular surface recognition: determination of geometric fit between proteins and their ligands by correlation techniques. Proc Natl Acad Sci U S A. 1992 Mar 15;89(6):2195-9.
3. Janin J. 2002. Welcome to CAPRI: A Critical Assessment of PRedicted Interactions. Proteins: Structure, Function, and Genetics Volume 47, Issue 3, 2002. Pages: 257

4. Krippahl L, Moura JJ, Palma PN. 2003. Modeling protein complexes with BiGGER. Proteins: Structure, Function, and Genetics. V. 52(1):19-23.
5. Dominguez C, Boelens R, Bonvin AM. HADDOCK: a protein-protein docking approach based on biochemical or biophysical information. J Am Chem Soc. 2003 Feb 19;125(7):1731-7.
6. Moont G., Gabb H.A., Sternberg M. J. E., Use of Pair Potentials Across Protein Interfaces in Screening Predicted Docked Complexes Proteins: Structure, Function, and Genetics, V35-3, 364-373, 1999
7. Pettigrew GW, Goodhew CF, Cooper A, Nutley M, Jumel K, Harding SE. 2003, The electron transfer complexes of cytochrome c peroxidase from Paracoccus denitrificans. Biochemistry. 2003 Feb 25;42(7):2046-55.
8. Pettigrew GW, Prazeres S, Costa C, Palma N, Krippahl L, Moura I, Moura JJ. 1999. The structure of an electron transfer complex containing a cytochrome c and a peroxidase. J Biol Chem. 1999 Apr 16;274(16):11383-9.
9. Pettigrew GW, Pauleta SR, Goodhew CF, Cooper A, Nutley M, Jumel K, Harding SE, Costa C, Krippahl L, Moura I, Moura J. 2003. Electron Transfer Complexes of Cytochrome c Peroxidase from Paracoccus denitrificans Containing More than One Cytochrome. Biochemistry 2003, 42, 11968-81
10. Morelli X, Dolla A., Czjzek M, Palma PN, Blasco, F, Krippahl L, Moura JJ, Guerlesquin F. 2000. Heteronuclear NMR and soft docking: an experimental approach for a structural model of the cytochrome c553-ferredoxin complex. Biochemistry 39:2530-2537.
11. Morelli X, Palma PN, Guerlesquin F, Rigby AC. 2001. A novel approach for assessing macromolecular complexes combining soft-docking calculations with NMR data. Protein Sci. 10:2131-2137.
12. Chen R. & Weng Z. 2002 Docking Unbound Proteins Using Shape Complementarity, Desolvation, and Electrostatics, Proteins 47:281-294
13. Ten Eyck, L. F., Mandell, J., Roberts, V. A., and Pique, M. E. Surveying Molecular Interactions With DOT. Proceedings of the 1995 ACM/IEEE Supercomputing Conference, San Diego
14. A. Vakser, C. Aflalo, 1994, Hydrophobic docking: A proposed enhancement to molecular recognition techniques, Proteins, 20, 320-329.
15. Krippahl L, Barahona P. PSICO: Solving Protein Structures with Constraint Programming and Optimisation, Constraints 2002, 7, 317-331
16. Impagliazzo, A., Transient protein interactions: the case of pseudoazurin and nitrite reductase. 2005. Doctoral Thesis, Leiden University

Maximum Constraint Satisfaction on Diamonds

Andrei Krokhin[1] and Benoit Larose[2]

[1] Department of Computer Science,
University of Durham,
Durham, DH1 3LE, UK
andrei.krokhin@durham.ac.uk
[2] Department of Mathematics and Statistics,
Concordia University,
Montréal, Qc, Canada, H3G 1M8
larose@mathstat.concordia.ca

Abstract. In this paper we study the complexity of the weighted maximum constraint satisfaction problem (MAX CSP) over an arbitrary finite domain. In this problem, one is given a collection of weighted constraints on overlapping sets of variables, and the goal is to find an assignment of values to the variables so as to maximize the total weight of satisfied constraints. MAX CSP is **NP**-hard in general; however, some restrictions on the form of constraints may ensure tractability. Recent results indicate that there is a connection between tractability of such restricted problems and supermodularity of the allowed constraint types with respect to some lattice ordering of the domain. We prove several results confirming this in a special case when the lattice ordering is as loose as possible, i.e., a diamond one.

1 Introduction

The main object of our study in this paper is the maximum constraint satisfaction problem (MAX CSP) where one is given a collection of constraints on overlapping sets of variables and the goal is to find an assignment of values to the variables that maximizes the number of satisfied constraints. A number of classical optimization problems including MAX k-SAT, MAX CUT and MAX DICUT can be represented in this framework, and it can also be used to model optimization problems arising in more applied settings, such as database design [11].

The Max-CSP framework has been well-studied in the Boolean case, that is, when the set of values for the variables is $\{0, 1\}$. Many fundamental results have been obtained, containing both complexity classifications and approximation properties (see, e.g., [10,18,20]). In the non-Boolean case, a number of results have been obtained that concern approximation properties (see, e.g., [11,14]). However, the study of efficient exact algorithms and complexity for subproblems of non-Boolean MAX CSP has started only very recently [8,21], and the present paper is a contribution towards this line of research.

We study a standard parameterized version of the MAX CSP, in which restrictions may be imposed on the types of constraints allowed in the instances.

The most well-known examples of such problems are MAX k-SAT and MAX CUT. In particular, we investigate which restrictions make such problems *tractable*, by allowing a polynomial time algorithm to find an optimal assignment. This setting (in several variations) has been extensively studied and completely classified in the Boolean case [6,10,20]. In contrast, we consider here the case where the set of possible values is an *arbitrary finite* set.

Let D denote a *finite* set with $|D| > 1$. Let $R_D^{(m)}$ denote the set of all m-ary *predicates* over D, that is, functions from D^m to $\{0,1\}$, and let $R_D = \bigcup_{m=1}^{\infty} R_D^{(m)}$. Also, let $\mathbb{Z}^+$ denote the set of all non negative integers.

Definition 1. *A constraint over a set of variables $V = \{x_1, x_2, \ldots, x_n\}$ is an expression of the form $f(\mathbf{x})$ where*

- *$f \in R_D^{(m)}$ is called the* constraint predicate*; and*
- *$\mathbf{x} = (x_{i_1}, \ldots, x_{i_m})$ is called the* constraint scope*.*

The constraint f is said to be satisfied *on a tuple $\mathbf{a} = (a_{i_1}, \ldots, a_{i_m}) \in D^m$ if $f(\mathbf{a}) = 1$.*

Definition 2. *For a finite $\mathcal{F} \subseteq R_D$, an instance of the* weighted MAX CSP($\mathcal{F}$) *problem is a pair (V,C) where*

- *$V = \{x_1, \ldots, x_n\}$ is a set of variables taking their values from the set D;*
- *C is a collection of constraints $f_1(\mathbf{x}_1), \ldots, f_q(\mathbf{x}_q)$ over V, where $f_i \in \mathcal{F}$ for all $1 \leq i \leq q$; each constraint $f_i(\mathbf{x}_i)$ is assigned a weight $\varrho_i \in \mathbb{Z}^+$.*

The goal is to find an assignment $\phi : V \to D$ that maximizes the total weight of satisfied constraints, that is, to maximize the function $f : D^n \to \mathbb{Z}^+$, defined by $f(x_1, \ldots, x_n) = \sum_{i=1}^{q} \varrho_i \cdot f_i(\mathbf{x}_i)$.

Note that throughout the paper the values 0 and 1 taken by any predicate will be considered, rather unusually, as integers, not as Boolean values, and addition will always denote the addition of integers. Throughout the paper, we assume that $\mathcal{F}$ is finite.

Example 1. The MAX CUT problem is the problem of partitioning the set of vertices of a given undirected graph with weighted edges into two subsets so as to maximize the total weight of edges with ends being in different subsets. Let neq_2 be the binary predicate on $\{0,1\}$ such that $neq_2(x,y) = 1 \Leftrightarrow x \neq y$. Then the MAX CUT problem is the same as MAX CSP($\{neq_2\}$). To see this, think of vertices of a given graph as of variables, and apply the predicate to every pair of variables x, y such that (x, y) is an edge in the graph. Let f_{dicut} be the binary predicate on $\{0, 1\}$ such that $f_{dicut}(x, y) = 1 \Leftrightarrow x = 0, y = 1$. Then MAX CSP($\{f_{dicut}\}$) is essentially the problem MAX DICUT which is the problem of partitioning the vertices of a digraph with weighted arcs into two subsets V_0 and V_1 so as to maximize the total weight of arcs going from V_0 to V_1. It is well known that both MAX CUT and MAX DICUT are **NP**-hard (see, e.g., [10]).

The main research problem we will study in this paper is the following:

Problem 1. What are the sets $\mathcal{F}$ such that MAX CSP($\mathcal{F}$) is tractable?

For the Boolean case, Problem 1 was solved in [9]. It appears that Boolean problems MAX CSP($\mathcal{F}$) exhibit a dichotomy in that such a problem either is solvable exactly in polynomial time or else is **NP**-hard (which cannot be taken for granted because of Ladner's theorem). The paper [9] also describes the boundary between the two cases.

Versions of Problem 1 for other non-Boolean constraint problems (including decision, quantified, and counting problems) have been actively studied in the last years, with many classification results obtained (see, e.g., [1–4,17]). Experience in the study of various forms of constraint satisfaction (see, e.g., [2,3]) has shown that the more general form of such problems, in which the domain is an arbitrary finite set, is often considerably more difficult to analyze than the Boolean case.

The algebraic combinatorial property of supermodularity (see Section 2) is a well-known source of tractable maximization problems [5,15]. In combinatorial optimization, this property (or the dual property of submodularity) is usually considered on subsets of a set or on distributive lattices [5,19]. However, it can be considered on arbitrary lattices, and this has proved useful in operational research [22]. Very recently [8], this general form of supermodularity was proposed as the main tool in tackling Problem 1. Indeed, for $|D| = 2$, this property was shown [8] to completely characterize the tractable cases of MAX CSP (originally, the characterization was obtained [9] in a different form), and moreover, this property also essentially characterizes the tractable cases for $|D| = 3$ [21].

Interestingly, the relevance of an ordering of the domain is not suggested in any way by the formulation of Problem 1. In this paper we determine the complexity of MAX CSP assuming that the domain has a lattice ordering, but the order is a diamond order, that is, it is as loose as a lattice order can possibly be.

The structure of the paper is as follows: in Section 2 we discuss lattices, supermodularity, and their relevance in the study of MAX CSP. In Section 3 we describe the structure of supermodular predicates on diamonds, which we use in Section 4 to show that MAX CSP with such constraints can be solved in cubic time. In Section 5 we show that a certain small set of supermodular constraints on diamonds gives rise to **NP**-hard problems when extended with any non-supermodular constraint.

2 Preliminaries

In this section we discuss the well-known combinatorial algebraic property of supermodularity [22] which will play a crucial role in classifying the complexity of MAX CSP problems.

A partial order on a set D is called a *lattice order* if, for every $x, y \in D$, there exists a greatest lower bound $x \sqcap y$ (called the *meet* of a and b) and a least upper bound $x \sqcup y$ (called the *join*). The corresponding algebra $\mathcal{L} = (D, \sqcap, \sqcup)$ is called a *lattice*. It is well-known that any finite lattice $\mathcal{L}$ has a greatest element $1_\mathcal{L}$ and a least element $0_\mathcal{L}$. A lattice is called *distributive* (also known as a *ring family*) if it can be represented by subsets of a set, the operations being set-theoretic intersection and union. For $n \geq 2$, an *n-diamond* (or simply a diamond), denoted $\mathcal{M}_n$, is a lattice on an $(n+2)$-element set such that all n elements in $\mathcal{M}_n \setminus \{0_{\mathcal{M}_n}, 1_{\mathcal{M}_n}\}$ are pairwise incomparable. The Hasse diagram of $\mathcal{M}_n$ is given in Fig. 1. Since every element of any finite lattice must be comparable with both

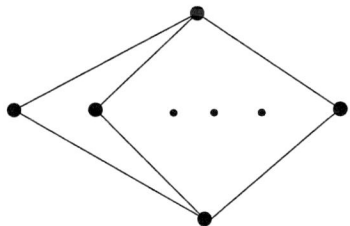

Fig. 1. A diamond lattice $\mathcal{M}_n$

the top and the bottom elements, diamonds are as unordered as lattices can possibly be. The middle elements of $\mathcal{M}_n$ are called *atoms*. Note that, for every pair of distinct atoms a and b, we have $a \sqcap b = 0_{\mathcal{M}_n}$ and $a \sqcup b = 1_{\mathcal{M}_n}$. It is well-known (and easy to see) that a distributive lattice cannot contain $\mathcal{M}_3$ (and hence any $\mathcal{M}_n$ with $n \geq 3$) as a sublattice. In the literature (e.g., [12]), the lattice $\mathcal{M}_3$ is often called *the* diamond. It is one of the two minimal non-distributive lattices. For more information on lattices and orders, see [12].

For tuples $\mathbf{a} = (a_1, \ldots, a_n)$, $\mathbf{b} = (b_1, \ldots, b_n)$ in D^n, let $\mathbf{a} \sqcap \mathbf{b}$ and $\mathbf{a} \sqcup \mathbf{b}$ denote the tuples $(a_1 \sqcap b_1, \ldots, a_n \sqcap b_n)$ and $(a_1 \sqcup b_1, \ldots, a_n \sqcup b_n)$, respectively.

Definition 3. *Let $\mathcal{L}$ be a lattice on D. A function $f : D^n \to \mathbb{R}$ is called* supermodular *on $\mathcal{L}$ if it satisfies*

$$f(\mathbf{a}) + f(\mathbf{b}) \leq f(\mathbf{a} \sqcap \mathbf{b}) + f(\mathbf{a} \sqcup \mathbf{b}) \tag{1}$$

for all $\mathbf{a}, \mathbf{b} \in D^n$, and f is called submodular *on $\mathcal{L}$ if the inverse inequality holds. The set of all supermodular predicates on $\mathcal{L}$ will be denoted* $\mathrm{Spmod}_\mathcal{L}$.

The standard definition of sub- and supermodular (set) functions [5,15] corresponds to the special case of the above definition when $|D| = 2$. Recall that a *chain* is a totally ordered lattice. Sub- and supermodular functions on finite chains have been studied in combinatorial optimization under the name of Monge and inverse Monge matrices and arrays (see survey [5]). Note that chains and diamonds represent "opposite" types of lattices: chains have all possible comparabilities, while diamonds have as few comparabilities as possible.

The following results have been previously obtained in classifying the complexity of MAX CSP.

Theorem 1 ([8]). *If $\mathcal{F}$ is supermodular on some distributive lattice on D, then* MAX CSP$(\mathcal{F})$ *is tractable.*

An *endomorphism* of $\mathcal{F}$ is a unary operation π on D such that, for all $f \in \mathcal{F}$ and all $(a_1, \ldots, a_m) \in D^m$, we have $f(a_1, \ldots, a_m) = 1 \Rightarrow f(\pi(a_1), \ldots, \pi(a_m)) = 1$. We will say that $\mathcal{F}$ is a *core* if every endomorphism of $\mathcal{F}$ is injective (i.e., a permutation). The intuition here is that if $\mathcal{F}$ is not a core then it has a non-injective endomorphism π, which implies that, for every assignment ϕ, there is another assignment $\pi\phi$ that satisfies all constraints satisfied by ϕ and uses only a restricted set of values, so the problem is equivalent to a problem over this smaller set.

Theorem 2 ([8,10,21]). *Let $|D| \leq 3$ and $\mathcal{F} \subseteq R_D$ be a core. If $\mathcal{F} \subseteq \text{Spmod}_\mathcal{C}$ for some chain $\mathcal{C}$ on D then* MAX CSP$(\mathcal{F})$ *is tractable. Otherwise,* MAX CSP$(\mathcal{F})$ *is NP-hard.*

Proofs of both theorems cited above enjoyed support of known results on classical submodular (set) functions and on Monge matrices and arrays. However, if we are unable to represent the lattice operations by set-theoretic ones then the analysis of supermodular functions becomes significantly more difficult.

We will now consider a form of supermodular constraints that can be defined on any lattice.

Definition 4. *A predicate $f \in R_D^{(n)}$ will be called* 2-monotone[1] *on a poset $\mathcal{P}$ on D if it can be expressed as follows*

$$f(\mathbf{x}) = 1 \Leftrightarrow ((x_{i_1} \sqsubseteq a_{i_1}) \wedge \ldots \wedge (x_{i_s} \sqsubseteq a_{i_s})) \vee ((x_{j_1} \sqsupseteq b_{j_1}) \wedge \ldots \wedge (x_{j_t} \sqsupseteq b_{j_t})) \quad (2)$$

where $\mathbf{x} = (x_1, \ldots, x_n)$, $a_{i_1}, \ldots, a_{i_s}, b_{j_1}, \ldots, b_{j_t} \in D$, and either of the two disjuncts may be empty (i.e., the value of s or t may be zero).

It is straightforward to check that every 2-monotone predicate on a lattice is supermodular on it. The next theorem is, to the best of our knowledge, the only one available on the complexity of supermodular constraints on arbitrary lattices.

Theorem 3 ([8]). *Let $\mathcal{L}$ be a lattice on a finite set D. If $\mathcal{F}$ consists of 2-monotone predicates on $\mathcal{L}$, then* MAX CSP$(\mathcal{F})$ *is tractable.*

3 The Structure of Supermodular Predicates on Diamonds

In the rest of this paper we consider supermodular constraints on diamonds $\mathcal{M}_n$. Throughout the rest of this paper, let $\mathcal{M}$ be an arbitrary (fixed) n-diamond, $n \geq 2$. In this section, we describe the structure of supermodular predicates on $\mathcal{M}$ by representing them as logical formulas involving constants (elements of $\mathcal{M}$) and the order relation $\sqsubseteq$ of $\mathcal{M}$.

---
[1] In [8], such predicates are called *generalized* 2-monotone.

For a subset $D' \subseteq D$, let $u_{D'}$ denote the predicate such that $u_{D'}(x) = 1 \Leftrightarrow x \in D'$. The following lemma can be easily derived directly from the definition of supermodularity.

Lemma 1. *A unary predicate $u_{D'}$ is in* $\text{Spmod}_{\mathcal{M}}$ *if and only if either both $0_{\mathcal{M}}, 1_{\mathcal{M}} \in D'$ or else $|D'| \leq 2$ and at least one of $0_{\mathcal{M}}, 1_{\mathcal{M}}$ is in D'.*

In the next theorem, the condition ($\mathbf{y} \sqsupseteq \mathbf{c}$), where $\mathbf{y}$ and $\mathbf{c}$ are tuples of the same length, will denote $\bigwedge (y_i \sqsupseteq c_i)$. The condition ($\mathbf{y} \sqsubseteq \mathbf{c}$) is defined similarly.

Theorem 4. *Every predicate $f(x_1, \ldots, x_m)$ in* $\text{Spmod}_{\mathcal{M}}$, *such that f takes both values 0 and 1, can be represented as one of the following logical implications:*

1. $[(x_i \sqsubseteq a_1) \vee \ldots \vee (x_i \sqsubseteq a_l)] \implies (x_i \sqsubseteq 0_{\mathcal{M}})$ *where the a_j's are atoms;*
2. $\neg(\mathbf{y} \sqsupseteq \mathbf{c}) \implies (\mathbf{z} \sqsubseteq \mathbf{d})$ *where $\mathbf{y}$ and $\mathbf{z}$ are some subsequences of $(x_1, \ldots, x_m)$, and $\mathbf{c}, \mathbf{d}$ are tuples of elements of $\mathcal{M}$ (of corresponding length) such that $\mathbf{c}$ contains no $0_{\mathcal{M}}$ and $\mathbf{d}$ no $1_{\mathcal{M}}$;*
3. $[(x_i \sqsubseteq b_1) \vee \cdots \vee (x_i \sqsubseteq b_k) \vee \neg(\mathbf{y} \sqsupseteq \mathbf{c})] \implies (x_i \sqsubseteq a)$ *where the b_j's are atoms, $\mathbf{y}$ does not contain x_i, and $a \neq 1_{\mathcal{M}}$;*
4. $\neg(x_i \sqsupseteq b) \implies [\neg(x_i \sqsupseteq a_1) \wedge \cdots \wedge \neg(x_i \sqsupseteq a_l) \wedge (\mathbf{y} \sqsubseteq \mathbf{c})]$ *where the a_j's are atoms, $\mathbf{y}$ does not contain x_i, and $b \neq 0_{\mathcal{M}}$;*
5. $\neg(\mathbf{y} \sqsupseteq \mathbf{c}) \implies \mathbf{false}$ *where $\mathbf{y}$ is a subsequence of $(x_1, \ldots, x_m)$ and $\mathbf{c}$ contains no $0_{\mathcal{M}}$;*
6. $\mathbf{true} \implies (\mathbf{y} \sqsubseteq \mathbf{c})$ *where $\mathbf{y}$ is a subsequence of $(x_1, \ldots, x_m)$ and $\mathbf{c}$ contains no $1_{\mathcal{M}}$.*

Conversely, every predicate that can be represented in one of the above forms belongs to $\text{Spmod}_{\mathcal{M}}$.

Example 2. The unary predicate of type (1) above is the same as $u_{D'}$ where $D' = D \setminus \{a_1, \ldots, a_l\}$. The predicates $u_{D'} \in \text{Spmod}_{\mathcal{M}}$ with $|D'| \leq 2$ are the unary predicates of types (5) and (6).

Remark 1. Note that constraints of types (2), (5), and (6) are 2-monotone on $\mathcal{M}$, while constraints of types (3) and (4) (and most of those of type (1)) are not.

Proof. It is straightforward to verify that all the predicates in the list are actually supermodular. Now we prove the converse. Consider first the case where the predicate f is *essentially unary*, i.e., there is a variable x_i such that $f(x_1, \ldots, x_m) = u_{D'}(x_i)$ for some $D' \subsetneq D$. If $D' = \{x : x \sqsubseteq a\}$ or $D' = \{x : x \sqsupseteq a\}$ for some atom a then f is of the form (5) or (6); otherwise both $0_{\mathcal{M}}$ and $1_{\mathcal{M}}$ are in D' by Lemma 1, and if $a_1, \ldots, a_l$ denote the atoms of the lattice that are not in D', then it is clear that f is described by the implication (1).

Now we may assume that f is not essentially unary. If it is 2-monotone, then it is easy to see that f must be described by an implication of type (2), (5) or (6). So now we assume that f is not essentially unary and it is not 2-monotone; we prove that it is described by an implication of type (3) or (4). We require a few claims:

Claim 0. *The set X of all tuples $\mathbf{u}$ such that $f(\mathbf{u}) = 1$ is a sublattice of $\mathcal{M}^m$, i.e. is closed under join and meet.*

This follows immediately from the supermodularity of f.

Claim 1. *There exist indices $1 \leq i_1, \ldots, i_k, j_1, \ldots, j_l \leq n$, atoms $e_1, \ldots, e_k$ and $b_1, \ldots, b_l$ of $\mathcal{M}$ such that $f(\mathbf{x}) = 1$ if and only if*

$$[\neg(x_{i_1} \sqsupseteq e_1) \wedge \cdots \wedge \neg(x_{i_k} \sqsupseteq e_k)] \bigvee [\neg(x_{j_1} \sqsubseteq b_1) \wedge \cdots \wedge \neg(x_{j_l} \sqsubseteq b_l)].$$

Notice first that the set Z of tuples $\mathbf{u}$ such that $f(\mathbf{u}) = 0$ is *convex* in $\mathcal{M}^m$, i.e. if $\mathbf{u} \sqsubseteq \mathbf{v} \sqsubseteq \mathbf{w}$ with $f(\mathbf{u}) = f(\mathbf{w}) = 0$ then $f(\mathbf{v}) = 0$. To show this we construct a tuple $\mathbf{v}'$ as follows: for each coordinate i it is easy to find an element v_i' such that $v_i \sqcap v_i' = u_i$ and $v_i \sqcup v_i' = w_i$. Hence $\mathbf{v} \sqcap \mathbf{v}' = \mathbf{u}$ and $\mathbf{v} \sqcup \mathbf{v}' = \mathbf{w}$ so by supermodularity of f neither $\mathbf{v}$ nor $\mathbf{v}'$ is in X. It follows in particular that neither $0_{\mathcal{M}^m}$ nor $1_{\mathcal{M}^m}$ is in Z; indeed, if $0_{\mathcal{M}^m} \in Z$, let $\mathbf{a}$ be the smallest element in X (the meet of all elements in X), which exists by Claim 0. Since Z is convex it follows that every element above $\mathbf{a}$ is in X so f is 2-monotone, a contradiction. The argument for $1_{\mathcal{M}^m}$ is identical.

Now let $\mathbf{w} \in Z$ be minimal, and let $\mathbf{v} \sqsubseteq \mathbf{w}$. As above we can find a tuple $\mathbf{v}'$ such that $\mathbf{v} \sqcup \mathbf{v}' = \mathbf{w}$; by supermodularity of f it follows that $\mathbf{v} = \mathbf{w}$ or $\mathbf{v}' = \mathbf{w}$. It is easy to deduce from this that there exists a coordinate s such that w_s is an atom of $\mathcal{M}$ and $w_t = 0_\mathcal{M}$ for all $t \neq s$. A similar argument shows that every maximal element of Z has a unique coordinate which is an atom and all others are equal to $1_\mathcal{M}$.

Since Z is convex, we have that $f(\mathbf{x}) = 0$ if and only if $\mathbf{x}$ is above some minimal element of Z and below some maximal element of Z; Claim 1 then follows immediately.

For each index $i \in \{i_1, \ldots, i_k\}$ that appears in the expression in Claim 1, there is a corresponding condition of the form

$$\neg(x_i \sqsupseteq e_{s_1}) \wedge \cdots \wedge \neg(x_i \sqsupseteq e_{s_r});$$

let I_i denote the set of elements of $\mathcal{M}$ that satisfy this condition. Obviously it cannot contain $1_\mathcal{M}$ and must contain $0_\mathcal{M}$. Similarly, define for each index $j \in \{j_1, \ldots, j_l\}$ the set F_j of all elements of $\mathcal{M}$ that satisfy the corresponding condition of the form

$$\neg(x_j \sqsubseteq b_{t_1}) \wedge \cdots \wedge \neg(x_j \sqsubseteq b_{t_q});$$

it is clear that $0_\mathcal{M} \notin F_j$ and $1_\mathcal{M} \in F_j$.

The condition of Claim 1 can now be rephrased as follows: $f(\mathbf{x}) = 1$ if and only if $x_i \in I_i$ for all $i \in \{i_1, \ldots, i_k\}$ or $x_j \in F_j$ for all $j \in \{j_1, \ldots, j_l\}$. It is straightforward to verify that since f is not 2-monotone, one of the I_i or one of the F_j must contain 2 distinct atoms. We consider the first case, and we show that the predicate f is of type (4). The case where some F_j contains two atoms is dual and will yield type (3).

Claim 2. *Suppose that I_i contains distinct atoms c and d for some $i \in \{i_1, \ldots, i_k\}$. Then (a) i is the only index with this property, (b) $\{j_1, \ldots, j_l\} = \{i\}$ and (c) F_i does not contain 2 distinct atoms.*

We prove (b) first. We have that

$$f(0_\mathcal{M}, \ldots, 0_\mathcal{M}, c, 0_\mathcal{M}, \ldots, 0_\mathcal{M}) = f(0_\mathcal{M}, \ldots, 0_\mathcal{M}, d, 0_\mathcal{M}, \ldots, 0_\mathcal{M}) = 1$$

(where c and d appear in the i-th position) and by supermodularity it follows that $f(0_\mathcal{M}, \ldots, 0_\mathcal{M}, 1_\mathcal{M}, 0_\mathcal{M}, \ldots, 0_\mathcal{M}) = 1$ also. Since I_i does not contain $1_\mathcal{M}$, we have that $x_j \in F_j$ for each $j \in \{j_1, \ldots, j_l\}$; since F_j never contains $0_\mathcal{M}$, (b) follows immediately. Since $\{j_1, \ldots, j_l\}$ is non-empty, (a) follows immediately from (b). Finally, if F_i contained distinct atoms then by dualising the preceding argument we would obtain that $\{i_1, \ldots, i_k\} = \{i\}$ from which it would follow that f would be essentially unary, contrary to our assumption. This concludes the proof of the claim.

Let b denote the minimal element in F_i, and for each index $s \in \{i_1, \ldots, i_k\}$ different from i let c_s denote the (unique) maximal element of I_s; then we can describe f as follows: $f(\mathbf{x}) = 1$ if and only if

$$[x_i \in I_i \wedge (\mathbf{y} \sqsubseteq \mathbf{c})] \vee (x_i \sqsupseteq b)$$

where $\mathbf{y}$ is a tuple of variables different from x_i and $\mathbf{c}$ is the tuple whose entries are the c_s defined previously. It remains to rewrite the condition $x_i \in I_i$. Suppose first that there exists at least one atom of $\mathcal{M}$ outside I_i, and let $a_1, \ldots, a_l$ denote the atoms outside I_i. Then it is clear that $x_i \in I_i$ if and only if $\neg(x_i \sqsupseteq a_1) \vee \cdots \vee \neg(x_i \sqsupseteq a_l)$ holds, so the predicate f is of type (4) (simply restate the disjunction as an implication). Now for the last possibility, where I_i contains all of D except $1_\mathcal{M}$; then it is easy to see that f can be described by the following:

$$[\neg(x_i \sqsupseteq b) \wedge (\mathbf{y} \sqsubseteq \mathbf{c})] \vee (x_i \sqsupseteq b)$$

and this completes the proof of the theorem. □

4 Supermodular Constraints on Diamonds are Tractable

In this section we prove the main tractability result of this paper. The proof technique extends ideas from the proof of Theorem 3.

Theorem 5. *If $\mathcal{F} \subseteq \text{Spmod}_\mathcal{M}$ then MAX CSP($\mathcal{F}$) can be solved (to optimality) in $O(t^3 \cdot |D|^3 + q^3)$ time where t is the number of variables and q is the number of constraints in an instance.*

Proof. We will show how the problem can be reduced to the well-known tractable problem MIN CUT.

Let $\mathcal{I} = \{\rho_1 \cdot f_1(\mathbf{x}_1), \ldots, \rho_q \cdot f_q(\mathbf{x}_q)\}$, $q \geq 1$, be an instance of weighted MAX CSP($\mathcal{F}$), over a set of variables $V = \{x_1, , \ldots, , x_n\}$.

Construction.
Let ∞ denote an integer greater than $\sum \rho_i$. For each constraint f_i, fix a representation as described in Theorem 4. In the following construction, we will refer to the type of f_i which will be a number from 1 to 6 according to the type of representation. Every condition of the form $(\mathbf{y} \sqsubseteq \mathbf{c})$ will be read as $\bigwedge (x_{i_s} \sqsubseteq c_{i_s})$, and every condition of the form $\neg(\mathbf{y} \sqsupseteq \mathbf{c})$ as $\bigvee \neg(x_{i_s} \sqsupseteq c_{i_s})$, where i_s runs through the indices of variables in $\mathbf{y}$. Moreover, we replace every (sub)formula of the form $\neg(x \sqsupseteq 1_\mathcal{M})$ by $\bigvee_{i=1}^n \neg(x \sqsupseteq a_i)$ where $a_1, \ldots, a_n$ are the atoms of $\mathcal{M}$.

We construct a digraph $G_\mathcal{I}$ as follows:

- The vertices of $G_\mathcal{I}$ are as follows
  - $\{T, F\} \cup \{x_d \mid x \in V, d \in \mathcal{M}\} \cup \{\bar{x}_d \mid x \in V, d \in \mathcal{M} \text{ is an atom}\} \cup \{e_i, \bar{e}_i \mid i = 1, 2, \ldots, q\}^2$.

  For each f_i of type (5), we identify the vertex e_i with F. Similarly, for each f_i of type (6), we identify the vertex $\bar{e}_i$ with T.

- The arcs of $G_\mathcal{I}$ are defined as follows:
  - For each atom c in $\mathcal{M}$ and for each $x \in V$, there is an arc from $x_{0_\mathcal{M}}$ to x_c with weight ∞, and an arc from $\bar{x}_c$ to $x_{1_\mathcal{M}}$ with weight ∞;
  - For each pair of distinct atoms c, d in $\mathcal{M}$ and for each $x \in V$, there is an arc from x_c to $\bar{x}_d$ with weight ∞;
  - For each f_i, there is an arc from $\bar{e}_i$ to e_i with weight ρ_i;
  - For each f_i of types (1-4), and each subformula of the form $(x \sqsubseteq a)$ or $\neg(x \sqsupseteq a)$ in the consequent of f_i, there is an arc from e_i to x_a or $\bar{x}_a$, respectively, with weight ∞;
  - For each f_i of types (1-4), and each subformula of the form $(x \sqsubseteq a)$ or $\neg(x \sqsupseteq a)$ in the antecedent of f_i, there is an arc from x_a or $\bar{x}_a$, respectively, to $\bar{e}_i$, with weight ∞;
  - For each f_i of type (5), and each subformula of the form $\neg(x \sqsupseteq a)$ in it, there is an arc from $\bar{x}_a$ to $\bar{e}_i$ with weight ∞;
  - For each f_i of type (6), and each subformula of the form $(x \sqsubseteq a)$ in it, there is an arc from e_i to x_a with weight ∞;

Arcs with weight less than ∞ will be called *constraint* arcs.

It is easy to see that $G_\mathcal{I}$ is a digraph with source T (corresponding to **true**) and sink F (corresponding to **false**). Note that paths of non-constraint arcs between vertices corresponding to any given variable $x \in V$ precisely correspond to logical implications that hold between the corresponding assertions.

Define the *deficiency* of an assignment ϕ as the difference between $\sum_{i=1}^{q} \rho_i$ and the evaluation of ϕ on $\mathcal{I}$. In other words, the deficiency of ϕ is the total weight of constraints not satisfied by ϕ. We will prove that minimal cuts in $G_\mathcal{I}$ exactly correspond to optimal assignments to $\mathcal{I}$. More precisely, we will show that, for each minimal cut in $G_\mathcal{I}$ with weight ρ, there is an assignment for $\mathcal{I}$ with deficiency at most ρ, and, for each assignment to $\mathcal{I}$ with deficiency ρ', there is a cut in $G_\mathcal{I}$ with weight ρ'.

The semantics of the construction of $G_\mathcal{I}$ will be as follows: the vertices of the form x_a or $\bar{x}_a$ correspond to assertions of the form $x \sqsubseteq a$ or $\neg(x \sqsupseteq a)$, respectively, and arcs denote implications about these assertions. Given a minimal cut in $G_\mathcal{I}$, we will call a vertex x_a *reaching* if F can be reached from it without crossing the cut. Furthermore, if a vertex x_a is reaching then this will designate that the corresponding assertion is false, and otherwise the corresponding assertion is true. A constraint is not satisfied if and only if the corresponding constraint arc crosses the cut.

---

[2] The vertices x_d will correspond to the expressions $x \sqsubseteq d$ and $\bar{x}_d$ to $\neg(x \sqsupseteq d)$.

Let C be a minimal cut in $G_\mathcal{I}$. Obviously, C contains only constraint arcs. First we show that, for every variable $x \in V$, there is a unique minimal element $a \in \mathcal{M}$ such that x_a is non-reaching. All we need to show is the following: if c, d are distinct atoms such that both x_c and x_d are both non-reaching then so is $x_{0_\mathcal{M}}$. Assume that, on the contrary, $x_{0_\mathcal{M}}$ is reaching. Then there is a path from $x_{0_\mathcal{M}}$ to F not crossing the cut. By examining the arcs of $G_\mathcal{I}$, it is easy to notice that such a path has to go through a vertex $\bar{x}_a$ for some atom $a \in \mathcal{M}$. However, we have an arc from at least one of vertices x_c, x_d to $\bar{x}_a$, and hence at least one of this vertices would have a path to F not crossing the cut, a contradiction.

Note that, for every $x \in V$, there are no arcs coming out of $x_{1_\mathcal{M}}$. Hence, for every $x \in V$, there is a unique minimal element $v \in \mathcal{M}$ such that F cannot be reached from x_v without crossing the cut.

Define an assignment ϕ_C as follows:

$\phi_C(x)$ is the unique minimal element a such that x_a is non-reaching.

We now make some observations. Note that, for all $x \in V$ and $a \in \mathcal{M}$, we have that $\phi_C(x) \sqsubseteq a$ if and only x_a is non-reaching. Moreover, if $\bar{x}_a$ is reaching then, for each atom $b \neq a$, we have an arc from x_b to $\bar{x}_a$ meaning that $\phi_C(x) \not\sqsubseteq b$, and hence $\phi_C(x) \sqsupseteq a$. Furthermore, if $\bar{x}_a$ is non-reaching then $\phi_C(x) \neq a$. Indeed, if $\phi_C(x) = a$ then x_b is reaching for all atoms $b \neq a$, and, since every path from x_b to F has to go through a vertex $\bar{x}_c$ for some c, we have that $\bar{x}_c$ is reaching. Then $c \neq a$, and there is an arc from x_a to $\bar{x}_c$, so x_a is reaching, a contradiction. To summarize,

- if a node of the form x_a or $\bar{x}_a$ is reaching then the corresponding assertion is falsified by the assignment ϕ_C;
- if a node of the form x_a is non-reaching then $\phi_C(x) \sqsubseteq a$;
- if a node of the form $\bar{x}_a$ is non-reaching then the truth value of the corresponding assertion is undecided.

Suppose that a constraint arc corresponding to a constraint f_i is not in the cut. We claim that f_i is satisfied by the assignment ϕ_C. To show this, we will go through the possible types of f_i.

If f_i is of type (1), (2), (5), or (6), then the claim is straightforward. For example, let f_i be of type (1). If the node $x_{0_\mathcal{M}}$ corresponding to the consequent is reaching, then so are all nodes corresponding to the antecedent. Hence, all atomic formulas in $f_i(\mathbf{x}_i)$ are falsified by the assignment ϕ_C, and the implication is true. If $x_{0_\mathcal{M}}$ is non-reaching, then $\phi_C(x) = 0_\mathcal{M}$, and the constraint is clearly satisfied. The argument for types (2), (5), (6) is very similar.

Let f_i be of type (3). Then, if the node corresponding to the consequent is non-reaching then the consequent is satisfied by ϕ_C, and so the constraint is satisfied. If this node is reaching then every node corresponding to the disjuncts in the antecedent is reaching. Then both antecedent and consequent are falsified by ϕ_C, and the constraint is satisfied.

Let f_i be of type (4), that is, of the form

$$\neg(x_i \sqsupseteq b) \implies [\neg(x_i \sqsupseteq a_1) \land \cdots \land \neg(x_i \sqsupseteq a_l) \land (\mathbf{y} \sqsubseteq \mathbf{c})].$$

If a node corresponding to some conjunct in the consequent is reaching, then the node corresponding to the antecedent is also reaching. So $\phi_C(x_i) \sqsupseteq b$, and the constraint is satisfied. More generally, if the node corresponding to the antecedent is reaching then the constraint is satisfied regardless of what happens with the consequent. Assume that all nodes corresponding to conjuncts in the consequent and in the antecedent are non-reaching. Then the conjunct $(\mathbf{y} \sqsubseteq \mathbf{c})$ is satisfied by ϕ_C. Furthermore, we know (see the observations above) that $\phi_C(x_i) \neq b$, and also that $\phi_C(x_i) \neq a_s$ for $1 \leq s \leq l$. If $\phi_C(x_i) = 1_\mathcal{M}$ then both the antecedent and the consequent of f_i are false, and hence f_i is satisfied. Otherwise, $\phi_C(x_i) \not\sqsupseteq b$ and $\phi_C(x_i) \not\sqsupseteq a_s$ for $1 \leq s \leq l$, so f_i is satisfied anyway.

Conversely, let ϕ be an assignment to $\mathcal{I}$, and let K be the set of constraints in $\mathcal{I}$ that are not satisfied by ϕ. Consider any path from T to F. It is clear that if all constraints corresponding to constraint arcs on this path are satisfied, then we have a chain of valid implications starting from **true** and finishing at **false**. Since this is impossible, at least one constraint corresponding to such an arc is not satisfied by ϕ. Hence, the constraints arcs corresponding to constraints in K form a cut in $G_\mathcal{I}$. Furthermore, by the choice of K, the weight of this cut is equal to the deficiency of ϕ.

It follows that the standard algorithm [16] for the MIN CUT problem can be used to find an optimal assignment for any instance of MAX CSP($\mathcal{F}$). This algorithm runs in $O(k^3)$ where k is the number of vertices in the graph. Since the number of vertices in $G_\mathcal{I}$ is at most $2(1 + t \cdot |D| + q)$, the result follows. □

5 A Partial Converse

We will now prove a partial converse to Theorem 5.

The following theorem shows that, in order to establish that a given function f is supermodular on a given lattice, it is sufficient to prove supermodularity of certain unary and binary functions derived from f by substituting constants for variables. This result was proved in [13] for submodular functions on lattices, but clearly it is also is true for supermodular functions because f is supermodular if and only if $-f$ is submodular.

Theorem 6 ([13]). *Let $\mathcal{L}$ be a finite lattice. An n-ary function f on $\mathcal{L}$ is supermodular on $\mathcal{L}$ if and only if it satisfies inequality (1) for all $\mathbf{a}, \mathbf{b} \in \mathcal{L}^n$ such that*

- $a_i = b_i$ *with one exception, or*
- $a_i = b_i$ *with two exceptions, and, for each i, the elements a_i and b_i are comparable in $\mathcal{L}$.*

Theorem 7. *Let $\mathcal{F}$ contain all at most binary 2-monotone predicates on $\mathcal{M}$. If $\mathcal{F} \subseteq \mathrm{Spmod}_\mathcal{M}$ then MAX CSP($\mathcal{F}$) is tractable. Otherwise, MAX CSP($\mathcal{F}$) is NP-hard.*

Proof. If $\mathcal{F} \subseteq \mathrm{Spmod}_\mathcal{M}$ then the result follows from Theorem 5. Otherwise, there is a predicate $f \in \mathcal{F}$ such that $f \notin \mathrm{Spmod}_\mathcal{M}$. First, we prove that we can assume f to be at most binary. By Theorem 6, we can substitute constants for all but at most two variables in such a way that the obtained predicate f' is not supermodular on $\mathcal{M}$. We now show that f' can be assumed to be in $\mathcal{F}$. We will consider the case when f' is binary, the other case (when f' is unary) is similar. Assume without loss of generality that $f'(x_1, x_2) = f(x_1, x_2, a_1, \ldots, a_p)$, and reduce MAX CSP$(\mathcal{F} \cup \{f'\})$ to MAX CSP$(\mathcal{F})$. Let $\mathcal{I}$ be an instance of MAX CSP$(\mathcal{F} \cup \{f'\})$ and W the total weight of all constraints in $\mathcal{I}$, plus 1. Transform $\mathcal{I}$ into an instance $\mathcal{I}'$ of MAX CSP$(\mathcal{F})$ as follows:

1. For each constraint $f_i(\mathbf{x}_i)$ in $\mathcal{I}$ such that $f_i = f'$
   – replace f' with f
   – keep the same first two variables as in the original constraint
   – introduce fresh variables $y_1^i, \ldots, y_p^i$ for the last p variables.
2. For every new variable y_s^i introduced in step 1, add
   – a constraint $y_s^i \sqsupseteq a_s$ with weight W, and
   – a constraint $y_s^i \sqsubseteq a_s$, with weight W.

Clearly this transformation can be performed in polynomial time, and the constraints added in step two above ensure that, in every optimal solution to $\mathcal{I}'$, every variable y_s^i takes the value a_s. Hence, optimal solutions to $\mathcal{I}$ and to $\mathcal{I}'$ precisely correspond to each other. So, indeed, f can be assumed to be at most binary. We consider the two cases separately.

<u>Case 1.</u> f is unary.
By Lemma 1, $f = u_{D'}$ for some non-empty $D' \subseteq D$ such that either $0_\mathcal{M}, 1_\mathcal{M} \notin D'$ or else $|D'| > 2$ and at least one of $0_\mathcal{M}, 1_\mathcal{M}$ is not in D'. If $f = u_{\{a\}}$ where a is an atom then we choose another atom b and consider the predicate $u_{\{1_\mathcal{M}, a, b\}}$. Note that the predicate $u_{\{1_\mathcal{M}, b\}}$ is 2-monotone on $\mathcal{M}$ (and hence belongs to $\mathcal{F}$), and $u_{\{1_\mathcal{M}, a, b\}}(x) = u_{\{1_\mathcal{M}, b\}}(x) + f(x)$. Hence, we may assume that $u_{\{1_\mathcal{M}, a, b\}} \in \mathcal{F}$, since, in any instance, this predicate can be replaced by the sum above. It follows that we can now assume that $f = u_{D'}$ where two distinct atoms a, b belong to D', but at least one of $0_\mathcal{M}, 1_\mathcal{M}$ (say, $0_\mathcal{M}$) does not. We will show how to reduce MAX CSP$(\{f_{dicut}\})$ (see Example 1) to MAX CSP$(\mathcal{F})$. Assume that the domain D for MAX CSP$(\{f_{dicut}\})$ is $\{a, b\}$ where a plays the role of 0 and b that of 1. Let $g \in \mathcal{F}$ be such that $g(x, y) = 1 \Leftrightarrow [(x \sqsubseteq a) \wedge (y \sqsubseteq b)]$.

Take an arbitrary instance $\mathcal{I}$ of MAX CSP$(\{f_{dicut}\})$. Replace each constraint $f_{dicut}(x, y)$ by $g(x, y)$ with the same weight. Let W be the total weight of all constraints in $\mathcal{I}$ plus 1. For every variable x in $\mathcal{I}$, add the constraint $f(x)$ with weight W and denote the obtained instance by $\mathcal{I}'$. Note that any solution to $\mathcal{I}'$ that assigns $0_\mathcal{M}$ to any variable is suboptimal because it violates one of the large-weight constraints. Moreover, if a solution assigns a value d to some variable, and $d \notin \{a, b\}$, then d can be changed to one of a, b without decreasing the total weight of the solution. Hence, there is an optimal solution to $\mathcal{I}'$ which uses only values a and b. Clearly, this solution is also optimal for $\mathcal{I}$. The other direction is similar, since any optimal solution to $\mathcal{I}$ is also an optimal solution to $\mathcal{I}'$, or else the transformation of solutions to $\mathcal{I}'$ such as described above would produce a better solution to $\mathcal{I}$.

Case 2. f is binary.
Note that, by Theorem 6, if we cannot use case 1 then the tuples $\mathbf{a} = (a_1, a_2)$ and $\mathbf{b} = (b_1, b_2)$ witnessing non-supermodularity of f can be chosen in such a way that a_i and b_i are comparable for $i = 1, 2$. For $i = 1, 2$, define functions $t_i : \{0, 1\} \to \{a_i, b_i\}$ by the following rule:

- if $a_i \sqsubseteq b_i$ then $t_i(0) = a_i$ and $t_i(1) = b_i$;
- if $b_i \sqsubseteq a_i$ then $t_i(0) = b_i$ and $t_i(1) = a_i$.

Then it is easy to check that the binary function $g' \in R_{\{0,1\}}$ such that $g'(x_1, x_2) = f(t_1(x_1), t_2(x_2))$ is a Boolean non-supermodular function. We will need unary functions c'_0, c'_1 on $\{0, 1\}$ which are defined as follows: $c'_i(x)$ is 1 if $x = i$ and 0 otherwise. It follows from Theorem 2 that MAX CSP($\mathcal{F}'$) on $\{0, 1\}$, where $\mathcal{F}' = \{g', c'_0, c'_1\}$, is **NP**-hard. (Note that that we include c'_0, c'_1 to ensure that $\mathcal{F}'$ is a core). We will give a polynomial time reduction from this problem to MAX CSP($\mathcal{F}$).

In the reduction, we will use functions $h_i(x, y)$, $i = 1, 2$, defined by the rule

$$h_i(x, y) = 1 \Leftrightarrow ((x \sqsubseteq 0) \wedge (y \sqsubseteq t_i(0))) \vee ((x \sqsupseteq 1) \wedge (y \sqsupseteq t_i(1))).$$

It is easy to see that these functions are 2-monotone on $\mathcal{M}$. In the rest of the proof we identify $0_\mathcal{M}, 1_\mathcal{M}$ with the corresponding elements $0, 1$ from the domain of $\mathcal{F}'$. Other functions used in the reduction are $u_{\{0\}}$, $u_{\{1\}}$, $u_{\{0,1\}}$, $u_{\{a_1,b_1\}}$, $u_{\{a_2,b_2\}}$. By Lemma 1, all these functions are supermodular on $\mathcal{M}$, and, in fact, they are 2-monotone (recall that a_i and b_i are comparable, so at least one of them is $0_\mathcal{M}$ or $1_\mathcal{M}$).

Let $f'(x_1, \ldots, x_n) = \sum_{i=1}^q \rho_i \cdot f'_i(\mathbf{x}_i)$ be an instance $\mathcal{I}'$ of MAX CSP($\mathcal{F}'$), over the set $V = \{x_1, \ldots, x_n\}$ of variables. Let $W = \sum \rho_i + 1$. Construct an instance $\mathcal{I}$ of MAX CSP($\mathcal{F}$) containing all variables from V and further variables and constraints as follows.

- For every $1 \leq i \leq q$ such that $f'_i(\mathbf{x}_i) = g'(x_{j_1}, x_{j_2})$, introduce
  - two new variables $y^i_{j_1}, y^i_{j_2}$,
  - constraint $f(y^i_{j_1}, y^i_{j_2})$ with weight ρ_i,
  - constraints $u_{\{a_1,b_1\}}(y^i_{j_1}), u_{\{a_2,b_2\}}(y^i_{j_2})$, each with weight W,
  - constraints $h_1(x_{j_1}, y^i_{j_1}), h_2(x_{j_2}, y^i_{j_2})$, each with weight W;
- for every $1 \leq i \leq q$ such that $f'_i(\mathbf{x}_i) = c'_0(x_{j_1})$, introduce constraint $u_{\{0\}}(x_{j_1})$ with weight ρ_i;
- for every $1 \leq i \leq q$ such that $f'_i(\mathbf{x}_i) = c'_1(x_{j_1})$, introduce constraint $u_{\{1\}}(x_{j_1})$ with weight ρ_i;
- for every variable $x_i \in V$, introduce constraint $u_{\{0,1\}}(x_i)$ with weight W.

It is easy to see that $\mathcal{I}$ can be built from $\mathcal{I}'$ in polynomial time. Let l be the number of constraints with weight W in $\mathcal{I}$.

For every assignment ϕ' to $\mathcal{I}'$, let ϕ be an assignment to $\mathcal{I}$ which coincides with ϕ' on V, and, for every variable $y^i_{j_s}$ ($s = 1, 2$), set $\phi(y^i_{j_s}) = t_s(\phi'(x_{j_s}))$. It is easy to see that ϕ satisfies all constraints of weight W. Moreover, every constraint of the form $c'_i(x_{j_1})$, $i \in \{0,1\}$, in $\mathcal{I}'$ is satisfied if and only if the corresponding constraint $u_{\{i\}}(x'_{j_1})$ in $\mathcal{I}$ is satisfied. It follows from the construction of the function g' and the choice of functions h_i and $u_{\{0,1\}}$ in $\mathcal{I}$ that a constraint $f'_i(\mathbf{x}_i)$ in $\mathcal{I}'$ with the constraint function g' is satisfied if and only if the corresponding constraint with constraint function f in $\mathcal{I}$ is satisfied. Hence, if the total weight of satisfied constraints in $\mathcal{I}'$ is ρ then the total weight of satisfied constraints in $\mathcal{I}$ is $l \cdot W + \rho$.

In the other direction, it is easy to see that every optimal assignment ϕ to $\mathcal{I}$ satisfies all constraints of weight W, therefore its weight is $l \cdot W + \rho$ for some $\rho < W$. In particular, it follows that $\phi(x) \in \{0,1\}$ for every $x \in V$. Let ϕ' be an assignment to $\mathcal{I}'$ that is the restriction of ϕ to V. Then the total weight of satisfied constraints in $\mathcal{I}'$ is ρ. Indeed, this follows from the fact that all constraints of the form h_i, $u_{\{i\}}$, and $u_{\{0,1\}}$ are satisfied, that all variables $y^i_{j_s}$, $s = 1, 2$, take values in the corresponding sets $\{a_s, b_s\}$, and these values can always be recovered from the values of the variables x_{j_s} by using the functions t_s. Thus, optimal assignments to $\mathcal{I}$ and to $\mathcal{I}'$ exactly correspond to each other, and the result follows. □

6 Conclusion

We have proved that the MAX CSP problem for constraints that are supermodular on diamonds is tractable. This is the first result about tractability of all supermodular constraints on non-distributive lattices. One natural extension of this line of research is to establish similar results for other classes of non-distributive lattices. It would be interesting to explore methods of proving tractability of MAX CSP other than via a reduction to submodular set function minimization (as in [8]) or via an explicit description of predicates (as in this paper). Can the technique of multimorphisms [6,7] be effectively used in the study of non-Boolean MAX CSP? Another interesting direction for future work is to study approximability of hard MAX CSP problems. It is known that, for $|D| \leq 3$, all hard problems MAX CSP($\mathcal{F}$) are **APX**-complete [10,21], that is, they do not admit a polynomial-time approximation scheme. Is this true for larger domains?

References

1. F. Börner, A. Bulatov, P. Jeavons, and A. Krokhin. Quantified constraints: Algorithms and complexity. In *CSL'03*, volume 2803 of *LNCS*, pages 58–70, 2003.
2. A. Bulatov. A dichotomy theorem for constraints on a 3-element set. In *FOCS'02*, pages 649–658, 2002.
3. A. Bulatov. Tractable conservative constraint satisfaction problems. In *LICS'03*, pages 321–330, 2003.
4. A. Bulatov and V. Dalmau. Towards a dichotomy theorem for the counting constraint satisfaction problem. In *FOCS'03*, pages 562–571, 2003.
5. R.E. Burkard, B. Klinz, and R. Rudolf. Perspectives of Monge properties in optimization. *Discrete Applied Mathematics*, 70:95–161, 1996.

6. D. Cohen, M. Cooper, and P. Jeavons. A complete characterization of complexity for Boolean constraint optimization problems. In *CP'04*, volume 3258 of *LNCS*, pages 212–226, 2004.
7. D. Cohen, M. Cooper, P. Jeavons, and A. Krokhin. Soft constraints: complexity and multimorphisms. In *CP'03*, volume 2833 of *LNCS*, pages 244–258, 2003.
8. D. Cohen, M. Cooper, P. Jeavons, and A. Krokhin. Identifying efficiently solvable cases of Max CSP. In *STACS'04*, volume 2996 of *LNCS*, pages 152–163, 2004.
9. N. Creignou. A dichotomy theorem for maximum generalized satisfiability problems. *Journal of Computer and System Sciences*, 51:511–522, 1995.
10. N. Creignou, S. Khanna, and M. Sudan. *Complexity Classifications of Boolean Constraint Satisfaction Problems*, SIAM, 2001.
11. M. Datar, T. Feder, A. Gionis, R. Motwani, and R. Panigrahy. A combinatorial algorithm for MAX CSP. *Information Processing Letters*, 85(6):307–315, 2003.
12. B.A. Davey and H.A. Priestley. *Introduction to Lattices and Order*. Cambridge University Press, 2nd edition, 2002.
13. B.L. Dietrich and A.J. Hoffman. On greedy algorithms, partially ordered sets, and submodular functions. *IBM J. of Research and Development*, 47(1):25–30, 2003.
14. L. Engebretsen and V. Guruswami. Is constraint satisfaction over two variables always easy? *Random Structures and Algorithms*, 25(2):150–178, 2004.
15. S. Fujishige. *Submodular Functions and Optimization*, North-Holland, 1991.
16. A. Goldberg and R.E. Tarjan. A new approach to the maximum flow problem. *J. ACM*, 35:921–940, 1988.
17. M. Grohe. The complexity of homomorphism and constraint satisfaction problems seen from the other side. In *FOCS'03*, pages 552–561, 2003.
18. J. Håstad. Some optimal inapproximability results. *J. ACM*, 48:798–859, 2001.
19. S. Iwata, L. Fleischer, and S. Fujishige. A combinatorial strongly polynomial algorithm for minimizing submodular functions. *J. ACM*, 48(4):761–777, 2001.
20. P. Jonsson. Boolean constraint satisfaction: Complexity results for optimization problems with arbitrary weights. *Theoret. Comput. Sci.*, 244(1-2):189–203, 2000.
21. P. Jonsson, M. Klasson, and A. Krokhin. The approximability of three-valued Max CSP. Technical Report cs.CC/0412042, CoRR, 2004.
22. D. Topkis. *Supermodularity and Complementarity*. Princeton Univ. Press, 1998.

Exploiting Unit Propagation to Compute Lower Bounds in Branch and Bound Max-SAT Solvers[*]

Chu Min Li[1], Felip Manyà[2], and Jordi Planes[3]

[1] LaRIA, Université de Picardie Jules Verne,
33 Rue St. Leu, 80039 Amiens Cedex 01, France
cli@laria.u-picardie.fr
[2] Artificial Intelligence Research Institute (IIIA-CSIC),
Campus UAB, 08193 Bellaterra, Spain
felip@iiia.csic.es
[3] Computer Science Department, Universitat de Lleida,
Jaume II, 69, E-25001 Lleida, Spain
jordi@eps.udl.es

Abstract. One of the main differences between complete SAT solvers and exact Max-SAT solvers is that the former make an intensive use of unit propagation at each node of the proof tree while the latter, in order to ensure optimality, can only apply unit propagation to a restricted number of nodes. In this paper, we describe a branch and bound Max-SAT solver that applies unit propagation at each node of the proof tree to compute the lower bound instead of applying unit propagation to simplify the formula. The new lower bound captures the lower bound based on inconsistency counts that apply most of the state-of-the-art Max-SAT solvers as well as other improvements, like the start rule, that have been defined to get a lower bound of better quality. Moreover, our solver incorporates the Jeroslow-Wang variable selection heuristic, the pure literal and dominating unit clause rules, and novel preprocessing techniques. The experimental investigation we conducted to compare our solver with the most modern Max-SAT solvers provides experimental evidence that our solver is very competitive.

1 Introduction

In recent years there has been a growing interest in defining formalisms and techniques for modeling and solving problems with soft constraints [13]. Even when most of the research has been around the Max-CSP problem, we observe an increasing activity around the Max-SAT problem and, in particular, in developing fast Max-SAT solvers [1,2,4,6,18,20].

Given the good results obtained in SAT on solving NP-complete decision problems in application areas as diverse as automatic test pattern generation, bounded model checking, planning, graph coloring and software verification, it

---

[*] Research partially supported by projects TIN2004-07933-C03-03 and TIC2003-00950 funded by the *Ministerio de Educación y Ciencia*. The second author is supported by a grant *Ramón y Cajal*.

seems sensible to believe that part of the technology that has been developed for SAT solvers like BerkMin [7], Chaff [21], Grasp [12], SATO [19], and Satz [11] could be adapted and incorporated into modern Max-SAT solvers in order to solve efficiently problems with soft constraints.

One of the main differences between complete SAT solvers and exact Max-SAT solvers is that the former make an intensive use of unit propagation at each node of the proof tree while the latter, in order to ensure optimality, can only apply unit propagation to a restricted number of nodes. In this paper, we describe a branch and bound Max-SAT solver that applies unit propagation at each node of the proof tree to compute the lower bound instead of applying unit propagation to simplify the formula. The new lower bound captures the lower bound based on inconsistency counts that apply most of the state-of-the-art Max-SAT solvers as well as other improvements, like the start rule, that have been defined to get a lower bound of better quality. Moreover, our solver incorporates the Jeroslow-Wang variable selection heuristic, the pure literal and dominating unit clause rules, and novel preprocessing techniques. The experimental investigation we conducted to compare our solver with the most modern Max-SAT solvers provides experimental evidence that our solver is very competitive.

The structure of the paper is as follows: we first give some notation and preliminary definitions, and describe a basic branch and bound algorithm for Max-SAT. Then, we give a detailed description of the Max-SAT solver we have developed, and report on the experimental investigation. Finally, we present some concluding remarks.

2 Notation and Definitions

In propositional logic a variable p_i may take values 0 (for false) or 1 (for true). A literal l_i is a variable p_i or its negation $\neg p_i$. A clause is a disjunction of literals, and a CNF formula is a conjunction of clauses. An assignment of truth values to the propositional variables satisfies a literal p_i if p_i takes the value 1 and satisfies a literal $\neg p_i$ if p_i takes the value 0, satisfies a clause if it satisfies at least one literal of the clause, and satisfies a CNF formula if it satisfies all the clauses of the formula.

The Max-SAT problem for a CNF formula ϕ is the problem of finding an assignment of values to propositional variables that minimizes the number of unsatisfied clauses (or equivalently, that maximizes the number of satisfied clauses). Max-SAT is called Max-k-SAT when all the clauses have k literals per clause.

3 Description of a Basic Max-SAT Solver

The space of all possible assignments for a CNF formula ϕ can be represented as a search tree, where internal nodes represent partial assignments and leaf nodes represent complete assignments. A branch and bound algorithm for Max-SAT explores the search tree in a depth-first manner. At every node, the algorithm compares the number of clauses unsatisfied by the best complete assignment found so far —called upper bound (UB)— with the number of clauses unsatisfied by the current partial assignment ($unsat$) plus an underestimation of the number of clauses that will become unsatisfied if we extend the current partial assignment into a complete assignment ($underestimation$). The sum $unsat + underestimation$ is called lower bound (LB). Obviously, if $UB \leq LB$, a better assignment cannot be found from this point in search. In that case, the algorithm prunes the subtree below the current node and backtracks to a higher level in the search tree. If $UB > LB$, it extends the current partial assignment by instantiating one more variable; which leads to the creation of two branches from the current branch: the left branch corresponds to assigning the new variable to false, and the right branch corresponds to assigning the new variable to true. In that case, the formula associated with the left (right) branch is obtained from the formula of the current node by deleting all the clauses containing the literal $\neg p$ (p) and removing all the occurrences of the literal p ($\neg p$); i.e., the algorithm applies the one-literal rule. The solution to Max-SAT is the value that UB takes after exploring the entire search tree.

Input: $max\text{-}sat(\phi, UB)$: A CNF formula ϕ and an upper bound UB
1: **if** $\phi = \emptyset$ or ϕ only contains empty clauses **then**
2:     return $empty\text{-}clauses(\phi)$
3: **end if**
4: **if** $LB(\phi) \geq UB$ **then**
5:     return ∞
6: **end if**
7: $p \leftarrow select\text{-}variable(\phi)$
8: $UB \leftarrow \min(UB, max\text{-}sat(\phi_{\neg p}, UB))$
9: return $\min(UB, max\text{-}sat(\phi_p, UB))$
Output: The minimal number of unsatisfied clauses of ϕ

Fig. 1. Basic branch and bound algorithm for Max-SAT

Figure 1 shows the pseudo-code of a basic branch and bound algorithms for Max-SAT. We use the following notation:

- $empty\text{-}clauses(\phi)$ is a function that returns the number of empty clauses of ϕ.
- $LB(\phi)$ is a lower bound for ϕ.
- UB is an upper bound of the number of unsatisfied clauses in an optimal solution. We assume that the initial value is ∞.
- $select\text{-}variable(\phi)$ is a function that returns a variable of ϕ following an heuristic.
- ϕ_p ($\phi_{\neg p}$) is the formula obtained by applying the one-literal rule to ϕ using the literal p ($\neg p$).

State-of-the-art Max-SAT solvers implement that basic algorithm augmented with preprocessing techniques, clever variable selection heuristics, powerful inference techniques, lower bounds of good quality, and efficient data structures.

4 Description of the Solver

Our solver implements the previous basic branch and bound algorithm augmented with a number of improvements that we explain below.

4.1 Preprocessing Techniques

We present the two preprocessing techniques of our solver. The first technique consists of computing an initial upper bound with a local search procedure. The second technique consists of simplifying the input formula by applying a resolution refinement to binary clauses.

Before starting to explore the search tree, we obtain an upper bound on the number of unsatisfied clauses in an optimal solution using the local search procedure GSAT [15]. This technique was first used by Borchers & Furman in their solver BF [5].

GSAT is a local search algorithm that starts with a randomly generated truth assignment for the input CNF formula, and tries to find a truth assignment that satisfies a maximal number of clauses by iteratively flipping the value of one propositional variable (i.e.; changing the value from true to false or vice versa). The selection of the variable to be flipped is based on the difference between the number of clauses satisfied by the new assignment and the number of clauses satisfied by the current assignment. This value, which is positive for those flips that cause an increment in the number of satisfied clauses, is called the score of the variable. In every step, a variable with maximal score is flipped. If there are several variables with maximal score, one of these is randomly selected. Our solver runs 10 tries, with 10.000 flips per try, and takes as initial upper bound the minimum number of unsatisfied clauses found.

It is worth to mention that GSAT found an optimal solution for most of the instances tested in our experimental investigation. For hardest instances, it would be useful to compute the initial upper bound with local search solvers that incorporate techniques to escape from local optima more sophisticated than the techniques implemented in GSAT.

Moreover, our solver does an additional action: if the initial upper bound is 1, we know that the input formula can only have 0 or 1 unsatisfied clauses. In this case, we solve the instance with Satz [10,11]. If Satz determines that the instance is satisfiable, then the solution to Max-SAT is 0. If Satz determines that the instance is unsatisfiable, then the solution to Max-SAT is 1. This way we take advantage of SAT techniques, like the sophisticated variable selection heuristic of Satz, that have not yet been extended to Max-SAT. We observed in the experiments that the run-time gains obtained with our preprocessing can be up to one order of magnitude.

Before the search starts, we also simplify the input formula by applying the resolution rule to a particular class of binary clauses. We replace every pair of clauses $l_1 \vee l_2$ and $\neg l_1 \vee l_2$ with the clause l_2. The advantage of this preprocessing is that we generate new unit clauses. Note that arbitrary binary resolution cannot be applied safely in Max-SAT. This rule was first introduced in [3].

4.2 Inference Techniques

We next define the inference rules that our solver applies at each node of the proof tree in order to simplify the formula associated with the node:

- Pure literal rule: If a literal only appears with either positive polarity or negative polarity, we delete the clauses containing that literal.
- Dominating Unit Clause (DUC) rule: DUC [14] is an inference rule that allows one to fix the truth value of a variable; i.e., it avoids to apply branching on that variable. DUC is defined as follows: If the number of clauses in which a literal p ($\neg p$) appears is not bigger than the number of unit clauses in which the literal $\neg p$ (p) appears, then the value of p can be set to false (true).
- Unit propagation: When branching is done, branch and bound algorithms for Max-SAT apply the one-literal rule (simplifying with the branching literal) instead of applying unit propagation as in most SAT solvers.[1] If unit propagation is applied at each node, the algorithm can return a non-optimal solution. For example, if we apply unit propagation to $p \wedge \neg q \wedge (\neg p \vee q) \wedge \neg p$ using the unit clause $\neg p$, we derive one empty clause while if we use the unit clause p, we derive two empty clauses. However, when the difference between the lower bound and the upper bound is one, unit propagation can be safely applied, because otherwise by fixing to false any literal of any unit clause we reach the upper bound. This inference technique, which was first used by Borchers & Furman [5], is also used in our solver. Nevertheless, the novel use of unit propagation that we introduce, in this paper, is explained below.

4.3 Variable Selection Heuristic

Our solver implements the variable selection heuristic known as Jeroslow-Wang rule (JW) [9,8]: Given a formula ϕ, for each literal l of ψ the following function is defined:

$$J(l) = \sum_{l \in C \in \phi} 2^{-|C|}$$

where $|C|$ is the length of clause C. JW selects a variable p of ϕ among those that maximize $J(p) + J(\neg p)$.

4.4 Computation of the Lower Bound

To compute an underestimation of the number of clauses that will become unsatisfied if we extend the current partial assignment into a complete assignment, our solver proceeds as follows:

1. Let ϕ be the current CNF formula
2. $underestimation := 0$
3. Apply the one-literal rule to the unit clauses of ϕ until an empty clause is derived.

---

[1] By unit propagation we mean the repeated application of the one-literal rule until a saturation state is reached.

4. If no empty clause can be derived, exit.
5. Let ϕ' be ϕ without the clauses that have been used to derive the empty clause.
6. $\phi := \phi'$
7. $underestimation := underestimation + 1$
8. go to 3

Example 1. Let ϕ be the following CNF formula:

$$x_1 \wedge x_2 \wedge x_3 \wedge x_4 \wedge (\neg x_1 \vee \neg x_2 \vee \neg x_3) \wedge \neg x_4 \wedge x_5 \wedge (\neg x_5 \vee \neg x_2) \wedge (\neg x_5 \vee x_2).$$

With our lower bound we are able to establish that the number of unsatisfied clauses in ϕ is at least 3. The steps performed are the following ones:

1. $\phi = \square \wedge x_4 \wedge \neg x_4 \wedge x_5 \wedge (\neg x_5 \vee \neg x_2) \wedge (\neg x_5 \vee x_2)$ and $underestimation = 1$, where the empty clause was derived from the clauses $x_1, x_2, x_3, \neg x_1 \vee \neg x_2 \vee \neg x_3$ by applying unit propagation.
2. $\phi = \square \wedge \square \wedge x_5 \wedge (\neg x_5 \vee \neg x_2) \wedge (\neg x_5 \vee x_2)$ and $underestimation = 2$, where the new empty clause was derived from the clauses $x_4, \neg x_4$ by applying unit propagation.
3. $\phi = \square \wedge \square \wedge \square$ and $underestimation = 3$, where the new empty clause was derived from the clauses $x_5, \neg x_5 \vee \neg x_2, \neg x_5 \vee x_2$ by applying unit propagation.

Given an unsatisfiable CNF formula $\phi = \phi_1 \cup \phi_2$, it is well-known that Max-SAT$(\phi) \geq$ Max-SAT$(\phi_1) +$ Max-SAT(ϕ_2). So, we have that if ϕ_1 are the clauses involved in the derivation of an empty clause by unit propagation, we can conclude that Max-SAT$(\phi) \geq 1+$ Max-SAT(ϕ_2). This is the idea behind our lower bound.

Most of the existing exact Max-SAT solvers use the following lower bound [17]:

$$\text{LB}(\phi) = unsat + \sum_{p \text{ occurs in } \phi} min(ic(p), ic(\neg p)),$$

where ϕ is the formula associated with the current partial assignment, and $ic(p)$ ($ic(\neg p)$) —inconsistency count of p ($\neg p$)— is the number of clauses that become unsatisfied if the current partial assignment is extended by fixing p to true (false); in other words, $ic(p)$ ($ic(\neg p)$) coincides with the number of unit clauses of ϕ that contain $\neg p$ (p). Note that our lower bound captures the lower bound based on inconsistency counts: if we apply that lower bound to the formula ϕ from Example 1, it is captured when we derive the empty clause from x_4 and $\neg x_4$. Observe that while our lower bound is 3, this lower bound is only 1.

With our approach we also capture more sophisticated rules that are not often applied during the search for an optimal solution not because they do not provide useful information but because the overhead of computing the rule with the data structures defined in most solvers does not compensate the benefits obtained. This is the case of the star rule [3]:[2] if we have a clause of the form $\neg l_1 \vee \cdots \vee \neg l_k$,

---

[2] The start rule defined in [3] was inspired by the so-called star rule in [14]. Nevertheless, the rule defined in [14] is not used to compute lower bounds.

where $l_1,\ldots,l_k$ are literals, and k unit clauses of the form $l_1,\ldots,l_k$, then the lower bound can be incremented by one. We considered this rule with a very low overhead: it is known that unit propagation can be computed in linear time with respect to the size of the formula. In the formula ϕ from Example 1, the star-rule is captured when we derive the empty clause from $x_1 \wedge x_2 \wedge x_3 \wedge (\neg x_1 \vee \neg x_2 \vee \neg x_3)$.

We also capture other situations that have not been described as rules. For example, when we derive the empty clause from $x_5 \wedge (\neg x_5 \vee \neg x_2) \wedge (\neg x_5 \vee x_2)$ in the formula ϕ from Example 1, it can be seen as that we replace $(\neg x_5 \vee \neg x_2) \wedge (\neg x_5 \vee x_2)$ with $\neg x_5$, as an application of the resolution refinement explained above, and then derive the empty clause from x_5 and $\neg x_5$.

5 Experimental Results

We conducted an experimental investigation in order to compare the performance of our Max-SAT solver with the following state-of-the-art solvers:

- BF [5]: a branch and bound Max-SAT solver which uses MOMS as dynamic variable selection heuristic, and it considers neither underestimations in the lower bound nor formula reduction preprocessing and DUC. It was developed by Borchers & Furman in 1999.
- GLMS [6]: a Max-SAT solver that encodes the input instance as a constraint network and solves that network with a state-of-the-art Max-CSP solver with a sophisticated and good performing lower bound. It was developed by Givry, Larrosa, Meseguer & Schiex in and presented at CP-2003.
- XZ [18]: a branch and bound Max-SAT solver developed by Xing & Zhang and presented at CP-2004. We used the second release of this solver which is known as MaxSolver.
- AGN [1]: a branch and bound Max-2-SAT solver. It was developed by Alber, Gramm & Niedermeier in 1998.
- ZSM [20]: a branch and bound Max-2-SAT solver. It was developed by Zhang, Shen & Manyà in 2003. Improved lower bounds for this solver are described in [16].
- Lazy [4]: a branch and bound Max-SAT solver with lazy data structures and a static variable selection heuristic. It was developed by Alsinet, Manyà & Planes and presented at SAT-2005.

In this section we refer to our solver as UP. As explained above, UP computes an initial upper bound with a local search solver. That upper bound is also provided as input to the rest of solvers.

As benchmarks we used randomly generated Max-2-SAT instances and the set of individual Max-SAT instances that were used as benchmarks by Givry, Larrosa, Meseguer & Schiex in their CP-2003 paper. These instances are Max-3-SAT, graph coloring and pigeon hole instances. The experiments were performed on a 2GHz Pentium IV with 512 Mb of RAM under Linux.

In our first experiment, we evaluated the impact of the new lower bound based on unit propagation. We compared UP with a version of UP (called IC in the plot) where the lower bound is computed by means of inconsistency counts, and with a version of UP (called Star in the plot) where the lower bound is computed by means of inconsistency counts and the star rule. As benchmark we used sets of random Max-2-SAT instances with 50 variables and a number of clauses ranging from 200 to 1000. Each set had 500 instances. The results obtained are shown in Figure 2. Along the horizontal axis is the number of clauses, and along the vertical axis is the mean number of backtracks (left plot) and the mean time (right plot), in seconds, needed to solve an instance of a set. Notice that we use a log scale to represent both backtracks and run-time. We observe that our lower bound outperforms dramatically the rest of lower bounds in both the number of backtracks and the time needed to solve an instance.

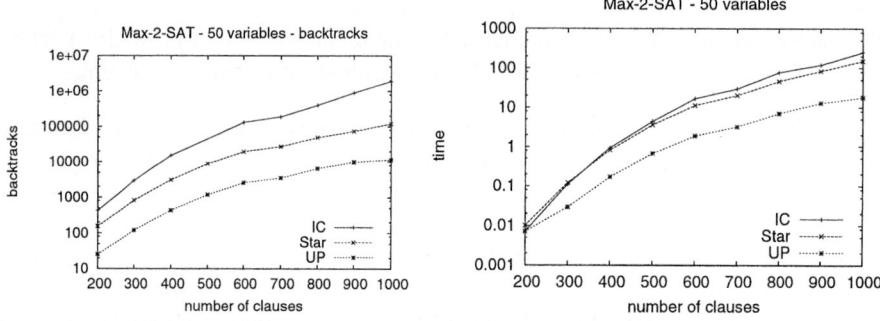

Fig. 2. Experimental results for 50-variable Max-2-SAT instances for evaluating the impact of the lower bound based on unit propagation

In our second experiment, we evaluated the impact of simplifying the input formula by applying, as a preprocessing, the resolution refinement defined in the previous section. We compared UP with a version of UP without that preprocessing. As benchmark we used sets of random Max-2-SAT instances with 100 variables and a number of clauses ranging from 200 to 800. Each set had 500 instances. The results obtained are shown in Figure 3. Along the horizontal axis is the number of clauses, and along the vertical axis is the mean number of backtracks (left plot) and the mean time (right plot), in seconds, needed to solve an instance of a set. We observe that the resolution refinement we have defined gives raise to substantial gains.

In our third experiment, we generated sets of random Max-2-SAT instances with 100 and 150 variables and a different number of clauses. Each set had 500 instances. The results of solving such instances with UP, BF, GLMS, XZ, AGN, ZSM and Lazy are shown in Figure 4. Along the horizontal axis is the number of clauses, and along the vertical axis is the mean time, in seconds, needed to solve an instance of a set. Notice that we use a log scale to represent run-time. Observe that UP outperforms the rest of solvers, including ZSM and AGN that are specifically designed to solve Max-2-SAT instances. XZ shows a good scaling behavior but UP is up to 6 times faster than XZ in the hardest instances.

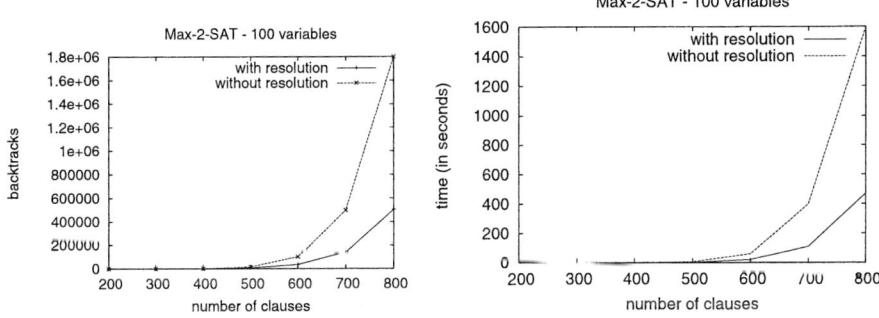

Fig. 3. Experimental results for 100-variable Max-2-SAT instances for evaluating the impact of the preprocessing based on a resolution refinement

It is worth mentioning that Givry, Larrosa, Meseguer & Schiex showed that their solver is much better than CPLEX and two pseudo-Boolean solvers (PBS and OPBDP) on randomly generated Max-2-SAT instances. Since UP outperforms GLMS, we could conclude that UP is better than CPLEX, PBS and OPBDP on Max-2-SAT instances.

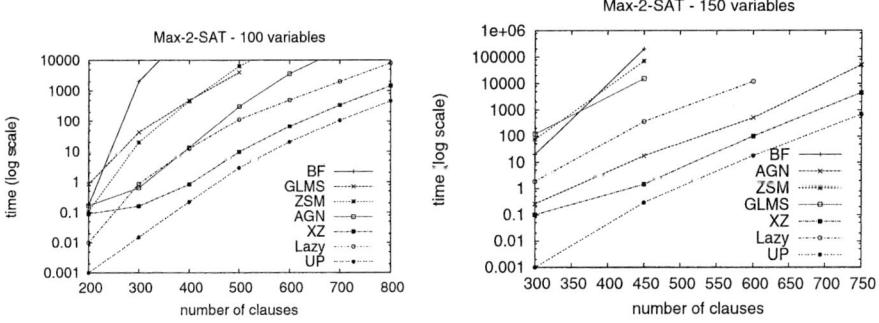

Fig. 4. Experimental results for 100-variable and 150-variable Max-2-SAT instances. Mean time (in seconds).

In our fourth experiment, we solved the Max-3-SAT (dubois and aim), graph coloring (Pret) and pigeon hole (hole) instances used by Givry, Larrosa, Meseguer & Schiex in their CP-2003 paper. We compared UP with GLMS, XZ, BF and Lazy. AGN and ZSM were not considered because they only admit Max-2-SAT instances. We used a cutoff of 600 seconds as in [6]. The results clearly indicate that UP is superior to the rest of solvers.[3] In this experiment, where the minimal number of unsatisfied clauses of each instance is one, it was crucial to get one as initial upper bound and then solve the instance with Satz.

---

[3] The results indicated by an hyphen (-) correspond to a segmentation fault.

Instance	BF	GLMS	XZ	Lazy	UP
Pret60_25	8.98	473	9.75	98	7.29
Pret60_40	9.03	455	9.43	98	7.49
Pret60_60	9.47	463	9.75	98	7.44
Pret60_75	8.94	466	9.75	98 1	7.28
dubois20	5.93	378	8.23	39	5.29
dubois21	12	>600	17	85	5.87
dubois22	22	>600	34	219	15
dubois23	45	>600	70	>600	42
dubois24	92	>600	140	>600	47
dubois25	194	>600	299	>600	127
dubois26	413	>600	>600	>600	339
dubois27	>600	>600	>600	>600	383
dubois28	>600	>600	>600	>600	>600
dubois29	>600	>600	>600	>600	>600
dubois30	>600	>600	>600	>600	>600
aim-50-1-6n1	0.11	0.01	0.08	0.01	0.01
aim-50-1-6n2	0.28	0.01	0.05	20	0.01
aim-50-1-6n3	0.14	0.01	0.10	3.84	0.01
aim-50-1-6n4	0.14	0.01	0.05	29	0.01
aim-50-2-6n1	0.16	0.01	0.09	43	0.01
aim-50-2-6n2	0.14	0.01	0.06	21	0.01
aim-50-2-6n3	0.15	0.01	0.08	24	0.01
aim-50-2-6n4	0.01	0.01	0.09	0.01	0.01
aim-100-1-6n1	>600	>600	450	>600	0.01
aim-100-1-6n2	297	287	79	>600	0.01
aim-100-1-6n3	>600	>600	519	>600	0.01
aim-100-1-6n4	>600	>600	197	>600	0.01
aim-100-2-6n1	182	>600	76	>600	0.01
aim-100-2-6n2	0.12	0.01	41	0.01	0.01
aim-100-2-6n3	0.14	0.01	33	0.01	0.01
aim-100-2-6n4	104	>600	44	>600	0.01
hole6	0.13	0.14	0.07	0.04	0.01
hole7	0.17	1.33	-	0.27	0.03
hole8	1.28	14	0.06	5.81	0.31
hole9	14	155	-	84	2.81
hole10	245	>600	0.07	>600	30

Fig. 5. Experimental results for Max-3-SAT, graph coloring and pigeon hole instances

The results of this paper indicate that the new lower bound based on unit propagation in combination with the other techniques we have incorporated into UP are a very competitive approach to solving Max-SAT. We are currently working on incorporating more powerful variable selection heuristics to UP and on applying more inference techniques at the formula associated with each node of the proof tree generated by UP. The results of this paper also provide experimental evidence that revisiting the solving techniques developed for SAT and trying to adapt them to Max-SAT could lead to good performing Max-SAT solvers.

References

1. J. Alber, J. Gramm, and R. Niedermeier. Faster exact algorithms for hard problems: A parameterized point of view. In *25th Conf. on Current Trends in Theory and Practice of Informatics*, LNCS, pages 168–185. Springer-Verlag, November 1998.
2. T. Alsinet, F. Manyà, and J. Planes. Improved branch and bound algorithms for Max-SAT. In *Proceedings of the 6th International Conference on the Theory and Applications of Satisfiability Testing*, 2003.
3. T. Alsinet, F. Manyà, and J. Planes. A Max-SAT solver with lazy data structures. In *Proceedings of the 9th Ibero-American Conference on Artificial Intelligence, IBERAMIA 2004, Puebla, México*, pages 334–342. Springer LNCS 3315, 2004.
4. T. Alsinet, F. Manyà, and J. Planes. Improved exact solvers for weighted Max-SAT. In *Proceedings of the 8th International Conference on the Theory and Applications of Satisfiability Testing, SAT-2005, St. Andrews, Scotland, UK*, pages 371–367. Springer LNCS 3569, 2005.
5. B. Borchers and J. Furman. A two-phase exact algorithm for MAX-SAT and weighted MAX-SAT problems. *Journal of Combinatorial Optimization*, 2:299–306, 1999.
6. S. de Givry, J. Larrosa, P. Meseguer, and T. Schiex. Solving Max-SAT as weighted CSP. In *9th International Conference on Principles and Practice of Constraint Programming, CP-2003, Kinsale, Ireland*, pages 363–376. Springer LNCS 2833, 2003.
7. E. Goldberg and Y. Novikov. BerkMin: A fast and robust SAT solver. In *Proceedings of Design, Automation and Test in Europe, DATE-2002, Paris, France*, pages 142–149. IEEE Computer Society, 2001.
8. J. N. Hooker and V. Vinay. Branching rules for satisfiability. *Journal of Automated Reasoning*, 15:359–383, 1995.
9. R. G. Jeroslow and J. Wang. Solving propositional satisfiability problems. *Annals of Mathematics and Artificial Intelligence*, 1:167–187, 1990.
10. C. M. Li and Anbulagan. Heuristics based on unit propagation for satisfiability problems. In *Proceedings of the International Joint Conference on Artificial Intelligence, IJCAI'97, Nagoya, Japan*, pages 366–371. Morgan Kaufmann, 1997.
11. C. M. Li and Anbulagan. Look-ahead versus look-back for satisfiability problems. In *Proceedings of the 3rd International Conference on Principles of Constraint Programming, CP'97, Linz, Austria*, pages 341–355. Springer LNCS 1330, 1997.
12. J. P. Marques-Silva and K. A. Sakallah. GRASP: A search algorithm for propositional satisfiability. *IEEE Transactions on Computers*, 48(5):506–521, 1999.
13. P. Meseguer, N. Bouhmala, T. Bouzoubaa, M. Irgens, and M. Sánchez. Current approaches for solving over-constrained problems. *Constraints*, 8(1):9–39, 2003.
14. R. Niedermeier and P. Rossmanith. New upper bounds for maximum satisfiability. *Journal of Algorithms*, 36:63–88, 2000.
15. B. Selman, H. Levesque, and D. Mitchell. A new method for solving hard satisfiability problems. In *Proceedings of the 10th National Conference on Artificial Intelligence, AAAI'92, San Jose/CA, USA*, pages 440–446. AAAI Press, 1992.
16. H. Shen and H. Zhang. Study of lower bound functions for max-2-sat. In *Proceedings of AAAI-2004*, pages 185–190, 2004.
17. R. Wallace and E. Freuder. Comparative studies of constraint satisfaction and Davis-Putnam algorithms for maximum satisfiability problems. In D. Johnson and M. Trick, editors, *Cliques, Coloring and Satisfiability*, volume 26, pages 587–615. 1996.

18. Z. Xing and W. Zhang. Efficient strategies for (weighted) maximum satisfiability. In *Proceedings of CP-2004*, pages 690–705, 2004.
19. H. Zhang. SATO: An efficient propositional prover. In *Conference on Automated Deduction (CADE-97)*, pages 272–275, 1997.
20. H. Zhang, H. Shen, and F. Manya. Exact algorithms for MAX-SAT. In *4th Int. Workshop on First order Theorem Proving*, June 2003.
21. L. Zhang, C. Madigan, M. Moskewicz, and S. Malik. Efficient conflict driven learning in a Boolean satisfiability solver. In *International Conference on Computer Aided Design, ICCAD-2001, San Jose/CA, USA*, pages 279–285, 2001.

Generalized Conflict Learning for Hybrid Discrete/Linear Optimization*

Hui Li and Brian Williams

Computer Science and Artificial Intelligence Laboratory,
Massachusetts Institute of Technology
{huili, williams}@mit.edu

Abstract. Conflict-directed search algorithms have formed the core of practical, model-based reasoning systems for the last three decades. At the core of many of these applications is a series of discrete constraint optimization problems and a conflict-directed search algorithm, which uses conflicts in the forward search step to focus search away from known infeasibilities and towards the optimal feasible solution. In the arena of model-based autonomy, deep space probes have given way to more agile vehicles, such as coordinated vehicle control, which must robustly control their continuous dynamics. Controlling these systems requires optimizing over continuous, as well as discrete variables, using linear as well as logical constraints.

This paper explores the development of algorithms for solving hybrid discrete/linear optimization problems that use conflicts in the forward search direction, carried from the conflict-directed search algorithm in model-based reasoning. We introduce a novel algorithm called Generalized Conflict-Directed Branch and Bound (GCD-BB). GCD-BB extends traditional Branch and Bound (B&B), by first constructing conflicts from nodes of the search tree that are found to be infeasible or sub-optimal, and then by using these conflicts to guide the forward search away from known infeasible and sub-optimal states. Evaluated empirically on a range of test problems of coordinated air vehicle control, GCD-BB demonstrates a substantial improvement in performance compared to a traditional B&B algorithm applied to either disjunctive linear programs or an equivalent binary integer programming encoding.

1 Introduction

Conflict-directed search algorithms have formed the core of practical, model-based reasoning systems for the last three decades, including the analysis of electrical circuits [1], the diagnosis of thousand-component circuits [5], and the model-based autonomous control of a deep space probe [10]. A conflict, also called nogood, is a partial assignment to a problem's state variables, representing sets of search states that are discovered to be infeasible, in the process of testing candidate solutions.

---

* This research is funded by The Boeing Company grant MIT-BA-GTA-1 and by NASA grant NNA04CK91A.

At the core of many of the above applications is a series of discrete constraint optimization problems, whose constraints are expressed in propositional state logic, and a set of conflict-directed algorithms, which use conflicts to focus search away from known infeasibilities and towards the optimal feasible solution.

In the arena of model-based autonomy, deep space probes have given way to more agile vehicles, including rovers, airplanes and legged robots [20], which must robustly control their continuous dynamics according to some higher level plan. Controlling these systems requires optimizing over continuous, as well as discrete variables, using linear as well as logical constraints. In particular, [22] introduces an approach for model-based execution of continuous, non-holonomic systems, and demonstrates this capability for coordinated air vehicle search and rescue, using a real-time hardware-in-the-loop testbed.

In this framework the air vehicle control trajectories are generated and updated in real-time, by encoding the plan's logical constraints and the vehicles continuous dynamics as a disjunctive linear program (DLP). A DLP [3] generalizes the constraints in linear programs (LPs) to clauses comprised of disjunctions of linear inequalities. A DLP is one instance of a growing class of hybrid representations that are used to encode mixed discrete/linear constraints, such as mixed linear logic programs (MLLPs) [13] and LCNF [16], in addition to the well known mixed integer programs (MIPs) and binary integer programs (BIPs).

In this paper we explore the development of algorithms for solving hybrid discrete/linear optimization problems (HDLOPs) that use conflicts in the forward search direction, similar to the conflict-directed A* algorithm [23]. We introduce an algorithm called Generalized Conflict-Directed Branch and Bound (GCD-BB) applied to the solution of DLPs. GCD-BB extends traditional Branch and Bound (B&B), by first constructing a conflict from each search node that is found to be infeasible or sub-optimal, and then by using these conflicts to guide the forward search away from known infeasible and sub-optimal states.

In the next section we begin by reviewing the DLP formulation. Second, we introduce the GCD-BB algorithm, including B&B for DLPs, generalized conflicts, conflict-directed search and the relaxation method. Third, we evaluate GCD-BB empirically on the test problems generated by the coordinated air vehicle path planner [22]. GCD-BB demonstrates a substantial improvement in performance compared to a traditional B&B algorithm applied to either DLPs or an equivalent BIP encoding. Finally, we conclude and discuss future work.

2 Disjunctive Linear Programs

A DLP is defined in Eq.1 [3], where x is a vector of decision variables, $f(x)$ is a linear cost function, and the constraints are a conjunction of n clauses, each of which (clause i) is a disjunction of (m_i) linear inequalities, $C_{ij}(x) \leq 0$.

$$Minimize\ f(x)$$
$$Subject\ to\ \bigwedge_{i=1,...,n} (\bigvee_{j=1,...,m_i} C_{ij}(x) \leq 0) \quad (1)$$

A DLP reduces to a standard Linear Program (LP) in the special case when every clause in the DLP is a *unit clause*, that is $m_i = 1, \forall i = 1, \ldots, n$. A clause is a unit clause if it only contains one linear inequality. For a DLP to be feasible, no clause in the DLP should be *violated*. A clause is violated if none of the linear inequalities in the clause is satisfied.

For example, in Fig.1 a vehicle has to go from point A to C, without hitting the obstacle B, while minimizing fuel use. Its DLP formulation is Eq. 2.

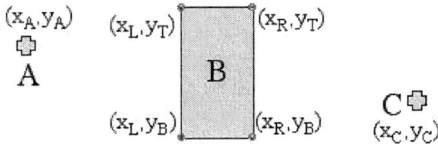

Fig. 1. A simple example of a hybrid discrete/linear optimization problem

$$\begin{aligned}
&Minimize\ f(x) \\
&Subject\ to\ \ g(x) \leq 0 \\
&\qquad x_t \leq x_L \ \vee\ x_t \geq x_R \ \vee\ y_t \leq y_B \ \vee\ y_t \geq y_T, \\
&\qquad \forall t = 1, \ldots, n
\end{aligned} \quad (2)$$

Here $\vee$ denotes logical *or*, and x is a vector of decision variables that includes, at each time step $t(= 1, \ldots, n)$, the position, velocity and acceleration of the vehicle. $f(x)$ is a linear cost function in terms of fuel use, and $g(x) \leq 0$ is a conjunction of linear inequalities on vehicle dynamics, and the last constraint keeps the vehicle outside obstacle B, at each time step t.

Note that HDLOPs can also be formulated in other ways: BIPs [17,15,14], MLLPs [13] and LCNF [16]. Our GCD-BB algorithm, though introduced in the context of DLPs, can be generalized to other formulations. Our focus is on the generalization of forward conflict-directed search to these hybrid problems, not on the DLP encoding in particular.

3 The GCD-BB Algorithm

The GCD-BB algorithm builds upon B&B and incorporates three key innovative features: first, Generalized Conflict Learning learns *conflicts* comprised of constraint sets that produce either infeasibility or sub-optimality; second, Forward Conflict-Directed Search guides the forward step of the search away from regions of state space corresponding to known conflicts; and third, Induced Unit Clause Relaxation uses unit propagation to form a relaxed problem and reduce the size of its unassigned problem. In addition, we compare different search orders: Best-first Search (BFS) versus Depth-first Search (DFS). In the following subsections, we develop these key features of GCD-BB in detail, including examples and pseudo code.

3.1 Branch and Bound for DLPs

GCD-BB builds upon B&B, which is frequently used by BIPs and MIPs, to solve problems involving both discrete and continuous variables. Instead of exploring the entire feasible set of a constrained problem, B&B uses bounds on the optimal cost, in order to avoid exploring subsets of the feasible set that it can prove are sub-optimal, that is, subsets whose optimal solution is not better than the *incumbent*, which is the best solution found so far. The algorithm for B&B applied to DLPs is Alg. 1.

Alg. 1 is special for DLPs, in mainly function Clause-Violated? and function Expand-Node. Clause-Violated? checks if any clause is violated by the relaxed solution. Note that a node in the search tree represents a set of unselected clauses and a set of selected unit clauses. At each node in the search tree, the selected unit

---

Algorithm 1. BB-DLP(DLP)

1: $upperBound \leftarrow +\infty$
2: $timestamp = 0$
3: put DLP into a FILO queue
4: **while** queue is not empty **do**
5:    $node \leftarrow$ remove from queue
6:    $node$.relaxedSolution $\leftarrow$ solveLP($node$.relaxedLP)
7:    **if** $node$.relaxedLP is infeasible **then**
8:      continue {$node$ is deleted}
9:    **else if** $node$.relaxedValue $\geq upperBound$ **then**
10:     continue {$node$ is deleted}
11:    **else**
12:     $expand =$ False
13:     **for** each clause in $node$.nonUnitClauses **do**
14:       **if** Clause-Violated?(*clause*, $node$.relaxedSolution) **then**
15:         $expand \leftarrow$ True
16:         break
17:       **end if**
18:     **end for**
19:     **if** $expand =$ False **then**
20:       $upperBound \leftarrow node$.relaxedValue {*a new incumbent was found*}
21:       $incumbent \leftarrow node$.relaxedSolution
22:     **else**
23:       put Expand-Node($node, timestamp$) in queue
24:       $timestamp \leftarrow timestamp + 1$
25:     **end if**
26:    **end if**
27: **end while**
28: **if** $upperBound < +\infty$ **then**
29:    return *incumbent*
30: **else**
31:    return INFEASIBLE
32: **end if**

clause set and the objective function form the relaxed LP to be solved[1]. While the search tree of B&B for BIPs branches by assigning values to the binary variables, in Expand-Node, B&B for DLPs branches by splitting clauses; that is, a tree node is expanded by selecting one of the DLP clauses, and then selecting one of the clauses' disjuncts for each of the child nodes. More detailed pseudo code can be found in [21].

3.2 Generalized Conflict Learning

Underlying the power of B&B is its ability to prune subsets of the search tree that correspond to relaxed subproblems that are identified as inconsistent or sub-optimal, as seen in line 7 and 9 in Alg.1. Hence two opportunities exist for learning and pruning. We exploit these opportunities by introducing the concept of generalized conflict learning, which extracts a description from each fathomed subproblem that is infeasible or sub-optimal. This avoids exploring subproblems with the same description in the future. To accomplish this we add functions Extract-Infeasibility and Extract-Suboptimality after line 7 and 9 in Alg. 1, respectively. It is valuable to have each conflict as compact as possible, so that the subspace that can be pruned is as large as possible.

In the related fields of model-based reasoning and discrete constraint satisfaction, conflict-directed methods, such as dependency-directed backtracking [1], backjumping [2], conflict-directed backjumping [8] and dynamic backtracking [7], dramatically improve the performance of backtrack (BT) search, by learning the source of each inconsistency discovered and using this information, called a conflict (or nogood), to prune additional subtrees that the conflict identifies as inconsistent. Similarly nogood learning is a standard technique for improving BT search, in CSP [6][19] and in SAT solvers [12].

Definition of a Conflict. In the context of DLPs, each *conflict* can be one of two types: an *infeasibility conflict*, or a *sub-optimality conflict*. An infeasibility conflict is a set of inconsistent constraints of an infeasible subproblem. An example is the constraint set {a,b,c,d} in Fig. 2(a). A sub-optimality conflict is a set of active constraints of a sub-optimal subproblem. An inequality constraint $g_i(x) \leq 0$ is active at a feasible point $\tilde{x}$ if $g_i(\tilde{x}) = 0$. An example of a sub-optimality conflict is the constraint set {a,b,d} in Fig. 2(b).

Definition of a Minimal Conflict. A conflict is *minimal* if none of its proper subsets is a conflict. For example, the constraint set {a,c,d} in Fig. 2(a) is a minimal conflict, as it is an inconsistent constraint set and every proper subset of it is consistent. Constraint set {a,d} in Fig. 2(b) is also a minimal conflict. Note that there can be more than one minimal conflict (possibly with different cardinalities) involved in one infeasibility or sub-optimality, and a minimal

---
[1] $p\prime$ is a relaxed LP of an optimization problem p, if the feasible region of $p\prime$ contains the feasible region of p, and they have the same objective function. Therefore if $p\prime$ is infeasible, then p is infeasible. Assuming minimization, if $p\prime$ is solved with an optimal value v, the optimal value of p is guaranteed to be greater than or equal to v. B&B uses relaxed problems to obtain lower bounds of the original problem.

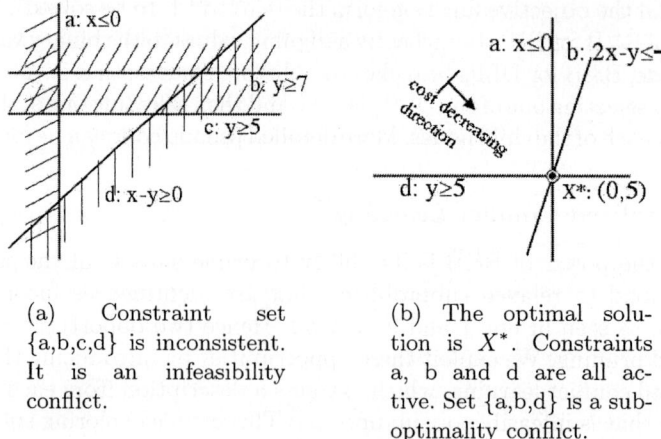

(a) Constraint set {a,b,c,d} is inconsistent. It is an infeasibility conflict.

(b) The optimal solution is X^*. Constraints a, b and d are all active. Set {a,b,d} is a sub-optimality conflict.

Fig. 2. Examples of conflicts

conflict is not guaranteed to have the *minimum* cardinality. We extract minimal conflicts instead of any conflicts, since minimal conflicts can prune larger portion of the state space. However, we do not try to extract the minimum conflict of a subproblem, because it is NP-complete.

Implementation. The function of extracting the minimal infeasibility conflict is provided by the commercial software CPLEX. Intuitively, A *dual* variable of an LP problem is the cost for violating a constraint in the LP. Thus the dual vector of an LP has the same dimension as the number of constraints in the LP. The presence of violation costs allows the constraints of the LP to be broken, and the goal is to minimize the violation costs. A constraint is consistent if and only if the costs can be minimized to zero. Therefore the set of non-zero dual variables of the infeasible LP corresponds to the set of the inconsistent constraints that forms a minimal infeasibility conflict.

For sub-optimality, we use the dual method of LP to extract minimal conflicts. According to Complementary Slackness [11] from linear optimization theory, the non-zero terms of the optimal dual vector correspond to the set of active constraints (assuming with cardinality k) at the optimal solution (assuming with dimension n) of the LP. When the optimal solution is non-degenerate, it is guaranteed that $k \leq n$ and the active constraint set is the minimal sub-optimality conflict; when there is degeneracy, we take any $min\{k, n\}$ constraints from the active constraint set to form the minimal sub-optimality conflict.

Once extracted, the minimal conflict is stored in a conflict database, *conflictDB*, indexed by a timestamp that marks its discovery time.

3.3 Forward Conflict-Directed Search

We use forward conflict-directed search to guide the forward step of search away from regions of the feasible space that are ruled out by known conflicts. Backward search methods also use conflicts to direct search, such as dependency-directed backtracking [1], backjumping [2], conflict-directed backjumping [8], dynamic backtracking [7] and LPSAT [16]. These backtrack search methods use conflicts both to select backtrack points and as a cache to prune nodes without testing consistency. In contrast, methods like conflict-directed A* [23] use conflicts in forward search, to move away from known bad states. Thus not only one conflict is used to prune multiple subtrees, but also several conflicts can be combined as one compact description to prune multiple subtrees. We generalize this idea to guiding B&B away from regions of state space that the known conflicts indicate as infeasible or sub-optimal. Our experimental results show that forward conflict-directed search significantly outperforms backtrack search with conflicts on a range of cooperative vehicle plan execution problems.

In terms of implementation, we replace function Expand-Node in Alg. 1 with function General-Expand-Node (Alg. 2). When there is no unresolved conflict[2], the normal Expand-Node is used, and when unresolved conflicts exist, forward conflict-directed search is performed. Forward conflict-directed search (Forward-

---

Algorithm 2. General-Expand-Node(*node*, *timestamp*, conflictDB)

1: $conflictSet \leftarrow$ conflictDB(*timestamp*)
2: **if** conflictSet is empty **then**
3:     Expand-Node(*node*, *timestamp*)
4: **else**
5:     Forward-CD-Search(*node*, *conflictSet*)
6: **end if**

CD-Search as in Alg. 2) includes three steps: 1) Generate-Constituent-Kernels, 2) Generate-Kernels (Alg. 3) and 3) Generate-And-Test-DLP-Candidates (Alg. 5). An example is shown in Fig. 3.

As shown in Generate-Kernels (Alg. 3), we use minimal set covering to generate the kernels. Fig. 4(b) demonstrates Generate-Kernels by continuing the example from Fig. 3. In particular, in Fig. 4(b) the tree branches by splitting on constituent kernels. In this example, each node represents a set of chosen constituent kernels: the root node is an empty set, and the leaf node on the right is $\{\neg c_1, \neg c_2\}$. At each node, consistency is checked (line 8 in Alg. 3), and then Generate-Kernels checks whether any of the existing kernels is a subset of the current node (line 10). If this is the case, there is no need to keep expanding the node, and it is removed. In this event, the leaf node is marked with an X in Fig. 4(b); otherwise, Generate-Kernels checks whether any conflict is unresolved at the current node (line 16): if yes, the node is expanded by splitting on the constituent kernels of the unresolved conflicts (line 17); otherwise, the node is added to the kernel list, while removing from the list any node whose set of

---

[2] A node *resolves* conflict C if at least one of the C's disjuncts is explicitly excluded in the relaxed LP of the node.

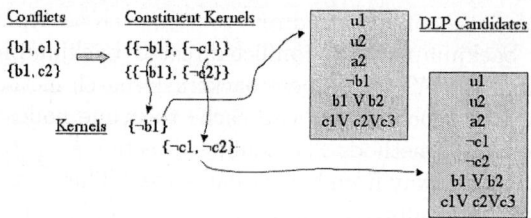

Fig. 3. Each conflict is mapped to a set of constituent kernels, which resolve that conflict alone. Kernels are generated by combining the constituent kernels using minimal set covering. A DLP candidate is formed for each kernel, and is checked for consistency.

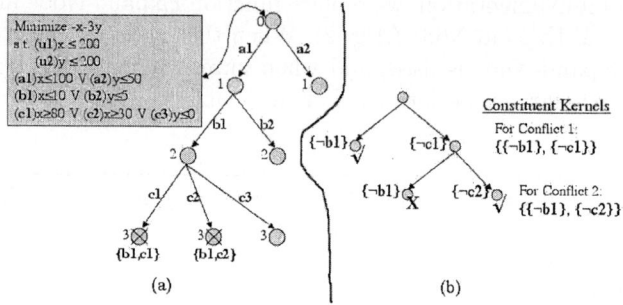

Fig. 4. (a) A partial tree of B&B for DLPs. The creation time of each node is shown on the left of the node. Two conflicts are discovered at the bottom. (b) The search tree for minimal set covering to generate kernels from constituent kernels.

constraints is a superset of another node (line 19). The node at the far left of Fig. 4(b) resolves all the conflict and, therefore, is not expanded.

A *constituent kernel* is a minimal description of the states that resolve a conflict. In the context of DLPs, a constituent kernel of a conflict is a linear inequality that is the negation of a linear inequality in the conflict. For example, one constituent kernel of the minimal infeasibility conflict in Fig. 2(a) is $\{x-y \leq 0\}$[3].

In [23] *kernels* are generated to resolve all known conflicts, by combining the constituent kernels using minimal set covering. It views minimal set covering as a search and uses A* to find the kernel containing the best utility state. In the context of DLPs, we similarly build up a kernel by incrementally selecting constituent kernels (which are linear inequalities) from discovered conflicts using minimal set covering. However, we do not use A* search to identify the best kernel. In order to evaluate the heuristic during A* search, we would need to solve an LP at each step as we build the kernels; this can be very costly. Instead GCD-BB generates a DLP candidate with each kernel, as shown in Fig. 3, and prunes

---
[3] It is not the strictly correct negation of $x - y \geq 0$, but in the context of linear programming, it is correct and convenient.

Algorithm 3. Generate-Kernels(*constituentKernelSet*)

1: root ← {}
2: root.unresolved ← *constituentKernelSet* {initializes *node*.unresolved}
3: put root in a queue
4: *kernelSet* ← {}
5: nodeDelete ← False {the flag to determine whether to delete a node}
6: **while** queue is not empty **do**
7:    *node* ← remove from queue
8:    **if** Consistent?(*node*) **then**
9:      **for** each E in *kernelSet* **do**
10:        **if** E ⊆ *node* **then**
11:          nodeDelete ← True {checks whether any of the existing kernels is a subset of the current node}
12:          break
13:        **end if**
14:      **end for**
15:      **if** nodeDelete = False **then**
16:        **if** Unresolved-Conflict?(*node*, *node*.unresolved) **then**
17:          put Expand-Conflict(*node*, *node*.unresolved) in queue {checks whether any conflicts are unresolved by *node*}
18:        **else**
19:          Add-To-Minimal-Sets(*kernelSet*, *node*) {avoids any node that is a superset of another in *kernelSet*}
20:        **end if**
21:      **end if**
22:    **end if**
23: **end while**
24: **return** *kernelSet*

Algorithm 4. Add-To-Minimal-Sets(*Set*, *S*)

  for each E in *Set* **do**
    if E ⊂ S **then**
      return *Set*
    else if S ⊂ E **then**
      remove E from *Set*
    end if
  end for
  return *Set* ∪ {S}

---

the DLPs that are propositionally unsatisfiable, using a fast unit propagation test before solving any relaxed LP, as shown in Alg. 5.

Finally, a timestamp is used to record the time that a node is created or a conflict is discovered. We use timestamps to ensure that each node resolves all conflicts, while avoiding repetition. This is accomplished through the following rules: 1. if {conflict time = node time}, there is no need to resolve the conflict

Algorithm 5. Generate-And-Test-DLP-Candidate(*kernelSet, DLP*)
1: $S \leftarrow DLP.unitClauses$
2: **for** each *kernel* in *kernelSet* **do**
3:    **if** Consistent?$(S \cup kernel)$ **then**
4:      $DLP.unitClauses \leftarrow S \cup kernel$ {checks whether *kernel* is consistent with the unit clause set of *DLP*}
5:      add *DLP* in DLPList
6:    **end if**
7: **end for**
8: **return** DLPList

when expanding the node. For example, in Fig. 4(a), node c_3 and its children (if any) are guaranteed to resolve the two conflicts $\{b_1, c_1\}$ and $\{b_1, c_2\}$. 2. If {conflict time > node time}, we expand the node in order to resolve the conflict using the conflict's constituent kernels. For example, node b_2 and a_2 are to be expanded using Forward-CD-Search. 3. If {conflict time < node time}, the conflict is guaranteed to be resolved by an ancestor node of the current node, and therefore, needs not to be resolved again.

3.4 Induced Unit Clause Relaxation

Relaxation is an essential tool for quickly characterizing a problem when the original problem is hard to solve directly; it provides bounds on feasibility and the optimal value of a problem, which are commonly used to prune the search space. Previous research [18] typically solves DLPs by reformulating them as BIPs, where a relaxed LP is formed by relaxing the binary constraint ($x \in \{0, 1\}$) to the continuous linear constraint ($0 \leq x \leq 1$).

An alternative way of creating a relaxed LP is to operate on the DLP encoding directly, by removing all non-unit clauses from the DLP. Prior work argues for the reformulation of DLP as BIP relaxation, with the rationale that it maintains some of the constraints of the non-unit clauses through the continuous relaxation from binary to real-valued variables, in contrast to ignoring all the non-unit clauses. However, this benefit is at the cost of adding binary variables and constraints, which increases the dimensionality of the search problem.

Our approach starts with the direct DLP relaxation. We overcome the weakness of standard DLP relaxation (loss of non-unit clauses) by adding to the relaxation unit clauses that are logically entailed by the original DLP. In the experiment section we compare our induced unit clause relaxation with the BIP relaxation and show a profound improvement on a range of cooperative vehicle plan execution problems.

In terms of implementation, as seen in Alg.6 and the example in Fig. 5, Induce-Unit-Clause performs unit propagation among the unit and non-unit clauses to induce more unit clauses and simplify a DLP. A relaxed LP is also formed by combining the objective function and the unit clause set (line 2).

Algorithm 6. Induce-Unit-Clause(DLP)

1: $\{DLP.\text{unitClauses}, DLP.\text{nonUnitClauses}\} \leftarrow$
   Unit-Propagation($\{DLP.\text{unitClauses}, DLP.\text{nonUnitClauses}\}$)
2: $DLP.\text{relaxedLP} \leftarrow <DLP.\text{objective}, DLP.\text{unitClauses}>$
3: return DLP

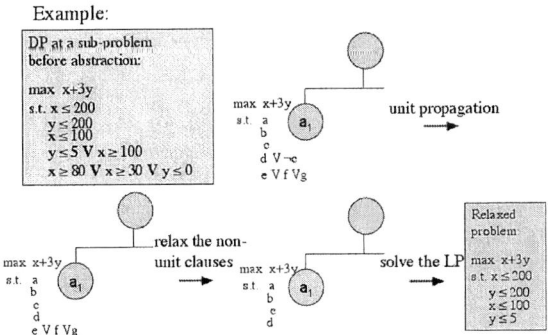

Fig. 5. A simple example of induced unit clause relaxation

3.5 Search Order: Best-First Versus Depth-First

Given a fixed set of heuristic information, [4] shows that best-first search is the most efficient algorithm in terms of time efficiency. Intuitively, this is because BFS does not visit any node whose heuristic value is worse than the optimum, and all nodes better than the optimum must be visited to ensure that the optimum is not missed. However, BFS can take dramatically more memory space than DFS. Nevertheless, with conflict learning and forward conflict-directed search, the queue of the BFS search tree can be significantly reduced. Our experimental results show that on a range of test problems BFS can take memory space similar to DFS, while taking significantly less time to find the optimum.

An additional issue for GCD-BB is that the concept of sub-optimality is rooted in maintaining an incumbent. Hence, it can be applied to DFS but not to BFS. To evaluate these tradeoffs, our experiments in the next section compare the use of BFS and conflict learning from infeasibility only, with DFS and conflict learning from both infeasibility and from suboptimality.

4 Experimental Performance Analysis

This section provides experimental results of the GCD-BB algorithm, compared with the benchmark B&B algorithm applied either to DLPs or to an equivalent BIP encoding, on a range of test problems of coordinated air vehicle control [22]. We also compare the effect of several algorithmic variants, in particular,

BFS versus DFS, infeasibility conflict learning versus sub-optimality conflict learning and forward search versus backtrack search. While each algorithmic variant terminates with the same optimal solution, GCD-BB achieves an order of magnitude speed-up over BIP-BB. In addition, the difference in performance increases as the problem size increases.

As the bulk of the computational effort expended by these algorithms is devoted to solving relaxed LP problems, the total number and average size of these LPs are representative of the total computational effort involved in solving the HDLOPs. Note that extracting infeasibility conflicts and sub-optimality conflicts can be achieved as by-products of solving the LPs, and therefore does not incur any additional LP to solve. We use the total number of relaxed LPs solved and the average LP size as our LP solver and hardware independent measures of computation time. To measure memory space use, maximum queue size is used.

Table 1. Comparison on the number of relaxed LPs

	Clause/Variable	80/36	700/144	1492/300	2456/480
	BIP-BB	31.5	2009	4890	8133
DLP BFS	without Conflict Learning	24.3	735.6	1569	2651
	Infeasibility Conflict	19.2	67.3	96.3	130.2
	Conflict-directed Backtrack	23.1	396.7	887.8	1406
DLP DFS	without Conflict Learning	28.0	2014	3023	4662
	Infeasibility Conflict	22.5	106.0	225.4	370.5
	Conflict-directed Backtrack	25.9	596.9	1260	1994
	Infeasibility+Suboptimality Conflict	22.1	76.4	84.4	102.9
	Suboptimality Conflict	25.8	127.6	363.7	715.0

We programmed BIP-BB, GCD-BB and its variations in Java. All used the commercial software CPLEX as the LP solver. Test problems were generated using the model-based temporal planner [22], performing multi-vehicle search and rescue missions. This planner takes as input a temporally flexible state plan, which specifies the goals of a mission, and a continuous model of vehicle dynamics, and encodes them in DLPs. The GCD-BB solver generates an optimal vehicle control sequence that achieves the constraints in the temporal plan. For each Clause/Variable set, 15 problems were generated and the average was recorded in the tables.

Table 1 records the number of relaxed LPs solved by each algorithm. In both the DLP BFS and the DLP DFS cases, the algorithm with conflict learning performs significantly better than the one without conflict learning. In addition, the difference increases with the test problem size. The backtrack algorithm, based on dependency-directed backtracking [1], uses infeasibility conflicts as a cache to check consistency of a relaxed LP before solving it. We observe that in both the BFS and the DFS cases, the forward algorithm performs significantly better than the backward algorithm. In order to show the reason for using our DLP relaxation instead of the continuous relaxation of BIP, we compare row "BIP-BB" with row "DLP DFS without Conflict Learning", and DLP performs significantly better than BIP. To address the tradeoffs of BFS and DFS, we observe that in terms of time efficiency, BFS performs better than DFS, in both the "without Conflict Learning" and the "Infeasibility Conflict" cases. Finally, "BFS Infeasibility Conflict" performs similar to "DFS Infeasibility+Suboptimality Conflict"; for large test problems, DFS performs better than BFS.

Table 2. Comparison on the average size of relaxed LPs

		Clause/ Variable	80/ 36	700/ 144	1492/ 300	2456/ 480
		BIP-BB	90	889	1909	3911
DLP BFS		without Conflict Learning	72	685	1460	2406
		Infeasibility Conflict	70	677	1457	2389
		Conflict-directed Backtrack	72	691	1461	2397
DLP DFS		without Conflict Learning	76	692	1475	2421
		Infeasibility Conflict	74	691	1470	2403
		Conflict-directed Backtrack	75	692	1472	2427
		Infeasibility+Suboptimality Conflict	73	691	1470	2403
		Suboptimality Conflict	74	692	1471	2410

Table 3. Comparison on the maximum queue size

		Clause/ Variable	80/ 36	700/ 144	1492/ 300	2456/ 480
		BIP-BB	8.4	30.8	46.2	58.7
DLP BFS		without Conflict Learning	19.1	161.1	296.8	419.0
		Infeasibility Conflict	6.4	18.3	38.4	52.5
		Conflict-directed Backtrack	15.6	101.7	205.1	327.8
DLP DFS		without Conflict Learning	6.1	18.7	25.1	30.3
		Infeasibility Conflict	6.5	21.4	45.0	57.3
		Conflict-directed Backtrack	6.1	18.4	23.5	28.1
		Infeasibility+Suboptimality Conflict	6.5	21.4	33.0	40.9
		Suboptimality Conflict	6.5	21.6	38.7	47.0

As seen in Table 2, the average size of LPs solved in BIP is much larger than that of the LPs solved for DLPs, and the difference grows larger as the problem size increases. Experiments also show that the average size of LPs solved by each DLP algorithm variant is similar to one another.

Maximum queue size of the search tree of each algorithm is recorded in Table 3. Our goal is to compare the memory use of BFS algorithms with that of DFS algorithms. BFS without Conflict Learning takes significantly more memory space than any other algorithm. Compared with DFS without Conflict Learning, its maximum queue size is from 68% to 90% larger. However, it is notable that using conflict learning, the memory taken by BFS is reduced to the same level as DFS.

5 Discussion

This paper presented a novel algorithm, Generalized Conflict-Directed Branch and Bound, that efficiently solves DLP problems through a powerful three-fold method, featuring *generalized conflict learning, forward conflict-directed search* and *induced unit clause relaxation*. The key feature of the approach reasons about infeasible or sub-optimal subsets of state space using conflicts, in order to guide the forward step of search, by moving away from regions of state space corresponding to known conflicts. Our experiments on model-based temporal plan execution for cooperative vehicles demonstrated an order of magnitude speed-up over BIP-BB.

The authors are in the process of applying GCD-BB to the BIP formulation, and empirically comparing GCD-BB with the cutting plane method and Benders Decomposition. Although GCD-BB can be applied to any MIPs and BIPs, our preliminary results show that there is not always significant improvement over the standard B&B. Future work will include experimenting on a wider range of test problems to understand better this behavior.

References

1. Stallman, R. and Sussman, G.J.: Forward Reasoning and Dependency-Directed Backtracking in a System for Computer-Aided Circuit Analysis. J. of Artificial Intelligence. **9** (1977) 135196
2. Gaschnig, J.: Experimental Case Studies of Backtrack vs. Waltz-type vs. New Algorithms for Satisfying Assignment Problems. Proceedings of The 2nd Canadian Conference on AI. (1978)
3. Balas, E.: Disjunctive programming. Annals of Discrete Math. **5** (1979) 3-51
4. Dechter, R. and Pearl, J.: Generalized Best-first Search Strategies and the Optimality of A*. J. of ACM. **32** (1985) 506-536
5. de Kleer, J. and Williams, B.: Diagnosis with Behavioral Modes. Proceedings of IJCAI. (1989)
6. Dechter, R.: Enhancement Schemes for Constraint Processing: Backjumping, Learning and Cutset Decomposition. J. of Artificial Intelligence. **41** (1990) 273-312
7. Ginsberg, M.: Dynamic Backtracking. J. of Artificial Intelligence Research. **1** (1993) 25-46
8. Prosser, P.: Hybrid Algorithms for the Constraint Satisfaction Problem. J. of Computational Intelligence. **9(3)** (1993) 268-299
9. Williams, B. and Cagan, J.: Activity Analysis: The Qualitative Analysis of Stationary Points for Optimal Reasoning. Proceedings of AAAI. (1994)
10. Williams, B. and Nayak, P.: A Model-based Approach to Reactive Self-Configuring Systems. Proceedings of AAAI. (1996)
11. Bertsimas, D. and Tsitsiklis, J.N.: Introduction to Linear Optimization. Athena Scientific. (1997)
12. Bayardo, R. J. and Schrag, R. C.: Using CSP Look-back Techniques to Solve Real-world SAT Instances. Proceedings of AAAI. (1997)
13. Hooker, J.N. and Osorio, M.A.: Mixed Logical/Linear Programming. J. of Discrete Applied Math. **96-97** (1999) 395-442

14. Kautz, H. and Walser, J.P.: State space planning by integer optimization. Proceedings of AAAI. (1999)
15. Vossen, T. and Ball, M. and Lotem, A. and Nau, D.: On the Use of Integer Programming Models in AI Planning. Proceedings of IJCAI. (1999)
16. Wolfman, S. and Weld, D.: The LPSAT Engine & Its Application to Resource Planning. Proceedings of IJCAI. (1999)
17. Schouwenaars, T. and de Moor, B. and Feron, E. and How, J.: Mixed Integer Programming for Multi-Vehicle Path Planning. Proceedings of European Control Conference. (2001)
18. Hooker, J.N.: Logic, Optimization and Constraint Programming. INFORMS J. on Computing. **14** (2002) 295-321
19. Katsirelos, G. and Bacchus, F.: Unrestricted Nogood Recording in CSP Search. Proceedings of CP. (2003)
20. Hofmann, A. and Williams, B.: Safe Execution of Temporally Flexible Plans for Bipedal Walking Devices. Plan Execution Workshop of ICAPS. (2005)
21. Li, H.: Generalized Conflict Learning for Hybrid Discrete Linear Optimization. Master's Thesis, M.I.T. (2005)
22. Léauté, T. and Williams, B.: Coordinating Agile Systems Through The Model-based Execution of Temporal Plans. Proceedings of AAAI. (2005)
23. Williams, B. and Ragno, R.: Conflict-directed A* and its Role in Model-based Embedded Systems. J. of Discrete Applied Math. (to appear 2005)

Parallel Local Search in Comet

Laurent Michel[1] and Pascal Van Hentenryck[2]

[1] University of Connecticut, Storrs, CT 06269-2155
[2] Brown University, Box 1910, Providence, RI 02912

Abstract. The availability of commodity multiprocessors offers significant opportunities for addressing the increasing computational requirements of optimization applications. To leverage these potential benefits, it is important however to make parallel processing easily accessible to a wide audience of optimization programmers. This paper addresses this challenge by proposing parallel programming abstractions that keep the distance between sequential and parallel local search algorithms as small as possible. The abstractions, that include parallel loops, interruptions, and thread pools, are compositional and cleanly separate the optimization program and the parallel instructions. They have been evaluated experimentally on a variety of applications, including facility location and coloring, for which they provide significant speedups.

1 Introduction

With the availability of commodity multiprocessors (e.g., dual Apple G5s) and the advent of multi-core chips (e.g., the 870 processor from AMD and the forthcoming Cell Architecture), parallel processing is becoming widely affordable. It also provides significant opportunities to meet the increasing computational requirements of optimization applications as the field moves towards large-scale, online, and stochastic optimization. Indeed, optimization applications often exhibit significant parallelism. For instance, multistart local search, hybrid local search, cooperating local search, and online stochastic optimization all involve multiple, largely independent, searches that only communicates loosely and asynchronously. Search in constraint programming can also be viewed as largely independent searches, communicating computation paths [3,9] or subproblems [8].

Unfortunately, a major obstacle in exploiting these opportunities is the additional expertise required to write parallel algorithms, since optimization applications already demand mathematical sophistication, domain expertise, and programming abilities. It is thus important to leverage the promises of multiprocessors as transparently as possible, imposing as small a burden as possible on optimization modelers and programmers.

This paper describes an attempt to address this challenge. It proposes high-level abstractions for parallel programming in COMET, an object-oriented language featuring a constraint-based architecture for local search. The parallel abstractions exploit multiprocessors in a transparent way and have a number of desirable properties. They are natural counterparts to sequential constructs, ensuring a small distance between the sequential and parallel versions of the same algorithm. The abstractions are general-purpose and widely applicable, yet they provide a natural vehicle to express a variety of parallel optimization algorithms. The abstractions are compositional and cleanly separate the optimization models from the parallel code, allowing modelers/programmers to reuse their existing models when exploiting parallelism. Finally, their implementation leverages the advanced control abstractions of COMET such as events and first-order closures [10] and is primarily based on source-to-source transformations.

The rest of the paper is organized as follows. Section 2 reviews the enabling technologies, i.e., threads and monitors. Section 3 describes the abstractions and their implementations. Section 4 describes the experimental results.

2 Enabling Concurrent Technologies

Threads and monitors are the enabling technology for the parallel abstractions of COMET. Although these concurrent programming extensions resemble those of Java, the subtle differences between them contribute in making COMET's abstractions natural, convenient, and easier to implement. In particular, threads exhibit a nice synergy with first-order closures, the foundation of many control abstractions of COMET [10]. Figure 1 illustrates both threads and monitors in COMET. The class Count (lines 1–6) encapsulates a counter. Due to the keyword synchronized, the class is a monitor: its method invocations execute in mutual exclusion. An instance of the class is declared in line 7. The core of the program is a loop creating two threads (lines 8-12). The body of each thread, executed upon the thread creation, increments the counter c 200 times, by 1 for the first thread (i=1) and by 2 for the second thread (i=2).

Threads have their own version of the COMET runtime, including a stack for function and method calls, and are implemented by native threads of the operating system. Threads are first-class objects in COMET but, unlike Java, they do not have to extend an existing class. Rather, upon creation, they execute a closure specified by their statement (e.g., lines 10–11 in Figure 1) and the current environment. This design decision, i.e., the ability to use a closure as the thread code, is fundamental in keeping the distance between sequential and parallel code small in COMET. Observe that, in Figure 1, the two threads naturally increment the counter by different amounts thanks to the use of closures.

Figure 2 shows a program implementing an (unordered) producer/consumer monitor. Class Buffer (lines 1–10) specifies a buffer than can store up to sz in-

```
1.    synchronized class Count {            7.    Count c(0);
2.        int c;                            8.    forall(i in 1..2) {
3.        Count(int i) { c = i; }          9.        thread
4.        void incr(int n) { c += n; }    10.            forall(k in 1..200)
5.        int get() { return c; }         11.                c.incr(i);
6.    }                                    12.    }
```

Fig. 1. Illustrating Threads and Monitors in COMET

```
1.  synchronized class Buffer {          21. int Buffer::consume() {
2.     int[] buffer;                     22.    if (nb == 0) empty.wait();
3.     int sz;                           23.    int v = buffer[--nb];
4.     int nb;                           24.    full.signal();
5.     Condition full;                   25.    return v;
6.     Condition empty;                  26. }
7.     Buffer(int s);
8.     void produce(int s);              27. Buffer b(2);
9.     int consume();                    28. thread consumer {
10. }                                    29.    for(int k=0;k<100;k++) {
11. Buffer::Buffer(int s) {              30.       int c = b.consume();
12.    sz = s;                           31.       cout << "-" << c << flush;
13.    nb = 0;                           32.    }
14.    buffer = new int[0..sz-1];        33. }
15. }                                    34. thread producer {
16. void Buffer::produce(int s) {        45.    for(int k=0;k<100;k++) {
17.    if (nb == sz) full.wait();        36.       b.produce(k);
18.    buffer[nb++] = s;                 37.       cout << "+" << k << flush;
19.    empty.signal();                   38.    }
20. }                                    39. }
```

Fig. 2. A Simple Producer/Consumer Pattern in COMET

tegers. Method produces stores an integer in the buffer, while method consumes retrieves an integer from it. The monitor uses two *conditions*, full and empty, to synchronize the producers and consumers. When the buffer is full, the producers wait until there is room in the buffer (line 17). When the buffer is empty, the consumers wait until some integer is available (line 22). The producers and consumers also notify their respective conditions when they produce and consume integers (lines 19 and 24 respectively). As is traditional, when a thread waits on a condition, it releases the monitor and must re-acquire it upon reactivation. Observe that, unlike Java, COMET may use several conditions inside a monitor which, once again, simplifies several concurrent programming patterns. Here is the beginning of the output of this COMET program when executed on an Apple G5 with 2 processors: +0+1-1-0+2+3-3-2+4+5-5-4+6+7-7-6+8+9-9-8...

3 Parallel Abstractions

The parallel abstractions of COMET support various parallel loops, interruptions, as well as thread and model pools.

3.1 Parallel Execution

COMET provides a parall construct, as the parallel counterpart to the sequential forall loop. Reconsider the counter example from Figure 1. It could be rewritten, and expanded, as follows:

```
1.   Buffer b(2);                        8.   {
2.   pardo {                             9.     forall(k in 0..99) {
3.     forall(k in 0..99) {              10.      b.produce(k);
4.       int c = b.consume();            11.      cout << "+" << k << flush;
5.       cout << "-" << c << flush;      12.    }
6.     }                                 13.  }
7.   } |
```

Fig. 3. Revisiting the Simple Producer/Consumer Pattern in COMET

```
1.  Count c(0);
2.  parall(i in 1..2)
3.    forall(k in 1..200)
4.      c.incr(i);
5.  cout << "value: " << c.get() << endl;
```

Lines 2–4 feature a parallel loop in COMET: the loop body may be executed in parallel for all values of the loop parameter. Operationally the `parall` instruction creates a thread to execute the loop body for each value of i. These threads are joined after the loop, i.e., the instruction following the loop is only executed after all threads completed their execution. Hence the COMET code displays the correct value (600) of the counter in line 5, since the output instruction is guaranteed to execute only after the completion of the `parall` instruction (which was not the case for the program in Figure 1). The instructions have the same effect as the sequential code:

```
1.  Count c(0);
2.  forall(i in 1..2)
3.    forall(k in 1..200)
4.      c.incr(i);
5.  cout << "value: " << c.get() << endl;
```

showing how easy it is to move from a sequential to a parallel implementation.

```
1.  synchronized class Count {         7.   Count c(0);
2.    int c;                           8.   forall(i in 1..2) {
3.    Count(int i) { c = i; }          9.     thread
4.    void incr(int n) { c += n; }     10.      forall(k in 1..200)
5.    int get() { return c; }          11.        c.incr(i);
6.  }                                  12.  }
```

Figure 3 revisits the producer/consumer pattern from Figure 2 and illustrates its implementation with the `pardo` construct of COMET. As is the case with the `parall` construct, the instruction following line 12 in the program (if any) only executes after completion of the `pardo` instruction.

Many optimization algorithms apply a local search multiple times. This is the case for multistart or iterated local searches that apply a local search repeatedly from (typically) different starting solutions; hybrid evolutionary algorithms and scatter search that apply a local search on a population of solutions; and on-line stochastic optimization where a local search produces solutions to a variety of scenarios before making a decision. These algorithms exhibit inherent parallelism which an optimization system should be able to exploit naturally, without requiring significant expertise in parallel programming. Consider uncapacitated facility location for which state-of-the-art algorithms are based on multistart tabu search [11] and hybrid heuristics [1]. The fragment

```
1.    Solution sol[1..nbTrials];
2.    parall(i in 1..nbTrials) {
3.       WarehouseLocation location(); location.state();
4.       sol[i] = location.search();
5.    }
6.    selectMax(i in 1..nbTrials)(sol[i].getValue())
7.       cout << "Solution at Cost: " << sol[i].getValue() << endl;
```

depicts the COMET implementation of a parallel multistart variable neighborhood search. Each execution of the body creates a facility location model and states its constraints (line 3), and searches for a high-quality solution from a randomly generated initial solution (line 4). The returned solution is stored in `sol[i]` (line 4 again). Once all executions are completed, the values of the best found solutions is displayed (lines 6-7). The parallel code enjoys some interesting properties. First, it provides a parallel counterpart to a natural sequential implementation: the `parall` instruction simply replaces the `forall` construct of COMET. Second, the modeling and search components of the application are independent from the parallel code: they have not been modified when moving from the sequential to the parallel implementation.

Some complex applications in scheduling and vehicle routing explore heterogeneous neighborhoods and may feature several distinct local search algorithms collaborating in finding a solution. For instance, the snippet

```
pardo exploreRNA() | exploreNB();
```

illustrates how the two neighborhoods of the jobshop algorithm of Dell'Amico and Trubian [5] can be explored in parallel. The exploration code in [10] uses a neighborhood selector that must now be a synchronized object. Once again, the effort of moving from a sequential to a parallel implementation is minimal.

The implementation of the `parall` construct uses a source-to-source transformation that creates a thread for each iteration and a barrier to join all the threads. For instance, the parallel COMET for facility location just described is transformed into the COMET code:

```
1.    Solution sol[1..nbTrials];
2.    Barrier joinPoint();
3.    forall(i in 1..nbTrials) {
4.       joinPoint.incr();
5.       thread {
6.          WarehouseLocation location(); location.state();
7.          sol[i] = location.search();
8.          joinPoint.decr();
```

```
9.    }
10.   }
11.   joinPoint.wait();
12.   selectMax(i in 1..nbTrials)(sol[i].getValue())
13.      cout << "Solution at Cost: " << sol[i].getValue() << endl;
```

During the transformation, the `parall` construct is replaced by a `forall` loop that creates a thread at each iteration (lines 4-9). As a consequence, $nbTrials + 1$ threads may be executing simultaneously: the master thread executing the `forall` instruction and the $nbTrials$ slave threads created during the loop. The master thread waits for the completion of all slaves after the loop (line 11) before proceeding to subsequent instructions. The synchronization is performed using a barrier declared in line 2. The monitor is incremented in line 4 to specify that a new thread is about to join the execution and is decremented in line 8, just before the thread completes its execution.

3.2 Thread Pools

The implementation of the `parall` instruction associates a thread with each iteration of the parallel loop. Since each thread has its own runtime control blocks and stacks, this implementation may induce some non-negligible overhead when the number of iterations is large. The concept of thread pool, i.e., a collection of cooperating threads, overcomes this limitation and allows COMET programs to map nicely onto the underlying architecture. The `parall` instruction can be parameterized by a thread pool which is then responsible for executing the loop iterations in parallel. The size of the thread pool can be determined according to the number of available processors or any other appropriate criterion.

Figure 4 depicts the implementation of the multistart local search for facility location in terms of thread pools. The pool is declared in line 1, used in the `parall` instruction (line 3), and closed after the loop (line 7). Observe the small distance between the sequential and parallel code and the clean separation between the model, the parallel code, and the mapping on the target architecture.

The implementation of the `parall` instruction over parallel pools (and thus thread pools) is also based on a source-to-source transformation. However, it

```
1.   ThreadPool tp(4);
2.   Solution sol[1..nbTrials];
3.   parall<tp>(i in 1..nbTrials) {
4.      WarehouseLocation location(); location.state();
5.      sol[i] = location.search();
6.   }
7.   tp.close();
8.   selectMax(i in 1..nbTrials)(sol[i].getValue())
9.      cout << ``Best Solution at Cost: '' << sol[i].getValue() << endl;
```

Fig. 4. The Parall Instruction over Thread Pools for a Multistart Local Search

```
1.   ThreadPool tp(4);
2.   Solution sol[1..nbTrials];
3.   Barrier joinPoint();
4.   forall(i in 1..nbTrials) {
5.     joinPoint.incr();
6.     closure cl {
7.       WarehouseLocation location(); location.state();
8.       sol[i] = location.search();
9.       joinPoint.decr();
10.    }
11.    tp.execute(cl);
12.  }
13.  joinPoint.wait();
14.  tp.close();
15.  selectMax(i in 1..nbTrials)(sol[i].getValue())
16.    cout << "Solution at Cost: " << sol[i].getValue() << endl;
```

Fig. 5. The Implementation of the Parall Instruction over Thread Pools

differs from the earlier implementation by not using threads. Instead it creates closures that are submitted to the pool for execution. Figure 5 depicts the result of the source-to-source transformation for the code presented in Figure 4. The main novelty is the creation, for each iteration of the parallel loop, of a closure (lines 6–10) which is submitted to the pool (line 11). The implementation is shown in Figure 6. Thread pools implement the interface `ParallelPool` and support a method `execute` on closures. Its core is the constructor (lines 4–13). It first constructs a producer/consumer buffer of closures whose implementation is similar to the COMET class in Figure 2. It then creates n threads that consume and execute closures. These closures are produced by the `parall` instruction for each iteration as shown in Figure 5 and the `execute` method of the thread pool simply "produces" a closure for the buffer. When the thread pool is closed (line 14), all threads are terminated, since method `terminate` on the producer/consumer buffer wakes all threads waiting for a closure. Note that first-class closures [10] are critical in implementing the abstractions.

3.3 Interruptions

Multistart local searches are also useful when for finding feasible solutions. Indeed, many algorithms use restarts to avoid being trapped in long unsuccessful runs. Contrary to optimization problems where all searches are potentially pertinent, a multistart local search for constraint satisfaction should terminate as soon as a feasible solution is found. Consider the code

```
1.   Boolean found(false);
2.   parall(i in Trials) {
3.     ProgressiveParty pp(); pp.state();
4.     found := pp.search();
5.   } until found;
```

```
1.   class ThreadPool implements ParallelPool {
2.     ClosureBuffer buffer;
3.     bool closed;
4.     ThreadPool(int n) {
5.       closed = false;
6.       buffer = new ClosureBuffer(n);
7.       forall(i in 1..n)
8.         thread b
9.           while (!closed) {
10.             Closure v = buffer.consume();
11.             if (v != null) call(v);
12.           }
13.     }
14.    void execute(Closure v) { buffer.produce(v); }
15.    void close() { closed = true; buffer.terminate(); }
16.  }
```

Fig. 6. The Implementation of the Thread Pool

which uses a multistart local search to solve the progressive party (see [7,13] for descriptions of the tabu-search algorithm). The code declares a Boolean variable found to denote whether a solution has been found (line 1). This variable is then used in line 5 to specify that the local searches must terminate as soon as found becomes true. Each loop iteration creates an instance of the model, states the constraints, and searches for a feasible solution from a random starting point.

This COMET code features a complete separation between the model and the parallel instructions, although the operational behavior of the model is fundamentally affected. There is no need in COMET to enhance the model to implement interruptions, showing the compositionality and the modularity promoted by the parallel abstractions. Observe also that interruptions are a fundamental abstractions for many applications: they may be used to interrupt local searches after some internal or external event as is frequently the case in online optimization or when cooperating local searches produces new improving solutions.

The implementation of interruptions relies on events [10] and is once again based on a source-to-source transformation. The rewriting is best understood as a two-step process. The first step rewrites the parall instruction into a forall loop featuring a break/when construct to terminate the threads, while the second step rewrites this construct into an event and an exception. For instance, Figure 7 depicts the rewriting for the multistart local search for the progressive party problem described earlier: the left and right columns show the result of the first and second phases respectively. The main novelty in the left column is the break/when instruction in lines 6–10: the new construct encapsulates the search and terminates when found becomes true. The right column shows how the break/when instruction is rewritten in terms of an event (lines 6b–6d) which monitors whether the Boolean variable is updated (line 6b) and interrupts the search by throwing an exception from inside the event-handler (line 6c) when the Boolean becomes true. It is important to highlight the operational behavior

```
1. Boolean found(false);              1. Boolean found(false);
2. Barrier joinPoint();               2. Barrier joinPoint();
3. forall(i in Trials:!found){        3. forall(i in Trials:!found){
4.    joinPoint.incr();               4.    joinPoint.incr();
5.    thread {                        5.    thread {
6.       break {                      6a.      try {
7.          ProgressiveParty pp();    6b.         whenever found@changes(){
8.          pp.state();               6c.            throw new Stop();
9.          found := pp.search());    6d.         } in {
10.      } when found;                7.             ProgressiveParty pp();
11.   joinPoint.decr();               8.             pp.state();
12. }                                 9.             found := pp.search();
13.}                                  10a.        }
                                      10b.     } catch (Stop e) {}
                                      11.   joinPoint.decr();
                                      12. }
                                      13.}
```

Fig. 7. The Implementation of Early Termination for a Multistart Local Search

induced by this implementation. Whenever the Boolean becomes true, an event is published to all the concerned threads, each of which now interrupts its execution by throwing an exception in their event-handlers. The ability of a thread to post events caught in other threads is fundamental in implementing interruptions and providing the desired compositionality and separation of concerns of the abstractions. Observe also that the novel whenever/in construct that specifies the scope in which the event is active. This generalization ensures that notifications only reach relevant events, which is essentially when the parallel code is embedded in outermost loops (as in the Golomb ruler discussed later).

3.4 Parallel Repeat Loop

Once thread pools are available, some additional parallel abstractions become natural. Reconsider the progressive party problem where the number of restarts is not chosen a priori. The multistart local search procedure can be implemented by the parallel counterpart to a repeat loop:

```
1.   Boolean found(false);
2.   ThreadPool tp(4);
3.   parrepeat<tp> {
4.      ProgressiveParty pp(); pp.state();
5.      found := found || pp.search();
6.   } until found;
7.   tp.close();
```

The parrepeat instruction uses the thread pool to execute its body in parallel until a feasible solution is found. Each time a thread completes a local search, it restarts a new search. Once a solution is obtained, all the threads in the pool

```
1.   Boolean found(false);
2.   ThreadPool tp(4);
3.   BoundedSemaphore sem(4);
4.   do {
5.     sem.incr();
6.     closure cl {
7.       break {
8.         ProgressiveParty pp(); pp.state();
9.         found := pp.search();
10.      } when found,
11.      sem.decr();
12.    };
13.    tp.execute(cl);
14.  } while (!found);
15.  tp.close();
```

Fig. 8. The Implementation of Parallel Repeat Loops

terminate, at which stage the parallel repeat also terminates. It is important to emphasize the novelty of the `parrepeat` construct: the automatic vectorization performed by automatic vectorization in compilers (e.g., the recent GCC-4 compiler) only applies to `for` loops. It is the availability of interuptions (and thus of events and closures) and the application domain that allow the parallelizations of loops with no apriori bounds on the number of iterations.

The implementation of the `parrepeat` construct is based on a source-to-source transformation and a bounded semaphore (i.e., a synchronization object that blocks when it is about to become negative or to exceed its upper bound). For instance, Figure 8 shows the rewriting for the progressive party problem. The implementation creates a bounded semaphore (line 3) ensuring that at most 4 threads are searching at any one time. The semaphore is incremented before creating a closure (line 5) and decremented upon completion of a search (line 12). The master thread (executing the loop) blocks as soon at the semaphore reaches its upper bound before moving to the next iteration to produce a new closure. Whenever a solution is found by some thread, all threads in the pool are interrupted and the master thread exits the loop.

3.5 Model Pools

Thread pools remove the one-to-one mapping between a thread and a loop iteration, avoid the overhead of running many threads, and allow for novel parallel abstractions. However, they do not avoid the overhead induced by creating many instances of the same model and stating the model constraints. For instance, the multistart local searches presented so far always construct a new model for each iteration of the parallel loops, an overhead which may be avoided by sequential restarts. This overhead, if non-negligible, can be remedied by model pools which are now responsible for executing the loop iterations. Consider again the multistart local search for facility location. With model pools, it becomes:

```
1.    ParallelModel model[1..4] = new WarehouseLocation();
2.    ModelPool mp(model);
3.    Solution s[Trials];
4.    parall<mp>(i in Trials) s[i] = mp.search();
5.    mp.close();
```

The COMET code creates an array of models (line 1), which are then used to define the model pool (line 2). The `parall` instruction is now parameterized by the model pool to implement the multistart local search. A particularly interesting feature of this COMET program is the way solutions are produced: the parallel loop requests the model pool to search for solutions, not individual models (line 4). This liberates programmers from keeping track of which models are now available and which are busy. As a consequence, the parallel abstractions promote elegant compositionality and separation of concerns, letting users focus on their (sequential) models, automating the synchronization aspects, and reusing the same models in sequential and parallel settings. Note also that the models in the pool may implement different search strategies as sometimes proposed in cooperating local search: it suffices to fill the `model` array with different models, showing the simplicity of parallelizing heterogeneous models.

To be included in a model pool, a model must implement the interface depicted in Figure 9. The interface contains methods for stating the model constraint, searching for a solution, searching for a solution from a given starting point, and searching for solutions using several existing solutions, as is typically the case in hybrid evolutionary algorithms and scatter search.

The problem of finding optimal, or near-optimal, Golomb rulers using hybrid evolutionary algorithms is an interesting illustration of model pools. The hybrid algorithm is organized as a series of searches, each of which finding a shorter ruler. More precisely, the basic step of the algorithm is to find a Golomb ruler whose length is smaller than l. This feasibility search is performed by an hybrid evolutionary algorithm applying a tabu search on solutions obtained by crossing existing solutions in the population. The initial population is simply a set of (infeasible) rulers of size smaller than l and the crossover operator combines two rulers by taking the first half of the first ruler and the second half of the second one. At each iteration, the hybrid algorithm has a population of n rulers and generates a new population of the same size by repeatedly choosing two rulers randomly, crossing them, and applying the tabu search. Each iteration is inherently parallel and can be implemented by the COMET code

```
1.  interface ParallelModel {
2.     void state();
3.     Solution search();
4.     Solution search(Solution s);
5.     Solution search(Solution s1,Solution s2);
6.     Solution search(Solution[] s);
7.  }
```

Fig. 9. The Interface of Parallel Models

```
1.   Solution o[k in Pop] = pop[k];
2.   parall<mp>(k in Pop) {
3.     select(i in Pop, j in Pop: i != j) {
4.       pop[k] = mp.search(o[i],o[j]);
5.       found := (pop[k].getValue() == 0);
6.     }
7.   } until found;
```

where mp is a model pool. The code uses a parallel loop, early termination, and model pools. The computation starts by storing the current population in o, making it the old population (line 1). The search for a feasible ruler uses a parall instruction over a model pool, terminating when found becomes true (lines 2-7). The model pool contains a number of Golomb ruler models that can be used simultaneously in the parallel loop. Each iteration selects two solutions in the old population, crosses them, searches for a solution using the model pool, and stores the resulting solution in pop[k], i.e., the kth element of the new population (line 4). If the ruler is feasible (i.e., its objective, which denotes the number of constraint violations, is zero), all threads are interrupted and the loop execution completes after the assignment in line 5. This code is included in an outermost loop, which will start a new search for a shorter ruler.

The resulting COMET code exhibits several desirable properties. First, the parallel code is almost identical to the sequential code. The only changes are, in

```
1. class ModelPool implements ParallelPool {
2.   bool closed;
3.   ModelBuffer mbuf;
4.   ClosureBuffer cbuf;
5.   ModelPool(ParallelModel[] models){
6.     closed = false;
7.     mbuf = new ModelBuffer(models.size());
8.     cbuf = new ClosureBuffer(models.size());
9.     forall(i in 1..models.size()) {
10.       models[i].state(); mbuf.produce(models[i]);
11.    }
12.    forall(i in 1..models.size())
13.      thread b { while (!closed) call(cbuf.consume()); }
14.  }
15.  void submit(Closure body) { cbuf.produce(body);}
16.  void close() { closed = true; mbuf.terminate(); cbuf.terminate(); }
17.  Solution search() {
18.    ParallelModel m = mbuf.consume();
19.    Solution s = m.search();
20.    mbuf.produce(m);
21.    return s;
22.  }
23.}
```

Fig. 10. The Implementation of Model Pools

fact, the parallel loop which replaces its sequential counterpart and the model pool which generalizes the single model of the sequential implementation. Second, the compositionality and separation of concerns promoted by the parallel abstractions ensure that the parallel implementation induces no changes to the basic model, i.e., the constraints, the tabu search, and the crossover operators. Only the generation of the new population is affected and it is precisely the code that is being parallelized. Observe that the COMET program has no explicit synchronization, thread management, or termination code.

Model pools use the same source-to-source transformation as thread pools, since both are implementations of parallel pools. The main difference is in the implementation of the pool itself which is depicted in Figure 10. In addition to the closure buffer, model pools also use a buffer to keep track of models available for execution. Initially, the pool states the constraints in all models and "produces" the models (lines 9–11). When a search instruction is executed (lines 17–22), the pool first "consumes" a model (line 18), applies the search on the so-obtained model (line 19), and "produces" the model back (line 20). Note that the implementation decouples the threads and models: coupling them is not correct when parallel loops also use parallel instructions.

4 Experimental Results

Table 1 presents preliminary experimental results on a Apple G5 with two processors. The table reports the solution quality $(min(S), max(S), avg(S))$, the average running time in seconds, and how much of the potential speedup (in percentage) is achieved by the parallel implementation. Note that the parallel implementation is unlikely to approach 100% because the operating systems is also running on one of the processors. The tested program includes a multi-start variable-neighborhood search for uncapacitated facility location (probably the most effective algorithm for this problem), the tabu-search algorithm for graph-coloring from [6] running for a large number of iterations, and an hybrid evolutionary algorithm for finding Golomb rulers. The facility location lines covers 30 benchmarks from the class FPP17, which requires a multistart strategy

Table 1. Experimental Results on a Dual Apple G5

Problem	$min(S)$	$avg(S)$	$max(S)$	$avg(T)$	$\%(S)$
Facility Location (//)	54526.00	54545.20	54557.00	63.97	
Facility Location (seq)	54526.00	54545.20	54557.00	49.92	44%
Coloring (5) (seq)	66.00	66.38	67.00	240.33	
Coloring (5) (//)	65.00	66.32	67.00	130.16	92%
Coloring (1c) (seq)	64.00	64.51	65.00	368.38	
Coloring (1c) (//)	64.00	64.34	65.00	209.16	86%
Golomb-11 (seq)	72.00	72.00	72.00	57.08	
Golomb-11 (//)	72.00	72.00	72.00	36.90	71%

to obtain high-quality results. Each benchmark is run 100 times, accounting for a total of 6,000 runs. The coloring algorithm was evaluated on the benchmarks R250.5.Col (250 vertices and 50% density) whose best-known solution is 65 and R250.1c.Col (250 vertices and 90% density) whose best-known solution is 64, accounting for 200 runs. The Golomb ruler program was run until the optimal solution (of length 72) was found, also accounting for 200 runs. The experimental results confirm the practicality of the extensions. On coloring, the parallel implementation produces 92% and 86% of the maximum speedups. On facility location, 44% of the potential speedup is realized. The smaller percentage is due partly due to differences in runtimes between several runs (decreasing in fact the maximum possible speedup) and the memory allocation necessary to maintain the best set of facilities to swap. Since both threads use the same memory pool and garbage collection, there is some contention for memory. The Golomb ruler produces 71% of the maximum speedup, which is quite impressive since there are considerable differences between runs and the execution also terminates as soon as the optimal solution is found. Overall these results are promising. Moreover, potential limitations have been isolated and can be remedied.

5 Related Work

The parallel abstractions of COMET share the same motivation as openMP, a preprocessor for parallel loops in C and Fortran [4,2]. Both systems aim at making parallel computing widely accessible by reducing the distance between sequential and parallel code. openMP supports instructions that resemble the parall and pardo constructs of COMET. However, the parallel abstractions of COMET are simpler and richer, primarily because of its advanced control abstractions: first-order closures and events. Unlike openMP, there is no need in COMET to specify the role of variables in parallel loop. The role of variables in COMET is uniform with respect to events [10], nondeterminism [12], and parallelism. Unlike openMP, COMET provides interruptions and parallel repeat/while loops which impose no a-priori bounds on the number of iterations. The concepts of parallel pools naturally support homogeneous and heterogeneous cooperating local searches and reduces the overhead that plagues simpler parallel loops. Finally, the parallel abstractions of COMET are modular and compositional, separates the optimization models from the parallel code, and imposes minimal requirements on the underlying implementation which remains simple and easily maintainable.

6 Conclusion

This paper proposed parallel programming abstractions to exploit the availability of commodity multiprocessors in COMET. The abstractions include parallel loops, interruptions, as well as thread and model pools. They address the need of making parallel constraint-based local search and hybrid algorithms as close as possible to their sequential counterparts. In particular, they are compositional, cleanly separates the parallel codes from the optimization models, and leverages the advanced control abstractions of COMET: events and first-order closures. Preliminary results on a variety of applications indicate that they can be implemented with minimal overhead. Future research will be devoted to a distributed implementation of COMET on networks of commodity computers.

Acknowledgments. Special thanks to the first reviewer for his detailed comments.

References

1. R. Aiex, S. Binato, and M. Resende. Parallel GRASP with Path-Relinking for Jobshop Scheduling. *Parallel Computing*, 29(4):393–430, 2003.
2. R. Chandra, L. Dagum, D. Kohr, D. Maydan, J. McDonald, and R. Menon. *Parallel Programming in OpenMP*. Morgan Kaufmann, 2000. ISBN:1558606718.
3. W.F. Clocksin and H. Alshawi. A Method for Efficiently Executing Horn Clause Programs Using Multiple Processors. *New Generation Computing*, 5:361–376, 1988.
4. L. Dagum and R. Menon. Openmp: An industry-standard api for shared-memory programming. *IEEE Computational Science and Engineering*, 5:46–55, 1998.
5. M. Dell'Amico and M. Trubian. Applying Tabu Search to the Job-Shop Scheduling Problem. *Annals of Operations Research*, 41:231–252, 1993.
6. R. Dorne and J.K. Hao. *Tabu Search for Graph Coloring, T-Colorings and Set T-Colorings*, chapter Meta-heuristics: Advances and Trends in Local Search Paradigms for Optimization, pages 77–92. Kluwer Academic Publishers, 1998.
7. L. Michel and P. Van Hentenryck. A Constraint-Based Architecture for Local Search. In *OOPSLA02*, pages 101–110, Seattle, November 2002.
8. L. Michel and P. Van Hentenryck. A Decomposition-Based Implementation of Search Strategies. *ACM Transactions on Computational Logic*, 5(2), 2004.
9. L. Perron. Search Procedures and Parallelism in Constraint Programming. In *CP'99*, pages 346–360, Alexandria, Virginia, October 1999.
10. P. Van Hentenryck and L. Michel. Control Abstractions for Local Search. In *CP'03*, pages 65–80, Cork, Ireland, 2003.
11. P. Van Hentenryck and L. Michel. *Constraint-Based Local Search*. The MIT Press, Cambridge, Mass., 2005.
12. P. Van Hentenryck and L. Michel. Nondeterministic Control for Hybrid Search. In *CP-AI-OR'05*, Prague, May 2005.
13. P. Van Hentenryck, L. Michel, and L. Liu. Constraint-Based Combinators for Local Search. In *CP'04*, pages 47–61, Toronto, Canada, October 2004.

Generating Corrective Explanations for Interactive Constraint Satisfaction

Barry O'Callaghan, Barry O'Sullivan, and Eugene C. Freuder

Cork Constraint Computation Centre,
Department of Computer Science, University College Cork, Ireland
{b.ocallaghan, b.osullivan, e.freuder}@4c.ucc.ie

Abstract. Interactive tasks such as online configuration and e-commerce can be modelled as constraint satisfaction problems (CSPs). These can be solved interactively by a user assigning values to variables. The user may require advice and explanations from a system to help him/her find a satisfactory solution. Explanations of failure in constraint programming tend to focus on conflict. However, what is really desirable is an explanation that is *corrective* in the sense that it provides the basis for moving forward in the problem-solving process. More specifically, when faced with a dead-end, or when a desirable value has been removed from a domain, we need to compute alternative assignments for a subset of the assigned variables that enables the user to move forward. This paper defines this notion of *corrective explanation*, and proposes an algorithm to generate such explanations. The approach is shown to perform well on both real-world configuration benchmarks and randomly generated problems.

1 Introduction

It is now generally accepted by the constraint processing community that "ease-of-use" is the next research challenge that must be tackled in order to ensure widespread adoption of constraint technology in industrial applications [14]. One of the most important aspects of such a challenge is the development of new approaches to generating explanations. In this paper we focus on supporting interactive constraint satisfaction, a setting where a user solves a problem interactively by adding constraints. For example, configuration problems are typically solved interactively by a user who assigns values, representing the various options that are available, to variables representing the features of the product being configured.

In such an application it is important that the user can be guided towards a desired solution without being forced to blindly backtrack [1]. Specifically, during the course of interactive problem solving the user may encounter difficulties such as inconsistency or desirable values being eliminated due to conflicts with previous decisions. In such situations it is desirable for the interactive system to generate an explanation that, rather than focusing on what has caused the problem, explains what can be done to overcome it. Explanations of failure in constraint satisfaction tend to focus on blame; what we often need is an explanation that is corrective in the sense that it provides the basis for moving forward. In particular, when faced with a dead-end, we want to find a set of assigned variables for which there are alternative assignments that allow a user to continue making consistent decisions.

To address this issue we introduce the notion of *corrective explanation*. To demonstrate the distinction between corrective explanations and more traditional blame-based "causal explanations", consider the example in Figure 1.

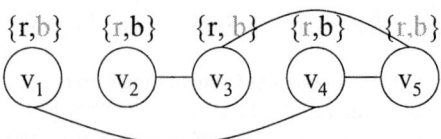

Fig. 1. An example of corrective versus causal explanations

This figure presents assignments of colours to variables in a colouring problem. We have assigned colours as shown to the first 4 variables (highlighted in black), only two colours are available, and for the purposes of this simple example, we are just running a basic backtracking algorithm. We have encountered a dead-end on variable v_5 at this point. A "causal explanation" algorithm would look to assign blame to a set of variables whose assignments are sufficient to leave us at this dead-end, because every value for v_5 is inconsistent with one of these assignments. In this case, v_3 and v_4 provide a causal explanation. However, v_3 and v_4 do not provide a corrective explanation because changing their instantiations alone is not sufficient to enable us to move forward and assign a consistent value to v_5.

Given this causal explanation, a backtrack search algorithm, or more importantly a human user making the choices in an interactive setting – imagine a customer trying to configure a product at an e-commerce website – would now go back to reconsider v_4, and finding no further alternatives there, would backtrack to v_3. There the customer could try b(lue) for v_3, but would be told that it is not consistent with the prior choice for v_2. At this point, the customer might understandably explode at the computer screen: "You told me the problem was my choices for v_3 and v_4, but now I've looked at all the other possible choices for these and you tell me that isn't good enough; what kind of an 'explanation' was that?" And imagine how the customer might feel if there had been dozens of other choices to consider at v_3 and v_4, none of which in fact allowed the customer to move forward to a successful choice for v_5.

A corrective explanation which does permit forward movement can be found based on $\{v_1, v_4\}$. Making v_1 b(lue) and v_4 r(ed) allows us to proceed to assign a value to v_5, blue. In general there might be more than one set of reassignments that allows us to proceed, and more than one set of corrective explanation variables. For example, another corrective explanation can be found here based on $\{v_2, v_3\}$. In general, we might expect to prefer shorter corrective explanations (fewer variables). However, we might have other "goodness" criteria, e.g. we might prefer not to change v_1.

The contributions of this paper are as follows:

1. We formally define the general notion of corrective explanation, which is a new form of explanation for constraint programming[1].

---

[1] We introduced the corrective explanation concept and the heuristic method earlier ourselves, but only in the context of a Doctoral Program abstract [11] and a poster [12].

2. We present a systematic algorithm, CORRECTIVEEXP, for finding minimal corrective explanations.
3. We demonstrate the utility of CORRECTIVEEXP on a number of real-world configuration problems and randomly generated instances, showing that corrective explanations can be found for these problems with effort close to the best-case theoretical performance of the algorithm.
4. We compare CORRECTIVEEXP with a branch-and-bound method for finding minimal corrective explanations and a heuristic method that finds corrective explanations, but does not guarantee minimality; we identify contexts in which CORRECTIVEEXP is the algorithm of choice.

The remainder of the paper is organised as follows. In Section 2 we formally define the notion of corrective explanation in the context of finite domain constraint satisfaction. We present an algorithm for computing minimal corrective explanations in Section 3, which is then evaluated in Section 4. The current state-of-the-art in explanation generation is surveyed in Section 5, highlighting the differences between existing methods and the type of explanation presented here, and outlining some important aspects of our research agenda. A number of concluding remarks are made in Section 6.

2 Corrective Explanation

A constraint satisfaction problem (CSP) is a 3-tuple $P \triangleq \langle \mathcal{X}, \mathcal{D}, \mathcal{C} \rangle$ where $\mathcal{X}$ is a finite set of variables $\mathcal{X} \triangleq \{x_1, \ldots, x_n\}$, $\mathcal{D}$ is a set of finite domains $\mathcal{D} \triangleq \{D(x_1), \ldots, D(x_n)\}$ where the the domain $D(x_i)$ is the finite set of values that variable x_i can take, and a set of constraints $\mathcal{C} \triangleq \{c_1, \ldots, c_m\}$. Each constraint c_i is defined by the ordered set $var(c_i)$ of the variables it involves, and a set $sol(c_i)$ of allowed combinations of values. An assignment of values to the variables in $var(c_i)$ *satisfies* c_i if it belongs to $sol(c_i)$. A *solution* to a constraint satisfaction problem is an assignment of a value from its domain to each variable such that every constraint in the network is satisfied.

In interactive constraint satisfaction it is often useful to partition the set of constraints, $\mathcal{C}$, into a set of background constraints, $\mathcal{B}$, and a set of user-specified constraints, $\mathcal{U}$, such that $\mathcal{C} \triangleq \mathcal{B} \cup \mathcal{U}$. The set of background constraints, $\mathcal{B}$, are those constraints that form the technical characteristics of the problem, such as compatibility constraints in configuration, routing constraints in travel planning, etc. Such constraints cannot be modified. On the other hand the set of user-specified constraints, $\mathcal{U}$, define the set of decisions made by the user during the interactive session and can, therefore, be modifed.

We assume that the set of background constraints are consistent, i.e. that $\langle \mathcal{X}, \mathcal{D}, \mathcal{B} \rangle$ is soluble. We furthermore assume that the constraints in $\mathcal{U}$ represent assignments of values to variables. This is a reasonable assumption in many interactive contexts such as configuration and travel planning where a user tries to find a satisfactory solution by specifying values for each variable in the problem. It is trivial to extend the work presented here to handle more general constraints.

Unless the system maintains global consistency after each decision, the user can reach a state where a consistent assignment for the current variable cannot be found. For example, if the system relies on checking the user's assignments for consistency against the constraints in the problem, a user may reach a dead-end just as in chronological backtrack search. On the other hand, if the system relies on some form of lookahead (e.g. forward checking or arc-consistency), then the user may not be able to find an assignment for the current variable that does not cause the wipe-out of the domain of some future variable. A corrective explanation should identify reassignments for a subset of the user's decisions that guarantee that consistency is recovered so that the user can continue making decisions about future variables. We refer to this set of assignments as a *corrective explanation of inconsistency*, since rather than focusing on explaining why the problem is inconsistent, it focuses on the more useful issue of how to overcome inconsistency.

We may also reach a point where the user would like to restore a value for a particular variable that was removed due to one or more of the user's previous decisions. A corrective explanation in this context should identify reassignments that guarantee that the desired value is restored so that it can be selected and consistency is maintained. We refer to this set of reassignments as a *corrective explanation for value restoration*. Note that both of these forms of explanation are semantically equivalent, the difference being how we want to move ahead: is any value for the current variable acceptable or is a specific value required? We now focus on the general notion of corrective explanation.

Formally, given a $P \triangleq \langle \mathcal{X}, \mathcal{D}, \mathcal{B} \cup \mathcal{U} \rangle$, let $X \triangleq vars(\mathcal{U})$, the set of variables for which the user has assigned values. Let $x \in \mathcal{X} - X$ be the current variable to which the user wishes to assign a value. If there does not exist a value, $v \in \mathcal{D}(x)$, such that $P' \triangleq \langle \mathcal{X}, \mathcal{D}, \mathcal{B} \cup \mathcal{U} \cup \{(x, v)\} \rangle$ can be extended to a solution then we need to compute a corrective explanation.

Definition 1 (Corrective Explanation). *Given* $P' \triangleq \langle \mathcal{X}, \mathcal{D}, \mathcal{B} \cup \mathcal{U} \cup \{(x, v)\} \rangle$ *which is inconsistent for all* $v \in \mathcal{D}(x)$, *where* x *is the current variable that the user wishes to assign, let* $\mathcal{E} = \{(e_1, v_{e_1}), \ldots, (e_k, v_{e_k})\}$ *be a set of assignments in* $\mathcal{U}$, *i.e.* $\mathcal{E} \subseteq \mathcal{U}$, *such that* $\langle \mathcal{X}, \mathcal{D}, \mathcal{B} \cup (\mathcal{U} - \mathcal{E}) \cup \{(x, v)\} \rangle$ *extends to a solution for some* $v \in \mathcal{D}(x)$. *A corrective explanation,* $\mathcal{E}'$, *is a reassignment of the variables in* $\mathcal{E}$ *such that* $\langle \mathcal{X}, \mathcal{D}, \mathcal{B} \cup (\mathcal{U} - \mathcal{E}) \cup \mathcal{E}' \cup \{(x, v)\} \rangle$ *has a solution. The length of the explanation is* $|\mathcal{E}'|$.

Informally, a corrective explanation is a reassignment of a subset of the user's unary decision constraints that enables the user to assign at least one more variable. For the moment we do not concern ourselves with preferred explanations [9]. This issue will be discussed later in this paper. However, we can focus on either finding any explanation or one that requires making a minimum number of changes to the user's set of decisions.

The problem of finding a corrective explanation, disregarding the number of changes to the user's decisions that it implies, is equivalent to solving the underlying CSP, and is therefore NP-complete. The problem of finding the corrective explanation that requires the minimum number of changes to the user's decisions is equivalent to the problem of finding the closest solution to his current partial assignment. This is equivalent to solving the MOSTCLOSE problem [8], which has been shown to be $FP^{NP[\log n]}$-complete.

However, rather than trying to find an explanation that is optimal, in the sense that it requires that a minimum number of changes are made to the user's decisions, we can consider finding *minimal length* corrective explanations. A minimal length corrective explanation is one for which any proper subset of its variables cannot be reassigned to provide a corrective explanation. It is this type of explanation that we will focus on in Section 3.

3 Computing Corrective Explanations

Our objective is to support users as they try to interactively solve problems by making assignments to variables in domains such as product configuration. While in practice many of the problems that are solved in this way are easy, maintaining global consistency in an online/real-time fashion may not be practical due to the need for fast response times. One could compile the problem into a data-structure that can maintain global consistency, such as an automaton [1], but this may not be necessary if the interactive solver can recover consistency in reasonable time when required. Furthermore, many compilation methods, which have the advantage of maintaining global consistency and generating explanations quickly, can have difficulties dealing with intensional constraints and dynamic problems, while also having worst-case exponential space complexity.

Explanations that are guaranteed to be corrective can be generated from solutions to the problem. These explanations can be calculated relatively cheaply, in terms of the number of constraint checks required to compute them. The objective when trying to greedily find a corrective explanation is to try to find a solution to the CSP that involves as many of the user's assignments as possible using carefully chosen variable and value ordering heuristics. Once a solution is found, the corrective explanation can be determined by simply comparing the assignments made by the user with the assignments in the solution. The corrective explanation that will be proposed to the user is simply the set of assignments to variables in the solution that differ from the user's original assignments. However, such explanations have no guarantee of being minimal.

Corrective explanations can also be regarded as diagnoses that can be computed using hitting-tree techniques [15]. However, diagnosis algorithms typically focus on finding all diagnoses, while in an interactive context we are usually interested in just finding a single explanation. Junker [9] points out the dualities of conflicts and relaxations, which are equivalent to diagnoses, and proposes an algorithm, QUICKXPLAIN, that focuses on detecting minimal conflicts. His algorithm can be readily modified to compute maximal relaxations. However, a corrective explanation is more than just the complement of a relaxation, i.e. those *variables* whose assignments must be modified in order to guarantee consistency. A corrective explanation also *proposes alternative assignments* for those variables that ensure a solution can be found.

3.1 Generating Corrective Explanations Using Relaxations

We adopt an approach similar to that taken by many others working on explanation generation [9]. Given a set of constraints that do not admit a solution, some constraints must be removed to restore consistency. As noted earlier, in this paper we focus on solving problems interactively where we have a set of background constraints, B, that we assume admit a solution, and a set of user constraints, U. Therefore, to recover consistency it is sufficient to remove some or all of the constraints in U.

Definition 2 (Relaxation). *Given a CSP, $P \triangleq \langle \mathcal{X}, \mathcal{D}, \mathcal{B} \cup \mathcal{U} \rangle$, we define P_r as $\langle \mathcal{X}, \mathcal{D}, \mathcal{B} \cup \mathcal{R} \rangle$ such that $\mathcal{R} \subseteq \mathcal{U}$ and P_r admits a solution. We refer to $\mathcal{R}$ as a relaxation of $\mathcal{U}$.*

We can define both optimal and maximal relaxations.

Definition 3 (Optimal and Maximal Relaxations). *A relaxation $\mathcal{R}$ is maximal if no superset of it is also a relaxation. A relaxation $\mathcal{R}$ is optimal if there does not exist a relaxation $\mathcal{R}'$ such that $|\mathcal{R}'| > |\mathcal{R}|$.*

A corrective explanation can be generated from a relaxation. If $\mathcal{R}$ is a relaxation of the user's constraints, $\mathcal{U}$, that is consistent with a solution, *sol*, the corresponding corrective explanation is $sol \Downarrow vars(\mathcal{U} - \mathcal{R})$, i.e. the set of assignments from *sol* for the variables in the constraints in $\mathcal{U}$ but not in $\mathcal{R}$. If $\mathcal{R}$ is an optimal (respectively, maximal) length relaxation, then the corresponding corrective explanation is optimal (respectively, minimal).

3.2 Algorithm

We propose a constructive algorithm for computing maximal relaxations, inspired by the conflict detection algorithm QUICKXPLAIN [9]. Since we need to find reassignments of the variables based on a relaxation of the user's assignments we do not employ a "divide-and-conquer" approach as in QUICKXPLAIN, but instead employ an approach based on binary search. The CORRECTIVEEXP algorithm is presented as Algorithm 1. An explanation is generated iff the set of constraints $\mathcal{B} \cup \mathcal{U}$ are inconsistent. The procedure CONSISTENT verifies that a solution exists. For tree structured CSPs arc-consistency is sufficient, but in general we need to resort to search. If an explanation is required, a call to CORRECTIVERELAX is made, presented as Algorithm 3. The assignments for the variables that form the corrective explanation are obtained from the last solution used to prove that $\mathcal{R}$ is a globally consistent relaxation of $\mathcal{U}$.

Algorithm 1. CORRECTIVEEXP($\mathcal{B},\mathcal{U}$)

Input: A set of background constraints $\mathcal{B}$, an ordered set of user constraints $\mathcal{U}$.
Output: A corrective explanation.
if CONSISTENT($\mathcal{B} \cup \mathcal{U}$) **then return** $\emptyset$;
else
    let $\mathcal{R} \leftarrow$ CORRECTIVERELAX($\emptyset, \mathcal{U}, \emptyset, \mathcal{B}$);
    $sol \leftarrow$ RESTORELASTSOLUTION;
    return $sol \Downarrow vars(\mathcal{U} - \mathcal{R})$;

CORRECTIVERELAX finds a maximal relaxation by removing, one-by-one, constraints that cause inconsistency. The algorithm performs a binary search on the set of user constraints, $\mathcal{U}$. Starting from an empty relaxation, its successively adds constraints from $\mathcal{U}$ to the relaxation while it remains consistent (i.e. a solution still exists). Upon attempting to add a set of constraints that are inconsistent, the algorithm identifies constraints that are responsible for the inconsistency and removes them individually, preventing their consideration again. This is correct, since if a constraint is inconsistent with a partial relaxation, it will be inconsistent with all of its extensions.

Algorithm 2. CONSISTENT($\mathcal{C}$)

Input: A set of constraints, $\mathcal{C}$.
Output: A Boolean: consistent or not consistent.
$sol \leftarrow$ FINDSOLUTION(C);
SAVESOLUTION sol;
if *not null(sol)* **then return** TRUE;
else return FALSE;

Algorithm 3. CORRECTIVERELAX($\mathcal{R}, \mathcal{U}, \mathcal{A}, \mathcal{B}$)

Input: $\mathcal{R}$ the set of constraints being tested in this invocation; $\mathcal{U}$ the ordered set of constraints yet to be tested; $\mathcal{A}$ the most recent additions to $\mathcal{R}$; and the set of background constraints $\mathcal{B}$.
Output: A maximal relaxation of $\mathcal{U}$.
if $\mathcal{U} = \emptyset$ **then**
  if CONSISTENT($\mathcal{R} \cup \mathcal{B}$) **then return** $\mathcal{R}$;
  else return $\mathcal{R} - \mathcal{A}$;
else if CONSISTENT($\mathcal{R} \cup \mathcal{B}$) **then**
  let $(\triangle_1, \triangle_2) \leftarrow$ SPLIT($\mathcal{U}$);
  return CORRECTIVERELAX($\mathcal{R} \cup \triangle_1, \triangle_2, \triangle_1, \mathcal{B}$);
else if $\mathcal{A} = \{a\}$ **then**
  let $(\triangle_1, \triangle_2) \leftarrow$ SPLIT($\mathcal{U}$);
  return CORRECTIVERELAX($(\mathcal{R} - \mathcal{A}) \cup \triangle_1, \triangle_2, \triangle_1, \mathcal{B}$);
else
  let $(\triangle_1, \triangle_2) \leftarrow$ SPLIT($\mathcal{A}$);
  return CORRECTIVERELAX($(\mathcal{R} - \mathcal{A}) \cup \triangle_1, \triangle_2 \cup \mathcal{U}, \triangle_1, \mathcal{B}$);

Algorithm 4. SPLIT($Ł$)

Input: An ordered set of constraints $Ł$.
Output: A partition of $Ł$.
let $\alpha_1, .., \alpha_n$ be an enumeration of $Ł$;
let k be $\lceil \frac{n}{2} \rceil$;
return $(\{\alpha_1, .., \alpha_k\}, \{\alpha_{k+1}, .., \alpha_n\})$;

The algorithm's SPLIT procedure, presented as Algorithm 4, splits a set of constraints in a binary search fashion. However, as for QUICKXPLAIN [9], there are a number of other possibilities that can be used there.

Theorem 1 (Correctness). *The algorithm* CORRECTIVEEXP *always terminates and always returns a corrective explanation of minimal length for* $\mathcal{B} \cup \mathcal{U}$.

Proof. (Sketch) An explanation is not required if $\mathcal{B} \cup \mathcal{U}$ is consistent, in which case CORRECTIVEEXP terminates with $\emptyset$. This is correct since no assignments in $\mathcal{U}$ need to be modified to recover consistency. If an explanation is required, CORRECTIVEEXP builds a maximal relaxation, $\mathcal{R}$, by adding assignments from a binary search on $\mathcal{U}$. Sets of assignments, $\mathcal{A}$, are removed from $\mathcal{U}$ and added to to $\mathcal{R}$ while they are consistent with $\mathcal{R}$. If inconsistency is detected, the most recent set of assignments to be added to the relaxation, i.e. $\mathcal{A}$, is repeatedly divided until all assignments inconsistent with $\mathcal{R}$ have been removed from $\mathcal{A}$. Each assignment inconsistent with the current relaxation is removed individually within CORRECTIVERELAX by the case "else if $\mathcal{A} = \{a\}$". We terminate when there are no more assignments in $\mathcal{U}$ to be considered. All assignments in $\mathcal{U}$ that are consistent with $\mathcal{B}$ will have been added to $\mathcal{R}$. Only those assignments in $\mathcal{U}$ that are inconsistent with $\mathcal{R}$ will have been removed, therefore ensuring that the resultant relaxation is of maximal length. It is easy to see that the corrective explanation computed in the last line of CORRECTIVEEXP is, therefore, of minimal length. □

The best case performance of CORRECTIVEEXP is similar to that of QUICKX-PLAIN. Finding a relaxation is equivalent to a binary search on the constraints in $\mathcal{U}$. If $k = |\mathcal{U}|$, then the path to any constraint has length $log\ k$. To find a relaxation of size r from amongst these k constraints, the best case is for all $k - r$ constraints not involved in the relaxation to be located in the same subtree of the binary search tree explored by the algorithm. Reaching the root of that subtree requires $log\ k - log\ (k - r)$ calls to CONSISTENT. To fully explore the subtree requires $2 \cdot (k - r)$ calls. Therefore, the best case number of calls to CONSISTENT required to find a maximal relaxation, and hence a minimal corrective explanation, is $2 \cdot (k - r) + log\ \frac{k}{k-r}$. If relaxations are relatively large with respect to the size of $\mathcal{U}$, the algorithm is quite efficient. Indeed, as we will see in the experimental evaluation, it is normally the case the the algorithm performs close to its best case.

4 Experiments

We present an evaluation of CORRECTIVEEXP. The primary objective of the evaluation was to study how the algorithm behaves when computing corrective explanations for a variety of different problem classes. In particular, we focused on the length and cost of corrective explanations. We also considered how close to finding explanations of optimal length we could get using CORRECTIVEEXP, as well as observing how close to its best-case behaviour could be achieved.

We ran a suite of experiments on a number of real-world configuration benchmark problems as well as random soluble binary CSPs. The solver we used in our experiments is based on generalised forward checking.

The real-world problems used were the Renault Megane Problem [1] and the Bike Configuration Problem [6]. The Renault Megane Configuration benchmark deals with the configuration of a family of cars. The problem consists of 101 variables, domain sizes vary from 2 to 43, and there are 113 constraints, almost all of which are non-binary. The number of solutions to the problem is over 1.4×10^{12}. The Bike problem deals with the configuration of bicycles. The problem consists of 34 variables, domain sizes vary from 2 to 16, and there are 40 constraints, many of which are non-binary. The number of solutions to the problem is over 1.3×10^8.

We also generated 500 random CSPs comprising 15 variables, with 10 values per domain, tightness 0.3 and density ranging from 0.3-0.6. These problems are all in the soluble region. These problems sizes were chosen as being representative of many problems one finds in interactive applications. For example, the standard benchmarks used in recommender systems and case-based reasoning systems typically have 10-15 features (variables) and 5-15 possible values for each.

We considered both the task of generating corrective explanations for consistency recovery and corrective explanations for value restoration. For each of the real-world problems studied, a set of 500 distinct test-points were generated for the experiment by simulating a user solving each problem, and recording the situations for which the user either required or requested corrective explanations. For the random problems we generated one test-point per problem. Test-points were generated for both the consistency recovery and value restoration tasks for each problem. The simulated user instantiated variables randomly and values lexicographically. In order to compare explanation generation techniques we generate explanations for the situations described by these test-points. This ensures that we compare the techniques fairly, as explanations are generated on the basis of the same search state. Further details of how test-points were generated are provided below when discussing each experiment.

We compare three approaches to generating corrective explanations:

1. A branch-and-bound search to find optimal (minimum) length explanation;
2. The CORRECTIVEEXP algorithm proposed in this paper;
3. A heuristic-based approach which returns a corrective explanation based on the first solution found for the problem [12].

In the third case above, using the heuristic-based approach, corrective explanations are found by returning any differences between the assignments made by the user and the assignments in a solution found using carefully chosen variable and value ordering heuristics. These heuristics attempt to maximise the number of user assignments in such a solution. The *value ordering heuristic* favours values chosen by the user during search, by selecting those first whenever possible, and uses random choices for the remaining ones. We partition the set of variables into two subsets: those that are user-assigned and those that are still unassigned. User-assigned variables are considered first, and within each subset of variables the min(dom/deg) ordering heuristic was used. The intuition here is that during search the user's choices are always considered first, so they are more likely to participate in the solution used to generate an explanation.

4.1 Results

Consistency Recovery. In this experiment we simulate a user who is simply trying to find a solution to the problem. Test-points are generated when the user reaches a variable for which a consistent assignment cannot be found. For each explanation we record its length, the depth at which the explanation was requested (reflecting the number of assignments the user has already made), and the cost of the explanation (measured by the number of constraint checks required to generate it). The results are averaged at various intervals in the depth. For example for the Megane problem the results are presented in steps of 10, i.e. the data for each explanation requested between 1 and 10 are averaged and presented at depth 10 in the graph, between 11 and 20, etc. The results for the experiments on the benchmark configuration problems are presented in Figures 2(a), 2(c), 3(a) and 3(c). We do not present results for the random problems for this experiment since each approach found, effectively, optimal explanations.

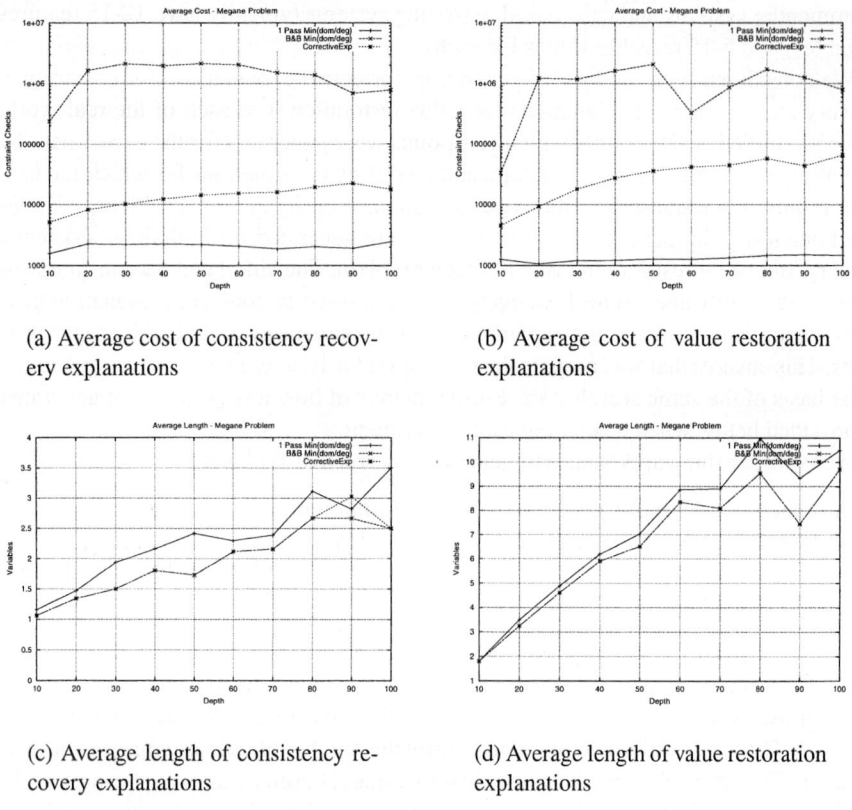

(a) Average cost of consistency recovery explanations

(b) Average cost of value restoration explanations

(c) Average length of consistency recovery explanations

(d) Average length of value restoration explanations

Fig. 2. Results for finding explanations for the Renault Megane Configuration Benchmark

Value Restoration. For each interaction in these experiments (attempt to make a variable assignment) there was a 10% chance that the user would ask to restore a value removed from the domain of the current variable. The explanation length, depth and cost are plotted as per the consistency restoration experiment. The results for the benchmark experiments are presented in Figures 2(b), 2(d), 3(b) and 3(d). Results for the experiments on the random problems are presented in Figure 4.

4.2 Discussion

We discuss our results in detail below, but first give a summary of our evaluation. We demonstrate that CORRECTIVEEXP almost always finds optimal length explanations without incurring the high costs associated with a branch-and-bound approach. While for the real-world benchmarks a heuristic approach often finds explanations that are close to optimal very cheaply, we show that in the more controlled context of random problems, CORRECTIVEEXP can find significantly shorter explanations. In almost every case CORRECTIVEEXP finds corrective explanations with effort close to the best-case theoretical performance of the algorithm.

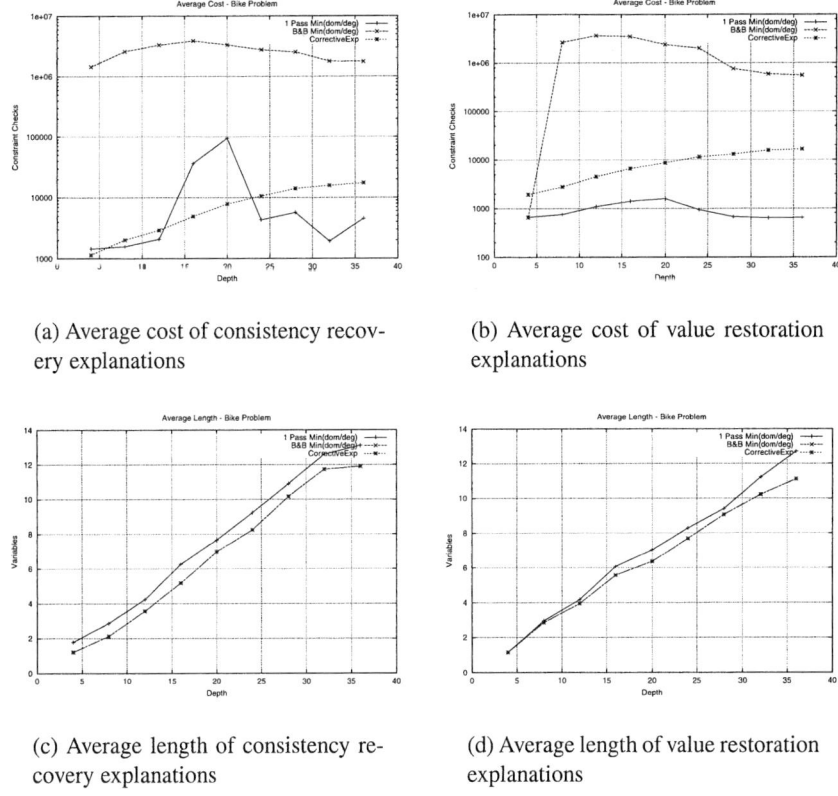

(a) Average cost of consistency recovery explanations

(b) Average cost of value restoration explanations

(c) Average length of consistency recovery explanations

(d) Average length of value restoration explanations

Fig. 3. Results for finding explanations for the Bike Configuration Benchmark

Benchmark Problems. We see that the CORRECTIVEEXP explanations are always close to optimal length for both tasks. In fact CORRECTIVEEXP found minimum explanations in every case in the experiments on the benchmark problems with the exception of some test cases for the Megane problem, when attempting to restore consistency at depths between 80 and 90. The heuristic search-based approach also performed well for the benchmark problems. Explanations of within one variable of optimal were generated for the Bike and Megane problems.

Explanations for the consistency recovery task tend to be shorter, as they aim only to allow the user to proceed with his/her search whereas the value restoration explanations may require modifying many more of the user's earlier decisions in order to accommodate a specific new preference.

In Figures 2(a) and 3(a) the average explanation costs for consistency recovery task are presented. The results for the value restoration task are shown in Figures 2(b) and 3(b). It should be noted that CORRECTIVEEXP always finds explanations using a number of constraint checks close to the best case for the algorithm. For example, consider Figure 2(a) when computing an explanation to recover consistency at depth 50. The average cost to find a solution is less that 2000 consistency checks, while CORREC-

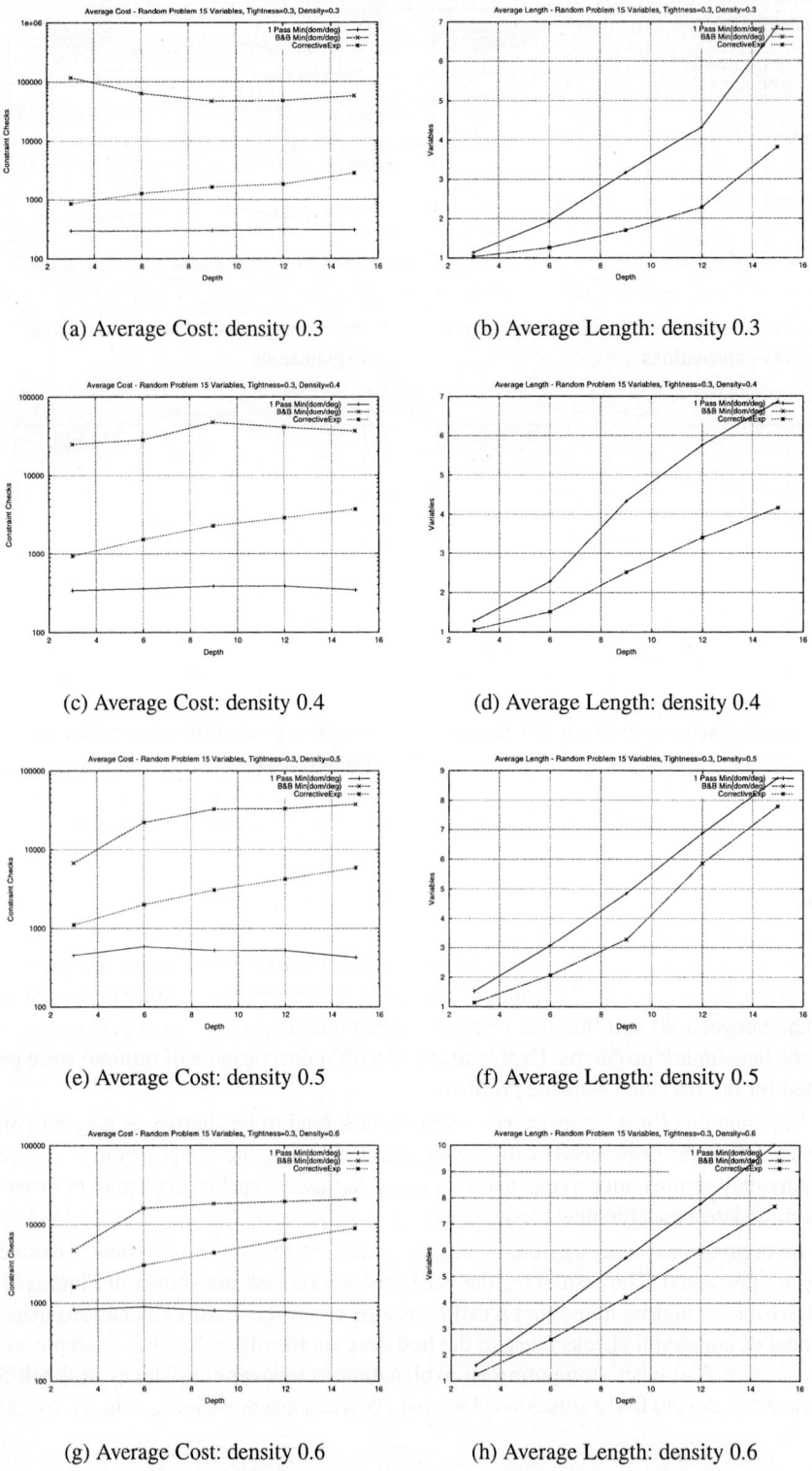

(a) Average Cost: density 0.3
(b) Average Length: density 0.3
(c) Average Cost: density 0.4
(d) Average Length: density 0.4
(e) Average Cost: density 0.5
(f) Average Length: density 0.5
(g) Average Cost: density 0.6
(h) Average Length: density 0.6

Fig. 4. Results for finding corrective explanations for value restoration for random binary problems (15 variables, 10 values, tightness 0.3)

TIVEEXP requires approximately 16000. The best case number of solutions required for CORRECTIVEEXP to find a minimal corrective explanation in this case is 8.

Minimum length explanations found using branch-and-bound tend to be very expensive to compute, as one would expect, while a greedy heuristic-based approach finds explanations quickly. CORRECTIVEEXP explanations are considerably cheaper (by orders of magnitude) than the branch-and-bound algorithm while still finding explanations of optimal length.

The greedy search-based explanation generation technique performs very well for the benchmark configuration problems. Close to optimal explanations (within one variable) are found very cheaply (1000's of constraint checks). CORRECTIVEEXP finds minimal explanations which are optimal in almost every case. For these problems it is doubtful whether the additional cost is warranted given how well a heuristic approach seems to perform. However, with modest additional search cost CORRECTIVEEXP will guarantee minimality and performs close to its theoretical best-case.

Random Problems. For random problems we only present results for the value restoration task, for reasons outlined earlier. For most of the problem densities we considered it is clear that a heuristic search-based approach is not as effective on these problems as it was on the real-world configuration benchmarks when we consider the length of the explanations found. However, CORRECTIVEEXP finds optimal length explanations in every case. From the perspective of search cost, CORRECTIVEEXP again is orders of magnitude better than a branch-and-bound approach, but not prohibitively worse than finding a single solution. Indeed, it is again performing close to its theoretical best-case.

Of particular interest is that for lower density problems a heuristic search-based approach generates explanations that can be considerably longer than optimal, but that guaranteeing minimality using CORRECTIVEEXP (and in these cases optimality) is not prohibitively more expensive than finding a single solution, which is encouraging.

While not reported here, we did run experiments on random problems at the phase transition with results consistent with those presented here. However, since solutions become rarer as the phase transition point is reached, it is to be expected that the heuristic-based approach starts to find explanations that are very close to optimal. Therefore, we argue that the experiment we have presented here is the most interesting from the perspective of explanation generation for interactive constraint satisfaction, since such problems tend to have many solutions.

5 Related Work

QUICKXPLAIN [9] is the current industry standard explanation algorithm. It is used as the explanation component of ILOG's Configurator product. However, QUICKXPLAIN does not compute corrective explanations, but minimal conflict sets. These can be regarded as minimal causal explanations discussed in the Introduction. The QUICKXPLAIN algorithm could be modified to find maximal relaxations, however this would simply provide us with a corrective set of variables, i.e. those variables that must be reassigned corrective values to give a corrective explanation. The CORRECTIVEEXP proposed here does essentially this, but directly. However, we acknowledge QUICKXPLAIN as providing motivation for developing a relaxation-based approach to finding corrective explanations.

There is a considerable amount of work on explanation in constraint satisfaction. For example, many researchers have addressed the generation of explanations in interactive constraint-based systems [1, 2, 4]. There has also been work on explanations that focus on explaining why a particular solution to a problem exists [10, 13, 16]. However, these existing approaches to generating explanations are primarily focused on conflict. While sometimes such conflict-based explanations may be helpful, in the context of interactive constraint satisfaction such explanations are of limited value to a user who wishes to progress through the interactive process by finding assignments that are guaranteed to yield a solution. Recent work on tradeoff generation [5] is closely related to the notion of corrective explanation. However, a tradeoff is essentially a binary constraint. A corrective explanation can be much more general.

We see our research developing along three fronts. Firstly, there are strong links between the notion of corrective explanation and that of a diagnosis in both model-based diagnosis [15] and ATMS [3]. However, while diagnosis algorithms focus on finding all diagnoses, we are interested in finding a single diagnosis which can be used to form the basis of an explanation. Building on the work of Junker [9], we plan to further explore the potential for relaxation-focused algorithms for finding corrective explanations. Secondly, we will address the issue of computing corrective explanations that take users' preferences into account. Thirdly, in this paper we considered one possible algorithm for finding corrective explanations, in addition to the heuristic approach we have proposed previously [12]. However, there are other search-based techniques that we could consider, for example, repair-based techniques [7] as well as techniques for solving dynamic CSPs [17].

6 Conclusion

Interactive tasks such as online configuration and e-commerce can be modelled as constraint satisfaction problems (CSPs). These can be solved interactively by a user assigning values to variables. In this paper we have characterised a class of explanations that have not been previously studied in the field of constraint satisfaction. Such explanations focus on how to overcome inconsistency, rather than explain its presence. We call these corrective explanations.

We have proposed an algorithm for generating minimal corrective explanations, and have demonstrated that such an approach is practical. We evaluated the approach on both real-world configuration benchmarks and randomly generated problems with encouraging results. Finally, we outlined aspects of our research agenda in this area.

Acknowledgements. This work has received support from Enterprise Ireland (Grant SC/2002/289) and Science Foundation Ireland (Grant 00/PI.1/C075). The authors would like to thank Alex Ferguson, Tudor Hulubei, Chavalit Likitvivatanavong and Nic Wilson for their comments on an earlier draft of this paper.

References

1. Jérôme Amilhastre, Hélène Fargier, and Pierre Marguis. Consistency restoration and explanations in dynamic csps – application to configuration. *Artificial Intelligence*, 135:199–234, 2002.
2. James Bowen. Using dependency records to generate design coordination advice in a constraint-based approach to concurrent engineering. *Computers in Industry*, 22(1):191–199, 1997.
3. Johan de Kleer. A comparison of ATMS and CSP techniques. In *Proceedings of IJCAI-89*, pages 290–296, 1989.
4. Eugene C. Freuder, Chavalit Likitvivatanavong, Manuela Moretti, Francesca Rossi, and Richard J. Wallace. Computing explanations and implications in preference-based configurators. In *Recent Advances in Constraints*, LNAI 2627, pages 76–92, 2003.
5. Eugene C. Freuder and Barry O'Sullivan. Generating tradeoffs for interative constraint-based configuration. In *Proceedings of CP-2001*, pages 590–594, 2001.
6. VeCoS Group. Clib: Configuration benchmarks. http://www.itu.dk/doi/VeCoS/clib/.
7. William D. Harvey and Matthew L. Ginsberg. Limited discrepancy search. In *Proceedings of IJCAI-95*, pages 607–615, 1995.
8. Emmanuel Hebrard, Brahim Hnich, Barry O'Sullivan, and Toby Walsh. Finding similar and diverse solutions in constraint programming. In *Proceedings of AAAI-2005*, pages 372–377, 2005.
9. Ulrich Junker. QUICKXPLAIN: Preferred explanations and relaxations for over-constrained problems. In *Proceedings AAAI-2004*, pages 167 – 172, 2004.
10. Narendra Jussien and Vincent Barichard. The PaLM system: explanation-based constraint programming. In *Proceedings of CP-2000 TRICS Workshop*, pages 118–133, 2000.
11. Barry O'Callaghan, Eugene C. Freuder, and Barry O'Sullivan. Useful explanations. In *Proceedings of CP-2003*, LNCS 2833, page 988, 2003.
12. Barry O'Sullivan, Barry O'Callaghan, and Eugene C. Freuder. Corrective explanation for interactive constraint satisfaction. In *Proceedings of IJCAI-2005*, 2005. Poster.
13. Samir Ouis, Narendra Jussien, and Patrice Boizumault. COINS: a constraint-based interactive solving system. In *Proceedings of ICLP-2002 Workshop on Logic Programming Environments*, pages 31 – 46, 2002.
14. Jean-Francois Puget. The next challenge for CP: Ease of use. Invited Talk at CP-2004.
15. Raymond Reiter. A theory of diagnosis from first principles. *Artificial Intelligence*, 32(1):57–95, 1987.
16. Mohammed H. Sqalli and Eugene C. Freuder. Inference-based constraint satisfaction supports explanation. In *Proceedings of AAAI-96*, pages 318–325, 1996.
17. Gérard Verfaillie and Thomas Schiex. Solution reuse in dynamic constraint satisfaction problems. In *Proceedings of AAAI-94*, pages 307–312, Seattle, 1994.

sPREAd:
A Balancing Constraint Based on Statistics

Gilles Pesant[1] and Jean-Charles Régin[2]

[1] ILOG, 1681 route des Dolines, 06560 Valbonne, France
[2] Computing and Information Science, Cornell University, Ithaca NY 14850 USA[*]
pesant@crt.umontreal.ca, jcregin@cs.cornell.edu

Abstract. Many combinatorial problems require of their solutions that they achieve a certain balance of given features. In the constraint programming literature, little has been written to specifically address this issue, particularly at the modeling level. We propose a new constraint dedicated to balancing, based on well-known and well-understood concepts in statistics. We show how it can be used to model different situations in which balance is important. We also design efficient filtering algorithms to guide the search towards balanced solutions.

1 Introduction

We have seen many advances in CP modeling in recent years. Useful problem substructures have been identified, leading to new constraints with efficient filtering algorithms. Soft constraints have been introduced to handle over-constrained problems. Lexicographic constraints have been designed to break problem symmetries. Efforts to automate the modeling process have also been made.

One aspect that has lacked a truly satisfying approach to date is the ability to balance certain features of a solution. Take for example the balanced academic curriculum problem [1], in which courses are assigned to periods so as to balance the academic load between periods. Because of additional constraints (prerequisite courses, minimum and maximum number of courses per period) and a varying number of credits per course, reaching perfect balance is generally impossible. Given that, some common ways of encouraging balance at the modeling level are:

  $a)$ to set reasonable bounds on each load, tolerating a certain deviation from the ideal value;
  $b)$ to minimize the greatest load, thus avoiding outliers (or at least those above the ideal value);
  $c)$ to take the least square error.

---

[*] Research conducted while the first author was on sabbatical leave from École Polytechnique de Montréal and while the second author was on sabbatical leave from ILOG.

The first two options both have the disadvantage of putting on an equal footing solutions with quite different balance:

a) If we require that loads belong to $[8, 12]$, aiming for an ideal load of 10, then sets of loads $\{10, 10, 10, 10, 9, 11\}$ and $\{8, 8, 8, 12, 12, 12\}$ both satisfy the restriction but the former is much more balanced. The situation could be corrected somewhat by only allowing deviations for a few of the loads, but which ones should it be? We run the risk of being unfair (ironically) or, even worse, of excluding legitimate solutions.

b) Loads $\{10, 10, 10, 10, 9, 11\}$ and $\{9, 9, 9, 11, 11, 11\}$ both have a greatest load of 11 but again the former is more balanced.

The last option corrects this by considering a combination of individual deviations. However it requires that we solve a discrete optimization problem, with a nonlinear objective as is the case for the second option. This may not be easy and, if other real objectives are present, we have to come up with suitable weights for the different terms of the objective function. Balance can also be dealt with in the search strategy: by keeping track of previous course assignments, we can favor certain future assignments that will improve the balance. This is helpful but using it on its own means that an important aspect of the problem is not present at all in the model itself.

Balance is often important in assignment problems or in problems with an assignment component. We give a few examples. In assembly line balancing the workload of the line operators must be balanced. In rostering we may talk of fairness instead of balance, because of the human factor. Here we want a fair distribution of weekends off or of night shifts among workers, for example. In vehicle routing one dimension of the problem is to partition the customers into the different routes — balancing the number of customers served on each route, the quantity of goods delivered, or the time required to complete the route may be of interest. In one of the few works specifically addressing balance in the context of constraint satisfaction, an earth observation satellite scheduling and sharing problem is used to investigate three ways of handling fairness among agents with competing observation requirements [3]. The first one applies a decomposition into individual problems, each with a fair share of observation windows, but overall efficiency suffers. The second one favors efficiency and sets a lower bound on individual shares for fairness (option *a)* above). The third one computes a set of Pareto-optimal solutions in the two-dimensional space of overall efficiency and fairness. To evaluate fairness, they use the Gini index, popular in microeconomics.

We could describe the balance we seek in the following way:

- the average value should be close to a given target, corresponding to the ideal value;
- there should be no outliers, as they would correspond to an unbalanced situation;
- values should be grouped around the average value.

We claim that statistics provide appropriate mathematical concepts to express this. We will propose a constraint expressing balance in a way similar to the method of least squares mentioned before but by setting limits on the deviation instead of minimizing an objective which must be weighted relative to other potential objectives.

The rest of this paper is organized as follows. Section 2 reviews some basic concepts and definitions in statistics. Section 3 defines the new constraint based on statistics that we propose and presents typical uses. Section 4 derives some inequalities bounding the number of variables taking extreme values and uses them to filter the domains of the variables. Section 5 builds up to another filtering algorithm, this one achieving bounds consistency.

2 Statistics Background

Given a collection of numbers, even simple summary statistics about them can be revealing. *Measures of location* tell us about the central tendency of the values. The most common such measures are the mode, the median, and the mean. The *mode* is the value(s) occurring most often in a given collection of numbers. The *median*, denoted $\tilde{x}$, is the smallest value such that at least half of the numbers are no larger than it, and at least half of the numbers are at least as large as it. We will prefer to use the mean because it is instrumental in telling us how many values may exceed a given threshold, which will prove useful to filter domains.

Definition 1 (Mean). *The* (arithmetic) mean *of a collection of values $\langle x_1, x_2, \ldots, x_n \rangle$, denoted μ, is computed as*

$$\mu = \frac{1}{n} \sum_{i=1}^{n} x_i. \tag{1}$$

Measures of spread tell us whether the values tend to be bunched together or spread out. The most common measures are the range, the semi-quartile range, and the standard deviation. The *range* is the size of the smallest interval containing all the values. Unfortunately that measure is highly sensitive to outliers. The *semi-quartile range*, half the size of the smallest interval containing fifty percent of the most central values, partially overcomes that drawback. We favor the more familiar standard deviation, partly for the same reason as the mean: we will be able to limit the number of values straying away from the center.

Definition 2 (Standard Deviation). *The* standard (or root-mean-square) deviation *of a collection of values $\langle x_1, x_2, \ldots, x_n \rangle$, denoted σ, is computed as*

$$\sigma = \left(\frac{1}{n} \sum_{i=1}^{n} (x_i - \mu)^2 \right)^{\frac{1}{2}}. \tag{2}$$

An alternate way of computing the standard deviation, which is more numerically stable, is obtained through the *Koenig-Huyghens relation*:

$$\sigma^2 = \frac{1}{n} \sum_{i=1}^{n} x_i^2 - \mu^2. \tag{3}$$

Measures of skewness tell us about the general shape of the distribution of values. Two collections of values with identical mean and standard deviation may nevertheless be significantly different. A perfectly symmetric *continuous* distribution will have its median and mean coincide. A distribution with a positive (resp. negative) bias will have $\tilde{x} < \mu$ (resp. $\tilde{x} > \mu$). The *Pearson coefficient*, computed as $3(\mu - \tilde{x})/\sigma$, is one way to measure skewness. The simpler form $\mu - \tilde{x}$ at least preserves the sign of the bias.

Two well-known inequalities for random variables can be recast for our purpose. They can be useful to derive filtering algorithms.

Theorem 1 (Markov's Inequality). *Consider a collection of non-negative values $\langle x_1, x_2, \ldots, x_n \rangle$ with mean μ, and some threshold τ. Then the fraction of these values that are greater or equal to τ is at most $\frac{\mu}{\tau}$.*

For example, if the threshold selected is three times the mean then at most one third of the values are no smaller than that threshold.

Theorem 2 (Bienaymé-Chebychev's Inequality). *Consider a collection of values $\langle x_1, x_2, \ldots, x_n \rangle$ with mean μ and standard deviation σ, and some positive number k. Then the fraction of these values that are $k\sigma$ or further from μ is at most $\frac{1}{k^2}$.*

This important result bounds the number of values that can be far from the mean. For example, at most 25% of the values may be two standard deviations away from the mean and at most 4% may be five standard deviations away.

3 The Spread Constraint

This section defines and discusses the constraint we propose. We first give some basic definitions and notation in constraint programming.

Definition 3 (Finite-Domain (Discrete) Variable). *A finite-domain (discrete) variable x takes a value in $D(x)$, a finite set called its* domain. *Whenever there is a total order defined on that set (e.g. when it is a subset of $\mathbb{N}$), we denote the smallest (resp. largest) value x may take as $x^{\min}$ (resp. $x^{\max}$).*

Definition 4 (Bounded-Domain (Continuous) Variable). *A bounded-domain (continuous) variable y takes a value in $I_D(y) = [y^{\min}, y^{\max}]$, an interval on $\mathbb{R}$ called its* domain *as well.*

Definition 5 (Relaxed Domain). *Given finite-domain variable x, we denote by $I_D(x)$ its domain relaxed to the continuous interval $[x^{\min}, x^{\max}]$. By extension for a union of domains $\mathcal{D} = \bigcup_{i=1}^{n} D(x_i)$, let $I_{\mathcal{D}}$ represent the continuous interval $[\min_{i=1}^{n} x_i^{\min}, \max_{i=1}^{n} x_i^{\max}]$.*

We are now ready to state the constraint:

Definition 6 (Spread Constraint). *Given a set of finite-domain variables $X = \{x_1, x_2, \ldots, x_n\}$ and bounded-domain continuous variables μ, σ, and $\tilde{x}$, constraint* $\mathtt{spread}(X, \mu, \sigma, \tilde{x})$ *states that the collection of values taken by the variables of X exhibits an arithmetic mean μ, a standard deviation σ, and a median $\tilde{x}$.*

There are clear advantages to this formulation. First, it is not affected by a permutation of the values given to the x_i's. No particular variable or subset of variables is a priori identified as taking a lower value than others, for example, which might be necessary with other approaches to fairness, ironically introducing a bias. Second, it is not affected by the sign of the deviation. The impact on the standard deviation of a value away from the mean is the same whether the value is above or below the mean. Finally, it is based on well-established concepts in statistics.

3.1 Typical Uses

We outline some typical uses of the constraint by focusing on how μ is constrained and illustrate them with examples taken from rostering. First note that if we set σ to 0, we are asking for perfect fairness: every x_i should be identical. If in essence we have a fixed number of balls to distribute as evenly as possible into a fixed number of boxes, μ is fixed since it corresponds to the ratio of the number of balls to the number of boxes. We constrain the variables by limiting σ. This situation occurs, for example, when night shifts should be evenly distributed among 10 staff members and we know that there are exactly 200 night shifts to cover:

$$\mathtt{spread}(X, 20, [0, 1], \tilde{x})$$

If on the contrary the number of balls is unknown, μ is not fixed. We may have some approximate idea of what the mean should be and in this case μ is constrained around that approximation. For example, weekends off should be evenly spread over the whole planning horizon in an individual schedule. Taking our variables to be the size of the gaps between such weekends and even given the number of them, the mean may not be known because of the uncertainty as to where the last weekend off falls. Nevertheless, we may wish for a typical gap of 3:

$$\mathtt{spread}(X, [2.8, 3.2], [0, 0.5], \tilde{x})$$

Other times we have no idea what the mean could be and μ is left free. For example, a weekend on which one day is worked and the other not is called a "broken" weekend, a generally undesirable feature. We often do not know in advance how many such weekends will occur in a schedule but we nevertheless wish the number of broken weekends to be evenly distributed among all staff members. Considering a roster over w weeks, we could state:

$$\mathtt{spread}(X, [0, w], [0, \frac{w}{3}], \tilde{x})$$

If two of the staff members have more seniority, their number of broken weekends should be about half that of the others:

$$y_1 = 2x_1, \; y_2 = 2x_2, \; y_i = x_i \; (3 \leq i \leq n), \quad \texttt{spread}(Y, [0, w], [0, \frac{w}{3}], \tilde{x})$$

Since broken weekends are undesirable, we could prefer instead that the distribution of values does not show a negative bias, i.e. there should not be a majority of staff members with an above-average number of such weekends:

$$0 \leq \tilde{x} \leq \mu \leq w, \quad \texttt{oproad}(X, \mu, [0, \frac{w}{3}], \tilde{x})$$

4 Fast Filtering

It would be difficult to efficiently achieve domain consistency on the spread constraint because even in the special case where μ is fixed, we are left with a linear Diophantine equation originating from Definition 1. In the case of Definition 2, it is not even linear. Bounds consistency is a common compromise in such a case. At a minimum, we can apply bounds consistency on (1) and (3).

Example 1. Consider a set of ten variables required to take integer values from $\{7, 8, \ldots, 13\}$ such that $\mu \in [9.5, 10.5]$. Suppose that at some point five of the variables are fixed to value 13. Bounds consistency on (1) alone will remove 13 from the domain of every other variable as there is no support for a sixth variable taking that value: $[9.5, 10.5] \cap (6 \times 13 + 4 \times [7, 13])/10 = [9.5, 10.5] \cap [10.6, 13] = \emptyset$.

Theorem 1 bounds the number of occurrences of values far from the mean. We could extend this result to filter the domains of the variables in X but it would not give us more than bounds consistency on (1). However Theorem 2 also bounds the number of occurrences of values far from the mean and we will show that it can lead to more filtering than bounds consistency on (1) and (3).

4.1 Exploiting Bienaymé-Chebychev's Inequality

We wish to derive a family of inequalities for consecutive integer thresholds away from the mean. The key observation is that the value k in the theorem need not be integer: we therefore use appropriate values of k that will provide the integer thresholds we need. By seeking these exact values we obtain the strongest possible bounds from the theorem.

Let $\mathcal{D} = \bigcup_{i=1}^n D(x_i)$ and $I_\mathcal{D} = [a, b]$. Define variables c_ℓ, $\ell \in \{a, a+1, \ldots, b\}$ as the number of times a variable from X takes value ℓ. First consider the case $\mu - a \geq b - \mu$. Since this means there is at least as much slack below μ as there is above, we focus on threshold values below, that is $a + j$ for $0 \leq j < \mu - a$. For each threshold $a + j$ we seek k such that $\mu - k\sigma = a + j$, in order to get the smallest bound $\frac{1}{k^2}$. Solving for k we obtain $k = \frac{\mu - a - j}{\sigma}$, yielding:

$$\sum_{\ell=a}^{a+j} c_\ell + \sum_{\ell=\mu^{\max}+\mu^{\min}-(a+j)}^{b} c_\ell \leq \lfloor \frac{\sigma^2}{(\mu-a-j)^2} \cdot n \rfloor \quad 0 \leq j < \mu - a \quad (4)$$

The lower limit in the second sum ensures that it only considers values that are at least $\mu - (a+j)$ away from the mean, as in the first sum.

Similarly when $\mu - a < b - \mu$, for each threshold $b - j$ we seek k such that $\mu + k\sigma = b - j$, yielding:

$$\sum_{\ell=a}^{\mu^{\min}-((b-j)-\mu^{\max})} c_\ell + \sum_{\ell=b-j}^{b} c_\ell \leq \lfloor \frac{\sigma^2}{(b-\mu-j)^2} \cdot n \rfloor \qquad 0 \leq j < b - \mu \quad (5)$$

These inequalities can lead to better filtering than bounds consistency on (1) and (3) because they simultaneously take into account μ and σ, as illustrated in the following example.

Example 2. Consider again the situation depicted in Example 1 with the additional restriction that $\sigma \in [0, 0.4]$. The left-hand side of (3) consequently lies in $[0, 0.16]$, which has plenty of overlap with the right-hand side ($10 \times [7^2, 13^2] - [9.5^2, 10.5^2])/10 \subset [-61.25, 78.75]$. It is easy to verify that (3) is bounds consistent: for example, checking value 7 only shrinks the right-hand side to $[-61.25, 66.75]$. Equation (1) is bounds consistent as well. However inequality (4) for $j = 1$ gives $c_7 + c_8 + c_{12} + c_{13} \leq \lfloor 0.7\bar{1} \rfloor = 0$. In other words, the domain of each x_i can be narrowed to $\{9, 10, 11\}$.

The c_ℓ variables are the same we would use in a global cardinality constraint except that here we do not bound them individually but in telescoping sums. We can maintain bounds consistency on each inequality in $\mathcal{O}(b-a)$ time and use an *upper bound constraint* (half of a gcc) between the c_ℓ's and the x_i's on which we maintain bounds consistency in $\mathcal{O}(n+t)$ time where t is the time required to sort the x_i's by their bounds [4]. (Note however that we do not necessarily achieve bounds consistency on the spread constraint as Example 3 will show.) The overall time complexity is $\mathcal{O}(n+t+(b-a)^2)$. Since n, the number of variables, is typically much larger than $b-a$, the span of the values, the algorithm runs in linear time under the reasonable assumption that $b-a$ is a small constant.

4.2 Median

Simple inequalities follow from the definition of the median:

$$\sum_{i=a}^{\tilde{x}^{\min}-1} c_\ell < \lfloor \frac{n}{2} \rfloor, \qquad \sum_{i=a}^{\tilde{x}^{\max}} c_\ell \geq \lceil \frac{n}{2} \rceil \quad (6)$$

$$\sum_{i=\tilde{x}^{\max}+1}^{b} c_\ell < \lfloor \frac{n}{2} \rfloor, \qquad \sum_{i=\tilde{x}^{\min}}^{b} c_\ell \geq \lceil \frac{n}{2} \rceil \quad (7)$$

We can maintain bounds consistency on them as well but here we should combine them with a (full) bounds consistent gcc constraint [4][2]. To filter on $\tilde{x}$, we can use the fact that $\tilde{x} = \min\{k \mid \sum_{i=a}^{k} c_\ell \geq \lceil \frac{n}{2} \rceil\} = \max\{k \mid \sum_{i=k}^{b} c_\ell \geq \lceil \frac{n}{2} \rceil\}$.

5   A Bounds Consistency Algorithm

The algorithm of the previous section did not consider the individual domains of the x_i's but worked instead from the smallest interval containing all of them. Even a very simple example like Example 3 is enough to show that some filtering may be missed when the domains are significantly different. This section describes an algorithm that takes into account the span of each individual domain of the x_i's and that achieves bounds consistency for the spread constraint.

Example 3. Consider two variables with respective domains $\{7, 8\}$ and $\{12, 13\}$ such that $\mu \in [9.5, 10.5]$ and $\sigma \in [0, 2]$. Equations (1) and (3) are bounds consistent and inequality (4) for $j = 0$ gives $c_7 + c_{13} \leq \lfloor 1.28 \rfloor = 1$ but there is clearly no solution with 7 or 13.

5.1   Establishing the Optimal Value

Definition 7. *Let $X = \{x_1, x_2, \ldots, x_n\}$ as before and define the following problem $\Pi(X, q)$ for some fixed number q:*

$$\min \sum_{i=1}^{n}(x_i - \frac{q}{n})^2 \text{ such that } \sum_{i=1}^{n} x_i = q, \quad x_i \in I_D(x_i) \; 1 \leq i \leq n.$$

We also define the more general problem $\Pi(X, [\ell_q, u_q])$:

$$\min \sum_{i=1}^{n}(x_i - \frac{q}{n})^2 \text{ such that } \sum_{i=1}^{n} x_i = q, \quad x_i \in I_D(x_i) \; 1 \leq i \leq n, \quad q \in [\ell_q, u_q].$$

We will denote by $\text{opt}(\Pi)$ the optimal value of the problem Π.

Definition 8. *An assignment $A : x \mapsto I_D(x)$ over X is said to be a ν-centered assignment when*

$$A(x) = \begin{cases} x^{\max}, & \text{if } x^{\max} \leq \nu \\ x^{\min}, & \text{if } x^{\min} \geq \nu \\ \nu, & \text{otherwise} \end{cases}$$

Lemma 1. *Any optimal solution to $\Pi(X, q)$ must be a ν-centered assignment.*

Proof. The objective function of $\Pi(X, q)$ can be rewritten as follows: $\sum(x_i - \frac{q}{n})^2 = (\sum x_i^2) - \frac{q^2}{n}$ because $\sum x_i = q$. Thus, for a given q the minimum value of $\sum(x_i - \frac{q}{n})^2$ can be deduced from the minimum value of $\sum x_i^2$. Consider an assignment A on X which is a solution to $\Pi(X, q)$ but not a ν-centered assignment. We prove that $\sum(A(x_i))^2$ is not optimal by constructing another assignment B such that $\sum(B(x_i))^2 < \sum(A(x_i))^2$. There are three ways in which A may fail to be a ν-centered assignment:

- $\exists \, i, j$ s.t. $x_i^{\min} < A(x_i) < x_i^{\max}$, $x_j^{\min} < A(x_j) < x_j^{\max}$, and $A(x_i) > A(x_j)$. Define B as $B(x_i) = A(x_i) - d$, $B(x_j) = A(x_j) + d$, $B(x_k) = A(x_k)$ for $k \neq i, j$,

Table 1. Relevant values computed from Example 4

I	$ES(I)$	$|M(I)|$	$V(I)$	$GC(I)$	q-opt($\Pi(X,I)$)	opt($\Pi(X,I)$)
$[0,1]$	13	2	$[13,15]$	18	15	19.5
$[1,2]$	12	3	$[15,18]$	24	18	12.0
$[2,3]$	14	2	$[18,20]$	21	20	$8.\bar{3}$
$[3,4]$	8	4	$[20,24]$	24	24	8.0
$[4,5]$	16	2	$[24,26]$	24	24	8.0
$[5,6]$	26	0	$[26,26]$	26	26	$9.\bar{3}$
$[6,9]$	20	1	$[26,29]$	24	26	$9.\bar{3}$

where $d = \frac{1}{2}\min((x_j^{\max} - A(x_j)), (A(x_i) - A(x_j)), (A(x_i) - x_i^{\min}))$. Then B is also a solution to $\Pi(X,q)$ from the definition of B and the choice of d. Now $(B(x_i))^2 + (B(x_j))^2 = (A(x_i) - d)^2 + (A(x_j) + d)^2 = (A(x_i))^2 + (A(x_j))^2 + 2d(A(x_j) - A(x_i) + d)$. Since $A(x_j) < A(x_i)$, $d > 0$ and $d \leq (A(x_i) - A(x_j))/2$ we have that $2d(A(x_j) - A(x_i) + d) < 0$. Thus $(B(x_i))^2 + (B(x_j))^2 < (A(x_i))^2 + (A(x_j))^2$ and B is a better assignment.

- $\exists\ i$ s.t. $A(x_i) = x_i^{\max} > \nu$ (and the symmetric case $A(x_i) = x_i^{\min} < \nu$). Take j s.t. $A(x_j) = \nu < x_j^{\max}$ (if we cannot find such a j then we are in the third case below). Build B as in the first case.
- $\exists\ i,j$ s.t. $A(x_i) = x_i^{\max}$, $A(x_j) = x_j^{\min}$, and $A(x_i) > A(x_j)$ (i.e. the two groups overlap). Build B as in the first case. □

To simplify the analysis, we first partition $I_\mathcal{D}$ into intervals in which the status of the relaxed domains of the x_i's does not vary: each either completely lies to the left or right, or completely contains the interval. We then exhibit a particular ν-centered assignment and show that it is an optimal solution to $\Pi(X,q)$. Finally we generalize for an unspecified value $q \in [\ell_q, u_q]$.

Definition 9. *Let $B(X)$ be the sorted sequence of bounds of the relaxed domains of the variables of X, in non-decreasing order and with duplicates removed. Define $\mathcal{I}(X)$ as the set of intervals defined by a pair of two consecutive elements of $B(X)$. The kth interval of $\mathcal{I}(X)$ is denoted by I_k.*

Example 4. Let $D(x_1) = [0,2]$, $D(x_2) = [1,4]$, $D(x_3) = [0,5]$, $D(x_4) = [3,5]$, $D(x_5) = [3,4]$, $D(x_6) = [6,9]$. Then $I_1 = [0,1]$, $I_2 = [1,2]$, $I_3 = [2,3]$, $I_4 = [3,4]$, $I_5 = [4,5]$, $I_6 = [5,6]$, $I_7 = [6,9]$.

Definition 10. $\underline{S}(X) = \sum_{x \in X} x^{\min}$ *and* $\overline{S}(X) = \sum_{x \in X} x^{\max}$.
Let I be an interval of $\mathcal{I}(X)$. Then
- $R(I) = \{x \mid x^{\min} \geq \max(I)\}$, *the variables lying to the right of I*
- $L(I) = \{x \mid x^{\max} \leq \min(I)\}$, *the variables lying to the left of I*
- $M(I) = \{x \mid I \subseteq I_D(x)\}$, *the variables overlapping I*
- $ES(I) = \sum_{x \in L(I)} x^{\max} + \sum_{x \in R(I)} x^{\min}$
- $V(I) = [ES(I) + \min(I) \times |M(I)|, ES(I) + \max(I) \times |M(I)|]$

Lemma 2. $ES(I_{k+1}) = ES(I_k) + (p_{k+1} - q_{k+1}) \times \max(I_k)$,
where $p_{k+1} = |L(I_{k+1})| - |L(I_k)|$ and $q_{k+1} = |R(I_k)| - |R(I_{k+1})|$.

Proof. $\forall x \in (R(I_k) - R(I_{k+1}))$ $x^{\min} = \min(I_{k+1})$ and $\forall x \in (L(I_{k+1}) - L(I_k))$ $x^{\max} = \max(I_k)$. From Def. 9 $\max(I_k) = \min(I_{k+1})$. $\square$

Proposition 1. $\forall a \in [\underline{S}(X), \overline{S}(X)]$ there exists $I \in \mathcal{I}(X)$ such that $a \in V(I)$.

Proof. We already have $\min(V(I_1)) = \underline{S}(X)$ and $\max(V(I_{|\mathcal{I}(X)|})) = \overline{S}(X)$. It is therefore sufficient to show that for any two consecutive intervals I_k, I_{k+1} from $\mathcal{I}(X)$, we have $\min(V(I_{k+1})) = \max(V(I_k))$, thus leaving no gaps. Let $m_k = |M(I_k)|$ and $m_{k+1} = |M(I_{k+1})|$. From Lemma 2, $\min(V(I_{k+1})) = ES(I_{k+1}) + m_{k+1} \min(I_{k+1}) = ES(I_k) + (p_{k+1} - q_{k+1}) \max(I_k) + m_{k+1} \min(I_{k+1})$. In addition, $m_{k+1} = m_k - p_{k+1} + q_{k+1}$ and $\min(I_{k+1}) = \max(I_k)$. Therefore $\min(V(I_{k+1})) = ES(I_k) + \max(I_k) \times |M(I_k)| = \max(V(I_k))$. $\square$

Definition 11. Given a value q such that $q \in [\underline{S}(X), \overline{S}(X)]$ and I such that $q \in V(I)$, define the following assignment $A_{q,I}$ on X:

$$A_{q,I}(x) = \begin{cases} x^{\max}, & x \in L(I) \\ x^{\min}, & x \in R(I) \\ (q - ES(I))/|M(I)|, & x \in M(I) \end{cases}$$

Lemma 3. Assignment $A_{q,I}$ is a feasible solution to $\Pi(X,q)$ and is ν-centered.

Proof. We first have to show that every variable is assigned a value within its relaxed domain. It is immediate in the first two cases but not so for $x \in M(I)$. Since $q \in V(I)$, we have $q - ES(I) \in [\min(I) \times |M(I)|, \max(I) \times |M(I)|]$ and so $(q - ES(I))/|M(I)| \in [\min(I), \max(I)] = I \subseteq I_D(x)$, by definition of $M(I)$. This also shows that $A_{q,I}$ is ν-centered with $\nu = (q - ES(I))/|M(I)|$. As for the sum, $\sum_{i=1}^{n} A_{q,I}(x) = ES(I) + |M(I)|(q - ES(I))/|M(I)| = q$. $\square$

Theorem 3. $A_{q,I}$ is an optimal solution to $\Pi(X,q)$.

Proof. Given lemmas 1 and 3, it is sufficient to show that $A_{q,I}$ is the unique feasible ν-centered assignment for $\Pi(X,q)$. Suppose A' is another such assignment. There is at least one variable x_j such that $A'(x_j) > A_{q,I}(x_j)$ because $A_{q,I}$ and A' are not equal but have the same sum. So, $A'(x_j) > x_j^{\min}$ and from Def. 8 for A' we have $\forall i$ s.t. $A'(x_i) < A'(x_j) : A'(x_i) = x_i^{\max} \geq A_{q,I}(x_i)$. Then, consider any variable x_i with $A'(x_i) \geq A'(x_j)$ and assume that $A_{q,I}(x_i) > A'(x_i)$. In this case, $A_{q,I}(x_i) > A_{q,I}(x_j)$ and since $x_j^{\max} \geq A'(x_j) > A_{q,I}(x_j)$ Def. 8 for $A_{q,I}$ implies that $A_{q,I}(x_i) = x_i^{\min}$ which is not possible because $A_{q,I}(x_i) > A'(x_i)$. Therefore $\forall i$ s.t. $A'(x_i) \geq A'(x_j): A'(x_i) \geq A_{q,I}(x_i)$. Thus, $\forall i = 1..n, i \neq j : A'(x_i) \geq A_{q,I}(x_i)$ and $A'(x_j) > A_{q,I}(x_j)$ so the sum of the elements of $A_{q,I}$ cannot be equal to the sum of the elements of A'. $\square$

Next we propose to do the same thing for the more general problem $\Pi(X, [\ell_q, u_q])$.

Theorem 4. *Given $I \in \mathcal{I}(X)$ and $GC(I) = n \times ES(I)/(n - |M(I)|)$. We will denote by q-opt$(\Pi(X, V(I)))$ the value of $q \in V(I)$ for which the objective value of $\Pi(X, V(I))$ is optimal. Then*
  (i) *If $GC(I) \in V(I)$ then q-opt$(\Pi(X, V(I))) = GC(I)$.*
  (ii) *If $GC(I) > \max(V(I))$ then q-opt$(\Pi(X, V(I))) = \max(V(I))$.*
  (iii) *If $GC(I) < \min(V(I))$ then q-opt$(\Pi(X, V(I))) = \min(V(I))$.*

Proof. Consider $q \in V(I)$ and $q' \in V(I)$ with $q \neq q'$. From Theorem 3 $A_{q,I}$ is an optimal solution of $\Pi(X,q)$, $A_{q',I}$ is an optimal solution of $\Pi(X,q')$. We have $\sum (x_i - \frac{q}{n})^2 = (\sum x_i^2) - \frac{q^2}{n}$ and let $D(q,q') = \sum (A_{q,I}(x) - \frac{q}{n})^2 - \sum (A_{q',I}(x) - \frac{q'}{n})^2$. The values q and q' belong to $V(I)$ so $\forall x \in (L(I) \cup R(I))$: $A_{q,I}(x) = A_{q',I}(x)$. Therefore the sums of the squares for $A_{q,I}$ and $A_{q',I}$ differ only for the elements of $M(I)$. If $M(I) = \emptyset$ then $\min(V(I)) = \max(V(I))$ so $q' \neq q$ does not exist. Let $m = |M(I)|$ and $e = ES(I)$. For $A_{q,I}$ we have $x \in M(I) \Rightarrow A_{q,I}(x) = (q-e)/m$, so $\sum_{x \in M(I)} A_{q,I}(x)^2 = \sum_{x \in M(I)}((q-e)/m)^2 = \frac{1}{m}(q^2 + e^2 - 2qe)$. Thus $D(q,q') = \frac{1}{m}(q^2 + e^2 - 2qe) - \frac{q^2}{n} - \frac{1}{m}((q')^2 + e^2 - 2q'e) + \frac{(q')^2}{n}$ or $D(q,q') = \frac{1}{nm}((n-m)(q^2 - (q')^2) - 2ne(q-q'))$. Let $q' = q - \alpha$ for some $\alpha \neq 0$ then $D(q, q - \alpha) = \frac{\alpha}{nm}[(n-m)(2q - \alpha) - 2ne] = \frac{2\alpha q(n-m)}{nm} - \frac{\alpha^2(n-m)}{nm} - \frac{2\alpha ne}{nm}$. Now, we can use this property to prove the theorem:

  (i) Let $q = GC(I) = \frac{ne}{n-m}$ then $D(q, q - \alpha) = \frac{-\alpha^2(n-m)}{nm}$ therefore since $n > m$ for all α such that $(q - \alpha) \in V(I)$, $D(q, q - \alpha) < 0$ so q-opt$(\Pi(X, V(I))) = q$.

  (ii) Let $q = max(V(I))$ then $D(q, q - \alpha) = \frac{2\alpha max(V(I))(n-m)}{nm} - \frac{\alpha^2(n-m)}{nm} - \frac{2\alpha ne}{nm}$. We have $GC(I) = \frac{ne}{n-m} > max(V(I))$ and $n > m$ and $q - \alpha < max(V(I)) \Rightarrow \alpha > 0$ so $\frac{2\alpha max(V(I))(n-m)}{nm} < \frac{2\alpha(ne/(n-m))(n-m)}{nm} = \frac{2\alpha ne}{nm}$. Therefore $D(q, q - \alpha) < \frac{-\alpha^2(n-m)}{nm} < 0$ because $n > m$. So q-opt$(\Pi(X, V(I))) = q = max(V(I))$.

  (iii) Let $q = min(V(I))$ then $D(q, q - \alpha) = \frac{2\alpha min(V(I))(n-m)}{nm} - \frac{\alpha^2(n-m)}{nm} - \frac{2\alpha ne}{nm}$. We have $GC(I) = ne/(n-m) < min(V(I))$ and $(n-m) > 0$ and $q - \alpha > min(V(I)) \Rightarrow \alpha < 0$ so $\alpha(n-m) < 0$ and $\frac{2\alpha min(V(I))(n-m)}{nm} < \frac{2\alpha(ne/(n-m))(n-m)}{nm} = \frac{2\alpha ne}{nm}$. Therefore $D(q, q - \alpha) < \frac{-\alpha^2(n-m)}{nm} < 0$ because $n > m$. So q-opt$(\Pi(X, V(I))) = q = min(V(I))$. □

Corollary 1. *Theorem 4 holds if $V(I)$ is replaced by $V(I) \cap [\ell_q, u_q]$ provided $V(I) \cap [\ell_q, u_q] \neq \emptyset$.*

5.2 Computing the Optimal Value

Given $\mathcal{I}$ and the x_i's sorted according to their bounds, Algorithm 1 computes q-opt$(\Pi(X, V(I)))$ and opt$(\Pi(X, V(I)))$ for all $I \in \mathcal{I}$ in linear time. Following the notation of Lemma 2 we have $p_k = |L(I_k)| - |L(I_{k-1})|$ and $q_k = |R(I_{k-1})| - |R(I_k)|$.

The two steps of the algorithm before the loop can certainly be performed in $O(n)$. We argue that each iteration of the loop can be computed in $O(p_k + q_k)$ time. Sets $L(I_k)$, $R(I_k)$, and $M(I_k)$ are obtained in p_k, q_k, and $p_k + q_k$ steps

SPREAD: A Balancing Constraint Based on Statistics   471

Algorithm 1. Computing q-opt($\Pi(X, V(I))$) and opt($\Pi(X, V(I))$) for all $I \in \mathcal{I}$

Compute $L(I_1)$, $R(I_1)$, $M(I_1)$, and $ES(I_1)$;
Compute q-opt($\Pi(X, V(I_1))$) and opt($\Pi(X, V(I_1))$) using Th. 4 and Def. 11 and 7;
for $k = 2$ to $|\mathcal{I}|$ do
  $L(I_k) \leftarrow L(I_{k-1}) \cup \{x \mid x^{\max} = \max(I_{k-1})\}$;
  $R(I_k) \leftarrow R(I_{k-1}) \setminus \{x \mid x^{\min} = \max(I_{k-1})\}$;
  $M(I_k) \leftarrow M(I_{k-1}) \setminus \{x \mid x^{\max} = \max(I_{k-1})\} \cup \{x \mid x^{\min} = \max(I_{k-1})\}$;
  $ES(I_k) \leftarrow ES(I_{k-1}) + (p_k - q_k) \times \max(I_{k-1})$;
  $V(I_k) \leftarrow [ES(I_k) \mid \min(I_k) \times |M(I_k)|, ES(I_k) + \max(I_k) \times |M(I_k)|]$;
  $GC(I_k) \leftarrow n \times ES(I_k)/(n - |M(I_k)|)$;
  Compute opt($\Pi(X, V(I_k))$) and opt($\Pi(X, V(I_k))$) using Th. 4, Def. 11 and 7;
---

respectively, which correspond to the number of elements added or deleted (each is obtained in constant time since the x_i's are sorted). From Lemma 2, $ES(I_k)$ can also be computed in $p_k + q_k$ steps. When all these values are known, $V(I_k)$ and $GC(I_k)$ can be computed in $O(1)$ so from Theorem 4 q-opt($\Pi(X, V(I_k))$) can be computed in $O(1)$. In addition, opt($\Pi(X, V(I_{k-1}))$) is known and $A_{q,I_{k-1}}$ has $p_k + q_k$ values different from A_{q',I_k} so opt($\Pi(X, V(I_k))$) can be computed with $O(p_k + q_k)$ operations using the formula $\sum (x_i - q)^2 = \sum (x_i)^2 - \frac{q^2}{n}$. Since $\sum_{k=1}^{n} p_k = n$ and $\sum_{k=1}^{n} q_k = n$, the total amount of time to compute q-opt($\Pi(X, V(I))$) and opt($\Pi(X, V(I))$) for all $I \in \mathcal{I}$ is in $O(n)$.

Therefore, if we are provided with a maximum value $\pi^{\max}$ for $\Pi(X, [\ell_q, u_q])$ then we can reduce the interval $[\mu^{\min}, \mu^{\max}]$ for μ since $q = n\mu$. Such a value can be easily obtained from σ^{max} because from Def. 2 and Def. 7 we have the relation $n(\sigma^{max})^2 = \pi^{max}$.

5.3   Bounds Reduction

We consider a variable x of X and we study the consequences of the modifications of the bounds of x. Of course if there is an interval I for which $A_{q,I}(x) = x^{\min}$ and opt($\Pi(X, V(I))$) is consistent with $\pi^{\max}$ (i.e. less than or equal to $\pi^{\max}$) then there is no need to consider any modification of the minimum, and the same reasoning can be applied to $x^{\max}$.

For a given interval I, we know how to compute efficiently the optimal solution opt($\Pi(X, V(I))$). Thus, we can study the consequences of the modification of the bounds of x for this interval, that is searching what are the minimum and the maximum values that x can take while opt($\Pi(X, V(I))$) $\leq \pi^{\max}$. Then, we can repeat this process for all the intervals. Efficiently computing the new possible bounds of x is not obvious because when x is changing the possible sum of the variables is also changing and this impacts the value $GC(I)$, and the optimal value of $\Pi(X, V(I))$ depends on it. The following propositions show how to compute them. For convenience let I be an interval, $m = |M(I)|$, $e = ES(I)$, $\delta = \pi^{\max} - $opt($\Pi(X, V(I))$). and $sol(a, b, c) = \frac{-b+\sqrt{b^2-ac}}{a}$.

Proposition 2. *Given $x \in R(I)$, let $\Pi(X', V'(I))$ be the problem obtained by setting $x' = x + d$, $V'(I)$ and $GC'(I)$ be the corresponding quantities for X'.*

(i) If $GC(I) < \min(V(I))$ then
$GC'(I) < \min(V'(I))$ *with* $d < d_1 = \frac{n-m}{m}(\min(V(I)) - GC(I))$ *and* $\max(d) = sol(a_1, b_1, c_1)$, *with* $a_1 = 1 - \frac{1}{n}$, $b_1 = x - \frac{\min(V(I))}{n}$, $c_1 = -\delta$

(ii) If $\min(V(I)) \leq GC(I) < \max(V(I))$ then
$\min(V'(I)) \leq GC'(I) < \max(V'(I))$ *with* $d < d_2 = \frac{n-m}{m}(\max(V(I)) - GC(I))$ *and* $\max(d) = sol(a_2, b_2, c_2)$, *with* $a_2 = 1 + \frac{m-n}{(n-m)^2}$, $b_2 = \frac{mES(I)}{n-m} + x - \frac{GC(I)}{n-m}$, $c_2 = -\delta$

(iii) If $GC(I) \geq \max(V(I))$ then
$GC'(I) \geq \max(V'(I))$ *with* $\max(d) = sol(a_3, b_3, c_3)$, *with* $a_3 = a_1$, $c_3 = c_1$ *and* $b_3 = x - \frac{\max(V(I))}{n}$

Proof. *(i)* $x \in R(I)$, so $ES'(I) = ES(I) + d$, $V'(I) = V(I) + d$, $M'(I) = M(I)$ and $GC'(I) = GC(I) + nd/(n-m)$. Then $GC'(I) < \min(V'(I))$ if $GC(I) + nd/(n-m) < \min(V(I)) + d$ that is $d < \frac{n-m}{m}(\min(V(I)) - GC(I))$. The optimal value for q' is $\min(V'(I)) = q + d$. Consider $opt' = \Pi(X', V'(I))$. Then $opt' = \sum_{j \neq i}(x'_j)^2 + (x'_i)^2 - \frac{q'^2}{n}$. In addition, $\forall x'_j \in R(I) \cup L(I)$ with $x'_j \neq x$: $x'_j = x_j$ and $\forall x'_j \in M'(I)$: $x'_j = (q' - ES'(I))/m = q - ES(I)/m = x_j$. Then, $opt' = \sum_{j \neq i}(x_j)^2 + (x_i + d)^2 - \frac{(q+d)^2}{n}$. So, the value of d for which $opt' = \pi^{max}$ is a root of the equation: $(1 - \frac{1}{n})d^2 + 2d(x - \frac{q}{n}) - \delta = 0$, which has only one positive root.

(ii) similar as *(i)* excepted that the variables of $M(I)$ have no longer the same value. If $x_j \in M(I)$ then $x'_j = (GC'(I) - ES'(I))/m = x_j + d/(n-m)$.

(iii) similar as *(i)* excepted that $q = \max(V(I))$. □

From this proposition and for a given interval I and a given variable $x \in R(I)$, we can define Function *compute-d* (see Algorithm 2) which computes the greatest possible value of d. It is called with x^{min} as parameter for x. Its time complexity is in $O(1)$ because the recursive call in line ln1 does not satisfy the *(i)* and the recursive call in line ln2 does not satisfy neither *(i)* or *(ii)*.

The following proposition just mirrors the previous one and an algorithm similar to Algorithm 2 can be derived from it.

Proposition 3. *Given $x \in L(I)$, let $\Pi(X', V'(I))$ be the problem obtained by setting $x' = x - d$, $V'(I)$ and $GC'(I)$ be the corresponding quantities for X'.*

(i) If $GC(I) > \max(V(I))$ then
$GC'(I) > \max(V'(I))$ *with* $d < d_1 = \frac{n-m}{m}(GC(I) - \max(V(I)))$ *and* $\max(d) = sol(a_1, -b_1, c_1)$, *with* a_1, b_1 *and* c_1 *as defined in Prop.2.(i).*

(ii) If $\max(V(I)) \geq GC(I) > \min(V(I))$ then
$\max(V'(I)) \geq GC'(I) > \min(V'(I))$ *with* $d < d_2 = \frac{n-m}{m}(GC(I) - \min(V(I)))$ *and* $\max(d) = sol(a_2, -b_2, c_2)$, *with* a_2, b_2 *and* c_2 *as defined in Prop.2.(ii).*

(iii) If $GC(I) \leq \min(V(I))$ then
$GC'(I) \leq \min(V'(I))$ *with* $\max(d) = sol(a_3, -b_3, c_3)$, *with* a_3, b_3 *and* c_3 *as defined in Prop.2.(iii).*

Algorithm 2. Adjusting the upper bound of $x \in R(I)$

Function compute-d$(V(I), ES(I), GC(I), m, x)$: number
if $GC(I) < \min(V(I))$ **then**
  Compute $max(d)$ as indicated in Proposition 2(i);
  $d_1 \leftarrow \frac{n-m}{m}(\min(V(I)) - GC(I))$
  if $max(d) < d_1$ **then**
    Return $max(d)$;
  else
    $x' \leftarrow x + d_1$; $V'(I) \leftarrow V(I) + d_1$, $ES'(I) \leftarrow ES(I) + d_1$; $GC'(I) \leftarrow \min(V'(I))$
    ln1: Return d_1+ compute-d$(V'(I), ES'(I), GC'(I), m, x')$;
if $\min(V(I)) \leq GC(I) < \max(V(I))$ **then**
  Compute $max(d)$ as indicated in Proposition 2(ii);
  $d_2 \leftarrow \frac{n-m}{m}(\max(V(I)) - GC(I))$;
  if $max(d) < d_2$ **then**
    Return $max(d)$;
  else
    $x' \leftarrow x + d_2$; $V'(I) \leftarrow V(I) + d_2$; $ES'(I) \leftarrow ES(I) + d_2$; $GC'(I) \leftarrow \max(V'(I))$
    ln2: Return d_2+ compute-d$(V'(I), ES'(I), GC'(I), m, x')$;
Compute $max(d)$ as indicated in Proposition 2(iii) and Return $max(d)$;

When $x \in M(I)$ the problem is more complex because if x is modified then the number of variables in $M(I)$ is also modified:

Proposition 4. *Given $x \in M(I)$, let $\Pi(X', V'(I))$ be the problem obtained by setting $x' = x + d$, $V'(I)$ and $GC'(I)$ be the corresponding quantities for X'.*

*(i) If $GC(I) < \min(V(I))$ then
$GC'(I) < \min(V'(I))$ with $d < d_1 = \frac{n-m+1}{m-1}[(\min(V(I)) - GC(I)) + \frac{ne}{(n-m)(m-1)}]$
and $max(d) = sol(a,b,c)$, with $q = \min(V(I))$ and $a = 1 - \frac{1}{n} + \frac{m}{(n-m+1)^2}$, $b = \frac{em}{(n-m)(n-m+1)} - \frac{em}{(n-m)(n-m+1)^2} - \frac{q}{n} + x$, $c = -\frac{m2e^2}{(n-m)^2(n-m+1)} + \frac{me^2}{(n-m)^2(n-m+1)^2} - \delta$*

*(ii) If $\min(V(I)) \leq GC(I) < \max(V(I))$ then
$\min(V'(I)) \leq GC'(I) < \max(V'(I))$ with $d < d_2 = \frac{n-m+1}{m-1}[(\max(V(I)) - GC(I)) + \frac{ne}{(n-m)(m-1)}]$ and $max(d) = sol(a,b,c)$, with $a = 1 + \frac{m-n}{(n-m+1)^2}$, $b = x + \frac{em}{(n-m)(n-m+1)} - \frac{GC(I)}{n-m+1} + \frac{e}{(n-m+1)^2}$, $c = -\frac{e^2}{(n-m)(n-m+1)^2} + \frac{2GC(I)e}{(n-m)(n-m+1)} - \frac{2me^2}{(n-m)^2(n-m+1)} - \delta$*

*(iii) If $GC(I) \geq \max(V(I))$ then
$GC'(I) \geq \max(V'(I))$ with $max(d) = sol(a,b,c)$ of (i) with $q = \max(V(I))$.*

From this proposition we can derive a function which computes the maximum value of d. This function is slightly different from the one of Algorithm 2, because if $x \in M(I)$ then after modifying x we have $x \in R(I)$. So after a modification the proposed function directly calls Function *compute-d* of Algorithm 2.

Proposition 5. *Given $x \in M(I)$, let $\Pi(X', V'(I))$ be the problem obtained by setting $x' = x - d$, $V'(I)$ and $GC'(I)$ be the corresponding quantities for X'.*

(i) If $GC(I) > \max(V(I))$ then
$GC'(I) > \max(V'(I))$ with $d < d_1 = \frac{n-m+1}{m-1}[(GC(I)-\max(V(I)))+\frac{ne}{(n-m)(m-1)}]$
and $max(d) = sol(a_1, -b_1, c_1)$, with a_1, b_1 and c_1 as defined in Prop.4.(i).

(ii) If $GC(I) \in V(I)$ then
$GC'(I) \in V'(I)$ with $d < d_1 = \frac{n-m+1}{m-1}[(GC(I) - \min(V(I))) + \frac{ne}{(n-m)(m-1)}]$ and
$max(d) = sol(a_2, -b_2, c_2)$, with a_2, b_2 and c_2 as defined in Prop.4.(ii).

(iii) If $GC(I) < \min(V(I))$ then
$GC'(I) < \min(V'(I))$ with $max(d) = sol(a_3, -b_3, c_3)$, with a_3, b_3 and c_3 as defined in Prop.4.(iii).

We can derive a similar algorithm from the previous propositions as we did from Proposition 4. Then, for each $x \in X$ we can compute for every interval $I \in \mathcal{I}$ the minimum and the maximum values of x denoted by $\min(x)$ and $\max(x)$ such that $opt(\Pi(X, V(I))) \leq \pi^{max}$. By taking the minimum value of $\min(x)$ among the values computed for every interval we obtain the new minimum value of $D(x)$, and by taking the maximum value of $\max(x)$ among the values computed for every interval we obtain the new maximum value of $D(x)$. Since the number of intervals is at most n, this process takes $O(n)$ time per variable. So we can achieve bounds consistency on the variables of X is in $O(n^2)$.

6 Conclusion

This paper introduced a new constraint to express balance among n variables in constraint programming models. It is based on the notions of mean, median, and standard deviation from statistics. We gave several examples showing how balance can be formulated with this constraint. Two efficient filtering algorithms were given. The first one runs in $\mathcal{O}(n)$ time under a reasonable assumption. The second one achieves bounds consistency in $\mathcal{O}(n^2)$ time.

Acknowledgments

This research was supported by the Natural Sciences and Engineering Research Council of Canada (NSERC), ILOG S.A., and the Intelligent Information Systems Institute at Cornell University.

References

1. Problem 30 of CSPLIB. (www.csplib.org).
2. I. Katriel and S Thiel. Fast Bound Consistency for the Global Cardinality Constraint. In *Proc. CP 2003*, pages 437–451. Springer-Verlag LNCS 2833, 2003.
3. M. Lemaître, G. Verfaillie, and N. Bataille. Exploiting a Common Property Resource under a Fairness Constraint: a Case Study. In *Proc. IJCAI*, Stockholm, Sweden, 1999.
4. C.-G. Quimper, P. van Beek, A. López-Ortiz, A. Golynski, and S. B. Sadjad. An Efficient Bounds Consistency Algorithm for the Global Cardinality Constraint. In *Proc. CP 2003*, pages 600–614. Springer-Verlag LNCS 2833, 2003.

Automatic Detection of Variable and Value Symmetries

Jean-François Puget

ILOG, 9 avenue de Verdun, 94253 Gentilly, France
puget@ilog.fr

Abstract. Many symmetry breaking techniques assume that the symmetries of a CSP are given as input in addition to the CSP itself. We present a method that can be used to detect all the symmetries of a CSP. This method constructs a graph that has the same symmetries as the CSP. Then, generators for the symmetry group are computed using a graph automorphism algorithm. This method improves and extends previous work in order to cover global constraints, arithmetic expressions and value symmetries. We show that this method is able to find symmetries for examples that were thought to be too convoluted for automated detection. We also show that the overhead of symmetry detection is quite negligible, even on very large instances. We present a comprehensive set of examples where automated symmetry detection is coupled with symmetry breaking techniques.

1 Introduction

Symmetry for a Constraint Satisfaction Problem (CSP) is a mapping of the CSP onto itself that preserves its solutions. If a CSP has some symmetry, it may be the case that all symmetrical variants of every dead end encountered during the search must be explored before a solution can be found. Even if the problem is easy to solve, all symmetrical variants of a solution are also solutions, and listing all of them may just be impossible in practice. Among symmetries, two categories have been studied in detail, variable symmetries, and value symmetries. A variable symmetry is a permutation of variables that leave a given CSP invariant. A value symmetry is a permutation of values that leave the CSP invariant. Both kinds of symmetries can be combined. There are even some symmetries that cannot be decomposed as the product of a variable and a value symmetry.

This paper focuses on symmetry detection. However, we will present some experiments where symmetry detection is coupled with some symmetry breaking technique in order to provide a fully automated procedure. Our approach, as well as its predecessors, relies on the efficient computations of the symmetries of a given graph. The idea is to construct a graph such that the automorphisms of the graph are symmetries of the CSP. Then a graph automorphism algorithm is used to compute these symmetries. These can be used in turn as an input for symmetry breaking techniques.

Before explaining our method in detail, let us introduce a simple example in order to give a flavor of it. We consider the Latin square problem. We want to fill a n by n square such that (i) every cell contains a value from 1 to n (ii) the values in each row are all different (iii) the values in each column are all different. A natural model for this is to have one variable per cell of the square with initial domain $\{1, 2, \ldots, n\}$. There is an all different constraint for variables in each row, and an all different constraint for variables in each column. There are many variable symmetries. Any row permutation is a symmetry, as well as any column permutation. Moreover, any reflection along a diagonal is also a symmetry. There are $2(n!)^2$ variable symmetries in fact.

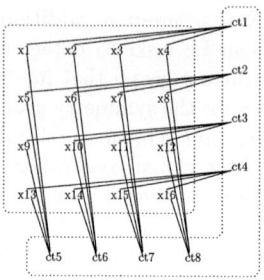

Fig. 1. Latin square graph

The graph corresponding to this CSP is given in figure 1. There is one node per variable, and one node per all different constraint. Edges link every constraint to the variables in its scope. Vertices are grouped into 2 classes, one for the variables, and one for the constraints. Symmetries can only map a vertex to a vertex in the same class. Labels for vertices are represented for the sake of clarity, but they are not relevant for defining symmetries. Our graph automorphism algorithm finds 1152 symmetries, which is what theory predicts.

The rest of the paper is organized as follows. Section 2 gives some background and discusses related work. Section 3 shows that we can routinely compute symmetries of graphs that have over a million edges. Section 4 describes how to extend the work of [17] to detect variable symmetries for any kind of CSP. Section 5 extends this in order to take into account any kind of symmetries, including value symmetries. Section 6 contains a set of experiments that show that the overhead of symmetry detection is quite negligible. We conclude in section 7.

2 Preliminaries

The symmetries we consider are permutations, i.e. one to one mappings (bijections) from a finite set onto itself. Without loss of generality, we can consider permutations of I^n, where I^n is the set of integers ranging from 0 to $n-1$. Let S^n be the set of all permutations of the set I^n. The image of i by the permutation σ is denoted i^σ.

A *constraint satisfaction problem* $\mathcal{P}$ (CSP) with n variables is a tuple $\mathcal{P} = (\mathcal{X}, \mathcal{V}, \mathcal{D}, \mathcal{C})$ where $\mathcal{X}$ is a finite set of variables $(x_i)_{i \in I^n}$, $\mathcal{V}$ is a finite set of values, $\mathcal{D}$ a finite set of finite sets $(\mathcal{D}_i)_{i \in I^n}$, and every constraint in $\mathcal{C}$ is a subset of the cross product $\bigotimes_{i \in I^n} \mathcal{D}_i$ such that $\mathcal{D}_i \subseteq \mathcal{V}$ for all i. Without loss of generality, we can assume that $\mathcal{V} = I^d$ for some d.

A *literal* is a statement of the form $x_i = j$ where $j \in \mathcal{D}_i$.

An *assignment* is a set of literals, one for each variable of the CSP. A *partial* assignment is a subset of an assignment.

A *solution* to $(\mathcal{V}, \mathcal{D}, \mathcal{C})$ is an assignment that is consistent with every member of $\mathcal{C}$.

A *symmetry* is a bijection from literals to literals that maps solutions to solutions.

A *variable symmetry* is a symmetry g such that there exists a permutation σ of the variables such that $(x_i = j)^g = (x_{i^\sigma} = j)$. In such case we will denote g by σ:

$$(x_i = j)^\sigma = (x_{i^\sigma} = j) \qquad (1)$$

A *value symmetry* is a symmetry g such that there exists a permutation θ of I^n such that $(x_i = j)^g = (x = j^\theta)$. In such case we will denote g by θ:

$$(x_i = j)^\theta = (x_i = j^\theta) \qquad (2)$$

Our definition of symmetries is similar to the one used in [9]. Other variable symmetry detection approaches are described in [4] and [23]. However these are quite ad hoc and do not cover all the symmetries we will exemplify in this paper. Others provide some language constructs in order to facilitate the description of the symmetries of the problem [11][7]. The use of graph automorphism for detecting symmetries for SAT problems has been proposed in [1]. This has been further extended in [17]. Graph automorphism has also been used in the mathematical programming community[13].

3 Graph Automorphism

The graphs we consider are simple (i.e. undirected without loops and multiple edges), and colored. A colored graph is a triple (V, E, c) where V is a finite set of vertices, E a set of edges between these vertices, and c a function from V to integers. An edge is a set of two vertices. An automorphism of the graph (V, E) is a one to one mapping (bijection) f from V to V such that:

$$\forall e \in E, f(e) \in E$$
$$\forall v \in V, \ c(f(v)) = c(v)$$

where $f(\{i, j\}) = \{f(i), f(j)\}$.

Finding whether such a nonidentity function exists is known as the graph automorphism (GA) problem. GA is in NP but it is not known whether it is in P or not [10]. Colors are used to restrict the symmetries of the graph. For

Table 1. SAT instances

Instance	Graph		Symmetry		Detection		Gain
Name	Vertices	Edges	Group	Gen	SAUCY	AUTOM	
2pipe	3575	14625	2.26E+45	68	0.06	0.0052	11.5
3pipe	10048	58556	7.29E+136	160	0.15	0.017	8.8
4pipe	21547	167942	1.08E+289	292	0.62	0.055	11.3
5pipe	38746	403799	2.51E+507	464	1.74	0.14	12.4
6pipe	65839	812525	1.34E+796	676	4.8	0.29	16.6
7pipe	100668	1498971	3.68E+1158	928	10.8	0.55	19.6

Table 2. MIP instances

Instance	Graph		Symmetry		Detection			Gain	
Name	Vertices	Edges	Group	Gen	NAUTY	SAUCY	AUTOM	N/A	S/A
p2756	9248	14674	1.18E+21	70	6.05	0.1	0.0045	1344	22.2
roll3000	8108	34033	1.92E+61	203	8.7	0.11	0.0048	1813	22.9
qiu	3872	5272	48	4	5.2	0.02	0.005	1040	4.0
seymour	6316	33549	2.78E+234	210	6.36	0.1	0.0052	1223	19.2
arki001	18062	36065	5.23E+44	37	29.65	0.05	0.0073	4062	6.8
air04	9727	82692	4.95E+12	41	22	0.04	0.0075	2933	5.3
a1c1s1	14000	17218	1	0	20.3	0.06	0.0091	2231	6.6
cap6000	17575	57642	120	4	49.6	0.05	0.0092	5391	5.4
swath	14675	41951	3.35E+816	461	79.47	0.64	0.011	7225	58.2
protfold	7448	26992	4	2	24.13	0.04	0.0148	1630	2.7
dano3mip	24927	87507	32768	15	84.7	0.06	0.02	4235	3.0
nsrand-ipx	13406	229311	1.04E+325	1007	601.92	4.23	0.029	20756	145.9
10teams	2255	12150	1.76E+13	19	3.81	0.08	0.031	123	2.6
mzzv11	34082	148946	4.57E+46	155	285.36	0.4	0.032	8918	12.5
mzzv42z	38468	167552	1.30E+33	110	206.41	0.38	0.037	5579	10.3
mod011	25629	32445	6.79E+3169	1698	2982.57	8.31	0.053	56275	156.8
fast0507	63516	409349	5.71E+254	834	5420.91	3.35	0.064	84702	52.3
net12	56875	109123	1	0	1742.56	0.22	0.077	22631	2.9
mkc	15863	24165	1.32E+77	190	725.85	0.56	0.084	8641	6.7
msc98-ip	82756	138681	4.27E+3700	5969	26881.46	86.13	0.106	253599	812.5
ds	68388	1024059	4.00E+00	2	3789.63	0.16	0.106	35751	1.5
nw04	87518	636666	3.65E+15872	41293		17446.6	0.188		92801.1
t1717	74436	325689	8.32E+54755	57457		16590.88	0.295		56240.3
rd-rplusc-21	133969	859562	2.33E+25647	71300		187313.56	0.326		574581.5
atlanta-ip	234210	421272	1.29E+4455	11694		736.61	0.42		1753.8
momentum3	270818	1149959	4.66E+36	55		1.74	0.45		3.9
stp3d	677539	975299	6.48E+178	594		136.85	2.56		53.5

instance, in the graph of figure 1, we have two colors, one for variables, and the other for constraints.

One of the most efficient procedure for computing colored graph automorphisms is NAUTY [12]. NAUTY is quite efficient for dense graphs, where the number of edges grows quadratically with the number of vertices. In [2] a sparse graph automorphism software called SAUCY is presented. It uses the same principles as NAUTY, but a spare graph representation is used. We have also implemented a graph automorphism software based on Nauty principles that uses sparsity (AUTOM). In order to asses its efficiency we have performed two experiments.

First we ran SAUCY and AUTOM on the graphs presented in [12]. Results are shown in Table 1. All the running times are expressed in seconds. They are obtained on a 1.4 GHz Pentium M laptop running Windows XP and ILOG Solver 6.1. We ran SAUCY and NAUTY on the same computer. The last column indicates the speedup of AUTOM over SAUCY.

We ran a second set of experiments on large graphs coming from MIPLIB examples. These are CSPs where all constraints are linear, and where variables are either integer or floating point variables. The graphs are constructed using the techniques described later in the paper. The point here is not to solve these problems using a constraint programming software. It is to show that we can efficiently detect all the symmetries on sparse graphs that have up to a million edges in few seconds. Results are shown in table 2. The last two columns show the speedup of AUTOM vs. NAUTY (N/A) and the speedup of AUTOM vs. SAUCY (S/A). NAUTY wasn't able to compute the automorphism of the largest graphs. SAUCY, despite its use of sparsity, is more than half a million times slower than AUTOM on one instance.

4 Detection of Variable Symmetries

The idea of the method is to construct a graph with one vertex per variable. For each constraint we add some vertices and some edges linking them to the variables. The resulting graph must have symmetries that are equivalent to the symmetries of the constraint. Then the graphs for all constraints are combined into a single graph.

4.1 One Extensional Constraint

Let us consider first the case where there is a single constraint in the CSP. The case of more complex CSPs will be described later. This constraint is given in extension, i.e. the set of assignments consistent with the constraint is given. The variables are $x_1, x_2, \ldots, x_n$. A consistent assignment $< x_1 = a_{i1}, x_2 = a_{i2}, \ldots, x_n = a_{in} >$ is described by a tuple $< a_{ij1}, a_{i2}, \ldots, a_{in} >$.

The graph for this constraint is constructed as follows. There is one vertex per variable. A vertex is added for each value a_{ij} in the domain of x_i. A vertex is added for each consistent assignment. A last vertex is added for the constraint. Variable vertices are of the same color. Assignment vertices are of the same color, different from the previous one. The constraint vertex is yet of another color. Value vertices are linked to the variable vertex. The constraint vertex is linked to every assignment vertex. The vertex for assignment $< a_{i1}, a_{i2}, \ldots, a_{in} >$ is linked to the vertices representing $a_{ij1}, a_{i2}, \ldots, a_{in}$. All the value vertices a_{ij} for a given value j are colored with a new color, different from the ones already used. This ensures that only variables symmetries can be detected.

Example 1. An equality constraint $x = y$ on two variables ranging from 1 to 3 is represented by the assignments $< 1, 1 >, < 2, 2 >, < 3, 3 >$. Its graph is represented in figure 2(a). There is one trivial symmetry in this graph. It swaps x and y and their values.

Example 2. An inequality constraint $x < y$ on two variables ranging from 1 to 3 is represented by the assignments $< 1, 2 >, < 1, 3 >, < 2, 3 >$. Its graph is represented in figure 2(b). There is no symmetry in this graph, given that values have different colors.

Example 3. A constraint arising in sports league scheduling. It relates 3 variables g, x and y, where g is a game, and where x, y are the teams of that game.

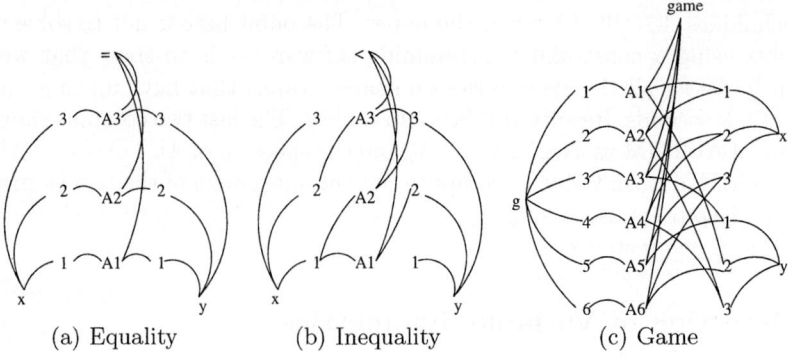

Fig. 2. Some symmetry graphs

The corresponding graph is represented in figure 2(c). For 3 teams, there are 3 games and 6 consistent assignments listed below. Assignment $< a, b, c >$ is noted $a = (b\ vs.\ c)$.

$1 = (1\ vs.\ 2),\ 2 = (1\ vs.\ 3),\ 3 = (2\ vs.\ 1),\ 4 = (2\ vs.\ 3), 5 = (3\ vs.\ 1),\ 6 = (3\ vs.2)$

When there are less inconsistent assignments than consistent ones, it is equivalent and more efficient to use inconsistent assignments for constructing the graph. For instance, the graph for $x \neq y$ can be the same as the one in figure 2(a), with the label of the constraint changed to $\neq$ instead of $=$.

It can be proved that the above graph construction is correct and complete. Indeed, the symmetries of the graph and the symmetries of the CSP are equivalent. We omit the proof.

4.2 One Intentional Constraint

In general, it is possible to create a simpler graph that still has the same symmetries than the constraint. For instance, the equality graph of figure 2(a) has one non trivial symmetry that swaps the two variables. A much simpler graph having the same symmetry is given in figure 3(a). Similarly, the inequality graph has no symmetry. A much simpler graph is given in figure 3(b). In this graph, a dummy vertex d is introduced to break the symmetry. All the dummy vertices corresponding to inequalities are colored with a new color distinct from all the colors used for the other nodes.

A global constraint can be also represented that way, instead of listing all the assignments consistent with it. For instance, an all different constraint can be represented with only one vertex, linked to every variable. Such graph has many symmetries: any variable permutation is a symmetry. This is precisely the set of symmetries allowed by the constraint.

Let us look at another global constraint, the global cardinality constraint $gcc(X, C, V)$ where X is a vector of variables $< x_1, \ldots, x_n >$, C another vector

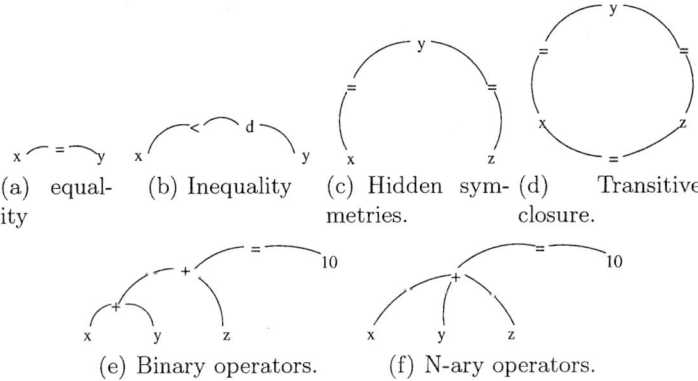

Fig. 3. Simpler graphs

of variables $< c_1, \ldots, c_m >$, and V a vector of values $< v_1, \ldots, v_m >$[18]. The constraint states that c_i is the number of occurrences of v_i in the vector X. A study of the constraint shows that the variables in X can be freely permuted, but not the variables in C. Indeed, the latter are linked to the values in V. A graph capturing these symmetries is the following. There is one vertex for the constraint, and one per value in V. Each variable in X is linked to the constraint. Each value in V is linked to the constraint. Each variable c_i in C is linked to the corresponding value v_i. Value nodes are colored with m different colors. This removes the symmetries among the c_i variables.

4.3 Handling Several Constraints

When a CSP contains several constraints, we simply add the nodes and edges described previously for each constraint. Vertices playing identical roles in different constraints are merged. For instance, constraints given in extension require the introduction of a vertex for every value in the domain of the variables in its scope. When there are several such constraints, all the value nodes corresponding to a given value in a given domain are merged. Colors are also merged for some vertices: all the constraints of the same kind have the same color. This enables symmetries that permute constraints as well as variables.

Example 4. Let us consider the Latin square problem presented in the introduction. The graph in figure 1 is constructed with one vertex per all different constraint. Each constraint is linked to the variables in its scope. All the vertices representing the all different constraints have the same color.

The above construction is correct : any symmetry of the graph is a symmetry of the CSP. We omit the proof because of lack of space. However, it is not complete. Indeed, there may be some symmetries of the CSP that are not equivalent to some symmetries of the graph.

Example 5. Let us consider the CSP $x = y \wedge y = z$. Its graph is depicted in figure 3(c). This graph has only one non trivial symmetry that swaps x and z.

This is indeed a symmetry of the CSP. However, any variable permutation is a symmetry of the CSP. In order to be able to detect these symmetries, a simple modification of the graph fixes the problem: it is sufficient to always take the transitive closure of the equality constraints. In our example, this means to add the vertex for the constraint $x = z$. The resulting graph is depicted in figure 3(d). Similarly, we take the transitive closure of the $\leq$ constraints. Moreover, when both $x \leq y$ and $y \leq$ are present, they are replaced by $x = y$. These transformations are applied until a fix point is reached.

4.4 Expressions

Many CP systems let the user create expressions with arithmetic operators $(+, \times, -, /)$ and logical operators $(\wedge, \vee, \neg)$. Then a simple approach is to construct a parse graph for each expression, as explained in [17]. The general idea is to create one vertex per operator. This vertex is linked to the vertices representing its operands. However, doing so could create false symmetries, because some operators $(-, /)$ do not accept symmetries among their operands. In order to avoid this, we decompose these operators with a unary inverse operator. The expression $x - y$ is handled as $x + (-y)$. Similarly, x/y is handled as $x \times (1/y)$.

Some care must be taken as well in order to avoid breaking symmetries unintentionally. For instance, consider the CSP $x + y + z = 10$. Obviously, any variable permutation defines a symmetry. However, depending on the associativity rule for the operator, the corresponding graph may not have that many symmetries. For instance, if the CSP is interpreted as $(x+y)+z$, then the graph is depicted in figure 3(e). Its non trivial symmetry swaps x and y. The other variable permutations are not symmetries of this graph. A simple fix is to use an $n - ary$ version of the operator, as depicted in figure 3(f). In this graph, any variable permutation is a symmetry. This grouping of associative operators was introduced in [17].

Example 6. Let us consider a simple example from [5]. We want to solve the following equation, where the letter represent different numbers from 1 to 9, and BC means $10B + C$, etc.

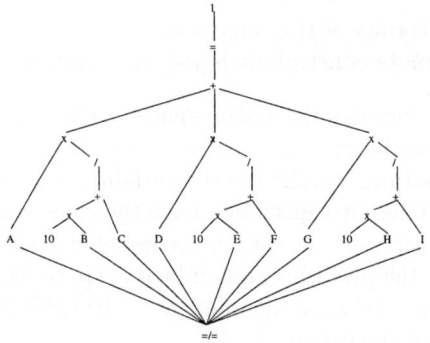

Fig. 4. $\frac{A}{BC} + \frac{D}{EF} + \frac{G}{HI} = 1$ puzzle

$$\frac{A}{BC} + \frac{D}{EF} + \frac{G}{HI} = 1$$

The corresponding graph is given in figure 4.4.

Another issue must be dealt with. The graph automorphism algorithm accepts only simple graphs, i.e. graphs where at most one edge can exist between any two vertices. However the constructs given so far may lead to non simple graphs when variables are repeated. For instance, the CSP $A \times A = 1$ will create the graph in figure 5(a). This can be dealt with a power operator. The resulting graph is given in figure 5(b).

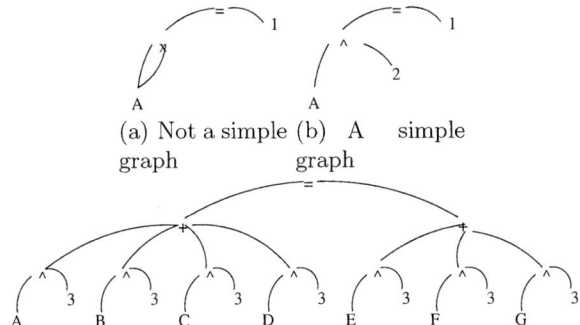

(a) Not a simple graph (b) A simple graph

Fig. 5. Handling expressions

Example 7. Let us consider the following example from [6]. Its graph is depicted in figure 5(c). There are 144 symmetries corresponding to the 24 permutations of A, B, C, D to the 6 permutations of E, F, G, and to their combinations.

$$A \times A \times A + B \times B \times B + C \times C \times C + D \times D \times D = E \times E \times E + G \times G \times G + H \times H \times H$$

5 Detection of All Symmetries

The constructs presented so far are geared towards the detection of variable symmetries. It is quite simple to extend these constructs for the detection of any symmetry, including value symmetries.

5.1 One Extensional Constraint

Let us first consider a CSP with a unique constraint described by the assignments consistent with it. Its symmetry graph is the similar to the one in section 4.1. The only difference is that now all the value vertices are of the same color. This yields some very interesting results. For instance, there are 12 symmetries for the graph of figure 2(a). They correspond to the swap of the two variables, the permutations of the 3 values, and their combinations.

The graph of figure 2(b) has one non trivial symmetry:

$$(x\ y)(1_x\ 3_y)(2_x\ 2_y)(3_x\ 1_y)(A1\ A3) \qquad (3)$$

This symmetry swaps x and y. It also maps value i to $3-i$. It is interesting to see that such non trivial symmetry is automatically detected.

5.2 One Intentional Constraint

The treatment of all constraints must take into account the values in the domains of the variables. For instance, it is no longer possible to simplify the graph from figure 2(b) to figure 3(b). Indeed, doing so would prevent us from discovering the symmetry (3).

The treatment of global constraints must be revisited as well. Indeed, we want to construct graphs that reflect all the symmetries allowed by a constraint, including value symmetries if any. We further want to be able to detect symmetries that are not a combination of variable and value symmetry. Our approach uses a hidden reformulation of the CSP with binary variables y_{ij} (variables with domains equal to $\{0, 1\}$). The variable y_{ij} equals 1 if and only if $x_i = j$. Therefore, we may denote the variable y_{ij} by $x_i = j$. The y_{ij} form a square matrix when all the x variables have the same domain. In the general case, there are holes in the y_{ij} matrix. Holes are filled with zeroes. Using these new variables does not change the solutions of the CSP, nor its symmetriesvalsym. Variable symmetries of $\mathcal{P}$ are equivalent to permutations of the rows of the y_{ij} matrix by (1). Value symmetries of $\mathcal{P}$ are equivalent to permutations of the columns of the same matrix by (2). By definition, the new variables satisfy:

$$\forall i\ \sum y_{ij} = 1$$

Then, many global constraints can be expressed with the y_{ij} variables. We construct the graph corresponding to these elementary constraints. In the graph, there is no node for the original variables of the CSP. There is one vertex per variable y_{ij}. These vertices are in fact the value vertices a_{ij} that we introduced in section 4.1. These vertices are linked to the graphs induced by the elementary constraints. Note that the variables y_{ij} are not added to the CSP. They are only used for the construction of the graph. The original CSP formulation is kept as it is.

Example 8. The graph corresponding to $x = y$ is represented in figure 6(a).

Example 9. The graph corresponding to $x < y$ is given figure 6(b).

Example 10. The graph corresponding to the game constraint $game(g, x, y)$ is the one given in figure 6(c).

Example 11. The all different constraint on the variables $x_1, \ldots, x_n$ can be expressed as:

$$\forall j\ \sum_i y_{ij} \leq 1 \qquad (4)$$

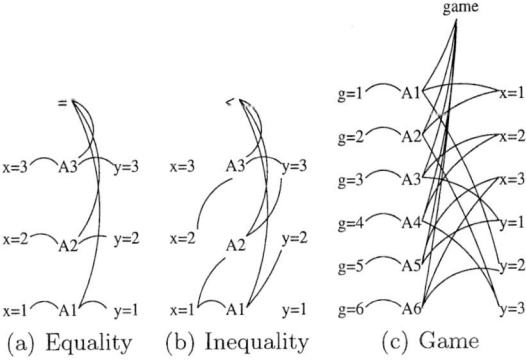

Fig. 6. Some symmetry graphs

If the number of variables is equal to the number of values, then the constraint can be stated by

$$\forall j \ \sum_i y_{ij} = 1 \qquad (5)$$

Then, depending on the case the vertices and edges for equation (4) or (5) are added.

Example 12. Let us consider the global cardinality constraint $gcc(X, C, V)$ where X is a vector of variables $< x_1, \ldots, x_n >$, C another vector of variables $< c_1, \ldots, c_m >$, and V a vector of values $< v_1, \ldots, v_m >$. Let y_{ij} be the variables corresponding to the values of the x_i variables, and let z_{kl} be the variables corresponding to the values of the c_k variables. Then the gcc constraint can be expressed by:

$$\forall j \ \sum_i y_{ij} = \sum_l l \times z_{jl} \qquad (6)$$

Indeed, we have that $\sum_i y_{ij} = c_j$ and that $c_k = \sum_l l \times z_{kl}$. Therefore, the vertices an edges corresponding to (6) are added.

5.3 Handling Expressions

The treatment of expressions is more complex. Indeed, one needs to be able to express the relationship between value vertices of x op y and the value vertices of x and y. A generic way is to replace expressions by constraints. For instance, an expression x op y where op is a binary operator can be replaced by a new variable z and a ternary constraint $op(z, x, y)$. Then this ternary constraint can be described in extension. This approach is correct: any symmetry of the resulting graph is a symmetry of the CSP. However, it may lead to extremely large graphs.

We have decided to only handle some simple expressions when detecting all symmetries. We handle expressions $f(x)$ involving only one occurrence of one variable x. Let y_j be the vertices representing $x = j$. Then the only possible values for $f(x)$ are given by $f(j)$ with j ranging over the domain of x. Then the vertices representing the values of $f(x)$ are of the form $f(c) = f(j)$, with j ranging over the domain of x. We then merge the vertex $f(x) = f(j)$ with the vertex $x = j$. Therefore, no additional vertices are needed to represent such expressions.

Example 13. Let us consider the expression $x + a$, where a is a constant. The vertex $(x + a) = j$ is the same as the vertex $x = (j - a)$. Therefore, no extra binary variables need to be introduced for the expression $x + a$.

Example 14. The n queen problem is usually represented by the following model. There are n variables x_i with domains $\{1, 2, \ldots, n\}$. There are three all different constraints stating that: the x_i are pair wise distinct, the $x_i + i$ are pair wise distinct, and the $x_i - i$ are pair wise distinct. The symmetry graph contains n^2 vertices of the form $x_i = j$. By construction, these nodes are linked to the elementary constraint $\sum_j x_{ij} = 1$. The all different constraint on the x_i is represented by the elementary constraints $\sum_j x_{ij} = 1$, after (5). The expressions $x_i + i$ are represented without additional vertices. Indeed, the vertex $(x_i + i) = j$ is the same as the vertex $x_i = (j - i)$. The all different constraint on the $x_i + i$ is represented by the equation $\sum_j ((x_i + i) = j) \leq 1$. This is the same as $\sum_j (x_i = (j - i)) \leq 1$, which yields $\sum_j y_{i,j-i} \leq 1$. Similarly, the all different constraint on the $x_i - i$ expressions results in $\sum_j y_{i,j+i} \leq 1$. The resulting graph has 8 symmetries. Let Y be the 2D matrix of the variables y_{ij}. Then $y_{ij} = 1$ if and only if there is a queen on square ij. The 8 symmetries are the symmetries of the square Y. This is rather interesting, because the authors of [7] claimed that automatic symmetry detection would not be able to detect the 8 square symmetries on the n queen example.

6 Experimental Results

We have implemented the graph constructions outlined in this paper, as well as the AUTOM algorithm described in section 3. This results in a fully automated procedure that takes as input a CSP and outputs generators for its group of symmetry. We have performed various experiments in order to assess the efficiency of our symmetry detection method.

Once symmetries are detected, various symmetry breaking techniques can be used. When the variables are subject to an all different constraint, then all variable symmetries can be removed by imposing a partial order on the variables (**VAR**). This partial order can be automatically computed from the symmetries we detect[15]. More general variable symmetries can be partially broken by stating a lexicographic ordering constraint for each generator of the symmetry group[2] (**GEN**). When the problem is a surjection, i.e. when each value appears in every solution, then all value symmetries can be broken using a partial order on the occurrences of the values [16] (**OCC**). More general cases of symmetries can be handled by generic methods that use the group of symmetry as input, such as **GAP-SBDD**[6], **GAP-SBDS**[5], **STAB**[14], and **GE-tree**[20].

We haven't implemented such methods yet. All results are given in table 3. For each example we give the number of symmetries, the time needed to detect symmetries, the symmetry breaking technique used, and the time needed to solve the problem with, and without symmetry breaking. The time to detect symmetries includes the time for constructing the graph and the time to run the automorphism algorithm. Results show that the time spent on finding symmetries is quite negligible.

Problem	Size	Break	Detection	Sym	No sym
Graceful	$K_3 \times P_2$	VAR+OCC	0	0.01	0.12
	$K_4 \times P_2$	VAR+OCC	0	0.27	13.6
	$K_5 \times P_2$	VAR+OCC	0	6.5	
	$K_6 \times P_2$	VAR+OCC	0	305	
$n \times n$ queen	5	VAR	0	0	0.06
	6	VAR	0.0	0	0.92
	7	VAR	0.02	0.11	268.03
	8	VAR	0.03	4.27	
Most Perfect	4	VAR	0.01	0.02	0.47
	8	VAR	0.09	0.39	
	12	VAR	0.44	22.2	
	16	VAR	4.6	275.6	
sport	6	VAR+OCC	0.00	0.04	
	8	VAR+OCC	0.01	0.15	
	10	VAR+OCC	0.05	35.15	

The examples used are the following ones. Unless otherwise stated, the search used to solve the examples is quite straightforward. It is a depth first search where one variable is selected at each node. The order in which variables is selected is the order given by variable indices. Values are tried in increasing order. Graceful graphs are taken from[15]. The sport scheduling examples are taken from[19]. We report results for finding all solutions. The $n \times n$ queen example is taken from [9]. The Most Perfect Magic Square example is taken from [20]. Besides running time results, some interesting observations can be made. In the graceful examples, all the variable symmetries are found. Moreover, the non trivial value symmetry is also found. This symmetry maps a to $n-a$ where n is a constant depending on the problem instance. We show in [16] that the automated symmetry detection combined with the **VAR** and **OCC** methods significantly outperforms the approach of [19] for sports league scheduling. For matrix models such as BIBD, the generators found by our algorithms correspond to the swap of two consecutive rows or two consecutive columns. Therefore the **GEN** method that states one lexicographic ordering constraint for each generator is equivalent to the double lex method of [3]. It is worth noticing that this is achieved without any input beside the usual CSP model for BIBD.

7 Conclusion

We have presented a fully automated symmetry detection method. This method constructs a graph that has the same symmetries as the CSP. Then, a graph automorphism algorithm computes a set of generators for the symmetry group. Our implementation is very efficient, and can handle graphs that have over a million edges in few seconds. We have described how to construct graphs for CSP that contains global constraints, arithmetic and logical expressions. We have also shown how to extend the method in order to detect value symmetries. Symmetries that are not combinations of variable and value symmetries such as the 8 square symmetries can be discovered. Some non trivial value symmetries can be automatically detected. For instance, symmetries of the form $a \to n - a$, where n is a constant, have been discovered in some examples. Experiments show that the time used for the detection of symmetries is small compared to the search for solutions. We used a simple value and variable ordering for our experiments, as little is known about which orderings are effective when searching for all solutions. It would be interesting to use the findings of [22] for this purpose.

Our method can be seen as a continuation of the work presented in [17]. We have extended this method to cover global constraints and value symmetries among other.

The method is powerful, but it is based on the syntactic expression of the CSP. This may prevent the discovery of some symmetries. We have described some new techniques, such as the use of transitivity of relations, to cope with that problem. The author welcomes examples of CSPs where it is believed that our method would miss some symmetries. It would be interesting to describe the class of CSPs for which our method detects all symmetries. For cases where some symmetries are not apparent in the syntax of the CSP, one can combine the symmetries detected by our method with symmetries given as input using systems such as the ones in [11][4][7].

References

1. Crawford, J., Ginsberg, M., Luks E.M., Roy, A. "Symmetry Breaking Predicates for Search Problems." In proceedings of KR'96, 148-159.
2. Paul T. Darga, Mark H. Liffiton, Karem A. Sakallah, Igor L. Markov: Exploiting structure in symmetry detection for CNF. DAC 2004: 530-534
3. P. Flener, A. M. Frisch, B. Hnich, Z. Kiziltan, I. Miguel, J. Pearson, T. Walsh.: "Breaking Row and Column Symmetries in Matrix Models. " Proceedings of CP'02, pages 462-476, 2002
4. Alan M. Frisch, Ian Miguel, Toby Walsh: CGRASS: A System for Transforming Constraint Satisfaction Problems. ERCIM/Colognet Workshop on Constraint Solving and Constraint Logic Programming 2002: 15-30
5. Gent, I.P., and Harvey, W., and Kelsey, T.: Groups and Constraints: Symmetry Breaking During Search, In proceedings of CP 2002, 415–430.
6. Gent, I.P., Harvey, W., Kelsey, T., Linton, S.: Generic SBDD Using Computational Group Theory. in proceedings of CP 2003, 333–437
7. Warwick Harvey, Tom Kelsey, and Karen Petrie, "Symmetry Group generation for CSPs" In proceedings of SymCon'03, 2003.
8. ILOG: ILOG Solver 6.0. User Manual. ILOG, S.A., Gentilly, France, September 2003

9. Kelsey, T, Linton, SA, Roney-Dougal, CM. New Developments in Symmetry Breaking in Search Using Computational Group Theory. In: Proceedings AISC 2004. Springer LNAI. 2004.
10. J. Kobler, U. Schoning, and J. Toran. *The Graph Isomorphism Problem: Its Structural Complexity*, Birkhauser, 1993.
11. McDonald, I: "NuSBDS: Symmetry Breaking made easy". In proceedings of SymCon'03, 2003.
12. Mc Kay, B.: "Practical Graph Isomorphism" Congr. Numer. 30, 45-87, 1981
13. F. Margot, "Exploiting Orbits in Symmetric ILP", Mathematical Programming Ser. B 98 (2003), 3–21.
14. Puget, J.-F.: "Symmetry Breaking Using Stabilizers", in proceedings of CP 03, Springer, 2003.
15. Puget, J.-F.: "Breaking symmetries in all different problems." to appear in proceedings of IJCAI 05.
16. Puget, J.-F.: "Breaking All Value Symmetries in Surjection Problems" To appear in proceedings of CP 05, Sitges, 2005.
17. A. Ramani, I. Markov.: "Automatically Exploiting Symmetries in Constraint Programming". In proceedings of SymCon 04.
18. J-C. Regin: "Generalized Arc Consistency for Global Cardinality Constraint", AAAI-96 Portland, OR, USA, pp 209–215, 1996
19. J-C. Regin, "Constraint Programming and Sports Scheduling Problems", Informs, May 1999, Cincinnati.
20. Roney-Dougal C.M., Gent, I.P., Kelsey T., Linton S.: "Tractable symmetry breaking using restricted search trees" In proceedings of ECAI'04.
21. Meinolf Sellmann and Pascal Van Hentenryck : Structural Symmetry Breaking To appear in proceedings of IJCAI 05.
22. Barbara Smith, Paula Sturdy "Value Ordering for Finding All Solutions". To appear in proceedings of IJCAI 2005.
23. Ven Hentenryck, P., Flener, P., Pearsons, J., and Agren, M.: "Compositional Derivation of Symmetries for Constraint Satisfaction" To appear in proceedings of SARA 05.

Breaking All Value Symmetries in Surjection Problems

Jean-François Puget

ILOG, 9 avenue de Verdun, 94253 Gentilly, France
puget@ilog.fr

Abstract. We propose a surprisingly simple new way of breaking all value symmetries with constraints. Our method requires the addition of one variable per value of the problem plus a linear number of binary constraints. The set of constraints is automatically computed from the symmetries of the problem using computational group theory. Our method applies to problems where every value is taken by at least one variable. Such problems occur frequently in practice. Various experiments show that our method is extremely effective when compared to previously published methods.

1 Introduction

A symmetry for a Constraint Satisfaction Problem (CSP) is a mapping of the CSP onto itself that preserves its structure as well as its solutions. If a CSP has some symmetries, it may be the case that all symmetrical variants of every dead end encountered during the search must be explored before a solution can be found. Even if the problem is easy to solve, all symmetrical variants of a solution are also solutions, and listing all of them may just be impossible in practice. Among symmetries, two categories have been studied in detail: variable symmetries, and value symmetries. A variable symmetry is a permutation of variables that leave a given CSP invariant. A value symmetry is a permutation of values that leave the CSP invariant. Both kind of symmetries can be combined. There are even some symmetries that cannot be decomposed as the product of a variable and a value symmetry.

Let us introduce an example that will be used throughout the paper. This problem is the sports league scheduling (problem 026 in the CSPLIB [6]). The problem is to schedule a tournament of n teams over $n-1$ weeks, with each week divided into $n/2$ periods. A game between two teams must occur every period of every week. A tournament must satisfy the following three constraints: every team plays once a week; every team plays at most twice in the same period over the tournament; every team plays every other team. A natural model for this problem is to introduce a matrix of variables x_{ij} representing the game played during period i of week j. The values of the variables are the possible games. Note that all possible games must be played. Problems having this property are called *surjection problems* because the mapping from variables to values is a surjection (onto mapping).

Here is a solution for $n = 6$ (note that games i vs. j and j vs. i are the same):

0 vs. 1	0 vs. 2	2 vs. 4	3 vs. 5	1 vs. 4
2 vs. 5	1 vs. 3	1 vs. 5	0 vs. 4	2 vs. 3
3 vs. 4	4 vs. 5	0 vs. 3	1 vs. 2	0 vs. 5

This problem has many symmetries. First of all, weeks can be exchanged. This means that the columns of the matrix can be freely exchanged. This is a variable symmetry. For instance, the following is a solution of the problem (the first two columns have been swapped):

0 vs. 2	0 vs. 1	2 vs. 4	3 vs. 5	1 vs. 4
1 vs. 3	2 vs. 5	1 vs. 5	0 vs. 4	2 vs. 3
4 vs. 5	3 vs. 4	0 vs. 3	1 vs. 2	0 vs. 5

Second, the periods can be exchanged. This means that the rows of the matrix can be freely permuted. This is a variable symmetry. For instance, the following is a solution (the first two rows have been swapped):

1 vs. 3	2 vs. 5	1 vs. 5	0 vs. 4	2 vs. 3
0 vs. 2	0 vs. 1	2 vs. 4	3 vs. 5	1 vs. 4
4 vs. 5	3 vs. 4	0 vs. 3	1 vs. 2	0 vs. 5

Third, the teams themselves can be exchanged. Any permutation of teams defines a permutation of the games. This is a value symmetry. For instance, the following is a solution (teams 1 and 2 have been swapped):

2 vs. 3	1 vs. 5	2 vs. 5	0 vs. 4	1 vs. 3
0 vs. 1	0 vs. 2	1 vs. 4	3 vs. 5	2 vs. 4
4 vs. 5	3 vs. 4	0 vs. 3	1 vs. 2	0 vs. 5

The three types of symmetries can be independently applied. Therefore, there are $(n-1)!(n/2)!n!$ symmetries in this problem, which is 4877107200 for $n = 8$. Listing all solutions may be impossible for $n = 8$, not to speak about larger values for n.

We focus in this paper on value symmetries. The paper is organized as follows. After some preliminaries in Section 2, we summarize the method of [14] for breaking variable symmetries. This method is then used in section 4 to break all value symmetries for surjection problems. In section 5 we discuss how to break value symmetries when there are also variable symmetries. In section 6 we perform a comparison of our method with previously published ones using various examples. We conclude with a discussion of related work and possible improvements in section 7.

2 Preliminaries

The symmetries we consider are permutations, i.e. one to one mappings (bijections) from a finite set onto itself. Without loss of generality, we can consider permutations of I^n, where I^n is the set of integers ranging from 0 to $n-1$. For instance, we can label the variables of a CSP with integers, such that any variable symmetry is completely described by a permutation of the labels of its variables. This is formalized as follows.

Let S^n be the set of all permutations of the set I^n. The image of i by the permutation σ is denoted i^σ. A permutation $\sigma \in S^n$ is fully described by the vector $[0^\sigma, 1^\sigma, \ldots, (n-1)^\sigma]$. The product of two permutations σ and θ is defined by $i^{(\sigma\theta)} = (i^\sigma)^\theta$.

A *constraint satisfaction problem* $\mathcal{P}$ (CSP) with n variables is a tuple $\mathcal{P} = (\mathcal{X}, \mathcal{V}, \mathcal{D}, \mathcal{C})$ where $\mathcal{X}$ is a finite set of variables $(x_i)_{i \in I^n}$, $\mathcal{V}$ is a finite set of values, $\mathcal{D}$ a finite set of finite sets $(\mathcal{D}_i)_{i \in I^n}$, and every constraint in $\mathcal{C}$ is a subset of the cross product $\bigotimes_{i \in I^n} \mathcal{D}_i$ such that $\mathcal{D}_i \subseteq \mathcal{V}$ for all i. Without loss of generality, we can assume that $\mathcal{V} = I^d$ for some d.

A *literal* is a statement of the form $x_i = j$ where $j \in \mathcal{D}_i$.

An *assignment* is a set of literals, one for each variable of the CSP. A *partial* assignment is a subset of an assignment.

A *solution* to $(\mathcal{V}, \mathcal{D}, \mathcal{C})$ is an assignment that is consistent with every member of $\mathcal{C}$.

A *symmetry* is a bijection from literals to literals that maps solutions to solutions.

A *variable symmetry* is a symmetry g such that there is a permutation σ of the variables such that $(x_i = j)^g = (x_{i^\sigma} = j)$. In such case, we will denote g by σ:

$$(x_i = j)^\sigma = (x_{i^\sigma} = j) \qquad (1)$$

A *value symmetry* is a symmetry g such that there exists a permutation θ of I^n such that $(x_i = j)^g = (x_i = j^\theta)$. In such case we will denote g by θ:

$$(x_i = j)^\theta = (x_i = j^\theta) \qquad (2)$$

Our definition of symmetries is similar to the one used in [10].

3 Breaking Variable Symmetries Using Computational Group Theory

The set of symmetries of a CSP forms a group, in the mathematical sense. Indeed, the composition of two symmetries is a symmetry, the identity function is a symmetry, and any symmetry can be inverted. This observation led to the publication of various symmetry breaking techniques that use the properties of the symmetry group. These use Computational Group Theory(CGT) [21] : GAP-SBDD [8], GAP-SBDS [7], and GE-tree [19]. In [14] we have used CGT to prove that all the variable symmetries of a CSP could be broken with at most $n-1$ binary constraints provided that all variables are pairwise different. The reminder of this section explains this method. First of all, let us introduce two useful notions.

Breaking All Value Symmetries in Surjection Problems

Given $i \in I^n$ and a permutation group $G \subseteq S^n$, the *orbit* of i in G, denoted i^G, is the set of elements to which i can be mapped to by an element of G:

$$i^G = \{i^\sigma | \sigma \in G\}$$

Given $i \in I^n$ and a permutation group $G \subseteq S^n$, the *stabilizer* of i in G, denoted i_G, is the set of permutations of G that leave i unchanged:

$$i_G = \{\sigma \in G | i^\sigma = i\}$$

Let us see how this method works on the example given in the introduction. This example can be modeled with a 3 by 5 matrix model as follows:

x_0	x_1	x_2	x_3	x_4
x_5	x_6	x_7	x_8	x_9
x_{10}	x_{11}	x_{12}	x_{13}	x_{14}

Variable symmetries are generated by column permutations and by row permutations. We will identify a variable and its index. We first consider the group of variable symmetries G_0. We compute the orbit of 0 in this group. This is the set of variables to which x_0 can be mapped to using any permutation of both row and columns. It is easy to see that any variable can be reached this way. Therefore, the orbit of 0 is the set of all variables:

$$U_0 = 0^{G_0} = \{0,1,2,3,4,5,6,7,8,9,10,11,12,13,14\}$$

We then consider the stabilizer G_1 of 0 in G_0. This is the set of symmetries that leave x_0 unchanged. Any symmetry in G_1 maps the first row to itself, and the first column to itself. The other row can be permuted, and the other columns can be permuted. Then we compute the orbit of 1 in G_1. It is easy to see that this is the first row except for 0. Therefore, the orbit of 1 in G_1 is :

$$U_1 = 1^{G_1} = \{1,2,3,4\}$$

We then compute the stabilizer of 1, etc. This yields

$$G_2 = 1_{G_1}, \; U_2 = 2^{G_2} = \{2,3,4\}$$
$$G_3 = 2_{G_2}, \; U_3 = 3^{G_3} = \{3,4\}$$
$$G_4 = 3_{G_3}, \; U_4 = 4^{G_4} = \{4\}$$
$$G_5 = 4_{G_3}, \; U_5 = 5^{G_5} = \{5,10\}$$
$$G_i = \{id\}, \; U_i = \{i\} \quad \forall i \geq 6$$

More generally, we compute the sequence of stabilizers and orbits defined by:

$$G_0 = G, \; G_i = (i-1)_{G_{i-1}}, \; U_i = i^{G_i}$$

By definition, $G_i = \{\sigma \in G | 0^\sigma = 0 \wedge \ldots \wedge (i-1)^\sigma = i-1\}$
Then we state the constraints:

$$\forall i, j \in I^n, (j \in U_i \wedge j \neq i) \rightarrow (x_i < x_j)$$

In our example, this yields the following constraints:

$$\forall i = 1, \ldots, 14, \ x_0 < x_i,$$
$$\forall i = 2, \ldots, 4, \ x_1 < x_i$$
$$\forall i = 3, 4, \ x_2 < x_i$$
$$x_3 < x_4$$
$$x_5 < x_{10}$$

Some constraints are redundant. For instance $x_0 < x_{10}$ is implied by $x_0 < x_5$ and $x_5 < x_{10}$. These can be removed as follows. Given $j \in I^n$, it may be the case that j belongs to several of the sets U_i. In such case, let us define r_j as the largest i different from j such that j belongs to U_i. If j belongs to no U_i other than U_j, then let $r_j = j$. Then, the main result of [14] states:

Theorem 1. [14] *With the above notation, given a CSP with n variables $x_0, \ldots, x_{n-1}$ such that all variables are pairwise distinct, then all variable symmetries can be broken by at most $n - 1$ binary constraints. These constraints are given by :*

$$\forall j \in I^n, \ r_j \neq j \rightarrow x_{r_j} < x_j \tag{3}$$

Theorem 1 can be slightly extended (see [15]) by relaxing the surjection condition into a weaker form where any pair of variables appearing in the same orbit are different :

$$\forall i, j, k, \ j \in U_i \wedge k \in U_i \rightarrow x_j \neq x_k \tag{4}$$

In our example, the constraints (3) are:

$$\forall i = 6, \ldots, 14, \ x_0 < x_i,$$
$$\forall i = 0, \ldots, 3, \ x_i < x_{i+1}$$
$$x_0 < x_5 < x_{10}$$

In other words, x_0 must be the smallest element in the matrix, the first row must be increasing, and the first column must be increasing. In this case, we find the same constraints as the ones given in [4]. There are only 30 solutions satisfying these constraints. Without these constraints, there are 21600 solutions, many of them being symmetric variants.

4 Breaking Value Symmetries

We are given a surjection CSP. The key idea of our method is to reason about the order in which values appear in the solution of the CSP $\mathcal{P}$. Let us select an arbitrary ordering on the variables of $\mathcal{P}$. Without loss of generality, we can rename the variables such that the ordering is $x_0, x_1, \ldots, x_n$. Let z_j be the index of the first variable equal to j:

$$\forall j \in I^d, \forall i \in I^n, \ z_j = min\{i \in I^n | x_i = j\} \tag{5}$$

Then, any value symmetry is a variable symmetry for the variables z_j. Indeed, let us define a new CSP $val(\mathcal{P})$. Its variables are the variables z_j. The domain of these variables is I^n. The constraints are:

$$\exists (x_i)_{i \in I^n} \ C \wedge (z_j = min\{i \in I^n | x_i = j\})$$

where C is the set of the constraints of $\mathcal{P}$. In other words, a solution of $val(\mathcal{P})$ is computed from a solution of $\mathcal{P}$ using (5). Then, we have:

Lemma 2. *Every value symmetry θ for $\mathcal{P}$ induces a variable symmetry of $val(\mathcal{P})$. This variable symmetry is defined by:*

$$(z_j = a)^\theta = (z_{j^\theta} = a)$$

Proof. Let us consider a solution s for $val(\mathcal{P})$. We want to prove that $\theta(s)$ is a solution of $val(\mathcal{P})$. s is of the form $z_j = min\{i | a_i = j\}$, where $x_i = a_i$ is a solution of $\mathcal{P}$. Then $x_i = a_i^\theta$ is also a solution of $\mathcal{P}$ because θ is a value symmetry for $\mathcal{P}$. The corresponding solution for $val(\mathcal{P})$ is given by $z_j = min\{i | a_i^\theta = j\}$. This is equivalent to $z_j = min\{i | a_i = j^{(\theta^{-1})}\}$. This, in turn, is equivalent to $z_{j^\theta} = min\{i | a_i = j\}$. □

Therefore, one can use any variable symmetry breaking technique on the z variables in order to break value symmetries on the CSP. One could, for instance, use the lexicographic constraints of [3]. The number of these constraints can grow exponentially with the number of variables z_j. Using the following result, we can significantly reduce the number of symmetry breaking constraints.

Lemma 3. *Let z_j be d variables satisfying (5). Then, we have that*

$$\forall i, j \in I^d, i \neq j \ \to \ z_i \neq z_j$$

Proof. Each variable x_i can take only one value. □

Therefore we can apply the symmetry breaking technique described in the previous section, which yields:

Theorem 4. *With the above notation, all value symmetries can be broken with at most $d - 1$ binary constraints on the z_j variables.*

Proof. Breaking all variable symmetries of $val(\mathcal{P})$ breaks all value symmetries by Lemma 2. The variables of $val(\mathcal{P})$ are pairwise different by Lemma 3. Therefore, Theorem 1 can be applied. □

Note that this is still valid if condition (4) holds.

The second idea used in our method is that the channeling constraint (5) can be enforced in a surprisingly simple way:

Theorem 5. *With the above notations, constraint (5) is equivalent to a linear number of binary constraints. These constraints are given by:*

$$\forall i \in I^n, j \in I^d, \ (x_i = j) \to (z_j \leq i) \tag{6}$$

$$\forall i \in I^n, j \in I^d, \ (z_j = i) \rightarrow (x_i = j) \tag{7}$$

Proof. The fact that the variables z_j satisfy both (6) and (7) is an immediate consequence of (5). We need to prove that the converse is true. Assume that the variables z_j satisfy both (6) and (7). Assume further that $x_i = a_i$ is a solution of $\mathcal{P}$. Let c_j be the value of z_j. Let us define $b_j = min\{i | x_i = j\}$. We want to prove that $c_j = b_j$. By (6) $z_j \leq i$ for each i such that $a_i = j$. Therefore $c_j \leq min\{i | x_i = j\}$, i.e. $c_j \leq b_j$. Conversely, by (7), $x_{c_j} = j$, therefore $c_j \geq b_j$. There are $2nd$ binary constraints in (6) and (7), which is linear in the size of the CSP. □

Let us look at our example. We introduce 15 variables z_i, and the corresponding channeling constraints (6)(7). Value symmetries are generated by team permutations as explained in the introduction. Applying the above results to this group of value symmetries yields the following constraints:

$$\forall i > 0, \quad z_0 < z_i$$
$$\forall i = 2 \ldots 8, \ z_1 < z_i$$
$$z_2 < z_3$$
$$z_3 < z_4$$

Adding these constraints to the problem leaves only 30 solutions instead of 21600. Note that these 30 solutions are not the same as the 30 solutions that satisfy the variable symmetry breaking constraints given in the previous section. In fact there is only one solution satisfying both set of constraints.

5 Breaking Both Variable and Value Symmetries

For the sake of clarity, we will refer to variable symmetry breaking constraints (such as the ones of Theorem 1) as **VAR**, and we will refer to the value symmetry breaking constraints of Theorem 4 and Theorem 5 as **OCC**.

The combination of variable symmetry breaking with value symmetry breaking has received some interest in the recent years, see [10] [20] [14] [4] for instance. It would be tempting to say that one can freely state **VAR** constraints with the **OCC** constraints. This can be wrong in general. For instance, let us consider a simple CSP with 2 variables x_0, x_1, a domain of 2 values, and the constraint $x_0 \neq x_1$. There are 2 solutions, $x_0 = 0 \land x_1 = 1$, and $x_0 = 1 \land x_1 = 0$. Variable symmetries can be broken by adding the **VAR** constraint $x_0 > x_1$. The only solution satisfying this constraint is $x_0 = 1 \land x_1 = 0$. For value symmetries, we introduce two variables z_0, z_1 and the channeling constraints (6)(7). Value symmetries can then be broken by $z_0 < z_1$. The only solutions satisfying this is $x_0 = 0 \land x_1 = 1$. On this example we see that there are no solutions that satisfy both the **VAR** constraints and the **OCC** constraints. In fact, the problem comes from the fact that we used incompatible order for the variables x_i when defining the symmetry breaking constraints.

Fortunately, both **VAR** and **OCC** constraints can be stated at the same time when the same variable ordering is used (X stands for the vector of variables x_i, and Z stands for the vector of variables z_j):

Theorem 6. *Let P be a CSP, G_1 its group of variable symmetries, and G_2 its group of value symmetries. The addition of the variables z_j, their channeling constraints (5) and the following constraints keep at least one solution in every solution orbit.*

$$\forall \sigma \in G_1, X \preceq X^\sigma \tag{8}$$
$$\forall \theta \in G_2, Z \preceq Z^\theta \tag{9}$$

This means that for any solution, there is a solution in its orbit (i.e. symmetrical to it) that satisfy (8) and (9). In particular, for surjection problems, we have seen that (9) is equivalent to the **OCC** constraints:

Corollary 7. *Let P be a surjection CSP, G_1 its group of variable symmetries, and G_2 its group of value symmetries. The addition of the variables z_j, their channeling constraints (5), the constraints (8) and the **OCC** constraints keep at least one solution in every solution orbit.*

Proof of theorem 6. It is shown in [4] how to transform $\mathcal{P}$ into a new CSP $\mathcal{P}'$ such that all value symmetries of $\mathcal{P}$ become variable symmetries of $\mathcal{P}'$. Although this was used for the case where any row permutation and any column permutation is a symmetry, this idea can be generalized to more general cases. The idea is to add $n \times d$ additional binary variables y_{ij} (variables with domains equal to $\{0,1\}$). We also add the following channeling constraints:

$$\forall i \in I^n, j \in I^d, (y_{ij} = 1) \leftrightarrow (x_i = j) \tag{10}$$

These constraints state that $y_{ij} = 1$ if and only if $x_i = j$. Adding these new variables does not change the solutions of the CSP. Variable symmetries of $\mathcal{P}$ are equivalent to permutations of the rows of the y_{ij} matrix by (1). Value symmetries of $\mathcal{P}$ are equivalent to permutations of the columns of the same matrix by (2).

Let Y be the vector obtained by concatenating the columns of the matrix y_{ij}. The variables y_{ij} are ranked in increasing values of j then increasing values of i in the vector Y. Let Y_j be the variables in the j-th column of the matrix. Since a variable x_i can only take one value, the columns of the y_{ij} matrix must be all different. More precisely, no two columns can have a variable equal to 1 in the same row. This means that it is sufficient to compare the index of the first occurrence of '1' in each column in order to compare lexicographically two columns Y_j and Y_k. These indices are precisely equal to the variables z_j and z_k that were introduced in the previous section. Therefore :

$$(Y_j \preceq Y_k) \leftrightarrow (z_j < z_k) \tag{11}$$

Let us consider a value symmetry θ for $\mathcal{P}$. Then θ is a permutation of the matrix columns. The value symmetry θ maps columns to columns. This is formalized as follows:

$$Y_j = (y_{0i}, y_{1j}, \ldots, y_{(d-1)j})$$
$$(Y^\theta)_j = (y_{0j^\theta}, y_{1j^\theta}, \ldots, y_{(d-1)j^\theta})$$

This symmetry is broken by the lexicographic constraint [3]:

$$Y \preceq Y^\theta$$

From the definition of $\preceq$, this is equivalent to the disjunction of the following constraints:

$$Y_0 < Y_{0\sigma}$$
$$Y_0 = Y_{0\sigma} \wedge Y_1 < Y_{1\sigma}$$
$$\vdots$$
$$Y_0 = Y_{0\sigma} \wedge \ldots \wedge Y_{d-2} = Y_{(d-2)\sigma} \wedge Y_{d-1} < Y_{(d-1)\sigma}$$
$$Y_0 = Y_{0\sigma} \wedge \ldots \wedge Y_{d-2} = Y_{(d-2)\sigma} \wedge Y_{d-1} = Y_{(d-1)\sigma}$$

By using (11), this is exactly equivalent to $Z \preceq Z^\theta$. This proves that:

$$(Y \preceq Y^\theta) \leftrightarrow (Z \preceq Z^\theta) \quad (12)$$

Similarly, one can prove that for any variable symmetry σ, we have:

$$(Y \preceq Y^\sigma) \leftrightarrow (X \preceq X^\sigma) \quad (13)$$

From [3], it is safe to add all possible lexicographic constraints on the Y variables. In particular, it is safe to add the following constraints:

$$\forall \sigma \in G_1, Y \preceq Y^\sigma$$
$$\forall \theta \in G_2, Y \preceq Y^\theta$$

By (13) and (12) these are equivalent to (8) and (9). □

6 Experimental Results

6.1 Implementation Hints

Our approach does not require any additional input beside the CSP. Both variable and value symmetries are automatically derived using the method of [16]. Then, the algorithm of [14] is applied for generating the constraints on the z_j variables.

All the running times are expressed in seconds. They are measured on a 1.4 GHz Pentium M laptop running Windows XP and ILOG Solver 6.1. Unless otherwise stated, the search used to solve the examples is quite straightforward. It is a depth first search where one variable is selected at each node. The order in which variables is selected is the order given by variable indices. Values are tried in increasing order.

6.2 Full Value Symmetry Group

Things get simpler when any value permutation is a symmetry. Typical examples include bin packing and graph coloring. In the latter, the exact color assigned to a vertex does not matter. What matter are the sets of vertices that have the same color. For problems where any value permutation is a value symmetry, our algorithm results in the following constraints:

$$\text{OCC} \begin{cases} \forall i \in I^n, j \in I^d, & x_i = j \to z_j \leq i \\ \forall i \in I^n, j \in I^d, & z_j = i \to x_i = j \\ \forall j \in I^{d-1} & z_j < z_{j+1} \end{cases}$$

Several methods have been published for breaking value symmetries in this case. A modified search strategy was proposed in [22]. See also [2] for a modified search strategy breaking value symmetries for graph coloring problems. A set of constraint achieving the same effect as the search of [22] is proposed in [5]. The idea is to introduce $2n$ variables m_i and r_i such that:

$$\text{IPG} \begin{cases} \forall i \in I^n, & m_i \in I^n \\ \forall i \in I^n, & r_i \in I^n \\ \forall i \in I^n, & x_i = x_{r_i} \\ \forall i \in I^n, & r_i = r_{r_i} \\ \forall i \in I^n, & r_i \leq i \\ & x_0 = 0 \\ & m_0 = 0 \\ & r_0 = 0 \\ \forall i \in I^n, i > 0 & m_i = max(m_{i-1}, x_i) \\ \forall i \in I^n, i > 0 & (r_i = i) \leftrightarrow (m_i - 1 = m_{i-1}) \end{cases}$$

These are much more complex and less efficient than our constraints (OCC).

Let us look at the $n \times n$ queen problem taken from [10]. The problem is to color a $n \times n$ chessboard with n colors, such that no line (row, column or diagonal) contains the same color twice. This can be seen as searching for n non intersecting solutions to the n queens problem. Each solution is given by the squares containing one of the n colors. This problem can be modeled with n^2 variables, one per square of the chess board, and one all different constraint per line. We assume that variables are ordered row by row.

x_0	x_1	...	x_{n-1}
x_n	x_{n+1}	...	x_{2n-1}
⋮	⋮	⋮	⋮
$x_{n(n-1)}$	...	...	x_{n^2-1}

Value symmetry breaking constraints are:

$$z_1 < z_2 < \ldots < z_{n-1} < z_n$$

There are also some variable symmetries corresponding to the 8 symmetries of a square. These can be broken by the following **VAR** constraints [15]:

$$x_0 < x_{n-1}, x_0 < x_{n(n-1)}, x_0 < x_{n^2-1}, x_1 < x_n$$

We can state both variable and value symmetry breaking constraints because of corollary 7. Results are shown in Table 1. First fail principle is used: the variable with the smallest domain size is selected during search. We also give the results of [10], where SBBD and GE-trees are used to break all the symmetries of the problem. These methods break all symmetries, but they are very expensive. Our technique is much more efficient. However, it does not break all symmetries, as shown by the number of solutions found. Our method breaks values symmetries and it breaks variable symmetries, but it does not break all their combinations. A possible explanation is the following. The propagation of value symmetry breaking constraints fixes the first row:

$$x_0 = 0, x_1 = 1, \ldots, x_{n-1} = n - 1$$

Then it is easy to see that all variable symmetry breaking constraints are trivially satisfied. This means that stating these constraints will not further reduce the number of solutions of the problem.

Table 1. Results for finding all solutions to the $n \times n$ queen problem

n	[10] sols	[10] time	VAR+OCC sols	VAR+OCC bt	VAR+OCC time
5	1	0.68	2	0	0
6	0	0.96	0	5	0
7	1	8.36	4	271	0.11
8	0	927.36	0	23794	4.27

6.3 Permutation Problems

Another special case of interest is when the variables of the CSP must be pairwise different, among other constraints. This class of problems is quite large. It includes the pigeon hole problem and the sports scheduling problem.

Most perfect magic squares, studied in [13], are given as an example of a CSP with convoluted value symmetries in [19]. In [13], it is proven that most perfect magic squares are in a one to one relationship with *reversible squares*. A reversible square of size $n \times n$ (where $n \equiv 0 \mod 4$) has entries $1 \ldots n^2$ such that:

1. The sum or the two entries at diagonally opposite corners of any rectangle or sub-square equals the sum of the other pair of diagonally opposite corners.
2. In each row or column, the sum of the first and last entries equals the sum of the next and the next to last number, etc.
3. Diametrically opposed numbers sum to $n^2 + 1$.

Any solution is one of $2^{n+1}((n/2)!)^2$ symmetric equivalent [13]. For $n = 16$, this is about 2.13e+14. The model of [19] for this problem has one variable per entry with its cell as value. In addition to the above constraints on entries, there is an all different constraint. Therefore, **OCC** constraints can be used. It is worth noting that in this case the channeling constraints of theorem 5 can be simplified into:

$$\forall i \in I^n, j \in I^d, \ (x_i = j) \leftrightarrow (z_j = i) \tag{14}$$

This means that the z_j variables are the variables corresponding to cells, with entries as values.

We report for various sizes the time used to compute the symmetry breaking constraints (CGT) as well as the time used for finding all non symmetrical solutions (search). We also report the results of [19], obtained with GAP-SBDD and with GE-tree on a computer about half the speed of ours. A direct comparison is difficult because they directly search for most perfect magic squares whereas we search for reversible squares. It is worth comparing the time spent in the symmetry computations though, because these deal with the same symmetry group. Our method spends much less time in symmetry computations because these need to be done only once before the search starts.

Table 2. Results for finding all solutions on the most perfect magic squares

		OCC		GAP-SBDD		GE-tree	
n	sols	CGT	search	CGT	search	CGT	search
4	3	0.01	0.02	0.3	0.3	0.2	0.1
8	10	0.09	0.39	5.4	125.4	0.7	90.0
12	42	0.44	22.2	2745	12518	29.1	10901.8
16	35	4.6	275.6				

6.4 Sports League Scheduling

The example given in the introduction has been solved using the model of [17]. In this model, some clever symmetry breaking constraint was added. The game (0 vs. i) must appear on week i. We compare this symmetry breaking constraint with the **VAR** constraints and the **OCC** constraints. Results are given in table 3. A "-" means that the program was still running after one hour. This shows that our automatically derived symmetry breaking constraints are more efficient than carefully thought ones.

Table 3. Results for finding all solutions on sports league scheduling

n	no sym		[17]		VAR		OCC		VAR+OCC	
	sols	bt time	sols	bt time	sols	bt time	sols	bt time	sols	bt time
6	21600	139454 9.89	60	448 0.11	30	220 0.09	30	480 0.2	1	18 0.04
8		-		-		-		-	1385	458073 157.5

In [18], a better model was proposed. The idea was to first ignore the constraint stating that each team must play at most twice in a given period. Then the problem is a round robin problem, for which solutions are known. The problem is then to rearrange the games within each week so that the period constraint is satisfied. Therefore, value symmetries are permutations of teams that map games to games in the same week. In [18], symmetries are broken by a fixing one game.

Table 4. Results for finding all solutions using 2nd model

n	[18]			VAR			OCC			VAR+OCC		
	sols	bt	time	sols	bt	time	sols	bt	time	sols	bt	time
6	2	12	0.04	5	17	0.06	3	8	0.05	1	4	0.04
8	96	407	0.21	112	1491	0.32	128	1202	0.32	18	274	0.15
10	169344	2266531	224.29	63504	2150549	232.04	307572	6727391	723.36	10357	327602	35.15

We report results for this improved model in table 4. Again, our automatically derived symmetry breaking constraints are more efficient than carefully thought ones.

We have also benchmarked the timings needed to find the first solution using the second model. We have used the variable ordering described in [18]. We have compared the timings with the symmetry breaking constraint of [18] and our combination of **VAR** and **OCC** constraints. We have not detected any measurable difference up to $n = 40$. The ILOG Solver code used for [17] and [18] are available from the author.

7 Related Work and Future Research

We have presented a surprisingly simple yet effective way of breaking all value symmetries for a large class of CSPs. These are CSPs where all values appear in every solution. Our method relies on the introduction of one variable per value of the problem. This variable represents the index of the first occurrence of the value. A surprisingly simple set of channeling constraints are sufficient to define the value of this variable. Channeling constraints can be expressed with a linear number of rather simple binary constraints. Then value symmetries are equivalent to variable symmetries for these newly added variables. Breaking these symmetries can be done with a linear number of constraints. We have further shown that it is safe to combine this new way of breaking value symmetries with symmetry breaking constraints.

Our method has been fully automated. First of all, the value symmetry group and the variable symmetry group are computed using graph automorphism packages [16]. Second, once the symmetry groups are given, symmetry breaking constraints are automatically derived using computational group theory. Various experiments show that our method is much more efficient than the previously published ones.

The idea of using channeling constraints for turning value symmetries in variable symmetries has been proposed in [4]. In that paper, it was proposed to replace the variables of the CSP by binary variables defined by equation (10). However this was only defined for problems where any value permutation is a symmetry. In [11] and [12], channeling constraints are proposed for matrix models. However, the channeling constraints are different from ours. In that work, a set variable is introduced for every value. This set variable represents the set of occurrences of the value (instead of the *first* occurrence in our case). Then symmetries are broken using lexicographic constraints on the matrix of set variables. When the group of value symmetries is not the full symmetry group, an exponential number of symmetry breaking constraints can be necessary for breaking all symmetries. This is to be contrasted with our approach that only requires a *linear* number of binary constraints for breaking all value symmetries. The method of [3] has been improved in [1]. In that work, a linear number of symmetry breaking constraints is stated, one for each generator of the symmetry group. However, these do not necessarily break all symmetries, contrarily to the ones we are using.

Our method breaks all value symmetries, provided all values appear in any solution of the problem. The method can still be applied when this is not true. First of all, the method can be applied provided condition (4) holds. Second, we can always extend a CSP so that the surjection condition becomes true. It is sufficient to add d dummy variables $x_n, x_{n+1}, \ldots, x_{n+d-1}$ with domains $D_{n+i} = \{i\}$. Adding these variables does not change the solutions of the CSP. However, the CSP is now a surjection: each value appears in at least one of the variables $x_0, x_1, \ldots, x_{n+d-1}$. Our method can then be applied. It is strong enough to still break all symmetries in a modified pigeon hole problem where variable domains are enlarged. However, it may not break all value symmetries in all problems. We plan to evaluate this technique on various non surjective problems.

Another possible improvement of the method is to look for cases where it would be easy to break the symmetries that are the product of a variable symmetry and a value symmetry. Indeed, we have provided various evidence that breaking variable symmetries and value symmetries separately still leaves many symmetries in the problems at hand.

Last, it would be interesting to see if the method can be extended to handle local symmetries, i.e. symmetries that appear during the search for solutions.

Acknowledgements

The author would like to thank Marie Puget and anonymous referees for their remarks. They greatly helped improving the readability of this paper.

References

[1] F. Aloul, I. Markov, and K. Sakallah "Efficient Symmetry-Breaking for Boolean Satisfiability". In *proceedings of IJCAI 03*, Acapulco, Mexico, pp. 271-282, 2003.
[2] Benhamou B., "Symmetry in Not-equals Binary Constraint Networks". *In Proceedings of SymCon'04*, pp. 2-8, Toronto, September 2004

[3] Crawford, J., Ginsberg, M., Luks E.M., Roy, A. "Symmetry Breaking Predicates for Search Problems". *In proceedings of KR'96*, pp. 148-159.
[4] P. Flener, A. M. Frisch, B. Hnich, Z. Kiziltan, I. Miguel, J. Pearson, T. Walsh.: "Breaking Row and Column Symmetries in Matrix Models". *In Proceedings of CP'02*, pp. 462-476, 2002
[5] Ian P. Gent "A Symmetry Breaking Constraint for Indistinguishable Values". *In proceedings of SymCon01*, a CP'01 workshop.
[6] I. Gent, T. Walsh, and B. Selman CSPLIB, A problem library for constraints http://www.csplib.org
[7] Gent, I.P., and Harvey, W., and Kelsey, T.: "Groups and Constraints: Symmetry Breaking During Search". *In proceedings of CP 2002*, pp. 415-430.
[8] Gent, I.P., Harvey, W., Kelsey, T., Linton, S.: "Generic SBDD Using Computational Group Theory". *In proceedings of CP 2003*, pp. 333-437
[9] ILOG: ILOG Solver 6.0. User Manual. ILOG, S.A., Gentilly, France, September 2003
[10] Kelsey, T, Linton, SA, Roney-Dougal, CM. "New Developments in Symmetry Breaking in Search Using Computational Group Theory". *In Proceedings AISC 2004*. Springer LNAI. 2004.
[11] Y. C. Law and J. H. M. Lee. "Expressing Symmetry Breaking Constraints Using Multiple Viewpoints and Channeling Constraints". *In Proceedings of SymCon 03* (held in conjunction with CP-2003), pages 127-141, 2003.
[12] Y. C. Law and J. H. M. Lee. "Breaking Value Symmetries in Matrix Models using Channeling Constraints". *In Proceedings of the 20th Annual ACM Symposium on Applied Computing (SAC-2005)*, pages 375-380, 2005.
[13] Dame Ollerenshaw, K. "On most perfect or complete 8x8 pandiagonal magic squares". *In Proceedings Royal Society London*, 407, 259-281, 1986.
[14] Puget, J.-F.: "Breaking symmetries in all different problems". To appear in proceedings of IJCAI 05.
[15] Puget, J.-F.: "Elimination de symetries dans les problmes injectifs." To appear in proceedings of JFPC 05 (in French).
[16] Puget, J.-F.: "Automatic detection of variable and value symmetries" To appear in the proceedings of CP 05, Sitges, 2005.
[17] J-C. Regin, "Modeling and Solving Sports League Scheduling with Constraint Programming", Informs, April 1998, Montreal.
[18] J-C. Regin, "Constraint Programming and Sports Scheduling Problems", Informs, May 1999, Cincinnati.
[19] Roney-Dougal C.M., Gent, I.P., Kelsey T., Linton S.: "Tractable symmetry breaking using restricted search trees" *In proceedings of ECAI'04*.
[20] Meinolf Sellmann and Pascal Van Hentenryck Structural Symmetry Breaking To appear in proceedings of IJCAI 05.
[21] Seress, A.: *Permutation Group Algorithms* Cambrige University Press, 2003.
[22] Van Hentenryck, P., *Constraint Satisfaction in Logic Programming*, MIT press, 1989.

AC-*: A Configurable, Generic and Adaptive Arc Consistency Algorithm

Jean-Charles Régin

Computing and Information Science, Cornell University, Ithaca NY 14850 USA
jcregin@cs.cornell.edu

Abstract. In this paper, we present AC-*, a new configurable, generic and adaptive algorithm for establishing arc consistency for binary constraints. AC-* is configurable, that is by combining some parameters AC-* corresponds to any existing AC algorithm: AC-3, AC-4, AC-6, AC-7, AC-2000, AC-2001, AC-8, AC-3_d, AC-3.2 and AC-3.3. AC-* is generic, like AC-5, because it may take into account the structure of the constraints.

AC-* is adaptive because the underlining algorithm can be changed during the computation in order to use the most efficient one. This new algorithm leads to a new nomenclature of the AC algorithms which is based on the different features used by the algorithm like the values that are reconsidered when a domain is modified, or the fact that bidirectionality is taken into account, or the way a new support is sought. This new nomenclature shows that several new possible combinations are now possible. That is, we can easily combine some ideas of AC-3 with some ideas of AC-7 and some ideas of AC-2001 with some ideas of AC-6. Some experimental results highlight the advantages of our approach.

1 Introduction

In this paper we focus our attention on binary constraints. For more than twenty years, a lot of algorithms establishing arc consistency (AC algorithms) have been proposed: AC-3 [6], AC-4 [7], AC-5 [9], AC-6 [1], AC-7, AC-Inference, AC-Identical [2], AC-8 [4], AC-2000: [3], AC-2001 (also denoted by AC-3.1 [10]) [3], AC-3_d [8], AC-3.2 and AC-3.3 [5]. Unfortunately, these algorithms are differently described and their comparison is not easy. Therefore, we propose a configurable, generic and adaptive AC algorithm, called AC-*.

Configurable means that the previous existing algorithms can be represented by setting some predefined parameters. This has some advantages:

- this unique algorithm can represent all known algorithms and it clearly shows the differences between them,
- some new arc consistency algorithms can be easily and quickly derived from AC-*, because some combinations of parameters have never been tested,
- AC-* leads to a new nomenclature which is much more explicit than the current one ("AC-" followed by a number.), because algorithms are now expressed by combinations of predefined parameters. For instance, AC-3 is renamed AC-pvD-sD and AC-6 becomes AC-pvΔs-last-sD.

Generic means that AC-* is also a framework that can be derived to take into account some specificity of some binary constraints. In other words, dedicated algorithms can be written, for functional constraints for instance. This corresponds to a part of the generic aspects of AC-5. In our case, the incremental behavior of the AC-5 is generalized.

Adaptive means that AC-* is able to use different algorithms successively as suggested in [3]. For instance, first AC-2001 can be used then AC-7 and then AC-2001 depending on which one seems to be the best for the current configuration of domains and delta domains. We think that **CP will be strongly improved if a filtering algorithm is in itself capable to select at each time its best version, instead of asking the user to do it a priori.**

This paper is organized as follows. First, we recall some definitions of CP. Then, we study all the existing algorithms, and we identify different concepts of the AC algorithms and detail the AC-* algorithm. A new nomenclature is proposed. Then, the adaptive behavior of AC-* algorithm is considered. At last, after studying some experiments, we conclude.

2 Preliminaries

A finite **constraint network** $\mathcal{N}$ is defined as a set of n **variables** $X = \{x_1, \ldots, x_n\}$, a set of current **domains** $\mathcal{D} = \{D(x_1), \ldots, D(x_n)\}$ where $D(x_i)$ is the finite set of possible **values** for variable x_i, and a set $\mathcal{C}$ of **constraints** between variables. A **constraint** C on the ordered set of variables $X(C) = (x_{i_1}, \ldots, x_{i_r})$ is a subset $T(C)$ of the Cartesian product $D(x_{i_1}) \times \cdots \times D(x_{i_r})$ that specifies the allowed combinations of values for the variables $x_{i_1}, \ldots, x_{i_r}$. An element of $D(x_{i_1}) \times \cdots \times D(x_{i_r})$ is called a **tuple** on $X(C)$ and $\tau[x]$ is the value of τ assigned to x. A value a for a variable x is often denoted by (x, a). (x, a) is **valid** iff $a \in D(x)$. Let C be a constraint. A tuple τ on $X(C)$ is **valid** iff $\forall x \in X(C), \tau[x] \in D(x)$; and τ is a **support** for (x, a) iff $\tau[x] = a$ and $\tau \in T(C)$. C is **consistent** iff $\exists \tau \in T(C)$ which is valid. A value $a \in D(x)$ is **consistent with** C iff $x \notin X(C)$ or there exists a valid support for (x, a). A constraint is **arc consistent** iff $\forall x \in X(C), D(x) \neq \emptyset$ and $\forall a \in D(x)$, a is consistent with C.

A **filtering algorithm** associated with a constraint C is an algorithm which may remove some values that are inconsistent with C; and that does not remove any consistent values. If the filtering algorithm removes all the values inconsistent with C then we say that it establishes arc consistency of C and that it is an AC algorithm.

The **delta domain** of a variable x with respect to a filtering algorithm F associated with a constraint C is the set of values that have been removed from the domain of x between two successive calls of F. It is denoted by $\Delta(x, F)$ and a value in $\Delta(x, F)$ is called a **delta value**. More information about delta domains can be found in [9] or in the manual of ILOG Solver. Note that the conjunction of the elements in the delta domains form the *waitingList* of AC-6 and AC-7 algorithms. Sometimes, all the filtering algorithms depending on the modifications of $D(x)$ are successively considered after the modifications of

x. Thus, if there is no side effect (that is x is not modified by these filtering algorithms), then all these filtering algorithms can share the same delta domain for x, and only one representation is needed. Therefore, there is no need to specify the filtering algorithm for identifying the delta domain associated with a filtering algorithm and the delta domain of x is denoted by $\Delta(x)$.

Propagation is the mechanism that consists of calling the filtering algorithm associated with the constraints involving a variable x each time the domain of this variable is modified. If every filtering algorithm associated with every constraint establishes arc consistency then we say that the propagation mechanism establishes arc consistency of the network.

Algorithm 1. function PROPAGATION

PROPAGATION()
    while $\exists y$ such that $\Delta(y) \neq \emptyset$ **do**
        pick y with $\Delta(y) \neq \emptyset$
        for each constraint C involving y **do**
            $(D(x), \Delta(x)) \leftarrow$ FILTER$(C, x, y, \Delta(y))$
            if $D(x) = \emptyset$ **then** return false
        $\Delta(y) \leftarrow \emptyset$
    return true

Function PROPAGATION of Algorithm 1 is a possible implementation of this mechanism when delta domains are shared.

The filtering algorithm associated with the constraint C defined on x and y corresponds to Function FILTER$(C, x, y, \Delta(y))$. This function removes some values of $D(x)$ that are not consistent with the constraint with respect to $\Delta(y)$. It also updates the delta domain of x. For a constraint C this function will also be called with the parameters $(C, y, x, \Delta(x))$.

3 Arc Consistency Algorithms

We will consider a constraint C defined on x and y for which we study the consequences of the modification of $D(y)$.

Definition 1. *Let x be a variable and F be a filtering algorithm aiming to remove some values of $D(x)$. We call **pending values** of x w.r.t. F, the set of **valid** values of x for which a valid support is sought by F when F is called.*

Thanks to this definition, and if every value which is not a pending value is consistent with the constraint then the principles of AC algorithms can be easily expressed:

Check whether there exists a valid support for every pending value and remove those that have none.

Algorithm 2. AC-* filtering algorithm

FILTER(**in** $C, x, y, \Delta(y)$): (domain,delta domain)
  get the parameters of C
  pvType← SELECTPVTYPE($C, x, y, \Delta(y)$,pvType)
  sType← SELECTSTYPE($C, x, y, \Delta(y)$,sType)
  (x, a) ← pvType.FIRSTPENDINGVALUE($C, x, y, \Delta(y)$)
  while $(x, a) \neq nil$ **do**
    if ¬ EXISTVALIDSUPPORT(C, x, a, y,sType) **then**
1 | $D(x) \leftarrow D(x) - \{a\}$
      | $\Delta(x) \leftarrow \Delta(x) \cup \{a\}$
      | **if** $D(x) = \emptyset$ **then return** $(\emptyset, \Delta(x))$
    (x, a) ← pvType.NEXTPENDINGVALUE($C, x, y, \Delta(y), a$)
  return $(D(x), \Delta(x))$

Algorithm 2 is a possible implementation of this principle. This is also the core of the generic AC-* algorithm. Functions SELECTPVTYPE and SELECTSTYPE can be ignored at this point. They will be detailed later. Functions FIRSTPENDINGVALUE and NEXTPENDINGVALUE identify the pending values, and Function EXISTVALIDSUPPORT searches for a valid support for these pending values.

We can now give the principles of these functions for each existing algorithm.

AC-3: The pending values are the values of $D(x)$, and $\Delta(y)$ is not used at all. All the values of $D(x)$ are considered and the search for a valid support is done by checking in $D(y)$ if there is a support for a value of $D(x)$. There is no memorization of the previous computations, so the same computations can be done several times. The search for a valid support of a value is in $O(d)$ and a value can be a pending value d times, so for one value the algorithm is in $O(d^2)$. Since there are d value, the time complexity for one constraint is in $O(d^3)$[1]. The advantage of this approach is that the space complexity is in $O(1)$ per constraint.

AC-4: In AC-4 the tuple set $T(C)$ of the constraint is pre-computed and stored in a structure that we call a **table**. This table contains for every value (x, a) a pointer to the next tuple involving (x, a). Therefore, the space complexity of AC-4 is in $O(d^2)$. The pending values are for each $(y, b) \in \Delta(y)$ all the valid values (x, a) such that $((x, a)(y, b)) \in T(C)$. The values that are not pending values are not compatible with the value of $\Delta(y)$, therefore there are consistent with the constraint. Note that a value (x, a) can be considered several times as a pending value for a given set $\Delta(y)$. The search for a valid support is immediate because Function EXISTVALIDSUPPORT can be implemented in $O(1)$ by associating with every value (x, a) a counter which counts the number of times

---

[1] In this paper, we will always express the complexities per constraint, because a constraint network can involved several types of constraints. The usual way to express complexities can be obtained by multiplying the complexity we give by the number of binary constraints of the network.

(x, a) has a support in $D(y)$. Then, each time this function is called the counter is decremented (because (x, a) lost a valid support) and if the counter is equal to zero then there is no longer any valid support. AC-4 was the first algorithm reaching the optimal $O(d^2)$ time complexity, because no computation is made twice. However, a lot of computations are systematically done.

AC-5: This algorithm is mainly a generic algorithm. It has been designed in order to be able to take into account the specificity or the structure of the considered constraints. In other words, Function EXISTVALIDSUPPORT can be specialized by the user in order to benefit from the exploitation of the structure of the constraint. For instance, functional constraints are more much simple and arc consistency for these constraints can be established in $O(d)$ per constraint. Function FILTER and the propagation mechanism we gave are similar to AC-5 ideas.

AC-6: AC-6 mixes some principles of AC-3 with some ideas of AC-4. AC-6 uses the idea of AC-4 to determine the pending values, but instead of considering all the values supported by the values in $\Delta(y)$, it exploits the fact that the knowledge of one support is enough. AC-6 can be viewed as a lazy computation of supports. AC-6 introduces another data structure which is a variation of the table: the **S-list**: for every value (y, b), S-list$[(y, b)]$ is the list of values that are currently supported by (y, b). Contrary to AC-4, in AC-6 the knowledge of only one support is enough, i.e. a value (x, a) is supported by **only one** value of $D(y)$. Hence there is at most one value of $D(y)$ that contains (x, a) in its S-list. Then, the pending values are the valid values contained in the S-lists of the values in $\Delta(y)$. If a value of $D(x)$ is not a pending value then it means that its support has not been deleted so the value is consistent with the constraint. If a new valid support (y, b) is found for a value (x, a) then (x, a) is removed from the S-list containing it and added to the S-list$[(y, b)]$. Note that, for a given $\Delta(y)$, a value (x, a) can be considered only once as a pending value. Function EXISTVALIDSUP-PORT is an improvement of the AC-3's one, because the checks in the domains are made w.r.t. an ordering and are started from the support that just has been lost. The space complexity of AC-6 is in $O(d)$ because a value belongs to at most one S-list and its time complexity is in $O(d^2)$, because a value can be a pending value only d times and the search for a valid support is done in $O(d)$ globally.

AC-7: This is an improvement of AC-6. AC-7 exploits the fact that if (x, a) is supported by (y, b) then (y, b) is also supported by (x, a). Then, for each pending value (x, a), AC-7 proposes to search first for a valid value in S-list$[(x, a)]$, and to remove from the S-list every non valid value which is reached. In this case, we say that the support is sought by **inference**. This idea contradicts an invariant of AC-6: a support found by inference is no longer necessarily the last value checked in $D(y)$ when searching for a valid support. Since this information is needed to avoid repeating some compatibility checks in Function EXISTVALIDSUPPORT, AC-7 introduces explicitly the concept of **last value** by the data **last** associated with every value in order to differentiate the concept of current support and the concept of last value returned by Function EXISTVALIDSUPPORT. AC-7 ensures the property: If $\text{last}[(x,a)] = (y,b)$ then there is no support (y,c) in $D(y)$ with $c < b$. If no support is found by inference, then AC-7 uses an improvement of the AC-6's method to find a support in $D(y)$. Negative compatibility checks can be avoided if $\text{last}[(y,b)] > (x,a)$, because in this case we know that (x,a) is a not a support of (y,b) and so that (y,b) is not a support for (x,a). The properties on which AC-7 is based are often called bidirectionalities. Hence, AC-7 is able to save some checks in the domain in regard to AC-6, while keeping the same space and time complexity.

AC-Inference: This algorithm uses the S-lists of AC-6 to determine in the same way the values for which a valid support must be sought, but the search for a new support is different from the AC-6's method. For every value (x,a), two lists of values are used: **P-list**$[(x,a)]$ and **U-list**$[(x,a)]$. P-list$[(x,a)]$ contains some supports of (x,a), where as U-list$[(x,a)]$ contains the values for which their compatibility with (x,a) has never been tested. When a valid support is sought for (x,a), it checks first if there is a valid value in P-list$[(x,a)]$, and every non valid value that is reached is removed from the P-list. If no valid value is found in the P-list, then the values of U-list$[(x,a)]$ are successively considered until a valid support is found. Every value of the U-list$[(x,a)]$ which is checked is removed from the U-list and added to the P-list if this value is a support. When a new support is found, then some inference rules can be applied to deduce new supports and the U-list and P-list are accordingly modified. The inference rules can be general like the AC-7's one or depending on the constraint like commutativity or reflexivity [2]. The space and time complexities are in $O(d^2)$ per constraint.

AC-Identical: This is an extension of AC-Inference which exploits the fact that the same constraint can be defined on different variables. In this case, any knowledge obtained from one constraint is inferred for the other similar constraints and the P-list and U-list are shared by similar constraints.

AC-2000: This is a modification of AC-3. The pending values are the values of $D(x)$ that have a support in $\Delta(y)$. No extra data is used, so it is costly to compute the pending values. Thus, AC-2000 uses this set of pending values only if $|\Delta(y)| < 0.2|D(x)|$; otherwise $D(x)$ is considered as in AC-3. Hence, AC-2000 is the first adaptive AC algorithm.

AC-2001: This algorithm is based on AC-3 and uses the "last value" concept of AC-6. That is, the pending values are the same as for AC-3 and function EXISTVALIDSUPPORT is similar as the AC-6'one, except that it is checked if the last value is valid. This algorithm inherits the space complexity of AC-6, without using the S-lists. Note also that this presentation of AC-2001 is original and simpler than the one given in [3].

AC-3.3: AC-3.3 is an improvement of AC-2001 which associates with every value (x,a) a counter corresponding to a lower bound of the size of S-list$[(x,a)]$. The algorithm does not use any S-list, but counters instead. When a valid support is sought for, the counter of (x,a) is first tested, if it is strictly greater than 0 then we know that a valid support exists. This valid support cannot be identified but we know that there is one. If (y,b) is deleted then the counters of all the values supported by (y,b) are decremented.

We will not consider AC-8 [4], AC-3_d [8], and AC-3.2 [5], because they mainly improve AC-3 by proposing to propagate the constraints w.r.t. specific orderings, and this is not our purpose.

The AC algorithms may use the following data structures:

Support: support$[(x,a)]$ is the current support of (x,a).
Last: the last value of (x,a) is represented by last$[(x,a)]$ which is a value of $D(y)$ or nil.
S-List, P-List, U-list: these are classical list data structures. For any list L we consider that we are provided with the following functions implemented in $O(1)$: ADD$(L,(x,a))$, which adds (x,a) to L, REMOVE$(L,(x,a))$, which removes (x,a) from L, and $|L|$ which computes the size of L.
Tuple counters: For each $a \in D(x)$: counter$[(x,a)]$ counts the number of valid tuples of $T(C)$ containing (x,a).
Table: A table is the set of tuples $T(C)$ associated with two functions implemented in $O(1)$: FIRSTTUPLE(C,y,b) which returns the first tuple of $T(C)$ containing (y,b) and NEXTTUPLE(C,y,b,τ) which returns the first tuple of $T(C)$ containing (y,b) and following τ. These functions return nil when no such specified tuple exists.

Now, we propose to identify the different concepts used by the existing algorithms instead of having one function per algorithm and one parameter corresponding to each specific algorithm. Thus, we will have a configurable algorithm from which every AC algorithm could be obtained by combining some parameters, each of them corresponding to a concept.

4 Pending Values

Finding efficiently a small set of pending values is difficult because pending values sets deal with two different concepts at the same time: validity and support. Thus, several sets of pending values have been considered. We identify four type of sets called pvType:

1. The values of $D(x)$ (like in AC-3, AC-2001, AC-3.3). This set is denoted by pvD.
2. The valid values lastly supported by the values of $\Delta(y)$, that is the AC-Inference, AC-Identical. It is denoted by pvΔs.
3. The values that belong to a tuple containing a value of $\Delta(y)$. A value is pending as many times as it is contained in such a tuple. AC-4 uses this set denoted by pvΔt.
4. The values of $D(x)$ compatible with at least one value of $\Delta(y)$, as in
5. AC-2000. This set is denoted by pvΔc.

Since we aim to have a generic algorithm, we propose to define a fifth type: pvG which represents any function given by the user. For instance, for $x < y$ only the modifications of the maximum value of $D(y)$ can lead to new deletions. Thus, the pending values are the values of $D(x)$ that are greater than the maximum value of $D(y)$.

Algorithm 3 is a possible implementation of the computation of pending values. Depending on the type of pending values, the algorithm traverses a particular set. Note that some functions require "internal data" (a data whose value is stored). We assume that FIRST$(D(x))$ returns the first value of $D(x)$ and NEXT$(D(x), a)$ returns the first value of $D(x)$ strictly greater than a. Function SEEKVALIDSUPPORTEDVALUE(C, x, a) returns a valid supported value belonging to the S-list$[(y, b)]$.

5 Existence of a Valid Support

Function EXISTVALIDSUPPORT also differentiates the existing algorithms. Almost each algorithm uses a different method. We identify eight ways to check whether a valid support exists for (x, a):

1. Check in the domain from scratch (AC-3, AC-2000.)
2. Check if the last value is still valid and if not check in the domain from the last value (AC-2001.)
3. Check in the domain from the last value (AC-6.)
4. Test if a valid support can be found in S-list$[(x, a)]$, then check in the domain from the last value. When searching in the domain, use the fact that last values are available to avoid explicit compatibility checks (AC-7.)
5. Check if there is a valid support in P-list$[(x, a)]$, if there is none check the compatibility with the valid values of U-list$[(x, a)]$. After checking some compatibilities, deduce the results of some other compatibility checks and update accordingly U-lists and P-lists (AC-Inference, AC-identical.)
6. Decrement the counter storing the number of valid supports and test if it is strictly greater than 0 (AC-4.)
7. Use a specific function dedicated to the constraint.
8. Use counters storing a lower bound of |S-list$[(x, a)]$|, and check in the domain from the last value (AC-3.3.)

The last point deserves a particular attention. The time complexity of using a counter of the number of elements in a list is the same as the management of the list. Moreover, AC-3.3 implies that the counters are immediately updated when a value is removed, which is not the case with AC-7, which uses a lazy approach to maintain the consistency of the S-list. This has been proved more efficient. Therefore, we will implement AC-3.3 with S-lists instead of lower bounds.

We propose to consider the following parameters:

- last: the search for a valid support uses the last data to restart the search from it. The last value is also used to avoid some negative checks (AC-6, AC-7, AC-Inference, AC-Identical, AC-2001, AC-3.3.)

Algorithm 3. Pending values selection based on *pvType*

$$\text{pvType} = \underline{\text{pvD}}$$

FIRSTPENDINGVALUE$(C, x, y, \Delta(y))$: return FIRST$(D(x))$
NEXTPENDINGVALUE$(C, x, y, \Delta(y), a)$: return NEXT$(D(x), a)$

$$\text{pvType} = \underline{\text{pv}\Delta\text{s}} \text{ (b is a local data)}$$

FIRSTPENDINGVALUE$(C, x, y, \Delta(y))$: value
  | $b \leftarrow$ FIRST$(\Delta(y))$
  | return TRAVERSES-LIST$(C, x, y, \Delta(y))$

NEXTPENDINGVALUE$(C, x, y, \Delta(y), a)$: value
  | return TRAVERSES-LIST$(C, x, y, \Delta(y))$

TRAVERSES-LIST$(C, x, y, \Delta(y))$: value
  | **while** $(y, b) \neq nil$ **do**
  | | $(x, a) \leftarrow$ SEEKVALIDSUPPORTEDVALUE(C, y, b)
  | | **if** $(x, a) \neq nil$ **then** return (x, a)
  | | $b \leftarrow$ NEXT$(\Delta(y), b)$
  | return nil

$$\text{pvType} = \underline{\text{pv}\Delta\text{t}} \text{ (b is a local data)}$$

FIRSTPENDINGVALUE$(C, x, y, \Delta(y))$: value
  | $b \leftarrow$ FIRST$(\Delta(y))$
  | $\tau \leftarrow$ FIRSTTUPLE(C, y, b)
  | return TRAVERSETUPLE$(C, x, y, \Delta(y), \tau)$

NEXTPENDINGVALUE$(C, x, y, \Delta(y), a)$: value
  | $\tau \leftarrow$ NEXTTUPLE$(C, x, y, b, ((x, a), (y, b)))$
  | return TRAVERSETUPLE$(C, x, y, \Delta(y), \tau)$

TRAVERSETUPLE$(C, x, y, \Delta(y), \tau)$: value
  | **while** $(y, b) \neq nil$ **do**
  | | **while** $\tau \neq nil$ **do**
  | | | **if** $\tau[x] \in D(x)$ **then** return $(x, \tau[x])$
  | | | $\tau \leftarrow$ NEXTTUPLE(C, x, y, b, τ)
  | | $b \leftarrow$ NEXT$(\Delta(y), b)$
  | | $\tau \leftarrow$ FIRSTTUPLE(C, x, y, b)
  | return nil

$$\text{pvType} = \underline{\text{pv}\Delta\text{c}}$$

FIRSTPENDINGVALUE$(C, y, \Delta(y))$: value
  | $a \leftarrow$ FIRST$(D(x))$
  | return SEEKCOMPATIBLE$(C, x, y, \Delta(y), a)$

NEXTPENDINGVALUE$(C, y, \Delta(y), a)$: value
  | $a \leftarrow$ NEXT$(D(x), a)$
  | return SEEKCOMPATIBLE$(C, x, y, \Delta(y), a)$

SEEKCOMPATIBLE$(C, x, y, \Delta(y), a)$: value
  | **while** $(x, a) \neq nil$ **do**
  | | **for** each $b \in \Delta(y)$ **do**
  | | | **if** $((x, a), (y, b)) \in T(C)$ **then** return (x, a)
  | | $(x, a) \leftarrow$ NEXT$(D(x), a)$
  | return nil

$$\text{pvType} = \underline{\text{pvG}}: \text{example of generic function: } < \text{constraint}$$

FIRSTPENDINGVALUE$(C, y, \Delta(y))$: value
  | return NEXT$(D(x), \max(D(y)) - 1)$

NEXTPENDINGVALUE$(C, x, y, \Delta(y), a)$: return NEXT$(D(x), a)$

Algorithm 4. Functions EXISTVALIDSUPPORT and SEEKVALIDSUPPORTED-VALUE

EXISTVALIDSUPPORT(C, x, a, y,sType): boolean
- **if** slist **then** REMOVE(S-list[support[(x,a)]], (x,a))
- $(y, b) \leftarrow nil$
- **if** last **and** last[(x,a)] $\in D(y)$ **then** $(y, b) \leftarrow$ last[(x,a)]
- **if** inf **and** $(y, b) = nil$ **then**
  - $(y, b) \leftarrow$ SEEKVALIDSUPPORTEDVALUE(C, x, a)
- **if** $(y, b) = nil$ **then**
  - $(y, b) \leftarrow$ sType.SEEKVALIDSUPPORT(C, x, a, y)
- **if** slist **and** $(y, b) \neq nil$ **then** ADD(S-list[(y,b)], (x,a))
- **if** $(y, b) \neq nil$ **then** support[(x,a)] $\leftarrow (y, b)$
- **return** ($(y, b) \neq nil$)

SEEKVALIDSUPPORTEDVALUE(C, x, a) : value
- **for** each value $(y, b) \in$ S-list[(x,a)] **do**
  - **if** $b \in D(y)$ **then return** (y, b)
  - REMOVE(S-list[(x,a)], y, b)
- **return** nil

- inf: the search for a valid support is first done by searching for a valid supported value in the S-list (AC-7, AC-3.3).
- slist: this parameter means that the S-lists are used.
- sD: the search for a valid support is made by testing the compatibility between (x, a) and the values in $D(y)$ (AC-3, AC-6, AC-7, AC-2000, AC-2001, AC-3.3.)
- sC: A valid support is sought by decrementing the counter of valid tuples and by checking if it is greater than 0 (AC-4.)
- sT: the search for a valid support is made by testing the validity of the values of P-list[(x,a)] and by checking if there is a value in U-list[(x,a)] which is valid and compatible with (x, a) (AC-Inference, AC-Identical.)
- sGen: the search for a valid support is defined by a function provided by the user and dedicated to the constraint.

From these parameters we can now propose a possible code for Function EXISTVALIDSUPPORT of AC-* algorithm (see Algorithm 4.) Possible instantiations of Function SEEKVALIDSUPPORT are given by Algorithm 5. An example is also given for constraint <.

6 Analysis of Different Methods

The main issue of AC algorithms is to deal with two different concepts: support and validity. It is difficult to handle these two concepts at the same time. Thus, the algorithms usually privilege one concept:

Algorithm 5. Functions seeking for a valid support

$sType = \underline{sD}$
SEEKVALIDSUPPORT(C, x, a, y) : value
  $b \leftarrow$ FIRST$(D(y))$
  if <u>last</u> **then**
    $b \leftarrow$ NEXT$(D(y),$last$[(x, a)])$
    while $b \neq nil$ **do**
      if last$[(y, b)] \leq (x, a)$ **and** $(a, b) \in T(C)$ **then**
        last$[(x, a)] \leftarrow (y, b)$
        return (y, b)
      $b \leftarrow$ NEXT$(D(y), b)$
  else
    while $b \neq nil$ **do**
      if $((x, a), (y, b)) \in T(C)$ **then** return (y, b)
      $b \leftarrow$ NEXT$(D(y), b)$
  return nil

$sType = \underline{sC}$
SEEKVALIDSUPPORT(C, x, a, y) : value
  counter$[(x, a)] \leftarrow$ counter$[(x, a)] - 1$
  if counter$[(x, a)] = 0$ **then** return nil
  else return $(y,$FIRST$(D(y)))$

$sType = \underline{sT}$
SEEKVALIDSUPPORT(C, x, a, y) : value
  for *each* $(y, b) \in$ P-list$[(x, a)]$ **do**
    REMOVE(P-list$[(x, a)], (y, b)$)
    if $b \in D(y)$ **then** return (y, b)
  for *each* $(y, b) \in$ U-list$[(x, a)]$ **do**
    REMOVE(U-list$[(x, a)], (y, b)$)
    REMOVE(U-list$[(y, b)], (x, a)$)
    if $((x, a), (y, b)) \in T(C)$ **then**
      ADD(P-list$[(y, b)], (x, a)$)
      if $b \in D(y)$ **then** return (y, b)
  return nil

$sType = \underline{sGen}$ example of generic function: $<$ constraint
SEEKVALIDSUPPORT(C, x, a, y) : return false

- When constructing the pending values set, <u>pvD</u> algorithms totally ignore the concept of support. The other algorithms try to combine the two concepts: <u>pvD</u> algorithms consider first the validity, whereas <u>pvΔt</u> algorithms deal first with all supports. And, <u>pvΔs</u> algorithms traverse the current supported values and check their validity.

- When searching for a new support, <u>sD</u> algorithms consider the valid values, and then check if they are support, whereas <u>sT</u> algorithms traverse the supports and check for their validity.

7 Nomenclature

From the different concepts we have identified we can propose a new nomenclature for the AC algorithms. Until now, the naming used the prefix "AC-" followed by a number or date. Excepted AC-Inference or AC-Identical which have tried to express a little bit some ideas of the algorithms, it is clearly impossible to understand the specificities of each algorithm from their name.

The nomenclature we propose still uses AC as prefix. The combinations of parameters corresponding to the AC algorithm are added to this AC prefix. For instance, AC-pvD-sD means that the pending values are the values of $D(x)$ and that a new valid support is sought in the domain by checking the compatibilities between values. This is exactly the description of AC-3. For the adaptive algorithms a "/" is used to differentiate the possibilities: AC-2000 is renamed AC-pvΔc/pvD-sD. We can describe all the existing algorithms:

name	new name
AC-3	AC-pvD-sD
AC-4	AC-pvΔt-sC
AC-6	AC-pvΔs-last-sD
AC-7	AC-pvΔs-last-inf-sD
AC-Inference or AC-Identical	AC-pvΔs-sT
AC-2000	AC-pvΔc/pvD-sD
AC-2001	AC-pvD-last-sD
AC-3.3	AC-pvD-last-inf-sD

8 Adaptive Algorithm

The advantage of adaptive algorithms is to avoid some pathological cases of each algorithm. The following property exactly differentiates AC-2001 and AC-6:

Property 1. *[3] The number of values that are considered to find the pending values in:*
- *a* pvD *oriented algorithm is* $|pvD| = |D(x)|$.
- *a* pvΔs *oriented algorithm is*
$$|pv\Delta s| = |\Delta(y)| + \sum_{b \in \Delta(y)} |S\text{-}list[(y,b)]|$$

These two numbers are sufficient to differentiate AC-2001 and AC-6 because they use both the same algorithm to find a support for a value. This is clearly shown by their new names that are respectively AC-pvD-last-sD and AC-pvΔs-last-sD. So, by considering the method to find the pending values that studies the smallest number of values we can define an algorithm which is better than any of two previous ones.

We can use first a pvΔs oriented algorithm and then switch to a pvD one and conversely. Unfortunately, it is difficult to quickly compute $|pv\Delta s|$, because the sum needs to consider every value of the delta domain independently. However, we immediately have: $|pv\Delta s| \geq 2|\Delta(y)|$, and $|\Delta(y)|$ can be incrementally maintained, thus we can consider that we know its value in $O(1)$. Algorithm 6 is a possible implementation of the functions selecting sType and pvType that is used by Algorithm 2 (AC-2000 is taken into account thanks to this function.)

Algorithm 6. Selection of pvType and sType

SELECTPVTYPE(C,x,y,$\Delta(y)$,pvType):pvType
$\quad$ | if $pvType$=pvΔc/pvD then
$\quad\quad$ | if $|\Delta(y)| < 0.2|D(x)|$ then return pvΔc
$\quad\quad$ | return pvD
$\quad$ | if $pvType$=pvD/pvΔs then
$\quad\quad$ | if $|D(x)| < 2.|\Delta(y)|$ then return pvD
$\quad\quad$ | if $|D(x)| < |\Delta(y)| + \sum_{b \in \Delta(y)}|S\text{-}list[(y,b)]|$ then return pvD
$\quad\quad$ | return pvΔs
$\quad$ | return $pvType$
SELECTSTYPE($C, x, a, sType$) : $sType$
$\quad$ | if $sType$=sD/sT then
$\quad\quad$ | if $|D(x)| < |P\text{-}list[(x,a)]|$ then return sD
$\quad\quad$ | return sT
$\quad$ | return $sType$

Switching from a type of algorithm to another one can also cause some other problems, because the different types of algorithms do not use the same data structures. When switching from an algorithm using a data structure to an algorithm that does not use it we have two possibilities: either the data structure is updated after switching, or it is systematically updated even if it is not used. For the S-lists, the cost to maintain them is $O(1)$ per deletion or addition therefore the second solution is simpler. For the U-lists and the P-lists there is no problem because they do not need to be updated.

We have seen that it is possible to change the way the pending values are computed. Two other possibilities are: we can use or not the inf parameter, or we can switch from sD and sT and conversely. However, it is much more complicated to find a good criterion of selection, because the lists are modified when using inf or sT. After some experiments it appears that the switch from inf to no inf does not change anything, and that it is sometimes effective to switch from sD to sT and conversely. If the size of the domain is smaller than the size of the P-list then sD is selected, else sT is selected. (see Algorithm 6.)

9 Experiments

We propose a comparison of the MAC version of the algorithms on the well-known RLFAPs benchmarks. We give the results only for instances SCEN#1, SCEN#8, SCEN#11 because the results are quite representative. For each algorithm we give the time (in s) needed by the algorithm to solve the problem with a Pentium II 300Mhz machine. A bullet means that the algorithm uses the corresponding parameter. An adaptive algorithm may have several bullets which means that it uses different modes.

	AC-4	AC-3	AC 2000	AC 2001	AC 3.3	AC-6	AC-7			AC Inf		
pvΔt	•											
pvΔc		•										
pvΔs						•	•	•	•	•	•	•
pvD		•	•	•			•	•		•		•
last				•	•	•	•	•	•	•		
inf					•		•	•	•			
sD		•	•	•	•	•	•	•	•			•
sC	•											
sT										•	•	•
#1	10.7	2.3	2.0	1.5	1.3	2.0	2.0	1.8	1.8	0.8	0.6	0.6
#8	1.42	1.64	1.62	1.2	1.15	0.5	0.46	0.1	0.09	0.1	0.03	0.02
#11	84.8	39.5	38.4	22.6	18.6	14.7	14.1	10.2	10.2	9.6	6.2	5.6

This results clearly show that adaptive algorithms perform better than non adaptive and that the sT algorithms are better than the others.

10 Conclusion

We have presented AC-* a new configurable, generic and adaptive algorithm, which is able to represent all existing algorithms that establish arc consistency for binary constraints. We have clearly differentiated all the existing algorithms thanks to the identification of the underlying concepts. We have proposed new combinations of concepts that perform well, as shown by some experimental results.

Acknowledgments

We would like to thank particularly Willem van Hoeve for his useful comments which helped improve this paper.

References

1. C. Bessière. Arc-consistency and arc-consistency again. *Artificial Intelligence*, 65(1):179–190, 1994.
2. C. Bessière, E.C. Freuder, and J-C. Régin. Using constraint metaknowledge to reduce arc consistency computation. *Artificial Intelligence*, 107(1):125–148, 1999.
3. C. Bessière and J-C. Régin. Refining the basic constraint propagation algorithm. In *Proceedings of IJCAI'01*, pages 309–315, Seattle, WA, USA, 2001.
4. A. Chmeiss and P. Jégou. Efficient path-consistency propagation. *Journal on Artificial Intelligence Tools*, 7(2):79–89, 1998.

5. C. Lecoutre, F. Boussemart, and F. Hemery. Exploiting multidirectionnality in coarse-grained arc consistency algorithm. In *Proceedings CP'03*, pages 480–494, Cork, Ireland, 2003.
6. A.K. Mackworth. Consistency in networks of relations. *Artificial Intelligence*, 8:99–118, 1977.
7. R. Mohr and T.C. Henderson. Arc and path consistency revisited. *Artificial Intelligence*, 28:225–233, 1986.
8. M.R. van Dongen. Ac-3d an efficient arc-consistency algorithm with a low space-complexity. In *Proc. CP'02*, pages 755–760, Ithaca, NY, USA, 2002.
9. P. Van Hentenryck, Y. Deville, and C.M. Teng. A generic arc-consistency algorithm and its specializations. *Artificial Intelligence*, 57:291–321, 1992.
10. Y. Zhang and R. Yap. Making ac-3 an optimal algorithm. In *Proceedings of IJCAI'01*, pages 316–321, Seattle, WA, USA, 2001.

Maintaining Arc Consistency Algorithms During the Search Without Additional Space Cost

Jean-Charles Régin

Computing and Information Science, Cornell University, Ithaca NY 14850 USA
jcregin@cs.cornell.edu

Abstract. In this paper, we detail the versions of the arc consistency algorithms for binary constraints based on list of supports and last value when they are maintained during the search for solutions. In other words, we give the explicit codes of MAC-6 and MAC-7 algorithms. Moreover, we present an original way to restore the last values of AC-6 and AC-7 algorithms in order to obtain a MAC version of these algorithms whose space complexity remains in $O(ed)$ while keeping the $O(ed^2)$ time complexity on any branch of the tree search, where d is the size of the largest domain and e is the number of constraints. This result outperforms all previous studies.

1 Introduction

In this paper we focus our attention on binary constraints. The MAC version of an algorithm establishing arc consistency (AC algorithm), is the maintaining of this AC algorithm during the search for a solution. For more than twenty years, a lot of AC algorithms have been proposed: AC-3 [6], AC-4 [7], AC-5 [12], AC-6 [1], AC-7, AC-Inference, AC-Identical [2], AC-8 [4], AC-2000: [3], AC-2001 (also denoted by AC-3.1 [13]) [3], AC-3_d [9], AC-3.2 and AC-3.3 [5]. Some AC algorithms, like AC-3 or AC-2000, are easy to maintain during the search whereas some others are much more complex. This is mainly the case for algorithms based on the concept of list of support (S-list) and on the concept of last support (last value). These algorithms, like AC-6, AC-7, or AC-2001, involve some data structures that need to be restored after a backtrack. Currently, there is no MAC version of these algorithms capable to keep the optimal time complexity on every branch of the tree search ($O(d^2)$ per constraint, where d is the size of the largest domain), without sacrificing the space complexity. More precisely, the algorithms AC-6, AC-7 and AC-2001 involve data structures that lead to a space complexity of $O(d)$ per constraint, but the MAC versions of these algorithms require to save some modifications of these data structures in order to restart the computations after a backtrack in a way similar as if this backtrack did not happen, and so they keep the same time complexity for any branch of the tree search as for one establishment of arc consistency. These savings have a cost which depends on the depth of the tree search and that is bounded by d. Therefore some authors have proposed algorithms having a $O(d\min(n, d))$ space complexity per constraint

[8,10,11], where n is the number of variables. Thus, the nice space complexity of these AC algorithms is lost for their MAC versions.

In this paper, we propose an original MAC version of the algorithms involving S-lists and last values with a space complexity in $O(d)$ per constraint while keeping the optimal time complexity ($O(d^2)$) for any branch of the tree search.

At this moment, our main goal is to close this open question and not to propose an algorithm outperforming MAC-6 or MAC-7.

This paper is organized as follows. First, we recall some definitions of CP and we give a classical backtrack algorithm associated with a propagation mechanism. Then, we give a classical AC algorithm using the S-List and last value data structures. Next, we identify the problems of the MAC version of this algorithm, and we propose a new MAC version without additional cost. At last, we conclude.

2 Preliminaries

A finite **constraint network** $\mathcal{N}$ is defined as a set of n **variables** $X = \{x_1, \ldots, x_n\}$, a set of current **domains** $\mathcal{D} = \{D(x_1), \ldots, D(x_n)\}$ where $D(x_i)$ is the finite set of possible **values** for variable x_i, and a set $\mathcal{C}$ of **constraints** between variables. A **constraint** C on the ordered set of variables $X(C) = (x_{i_1}, \ldots, x_{i_r})$ is a subset $T(C)$ of the Cartesian product $D(x_{i_1}) \times \cdots \times D(x_{i_r})$ that specifies the **allowed** combinations of values for the variables $x_{i_1}, \ldots, x_{i_r}$. An element of $D(x_{i_1}) \times \cdots \times D(x_{i_r})$ is called a **tuple on** $X(C)$ and $\tau[x]$ is the value of τ assigned to x. A value a for a variable x is often denoted by (x, a). (x, a) is **valid** iff $a \in D(x)$. Let C be a constraint. A tuple τ on $X(C)$ is **valid** iff $\forall x \in X(C), \tau[x] \in D(x)$; and τ is a **support** for (x, a) iff $\tau[x] = a$ and $\tau \in T(C)$. C is **consistent** iff $\exists \tau \in T(C)$ which is valid. A value $a \in D(x)$ is **consistent with** C iff $x \notin X(C)$ or there exists a valid support for (x, a). A constraint is **arc consistent** iff $\forall x \in X(C), D(x) \neq \emptyset$ and $\forall a \in D(x)$, a is consistent with C.

A **filtering algorithm** associated with a constraint C is an algorithm which may remove some values that are inconsistent with C; and that does not remove any consistent values. If the filtering algorithm removes all the values inconsistent with C then we say that it establishes arc consistency of C and that it is an AC algorithm.

The delta domain of a variable x with respect to a filtering algorithm F associated with a constraint C is the set of values that have been removed from the domain of x between two successive calls of F. It is denoted by $\Delta(x, F)$ and a value in $\Delta(x, F)$ is called a **delta value**. More information about delta domains can be found in [12] or in the manual of ILOG Solver. Note that the conjunction of the elements in the delta domains form the *waitingList* of AC-6 and AC-7 algorithms. Sometimes, all the filtering algorithms depending on the modifications of $D(x)$ are successively considered after the modifications of x. Thus, if there is no side effect (that is x is not modified by these filtering algorithms), then all these filtering algorithms can share the same delta domain for x, and only one representation is needed. Therefore, there is no need to specify the filtering algorithm for identifying the delta domain associated with a filtering algorithm and the delta domain of x is denoted by $\Delta(x)$.

Propagation is the mechanism that consists of calling the filtering algorithm associated with the constraints involving a variable x each time the domain of this variable is modified. If every filtering algorithm associated with every constraint establishes arc consistency then we say that the propagation mechanism establishes arc consistency of the network.

Algorithm 1. function SEARCHFORSOLUTION

SEARCHFORSOLUTION(x, a)
    ADDCONSTRAINT$(x = a)$
    if *all variables are instantiated* **then** PRINTSOLUTION()
    else
        if PROPAGATION() **then**
            do
                $y \leftarrow$ SELECTVARIABLE()
                $b \leftarrow$ SELECTVALUE(y)
                SEARCHFORSOLUTION(y, b)
                REMOVEFROMDOMAIN(y, b)
            while $D(y) \neq \emptyset$ **and** PROPAGATION()
    RESTORECN()

PROPAGATION()
    while $\exists y$ *such that* $\Delta(y) \neq \emptyset$ **do**
        pick y with $\Delta(y) \neq \emptyset$
        for *each constraint C involving y* **do**
            $(D(x), \Delta(x)) \leftarrow$ FILTER$(C, x, y, \Delta(y))$
            if $D(x) = \emptyset$ **then return** false
        $\Delta(y) \leftarrow \emptyset$
    return true

Function PROPAGATION of Algorithm 1 is a possible implementation of this mechanism when delta domains are shared.

The filtering algorithm associated with the constraint C defined on x and y corresponds to Function FILTER$(C, x, y, \Delta(y))$. This function removes some values of $D(x)$ that are not consistent with the constraint with respect to $\Delta(y)$. It also updates the delta domain of x. For a constraint C this function will also be called with the parameters $(C, y, x, \Delta(x))$.

Algorithm 1 also contains a classical recursive search procedure which selects a variable, then a value for this variable and call the propagation mechanism. Function RESTORECN restores the data structures used by the constraint when a backtrack occurs. We assume that Function SEARCHFORSOLUTION is called first with a dummy variable x and a dummy value a such that the constraint $x = a$ has no effect.

3   Arc Consistency Algorithms

We will consider a constraint C defined on x and y for which we study the consequences of the modification of $D(y)$. For the sake of clarity, we will avoid adding systematically C as a parameter of every data structure. For instance, we will denote by data$[(x, a)]$ a value linked to (x, a) instead of data$[C, (x, a)]$.

Definition 1. *Let x be a variable and F be a filtering algorithm aiming to remove some values of $D(x)$. We call* **pending values** *of x w.r.t. F, the set of* **valid** *values of x for which a valid support is sought by F when F is called.*

Thanks to this definition, and if every value which is not a pending value is consistent with the constraint then the principles of AC algorithms can be easily expressed:

Check whether there exists a valid support for every pending value and remove those that have none.

Algorithm 2. An AC algorithm

FILTER(**in** $C, x, y, \Delta(y)$): (domain,delta domain)
   $(x, a) \leftarrow$ FIRSTPENDINGVALUE$(C, x, y, \Delta(y))$
   while $(x, a) \neq nil$ **do**
   | **if** $\neg$ EXISTVALIDSUPPORT$(C, x, a, y, GET\Delta$VALUE$(C))$ **then**
   | | $D(x) \leftarrow D(x) - \{a\}$
   | | $\Delta(x) \leftarrow \Delta(x) \cup \{a\}$
   | | **if** $D(x) = \emptyset$ **then** return $(\emptyset, \Delta(x))$
   | $(x, a) \leftarrow$ NEXTPENDINGVALUE$(C, x, y, \Delta(y), a)$
   return $(D(x), \Delta(x))$

Algorithm 2 is a possible implementation of this principle. Functions FIRST-PENDINGVALUE and NEXTPENDINGVALUE identify the pending values, and Function EXISTVALIDSUPPORT searches for a valid support for these pending values. We can now detail the principles of these functions for AC-6 and AC-7 algorithms.

AC-6: AC-6 introduces the **S-list** data structure: for every value (y, b), the S-list associated with (y, b), denoted by S-list$[(y, b)]$, is the list of values that are currently supported by (y, b). A value (x, a) is supported by **only one** value of $D(y)$, so there is at most one value of $D(y)$ that contains (x, a) in its S-list. Then, the pending values are the valid values contained in the S-lists of the values in $\Delta(y)$. If a value of $D(x)$ is not a pending value then it means that its support has not been deleted so the value is consistent with the constraint. The search for a valid support (Function EXISTVALIDSUPPORT) is done by checking in $D(y)$ whether there is a support for (x, a). These checks are made w.r.t an ordering and are started from the support that just has been lost, which is the delta value containing the current value in its S-list. The space complexity of AC-6 is in $O(d)$ because a value belongs to at most one S-list and its time complexity is in $O(d^2)$, because a value can be a pending value only d times and the search for a valid support is done in $O(d)$ globally.

AC-7: AC-7 improves AC-6 by exploiting the fact that if (x, a) is supported by (y, b) then (y, b) is also supported by (x, a). Thus, when searching for a valid support for (x, a), AC-7 proposes, first, to search for a valid value in S-list$[(x, a)]$, and every non valid value which is reached is removed from the S-list. We say that the valid support is sought by **inference**. This idea contradicts an invariant of AC-6: a valid support found by inference is no longer necessarily the latest checked value in $D(y)$. Therefore, AC-7 introduces explicitly the concept of **last value** by the data **last** associated with every value. AC-7 ensures the property: If last$[(x, a)] = (y, b)$ then there is no support (y, c) in $D(y)$ with $c < b$. If no support is found by inference, then AC-7 uses an improvement of the AC-6's method to find a support in $D(y)$. When we want to know whether (y, b) is a support of (x, a), we can immediately give a negative answer if last$[(y, b)] > (x, a)$, because in this case we know that (x, a) is a not a support of (y, b) and so that (y, b) is not a support for (x, a). The property on which AC-7 is based are often called bidirectionality. Hence, AC-7 is able to save some checks in the domain in regard to AC-6, while keeping the same space and time complexity.

The MAC version of AC-6 needs an explicit representation of the latest checked value, thus the AC-6 and AC-7 algorithms use the following data structures:

last: the last value of (x, a) for a constraint C is represented by last$[(x, a)]$ which is equal to a value of y or nil.
S-List: these are classical list data structures.

Algorithm 3. Pending values computation

// b is an internal data
FIRSTPENDINGVALUE$(C, x, y, \Delta(y))$: value
| $b \leftarrow$ FIRST$(\Delta(y))$
| return TRAVERSES-LIST$(C, x, y, \Delta(y))$

NEXTPENDINGVALUE$(C, x, y, \Delta(y), a)$: value
| return TRAVERSES-LIST$(C, x, y, \Delta(y))$

TRAVERSES-LIST$(C, x, y, \Delta(y))$: value
| while $(y, b) \neq nil$ do
| | $(x, a) \leftarrow$ SEEKVALIDSUPPORTEDVALUE(C, y, b)
| | if $(x, a) \neq nil$ then return (x, a)
| | $b \leftarrow$ NEXT$(\Delta(y), b)$
| return nil
GETΔVALUE$(C, x, y, \Delta(y))$: return b

We can give a MAC version of AC-6 and AC-7:

Algorithm 3 is a possible implementation of the computation of pending values. We assume that FIRST$(D(x))$ returns the first value of $D(x)$ and NEXT$(D(x), a)$ returns the first value of $D(x)$ strictly greater than a.

Function SEEKVALIDSUPPORTEDVALUE(C, x, a) returns a valid supported value belonging to the S-list$[(y, b)]$ (see Algorithm 5.) Algorithm 4 gives a possible implementation of Function EXISTVALIDSUPPORT and Function SEEKVALID-SUPPORT.

The S-list representation will be detailed in a specific section, notably because it has to be carefully designed in order to be efficiently maintained during the search.

Algorithm 4. Search for a valid support

EXISTVALIDSUPPORT($C, x, a, y, \delta y$): boolean
    if last$[(x, a)] \in D(y)$ then $(y, b) \leftarrow$ last$[(x, a)])$
    if AC-7 and $(y, b) = nil$ then
        $(y, b) \leftarrow$ SEEKVALIDSUPPORTEDVALUE(C, x, a)
    if $(y, b) = nil$ then
        $(y, b) \leftarrow$ SEEKVALIDSUPPORT(C, x, a, y)
    UPDATES-LIST($C, x, a, y, \delta y, b$)
    return $((y, b) \neq nil)$

SEEKVALIDSUPPORT(C, x, a, y): value
    $b \leftarrow$NEXT($D(y)$,last$[(x, a)]$)
    while $b \neq nil$ do
        if last$[(y, b)] \leq (x, a)$ ***and*** $((x, a), (y, b)) \in T(C)$ then
            last$[(x, a)] \leftarrow (y, b)$
            return (y, b)
        $b \leftarrow$NEXT($D(y), b$)
    return nil

---

4 Maintenance During the Search

In this section, we propose a MAC version of an AC algorithm using S-lists and/or last values having the same space and time complexity as the AC algorithm.

Two types of data structures can be identified for a filtering algorithm (like an AC algorithm for instance) :

- the **external data structures**. These are the data structures from which the constraint of the filtering algorithm is stated, for instance the variables on which the constraint is defined or the list of combinations allowed by the constraint.
- the **internal data structures**. These are the data structures needed by the filtering algorithm. The space complexity of the filtering algorithm is usually based on these data structures. For instance, AC-6 and AC-7 require data structures in $O(d)$.

There is no particular problem when we go down to the search tree, because the instantiations of variables lead only to the deletion of values. The main difficulty is to manage the internal data structures when a failure occurs, that is when there is a backtrack.

Consider that N is the current node of the search. The internal data structures associated with an AC algorithm contain certain values. These values are called the **state** of the internal data structures. Then, assume that the search is continued from N and then backtracked to N. In this case, two possibilities have been identified [8]:

- the state of the internal data structure at the node N is exactly restored
- an equivalent state is restored.

4.1 Exact Restoration of the State

This method saves the modifications of the state of an AC algorithm in order to restore exactly this state after a backtrack. In other words, every data contains the same value as it had when N was the current node. This implies that every modification of a data has to be saved in order to be restored after a backtrack. Every S-list and every last value can be modified d times per constraint during the search. Thus, the space complexity is multiplied by a factor of d. So, this possibility cannot lead to a MAC version without additional cost.

4.2 Restoration of an Equivalent State

The algorithms have an optimal time complexity when some properties are satisfied. What is important is not the way they are satisfied, but only the fact that they are satisfied. For some data structures it is not necessary to restore exactly the values they contained before. For instance, if (y, b) was the current support of (x, a) for the node N and if this support changes to become (y, c) then (y, c) can be the current support of (x, a) when all the nodes following N are backtracked. This means that there is no need to change the elements in the S-list when backtracking. It is only required to add some values that have been removed.

We propose, in the next sections, to study how the S-Lists and the last values can be managed in order to restore only an equivalent state.

5 S-List Management

If an equivalent state is accepted after backtracking, then there is no need to save the modifications of supports, because they do not need to be restored. However, in order to keep an optimal time complexity for every branch of the tree search, the MAC version of AC-6 and AC-7 needs to remove from S-lists the values that are traversed and that are not valid to avoid considering them several times.

Function SEEKVALIDSUPPORTEDVALUE manages this deletion. So, this function deserves a particular attention.

This function is called during the computation of the pending values or when a valid support is sought by inference (AC-7). When it is called for a value (x,a) it traverses the S-list of (x,a) until a valid value is found and removes from this S-list the non valid values that are reached. In the MAC version, a specific restoration of the S-list is needed. More precisely, if (y,b) is reached when traversing S-list$[(x,a)]$ then (x,a) is the current valid support for (y,b) for this constraint. Thus, if (y,b) is no longer valid when it is reached, then (y,b) is removed from S-list$[(x,a)]$, but after backtracking the node of the tree search that led to the deletion of (y,b) it is necessary to restore (y,b) in S-list$[(x,a)]$, because at this moment (y,b) will be valid and (y,b) needs to have a valid support. Therefore, when an element is removed from the S-list when traversing it, it is necessary to save this information in order to restore it later.

In order to avoid unnecessary memory consumption we propose to represent the S-list as follows :

- The first element of an S-list of a value (y,b) is denoted by firstS$[(y,b)]$ which is equal to a value of x or nil.
- The S-lists exploit the fact that for a constraint, each value (x,a) can be in at most one S-list. So, every value (x,a) is associated with a data nextInS$[(x,a)]$ which is the next element in the S-list of the support of (x,a). For instance, S-list$[(y,b)] = ((x,a),(x,d),(x,e))$ will be represented by : firstS$[(y,b)] = (x,a)$; nextInS$[(x,a)] = (x,d)$; nextInS$[(x,d)] = (x,e)$; nextInS$[(x,e)] = nil$. The nextInS data are systematically associated with every value so they are **preallocated**.

The saving-restoration of a support by MAC, can be easily done by adding a data to every value (x,a): restoreSupport$[(x,a)]$. This data contains the support of (x,a) if (x,a) has been removed from the S-list of its support, otherwise it contains nil. This data will be used to restore (x,a) in the S-list of its support when a will be restored in $D(x)$. More precisely, assume that (y,b) is the support of (x,a) and that (x,a) has been removed from S-list$[(y,b)]$ when searching for a valid support of (y,b) by inference. Then, the data restoreSupport$[(x,a)]$ will be set to (y,b). And, when (x,a) will be restored in the domain of its variable after backtracking, then (x,a) will be added to the S-list of restoreSupport$[(x,a)]$. Of course, if restoreSupport$[(x,a)]$ is nil then nothing happens.

Another point must also be considered. Function EXISTVALIDSUPPORT calls Function UPDATES-LIST in order to update the S-list when a new valid support is found. Conceptually there is no problem, if a new valid support (y,b) is found for a value (x,a) then (x,a) is added to S-list$[(y,b)]$. However, before being added to a S-list, (x,a) must be removed from the S-list of its current support. This deletion causes some problems of implementation because the S-lists are unidirectional lists and to perform a deletion it is necessary to know the previous element. In order to avoid this problem, we have decided to systematically remove all the reached elements from the S-list. Thus, every element which is considered is the first element of the list and so there is no longer any problem to remove it. Function UPDATES-LIST implements that idea and Algorithm 5 gives a possible implementation of the management of S-lists.

Algorithm 5. Management of Supported Values Lists

SEEKVALIDSUPPORTEDVALUE(C, x, a) : value
    while $firstS[(x, a)] \neq nil$ **do**
        $(y, b) \leftarrow firstS[(x, a)]$
        if $b \in D(y)$ **then** return (y, b)
        $firstS[(x, a)] \leftarrow nextInS[(y, b)]$
        $restoreSupport[(y, b)] \leftarrow (x, a)$
    return nil

UPDATES-LIST$(C, x, a, y, \delta y, b)$
    $firstS[(y, \delta y)] \leftarrow nextInS[(x, a)]$
    if $(y, b) = nil$ **then** $restoreSupport[(x, a)] \leftarrow (y, \delta y)$
    else
        $nextInS[(x, a)] \leftarrow firstS[(y, b)]$
        $firstS[(y, b)] \leftarrow (x, a)$

RESTORESUPPORTS$(C, (x, a))$
    // the value a is restored in $D(x)$
    $(y, b) \leftarrow restoreSupport[(x, a)]$
    if $restoreSupport[(x, a)] \neq nil$ **then**
        // (x, a) is added to the S-list of its support (y, b)
        $nextInS[(x, a)] \leftarrow firstS[(y, b)]$
        $firstS[(y, b)] \leftarrow (x, a)$
        $restoreSupport[(x, a)] \leftarrow nil$

6 Last Management

First, when an equivalent state is restored, it is necessary to slightly modify the AC algorithm. The last value of (x, a) can indeed be valid and not be the current support of (x, a), because the supports are not systematically restored. Thus, it is necessary to check the validity of the last value in the MAC version of an AC algorithm (See first line of Function EXISTVALIDSUPPORT.)

The concept of last value is necessary for AC-6 and AC-7 algorithms to have an $O(d^2)$ time complexity per constraint. Any last value satisfies the following property:

Property 1. Let $(y, b) = last[(x, a)]$ then
    (i) $\forall c \in D(y), c < b \Rightarrow ((x, a), (y, c)) \notin T(C)$.
    (ii) Function SEEKVALIDSUPPORT has never checked the compatibility between (x, a) and any element $d \in D(y)$ with $d > b$.

This property ensures that the compatibility between two values will never be checked twice.

If the last values are not restored after backtracking then the time complexity of AC-6 and AC-7 algorithms is in $O(d^3)$. We can prove that claim with the following example. Consider a value (x, a) that has exactly ten supports among the 100 values of y: $(y, 91), (y, 92)..., (y, 100)$; and a node N of the tree search for which the valid support of (x,a) is $(y,91)$. If the last value is not restored after a backtrack then there are two possibilities to define a new last value:

- the new last value is recomputed from the first value of the domain
- the new last value is defined from the current last value, but the domains are considered as circular domains: the next value of the maximum value is the minimum value.

For the first case, it is clear that all the values strictly less than $(y,91)$ will have to be reconsidered after every backtrack for computing a valid support.
For the second possibility, we can imagine an example for which before backtracking $(y,100)$ is the current support; then after the backtrack and since the domains are considered as circular domains it will be necessary to reconsidered again all the values that are strictly less than $(y,91)$.

Note also, that if the last value is not correctly restored it is no longer possible to totally exploit the bidirectionality. So, it is necessary to correctly restore the last values.

6.1 Saving-Restoration of Last Values

The simplest way is to save the current value of last each time it is modified and then to restore these values after a backtrack. This method can be improved by remarking that it is sufficient to save only the first modification of the last value for a given node of the tree search. In this case, the space complexity of AC-6 and AC-7 algorithms is multiplied by $\min(n,d)$ where n is the maximum of the tree search depth [8,10,11].

6.2 Recomputation of Last Values

We propose an original method to restore the correct last value. Instead of being based on savings this method is based on recomputations.

Consider a node $N+1$ of the tree search obtained from a node N. We will denote by $D_N(y)$ (resp. $D_{N+1}(y)$) the domain of the variable y at node N (resp. $N+1$). Then, we have the following proposition on which our algorithm is based:

Proposition 1. *Let $D_R(y) = D_N(y) - D_{N+1}(y)$ and $K(x,a)$ be the set of values of y that are compatible with (x,a) w.r.t. C. If $last[(x,a)]$ satisfies Property 1 for node $N+1$ then $\min(last[(x,a)], \min(K(x,a) \cap D_R(y))$ is a possible value of $last[(x,a)]$ for node N.*

proof: It is sufficient to prove that $\min(last[(x,a)], \min(K(x,a) \cap D_R(y)))$ satisfies Property 1:

(i) : Let $b = last[(x,a)]$. We have $D_N(y) = D_{N+1}(y) \cup D_R(y)$ and by Property 1.(i) $\forall c \in D_{N+1}(y), c < b \Rightarrow ((x,a),(y,c)) \notin T(C)$. Thus, if $\forall c \in D_R(y), c < b \Rightarrow ((x,a),(y,c)) \notin T(C)$ then $last[(x,a)]$ also satisfies Property 1.(i). On the other hand, if $\exists c \in D_R(y)$ with $c < b$ and $((x,a),(y,c)) \in T(C)$ then $d = \min(K(x,a) \cap D_R(y))$ satisfies Property 1.(i).

(ii) If $\min(\text{last}[(x,a)], \min(K(x,a) \cap D_R(y))) = \text{last}[(x,a)]$ then $\text{last}[(x,a)]$ has the same value for node $N+1$ and for node N. Property 1.(ii) is satisfied by $\text{last}[(x,a)]$ for node $N+1$ therefore it is also satisfied by $\text{last}[(x,a)]$ for node N.

If $\min(\text{last}[(x,a)], \min(K(x,a) \cap D_R(y))) = \min(K(x,a) \cap D_R(y)) = d$ then suppose that Function SEEKVALIDSUPPORT has reached a value $c > d$ of y when seeking for a new support for the value (x,a) in the branch of the tree search going from the root to node N. The value a is still in $D_N(x)$, so it means that Function SEEKVALIDSUPPORT found a valid support for (x,a) which is greater than c and so greater than d. Since d is a support and $d \in D_N(y)$ this is not possible. So, Property 1.(ii) holds. ⊙

This proposition is used to restore the last values for the node N, that is when the node $N+1$ is backtracked.

Example: Consider the following last values for node N: $\text{last}[(x,0)] = (y,0)$, $\text{last}[(x,1)] = (y,1)$, $\text{last}[(x,2)] = (y,2)$; and the following domains $D_N(x) = \{0,1,2\}$ and $D_N(y) = \{0,1,3..,50\}$. Now, suppose that the last values for node $N+1$ are $\text{last}[(x,0)] = (y,0)$, $\text{last}[(x,2)] = (y,20)$, $\text{last}[(x,3)] = (y,20)$; and the domains are $D_{N+1}(x) = \{0,1\}$ and $D_{N+1}(y) = \{0,3..20,30..50\}$, so $D_R(y) = \{1,2,21..29\}$. From Proposition 1, when node $N+1$ is backtracked the last values will be recomputed as follows: $\text{last}[(x,0)] = \min((y,0), \min(K(x,0) \cap D_R(y))) = (y,0)$, because 0 is less than any value of $D_R(y)$. Then $\text{last}[(x,1)]$ is equal to $\min((y,20), \min(K(x,1) \cap D_R(y)))$ and value $(y,1)$ is the minimum so $\text{last}[(x,1)] = (y,1)$. For $\text{last}[(x,2)]$ an interesting result is obtained: $\min(\text{last}[(x,2)], \min(K(x,2) \cap D_R(y))) = (y,20)$ because the values less than 2 are not possible (in node N we had $\text{last}[(x,2)] = (y,2)$) and $2 \notin D_N(y)$ and all the values less than 20 have been negatively checked (because they are still in the domains of $D_{N+1}(y)$).

This example shows that the values that are restored by recomputation can be different from the ones that would had been restored by savings. In fact they are greater than or equal to the ones restored by savings. So, **the backtrack to the node N may benefit from the computations that have been performed after the node N.** Therefore, a lot of computations can be avoided. For our example, for $(x,2)$ the values of $D(y)$ less than 20 will no longer be considered for the next subtrees whose root is N.

Algorithm: Only the values of $D(x) \cup D_R(x)$ needs to have their last value restored (See Algorithm 6.) Function RECOMPUTELAST is called for every variable of every constraint after every backtrack.

Time Complexity of Function RECOMPUTELAST: For one restoration and for one variable of a constraint its time complexity is in $O(|D(x)| \times |D_R(y)|)$. Thus, for one branch of the tree search its time complexity is in $O(\sum_i |D_0(x)| \times |D_{Ri}(y)|) = O(|D_0(x)| \times \sum_i |D_{Ri}(y)|)$. Moreover, the set $D_{Ri}(y)$ are pairwise disjoint for one branch of the tree search and their union is included in $D(y)$. Therefore we have $\sum_i |D_{Ri}(y)| \leq |D_0(y)|$ and the time complexity is in $O(|D_0(x)| \times |D_0(y)|) = O(d^2)$ per constraint, that is the same time complexity as for AC-6 or AC-7 algorithms.

Algorithm 6. Restoration of last values by recomputation

RECOMPUTELAST(C, x)
for each $a \in (D(x) \cup D_R(x))$ do
  for each $b \in D_R(y)$ do
    if $((x, a), (y, b)) \in T(C)$ then
      $\text{last}[(x, a)] \leftarrow \min(\text{last}[(x, a)], (y, b))$

6.3 Improvements

The previous algorithm needs to be improved to be efficient in practice.

Improvement of Function RECOMPUTELAST:

• the values of $D_R(y)$ can be ordered to reduce the number of tests. If the complexity of one sort is in $d \log(d)$ then the time complexity of all the sorts for one branch of the tree search will be equal to $\sum_i |D_{Ri}(y)| \log(|D_{Ri}(y)|) \leq \sum_i |D_{Ri}(y)| \log(d) \leq \log(d) \sum_i |D_{Ri}(y)| \leq d \log(d) \leq d^2$.

• if $(x, a) \in D_R(x)$, then a new data storing the first value of a last for the current node (that is only one data is introduced per value) can be used. This new data saves the last value that has to be restored for the values that are removed by the current node. So, the last of these values can be restored in $O(1)$ per value.

• if $(x, a) \in D(x)$ and $\text{last}[(x, a)] \notin D(y)$ and $\text{last}[(x, a)] \notin D_R(y)$ then the last is correct and no restoration is needed. In order to avoid considering these values, a global list LM of values of variables is associated with every constraint. If $\text{last}[(x, a)]$ is modified by Function SEEKVALIDSUPPORT or by Function RECOMPUTELAST then (x, a) is added to the head of LM. If (x, a) was already in the list then it is first removed from it before adding it again (that is the ordering of the list is changed). In addition an added value is marked with the current node of the tree search. Then, when node N is backtracked only the values of the list associated with node N have to be considered. These values are at the beginning of the LM list. This method does not change the space complexity, because a value can be in the LM list of a constraint at most once.

Reduction of the Number of Studied Constraints: when a node N is backtracked, it is useless to call Function RECOMPUTELAST for constraints that have not been propagated at node N. A constraint can be propagated at most d times, because to be propagated at least one value must have been removed. Thus, we can associate with every node of the tree search the list of the constraints that have been propagated for this node without changing the space complexity. Then when node N is backtracked, Function RECOMPUTELAST is called only for the constraints belonging to the list of propagated constraints associated with N.

7 Discussion and Experiments

We tested our algorithm on different kinds of problems and compared it to a MAC version explicitly saving the last values. For some problems like n-queens there is almost no difference, but for some other problems like the RLFAPs and mainly instance 11, the improvements we give are really worthwhile. Without these improvements a factor of 15 is observed, but with these improvements the new algorithm is slower by only a factor of 2 and this is the worst result we have observed. For a lot of instances only 30% is lost. At last, this new algorithm always performs better than MAC-3, MAC-4 and MAC-2001. In addition, there is still room for improvement.

This method could also be worthwhile for the implementation of non binary constraints. Non binary constraints imply the explicit creation of tuples, whereas with binary constraints we can only work with domains. Moreover, a tuple can support several values. So, the memory management of the creation/deletion of tuples is difficult. Our method should lead to simpler algorithms.

8 Conclusion

In this paper we have presented MAC versions of AC-6 and AC-7 algorithms. We have also given a new method to restore the last value that lead to MAC-6 and MAC-7 algorithms having the same space complexity as AC-6 and AC-7. This result improves all the previous studies and closes an open question. In addition this work can be seen as a step toward a better understanding of AC algorithms and could lead to new improvements to existing algorithms. For instance, we have given an example for which our method saves a lot of checks in regards to the classical MAC algorithm.

References

1. C. Bessière. Arc-consistency and arc-consistency again. *Artificial Intelligence*, 65(1):179–190, 1994.
2. C. Bessière, E.C. Freuder, and J-C. Régin. Using constraint metaknowledge to reduce arc consistency computation. *Artificial Intelligence*, 107(1):125–148, 1999.
3. C. Bessière and J-C. Régin. Refining the basic constraint propagation algorithm. In *Proceedings of IJCAI'01*, pages 309–315, Seattle, WA, USA, 2001.
4. A. Chmeiss and P. Jégou. Efficient path-consistency propagation. *Journal on Artificial Intelligence Tools*, 7(2):79–89, 1998.
5. C. Lecoutre, F. Boussemart, and F. Hemery. Exploiting multidirectionnality in coarse-grained arc consistency algorithm. In *Proceedings CP'03*, pages 480–494, Cork, Ireland, 2003.
6. A.K. Mackworth. Consistency in networks of relations. *Artificial Intelligence*, 8:99–118, 1977.
7. R. Mohr and T.C. Henderson. Arc and path consistency revisited. *Artificial Intelligence*, 28:225–233, 1986.

8. J-C. Régin. *Développement d'outils algorithmiques pour l'Intelligence Artificielle. Application à la chimie organique.* PhD thesis, Université de Montpellier II, 1995.
9. M.R. van Dongen. Ac-3d an efficient arc-consistency algorithm with a low space-complexity. In *Proc. CP'02*, pages 755–760, Ithaca, NY, USA, 2002.
10. M.R. van Dongen. Lightweight arc consistency algorithms. Technical Report TR-01-2003, Cork Constraint Computation Center, University College Cork, 2003.
11. M.R. van Dongen. Lightweight mac algorithms. Technical Report TR-02-2003, Cork Constraint Computation Center, University College Cork, 2003.
12. P. Van Hentenryck, Y. Deville, and C.M. Teng. A generic arc-consistency algorithm and its specializations. *Artificial Intelligence*, 57:291–321, 1992.
13. Y. Zhang and R. Yap. Making ac-3 an optimal algorithm. In *Proceedings of IJCAI'01*, pages 316–321, Seattle, WA, USA, 2001.

Weak Composition for Qualitative Spatial and Temporal Reasoning

Jochen Renz[1] and Gérard Ligozat[2]

[1] National ICT Australia*, Knowledge Representation and Reasoning Group,
UNSW Sydney, NSW 2052, Australia
jochen.renz@nicta.com.au
[2] LIMSI-CNRS, Université Paris-Sud, 91403 Orsay, France
ligozat@limsi.fr

Abstract. It has now been clear for some time that for many qualitative spatial or temporal calculi, for instance the well-known RCC8 calculus, the operation of composition of relations which is used is actually only weak composition, which is defined as the strongest relation in the calculus that contains the real composition. An immediate consequence for qualitative calculi where weak composition is not equivalent to composition is that the well-known concept of path-consistency is not applicable anymore. In these cases we can only use algebraic closure which corresponds to applying the path-consistency algorithm with weak composition instead of composition.

In this paper we analyse the effects of having weak compositions. Starting with atomic CSPs, we show under which conditions algebraic closure can be used to decide consistency in a qualitative calculus, how weak consistency affects different important techniques for analysing qualitative calculi and under which conditions these techniques can be applied. For our analysis we introduce a new concept for qualitative relations, the "closure under constraints". It turns out that the most important property of a qualitative calculus is not whether weak composition is equivalent to composition, but whether the relations are closed under constraints. All our results are general and can be applied to all existing and future qualitative spatial and temporal calculi. We close our paper with a road map of how qualitative calculi should be analysed. As a side effect it turns out that some results in the literature have to be reconsidered.

1 Introduction

The domain of qualitative temporal reasoning underwent a major change when Allen [1] proposed a new calculus which up to a degree resulted in embedding it in the general paradigm of constraint satisfaction problems (CSPs). CSPs have their well-established sets of questions and methods, and qualitative temporal reasoning, and more recently qualitative spatial reasoning, has profited significantly from developing tools and methods analogous to those of classical constraint satisfaction. In particular, a central question for classical constraint networks is the consistency problem: is the set of constraints

---

* National ICT Australia is funded through the Australian Government's *Backing Australia's Ability* initiative, in part through the Australian Research Council.

specified by the constraint network consistent, that is, can the variables be instantiated with values from the domains in such a way that all constraints are satisfied?

Part of the apparatus for solving the problem consists of filtering algorithms which are able to restrict the domains of the variables without changing the problem, while remaining reasonably efficient from a computational point of view. Various algorithms such as arc consistency, path consistency, and various notions of k-consistency have been extensively studied in that direction. Reasoning about temporal or spatial qualitative constraint networks on the same line as CSPs has proved a fruitful approach. Both domains indeed share a general paradigm. However, there is a fundamental difference between the two situations:

- Relations in classical CSPs are finite relations, so they can be explicitly manipulated as sets of tuples of elements of a finite domain. In other terms, relations are given and processed in an extensional way.
- By contrast, relations in (most) qualitative temporal and spatial reasoning formalisms are provided in intentional terms – or, to use a more down-to-earth expression, they are infinite relations, which means that there is no feasible way of dealing with them extensionally.

But is that such an important point? We think it is, although this was not apparent for Allen's calculus. The differences began to appear when it became obvious that new formalisms, such as for instance the RCC8 calculus [19], could behave in a significantly different way than Allen's calculus. The differences have to do with changes in the notion of composition, with the modified meaning of the the classical concept of path-consistency and its relationship to consistency, and with the inapplicability of familiar techniques for analysing qualitative calculi.

1.1 Composition

Constraint propagation mainly uses the operation of composition of two binary relations. In the finite case, there is only a finite number of binary relations. In Allen's case, although the domains are infinite, the compositions of the thirteen atomic relations are themselves unions of atomic relations. But this is not the case in general, where insisting on genuine composition could lead to considering an infinite number of relations, whereas the basic idea of qualitative reasoning is to deal with a finite number of relations. The way around the difficulty consists in using weak composition, which only approximates true composition.

1.2 Path Consistency and Other Qualitative Techniques

When only weak composition is used then some algorithms and techniques which require true composition can only use weak composition instead. This might lead to the inapplicability of their outcomes. Path-consistency, for example, relies on the fact that a constraint between two variables must be at least as restrictive as every path in the constraint network between the same two variables. The influence of the paths depends on composition of relations on the path. If we use algebraic closure instead of path-consistency, which is essentially path-consistency with weak composition, then we might not detect restrictions imposed by composition and therefore the filtering effect of algebraic closure is weaker than that of path-consistency. As a consequence it might not be possible to use algebraic closure as a decision procedure for certain calculi. Likewise, commonly used reduction techniques lose their strength when using only weak composition and might not lead to valid reductions.

The main goal of this paper is to thoroughly analyse how the use of weak composition instead of composition affects the applicability of the common filtering algorithms and reduction techniques and to determine under which conditions their outcomes match that of their composition-based counterparts.

1.3 Related Work

The concepts of weak composition and algebraic closure are not new. Although there has not always been a unified terminology to describe these concepts, many authors have pointed out that composition tables do not necessarily correspond to the formal definition of composition [4,5,8,13]. Consequently, many researchers have been interested in finding criteria for (refutation) completeness of compositional reasoning, and Bennett et al. ([4,5]) posed this as a challenge and conjectured a possible solution. Later work focused on dealing with this problem for RCC8 [6,11]. In particular Li and Ying ([11]) showed that no RCC8 model can be interpreted extensionally, i.e., for RCC8 composition is always only a weak composition, which gives a negative answer to Bennett et al.'s conjecture. Our paper is the first to give a general account on the effects of having weak composition and a general and clear criterion for the relationship between algebraic closure and consistency. Therefore, the results of this paper are important for establishing the foundations of qualitative spatial and temporal reasoning and are a useful tool for investigating and developing qualitative calculi.

The structure of the paper is as follows: Section 2 introduces the main notions and terminology about constraint networks, various notions of consistency and discusses weak composition and algebraic closure. Section 3 provides a characterisation of those calculi for which algebraic closure decides consistency for atomic networks. Section 4 examines the conditions under which general techniques of reduction can be applied to a qualitative calculus. Finally, Section 5 draws general conclusions in terms of how qualitative calculi should be analysed, and shows that some existing results have to be revisited in consequence.

2 Background

2.1 Constraint Networks

Knowledge between different entities can be represented by using constraints. A *binary relation* R over a domain $\mathcal{D}$ is a set of pairs of elements of $\mathcal{D}$, i.e., $R \subseteq \mathcal{D} \times \mathcal{D}$. A binary *constraint* xRy between two variables x and y restricts the possible instantiations of x and y to the pairs contained in the relation R. A *constraint satisfaction problem* (CSP) consists of a finite set of variables $\mathcal{V}$, a domain $\mathcal{D}$ with possible instantiations for each variable $v_i \in \mathcal{V}$ and a finite set $\mathcal{C}$ of constraints between the variables of $\mathcal{V}$. A *solution* of a CSP is an instantiation of each variable $v_i \in \mathcal{V}$ with a value $d_i \in \mathcal{D}$ such that all constraints of $\mathcal{C}$ are satisfied, i.e., for each constraint $v_i R v_j \in \mathcal{C}$ we have $(d_i, d_j) \in R$. If a CSP has a solution, it is called *consistent* or *satisfiable*. Several algebraic operations are defined on relations that carry over to constraints, the most important ones being *union* ($\cup$), *intersection* ($\cap$), and *complement* ($\overline{\cdot}$) of a relation, defined as the usual set-theoretic operators, as well as *converse* ($\cdot^{-1}$) defined as $R^{-1} = \{(a, b) | (b, a) \in R\}$ and *composition* ($\circ$) of two relations R and S which is the relation $R \circ S = \{(a, b) | \exists c : (a, c) \in R \text{ and } (c, b) \in S\}$.

2.2 Path-Consistency

Because of the high complexity of deciding consistency, different forms of local consistency and algorithms for achieving local consistency were introduced. Local consistency is used to prune the search space by eliminating local inconsistencies. In some cases local consistency is even enough for deciding consistency. Montanari [15] developed a form of local consistency which Mackworth [14] later called path-consistency. Montanari's notion of path-consistency considers all paths between two variables. Mackworth showed that it is equivalent to consider only paths of length two, so path-consistency can be defined as follows: a CSP is *path-consistent*, if for every instantiation of two variables $v_i, v_j \in \mathcal{V}$ that satisfies $v_i R_{ij} v_j \in \mathcal{C}$ there exists an instantiation of every third variable $v_k \in \mathcal{V}$ such that $v_i R_{ik} v_k \in \mathcal{C}$ and $v_k R_{kj} v_j \in \mathcal{C}$ are also satisfied. Formally, for every triple of variables $v_i, v_j, v_k \in \mathcal{V}$: $\forall d_i, d_j : [(d_i, d_j) \in R_{ij} \rightarrow \exists d_k : ((d_i, d_k) \in R_{ik} \wedge (d_k, d_j) \in R_{kj})]$. Montanari also developed an algorithm that makes a CSP path-consistent, which was later simplified and called *path-consistency algorithm* or *enforcing path-consistency*. A path-consistency algorithm eliminates locally inconsistent tuples from the relations between the variables by successively applying the following operation to all triples of variables $v_i, v_j, v_k \in \mathcal{V}$ until a fixpoint is reached: $R_{ij} := R_{ij} \cap (R_{ik} \circ R_{kj})$. If the empty relation occurs, then the CSP is inconsistent. Otherwise the resulting CSP is path-consistent.

2.3 Varieties of k-Consistency

Freuder [7] generalised path-consistency and the weaker notion of arc-consistency to k-consistency: A CSP is *k-consistent*, if for every subset $\mathcal{V}_k \subset \mathcal{V}$ of k variables the following holds: for every instantiation of $k - 1$ variables of $\mathcal{V}_k$ that satisfies all constraints of $\mathcal{C}$ that involve only these $k - 1$ variables, there is an instantiation of the remaining variable of $\mathcal{V}_k$ such that all constraints involving only variables of $\mathcal{V}_k$ are satisfied. So if a CSP is k-consistent, we know that each consistent instantiation of $k - 1$ variables can be extended to any k-th variable. A CSP is strongly k-consistent, if it is i-consistent for every $i \leq k$. If a CSP with n variables is strongly n-consistent (also called *globally consistent*) then a solution can be constructed incrementally without backtracking. 3-consistency is equivalent to path-consistency, 2-consistency is equivalent to arc-consistency.

2.4 Qualitative Spatial and Temporal Relations

The main difference of spatial or temporal CSPs to normal CSPs is that the domains of the spatial and temporal variables are usually infinite. For instance, there are infinitely many time points or temporal intervals on the time line and infinitely many regions in a two or three dimensional space. Hence it is not feasible to represent relations as sets of tuples, nor is it feasible to apply algorithms that enumerate values of the domains. Instead, relations can be used as symbols and reasoning has to be done by manipulating symbols. This implies that the calculus, which deals with extensional relations in the finite case, becomes intensional in the sense that it manipulates symbols which stand for infinite relations. The usual way of dealing with relations in qualitative spatial and temporal reasoning is to have a finite (usually small) set $\mathcal{A}$ of jointly exhaustive and pairwise disjoint (JEPD) relations, i.e., each possible tuple $(a, b) \in \mathcal{D} \times \mathcal{D}$ is contained in exactly one relation $R \in \mathcal{A}$. The relations of a JEPD set $\mathcal{A}$ are called *atomic relations*. The full set of available relations is then the powerset $\mathcal{R} = 2^\mathcal{A}$ which enables us to represent indefinite knowledge, e.g., the constraint $x\{R_i, R_j, R_k\}y$ specifies that the relation between x and y is one of R_i, R_j or R_k, where R_i, R_j, R_k are atomic relations.

2.5 Composition and Weak Composition

Using these relations we can now represent qualitative spatial or temporal knowledge using CSPs and use constraint-based methods for deciding whether such a CSP is consistent, i.e., whether it has a solution. Since we are not dealing with explicit tuples anymore, we have to compute the algebraic operators for the relations. These operators are the only connection of the relation symbols to the tuples contained in the relations and they have to be computed depending on the tuples contained in the relations. Union, complement, converse, and intersection of relations are again the usual set-theoretic operators while composition is not as straightforward. Composition has to be computed only for pairs of atomic relations since composition of non-atomic relations is the union of the composition of the involved atomic relations. Nevertheless, according to the definition of composition, we would have to look at an infinite number of tuples in order to compute composition of atomic relations, which is clearly not feasible. Fortunately, many domains such as points or intervals on a time line are ordered or otherwise well-structured domains and composition can be computed using the formal definitions of the relations. However, for domains such as arbitrary spatial regions that are not well structured and where there is no common representation for the entities we consider, computing the true composition is not feasible and composition has to be approximated by using *weak composition* [6]. Weak composition ($\diamond$) of two relations S and T is defined as the strongest relation $R \in 2^\mathcal{A}$ which contains $S \circ T$, or formally, $S \diamond T = \{R_i \in \mathcal{A} | R_i \cap (S \circ T) \neq \emptyset\}$. The advantage of weak composition is that we stay within the given set of relations $\mathcal{R} = 2^\mathcal{A}$ while applying the algebraic operators, as $\mathcal{R}$ is by definition closed under weak composition, union, intersection, and converse.

In cases where composition cannot be formally computed (e.g. RCC8 [19]), it is often very difficult to determine whether weak composition is equivalent to composition or not. Usually only non-equality can be shown by giving a counterexample, while it is very difficult to prove equality. However, weak composition has also been used in cases where composition could have been computed because the domain is well-structured and consists of pairs of ordered points, but where the authors did not seem to be aware that $\mathcal{R}$ is not closed under composition (e.g. INDU, PDN, or PIDN [17,16,18]).

Example 1 (Region Connection Calculus RCC8 [19]). RCC8 is a topological constraint language based on eight atomic relations between extended regions of a topological space. Regions are regular subsets of a topological space, they can have holes and can consist of multiple disconnected pieces. The eight atomic relations DC (disconnected), EC (externally connected), PO (partial overlap), EQ (equal), TPP (tangential proper part), $NTPP$ (non-tangential proper part) and their converse relations $TPPi$, $NTPPi$ were originally defined in first-order logic. It was shown by Düntsch [6], that the composition of RCC8 is actually only a weak composition. Consider the consistent RCC8 constraints $B\{TPP\}A$, $B\{EC\}C$, $C\{TPP\}A$. If A is instantiated as a region with two disconnected pieces and B completely fills one piece, then C cannot be instantiated. So TPP is not a subset of $EC \circ TPP$ [11] and consequently RCC8 is not closed under composition.

2.6 Algebraic Closure

When weak composition differs from composition, we cannot apply the path-consistency algorithm as it requires composition and not just weak composition. We can, however, replace the composition operator in the path-consistency algorithm with the weak composition operator. The resulting algorithm is called the *algebraic closure algorithm* [12] which makes a network *algebraically closed* or *a-closed*.

If weak composition is equal to composition, then the two algorithms are also equivalent. But whenever we have only weak composition, an a-closed network is not necessarily path-consistent as there are relations S and T such that $S \circ T \subset S \diamond T$. So there are tuples $(u, v) \in S \diamond T$ for which there is no w with $(u, w) \in S$ and $(w, v) \in T$, i.e., for which $(u, v) \notin S \circ T$. This contradicts the path-consistency requirements given above.

Path-consistency has always been an important property when analysing qualitative calculi, in particular as a method for identifying tractability. When this method is not available, it is not clear what the consequences of this will be. Will it still be possible to find calculi for which a-closure decides consistency even if weak composition differs from composition? What effect does it have on techniques used for analysing qualitative calculi which require composition and not just weak composition? And what is very important, does it mean that some results in the literature have to be revised or is it enough to reformulate them? These and related questions will be answered in the remainder of the paper. As an immediate consequence, unless we have proven otherwise, we should for all qualitative spatial and temporal calculi always assume that we are dealing with weak composition and that it is not equivalent to composition.

3 Weak Composition and Algebraic Closure

For analysing the effects of weak composition, we will mainly focus on its effects on the most commonly studied reasoning problem, the consistency problem, i.e., whether a given set Θ of spatial or temporal constraints has a solution. Recall that consistency means that there is at least one instantiation for each variable of Θ with a value from its domain which satisfies all constraints. This is different from global consistency which

Table 1. Does a-closure decide atomic CSPs depending on whether weak composition differs from composition?

	a-closure sufficient	a-closure not sufficient
weak composition = composition	Interval Algebra [1] rectangle algebra [9] block algebra [3]	STAR calculus [21] containment algebra [10] cyclic algebra [2]
weak composition $\neq$ composition	RCC8 [19], discrete IA	INDU [17], PDN [16], PIDN [18]

requires strong k-consistency for all k. Global consistency cannot be obtained when we have only weak composition as we have no method for even determining 3-consistency. For the mere purpose of deciding consistency it actually seems overly strong to require any form of k-consistency as we are not interested in whether *any* consistent instantiation of k variables can be extended to $k + 1$ variables, but only whether there exists *at least one* consistent instantiation. Therefore it might not be too weak for deciding consistency to have only algebraic closure instead of path-consistency.

In the following we restrict ourselves to atomic CSPs, i.e., CSPs where all constraints are restricted to be atomic relations. If a-closure does not even decide atomic CSPs, it will not decide more general CSPs. We will later see how the results for atomic CSPs can be extended to less restricted CSPs. Let us first analyse for some existing calculi how the two properties whether a-closure decides atomic CSPs and whether weak composition differs from composition relate. We listed the results in Table 1 and they are significant:

Proposition 1. *Let $\mathcal{R}$ be a finite set of qualitative relations. Whether a-closure decides consistency for atomic CSPs over $\mathcal{R}$ is independent of whether weak composition differs from composition for relations in $\mathcal{R}$.*

This observation shows us that whether or not a-closure decides atomic CSPs does not depend on whether weak composition is equivalent to composition or not. Instead we will have to find another criterion for when a-closure decides atomic CSPs. In order to find such a criterion we will look at some examples where a-closure does not decide atomic CSPs and see if we can derive some commonalities.

Example 2 (STAR calculus [21]). Directions between two-dimensional points are distinguished by specifying an arbitrary number of angles which separate direction sectors. The atomic relations are the sectors as well as the lines that separate the sectors (see Figure 1 left). The domain is ordered so it is possible to compute composition. The relations are closed under composition. If more than two angles are given, then by using constraint configurations involving four or more variables, it is possible to refine the atomic relations that correspond to sectors to different particular angles (see Figure 1 right). By combining configurations that refine the same atomic relation to different angles, inconsistencies can be constructed that cannot be detected by a-closure. In this example we can see that even true composition can be too weak. Although we know the composition and all relations are closed under composition, it is possible to refine atomic relations using networks with more than three nodes.

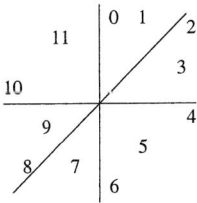 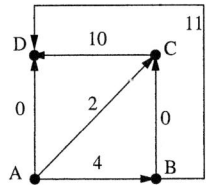

Fig. 1. A STAR calculus with 3 angles resulting in 13 atomic relations (left). The right picture shows an atomic CSP whose constraints enforce that D must be 45 degrees to the left of B, i.e., the constraint $B\{11\}D$ is refined by the other constraints to the line orthogonal to relation 2. Therefore, the atomic relation 11 can be refined to a subatomic relation using the given constraints.

Example 3 (INDU calculus [17]). Allen's 13 interval relations are combined with relative duration of intervals given in the form of a point algebra, i.e., INDU relations are of the form $R = I_\delta$ where I is an interval relation (precedes p, meets m, during d, starts s, overlaps o, finishes f, equal =, and the converse relations fi,oi,si,di,mi,pi) and δ a duration relation ($<, >, =$). This leads to only 25 atomic relations as some combinations are impossible, e.g., $a\{s\}b$ enforces that the duration of a must be less than that of b. Only weak composition is used, as for example the triple $a\{s_<\}b, a\{m_<\}c, c\{f_<\}b$ enforces that $a < 0.5 * b$ and $c > 0.5 * b$. So an instantiation where $a = 0.5 * b$ cannot be extended to a consistent instantiation of c. In the same way it is possible to generate any metric duration constraint of the form $duration(x) \, R \, \alpha * duration(b)$ where $R \in \{<, >, =\}$ and α is a rational number. Consequently, it is possible to construct inconsistent atomic CSPs which are a-closed.

In both examples it is possible to refine atomic relations to subatomic relations that have no tuples in common, i.e., which do not overlap. This can be used to construct inconsistent examples which are still a-closed. Note that in the case of the interval algebra over integers it is possible to refine atomic relations to subatomic relations, e.g., $a\{p\}b, b\{p\}c$ leads to $a\{p+2\}c$, where $p+2$ indicates that a must precede c by at least 2 more integers than is required by the precedes relation. But since these new subatomic relations always overlap, it is not possible to construct inconsistencies which are a-closed. Let us formally define these terms.

Definition 1 (refinement to a subatomic relation). *Let Θ be a consistent atomic CSP over a set $\mathcal{A}$ and $xRy \in \Theta$ a constraint. Let R' be the union of all tuples $(u, v) \in R$ that can be instantiated to x and y as part of a solution of Θ. If $R' \subset R$, then Θ refines R to the subatomic relation R'.*

Definition 2 (closure under constraints). *Let $\mathcal{A}$ be a set of atomic relations. $\mathcal{A}$ is closed under constraints if no relation $R \in \mathcal{A}$ can be refined to non-overlapping subatomic relations, i.e., if for each $R \in \mathcal{A}$ all subatomic relations $R' \subset R$ to which R can be refined to have a nonempty intersection.*

In the following theorem we show that the observation made in these examples holds in general and we can prove in which cases a-closure decides atomic CSPs, which is independent of whether weak composition differs from composition and only depends on whether the atomic relations are closed under constraints. Therefore, the new concept of closure under constraints turns out to be a very important property of qualitative reasoning.

Theorem 1. *Let $\mathcal{A}$ be a finite set of atomic relations. Then a-closure decides consistency of CSPs over $\mathcal{A}$ if and only if $\mathcal{A}$ is closed under constraints.*

Proof Sketch. $\Rightarrow$: Given a set of atomic relations $\mathcal{A} = \{R_1, \ldots, R_n\}$. We have to prove that if $\mathcal{A}$ is not closed under constraints, then a-closure does not decide consistency over $\mathcal{A}$. $\mathcal{A}$ is not closed under constraints means that there is an atomic relation $R_k \in \mathcal{A}$ which can be refined to non-overlapping subatomic relations using atomic sets of constraints over $\mathcal{A}$. We will prove this by constructing an a-closed but inconsistent set of constraints over $\mathcal{A}$ for those cases where $\mathcal{A}$ is not closed under constraints. We assume without loss of generality that if $\mathcal{A}$ is not closed under constraints, there are at least two non-overlapping subatomic relations R_k^1, R_k^2 of R_k which can be obtained using the atomic sets of constraints Θ^1, Θ^2 (both are a-closed and consistent and contain the constraint xR_ky). We combine all tuples of R_k not contained in R_k^1 or R_k^2 to R_k^m and have that $R_k^1 \cup R_k^2 \cup R_k^m = R_k$ and that R_k^1, R_k^2, R_k^m are pairwise disjoint.

We can now form a new set of atomic relations $\mathcal{A}'$ where R_k is replaced with R_k^1, R_k^2, R_k^m (analogous for R_k^{-1}). All the other relations are the same as in $\mathcal{A}$. The weak composition table of $\mathcal{A}'$ differs from that of $\mathcal{A}$ for the entries that contain R_k or R_k^{-1}. Since R_k^1 and R_k^2 can be obtained by atomic sets of constraints over $\mathcal{A}$, the entries in the weak composition table of $\mathcal{A}'$ cannot be the same for R_k^1 and for R_k^2. Therefore, there must be a relation $R_l \in \mathcal{A}$ for which the entries of $R_l \diamond R_k^1$ and of $R_l \diamond R_k^2$ differ. We assume that $R_l \diamond R_k = S$ and that $R_l \diamond R_k^1 = S \setminus S_1$ and $R_l \diamond R_k^2 = S \setminus S_2$, with $S, S_1, S_2 \in 2^{\mathcal{A}}$ and $S_1 \neq S_2$. We chose a non-empty one, say S_1, and can now obtain an inconsistent triple xR_k^1y, zR_lx, zS_1y for which the corresponding triple xR_ky, zR_lx, zS_1y is consistent. Note that we use $\mathcal{A}'$ only for identifying R_l and S_1.

If we now consider the set of constraints $\Theta = \Theta^1 \cup \{zR_lx, zS_1y\}$ (where z is a fresh variable not contained in Θ^1), then Θ is clearly inconsistent since Θ^1 refines xR_ky to xR_k^1y and since $R_l \diamond R_k^1 = S \setminus S_1$. However, applying the a-closure algorithm to Θ (resulting in Θ') using the weak composition table of $\mathcal{A}$ does not result in an inconsistency, since a-closure does not see the implicit refinement of xR_ky to xR_k^1y.

$\Leftarrow$: Proof by induction over the size n of Θ. Induction hypothesis: $P(n) = \{$For sets Θ of atomic constraints of size n, if it is not possible to refine atomic relations to non-overlapping subatomic relations, then a-closure decides consistency for Θ.$\}$ This is clear for $n \leq 3$. Now take an a-closed atomic CSP Θ of size n+1 over $\mathcal{A}$ and assume that $P(n)$ is true. For every variable $x \in \Theta$ let Θ_x be the atomic CSP that results from Θ by removing all constraints that involve x. Because of $P(n)$, Θ_x is consistent for all $x \in \Theta$. Let R_x be the subatomic relation to which R is refined to in Θ_x and let R' be the intersection of R_x for all $x \in \Theta$. If R' is non-empty for every $R \in \mathcal{A}$, i.e., if it is not possible to refine R to non-overlapping subatomic relations, then we can choose a consistent instantiation of Θ_x which contains for every relation R only tuples of R'. Since no relation R of Θ_x can be refined beyond R' by adding constraints of Θ that involve x, it is clear that we can then also find a consistent instantiation for x, and thereby obtain a consistent instantiation of Θ. ∎

This theorem is not constructive in the sense that it does not help us to prove that a-closure decides consistency for a particular calculus. But such a general constructive theorem would not be possible as it depends on the semantics of the relations and on the domains whether a-closure decides consistency. This has to be formally proven in a different way for each new calculus and for each new domain. What our theorem gives us, however, is a simple explanation why a-closure is independent of whether weak composition differs from composition: It makes no difference whatsoever whether non-overlapping subatomic relations are obtained via triples of constraints or via larger constellations (as in Example 2). In both cases a-closure cannot detect all inconsistencies. Our theorem also gives us both, a simple method for determining when a-closure does not decide consistency, and a very good heuristic for approximating when it does. Consider the following heuristic:

> Does the considered domain enable more distinctions than those made by the atomic relations, and if so, can these distinctions be enforced by a set of constraints over existing relations?

This works for the three examples we already mentioned. It also works for any other calculus that we looked at. Take for instance the containment algebra which is basically the interval algebra without distinguishing directions [10]. So having directions would be a natural distinction and it is easy to show that we can distinguish relative directions by giving constraints: If a is disjoint from b and c touches b but is disjoint from a, then c must be on the same side of a as b. This can be used to construct a-closed inconsistent configurations. For RCC8, the domain offers plenty of other distinctions, but none of them can be enforced by giving a set of RCC8 constraints. This gives a good indication that a-closure decides consistency (which has been proven in [22]). If we restrict the domain of RCC8, e.g., to two-dimensional discs of the same size, then we can find distinctions which can be enforced by giving constraints.

When defining a new qualitative calculus by defining a set of atomic relations, it is desirable that algebraic closure decides consistency of atomic CSPs. Therefore, we recommend to test the above given heuristic when defining a new qualitative calculus and to make sure that the new atomic relations are closed under constraints. In section 5 we discuss the consequences of having a set of relations which is not closed under constraints.

4 Effects on Qualitative Reduction Techniques

In the analysis of qualitative calculi it is usually tried to transfer properties such as tractability or applicability of the a-closure algorithm for deciding consistency to larger sets of relations and ideally find the maximal sets that have these properties. Such general techniques involve composition of relations in one way or another and it is not clear whether they can still be applied if only weak composition is known and if they have been properly applied in the literature. It might be that replacing composition with weak composition and path-consistency with a-closure is sufficient, but it might also be that existing results turn out to be wrong or not applicable. In this section we look at two important general techniques for extending properties to larger sets of relations.

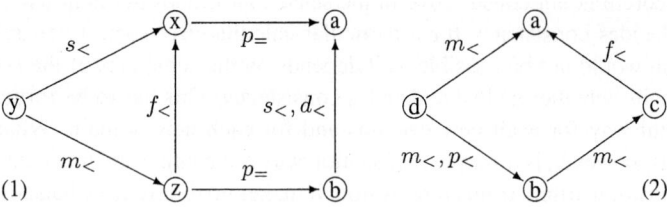

Fig. 2. (1) A consistent INDU network which becomes inconsistent when replacing $b\{s_<, d_<\}a$ with (2). From (1) we get $b > 0.5 * a$ and from (2) we get $b < 0.5 * a$.

The first technique is very widely used and is based on the fact that a set of relations $S \subseteq 2^A$ and the closure $\widehat{S}$ of S under composition, intersection, and converse have the same complexity. This results from a proof that the consistency problem for $\widehat{S}$ (written as $\mathsf{CSPSAT}(\widehat{S})$) can be polynomially reduced to $\mathsf{CSPSAT}(S)$ by inductively replacing each constraint xRy over a relation $R \in \widehat{S} \setminus S$ by either $xSy \wedge xTy$ or by $xSz \circ zTy$ for $S, T \in S$ [22]. If we have only weak composition, then we have two problems. First, we can only look at the closure of S under intersection, converse, and weak composition (we will denote this *weak closure* by $\widehat{S}_w$). And, second, we can replace a constraint xRy over a relation $R \in \widehat{S}_w \setminus S$ only by $xSy \wedge xTy$ or by $xSz \diamond zTy$ for $S, T \in S$. For $xSz \diamond zTy$ we know that it might not be a consistent replacement for xRy. In Figure 2 we give an example for a consistent set of INDU constraints which becomes inconsistent if we replace a non-atomic constraint by an intersection of two weak compositions of other INDU relations.

So it is clear that this widely used technique does not apply in all cases where we have only weak composition. In the following theorem we show when it can still be applied.

Theorem 2. *Let $\mathcal{R}$ be a finite set of qualitative relations and $S \subseteq \mathcal{R}$ a set of relations. Then $\mathsf{CSPSAT}(\widehat{S}_w)$ can be polynomially reduced to $\mathsf{CSPSAT}(S)$ if a-closure decides consistency for atomic CSPs over $\mathcal{R}$.*

Proof Sketch. Consider an a-closed set Θ of constraints over $\widehat{S}_w$. When inductively replacing constraints over $\widehat{S}_w$ with constraints over S, i.e., when replacing xRy where $R \in \widehat{S}_w$ with xSz and zTy where $S \diamond T = R$ and $S, T \in S$ and z is a fresh variable, then potential solutions are lost. However, all these triples of relations (R, S, T) are minimal, i.e., every atomic relation of R can be part of a solution of the triple. No solutions are lost when replacing constraints with the intersection of two other constraints or by a converse constraint. Let Θ' be the set obtained from Θ after inductively replacing all constraints over $\widehat{S}_w$ with constraints over S. Since potential solutions are lost in the transformation, the only problematic case is where Θ is consistent but Θ' is inconsistent. If Θ is consistent, then there must be a refinement of Θ to a consistent atomic CSP Θ_a. For each constraint xRy of Θ which is replaced, all the resulting triples are minimal and are not related to any other variable in Θ. Note that due to the inductive replacement, some constraints will be replaced by stacks of minimal triples. Therefore, each R can be replaced with any of its atomic relations without making the resulting stacks inconsistent. Intersecting Θ' with Θ_a followed by computing a-closure will always result in an a-closed set. Since the stacks contain only minimal triples, it is clear that they can be subsequently refined to atomic relations. The relations between the fresh variables and the variables of Θ can also be refined to atomic relations as they were unrelated before applying a-closure. The resulting atomic CSP will always be a-closed, so Θ' must be consistent if a-closure decides atomic CSPs. ∎

This covers all the cases in the middle column of Table 1 such as RCC8, but does not cover those cases in the bottom right cell. This result is very important for all existing and future calculi where only weak composition is used. We know now that for all calculi where a-closure decides atomic CSPs, complexity results can be transferred between a set of relations and its closure, independent of whether we are using weak composition or composition. This also resolves all doubts (Düntsch, personal communication) about applying this technique to RCC8. On the other hand, we cannot use this popular method of transferring complexity results in cases where we have only weak composition and a-closure does not decide atomic CSPs. For all existing calculi that fall into this category, we should reconsider the complexity analysis. In the following section we will have a look at the complexity results of INDU and PIDN and it turns out that some of the complexity results in the literature are wrong.

The second general technique which is very useful for analysing computational properties and identifying large tractable subsets is the refinement method [20]. It gives a simple algorithm for showing if a set $\mathcal{S} \subseteq 2^{\mathcal{A}}$ can be refined to a set $\mathcal{T} \subseteq 2^{\mathcal{A}}$ in the sense that for every path-consistent set of constraints Θ over $\mathcal{S}$ and every relation $S \in \mathcal{S}$ we can always refine S to a subrelation $T \subseteq S$ with $T \in \mathcal{T}$. If path-consistency decides consistency for $\mathcal{T}$ then it must also decide consistency for $\mathcal{S}$.

Theorem 3. *Let $\mathcal{R}$ be a finite set of qualitative relations for which a-closure decides atomic CSPs. The refinement method also works for weak composition by using the a-closure algorithm instead of the path-consistency algorithm.*

Proof Sketch. Any a-closed triple of variables is minimal. So if a relation S can be refined to T in any a-closed triple that contains S, then the refinement can be made in any a-closed network without making the resulting network not a-closed. If a-closure decides the resulting network, then it also decides the original network. ∎

Note that the refinement method only makes sense if a-closure decides atomic CSPs as the whole purpose of the refinement method is to transfer applicability of a-closure for deciding consistency from one subset of $\mathcal{R}$ to another.

5 A Road Map for Analysing Qualitative Calculi

Using the results of our paper we can now analyse new and revisit existing qualitative spatial and temporal calculi. When defining a new set of atomic relations and the domain is not ordered, we have to assume that we have only weak composition unless we can prove the contrary. The most important step is to prove whether a-closure decides atomic CSPs for our new calculus. It is possible to use the heuristic given in the previous section, but if a-closure decides atomic CSPs, then this has to be proven using the semantics of the relations. If it turns out that a-closure decides atomic CSPs then we can proceed by applying the techniques we discussed in the previous section, i.e., we can identify larger tractable subsets by using the refinement method and by computing the closure of known tractable subsets under intersection, converse and (weak) composition. But what if it does not?

5.1 When A-Closure Does Not Decide Atomic CSPs

This is the case for many calculi in the literature (see e.g. Table 1) and will probably be the case for many future calculi. As shown in Theorem 1 this means that it is possible to enforce non-overlapping subatomic relations. If we only get finitely many non-overlapping subatomic relations, as, e.g., for the containment algebra, then it is best to study the calculus obtained by the finitely many new atomic relations and treat the original calculus as a subcalculus of the new calculus. If we do get infinitely many non-overlapping subatomic relations, however, then we suggest to proceed in one of two different ways. Let us first reflect what it means to have infinitely many non-overlapping subatomic relations: An important property of a qualitative calculus is to have only finitely many distinctions. So if we have to make infinitely many distinctions, then we do not have a qualitative calculus anymore! Therefore we cannot expect that qualitative methods and techniques that are only based on (weak) compositions help us in any way. This is also the reason why we analysed the techniques in the previous section only for cases where a-closure decides atomic CSPs, i.e., where we do have qualitative calculi.[1]

One way of dealing with these calculi is to acknowledge that we do not have a qualitative calculus anymore and to use algorithms that deal with quantitative calculi instead. It might be that consistency can still be decided in polynomial time using these algorithms. Another way is to find the source that makes the calculus quantitative and to eliminate this source in such a way that it has no effect anymore, e.g., by combining atomic relations to form coarser atomic relations. Both of these ways were considered for the STAR calculus [21]. A third way, which is sometimes chosen, but which we discourage everyone from taking, is to look at 4-consistency.

5.2 Problems with Using 4-Consistency

We sometimes see results in the literature of the form "4-consistency decides consistency for a set of relations $\mathcal{S} \subseteq 2^{\mathcal{A}}$ and therefore $\mathcal{S}$ is tractable." What we have not seen so far is a proper 4-consistency algorithm. For infinite domains where we only manipulate relation symbols, a 4-consistency algorithm must be based on composition of real ternary relations. The question then is how can we show that the composition of the ternary relations is not just a weak composition. Just like computing composition for binary relations, we might have to check an infinite number of domain values. Consequently, there could be no 4-consistent configurations at all or it could be NP hard to show whether a configuration is 4-consistent. This makes these results rather

---

[1] It is unlikely to find a version of Theorem 2 for cases where a-closure does not decide atomic CSPs. As a heuristic, the following property could be considered: xRy can only be replaced with xSz, zTy if for all weak compositions $R_i \diamond R_j$ that contain R the intersection of all real compositions $R_i \circ R_j$ is nonempty.

useless from a practical point of view and certainly does not allow the conclusion that these sets are tractable. We illustrate this using an example from the literature where 4-consistency was wrongly used for proving that certain subsets of INDU or PIDN [17,18] are tractable.

1. 4-consistency decides consistency for $\mathcal{S} \subseteq 2^{\mathcal{A}}$
2. Deciding consistency is NP-hard for $\mathcal{T} \subseteq \mathcal{S}$

The first result was proven for some subsets of INDU and PIDN [17,18]. We obtained the second result by a straightforward reduction of the NP-hard consistency problem of PDN [16] to INDU and PIDN. It is clear from this example that 4-consistency results cannot be used for proving tractability. Validity and applicability of similar results in the literature should be reconsidered as well.

6 Conclusions

We started with the well-known observation that in many cases in qualitative spatial and temporal reasoning only weak composition can be determined. This requires us to use a-closure instead of path-consistency. We thoroughly analysed the consequences of this fact and showed that the main difficulty is not whether weak composition differs from composition, but whether it is possible to generate non-overlapping subatomic relations, a property which we prove to be equivalent to whether a-closure decides atomic CSPs. Since this occurs also in cases where weak composition is equal to composition, our analysis does not only affect cases where only weak composition is known (which are most cases where the domains are not ordered) but qualitative spatial and temporal calculi in general. We also showed under which conditions some important techniques for analysing qualitative calculi can be applied and finally gave a roadmap for how qualitative calculi should be developed and analysed. As a side effect of our analysis we found that some results in the literature have to be reconsidered.

References

1. J. F. Allen. Maintaining knowledge about temporal intervals. *Communications of the ACM*, 26(11):832–843, 1983.
2. P. Balbiani and A. Osmani. A model for reasoning about topologic relations between cyclic intervals. In *Proceedings of KR-2000*, Breckenridge, Colorado, 2000.
3. P. Balbiani, J.-F. Condotta, and L. Farinas del Cerro. A tractable subclass of the block algebra: constraint propagation and preconvex relations. In *Proceedings of the 9th Portuguese Conference on Artificial Intelligence*, pages 75–89, 1999.
4. B. Bennett. Some observations and puzzles about composing spatial and temporal relations. In *Proceedings ECAI-94 Workshop on Spatial and Temporal Reasoning*, 1994.
5. B. Bennett, A. Isli, and A.G. Cohn. When does a composition table provide a complete and tractable proof procedure for a relational constraint language? In *Proceedings of the IJCAI-97 Workshop on Spatial and Temporal Reasoning*, Nagoya, Japan, 1997.
6. I. Düntsch, H. Wang, and S. McCloskey. A relation - algebraic approach to the region connection calculus. *Theoretical Computer Science*, 255(1-2):63–83, 2001.

7. E.C. Freuder. Synthesizing constraint expressions. *Communications of the ACM*, 21(11):958–965, 1992.
8. M. Grigni, D. Papadias, and C. Papadimitriou. Topological inference. In *Proceedings of the 14th International Joint Conference on Artificial Intelligence*, pages 901–906, Montreal, Canada, August 1995.
9. H. Guesgen. Spatial reasoning based on Allen's temporal logic. Technical Report TR-89-049, ICSI, Berkeley, CA, 1989.
10. P. B. Ladkin and R. D. Maddux. On binary constraint problems. *Journal of the ACM*, 41(3):435–469, 1993.
11. S. Li and M. Ying. Region connection calculus: Its models and composition table. *Artificial Intelligence*, 145(1-2):121–146, 2003.
12. G. Ligozat and J. Renz. Qualitative calculi: a general framework. In *Proceedings of PRICAI'04*, pages 53–64, 2004.
13. G. Ligozat. When tables tell it all: Qualitative spatial and temporal reasoning based on linear orderings. In *Spatial Information Theory: Foundations of Geographic Information Science, International Conference, COSIT 2001*, pages 60–75, 2001.
14. A. K. Mackworth. Consistency in networks of relations. *Artificial Intelligence*, 8:99–118, 1977.
15. U. Montanari. Networks of constraints: Fundamental properties and applications to picture processing. *Information Sciences*, 7:95–132, 1974.
16. I. Navarrete, A. Sattar, R. Wetprasit, and R. Marin. On point-duration networks for temporal reasoning. *Artificial Intelligence*, 140(1-2):39–70, 2002.
17. A. K. Pujari, G. Vijaya Kumari, and A. Sattar. INDU: An Interval and Duration Network. In *Australian Joint Conference on Artificial Intelligence*, pages 291–303, 1999.
18. A. K. Pujari and A. Sattar. A new framework for reasoning about points, intervals and durations. In Dean Thomas, editor, *Proceedings of the 16th International Joint Conference on Artificial Intelligence (IJCAI'99)*, pages 1259–1267. Morgan Kaufmann Publishers, 1999.
19. D. Randell, Z. Cui, and T. Cohn. A spatial logic based on regions and connection. In *Proceedings of KR-92*, pages 165–176, San Mateo, CA, 1992. Morgan Kaufmann.
20. J. Renz. Maximal tractable fragments of the region connection calculus: A complete analysis. In *Proceedings of IJCAI'99*, pages 448–455, 1999.
21. J. Renz and D. Mitra. Qualitative direction calculi with arbitrary granularity. In *Proceedings of PRICAI'04*, pages 65–74, 2004.
22. J. Renz and B. Nebel. On the complexity of qualitative spatial reasoning: A maximal tractable fragment of the Region Connection Calculus. *Artificial Intelligence*, 108(1-2):69–123, 1999.

Boosting Distributed Constraint Satisfaction

Georg Ringwelski[1,*] and Youssef Hamadi[2]

[1] 4C, University College Cork, Ireland
g.ringwelski@4c.ucc.ie
[2] Microsoft Research, 7 J J Thomson Avenue,
Cambridge CB3 0FB, United Kingdom
youssefh@microsoft.com

Abstract. Competition and cooperation can boost the performance of search. Both can be implemented with a portfolio of algorithms which run in parallel, give hints to each other and compete for being the first to finish and deliver the solution. In this paper we present a new generic framework for the application of algorithms for distributed constraint satisfaction which makes use of both cooperation and competition. This framework improves the performance of two different standard algorithms by one order of magnitude and can reduce the risk of poor performance by up to three orders of magnitude. Moreover it greatly reduces the classical idleness flaw usually observed in distributed hierarchy-based searches. We expect our new methods to be similarly beneficial for any tree-based distributed search and describe ways on how to incorporate them.

1 Introduction

In many application domains constraint-based tree-search methods are the technology of choice to solve NP-complete problems today. However, when actually applying the algorithms without further customization, we have often experienced unacceptable performance. This results from various well-investigated factors including bad modelling and the choice of a wrong labelling strategy. The solution for bad modelling often resides in a good understanding of the constraint processing which results in the application of well known modelling patterns (channeling constraints, redundant modelling, etc). Finding a good labelling strategy is not obvious and usually requires long and expensive preliminary experiments on a set of realistic problem instances. Performing those experiments or defining realistic input samples is far from being simple for today's large scale real life applications. Ideally we would not have to make a choice for a labelling strategy at all and rather be able to use an algorithm "out-of-the-box" which finds the best strategy itself [Pug04].

The previous observations are emphasized in the processing of distributed constraint satisfaction problems (DisCSPs). Indeed, the distributed nature of

---

* This work has received support from the Embark Initiative of the Irish Research Council of Science Engineering and Technology under Grant PD2002/21. We'd like to thank Rick Wallace and Mark Hennesy of 4C for providing the problems.

those problems makes any preliminary experimental step difficult since constrained problems usually emerge from the interaction of independent and disconnected agents transiently agreeing to look after a set of globally consistent local solutions [FM02].

This work targets on those cases where bad performance in DisCSP can be prevented by choosing a good labelling strategy and executing it in a benefiting order within the agents. In this paper we define a notion for the risk we have to face when choosing an agent-ordering and present the new "M-" framework[1] for the execution of distributed search. An M- portfolio executes several distributed search strategies in parallel and let them compete and cooperate for being the first to finish. We apply the framework in two case studies where we define the algorithms "M-ABT" and "M-IDIBT" which improve their counterparts ABT [YDIK92] and IDIBT [Ham02] significantly. With these case studies we can show the benefit of competition and cooperation for the underlying distributed search algorithms. We expect the "M-" framework to be similarly beneficial for other tree-based DisCSP algorithms. Cooperation of distributed searches is implemented with the aggregation of knowledge within agents and thus yields no extra communication. The knowledge gained from *all* the parallel searches is used by the agents for their local decision making in each single search. We present two principles of aggregation and employ them in methods which are applicable to the limited scope of the agents in DisCSP.

In the next section we define the risks we have to face in search. This can be used as another metric (besides performance) to evaluate algorithms. In Section 3 we present the new "M-" framework. Section 4 describes our case studies and Section 5 their empirical evaluation. Then we discuss related work, summarize the results and outline some ideas for future work.

2 Risks in Search

Here we present two definitions of *risk* is search. The first notion called *randomization risk* is related to the changes in performances when the same algorithm is applied multiple times to a single problem instance. The second notion called *selection risk* represents the risk of selecting the wrong algorithm, i.e., the one which performs poorly on the considered instance.

2.1 Randomization Risk

In [GS01] "risk" is defined as the standard deviation of the performance of one algorithm applied to one problem multiple times. This risk increases when more randomness is used in the algorithms.

Definition 1. *The R-Risk is the standard deviation of the performance of one algorithm applied multiply to one problem.*

---

[1] M stands for Multi-Directional. "M-" searches in multiple directions, namely agent topologies, at the same time.

Reducing the R-Risk leads in many cases to trade-offs in performance [GSK98], such that the reduction of this risk is in general not desirable. For instance, we would in most cases rather wait between 1–10 seconds for a solution than waiting 7–8 seconds. In the latter case the risk is lower but we do not have the chance to get the best performance.

In asynchronous and distributed systems we are not able to eliminate randomness at all. Besides intended randomness (e.g. in value selection functions) it emerges from external factors including the CPU scheduling to agents or unpredictable times for message passing [ZM03].

To get a standpoint of the R-Risk in DisCSP we made a preliminary experiment, where randomness emerged from distribution only. We solved binary DisCSPs with the IDIBT and ABT algorithms with random message delays and unpredictable agent-activation. It turned out that the R-Risk is in general very high (compared to monolithic systems). Even with completely deterministic value-selection functions the performance of different runs of the algorithm on the same problem differed significantly. For instance, the ABT algorithm with lexicographic labelling applied 100 times to the 10-queens problem could find one solution in 297–5374 ms while IDIBT applied 100 times took 1640–1984 ms. The R-Risk resulting exclusively from distribution was 807 for ABT and 96 for IDIBT.

2.2 Selection Risk

The risk we take when we select a certain algorithm or a heuristic to be applied within an algorithm to solve a problem will always be that this is the wrong choice. For most problems we do not know in advance, which the best algorithm or heuristic will be and may select one which performs much worse than others. We'll refer to this risk as to the Selection-Risk (S-Risk).

Definition 2. *The S-Risk of a set of algorithms A is the standard deviation of the performance of each $a \in A$ applied the same number of times to one problem.*

We investigated the S-Risk emerging from the chosen agent ordering in IDIBT in a preliminary experiment on small, fairly hard random problems (15 variables, 5 values, density 0.3, tightness 0.4). We used one variable per agent and could thus implement variable-orderings in the ordering of agents. We used lexicographic value selection and four different static variable-ordering heuristics: a well-known "intelligent" heuristic, its inverse (which should be bad) and two different blind heuristics. As expected, we could observe that the intelligent heuristic dominates in average but that it is not always the best. It was the fastest in 59% of the tests, but it was also the slowest in 5% of the experiments. The second best heuristic (best in 18%) was also the second worst (also 18%). The "anti-intelligent" heuristic turned out to be the best of the four in 7% after all. The differences between the performances were quite significant with a factor of up to 5. Applied to the same problems, ABT gave very similar results with a larger performance range of up to factor 40.

3 Multi-directional Distributed Search

By a direction in search we refer to a variable ordering. In this paper we consider only static orderings but the "M-" framework can be used with dynamic orderings as well. In DisCSP the variable ordering implies the agent topology. Assume that each agent hosts one variable, for each constraint a *directed* connection between two agents/variables is imposed. The direction defines the priority of the agents and thus in which direction backtracking is performed. In Figure 1 we show two different static agent-topologies emerging from two different variable-ordering heuristics in DisCSP.

The idea of Multi-Directional search is that several variable orderings and thus several agent topologies are used by concurrent searches. We refer to this idea as to the "M-" framework for DisCSP. Applied to an algorithm X it defines a DisCSP algorithm M-X which applies X multiply in parallel. Each search operates in its usual way on one of the previously selected topologies. In each agent the multiple searches use separate contexts to store the various pieces of information they require. These include for example adjacent agents, their current value or their beliefs about the current values of other agents. Given the topologies in Figure 1, agent X3 for example, would contain two contexts. In the one which is related to maxDegree it would store X7 as lower prioritized adjacent agent and in the other it would store X1. In ABT or IDIBT it would thus address messages that notify others of new values (*ok?* in ABT, *infoVal* in IDIBT) to agent X7 in one search effort and to X1 in the other.

In a set of such agents *different* search-efforts can be made in parallel. Each message will refer to a context and will be processed in the scope of this context. The first search to terminate will deliver the solution or report failure. Termination detection has thus to be implemented for each of the contexts separately. This does not yield any extra communication as shown for the multiple contexts of IDIBT in [Ham02].

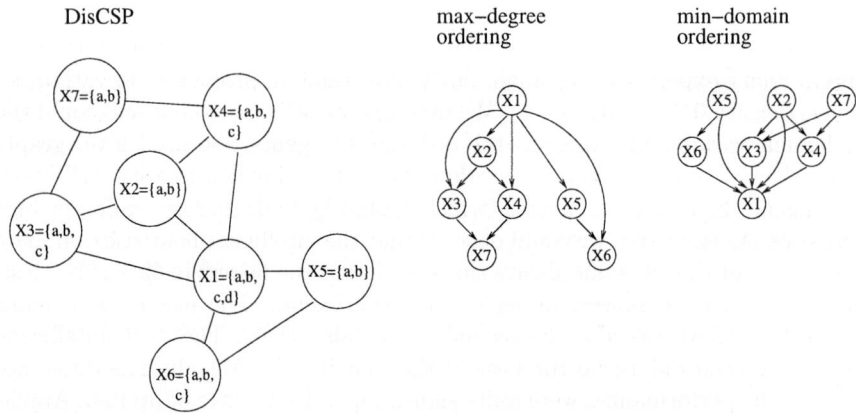

Fig. 1. DisCSP and agent topologies implied by variable orderings

One motivation for this is to reduce the S-Risk by adding more diversity to the used portfolio. Assuming we do not know anything about the quality of orderings, the chance of including a good ordering in a set of M different orderings is $|M|$-times higher than selecting it for execution in one search. When we know intelligent heuristics we should include them but the use of many of them will reduce the risk of bad performance for every single problem instance (cf. experiment in Section on S-Risk). Furthermore the expected performance is improved with the "M-" framework since always the best heuristic in the portfolio will deliver the solution or report failure. If we have a portfolio of orderings M where the expected runtime of each $m \in M$ is $t(m)$ then ideally (if no overhead emerges) the system terminates after $min(\{t(m)|m \in M\})$. The resulting trade-offs and overheads for this are investigated in this paper.

The trade-off in space is linear in the number of applied orderings. Thus, it clearly depends on the size of the data structures that need to be duplicated for the contexts. This will include only internal data structures which are related to the state of search. "M-" does not duplicate the whole agent. The data structures for communication for instance are jointly used by all the concurrent search efforts.

The trade-off in computational costs will be described in detail in the Section on the Empirical Evaluation.

3.1 Aggregation

Besides the idea of letting randomized algorithms compete to become "as good as the best" the "M-" framework can also use cooperation. With this we may be able to be even "better than the best", by accelerating the best search effort even more by providing it with useful knowledge others have found. Cooperation is implemented in the aggregation of knowledge within the agents. The agents use the information gained from one search to make better decisions (value selection) in another search. This enlarges the amount of knowledge on the basis of which local decisions are made.

In distributed search, the only information that agents can use for aggregation is their view to the global system. With multiple contexts, the agents have multiple views and thus more information available for their local reasoning. In this setting, the aggregation yields no extra communication costs. It can be performed locally and does not require any messages or blackboard-access.

In order to implement Aggregation we have to make two design decisions: first, which knowledge is used and second, how it is used. As mentioned before we use knowledge that is available for free from the internally stored data of the agents. In particular this may include:

Usage. Each agent knows the values it currently has selected in each search.
Support. Each agent can store currently known values of other agents (agent-view) and the constraints that need to be satisfied with these values.
Nogoods. Agents may store partial assignments that are found to be inconsistent.

Effort. Each agent knows for each search how much effort in terms of the number of backtracks it has already invested.

The interpretation of this knowledge can follow two orthogonal principles: **diversity** and **emulation**. Diversity implements the idea of traversing the search space in different parts simultaneously in order not to miss the part in which a solution can be found. The concept of emulation implements the idea of cooperative problem solving, where agents try to combine (partial) solutions in order to make use of work which others have already done.

With these concepts of providing and interpreting knowledge we can define the portfolio of aggregation methods shown in Table 1. In each box we provide a name (to be used in the following) and a short description of which value is preferably selected by an agent for a search.

Table 1. Methods of aggregation

	diversity	emulation
usage	*minUsed*: the value which is used the least in other searches	*maxUsed*: the value which is used most in other searches
support	–	*maxSupport*: the value that is most supported by constraints wrt. current agent-views
nogood	*differ*: the value which is least included in nogoods	*share*: always use nogoods of all searches
effort	*minBt*: a value which is not the current value of searches with many backtracks	*maxBt*: the current value of the search with most backtracks

4 Algorithms

As a case study to investigate the benefit of competition and cooperation in distributed search we implemented M-IDIBT and M-ABT.

M-IDIBT. This algorithm incorporates IDIBT [Ham02] in the "M-" framework. IDIBT already uses multiple contexts to perform parallel search (i.e., splitting of search tree). We use the contexts for different variable-orderings but apply each of them to the complete search tree. In order to prevent the required pre-processing of the agent topology with DisAO [Ham02] we changed the algorithm to add the required extra links between agents dynamically during search (similar to the processing of "addLink"-messages in ABT). Finally we extended the algorithm to support dynamic value selection which is essential for Aggregation.

M-ABT. This algorithm incorporates ABT [YDIK92] in the "M-" framwork. For this we implemented contexts by duplicating the local storage of current value, agent-view and nogood-store. Storing the nogood-store multiply may have large trade-offs in space, but sharing it means applying Aggregation and is thus considered separately. In M-ABT every message carries additionally the id of its related search. No other changes were made to the original algorithm.

5 Empirical Evaluation

For the empirical evaluation of the "M-" framework we processed more than 180000 DisCSPs with M-IDIBT and M-ABT. We solved random binary problems (15 variables, 5 values), n-queens-problems with n up to 20 and quasi-group completion problems with up to 81 agents. To compare the performance of the algorithms we counted overall constraint checks (cc), concurrent constraint checks(ccc), the overall number of messages(mc), the longest path of sequential messages(smc) and the run time (t) given in seconds. The runtime represents the "parallel time", i.e., the CPU+System time of the slowest agent.

All tests were run in a Java multi-threaded simulator where each agent implements a thread using random message delays and unpredictable thread-scheduling. All the threads were executed in one process and thus on one processor (2 Ghz Windows PC).

5.1 Basic Performance

In Figure 2 we show the median numbers of messages sent and the runtime to find one solution by different sized portfolios on fairly hard instances (density 0.3, tightness 0.4) of random problems (sample size 300). No aggregation was used in these experiments. The best known[2] variable-ordering (maxDegree) was used in each portfolio including those of size 1 which are equivalent to the basic algorithms. In the larger portfolios blind orderings (lex and random) and more instances of maxDegree were added. It can be seen that with increasing portfolio-size there is more communication (sent messages) between agents. In the same Figure we show the run time, which correlated strongly to smc and ccc. It can be seen that the performance improves up to a certain point when larger portfolios are used. In our experimental setting this point is reached with size 10. With larger portfolios no further speedup can be achieved which would make up the communication cost and computational overhead.

5.2 Risks

To evaluate the risks we used the same experimental setting as before but with random variable orderings and lexicographic value selection. This static value selection would reduce the R-Risk as widely as possible. Using random orderings would eliminate the effects we get from knowledge about heuristics and allow for a non-biased evaluation. Each portfolio was applied 100 times to one hard random problem instance. The standard-deviation of the runtime is shown in Figure 3 on a logarithmic scale. It can be seen that the risk is reduced significantly with the use of portfolios. With portfolio size 20, for instance, the risks

---
[2] We made preliminary experiments to determine this.

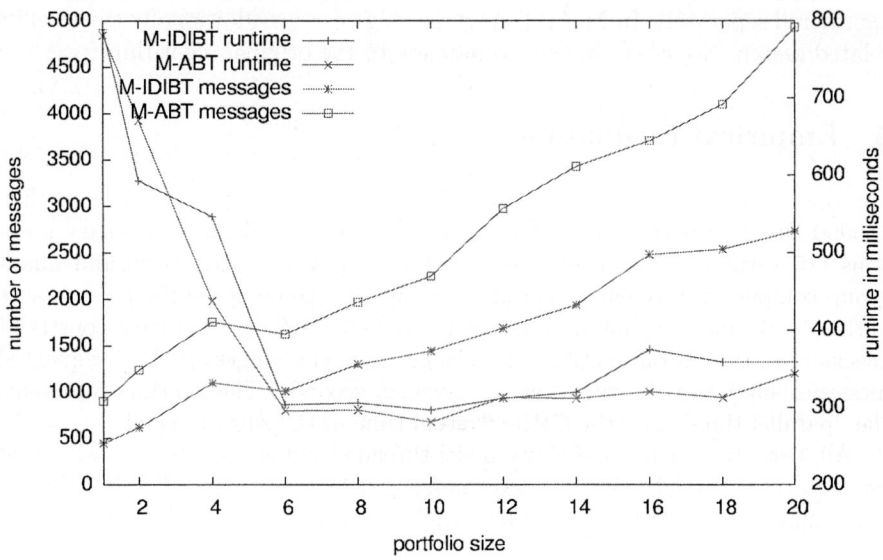

Fig. 2. Communication and runtime in portfolios

of M-IDIBT and M-ABT are 344 and 727 times smaller than the ones of IDIBT and ABT, respectively.

5.3 Performance with Aggregation

The benefit of Aggregation which is implemented with the different value selection heuristics is presented in Table 2. Each column in the table shows the median values of at least 100 samples solved with M-IDIBT with a portfolio of size 10 applied to 30 different hard random and quasigroup completion problems. The latter class of problems (cf. [GS01]) were encoded in a straightforward model: N^2 variables, one variable per agent, no symmetry breaking, binary constraints only. We solved problems with a 42% ratio of pre-assigned values which is the peak value in the phase transition for all orders, i.e., we used the hardest problem instances for our test.

In the table we refer to the aggregation methods introduced in Table 1, the bottom line shows the performance with random value selection (and thus no aggregation). When we consider the running time, it seems that the choice of the best method depends on the problem. For the quasigroup, aggregation based on the emulation principle seems to be better, on random problems not.

Interestingly, message passing operations present a different picture. It can be seen that *maxSupport* uses by far the least messages. These operations are reduced by a factor of 7 (resp. 38) for random (resp. quasigroups) problems. However, it cannot outperform the others significantly since the computation of this aggregation method is relatively costly. To this respect there is, however,

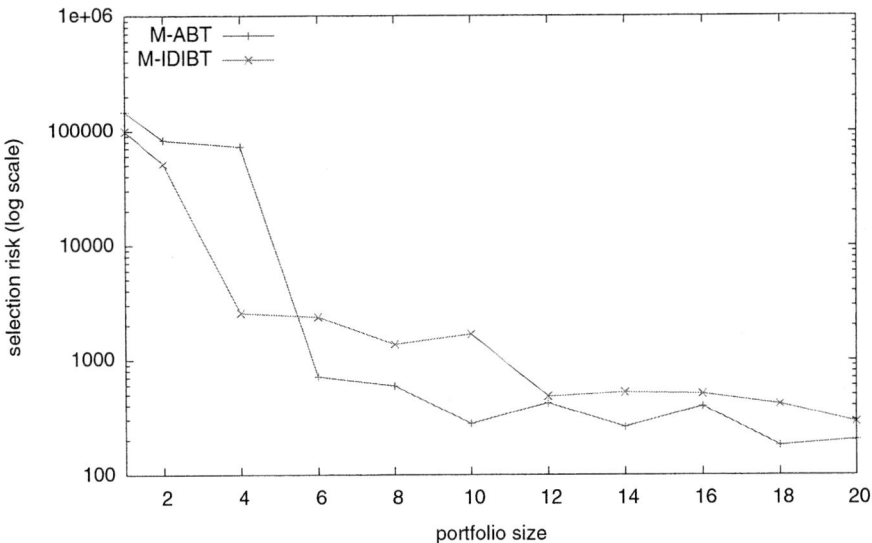

Fig. 3. S-Risk including the R-Risk emerging from distribution

Table 2. Performance of aggregation methods

	random			quasigroups		
	smc	ccc	t	$\frac{smc}{1000}$	$\frac{ccc}{1000}$	t
minUsed	367	2196	1.563	102	1625	448
maxUsed	379	**2118**	**1.437**	40	**635**	182
minBt	392	2281	1.640	104	1330	367
maxBt	433	2541	1.820	43	694	171
maxSupp	**57**	5718	1.922	**1.9**	3727	**143**
random	409	2406	1.664	73	1068	298

potential since we do not use an incremental algorithm for this. Moreover, message passing are the most critical operations in real systems and this for either long latencies or high energy consumption (e.g., ad-hoc networks [FM02]). The previous remark makes the *maxSupport* aggregation method really promising.

5.4 Overall Performance

In order to evaluate the relevance of the "M-" framework we investigated how it scales in larger and more structured problems. For this we applied good configurations found in the previous experiments to the well-known quasigroup completion problem.

Table 3 shows the experimental results of distributed search algorithms on problems of different orders (each column represents an order). ABT and IDIBT used the domain/degree variable ordering, which was tested best in preliminary experiments. In the larger portfolios we used domain/degree and additional other heuristics including maxDegree, minDomain, lex and random. In all portfolios Aggregation with the method *maxUsed* was applied. For each order (column) we show the median runtime (in seconds) to solve 20 different problems (once each) and the number of solved problems. When less than 10 instances could be solved within a timeout of two hours we naturally cannot provide meaningful median results. In the experiments with M-ABT we have also observed runs which were aborted because of memory problems in our simulator. For order 8 these were about one third of the unsolved problems, for order 9 this problem occurred in all unsuccessful tests. This memory problem arising from the nogood-storage of ABT was addressed in [BBMM05] and is not subject to this research.

Table 3. Median performance and instances solved (out of 20) of quasigroup completion problems with 42% pre-assigned values

	5	6	7	8	9
ABT	0.3, 20	-, 8	-, 1	-, 0	-, 0
size 5	0.5, 20	5.9, 19	35.8, 14	-, 2	-, 0
size 10	0.6, 20	6.1, 20	40.6, 17	-, 8	-, 1
IDIBT	1.8, 20	12.4, 20	234, 20	4356, 16	-, 5
size 5	**0.2, 20**	**0.9, 20**	9.3, 20	709, 20	-, 6
size 10	0.3, 20	1.7, 20	**8.2, 20**	**339, 20**	-, 8

From the successful tests it can be seen that portfolios improve the median performance of IDIBT significantly. In the problems of order 7 a portfolio of 10 was 28 times faster than the regular IDIBT. Furthermore, portfolios seem to become more and more beneficial in larger problems as the portfolio of size 10 seems to scale better than smaller one. ABT does not benefit in the median runtime but the reduced risk makes a big difference. With the portfolio we could solve 14 resp. 17 instances of order 7 problems whereas the plain algorithm could only solve one.

5.5 Idle Time

To complete the presentation of our experimental results let us consider time utilization in distributed search. It appears that both considered classical algorithms underuse available resources. This is figured in the first two columns of Table 4 for various problem classes. The numbers represent the average idle times (10-100 samples) of the agents.

We can observe that ABT and IDIBT are most of the time idle. This idleness comes from the inherent disbalance of work in DisCSPs. Indeed, it is well known that the hierarchical ordering of the agents makes low priority agents (at the bottom) more active than high priority ones. Ideally the work should be balanced. Ideally one agent on the top of the hierarchy in context 1 should be in the bottom in context 2, etc (e.g., see agent in charge of variable X_1 in figure 1). Obviously, since we use well known variable ordering heuristics we cannot enforce such a property. However, the previous is an argument for multi-directional

Table 4. Idle times of agents in DisCSP

problem class	idle time of agents			
	ABT	IDIBT	M-ABT	M-IDIBT
easy random	87%	92%	56%	47%
hard random	92%	96%	39%	59%
n-queens	91%	94%	48%	52%
hard quasigroups	87%	93%	28%	59%

search which can use the previous idle time "for free" in order to perform further computations in concurrent search efforts. This is figured in the last two columns of the table where the M- framework with a portfolio of size 10 applied to the same problems makes a better use of computational resources and this can be understood as an important decrease in idle times for either M-ABT or M-IDIBT.

6 Related Work

The benefit of cooperating searches executed in parallel was first investigated for CSP in [HH93]. They used multiple agents, each of which executed one monolithic search algorithm. Agents cooperated by writing/reading hints to/from a common blackboard. The hints were partial solutions or nogoods its sender has found and the receiver could re-use them in its efforts. In contrast to our work, this multi-agent system was an artefact created for the cooperation. Thus the overhead it produced, especially when not every agent could use its own processor, added directly to the overall performance. Another big difference between Hogg's work and ours is that DisCSP agents do not have a global view of the searches and can thus only communicate what's in their agent-view which usually captures partial solutions for comparably few variables only.

Later the expected performance and the expected (Randomization-) risk in portfolios of algorithms was investigated in [GS97, GS01]. No cooperation between the processes was used here. In the newer paper the authors concluded that portfolios, provided there are enough processors, reduce the risk and improve the performance. When algorithms do not run in parallel (i.e., when not each search can use its own processor) the portfolio approach becomes equivalent to random restarts [GSK98]. Using only one processor, the expected performance and risk of both are equivalent. In contrast to Gomes and Selman we cannot allocate search processes to CPUs. In DisCSP we have to allocate each agent, which participates in every search, to one process. Thus the load-balancing is performed by the agents and not by the designer of the portfolio. In this paper we consider agents that do this on a first-come-first-serve basis. Furthermore we use cooperation between the agents and the parallelism is not an overhead-prune artefact.

Recent work on constraint optimization [CB04] has shown that letting multiple search algorithms compete and cooperate can be very beneficial without having to know much about the algorithms themselves. They successfully use various optimization methods on one processor which compete for finding the next best solutions. Furthermore they cooperate by interchanging the best known feasible solutions. However, this method of cooperation cannot be applied to our distributed constraint satisfaction settings.

A different research trend performs "algorithm selection" [Ric76]. Here, portfolio does not represent competing methods but complementary ones. The problem is then to select from the portfolio the best possible method in order to tackle some incoming instance. [LBNA+03] applies the previous to combinatorial optimization. The authors use portfolios which combine algorithms with uncorrelated easy inputs. Their approach requires an extensive experimental step. It starts with the identification of problem's features which are representative of runtime performances. These features are used to generate a large set of problem instances which allow the collection of runtime data for each individual algorithm. Finally, statistical regression is used to learn a real-valued function of the features which allows runtime prediction. In real situation, the previous function predicts each algorithm's running time and the real instance is solved with the algorithm identified as the fastest one. The key point is to combine uncorrelated methods in order to exploit their relative strengths. The most important drawback here is the extensive offline step. This step must be performed for each new domain space. Moreover a careful analysis of the problem must be performed by the end-user to identify key parameters. The previous makes this approach highly unrealistic in a truly distributed system made by opportunistically connected components [FM02]. Finally knowledge sharing is not possible in this approach.

7 Conclusion and Future Work

In this paper we have presented a new generic framework for the execution of DisCSP algorithms. We have tested it with two standard methods but any tree-based distributed search should easily fit in the M- framework. The framework executes a portfolio of cooperative DisCSP algorithms with different agent-orderings concurrently until the first of them terminates. In real (truly distributed) applications, our framework will have to start with the computation of different orderings. The generic Distributed Agent Ordering heuristic (DisAO) [HBQ98] could easily be generalized at no extra message passing cost to concurrently compute several distributed hierarchies. The main idea is to simultaneously exchange several heuristic evaluation of a sub-problem instead of one.

This use of heterogeneous portfolios is shown to be very beneficial. It improves the performance and reduces the risk of distributed search. With our framework we were able to achieve a speedup of one order of magnitude while reducing the risk by up to three orders of magnitude compared to the traditional execution of the used algorithm.

The portfolios seem to make a better use of computational resources by reducing the idle time of agents. This is the first of two special advantages of the application of portfolios in DisCSP: we do not have to artificially add parallelism and the related overhead but can use idle resources instead. The M- framework can be seen as a solution to the classical "work unbalance" flaw of tree-based distributed search algorithms.

We analysed and defined distributed cooperation (Aggregation) with respect to two orthogonal principles *diversity* and *emulation*. Each principle was applied without overhead within the limited scope of each agent's knowledge. This is the second special advantage of using Aggregation in DisCSP: it yields no communicational costs and preserves privacy because processes are not related to search efforts but to agents instead. Our experiments identified the emulation-based *maxSupport* heuristic as the most promising one. Indeed, it is able to efficiently aggregate partial solutions which brings a large reduction in message passing operations.

Our present results greatly improve the applicability of DisCSP algorithms by providing greater efficiency and robustness to two classical tree search algorithms. In future work we would like to investigate how portfolios are best composed and how they could implement a more informed Aggregation (beyond agent's scope). The composition could be studied with different hand or system made portfolios or by dynamic adaptation during search. The latter could provide more resources to the most promising efforts. The former could take advantage of heterogeneous portfolios involving various tree- and local-search combined with some distributed consistency-enforcement method (e.g., [Ham99]). Finally, knowledge Aggregation could be easily improved at no cost by adding extra information to existing message passing operations (search effort, etc). This would give a more informed view of the distributed system which could be used by the Aggregation methods.

References

[BBMM05] C. Bessiere, I. Brito, A. Maestre, and P. Meseguer. Asynchronous backtracking without adding links: A new member in the ABT family. *Artificial Intelligence*, 161:7–24, 2005.

[CB04] T. Carchrae and J. C. Beck. Low knowledge algorithm control. In *Proc. AAAI'04*, 2004.

[FM02] S. Fitzpatrick and L. Meertens. Scalable, anytime constraint optimization through iterated, peer-to-peer interaction in sparsely-connected networks. In *Proc. IDPT'02*, 2002.

[GS97] C.P. Gomes and B. Selman. Algorithm portfolio design: Theory vs. practice. In *Proc. UAI'97*, pages 190–197, 1997.

[GS01] C.P. Gomes and B. Selman. Algorithm portfolios. *Artificial Intelligence*, 126:43–62, 2001.

[GSK98] C.P. Gomes, B. Selman, and H. Kautz. Boosting combinatorial search through randomization. In *Proc. AAAI'98*, pages 431–438. AAAI Press, 1998.

[Ham99] Y. Hamadi. Optimal distributed arc-consistency. In *Proc. CP'99*, pages 219–233, 1999.

[Ham02]   Y. Hamadi. Interleaved backtracking in distributed constraint networks. *International Journal on Artificial Intelligence Tools*, 11(2):167–188, 2002.

[HBQ98]   Y. Hamadi, C. Bessiere, and J. Quinqueton. Backtracking in distributed constraint networks. In *Proc. ECAI'98*, pages 219–223, 1998.

[HH93]   T. Hogg and B. A. Huberman. Better than the best: The power of cooperation. In *1992 Lectures in Complex Systems*, volume V of *SFI Studies in the Sciences of Complexity*, pages 165–184. Addison-Wesley, 1993.

[LBNA+03]   K. Leyton-Brown, E. Nudelman, G. Andrew, J. McFadden, and Y. Shoham. A portfolio approach to algorithm selection. In *Proc. IJCAI'03*, page 1542, 2003.

[Pug04]   J. F. Puget. Some challenges for constraint programming: an industry view. In *Proc. CP'04, invited talk*, pages 5–9. Springer LNCS 3258, 2004.

[Ric76]   J. R. Rice. The algorithm selection problem. *Advances in Computers*, 15:65–118, 1976.

[YDIK92]   M. Yokoo, E. H. Durfee, T. Ishida, and K. Kuwabara. Distributed constraint satisfaction for formalizing distributed problem solving. In *Proc. ICDCS'92*, pages 614–621, 1992.

[ZM03]   R. Zivan and A. Meisels. Synchronous vs asynchronous search on DisCSPs. In *Proc. EUMAS'03*, 2003.

Depth-First Mini-Bucket Elimination

Emma Rollon and Javier Larrosa

Universitat Politecnica de Catalunya,
Jordi Girona 1-3, 08034 Barcelona, Spain
{erollon, larrosa}@lsi.upc.edu

Abstract. Many important combinatorial optimization problems can be expressed as *constraint satisfaction problems* with *soft constraints*. When problems are too difficult to be solved exactly, approximation methods become the best option. *Mini-bucket elimination* (MBE) is a well known approximation method for combinatorial optimization problems. It has a control parameter z that allow us to trade time and space for accuracy. In practice it is the space and not the time that limits the execution with high values of z. In this paper we introduce a set of improvements on the way MBE handles memory. The resulting algorithm dfMBE may be orders of magnitude more efficient. As a consequence, higher values of z can be used which, in turn, yields significantly better bounds. We demonstrate our approach in scheduling, probabilistic reasoning and resource allocation problems.

1 Introduction

Constraint satisfaction problems (CSPs) involve the assignment of a set of variables subject to a set of constraints. The addition of *soft constraints* [1] extend the CSP framework to optimization tasks (we will assume optimization as minimization). Many problems in a variety of domains such as *probabilistic reasoning* [2], *bioinformatics* [3], *scheduling* [4], *etc*, can be naturally expressed as soft CSPs. In recent years a big effort has been made in the development of algorithms to solve this type of problems. In some cases, specialized algorithms can be designed to solve more efficiently particular problems. Nevertheless in this paper we will focus on general techniques.

There are two main approaches to solving soft CSPs: search and inference. *Search* algorithms traverse the tree of possible assignments typically following the deph-first branch-and-bound (BnB) principle [5,6]. *Inference* algorithms solve the problem by a sequence of reductions following the dynamic programming principle [7]. A well known inference algorithm is *bucket elimination* (BE) [8]. It falls into the category of the so-called *decomposition methods* [7]. In general, solving a soft CSP is NP-hard. Therefore, all known algorithms require exponential resources in the worst case, which means that many instances cannot be solved with current technology. Given the practical importance of this type of problems, when exact methods fail, algorithms that approximate the solution become very desirable.

When an instance is too difficult to be solved exactly, both search and inference, can be adapted to approximate its solution. BnB maintains during the search an upper bound of the optimum. Thus, it can be seen as an any-time algorithm providing increasingly better upper bounds. Alternatively, if BnB is executed in an iterative deepening manner it provides an increasing sequence of lower bounds. Both of these approaches are polynomial in space, and the time can be adjusted to the user needs. The BE algorithm can also be approximated which results in the *mini-buckets elimination* algorithm (MBE) [9]. In its more general formulation, the outcome of MBE is a lower and an upper bound of the optimum. It is arguably one of the best-known general approximation algorithms for soft CSPs and it has shown to be effective in a variety of domains including several probabilistic tasks in bayesian networks. It uses a control parameter z that allow us to trade time and space for accuracy. The time and space complexity of MBE is exponential in z and it is important to note that, with current computers, it is the space, rather than the time, that prohibits the execution of the algorithm beyond certain values of z.

In this paper, we show how to decrease the space demands of MBE. Our approach is based on the concept of *computation tree* (CT). A CT provides a graphical view of the MBE execution and can be computed as a pre-process. It is somewhat similar to the tree-decomposition in decomposition methods [9], where the first step is to build the tree-decomposition and the second step is to solve the problem. Our first contribution is a set of local transformations to the CT with which a more rational use of memory is achieved. They include: *i*) *branch re-arrangement* (nodes are moved upwards along a branch which means that the elimination of a variable is anticipated) and, *ii*) *vertical tree compaction* (adjacent nodes are joined which means that a sequence of operations is performed in a single step).

The second contribution is the exploitation of *memory deallocation* of intermediate functions when they become redundant. By construction of CT, MBE can be seen as a top-down traversal of the CT. The order of the traversal is imposed by the order in which variables are eliminated. We make the observation that any top-down traversal of the CT would produce the same outcome. Then, we propose to traverse the CT in a *depth-first* manner in order to decrease the number of intermediate functions that must be simultaneously stored. We show that with a depth-first traversal of the CT, the order of children has an impact in the space complexity which provides an additional source of improvement. We also discuss the benefits of *horizontal node compaction*. It is important to note that none of these transformations risk the accuracy of the algorithm.

The new algorithm that incorporates all these techniques is called depth-first mini-bucket elimination dfMBE. Our experiments show in a number of domains that dfMBE may provide important space savings. The main consequence is that in a given computer (namely, for a fixed amount of memory), dfMBE(z) can be executed with a higher value of z than MBE(z) which, in turn, may yield better lower bounds.

The structure of the paper is as follows: Section 2 provides preliminary definitions, Section 3 introduces CTs and two local transformations, Section 4 introduces dfMBE and additional CT transformations, Section 5 reports our experimental results and, finally, Section 6 gives conclusions and discusses future work.

2 Preliminaries

2.1 Soft CSPs

Let $\mathcal{X} = (x_1, \ldots, x_n)$ be an ordered set of variables and $\mathcal{D} = (D_1, \ldots, D_n)$ an ordered set of domains. Domain D_i is a finite set of potential values for x_i. The assignment (i.e, instantiation) of variable x_i with $a \in D_i$ is noted $(x_i \leftarrow a)$. A *tuple* is an ordered set of assignments to different variables $(x_{i_1} \leftarrow a_{i_1}, \ldots, x_{i_k} \leftarrow a_{i_k})$. The set of variables $(x_{i_1}, \ldots, x_{i_k})$ assigned by a tuple t, noted $var(t)$, is called its *scope*. The size of $var(t)$ is the *arity* of t. We focus on two basic operations over tuples: The *projection* of t over $A \subseteq var(t)$, noted $t[A]$, is a sub-tuple of t containing only the instantiation of variables in A. Let t and s be two tuples having the same instantiations to the common variables. Their *join*, noted $t \cdot s$, is a new tuple which contains the assignments of both t and s. Projecting a tuple t over the empty set $t[\emptyset]$ produces the empty tuple λ. We say that a tuple t is a *complete instantiation* when $var(t) = \mathcal{X}$. Sometimes, when we want to emphasize that a tuple is a complete instantiation we will call it X.

A *soft CSP* is a triple $(\mathcal{X}, \mathcal{D}, \mathcal{F})$, where $\mathcal{X} = \{x_1, \ldots, x_n\}$ and $\mathcal{D} = \{D_1, \ldots, D_n\}$ are sets of variables and domains. $\mathcal{F} = \{f_1, \ldots, f_r\}$ is a set of functions that form an objective function. *Function* f_i over $S \subseteq \mathcal{X}$ associates valuations to tuples t such that $var(t) = S$. The set of variables S is the *scope* of f and is noted $var(f_i)$. Abusing notation, when $var(f_i) \subset var(t)$, $f_i(t)$ will mean $f_i(t[var(f_i)])$. Functions may be given explicitly as tables or implicitly as mathematical expressions or computer procedures. The space complexity of explicitly storing a function f_i is $sp(f_i) = \prod_{x_j \in var(f_i)} |D_j|$.

Different soft CSP frameworks differ in: the set of possible valuations, the way functions are combined in order to form the objective function, and the task required of the objective function [1]. For simplicity, in the following we will assume weighted CSPs. In the weighted CSP (WCSP) model, valuations are natural numbers, the objective function is the sum of the functions,

$$F(X) = \sum_{i=1}^{r} f_i(X)$$

and it has to be *minimized*.

2.2 Bucket and Mini-Bucket Elimination

Bucket elimination (BE)[8,10] is a well-known algorithm for soft CSPs. It uses the following two operations on functions:

function BE($\mathcal{X}, \mathcal{D}, \mathcal{F}$)
1. **for each** $i = n..1$ **do**
2. $\mathcal{B}_i := \{f \in F| \; x_i \in var(f)\}$
3. $g_i := (\sum_{f \in \mathcal{B}_i} f) \downarrow x_i$;
4. $F := (F \cup \{g_i\}) - \mathcal{B}_i$;
5. **endfor**
6. $t := \lambda$;
7. **for each** $i = 1..n$ **do**
8. $v := \operatorname{argmin}_{a \in D_i} \{(\sum_{f \in \mathcal{B}_i} f)(t \cdot (x_i \leftarrow a))\}$
9. $t := t \cdot (x_i \leftarrow v)$;
10. **endfor**
11. **return**(g_1, t);
endfunction

Fig. 1. Bucket Elimination. Given a WCSP ($\mathcal{X}, \mathcal{D}, \mathcal{F}$), the algorithm returns a constant function g_1 (i.e, $var(g_1) = \emptyset$) with the optimal cost, along with one optimal assignment t.

- The *sum* of two functions f and g denoted $(f + g)$ is a new function with scope $var(f) \cup var(g)$ which returns for each tuple the sum of costs of f and g,

$$(f + g)(t) = f(t) + g(t)$$

- The *elimination* of variable x_i from f, denoted $f \downarrow x_i$, is a new function with scope $var(f) - \{x_i\}$ which returns for each tuple t the minimum cost extension of t to x_i,

$$(f \downarrow x_i)(t) = \min_{a \in D_i} \{f(t \cdot (x_i \leftarrow a))\}$$

where $t \cdot (x_i \leftarrow a)$ means the extension of t so as to include the assignment of a to x_i. Observe that when f is a unary function (*i.e.*, arity one), eliminating the only variable in its scope produces a constant.

The result of summing functions or eliminating variables cannot, in general, be expressed intensionally. Therefore, we store functions as tables.

BE (Figure 1) uses an arbitrary variable ordering o that we assume, without loss of generality, lexicographical (i.e, $o = (x_1, x_2, \ldots, x_n)$). It works in two phases. In the first phase (lines 1-5), the algorithm eliminates variables one by one, from last to first, according to o. The elimination of variable x_i is done as follows: $\mathcal{F}$ is the set of current functions. The algorithm computes the so called *bucket* of x_i, noted $\mathcal{B}_i$, which contains all cost functions in $\mathcal{F}$ having x_i in their scope (line 2). Next, BE computes a new function g_i by summing all functions in $\mathcal{B}_i$ and subsequently eliminating x_i (line 3). Then, $\mathcal{F}$ is updated by removing the functions in $\mathcal{B}_i$ and adding g_i (line 4). The new $\mathcal{F}$ does not contain x_i (all functions mentioning x_i were removed) but preserves the value of the optimal cost. The elimination of the last variable produces an empty-scope function (*i.e.*, a constant) which is the optimal cost of the problem. The second phase (lines 6-11) generates an optimal assignment of variables. It uses the set of buckets that were computed in the first phase. Starting from an empty assignment t (line 6), variables are assigned from first to last according to o. The optimal value for x_i is the best value regarding the extension of t with respect to the sum of functions in $\mathcal{B}_i$ (lines 8,9). We use argmin to denote the argument producing the minimum valuation. The time and space complexity of BE is exponential in a structural parameter called *induced width*. In practice, it is the space and not the time what makes the algorithm unfeasible in many instances.

Mini-bucket elimination (MBE) [9] is an approximation of BE that can be used to bound the optimum when the problem is too difficult to be solved exactly. Given a control parameter z, MBE partitions buckets into smaller subsets called mini-buckets such that their arity is bounded by $z+1$. Each mini-bucket is processed independently. At the end of the first phase, MBE has a lower bound of the problem optimum. In the second phase MBE computes a (non-necessarily optimal) assignment t. The evaluation of t on the objective function $F(t)$ constitutes an upper bound of the problem optimum. The pseudo-code of MBE is the result of replacing lines 3 and 4 in the algorithm of Figure 1 by,

3. $\{\mathcal{P}_{i_1}, \ldots, \mathcal{P}_{i_k}\} := \text{Partition}(\mathcal{B}_i);$
3b.   **for each** $j = 1..k$ **do** $g_{i_j} := (\sum_{f \in \mathcal{P}_{i_j}} f) \downarrow x_i;$
4. $F := (F \cup \{g_{i_1}, \ldots, g_{i_k}\}) - \mathcal{B}_i;$

The time and space complexity of MBE is exponential in z. Parameter z allows to trade time and space for accuracy, because greater values of z increment the number of functions that can be included in each mini-bucket. Therefore, the bounds will be presumably tighter.

Consider as a example a WCSP instance with seven variables and the following set of cost functions,

$$\mathcal{F} = \{f_1(x_6, x_5, x_4), f_2(x_6, x_5, x_3), f_3(x_5, x_3, x_2), f_4(x_6, x_4, x_2), f_5(x_7, x_2, x_1),$$
$$f_6(x_7, x_6, x_1)\}$$

One possible execution of MBE(3) along the lexicographical variable ordering leads to the following trace,

$Bucket_7$:	$f_6(x_7, x_6, x_1), f_5(x_7, x_2, x_1)$
$Bucket_6$:	$g_{7_1}(x_6, x_2, x_1) = (f_6 + f_5) \downarrow x_7,$
	$f_4(x_6, x_4, x_2), f_2(x_6, x_5, x_3), f_1(x_6, x_5, x_4)$
$Bucket_5$:	$g_{6_1}(x_5, x_4, x_3) = (f_1 + f_2) \downarrow x_6, f_3(x_5, x_3, x_2)$
$Bucket_4$:	$g_{6_2}(x_4, x_2, x_1) = (f_4 + g_{7_1}) \downarrow x_6,$
	$g_{5_1}(x_4, x_3, x_2) = (f_3 + g_{6_1}) \downarrow x_5$
$Bucket_3$:	$g_{4_1}(x_3, x_2, x_1) = (g_{6_2} + g_{5_1}) \downarrow x_4$
$Bucket_2$:	$g_{3_1}(x_2, x_1) = g_{4_1} \downarrow x_3$
$Bucket_1$:	$g_{2_1}(x_1) = g_{3_1} \downarrow x_2$
Result:	$g_{1_1}() = g_{2_1} \downarrow x_1$

3 Improving MBE Memory Usage

The first phase of MBE (as well as BE) can be seen as an algebraic expression that combines sums and variable eliminations. For instance, the execution of MBE(3) in the previous example is equivalent to the computation of the following expression,

$$((f_3 + (f_1 + f_2) \downarrow x_6) \downarrow x_5 + (f_4 + (f_6 + f_5) \downarrow x_7) \downarrow x_6) \downarrow x_4 \downarrow x_3 \downarrow x_2 \downarrow x_1$$

Note that each function appears only once in the formulae.

A *computation tree* (CT first introduced in [11]) provides a graphical view of the algebraic expression. The leaves are the original functions (arguments of the formulae) and internal nodes represent the computation of intermediate functions. If the node has only one child, the only operation performed is the elimination of one variables. Otherwise, all the children are summed and one variable is eliminated. Figure 2.A depicts the CT of the previous example. Dotted lines emphasize tree-leaves, which are associated to original functions. Even when original function are given explicitely as tables, do not include their space in the MBE cost. Adjacent to each internal node we indicate the variable that is eliminated. Although CTs are somehow related to decomposition-trees, they differ in the way they represent original functions. Besides, since CTs originate from MBE executions, they do not need to satisfy the running intersection property [7].

In the following we distinguish the computation of the CT from the evaluation of its associated expression. Given the scope of the original functions, a variable ordering, a policy for mini-bucket partitioning and a value for z, it is possible to compute the corresponding CT as a pre-process. Computing the CT is no more than finding the set of computations that the algorithm will perform in order to evaluate the formula.

One advantage of computing the CT in a pre-process is that it makes it easy to obtain the exact memory demands of MBE by summing the space requirements of every internal node of the CT. For instance, the CT in Figure 2.A, will need to store 5 functions of arity 3, 1 functions of arity 2, 1 function of arity 1 and 1 function of arity 0. Assuming domains of size 10, MBE will need to store $5 \times 10^3 + 1 \times 10^2 + 1 \times 10^1 + 1 \times 10^0 = 5111$ table entries.

CTs allow us to identify and remedy some space inefficiencies of MBE. In the following we describe two local transformations of CTs that improve their space requirements.

3.1 Branch Re-Arrangement

Consider again the CT in Figure 2.A. Observe that if we follow any branch in top-down order, variables are eliminated in decreasing order, because this is the order used by MBE. As a consequence, the elimination of x_1 is left to the end. However, this variable only appears in the two leftmost leaves. It is inefficient to carry it over down to the CT root, since it could have been eliminated higher up.

Consider a node v of a CT with a single child. Let x_i be the variable that is eliminated at v. Let u be the first descendent of v with $k > 1$ children. If only

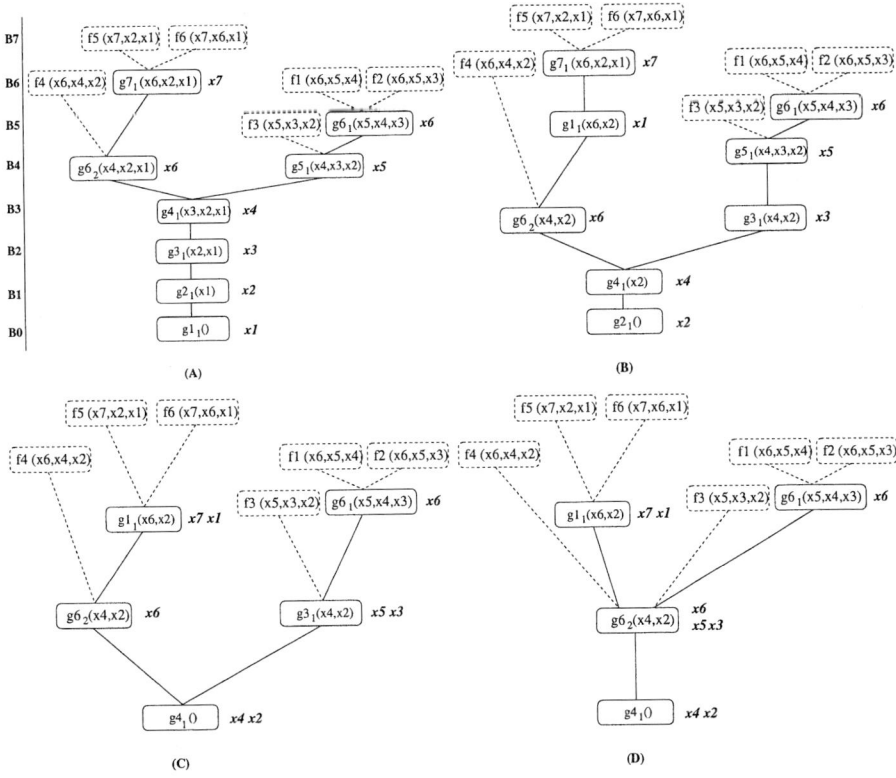

Fig. 2. Four different computation trees: *A)* original CT, *B)* after branch re-arrangement, *C)* after vertical compaction, *D)* after horizontal compaction

one child w of u has x_i in its scope, node v (namely, the elimination of x_i) can be moved in between w and u. We only perform the change if w is not a leaf. *Branch re-arrangement* is the process of applying the previous rule in a bottom-up order, moving nodes as close to the leaves as possible. The benefit of branch re-arrangement is that x_i disappears from the scope of intermediate functions earlier in the tree. In the CT of Figure 2.A, the leftmost branch can be re-arranged: variable x_1 can be eliminated right after x_7. Moreover, the rightmost branch can also be re-arranged: variable x_3 can be eliminated right after x_5. Figure 2.B shows the resulting CT. The space requirements of the new CT are decreased from 5111 to 3311. Observe that branch re-arrangement can never increase the space requirements of a CT.

3.2 Vertical Compaction

Consider the CT in Figure 2.B. There are two single-child nodes. In single-child nodes the only associated computation is a variable elimination. MBE considers each variable elimination as an independent operation because they take place in different buckets. However, a sequence of variable eliminations can be performed simultaneously in a single step without changing the outcome or increasing the time complexity. The advantage is that intermediate functions do not need to be stored.

Vertical compaction is the process of merging *internal linear paths* into one node representing the sequence of computations. An internal linear path is a path between an internal node v and one of its ancestors w, $(v, v_1 \ldots, v_k, w)$, such that every node in the path except v has only one child. After the compaction every internal node of the CT has $k > 1$ children. There is one exception: there may be internal nodes with only child if the child is a leaf. Figure 2.C depicts the result of applying vertical compaction to the CT of Figure 2.B. The space requirements of the new CT are decreased from 3311 to 1301. It is clear that the compaction of a CT may produce space saving and can never increase the space requirements of a CT.

4 Depth-First MBE

A CT can be traversed in any top-down order. A node can be computed as soon as all its children are available. Whatever traversal strategy is used it has to keep all intermediate functions because they are used in the second phase of the algorithm in order to compute the upper bound. However, the space consumption of the traversal can be drastically reduced if we sacrifice the upper bound and deallocate the memory used by intermediate functions when they become redundant. A function becomes redundant as soon as its parent has been computed. Note that an alternative solution that we do not explore in this paper is to store redundant functions in the hard-disk. Thus, the upper bound is not lost.

Without memory deallocation the traversal order has no effect on the space complexity, but this is no longer true when memory is deallocated. Traversing the CT depth-first has the advantage of only demanding the space of the current branch: computing a node only requires to have available its children, so they have to be sequentially and recursively computed. We denote by dfMBE the algorithm that traverses depth-first the CT and deallocates memory when intermediate functions become redundant. The space complexity of dfMBE can be formalized by means of a recurrence. Let v be a node, g_v the associated function and $(w_1, \ldots, w_k)$ its ordered set of children. $R(v)$ is the space complexity of computing the sub-tree rooted by a CT node v and is given by,

$$R(v) = \max_{i=1}^{k+1} \{ \sum_{j=1}^{i-1} sp(g_{w_j}) + R(w_i) \}$$

where $R(w_{k+1}) = sp(g_v)$ by definition. Also, the space $sp()$ of original functions is 0 because we do not count it as used by the algorithm. The space complexity of dfMBE is obtained by evaluating $R(v)$ at the root of the CT. In words, the recursion indicates that the space required to compute node v is the maximum among the space required to compute its children. However, when computing a given child, the space occupied by all its previous siblings must be added because they need to be available for the final computation of v.

Consider the CT of Figure 2.C. We showed in the previous Section that, with no memory deallocation, the space cost of internal nodes was 1301. If the CT is traversed depth-first, the cost (disregarding original functions) is,

$$\max\{R(g_{6_2}), sp(g_{6_2}) + R(g_{3_1}), sp(g_{6_2}) + sp(g_{3_1}) + sp(g_{4_1})\} =$$
$$\max\{200, 100 + 1100, 100 + 100 + 1\} = 1200$$

Observe that the order of children affects the space complexity of dfMBE. For instance, if we reverse the two children of the root in Figure 2.C, the space complexity of dfMBE is decreased to,

$$\max\{R(g_{3_1}), sp(g_{3_1}) + R(g_{6_2}), sp(g_{3_1}) + sp(g_{6_2}) + sp(g_{4_1})\} =$$
$$\max\{1100, 100 + 200, 100 + 100 + 1\} = 1100$$

In our implementation of dfMBE we make an additional optimization of the CT by processing nodes from leaves to the root. At each node, we swap the order of two of its children if it brings a space improvement.

Consider now the two children of the root-node in the CT of Figure 2.C. The scope of the associated functions g_{6_1} and g_{6_2} is the same. Since they will be summed up, one table can be shared to stored both of them as follows: the table entries are initialized to 0, the two functions are computed sequentially, and each function value is added to the table current value. Figure 2.D illustrates this idea. The cost of dfMBE with this new CT is,

$$\max\{R(g_{6_2}), sp(g_{6_2}) + sp(g_{4_1})\} =$$
$$\max\{\max\{100, 100 + 100, 100 + 1000, 100 + 1000\}, 100 + 1\} = 1100$$

which brings no gain over the CT in Figure 2.C. However, in some cases it may bring significant benefits. Note that $R(g_{6_2}) = \max\{R(g_{1_1}), sp(g_{1_1}) + sp(g_{6_2}), sp(g_{6_2}) + R(g_{6_1}), sp(g_{6_2}) + sp(g_{6_1})\}$. In our implementation, we check siblings pair-wise. If sharing their storing table produces space savings we take such an action.

5 Experimental Results

We have tested our approach in three different domains. We compare the memory requirements for MBE, MBE' (i.e, mini-buckets under the computation tree resulting from branch re-arrangement and vertical compaction), and dfMBE in a given computer (in other words, with a fixed amount of memory). For each domain we execute MBE(z_1), MBE'(z_2) and dfMBE(z_3), where z_1, z_2 and z_3 are the highest feasible values of the control parameter for each algorithm, given the available memory.

In all our experiments, the original CT was obtained assuming a MBE execution in which the order of variable elimination was established with the *min-degree* heuristic. For the elimination of each variable, mini-buckets are constructed one by one with the following process: Select one original function (or a non-original function if there are no original functions left). Choose among the remaining functions the one that adds the least number of variables to the mini-bucket until no more functions can be included in that mini-bucket.

In our benchmarks domain sizes range from 2 to 44, and some instances have variables with different domain size. Consequently, the arity of a function is not a proper way to indicate its spacial cost, which means that the control parameter z of MBE may be misleading (it forbids a function of arity $z+1$ with binary domains and allows a function of arity z with domains of size 4 that is much more costly to store). We overcome this problem by modifying the meaning of z: In the original formulation of MBE, the *arity* of intermediate functions is bounded by z, but in our implementation the *size* of intermediate functions is bounded by 2^z.

5.1 Scheduling

For our first experiment, we consider the scheduling of an earth observation satellite. Given a set of candidate photographs, the problem is to select the best subset that the satellite will actually take. The selected subset of photographs must satisfy a large number of imperative constraints and at the same time maximize the importance of selected photographs. We experimented with instances from the Spot5 satellite [4] that can be trivially translated into the WCSP framework. These instances have unary, binary and ternary constraints, and domains of size 2 and 4. Some instances include in their original formulation an additional capacity constraint imposed by the on-board storage limit. In our experiments we discarded such constraint.

Figure 3 reports the results that we have obtained assuming a computer with a memory limit of 1.5 Gigabytes. The first column identifies the instance. The second column indicates the induced width with the min-degree ordering. The third, fourth and fifth columns report the memory requirements in Megabytes with the three algorithms for different values of z. If the number is given in italics it means that it surpasses the space limit of the computer and the algorithm could not be executed (the memory requirement was obtained from the analysis of the CT). The sixth and seventh column indicate the value of z and the lower bound that is obtained. For each instance, we report results for three increasing values of z: the limit for MBE, MBE' and dfMBE. It can be observed that MBE' requires from 2 to 10 times less memory than MBE, which allows the execution with values of z up to 4 units higher. However, the most impressive results are obtained with dfMBE, which may require 275 times less space than MBE (e.g. instance 1405). As a consequence dfMBE can be executed with values of z up to 9 units higher (e.g. instance 1506), which in turn yields lower bounds up to 20% higher (e.g. instance 507). The mean space gain from MBE to dfMBE is 113.34, the mean increment of z is 7 and the mean increment of the lower bound is 8.74%.

Instance	w^*	Memory Requirement (Mb)			z	Lower Bound
		CT_{MBE}	$CT_{MBE'}$	CT_{dfMBE}		
1504	43	17161	10373	1052	27	158274
		1945	911	65	23	148259
		1240	577	34	22	142257
1506	51	227707	50435	1310	27	180356
		5503	1099	24	21	180316
		1185	214	4	18	166305
1401	156	137825	11250	524	26	210085
		11430	874	40	22	203083
		1286	131	6	19	196080
1403	156	237480	28144	1048	27	223189
		13416	1277	36	22	193185
		1153	125	5	18	189180
1405	156	325213	54378	1179	27	219302
		7226	1317	24	21	214283
		1548	289	3	18	203268
28	139	113739	14764	1048	27	141105
		8374	1424	65	23	141105
		694	109	5	19	148105
42	51	22558	6032	1572	28	125050
		2112	1123	147	24	135050
		1090	590	65	23	133050
5	83	82823	38425	917	27	206
		1861	843	16	21	192
		536	253	4	18	186
408	60	17903	7966	1048	27	5197
		2609	1355	163	24	6195
		1408	752	5	23	5197
412	61	58396	24513	1179	27	14258
		2771	882	40	22	17224
		1420	434	16	21	14220
414	144	172071	24566	1048	27	19295
		8605	1205	49	22	18301
		1154	166	4	19	18292
505	39	15833	8644	1067	27	18231
		2834	1534	139	24	19217
		1488	800	65	23	19206
507	91	76346	16932	1310	27	15286
		6222	1571	81	23	15280
		1217	250	10	20	12255
509	151	130553	26671	1114	27	18286
		6812	1008	40	22	17285
		946	162	4	19	17267

Fig. 3. Spot5 results. Memory bound of 1.5 Gb.

5.2 Probabilistic Reasoning

Bayesian Networks provides a formalism for reasoning about partial beliefs under conditions of uncertainty [2]. They are defined by a directed acyclic graph over nodes representing variables of interest. The arcs indicate the existence of direct causal influences between linked variables quantified by conditional probability tables (CPTs) that are attached to each cluster of parents-child nodes in the network. There are several possible tasks over a belief network. We tested the performance of our scheme for solving the *most probable explanation* (MPE) task: given evidence $x_1 \leftarrow v_1, \ldots, x_p \leftarrow v_p$ (i.e., some variable assignments), its MPE is the *maximization* of the objective function,

$$P(X) = \prod_{i=1}^{r} f_i(X)$$

subject to tuples that respect the evidence. It is easy to see that MPE can be expressed as a WCSP by replacing probability tables by their logarithm. We use two types of belief networks: Random and Noisy-OR Networks [12].

		Uniform Random Bayesian Networks					
		Memory Requirement (Mb)				Lower	
N, C, P	w^*	CT_{MBE}	$CT_{MBE'}$	CT_{dfMBE}	z	Bound	% better
128, 85, 4	31.71	3635	598	239	26.36	18.61	40
		2579	315	171	25.75	18.35	90
		370	84	45	22.95	17.56	-
128, 95, 4	43.96	4144	999	205	26.21	20.68	50
		1941	317	146	24.9	20.34	90
		335	94	43	22.5	19.51	-
128, 105, 4	38.71	4537	825	264	26.2	23.58	60
		2192	391	185	25.3	23.27	95
		358	89	48	22.7	22.16	-
128, 115, 4	48.32	4114	807	261	25.85	26.22	60
		1823	345	172	24.7	25.61	100
		355	99	43	22.5	24.69	-

		Noisy-OR $P_{noise} = 0.40$				
		Memory Requirement (Mb)				
N, C, P	w^*	CT_{MBE}	$CT_{MBE'}$	CT_{dfMBE}	z	% solved
128, 85, 4	35.39	4777	662	164	26.35	73
		2805	256	153	25.6	68
		331	68	29	22.65	47
128, 95, 4	38.61	4331	681	222	26.25	84
		2545	308	169	25.35	84
		340	74	34	22.55	58
128, 105, 4	43.06	3125	683	260	25.55	50
		1646	285	136	24.6	50
		364	91	45	22.45	15
128, 115, 4	46.51	4446	918	199	25.95	65
		1530	352	149	24.75	50
		340	102	46	22.55	25
		Noisy-OR $P_{noise} = 0.50$				
128, 85, 4	40.74	4780	631	242	26.45	75
		3154	330	177	25.7	75
		384	71	33	22.8	60
128, 95, 4	38.12	3663	356	243	25.89	55
		2170	309	158	25.15	55
		368	76	49	22.63	25
128, 105, 4	43.04	5080	952	245	26.4	65
		2006	329	109	24.8	65
		371	79	33	22.6	45
128, 115, 4	46.25	3506	964	227	26.05	60
		1552	342	176	24.7	45
		384	94	43	22.5	35

Fig. 4. MPE on bayesian networks. 20 samples. Memory bound of 512 Mb.

Uniform random bayesian networks and *noisy-OR* networks are generated using parameters (N, K, C, P), where N is the number of variables, K is their domain size, C is the number of conditional probability tables, and P is the number of parents in each conditional probability table. Instances are generated by selecting C variables at random. For each selected variable x_i, P parents are randomly selected from the set of variables with index less than i (if $i \leq P$ only $i-1$ parents are selected).

For random bayesian networks, each probability table is randomly generated using a uniform distribution. For noisy-OR networks, each probability table represents a noisy OR-function. For each CPT, we randomly assign to each parent variable y_j a value $P_j \in [0..P_{noise}]$. The CPT is then defined as, $P(x = 0|y_1,\ldots,y_P) = \prod_{y_j=1} P_j$ and $P(x = 1|y_1,\ldots,y_P) = 1 - P(x = 0|y_1,\ldots,y_P)$.

Fig 4 present results of random and noisy-OR networks assuming a computer with a memory limit of 512 Megabytes. In each table we fix parameters N, K and P and change the value of C in order to control the network's sparseness. For each parameter setting we generate and solve a sample of 20 instances. We always assumed empty evidence and report mean values.

It can be observed that dfMBE requires from 15 to 29 times less memory than MBE, which allows the execution with values of z up to 3 units higher. The mean space gain from MBE to dfMBE is 18.56, the mean increment of z is 3.51 and the mean increment of the lower bound is 5.75%. For uniform random networks we also report the mean number of instances executed with $CT_{MBE'}$ and CT_{dfMBE} in which the lower bound increases with respect its execution with CT_{MBE} and $CT_{MBE'}$, respectively (i.e., %*better* column).

With random networks we also executed the efficient WCSP branch-and-bound solver TOOLBAR [1] initializing its upper bound with the lower bound given by dfMBE and observed that it did not terminate with a time limit of one hour. Considering that dfMBE with the highest z value takes less than 300 seconds in this domain, we conclude that dfMBE is a better approach than iterative deepening branch and bound.

We observed that noisy-OR networks could be easily solved to optimality with TOOLBAR. Therefore, we also report for each parameter setting and each value of z, how many instances are solved to optimality with MBE, MBE' and dfMBE.

5.3 Resource Allocation

For our third experiment, we consider the *frequency assignment problem* where the task is to assign non-interfering frequencies to a set of communication links. We experimented with some instances of the so-called *radio link frequency assignment problem* [13] that can be expressed as WCSP. The optimization task is to provide the assignment with minimum global interference. In its usual formulation, these instances have binary cost functions and domains of size up to 44. We experimented with CELAR6, CELAR7 and graph instances. For lack of space, Fig 5 only reports graph instances where we obtained the best results. It can be observed that dfMBE is also very effective in this domain. It can require on average by 430.25 times less memory than MBE, which allows the execution with values of z up to 5.25 units larger.

---

[1] http://mulcyber.toulouse.inra.fr/projects/toolbar/

Instance	w^*	Memory Requirement (Mb)			z
		CT_{MBE}	$CT_{MBE'}$	CT_{dfMBE}	
graph05	135	*15955*	*1992*	49	28
		12880	1102	86	27
		1483	201	25	24
graph06	296	*30364*	*2544*	300	28
		17291	1320	300	27
		1354	117	10	23
graph07	146	*14797*	*1866*	527	28
		8187	266	49	27
		1511	180	45	24
graph11reduc	275	*30331*	*2044*	113	28
		15630	1183	113	27
		1267	154	22	23
graph11	495	*55260*	*3079*	22	28
		5935	338	30	25
		547	83	11	21
graph12	234	*23532*	*3570*	692	28
		3399	493	134	26
		1379	230	21	24
graph13reduc	619	*67123*	*6447*	723	28
		9964	1070	121	25
		1572	141	13	22
graph13	706	*89091*	*6828*	1067	28
		7354	515	24	25
		806	161	11	21

Fig. 5. RLFAP. Memory bound of 1.5 Gb.

6 Conclusions and Future Work

Mini-bucket elimination (MBE) is a well-known approximation algorithm for combinatorial optimization problems. Its output is an upper and lower bound of the problem optimum. It has a control parameter with which the user can trade computing resources (namely, cpu time and memory) for approximation accuracy. With current computers it is usually the space rather than the cpu time what imposes a technological limit to the control parameter.

In this paper we have introduced a set of improvements to the spatial cost of MBE. Our approach is based on the concept of computation trees (CT), which provide a pictorical view of the MBE execution. We show that CTs uncover some space inefficiencies of MBE. Such inefficiencies can be overcome by local transformations of the CT that preserve the outcome of the algorithm and its time complexity. In particular, we introduce the concepts of branch re-arrangement and vertical compaction of CTs.

Besides, we show that if we sacrifice the upper bound we can deallocate intermediate computations that are very space consuming. In this context, we introduce depth-first MBE (dfMBE), that traverses the CT in a depth-first manner. The space demands of dfMBE can also be reduced by additional CT transformations such as children re-ordering and children merging.

We demonstrate the relevance of dfMBE in scheduling, probabilistic reasoning and resource allocation where we show that dfMBE can divide the space demand of MBE by a factor of 18.56 to 430.25 depending on the domain. Such space decrement allows the execution of dfMBE with higher values of the control parameter, which in turn, may yield better bounds.

In our future work we want to investigate more compact encodings for cost tables. A simple approach is to establish a default cost and store (e.g. in a hash table) only those tuples with non-default cost. A more sophisticated approach is to explore encodings based on Binary Decision Diagrams (BDDs), a graph based representation for boolean function manipulation. In this paper we have assumed a given mini-bucket partition policy. In our experiments, we observed that the chosen policy may have a big influence in both the topology of the CT and the quality of the reported bounds. We want to improve our understanding of such phenomenon and establish robust and effective policies.

References

1. Bistarelli, S., Fargier, H., Montanari, U., Rossi, F., Schiex, T., Verfaillie, G.: Semiring-based CSPs and valued CSPs: Frameworks, properties and comparison. Constraints **4** (1999) 199–240
2. Pearl, J.: Probabilistic Inference in Intelligent Systems. Networks of Plausible Inference. Morgan Kaufmann, San Mateo, CA (1988)
3. Gilbert, D., Backofen, R., Yap, R., eds.: Constraints: an International Journal (Special Issue on Bioinformatics). Volume 6(2-3). Kluwer (2001)
4. Bensana, E., Lemaitre, M., Verfaillie, G.: Earth observation satellite management. Constraints **4(3)** (1999) 293–299
5. Lawler, E.L., Wood, D.E.: Branch-and-bound methods: A survey. Operations Research **14(4)** (1966) 699–719
6. Larrosa, J., Schiex, T.: Solving weighted csp by maintaining arc-consistency. Artificial Intelligence **159** (2004) 1–26
7. Gottlob, G., Leone, N., Scarcello, F.: A comparison of structural csp decomposition methods. Artificial Intelligence **124** (2000) 243–282
8. Dechter, R.: Bucket elimination: A unifying framework for reasoning. Artificial Intelligence **113** (1999) 41–85
9. Dechter, R., Rish, I.: Mini-buckets: A general scheme for bounded inference. Journal of the ACM **50** (2003) 107–153
10. Bertele, U., Brioschi, F.: Nonserial Dynamic Programming. Academic Press (1972)
11. Larrosa, J.: On the time complexity of bucket elimination algorithms. Technical report, University of California at Irvine (2001)
12. Kask, K., Dechter, R.: A general scheme for automatic generation of search heuristics from specification dependencies. Artificial Intelligence **129** (2001) 91–131
13. Cabon, B., de Givry, S., Lobjois, L., Schiex, T., Warners, J.: Radio link frequency assignment. Constraints **4** (1999) 79–89

Using SAT in QBF

Horst Samulowitz and Fahiem Bacchus*

Department of Computer Science, University of Toronto, Canada
{horst, fbacchus}@cs.toronto.edu

Abstract. QBF is the problem of deciding the satisfiability of quantified boolean formulae in which variables can be either universally or existentially quantified. QBF generalizes SAT (SAT is QBF under the restriction all variables are existential) and is in practice much harder to solve than SAT. One of the sources of added complexity in QBF arises from the restrictions quantifier nesting places on the variable orderings that can be utilized during backtracking search. In this paper we present a technique for alleviating some of this complexity by utilizing an order unconstrained SAT solver during QBF solving. The innovation of our paper lies in the integration of SAT and QBF. We have developed methods that allow information obtained from each solver to be used to improve the performance of the other. Unlike previous attempts to avoid the ordering constraints imposed by quantifier nesting, our algorithm retains the polynomial space requirements of standard backtracking search. Our empirical results demonstrate that our techniques allow improvements over the current state-of-the-art in QBF solvers.

1 Introduction

QBF is the problem of deciding the satisfiability of a quantified boolean formula where variables can be either universally or existentially quantified. It generalizes SAT in which all variables are (implicitly) existentially quantified. Constraint satisfaction problems (CSPs) can be similarly generalized from their purely existential version to QCSP where some of the variables become universal [5].

Adding universally quantified variables yields a considerable increase in expressive power, and consequently QBF and QCSPs can compactly represent a much wider range of problems than SAT and ordinary CSPs. These include problems like conditional planning, non-monotonic reasoning, problems in electronic design automation, scheduling, model checking and verification, see, e.g., [6,12,21].

However, this added expressiveness comes with a price. Namely QBF is much more difficult to solve than SAT. From the point of view of complexity theory QBF is PSPACE-complete where as SAT is "only" NP-complete [23]. Despite this intrinsically high complexity the goal of developing practically useful QBF solvers still seems to be feasible given sufficient conceptual and technical advances. This paper presents some new techniques that make progress towards this goal.

Most current QBF solvers, e.g., QuBE [15], Semprop [17], Quaffle [25] are adaptations of the classic DPLL backtracking search algorithm originally developed for solving SAT [10]. There are two main properties of QBF that must be accommodated by

---

* This work has been supported by Natural Science and Engineering Research Council Canada.

the search. First, the search must solve both settings of every universal variable, and second the variable ordering followed during search must respect the ordering imposed by quantifier nesting. Both of these properties make QBF solving slower than SAT. The first property is intrinsic to QBF, and must be accommodated in some fashion by any QBF solver. The second property is, however, somewhat more tractable, and various attempts have been made to avoid the variable ordering constraint. To date, however, all techniques for avoiding this constraint require exponential space in general, e.g., the Skolemization/expansion approach used by the Quantor [4] and Skizzo [3] solvers and the BDD technique used in [1].

In this paper we develop an algorithm that makes extensive use of order-free SAT solving in an attempt to alleviate (but not completely remove) the variable ordering constraint. Our algorithm retains the important polynomial space property of backtracking search. It can also use any extra space that can be provided to improve its performance, but extra space is not required for correctness (this is a common feature with current SAT and QBF backtracking solvers).

We utilize a backtracking SAT solver in a backtracking QBF solver. Because both solvers are doing backtracking search we are able to develop techniques to integrate them very tightly. For example, both solvers search the same tree and share all of their datastructures, including using the same stack to store the current path. The key innovation of our method lies in techniques for sharing information between the two solvers so that information computed during SAT solving can be used to improve QBF solving and vice versa. The result is a QBF solver that is able to improve on current state of the art on a number of benchmark suites.

In the rest of the paper we first present some necessary background, and set the context for our algorithm. We then present the details of our algorithm, prove some results about the algorithm's formal behavior and provide empirical evidence of its effectiveness. We close with a discussion of previous work, directions for future work, and some conclusions.

2 Background

A quantified boolean formula has the form $Q.F$, where F is a propositional formula expressed in CNF and Q is a sequence of quantified variables ($\forall x$ or $\exists x$). We require that no variable appears twice in Q and that the set of variables in F and Q is identical.

A **quantifier block** qb of Q is a maximal subsequence of Q where every variable in qb has the same type of quantifier. We order the quantifier blocks by their sequence of appearance in Q: $qb_1 < qb_2$ iff qb_1 appears before qb_2 in Q.

Each variable x in F appears in some quantifier block, which we denote as $qb(x)$, and the ordering of the quantifier blocks imposes a partial order on the variables. For two variables x and y we say that $x <_{qb} y$ iff $qb(x) < qb(y)$. Note that the variables in the same quantifier block are unordered, so we write $x \leq_{qb} y$ iff $qb(x) \leq qb(y)$. We also say that x is **universal** (**existential**) if its quantifier in Q is $\forall$ ($\exists$).

For example, $\exists e_1 e_2.\forall u_1 u_2.\exists e_3 e_4.(e_1, u_2, e_4) \wedge (\neg u_2, \neg e_4)$ is a QBF with $Q = \exists e_1 e_2.\forall u_1 u_2.\exists e_3 e_4$ and F equal to the two clauses (e_1, u_2, e_4) and $(\neg u_2, \neg e_4)$. The quantifier blocks in order are $\exists e_1 e_2$, $\forall u_1 u_2$, and $\exists e_3 e_4$, and we have that, e.g., $e_1 <_{qb} e_3$, $u_1 <_{qb} e_4$, u_1 is universal, and e_4 is existential.

A SAT model $\mathcal{M}_S$ of a CNF formula F is a truth assignment π to the variables of F that satisfies every clause in F. We denote the value of a variable v in π by $\pi(v)$. In contrast a QBF model (**Q-model**) $\mathcal{M}_Q$ of a quantified formula $Q.F$ is a **tree** of truth assignments in which the root is the empty truth assignment, and every node n assigns a truth value to a variable of F not yet assigned by one of n's ancestors. The tree $\mathcal{M}_Q$ is subject to the following conditions. (1) For every node n in $\mathcal{M}_Q$, if n assigns a truth value to a universal variable x then n has exactly one sibling that assigns the opposite truth value to x, and if n assigns a truth value to an existential variable then n has no siblings. For every sequence of truth assignments π from the root to a leaf of $\mathcal{M}_Q$ we have: (2) π must assign the variables in an order that respects $<_{qb}$. That is if n assigns x and one of n's ancestors assigns y then we must have that $y \leq_{qb} x$. And (3) π is a SAT model of F. A Q-model has a path for every possible setting of the universal variables of Q, and thus has size exponential in the number of universals contained in Q. We say that a QBF $Q.F$ is QSAT if it has a Q-model. The QBF problem is to determine whether or not $Q.F$ is QSAT.

DPLL works on the principle of assigning variables, simplifying the formula to account for that assignment and then recursively solving the simplified formula. The **reduction** of a formula $Q.F$ by a literal ℓ (denoted by $Q.F|_\ell$) is the new formula $Q'.F'$ where F' is F with all clauses containing ℓ marked as being satisfied (implicitly removed) and $\neg\ell$ marked as falsified in all remaining clauses (implicitly ℓ has been removed from these clauses), and Q' is Q with the variable of ℓ and its quantifier removed. For example, $(\forall xz.\exists y.(\neg y, x, z) \land (\neg x, y))|_{\neg x} = \forall z.\exists y(\neg y, z)$, where $(\neg x, y)$ has been marked as satisfied and x has been marked as falsified in $(\neg y, x, z)$. An alternative view of conditions (2) and (3) on a Q-model given above is that the subtree below every node n must be a Q-model of the formula $Q.F|_{\pi_n}$ where π_n is the sequence of literals made true on the path from the root to (and including) n.

From the definition of a Q-model it follows that if F' is logically equivalent to F (F' has the same SAT models as F) then $Q.F$ is QSAT if and only if $Q.F'$ is QSAT: condition 3 above is invariant for F and F'. Thus unit propagation and clause learning can be performed without changing $Q.F$'s QSAT status: both of these transform F to a logically equivalent F'. A QSAT preserving (but not SAT preserving) transformation that can additionally be performed on $Q.F$ is **universal reduction**. The universal reduction of a clause c is to remove all universal variables v from c such that for every other variable x in c we have $x \leq_{qb} v$. Such universals are called tailing. The intuition is as follows. Say that $v \in c$ is a tailing universal, then in any Q-Model, c must be satisfied along any path prior to v being instantiated. (Thus c with v removed imposes the same constraint on the set of Q-models as does c). If not then since v is universal, any path that fails to satisfy c prior to instantiating v must have an extension in which v is set to false: but then that extension will falsify c and violate condition (3).

We call the application of unit propagation and universal reduction until closure **Q-propagation**, and denote by $QProp(Q.F)$ the new formula that results from Q-propagation. In Q-propagation any universal reduction steps are always performed prior to any unit propagation steps: a unit clause containing only a universal variable should yield the empty clause rather than forcing the universal.

The algorithm utilized in modern SAT solvers (e.g., [18]) can be adapted to solve QBF. A recursive version of this algorithm is shown in Fig. 1. Modern backtracking QBF solvers employ two non-chronological backtracking schemes: conflict analysis and solution analysis. Conflict analysis is a standard SAT technique that involves learning new clauses via a resolution process. A failure deadend (line 2) is reached when F contains a clause in which all literals have been falsified by some subset of the literals that reduced F at the previous levels (the prefix). From this falsified clause a new falsified clause c can be learned via a process of resolution and universal reduction (conflict analysis). DPLL-QBF will then backtrack to the **asserting** level of c, which is the level where all but one of the literals in c have been falsified. This is the level where c is made unit (line 4). After returning from all levels deeper than *BTLevel* (line 13-14 or 19-20), the solver arrives at line 12 or line 19, where we now have that the new clause c is unit and forces ℓ. Notice that the solver does not actually undo the original decision made at this level (the setting of the variable v chosen at line 9). Rather it simply augments the reduction of $Q.F$ by the new unit implicant ℓ (line 11 and 18). Thus the solver might return to this level on failure a number of times: each time it discovers that another literal is implied at this level. Eventually, the recursive call at line 12 returns success at this level or returns to a higher level. (Each failure return sets another variable, so a failure return to this level at line 12 can only occur a finite number of times.)

```
 1: ⟨bool Result, literal forced, int BTLevel⟩ QBF-DPLL(Q.F, Level)
 2: if F contains a falsified clause then
 3:     Compute new clause c by Conflict Analysis
 4:     forced = deepest literal in c and BTLevel = level c is made unit
 5:     return ⟨FAIL, forced, BTLevel⟩
 6: if all clauses of F are satisfied then
 7:     Compute Backtrack Level (BTLevel) by Solution (Cube) Analysis
 8:     return ⟨SUCCEED, –, BTLevel⟩
 9: Pick v from the first quantifier block and let ℓ = v or ¬v
10: repeat
11:     Q.F = QProp(Q.F|ℓ)
12:     ⟨Result, ℓ, BTLevel⟩ = QBF-DPLL(Q.F, Level + 1)
13:     if BTLevel < Level then
14:         return ⟨Result, ℓ, BTLevel⟩
15: until Result == SUCCEED      /* v must be universal for this to happen */
16: let ℓ be v's opposite value from line 9.
17: repeat
18:     Q.F = QProp(Q.F|ℓ)
19:     ⟨Result, ℓ, BTLevel⟩ = QBF-DPLL(Q.F, Level + 1)
20:     if BTLevel < Level then
21:         return ⟨Result, ℓ, BTLevel⟩
22: until TRUE     /* line 19 will eventually return BTLevel < Level */
```

Fig. 1. DPLL for QBF

Success returns occur as a consequence of solution analysis (line 7). Solution analysis is a technique particular to QBF that identifies a subset of the assignments that are sufficient to make the QBF QSAT. This subset of assignments is called a cube. The solver can then backtrack to the deepest universal in the cube, skipping other universals not mentioned in the cube and any existentials irrespective of whether or not they are in the cube. Thus line 16 (success return) can be reached only if v is universal. A cube containing one setting of a universal can be combined with another cube containing the other setting to obtain a new cube in a cube resolution process akin to the resolution of clauses. In particular, if the deepest universal in the cube has already had its other value solved, the solver will combine these two cubes and remove the deepest universal. Hence, on success the solver always backtracks to a universal variable whose other side is not yet solved (line 12), and thus the recursive call on line 19 can never return with a successful result. We can, however, return from the call at line 19 a number of times with newly implied literals learned from failures by conflict analysis.

One additional aspect of solution and conflict analysis is that the new clauses and cubes can be stored (learned), reused along other paths in the search, and combined together to produce more powerful clauses and cubes. Cube and clause learning is essential in achieving state of the art performance in QBF solving. In Fig. 1 lines 2-4 and 6-7 would be modified to take into account learned clauses and cubes (e.g., at line 2 we would also fail if any learned clause was falsified, and at line 6 we would also succeed if any learned cube became true, similarly the backtrack level computed at lines 4 and 7 would take into account the already learned cubes and clauses). Cube and clause learning is developed in more detail in, e.g., [14,16,24,25]. With the enhancements of cube and clause learning QBF-DPLL as specified in Fig. 1 is quite close to state of the art solvers like Quaffle [25] and QuBE [15].

Finally note that QBF-DPLL requires only linear space (in the number of variables n), and only quadratic space (in n) when it utilizes non-chronological conflict and solution backtracking.[1] However, when clause and/or cube learning is employed (i.e., the cubes and clauses are stored) the algorithm can consume as much space as can be provided. Nevertheless, learning clauses and cubes does not affect the soundness or completeness of the algorithm, it only helps to improve performance. In particular, we can adopt any strategy for deleting these learned clauses and cubes when we run out of space, without affecting the correctness of the algorithm. In this sense QBF-DPLL, like most current SAT solvers, is an "any-space algorithm," it can utilize any space provided above and beyond its basic polynomial space requirements, but it can also work under any fixed space bound (above its basic requirements).

At line 9 we see that QBF-DPLL must always branch on a variable from the outermost quantifier block. This imposes a constraint on the possible variable orderings the search can use. We now turn to a new algorithm S-QBF that tries to alleviate this constraint on variable ordering imposed by the quantifier prefix Q.

---

[1] In the worst case with conflict and solution backtracking we must store a clause (cube) for every failed existential value (successful universal value) along the current path being explored. These clauses (cubes) have maximum size equal to the number variables n, and the current path can contain at most n literals.

3 S-QBF

As explained in the introduction there is no escaping the fact that in QBF we have to ensure that both settings of each universal variable are solvable.[2] The constraint on variable ordering imposed by the quantifier sequencing can also be a significant impediment to performance. In SAT, e.g., it is provable that an inflexible variable ordering can cause an exponential explosion in the size of the backtracking search tree. That is, there exist families of UNSAT problems for which **any** DPLL search tree where each branch follows a fixed variable ordering is exponential in size, whereas a quasi-polynomially ($O(n^{\log n})$) sized DPLL search tree exists when a dynamic ordering is used [8,2].

This observation (also bolstered by empirical observations of the tremendous impact variable ordering has on DPLL SAT search), is the underlying motivation for our approach. In particular, consider a QBF formula $Q.F$ in which the body F is UNSAT. If all of quantifier blocks have size 1, QBF-DPLL will be forced to follow a fixed static variable ordering in proving $Q.F$ to be UNQSAT. On the other hand an order unrestricted SAT solver might be able to determine that F is UNSAT very quickly, which will immediately tell us that $Q.F$ is UNQSAT.

The idea of testing the body of the formula, F, can be used recursively at every invocation of QBF-DPLL, just before line 9 prior to recursively solving the entire formula (body plus quantifier) with the order constrained QBF search. If the body F is UNSAT, we can backtrack immediately. If F is SAT, then we still do not know whether or not $Q.F$ is QSAT, so we have to continue recursively solving $Q.F$ with our QBF solver.

Furthermore, if F is SAT our SAT solver will find a satisfying truth assignment for F. This truth assignment is a sensible candidate for the left-most path in a Q-model. So after we obtain the SAT solution we can follow this solution in the QBF solver during its first (left-most) descent. It can, however, be the case that the SAT truth assignment is not in fact a feasible left-most path for the QBF solver. In particular, this truth assignment might not survive the stronger Q-propagation performed by the QBF solver. For example, if $Q.F = \forall a, b. \exists c. (a, c) \wedge (b, \neg c)$, then the SAT solver could return $\pi = \langle \neg a, b, c \rangle$ as SAT truth assignment for F. However, the QBF solver following this solution would first instantiate $\neg a$ which by Q-Propagation (unit-propagation plus universal reduction) would reduce $Q.F$ to $\forall b.()$, i.e., F would contain an empty clause.

Putting these pieces together we obtain the S-QBF algorithm given in Fig. 2. The algorithm is a modification of QBF-DPLL. S-QBF is first invoked with the input formula $Q.F$, *Level* equal to 1, and $\pi = \{\}$. Its first task is to find a SAT solution (line 4-8). The SAT solver might discover a number of literals implied at higher levels. Literals implied at higher levels cause S-QBF to backtrack, assert those literals, and then proceed downwards again. The SAT solver might also discover literals implied at the current level. These literals are used to reduce the input formula $Q.F$ (line 8) via Q-propagation: these literals are independent of any choices made by the SAT solver so their consequences need to be accounted for by the QBF solver. After Q-propagating these implied literals the SAT solver is called again to see if it can find a SAT solution in light of these added constraints on F.

---

[2] Cube learning is specifically designed to improve the efficiency of achieving this.

1: ⟨bool *Result*, literal *forced*, int *BTLevel*⟩ **S-QBF**(*Q.F*, *Level*, π)
2: **if** *F* contains a falsified clause or if all of its clauses are satisfied. **then**
3:     Perform non-chronological backtracking using conflict or solution analysis as in QBF-DPLL lines 2-8.
4: **while** $\pi == \{\}$ **do**   /* *No current SAT solution* */
5:     ⟨$\pi, \ell, BTLevel$⟩ = **SAT**(*F*, *Level*)
6:     **if** *BTLevel* < *Level* **then**   /* *SAT can cause S-QBF to backtrack* */
7:         **return** ⟨*FAIL*, ℓ, *BTLevel*⟩
8:     $Q.F = QProp(Q.F|_\ell)$
9: Pick v from the first quantifier block and let $\ell = \pi(v)$.
10: **repeat**   /* *Second and subsequent invocations of S-QBF need to find new SAT solution* */
11:     $Q.F = QProp(Q.F|_\ell)$
12:     ⟨*Result*, ℓ, *BTLevel*⟩ = **S-QBF**($Q.F$, *Level* + 1, π)
13:     **if** *BTLevel* < *Level* **then**
14:         **return** ⟨*Result*, ℓ, *BTLevel*⟩
15:     $\pi = \{\}$
16: **until** *Result* == SUCCEED
17: let ℓ be v's opposite value from line 9.
18: **repeat**   /* *First and all subsequent invocations of S-QBF need to find new SAT solution* */
19:     $Q.F = QProp(Q.F|_\ell)$
20:     ⟨*Result*, ℓ, *BTLevel*⟩ = **S-QBF**($Q.F$, *Level* + 1, $\{\}$)
21:     **if** *BTLevel* < *Level* **then**
22:         **return** ⟨*Result*, ℓ, *BTLevel*⟩
23: **until** TRUE   /* *line 20 will eventually return BTLevel < Level* */

Fig. 2. S-QBF

Eventually, the SAT solver finds a SAT solution (π is returned containing this solution), or causes a backtrack to a higher level in the QBF solver. If a solution is found, the QBF solver *heuristically* tries to follow this solution (in quantifier order) by choosing a value for v that agrees with π (line 9). The SAT solution π is passed down to the next recursion where it is followed as far as possible, either to a failure or a Q-solution at line 2-3.[3] Any conflicts encountered will cause a backtrack which will return to line 20 or 12 of some invocation after which the next invocation will call the SAT solver again. Thus the SAT solver is being used to refute UNSAT subtrees, and more importantly to compute new conflict clauses that can (a) cause the QBF solver to backtrack and (b) discover that various literals are implied at previous levels of the search. All of this information, computed by the SAT solver, is sound for the QBF solver: UNSAT subtrees are UNQSAT, any new clause learned by the SAT solver is a valid new clause for the QBF solver, and if a literal ℓ is SAT implied at a previous level of the tree then ℓ is Q-SAT implied at that level as well.

It should be noted that the SAT solver can also make an S-QBF invocation backtrack from line 20, even though we know that the other side of the universal branched on in

---
[3] Q-propagation might cause S-QBF to fail while following π even though π is a SAT solution. Note that Q-Propagation cannot be applied in the SAT solver since Q-Propagation is only valid when the variables are instantiated in quantifier order whereas the SAT solver is order unconstrained.

that invocation has already been successfully solved. This might seem strange, since at this point we already know that the current prefix (above the *Level* of this invocation) contains at least one satisfying assignment below it. Thus one might think that the SAT solver could never then conclude that the prefix is contradictory. However, although the prefix is not SAT contradictory, it could still be QBF contradictory. For example, say that the prefix contains the literal a, the body F contains the clauses $(\neg a, \neg b, c, d)$, $(\neg a, \neg b, c, \neg d)$, $(\neg a, \neg b, \neg c, d)$, $(\neg a, \neg b, \neg c, \neg d)$, b is universal, $b <_{qb} c$, and $b <_{qb} d$. The QBF solver will be able to solve the setting $\neg b$ without difficulty, as this setting satisfies all of these clauses. However, when at line 20 the setting b is made these four clauses become contradictory. Q-propagation cannot detect the contradiction so the SAT solver will be invoked in the next recursive S-QBF call. SAT will be able to learn the new clause $(\neg a, \neg b)$, which after universal reduction becomes $(\neg a)$. This will cause the QBF solver to backtrack all the way to the point where a was added to the prefix.

Integration of SAT and QBF. In our implementation of S-QBF we built our own SAT solver (utilizing all of the modern techniques like 1-UIP clause learning, watched literals, etc. [18]). In this way we were able to obtain a much tighter integration between the SAT solver and the QBF solver, e.g., sharing of datastructures.

Clause learning is the basic unit of communication between the two solvers. As pointed out above, learned clauses are not necessary for correctness, but they are very helpful for efficiency. In particular, both the QBF solver, via contradictions generated via Q-propagation, and the SAT solver via contradictions generated via unit propagation can learn clauses. Universal reduction is applied to these learned clauses to make them more powerful. All of these learned clauses arise from sequences of Q-resolution steps, thus as shown in [7] they are all logical consequences of the input QBF. That is, they do not alter the QSAT status of the input. This means that any clause learned by either solver can be used by both solvers to prune paths from the search space they explore.

This is useful as each solver is able to learn different kinds of clauses. In particular, since the SAT solver is order unrestricted it can learn powerful clauses via its VSIDS heuristic which would never be learned by the order restricted QBF solver. These clauses can significantly prune the set of paths explored by the QBF solver. On the other hand the QBF solver is able to employ stronger Q-propagation and so it also can learn clauses that the SAT solver could never learn. These clauses allow the SAT solver to prune paths that are fine from the point of view of SAT but which are contradictory with respect to QBF.

Another way that the SAT and QBF solvers are integrated involves techniques for finding "good" SAT solutions (if any exist) [13]. In particular, a good SAT solution is a solution that will allow the QBF solver to generate a good cube (at line 3) if the QBF solver is able to follow the SAT solution down to a leaf. Our technique here is to alter the SAT heuristic for choosing the next decision literal so as to minimize the number of clauses satisfied only by universal variables in the solution. In our implementation we try to branch on existentials that appear in clauses currently only satisfied by universals. Thus, this heuristic tries to ensure that as many clauses as possible are satisfied by existentials. This will result in a smaller cube being generated during solution analysis.

Finally, unlike the rigid prescription of Fig.2, our implementation employs some additional heuristic flexibility in deciding when to invoke the SAT solver. The most important difference is that on many problems the SAT solver will return a SAT solution that fails when we try to follow it using the stronger Q-propagation. This failure then invokes another call to SAT which returns another SAT solution which again fails as we follow it. This sequence of "SAT-ok", "QBF-bad" solutions returned by SAT can be quite long and time consuming. Hence, if this happens more than a certain number of times (5 in our implementation) we give up on SAT solving for this descent and instead try to find a solution using the QBF solver and Q-propagation. In most such cases Q-propagation is able to quickly descend to a leaf from which point we continue with S-QBF. Otherwise the Q-propagation descent learns a conflict, we backtrack, and again continue with S-QBF.

Formal Results

Theorem 1. *S-QBF is sound and complete.*

A sketch of the proof is as follows. First by relating the operations performed by QBF-DPLL on failure return to Q-resolution steps [7] it can be shown that QBF-DPLL will backtrack from the *root* of the search tree with *FAIL* only if its input is Q-UNSAT. Similarly it can be show that any recursive invocation of QBF-DPLL backtracks with *SUCCESS* only if its input is QSAT. Thus QBF-DPLL is sound. That it is also complete follows from the fact that no recursive call has exactly the same prefix of assignments as another call (after a failure a new literal is added to the prefix, and after a success the prefix has a different value for one of the universal variables). Since there are only a finite number of sets of assignments, there can only be a finite number of recursive calls, and the root QBF-DPLL invocation must eventually return (with the correct answer).

SAT in S-QBF only allows S-QBF to backtrack on failure, it does not affect success backtracking. Thus, *SUCCESS* returns continue to correctly prove QSAT. Furthermore, all operations performed by SAT during failure backtracking are sound Q-resolution steps, so S-QBF also preserves the property that it backtracks from the root with *FAIL* only if its input is Q-UNSAT. That is, S-QBF retains QBF-DPLL's soundness property.

Observation 1. *S-QBF is systematic. That is, it never revisits the same set of assignments.*

The previous argument still holds so S-QBF retains the systematic property of QBF-DPLL. This also means that S-QBF is complete.

4 Empirical Results

4.1 Benchmark Settings

We compared an implementation of our approach with two state of the art search based QBF solvers—Quaffle [25] (version as of Feb. 2005) and Qube (release 1.3) [15]. We also ran experiments with the non search based solver Quantor [4] (version as of Jan 2004). Like these solvers our implementation also utilizes techniques for detecting monotone literals, heuristics for guiding cube resolution, and some other standard improvements over the basic algorithm given in Fig.2.

Table 1. Summary of results reported in Table 2. Shown are the percentage of failed runs and the CPU time used (for each benchmark family and in total).

Solver	Blocks	Chain	Comp	Game	K	Robots	Term	Toilet	Total
S-QBF	0%	66%	25%	0%	37%	0%	0%	0%	22%
	2,991s	10,493s	5,000s	1,345s	70,848s	959s	2,577s	672s	26h
Qube	20%	0%	75%	57%	25%	0%	66%	50%	31%
	10,305s	3,499s	16,030s	39,723s	59,594s	2,373s	12,566s	11,057s	43h
Quaffle	20%	33%	0%	71%	50%	0%	0%	25%	43%
	5,709s	9,978s	69s	50,217s	96,251s	410s	299s	6,057s	47h
S⁻	0%	66%	50%	57%	43%	0%	0%	25%	40%
	4,932s	10,439s	10,000s	42,548s	84,279s	2,400s	3,246s	9,486s	45h

We used the following benchmark families from QBFLib: Adder, FlipFlop, Von-Neumann, Counter, Toilet c/g, Robots_D2, Term, Comp, Z4ml, S1169, S1196, S298 and all instances provided by Pan and Rintanen ($\approx$ 350 instances). In addition, we used a benchmark family introduced in [20] called Game (120 instances).

We excluded the families Mutex, Szymanski and Tree since all of them can be trivially solved by simple preprocessing. Further details will be discussed in a subsequent paper. We also excluded all of the other families from QBFLib (2004), e.g., Jmc and Uclid, because only one or two of their instances could be solved by any of the search based solvers.

Due to space limitations we exclude results on any instance that had one of the following properties: (1) the difference in solving time between all search based solvers is small (less than either 200 seconds or within 10% of the fastest time); or (2) no search based solver can solve it in under 5,000 seconds. The remaining results are shown in Table 2. All experiments were performed on a 2.4 GHz Pentium IV with 3GB of RAM.

A summary of these results is presented in Table 4.1. In this table we show the total time used by each solver for all instances in each benchmark family (among those instances shown in Table 2. The "Total" column show the sum of the time over all benchmarks. To obtain a time in the presence of failures we added a penalty of 5,000 seconds per failure. (Thus the times should be used only for qualitative comparisons). In addition, the table shows the percentage of failed instances for each benchmark family and in total.

4.2 Discussion

Table 4.1 shows that our new approach improves the current state of the art in search based solvers, in aggregate solving the most problems and taking the least time of any of the solvers. S-QBF is not always the fastest solver, but it does improve on Quaffle and Qube on 21 out of the 68 problems reported on in Table 2. In many of the other cases it is very competitive, being the worst solver of the three search based solvers on only 9 of the 68 problems. As noted above we experimented with many other benchmarks, but on these the solvers could not be effectively discriminated.

To obtain a more accurate assessment of the benefit provided specifically by our new techniques for using SAT (vs. differences in implementation and heuristics), we built a derivative of S-QBF. This derivative (denoted S⁻) used the same code base, the same variable ordering heuristic, the same cube learning and clause learning techniques, etc. S^- is simply S-QBF without the SAT solver. This provided us with a much more accurate control against which to assess our new techniques. The summary performance of S^-, shown in Table 4.1, demonstrates that although our base QBF solver is quite effective, our new techniques for using SAT yield clear performance advantages. Table 2 shows in more detail the time taken by the different solvers on individual problems (columns S^-, *S-QBF*, *Quaffle*, and *QuBE*).

It is also useful to examine the effect SAT has on the size of the QBF search tree. Columns *SAT-dec*, *Q-dec*, S^- *Q-dec* of Table 2 show the number of decisions made by the SAT solver, the number of decisions made by the QBF solver (in S-QBF), and the number of decisions made by S^- (where SAT is not used). In most cases we see that the SAT solver is able to significantly reduce the number of decisions the QBF solver needs to make (comparing columns *Q-dec* and S^- *Q-dec*). In fact, in many cases the sum of the SAT and QBF decisions in S-QBF is less than the number of QBF decisions used by the pure QBF solver S^-.

QBF decisions are more expensive than SAT decisions as they require extra work (e.g., triggering of cubes, detecting monotone literals, detecting the empty theory). Hence reducing the number of QBF decisions has a strong impact on the run-time (e.g, in the *Blocks*, *Game*, and *Toilet* benchmarks). In our implementation SAT decisions are made 5 to 10 times faster than QBF decisions depending on the problem instance. This means that using SAT can yield improvements even when the sum of decisions in SAT and QBF is higher than the number of decision made by pure QBF (in S^-) (e.g., the K benchmarks).

The SAT solver can, however, sometimes be a waste of time. For example the *Chain* benchmarks contain Q-propagation implication chains under which a QBF solver will never encounter a failure. Thus it is pointless to use a SAT solver to detect failures, and we see that on *chain16v.17* S-QBF performs the same number of Q-decisions as S^-. S^- fails on the two larger chain problems, even without the slow down of extraneous SAT solving. This is because the low-level efficiency of our solver is not as optimized as Qube or Quaffle. In some cases SAT solving can even be harmful, as following its solutions can be misleading. For example, on $k\_d4\_p\text{-}6$ S-QBF makes many more QBF decisions than when SAT is not used (S^-). But in the vast majority of the cases SAT is more informative than misleading.

Quantor is another state of the art QBF solver, but it is not based on backtracking search. Instead Quantor utilizes a variable elimination scheme based on the original resolution procedure of Davis-Putnam [11] and an additional scheme of universal expansion. It falls into the class of worst case space exponential algorithms. Quantor's approach often superior on these benchmarks. However, its failure rate is 24% which is slightly higher than that achieved by S-QBF. Furthermore, while we expect a few more problems could be solved by S-QBF given more time, Quantor is exhausting addressable memory on most of its failures. Overall, space exponential algorithms have the disadvantage that space is a much less flexible resource than time.

The question of whether space intensive algorithms like Quantor, Skizzo [3], or QMRES [19] will eventually be the best way to solve QBF remains open. However, we are more optimistic about search based methods. In particular, the wide variance in the times achieved by search based solvers shows that there is a lot of room for

Table 2. Benchmark Results

Problem Instance	QSAT?	SAT-dec	Q-dec	S^- Q-dec	S^-	S-QBF	Quaffle	QuBE	Quantor
blocks3i.5.3	0	37779	50482	439625	32.05	4.53	158.25	453.98	0.36
blocks3i.5.4	1	47300	62403	298121	11.85	3.12	11.08	4626.19	0.38
blocks4i.6.4	0	7367	6438	19931487	3116.49	0.95	fail	203.99	0.31
blocks4ii.6.3	0	6087	5685	6409879	1042.46	1.1	208.19	21.02	22.63
blocks4ii.7.2	0	1804960	1444039	2860315	729.34	2981.66	312.28	fail	43.23
chain16v.17	1	65519	131582	131582	439.97	493.32	129.3	71.14	0.04
chain19v.20	1	-	-	-	fail	fail	4849.32	1123.53	0.07
chain20v.21	1	-	-	-	fail	fail	fail	2304.390	0.08
comp_1_1.0_0_o	0	3401	755	-	fail	0.12	1.92	fail	0.02
comp_1_1.0_1_o	1	0	34	34	0	0	0	1030.88	0.04
comp_1_0.2_1_o	1	0	58	58	0.01	0.01	0	fail	0.03
comp_1_0.2_0_o	0	-	-	-	fail	fail	67.63	fail	0.05
game20_20_40_2	1	3855587	4425993	2754583	260.23	440.94	fail	98.26	0.08
game20_25_25_1	1	4517800	2213579	-	fail	309.46	fail	369.5	fail
game20_25_25_2	1	2109107	1168113	-	fail	125.29	fail	2874.96	fail
game20_25_25_3	1	920314	413170	2027831	326.64	40.06	fail	1150.51	fail
game20_25_25_4	1	3298510	1680483	-	fail	222.13	fail	1651.43	fail
game20_25_50_1	1	3298510	1680483	-	fail	221.74	fail	1657.63	fail
game50_25_25_1	1	2452664	954186	12368548	477.79	64.22	fail	1869.7	fail
game50_25_25_3	1	188743	66888	6182150	220.99	4.13	fail	fail	fail
game50_25_25_4	1	72203	34183	-	fail	1.63	fail	51.48	fail
game100_25_25_2	1	36165	24291	-	fail	0.73	fail	fail	9.26
game100_25_25_3	1	32923	16184	-	fail	0.63	4.06	fail	0.04
game150_25_25_1	0	0	21	21	0	0	0	fail	0.01
game150_25_25_2	1	208546	175239	-	fail	4.22	4.34	fail	0.01
game150_25_25_4	1	14604	13567	41798186	1262.76	0.3	208.79	fail	0.01
k_branch_p-5	1	-	-	-	fail	fail	fail	3854.78	fail
k_d4_p-6	0	5542611	55260801	2005	0.42	1689.13	fail	837.45	1.43
k_dum_n-6	1	1876929	1639193	1692680	221.21	122.79	fail	117.42	0.02
k_dum_n-8	1	-	-	-	fail	fail	fail	2916.89	0.06
k_dum_p-11	0	-	-	-	fail	fail	871.44	1014.83	5.32
k_grz_n-9	1	366963	294974	736851	117.68	22.32	3534.32	67.06	3.86
k_grz_n-12	1	1231288	1106900	2884937	3093.12	285.7	fail	250.53	10.3
k_grz_n-13	1	1420342	1277434	3339392	4046.65	353.39	fail	253.01	11.29
k_grz_n-16	1	5110635	4232820	-	fail	711.97	fail	1253.97	32.15
k_grz_n-17	1	6310863	5229135	-	fail	1396.91	fail	1321.97	20.7
k_grz_p-10	0	-	-	-	fail	fail	fail	164.81	6.78
k_grz_p-14	0	-	-	-	fail	fail	fail	1270.28	17.19
k_grz_p-16	0	-	-	-	fail	fail	2481.57	1694.67	27.73
k_grz_p-17	0	-	-	-	fail	fail	3107.51	1922.98	21.37
k_lin_n-7	1	1836874	900248	174011	404.32	194.34	169.26	49.75	454.34
k_lin_n-14	1	4503632	2422960	-	fail	4030.32	2525.31	1353.86	fail
k_lin_n-15	1	-	-	-	fail	fail	3008.53	2108.53	fail
k_path_n-5	1	3814468	3658630	3037899	473.3	493.5	fail	158.02	0
k_path_n-6	1	-	-	-	fail	fail	fail	1514.29	0.01
k_path_p-6	0	2895489	2490412	823834	101.87	406.71	270.42	30.26	0.01
k_ph_n-15	1	-	-	4072609	3731.09	fail	283.51	158.02	2962.78
k_poly_n-3	1	4702368	2945933	5078474	1445.27	426.24	fail	151.16	0
k_poly_n-4	1	-	-	-	fail	fail	fail	1651.2	0
k_poly_p-7	0	0	83	83	0	0	0	fail	0.01
k_poly_p-8	0	0	99	99	0	0	0	fail	0.02
k_poly_p-10	0	0	123	123	0	0	0	fail	0.04
k_poly_p-11	0	0	131	131	0.01	0.01	0	fail	0.03
k_poly_p-12	0	0	147	147	0.01	0.01	0	fail	0.03
k_poly_p-14	0	0	171	171	0.01	0.01	0	fail	0.03
k_poly_p-17	0	0	203	203	0.01	0.01	0	fail	0.03
k_t4p_n-2	1	2400994	2228055	1410656	645.73	709.56	fail	84.11	0.02
k_t4p_p-4	0	-	-	-	fail	fail	fail	194.57	0.1
robots1_5_2_72.7	1	21720	3002426	313292	44.14	221.7	19.64	1385.68	fail
robots1_5_2_42.7	0	29395	7713081	4458791	1519.08	672.14	288.06	565.01	fail
robots1_5_2_61.6	0	17992	4529115	4619291	836.47	268.29	99.34	424.87	fail
term1_1_0.2_0_i	0	2708395	2655162	2906302	3238.12	2555.78	296.52	fail	fail
term1_1_1.0_1_o	1	129	88	722	0.03	0.02	0.06	2566.76	0.07
term1_1_1.0_0_o	0	36105	6769	7276	7.86	18.65	3.11	fail	1.57
toilet6.1.11	0	54468	44831	108215	48.5	22.47	9.21	307.92	0.09
toilet7.1.13	0	347166	273852	1225940	3570.54	617.92	39.76	fail	1.14
toilet7.1.14	1	888	1097	712183	867.72	0.32	45.65	749.85	0.02
toilet10.1.20	1	57	264	-	fail	0.1	fail	fail	fail

improvements in heuristics. Several instances in the *Game* benchmark family illustrate this point. Some can be solved in only a few seconds by S-QBF but cause Quantor to exhaust available memory.

5 Relation to Previous Work

A number of other approaches have been proposed for escaping from the ordering constraints imposed by the quantifier prefix. Quantor [4], and Skizzo [3] both employ the device of removing universal variables by adding multiple copies of their scoped existentials. (A process akin to Skolemization in first-order logic). Once all universals have been removed the transformed theory becomes an order unconstrained SAT theory.

As our empirical results demonstrate this technique can be very effective, but in general it requires exponential space. Our empirical results also demonstrate that it is not difficult to find problems solvable by QBF-DPLL that are unsolvable by Quantor (Skizzo was not yet available for experimentation).

A more recent order unconstrained approach is based on a BDD representation of a Q-model [1]. The idea here is to generate arbitrary SAT solutions with a SAT solver, adding those solutions to the BDD. The BDD will eventually collapses to TRUE if the set of added SAT solutions suffice to form all paths in a Q-model. However, the BDD can grow to an exponential size prior to collapsing. Furthermore, the SAT solver can generate SAT solutions that form paths in disjoint Q-models—thus the BDD might be even larger as it has to represent multiple distinct Q-models before one collapses to a solution. The empirical results reported in [1] do not improve on the state of the art.

The idea of utilizing a SAT solver within QBF was first presented in [9]. SAT solving was employed to determine trivial truth (satisfiability after removing all universals from every clause) and trivial falsity (unsatisfiability of the subset of clauses that contain only existentials) at every recursive call. Trivial truth is a very strong condition: the remaining theory can easily be QSAT even though it is not trivially true. Furthermore, because a different clause set is being used, the satisfiability testing employed in trivial truth cannot be used to learn clauses for the remaining QBF search. Trivial falsity on the other hand is strictly weaker than the SAT testing we employ. Trivial falsity tests SAT on a subset of the clauses, hence whenever it reports UNSAT our SAT testing will also report UNSAT. Furthermore, our SAT testing can report UNSAT even on formulas that are not trivially false.

In more closely related work an incomplete SAT solver was used [13]. If a SAT solution was found it could be heuristically followed in an attempt to reach a successful leaf in the QBF search. This is quite different from our motivation which is to refute UNSAT subtree. This requires a complete SAT solver as well as a tighter integration between the SAT and QBF solvers. Empirically the WalkQSat solver reported in [13] did not display good performance. Independently to our work [22] utilized a complete SAT solver (ZChaff [18]). It allows the pruning of UNSAT subtrees and the computed reason for this conflict is used in the QBF solver to apply backtracking. However, the integration of the two solvers is not as tight as it is in our approach. For instance, the solvers operate on two distinct representations of the formula so that except for backtracking no exchange of learned clauses takes place between the SAT and QBF solvers. Furthermore, operations like the propagation of variable (un)assignments has to be performed twice.

6 Conclusions

We have presented an approach for integrating order unconstrained SAT solving within an order constrained QBF solver. By utilizing clause learning techniques, and the fact that a SAT learned clause is valid for QBF, we have been able to achieve a tight integration between the SAT solver and the QBF solver so that information computed in each part can be used to improve the performance of the other part.

A number of natural questions remain, most of which center around the issue of obtaining more information from the SAT solving computations. Our techniques mainly take advantage of failure information computed by the SAT solver, and we have shown that this can make a tremendous difference in performance. We have also found that the heuristic technique of guiding the SAT solver to find a "good cube" solution can have a large impact on performance. In general, however, there is considerable room for improvement in the whole area of heuristics for QBF, and an intriguing open question is whether or not useful heuristic information could be gathered during SAT solving.

References

1. G. Audemard and L. Saïs. A symbolic search based approach for quantified boolean formulas. to be published at SAT 2005.
2. P. Beame, H. Kautz, and A. Sabharwal. Towards understanding and harnessing the potential of clause learning. *Journal of Artificial Intelligence Research*, 22:319–351, 2004.
3. M. Benedetti. skizzo: a qbf decision procedure based on propositional skolemization and symbolic reasoning. Technical Report TR04-11-03, 2004.
4. A. Biere. Resolve and expand. In *Seventh International Conference on Theory and Applications of Satisfiability Testing (SAT)*, pages 238–246, 2004.
5. Lucas Bordeaux and Eric Monfroy. Beyond np: Arc-consistency for quantified constraints. In *Principles and Practice of Constraint Programming*, pages 371–386, 2002.
6. R. Bryant, S. Lahiri, and S. Seshia. Convergence testing in term-level bounded model checking. Technical Report CMU-CS-03-156, Carnegie Mellon University, 2003.
7. H. K. Büning, M. Karpinski, and A. Flügel. Resolution for quantified boolean formulas. *Inf. Comput.*, 117(1):12–18, 1995.
8. Joshua Buresh-Oppenheim and Toniann Pitassi. The complexity of resolution refinements. In *IEEE Symposium on Logic in Computer Science*, pages 138–147, 2003.
9. M. Cadoli, A. Giovanardi, and M. Schaerf. An algorithm to evaluate quantified boolean formulae. In *Proceedings of the AAAI National Conference (AAAI)*, pages 262–267, 1998.
10. M. Davis, G. Logemann, and D. Loveland. A machine program for theorem-proving. *Communications of the ACM*, 4:394–397, 1962.
11. M. Davis and H. Putnam. A computing procedure for quantification theory. *Journal of the ACM*, 7:201–215, 1960.
12. Uwe Egly, Thomas Eiter, Hans Tompits, and Stefan Woltran. Solving advanced reasoning tasks using quantified boolean formulas. In *AAAI/IAAI*, pages 417–422, 2000.
13. I.P. Gent, H.H. Hoos, A.G.D. Rowley, and K. Smyth. Using stochastic local search to solve quantified boolean formulae. In *Principles and Practice of Constraint Programming — CP'2003*, pages 348–362, 2003.
14. E. Giunchiglia, M. Narizzano, and A. Tacchella. Backjumping for quantified boolean logic satisfiability. In *Proceedings of the International Joint Conference on Artifical Intelligence (IJCAI)*, pages 275–281, 2001.

15. E. Giunchiglia, M. Narizzano, and A. Tacchella. QUBE: A system for deciding quantified boolean formulas satisfiability. In *International Joint Conference on Automated Reasoning (IJCAR)*, pages 364–369, 2001.
16. E. Giunchiglia, M. Narizzano, and A. Tacchella. Learning for quantified boolean logic satisfiability. In *Eighteenth national conference on Artificial intelligence*, pages 649–654, 2002.
17. Reinhold Letz. Lemma and model caching in decision procedures for quantified boolean formulas. In *TABLEAUX '02: Proceedings of the International Conference on Automated Reasoning with Analytic Tableaux and Related Methods*, pages 160–175, 2002.
18. M. Moskewicz, C. Madigan, Y. Zhao, L. Zhang, and S. Malik. Chaff: Engineering an efficient sat solver. In *Proc. of the Design Automation Conference (DAC)*, 2001.
19. G. Pan and M. Y. Vardi. Symbolic decision procedures for qbf. In *Principles and Practice of Constraint Programming*, number 3258 in Lecture Notes in Computer Science, pages 453–467. Springer-Verlag, New York, 2004.
20. A. Remshagen and K. Truemper. An effective algorithm for the futile questioning problem. *Journal of Automated Reasoning*, to be published.
21. Jussi Rintanen. Constructing conditional plans by a theorem-prover. *Journal of Artificial Intelligence Research*, 10:323–352, 1999.
22. A.G.D. Rowley. *Forthcoming*. PhD thesis, University of St. Andrews, 2005.
23. L.J. Stockmeyer and A.R. Meyer. Word problems requiring exponential time. *Journal of the ACM*, pages 1–9, 1973.
24. L. Zhang, C. F. Madigan, M. W. Moskewicz, and S. Malik. Efficient conflict driven learning in a Boolean satisfiability solver. In *International Conference on Computer-Aided Design (ICCAD'01)*, pages 279–285, November 2001.
25. L. Zhang and S. Malik. Towards symmetric treatment of conflicts and satisfaction in quantified boolean satisfiability solver. In *Principles and Practice of Constraint Programming (CP2002)*, pages 185–199, 2002.

Tree Decomposition with Function Filtering

Martí Sánchez[1], Javier Larrosa[2], and Pedro Meseguer[1]

[1] Institut d'Investigació en Intel.ligència Artificial,
Consejo Superior de Investigaciones Científicas,
Campus UAB, 08193 Bellaterra, Spain
{marti, pedro}@iiia.csic.es

[2] Dep. Llenguatges i Sistemes Informàtics,
Universitat Politècnica de Catalunya,
Jordi Girona, 08028 Barcelona, Spain
larrosa@lsi.upc.es

Abstract. Besides search, complete inference methods can also be used to solve soft constraint problems. Their main drawback is the high spatial complexity. To improve its practical usage, we present an approach to decrease memory consumtion in tree decomposition methods, a class of complete inference algorithms. This approach, called function filtering, allows to detect and remove some tuples that appear to be consistent (with a cost below the upper bound) but that will become inconsistent (with a cost exceeding the upper bound) when extended to other variables. Using this idea, we have developed new algorithms CTEf, MCTEf and IMCTEf, standing for cluster, mini-cluster and iterative mini-cluster tree elimination with function filtering. We demonstrate empirically the benefits of our approach.

1 Introduction

In constraint satisfaction, inference is widely used but in a very limited form. A simple example is arc consistency: by the inspection of constraints and domains, it is able to deduce that some values will never be in a solution so they can be removed. Arc consistency is incomplete inference since it cannot always produce a solution. Inference can also be complete. Some algorithms are adaptive consistency [8], cluster tree methods [9] and bucket elimination [10]. Their temporal and spatial complexities are exponential in some parameters of the constraint graph (see [6] for details). When compared with search methods (exponential complexity in time but lineal complexity in space), they look unattractive, especially when search is enhanced with the powerful machinery of local consistency coupled with global constraints.

In the soft constraints realm, satisfaction is replaced by optimization. This causes that problems with soft constraints become more difficult to solve than their hard counterparts. The same solving ideas are recreated here. Search methods, based on a branch-and-bound schema, are combined with soft local consistencies to filter domains [15]. Complete inference methods are easily adapted to compute the optimum, at the cost of dragging large arity constraints. Their high spatial complexity is the main drawback to be used in practice. Nevertheless, this issue is not always unavoidable: when there are ways to control the spatial complexity, complete inference can provide excellent performance [14].

The simplest form to control space complexity is the use of an upper bound of the optimal cost. This allows one to remove tuples whose cost exceed the upper bound, because their will never contribute to the optimum. Good upper bounds can be found by problem inspection, sampling or local search. In addition to upper bound usage, the basic operation of complete inference, constraint combination, should be handled with extreme care due to its multiplicative nature. Strategies that anticipate if some tuples will not produce a solution should be used, to limit as much as possible the combinatorial explosion. This is the subject of this paper. In the field of Bayesian Inference a work in a similar direction exists [11].

In this paper, we present a new strategy to decrease the memory consumption of tree decomposition methods, a class of complete inference algorithms, when applied to weighted CSP. Tree decomposition methods work on a decomposition of the problem with a tree structure. They solve subproblems or "parts", sending the result of one part to the rest of the problem. The tree structure permits an orderly exchange of information. The key idea we have pursued is as follows. When combining constraints in one part of the problem, if it happens that some of the resulting tuples would become unacceptable after sending them to another part, would it not be better to detect those tuples before sending, and eliminate them once and for all? In some cases we are able to detect that some tuples, apparently acceptable when solving a subproblem (that is, with a cost below the upper bound), will become unacceptable (with a cost exceeding the upper bound) when used in another subproblem, so we can remove them and decrease the memory usage. Obviously, it is possible to find problems where our method causes no benefits, but in this case it causes no harm as well. [1]

This technique is called *function filtering*, and it has been applied to hard constraints [16]. In the soft case, approximation techniques that limit the arity of the subproblem to solve can be successfully combined with function filtering, so successive iterations can increment the size of the subproblem to solve without increasing memory usage.

The paper structure is as follows. In Section 2 we summarize the notions used in the rest of the paper. In Section 3, we present the idea of function filtering. In Section 4 we apply function filtering to tree decomposition methods, producing the CTEf, MCTEf and IMCTEf algorithms, that stand for cluster, mini-cluster and iterative mini-cluster tree elimination with function filtering. Experimental results appear in Section 5, showing the obtained benefits on a set of benchmarks. Finally, Section 6 contains some conclusions.

---

[1] A similarity with arc-consistency (AC) can be stated here. You can find problems on which AC causes no change, but this does not invalidate AC as a extremely useful notion in constraint reasoning.

2 Preliminaries

2.1 Weighted CSP

Valuation structures are algebraic entities to specify costs in valued CSP. We use a particular structure $S(k)$ [13], for weighted CSP. Formally,

Definition 1. *A valuation structure is a triple $S = \langle E, \oplus, \succeq \rangle$, where E is the set of costs totally ordered by $\succeq$, and $\oplus$ is the binary internal operation to combine costs. The maximum and minimum costs are denoted as $\top$ and $\bot$. $\oplus$ is commutative, associative, monotone, $\bot$ is the neutral element and $\top$ is the annihilator.*

Definition 2. *The valuation structure $S(k)$ is a triple $\langle [0, 1, ..., k], \oplus, \geq \rangle$ where $\top = k$, $\bot = 0$ and*

- $k \in [1, \ldots, \infty]$,
- $a \oplus b = min\{k, a + b\}$, and
- $\geq$ *is the standard order among naturals.*

Definition 3. *A Weighted CSP (WCSP) is a tuple $\langle X, D, C, S(k) \rangle$ where,*

- $X = \{x_1, ..., x_n\}$ *is a set of n variables;*
- $D = \{D_1, ..., D_n\}$ *is a set of finite domains, each variable $x_i \in X$ taking its values in D_i;*
- *C is a finite set of constraints as cost functions. Each function $f \in C$ relates a number of variables $var(f) = \{x_{i_1}, \ldots x_{i_r}\}$ called its scope, and assigns costs to tuples $t \in \prod_{x_i \in var(f)} D_i$ such that,*

$$f(t) = \begin{cases} 0 & \text{if } t \text{ is allowed} \\ [1 \ldots k\text{-}1] & \text{if } t \text{ is partially allowed} \\ k & \text{if } t \text{ is totally forbidden} \end{cases}$$

- *$S(k)$ is a valuation structure.*

An *assignment* or tuple t_S on a sequence of variables $S = (x_1, x_2, \ldots, x_k)$, is a sequence of values $(a_1, a_2, \ldots, a_k)$ such that a_1 is the value for x_1, a_2 is the value for x_2 and so on. An assignment t_S is complete if $S = X$. Given $S' \subset S$, $t_S[S']$ is the tuple obtained removing from t_S the values of variables in $S - S'$. If S is implicitly assumed or irrelevant, we write directly t. For clarity, we assume that $f(t_S)$ (with $var(f) \subset S$) always means $f(t_S[var(f)])$, so we select from tuple t_S the values of variables in f and ignore the others. The concatenation of two tuples t_S and t'_T, noted $t.t'_{S \cup T}$, is a new tuple on $S \cup T$ formed by the union of its values, and it is only defined if common variables coincide in their corresponding values. A complete assignment t_S is *consistent* if $\bigoplus_{f \in C} f(t) < k$. Else t_S is *inconsistent*. A *solution* of a WCSP is a complete consistent assignment with minimum cost. The problem of finding a solution is NP-hard. It is easy to check that WCSP with $k = 1$ reduces to classical CSP.

We define two operations on functions:

- **Projecting out.** Given a function f, projecting out variable $x \in var(f)$, denoted $f_{\downarrow x}$, is a new function with scope $var(f) - x$. Every tuple removing x component is present in the projection and its cost is the minimum among all permitted x extensions: $f_{\downarrow x}(t) = \min_{a \in D_x}(f(a.t))$. Projecting out the variable of a unary function produces a constant. Any constant can be considered an empty scope function.
- **Sum.** Given two functions f and g, its sum $f + g$ is a new function with scope $var(f) \cup var(g)$ and $\forall t \in \prod_{x_i \in var(f)} D_i$, $\forall t' \in \prod_{x_j \in var(g)} D_j$ such that $t.t'$ is defined, $(f+g)(t.t') = f(t) \oplus g(t')$.

Definition 4. *Function g is a lower bound of function f, denoted $g \leq f$, if $var(g) \subseteq var(f)$ and for all possible tuples t of f, $g(t) \leq f(t)$. Abusing notation, a set of functions G is a lower bound of function f iff $(\sum_{g \in G} g) \leq f$*

Property 1. For any function f, $(f_{\downarrow x})$ is a lower bound of f.

Property 2. $\sum_{f \in F}(f_{\downarrow x}) \leq (\sum_{f \in F} f)_{\downarrow x}$ holds.

2.2 Tree Decomposition

A tree decomposition of a WCSP is a clustering of the functions in C such that clusters are linked if they share variables and form an acyclic tree network.

Definition 5. *A tree decomposition for a WCSP $\langle X, D, C, S(k) \rangle$ is a triplet $\langle T, \chi, \psi \rangle$, where $T = \langle V, E \rangle$ is a tree. χ and ψ are labeling functions which associate with each vertex $v \in V$ two sets, $\chi(v) \subseteq X$ and $\psi(v) \subseteq C$ that satisfy the following conditions:*

1. *For each function $f \in C$, there is exactly one vertex $v \in V$ such that $f \in \psi(v)$. In addition, vertex v satisfies $var(f) \subseteq \chi(v)$.*
2. *For each variable $x \in X$, the set $\{v \in V | x \in \chi(v)\}$ induces a connected subtree of T.*

Tree decompositions for CSP often relax condition (1) by requiring that any function $f \in C$ must appear in *at least* one vertex $v \in V$ of the decomposition (see [6]). For WCSP, if function f appears in two vertices, tree decomposition methods could add twice its contribution, so the *exactly* condition is required.

Definition 6. *The tree-width of a tree decomposition is the maximum number of variables in a vertex minus one $tw = max_{v \in V} |\chi(v)| - 1$. Let (u,v) be an edge of a tree-decomposition, the separator of u and v is $sep(u,v) = \chi(u) \cap \chi(v)$, formed by the common variables between two vertices of the decomposition. We will call s the maximum separator size $s = max_{(u,v) \in E} |sep(u,v)|$. The eliminator of u and v is defined as $elim(u,v) = \chi(u) - sep(u,v)$, and represent the variables in u that are not present in v.*

In [5] tree decomposition is defined only for binary graphs and hyper-tree decomposition for hyper-graphs. Following [6] we use the concept of tree decomposition of a CSP referring to an hyper-tree decomposition of the hyper-graph formed by the functions of the CSP. We also extend this definition for WCSP imposing that every constraint must appear exactly once in all clusters.

Example 1. The crossword puzzle of Figure 1 is a WCSP $\langle\{x_0, \ldots, x_9\}, \{a, \ldots, z\},$ $\{f_1, \ldots, f_4\}, S(k)\rangle$, with a variable per cell, functions correspond to vertical and horizontal slots and accepts words of numbers from "zero" to "ten", that can also be reversed. The cost of each word is its number or its number plus one, if reversed. Any other word costs k.

For example: $f_1(x_1, x_2, x_3, x_4) = \{$(zero,0), (orez,1), (four,4), (rouf,5), (five,5), (evif,6), (nine,9), (enin,10)$\}$ and $f_2(x_7, x_8, x_9) = \{$(one,1), (eno,2), (two,2), (owt,3), (six,6), (xis,7), (ten,10), (net,11)$\}$. An optimal solution tuple is $\{(x_0, z), (x_1, z),$ $(x_2, e), (x_3, r), (x_4, o), (x_5, r), (x_6, n), (x_7, o), (x_8, n), (x_9, e)\}$ with cost 2.

f_1	x_1	x_2	x_3	x_4		f_2	x_7	x_8	x_9		f_3	x_0	x_2	x_5	x_7		f_4	x_4	x_6	x_9
0	z	e	r	o		1	o	n	e		0	z	e	r	o		1	o	n	e
1	o	r	e	z		2	e	n	o		1	o	r	e	z		2	e	n	o
4	f	o	u	r		2	t	w	o		4	f	o	u	r		2	t	w	o
5	r	u	o	f		3	o	w	t		5	r	u	o	f		3	o	w	t
5	f	i	v	e		6	s	i	x		5	f	i	v	e		6	s	i	x
6	e	v	i	f		7	x	i	s		6	e	v	i	f		7	x	i	s
9	n	i	n	e		10	t	e	n		9	n	i	n	e		10	t	e	n
10	e	n	i	n		11	n	e	t		10	e	n	i	n		11	n	e	t

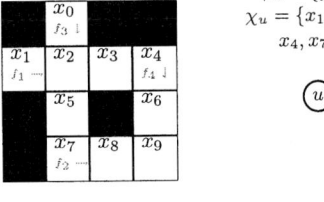

$\psi_u = \{f_1, f_2\}$
$\chi_u = \{x_1, x_2, x_3,$
$x_4, x_7, x_8, x_9\}$

$\psi_v = \{f_3, f_4\}$
$\chi_v = \{x_0, x_2, x_5$
$x_7, x_4, x_6, x_9\}$

Fig. 1. Upper: crossword functions. Lower left: the crossword puzzle. Lower right: a possible tree decomposition.

2.3 Cluster and Mini-Cluster Tree Elimination

Cluster-Tree Elimination (CTE) is a generic algorithm that can be used for CSP solving and unifies other inference algorithms such as Bucket Elimination [3,10]. CTE also solves a constraint optimization problem by sending messages along every edge of a tree decomposition of the problem. Concepts of this Section are more extensively described in [6].

Given a tree decomposition $\langle\langle V, E\rangle, \chi, \psi\rangle$, every edge $(u, v) \in E$ has associated two *CTE messages* denoted $m_{(u,v)}$, from u to v, and $m_{(v,u)}$, from v to u.

procedure CTE($\langle X, D, C, k \rangle$, $\langle \langle V, E \rangle, \chi, \psi \rangle$)
1 **for each** $(u, v) \in E$ s.t. all $m_{(i,u)}, i \neq v$ have arrived **do**
2     $B \leftarrow \psi(u) \cup \{m_{(i,u)} \mid (i, u) \in E, i \neq v\}$;
3     $m_{(u,v)} \leftarrow (\sum_{f \in B} f) \Downarrow_{elim(u,v)}$;
4   send $m_{(u,v)}$;

Fig. 2. The CTE algorithm. $\langle X, D, C, k \rangle$ is a WCSP instance and $\langle \langle V, E \rangle, \chi, \psi \rangle$ is its tree decomposition.

Message $m_{(u,v)}$ is a function computed summing all functions in $\psi(v)$ with all incoming CTE messages except from $m_{(v,u)}$ and then projecting out the variables in u not mentioned by v, that is variables in $elim(u, v)$. $m_{(u,v)}$ has scope $sep(u, v)$. In Figure 2 we present the CTE algorithm. Line 1 is a loop that looks for edges such that all their incoming messages but one have arrived. Lines 2 gathers the set of functions to be summed. Line 3 performs the sum and projection. Let $T(u, v)$ (resp. $T(v, u)$) denote the subtree of T containing the connected component containing vertex u (resp. v) after the removal of edge (u, v).

Property 3. $m_{(u,v)}(t)$ is equal to the minimum cost of extending tuple t to the subproblem induced by $T(u, v)$. This is guaranteed by the correctness of the algorithm.

The complexity of CTE is time $O((|C|+|V|).deg.d^{tw+1})$ and space $O(|V|.d^s)$ where tw is the tree-width, $|C|$ is the number of constraints, $|V|$ is the number of nodes of the tree decomposition, deg is the maximum degree in the tree decomposition, d is largest domain size and s is maximum separator size. In Figure 3 we can see an execution of CTE on example 1. Original functions have size 8. Once the messages have been sent we can compute the solution in any of the two nodes. For example, in v the minimum cost of $f_2 + f_3 + m_{(u,v)}$ is the optimal solution.

Mini-Cluster-Tree Elimination (MCTE(r)) approximates the exact CTE algorithm. When the number of variables in a cluster is too high, it is not possible to compute a single message that captures the joint effect of all functions of the cluster plus all incoming messages due to memory limitations. In this case, MCTE(r) computes a lower bound of the problem by limiting by a constant r the arity of the functions sent in the messages. This is because we can not afford to compute one single function that will be of high arity and then project it.

A *MCTE(r) message*, noted $M_{(u,v)}$, is a set of functions that approximate the corresponding CTE message $m_{(u,v)}$ (namely $M_{(u,v)} \leq m_{(u,v)}$). It is computed as $m_{(u,v)}$ but instead of summing all functions of set B (line 2 of CTE algorithm in Figure 2), it computes a partition $P = \{B_1, B_2, \ldots, B_p\}$ of B such

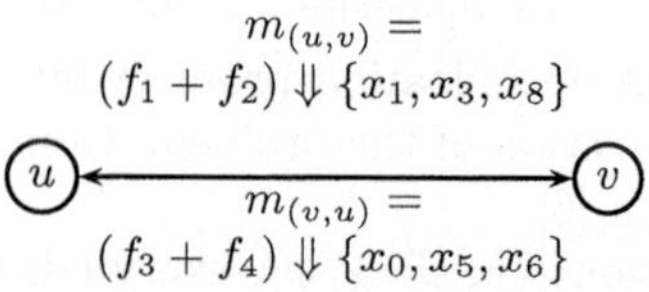

$$m_{(u,v)} = (f_1 + f_2) \Downarrow \{x_1, x_3, x_8\}$$

$$u \xleftarrow{\qquad} v$$

$$m_{(v,u)} = (f_3 + f_4) \Downarrow \{x_0, x_5, x_6\}$$

Fig. 3. The 2 CTE messages of edge (u, v) of example 1

that the sum of the functions in every B_i does not exceed arity r. We compute $M_{(u,v)}$ from P by summing all functions in every partition and project out from each resulting function the variables not mentioned by node v. The MCTE(r) algorithm is obtained replacing line 3 of the CTE algorithm by the following lines,

3.1 $P \leftarrow partitioning(B, r)$;
3.2 $M_{(u,v)} \leftarrow \{(\sum_{f \in B_i} f) \Downarrow elim(u,v) | B_i \in P\}$;

MCTE(r) time complexity is $O((|C| + |V|).deg.d^r)$ and space is $O(|V|.d^r)$.

3 Function Filtering

A *nogood* is a tuple t that cannot be extended into a complete consistent assignment. Nogoods are useless for solution generation, so they can be eliminated as soon as are detected.

Typically, a cost function f is stored in an array T_f, where tuples t are the indexes and $T_f[t]$ stores $f(t)$, the cost of t. The space used by T_f is $\Theta(\prod_{i \in var(f)} |D_i|)$. Costs can be retrieved in constant time. An alternative is to store function f as a set S_f containing all pairs $(t, f(t))$ with cost less than k, $S_f = \{(t, f(t)) | t \in \prod_{x_i \in var(f)} D_i, f(t) < k\}$. We define the *size* of a function f, denoted $|f|$, as the number of tuples with cost less than k. The space used by S_f is $\Theta(|f|)$, which can be smaller than the space of T_f if f contains many inconsistent tuples. If S_f is implemented as a hash table, $f(t)$ can be retrieved in constant time.

In the following, we will assume that functions are stored as sets of pairs. Then, computing $f \Downarrow_x$ has time complexity $O(|f|)$. Regarding the sum of two functions $f + g$, there are two basic ways to compute it: (i) iterate over all the combinations of $(t, f(t)) \in S_f$ and $(t', g(t')) \in S_g$ and, if they match, compute $(t \cdot t', f(t) \oplus g(t'))$, which has complexity $O(|f||g|)$, and (ii) compute every tuple t over $var(f) \cup var(g)$ and retrieve from S_f and S_g the $f(t)$ and $g(t)$ values, which has complexity $O(exp(|var(f) \cup var(g)|))$. Since one can choose the best option beforehand, the cost is $O(\min\{|f||g|, exp(|var(f) \cup var(g)|)\})$. Observe that the efficiency of computing the previous operations depends on the size of the functions.

We now introduce the *function filtering* operation, which allows us to reduce the size of a function f before operating with it. The idea is to anticipate the detection of nogoods of f in order to remove them from S_f as soon as possible.

Definition 7. *The* function filtering *operation applied to a function f from a set of functions H, noted $\overline{f}^H$, is the process of performing a consistency test to every tuple t of f after adding the contribution of every function in H. Every tuple that reaches the upper bound k is removed from S_f.*

$$\overline{f}^H(t) = \begin{cases} f(t) & if \left(\bigoplus_{h \in H} h(t) \right) \oplus f(t) < k \\ k & otherwise \end{cases}$$

Suppose that we know that f will be eventually summed with g. If there is a tuple $t, (t, f(t)) \in S_f$ such that $t \cdot t'$ will become a nogood after the sum for any $t', (t', g(t')) \in S_g$, we can safely remove $(t, f(t))$ from S_f right away. The following Property formalizes the previous observation.

Property 4. Let f (resp. g) be a function and F (resp. G) a lower bound. When summing f and g, if previously we filter each function with the lower bound of the other function, the result is preserved. Namely,

$$\overline{f}^G + \overline{g}^F = f + g$$

Besides, the sum is done with functions of smaller size. Thus, it is presumably done more efficiently.

Example 2. Consider node u of tree decomposition of example 1 with $\psi_u = \{f_1, f_2\}$. Potentially $|f_1| = 26^4$ but as we record consistent tuples only ($k = \infty$) we have $|f_1| = |f_2| = 8$. They do not share any variable so $|f_1 + f_2| = 64$. If we set $k = 5$, this causes that some tuples of f_1 and f_2 become nogoods and they can be eliminated. Now, $|f_1| = 3$, $|f_2| = 4$. To make $|f_1 + f_2| = 8$, we need $3 * 4 = 12$ operations. To use Property 4, we take as G the set formed by the function $f_2 \Downarrow \{x_7, x_8, x_9\}$, that is, $G = \{f_2 \Downarrow \{x_7, x_8, x_9\}\} = \{1\}$ (G is a lower bound of f_2 by Property 1). $|\overline{f_1}^G| = 2$. Filtering with G allows us to add 1 to every tuple of f_1, which causes that tuple $(four, 4)$ becomes a nogood (it reaches $k = 5$) and can be eliminated. Therefore, we only need $2 * 4 = 8$ operations to compute the sum.

The following property shows that filtering functions can be safely brought inside summations, anticipating the detection of nogoods and reducing the size of functions.

Property 5. Let f and g be two functions and H a set of functions, $f \notin H, g \notin H$:

$$\overline{f+g}^H = \overline{f}^H + \overline{g}^H$$

Example 3. We show an application of the previous property:

Take H as a lower bound of a function h that has to be added with f and g. In the example 1 solved by CTE, functions f_1 and f_2 of node u have to be added with $m_{(v,u)}$. Functions in node v projecting out variables in $elim(v, u)$ form a set that is a lower bound of $m_{(v,u)}$ (see Properties 1 and 2). So we take $H = \{f_3 \Downarrow \{x_0, x_5\}, f_4 \Downarrow \{x_6\}\}$:

$f_3 \Downarrow_{\{x_0,x_5\}}$	x_2 x_7
0	e o
1	r z
4	o r
5	u f
5	i e
6	v f
10	n n

$f_4 \Downarrow_{x_6}$	x_4 x_9
1	o e
2	e o
2	t o
3	o t
6	s x
7	x s
10	t n
11	n t

To compute $\overline{f_1 + f_2}^H$, we first compute $f_1 + f_2$. Since they have no variables in common $|f_1+f_2| = 64$. Applying filtering with H, we realize that values z, r, f for

x_4 are not permitted by $f_4 \Downarrow_{x_6}$, so all tuples including them are eliminated (32 tuples). We also realize that values t, s, x are not permitted by $f_3 \Downarrow_{\{x_0, x_5\}}$, so all remaining tuples including them are eliminated (16 tuples). Now $|\overline{f_1 + f_2}^H| = 16$. As Property 5 says, we could realize this fact by filtering functions f_1 and f_2 in advance, and then filtering their sum. Filtering f_1 removes tuples with forbidden values for x_4, $|\overline{f_1}^H| = 4$, and filtering f_2 removes tuples with forbidden values for x_7, $|\overline{f_2}^H| = 4$. Then, $|\overline{f_1}^H + \overline{f_2}^H| = 16$, and additional filtering causes no removals. So the application of Property 5 allows us to save $64 - 16 = 48$ tuples, a 75% of the initial memory.

Previous discussion implicitly assumes $k = \infty$. Lower values of k causes further savings. For instance, let us assume $k = 5$. Then, $|f_1 + f_2| = 8$. Filtering with H causes to remove all tuples with z for x_4 and t for x_7 (5 tuples). In addition, the cost of two tuples reaches k so they are eliminated. Now, $|\overline{f_1 + f_2}^H| = 1$. Applying Property 5, we first filter f_1 and f_2 with H, which leaves a single tuple in each function $|\overline{f_1}^H| = |\overline{f_2}^H| = 1$, and additional filtering causes no removals. So the application of Property 5 allows us to save $8 - 1 = 7$ tuples, a 87% of the initial memory.

4 CTE and MCTE with Function Filtering

Now we integrate the idea of filtering into the CTE schema. First, we define a *filtering* tree-decomposition which adds a new labelling ϕ to a tree-decomposition that will be used for filtering purposes.

Definition 8. *A filtering tree-decomposition of a WCSP is a tuple $\langle T, \chi, \psi, \phi \rangle$ where:*

- $\langle T, \chi, \psi \rangle$ *is a tree-decomposition as in definition 5.*
- ϕ *is a labelling. $\phi(u, v)$ is a set of functions associated to edge $(u, v) \in E$ with scope included in $sep(u, v)$. $\phi(u, v)$ must be a lower bound of the corresponding $m_{(u,v)}$ CTE message (namely, $\phi(u, v) \leq m_{(u,v)}$).*

The new algorithms CTEf and MCTEf(r) use a filtering tree decomposition. They are essentially equivalent to CTE and MCTE(r) except in that they use $\phi(u, v)$ for filtering functions before computing the message $m_{(u,v)}$ or $M_{(u,v)}$. The pseudo-code of CTEf is obtained by replacing line 3 of the algorithm by line,

3     $m_{(u,v)} \leftarrow \overline{\sum_{f \in B} f}^{\phi(u,v)} \Downarrow_{elim(u,v)};$

Besides, the computation of the new line 3, will make discretional use of Property 5. Similarly for MCTEf(r) we replace line 3 by two lines,

3.1 $P \leftarrow partitioning(B, r);$
3.2 $M_{(u,v)} \leftarrow \{\overline{(\sum_{f \in B_i} f)}^{\phi(u,v)} \Downarrow_{elim(u,v)} |B_i \in P\};$

procedure IMCTE($\langle X, D, C, k \rangle, \langle \langle V, E \rangle, \chi, \psi \rangle$)
1 **for each** $(u,v) \in E$ **do** $\phi(u,v) := \{\emptyset\}$;
2 $r := 1$;
3 **repeat**
4 $\quad$ MCTEf(r);
5 $\quad$ **for each** $(u,v) \in E$ **do** $\phi(u,v) := M_{(u,v)}$;
6 $\quad$ $r := r + 1$;
7 **until** exact solution or exhausted resources

Fig. 4. The IMCTE algorithm. $\langle X, D, C, k \rangle$ is a WCSP instance and $\langle \langle V, E \rangle, \chi, \psi \rangle$ is its tree decomposition.

The effectiveness of the new algorithms will depend on the ability of finding good lower bounds $\phi(u,v)$ for the messages $m_{(u,v)}$ (resp. $M_{(u,v)}$). If we use dummy lower bounds (i.e, $\phi(u,v) = \emptyset$, for all $(u,v) \in E$), CTEf (resp. MCTEf(r)) is clearly equivalent to CTE (resp. MCTE(r)). It is important to note that the algorithms will be correct as long as $\phi(u,v)$ is a true lower bound which can be computed with either a domain-specific or general technique (see [5] [4] [7] for a collection of general lower bound techniques). An option is to include in $\phi(u,v)$ all the original functions used to compute $m_{(v,u)}$ properly projected,

$$\phi(u,v) = \{f \Downarrow_S \mid f \in \psi(w), w \in T(u,v), S = var(f) - \chi(u)\}$$

Our CTEf and MCTEf implementations use this lower bound. Another option for CTEf is to include in $\phi(u,v)$ a message $M_{(v,u)}$ from a previously computed execution of MCTE(r). When we apply the previous idea to MCTEf, we obtain a recursive algorithm which naturally produces an elegant iterative approximating method that we call iterative MCTEf (IMCTEf). The idea is to execute MCTEf(r) using as lower bounds $\phi(u,v)$ the messages $M^{r-1}_{(v,u)}$ computed by MCTEf($r-1$) which, recursively, uses the messages $M^{r-2}_{(v,u)}$ computed by MCTEf($r-2$), an so on. Algorithm 4 develops this idea. Starting from dummy lower bounds (line 1), we execute MCTEf(r) for increasing values of r (line 4). The lower bounds computed by MCTEf(r) will be used to detect and filter nogoods during the execution of MCTEf($r+1$) (line 5). The algorithm follows this process until the exact solution is computed (namely, MCTEf does not break messages into smaller functions), or the available resources are exhausted.

5 Experimental Results

Experiments are focused in two aspects:

1. Showing that CTEf versus state of the art CTE uses less tuples to find the exact solution.
2. Inside an approximation schema we show that MCTEf(r), exhausts resources at a smaller r and finds worst LB than the iterative version IMCTEf where the previous messages of MCTEf(r) execution are used as filters.

Table 1. Columns are: instance, number of variables, number of constraints, maximum domain size, maximum separator size, tuples consumed by CTE algorithm, tuples consumed by CTEf algorithm (- denotes exhausted memory), arity r reached by MCTE(r), LB computed by MCTE(r), arity r reached by IMCTEf, LB computed by IMCTE (before resources exhausted), optimal UB of the problem. When marked with (*) means that the instance is optimally by at least one of the algorithms.

							MCTEf(r)		IMCTEf		
	$|X|$	$|C|$	d	sep	CTE	CTEf	r	LB	r	LB	UB
dubois100	75	200	2	3	3k	2k					1*
wp2100	50	95	2	9	6k	1k					16*
wp2150	50	138	2	15	302k	40k					34*
wp2200	50	186	2	19	-	733k					69*
wp2250	50	233	2	24	-	-	23	71	25	96	96*
wp2300	50	261	2	26	-	-	22	84	26	132	132*
wp2350	50	302	2	30	-	-	21	129	21	159	212
wp2400	50	340	2	30	-	-	20	70	20	137	212
wp2450	50	378	2	31	-	-	20	130	20	187	257
wp2500	50	418	2	34	-	-	20	168	20	251	318
spot54	67	271	4	11	754k	16k					37*
spot29	82	462	4	14	-	63k					8059*
spot503	143	635	4	8	-	34k					11113*
spot404	100	710	4	20	-	306k					115*
spot505	240	2242	4	22	-	-	12	8044	15	19217	21254
spot42	190	1394	4	26	-	-	13	116001	15	127050	155051

We have tested CTE, CTEf, MCTEf(r) and IMCTEf on DIMACS dubois Max-Sat instances, Borchers Weigthed Max-Sat (can be obtained at [2]) instances and SPOT instances (described in [12]). Tree decompositions where computed using the ToolBar library (available at [1]) that implements a min fill heuristic for this purpose and visualized with LEDA library.

The efficiency of inference algorithms strongly relies on achieving a good tree decomposition of the problem, ideally one with small maximum separator size, the bottleneck of CTE based algorithms. The number of edges of the decomposition is important for IMCTE algorithm because it has to store all the messages in both directions. Two instances and its corresponding tree decompositions are drawn in figure 6.

State of the art CTE always assumes that the memory spent by the algorithm is always equal to the worst case d^s for every sent message. So here we assume that we always use the upper bound of the problem to filter tuples. We want to prove that assuming that functions only store consistent tuples with the joint effect of applying filtering techniques to anticipate inconsistent tuples, the memory stored in the solving process is actually much less than the worst

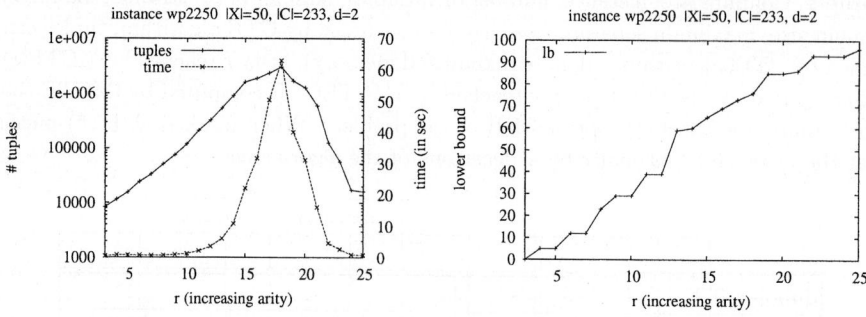

Fig. 5. IMCTEf execution in Borchers instance wp2250. On the left, y-axis is the total number of computed tuples and time respectively. On the right, y-axis is the lower bound achieved for each arity r.

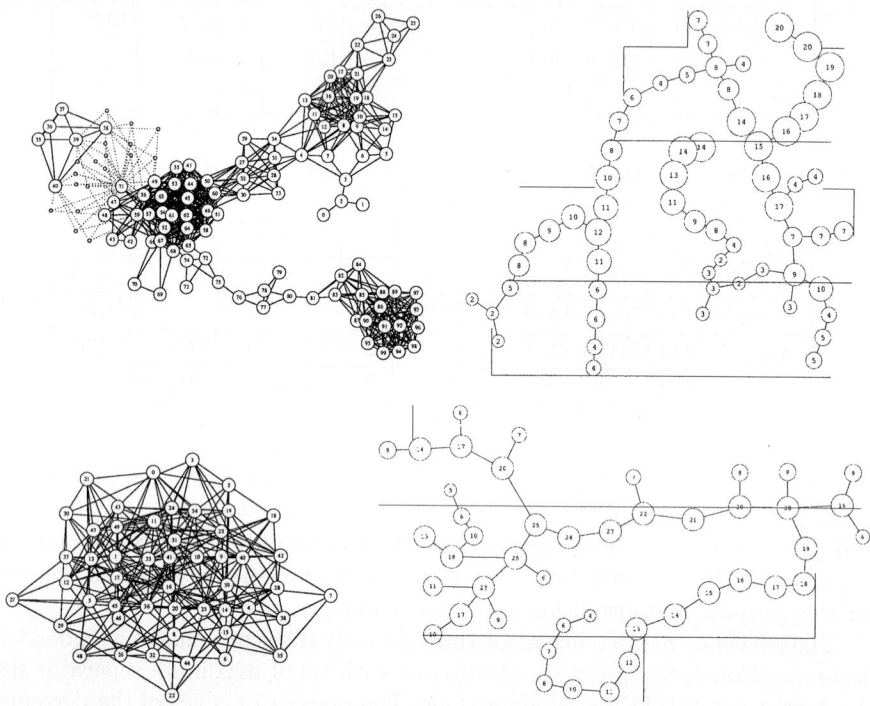

Fig. 6. On the left column visualization of the SPOT404 and wp2250 instances where small dots represent ternary constraints. On the right column the corresponding tree decomposition where each node is drawn proportionally to the number of variables $|\chi(v)|$ which is plotted inside the node.

case space complexity assumed by usual CTE. When d^s is small usual CTE is feasible. For example in dubois100 we have $2^3 = 8$ and we can hardly see the improvement of CTEf. In instances where both CTE and CTEf are feasible (see the first Borcher's and first SPOT instances) the latter solves the problem with one order of magnitude less tuples. As the separator size increases CTE becomes at some point infeasible. This happens in wp2200 where we have $d^s = 2^{19}$ and however CTEf is still feasible spending 733k tuples. In instances wp2250 and wp2300 an interesting thing happens; neither CTE nor CTEf can solve them, but the iterative version IMCTEf can solve it. In figure 5 the execution of the algorithm is plotted for instance wp2250. Each new execution with a bigger arity uses the previous computed messages as filtering functions. The total number of tuples for a particular execution is computed summing all the tuples of the sent messages. We can see that there is a critical arity where a maximum of tuples is generated. Iterations corresponding to last r's generate less tuples, this is due to the good increasing quality of previous messages. On the right of the same figure the computed lower bound for each arity is plotted.

When the separator size increases and instances cannot be optimally solved by any algorithm (CTE, CTEf, MCTEf, IMCTEf) the latter approximates the problem with a higher lower bound in all cases and reaches a higher arity in some of them.

When sending a particular message an important fact is how we sum all the available functions for that message. The direct way is to sum them two by two if the arity limit permits, applying filtering at each sum with all possible available filters. We must be careful with summing first functions with low cost, because they can quickly exhaust memory since almost no tuple will reach the level to be detected as inconsistent. So at this point some heuristics have been tested to select the pairs of functions to be summed. The two giving the best results are the following ones: (i) minimize mean cost of function tuples and (ii) minimum arity of the generated function. When minimum arity coincides then we minimize cost.

6 Conclusions

We have presented the idea of function filtering for WCSP case, where constraints are cost functions, inside a complete inference schema. This idea has been nicely combined with tree decomposition algorithms, producing new algorithms which experimentally require far less memory than their original counterparts. This represent an important step forward the practical applicability of complete inference for WCSP solving.

So far, the use of upper and lower bounds for WCSP solving was limited to search methods, namely branch-and-bound search. This is the first time that are used inside complete inference methods, to speed up their execution and to reduce their memory consumption. As results show, this combination has been quite beneficial. Combining other inference methods with bounds usage seems a promising line of research and deserves further exploration in the future.

References

1. http://carlit.toulouse.inra.fr/cgi-bin/awki.cgi/softcsp.
2. http://www.nmt.edu/~borchers/maxsat.html.

3. U. Bertele and F. Brioschi. *Nonserial Dynamic Programming.* AC. Press, 1972.
4. B. Cabon, S. Givry, and G. Verfaillie. Anytime lower bounds for constraint violation minimization problems. In *Proceedings of the 4th Conference on Principles and Practice of Constraint Programming*, volume 1520, pages 117–131, 1998.
5. S. de Givry, G. Verfaillie, and T. Schiex. Bounding the optimum of constraint optimization problems. In *Proceedings of the 3th Conference on Principles and Practice of Constraint Programming*, pages 405–419, Schloss Hagenberg, Austria.
6. R Dechter. *Constraint Processing.* Elsevier, 2003.
7. R. Dechter, K. Kask, and J. Larrosa. A general scheme for multiple lower bound computation in constraint optimization. In *Proceedings of the 6th Conference on Principles and Practice of Constraint Programming*, pages 346–360, 2001.
8. R. Dechter and J. Pearl. Network-based heuristics for constraint satisfaction problems. *Artificial Intelligence*, 34:1–38, 1987.
9. R. Dechter and J. Pearl. Tree clustering for constraints networks. *Artifical Intelligence*, 38, 1989.
10. Rina Dechter. Bucket elimination: A unifying framework for reasoning. *Artifical Intelligence*, 113:41–85, 1999.
11. D.Larkin and R.Dechter. Bayesian inference in the presence of determinism. 2003.
12. E.Bensana, M.Lemaitre, and G.Verfaillie. Earth observation satellite management. *Constraints*, 4:293–299, 1999.
13. J.Larrosa. Node and arc consistency in weighted csp. In *Proc. AAAI*, 2002.
14. J.Larrosa, E.Morancho, and D.Niso. On the practical applicability of bucket elimination: Still-life as a case study. *Journal of Artificial Intelligence Research*, 2005.
15. J. Larrosa and T. Schiex. Solving weighted csp by maintaining arc consistency. *Artificial Intelligence*, 159, 2004.
16. M. Sanchez, P. Meseguer, and J. Larrosa. Improving the applicability of adaptive consistency. In *Proceedings of the 10th Conference on Principles and Practice of Constraint Programming*, Toronto, Canda, 2004.

On Solving Soft Temporal Constraints Using SAT Techniques

Hossein M. Sheini, Bart Peintner, Karem A. Sakallah, and Martha E. Pollack

University of Michigan, Ann Arbor, MI 48109, USA
{hsheini, bpeintne, karem, pollackm}@eecs.umich.edu

Abstract. In this paper, we present an algorithm for finding utilitarian optimal solutions to Simple and Disjunctive Temporal Problems with Preferences (STPPs and DTPPs) based on Benders' decomposition and adopting SAT techniques. In our approach, each temporal constraint is replaced by a Boolean *indicator* variable and the decomposed problem is solved by a tightly integrated STP solver and SAT solver. Several hybridization techniques that take advantage of each solver's strengths are introduced. Finally, empirical evidence is presented to demonstrate the effectiveness of our method compared to other algorithms.

1 Introduction

Temporal Constraint Satisfaction Problems (TCSPs) [1] are a subclass of constraint satisfaction problems that model constraints over variables with temporal domains. Several TCSP subproblems have been used successfully as components in planning and scheduling applications such as NASA's Mars Rover [2] and Autominder [3]. In planning and scheduling domains, the variables in TCSPs represent events to be scheduled or executed by an agent, and the constraints specify allowable times and temporal differences between those events. The main task for these systems, when given a TCSP, is to assign to all variables times that respect all constraints.

Over the last decade, efficient algorithms have been developed for reasoning about TCSP subproblems, which include Simple Temporal Problems (STPs)[1], Binary TCSPs (bTCSPs) [1] and Disjunctive Temporal Problems (DTPs) [4,5,6]. The most expressive of these, the DTP, has received considerable attention due to its ability to express relationships found in temporal planning problems.

Recent efforts have extended STPs and DTPs to include soft constraints, or preferences [7,8,9,10,11]. Preferences, which are represented as functions that map temporal assignments to a *local preference value*, denote how well an assignment satisfies the constraint to which it is attached. By aggregating the local preference values, the value of the entire set of assignments (a solution) can be quantified. Preferences change the problem to one of finding *optimal* solutions, i.e., solutions that maximize the aggregated preference value. Three different types of aggregation have been explored in the STP case, which result in three types of optimality: maximin optimality, where the lowest local preference value is maximized; utilitarian optimality, where the sum of local preference values is maximized; and stratified egalitarian optimality, where the Pareto-optimal maximin solution is found. For the DTP case, only a solution for the maximin case has been published [10][1]. In this paper, we present a single solution to the problems of finding utilitarian-optimal solutions to both STPs with Preferences (STPPs) and DTPs with Preferences (DTPPs).

To solve STPPs and DTPPs, we adapt a recent SAT-based algorithm [15] designed for solving Mixed Logical Linear Programming (MLLP) problems involving two types of constraints: logical constraints over Boolean variables, and Unit-Two-Variable-Per-inequality (UTVPI) integer constraints of the form $ax - by \leq d$, where $a, b \in \{-1, 0, 1\}$. The temporal constraints of the form $x - y \leq d$, where x and y represent times assigned to events, and d is a real bound on their temporal difference, can be safely solved using the same UTVPI solver of [15]. This algorithm is implemented in the Ario Satisfiability Modulo Theories (SMT) Solver [16]. To encode the STPPs and DTPPs as MLLPs, we adopt a recent strategy for approximating preference functions in an STPP or DTPP with a set of temporal difference constraints [11] and show how to encode the relationships between the temporal constraints and the logical constraints. The result is an MLLP SAT problem with an objective function. We adapt the SAT-based algorithm of Ario to reason about the objective function and exploit the structure in the STPPs and DTPPs.

This paper presents the first algorithm (to our knowledge) for finding utilitarian-optimal solutions to DTPPs. While this is the main contribution of the paper, we emphasize that the DTPP is a restricted form of the problems solvable by our algorithm. Adding non-temporal logical constraints requires no modification. In fact, Ario is optimized to handle them, having been built on the recent advances in SAT solvers. In the future work section, we discuss other uses for the solver.

2 Background

A Simple Temporal Problem (STP) is a pair $\langle X, C \rangle$, where X is a set of events, and C is a set of temporal constraints of the form: $x - y \in [c, d]$, $x, y \in X$ and $c, d \in \Re$. Often, STP constraints are single-bounded, i.e. in the form $x - y \leq d$. The dual-bounded version can be represented as a pair of single-bounded constraints: $x - y \leq d \wedge y - x \leq -c$. While there is no difference in the expressive power of STPs that use the single- or dual-bounded constraints, the dual-bounded variety are more convenient when preferences are involved.

An STP *solution* is an assignment of times to events that satisfies all constraints. An STP is *consistent* if at least one solution exists. Checking consistency requires $O(|X|^3)$ time, using an all-pairs shortest path algorithm.

To extend an STP to an STPP, each constraint is assigned a preference function that maps a temporal difference between the constraint's events to a

---

[1] Tractable DTP subproblems have been identified [12,13], as have tractable instances of soft constraint problems [14]. However, in this paper, we are interested in arbitrary DTPs with preferences–a more expressive, but intractable class of problems.

preference value, a quantitative measure of the difference's desirability. STPP constraints thus have the form: $\langle x - y \in [a,b], f : t \in [a,b] \rightarrow \{0, \Re+\}\rangle$.

As noted above, once preference functions are added, the challenge becomes one of finding an *optimal* solution. We evaluate a solution with an objective function that aggregates the values from each constraint's preference function. In this paper, we use the *sum* function, which results in *utilitarian* optimality.

A DTP is also described as a pair $\langle X, C \rangle$, only each constraint is a disjunction of the STP constraints just described. A DTP *solution* is an assignment of times to events that satisfy at least one disjunct of all constraints. A DTP is *consistent* if at least one solution exists. Checking the consistency of a DTP is NP-Hard, but recent techniques have substantially improved their average-case performance.

We extend a DTP to a DTPP by adding a preference function to the disjuncts in each constraint. If multiple disjuncts in a constraint are satisfied by a solution, the constraint's local preference value is taken from the highest valued disjunct.

3 Motivating Example

We describe a very simple example of an STPP based on the Mars rover domain [9], taken directly from [11]. We then extend the example to the DTPP case and discuss why the DTPP case is so much more difficult.

The daily plan for a Mars rover must satisfy a set of constraints that ensure the safety of the rover while maximizing the scientific value of the experiments it performs. Imagine a very simple scenario in which two events need to be optimally scheduled: the start- and end-time of a single experiment (events S and E). The experiment can begin immediately after the instrument it requires becomes available (event A, set to time 0), but it is preferable that some time separates A and S to allow the instrument to cool. This preference is expressed as MC1 (Mars constraint 1) in Figure 1(a); the horizontal axis represents the difference between events A and S, while the vertical axis represents the preference value assigned to each temporal difference.

The scientific value of the experiment changes irregularly with time spent running it (E-S), but is mitigated by the instrument's significant power usage. The net value is expressed by the function in Figure 1(b). Finally, since other experiments can begin once the current experiment ends, it is preferred that the experiment finish as early as possible. Figure 1(c) expresses this relationship.

A legal solution in this example is one in which $E < 12$ and $1 \leq E - S < 7$; that is, one in which all preference functions map to a nonnegative value. For

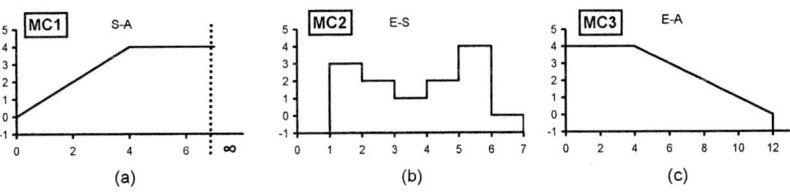

Fig. 1. Example preference functions for the Mars Rover example

a solution $\{A = 0, S = 3, E = 6\}$, constraints MC1, MC2, and MC3 have respective preference values 3, 1, and 3, for a utilitarian value of 7. An optimal solution, with a utilitarian value 10, is $\{A = 0, S = 4, E = 5\}$.

Notice that even with such a trivial example, it is not immediately apparent whether a given solution is optimal. In fact, unless all preference functions are convex, the problem of finding the optimal solution is NP-Hard.

Extending to the DTPP case makes the problem even more difficult. Imagine that the number of experiments to schedule in our Mars rover example increases from one to three: the one originally described (which uses the same instrument as the previous experiment), and two others that use a second instrument. The three experiments can be executed in any order, but they cannot overlap. Therefore, three constraints are needed to express that each pair cannot overlap, i.e. DTPP constraints are needed to express sentiments such as "Experiment 1 can end before Experiment 2 begins or start after Experiment 2 ends" and to designate which option is more preferable.

Whereas the STPP case had only a single ordering possible for the events to be scheduled, the new situation allows six different orderings for the experiments. If we were scheduling four experiments, the six disjunctive constraints needed would allow 24 different orderings. This exponential increase in possible orderings is intuitive evidence of why finding utilitarian optimal solutions to DTPPs is so much more difficult than the STPP case.

4   Solving MLLPs

Mixed Logical Linear Programming (MLLP) problems [17] consist of logical constraints over Boolean variables and temporal difference constraints over temporal variables, i.e. STP constraints. Disjunctions involving both Boolean variables and STP constraints allow the representation of conditional STP constraints.

One common method for solving an MLLP problem is Benders' Decomposition [18], which partitions the problem into a master subproblem containing only Boolean variables and logical formulas, and a subproblem containing the STP constraints. The two subproblems are linked using indicator variables, which are Boolean variables that represent whether a particular STP constraint is asserted. Every reference to an STP constraint in the original problem is replaced with the constraint's indicator variable, converting all disjunctions that involve temporal constraints into pure Boolean formulas. An MLLP solution is an assignment to all variables, Boolean and temporal, in which all constraints are satisfied.

A simple MLLP containing 2 Boolean variables, 3 STP constraints, and 3 logical constraints is listed below, along with its Benders' decomposition:

MLLP	Benders' decomposition	
$A_1 \vee (x - y \leq 3)$	$A_1 \vee B_1$	
$y - z \leq 5$	B_2	Boolean subproblem
$\neg A_1 \vee \neg A_2 \vee (y - x \leq 5)$	$\neg A_1 \vee \neg A_2 \vee B_3$	
	$B_1 \rightarrow (x - y \leq 3)$	
	$B_2 \rightarrow (y - z \leq 5)$	STP subproblem
	$B_3 \rightarrow (y - x \leq 5)$	

In the most straight-forward application of Benders' decomposition, the two subproblems are solved separately. First, a SAT solver finds a consistent set of assignments for all Boolean variables. Then, all STP constraints whose indicator variables are set to true are gathered and checked for consistency. If the set of STP constraints is consistent, then a solution is found and the algorithm exits. If inconsistent, the set of STP constraints causing the inconsistency is determined. Since the set of inconsistent STP constraints cannot participate in any solution, they represent a conflict, which can be encoded as a clause in the Boolean part (known as a Benders' Cut). The conflict clause states that the combination of indicator variables associated with those STP constraints cannot all be true at once. The process continues, attempting to find an alternative solution to the Boolean subproblem augmented with the Benders' Cut.

Despite the fact that satisfiability checking is NP-complete, recent enhancements in modern backtrack SAT algorithms have made them very efficient and scalable. At a high-level, SAT solvers operate by assigning values to the Boolean variables and detecting possible implications and conflicts caused by the assigned values. The SAT problem is encoded in *Conjunctive Normal Form*, which is a conjunction of clauses. A clause is the disjunction of literals, and a literal is a Boolean variable or its negation. Upon assigning a literal, consequent implications are detected by adopting a *two-watched-literal* strategy where each clause is only propagated if one of its two *watched* literals is assigned to false [19]. In case of a conflict, where all literals in a clause are false, a new clause is learned to prevent the conflict from being encountered again. Conflict analysis is performed by backward traversal of the implication graph that can result in non-chronological backtracking. For more details, the reader is referred to [20].

4.1 Integrated Solving

A recent algorithm has improved performance by solving both subproblems together. The algorithm, found in [15] and implemented in the Ario SMT solver [16] (hereafter, the Ario algorithm), tightly integrates both solvers.

In this algorithm, each time an assignment is made to a Boolean indicator variable during search, its corresponding STP constraint is activated and checked for consistency with other activated STP constraints. This is achieved using the incremental algorithm of Jaffar et. al. [21] for solving problems involving UTVPI integer constraints, which are slightly more general than STP constraints. Each time a new STP constraint is added to the STP solver, it generates a set of new STP constraints that are implied by the addition. For instance, adding the STP constraint $y - z \leq d_2$ to the set $\{x - y \leq d_1\}$ will result in generating the implied STP constraint $x - z \leq d_1 + d_2$. If a newly generated STP constraint is equivalent to or stronger than the STP constraint implied by an indicator variable, the indicator variable is assigned to true. Any conflict detected in the activated STP constraints can be encoded as a clause on the Boolean side. However, given that the integrated solver checks the consistency of the temporal side as it makes assignments, such conflicts will often be found much sooner.

4.2 Encoding a DTP as an MLLP

DTPs (and by extension STPs) can be directly encoded as MLLP problems. DTPs are simply MLLPs that do not include any Boolean variables. During Benders' decomposition, each disjunct i of DTP constraint k, denoted $C_{\langle k,i \rangle}$, is given an indicator variable $B_{\langle k,i \rangle}$ on the Boolean side, and the disjunctive constraint will have the Boolean form of $\bigvee_i B_{\langle k,i \rangle}$.

The MLLP algorithm of Ario bears a strong resemblance to the meta-CSP concept used by many DTP solvers. To create the meta-CSP of a DTP, a CSP variable is created for each DTP constraint; the domain of the CSP variable includes one value for each disjunct in the DTP constraint. During search, assignments are made to the meta-CSP variables. After a variable is assigned a value, the disjunct associated with that value (i.e. an STP constraint) is added to an incremental STP solver, much like the Jaffar solver mentioned above. This act resembles the process of assigning an indicator variable to true and adding the indicated STP constraint to the Jaffar solver.

Given the strong similarity of the two methods, it is unsurprising that many techniques in one apply to the other. In fact, many of the efficiency techniques used to prune the search of Meta-CSPs have an analogue in the Ario algorithm. For example, the method of incorporating conflicts detected on the STP side into the Boolean side has a CSP analogue called no-good learning. A method called *removal of subsumed variables* in DTP solvers identifies disjuncts that are already satisfied (without being inserted into the STP solver) and assigns them to their meta-CSP variables. This technique is an integral part of the Ario algorithm, which sets indicator variables to true when the STP constraints they imply are subsumed by the implied constraints discovered by the STP solver.

These techniques help reduce the role of the relatively slow STP solver by shifting more work toward the efficient SAT solver. When describing our modifications to the Ario algorithm, we will show how to incorporate another technique found in DTP solvers, called *semantic branching*.

5 Solving DTPPs

To extend Ario's MLLP algorithm into a DTPP solver, we address three issues: how to represent arbitrary preference functions in an MLLP; how to convert the solver from a *satisfaction* algorithm to an *optimization* algorithm; and how to improve performance by taking advantage of the structure of DTPPs.

5.1 Encoding Preference Functions as an MLLP

In the preceding section, we described how STP constraints are linked to Boolean variables using the conditional form of $B_i \rightarrow x - y \leq d$. We can use the same mechanism to reason about arbitrary preference functions. In other words, we can represent a DTPP with arbitrary preference functions as an MLLP.

If the preference functions are restricted to be convex, they can be easily represented (or at least approximated) by a set of linear functions [9]. However,

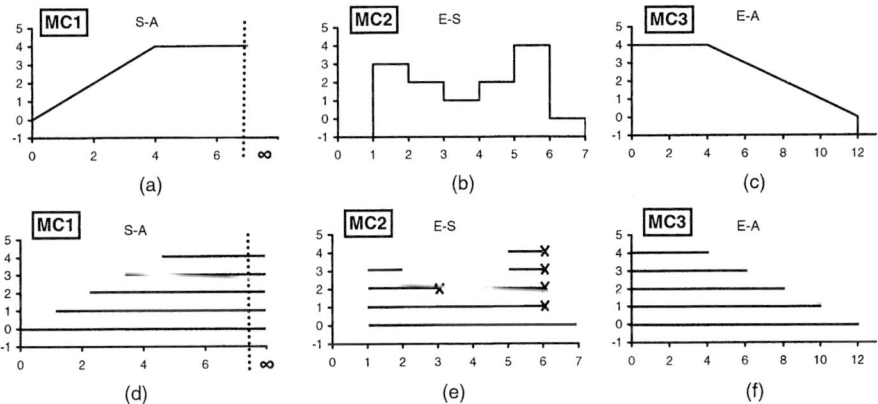

Fig. 2. The preference projections for each constraint in the Mars rover example (see Section 3). Each line segment at level l represents intervals for which the value of the preference function is l or greater. "X" marks ends of open intervals.

when arbitrary, non-convex preference functions exist (such as the one in Figure 2(b)), more complicated schemes are required. For our purposes, we adopt the scheme presented in [11], which approximates arbitrary preference functions using a set of hard STP constraints, called a *preference projection* [11][2]. After creating the preference projections, we assign an indicator variable to each element of the preference projection (i.e. to each hard STP constraint) and show how to define Boolean formulas that will ensure that any solution to the MLLP is a solution to the DTPP and vice-versa.

To obtain a preference projection for a DTPP constraint, we first discretize the range of its preference functions into a finite set of real values A, called a *preference value set* ($\{0, 1, 2, 3, 4\}$ in our Mars rover example). Then, we project each disjunct (STPP constraint) at each level $l \in A$ into a set of hard STP constraints. In the end, each function will be represented as a set of hard STP constraints. Again, we refer to disjunct i of DTPP constraint k as $C_{\langle k,i \rangle}$.

The projection of disjunct $C_{\langle k,i \rangle}$ at preference level l is a list of STP constraints representing the intervals at which $C_{\langle k,i \rangle}$ is satisfied at preference level l or higher. Figure 2(d)-(f) shows the preference projection for each constraint in our Mars rover example (Figure 2(a)-(c)). Each horizontal line segment in Figure 2(d)-(f) is an STP constraint in the preference projection. For example, the line segment at preference level 3 in Figure 1(f) denotes that if $0 \leq E - A \leq 6$, then the preference value for constraint MC3 will be 3 or greater.

Once we have a list of STP constraints for each disjunct of each DTPP constraint, we union the lists for all disjuncts that belong to the same DTPP constraint and level. Therefore, we end with a list of STP constraints for each level

---

[2] Although the method only approximates functions, the degree of approximation can be controlled by varying the number of preference levels.

and each DTPP constraint. The following two definitions formalize the idea of a preference projection for STPP and DTPP constraints.

Definition 1 (STPP Preference Projection). *(From [11]) Given an STPP constraint $C_{\langle k,i \rangle} = \langle x-y \in [a,b], f \rangle$, the **preference projection** at level l is $\mathcal{P}_{\langle k,i \rangle}[l] = \{c_1, c_2, \ldots, c_n\}$, where $c_p = \langle x - y \in [a_p, b_p] \rangle$, $b_p < a_{p+1}$ for $0 \leq p < n$ and $\bigcup_{p=1}^{n}[a_p, b_p] = \{t | f(t) \geq l\}$. The **STPP preference projection** is $\mathcal{P}_{\langle k,i \rangle} = \bigcup_{l \in A} \mathcal{P}_{\langle k,i \rangle}[l]$.*

That is, the preference projection at level l for an STPP constraint is the unique set of maximal intervals for which the constraint receives preference $\geq l$.

Definition 2 (DTPP Preference Projection). *Given a DTPP constraint $C_k = C_{\langle k,1 \rangle} \vee C_{\langle k,2 \rangle} \vee \ldots \vee C_{\langle k,n \rangle}$, the preference projection for C_k at level l is $\mathcal{P}_k[l] = \bigcup_{i=1}^{n} \mathcal{P}_{\langle k,i \rangle}[l]$. We refer to the set of all hard STP constraints projected from C_k using preference value set A as the **preference projection** for C_k, denoted $\mathcal{P}_k = \bigcup_{l \in A} \mathcal{P}_k[l]$.*

Thus, for each DTPP constraint C_k and each level l, the list of dual-bounded STP constraints is denoted as $\mathcal{P}_k[l]$. Using the definitions, we can show that if an assignment of times to each temporal variable satisfies at least one STP constraint in $\mathcal{P}_k[l]$, then DTPP constraint C_k will be satisfied at level l or greater. If we find the maximum l for which some STP constraint in $\mathcal{P}_k[l]$ is satisfied, we say that the assignment satisfies the DTPP constraint at level l. If we sum this value for all DTPP constraints in the problem, we have the utilitarian value of the assignment. Therefore, the utilitarian value of any assignment can be approximated[3] by finding the highest valued satisfied STP constraint in each DTPP constraint's preference projection.

We can define an indicator variable $B_{\langle k,l,p \rangle}$ to imply the pth element of $\mathcal{P}_k[l]$. Just as in the DTP case, a solution exists when at least one B variable for each DTPP constraint is "true" and the STP constraints implied by the true B variables represent a consistent STP. In terms of indicator variables, the following Boolean constraint must be satisfied: $\bigwedge_k \bigvee_l \bigvee_p B_{\langle k,l,p \rangle}$.

When preferences are present, we are not content with finding any assignment to the indicator variables that satisfies the above Boolean constraint; we want the assignment that maximizes an objective function. To prepare for encoding the objective function, we factor the above constraint by introducing an intermediate variable for each DTPP constraint and level: $B_{\langle k,l \rangle} = \bigvee_p B_{\langle k,l,p \rangle}$. In the next section, we show how to tie these intermediate variables to the objective function.

As an example, consider the preference projection for $MC2$ in Figure 2(e). There are 7 STP constraints in the projection: 1 at level 0, $B_{\langle 2,0,0 \rangle}$; 1 at level 1, $B_{\langle 2,1,0 \rangle}$; 2 at level 2, $B_{\langle 2,2,0 \rangle}$ and $B_{\langle 2,2,1 \rangle}$; 2 at level 3, $B_{\langle 2,3,0 \rangle}$ and $B_{\langle 2,3,1 \rangle}$; and 1 at level 4, $B_{\langle 2,4,0 \rangle}$. The Boolean constraints in the first column below represent this preference projection:

---

[3] Subject to the approximation error of the discretization process.

$B_{\langle 2,4\rangle} = B_{\langle 2,4,0\rangle}$	$M_{\langle 2,4\rangle} = B_{\langle 2,4\rangle}$
$B_{\langle 2,3\rangle} = B_{\langle 2,3,0\rangle} \lor B_{\langle 2,3,1\rangle}$	$M_{\langle 2,3\rangle} = B_{\langle 2,3\rangle} \land \neg B_{\langle 2,4\rangle}$
$B_{\langle 2,2\rangle} = B_{\langle 2,2,0\rangle} \lor B_{\langle 2,2,1\rangle}$	$M_{\langle 2,2\rangle} = B_{\langle 2,2\rangle} \land \neg B_{\langle 2,3\rangle}$
$B_{\langle 2,1\rangle} = B_{\langle 2,1,0\rangle}$	$M_{\langle 2,1\rangle} = B_{\langle 2,1\rangle} \land \neg B_{\langle 2,2\rangle}$
$B_{\langle 2,0\rangle} = B_{\langle 2,0,0\rangle}$	$M_{\langle 2,0\rangle} = B_{\langle 2,0\rangle} \land \neg B_{\langle 2,1\rangle}$

To ensure every DTPP constraint is satisfied, a final Boolean equivalent to the unfactored Boolean constraint above is required: $\bigwedge_k \bigvee_l B_{\langle k,l\rangle}$.

5.2 Finding the Optimal Solution to the MLLP

The optimal solution to a DTPP is an assignment of times to temporal variables that produces the highest utilitarian value. The utilitarian value is calculated by finding a true indicator variable from each DTPP constraint and summing their l values. If more than one indicator variable is true for a given DTPP constraint, the one with the maximum l value is used.

To find the maximum l value for each DTPP constraint k, we add Boolean constraints of the form $M_{\langle k,l\rangle} = B_{\langle k,l\rangle} \land \neg B_{\langle k,l+1\rangle}$, where the variable $M_{\langle k,l\rangle}$ becomes true if l is the highest level satisfied for constraint k[4]. The second column in the table above shows the M variables and constraints for our example.

The objective function for the optimization problem is therefore a sum consisting of one term for each level of each DTPP constraint: $l \cdot M_{\langle k,l\rangle}$. Thus, the objective function for the MLLP is the following: $\max \sum_k \sum_l l \cdot M_{\langle k,l\rangle}$.

We perform the optimization by solving a sequence of satisfaction problems. We encode the objective function as a special linear constraint: $\sum_k \sum_l l \cdot M_{\langle k,l\rangle} \geq lowerBound$, where $lowerBound$ is a constant that we increase after each problem in the sequence is solved. The search starts by solving the satisfaction problem in which $lowerBound$ is set to 0. If the solver finds a solution, and the objective evaluation of that solution is some value v, then we update the $lowerBound$ value in the special constraint to $v+1$, and re-solve the problem. At each iteration the lower bound is updated and the search terminates when the problem becomes unsatisfiable. The last satisfiable $lowerBound$ then will be the maximum value of the objective function.

5.3 Exploiting the DTPP Structure

Thus far, we have described a method for finding the optimal solution to a DTPP by encoding the STP constraints in the preference projection as an MLLP and by solving a sequence of MLLPs with a special constraint encoding the objective function. We now discuss how to take advantage of the structure of the DTPP and its objective function to improve performance.

---

[4] For each DTPP constraint's top-level M variable, the included Boolean constraint is $M_{\langle k,l\rangle} = B_{\langle k,l\rangle}$.

Semantic Branching. One method used by meta-CSP solvers that did not already exist in our MLLP solver is *semantic branching*. In semantic branching, as soon as the solver finds that enforcing an STP constraint cannot lead to any solution, it infers that the negation of that STP constraint should hold in any solution. Enforcing the negation of the STP constraint further prunes the search, possibly detecting dead ends in the search sooner than otherwise possible. In our method, each time an indicator variable for an STP constraint is set to false, the temporal solver can enforce the negation of the STP constraint. A similar method was also successfully used in another SAT-based DTP solver [6].

Relationships Among STP Constraints. STP constraints projected from a single DTPP disjunct are closely related. Note that each interval of a preference projection constraint is a subset of an interval in every level below it. Therefore, if a set of assignments satisfies a projected STP constraint at level l, then at least one STP constraint is satisfied at all lower levels. Conversely, if no STP constraint at level l is satisfied, then no STP constraint at any higher level can be satisfied. We encode this relationship using the Boolean formulas $\neg B_{(k,l)} \rightarrow \neg B_{(k,l+1)}$.

Efficient Processing of Objective Function. Each time a Boolean variable is assigned or unassigned, the value of the objective function may change. To avoid constantly updating the objective value, our algorithm instead monitors an *upper bound* for the objective function, which changes much less often. To calculate the upper bound, we first locate the highest non-false M variable for each DTPP constraint, i.e., the non-false M variable with the highest l value. We refer to this set as the *watched M* variables. Then, we sum the l value of all watched variables to produce the upper bound. The upper bound only needs to be updated when one of the watched M variables is assigned to false.

When the upper bound becomes equal to the *lowerBound* value in the objective function, all the corresponding watched variables should be implied to true. On the other hand, if the upper bound becomes less than *lowerBound*, a conflict is detected. The reason for the conflict is the set of M variables whose assignment to false resulted in the drop of the *watched-sum* below its *lowerBound*. The conflict set is passed to the SAT Solver as a new clause, and backtracking occurs. This method incorporates standard branch-and-bound concepts.

Pruning Using Slack. We use the difference between the upper and lower bounds to help prune the search. We use this difference, called the *slack*, to prune disjuncts that are projected from the lower preference levels. Consider our Mars Rover example and the case where the *lowerBound* = 8 and the watched variables are $M_{\langle 1,4 \rangle}$, $M_{\langle 2,2 \rangle}$ and $M_{\langle 3,4 \rangle}$. The upper bound in this case is 10 (4+2+4), resulting in a slack of 2. When choosing an indicator variable to assert in constraint 1, all indicator variables at level 1 or lower can be ignored because they would lower the upper bound by an amount greater than the available slack; therefore, we can safely assign false to the variables $M_{\langle 1,0 \rangle}$ and $M_{\langle 1,1 \rangle}$.

In general, any $M_{\langle k,l \rangle}$ variable will be assigned to false if it is detected that assigning $M_{\langle k,l \rangle}$ to true would prevent the sum in the objective function from reaching the lower bound. In short, if for some DTPP constraint k, the watched element of the objective function is $M_{\langle k, l^* \rangle}$, then all variables $M_{\langle k, l \rangle}$ in which $l < (l^* - slack)$, should be assigned to false.

When the lowest M variables are implied to false, it effectively raises the minimum level at which the DTPP constraint must be satisfied. In the above case, the minimum level was raised to 2. To encode this explicitly, we simply set $B_{\langle 3, 2 \rangle}$ to true. The same effect can be produced by adding a set of Boolean constraints of the form: $\bigwedge_{a=0}^{l} \neg M_{(k,a)} \rightarrow B_{(k,l+1)}$ to the problem.

6 Experimental Results

Our algorithm for optimally solving the DTPPs is incorporated into the SMT-solver Ario [16]. Its STP algorithm is a specialization of its UTVPI engine fully explained in [15]. All experiments were conducted on a Pentium-IV 2800MHz machine with 1 GB of RAM running Linux.

6.1 Generating Random DTPPs

For the tests described in this section, we generated random DTPPs using a set of parameters $\langle E, C, D_-, D_+, L, R_-, R_+, S \rangle$, where E is the number of events, C is the number of constraints, D_- and D_+ are the minimum and maximum bounds on any constraint, and the remaining elements define the preference functions.

We first generate a set of events $\{x_1, x_2, \ldots, x_E\}$. Then, we generate a set of C 2-disjunct DTP constraints (without preference functions) by creating one disjunct at a time. For each disjunct of each constraint, we randomly choose a pair of events, and then randomly choose an upper and lower bound for the temporal difference between the events from the interval $[D_-, D_+]$.

Once the hard DTP constraints are formed, we create a preference function for each disjunct. Instead of creating the functions directly, we create the constraints of its function's preference projection. The lowest level of the preference projection is formed using the bounds that were chosen for the underlying STP constraint. To form a new constraint at the next level, we first calculate the width of the new constraint's interval by multiplying the width of the previous constraint's interval by a reduction factor, chosen from the interval $[R_-, R_+] \subset [0, 1]$. An interval of the newly calculated width is created and placed randomly within the original interval. With probability S, the new interval is split into two parts, and each interval is randomly placed. When S is 0, the interval never splits, and the result is a preference function that is semi-convex[5], as in Figure 2(d). When S is greater than 0, functions such as those in Figure 2(e) are created. We continue creating new preference levels until the calculated interval width for a new level is 0 (occurs often because we round to the nearest integer) or we hit the maximum number of preference levels defined by L.

---

[5] A funtion f is semi-convex if the set $\{X : f(X) \geq Y\}$ forms an interval for all Y[7].

6.2 Experiment 1: Varying Problem Size

Given that no other algorithm exists for finding utilitarian-optimal solutions to DTPPs, our first set of experiments evaluates Ario in terms of the different parameters in the DTPP problem, generated as previously explained. For each problem, we fixed the following parameters: $\{D_- = -50, D_+ = 100, R_- = 0.5, R_+ = 0.9, S = 0\}$. In the first run, we fixed the number of preference levels (L) to 5 and varied the number of 2-disjunct constraints (C) from 10 to 70. In the second run, we fixed C to 35 and varied L from 2 to 9. In both runs, the number of events (E) was set to $\frac{4}{5}C$ (constant constraint density). Figure 3 shows the average and median running times for 20 trials of each problem size.

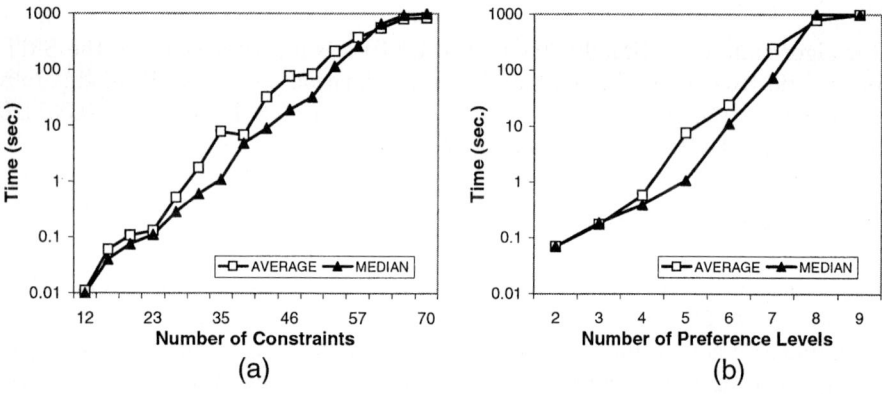

Fig. 3. Running times for 20 trials solving problems with different numbers of constraints and preference levels. (a) number of preference levels fixed at 5. (b) number of constraints fixed to 35. (Timeout set to 1000s).

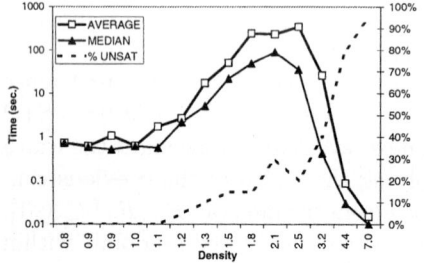

Fig. 4. Median and average running times of ARIO for DTPPs with varying density. The dotted line denotes the percentage of problems with no solution.

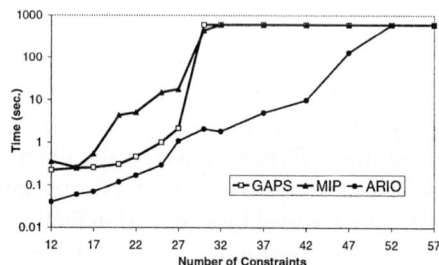

Fig. 5. Median running times of the ARIO, GAPS and MIP methods on STPP problems with 5 preference levels. (Timeout set at 600s).

As expected, the running time increases exponentially with problem size. However, it is much more sensitive to an increase in the number of preference levels than the number of constraints. Fortunately, the number of preference levels is controllable; we choose this number when we create the preference projection. Thus, the knowledge engineer can trade off accuracy (number of preference levels) for speed. The number of constraints is problem dependent, so practically it is more important that we do well in this dimension.

In a third run, we held the problem size constant ($C = 35$, $L = 5$) and varied the constraint density by varying E from 8 to 44. The result, shown in Figure 4, qualitatively resembles the result of many CSP density tests: for over- or under-constrained problems, finding the optimal solution is fairly easy, while problems in the middle range are much more difficult. Note that the previous two runs in this experiment used a density of 1.25 ($E = \frac{4}{5}C$), which is in the difficult range.

6.3 Experiment 2: Performance on STPPs

We compared Ario's performance on STPPs to two methods for solving STPPs:

1. Simplex-based MIP method using the solver XPRESS-MP [22]. In this method, the disjunction between the temporal constraints associated with each preference level was removed using the *Big-M* method. Specifically, each temporal constraint of the form $d_1 \leq x-y \leq d_2$ in the preference projections was replaced by the following two constraints:

$$x - y \leq d_2 + M(1 - B_{\langle k,l,p \rangle})$$
$$x - y \geq d_1 - M(1 - B_{\langle k,l,p \rangle})$$

where M is the Big-M parameter and $B_{\langle k,l,p \rangle}$ is a binary variable representing the projected constraint. Since each constraint k should be individually satisfied, a constraint of the form $\sum_l \sum_p B_{\langle k,l,p \rangle} = 1$ is also entered for each constraint k. The objective function is encoded as below:

$$\max \sum_k \sum_l \sum_p l \cdot B_{\langle k,l,p \rangle}$$

2. GAPS[11]. GAPS was the first algorithm specifically-designed for solving STPPs with unrestricted preference functions. Although GAPS was designed to maximize anytime performance, it is also complete, which allows us to compare against it. GAPS executes a greedy search in the space defined by the STPP preference projection. Each point in the search space is a *component STP*, which is an STP formed by selecting a single STP constraint from each preference projection. It starts with the component STP formed by selecting the STP constraint at the lowest preference level of each projection, and incrementally improves it by replacing one STP constraint in the component STP with another from a higher preference level. Once the greedy search finds a component STP that cannot be improved, it is finished with the first iteration. The first greedy solution is used to partition the problem into several smaller STPPs, each of which can be searched using the same greedy search. Each partition prunes much of the search space and prevents previously visited parts of the space from being revisited.

In this test, we used to the same fixed parameters as the first run in Experiment 1, except we increased S to 0.05, resulting in non-convex preference functions. Figure 5 shows that Ario outperforms both MIP and GAPS methods for the cases in which the number of preference levels is 5.

7 Conclusions and Future Work

In this paper, we presented an algorithm for finding utilitarian optimal solutions to STPPs and DTPPs based on Benders' decomposition and adopting SAT techniques. In our approach, we adopt the technique of representing each preference function as a set of hard STP constraints called a preference projection. Each temporal constraint in the preference projection is replaced by a Boolean indicator variable and the decomposed problem is solved by a tightly integrated STP solver and a SAT solver. We showed empirically that our method finds an optimal solution to STPPs much faster than the most recent algorithm, and showed how the running time of our algorithm on DTPPs varied with problem size.

As we mentioned in the introduction, STPPs and DTPPs only take advantage of part of the expressive power of Ario. Many real world problems contain not only temporal constraints, but logical constraints as well, which Ario can represent and reason about with no modification. Allowing logical constraints enables the representation of optional constraints, conditional constraints, and temporal constraints with variable bounds. Using such devices, we can extend our Mars rover example to include optional experiments, experiments that can only take place if some environmental condition holds, and experiments whose duration depends on the amount of sunlight available or amount of power remaining.

References

1. Dechter, R., Meiri, I., Pearl, J.: Temporal constraint networks. Artificial Intelligence **49** (1991) 61–95
2. Muscettola, N., Nayak, P.P., Pell, B., Williams, B.C.: Remote agent: To boldly go where no AI system has gone before. Artificial Intelligence **103** (1998) 5–47
3. Pollack, M.E., Brown, L., Colbry, D., McCarthy, C.E., Orosz, C., Peintner, B., Ramakrishnan, S., Tsamardinos, I.: Autominder: An intelligent cognitive orthotic system for people with memory impairment. Robotics and Autonomous Systems **44(3-4)** (2003) 273–282
4. Stergiou, K., Koubarakis, M.: Backtracking algorithms for disjunctions of temporal constraints. Artificial Intelligence **120** (2000) 81–117
5. Tsamardinos, I., Pollack, M.E.: Efficient solution techniques for Disjunctive Temporal Reasoning Problems. Artificial Intelligence **151(1-2)** (2003) 43–90
6. Armando, A., Castellini, C., Giunchiglia, E., Maratea, M.: A SAT-based decision procedure for the boolean combination of difference constraints. In: 7th International Conference on Theory and Applications of Satisfiability Testing. (2004)
7. Khatib, L., Morris, P., Morris, R., Rossi, F.: Temporal constraint reasoning with preferences. In: 17th International Joint Conference on Artificial Intelligence. (2001) 322–327

8. Khatib, L., Morris, P., Morris, R., Venable, K.B.: Tractable pareto optimal optimization of temporal preferences. In: 18th International Joint Conference on Artificial Intelligence. (2003) 1289–1294
9. Morris, P., Morris, R., Khatib, L., Ramakrishnan, S., Bachmann, A.: Strategies for global optimization of temporal preferences. In: Tenth International Conference on Principles and Practice of Constraint Programming. (2004) 408–422
10. Peintner, B., Pollack, M.E.: Low-cost addition of preferences to DTPs and TCSPs. In: 19th National Conference on Artificial Intelligence. (2004) 723–728
11. Peintner, B., Pollack, M.E.: Anytime, complete algorithm for finding utilitarian optimal solutions to STPPs. In: 20th National Conference on Artificial Intelligence. (2005) 443–448
12. Koubarakis, M.: Tractable disjunctions of linear constraints: basic results and applications to temporal reasoning. Theoretical Computer Science **266** (2001) 311–339
13. Jonsson, P., Bāckström, C.: A unifying approach to temporal constraint reasoning. Artificial Intelligence **102** (1998) 143–155
14. Cohen, D.A., Cooper, M.C., Jeavons, P., Krokhin, A.A.: A maximal tractable class of soft constraints. Journal Artificial Intelligence Research **22** (2004) 1–22
15. Sheini, H.M., Sakallah, K.A.: A SAT-based decision procedure for Mixed Logical/Integer Linear Problems. In: Integration of AI and OR Techniques in Constraint Programming for Combinatorial Optimization Problems. (2005) 320–335
16. (Ario SMT Solver) http://www.eecs.umich.edu/~ario/.
17. Hooker, J.N., Ottosson, G., Thorsteinsson, E.S., Kim, H.J.: On integrating constraint propagation and linear programming for combinatorial optimization. In: 16th National Conference on Artificial Intelligence. (1999) 136–141
18. Hooker, J.N.: Logic-Based Methods for Optimization: Combining Optimization and Constraint Satisfaction. Wiley, New York, NY (2000)
19. Moskewicz, M.W., Madigan, C.F., Zhao, Y., Zhang, L., Malik, S.: Chaff: engineering an efficient SAT solver. In: 38th Design Automation Conference. (2001) 530–535
20. Marques-Silva, J.P., Sakallah, K.A.: GRASP: A search algorithm for propositional satisfiability. IEEE Trans. Comput. **48** (1999) 506–521
21. Jaffar, J., Maher, M.J., Stuckey, P.J., Yap, R.H.C.: Beyond finite domains. In: Proceedings of the Second International Workshop on Principles and Practice of Constraint Programming, Springer-Verlag (1994) 86–94
22. Dash Inc.: (XPRESS-MP version 15.25.03) http://www.dashoptimization.com/.

Eplex: Harnessing Mathematical Programming Solvers for Constraint Logic Programming

Kish Shen and Joachim Schimpf

IC-Parc, Imperial College London, London SW7 2AZ, United Kingdom
{k.shen, j.schimpf}@icparc.ic.ac.uk

Abstract. The *eplex* library of the ECL^iPS^e Constraint Logic Programming platform allows the integration of Mathematical Programming techniques with its native Constraint Logic Programming techniques within the same unified framework. It provides an interface to state-of-the-art Mathematical Programming solvers, and a set of programming primitives that allow 'hybrid' techniques to be easily expressed. This paper presents these facilities, and discusses some associated implementation issues.

1 Introduction

Constraint Programming (CP) and Mathematical Programming (MP) are two approaches that have been used to tackle large scale Combinatorial Optimisation problems. In recent years, there has been significant research effort [19] to combine the two, exploiting their complementary strengths, to develop 'hybrid' algorithms that can tackle problems that are difficult for either approach alone.

Much of the recent algorithmic research and development work at IC-Parc has been focused on this hybrid approach. The ECL^iPS^e Constraint Logic Programming (CLP) platform is the programming environment used for this development work. As developers of ECL^iPS^e, we aim to provide a unified high-level platform for programmers to explore different approaches to solving their problems. To allow the exploration of hybrid and MP techniques from a CLP perspective, we developed the *eplex* library for ECL^iPS^e, whose first version was released in 1997 and which has been under continuous development since, mainly driven by application requirements.

In this paper, we present the *eplex* library in its current form. Our aim is to highlight the facilities provided which enable the MP/hybrid algorithms to be developed in ECL^iPS^e, rather than describing the algorithms themselves. We also assume that the reader has some familiarity with CLP languages and concepts.

2 Motivation and Objectives

With this work, we pursued the following objectives

- make the convenience of CLP available for modelling MP problems
- make state-of-the-art implementations of MP solvers accessible and provide a unified interface to them

– provide the means to safely combine standard MP optimisation solvers and propagation-based CP solvers

While the first two objectives give rise to relatively straightforward engineering tasks, everyone who wants to smoothly integrate CP and MP faces the dilemma that the standard solution techniques exhibit quite fundamental differences:

In CP, problems are solved by a combination of propagation (the systematic exclusion of non-solutions from the search space) and search (the heuristic partitioning of the search space into smaller, more manageable sub-spaces). This principle is very general and not specific to a particular problem class. It is however aimed at constraint satisfaction, i.e. at finding all solutions that satisfy the constraints. If an objective function is given, and optimisation is required, then this is usually achieved by applying a bounding method on top of the all-solutions method, i.e. incrementally looking for solutions that are better than a previously found one.

In MP, we deal with two particular problem classes: linear programming problems (LP, linear constraints over continuous variables), and (mixed) integer problems (MIP, where some or all of the variables are required to take integral values).

For LP, we have very good algorithms (simplex and interior point methods) which, given a constraint system and an additional objective, can find one (of possibly many) optimal solutions quite efficiently. But unlike constraint propagation techniques, these algorithms do not compute a representation of a reduced search space, and can therefore not straightforwardly be integrated into a CP system.

MIP solution techniques are also difficult to integrate with CP, but for a different reason. Like for general CP, there is no efficient direct algorithm for solving MIPs. MIPs are therefore solved by a combination of branch-and-bound search with an underlying LP solver. When integrating with CP, we face the problem of having to merge the CP and the MIP search. Because the MIP search is usually implemented as a black box, this is difficult to achieve.

3 Functionality

Like other solvers in ECL^{i}PS^e, *eplex* is implemented in the form of a library. The *eplex* library allows MP problems to be modelled in ECL^{i}PS^e, and solved (optimised) by an external MP solver. In terms of solving, we provide two interfaces, a low-level procedural one that is close to the MP solver's given API, and a safe, logical one that is close to the concepts used in propagation-based CP solvers. In either case, our interfaces try to hide as much as possible the differences between the different brands of MP solvers that we interface to.

3.1 Declarative Modelling

Problems are modelled in the same way as with other ECL^{i}PS^e solvers, i.e. by specifying a logic program where some of the predicates represent the constraints to be satisfied. The constraints that *eplex* supports are equalities and inequalities ($=/2, $>=/2, $=</2) over linear arithmetic expressions, the integrality constraint (integers/1) and the bounds constraint ($::/2) which is just a special case of inequalities. They are used as in the following examples:

```
:- lib(eplex).

model1([X,Y], X) :-
    X $= Y + 1,
    integers([X]),
    X + Y $>= 4.

model_knapsack(Bools, Weights, Profits, Cap, Profit) :-
    Bools $:: 0..1,
    integers(Bools),
    Bools*Weights $=< Cap,    % List*List (dot product)
    Bools*Profits $= Profit.
```

The first example, model1, defines a problem with two variables, one equality, one inequality and one integrality constraint. The second example, model_knapsack, is a model for a knapsack problem, consisting of the declaration of a list of boolean variables, and stating a capacity constraint and a profit equation, using the given lists of item weights and profits.

Note that this modelling code is solver-independent, in particular, it is completely identical to the modelling code that would be used for ECL^{i}PS^e's interval and finite-domain propagation solver *ic*!

3.2 Procedural Solver Interface

Once a problem has been modelled by means of constraints, we want to solve it. We first present a conventional, procedural interface that is very close to the API provided by the MP solvers, and not too different from the way an imperative language would interface to such a solver. In addition to the constraint predicates that are used in the problem model, we simply provide additional primitives for (i) specifying the objective, (ii) invoking the solver, and (iii) accessing solution information. The model above can then be solved using this additional code:

```
solve :-
    model1([X,Y], Cost),
    eplex_solver_setup(min(Cost)),
    eplex_solve(Opt),
    eplex_var_get(X, solution, OptX),
    eplex_var_get(Y, solution, OptY),
    printf("Solution X=%f, Y=%f at cost %f%n", [OptX,OptY,Opt]).
```

Setup and solving. Solver setup is performed via the eplex_solver_setup/1, which initialises the MP solver for this problem. Constraints can be stated before or after solver setup. In this case, we stated the constraints before solver setup. Operationally, constraints stated before solver setup are delayed, and during solver setup, the objective is set, and all constraints stated so far are collected and passed to the solver in one batch. No solving is performed at this time: this is the job of the separate eplex_solve/1 predicate, which invokes the MP solver and either fails (if the problem is infeasible) or returns the optimal objective value. The point of separating setup and solving functionalities is to enable repeated re-solving of the problem, usually with a slightly modified problem. After the initial problem setup, additional constraints and variables can be incrementally added to the problem (and indeed be removed on backtracking) in the same way this would happen with the constraints of a CP solver. Problem modification can be interleaved with new calls to the solver.

Accessing results. Apart from computing the optimal objective, the solver also finds one set of solution values for the problem variables. These values must be explicitly retrieved using the eplex_var_get/3 predicate. This may seem surprising at first - why are the variables not instantiated to their solution values? There are two reasons: First, the MP solver delivers only one of possibly many solutions, so it would not be logically correct to assign this value. In particular, this initial solution may no longer be feasible once additional constraints are added and the problem is re-solved.

A second problem is that MP solvers are typically implemented using floating-point arithmetic, making the results subject to rounding errors. This means that with non-integral variables, the floating-point values that the solver considers a solution will usually not be suitable to serve as actual variable instantiations. In particular when equality constraints are involved, passive checking of the constraints with floating-point solutions filled in will usually fail (because we are violating the golden programmer's rule of never comparing floating-point values for equality). All non-integral solutions from an MP solver should therefore always be considered as approximations. A good use for them is as a labelling heuristics within a search routine.

The eplex_var_get/3 predicate is also used to retrieve other variable-related solver information, like the reduced costs, which are useful to do cost-based filtering [12]. Similar interface predicates give access to further information from the solver, for instance dual values for the constraints.

3.3 Logical Integration with CLP

The problem with the procedural interface described above is that the semantics of the posted constraints is only respected when the programmer explicitly invokes the eplex_solve/1 predicate in the right places of the code.

The programming paradigm of a CP system is however that the constraints 'take care of themselves', i.e. once they have been posted, the system should automatically make sure that they are not violated. And not only that: much of the power of CP derives from the data-driven way in which the consequences of changes are propagated through a constraint network. Each CP constraint is represented by one or more propagators, which are suspended awaiting specific events (which generally involve changes to the variables in the constraint) that will trigger their execution.

We now combine the availability of the MP solver with the idea of event-driven execution in order to achieve a logically correct implementation of our linear constraints, to detect inconsistency as soon as possible, and even to propagate information in case of consistency. We just need to make sure that the solver is automatically invoked whenever the corresponding constraint system has changed, more precisely, if it was tightened in a way that invalidates the previously found solution. This may happen through

- the addition of new linear constraints (`new_constraint`)
- new, tighter variable bounds that exclude the solution value (`deviating_bounds`)
- instantiation of variables to a value different from its solution value (`deviating_inst`)

The *eplex* library supports all these (and a few more) trigger conditions, which can be specified as parameters to an extended version of the `eplex_solver_setup` predicate. Note that the laziest trigger condition that still achieves logically correct handling of the constraints is the `deviating_inst`-condition: when variables are instantiated to a non-solution value, the solver is reinvoked. In particular, it is guaranteed that the constraints will have been checked (and inconsistency detected) once all variables are instantiated. Additional trigger conditions will make the system more eager: when using all three conditions above, inconsistency will be detected as soon as possible.

Additionally, the programmer can specify their own triggering conditions based on the general suspend and resume mechanism of ECL^{i}PS^e. The MP solver can thus be made to trigger only on 'interesting' problem changes, reducing unnecessary computation in case the predefined trigger conditions turn out to trigger too eagerly.

An automatically triggered solver can do more than just detecting inconsistency: it computes an optimum cost for the current state of the constraint system. Since the constraints can only get tighter later, this cost can be used as a lower bound (in case of minimisation) on the cost variable (C in the example code). The MP solver thus acquires the characteristics of a propagation constraint: it reacts to e.g. bound changes in its problem variables, and imposes a new bound on its cost variable. It can therefore take part in propagation sequences, and it can be considered as a compound constraint, representing the whole MP problem with all its variables.

In a setting where (cheap) interval-propagation constraints are mixed with (expensive) MP-solver constraints, we prioritise the execution such that the expensive constraints are only executed once the cheap constraints have reached a fixpoint. That way, MP solving is done only as many times as absolutely necessary.

Another way in which a solver can perform propagation is by pruning variable bounds using reduced cost information [12]. This feature is available as a further solver setup option. Other information from the MP solve can be used to assist the CP solve more indirectly, e.g. using the solution values for labelling the variables.

3.4 Multiple Subproblems

Since the constraint syntax is identical for different solvers, in a hybrid program it becomes necessary to specify which solver a constraint is intended for. This is syntactically solved by prefixing the constraint with the solver name (which is in fact simply an ECL^{i}PS^e module name), e.g. with `ic:(X+Y $>= 4)` the constraint is posted to the *ic* interval CP solver, with `eplex:(X+Y $>= 4)` the constraint is posted to the *eplex* MP solver.

We also wanted to provide the flexibility to group *eplex* constraints into separate subproblems that can then be handled as independent subproblems by an MP solver. This is done through the concept of *eplex* instances. The constraints are prefixed with instance names to group them into different subproblems. The following example defines two overlapping subproblems, corresponding to the two declared *eplex* instances 'lp' and 'mip':

```
:- eplex_instance(mip).
:- eplex_instance(lp).

model2([X,Y,Z]) :-
    [lp,mip]: (X $= Y + 1),
    mip: integers([X]),
    [lp,mip]: (X + Y $>= 4).
```

Each constraint here is posted to one or both solver instances. Note that not only constraints, but also the solver setup, solve and access predicates can be prefixed by an instance name in order to make them apply to a particular instance. The solver-prefix is first-class, i.e. it can be a variable and specified at runtime.

3.5 Branch-and-Cut

Using the automatic triggering mechanism, the solving of an *eplex* problem can be tightly integrated into the CP system's constraint propagation and search process. The most natural example of this is the implementation of a branch-and-cut search. Here, some of the constraints of the full problem are initially relaxed. Branching is then done by adding different constraints to the problem on each branch of a search node.

The simplest example of this in MP is the MIP search. It is used to obtain the optimal integral solution to a problem, where at each node, a relaxed linear problem is solved, and in each branch constraints are added to push integer variables away from non-integer solution values. This search can be implemented in ECL^{i}PS^e, using *eplex* to solve the relaxed problem automatically when required:

```
example_mip(Vars, Opt) :-
    model(Vars, Ints, Obj),                    % problem specification
    eplex_solver_setup(min(Obj), Opt, [], [deviating_bounds]),
    bb_min((branch(Ints),eplex_get(cost,Opt)), Opt, _).    % (A)

branch(Ints) :-
    (
        member(X, Ints),                        %
        eplex_var_get(X, solution, Sol),        % (B)
        abs(Sol - round(Sol)) >= 1e-5           %
    ->
        ( X $=< floor(Sol) ; X $>= ceiling(Sol) ),    % (C)
        branch(Ints)
    ;
        true                                    % integer solution found
    ).
```

For this program, we are using two features of ECL^{i}PS^e to perform the required search: Disjunctions ';' with automatic depth-first search to explore all alternatives (line C), and the generic branch-and-bound control procedure bb_min to impose cost bounds and locate an optimal solution (line A).

We use the MP solver only to solve the continuous relaxation of the problem, and take care of integrality constraints explicitly. At each search node, we select a variable whose value should be integral, but is indeed fractional in the current solution to the continuous relaxation (lines B). The program then branches by adding (bounds-) constraints to the problem to push the solution away from the non-integral value (line C).

The *eplex* problem is set up with a call to eplex_solver_setup/4, which allows the user to customise the solver setup. The last argument specifies the pre-built deviating_bounds trigger condition, so the solver is triggered by the exact condition we need to push the solution value of an integer value away from its fractional value: if it is fractional and is outside the new bound, the solver would be invoked. By default, if trigger conditions are specified, then the problem will be solved once immediately after set up, so that there is a solution available when the solver is triggered. Also, in general, if a branching decision does not affect the MP problem variables (as specified by the trigger condition), then the solver is not invoked.

The above example is a very simple implementation of a MIP search and is of course not competitive with the MIP search built into the MP solver. However, this search framework can be used to implement more flexible and elaborate search strategies that cannot be performed by the black-box MP solver alone. Indeed the subproblem solved at each node can be a MIP or any of the problem types supported by the MP solver. Examples of this more involved search are probe backtrack search [9] and its generalisation [2], which was used to implement a commercial transportation application.

4 Implementation Considerations

4.1 Outline of Implementation

The *eplex* library is written in both ECL^{i}PS^e and C, corresponding to the logical and low-level interfaces outlined in section 3. Two MP solvers are currently supported: Dash Optimization's Xpress-MP [15], and ILOG CPLEX [17]. Because of the differences between the two solvers' API and because not all *eplex* features are directly supported by both solvers, the C layer contains some solver dependent code. The ECL^{i}PS^e layer is almost completely solver independent.

Each eplex instance is implemented as a problem instance of the MP solver. The problem instance is created when eplex_solver_setup is called, using the objective function and any constraints that have been posted to the eplex instance. In this phase, the main job of the eplex interface is to convert the ECL^{i}PS^e modelling level representation of the problem's variables and constraints into the form required by the MP solver, namely a compact row- or column-wise matrix representation. Constraints posted *after* initial solver setup are added to the problem instance incrementally.

In terms of data structures, each *eplex* problem is represented by a problem handle at the ECL^{i}PS^e level. This is simply a Prolog structure storing a reference to the MP solver instance plus various information associated with the problem, e.g. the solution values for the variables. The ECL^{i}PS^e level variables are linked to the solver by means of variable attributes (now a feature of several popular Prolog implementations): each problem variable is given an *eplex* attribute which refers to the problem handle. If a variable occurs in more than one eplex instance, a chain of *eplex* attributes is created, one for each eplex instance.

The data-driven triggering of the MP solver is implemented using the suspension (delayed goal) mechanism of ECL^iPS^e. A 'demon' goal which invokes the MP solver is created, which is woken and executed whenever the specified triggering conditions are met.

Any changes made to a problem after setup (e.g. adding constraints, changing variable bounds), need to be undone on backtracking to maintain the 'logical behaviour' of the whole system. As far as ECL^iPS^e level data structures are concerned, this undoing is automatic. The challenge for the *eplex* interface is to make changes in the external MP solver behave in the same way. This is done at the C level with ECL^iPS^e's 'trail undo' facility, which allows a C function call to be trailed on forward execution, and executed when it is untrailed. Several changes are undone this way, the most important is to restore the original problem matrix after backtracking. As constraints posted after problem setup are appended to the end of the matrix, the original matrix is restored simply by resetting the matrix to its former size. It should be noted that for some types of incremental changes, the use of a time-stamping technique[1] is essential in order to avoid excessive trailing.

None of the features required to implement the *eplex* library are specific to ECL^iPS^e: an interface to C/C++, suspension, attributed variables, and a 'trail undo' facility, are supported by other CLP systems. It should thus be possible to implement the *eplex* library in other CLP languages, although not trivial due to lack of standardisation.

4.2 Overheads of Performing Search in ECL^iPS^e

A main concern is the efficiency of the common scenario of conducting search in ECL^iPS^e while solving multiple subproblems. Can a high-level language like ECL^iPS^e efficiently maintain the search-tree needed and can it allow an MP problem to be efficiently modified and solved repeatedly?

An issue is how the successive subproblems are produced. In many cases, the successive subproblems are derived from each other with small changes, and *eplex* will allow the same MP problem to be incrementally changed and re-solved. This should be more efficient than the alternative, which is to construct each subproblem afresh for each solve.

We tried to measure the impact of incremental modifications and maintaining the search-tree in ECL^iPS^e by timing various ways of performing MIP, the most common MP search method. Firstly, we perform the MIP search using the MP solver. Secondly, we perform the MIP search in ECL^iPS^e, using the MP solver as a linear solver at each node, and allowing the problem to be incrementally modified. Thirdly, we perform the MIP search in ECL^iPS^e as before, but construct the problem afresh at each node.

The MIP problem used for this study is taken from a set of examples that originated from MIPLIB [4], a standard MIP benchmark suite.

The results, obtained on a 900MHz Pentium III Linux box with 256M of memory, running ECL^iPS^e 5.8 with CPLEX 8.1.1, are presented in Figure 1. For each problem,

Program	vars	cons	CPLEX mip nodes	node^{-1}	ECLiPSe incr. mip calls	node^{-1}	ECLiPSe non-incr mip nodes	node^{-1}	load
flugpl	18	17	70	0.393	4957	0.339	5221	3.33	1.74
flugplan	18	17	70	0.404	1986	0.393	2187	3.22	1.65
sample2	67	45	75	1.79	353	0.652	345	6.58	4.47
noswot	128	182	1	55.1	1127	1.63	32786	17.0	13.3
bell3a-nonred	133	111	18845	1.19	142583	1.45	162027	14.2	9.44

Fig. 1. Performing MIP search in ECL^{i}PS^e

its size in terms of number of variables (vars) and constraints (cons) are given. For most of the problems with the solver MIP and incremental MIP, the solving is repeated 10 to 100 times to get a more accurate timing, and each timing is done 3 times.

In the table, we give either the number of nodes in the MIP search tree (including the root node), or (in the incremental case, where there is one solver call per MIP node), the number of solver calls, and the derived average time spent per node (runtime divided by the number of nodes) of the search tree. In addition, the last column in the table is the time needed to load the initial problem once into the MP solver, all timings are in ms. The problem is constructed and loaded 1000 times, to simulate the construction of the problem in the non-incremental MIP search.

MIP search-tree size. A simple depth-first branch-and-bound search similar to that outlined in section 3.5 was used for the ECL^{i}PS^e MIP. The MP MIP search benefits from good branching decisions and other optimisations, and its MIP search-trees are significantly smaller than ECL^{i}PS^e's. Our interest in this study is not how good the MP's MIP strategy is, but in the overheads in performing a search in ECL^{i}PS^e. For this, the time spent on each node of the search-tree is a more accurate reflection of the overheads associated with implementing the search.

Incremental vs. non-incremental search. Even for small problems like the ones tested, the ECL^{i}PS^e incremental MIP search is about 10 times faster per node than the non-incremental version. Modifying an existing problem is much less costly than constructing the problem anew, as loading the problem is relatively expensive. In addition, the incremental case is able to 'warm start' a problem when the modified problem is resolved – the solver will not start solving from scratch, but instead will try to reuse information from the previous solve.

ECL^{i}PS^e search vs. MP search. Comparing the incremental search with the MP solver's MIP search is somewhat more complicated: the MP's MIP search is tightly integrated with its linear solver, and this should result in lower overheads in the solving of each node, for example, adding the constraints at each node can be done more directly. Furthermore, some optimisations can be done once at the start of the MP solver's MIP search, rather than repeatedly at each node, as is the case for the ECL^{i}PS^e MIP search. At each node, the MP MIP search can also take advantage of the knowledge that it is performing a MIP search, for example by posting extra cuts that would be invalid for the LP problem and the problem may even be solved more than once per node to drive it closer to an integer solution. However, the effect of this may be more to reduce the search-tree size, rather than make the solve at each node faster: the noswot result is a striking example of this: the MP MIP solves the problem with a single node, but this solve itself is relatively expensive, even taking into account the cost of loading the problem. Thus, the time per node comparison presented in the results should be taken with care.

As the size of the MIP search-tree is so small for many of the MP MIP search, it is not too meaningful to use the per node time for comparison: the cost of loading the problem into the solver, and the cost of performing the initial solve, which is likely to be more expensive because it does not benefit from a warm start, will skew the results too much. However, for bell3a-nonred, where the search-tree is sufficiently large, the time per node for the MP MIP and incremental MIP are quite similar, suggesting that the cost of using ECL^iPS^e to control the MIP search is not prohibitive.

Impact on real applications. This ability to solve multiple problems, and to repeatedly modify and solve problems has been used to good effect to solve very large problems. In some applications, over a million subproblems were solved in a single program, e.g. [7], which performs a complex search and at each node solves a series of subproblems, including some that have a quadratic objective.

4.3 Memory Considerations

Multiple representation of problem. For large problems, the memory required to represent the MP problem can be significant. Moreover, the problem may be represented in different forms at the same time during the execution. At the ECL^iPS^e level, the constraints for the problem are initially represented as expressions. When they are added to the MP solver, they are first converted to a normalised form, and then passed to the C level to construct the data structures required by the MP solver API. Both the C data structures and the normalised form are only required temporarily, and the memory used can be recovered once the constraints have been passed to the MP solver.

If a constraint is required by the MP solver and another ECL^iPS^e solver, then it has to be represented in both. If it is only required by the MP solver, then the ECL^iPS^e representation can be dropped once it has been passed to the MP solver. This is done automatically by ECL^iPS^e if the constraint is posted incrementally to the MP solver and then not referred to elsewhere in the program.

For most applications, the constraints for *eplex* are not given statically in the model code, but are computed from some sort of abstract representation of the problem, e.g. a graph. This will impose extra memory usage on the program.

MP representation of the problem. The MP solver stores the problem in a compact form, with only the non-zero coefficients of the constraints stored (along with their location in the problem matrix). In ECL^iPS^e, the constraint are represented as expressions, which also normally contain only non-zero coefficients. However, more memory is required to store the expression as it is designed for ease of manipulation rather than minimise memory usage. The exact amount of memory required depends on the actual expressions used, but is roughly about 4 to 5 times greater than that of the compact form.

A concrete example. We examined Thorsten Winterer's Swapper program from his thesis [24], which is an application to swap aircrafts for scheduled flights. We examine his single MIP formulation of the problem, and the largest problem instance he used: this extracted a MIP problem from a graph constructed from the raw flight data, and has 421473 constraints and 145278 variables. As written, the program first constructs all the constraints, before posting them all to the MP solver in one go.

However, as the constraints are not used elsewhere at the ECL^iPS^e level, and most of the constraints can be extracted without looking at the whole graph, they can be posted to the MP solver immediately. We modified the program to do this, and the peak memory usage was greatly reduced: from about 400M to 150M. The execution time (to the point where the problem have been loaded into the MP solver), however, increased slightly from 102 seconds to 126 seconds (on a Pentium 4 2GHz Linux box with 1G of memory, running CPLEX 9.0). This is probably due to the increase in memory management in the solver when the constraints are added to it incrementally.

In summary, while the ECL^iPS^e representation of the problem is less compact than the compact matrix representation, it is often not necessary to represent the whole problem at the ECL^iPS^e level. In addition, even though the ECL^iPS^e representation is less compact, it still avoids representing the non-zero coefficients, and would use far less memory than a full, non-sparse matrix for the problem, so it is still possible to represent quite large problems. At IC-Parc, *eplex* has been used successfully to solve problems that approach 1 million constraints and variables e.g. [25] (627168 variables, 947967 constraints).

5 Related Work

5.1 Extensions of *eplex*

In addition to direct use of *eplex* in applications, *eplex* is also used at IC-Parc to develop various hybridisation forms, such as column generation [10], Bender's decomposition [11] and Lagrangian relaxation [20]. Of these, column generation is now packaged as an ECL^iPS^e library. In addition to the facilities described in this paper, *eplex* provides additional low-level support for the *colgen* library, for example, adding new columns with non-zero coefficients in existing rows of the matrix.

5.2 CLP Systems that Perform MP Solving

An alternative to providing an interface to an external MP solver is to implement an MP solver. In this case, it should be possible to achieve much tighter coupling between the MP solving and the rest of the CLP system, e.g., there may be no need to construct a separate representation of the problem for the MP solver as in *eplex*. In fact, this is the approach taken by many of the earlier CLP systems that have constraint solvers over the real domain, such as CLP($\mathcal{R}$) [18], and clp(Q,R) [16], both of which implemented their own Simplex solvers.

For CLP($\mathcal{R}$), the solver is used to determine the feasibility of a set of constraints, rather than finding an optimal. The tighter integration of the solver with the rest of the

CLP system allows the posted constraints to be actively simplified as new constraints are added. However, this ability to rewrite constraints means more complex backtracking actions are required to restore the constraints: unlike in *eplex*, where the problem matrix can simply be restored to its original size on backtracking. The Q variant of clp(Q,R) performs all calculations with rational rather than floating point values, avoiding imprecision problems at the cost of increased time and memory. Another difference with *eplex* is that both CLP($\mathcal{R}$) and clp(Q,R) do not provide mechanisms for separating the constraints into different subproblems that are solved independently.

Performance comparison. A motivation for the *eplex* interface is that an external MP solver would be more efficient than trying to implement an MP solver directly – considerable effort and specialist knowledge have been devoted to implementing MP solvers such as CPLEX and Xpress, and it is unlikely that similar effort (and indeed the specialist knowledge) can be devoted to a single component in a CLP system. To see if this belief is correct, we compared *eplex* using both the CPLEX and Xpress MP solvers against clp(Q,R). clp(Q,R) has a Simplex solver implemented in Prolog with attributed variables, and can optimise LP and MIP problems. It is available with several CLP systems, including ECL^{i}PS^e. Some effort was spent to implement an efficient Simplex solver, although the MIP search implementation is still quite a simple one.

Program	clpr,eclipse lp	clpr,eclipse mip	eplex,CPLEX lp	eplex,CPLEX mip	eplex,xpress lp	eplex,xpress mip
flugpl	0.0087s	2.43s	1.43×	88.4×	1.21×	33.4×
flugplan	0.0089s	0.99s	1.56×	35.0×	1.27×	13.5×
sample2	0.17s	4.31s	12.7×	32.2×	12.7×	29.3×
noswot	2.95s	–	78.5× (0.0551s)		67.8× (2.31s)	
bell3a-nonred	4.53s	20472s	164×	913×	168×	957×

Fig. 2. Speedup comparison of clp(Q,R) with eplex

Figure 2 shows the speedups of solving the same problems used in the search comparison (section 4.2) with *eplex* (using CPLEX 8.1.1 and Xpress MP 14.27), relative to the performance of the R solver of clp(Q,R). The results were obtained using a 900MHz Pentium III Linux box running ECL^{i}PS^e 5.8. The problems are solved as both LP (where the integer constraints are dropped) and MIP problems, and the timings are presented for clp(Q,R) (in seconds) and for the MIP noswot times for CPLEX and Xpress, as the clp(Q,R) was unable to solve this problem due to stack overflow.

Except for the smallest problems (flugpl and flugplan), *eplex* with the two MP solvers was significantly faster than clp(Q,R) running on ECL^{i}PS^e: between 1 and 2 orders of magnitudes for the linear problems, and 1 and 3 orders of magnitudes for the MIP problems.[1] In addition, the difference is greater for the larger problems, so the

---

[1] The performance of the ECL^{i}PS^e version of clp(Q,R) is quite comparable to that on other CLP systems. For example, the measured difference in execution time between ECL^{i}PS^e and SICStus Prolog (version 3.11.2) running these problems is at most 25%.

difference would likely even be greater for the type of application problems that have been tackled using *eplex*.

In addition to the performance advantages, the external MP solvers offer more options. For example, both Primal and Dual Simplex and interior point methods are available for solving problems, and quadratic problems (i.e. problems with quadratic objectives) can be solved.

5.3 Other Ways of Combining CP and MP

Using problem files. Instead of interfacing to the callable library of the MP solver, an alternative would be to generate a file specifying the problem in one of the standard formats (MPS or LP) that can then be read in and solved by an MP solver. The solution is written to a file and read back by the user program. This provides a looser coupling between the CLP language and the MP solver, and is probably easier to implement for solving individual MP problems. This approach was used initially to interface ECL^{i}PS^e to an MP solver [14], before the development of *eplex*, and was also used by COSYTEC to combine CHIP [3] with Xpress MP to solve a part of a train schedule problem.[2] However, it is less flexible than using the callable library. For example, it would be difficult to repeatedly modify and resolve the same problem, without creating the problem anew each time, and it would be difficult to achieve tight co-operation between the MP solver and other solvers in the CLP system.

Other high-level languages combining MP and CP. Eplex allows MP and CP problems to be modelled in a high-level language. In the MP community, the need for a easy-to-use way of modelling MP problem lead to the development of modelling languages such as AMPL [13] and GAMS [5]. This in turn lead to the development of OPL [22], which extended MP modelling languages to model and solve CP problems as well. However, like other MP modelling languages, OPL lacks the flexibility of a full-blown programming language, and to allow a problem to be decomposed into subproblems that are solved separately, a scripting language, OPL Script [23], was introduced. As each subproblem can be solved by different methods, it does allow some hybrid solving. Additionally, limited predefined ways of combining CP and MP solving in the same OPL model is also possible, but as OPL Script is separate from the OPL model, more programmatic control is not possible within the search specification. In addition, the only way available to modify a problem and re-solve it is to change the data (constraints) associated with the OPL model using OPL script, and then re-initialise the model. This appears to create a new instance of the problem, which can be much more expensive than incremental changes of the problem, as discussed in section 4.2.

Although OPL/OPL Script is solver independent, it is currently available with ILOG CPLEX and Solver only.

Xpress-Mosel [8] offers high-level language functionality with Xpress-MP, and with the announcement of the constraint-base module Xpress-CP, which uses the constraint engine of CHIP, similar functionality to OPL is available.

---

[2] Personal communication with Helmut Simonis, 2004.

Combining MP and CP in an imperative language. Using a high-level language to combine CP and MP is not the only possibility. Much existing hybrid research work is done using C/C++, interfacing to MP solvers such as ILOG CPLEX and CP solvers such as ILOG Solver. In fact, ILOG provides Concert Technology [17], a common C++ classes and functions for Solver and CPLEX, to aid the writing of such code. With this approach, the user would not benefit from the high-level ease of programming provided by a language such as ECL^iPS^e or OPL, and furthermore, the programs are no longer solver independent.

5.4 Other Common Solver Interfaces

The MP modelling languages like GAMS and AMPL are both available for use with different MP solvers. Unlike OPL, however, they do not provide a CP solving component.

The Open Solver Interface (OSI) from the COIN-OR project [6, 21] is a uniform API in C++ for calling MP solvers. This allows solver independent program code to be written in C++. In 2004, we investigated if *eplex* can use OSI as the API, rather than directly the CPLEX and Xpress API, for accessing the MP solvers. This would also give *eplex* immediate access to other solvers such as GNU's GLPK. A prototype *eplex*-like interface, implementing the minimal required functionality, was developed. However, at the time, the OSI API was not flexible enough, particularly for MIP problems, to replace our existing interface.

6 Conclusion

We believe that *eplex* provides a very powerful and flexible interface for users to solve problems with MP and hybridisation techniques within a CLP language. While it is now implemented for ECL^iPS^e, it should be possible to adapt it for other CLP languages.

The interface is still evolving to meet the needs of our users. In the short term, we plan to add support for globally valid constraint pools ('global cuts' pools) – once added to the pool, these constraints will apply to all subsequent solving of the problem, even after backtracking.

We also plan to support Bender's Decomposition and Lagrangian Relaxation as libraries for ECL^iPS^e, so that the techniques can be used by the general users without reprogramming these techniques on their own.

Acknowledgements

The authors gratefully acknowledge the invaluable help we got from our colleagues at IC-Parc, in particular Andy Eremin, through their feedback and discussions on the development of eplex. We also thank Andy Eremin and Andy Cheadle for their comments on drafts of this paper. Many thanks also to Roland Yap for providing us with CLP($\mathcal{R}$), and answering our questions about it. Finally, we would like to thank Dash Optimization, for their help and support with our use of the Xpress MP solver.

References

[1] A. Aggoun and N. Beldiceanu. Time Stamps Techniques for the Trailed Data in Constraint Logic Programming Systems. In *Actes du Séminaire 1990 - Programmation en Logique*, 1990.
[2] F. Ajili and H. El Sakkout. A Probe-based Algorithm for Piecewise Linear Optimization in Scheduling. *Annuals of Operations Research*, 118, 2003.
[3] N. Beldiceanu, H. Simonis, P. Kay, and P. Chan. The CHIP System. White Paper COSY/WHITE/002, COSYTEC SA, 1997.
[4] R. E. Bixby, C. M. M. S. Ceria, and M. W. P. Savelsbergh. An Updated Mixed Integer Programing Library: MIPLIB 3.0. Technical Report TR98-03, The Department of Computational and Applied Mathematics, Rice University, 1998.
[5] A. Brooke, D. Kendrick, A. Meeraix, and R. Raman. *GAMS A User's Guide*, 1998.
[6] COIN-OR Foundation. COIN-OR Website http://www.coin-or.org.
[7] W. Cronholm and F. Ajili. Strong Cost-Based Filtering for Lagrange Decomposition Applied to Network Design. In *CP 2004*, 2004.
[8] Dash Optimization. *Xpress-Mosel User Guide*, 2004.
[9] H. El Sakkout and M. G. Wallace. Probe Backtrack Search for Minimal Perturbation in Dynamic Scheduling. *Constraints*, 5(4):359–388, 2000.
[10] A. Eremin. *Using Dual Values to Integrate Row and Column Generation into Constraint Logic Programming*. PhD thesis, IC-Parc, Imperial College London, 2003.
[11] A. Eremin and M. Wallace. Hybrid Benders Decomposition Algorithms in Constraint Logic Programming. In *CP 2001*, 2001.
[12] F. Focacci, A. Lodi, and M. Milano. Cost-based Domain Filtering. In *CP 1999*, 1999.
[13] R. Fourer, D. M. Gay, and B. W. Kernighan. A Modeling Language for Mathematical Programming. *Management Science*, 36, 1990.
[14] M. T. Hajian, H. El-Sakkout, M. Wallace, J. M. Lever, and E. B. Richards. Towards a closer integration of finite domain propagation and simplex-based algorithms. *Annals of Operations Research*, 1998.
[15] S. Heipcke. *Applications of Optimization with Xpress^{MP}*. DASH Optimization Ltd., 2002. Translated and revised from the French Language.
[16] C. Holzbaur. Ofai clpq(q,r) manual, edition 1.3.3. Technical Report TR-95-09, Austrian Research Institute for Arificial Intelligence, Vienna, 1995.
[17] ILOG, Inc. ILOG Products Web Page: http://www.ilog.com/products/.
[18] J. Jaffar, S. Michaylov, P. Stucky, and R. Yap. The CLP(R) Language and System. *ACM Transaction on Programming Language Systems*, 14(3), 1992.
[19] M. Milano, editor. *Constraint and Integer Programming: Toward a Unified Methodology*. Kluwer Academic Publishers, 2004.
[20] W. Ouaja Ajili. *Integrating Lagrangian Relaxation and Constraint Programming for Multicommodity Network Routing*. PhD thesis, IC-Parc, Imperial College London, 2004.
[21] T. Ralphs. COIN-OR: Software Tools for Optimization. Tutorial at CORS/INFORMS Joint International Meeting, May 2004.
[22] P. Van Hentenryck. *The OPL Optimization Programming Language*. The MIT Press, 1999.
[23] P. Van Hentenryck and L. Michel. OPL Script: Composing and Controlling Methods. In *New Trends in Constraints*, 2000.
[24] T. J. Winterer. *Requested Resource Reallocation with Retiming: An Algorithm for Finding Non-Dominated Solutions with Minimal Changes*. PhD thesis, IC-Parc, Imperial College London, 2004.
[25] Q. Xia. Traffic Diversion Problem: Reformulation and New Solutions. In *Proceedings of the Second International Network Optimization Conference*, 2005.

Caching Search States in Permutation Problems

Barbara M. Smith

Cork Constraint Computation Centre, University College Cork, Ireland
b.smith@4c.ucc.ie

Abstract. When the search for a solution to a constraint satisfaction problem backtracks, it is not usually worthwhile to remember the assignment that failed, because the same assignment will not occur again. However, we show that for some problems recording assignments is useful, because other assignments can lead to the same state of the search. We demonstrate this in two classes of permutation problem, a satisfaction problem and an optimization problem. Caching states visited has proved effective in reducing both search effort and run-time for difficult instances of each class, and the space requirements are manageable.

1 Introduction

The aim of this paper is to show that for some types of constraint problem it can be worthwhile to cache information about the assignments visited during the search for solutions; this information can be used to prune parts of the search visited later and avoid wasted effort.

When a constraint satisfaction problem (CSP) is solved by depth-first backtracking search, and the search backtracks, the failure of the current assignment is due to some inconsistency that is not explicitly stated in the constraints. The search has discovered that the assignment cannot be extended to a solution; it is a *nogood*. There is no point in recording the assignment itself, in order to avoid it in future, because the search will never revisit it anyway. However, in some problems, assignments can occur later in the search that are *equivalent* to the failed assignment, in the sense that they leave the remaining search in the same state, and hence whether or not the equivalent assignment will fail can be determined from the failed assignment.

In such a case, if assignments are recorded and an assignment occurs later in the search that is equivalent to one that has already failed, the search can immediately backtrack without rediscovering the same failure. Permutation problems are a promising type of problem where equivalent states might occur. We demonstrate the value of recording assignments in two classes of permutation problem, where both search effort and run-time can be considerably reduced.

Previous work on recording nogoods has depended on identifying a subset of the failed assignment that is responsible for the failure and adding this smaller nogood to the CSP as a new constraint; although the assignment will not occur again during the search, the subset may. For instance, Frost and Dechter [5] use a backjumping algorithm that identifies a conflict set causing the failing assignment. Katsirelos and Bacchus [10] adapt the nogood recording techniques successful in SAT, by keeping a record of the reasons for removing a value from the domain of a variable and using these reasons, with the constraints that each variable must have a value, to construct nogoods on failure. Bayardo and Mirankar [1] discuss the fact that the space requirements of these methods of learning nogoods during search can be prohibitive without some restriction on the nogoods learnt, or some way of deleting nogoods no longer considered useful.

In comparison to these methods, the ideas discussed here are specific to a particular type of problem. On the other hand, they have the advantage that it is not necessary to identify a reason for a failure. Furthermore, the process of matching an assignment with the cache is simplified by the fact that matching assignments can only occur at the same level of the search tree. The results will show that for the examples considered, the space requirements are manageable, even for the most difficult problems requiring extensive search.

Two classes of permutation problem are considered below: a satisfaction problem and an optimization problem. In both cases, caching is very beneficial in speeding up the solution of difficult problems. It is slightly more complex to incorporate caching into the search for optimal solutions, but essentially the same method is used. Other applications of the same idea are also discussed.

2 Permutation Problems and Caching

In this section, we discuss how equivalent assignments can arise in permutation problems. Two assignments can be considered equivalent if they leave the search in the same state, i.e. the subproblems consisting of the not-yet-assigned variables and their current domains (after any constraint propagation) are the same and the assignments to the future variables that are consistent with the assignments already made are the same in both cases. Hence, if an assignment cannot be extended to a complete solution, i.e. is a nogood, neither can any equivalent assignment. Two assignments can only be equivalent if they involve the same set of variables, because the set of variables that have not yet been assigned must be the same. Since equivalent assignments leave the search in the same state, we can think of a set of equivalent assignments as a (search) state; and they will be referred to as states below.

A *permutation problem* is a CSP with the same number of values as variables in which the constraints restrict every variable to have a different value [8]. If the search algorithm assigns the variables in lexicographic order, an assignment of size k consists of k of the values assigned to the first k variables. For some permutation problems, whether or not the assignment can be extended to a complete solution depends only on the *set* of values assigned, rather than on the order in which they are assigned to the variables, together with possibly a few other features of the assignment. In the 'Black Hole' problem discussed in the next section, for instance, two assignments to the first k variables are equivalent if the set of values assigned to the first $k-1$ variables is the same, and the kth variable is assigned the same value in both. Recording the set of values, along with the other features, if any, can then allow the inconsistency of future assignments using the same set of values to be recognised without further search.

3 The Game of 'Black Hole'

The first problem class examined is a class of satisfaction problems, i.e. just one solution is required, or determination that there is no solution. It arises from a game of Patience or Solitaire, that can be straightforwardly modelled in constraint programming. 'Black Hole' was invented by David Parlett, who describes it thus:

> *Layout* Put the Ace of spades in the middle of the board as the base or 'black hole'. Deal all the other cards face up in seventeen fans of three, orbiting the black hole.
> *Object* To build the whole pack into a single suite based on the black hole.
> *Play* The exposed card of each fan is available for building. Build in ascending or descending sequence regardless of suit, going up or down ad lib and changing direction as often as necessary. Ranking is continuous between Ace and King. For example, a start might be made as follows: A-K-Q-K-A-2-3-4-3- and so on."

The table below shows an instance of the game: the 17 columns represent the 17 'fans' of 3 cards each:

7♠	3◇	5♠	T♣	6♠	J♣	J♠	4◇	7♡	9◇	7◇	2♣	3♡	7♣	3♠	6◇	9♣
J♡	4♠	K◇	Q◇	T♠	T◇	A♣	9♠	9♡	Q♠	K♠	Q♡	5♡	K♣	8♡	J◇	2◇
2♡	5♣	T♡	3♣	8♣	A♡	2♠	8♠	5◇	K♡	Q♣	4♡	6♣	6♡	A◇	4♣	8◇

We can represent a solution as a sequence of the 52 cards in the pack, starting with the ace of spades, the sequence representing the order in which the cards will be played into the Black Hole. The top card in each column is available to add to the sequence of cards being built. A solution to this game is:

A♠-2♣-3♠-4◇-5♠-6♠-7♠-8♡-9♠-8♠-9♣-T♠-J♠-Q♡-J♡-T♣-J♣-Q◇-K◇-A♣-2♠-3♡-2◇-3♣-4♡-5♡-6♣-7♡-8♣-7♣-6◇-7◇-8◇-9◇-T♡-9♡-T◇-J◇-Q♠-K♠-A♡-K♡-Q♣-K♣-A◇-2♡-3◇-4♠-5♣-6♡-5◇-4♣

A constraint programming model for this problem is described in [6]. It is modelled as a permutation problem: the cards are numbered 0 (the ace of spades) to 51 and the sequence of cards is represented as a permutation of these numbers. There are two sets of dual variables: x_i represents position i in the sequence, and its value represents a card; y_j represents a card and its value is the position in the sequence where that card occurs. These are linked by the usual channelling constraints: $x_i = j$ iff $y_j = i$, $0 \leq i, j \leq 51$. The constraints that a card covering another card must be played before it are represented by $<$ constraints on the corresponding y_j variables. Constraints between x_i and x_{i+1}, $0 \leq i < 51$, ensure that each card must be followed by a card whose value is one higher or one lower.

We set $x_0 = 0$, i.e. the ace of spades is the first card in the sequence. The search strategy assigns values to the variables $x_i, i = 1, 2, ..., 51$ in order, i.e. the sequence of cards is built up as it would be played in the game. Some equivalent sequences that would result from exchanging two cards of the same rank but different suits are eliminated by *conditional symmetry breaking* constraints, as described in [7]; a conditional symmetry holds only within a subproblem of the CSP. Eliminating the conditional symmetry has a huge impact on the search, for any instance that requires a significant amount of backtracking to find a solution.

This model has been implemented in ILOG Solver 6.0 and applied to 2,500 randomly generated instances that were used to produce the results in [6]. The performance of the CP model is highly skewed: half of the instances take fewer than 100 backtracks to solve, or to prove unsatisfiable, whereas the most difficult instances take millions of backtracks. This is shown in Figure 1, where the instances are sorted by search effort. About 12% of the instances are unsatisfiable; for most of these, the proof is trivial (for instance, the game cannot be won if the top layer of cards contains neither a 2 nor a King). On the other hand, the instances that are most difficult for the CP model are also unsatisfiable.

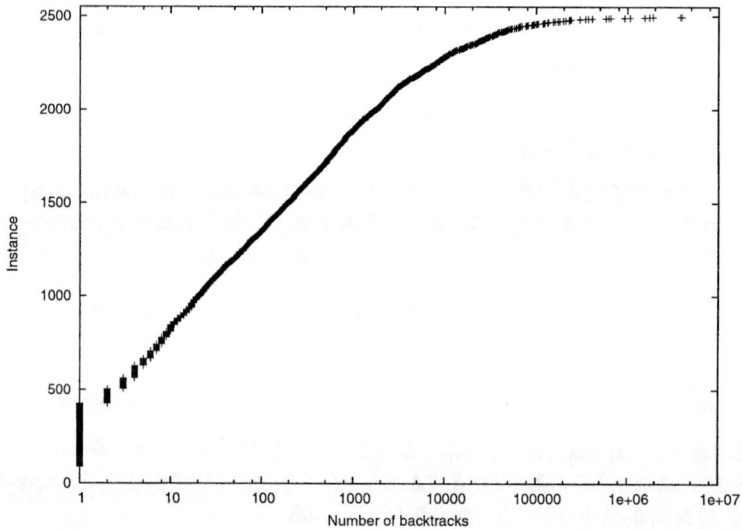

Fig. 1. Number of backtracks to solve 2500 random instances of 'Black Hole'

4 Caching States in 'Black Hole'

At any point during search where the current assignment is about to be extended, a valid sequence of cards has been built up, starting from the ace of spades. Whether or not the sequence can be completed depends only on the cards that have been played and the last card; apart from the last card, the order of the previously-played cards is immaterial.

For instance, suppose the following sequence of cards occurs during search (assuming that in some game the sequence is possible, given the initial layout of the cards):

A♠-2♣-3♠-4◇-5♠-4♣-3♣-2♠-A♣-K◇-A◇-2◇-3◇

If at some later point in the search, the following sequence occurs:

A♠-K◇-A◇-2♣-3♠-2♠-A♣-2◇-3♣-4♣-5♠-4◇-3◇

the second sequence will not lead to a solution. The set of cards in both sequences is the same, and they end with the same card. Hence, in both cases, the remaining cards and their layout are the same. Since the first sequence did not lead to a solution (otherwise the search would have terminated), the second will not either.

Based on this insight, the search algorithm in Solver has been modified to record and use the relevant information. The search seeks to extend the current sequence of cards at *choice points*. Suppose that the first unassigned variable is x_k and the values of the earlier variables are $x_0 = 0, x_1 = v_1, ..., x_{k-1} = v_{k-1}$. (Some of these values may have been assigned by constraint propagation rather than previous choices.) The search is about to extend this assignment by assigning the value v_k to x_k. A binary choice is created between $x_k = v_k$ and $x_k \neq v_k$, for some value v_k in the domain of x_k. The set of cards played so far, $\{v_1, v_2, ..., v_{k-1}\}$ and the card about to be played, v_k, are then compared against the states already cached. If the search has previously assigned $\{v_1, v_2, ..., v_{k-1}\}$ to the variables $x_1, x_2, ..., x_{k-1}$, in some order, and v_k to x_k, then the branch $x_k = v_k$ should fail. If no match is found, a new state is added to the cache, consisting of the set of cards already played and the card about to be played, and the search continues. In the example, when the 3◇ is about to be added to the sequence, the set $\{2♠, 3♠, 5♠, A◇, 2◇, 4◇, K◇, A♣, 2♣, 3♣, 4♣\}$, and $x_{12} = 3◇$, would be compared with the states already visited.

(Note that constraint propagation may also have reduced the domains of some future variables to a single value, which will therefore have been assigned, but this can be considered as part of the state of the remaining search left by the sequence $x_0 = 0, x_1 = v_1, ..., x_{k-1} = v_{k-1}$.)

The implementation represents the set of cards in the current sequence, excluding the A♠, as a 51-bit integer, where bit $i = 1$ if card i is in the set, $1 \leq i \leq 51$. The current state can only match a state in the cache if both the number of cards played $(k-1)$ and the current card (v_k) match. Hence, the cache is indexed by these items. It is stored as an array of extensible arrays, one for each possible combination of $k-1$ and v_k: this is a somewhat crude storage system, but has proved adequate for this problem. Within the relevant extensible array, the integer representing $\{v_1, v_2, ..., v_{k-1}\}$ is compared with the corresponding stored integers, until either a match is found, or there is no match. In the former case, the search backtracks: the current state cannot lead to a solution. Otherwise, the integer representing $\{v_1, v_2, ..., v_{k-1}\}$ is added to the array, $x_k = v_k$ is added to the sequence being built and the search continues.

When an assignment of length k fails, it would in theory be possible to represent this information as a k-ary constraint. In 'Black Hole', the failure has revealed that assigning $\{v_1, v_2, ..., v_{k-1}\}$ to $\{x_1, x_2, ..., x_{k-1}\}$, in any order, and v_k to x_k is inconsistent, and a constraint expressing this could be added to the CSP. However, as will be seen, tens of thousands of states may be cached in solving an instance of 'Black Hole'; storing and processing so many constraints added during search would undoubtedly take more space and time than the caching proposed here.

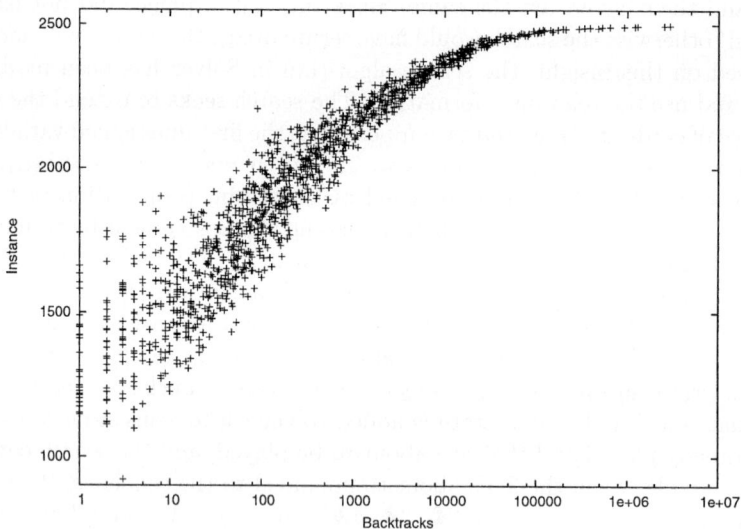

Fig. 2. Solving 2500 random instances of 'Black Hole': difference in number of backtracks between the original search and the search with cached states, instances in the same order as Figure 1

Figure 2 shows the reduction in the number of backtracks required to solve the 2,500 instances resulting from caching states. Only the instances which take fewer backtracks with caching than without are shown, but the instances are given the same numbering as in Figure 1 (so that the most difficult instance from Figure 1 is still shown as instance 2500). It is clear that the saving in search effort increases with the search effort originally expended.

For all but 15 of the 1,206 instances that take 50 or fewer backtracks to find a solution, caching states visited makes no difference to the search effort. However, since few states are cached in these cases, the run-time is hardly affected either. Solver occasionally reports a longer run-time with caching than without, by up to 0.01 sec., but only for instances that take little time to solve in either case.

At the other end of the scale, the instances that take more than 1 million backtracks with the original search are shown in Table 1; these instances have

Table 1. Number of backtracks and run-time in seconds (on a 1.7GHz Pentium M PC, running Windows 2000) to solve the most difficult of the 2,500 'Black Hole' instances, with and without caching states visited

No caching		Caching	
Backtracks	Time	Backtracks	Time
3,943,901	1,427.93	1,020,371	431.33
3,790,412	1,454.16	1,259,151	509.94
1,901,738	721.07	606,231	251.01
1,735,849	681.57	528,379	233.40
1,540,321	582.71	619,735	257.95
1,065,596	398.44	423,416	176.01

no solution. For these instances, caching states visited reduces the search effort by at least 60%; for the most difficult instance, the reduction is nearly 75%. In spite of the unsophisticated storage of the cache, the saving in run-time is nearly as great; more than 55% for all six instances, and 70% for the most difficult instance.

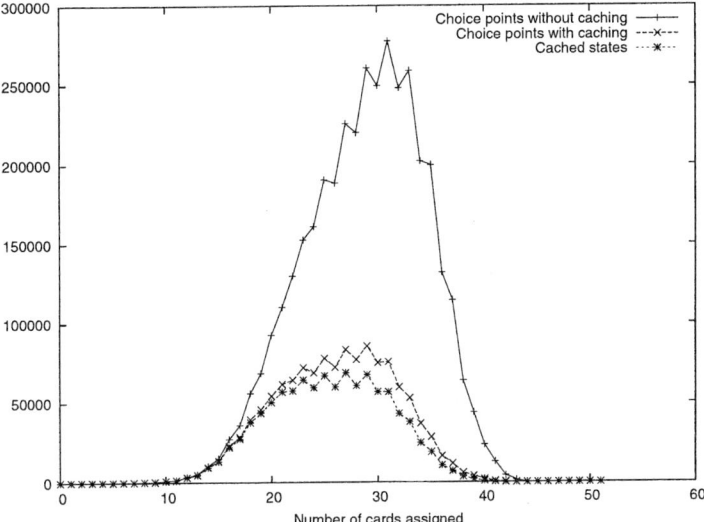

Fig. 3. Proving insolubility for the most difficult 'Black Hole' instance in the sample, with and without caching

To show more clearly how caching affects the search, Figure 3 shows the search profile for the most difficult instance of the 2,500 for the original search. The number of choice points is plotted against the number of variables assigned when the choice point is created, so showing the depth in the search where the choice point occurs. The number of cached states at each depth is also shown;

this is equal to the number of choice points where no matching state is found in the cache and the search is allowed to continue.

The total number of cached states for the instance shown in Figure 3 is about 1.25 million ($< 2^{21}$). In a permutation problem, the number of possible assignments is at most the number of subsets of the values, i.e. 2^n, where n is the length of the sequence, in this case effectively 51; hence, this is an upper bound on the number of states that need to be cached during the course of search. However, in this case, most of the subsets of the cards are not feasible states, since a valid sequence cannot be constructed in which the cards follow each other correctly in ascending or descending rank. Hence, the number of possible cached states is much less than 2^{51}, even for the difficult unsatisfiable instances.

5 An Optimization Problem: Talent Scheduling

In this section, the application of these ideas to an optimization problem is considered. The rehearsal problem is prob039 in CSPLib: constraint programming approaches to solving it have been discussed in [11]. The talent scheduling problem [2] is a generalization of the rehearsal problem, arising in film production. A film requires a certain number of days of filming, which can be shot in any order. Each day's filming (called a 'scene' below) requires some subset of the actors. Actors are paid from the first day that they are required to the last day, including any day when they are not working. Hence, the schedule should minimize the cost of paying actors while they are waiting for their next scene but not working; actors are paid different rates, so the cost is the waiting time, weighted by the pay rates of the actors. The rehearsal problem is similar, except that it is simply the total waiting time that is minimized: this is equivalent to the actors all being paid the same rate.

Again this is a permutation problem: a schedule is a permutation of the scenes. As before, we can define two sets of dual variables: s_i represents position i in the sequence, and its value represents a scene; d_j represents a scene and its value is the position in the sequence where that scene occurs. The channelling constraints are: $s_i = j$ iff $d_j = i$, $1 \leq i, j \leq n$, where n is the number of scenes to be shot and hence the length of the sequence. There are constraints in the model to allow the waiting time for each actor to be derived from the sequence of scenes: these are described in [11]. The model used for the experiments described in this paper differs slightly from the one described in [11]: in that case dominance rules were added as constraints to the CP model whenever there is a pair of scenes i and j such that every actor required for i is required for j, and j requires one additional actor, a. The rules specify that if scene i is before scene j in the sequence, actor a must not be required until after scene i. For the experiments described in this paper, similar rules are used to cover the case that scene j requires *two* additional actors.

An optimal solution is found using the default optimization strategy provided by ILOG Solver; the cost of the best sequence found so far becomes an upper bound on the cost of any sequence found in future. As the search proceeds, this constraint on the cost becomes increasingly tight, so that eventually no further sequence can be found with cost less than the incumbent solution, which has therefore been proved optimal. Because any permutation of the scenes is a feasible schedule, the first solution is found immediately, simply sequencing the scenes according to the order that they appear in the data.

The search strategy used in [11] is to assign scenes from the ends to the middle of the sequence, i.e. the variables are assigned in the order $s_1, s_n, s_2, s_{n-1}, \ldots$. The advantage of this over building up the sequence consecutively from the start is that if an actor is assigned to a scene in the first part of the sequence and also to a scene in the second part of the sequence, that actor's total waiting time is known: it does not depend on the order of the remaining scenes. Hence, partial sequences that will be more expensive than the best solution found so far can be pruned early.

For this problem, with this search strategy, a state consists of the set of scenes already placed at the start of the sequence, and the set of scenes scheduled at the end of the sequence. Because it is an optimization problem, we also need to record the cost associated with the partial sequence: that is, the waiting cost during the scenes already sequenced that is incurred for actors that are on set but not working during those scenes.

In the 'Black Hole' problem, if a search state matches one of those in the cache, this branch of the search can be pruned. In this case, however, if there is a matching state in the cache, but the current state is cheaper, then it may lead to a better complete solution than the best found so far, and so the search should continue. In that case, the cost associated with the cached state is replaced by the cost of the current partial sequence.

The cache is indexed only by the total number of scenes sequenced, corresponding to the depth in the search tree where the state occurs. Given the search strategy, if this number is even, say $2m$, then m scenes have been sequenced in the first part of the sequence and m in the last part; if the number is odd, say $2m+1$, then $m+1$ scenes are in the first part and m in the second. For problems that require a lot of search to find an optimal solution, there can be many states cached at some levels of search. To speed up the search for a matching state, the cache at each level is divided between a fixed number of extensible arrays, and the states are distributed evenly over these arrays using a hash function. Applying the hash function to the current state gives the index of the array where any possible matching state will be stored. Again, this method could be made more sophisticated so that matching is faster, but as will be seen from the results, this method is good enough to speed up search significantly and so demonstrate that caching is worthwhile.

When a state is stored in the cache, the search continues and tries to complete the sequence at a cost lower than the best solution so far. If this can be done, then conceivably it would be worth storing the cost of completing the sequence in the cache. Then if any future partial sequence matches the cached state, with lower cost than the cost of the stored partial sequence, the cost of completing it can be immediately known, and so whether it can beat the incumbent solution.

This might allow some states whose cost is lower than the previous occurrence of the same state to be pruned, because the minimum cost of a complete sequence based on this partial sequence cannot beat the incumbent solution. This has not been done for several reasons; first, it would complicate the algorithm to return to the cache to store completion costs for all partial sequences leading to each new solution, and would mean that satisfaction and optimization problems would be treated very differently. Secondly, relatively few solutions of successively lower cost are found during the course of the search; most sequences are never completed, because at some point their cumulative cost is higher than the best known solution. Hence, storing the completion cost in the cache seems unlikely to give a great reduction in search, and would certainly complicate the algorithm and make it more difficult to generalize.

6 Talent Scheduling Results

In this section, the results of using caching are presented, both for the rehearsal problem described in CSPLib, and for a number of talent scheduling problems, which are much more difficult to solve. The 'Mob Story' problem is derived from the problem in [2] (based on a film of that name); the data for this problem is also given in CSPLib. It has 20 scenes to sequence. The 'Mob Story$x$' instances are derived from it by taking the first x scenes in the data.

Tables 2 and 3 show the effect of caching states for these relatively small problems together with the rehearsal problem. In Table 2, as in [11], the sequence is built from the ends to the middle, as described earlier. In Table 3, the sequence is built from the start to the end, i.e. the search variables are assigned in the order $s_1, s_2, ..., s_n$. This makes implementing caching simpler, since the state consists of only the set of scenes at the start of the sequence.

Table 2. Solving small instances of the talent scheduling problem, with and without caching, building the sequence from both ends to the middle

Problem	No caching		Caching		
	Backtracks	Time	Backtracks	Time	Cached states
rehearsal	286	0.04	276	0.04	204
Mob Story10	289	0.05	281	0.06	236
Mob Story12	2,859	0.27	2,579	0.33	1,670
Mob Story14	15,598	1.64	10,439	1.48	5,597
Mob Story15	41,796	4.71	23,565	3.51	10,833
Mob Story	1,026,328	132.93	405,888	64.71	136,765

As already claimed, building the sequence from the ends to the middle is much faster than building from start to end. However, caching states makes a much greater difference when the worse variable ordering is used; caching with the poor variable ordering is better than the 'ends-to-middle' variable ordering without caching. Caching is still very worthwhile for the larger instances

Table 3. Solving small instances of the talent scheduling problem, with and without caching, building the sequence from start to end

Problem	No caching		Caching		
	Backtracks	Time	Backtracks	Time	Cached states
rehearsal	1,734	0.12	967	0.07	301
Mob Story10	1,054	0.17	838	0.13	291
Mob Story12	11,613	1.46	6,765	0.64	1,387
Mob Story14	350,991	56.19	68,134	6.09	7,341
Mob Story15	758,270	143.84	109,381	10.98	11,781
Mob Story	13,614,469	1,917.92	658,784	83.93	72,382

Table 4. Solving larger instances of the talent scheduling problem, with and without caching, and with both variable orders

	Build sequence start to end, with caching			Build sequence ends to middle				
				No caching		Caching		
Problem	Backtracks	Time (sec.)	Cached states	Backtracks	Time (sec.)	Backtracks	Time (sec.)	Cached states
film105	536,299	51.18	61,100	459,071	48.10	118,361	16.07	40,511
film116	1,160,295	143.72	81,084	2,102,591	277.96	744,481	125.8	225,314
film119	1,505,228	97.49	127,459	1,493,988	171.47	526,392	70.80	144,226
film118	2,333,385	178.22	201,115	2,618,066	315.74	606,591	93.10	205,190
film114	2,569,252	217.21	162,027	4,909,250	472.79	1,032,902	127.00	267,526
film103	4,723,274	313.18	215,354	2,628,434	250.42	607,935	76.69	180,133
film117	6,303,052	396.04	193,163	4,078,225	384.52	651,781	76.86	174,100

with the 'ends-to-middle' variable ordering, and the combination gives the best performance overall. However, with this variable ordering, caching reduces the run-time only by half for the Mob Story problem, compared with an order of magnitude reduction with the poor variable ordering. Evidently, the better variable ordering already leads to less wasted search, and so gives less scope for further reductions from caching.

Finally, Table 4 gives results on randomly-generated instances based on the characteristics of the Mob Story problem. These instances were generated with originally 20 scenes, as in the Mob Story problem. However, two scenes requiring the same set of actors can clearly be treated as one scene taking two days to shoot: requiring these scenes to be sequenced consecutively will not affect the optimality of any solution. After merging scenes in this way, most of these instances have slightly fewer than 20 scenes. Even so, they proved to be more difficult than the original Mob Story problem, overall, and so have not been attempted with 'start-to-end' variable ordering and no caching.

As with the Mob Story problem, the poor variable ordering with caching states gives better performance on the whole than the better variable ordering without caching, and the 'ends-to-middle' ordering with caching gives better results still. The size of the cache does not present any difficulty for these instances. However, the cache size is much closer to 2^n than in the 'Black Hole' problems:

since every sequence represents a feasible schedule, a greater proportion of the possible subsets is likely to be met during search than in the 'Black Hole' problems, where many subsets cannot form feasible sequences. The 'ends-to-middle' ordering does not require more states to be cached, on average, than 'start-to-end' ordering. This is somewhat surprising, since the total number of possible states is larger, if the state consists of two subsets of the scenes (representing the first and last parts of the sequence) rather than one.

Figure 4 gives a similar search profile to Figure 3 for this problem class: it is based on the most difficult instance shown in Table 4. Recall that the search can extend an assignment even when it matches a state in the cache, provided that the cost of the assignment is lower than the stored cost. Hence, cached states can be 're-used' when their associated costs are updated, and so the number of cached states in relation to the number of choice points is much smaller than in the 'Black Hole' problems.

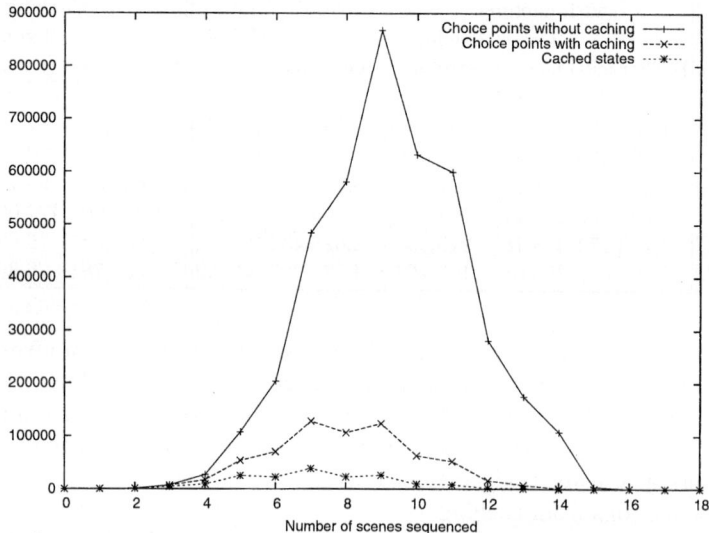

Fig. 4. Profile of number of choice points, with and without caching, and number of states cached, at each depth in search, for the random instance film117

7 Discussion

Caching would be a potentially valuable way of avoiding wasted search in other permutation problems, as well as those discussed here, though not all are suitable. For instance, Langford's problem (prob024 in CSPLib) is not a suitable candidate: if we consider a partial assignment to the first k variables representing the positions in the sequence, then whether or not the assignment can be extended to a solution depends on the order of the values assigned to the variables and not just the set of values. On the other hand, Fink and Voss [3] discuss a number of sequencing problems that could potentially be modelled as permutation problems and are suitable for caching. The problems that they discuss are related to the talent scheduling problem, but have a variety of different objectives. For instance, 'minimization of the number of simultaneously open stacks' is equivalent to the talent scheduling problem but with the objective to minimize the maximum number of actors on set (either acting in the current scene or waiting) at any time. We could expect that caching could be useful for this problem, just as in the talent scheduling problem itself.

Focacci and Shaw [4] describe a similar approach to that in this paper, in the context of the Travelling Salesman Problem and the TSP with Time Windows (which are again permutation problems). They record nogoods during search and use local search to test whether the current assignment (a sequence of cities) can be rearranged to give a lower cost assignment that is an extension of a nogood; if so, the current assignment can be pruned.

Jefferson, Miguel, Miguel and Tarim [9] discuss the game of Peg Solitaire, modelled as a CSP. The game is played with pegs on a board studded with holes; a peg can jump over a neighbouring peg into a hole beyond, and the jumped-over peg is removed. The aim is to start from a state where all the holes but one are filled, to a state where only one peg is left. This is not a permutation problem, but it has some similarities and the authors noted that the same state of the board can be reached in multiple ways.

Jefferson et al. consider the existence of different paths to the same state as a form of symmetry, and sets of equivalent paths as symmetry equivalence classes. However, this does not seem a useful point of view, since the 'symmetries' are not identified, only equivalent paths. They attempted to deal with equivalent board states by preprocessing to find sets of equivalent paths and adding constraints to forbid all but one path in each set, as in conventional symmetry breaking. They found the sets by exhaustive search, which is only practicable for short paths. As a result, they could only eliminate equivalent board states occurring near the top of the search tree, which did not lead to great benefits.

On the other hand, Peg Solitaire seems a good candidate for caching states dynamically as they are encountered during the search, as described in this paper, even though this is not a permutation problem. Whether or not the game can be completed from a given board state does not depend on how that state was reached, so that this is similar to 'Black Hole'. Moreover, a given board state can only occur at a particular depth in the search (games require a fixed number of moves to complete). Hence, a cache of board states could be indexed by the depth in search, just as in the 'Black Hole' and talent scheduling examples. This example suggests that caching states during search could have wider application than permutation problems; the key feature is that different assignments should lead to the same state of the search.

The method described in this paper assumes that variables will be assigned in a static order. In the 'Black Hole' problem, for instance, an assignment to a subset of the variables that does not represent a consecutive sequence of cards would not leave the search in the same state as an assignment of the same values to these variables in a different order. The requirement of a static variable ordering is not a restriction, however, since a static ordering that builds up the sequence consecutively is a good search strategy for problems requiring the construction of a sequence, such as 'Black Hole', talent scheduling, Peg Solitaire and so on.

The space requirements of the cache are not an issue for the problems investigated in this paper. For 'Black Hole', especially, many of the potentially 2^{51} states are not feasible, and so are never visited and never cached. Space is potentially more likely to present difficulties for the talent scheduling problem, where in theory every possible state could be visited, although since assignments that already exceed the current cost bound fail, this cannot happen in practice. The instances reported here are near the limit of what can be solved in a reasonable time with the current model and search strategy, so that solving larger instances, and thereby needing a larger cache, is not practicable. However, a better value ordering heuristic, for instance based on that described by Cheng et al. [2], should mean that the first solution found would be much closer to optimal than at present. This would allow larger instances to be solved; but at the same time the better cost bound would also limit the number of states cached. Future work will investigate the overall effect on the size of the cache. If the cache size ever becomes too large, it would be possible to limit its size, for instance by simply not saving more states when the cache reaches a preset size, thus trading a smaller reduction in run-time for space.

8 Conclusion

It has been shown that in some classes of problem, two assignments to the same set of variables can leave the search in the same state; hence if one assignment is a nogood, so is the other. By caching the problem-specific details that will allow equivalent states to be recognised, wasted search exploring equivalent assignments can be avoided. In satisfaction problems, such as the 'Black Hole' problem, if the current assignment matches one in the cache, an equivalent assignment has already failed; hence the current assignment will also fail and the search should backtrack. In optimization problems, such as the talent scheduling problem, the cost of the current assignment should also be compared with the cost associated with the cached state; the current assignment should fail if it is at least as expensive as the cached state. The two case studies considered in this paper have shown that caching can reduce the run-time for difficult instances by at least half, and sometimes by an order of magnitude, depending on the problem and the instance. It does not always give any benefit for instances that are already easy to solve, but in those cases does not increase run-time either. Although in previous work, recording nogoods has been problematic because of the very large number of nogoods generated, the number of states cached has not presented any difficulty for the cases investigated here, and looking for a matching state in the cache has not incurred a heavy overhead, in spite of somewhat crude storage methods. Permutation problems in general seem most likely to give rise to equivalent states; the example of Peg Solitaire, which is not a permutation problem, shows that caching states could also have wider application.

Acknowledgments

I am grateful to Paul Shaw for providing Solver 6.0 code for the rehearsal problem and to Ian Miguel and Peter Stuckey for helpful discussions. This material is based on works supported by the Science Foundation Ireland under Grant No. 00/PI.1/C075.

References

1. R. J. Bayardo, Jr. and D. P. Miranker. A Complexity Analysis of Space-Bounded Learning Algorithms for the Constraint Satisfaction Problem. In *Proceedings AAAI-96*, pages 298–304, 1996.
2. T. Cheng, J. Diamond, and B. Lin. Optimal scheduling in film production to minimize talent hold cost. *J. Optimiz. Theory & Apps*, 79:197–206, 1993.
3. A. Fink and S. Voss. Applications of modern heuristic search methods to pattern sequencing problems. *Computers & Operations Research*, 26:17–34, 1999.
4. F. Focacci and P. Shaw. Pruning sub-optimal search branches using local search. In N. Jussien and F. Laburthe, editors, *Proceedings of the Fourth International Workshop on Integration of AI and OR Techniques in Constraint Programming for Combinatorial Optimisation Problems (CP-AI-OR'02)*, pages 181–189, 2002.
5. D. Frost and R. Dechter. Dead-end driven learning. In *Proceedings AAAI'94*, pages 294–300, 1994.
6. I. Gent, C. Jefferson, I. Lynce, I. Miguel, P. Nightingale, B. Smith, and A. Tarim. Search in the Patience Game 'Black Hole'. Technical Report CPPod-10-2005, CPPod Research Group, 2005. Available from http://www.dcs.st-and.ac.uk/~cppod/publications/reports/.
7. I. P. Gent, T. Kelsey, S. A. Linton, I. McDonald, I. Miguel, and B. M. Smith. Conditional Symmetry Breaking. In P. van Beek, editor, *Principles and Practice of Constraint Programming - CP 2005*, LNCS. Springer, 2005.
8. B. Hnich, B. M. Smith, and T. Walsh. Dual Models of Permutation and Injection Problems. *JAIR*, 21:357–391, 2004.
9. C. Jefferson, A. Miguel, I. Miguel, and S. A. Tarim. Modelling and Solving English Peg Solitaire. *Computers & Operations Research*, 2005. In Press.
10. G. Katsirelos and F. Bacchus. Unrestricted Nogood Recording in CSP Search. In F. Rossi, editor, *Principles and Practice of Constraint Programming - CP 2003*, LNCS 2833, pages 873–877. Springer, 2003.
11. B. M. Smith. Constraint Programming in Practice: Scheduling a Rehearsal. Technical Report APES-67-2003, APES Research Group, September 2003. Available from http://www.dcs.st-and.ac.uk/~apes/apesreports.html.

Repair-Based Methods for Quantified CSPs

Kostas Stergiou

Department of Information and Communication Systems Engineering,
University of the Aegean, Samos, Greece
konsterg@aegean.gr

Abstract. The Quantified CSP (QCSP) is a generalization of the CSP which allows for universally quantified variables. For each possible sequence of assignments to such variables, we have to find a way to set the values of the remaining, existentially quantified, variables so that all the constraints are satisfied. Such problems arise in areas such as planning under uncertainty, model checking, and adversary game playing. QCSPs are starting to attract interest following the development of numerous efficient solvers for the closely related area of QBF. Two approaches have been studied so far; the encoding of QCSPs into QBF, and the generalization of well-known search procedures for CSPs, like FC and MAC, to the quantified case. In this paper we introduce a new approach which utilizes repair-based techniques. We describe a framework for a QCSP solver in which complete and incomplete repair-based methods can be incorporated. We also evaluate such a solver that applies backtracking and local search methods based on the min-conflicts heuristic. Experimental results demonstrate that even simple repair-based techniques can outperform the state-of-the-art solver QCSP-Solve.

1 Introduction

The standard CSP framework has been extended in many ways to deal with problems that contain uncertainty. The Quantified Constraint Satisfaction Problem (QCSP) is such an extension in which some of the variables may be universally quantified. Universal variables are used to model actions or events for which we are uncertain. For example, user choices in a configuration problem, or opponent moves in an adversary game. In a QCSP we try to find a strategy, defining the values of the existential variables for all possible sequences of instantiations for the universal variables, so that all the constraints in the problem are satisfied. The QCSP can be used to model PSPACE-complete decision problems from areas such as planning under uncertainty, design, adversary game playing, and model checking. For example, in game playing we may want to find a winning strategy for all possible moves of the opponent. In a design problem it may be required that a configuration must be possible for all possible sequences of user choices. As a final example, when planning in a safety critical environment, such as a nuclear station, we require that an action is possible for every eventuality.

Although there is a significant body of work on quantified problems with continuous domains (e.g. [1,9]), little work has been done on QCSPs with discrete finite domains. Interest in such problems has very recently started to grow, following the development of numerous efficient solvers in the closely related area of Quantified Boolean Formulae (QBF or QSAT). Currently, there are two general approaches to solving QCSPs: 1) The direct approach where techniques from CSPs are extended to deal with quantification [2,7,5], and 2) the approach based on encoding QCSPs as QBFs and solving the encoded problem using a QBF solver [4]. Gent et.al. [5] showed that QCSP-Solve, an advanced solver that follows the first approach, significantly outperforms the second approach of [4].

In this paper we introduce an alternative approach to QCSP solving, based on techniques for repairing variable assignments. Repair-based methods, such as min-conflicts and WSAT, have been successfully applied in CSPs and SAT to solve large hard problems. Many variations have been proposed, either coupled with local search (incomplete ones), or with backtracking (complete ones). An incomplete repair-based method, called WalkQSAT, has also been developed and applied in QBF [3]. As explained in [3], a search state in QBF (and QCSP) is not merely an assignment of values to variables, in which case the application of standard repair methods would be straightforward. A search state is best described as a strategy where we try to set the existential variables so that for all values of the universals there is a solution. At a first glance, this makes the use of repair-based methods (and especially incomplete ones) counterintuitive. However, as we will explain, the process of solving a QCSP (or a QBF) involves many searches (in the standard sense) for consistent assignments of closely related CSP instances. This property was exploited in [3] to obtain a QBF solver based on local search.

This paper describes a framework for the implementation of repair-based techniques for QCSPs. Following [3], this framework is built on top of a standard backtracking algorithm. We demonstrate how complete and incomplete variations of a simple repair-based technique that utilizes the min-conflicts heuristic can be implemented within the proposed framework, resulting in an efficient QCSP solver. After giving some preliminary background about QCSPs and repair-based methods for CSPs, we present a framework that combines standard backtracking search with a repair-based procedure. Then we discuss various implementations of the framework. Finally, we present an experimental evaluation of the introduced techniques. Results demonstrate that repair-based methods display promising performance, they can be competitive, and often better, than QCSP-Solve.

2 Preliminaries

In standard CSPs all variables are existentially quantified. QCSPs are more expressive than CSPs in that they allow universally quantified variables. They enable the formulation of problems where all contingencies must be allowed for.

Definition 1. A *Quantified Constraint Satisfaction Problem* (QCSP) is a formula of the form QC where Q is a sequence of quantifiers $Q_1 x_1 \ldots Q_n x_n$, where each Q_i quantifies ($\exists$ or $\forall$) a variable x_i and each variable occurs exactly once in the sequence. C is a conjunction of constraints $(c_1 \wedge \ldots \wedge c_m)$ where each c_i involves some variables among $x_1, \ldots, x_n$.

The semantics of a QCSP QC can be defined recursively as follows. If C is empty then the problem is true. If Q is of the form $\exists x_1 Q_2 x_2 \ldots Q_n x_n$ then QC is true iff there exists some value $a \in D(x_1)$ such that $Q_2 x_2 \ldots Q_n x_n C[(x_1, a)]$[1] is true. If Q is of the form $\forall x_1 Q_2 x_2 \ldots Q_n x_n$ then QC is true iff for each value $a \in D(x_1)$, $Q_2 x_2 \ldots Q_n x_n C[(x_1, a)]$ is true. In a binary QCSP, each constraint, denoted by $c(x_i, x_j)$, involves two variables (x_i and x_j) which may be universally or existentially quantified. As an example of a realistic problem that can be modelled as a QCSP consider the following.

Example 1. Imagine an interactive configuration problem (for example, in PC or car configuration) where a system is built step by step. There are various components, some of which are selected by the user while others must be filled in by the configurator based on various constraints regarding the connections between components. Each time the user selects a specific component, the system must complement the selected part with any extra components required by the specifications. There are 3 components, x_1, x_2, x_3, which the user must specify. Each of them can be implemented in 3 different ways, denoted by x_{11}, x_{12}, and x_{13} for x_1, and accordingly for the other components. For instance, the 3 components might correspond to hard disk, RAM, and motherboard in PC configuration. There are also 3 extra components, y_1, y_2, y_3, required. The implementation of these components depends on the choices of implementation for components x_1, x_2, and x_3. Again each of them can be implemented in 3 different ways. Assume that y_1 and y_2 must be placed adjacent to x_1 according to the system's specification, y_2 must also be adjacent to x_2, and y_3 must be placed adjacent to x_2 and x_3. Also, there are constraints with respect to the compatibility between adjacent components. For example, "if x_{11} is selected for x_1 then y_{12} must be selected for y_2".

Initially the user must select one of the 3 possible implementations of x_1. Now the configurator must specify the implementation of component y_1 according to the constraint on the connection between x_1 and y_1. Then the user must specify the implementation of x_2 and the system will add component y_2 according to the restrictions on the connections of y_2 to x_1 and x_2. Finally, the user must specify the implementation of x_3 and the system will add the appropriate implementation of y_3.

An interesting question for the system provider is whether a configuration exists for all possible sequences of user choices. This question can be modelled as QCSP where components chosen by the user correspond to universal variables and the extra components correspond to existential variables. The domain of a variable consists of the possible implementations of the corresponding component. Each compatibility restriction on the connection between components is

---

[1] $D(x_1)$ and (x_1, a) denote the domain of variable x_1 and the assignment of value a to x_1 respectively.

modelled as a constraint between the corresponding variables. The above problem can be modelled by the following QCSP:

$\forall x_1 \exists y_1 \forall x_2 \exists y_2 \forall x_3 \exists y_3 (c(x_1, y_1), c(x_1, y_2), c(x_2, y_2), c(x_2, y_3), c(x_3, y_3))$

The QCSP is a problem that only recently started to attract interest, and as a result very few solution methods have been proposed. In [2] Bordeaux and Monfroy introduced ways to implement arc consistency in QCSPs. Algorithms for arc consistency, forward checking and MAC in binary QCSPs were described in [7]. A solution method based on encoding QCSPs as QBFs was proposed and evaluated in [4]. Finally, an advanced solver for QCSPs that incorporates various look-ahead and look-back methods was presented in [5].

In the rest of the paper we will sometimes refer to universally and existentially quantified variables as *universals* and *existentials* respectively.

2.1 Repair-Based Methods

Many repair-methods for CSPs have been proposed in the literature. Typically, these methods begin by giving tentative values to all variables resulting in a complete, but inconsistent, assignment. Then they try to repair the initial assignment either by using it to guide a backtracking-based search, or by making local moves (i.e. changes of some variable assignments). The former methods are typically complete while the latter are incomplete.

Incomplete repair-based methods, such as min-conflicts [8] and WSAT [11], have been widely used in CSPs and SAT to tackle large hard problems where standard backtracking-based methods are inefficient. Such a method, called WalkQSAT, has also been developed and applied in QBF [3]. Although the application of incomplete local search in QBF looks counterintuitive at a first glance, WalkQSAT was found to be competitive with state-of-the-art QBF solvers on some hard instances. However, local search methods suffer from their inherent incompleteness. That is, they cannot guarantee that a solution will be returned, if one exists, or that a proof of insolubility will be provided when no solution exists.

To overcome this, some repair strategies have been combined with backtracking search to achieve completeness and at the same time yield the benefits that search in the space of repairs may offer (for example [8,13,12]). Also, many methods that combine local and backtracking search and utilize repairs have been proposed (for example [10,6]).

3 A Framework for Repair-Based Methods in QCSPs

In this section we describe a general framework that can be used to implement repair-based methods for QCSPs. First, we briefly discuss how a direct backtracking-based solver works. Then we show how repair-based methods can be implemented on top of such a solver.

3.1 Backtracking Search in QCSPs

A basic backtracking algorithm for QCSPs works as follows: Variables are instantiated one by one in the order they appear in Q[2]. If a consistent leaf node is reached then the algorithm backtracks to the last universal and assigns it its next available value. If the current variable is universal and paths to consistent leaf nodes have been found for all of its values, then the algorithm backtracks to the last universal to check its next value. Whenever a dead-end occurs the algorithm backtracks to the previously instantiated existential and tries another assignment. The algorithm terminates successfully if paths to consistent leaf nodes have been found for all the values of the first universal in Q. The algorithm terminates unsuccessfully if there is a backtrack from the first existential. In this case there is no way to set the values of the existentials so that for all values of the universals there is a consistent assignment.

All direct algorithms for QCSPs are based on the above scheme to systematically traverse the search space. QCSP-Solve significantly enhances the basic algorithm with various look-ahead and look-back features. QCSP-Solve's main features are the following: Arc consistency is applied during preprocessing to remove all constraints of the form $\exists\, x_i \forall\, x_j, c(x_i, x_j)$ and $\forall\, x_i \forall\, x_j, c(x_i, x_j)$ and also prune the domains of existentials. Forward checking (or arc consistency) is applied after each variable instantiation to prune the domains of future existential variables and discover dead-ends early. Before assigning a value to a universal variable, QCSP-Solve performs forward checking (or arc consistency) for *all* the available values of the variable. These variations of FC and MAC, called FC1 and MAC1 in [5], can discover dead-ends earlier than the standard versions. The *pure value* rule, which is the equivalent of the pure literal rule for QBF, is also applied during search. According to this rule, if a value of an existential has no conflicts with values of future variables then the existential is immediately assigned with that value. If a value of a universal has no conflicts with values of future variables then it is removed from the domain of the universal.

When encountering a dead-end, QCSP-Solve applies conflict-based backjumping (CBJ) to backjump to a variable that is responsible for the dead-end. After reaching a consistent leaf node, solution-directed pruning (SDP) is applied to the last universal (and possibly others further back) to avoid redundant search. SDP identifies the values of the last universal that are compatible with all the assignments of the future existentials in the previous path to a consistent leaf node, and avoids running a search for them. If there are no more values for the last universal, SDP is applied for the universal immediately before the last in Q. This is repeated recursively until a universal is found with at least one value for which SDP does not apply. QCSP-Solve then backjumps to this universal.

3.2 Motivation

Before describing the framework for repair-based search, let us first discuss the motivation behind the application of such methods. As mentioned in the Intro-

---

[2] Note that consecutive existentials or universals can be instantiated in any order.

duction, solving a QCSP involves solving a large number of similar standard CSPs. What does this mean? Consider a QCSP QC where there are k existentials after the last universal x_i in Q. When variable x_i is reached for the first time by a backtracking algorithm, it will be assigned its first value, say a, and then essentially a standard search will commence in the CSP comprising of the remaining k existentials. Assuming a solution is found, the algorithm will backtrack to x_i, assign it its next value, say b, and start another search in the CSP comprising of the k existentials. These two searches will be performed in two CSPs that are very similar. The only difference is that x_i takes value a in the first, and value b in the second. Now, since we already have a solution for the first CSP, the only way that this not a solution for the second CSP as well, is if assignment (x_i, b) is in conflict with a subset of the assignments that the k existentials have in the first solution. If this subset is small, it is reasonable to try to repair it (i.e. change the assignments of the variables involved in it so that they become consistent), instead of starting search from scratch.

The following example illustrates the above point, and shows how search effort can be saved using repair-based techniques.

Example 2. Consider a QCSP QC where $Q = \forall x_1 \exists x_2 \exists x_3 \exists x_4$, and $D(x_1) = \{0,1\}$, $D(x_2) = D(x_3) = D(x_4) = \{0,1,2\}$. Assume that after instantiating x_1 to 0, a solution is found with $x_2 = x_3 = x_4 = 2$. A standard search algorithm like QCSP-Solve will now backtrack to x_1, assign it value 1 and try to find a consistent instantiation of the existentials. Assuming that the only consistent instantiation is $(x_2 = 2, x_3 = 2, x_4 = 1)$, QCSP-Solve will exhaustively search the subtrees rooted at the circled nodes in Figure 1 before discovering this. On the other hand, a repair-based method will use the previous solution $(x_2 = x_3 = x_4 = 2)$ to guide a (complete or incomplete) search in the space of repairs. Assume that value 1 of x_1 is consistent with value 2 of both x_2 and x_3. Also, it is in conflict with values 0 and 2 of x_4, but consistent with value 1. Finally, value 1 of x_4 is consistent with value 2 of both x_2 and x_3. A repair-based method can proceed as follows: Since the assignments in the guiding previous solution of both x_2 and x_3 are consistent with the new assignment of x_1, it will try to repair the inconsistent assignment of x_4. The only consistent value of x_4 is 1, which will be assigned to it and the algorithm will terminate avoiding fruitless search. Note that the SDP feature of QCSP-Solve cannot detect this since value 1 of x_1 is not consistent with the previous assignments of *all* existentials after x_1.

It is important to point out that the applicability of repair-based methods is not restricted to the last universal in Q, or to universals only. Consider an arbitrary universal x_i that has been assigned its first value a. If the algorithm determines that the future problem is consistent then it will backtrack to x_i and assign it its next value b. A repair-based method can use the assignments of the variables after x_i, along the previously discovered path to a consistent leaf node, as a tentative initial assignment for these variables. This assignment will guide search, in the space of repairs, for a path to a consistent leaf node, which will now include assignment (x_i, b). The process can work in a similar way for

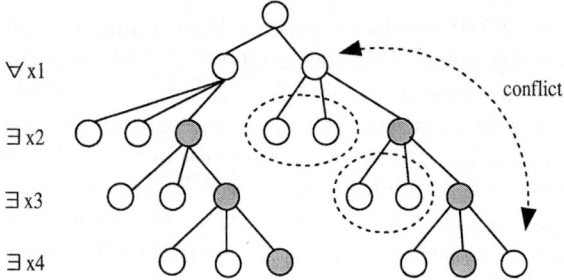

Fig. 1. Search tree of Example 2. Dark nodes are instantiations for existentials that are along solution paths. The subtrees below the nodes in the dashed circle are skipped by the repair-based method, while QCSP-Solve has to explore them exhaustively.

existentials. This is similar to the way WalkQSAT operates in QBF. These issues will be clarified below, after the framework for repair-based search is presented.

3.3 Repair-Based Search

A high level description of a framework for repair-based search in QCSPs, called RB-Schema (from Repair-Based-Schema), is shown in Figure 2. It takes a QCSP QC and returns TRUE if the problem is satisfiable, and FALSE otherwise. Note that if the repair-based method used is incomplete then FALSE will not necessarily mean that the problem is unsatisfiable. RB-Schema is based on a standard backtracking search procedure as described above. The main difference with the existing algorithms, such as QCSP-Solve, is that whenever a backtrack to a universal or existential variable is performed, RB-Schema tries to reach a consistent leaf node by repairing the assignments of the variables in the previously discovered solution. In Figure 2,

- c_var is the current variable and $prev\_var$ is the variable that was visited by the algorithm immediately before c_var. That is, if the algorithm is moving forward, $prev\_var$ is $c\_var - 1$. If the algorithm backtracks from a variable x_i to c_var then $prev\_var$ is x_i.
- Propagate() is a function that propagates the current variable assignment to the future (unassigned) variables ($future\_vars$). It can be instantiated to forward checking, arc consistency, or any other propagation method.
- Repair() is a function that implements a repair-based method for CSPs. It takes as input the set of future variables and the previously found solution ($prev\_sol$), and it tries to repair $prev\_sol$ so that it is consistent with the new assignment of c_var (and all assignments of variables before c_var). For reasons of simplicity we do not include the updates of $prev\_sol$ in the pseudocode. The actual implementation of function Repair() depends on the repair-based method used.

RB-Schema operates in exactly the same way as a standard backtracking algorithm until it reaches the first consistent leaf node. Lines 12 and 26 ensure

Boolean **RB-Schema** (Q, C)
1: $c\_var \leftarrow$ leftmost variable in the quantification formula
2: **while** there is no backtrack from the first existential or universal
3:    **if** c_var is existential
4:      **if** no more values in $D(c\_var)$
5:        $c\_var \leftarrow$ previously assigned existential variable
6:      **else**
7:        assign c_var with next available value $a \in D(c\_var)$
8:        Propagate($future\_vars,(c\_var, a)$)
9:        **if** there is no domain wipe-out
10:         **if** c_var is the last variable in Q
11:           $c\_var \leftarrow$ previously assigned universal variable
12:         **else if** $c\_var > prev\_var$ **or** no consistent leaf node has been found
13:           $c\_var \leftarrow$ next unassigned variable
14:         **else** //a backtrack to c_var was performed//
15:           $SOLUTION\_FOUND =$ Repair($future\_vars,prev\_sol$)
16:           **if** $SOLUTION\_FOUND = TRUE$
17:             $c\_var \leftarrow$ last variable in Q
18:   **else** //c_var is universal//
19:     **if** no more values in $D(c\_var)$
20:       **if** c_var is the first universal **return** TRUE
21:       **else** $c\_var \leftarrow$ previously assigned universal variable
22:     **else**
23:       assign c_var with next available value $a \in D(c\_var)$
24:       Propagate($future\_vars,(c\_var, a)$)
25:       **if** there is no domain wipe-out
26:         **if** $c\_var > prev\_var$
27:           $c\_var \leftarrow$ next unassigned variable
28:         **else** //a backtrack to c_var was performed//
29:           $SOLUTION\_FOUND =$ Repair($future\_vars,prev\_sol$)
30:           **if** $SOLUTION\_FOUND = TRUE$
31:             $c\_var \leftarrow$ last variable in Q
32:           **else**
33:             $c\_var \leftarrow$ previously assigned existential variable
34:       **else**
35:         $c\_var \leftarrow$ previously assigned existential variable
36: **if** there is a backtrack from the first existential **return** FALSE
37: **return** TRUE

Fig. 2. A framework for repair-based methods in QCSPs

this by preventing calls to Repair() unless a consistent leaf node has been found. Thereafter, RB-Schema works as follows.

After a backtrack to a universal variable, there are two cases. If there are no values left in the domain of c_var, the algorithm backtracks to the previous universal (line 21), unless c_var is the first universal, in which case RB-Schema terminates successfully (line 20). If there are values left then c_var is assigned its next value and the assignment is propagated (lines 23-24). If there is a domain wipe-out, the algorithm backtracks to the last existential (line 35). Otherwise, it calls function `Repair()` to repair the previous solution under the new assignment of c_var (line 29). If this is successful, the last variable in Q becomes the new current variable (line 31) to initiate a new search for the next value of the last universal in Q. If `Repair()` is unsuccessful[3], the algorithm backtracks to the last existential (line 33).

After a backtrack to an existential, there are two cases. If there are no values left in the domain of c_var, the algorithm backtracks to the previous existential (line 5). If a backtrack from the first existential is performed then RB-Schema terminates unsuccessfully. If there are values left then c_var is assigned its next value and the assignment is propagated (lines 7-8). If there is a domain wipe-out, the next value of c_var will be tried in the next iteration of the **while** loop. Otherwise, if c_var is the last variable in Q, the algorithm backtracks to the previous universal (line 11). If it is not the last variable, function `Repair()` is called to repair the previous solution under the new assignment of c_var (line 15). If this is successful, the last variable in Q becomes the new current variable (line 17) to initiate a new search for the next value of the last universal in Q. If `Repair()` is unsuccessful, the next value of c_var will be tried in the next iteration of the **while** loop.

Note that when `Repair()` is called (line 15 or 29) there are two alternative ways in which the future subproblem (i.e. the problem defined by variables after c_var in Q) can be viewed by the repair-based method:

1. All variables in the future subproblem, including universals, can be viewed as existentials. In this case, the repair-based method will be free to change the assignment of any variable while trying to repair the previous solution. This is the approach followed in [3].
2. All universals in the future subproblem can be can be viewed as fixed to the assignment they had in the previous solution. In this case, the repair-based method will only be able to change the assignments of existential variables while repairing the previous solution.

The only practical difference between the two approaches is that they may iterate through the domains of some universals in different orders.

The currently implemented instantiations of RB-Schema incorporate FC1 look-ahead and the pure value rule. In order to keep the pseudocode simple, these features are not shown in Figure 2, but we should note that embedding them into RB-Schema is straightforward. Also, SDP is subsumed by any repair-based technique. However, CBJ has not yet been implemented within RB-Schema.

Example 3. Consider a QCSP QC, where $Q = \forall x_1 \exists x_2 \exists x_3 \forall x_4 \exists x_5 \exists x_6$ and all variables have $\{0,1\}$ domains. Assume that there are some constraints, which we do not mention for simplicity reasons. Figure 3 depicts a series of states during search that illustrate the way SB-Schema operates.

Starting with x_1, SB-Schema will proceed to assign values to variables, just like a standard backtracking algorithm, until the first consistent leaf node is

---

[3] This means that either a complete method proved that there is no solution, or an incomplete method terminated without finding a solution.

found. The path to this node includes the gray nodes of Figure 3a. Now the algorithm will backtrack to the last universal (x_4), assign it its next value, propagate the assignment, and call function Repair() to search for a consistent assignment of the future variables x_5 and x_6. The repair-based method implemented by function Repair() will use the values that x_5 and x_6 had in the previous solution as a tentative assignment that will be repaired. The repaired assignment is depicted in Figure 3b. The numbers beside nodes $(x_5, 1)$ and $(x_6, 1)$ give the values of the variables in the initial tentative assignment.

Since there are no more values in $D(x_4)$, SB-Schema will backtrack further back to x_1, assign it its next value, propagate the assignment, and call function Repair() to search for a consistent assignment of the future variables based on the previous solution. The repaired assignment is depicted in Figure 3c. Since SB-Schema has reached a consistent leaf node, it will backtrack to the previous universal (x_4) and assign it its next value (0). Let us assume that the propagation of this assignment results in a fail (i.e. a domain wipe-out of some future variable), as depicted in Figure 3d. SB-Schema will backtrack to the previous existential (x_3), assign it its next value, propagate the assignment, and call Repair() to search for a consistent assignment of the future variables. The repaired assignment is depicted in Figure 3e. Note that the assignment of x_4 has changed compared to the initial tentative assignment. This is because we assume that Repair() views all variables in the future subproblem as existentials when trying to repair the previous solution. Therefore, such a change is possible. Finally, SB-Schema will backtrack to x_4, assign it its next value, propagate the assignment, and call Repair() to search for a consistent assignment of the future variables. The resulting assignment is depicted in Figure 3f.

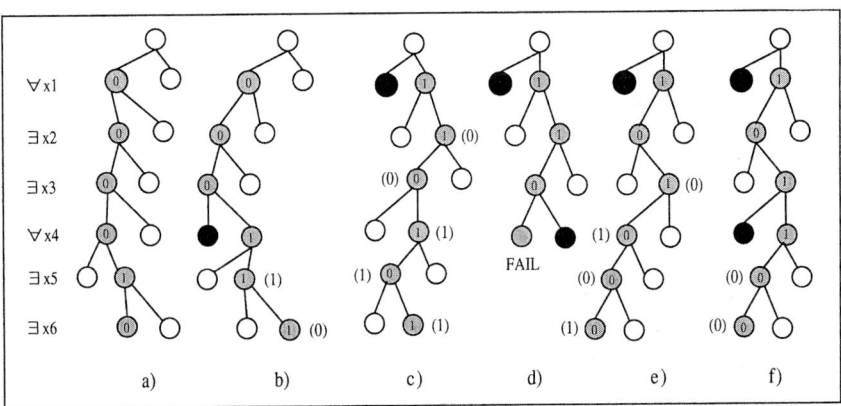

Fig. 3. Search states in the problem of Example 3. Gray nodes denote the current instantiations at each stage of search. Black nodes correspond to past assignments of universals. The number in brackets beside a gray node is the value that the corresponding variable had in the previous solution.

4 Instantiations of the Framework

In this section we show how the framework described above can be instantiated to yield complete or incomplete repair-based methods for QCSPs. We first describe a complete backtracking-based method and then an incomplete local search one. Both utilize the min-conflicts heuristic to guide the selection of variable assignment repairs. Finally, we discuss how the application of repair techniques can be modified to yield a more efficient algorithm.

A Backtracking-Based Method. Various complete repair-based methods for CSPs have been proposed ([8,13,12]). Any of them can be used in the context of RB-Schema by implementing it as function Repair(). We have experimented with one the simplest methods; *min-conflicts backtracking* (originally called *informed backtrack* in [8]). We now describe how it operates within RB-Schema.

Assume that function Repair() is called after a backtrack to some universal or existential variable x_i. The assignments of the variables after x_i on the previously discovered path to a consistent leaf node are passed to Repair(). These comprise the initial tentative assignment that will be used to guide search in the space of repairs. Initially, all variables are in list VARS-LEFT, and as they are repaired, they are placed in list VARS-DONE. The values of all variables are ordered according to the min-conflicts heuristic. That is, in ascending order according to the number of conflicts with the assignments of variables in VARS-LEFT. If there is no way to repair the assignment of a variable without conflicting with the assignment of a variable in VARS-DONE, the algorithm backtracks to the previously repaired variable and undoes its assignment. Min-conflicts backtracking is essentially a complete backtracking algorithm that uses the min-conflicts heuristic for value ordering. In our implementation, we augmented the simple backtracking algorithm with forward checking and the pure value rule.

A Local Search Method. Local search methods for CSPs have been widely studied and applied on large hard problems (for example, [8,11]). Any of them can be used in the context of RB-Schema by implementing it as function Repair(). We have experimented with one the simplest methods; *min-conflicts hill-climbing* [8]). This algorithm tries to repair the initial tentative assignment by making a series of local moves. At each such move a variable that is in conflict is randomly selected and it is given the value which minimizes the number of conflicts with other variables. This process repeats until a consistent total assignment is found, or a local optimum is reached (i.e. no change in variable assignments can decrease the number of conflicts). In the former case, Repair() returns TRUE, and in the latter FALSE. Although many techniques for escaping local optima have been proposed, for the purposes of this paper we only implemented the basic min-conflicts procedure. Since min-conflicts hill-climbing is incomplete, RB-Schema instantiated with this method is also incomplete.

Min-conflicts hill-climbing can be easily modified to return UNKNOWN instead of FALSE when it gets stuck in a local optimum. This will help determine if the QCSP is actually unsatisfiable or the result is unspecified due to the solver's incompleteness. Like WalkQSAT for the case of QBF, an incomplete instantiation of RB-Schema can sometimes determine unsatisfiability because it performs constraint propagation. The most trivial case is the one where the first variable in Q is universal and, when propagated, all its possible assignments result in a domain-wipeout.

Modifying the Repair-Based Approach. RB-Schema calls function `Repair()` each time a backtrack is performed. However, as we discovered empirically, this is not always efficient. One of the reasons is that the interplay between the underlying backtracking algorithm and function `Repair()` adds a lot of cpu time overhead, due to various data structures that need to be maintained. We discovered that RB-Schema, instantiated in any of the above ways, becomes much more efficient when restricted in the following way: For any block of consecutive universals $\forall x_i \ldots \forall x_j$, `Repair()` is called only for the last one (x_j). Universals $x_i, \ldots, x_{j-1}$ are assigned one by one as usual. Apart from avoiding the overheads explained above, this can result in earlier domain wipe-out detection. Assume that the propagation of all possible assignments of variable x_{i+1} results in a domain wipe-out. Standard RB-Schema will discover this when the first backtrack to x_{i+1} occurs and FC1 is applied. This means that all assignments of variables $x_{i+2}, \ldots, x_j$ will be tried first. On the other hand, the restricted version of RB-Schema will first instantiate x_i and then move on to x_{i+1}. At this point FC1 will be applied and the dead end will be discovered. All the experiments reported in the following section were performed with this version of RB-Schema.

Apart from its inherent incompleteness, RB-Schema instantiated with an incomplete repair-based method suffers from another drawback. Consider the case where c_var is universal and `Repair()` returns FALSE (or UNKNOWN) while there actually exists a solution in the future subproblem. This will force a backtrack to the previous existential which may cause the exploration of a large portion of the search space. On the other hand, it is possible that a complete method, which identified the solution, could proceed to prove the satisfiability of the QCSP in a few steps. To avoid such phenomena, we experimented with a simple variation of RB-Schema where a call to `Repair()` initiates a min-conflicts hill climbing search, and in case of failure, min-conflicts backtracking is then called. This ensures that the algorithm is complete.

5 Experiments

In this section we present indicative results from an experimental comparison between repair-based techniques and QCSP-Solve on randomly generated problems. We only experimented with random problems because, currently, QCSP-Solve can only deal with binary and ternary constraints. This limitation, which is unrelated to the approach presented in this paper, prohibits us, for the time being, from using realistic QCSPs from areas such as configuration and game playing, where non-binary constraints of high arities are present.

Random problems were created using the generation model proposed in [5]. In this model variables are quantified in three blocks, a block of existentials followed by a block of universals, then another block of existentials. The generator takes 7 parameters: $< n, n_\forall, n_{pos}, d, p, q_{\forall\exists}, q_{\exists\exists} >$ where n is the total number of variables, $n_\forall$ is the number of universals, n_{pos} is the position of the first universal in Q, d is the uniform domain size, and p is the number of binary constraints as a fraction of all possible constraints. All constraints are of type $\exists x_i \exists x_j, c(x_i, x_j)$ or $\forall x_i \exists x_j, c(x_i, x_j)$. Constraints of type $\exists x_i \forall x_j, c(x_i, x_j)$ and $\forall x_i \forall x_j, c(x_i, x_j)$ can be removed by applying arc consistency as a preprocessing step [7], and therefore, no such constraints are generated. $q_{\exists\exists}$ specifies the number of allowed tuples in $\exists x_i \exists x_j, c(x_i, x_j)$ constraints as a fraction of all possible tuples. For $\forall x_i \exists x_j, c(x_i, x_j)$ constraints, a random total bijection from $D(x_i)$ to $D(x_j)$ is generated and $q_{\forall\exists}$ specifies the fraction of allowed tuples from the d tuples in the bijection. All tuples not in the bijection are allowed. This feature of the generation model ensures that, under certain parameter settings, the generated instances are free from a flaw of the generation model used in [7].

Apart from problems where variables are quantified in three blocks, we also experimented with problems where there are five blocks of variables with alternating quantification, starting with a block of existentials. Such problems were generated in a way similar to the one described above. Figures 4 and 5 compare the performance of QCSP-Solve to various repair-based methods. SB-Schema-MCback and SB-Schema-MChc stand for SB-Schema where function `Repair()` is instantiated to min-conflicts backtracking and min-conflicts hill climbing respectively. SB-Schema-MCcomb is the version which combines the two methods. In the problems of Figure 4 variables are quantified in three blocks, while in those of Figures 5 variables are quantified in five blocks, with each block containing four variables. Both figures give average cpu times over 100 instances.

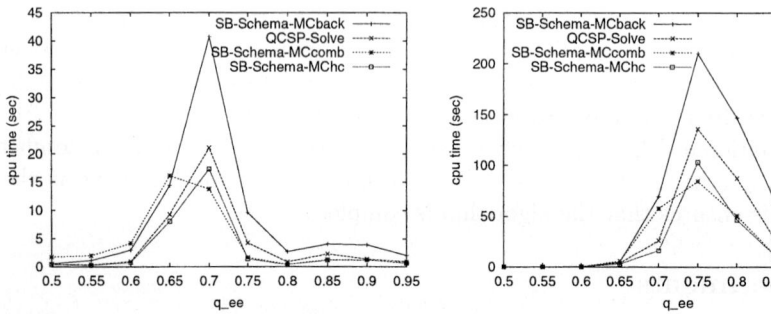

Fig. 4. $n = 21$, $n_\forall = 7$, $n_{pos} = 7$, $d = 8$, $p = 0.20$, $q_{\forall\exists} = 0.50$

Fig. 5. $n = 25$, $n_\forall = 10$, $n_{pos} = 5$, $d = 8$, $p = 0.20$, $q_{\forall\exists} = 0.50$

From Figures 4 and 5 we can make the following observations:

- SB-Schema-MCback is constantly slower (around 2-3 times) than QCSP-Solve. SB-Schema-MCback reduces slightly the numbers of node visits compared to QCSP-Solve, but the reduction is not enough to overcome the

overheads caused by the interaction between the underlying backtracking procedure and the repair-based method. However, we have to keep in mind that min-conflicts backtracking is a rather simplistic algorithm. Other, more advanced, complete methods can potentially be competitive with QCSP-Solve.
- SB-Schema-MChc is constantly faster than QCSP-Solve. For high values of $q_\exists$ (≥ 0.75), where all problems are satisfiable, SB-Schema-MChc successfully solves all instances. However, for low values of $q_\exists$ (≤ 0.60), where all problems are unsatisfiable, SB-Schema-MChc returns UNKNOWN (i.e. it is unable to determine unsatisfiability) for the majority of instances. Similarly, at the phase transition region there are many unsatisfiable instances for which SB-Schema-MChc returns UNKNOWN. Around the phase transition there are also a few instances for which SB-Schema-MChc displays the problematic behavior explained in Section 4. Because of them the average run times of SB-Schema-MChc are not much better than QCSP-Solve, despite the fact that for the majority of instances SB-Schema-MChc is much faster.
- SB-Schema-MCcomb is slower than QCSP-Solve in the insoluble region and faster in the soluble one and at the phase transition. This can be explained if we consider that for insoluble problems SB-Schema-MCcomb makes a lot of calls to the min-conflicts backtracking procedure because min-conflicts hill climbing fails very often. For soluble ones the calls to min-conflicts hill climbing find a solution fast most of the times, avoiding calls to min-conflicts backtracking. Also, at the phase transition the call to min-conflicts backtracking after a failed min-conflicts hill climbing ensures that the problematic behavior of SB-Schema-MChc is alleviated.

Overall, we can see that simple repair-based methods can outperform (though not significantly) the state-of-the-art solver QCSP-Solve, especially for satisfiable instances. We conjecture that the performance of SB-Schema can be significantly enhanced by applying more advanced repair-based techniques and augmenting the underlying backtracking algorithm with capabilities such as CBJ.

6 Conclusion

In this paper we studied repair-based methods for QCSPs. We demonstrated that such methods are promising because QCSPs involve many searches in very similar CSPs. We showed how a flexible framework, within which any repair-based method can be implemented, can be built on top of a standard backtracking algorithm. Preliminary experiments showed that simple implementations of the framework based on the min-conflicts heuristic can outperform QCSP-Solve, a state-of-the-art QCSP solver. As future work we intend to consider more advanced backtracking and local search instantiations of the repair-based framework. Also, we plan to investigate hybrid algorithms that, depending on the problem properties, either apply standard search or repair-based methods.

References

1. F. Benhamou and F. Goualard. Universally Quantified Interval Constraints. In *Proceedings of CP-2000*, pages 67–82, 2000.
2. L. Bordeaux and E. Monfroy. Beyond NP: Arc-consistency for Quantified Constraints. In *Proceedings of CP-2002*, 2002.
3. I. Gent, H. Hoos, A. Rowley, and K. Smyth. Using Stochastic Local Search to Solve Quantified Boolean Formulae. In *Proceedings of CP-2003*, pages 348–362, 2003.
4. I. Gent, P. Nightingale, and A. Rowley. Encoding Quantified CSPs as Quantified Boolean Formulae. In *Proceedings of ECAI-2004*, pages 176–180, 2004.
5. I. Gent, P. Nightingale, and K. Stergiou. QCSP-Solve: A Solver for Quantified Constraint Satisfaction Problems. In *Proceedings of IJCAI-2005 (to appear)*, 2005.
6. N. Jussien and O. Lhomme. Local Search with Constraint Propagation and Conflict-based Heuristics. *Artificial Intelligence*, 139:21–45, 2002.
7. N. Mamoulis and K. Stergiou. Algorithms for Quantified Constraint Satisfaction Problems. In *Proceedings of CP-2004*, pages 752–756, 2004.
8. S. Minton, A. Philips, M. Johnston, and P. Laird. Minimizing conflicts: A heuristic repair method for constraint-satisfaction and scheduling problems. *Journal of Artificial Intelligence Research*, 1:1–15, 1993.
9. S. Ratschan. Quantified Constraints under Perturbations. *Journal of Symbolic Computation*, 33(4):493–505, 2002.
10. A. Schaerf. Combining Local Search and Look-ahead for Scheduling and Constraint Satisfaction Problems. In *Proceedings of IJCAI-97*, pages 1254–1259, 1997.
11. B. Selman and H. Kautz. Domain-independent Extensions to GSAT: Solving Large Structured Satisfiability Problems. In *Proceedings of IJCAI-93*, pages 290–295, 1993.
12. G. Verfaillie and T. Schiex. Solution Reuse in Dynamic Constraint Satisfaction Problems. In *Proceedings of AAAI-94*, pages 307–312, 1994.
13. M. Yokoo. Weak-commitment Search for Solving Constraint Satisfaction Problems. In *Proceedings of AAAI-1994*, pages 313–318, 1994.

Handling Implication and Universal Quantification Constraints in FLUX

Michael Thielscher

Dresden University of Technology, 01062 Dresden, Germany
mit@inf.tu-dresden.de

Abstract. FLUX is a CLP-approach for programming agents that reason about actions under incomplete state knowledge. FLUX is based on the solution to the fundamental frame problem in the fluent calculus. The core is a set of Constraint Handling Rules for the constraints that are used to encode state knowledge. In order to allow for efficient constraint solving, the original expressiveness of state representations in FLUX has been carefully restricted. In this paper, we enhance the expressiveness by adding both implication and universal quantification constraints. We do so without losing the computational merits of FLUX. We present a set of Constraint Handling Rules for these new constraints and prove their correctness against the fluent calculus.

1 Introduction

Reasoning about actions is one of the central issues in Artificial Intelligence [1]. The classical formalism for representing knowledge of actions and their effects is the situation calculus [2]. A fundamental challenge in this context is raised by the classical *frame problem*, which means to find an efficient way of inferring what changes and what does not change as a result of an action [3]. Simple solutions to this problem, such as STRIPS [4], apply only to the special case of complete knowledge. Solutions to the frame problem for the general case of incomplete states have recently evolved into logic programming approaches, e.g., [5,6] based on the situation calculus and the event calculus, respectively. These allow to program agents who use an internal world model for decision making and who reason about their actions in order to keep this model up to date as they move along. However, both of the aforementioned approaches lack an explicit notion of states. Knowledge of the current state is represented indirectly via the initial conditions and the actions which the agent has performed up to now. As a consequence, the entire history of actions is needed when evaluating a condition in an agent program [7]. This problem has been overcome in the language FLUX [8], where an incomplete state is explicitly represented by a list (of atomic state components) along with constraints. Actions are specified in terms of how they affect a state, which allows agents to *progress* the state whenever they execute an action and, hence, to directly evaluate conditions in agent programs against the current world model. This is necessary if we aim at programs that scale up to non-trivial domains in which agents need to perform long sequences of actions [8].

The core of FLUX is a set of Constraint Handling Rules [9] for the constraints that are used to describe (incomplete) states. The semantics of FLUX, and in particular of the constraint solver, is given by the fluent calculus—an action formalism which can be viewed as an extension of the classical situation calculus by the basic notion of a state [10]. In order to obtain an efficient constraint solver, the expressiveness of FLUX as presented in [11] has been carefully restricted: States are composed of finitely many atomic state components, so-called fluents, accompanied by constraints for (possibly universally quantified) negated single fluents and for disjunctions of fluents. These restrictions allow for efficient constraint solving based on *unit resolution*, so that evaluating a new constraint is linear in the size of the constraint store. This is necessary if we aim at a system which scales up gracefully to domains with a large state space [8].

However, the restrictions imposed on the state representation in FLUX are too weak to cover two important phenomena: Firstly, if an action has conditional effects and the condition is unknown at the time when the action is performed, then a complete encoding of what is known after the action requires *implication constraints*. Secondly, a state in which infinitely many instances of a fluent hold cannot be expressed in a finite list. In this paper, we will overcome these restrictions by extending FLUX to both implication constraints and constraints for universal quantification. We will develop a set of Constraint Handling Rules which again is carefully designed so as to retain the linear complexity of constraint solving in FLUX. Correctness of these rules is formally proved against the semantics of the fluent calculus.

2 Reasoning About Actions with FLUX

2.1 The Fluent Calculus

The fluent calculus [10] is a predicate logic language which extends the classical situation calculus [2]. The latter builds on the basic notions of actions (i.e., primitive behaviors of an agent), situations (i.e., sequences of actions), and fluents (i.e., atomic state components). To this, the fluent calculus adds the notion of states (i.e., collections of fluents).

Definition 1. *A fluent calculus signature consists of a finite set $\mathcal{A}$ of functions into sort* ACTION *and a finite set $\mathcal{F}$ of functions into sort* FLUENT. *Sort* FLUENT *is a sub-sort of* STATE. *Furthermore,*

$$S_0 : \text{SIT} \qquad\qquad \emptyset : \text{STATE}$$
$$Do : \text{ACTION} \times \text{SIT} \mapsto \text{SIT} \qquad \circ : \text{STATE} \times \text{STATE} \mapsto \text{STATE}$$
$$State : \text{SIT} \mapsto \text{STATE}$$

Inherited from the situation calculus, constant S_0 denotes the initial situation and $Do(a,s)$ denotes the situation after performing action a in situation s.

The term $State(s)$ denotes the state in situation s. Constant $\emptyset$ denotes the empty state. Finally, every fluent is a (singleton) state, and if z_1 and z_2 are states then so is $z_1 \circ z_2$.[1] A fluent f is defined to *hold* in a state z just in case z can be decomposed into two states one of which is the singleton f. For notational convenience, the following macro is used as an abbreviation for the corresponding equational formula:

$$Holds(f, z) \stackrel{\text{def}}{=} (\exists z') \, z = f \circ z' \qquad (1)$$

The foundational axioms of the fluent calculus stipulate that function "$\circ$" shares essential properties with the union operation for sets:

Definition 2. *The* foundational axioms $\mathcal{F}_{state}$ *of the fluent calculus include:*

1. *Associativity and commutativity,*

$$(z_1 \circ z_2) \circ z_3 = z_1 \circ (z_2 \circ z_3) \qquad z_1 \circ z_2 = z_2 \circ z_1 \qquad (2)$$

2. *Empty state axiom,*

$$\neg Holds(f, \emptyset) \qquad (3)$$

3. *Irreducibility and decomposition,*

$$Holds(f_1, f) \supset f_1 = f \qquad (4)$$
$$Holds(f, z_1 \circ z_2) \supset Holds(f, z_1) \vee Holds(f, z_2) \qquad (5)$$

Associativity allows us to omit parentheses in nested applications of "$\circ$".[2]

Based on the notion of a state, the frame problem is solved in the fluent calculus by axioms which define the effects of an action $A(\overline{x})$ in situation s in terms of how $State(s)$ is updated to the successor $State(Do(A(\overline{x}), s))$. To this end, two functions "$-$" and "$+$" are used which denote, respectively, removal and addition of fluents to states. They have a purely axiomatic characterization: Let ϑ^-, ϑ^+ be finitely many FLUENT terms connected by "$\circ$", then

$$z_1 - \emptyset = z_2 \stackrel{\text{def}}{=} z_2 = z_1$$
$$z_1 - (f \circ \vartheta^-) = z_2 \stackrel{\text{def}}{=} (\exists z)((z = z_1 \vee z \circ f = z_1) \wedge \neg Holds(f, z)$$
$$\wedge z - \vartheta^- = z_2)$$
$$z_2 = (z_1 - \vartheta^-) + \vartheta^+ \stackrel{\text{def}}{=} (\exists z)(z_1 - \vartheta^- = z \wedge z_2 = z \circ \vartheta^+)$$

The crucial item is the second one, which inductively defines removal of fluents f using a case distinction: Either $z_1 - f$ equals z_1 (which applies in case $\neg Holds(f, z_1)$), or $(z_1 - f) \circ f$ equals z_1 (which applies in case $Holds(f, z_1)$).

---

[1] Throughout the paper, free variables in formulas are assumed to be universally quantified. Variables of sorts fluent, state, action, and situation shall be denoted by the letters f, z, a, and s, respectively. The function "$\circ$" is written in infix notation. A (possibly empty) sequence of variables is denoted by $\overline{x}$. We use the standard logical connectives $\neg$, $\wedge$, $\vee$, $\supset$ (implication), and $\equiv$ (equivalence).

[2] The full axiomatic foundation of the fluent calculus contains two further axioms [8], which, however, are not needed in the present paper. By the foundational axioms, states are essentially *flat* sets (of fluents), i.e., which do not contain sets as elements.

2.2 FLUX

The basic data structure in FLUX is that of an incomplete state, which represents what an agent knows of the state of its environment in a specific situation. An incomplete state is encoded as a fluent list which carries a tail variable; e.g.,

```
Z0 = [solution(a),solution(b),litmus(p1) | Z]
```

shall encode the knowledge that there are at least the two (chemical) solutions a,b and the litmus paper p1. In addition to knowledge of fluents that hold in a state, FLUX—as presented in [11]—allows to encode negative and disjunctive state information as *constraints* on the tail variable. For example,

```
not_holds(red(p1),Z), or_holds([acidic(a),acidic(b)],Z),
not_holds_all(solution(_),Z)
```

encodes the knowledge that the litmus paper is not red, that one of the two solutions is acidic, and that there are no other solutions available. The semantics of a FLUX state specification is given by an equational fluent calculus formula, here $(\exists Z)(Z0 = solution(a) \circ solution(b) \circ litmus(p1) \circ Z)$, along with formulas corresponding to the semantics of the constraints:

constraint	semantics	
not_holds(F,Z)	$\neg Holds(F,Z)$	
not_holds_all(F,Z)	$(\forall \overline{x}) \neg Holds(F,Z)$, $\overline{x}$ variables in F	(6)
or_holds([F$_1$,...,F$_k$],Z)	$\bigvee_{i=1}^{k} Holds(F_i, Z)$	

In [11], a set of *Constraint Handling Rules* (CHRs) [9] has been developed for the FLUX constraints. CHRs are of the form

```
H1,...,Hm <=> G1,...,Gk | B1,...,Bn.
```

where the *head* $H_1, \ldots, H_m$ are constraints ($m \geq 1$); the *guard* $G_1, \ldots, G_k$ are Prolog literals ($k \geq 0$); and the *body* $B_1, \ldots, B_n$ are constraints ($n \geq 0$). An empty guard is omitted; the empty body is denoted by true. The declarative interpretation of a CHR is given by the formula

$$(\forall \overline{x})(G_1 \wedge \ldots \wedge G_k \supset [H_1 \wedge \ldots \wedge H_m \equiv (\exists \overline{y})(B_1 \wedge \ldots \wedge B_n)]) \quad (7)$$

where $\overline{x}$ are the variables in both guard and head and $\overline{y}$ are the variables which additionally occur in the body. The procedural interpretation of a CHR is given by a transition in a constraint store: If the head can be matched against elements of the constraint store and the guard can be derived, then the constraints of the head are replaced by the constraints of the body.

The two main computation mechanisms for constraint solving in FLUX are propagation and unit resolution. Figure 1 depicts two out of the total of 18 rules, each of which has been verified against the foundational axioms of the fluent calculus. The first example CHR *propagates* a negation constraint through a list

```
not_holds(F,[F1|Z])        <=> neq(F,F1), not_holds(F,Z).

not_holds(F,Z) \ or_holds(V,Z) <=> member(G,V,W), F==G | or_holds(W,Z).
```

Fig. 1. Two example CHRs for the FLUX constraints. The auxiliary predicate neq(F, G) defines the inequality of F and G by a finite domain constraint [12] among the arguments of the two fluents. Predicate member(X, Y, Z) is true if X occurs in list Y and if Z is Y without X. Notation H1 \ H2 <=> G | B abbreviates H1,H2 <=> G | H1,B.

of fluents. Suppose, say, that tail variable Z of our example state were substituted by [red(X)|Z1], then not_holds(red(p1),[red(X)|Z1]) reduces to finite domain constraint p1 ≠ X along with not_holds(red(p1),Z1). The second CHR *resolves* a disjunction in the presence of a negation constraint. Suppose, for instance, we add the constraint not_holds(acidic(b),Z) to our example state, then or_holds([acidic(a),acidic(b)],Z) reduces to the singleton or_holds([acidic(a)],Z).[3]

Actions are specified in FLUX by *state update axioms*. Two examples are,

```
state_update(Z1,get_litmus_paper(P),Z2,[]) :-
    update(Z1,[litmus(P)],[],Z2).

state_update(Z1,sense_paper(P),Z2,[Red]) :-
    ( Red=true,  holds(red(P),Z1) ;
      Red=false, not_holds(red(P),Z1) ), Z2 = Z1.
```

The semantics of the auxiliary predicate update(Z1,P,N,Z2) is given by the fluent calculus update equation $Z2 = (Z1 - N) + P$. The last argument of state_update being empty indicates that action get_litmus_paper does not involve sensing. The action of sensing the status of a litmus paper, on the other hand, does not cause any physical effect, hence the state equality Z2=Z1. Recall, for instance, the initial state from above, then

```
?- state_update(Z0,get_litmus_paper(p2),Z1,[]),
   state_update(Z1,sense_paper(p2),Z2,[true]).

Z2 = [litmus(p2),solution(a),solution(b),litmus(p1),red(p2)|Z]
Constraints:
not_holds(red(p1),Z)
or_holds([acidic(a),acidic(b)],Z)
not_holds_all(solution(_),Z)
...
```

---

[3] It is worth mentioning that the guard in the second CHR of Figure 1 cannot be simplified to member(F, V, W) because constraints may contain variables. For example, ($\exists X$) ¬*Holds*(acidic(X), Z) and *Holds*(acidic(a), Z) ∨ *Holds*(red(p), Z) do *not* imply *Holds*(red(p), Z).

The constraint solver and the definition of state update provide the basis for agent programs in which an internal model of the environment is used for decision making and where this model is updated through the execution of actions.

3 Handling Implication Constraints

3.1 Why Implication Constraints?

The constraints and CHRs for FLUX presented in [11] have been carefully designed to allow for efficient constraint solving. This has been achieved by restricting disjunctions to positive atoms only, which allows to apply unit resolution. As a consequence, the computational effort of evaluating a new constraint is *linear* in the size of the constraint store. A disadvantage, however, is that the restricted expressiveness is too weak for solving problems which involve actions with conditional effects and where the condition is unknown at execution time. As an example, consider the action dip(P,X) of dipping litmus paper P into solution X, of which it is not known whether it is acidic or not. With the given restricted expressiveness, FLUX requires to specify this action by the following state update axiom:

```
state_update(Z1,dip(P,X),Z2,[]) :-
   \+ not_holds(acidic(X),Z1) -> update(Z1,[red(P)],[],Z2) ;
   \+ holds(acidic(X),Z1)     -> update(Z1,[],[red(P)],Z2) ;
   cancel(red(P),Z1,Z2).
```

That is, if state Z1 contains sufficient information to conclude that acidic(X) cannot be false, then the agent can update its state knowledge by +red(P). Conversely, if the agent knows that acidic(X) cannot hold, then it updates its state by −red(P). If, however, the status of acidic(X) is not known in Z1, then cancel(F,Z1,Z2) means that state Z2 is as state Z1 except that any constraint on fluent F is cancelled. With this, the essence of the Litmus Test cannot be expressed, because testing a solution and afterwards checking the color of the paper does not enable the agent to infer the status of the solution. Recall, for example, the initial state Z0 in Section 2, then

```
?- state_update(Z0,dip(p1,a),Z1,[]),
   state_update(Z1,sense_paper(p1),Z2,[true]).

Z2 = [solution(a),solution(b),litmus(p1),red(p1) | _]
```

Although fluent red(p1) is known to be true now, it does not follow that solution a is acidic. The reason is that initially the status of the solution is unknown, and hence the only inferred effect of applying the state update axiom for dip(p1,a) is that paper p1 is no longer known not to be red. The restricted expressiveness of FLUX does not allow to encode the effect of this action in such a way that the logical dependency between redness of the paper and acidity of the solution is captured in the successor state. This is a general limitation of the existing FLUX when it comes to actions with conditional effects.

```
if_then_holds(F,G1,Z)     <=> if_then_or_holds(F,[G1],Z).              %1

if_then_or_holds(F,[],Z)  <=> not_holds(F,Z).                          %2
if_then_or_holds(_,_,[])  <=> true.                                    %3
if_then_or_holds(_,V,Z)   <=> member(eq(X,Y),V),                       %4
                              or_neq(exists,X,Y,D), \+ call(D) | true.
if_then_or_holds(F,V,Z)   <=> member(eq(X,Y),V,W),                     %5
                              \+ (and_eq(X,Y,D), call(D))
                              | if_then_or_holds(F,W,Z).
```

Fig. 2. Simplification CHRs for implication constraints. The auxiliary predicates or_neq(exists, $\overline{X}, \overline{Y}, D$) and and_eq($\overline{X}, \overline{Y}, D$) define D to be a finite domain constraint that encodes, respectively, inequality $\overline{X} \neq \overline{Y}$ and equality $\overline{X} = \overline{Y}$ (see [11] for details).

3.2 Handling Implication Constraints

In this section, we will extend FLUX by a constraint for disjunctions containing a negative literal. A special case of this will be an auxiliary constraint for implicational dependencies between two fluents:

constraint	semantics
if_then_or_holds(F,[G_1,...,G_k],Z)	$Holds(F, Z) \supset \bigvee_{i=1}^{k} Holds(G_i, Z)$ (8)
if_then_holds(F,G,Z)	$Holds(F, Z) \supset Holds(G, Z)$

We incorporate the new constraint into FLUX by adding a set of Constraint Handling Rules. Each of the new CHRs, too, constitutes either a simplification, propagation, or unit resolution step, so that evaluating a new constraint is still linear in the size of the constraint store. The first part of the new set of CHRs is depicted in Figure 2. The solver employs an extended notion of an implication constraint where the disjunctive part may include atoms of the form eq(X,Y) and neq(X,Y) with X and Y being lists of equal length. The meaning of this general constraint if_then_or_holds(F,[G_1,...,G_k],Z) is

$$Holds(\text{F}, Z) \supset \bigvee_{i=1}^{k} \begin{cases} Holds(G_i, Z) & \text{if } G_i \text{ is a fluent} \\ X = Y & \text{if } G_i \text{ is eq(X,Y)} \\ X \neq Y & \text{if } G_i \text{ is neq(X,Y)} \end{cases} \qquad (9)$$

This generalization is needed for propagating an implication constraint containing fluents with variable arguments, as will be shown below.

To begin with, CHR 1 defines if_then_holds in terms of the general implication constraint. CHRs 2–5 are simplification rules. Consider, say, the implication constraint if_then_or_holds(acidic(a),[eq([p1],[p2])],Z), which has a singleton, equational disjunction. To this, CHR 5 applies since p1 = p2 fails. The application of the rule yields if_then_or_holds(acidic(a),[],Z), which by CHR 2 gets reduced to not_holds(acidic(a),Z).

The four CHRs in Figure 3 encode unit resolution steps. Specifically, CHRs 6 and 7 solve an implication whose antecedent is implied by a negation constraint.

```
not_holds(F,Z)       \ if_then_or_holds(G,_,Z) <=> F==G    | true.       %6
not_holds_all(F,Z)   \ if_then_or_holds(G,_,Z) <=> inst(G,F) | true.     %7

not_holds(F,Z)       \ if_then_or_holds(C,V,Z) <=>                       %8
                       member(G,V,W), F==G    | if_then_or_holds(C,W,Z).
not_holds_all(F,Z)   \ if_then_or_holds(C,V,Z) <=>                       %9
                       member(G,V,W), inst(G,F) | if_then_or_holds(C,W,Z).
```

Fig. 3. Unit resolution CHRs for implication constraints. Predicate inst(G,F) means that fluent term G is an instance of F.

CHRs 8 and 9 resolve an implication containing a disjunct that unifies with a negation constraint. For example, in the presence of not_holds(red(p1),Z), implication if_then_or_holds(acidic(a),[red(p1)],Z) reduces, by CHR 8, to if_then_or_holds(acidic(a),[],Z).

Crucial for constraint solving in FLUX is the propagation through a list of fluents. It is needed whenever the variable state argument is substituted by an (incomplete) list. This happens when an agent performs actions or acquires new information about the world. In general, propagating a constraint through a list of fluents requires us to evaluate these fluents against those that occur in the constraint. CHRs 10–12 in Figure 4 model the propagation of our new implication constraint. Specifically, the first case in CHR 10 applies if the antecedent of the implication is true in the given state. The other two cases employ the 4-ary constraint if_then_or_holds(C,[G_1,...,G_k],[H_1,...,H_l],[F|Z]), whose intended semantics is

$$Holds(C,Z) \supset \bigvee_{i=1}^{k} \begin{cases} Holds(G_i, F \circ Z) & \text{if } G_i \text{ is a fluent} \\ X = Y & \text{if } G_i \text{ is eq(X,Y)} \\ X \neq Y & \text{if } G_i \text{ is neq(X,Y)} \end{cases} \vee \bigvee_{j=1}^{l} \begin{cases} Holds(H_j, Z) & \text{if } H_j \text{ is a fluent} \\ X = Y & \text{if } H_j \text{ is eq(X,Y)} \\ X \neq Y & \text{if } H_j \text{ is neq(X,Y)} \end{cases} \quad (10)$$

Hence, the G_i's are the fluents that have not yet been evaluated against the head F of the state list, while the H_j's are those fluents that have been evaluated. For example, $Holds(G, F(x) \circ z) \supset Holds(F(a), F(x) \circ z) \vee Holds(F(b), F(x) \circ z)$ is equivalent to $Holds(G, z) \supset x = a \vee x = b \vee Holds(F(a), z) \vee Holds(F(b), z)$ according to the foundational axioms of decomposition and irreducibility and given the unique-name axiom $F(x) = F(y) \supset x = y$. Correspondingly,

```
    if(g,[f(a),f(b)],[f(X)|Z])
<=> if(g,[f(a),f(b)],[],[f(X)|Z])
<=> if(g,[f(b)],[eq([a],[X]),f(a)],[f(X)|Z])
<=> if(g,[],[eq([b],[X]),f(b),eq([a],[X]),f(a)],[f(X)|Z])
<=> if(g,[eq([b],[X]),f(b),eq([a],[X]),f(a)],Z)
```

(where if abbreviates if_then_or_holds). The third case in CHR 10 applies when the antecedent of an implication constraint unifies with the head of a state.

```
if_then_or_holds(C,V,[F|Z]) <=>                                              %10
    C==F -> or_holds(V,[F|Z]) ;
    C\=F -> if_then_or_holds(C,V,[],[F|Z]) ;
    C=..[_|ArgX], F=..[_|ArgY], or_holds([neq(ArgX,ArgY)|V],[F|Z]),
                        if_then_or_holds(C,V,[],[F|Z]).

if_then_or_holds(C,[G|V],W,[F|Z]) <=>                                        %11
    G==F -> true ;
    G\=F -> if_then_or_holds(C,V,[G|W],[F|Z]) ;
    G=..[_|ArgX], F=..[_|ArgY],
        if_then_or_holds(C,V,[eq(ArgX,ArgY),G|W],[F|Z]).

if_then_or_holds(C,[],W,[_|Z]) <=> if_then_or_holds(C,W,Z).                  %12
```

Fig. 4. Propagation CHRs for implication constraints

For example, $Holds(F(a), F(x) \circ z) \supset Holds(G, F(x) \circ z)$ is equivalent to

$$[a \neq x \vee Holds(G, z)] \wedge [Holds(F(a), z) \supset Holds(G, z)]$$

Correspondingly, `if_then_or_holds(f(a),[g],[f(X)|Z])` is reduced to

```
or_holds([neq([a],[X]),g],Z)
if_then_or_holds(f(a),[g],Z)
```

3.3 Correctness

In the following we prove the formal correctness of the new Constraint Handling Rules against the underlying theory of the fluent calculus. The proof is based on the declarative interpretation of CHRs (see (7)) and the semantics of the constraints in terms of the fluent calculus, given by (6) and (8)–(10).

Theorem 1. *CHRs 1–12 are correct under the foundational axioms $\mathcal{F}_{state}$ and the assumption of uniqueness-of-names (UNA) for all fluents.*

Proof. The logical reading of the rules are given by these formulas:

1. $[Holds(f, z) \supset G_1] \equiv [Holds(f, z) \supset \bigvee_{i=1}^{1} G_i]$;
2. $[Holds(f, z) \supset \bigvee_{i=1}^{0} G_i] \equiv \neg Holds(f, z)$;
3. $[Holds(f, \emptyset) \supset \bigvee_{i=1}^{k} G_i] \equiv \top$;
4. If $\neg \overline{x} \neq \overline{y}$ then $[Holds(f, z) \supset \overline{x} = \overline{y} \vee \bigvee_{i=1}^{k} G_i] \equiv \top$;
5. If $\neg \overline{x} = \overline{y}$ then $[Holds(f, z) \supset \overline{x} = \overline{y} \vee \bigvee_{i=1}^{k} G_i] \equiv [Holds(f, z) \supset \bigvee_{i=1}^{k} G_i]$;
6. If $\neg Holds(f, z)$ then $[(Holds(f, z) \supset \bigvee_{i=1}^{k} G_i] \equiv \top$;
7. If $(\forall \overline{x}) \neg Holds(f, z)$ and g is an instance of f then
   $[(Holds(g, z) \supset \bigvee_{i=1}^{k} G_i] \equiv \top$;
8. If $\neg Holds(f_1, z)$ then
   $[Holds(f, z) \supset Holds(f_1, z) \vee \bigvee_{i=1}^{k} G_i] \equiv [Holds(f, z) \supset \bigvee_{i=1}^{k} G_i]$;

9. If $(\forall \overline{x}) \neg Holds(f_1, z)$ and g is an instance of f_1 then
   $[Holds(f, z) \supset Holds(g, z) \vee \bigvee_{i=1}^{k} G_i] \equiv [Holds(f, z) \supset \bigvee_{i=1}^{k} G_i]$;
10. The following corresponds to the three cases in CHR 10:
   (a) $[Holds(f, f \circ z) \supset \bigvee_{i=1}^{k} G_i] \equiv \bigvee_{i=1}^{k} G_i$;
   (b) If $f \neq f_1$ then $[Holds(f, f_1 \circ z) \supset \bigvee_{i=1}^{k} G_i] \equiv [Holds(f, z) \supset \bigvee_{i=1}^{k} G_i]$;
   (c) $[Holds(F(\overline{x}), F(\overline{y}) \circ z) \supset \bigvee_{i=1}^{k} G_i] \equiv$
       $[(\overline{x} \neq \overline{y} \vee \bigvee_{i=1}^{k} G_i) \wedge (Holds(F(\overline{x}), z) \supset \bigvee_{i=1}^{k} G_i)]$;
11. The following corresponds to the three cases in CHR 11:
   (a) $[Holds(f, z) \supset Holds(f_1, f_1 \circ z) \vee \bigvee_{i=1}^{k} G_i \vee \bigvee_{j=1}^{l} H_j] \equiv \top$;
   (b) If $g \neq f_1$ then $[Holds(f, z) \supset (Holds(g, f_1 \circ z) \vee \bigvee_{i=1}^{k} G_i) \vee \bigvee_{j=1}^{l} H_j] \equiv$
       $[Holds(f, z) \supset \bigvee_{i=1}^{k} G_i \vee (Holds(g, z) \vee \bigvee_{j=1}^{l} H_j)]$;
   (c) $[Holds(f, z) \supset (Holds(F(\overline{x}), F(\overline{y}) \circ z) \vee \bigvee_{i=1}^{k} G_i) \vee \bigvee_{j=1}^{l} H_j] \equiv$
       $[Holds(f, z) \supset \bigvee_{i=1}^{k} G_i \vee (\overline{x} = \overline{y} \vee Holds(F(\overline{x}), z) \vee \bigvee_{j=1}^{l} H_j)]$;
12. $[Holds(c, z) \supset \bigvee_{i=1}^{0} G_i \vee \bigvee_{j=1}^{l} H_j] \equiv [Holds(c, z) \supset \bigvee_{j=1}^{l} H_j]$.

Let $\mathcal{F}$ be the underlying fluent functions, then $\mathcal{F}_{state} \cup UNA[\mathcal{F}]$ [4] entails each of the formulas above: Claims 1, 2, 4–9, and 12 are tautologies. Claim 3 follows by the foundational axiom on the empty state, (3). Claims 10(a) and 11(a) follow by the definition of Holds, (1). Claim 10(b) follows by the foundational axioms of decomposition, (5), and irreducibility, (4). Regarding 10(c), by decomposition and irreducibility $Holds(F(\overline{x}), F(\overline{y}) \circ z) \supset \bigvee_{i=1}^{k} G_i$ is equivalent to $[\overline{x} \neq \overline{y} \wedge \neg Holds(F(\overline{x}), z)] \vee \bigvee_{i=1}^{k} G_i$. This, in turn, is equivalent to the conjunction $[\overline{x} \neq \overline{y} \vee \bigvee_{i=1}^{k} G_i] \wedge [\neg Holds(F(\overline{x}), z) \vee \bigvee_{i=1}^{k} G_i]$, which implies the claim. Regarding 11(b), if $g \neq f_1$ then by decomposition and irreducibility $Holds(g, f_1 \circ z)$ is equivalent to $Holds(g, z)$, which implies the claim. Regarding 11(c), finally, by decomposition, $UNA[\mathcal{F}]$, and irreducibility $Holds(F(\overline{x}), F(\overline{y}) \circ z)$ is equivalent to $\overline{x} = \overline{y} \vee Holds(F(\overline{x}), z)$, which implies the claim.

While the extended set of CHRs is provably correct, a limitation is inherited from the original solver: Agents are not able to draw all conclusions that follow logically from a state specification if the underlying arithmetic solver trades full inference capabilities for efficiency; we refer to [11] for details.

3.4 Using the Implication Constraint

The new constraint allows to encode the logical dependencies that result from applying an action with conditional effects in situations where it is unknown whether the condition holds. The crucial action in the Litmus Test example can thus be encoded in such a way as to retain the dependency of cause and effect in case the status of the chemical solution in question is unknown. By the following update specification for action dip(P,X), first any knowledge of fluent red(P) is cancelled in state Z1, since this fluent may be affected by the action, and then the effect of the action is that red(P) is true in case acidic(X) holds and false in case acidic(X) does not hold:

---
[4] $UNA[f_1, \ldots, f_n] \stackrel{\text{def}}{=} \bigwedge_{i<j} f_i(\overline{x}) \neq f_j(\overline{y}) \wedge \bigwedge_i [f_i(\overline{x}) = f_i(\overline{y}) \supset \overline{x} = \overline{y}]$.

```
state_update(Z1,dip(P,X),Z2,[]) :-
   cancel(red(P),Z1,Z2),
   if_then_holds(acidic(X),red(P),Z2),
   if_then_holds(red(P),acidic(X),Z2).
```

Recall, e.g., the scenario discussed in Section 3.1, where it is given that either of two solutions is acidic and where the litmus paper is dipped into one of them:[5]

```
init(Z0) :- Z0 = [solution(a),solution(b),litmus(p1) | Z],
            not_holds(red(p1),Z),
            or_holds([acidic(a),acidic(b)],Z),
            not_holds_all(solution(_),Z),
            duplicate_free(Z0).

?- init(Z0), state_update(Z0,dip(p1,a),Z1,[]).

Z1 = [solution(a),solution(b),litmus(p1) | Z]
Constraints:
or_holds([acidic(a),acidic(b)],Z),
if_then_or_holds(acidic(a),[red(p1)],Z)
if_then_or_holds(red(p1),[acidic(a)],Z)
...
```

Suppose, now, that the subsequent test of the litmus paper reveals that it turned red. The update axiom for action sense_paper (cf. Section 2) effects a substitution of state variable Z by [red(p1)|_]. The extended FLUX constraint solver is then able to reduce the two implication constraints from above:

```
?- init(Z0),
   state_update(Z0,dip(p1,a),Z1,[]),
   state_update(Z1,sense_paper(p1),Z2,[true]).

Z2 = [solution(a),solution(b),litmus(p1),red(p1),acidic(a) | _]
```

Thus it follows that solution a must be acidic. Conversely, suppose that the test of the litmus paper reveals that it did not turn red. In this case the update axiom for action sense_paper adds the constraint not_holds(red(p1),Z). Again the extended FLUX constraint solver is able to reduce the two implication constraints from above. Furthermore, the disjunction is solved:

```
?- init(Z0),
   state_update(Z0,dip(p1,a),Z1,[]),
   state_update(Z1,sense_paper(p1),Z2,[true]).

Z2 = [solution(a),solution(b),litmus(p1),acidic(b) | _]
```

Thus it follows that solution b must be acidic.

---

[5] Auxiliary constraint duplicate_free(Z) ensures that no fluent occurs twice in Z.

3.5 Why Not General Disjunctions?

Read as disjunction, the new implication constraint allows to encode disjunctive clauses which include one negative literal (namely, the antecedent). This immediately raises the question of introducing general disjunctions with two or more negative literals. This, however, can only be done either by defining a highly incomplete constraint solver, or by worsening the complexity to exponential. To see why, consider a disjunctive statement with two negations, like

$$\neg Holds(F(a), F(x_1) \circ \ldots \circ F(x_n) \circ z) \vee \neg Holds(F(b), F(x_1) \circ \ldots \circ F(x_n) \circ z)$$

Using propagation through the first element of the state, $F(x_1)$, this formula is equivalent to the conjunction of these four constraints:

$a \neq x_1 \vee b \neq x_1$
$a \neq x_1 \vee \neg Holds(F(b), F(x_2) \circ \ldots \circ F(x_n) \circ z)$
$b \neq x_1 \vee \neg Holds(F(a), F(x_2) \circ \ldots \circ F(x_n) \circ z)$
$\neg Holds(F(a), F(x_2) \circ \ldots \circ F(x_n) \circ z) \vee \neg Holds(F(b), F(x_2) \circ \ldots \circ F(x_n) \circ z)$

Assuming uniqueness-of-names, the first disjunction is trivially true, but the other three constraints need to be propagated further. Propagation through the remaining $n-1$ fluents will result in $2^n - 1$ constraints. Hence, either constraint solving becomes exponential, or the solver avoids propagating a general disjunction. The latter, however, would render the solver powerless.

4 Handling Universal Quantification Constraints

A second limitation of the constraint solver presented in [11] is that it lacks universally quantified positive information. In this section, we will extend FLUX further by a constraint `all_holds(F,C,Z)` with the intended semantics

$$(\forall \overline{x}) \, (\text{C}[\overline{x}] \supset Holds(\text{F}, \text{Z})) \tag{11}$$

where $\overline{x}$ are the variables occurring in fluent F and where $\text{C}[\overline{x}]$ is a finite domain constraint over $\overline{x}$. The special case of unconstrained universal quantification shall be encoded by `all_holds(F,Z)`, meaning $(\forall \overline{x}) \, Holds(\text{F}, \text{Z})$. In a similar way, we generalize universally quantified negation to `all_not_holds(F,C,Z)` with the intended semantics

$$(\forall \overline{x}) \, (\text{C}[\overline{x}] \supset \neg Holds(\text{F}, \text{Z})) \tag{12}$$

where $\overline{x}$ are the variables occurring in fluent F and where $\text{C}[\overline{x}]$ is a finite domain constraint over $\overline{x}$. In the following, we present a set of CHRs for the new universal quantification constraints. Lack of space, however, will prevent us from discussing this extension as thoroughly as in the preceding section.

```
all_holds(F,Z) <=> all_holds(F,(0#=0),Z).

all_holds(F,C,Z), not_holds(G,Z) ==>                                    %1
    copy_fluent(F,C,F1,C1) | F1=G, call(#\+C1).
all_holds(F,C,Z), all_not_holds(G,D,Z) <=>                              %2
    copy_fluent(F,C,F1,C1), copy_fluent(G,D,G1,D1),
    F1=G1, call(C1#/\D1) | false.
all_holds(F,C,Z) \ or_holds(V,Z) <=>                                    %3
    member(G,V), copy_fluent(F,C,F1,C1), F1=G, \+ call(#\+C1) | true.
all_holds(F,C,Z) \ if_then_or_holds(G,V,Z) <=>                          %4
    copy_fluent(F,C,F1,C1), F1=G, \+ call(#\+C1) | or_holds(V,Z).
all_holds(F,C,Z) \ if_then_or_holds(_,V,Z) <=>                          %5
    member(G,V), copy_fluent(F,C,F1,C1), F1=G, \+ call(#\+C1) | true.
all_holds(F,C,[G|Z]) <=>                                                %6
    \+ (F=G, call(C)) -> all_holds(F,C,Z) ;
    F=..[_|ArgX], G=..[_|ArgY],
    or_neq(exists,ArgX,ArgY,C1), all_holds(F,(C#/\C1),Z).
```

Fig. 5. The CHRs for universal quantification constraints. Following the syntax of Eclipse Prolog, the symbol # is used to identify the operators for composing finite domain constraints. The auxiliary predicate copy_fluent(F, C, F1, C1) defines F1 and C1 to be variable-disjoint variants of, respectively, fluent F and constraint C. CHR 1 is a so-called propagation rule, where the constraints in the head are not removed from the constraint store.

4.1 Handling the Universal Constraint

Figure 5 depicts unit resolution and propagation rules for constraint all_holds. Specifically, CHRs 1 and 2 model unit resolution wrt. negation constraints. For example, the constraints all_holds(f(X),X#>5,Z) and not_holds(f(8),Z) together imply, by CHR 1, the finite domain constraint #\+ 8#>5, which fails (since 8 > 5). CHR 3 models the subsumption of a disjunctive constraint by a universal one. For example, given all_holds(f(X),X#>5,Z) the disjunctive constraint or_holds([f(3),f(7)],Z) is true (since 7 > 5). CHR 4 models unit resolution wrt. an implication constraint whose antecedent is implied by a universal constraint, whereas CHR 5 solves an implication constraint whose succedent is subsumed by a universal constraint. Finally, CHR 6 defines the propagation of a universal constraint through a state list: In case the head fluent g of the state is within the range of the universal constraint, this range is restricted so as to be unequal to g. For example, propagation applied to all_holds(f(X),X#>5,[f(6)|Z]) yields all_holds(f(X),X#>6,Z).

A similar set of CHRs for negated universal quantification is given in Figure 6. Altogether the rules can be shown to be correct wrt. the foundational axioms of the fluent calculus.

Theorem 2. *CHRs 1–11 in Figures 5 and 6 are correct under the foundational axioms $\mathcal{F}_{state}$ and the assumption of uniqueness-of-names for all fluents.*

```
not_holds_all(F,Z) <=> all_not_holds(F,(0#=0),Z).

all_not_holds(F,C,Z) \ not_holds(G,Z) <=>                              %7
    copy_fluent(F,C,F1,C1), F1=G, \+ call(#\+C1) | true.
all_not_holds(F,C,Z) \ or_holds(V,Z) <=>                               %8
    member(G,V,W), copy_fluent(F,C,F1,C1), F1=G, \+ call(#\+C1)
    | or_holds(W,Z).
all_not_holds(F,C,Z) \ if_then_or_holds(G,_,Z) <=>                     %9
    copy_fluent(F,C,F1,C1), F1=G, \+ call(#\+C1) | true.
all_not_holds(F,C,Z) \ if_then_or_holds(F2,V,Z) <=>                    %10
    member(G,V,W), copy_fluent(F,C,F1,C1), F1=G, \+ call(#\+C1)
    | if_then_or_holds(F2,W,Z).
all_not_holds(F,C,[G|Z]) <=>                                           %11
    (\+ (F=G, call(C)) -> true ;
    copy_fluent(F,C,F1,C1), F1=G, call(#\+C1)), all_not_holds(F,C,Z).
```

Fig. 6. CHRs for universally quantified negation

4.2 Using the Universal Constraints

The new universal constraints can be used for domains with states in which infinitely many instances of a fluent are true and, at the same time, infinitely many of its instances are false. We conclude this section with a small example of a fluent F which, initially, is known to be true for all integers greater than 2 and false for all negative integers. The agent then performs several actions which affect specific instances of the fluent:

```
init(Z0) :- all_holds(f(X),X#>2,Z0),
            all_not_holds(f(X),X#<0,Z0), duplicate_free(Z0).

state_update(Z1,set(X),   Z2,[]) :- update(Z1,[f(X)],[],Z2).
state_update(Z1,reset(X),Z2,[]) :- update(Z1,[],[f(X)],Z2).

?- init(Z0),
   state_update(Z0,set(-2), Z1,[]),
   state_update(Z1,reset(5),Z2,[]),
   state_update(Z2,set(0),  Z3,[]).

Z3 = [f(0),f(-2) | Z]
Constraints:
all_holds(f(X),X#>2 #/\ X#\=5,Z)
all_not_holds(f(X),X#<0,Z)
not_holds(f(5),Z)
not_holds(f(0),Z)
duplicate_free(Z)
```

5 Summary

We have enriched significantly the expressiveness of state representations in FLUX by introducing both implication and universal quantification constraints. We have presented a set of Constraint Handling Rules based solely on simplification, propagation, and unit resolution, so that the efficiency of constraint solving in FLUX is retained. The rules have been formally verified against the fluent calculus.

The closest work is the logic program presented in [5] for GOLOG with incomplete states. The main difference is that states are only indirectly represented in GOLOG and that regression through the history of actions is used to evaluate conditions in agent programs. In contrast, FLUX uses explicit representations of incomplete states along with the computation mechanism of progression, which allows to evaluate conditions directly against the updated state. A further difference is that the GOLOG variant of [5] employs a general theorem prover for evaluating a regressed condition (against the initial state knowledge). In contrast, the motivation for FLUX is to retain a restricted expressiveness in order to be able to employ efficient inference techniques. Benchmark problems have shown that FLUX scales much better to domains with large state space and in which agents perform long sequences of actions [8,7].

References

1. McCarthy, J.: Programs with common sense. In: Proc. of the Symposium on the Mechanization of Thought Processes. Volume 1, London (1958) 77–84.
2. McCarthy, J.: Situations and Actions and Causal Laws. Stanford Artif. Intell. Project, Memo 2, Stanford University, CA (1963)
3. McCarthy, J., Hayes, P.J.: Some philosophical problems from the standpoint of artificial intelligence. Machine Intell. **4** (1969) 463–502
4. Fikes, R.E., Nilsson, N.J.: STRIPS: A new approach to the application of theorem proving to problem solving. Artif. Intell. **2** (1971) 189–208
5. Reiter, R.: On knowledge-based programming with sensing in the situation calculus. ACM Transactions on Computational Logic **2** (2001) 433–457
6. Shanahan, M., Witkowski, M.: High-level robot control through logic. In Castelfranchi, C., Lespérance, Y., eds.: Proc. of the Internat. Workshop on Agent Theories Architectures and Languages. Vol. 1986 of LNCS, Springer (2000) 104–121
7. Thielscher, M.: Pushing the envelope: programming reasoning agents. In Baral, C., ed.: *AAAI Workshop on Cognitive Robotics*. AAAI Press (2002) 110–117
8. Thielscher, M.: FLUX: A logic programming method for reasoning agents. Theory and Practice of Logic Programming (2005). Available at: www.fluxagent.org
9. Frühwirth, T.: Theory and practice of constraint handling rules. Journal of Logic Programming **37** (1998) 95–138
10. Thielscher, M.: From situation calculus to fluent calculus: State update axioms as a solution to the inferential frame problem. Artif. Intell. **111** (1999) 277–299
11. Thielscher, M.: Reasoning about actions with CHRs and finite domain constraints. In Stuckey, P., ed.: Proc. of ICLP. Vol. 2401 of LNCS, Springer (2002) 70–84
12. Van Hentenryck, P.: Constraint Satisfaction in Logic Programming. MIT Press (1989)

Solving Simple Planning Problems with More Inference and No Search

Vincent Vidal[1] and Héctor Geffner[2]

[1] CRIL & Université d'Artois,
rue de l'université - SP16, 62307 Lens Cedex, France
`vidal@cril.univ-artois.fr`
[2] ICREA & Universitat Pompeu Fabra,
Paseo de Circunvalacion 8, 08003 Barcelona, Spain
`hector.geffner@upf.edu`

Abstract. Many benchmark domains in AI planning including Blocks, Logistics, Gripper, Satellite, and others lack the interactions that characterize puzzles and can be solved non-optimally in low polynomial time. They are indeed easy problems for people, although as with many other problems in AI, not always easy for machines. In this paper, we address the question of whether simple problems such as these can be solved in a simple way, i.e., without search, by means of a domain-independent planner. We address this question *empirically* by extending the constraint-based planner CPT with additional domain-independent inference mechanisms. We show then for the first time that these and several other benchmark domains can be solved with no backtracks while performing only polynomial node operations. This is a remarkable finding in our view that suggests that the classes of problems that are solvable without search may be actually much broader than the classes that have been identified so far by work in Tractable Planning.

1 Introduction

Simple problems can be hard for a general problem solver when the structure of the problems is not exploited. Domains like Blocks, Logistics, Satellite and others, for example, have all a low polynomial complexity (once the optimality requirement is dropped) and yet they all have been challenging for domain-independent planners until quite recently. Current planners solve these and other problems by exploiting structure in the form of heuristic functions that are extracted automatically and guide the search for plans [1,2].

In this paper, we address the question of whether these and other simple, tractable domains can be solved by a domain-independent planner *with no search at all* by performing polynomial node operations only. The work in Tractable Planning addresses a related question by studying fragments of general planning languages such as Strips over which planning is polynomial [3–6]. Unfortunately, the fragments that have been identified so far as tractable remain somehow narrow and do not account for the tractability of the standard benchmarks.

In this work we approach this problem in a different way – *empirically* – by developing a general planning algorithm and showing that it solves these and other domains backtrack free, suggesting thus that the classes of problems that can be solved with no search by means of a domain-independent planner may be much broader than the ones that have been identified *theoretically* so far. Closing the gap between the empirical results and the theoretical accounts arises then as a key challenge that we hope to approach elsewhere.

The planning algorithm that we use for solving the various domains backtrack-free is an extension of the constraint-based planner CPT, an optimal temporal planner that combines a POCL branching scheme (for Partial Order Causal Link Planning [7]) with strong pruning mechanisms [8]. The extension is modular and takes the form of additional domain-independent constraints and inference mechanisms. We will refer to domain-independent planners that aim to solve simple problems in a backtrack-free manner by performing low polynomial operations in every node, as *easy planners*. The development of easy planners, we believe, is a crisp and meaningful goal, which may yield insights that an exclusive focus on performance may not, like the identification of broader tractable planning fragments, and the process by which people actually plan. Humans indeed are quite good at solving these simple problems, and while it is often assumed that this ability is the result of domain-dependent strategies, our results suggest that they may also result from simple but general inference mechanisms.

By itself, CPT like other SAT and constraint-based optimal planners [9–11], does not make for a good suboptimal planner and much less for an easy planner. Indeed, while SAT and constraint-based planners can be used with large, non-optimal planning horizons (which are upper bounds on the makespan of the plan), they face two problems: 1) SAT and CSP encodings based on one variable per time point, as normally used, become too large to handle for large planning horizons; and 2) the constraint that requires the goals to be true at the planning horizon becomes ineffective when the horizon is set too high.

In CPT the first is not a problem because, being a temporal planner, CPT uses temporal rather than boolean encodings; i.e. for each action in the domain, a single variable represents the starting time of the action in the plan. Thus, the use of a large bound on the admissible makespan of plans has a direct effect on the *upper bounds* of the temporal variables but not in their *number*.

CPT, on the other hand, does not escape from Problem 2: with a large bound on the makespan, the search becomes less constrained and focused, and even problems that are solved backtrack free with the optimal bound are not solved at all after thousands of backtracks when a larger bound is used instead. In this work, we tackle this problem by extending the inferential capabilities of CPT so that it relies less on inferences drawn from the bounding constraint and more on domain-independent inferences not captured by CPT. The new version of CPT, that we call eCPT, does simple but more extensive reasoning, making use and adapting techniques like landmarks [12,13] and distances [14] among others.

The paper is organized as follows. We first review the CPT planner, discuss its strength as an optimal planner and its weakness as a suboptimal planner, and introduce extensions of the inferential machinery of CPT that render the search backtrack-free over a wide range of domains. We then evaluate the resulting planner, eCPT, and discuss implications and open ends.

2 CPT

CPT is a domain-independent temporal planner that combines a branching scheme based on Partial Order Causal Link (POCL) Planning with powerful and sound pruning rules implemented as constraints [8]. The key novelty in CPT in relation to other formulations [7,15,16] is the ability to reason about supports, precedences, and causal links involving actions that are not in the plan. In this way, CPT can prune the start time and supports of actions that are not yet in the plan, rule out actions from the plan, detect failures early on, etc. The inferences in CPT are supported by a convenient representation of POCL plans in terms of variables and constraints. For example, for each action a in the domain there is a variable $T(a)$ that represents the starting time of a, and for each precondition p of a, a variable $S(p, a)$ that represents the supporter of precondition p of a. A causal link $a'[p]a$ is thus represented by the constraint $S(p, a) = a'$, while its negation is represented by the constraint $S(p, a) \neq a'$ which means that a' cannot produce p for a, i.e. the causal link $a'[p]a$ is forbidden. Unlike other POCL planners based on constraints however, [17–20], CPT represents and reasons with all these variables, whether or not the action a is part of the current plan.

CPT uses a simple extension of the Strips language that accommodates concurrent actions with integer durations. A temporal planning problem is a tuple $P = \langle A, I, O, G \rangle$ where A is a set of ground atoms, $I \subseteq A$ and $G \subseteq A$ represent the initial and goal situations, and O is the set of ground Strips operators, each with precondition, add, and delete list $pre(a)$, $add(a)$, and $del(a)$, and *duration* $dur(a)$. As is common in POCL planning, there are also the dummy actions *Start* and *End* with zero durations, the first with an empty precondition and effect I; the latter with precondition G and empty effects. As in GRAPHPLAN [21], two actions a and a' interfere when one deletes a precondition or positive effect of the other. CPT follows the simple model of time in [22] where interfering actions cannot overlap, and produces valid plans with minimum *makespan*.

The basic formulation of the CPT planner can be described in four parts: *preprocessing, variables, constraints,* and *branching*. After the preprocessing, the variables are created and the constraints are asserted and propagated. If an inconsistency is found, no valid plan for the problem exists. Otherwise, the constraint $T(End) = B$ for the bound B on the makespan, set to the earliest possible starting time of the action End (i.e.; $B = T_{min}(End)$ which is determined by preprocessing, see below), is asserted and propagated. The branching scheme then takes over and if no solution is found, the process restarts by retracting the constraint $T(End) = B$ and replacing it with $T(End) = B + 1$ (1 being the smallest time unit). The search is then restarted from scratch with the new bound, and this is repeated until a solution is found. For simplicity, we follow [8] and assume that no action in the domain can be done more than once in the plan. This restriction is removed in the last version of CPT, which is the one

2.1 Preprocessing

In the preprocessing phase, CPT computes the heuristic values $h_T^2(a)$ and $h_T^2(\{p,q\})$ for each action $a \in O$ and each atom pair $\{p,q\}$ as in [24]. The values provide lower bounds on the times to achieve the preconditions of a and the pair of atoms p, q, from the initial situation I. The *(structural) mutexes* (pairs of atoms that cannot be true in a world situation) are then identified as the pairs of atoms p, q for which $h_T^2(\{p,q\}) = \infty$. An action a is said to *e-delete* an atom p when either a deletes p, a adds an atom q such that q and p are mutex, or a precondition r of a is mutex with p and a does not add p. In all cases, if a e-deletes p, p is false after doing a; see [25]. Finally, $T_{min}(End) = \max_{\{p,q\} \subseteq G} h_T^2(\{p,q\})$.

In addition, the simpler heuristic h_T^1 is used for defining *distances* between actions [14]. For each action $a \in O$, the h_T^1 heuristic is computed from an initial situation I_a that includes all facts *except those that are e-deleted by* a. The distances $dist(a, a')$ are then set to the resulting $h_T^1(a')$ values. These distances encode lower bounds on the *slack* that must be inserted between the completion of a and the start of a' in any legal plan in which a' follows a. They are not symmetric in general and their calculation, which remains polynomial, involves the computation of the h_T^1 heuristic $|O|$ times.

2.2 Variables and Domains

The state of the planner is given by a collection of variables, domains, and constraints. As emphasized above, the variables are defined for each action $a \in O$ and not only for the actions in the current plan. Moreover, variables are created for each precondition p of each action a as indicated below. The domain of variable X is indicated by $D[X]$ or simply as $X :: [X_{min}, X_{max}]$ if X is a numerical variable. The variables, their initial domains, and their meanings are:

- $T(a) :: [0, \infty]$ encodes the starting time of each action a, with $T(Start) = 0$
- $S(p, a)$ encodes the support of precondition p of action a with initial domain $D[S(p, a)] = O(p)$ where $O(p)$ is the set of actions in O that add p
- $T(p, a) :: [0, \infty]$ encodes the starting time of $S(p, a)$
- $InPlan(a) :: [0, 1]$ indicates the presence of a in plan; $InPlan(Start) = InPlan(End) = 1$ (true)

In addition, the set of actions in the current plan is kept in the variable *Steps*; i.e., $Steps = \{a \mid InPlan(a) = 1\}$. Variables $T(a)$, $S(p, a)$, and $T(p, a)$ associated with actions a which are either in or out of the current plan (i.e., actions for which the $InPlan(a)$ variable is not set to either 0 or 1 yet) are *conditional* in the following sense: these variables and their domains are meaningful only under the assumption that they will be part of the plan. In order to ensure this interpretation, some care needs to be taken in the propagation of constraints as explained in [8].

2.3 Constraints

The constraints correspond basically to disjunctions, rules, and precedences, or their combination. Temporal constraints are propagated by bounds consistency [26]. The constraints apply to all actions $a \in O$ and all $p \in pre(a)$; we use $\delta(a, a')$ to stand for $dur(a) + dist(a, a')$.

- **Bounds:** For all $a \in O$, $T(Start) + \delta(Start, a) \leq T(a)$ and $T(a) + \delta(a, End) \leq T(End)$
- **Preconditions:** Supporter a' of precondition p of a must precede a by an amount that depends on $\delta(a', a)$:

$$T(a) \geq \min_{a' \in D[S(p,a)]} (T(a') + \delta(a', a))$$

$$T(a) \geq T(p, a) + \min_{a' \in D[S(p,a)]} \delta(a', a)$$

$$T(a') + \delta(a', a) > T(a) \to S(p, a) \neq a'$$

- **Causal Link Constraints:** For all $a \in O$, $p \in pre(a)$ and a' that e-deletes p, a' precedes $S(p, a)$ or follows a

$$T(a') + dur(a') + \min_{a'' \in D[S(p,a)]} dist(a', a'') \leq T(p, a) \;\vee\; T(a) + \delta(a, a') \leq T(a')$$

- **Mutex Constraints:** For effect-interfering a and a'[1]

$$T(a) + \delta(a, a') \leq T(a') \;\vee\; T(a') + \delta(a', a) \leq T(a)$$

- **Support Constraints:** $T(p, a)$ and $S(p, a)$ related by

$$S(p, a) = a' \to T(p, a) = T(a')$$

$$T(p, a) \neq T(a') \to S(p, a) \neq a'$$

$$\min_{a' \in D[S(p,a)]} T(a') \leq T(p, a) \leq \max_{a' \in D[S(p,a)]} T(a')$$

2.4 Branching

As in POCL planning, branching in CPT proceeds by iteratively selecting and fixing flaws in non-terminal states σ, backtracking upon inconsistencies. A state σ is given by the variables, their domains, and the constraints involving them. The initial state σ_0 contains the variables, domains, and constraints above, along with the *bounding constraint* $T(End) = B$ where B is the current bound on the makespan, which in the optimal setting is set to a lower bound and is then increased until a plan is found. A state is inconsistent when a non-conditional variable has an empty domain, while a consistent state σ with no flaws is a *goal state* from which a valid plan P with bound B can be extracted by scheduling the in-plan variables at their earliest starting times.

The definition of 'flaws' parallels the one in POCL planning expressed in terms of the temporal and support variables, with the addition of 'mutex threats':

---

[1] Two actions are effect-interfering in CPT when one deletes a positive effect of the other, and neither one *e-deletes* a precondition of the other.

- **Support Threats:** a' *threatens a support* $S(p, a)$ when both actions a and a' are in the current plan, a' e-deletes p, and neither $T_{min}(a') + dur(a') \leq T_{min}(p, a)$ nor $T_{min}(a) + dur(a) \leq T_{min}(a')$ hold,
- **Open Conditions:** $S(p, a)$ is an *open condition* when $|D[S(p, a)]| > 1$ holds for an action a in the plan,
- **Mutex Threats:** a and a' constitute a *mutex threat* when both actions are in the plan, they are effect-interfering, and neither $T_{min}(a) + dur(a) \leq T_{min}(a')$ nor $T_{min}(a') + dur(a') \leq T_{min}(a)$ hold.

Flaws are selected for repair in the following order: first Support Threats (ST's), then Open Conditions (OC's), and finally Mutex Threats (MT's). ST's and MT's are repaired by posting precedence constraints, while OC's are repaired by choosing a supporter, as usual in POCL planning.

3 eCPT

CPT is an optimal temporal planner with good performance which is competitive with the best SAT parallel planners when actions have uniform durations [8]. At the same time, for non-optimal planning, CPT has the advantage that the size of the encodings does not grow with the bound; indeed the bound in CPT enters only through the constraint $T(End) = B$, which affects the domain upper bounds of the variables but not their number. In spite of this, however, CPT does not make for a good suboptimal planner, because like SAT and CSP planners it still relies heavily on the bounding constraint which becomes ineffective for large values of B.

Figure 1 shows the performance of CPT for the Tower-n problem for several values of n and several horizons B. Tower-n is the problem of assembling a specific tower of n blocks which are initially on the table. This is a trivial problem for people, but as shown in [8], it is not trivial for most optimal planners. CPT, however, solves this problem optimally *backtrack free* for any value of n. As the figure shows, however, the times and the number of backtracks increase when the horizon B is increased *above* the optimal bound, and for large values of B, CPT cannot solve these problems after thousands of seconds and backtracks.

The figure also shows the performance of eCPT, the extension of CPT described in this paper. It can be seen that while the performance of CPT degrades with the increase of the bound B, the performance of eCPT remains stable, and actually *backtrack free* for the different values of B. eCPT exploits the flexibility afforded by the Constraint-Programming formulation underlying CPT, extending it with inferences that do not rely as much on the bound, and which produce a backtrack-free behavior across a wide range of domains. In this section we focus on such inferences.

3.1 Impossible Supports

Many supports can be eliminated at preprocessing avoiding some dead-ends during the search. For example, the action $a' = putdown(b1)$ can never support

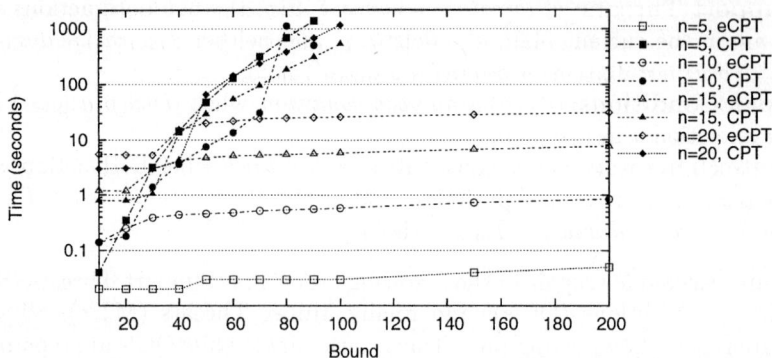

Fig. 1. Performance of CPT and eCPT over Tower-n for various numbers of blocks n and bounds B. Curves that diverge correspond to CPT; curves that remain stable to eCPT.

the precondition $p = handempty$ of an action like $a = unstack(b1, b3)$. This is because action a has another precondition $p' = on(b1, b3)$ which is e-deleted by a' (false after a') and which then would have to be reestablished by another action b before a. Yet it can be shown that in this domain, any such action b e-deletes p and is thus incompatible with the causal link $a'[p]a$.

More generally, let $dist(a', p, a)$ refer to a lower bound on the slack between actions a' and a in any valid plan in which a' *is a supporter of precondition p of a*. We show that for some cases, at preprocessing time, it can be shown that $dist(a', p, a) = \infty$, and hence, that a' can be safely removed from the domain of the variable $S(p, a)$ encoding the support of precondition p of a.

This actually happens when some precondition p' of a is not *reachable* from the initial situation that includes all the facts except those e-deleted by a' and where *the actions that either add or delete p are excluded*. The reason for this exclusion is that if a' supports the precondition p of a then it can be assumed that no action adding or deleting p can occur between a' and a (the first part is the systematicity requirement [7]). By a proposition being reachable we mean that it makes it into the so-called relaxed planning graph; the planning graph with the delete lists excluded [27].

This simple test prunes the action $putdown(b_1)$ as a possible support of the precondition $handempty$ of action $unstack(b_1, b_3)$, the action $stack(b_1, b_3)$ as a possible support of precondition $clear(b_1)$ of $pickup(b_1)$, etc.

3.2 Unique Supports

We say that an action *consumes* an atom p when it requires and deletes p. For example, the actions $unstack(b_3, b_1)$ and $pickup(b_2)$ both consume the atom $handempty$. In such cases, if the actions make it into the plan, it can be shown that their common precondition p must have different supports. Indeed, if an action a deletes a precondition of a', and a' deletes a precondition of a, a and a'

are incompatible and cannot overlap in time according to the semantics. Then either a must precede a' or a' must precede a, and in either case, the precondition p needs to be established at least twice: one for the first action, and one for the second. The constraint $S(p, a) \neq S(p, a')$ for pairs of actions a and a' that consume p, ensures this, and when one of the support variables $S(p, a)$ or $S(p, a')$ is instantiated to a value b, b is immediately removed from the domain of the other variable.

3.3 Distance Boosting

The distances $dist(a, a')$ precomputed for all pairs of actions a and a' provide a lower bound on the slack between the end of a and the beginning of a'. In some cases, this lower bound can be easily improved, leading to stronger inferences. For example, the distance between the actions $putdown(b_1)$ and $pickup(b_1)$ is 0, as it is actually possible to do one action after the other. Yet the action $putdown(b_1)$ followed by $pickup(b_1)$ makes sense only if some other action using the effects of the first, occurs between these two, as when block b_1 is on block b_2 but needs to be moved on top of the block beneath b_2.

Let us say that an action a *cancels* an action a' when 1) every atom added by a' is e-deleted by a, and 2) every atom added by a is a precondition of a'. Thus, when a cancels a', the sequence a', a does not add anything that was not already true before a'. For example, $pickup(b_1)$ cancels the action $putdown(b_1)$.

When an action a cancels a', and there is a precondition p of a that is made true by a' (i.e., p is added by a' and is mutex with some precondition of a'), the distance $dist(a', p, a)$ introduced above becomes ∞ if all the actions that use an effect of a' e-delete p. In such case, as before, the action a' can be excluded from the domain of the $S(p, a)$ variable. Otherwise, the distance $dist(a', a)$ can be increased to $\min_b[dist(a', b) + dist(b, a)]$ with b ranging over the actions different than a and a' that either use an effect of a' but do not e-delete p or do not use necessarily an effect of a' but add p (because a' may be followed by an action c before a that e-deletes p but only if there is another action b between c and a that re-establishes p).

In this way, the distance between the actions $putdown(a)$ and $pickup(a)$ in Blocks is increased by 2, the distance between $sail(a, b)$ and $sail(b, a)$ in Ferry is increased by 1, etc. The net effect is similar to pruning cycles of size two in standard heuristic search. Pruning cycles of larger sizes, however, appears to be more difficult in the POCL setting, although similar ideas can potentially be used for pruning certain sequences of commutative actions.

3.4 Qualitative Precedences

Unlike traditional POCL planners, CPT reasons with *temporal precedences* of the form $T(a) + \delta(a, a') \leq T(a')$ rather than with *qualitative precedences*. CPT is a CP-based temporal planner and such a choice arises naturally from the representation used. Yet, the constraint propagation mechanism, bounds consistency, is incomplete, and in a planning context, it is often too weak. In particular, bounds consistency does not capture *transitivity:* namely from the constraints $A < B$ and $B < C$, it does not entail $A < C$. Indeed if the initial domains of the variables A, B, and C is $[1, \ldots, 100]$, bounds consistency reduces the domains to $[1, \ldots, 98]$, $[2, \ldots, 99]$, and $[3, \ldots, 100]$ respectively, which do not make $A < C$ true for all value combinations. Transitivities, however, are important in planning, and thus eCPT incorporates, in addition to temporal precedences, qualitative precedences of the form $a \prec a'$ *not limited to the actions a and a' in the plan*. Such qualitative precedences are obtained every time a temporal precedence is asserted or entailed, and are kept closed under transitivity.[2] When a new qualitative precedence $a \prec a'$ is found, the transitive closure is computed as follows: if a belongs to the current partial plan, then for all a'' such that $a'' \prec a$, $a'' \prec a'$ is recorded; and if a' belongs to the plan, then for all a'' such that $a' \prec a''$, $a \prec a''$ is recorded. The same updates are incrementally performed for an existing relation $a \prec a'$ with a or a' not in the plan, as soon as a or a' make it into the plan.

Then two inference rules make use of these qualitative precedences for pruning further the domains of the support variables:

- for an action a' in the plan that adds a precondition p of an action a: if $a \prec a'$ then $S(p, a) \neq a'$
- for an action a' that adds a precondition p of an action a and an action b in the plan that e-deletes p: if $a' \prec b$ and $b \prec a$, then $S(p, a) \neq a'$

3.5 Action Landmarks

Like all POCL planners, CPT starts with a partial plan with two actions only: *Start* and *End*. In many cases, however, it is possible to infer easily that certain other actions must be in the plan as well. For example, if a block b_1 must be moved but is beneath two blocks b_3 and b_2 in that order, then the actions $unstack(b_3, b_2)$ and $unstack(b_2, b_1)$ will have to be taken at some point, and moreover, the first must precede the second. In eCPT we identify such necessary actions and a partial order on them in a preprocessing step, following the idea of *landmarks* introduced in [12], in the form presented in [13]. An action a is a *landmark* if the action *End* is not *reachable* when the action a is excluded from the domain (as mentioned above, an action a is reachable when it makes it into the relaxed planning graph). Also, a landmark action a *precedes* a landmark action b, when b is not reachable when the action a is excluded. Action landmarks and the partial order on them are computed in the preprocessing step and are included in the initial state of the planner along with the actions *Start* and *End*. This involves the calculation of $|O|$ relaxed planning graphs, one for each action in the domain.

---

[2] Temporal precedences are asserted as a result of the branching decisions corresponding to support and mutex threats, and are inferred when either supports are asserted or inferred, or when one of the disjuncts in a causal link or mutex constraint becomes false.

3.6 Branching and Heuristics

eCPT retains the same branching scheme as CPT and the same ordering: it first branches on support threats (ST's), then on open conditions (OC's), and finally on mutex threats (MT's). The heuristic for selecting the support threats and open conditions however, is slightly different.

Support threats $\langle a', S(p,a) \rangle$ are selected in eCPT minimizing $T_{min}(a)$, breaking ties by first minimizing $T_{max}(p,a)$, and then with the slack based criterion used in CPT. Open supports $S(p,a)$ are selected minimizing $T_{max}(p,a)$, breaking ties minimizing $slack(a',a)$ where a' is the producer of a in $D[S(p,a)]$ with min $T_{min}(a')$. Also the constraint posted in the second case is $S(p,a) = a'$, and if that fails, $S(p,a) \neq a'$.

4 Experimental Results

While our motivation behind the development of eCPT is to study empirically the possibility of solving a wide variety of planning benchmarks with no search, we report also results that are illustrative for assessing eCPT as either an optimal or suboptimal planner in relation with state-of-the-art systems such as FF or SATPLAN04. FF [27] is a suboptimal, sequential planner winner of the 2nd Int. Planning Competition, while SATPLAN04 [9] is an optimal parallel planner winner of the Optimal Track of the 4th and last Int. Planning Competition that relies on the Siege SAT solver [28]. The instances and domains are all from the 2nd and 3rd Int. Planning Competitions [29,30], and the results have been obtained using a Pentium IV machine running at 2.8Ghz, with 1Gb of RAM, under Linux. The time limit for each problem is 30 minutes, and all times include preprocessing. Since FF and SATPLAN04 cannot handle temporal domains, we consider only the formulation in which all actions have unit duration. The bound B on the makespan for suboptimal eCPT is then set to 200 which is well above the optimal makespan in these benchmarks.

Table 1 shows for each domain, the total number of instances, the number of instances solved by eCPT, the number of instances solved backtrack free (and in parenthesis, the max number of backtracks over problems solved with backtracks), and the max number of nodes generated (in POCL planning, this number is different than the number of actions in the plan). For illustration purposes, the number of instances solved and the corresponding max number of nodes generated are reported also for FF [27]. As it can be seen, eCPT *solves* 339 *out of* 350 *instances,* 336 *of them backtrack free, including all the instances of Blocks, Ferry, Logistics, Gripper, Miconic, Rovers and Satellite* (the 11 unsolved instances are actually all caused by memory limitations in the Claire language rather than time). This is quite remarkable; these are instances that were challenging until very recently. eCPT solves actually 3 instances more than FF over this set of problems, eCPT having best relative coverage in Blocks and DriverLog, and FF in Depots and Zeno. In the last domain from IPC-3, Freecell, FF solves more instances than eCPT, which no longer exhibits a backtrack-free behavior.

Table 1. eCPT vs. FF: Coverage over various simple domains, showing # problems solved, backtrack free (max # backtracks), and max # of nodes generated

		eCPT			FF	
	#pbs	solved	b.-free (max b.)	max nd	solved	max nd
blocks	50	50	50 (0)	275	42	146624
depots	20	18	16 (4)	285	19	166141
driver	20	17	16 (5)	176	15	4657
ferry	50	50	50 (0)	1176	50	201
gripper	50	50	50 (0)	201	50	200
logistics	50	50	50 (0)	273	50	2088
miconic	50	50	50 (0)	131	50	76
rovers	20	20	20 (0)	207	20	3072
satellite	20	20	20 (0)	249	20	5889
zeno	20	14	14 (0)	70	20	933

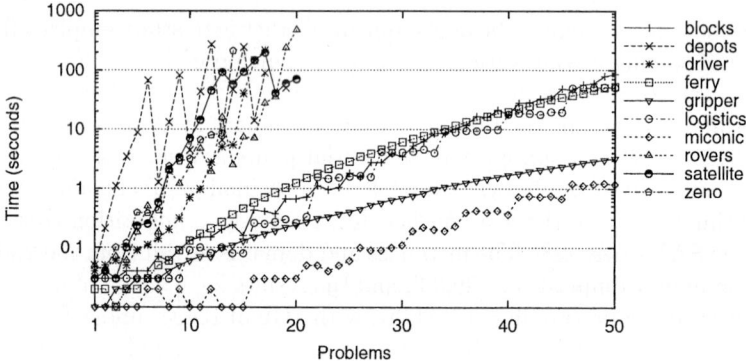

Fig. 2. eCPT running times on all domains

This domain, however, causes difficulties to FF as well due to the presence of dead-ends [31].

Not all the new inference rules are needed to generate the backtrack free behavior in every domain; yet Impossible Supports appears to be critical for Depots, Distance Boosting for Depots, DriverLog and Ferry, Qualitative Precedences for all domains except Blocks, and Action Landmarks for Blocks. In addition, often some disjunctions of rule sets are critical as well. For example, while either Qualitative Precedences or Unique Supports can be removed in Blocks without generating additional backtracks, the removal of both sets of rules does cause backtracks. Also, the modified heuristics are crucial for all domains.

Information about the runtime of eCPT over the various domains can be seen in Figure 2, with Table 2 providing additional details for selected instances in comparison with FF. As it can be seen, the runtimes for eCPT tend to scale well although they do not compete with the runtimes of FF (except for a few Depots instances): FF generates many more nodes but does so faster. Plan quality measured in the number of actions in the plan is better for FF in domains like

Table 2. eCPT vs. FF: further details on a few instances

	CPU time (sec.) eCPT	CPU time (sec.) FF	Actions eCPT	Actions FF	Nodes eCPT (bkts)	Nodes FF
bw-ipc48	59.51	-	74	-	281 (0)	-
bw-ipc49	78.37	-	80	-	282 (0)	-
bw-ipc50	85.09	0.02	88	86	235 (0)	195
log-ipc48	50.56	0.20	164	142	261 (0)	515
log-ipc49	51.54	0.50	176	171	273 (0)	1252
log-ipc50	50.39	0.43	161	154	245 (0)	1147
depots06	66.23	-	68	-	160 (0)	-
depots07	1.27	0.01	28	25	68 (0)	142
depots08	13.13	579.89	75	43	206 (0)	172478
driver14	5.40	0.09	48	45	75 (0)	1209
driver15	39.91	0.03	69	44	130 (0)	161
driver16	147.15	-	107	-	163 (5)	-

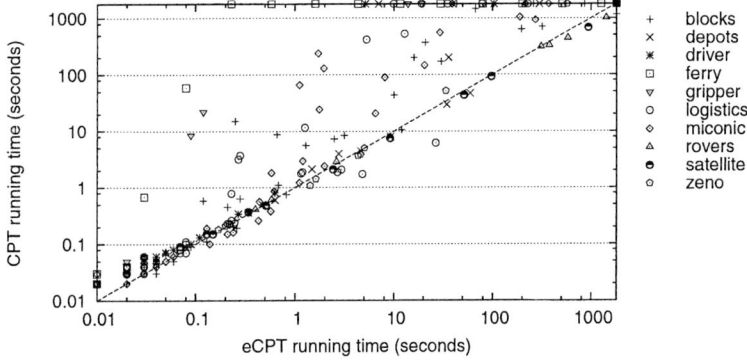

Fig. 3. eCPT vs. CPT for optimal planning

Logistics or DriverLog, which may have to do with the fact that eCPT computes concurrent plans.

The scatter plots in Figures 3 and 4 compare eCPT respectively with CPT and SATPLAN04 as *optimal* planners; dots above (below) the diagonal indicate instances where eCPT is faster (resp. slower), while dots on the right (top) border are unsolved by eCPT (resp. the other planner). eCPT solves 207 out of the 350 instances, while CPT and SATPLAN04 solve 179 and 180 instances respectively. eCPT generates many fewer nodes than CPT, often running orders-of-magnitude faster (although not always so as the additional overhead does not always pay off).

As *suboptimal planners*, eCPT solves 339 out of the 350 instances, while CPT solves only 66 instances, with runtimes often above 1000 seconds, resulting usually in poor plans. This is because, as mentioned above, CPT behavior degrades quickly as the bound on the makespan is pushed above the optimal value leaving the problems unconstrained and the search unfocused.

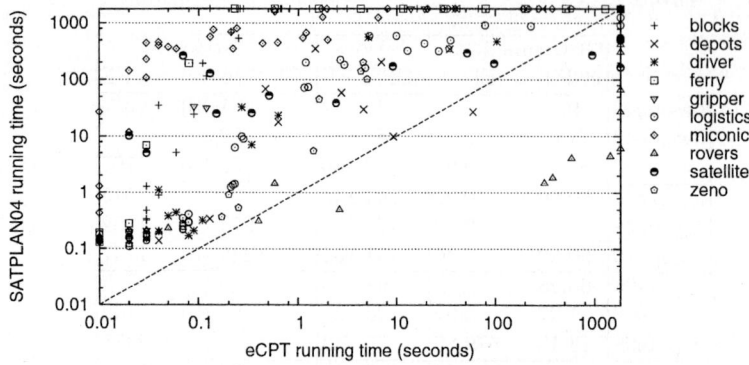

Fig. 4. eCPT vs. SATPLAN04 for optimal planning

5 Discussion

The task of solving simple planning problems in a *domain-independent* way with no search, by performing low polynomial operations in every node, is a crisp and meaningful goal, which may yield insights that an exclusive focus on performance may not, like the identification of broader tractable planning fragments, and the process by which people actually plan. In this work we have shown that a suitable extension of the temporal planner CPT achieves this behavior over a wide range of benchmark domains. The new constraints and inference mechanisms have been obtained from observing the behavior of CPT over various domains. The fact that this fine grain analysis is possible, and that the results can be easily incorporated into the planner, is a clear benefit of the CP formulation, which thus provides a way for making use of (human) *domain-specific* analysis for improving the performance of a *domain-independent* planner. We have also empirically evaluated the resulting planner eCPT, as a suboptimal and optimal planner, and have shown significant gains over CPT.

The finding that a few *inference rules* is all that it takes to render the search backtrack free in domains which until recently were considered challenging for planners, bears some similarity with the *empirical observation* in [2] that a simple domain-independent *heuristic function* can effectively guide the search for plans in many domains, an idea exploited in many current planners. The two devices for taming the search, however, are different: heuristic estimators provide *numeric* information to weight alternatives, the inference rules provide *structural* information to discard alternatives. We believe that it should be possible to *prove* some domains backtrack free for eCPT, and in this way identify new abstract classes of tractable problems. Current classes, as defined in [3–6] remain somewhat narrow, and do not account for the tractability of existing benchmarks [32]. In the future, we want to investigate the gap between the empirical results and current theoretical tractability accounts, and explore the possibility of obtaining the behavior of eCPT from a *general inference engine* and not a customized implementation.

Last but not least, we have recently studied in detail the traces for some of the problems considered, and noticed that in several cases, some of the decisions taken are the result of ties. Since we are interested in making the planning process transparent such ties pose a problem for justifying the decisions that are taken. We decided then to explore *all* the branches that are tied, rather than selecting the first branch only, hoping that all tied branches would lead to backtrack-free solutions. We discovered however that in some problems, this was not the case; namely, in some cases the way in which the code was breaking ties mattered, and in such cases, this had to do, for example, with the order of the actions in the PDDL file. Our next goal is thus not only to extend the range of domains that are solved backtrack-free but to do so in a *robust* way, meaning that decisions that are found to be equally good according to the criteria that are *explicit* in eCPT, should all lead equally well to the solution (namely backtrack free). This requires refining the rules and the selection criterion in eCPT still further. The most recent results that we have obtained, suggest that this is possible too.

Acknowledgments

V. Vidal is partially supported by the "IUT de Lens", the CNRS and the "région Nord/Pas-de-Calais" under the COCOA program. H. Geffner is partially supported by Grant TIC2002-04470-C03-02, MCyT, Spain.

References

1. McDermott, D.: A heuristic estimator for means-ends analysis in planning. In: Proceedings of AIPS-96. (1996) 142–149
2. Bonet, B., Loerincs, G., Geffner, H.: A robust and fast action selection mechanism for planning. In: Proceedings of AAAI-97, MIT Press (1997) 714–719
3. Bylander, T.: The computational complexity of STRIPS planning. Artificial Intelligence **69** (1994) 165–204
4. Bäckström, C., Nebel, B.: Complexity results for SAS^+ planning. Computational Intelligence **11** (1995) 625–655
5. Jonsson, P., Bäckstrom, C.: Tractable planning with state variables by exploiting structural restrictions. In: Proceedings of AAAI-94. (1994) 998–1003
6. Brafman, R., Domshlak, C.: Structure and complexity of planning with unary operators. JAIR **18** (2003) 315–349
7. McAllester, D., Rosenblitt, D.: Systematic nonlinear planning. In: Proceedings of AAAI-91, Anaheim, CA, AAAI Press (1991) 634–639
8. Vidal, V., Geffner, H.: Branching and pruning: An optimal temporal POCL planner based on constraint programming. In: Proceedings of AAAI-2004. (2004) 570–577
9. Kautz, H., Selman, B.: Unifying SAT-based and Graph-based planning. In Dean, T., ed.: Proceedings of IJCAI-99, Morgan Kaufmann (1999) 318–327
10. Rintanen, J.: A planning algorithm not based on directional search. In: Proceedings of KR'98, Morgan Kaufmann (1998) 617–624
11. Do, M.B., Kambhampati, S.: Solving planning-graph by compiling it into CSP. In: Proceedings of AIPS-00. (2000) 82–91

12. Porteous, J., Sebastia, L., Hoffmann, J.: On the extraction, ordering, and usage of landmarks in planning. In: Proceedings of ECP-01. (2001) 37–48
13. Zhu, L., Givan, R.: Heuristic planning via roadmap deduction. In: 4th. Int. Planning Competition Booklet (ICAPS-04). (2004)
14. Van Beek, P., Chen, X.: CPlan: a constraint programming approach to planning. In: Proceedings AAAI-99. (1999) 585–590
15. Kambhampati, S., Knoblock, C., Yang, Q.: Planning as refinement search: A unified framework for evaluating design tradeoffs in partial-order planning. Artificial Intelligence **76** (1995) 167–238
16. Weld, D.S.: An introduction to least commitment planning. AI Magazine **15** (1994) 27–61
17. Laborie, P., Ghallab, M.: Planning with sharable resources constraints. In Mellish, C., ed.: Proceedings of IJCAI-95, Morgan Kaufmann (1995) 1643–1649
18. Joslin, D., Pollack, M.E.: Is "early commitment" in plan generation ever a good idea? In: Proceedings of AAAI-96. (1996) 1188–1193
19. Penberthy, J.S., Weld, D.S.: Temporal planning with continous change. In: Proceedings of AAAI-94. (1994) 1010–1015
20. Jonsson, A., Morris, P., Muscettola, N., Rajan, K.: Planning in interplanetary space: Theory and practice. In: Proceedings of AIPS-2000. (2000) 177–186
21. Blum, A., Furst, M.: Fast planning through planning graph analysis. In: Proceedings of IJCAI-95, Morgan Kaufmann (1995) 1636–1642
22. Smith, D., Weld, D.S.: Temporal planning with mutual exclusion reasoning. In: Proceedings of IJCAI-99. (1999) 326–337
23. Vidal, V., Geffner, H.: Branching and pruning: An optimal temporal POCL planner based on constraint programming (long version). Technical report (2004)
24. Haslum, P., Geffner, H.: Heuristic planning with time and resources. In: Proceedings of European Conference of Planning (ECP-01). (2001) 121–132
25. Nguyen, X.L., Kambhampati, S.: Reviving partial order planning. In: Proceedings of IJCAI-01. (2001) 459–466
26. Marriot, K., Stuckey, P.: Programming with Constraints. MIT Press (1999)
27. Hoffmann, J., Nebel, B.: The FF planning system: Fast plan generation through heuristic search. Journal of Artificial Intelligence Research **2001** (2001) 253–302
28. Ryan, L.: Efficient algorithms for clause-learning sat solvers. Master's thesis, Simon Fraser University (2003)
29. Bacchus, F.: The 2000 AI Planning Systems Competition. Artificial Intelligence Magazine **22** (2001) 47–56
30. Long, D., Fox, M.: The 3rd international planning competition: Results and analysis. Journal of Artificial Intelligence Research **20** (2003) 1–59
31. Hoffmann, J.: Local search topology in planning benchmarks: An empirical analysis. In: Proc. IJCAI-2001. (2001) 453–458
32. Helmert, M.: Complexity results for standard benchmark domains in planning. Artificial Intelligence **143** (2003) 219–262

Solving Large-Scale Nonlinear Programming Problems by Constraint Partitioning[*]

Benjamin W. Wah and Yixin Chen

Department of Electrical and Computer Engineering
and the Coordinated Science Laboratory,
University of Illinois, Urbana-Champaign,
Urbana, IL 61801, USA
{wah, chen}@manip.crhc.uiuc.edu
http://www.manip.crhc.uiuc.edu

Abstract. In this paper, we present a constraint-partitioning approach for finding local optimal solutions of large-scale mixed-integer nonlinear programming problems (MINLPs). Based on our observation that MINLPs in many engineering applications have highly structured constraints, we propose to partition these MINLPs by their constraints into subproblems, solve each subproblem by an existing solver, and resolve those violated global constraints across the subproblems using our theory of extended saddle points. Constraint partitioning allows many MINLPs that cannot be solved by existing solvers to be solvable because it leads to easier subproblems that are significant relaxations of the original problem. The success of our approach relies on our ability to resolve violated global constraints efficiently, without requiring exhaustive enumerations of variable values in these constraints. We have developed an algorithm for automatically partitioning a large MINLP in order to minimize the number of global constraints, an iterative method for determining the optimal number of partitions in order to minimize the search time, and an efficient strategy for resolving violated global constraints. Our experimental results demonstrate significant improvements over the best existing solvers in terms of solution time and quality in solving a collection of mixed-integer and continuous nonlinear constrained optimization benchmarks.

1 Introduction

In this paper, we study mixed-integer nonlinear programming problems (MINLPs) of the following general form:

$$(P_m): \quad \min_z \; f(z), \tag{1}$$

$$\text{subject to } h(z) = 0 \text{ and } g(z) \leq 0,$$

where variable $z = (x, y)$, and $x \in \mathbb{R}^v$ and $y \in \mathbb{D}^w$ are, respectively, the continuous and the discrete parts. The objective function f is continuous and differentiable with respect to x, whereas the constraint functions $h = (h_1, \ldots, h_m)^T$ and $g = (g_1, \ldots, g_r)^T$ are general functions that can be discontinuous, non-differentiable, and not in closed form.

---
[*] Research supported by National Science Foundation Grant IIS 03-12084.

MINLPs defined by P_m include discrete problems and continuous nonlinear programming problems (CNLPs) as special cases. Ample applications exist in production management, operations research, optimal control, and engineering designs.

Because there is no closed-form solution to P_m, we aim at finding local optimal solutions to the problem. We, however, focus on solving some of the more difficult instances that cannot be solved by existing solvers.

An example MINLP that cannot be solved by existing solvers is TRIMLON12. This is an instance of the TRIMLON benchmark [9] with $I = J = 12$. The goal is to produce a set of product paper rolls from raw paper rolls by assigning continuous variables $m[j]$ and $y[j]$ and integer variables $n[i, j]$, where $i = 1, \ldots, I$ and $j = 1, \ldots, J$, in order to minimize f as a function of the trim loss and the overall production cost.

objective: $\min_{z=(y,m,n)} f(z) = \sum_{j=1}^{J}(c[j] \cdot m[j] + C[j] \cdot y[j])$ (OBJ)
subject to: $B_{min} \leq \sum_{i=1}^{I}(b[i] \cdot n[i,j]) \leq B_{max}$ (C1)
$\sum_{i=1}^{I} n[i,j] - N_{max} \leq 0$ (C2)
$y[i] - m[j] \leq 0$ (C3)
$m[j] - M \cdot y[j] \leq 0$ (C4)
$Nord[i] - \sum_{j=1}^{J}(m[j] \cdot n[i,j]) \leq 0.$ (C5)

An instance can be specified by defining I and J, leading to $(I+2)J$ variables and $5J+I$ constraints. For example, there are 168 variables and 72 constraints in TRIMLON12.

A key observation we have made on many application benchmarks, including TRIMLON12, is that their constraints do not involve variables that are picked randomly from their variable sets. Invariably, many constraints in these benchmarks are highly structured because they model relationships that have strong spatial or temporal locality, such as those in physical structures and task scheduling.

Figure 1a illustrates this point by depicting the constraint structure of TRIMLON12. It shows a dot where a constraint (with a unique ID on the x axis) is related to a variable (with a unique ID on the y axis). With the order of the variables and the constraints arranged properly, the figure shows a strong regular structure of the constraints. Figures 1b and 1c further illustrate the regular constraint structure of two other benchmarks.

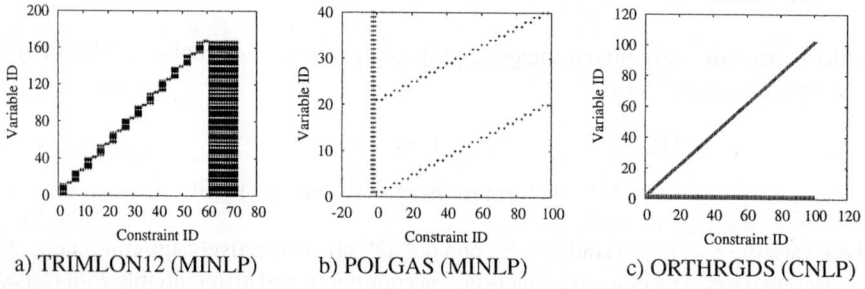

a) TRIMLON12 (MINLP)　　b) POLGAS (MINLP)　　c) ORTHRGDS (CNLP)

Fig. 1. Regular structures of constraints in some MINLP and CNLP benchmarks. A dot in each graph represents a variable associated with a constraint.

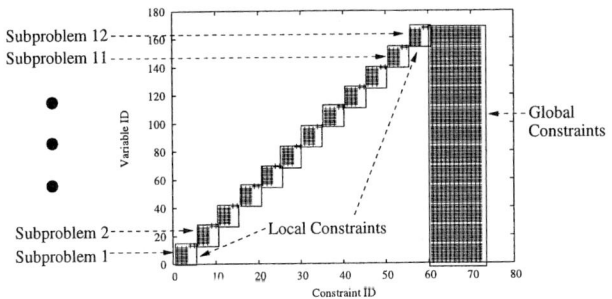

Fig. 2. An illustration of the partitioning of the constraints in TRIMLON12 into 12 subproblems

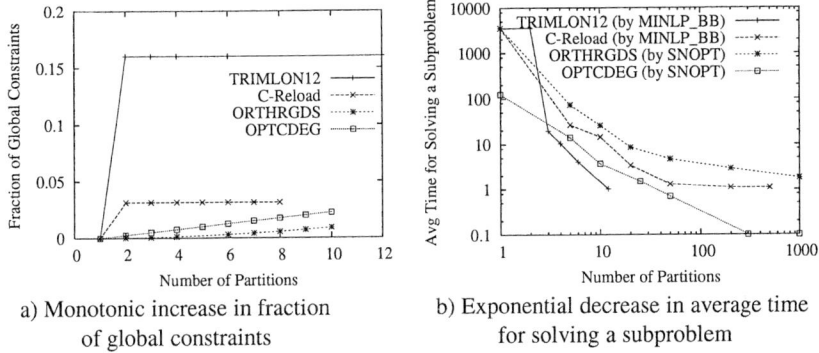

a) Monotonic increase in fraction of global constraints

b) Exponential decrease in average time for solving a subproblem

Fig. 3. Trade-offs between the number of global constraints to be resolved and the average time for evaluating a subproblem. As the number of partitions increases, the number of global constraints to be satisfied increases, while the average time to solve a subproblem decreases.

Based on the regular constraint structure of a problem instance, we can cluster its constraints into multiple loosely coupled partitions. To illustrate the idea, consider the partitioning of the constraints in TRIMLON12 by index $j \in S_J = \{1, \cdots, 12\}$. Suppose S_J is partitioned into N disjoint subsets in such a way that $S_1 \cup \cdots \cup S_N = S_J$. Then the kth subproblem, $k = 1, \ldots, N$, has variables $y[j], m[j], n[j, i]$, where $i = 1, \cdots, I$, $j \in S_k$, and a common objective function (OBJ). (C1)-(C4) are its local constraints because each involves only local indexes on j. (C5), however, is a global constraint because it involves a summation over all j.

Figure 2 illustrates the decomposition of TRIMLON12 into $N = 12$ partitions, where S_J is partitioned evenly and $S_k = \{k\}$. Of the 72 constraints, 60 are local and 12 are global. Hence, the fraction of constraints that are global is 16.7%.

The fraction of constraints that are global in a problem instance depends strongly on its constraint structure and the number of partitions. Using the straightforward scheme in TRIMLON12 to partition the constraints evenly, Figure 3a illustrates that the fraction of global constraints either increases monotonically or stays unchanged with respect to the number of partitions for four benchmarks.

In contrast, the time required to solve a subproblem decreases monotonically as the number of partitions is increased. When a problem is partitioned by its constraints,

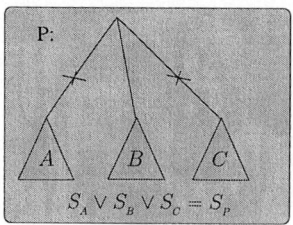 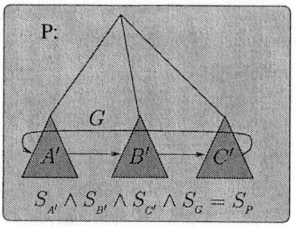

a) Subspace partitioning b) Constraint partitioning

Fig. 4. An illustration of subspace partitioning and constraint partitioning. Subspace partitioning decomposes P into a disjunction ($\vee$) of subproblems, where the complexity of each subproblem is similar to that of P. In contrast, constraint partitioning decomposes P into a conjunction ($\wedge$) of subproblems and a set of global constraints (G) to be resolved, where the complexity of each subproblem is substantially smaller than that of P.

each subproblem is much more relaxed than the original problem and can be solved in exponentially less time than the original. Figure 3b illustrates this exponential decrease of the average time for solving a subproblem with increasing number of partitions. The overheads between no partitioning and partitioning can be several orders of magnitude.

The partitioning of a problem by its constraints creates a new issue not addressed in past studies, namely, the resolution of global constraints relating the subproblems.

Traditional methods solve MINLPs by *subspace partitioning*. This decomposes a problem by partitioning its variable space into a disjunction ($\vee$) of subspaces and by exploring each subspace one at a time until the problem is solved (Figure 4a). Although pruning and ordering strategies can make the search more efficient by not requiring the search of every subspace, the complexity of searching each subspace is very similar to that of the original problem. In contrast, constraint partitioning decomposes the constraints of a problem into a conjunction ($\wedge$) of subproblems that must all be solved in order to solve the original problem. Each subproblem is typically much more relaxed than the original and requires significantly less time to solve (Figure 3b). However, there are global constraints (S_G in Figure 4b) that may not be satisfied after solving the subproblems independently. These global constraints include constraints in P that span across variables in multiple subproblems and new constraints added to maintain the consistency of shared variables across the subproblems. As a result, the subproblems may need to be solved multiple times in order to resolve any violated global constraints. The number of times that the subproblems are to be solved depends strongly on the difficulty in resolving the violated global constraints.

The keys to the success of using constraint partitioning to solve MINLPs and CNLPs, therefore, depend on the identification of the constraint structure of a problem instance and the efficient resolution of its violated global constraints. To this end, we study four related issues in this paper.

a) *Automated analysis of the constraint structure of a problem instance and its partitioning into subproblems.* We present in Section 4.1 the analysis of an instance specified in some standard form (such as AMPL [5] and GAMS). We show methods for determining the structure of an instance after possibly reorganizing its variables and its constraints, and identify the dimension by which the constraints can be partitioned.

b) *Optimality of the partitioning.* The optimality relies on trade-offs between the number of violated global constraints to be resolved (Figures 3a) and the overhead for evaluating a subproblem (Figure 3b). We present in Section 4.1 a metric for comparing the various partitioning schemes and a simple and effective heuristic method for selecting the optimal partitioning according to the metric.

c) *Resolution of violated global constraints.* We present in Section 3 the theory of extended saddle points (ESP) for resolving violated global constraints. The theory was originally developed for solving AI planning problems [15] whose constraints are not necessarily continuous, differentiable, and in closed form. Since continuity and differentiability of the continuous subspace is generally true in CNLPs and MINLPs, they can be exploited to speed up tremendously the solution of each subproblem.

d) *Demonstration of improvements over existing solvers.* We demonstrate the success of our approach in Section 5 by solving some large-scale CNLP and MINLP benchmarks that cannot be solved by other leading solvers.

2 Previous Work

In this section, we survey existing penalty methods for solving CNLPs and MINLPs and partitioning methods for decomposing large problems into subproblems.

Penalty Methods for Constrained Programming. Penalty methods belong to a general approach that can solve continuous, discrete, and mixed constrained optimization problems, with no continuity, differentiability, and convexity requirements. A penalty function of P_m is a summation of its objective and constraint functions (possibly under some transformations) weighted by penalties. The goal of a penalty method is to find suitable penalty values in such a way that the z^* which minimizes the penalty function corresponds to a local optimal solution of P_m.

Penalty methods can be classified into global (*resp.*, local) optimal penalty methods that look for constrained global (*resp.*, local) optimal solutions.

Global optimal penalty methods rely on the one-to-one correspondence between a *constrained global minimum* (CGM) of P_m and a global minimum z^* of the following penalty function with non-negative (transformed) constraint functions [13]:

$$L_s(z, c) = f(z) + c \cdot \left[\sum_{i=1}^{m} (h_i(z))^\rho + \sum_{i=1}^{r} (\max(0, g_i(z)))^\rho \right], \qquad (2)$$

where ρ is a constant no less than 1, and c is a positive penalty parameter that is larger than a finite c^*. Here, c^* can be finite or infinite, depending on the value of ρ, and can be statically chosen or dynamically adjusted.

Methods based on finding the global minimum of (2) are of limited practical importance because the search of a global minimum of a nonlinear function is very computationally expensive. Techniques like simulated annealing are too slow because they only achieve global optimality with asymptotic convergence.

To avoid expensive global optimization, *local optimal penalty methods* have been developed for finding *constrained local minima* (CLM) instead of CGM. One approach is the Lagrange-multiplier method developed for solving CNLPs with continuous and differentiable objective and constraint functions. It relies on the *Karush-Kuhn-Tucker*

(KKT) condition [1], a first-order necessary condition on a CLM that is also a regular point. Because the condition is expressed as a system of simultaneous equations, its solution leads to unique Lagrange multipliers at a CLM. When the condition is nonlinear and not solvable in closed form, iterative procedures have been developed. However, there is no efficient solution procedure for resolving inconsistent assignments when the nonlinear equations are partitioned into subproblems and solved independently.

Another local optimal penalty method for solving CNLPs is the ℓ_1-penalty method based on the following ℓ_1-penalty function [8]:

$$\ell_1(z,c) = f(z) + c \cdot \max\left(0, |h_1(z)|, \cdots, |h_m(z)|, g_1(z), \cdots, g_q(z)\right). \tag{3}$$

Its theory shows that there is a one-to-one correspondence between a CLM and an unconstrained local minimum of (3) when c is larger than a finite c^*. The method cannot support the constraint partitioning of P_m for two reasons. First, the theory was derived under the continuity and differentiability assumptions on constraints similar to those in the first-order KKT condition. In fact, c^* can be proved to be the maximum of all Lagrange multipliers of the corresponding Lagrangian formulation. Second, since there is only one penalty c on the maximum of all constraint violations, it is difficult to partition (3) by its constraints and to reach a consistent value of c across the subproblems.

Existing Partitioning Methods. Partitioning is popular in existing methods for solving NLPs. Many MINLP solution methods are based on subspace partitioning and decompose the search space of a problem instance into subproblems. Examples include the following. a) *Generalized Benders decomposition (GBD)* [6] decomposes a problem space into multiple subspaces by fixing the values of its discrete variables, and by using a master problem to derive bounds and to prune inferior subproblems. b) *Outer approximation (OA)* [4] is similar to GBD except that the master problem is formulated using primal information and outer linearization. c) *Generalized cross decomposition (GCD)* [10] iterates between a phase solving the primal and dual subproblems and a phase solving the master problem. d) *Branch-and-reduce methods* [14] solve MINLPs and CNLPs by a branch-and-bound algorithm and exploit factorable programming to construct relaxed problems. All these methods require the original problem to have special decomposable structures and the subproblems to have some special properties, such as nonempty and compact subspaces with convex objective and constraint functions.

Another class of decomposition methods is *separable programming methods* based on duality [1]. By decomposing a large problem into multiple much simpler subproblems, they have similar advantages as our constraint partitioning approach. However, they are limited in their general applications because they have restricted assumptions, such as linearity or convexity of functions. In this paper, we study a general constrained optimization approach with no restricted assumptions on constraint functions. Instead of using duality, we build our theoretical foundation on a novel penalty formulation discussed in the next section.

3 Constraint Partitioning by Penalty Formulations

In this section, we summarize our theory of extended saddle points (ESP). Our goal in solving P_m is to find a constrained local minimum $z^* = (x^*, y^*)$ with respect to

$\mathcal{N}_m(z^*)$, the mixed neighborhood of z^*. Due to space limitations, we only summarize some high-level concepts without the precise formalism [15].

Definition 1. *A mixed neighborhood $\mathcal{N}_m(z)$, $z = (x, y)$, in mixed space $\mathbb{R}^v \times \mathbb{D}^w$ is:*

$$\mathcal{N}_m(z) = \left\{ (x', y) \mid x' \in \mathcal{N}_c(x) \right\} \cup \left\{ (x, y') \mid y' \in \mathcal{N}(y) \right\}, \tag{4}$$

where $\mathcal{N}_c(x) = \{x' : \|x' - x\| \le \epsilon \text{ and } \epsilon \to 0\}$ is the continuous neighborhood of x, and the discrete neighborhood $\mathcal{N}(y)$ is a finite user-defined set of points $\{y' \in \mathbb{D}^w\}$.

Definition 2. *Point z^* is a CLM_m, a constrained local minimum of P_m with respect to points in $\mathcal{N}_m(z^*)$, if z^* is feasible and $f(z^*) \le f(z)$ for all feasible $z \in \mathcal{N}_m(z^*)$.*

Definition 3. *The penalty function of P_m with penalty vectors $\alpha \in \mathbb{R}^m$ and $\beta \in \mathbb{R}^r$ is:*

$$L_m(z, \alpha, \beta) = f(z) + \alpha^T |h(z)| + \beta^T \max(0, g(z)). \tag{5}$$

Theorem 1. *Necessary and sufficient ESPC on CLM_m of P_m [15]. Assuming $z^* \in \mathbb{R}^v \times \mathbb{D}^w$ of P_m satisfies a constraint-qualification condition (not shown due to space limitations), then z^* is a CLM_m of P_m iff there exist finite $\alpha^* \ge 0$ and $\beta^* \ge 0$ that satisfies the following extended saddle-point condition (ESPC):*

$$L_m(z^*, \alpha, \beta) \le L_m(z^*, \alpha^{**}, \beta^{**}) \le L_m(z, \alpha^{**}, \beta^{**}) \tag{6}$$

for any $\alpha^{**} > \alpha^*$ and $\beta^{**} > \beta^*$ and for all $z \in \mathcal{N}_m(z^*)$, $\alpha \in \mathbb{R}^m$, and $\beta \in \mathbb{R}^r$.

Note that the condition in (6) is rather loose because it only needs to be satisfied for any α^{**} and β^{**} that are larger than some critical α^* and β^*. The theorem is important because it establishes a one-to-one correspondence between a CLM_m z^* of P_m and an ESP of the corresponding unconstrained penalty function in (5) when penalties are sufficiently large. Moreover, it leads to a way for finding CLM_m. Since an ESP is a local minimum of (5) (but not the converse), z^* can be found by increasing gradually the penalties of violated constraints in (5) and by finding repeatedly local minima of (5) until a feasible solution to P_m is obtained. This is practical because there exist many search algorithms for locating the local minima of unconstrained nonlinear functions.

The ESPC in Theorem 1 has two features that distinguish it from the traditional penalty theory. First, because the ESPC can be satisfied by many possible penalty values, the search of these penalties can be carried out in a partitioned fashion in which each subproblem is solved by looking for any penalty values that are larger than α^* and β^*. This is not possible if the search were formulated as the solution of a system of nonlinear equations as in the KKT condition, or as the search of a single penalty term in the ℓ_1-penalty function in (3). Second, the condition is developed for general constraint functions and does not require continuity and differentiability as in the KKT condition. Further, it can be implemented by looking for the local minima of a nonlinear penalty function, and not for the global minima as in the general penalty theory.

Consider P_t, a version of P_m whose constraints can be partitioned into N stages. Stage t, $t = 1, \ldots, N$, has local state vector $z(t) = (z_1(t), \ldots, z_{u_t}(t))^T$, where $z(t)$

includes all the variables that appear in any of the local constraints in stage t. Note that since the partitioning is by constraints, $z(1), \ldots, z(N)$ may overlap with each other.

$$(P_t): \quad \min_z \; J(z) \tag{7}$$

$$\text{subject to} \quad h^{(t)}(z(t)) = 0, \quad g^{(t)}(z(t)) \leq 0 \quad \text{(local constraints)}$$
$$\text{and} \quad H(z) = 0, \quad G(z) \leq 0 \quad \text{(global constraints)}.$$

Here, $h^{(t)} = (h_1^{(t)}, \ldots, h_{m_t}^{(t)})^T$ and $g^{(t)} = (g_1^{(t)}, \ldots, g_{r_t}^{(t)})^T$ are local-constraint functions in stage t that involve $z(t)$; and $H = (H_1, \ldots, H_p)^T$ and $G = (G_1, \ldots, G_q)^T$ are global-constraint functions that involve $z \in \mathcal{X} \times \mathcal{Y}$.

Without showing the details [15], we first describe intuitively $\mathcal{N}_b(z)$, the mixed neighborhood of z in P_t. $\mathcal{N}_b(z)$ is made up of N neighborhoods, each perturbing z in one of the stages of P_t, while keeping the overlapped variables consistent across the other stages. Next, by considering P_t as a MINLP and by defining the corresponding penalty function, we apply Theorem 1 and derive the ESPC of P_t. Finally, we decompose the ESPC into N necessary conditions, one for each stage, and an overall necessary condition on the global constraints across the subproblems.

The partitioned condition in stage t can be satisfied by finding the ESPs in that stage. Because finding an ESP is equivalent to solving a MINLP, we can reformulate the search in stage t as the solution of the following optimization problem:

$$\left(P_t^{(t)}\right): \quad \min_{z(t)} \; J(z) + \gamma^T |H(z)| + \eta^T \max(0, G(z)) \tag{8}$$

$$\text{subject to} \quad h^{(t)}(z(t)) = 0 \quad \text{and} \quad g^{(t)}(z(t)) \leq 0.$$

The weighted global-constraint violations in the objective of $P_t^{(t)}$ are important because they lead to points that minimize such violations. When they are large enough, solving $P_t^{(t)}$ will lead to points, if they exist, that satisfy the global constraints.

4 Partitioning and Resolution Strategies

Figure 5 presents CPOPT, a partition-and-resolve procedure for solving P_t. It first partitions the constraints into N subproblems (Line 2 of Figure 5b, discussed in Section 4.1). With fixed γ and η, it then solves $P_t^{(t)}$ in stage t using an existing solver (Line 6). To allow $P_t^{(t)}$ to be solvable by an existing solver that requires a differentiable objective function, we transform $P_t^{(t)}$ into the following equivalent MINLP:

$$\min_{z(t)} \; J(z) + \gamma^T a + \eta^T b \tag{9}$$

$$\text{subject to} \quad h^{(t)}(z(t)) = 0 \quad \text{and} \quad g^{(t)}(z(t)) \leq 0,$$
$$-a \leq H(z) \leq a \quad \text{and} \quad G(z) \leq b,$$

where a and b are non-negative auxiliary vectors. After solving each subproblem, we increase γ and η on the violated global constraints (Line 7, discussed in Section 4.2). The process is repeated until a CLM_m to P_t is found or when γ and η exceed their maximum bounds (Line 9, discussed in Section 4.2).

We describe below the partitioning of the constraints and the update of the penalties.

$$L_m(z, \alpha, \beta, \gamma, \eta) \uparrow_{\gamma,\eta} \text{ to find } \gamma^{**} \text{ and } \eta^{**}$$

$(P_t^{(1)})$: $\min_{z(1)} J(z) + \gamma^T |H(z)| + \eta^T \max(0, G(z))$
subject to $h^{(1)}(z(1)) = 0$ and $g^{(1)}(z(1)) \leq 0$

$\cdots$

$(P_t^{(N)})$: $\min_{z(N)} J(z) + \gamma^T |H(z)| + \eta^T \max(0, G(z))$
subject to $h^{(N)}(z(N)) = 0$ and $g^{(N)}(z(N)) \leq 0$

a) The partition-and-resolve framework to look for CLM_m of P_t

1. **procedure** CPOPT
2.   **call** *automated_partition()*; // automatically partition the problem //
3. $\gamma \longleftarrow \gamma_0$; $\eta \longleftarrow \eta_0$; // initialize penalty values for global constraints//
4.   **repeat**   // outer loop //
5.   **for** $t = 1$ **to** N // iterate over all N stages to solve $P_t^{(t)}$ in stage t //
6.   apply an existing solver to solve $P_t^{(t)}$;
7.   **call** *update_penalty()*; // update penalties of violated global constraints //
8.   **end_for**;
9.   **until** stopping condition is satisfied;
10. **end_procedure**

b) CPOPT: Implementation of the partition-and-resolve framework

Fig. 5. The partition-and-resolve procedure to look for CLM_m of P_t

4.1 Strategies for Partitioning Constraints into Subproblems

Our goal in Line 2 of Figure 5b is to partition the constraints in such a way that minimizes the overall search time. Since the enumeration of all possible ways of partitioning is computationally prohibitive, we restrict our strategy to only partitioning by index vectors of problems modeled by the AMPL language [5].

Definition 4. *An index vector V in an AMPL model is a finite ordered array of discrete elements that are used to index variables and constraints.*

For example, TRIMLON12 described in Section 1 has two index vectors: $I = J = \{1, \cdots, 12\}$. A variable or a constraint function can be indexed by one or more index vectors: $n[i, j], i \in I, j \in J$, is indexed by I and J; and (C5) is indexed by I alone.

Definition 5. *A partitioning index vector (PIV) of an AMPL model is an index vector in the model that is used for partitioning the constraints.*

Definition 6. *Constraint partitioning by PIV. Given a PIV of an AMPL model, an N-partition by the PIV is a collection of subsets of the PIV, $S_1, \cdots, S_N$, where a) $S_i \in PIV$; b) $S_1 \cup \cdots \cup S_N = PIV$; and c) $S_i \cap S_j = \emptyset$ for $i \neq j$ and $i, j = 1 \ldots N$.*

The constraints of a problem can be partitioned along one or more index vectors. With multiple index vectors, the Cartesian-product space of the PIVs is partitioned into subsets. For instance, we have shown in Section 1 the partitioning of TRIMLON12 by J into $N = 12$ subproblems; that is, PIV = $\{J\}$, and $S_1 = \{1\}, \cdots, S_{12} = \{12\}$. This allows all the constraints indexed by J (C1 to C4) to be grouped into local constraints, and those not indexed by J (C5) to be the global constraints.

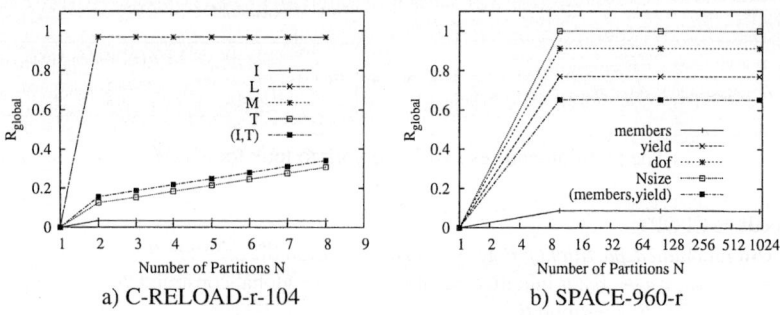

Fig. 6. Ratio of global constraints when partitioned by different PIVs for two MINLPs

We argue that it is reasonable and effective to partition constraints by their index vectors. First, indexing is essential in modeling languages like AMPL and GAMS for representing a complex problem in a compact form. Without it, it will be very cumbersome to use a unique name for each variable, especially when there are thousands of variables and constraints. Second, index vectors in large application problems are typically associated with physical entities. When constraints are partitioned by their index vectors, the partitions can be interpreted meaningfully. For example, index vector J in TRIMLON12 corresponds to the possible cuts of paper rolls, and a subproblem partitioned by J entails the optimization of the individual paper production in each cut.

Given a MINLP specified in AMPL, we present in the following our approach to automatically partition the problem by its constraints. We propose a metric to measure the quality of partitioning, present an algorithm to select the optimal PIV, illustrate the trade-offs between the number of partitions and the overall complexity, and show an efficient heuristic for determining the optimal number of partitions.

a) *Metric of partition-ability.* Since the time to solve a partitioned problem is largely driven by the overhead in resolving its inconsistent global constraints, we define R_{global} to be the ratio of the number of global constraints to the number of all constraints. This metric also needs to account for the shared variables in multiple subproblems that must be consistent with each other. For simplicity, we assume each shared variable v that appears in k subproblems to be equivalent to $k-1$ global constraints, where the ith constraint involves the consistency between the ith copy and the $i+1^{st}$ copy. Note that the metric is heuristic because the exact overhead depends on the difficulty of resolving the inconsistent global constraints and not on the number of global constraints.

b) *Selection of PIV.* To select the best PIV that minimizes R_{global}, we observe from the benchmarks tested that the best PIV for a problem instance is independent of the number of partitions N. To illustrate this observation, Figure 6 plots the value of R_{global} for various PIVs as a function of N for two benchmarks. It shows that the best PIV that minimizes R_{global} is the same for all N. Based on this property, we first fix an arbitrary value of N in our implementation. As there are usually less than five index vectors in a model file, we just enumerate all possible combinations of PIVs, compute R_{global} for each case, and pick the one that minimizes R_{global}.

c) *Number of partitions.* Based on the best PIV selected, we decide next the number of partitions. Experimentally, we have observed a convex relationship between N and

Table 1. Trade-offs between N and the total solution time on the SPACE-960-r MINLP

Number of partitions N	1	15	30	60	120	240	480
Time per subproblem	>3600	8.4	3.3	3.1	2.8	2.7	2.6
Time per iteration	>3600	126	99	186	336	648	1248
Number of iterations	1	1	1	2	2	2	5
Total time to solve problem	>3600	126	99	372	672	1296	6240

1. **procedure optimal_number_of_partitions** (PIV)
2. $N \longleftarrow |PIV|$; $last\_time \longleftarrow \infty$;
3.   **repeat**
4.   evaluate a subproblem under N partitions, and record the solution time $T_p(N)$;
5. $overall\_time \longleftarrow T_p(N) \cdot N$;
6.   **if** ($overall\_time > last\_time$) **then return** ($2N$);
7. $last\_time \longleftarrow overall\_time$;
8. $N \longleftarrow N/2$;
9.   **end_repeat**
10. **end_procedure**

Fig. 7. An iterative algorithm to estimate the optimal number of partitions

the total solution time. We illustrate this observation in Table 1 for various values of N on the SPACE-960-r MINLP from the MacMINLP library [12]. It shows the average time to solve a subproblem, the total time to solve N subproblems in one iteration, the number of iterations needed to resolve the inconsistent global constraints, and the overall time to solve the problem. The best N for this problem is 30.

The convex relationship is intuitively reasonable. When the number of partitions is small or when there is no partitioning, the global constraints will be few in number and easy to revolve, but each subproblem is large and expensive to evaluate. On the other hand, when there are many partitions, each subproblem is small and easy to evaluate, but there will be many global constraints that are hard to resolve.

The convex relationship allows us to determine an optimal number of partitions that minimizes the overall solution time. We start with the maximum number of partitions in the original problem (Line 2 of Figure 7) and evaluate a few subproblems in order to estimate $T_p(N)$, the average time to solve a subproblem when there are N partitions (Line 4). We also evaluate $overall\_time$, the time to solve all the subproblems once (Line 5). Assuming the number of iterations for resolving the global constraints to be small, $overall\_time$ will be related to the time to solve the original problem by a constant factor. This assumption is generally true for the benchmarks tested when N is close to the optimal value (as illustrated in Table 1). Next, we reduce N by half (Line 8) and repeat the process. We stop the process when we hit the bottom of the convex curve and report $2N$ that leads to the minimum $overall\_time$ (Line 6).

The algorithm requires $T_p(N)$, which can be estimated accurately based on the observation that it has little variations when the constraints are partitioned evenly. Table 2 illustrates this observation and shows that the standard deviation of the time to evaluate a subproblem is very small for two values of N. As a result, we only evaluate one subproblem in each iteration of Figure 7 in order to estimate $T_p(N)$ (Line 4).

Table 2. Average and standard deviation of solution time per subproblem for two benchmarks

Problem instance	ORTHRGDS		SPACE-960-r	
Number of partitions N	1000	20	100	10
Avg. time per subproblem ($T_p(N)$)	1.8	8.5	2.8	9.4
Std. dev. of time per subproblem	0.021	0.31	0.013	0.015

For the SPACE-960-r MINLP in Table 1, we set N to 480, 240, 120, 60, 30, 15. We stop at $N = 15$ and report $N = 30$ when *overall_time* starts to increase. The total time for solving the six subproblems is only 22.9 seconds, which is small when compared to the 160.45 seconds required by CPOPT for solving the original problem (see Table 3).

4.2 Strategies for Updating Penalty Values

After solving each subproblem, we use the following formulas to update the penalty vectors γ and μ of violated global constraints (Line 7 of Figure 5b):

$$\gamma \longleftarrow \gamma + \rho^T |H(z)|, \qquad \eta \longleftarrow \eta + \varrho^T \max(0, G(z)), \qquad (10)$$

where ρ and ϱ are vectors for controlling the rate of updating γ and η.

We update each element of ρ and ϱ dynamically until the corresponding global constraint is satisfied. Vector ρ is initialized to ρ_0 and is updated as follows. For each global constraint H_i, $i = 1, \cdots, p$, we use c_i to count the number of consecutive subproblem evaluations in which H_i is violated since the last update of ρ_i. After solving a subproblem, we increase c_i by 1 if H_i is violated; if c_i reaches threshold K, which means that H_i has not been satisfied in K consecutive subproblem evaluations, we increase ρ_i by:

$$\rho_i \longleftarrow \rho_i \cdot \alpha, \qquad \text{where } \alpha > 1, \qquad (11)$$

and reset c_i to 0. If H_i is satisfied, we reset ρ_i to ρ_0 and c_i to 0. In our implementation, we choose $\rho_0 = 0.01$, $K = 3$ and, $\alpha = 1.25$. We update ϱ in the same manner.

The procedure in Figure 5 may generate fixed points of (5) that do not satisfy Theorem 1. This happens because an ESP is a local minimum of (5) but not the converse. One way to escape from infeasible fixed points of (5) is to allow periodic decreases of γ and η (Line 7 of Figure 5b). These decreases "lower" the barrier in the penalty function and allow local descents in the inner loop to escape from an infeasible region. In our implementation, we scale down γ and η by multiplying each penalty by a random value between 0.4 and 0.6 if we cannot decrease the maximum violation of the global constraints or improve the objective after solving five consecutive subproblems.

Example. Consider the partitioning of TRIMLON12 into 12 subproblems along index J and the solution of the following $P_t^{(t)}$ in Stage j:

$$\min_{z=(y,m,n)} f(z) + \sum_{i=1}^{I} \left(\eta[i] \cdot \max \left(0, Nord[i] - \sum_{j=1}^{J} m[j] \cdot n[i,j] \right) \right)$$

subject to: local constraints (C1) - (C4) for Subproblem j, $j = 1, \cdots, 12$,

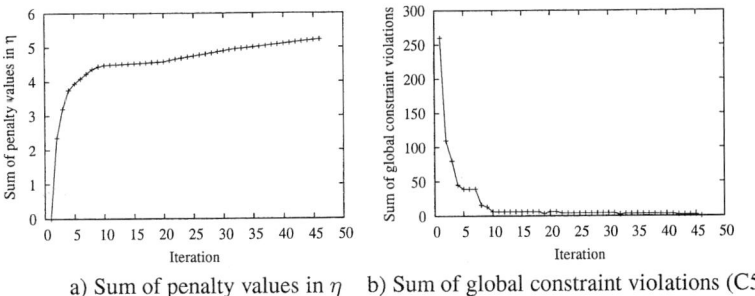

a) Sum of penalty values in η b) Sum of global constraint violations (C5)

Fig. 8. Illustration of solving TRIMLON12 by CPOPT

where η is the penalty vector for the global constraints (C5). Using the penalty update strategy discussed, Figure 8 shows the change on the sum of all penalty values in η and the sum of the violations on the global constrains as CPOPT is run. The search terminates in 46 iterations when all the global constraints are resolved.

5 Experimental Results

In this section, we compare the performance of CPOPT to that of other leading solvers. In CPOPT, if $P_t^{(t)}$ is a MINLP, CPOPT first generates a good starting point by solving it as a CNLP using SNOPT [7] without the integrality requirement, before solving it by MINLP_BB [11]. If $P_t^{(t)}$ is a CNLP, CPOPT applies SNOPT to solve it directly.

We have compared CPOPT to two of the best MINLP solvers, MINLP_BB [11] and BARON [14], on a collection of MINLP benchmarks from the MacMINLP library [12]. MINLP_BB implements a branch-and-bound algorithm with a sequential-quadratic-programming (SQP) solver for solving continuous subproblems, whereas BARON is a mixed-integer constrained solver implementing the branch-and-reduce algorithm. Of the 43 benchmarks in MacMINLP, we only show the results on 22 in Table 3. The remaining 21 benchmarks are all small problems and can be solved easily by all three solvers in tens of seconds or less. For these 21 benchmarks, the average solution times for CPOPT, BARON, and MINLP_BB are, respectively 8.40 seconds, 4.59 seconds, and 5.45 seconds. CPOPT is slower in solving these small problems due to its overhead in partitioning and in resolving the violated global constraints.

Note that although branch-and-bound methods, such as BARON and MINLP_BB, are theoretically complete methods that will converge to global optima, it is difficult to achieve global optimality in practice. BARON reports the best feasible solution found during its search until it times out in the 3600-sec time limit. For large problems, the gap between the lower and upper bounds usually does not vanish before termination, which implies that the solution found may not be optimal. Similarly, MINLP_BB reports the best solution found before it times out or runs out of memory.

We have also compared CPOPT to two of the best CNLP solvers, Lancelot (a solver implementing an augmented Lagrangian method) [3] and SNOPT (an SQP solver) [7] on the CNLPs from the CUTE library [2]. Table 3 summarizes only the results on

Table 3. Results on solving MINLP benchmarks from the MacMINLP library [12] and CNLP benchmarks from the CUTE library [2]. Results on MINLP_BB and BARON were obtained by submitting jobs to the NEOS server (*http://www-neos.mcs.anl.gov/neos/*) and BARON's site (*http://archimedes.scs.uiuc.edu/baron/baron.html*), respectively; results of other solvers were collected on an AMD Athlon MP2800 PC running RH Linux AS4 and a time limit of 3,600 sec. All timing results are in sec and should be compared only within a solver. For each instance, n_c and n_v represent, respectively, the number of constraints and the number of variables. Solutions with the best quality are boxed. "−" means that no feasible solutions were found in the time limit.

ID	n_c	n_v	Quality	Time	Quality	Time	Quality	Time
MINLP Test Problem			MINLP_BB		BARON		CPOPT(MINLP_BB)	
C-RELOAD-q-49	1430	3733	−	−	−	−	−1.13	69.45
C-RELOAD-q-104	3338	13936	−	−	−	−	−1.14	353.74
Ex12.6.3	57	92	⌈19.6⌉	23	19.6	423.1	19.6	13.43
Ex12.6.4	57	88	⌈8.6⌉	70	8.6	478.2	8.6	2.94
Ex12.6.5	76	130	15.1	4	⌈10.3⌉	845.5	10.6	3.33
Ex12.6.6	97	180	⌈16.3⌉	18	16.3	937.4	16.3	149.40
PUMP	34	24	−	−	131124	977	130788	84.53
SPACE-960-i	6497	5537	−	−	−	−	7.65E6	187.43
SPACE-960-ir	3617	2657	−	−	−	−	7.64E6	145.76
SPACE-960	8417	15137	−	−	−	−	7.84E6	1206.43
SPACE-960-r	5537	12257	−	−	−	−	5.13E6	160.45
STOCKCYCLE	97	480	−	−	436341	n/a	119948.7	6.45
TRIMLON4	24	24	12.2	10	⌈8.3⌉	11.0	8.3	2.73
TRIMLON5	30	35	12.5	14	⌈10.3⌉	55.3	10.3	24.5
TRIMLON6	36	48	18.8	19	⌈15.6⌉	1092.9	15.6	15.94
TRIMLON7	42	63	−	−	⌈17.5⌉	990.7	18.1	65.34
TRIMLON12	72	168	−	−	−	−	95.5	345.50
TRIMLOSS4	64	105	10.8	99	−	−	10.6	9.76
TRIMLOSS5	90	161	12.6	190	−	−	10.7	76.85
TRIMLOSS6	120	215	−	−	−	−	22.1	69.03
TRIMLOSS7	154	345	−	−	−	−	26.7	59.32
TRIMLOSS12	384	800	−	−	−	−	138.8	323.94
CNLP Test Problem			Lancelot		SNOPT		CPOPT(SNOPT)	
CATENARY	166	501	-	-	-	-	−1.35E5	245.64
DTOC6	5000	10001	-	-	-	-	1.02E6	58.05
EIGMAXB	101	101	⌈0.91⌉	1.34	-	-	1.87	24.33
GILBERT	1000	1000	2459.46	1.12	4700.61	689.18	2454.67	39.55
HADAMARD	256	129	-	-	-	-	0.99	7.88
KISSING	903	127	0.84	123.43	-	-	0.77	73.45
OPTCDEG	4000	6001	-	-	⌈45.76⌉	10.23	46.98	19.65
ORTHREGC	5000	10005	-	-	3469.05	557.98	2614.34	143.65
ORTHREGD	5000	10003	-	-	8729.64	208.27	7932.92	123.49
ORTHRGDM	5000	10003	⌈1513.80⌉	4.56	10167.82	250.00	2340.34	20.34
ORTHRGDS	5000	10003	912.41	4.20	-	-	894.65	105.34
VANDERM1	199	100	-	-	-	-	0.0	45.34
VANDERM3	199	100	-	-	-	-	0.0	36.70
VANDERM4	199	100	-	-	-	-	0.0	52.33

the 14 CUTE benchmarks that either Lancelot or SNOPT has difficulty with. For the remaining CUTE benchmarks that are easy to solve, the average solution times for Lancelot, SNOPT, and CPOPT are, respectively, 23.43 seconds, 13.04 seconds, and 19.34 seconds. For the same reason as before, CPOPT is slower in solving those small problems due to its additional overhead. The results show that, for those difficult-to-solve CUTE benchmarks, CPOPT can find the best solution, that it is one to two orders of magnitude faster, and that it scales well.

References

1. D. P. Bertsekas. *Nonlinear Programming*. Athena Scientific, Belmont, Massachusetts, 1999.
2. I. Bongartz, A. R. Conn, N. Gould, and P. L. Toint. CUTE: Constrained and unconstrained testing environment. *ACM Trans. on Mathematical Software*, 21(1):123–160, 1995.
3. A. R. Conn, N. Gould, and Ph. L. Toint. Numerical experiments with the LANCELOT package (Release A) for large-scale nonlinear optimization. *Mathematical Programming*, 73:73–110, 1996.
4. M. A. Duran and I. E. Grossmann. An outer approximation algorithm for a class of mixed-integer nonlinear programs. *Mathematical Programming*, 36:306–307, 1986.
5. R. Fourer, D. M. Gay, and B. W. Kernighan. *AMPL: A Modeling Language for Mathematical Programming*. Brooks Cole Publishing Company, 2002.
6. A. M. Geoffrion. Generalized Benders decomposition. *J. Optim. Theory and Appl.*, 10(4):237–241, 1972.
7. P. E. Gill, W. Murray, and M. Saunders. SNOPT: An SQP algorithm for large-scale constrained optimization. *SIAM Journal on Optimization*, 12:979–1006, 2002.
8. N. I. M. Gould, D. Orban, and Ph. L. Toint. An interior-point ℓ_1-penalty method for nonlinear optimization. Technical report, RAL-TR-2003-022, Rutherford Appleton Laboratory Chilton, Oxfordshire, UK, 2003.
9. I. Harjunkoski, T. Westerlund, R. Pörn, and H. Skrifvars. Different transformations for solving non–convex trim loss problems by MINLP. *European Journal of Operations Research*, 105:594–603, 1998.
10. K. Holmberg. On the convergence of the cross decomposition. *Mathematical Programming*, 47:269–316, 1990.
11. S. Leyffer. Mixed integer nonlinear programming solver. *http://www-unix.mcs.anl.gov/~leyffer/solvers.html*, 2002.
12. S. Leyffer. MacMINLP: AMPL collection of MINLP problems. *http://www-unix.mcs.anl.gov/~leyffer/MacMINLP/*, 2003.
13. R. L. Rardin. *Optimization in Operations Research*. Prentice Hall, 1998.
14. N. V. Sahinidis. BARON: A general purpose global optimization software package. *Journal of Global Optimization*, 8(2):201–205, 1996.
15. B. Wah and Y. X. Chen. Fast temporal planning using the theory of extended saddle points for mixed nonlinear optimization. *Artificial Intelligence*, (accepted for publication) 2005.

Factor Analytic Studies of CSP Heuristics

Richard J. Wallace

Cork Constraint Computation Centre and Department of Computer Science,
University College Cork, Cork, Ireland
r.wallace@4c.ucc.ie

Abstract. Factor analysis is a statistical technique for reducing the number of factors responsible for a matrix of correlations to a smaller number of factors that may reflect underlying variables. In this study factor analysis was used to determine if variation in search efficiency due to different variable ordering heuristics could be analyzed by this method to reveal basic sources of variation. It was found that the variation could be ascribed to two major factors, which appear to be related to contention (immediate failure) and to forward propagation (future failure). This was most clearcut with homogeneous random problems, but similar factor patterns were demonstrated for problems with small-world characteristics. Heuristics can be classified in terms of whether they tend to support one or the other strategy, or whether they balance the two; these differences are reflected in the pattern of loadings on the two major factors. Moreover, improvements in efficiency can be obtained by heuristic combinations ("heuristic synergy") only if the combination includes heuristics that are highly correlated with each factor; therefore, two such heuristics are sufficient. This work represents a step toward understanding the action of heuristics as well as suggesting limits to heuristic performance.

1 Introduction

Variable ordering heuristics are an effective means of reducing search effort. Numerous heuristics have been devised, and many others are conceivable. At present, there is no effective way to classify them other than in terms of features of the problem that they discriminate, such as domain size or number of constraints associated with a variable, or their overall effect on efficiency (which allows us to speak of heuristics and anti-heuristics, with respect to efficiency under random selection).

Outstanding open questions in this domain include,

1. To what degree are heuristics doing different things?,
2. How many factors serve to differentiate heuristics? In other words, how many distinguishable heuristic actions or strategies are there?

Related to the latter is the question, are better heuristics better because they're doing something new, or are they just better with respect to some fundamental factor like responsiveness to conflict?

At present, we have not really begun to address such questions let alone answer them cogently. In particular, there has been no attempt to analyze variability in performance in order to link it to differences in heuristics, except to say that heuristic X is more efficient than Y (on problem P). Contemporary discussions of experimental analysis of algorithms are almost entirely concerned with the latter question (e.g. [1]).

However, statistical methods exist that are designed to analyze variation across a set of measures by attempting to associate the total variance with a small number of common factors (ideally a much smaller number than the number of original measures). These techniques, collectively known as factor analysis, may be well-suited for the present task.

This approach is based on inter-problem variation. As will be shown, heuristics can be distinguished by the pattern of variation in search effort across problems. If the action of two heuristics is due to a common strategy, then the pattern of variation should be similar.

As far as the author is aware, factor analysis has not been used before in the analysis of algorithms. It may, in fact, be well-suited to the study of non-deterministic search, because the latter appears to be affected by many rather ill-defined features. This work is therefore also meant to contribute to the development of a proper experimental science in constraint satisfaction and related areas.

The next section gives a brief, general description of the basic technique and discusses its use in this domain. Section 3 outlines the experiment methodology. Section 4 describes some representative results of this analysis, and clarifies some 'anomalies' that can occur in the factor loadings. Section 5 shows the generality of the basic factor pattern across different types of problems and algorithms. Section 6 discusses hypotheses regarding the factors obtained from this analysis. Section 7 considers other problem classes. Section 8 evaluates some recently proposed heuristics in terms of the basic factors observed. Section 9 gives conclusions.

2 Background: Factor Analysis

"Factor analysis" refers to a collection of methods for reducing a set of variables to a smaller set that is equivalent in the sense that the set of measurements associated with the original variables can be derived from linear combinations of the new variables. This allows the investigator to reinterpret the original measurements in terms of a smaller set of possibly more basic variables. For details on these procedures see [2] [3].

The basic model can be described in this form (taken from [2]),

$$z_j = a_{j1}F_1 + a_{j2}F_2 + \ldots + a_{jm}F_m + d_j U_j \quad (j = 1, 2, \ldots, n),$$

for the jth measure, where the F_i are *common factors*, i.e. factors common to all measures and U_j a *unique factor* associated with measure j. Usually $m \ll n$. The coefficients a_{jk} are often referred to as "loadings". The square of the coefficient of U_j is referred to as the "uniqueness", because this is the portion of the variance unique to measure j.

Factor analysis is based on correlation coefficients and, thus, on measures of variance and covariance. Here, it is important to understand the meaning of the correlation coefficient itself - and not just the rough-and-ready intuition of relatedness that it is meant to support. The formula for the correlation coefficient can be written

$$\frac{1}{S_x S_y} \sum_{i=1}^{N} \frac{(X_i - \bar{X})(Y_i - \bar{Y})}{N}$$

In this case, the product of the standard deviations of variates X and Y has been factored out of the summation, leaving the formula for covariance. Since the former is the product of the average deviation from the mean for each variate, the latter can only equal it when the deviations of X_i and Y_i are of equal magnitude and all are either in the same direction (all positive or all negative products). The coefficient is, therefore, a kind of normalized covariance. It can be interpreted as indicating the accuracy of prediction of variable Y, given X (or vice versa), or the reduction in variance of variable Y when the value of variable X is known [4]. In the present context, the correlation between two measurements determines the extent to which they are loaded on the same factor [2].

Factor analysis begins with a matrix of correlations derived from a sample of n values for each variable. For example, if the variables were cognitive or personality tests, the matrix would be composed of correlations between all pairs of tests across n individuals. A factor extraction process is applied, which (for the analyses of concern here) extracts a set of *uncorrelated* factors which together account for a maximal amount of the variance in the original matrix. In this case, the a_{jk} above are equal to the correlation coefficient between z_j and F_k [2].

There are many methods of factor extraction. Here, the maximum-likelihood method was used, which starts from a hypothesis of m common factors and determines maximum likelihood estimates using the original correlation matrix [3] [2]. Once obtained, the set of factors, which forms a basis for an m-space, can be rotated according to various criteria. Here varimax rotation was used; this method tries to eliminate negative loadings while producing maximal loadings on the smallest set of measures possible.

In interpreting patterns of differences, one cannot assume that causal factors behave additively, only that patterns of variation can be expressed as additive combinations. Although factor analysis can thereby identify independent sources of variation, their interpretation requires further investigation.

2.1 Illustrative Example

The following example, based on a textbook demonstration in [5], shows the power of this approach. It involves a set of 100 randomly generated rectangles with length and width between 1 and 50 inclusive. The original variables are nine formulas based on length (L) and width (W):

1. $y_1 = L$
2. $y_2 = W$
3. $y_3 = 10L$
4. $y_4 = 10W$
5. $y_5 = 20L + 10W$
6. $y_6 = 20L + 20W$
7. $y_7 = 10L + 20W$
8. $y_8 = 40L + 10W$
9. $y_9 = 10L + 30W$

For each rectangle, an estimate or 'measurement' of y_i was obtained by calculating the formula from the dimensions of that rectangle and adding a random error. (The latter introduces unrelated ('spurious') patterns of variation, which should obscure the effect of basic variables.) Using the software package described below, results were obtained that corresponded closely to the original textbook example, despite differences in the procedure for extracting factors. (The method of principal components was used in the reference cited.) In both cases, two factors accounted for a large proportion of the variance. Since all variables in which length predominated loaded highly on one of these factors, while all variables in which width predominated loaded highly on the other (Table 1), these factors could be identified with the variables of length and width in the original formulas. The same pattern of factor loadings was apparent even when observations included large errors (Table 1).

Table 1. Factor analysis of rectangle 'measurements'

formula	error 20/100			error 50/250			error 100/500		
	factor 1	factor 2	unique	factor 1	factor 2	unique	factor 1	factor 2	unique
1	**0.936**		0.124		**0.679**	0.538		0.511	**0.730**
2		**0.938**	0.119	**0.725**		0.466	0.444		**0.803**
3	**0.982**		0.035		**0.877**	0.222		**0.761**	0.411
4		**0.983**	0.034	**0.910**		0.171	**0.682**		0.535
5	**0.890**	0.449	0.007	0.442	**0.869**	0.049	0.485	**0.793**	0.136
6	**0.695**	**0.716**	0.005	**0.722**	**0.672**	0.027	**0.683**	**0.667**	0.089
7	0.440	**0.894**	0.007	**0.889**	0.408	0.044	**0.815**	0.354	0.211
8	**0.970**	0.235	0.005	0.207	**0.967**	0.022	0.335	**0.878**	0.116
9	0.303	**0.951**	0.005	**0.950**	0.276	0.021	**0.921**	0.207	0.108

Notes. Error values are maximum error for first two and last seven formulas, respectively. Columns show loadings on two factors and unique factor coefficients for each measure. Unless otherwise noted, in this and later tables blank cells indicate factor loadings $< |0.1|$, which are not printed by the program. Factors are shown in descending order by amount of variance accounted for. (In these analyses amounts for the two factors were nearly identical.) In this and later tables, factor loadings ≥ 0.6 are in boldface. For these analyses, the proportion of variance accounted for by two factors was 0.962, 0.827 and 0.651, respectively.

In the analysis of algorithms there is no error in measurement as typically occurs in empirical science. But there may be problem-specific features and details of search that act to obscure whatever basic variables are present. Hence, the robustness of factor analysis in the face of irrelevant variation may be important in this domain as well.

3 Experimental Methods

3.1 Factor Analysis

System R was used in this work, downloaded from http://www.r-project.org. The factanal() function was used for the factor analysis. This program uses the maximum likelihood method for finding factors [3].

As noted in Section 2, maximum likelihood methods require the number of factors as input. Since the number of significant factors was not known beforehand, various numbers of factors were tested, first, to determine at what point factor extraction ceased to account for any significant part of the variance, second, to determine which number of factors gave strong, reliable results.

If there are other sources of variation than the ones emphasized here, since they are less important in their effects and less reliable across experiments, they are likely to be related to features of specific problem sets interacting with vagaries of the search process. In addition, the possible existence of further factors does not diminish the importance of the ones demonstrated here.

The present analyses were done with 100 or 500 problems. In comparisons between these sample sizes, the proportion of variance accounted for by successive factors and the factor loadings were similar for both problem sets; hence, the results described in this paper are all based on sets of 100 problems.

3.2 Heuristics, Problems, and Procedure

Heuristics used in basic tests included well-known heuristics based on simple CSP parameters, heuristics chosen for their analytic properties with respect to features of search (the FFx series [6] and the promise variable ordering heuristic [7]), and a few other heuristics that have been used in a project on learning heuristics [8].

The initial analyses were based on a set of twelve heuristics (abbreviations in parentheses are those used in the following tables):

- Minimum domain size (dm). Choose a variable with the smallest current domain size
- Minimum domain over static degree (d/dg). Choose a variable for which this quotient is minimal.
- Minimum domain over forward degree (d/fd). Choose a variable for which this quotient is minimal.
- Maximum forward degree (fd). Choose a variable with the largest number of neighbors (adjacent nodes) in the set of uninstantiated variables.
- Maximum backward degree (bkd). Choose the variable with largest number of neighbors in the set of instantiated variables.
- Maximum product of static degree and forward degree (dg*fd).
- Maximum (future) edgesum (edgsm). Choose an edge between future (uninstantiated) variables for which the sum of the degrees of the two adjacent variables is maximal, then choose the variable in this pair with the largest forward degree.
- FF2 (ff2) See [6] for descriptions of the FFx heuristics.
- FF3 (ff3)
- FF4 (ff4)
- Maximum promise (prom). Choose the variable with the largest summed promise values across its domain. (Promise for a value is the product ($\prod$) of the supporting values taken across all domains of neighboring future variables. Geelen's heuristic chose the smallest sum, but this proved to be an anti-heuristic, at least when used with lexical value ordering.)
- Maximum static degree (stdeg). Order variables by descending degree in the constraint graph.

All but the last heuristic involve dynamic features of the problem. In all cases, ties were broken according to the lexical order of the variable labels. Values were chosen according to their lexical order.

Initial tests were done with homogeneous random CSPs (soluble unless otherwise noted). Problems were generated according to a probability-of-inclusion model for possible constraints, domain elements and constraint tuples (cf. [9]). In all cases graphs were fully connected. Densities given are graph densities.

Later tests were based on other problem classes: geometric problems, which are random problems with small-world characteristics, and quasigroups-with-holes. Geometric problems are generated by choosing n points with random coordinates within the unit square to represent the n variables, and adding edges between all pairs of variables whose points are separated by a distance less than some threshold. In addition, connectivity is ensured by checking for connected components and if there is more than one, connecting them by adding an edge between variables in two components with the smallest separation of any pairs of points in those components.

The algorithms used in these experiments were MAC-3 and forward checking. The main tests were based on (i) nodes visited during search, (ii) constraint checks. Since both measures produced similar patterns of factor loadings, results in this paper are restricted to search nodes.

4 Factor Patterns for CSP Heuristics

4.1 Basic Results

Table 2 shows a typical correlation matrix for this set of heuristics, based on nodes searched. The size of the coefficients varies greatly; more importantly, there are indications of clusters of heuristics with high inter-correlations, although such clustering is not clearcut.

Table 2. Sample Correlation Matrix for Nodes Searched

	dm	d/dg	d/fd	fd	bkd	dg*fd	edsm	ff2	ff3	ff4	prom
dm											
d/dg	.171										
d/fd	.153	.987									
fd	.099	.842	.858								
bkd	.743	.295	.256	.255							
dg*fd	.096	.854	.870	.975	.252						
edgsm	.066	.823	.840	.975	.213	.951					
ff2	.238	.881	.866	.710	.295	.730	.695				
ff3	.269	.847	.824	.703	.369	.717	.688	.953			
ff4	.267	.862	.839	.729	.379	.746	.700	.919	.937		
prom	-.049	.690	.713	.832	.123	.842	.831	.582	.585	.589	
sdeg	.113	.839	.858	.952	.245	.977	.929	.715	.705	.730	.824

Notes. Based on 100 <30,8,0.31,0.34> problems. Half-matrix with ones on diagonal omitted.

The most important result of the initial analyses was that every test yielded two main factors which produced a similar pattern of loadings for the heuristics and which together accounted for most of the variance ($\geq 70\%$) (Table 3). In most tests, the bulk of the remaining variance was associated with high unique factor loadings for minimum domain size and maximum backward degree.

Table 3. Factor Analysis for CSP heuristics

heuristic	<30,8,0.31,0.34>				<50,10,0.18,0.37>			
	nodes	factor 1	factor 2	unique	nodes	factor 1	factor 2	unique
dom	261		0.310	**0.904**	11334	0.146	0.281	**0.900**
d/dg	143	**0.695**	**0.638**	0.018	2076	**0.913**	0.394	0.011
d/fd	130	**0.726**	**0.599**	0.114	1621	**0.909**	0.404	0.010
fd	164	**0.940**	0.300	0.027	2625	0.443	**0.873**	0.042
bkd	481	0.154	0.316	**0.876**	27391	0.107	0.224	**0.938**
dg*fd	151	**0.937**	0.322	0.018	2418	0.436	**0.897**	0.005
edgsm	160	**0.925**	0.286	0.062	2840			
ff2	163	0.488	**0.846**	0.046	3148	**0.801**	0.364	0.225
ff3	154	0.475	**0.847**	0.057	2579	**0.635**	0.448	0.396
ff4	122	0.519	**0.798**	0.095	1562	**0.734**	0.445	0.263
prom	232	**0.823**	0.212	0.278	7777	0.380	**0.702**	0.363
stdeg	147	**0.923**	0.315	0.050	2000	0.486	**0.835**	0.067

Notes. Numbers under "nodes" are averages. Not all 12 heuristics could be analyzed together in second set of problems, so edgesum was omitted.

There are no simple relations between average performance and loading on a particular factor. However, the difference between min domain and backward degree and the remaining heuristics does have a definite relation to the pattern of loadings, as indicated by the results in the next section.

4.2 Resolution of Anomalous Loadings for Specific Heuristics

On the basis of selection strategy, it is not clear why minimum domain size and maximum backward degree show distinct patterns of variation, reflected in high uniquenesses. One possible explanation is that these heuristics, unlike the others, 'start out blind', since at the top level(s) of search the features they use do not distinguish among variables. For domain size, this is true because the problems had equal domains initially, and few or no values were filtered before the first assignment. For backward degree, at the top of the search tree all variables have a backward degree of zero, and it may be necessary to instantiate several variables before the remaining ones can be usefully distinguished with respect to this feature. As a result, the pattern of variation associated with these heuristics may be related to lexical choices at the top of the search tree.

To evaluate this hypothesis, tests were carried out in which the first k variable choices were made according to their lexical order, and the remaining choices were made using one of the 12 heuristics. The rationale for this is that under this condition all tests begin the same way, so differences in the pattern of variation cannot be due to a distinct pattern of choices at the beginning of search.

The results of these tests are shown in Table 4. It can be seen that this manipulation served to eliminate the high unique factor loadings, first for domain size and then for backward degree as well. When this occurred, both heuristics showed high correlations (loadings) with one of the main factors. This manipulation did not have a marked effect on the difference in search efficiency between the two 'anomalous' heuristics and the others, so the change in the factor pattern cannot be ascribed to an elimination of this difference.

Table 4. Factor Analysis for Heuristics after k Lexical Choices

heuristic	$k=1$				$k=3$			
	nodes	factor 1	factor 2	unique	nodes	factor 1	factor 2	unique
dom	11378	**0.787**	0.301	0.290	19587	**0.804**	0.565	0.034
d/dg	2738	**0.956**	0.271	0.013	7712	**0.752**	0.652	0.010
d/fd	2192	**0.952**	0.272	0.019	6473	**0.744**	0.660	0.011
fd	3762	0.575	0.571	0.343	9551	0.602	**0.796**	0.005
bkd	27391	0.526	0.312	**0.626**	37536	**0.708**	0.488	0.261
dg*fd	5456	0.315	**0.946**	0.005	8567	0.626	**0.775**	0.008
edgsm	6377	0.295	**0.939**	0.032	9462	0.617	**0.783**	0.007
ff2	5499	**0.824**	0.311	0.224	11583	**0.802**	0.587	0.012
ff3	4559	**0.831**	0.294	0.223	10402	**0.794**	0.602	0.008
ff4	2851	**0.798**	0.352	0.239	6435	**0.789**	0.607	0.009
prom	9564	0.581	0.483	0.430	21344	0.588	**0.763**	0.073
stdeg	4839	0.311	**0.937**	0.024	7980	0.648	**0.752**	0.015

Notes. <50,10,0.18,0.37> problems. To better distinguish the highest loadings, in the columns under k=3 only those ≥ 0.7 are in boldface.

When the first three choices were lexical, the proportion of variance accounted for by the first two factors was 0.96. This is evidence that for these problems and heuristics, the pattern of variation in search efficiency can be ascribed to a very small number of distinct factors - in the causal sense.

As expected, increasing the number of lexical choices caused performance to deteriorate. Despite differences in degree of deterioration, the basic pattern of factor loadings remained the same, although there were changes in the size of the loadings.

In another test, using the <30,8.0.31,0.34> problems, data from search based on lexical ordering were added to the original set of data. In this case, the pattern of loading on the first two factors was essentially unchanged, while a distinct third factor emerged with high loadings (0.84-0.85) for min domain, max backward degree, and the lexical ordering. This supports the hypothesis that the pattern of variation associated with these heuristics is related to the initial lexical choice in the variable ordering.

Another way to evaluate the original loadings for min domain is to vary domain size. This was done using the same parameters as with the original 50-variable problems, but generating problems with an *expected* domain size of ten rather than a fixed domain size. (The maximum domain size was set to 20 and each potential domain element was chosen with a probability of 1/2.) With these problems, a factor analysis for two (or more) factors resulted in higher loading (0.55) for min domain on the same factor as in the tests with initial lexical choices, although there was still a moderately high unique factor loading ($\hat{d}_j = 0.58$).

4.3 Analysis of Easy Problems

In tests with easy problems (one run per problem), the factors described in previous sections were not clearcut. There were fewer substantial loadings, and the proportion of variance accounted for by these factors was greatly diminished. For most heuristics, the unique factor loading was very high. Table 5 shows an example for 50-variable problems with parameters similar to those in the previous section but with looser constraints.

Obviously, differences among heuristics must be due to different variable selections at some point in search. For problems with many solutions, it is more likely that this in turn leads to differences in value selections and thus to different solutions. As a result, each heuristic will show a more distinct pattern of variation across problems than with harder problems.

In this case, if there are basic variables affecting heuristic performance, it may be possible to average out peculiarities due to differences in value selection by testing problems repeatedly and choosing values at random. This was done, testing each problem 100 times with each heuristic. In this case, the simple factor structure observed earlier was apparent (Table 5, right-hand columns). Note that, at the same time the high unique factor loading for min domain and max backward degree remain; this is expected, since these heuristics still choose variables randomly at the top of the search tree. (The high unique loading for the promise heuristics cannot at present be explained.)

Table 5. Factor Analysis for Easy Problems

heuristic	nodes	1 run/problem w. lexical value			100 runs/problem, rand. value		
		factor 1	factor 2	unique	factor 1	factor 2	unique
dom	93			**0.992**	0.523	0.284	**0.646**
d/dg	63		**0.814**	0.331	**0.819**	0.331	0.220
d/fd	62		0.464	**0.784**	**0.828**	0.377	0.172
fd	67	**0.920**		0.154	0.409	**0.811**	0.174
bkd	166			**0.994**	0.339	0.206	**0.842**
dg*fd	68	0.620		0.616	0.460	**0.708**	0.288
edgsm	70	**0.828**		0.314	0.515	**0.674**	0.280
ff2	68	0.243	0.326	**0.835**	**0.883**	0.252	0.156
ff3	68		-0.121	**0.982**	**0.754**	0.192	0.395
ff4	57		-0.133	**0.981**	**0.878**	0.241	0.170
prom	109	0.335	0.228	**0.836**		0.340	**0.884**
stdeg	63	0.365		**0.865**	**0.649**	0.511	0.318

Note. Problem parameters were <50,10,0.184,0.32>.

From this and the previous analysis, we can posit a rule-of-thumb for interpreting factor patterns in this domain. This is that high unique factor loadings tend to be associated with random selection in some form. In this and the previous section it was shown that when differences due to random selection are eliminated, the high unique factor loadings vanish. On the basis of this rule-of-thumb, we can tentatively ascribe the anomalous result for the promise heuristic in Table 5 to some kind of random selection.

By resolving these anomalies, we have additional evidence that factor analysis produces reasonable patterns of results in this domain. In most cases, when the analysis showed deviations from a simple structure, it was possible to delineate features of the solving process that could be expected to produce deviations under these circumstances, leading, in particular, to significant loadings on unique factors.

5 Generality of Factor Patterns

5.1 Soluble and Insoluble Problems

The results in Table 6 show that a similar pattern of factor loadings is also found for insoluble problems and for a set of problems with singleton solution sets (obtained by generating problems in the usual manner and collecting only those with a single solution). In the latter test, differences in the pattern of variation across problems cannot be due to differences in the solution found.

Table 6. Factor Analysis: All Solutions, No Solutions

heuristic	soluble/all solutions			insoluble			singleton soln set		
	factor 1	factor 2	unique	factor 1	factor 2	unique	factor 1	factor 2	unique
dom	**0.610**	**0.672**	0.177	0.378	0.396	**0.701**		0.310	**0.904**
d/dg	**0.639**	**0.760**	0.014	**0.667**	**0.650**	0.132	**0.695**	**0.638**	0.109
d/fd	**0.685**	**0.723**	0.008	**0.684**	**0.637**	0.127	**0.726**	**0.599**	0.114
fd	**0.787**	**0.615**	0.005	**0.856**	0.416	0.094	**0.940**	0.300	0.027
bkd	**0.598**	**0.612**	0.268	0.375	0.191	**0.823**	0.154	0.316	**0.876**
dg*fd	**0.750**	**0.656**	0.007	**0.867**	0.458	0.039	**0.937**	0.322	0.018
edgsm	**0.787**	**0.615**	0.005				**0.925**	0.286	0.062
ff2	**0.636**	**0.760**	0.019	0.414	**0.882**	0.052	0.488	**0.846**	0.046
ff3	**0.700**	**0.702**	0.017	0.465	**0.854**	0.053	0.475	**0.847**	0.057
ff4	**0.737**	**0.658**	0.024	0.430	**0.832**	0.123	0.519	**0.798**	0.095
prom	**0.741**	**0.648**	0.030	**0.819**	0.412	0.159	**0.823**	0.212	0.278
stdeg	**0.721**	**0.683**	0.015	**0.831**	0.497	0.062	**0.923**	0.315	0.050

Note. For first two analyses, <30,8,0.31,0.34>, for third <30,8,0.31,0.37>.

In addition, the <30,8,0.31,0.34> problems were tested when the search was for all solutions. In this case, the pattern of loadings was quite different, although again two factors accounted for $\geq$ 95% of the variance in tests with 2 or 3 factors. One problem in evaluating this condition is that some variation must be due to differences in the size of subtrees containing only solutions. (The average number of solutions was about 500 for these problems.)

5.2 MAC and Forward Checking

Tests with forward checking give the same pattern of factor loadings as with MAC, despite the fact that max forward degree and other heuristics that load highly on the same factor perform poorly when used with this algorithm. Table 7 shows results from a composite test that included both MAC and forward checking for selected heuristics. Since the loadings are very similar with each algorithm, there are still only two major factors. In this case min domain and max backward degree are each associated with a separate factor in which they are the only heuristics with high loadings.

Table 7. Combined Analysis for MAC and FC

heuristic	nodes	factor 1	factor 2	factor 3	factor 4
		MAC			
dom	11,334	0.126	0.114	**0.886**	0.188
d/dg	2076	**0.864**	0.398	0.138	
fd	2625	0.451	**0.848**	0.167	
bkd	27,391		0.114	0.297	**0.851**
ff3	2579	**0.718**	0.383	0.121	
ff4	1562	**0.784**	0.404		0.174
stdeg	2000	0.493	**0.819**	0.159	
		forward checking			
dom	212,389		0.136	**0.956**	0.246
d/dg	32,368	**0.896**	0.322		
fd	38,568,409	0.373	**0.680**		
bkd	7,101,104		0.128	0.150	**0.943**
ff3	151,893	**0.744**	0.388		
ff4	43,416	**0.786**	0.379		0.186
stdeg	2,450,958	0.384	**0.761**		0.105

Notes. <50,10,0.184,0.37> problems, selected heuristics.

6 Interpreting the Factors

To assess the significance of the two major factors, we first consider the heuristics most closely associated with each of them. Since the FF (fail-first) heuristics always have high loadings on the same factor, and these pseudo-heuristics are designed to select for failure, we will tentatively label this factor as a "current failure" or "contention" factor. This is also supported by the high loading of backward degree on this factor once the effect of random selection has been removed, since this heuristic chooses according to the number of constraints with previous variables and does not consider future variables at all. The association of min domain with this factor suggests a relation to amount of branching, but this is contradicted by results for the FF heuristics with forward checking; here the branching factor is very high.

High loadings on the other major factor always seem to involve future variables, either directly adjacent (max forward degree) or one edge away (edgesum). It is also significant that the diagnostic heuristic, max summed promise, which is based entirely on look-ahead assessment, usually loads highly on this factor.

Increasing the number of future variables adjacent to the current variable could have either of two effects. It could lead to eventual failure through greater propagation (because more variables are adjacent to the variable just assigned a value). It might also enhance the promise of the heuristic (adherence to the "promise policy" [10]), since there are now more small domains among the future variables and, therefore, less chance for choosing invalid assignments. However, the latter hypothesis cannot account for the presence of this factor when problems are insoluble (Table 6). Hence, the second factor will be tentatively labeled as a "propagation" or "future failure" factor.

Most heuristics have at least moderate loadings on both factors. This is not surprising, since most heuristics would be expected to affect both current and future failure.

Here, it is critical to note that factor analysis guarantees that the factors are uncorrelated. This gives us reason to think that there may be two separate *causal* factors, despite the tendency of most heuristics to be associated with both (factor analysis) factors, even in some cases to a similar degree.

6.1 Evidence from Heuristic Synergies

A separate line of evidence comes from the analysis of heuristic 'synergies', especially in the form of weighted sums of ranked selections by different heuristics (as first described in [8]). This work has shown that weighted sums of ranked selections by different heuristics can sometimes outperform any of the individual heuristics in isolation.

Table 8. Results for Heuristic Combinations

heur/combinat	nodes	combinat	nodes	combinat	nodes
dom	11,334	dom+d/dg	2327	dom+fd+bkwd	1430
d/dg	2076	dom+fd	1317	dom+fd+stdeg	1374
fd	2625	dom+bkwd	12,521	dom+bkwd+stdeg	1822
bkd	27,391	dom+stdeg	1427	fd+bkwd+stdeg	1991
stdeg	2000	fd+stdeg	2344	dom+d/dg+fd+stdeg	1374
		bkwd+stdeg	1876	dom+d/dg+bkwd+stdeg	1834
				all five heuristics	1470

Note. <50,10,0.184,0.37> problems.

Sample results are shown in Table 8, for five heuristics and for heuristic "combinations". The latter were obtained by rating each choice with respect to each heuristic on a descending scale from 10 to 1 and then adding these ratings, weighted according to the heuristic. For the results in Table 8, heuristics were given equal weights.

These results show that some combinations do better, in terms of number of search nodes, than any heuristic used by itself. Other combinations yield no improvement over the best heuristic in the mix. The most significant finding is that whether or not there is marked improvement can be predicted from the factor loadings for the heuristics (cf. Table 3). In fact, all instances of heuristic synergy occurred when the heuristics in combination loaded highly on different major factors. Moreover, the best results for combinations of two heuristics were as good as any results for combinations of three or more. This is consistent with the conclusion that there are only two significant causal factors that distinguish heuristic performance.

From this, it can also be concluded that successful combinations (synergies) involve both of the major factors. Here it may be noted that domain/degree, one of the most efficient heuristics known, is itself a combination of heuristics which are associated with different major factors.

6.2 Analysis of Fail-First Measures

Data on five measures related to failure during search were collected for the <50,10, 0.184, 0.37> problems. These data are based on all-solutions runs, to avoid confounding effects of differences in promise (cf. [9]). The measures (means or counts per problem) were mistake-tree size (mistake-trees are insoluble subtrees rooted at the first bad assignment or "mistake"; this gives the most adequate measure of fail-firstness [cf. [9]]), number of mistakes (initial bad assignments, which must eventually be retracted; this is the number of mistake-trees), faildepth (depth at which an assignment 'fails', i.e. leads to a domain wipeout), fail-length (difference between the level of a mistake and the level of subsequent failure), and number of failures.

When factor analysis was applied to these measures, using the 12 heuristics and the MAC algorithm, the same factor patterns were found as for number of nodes, with the exception of number of mistakes. In other words, all measures related to fail-firstness (the tendency to fail as soon as possible *given that one is in an insoluble subtree*, [9]) gave the same factors and loading patterns as the analysis based on search efficiency.

For mistakes, most heuristics loaded about equally on both factors. Moreover, in a one-factor analysis based on this measure, the single factor accounted for 94% of the variance. Since this measure reflects the promise of a heuristic [10], this suggests that for these problems all heuristics behaved similarly with respect to promise.

These results support the hypothesis that the two basic variables are, indeed, immediate and future failure. They also confirm that, at least for problems in critical complexity regions, a two-fold classification of heuristics based on their association with one or the other factor is sufficient to account for nearly all the variation in performance.

7 Results for Other Problem Classes

The factor analysis with geometric problems gave results similar to those with homogeneous random problems; in particular, the pattern of loadings suggested that the contention and propagation effects were also the most important variables affecting patterns of variation in search. However, there were three important differences: (1) the domain/degree heuristics loaded highly on a separate (third) factor, (2) the promise heuristic did not load highly on a major factor and showed a high unique factor loading, (3) in these single-heuristic tests, min domain loaded highly on the 'contention' factor.

These differences must have to do with the graph topology of these problems. (While these problems were denser than the random problems discussed earlier, tests with random problems of greater density gave results similar to the latter.) Presumably, with the min domain heuristic search will tend to stay within a cluster of variables, while the forward-degree heuristics are likely to move search to other clumps where the number of uninstantiated neighbors is greater. The domain/degree heuristics should behave in an intermediate fashion. This is borne out by the patterns of correlation: while the FF heuristics and the forward-degree heuristics were highly correlated among themselves, domain/degree heuristics were almost equally well-correlated with both of these groups. It is therefore possible that the better balance between contention and propagation that would be expected in the domain/degree heuristics results in a distinct pattern of variation in search efficiency for these problems.

Evaluating tests with quasigroups was not straightforward. This was partly because some heuristics could not be used, since they either did not discriminate among variables (max static degree) or they were equivalent to other heuristics (e.g. domain/static degree, degree * forward-degree, backward degree, and less obviously, the edgesum heuristic). In addition, in cases involving forward-degree heuristics, the heuristic/anti-heuristic roles were reversed, so min forward degree and min promise became the heuristics; but these heuristics cannot be considered to enhance propagation.

A three-factor analysis gave the most reasonable results, with min domain and min domain/forward degree loading highly on the first factor, ff2 and ff3 on the second and ff4 on the third, while min forward degree and min promise had high unique factor loadings. Since min forward degree's heuristic effects are apparently based on search remaining within a partly instantiated clique, this may represent a contention strategy distinct from that of min domain, which should not be as clique-bound. This suggests that for highly structured problems, factor analysis may produce further (meaningful) factors when some heuristics make selections in relation to structural features.

8 Analysis of Some Recently Proposed Heuristics

Naturally, it is of interest to know how recently proposed heuristics fit into this framework. To this end, the min kappa heuristic [11], an extended DVO heuristic (H_1_DD_*) [12], and the weighted degree heuristic of [13] were tested with the <50,10,0.18,0.37> problems, and the results incorporated into the original factor analysis for these problems. In this analysis, min kappa loaded highly on the 'propagation' factor, while min weighted degree loaded highly on the 'contention' factor. The DVO* heuristic had a loading between 0.6 and 0.7 on the contention factor and a loading of about 0.5 on the propagation factor. It appears that the behavior of these heuristics can be accounted for in terms of the two basic factors. On the basis of the present analysis, the DVO* heuristic appears to have properties most consistent with heuristic efficiency. (It also had the lowest mean node count of any heuristic tested with these problems).

9 Conclusions and Open Questions

The usefulness of factor analysis is that it gives us hints about where to look for meaningful causal relations. It has the added strength of 'bounding our quest' by giving us some idea of the number of significant variables involved in a domain of study, such as the basis for differences among heuristics with respect to search efficiency.

In the present work this technique has allowed us to delineate two basic factors that account for much of the variation in search efficiency for a set of variable ordering heuristics. Further experimentation has allowed us to associate these factors with two causal factors, immediate and future failure. This leads to a new basis for classifying variable ordering heuristics. Evidence has also been adduced to show that heuristic selection can improve performance when both factors are taken into account.

In this analysis, the absolute magnitude of search efficiency is not reflected in the factors or the patterns of loadings. This occurs because all distributions are standardized before the analysis. This is both a strength and a limitation. It allows the analysis to delineate similar patterns of variation despite great differences in overall efficiency (as in the MAC/FC analysis). At the same time, further analysis is needed to account for differences in overall efficiency, as in the case of FC and propagation heuristics.

In this domain, factor analysis not only gives evidence (when properly interpreted) for basic heuristic strategies, but it also shows that problems are differentially affected by each strategy; otherwise, there would not be discernible differences in the pattern of variation under heuristics that emphasize one or the other strategy.

The study of heuristics now has three aspects:

- adherence to an ideal (optimal) policy [9]
- measureable features of heuristics such as the branching factor or mistake-tree size
- differences in heuristic action that cause heuristics to discriminate among problems and which are reflected in the "factors" derived from factor analysis

An important goal of future studies is to better understand the relations among these features of heuristic search.

Acknowledgment. This work was supported by Science Foundation Ireland under Grant 00/PI.1/C075. R. Heffernan assisted during the early stages of this project.

References

1. Barr, R.S., Golden, B.L., Kelly, J.P., Resende, M.G.C., Stewart, W.R.: Designing and reporting on computational experiments with heuristic methods. Journal of Heuristics **1** (1995) 9–32
2. Harman, H.H.: Modern Factor Analysis. 2nd edn. University of Chicago, Chicago and London (1967)
3. Lawley, D.N., Maxwell, A.E.: Factor Analysis as a Statistical Method. 2nd edn. Butterworths, London (1971)
4. McNemar, Q.: Psychological Statistics. 4th edn. John Wiley, New York (1969)
5. Cooley, W.W., Lohnes, P.R.: Multivariate Data Analysis. John Wiley, New York (1971)
6. Smith, B.M., Grant, S.A.: Trying harder to fail first. In: Proc. Thirteenth European Conference on Artificial Intelligence-ECAI'98, John Wiley & Sons (1998) 249–253
7. Geelen, P.A.: Dual viewpoint heuristics for binary constraint satisfaction problems. In: Proc. Tenth European Conference on Artificial Intelligence-ECAI'92. (1992) 31–35
8. Epstein, S.L., Freuder, E.C., Wallace, R., Morozov, A., Samuels, B.: The adaptive constraint engine. In van Hentenryck, P., ed.: Principles and Practice of Constraint Programming - CP2002. LNCS. No. 2470, Berlin, Springer (2002) 525–540
9. Beck, J.C., Prosser, P., Wallace, R.J.: Trying again to fail-first. In: Recent Advances in Constraints. Papers from the 2004 ERCIM/CologNet Workshop-CSCLP 2004. LNAI No. 3419, Berlin, Springer (2005) 41–55
10. Beck, J.C., Prosser, P., Wallace, R.J.: Variable ordering heuristics show promise. In: Principles and Practice of Constraint Programming-CP'04. LNCS No. 3258. (2004) 711–715
11. Gent, I., MacIntyre, E., Prosser, P., Smith, B., Walsh, T.: An empirical study of dynamic variable ordering heuristics for the constraint satisfaction problem. In: Principles and Practice of Constraint Programming-CP'96. LNCS No. 1118. (1996) 179–193
12. Bessière, C., Chmeiss, A., Saïs, L.: Neighborhood-based variable ordering heuristics for the constraint satisfaction problem. In: Principles and Practice of Constraint Programming-CP'01. LNCS No. 2239. (2001) 565–569
13. Boussemart, F., Hemery, F., Lecoutre, C., Saïs, L.: Boosting systematic search by weighting constraints. In: Proc. Sixteenth European Conference on Artificial Intelligence-ECAI'04. (2004) 146–150

Lookahead Saturation with Restriction for SAT

Anbulagan[1] and John Slaney[1,2]

[1] Logic and Computation Program, National ICT Australia Ltd., Canberra, Australia
[2] Computer Sciences Laboratory, Australian National University, Canberra, Australia
{anbulagan, john.slaney}@nicta.com.au

Abstract. We present a new and more efficient heuristic by restricting lookahead saturation (LAS) with NVO (neighbourhood variable ordering) and DEW (dynamic equality weighting). We report on the integration of this heuristic in Satz, a high-performance SAT solver, showing empirically that it significantly improves the performance on an extensive range of benchmark problems that exhibit hard structure.

1 Introduction

During the last decade, many new techniques have been proposed to enhance the performance of the DPLL procedure for solving various hard real-world problems represented in conjunctive normal form (CNF). One of the main improvements of this decision procedure has been the development of better branching variable selection through the use of unit propagation (UP) heuristics [1], which detect failed literals through a one-step lookahead. The effect of integrating the UP heuristic into DPLL is to prune the search tree earlier.

In this paper, we provide a new heuristic, DEW-NVO-LAS, which restricts lookahead saturation (LAS) with NVO (neighbourhood variable ordering) and DEW (dynamic equality weighting). DEW weighs equality literals during NVO-restricted lookahead saturation, firstly to restrict the variables to be propagated through the lookahead process, and secondly so that the next branching variable chosen can be the one having the highest score. We report on the integration of the DEW-NVO-LAS heuristic into Satz, showing empirically that it significantly improves Satz's performance on a range of benchmark problems, such as bounded model checking, cryptographic key search, FPGA routing, equivalence checking in circuits, and, particularly, the challenging 32-bit parity learning problems. The same problems are used for a comparative study between Dew_Satz, the DEW-NVO-LAS-enhanced Satz solver, and other state-of-the-art SAT solvers.

2 Lookahead Saturation with Restriction

Lookahead saturation (LAS) based DPLL was studied in [2]. The key idea underlying LAS is to choose a branching variable which is really the best from an irreducible sub-formula at a given node of search tree. LAS is very similar to the "singleton arc consistency" (SAC) algorithm in CSP reasoning [3].

Intuitively, although a reasoning-intensive process such as LAS can reduce the search tree size enormously, this increased efficiency is outweighed by the cost in terms of runtime. For that reason, we restrict the LAS process using the NVO and DEW heuristics. While the NVO heuristic concentrates on restricting the number of variables to be examined in the next iterative lookahead process by considering only the neighbours of the currently assigned variable in the currently size-reduced clauses, the DEW heuristic restricts the number of literals to be examined during the iterative lookahead process. DEW alone is not particularly useful in this regard, it must be incorporated into NVO-LAS to be really effective.

The basic concept of DEW is as follow. Whenever the binary equality clause $x_i \Leftrightarrow x_j$, which is equivalent to 2 CNF clauses $\bar{x}_i \vee x_j$ and $x_i \vee \bar{x}_j$, occurs in the formula at a node, Satz needs to perform the lookahead process on x_i, $\bar{x}_i$, x_j, and $\bar{x}_j$. As result, variables x_i and x_j will be associated the same weight, (i.e. 3 following the computation at line 25 of Algorithm 1). Clearly, the processing of x_j and $\bar{x}_j$ is redundant, so avoid it by assigning the implied literal $\bar{x}_j$ (x_j's) the weight of its parent literal $\bar{x}_i$ (x_i's), and then by restricting the lookahead process to literals with weight zero. By doing so, we save two lookahead processes.

To clarify the concept, we present a concrete example. Consider the following simple formula with binary equality clauses: $(x_1 \Leftrightarrow x_2) \wedge (x_2 \Leftrightarrow x_3) \wedge (x_1 \Leftrightarrow x_4)$. The Satz solver evaluates iteratively each variable of the formula by two forced unit propagations, where there is no failed literal found. Each literal of the formula gets the same weight, i.e. 3. Intuitively, we do not need to lookahead on variables x_2, x_3 and x_4 after performing lookahead on x_1: all three get the weight of the parent x_1. The effect of the DEW heuristic is that the weight of each implied literal accumulates dynamically during the lookahead process, and if it is greater than zero then no lookahead process is done on that literal. The DEW heuristic is executed only whenever binary equality clauses occur in the current state formula.

Our main observation is that DEW benefits markedly from NVO-LAS. We integrate DEW-NVO-LAS heuristic into Satz, and call the new solver by Dew_Satz. Intuitively, the merged heuristic will enhance the performance of NVO-LAS by avoiding the redundant lookahead process, which is computed by DEW. At the same time the DEW heuristic benefits from NVO-LAS as this dynamically bounds the number of variables to be weighed. The two mutually compatible heuristics work together to improve lookahead-based DPLL. Dew_Satz also inherits from Satz a preprocessor for saturating the input clauses under resolution with the restriction to clauses of length ≤ 3, removing subsumed clauses and tautologies along the way. In certain cases, the preprocessor may remove some equality clauses.

Algorithm 1 sketches the branching rule of Dew_Satz. The procedure Compute_DEW(x_i) is called for weighting the implied literals of the parent variable x_i. The function UP($\mathcal{F}_i$) at line 7 (10) of Algorithm 1 is executed if $w(x_i)=0$ ($w(\bar{x}_i)=0$). When there is no conflict found during the two unit propagations, then variable x_i will be piled into the branching variable candidates stack $\mathcal{B}$.

Algorithm 1. DEW-NVO-LAS-BranchingRule($\mathcal{F}$)

1: Push each variable $x_i \in \mathcal{V}$ to NVO_STACK;
2: **repeat**
3:     $\mathcal{B} := \emptyset$; $\mathcal{F}_{init} := \mathcal{F}$;
4:     **for** each variable $x_i \in$ NVO_STACK **do**
5:       Let $\mathcal{F}'_i$ and $\mathcal{F}''_i$ be two copies of $\mathcal{F}$;
6:       **if** $w\{x_i\} = 0$ **then**
7:         $\mathcal{F}'_i := \text{UP}(\mathcal{F}'_i \cup \{x_i\})$;
8:       **end if**
9:       **if** $w\{\bar{x}_i\} = 0$ **then**
10:       $\mathcal{F}''_i := \text{UP}(\mathcal{F}''_i \cup \{\bar{x}_i\})$;
11:       **end if**
12:       **if** empty clause $\in \mathcal{F}'_i$ **and** empty clause $\in \mathcal{F}''_i$ **then**
13:         **return** "unsatisfiable";
14:       **else if** empty clause $\in \mathcal{F}'_i$ **then**
15:         $\mathcal{F} := \mathcal{F}''_i$; NVO($x_i$);
16:       **else if** empty clause $\in \mathcal{F}''_i$ **then**
17:         $\mathcal{F} := \mathcal{F}'_i$; NVO($x_i$);
18:       **else**
19:         $w(x_i) := \text{diff}(\mathcal{F}'_i, \mathcal{F})$; $w(\bar{x}_i) := \text{diff}(\mathcal{F}''_i, \mathcal{F})$;
20:         $\mathcal{B} := \mathcal{B} \cup \{x_i\}$; Compute_DEW($x_i$);
21:       **end if**
22:     **end for**
23: **until** $\mathcal{F} = \mathcal{F}_{init}$
24: **for** each variable $x_i \in \mathcal{B}$ **do**
25:     $\mathcal{W}(x_i) := w(x_i) * w(\bar{x}_i) + w(x_i) + w(\bar{x}_i)$;
26: **end for**
27: NVO(x_i);
28: **return** x_i with highest $\mathcal{W}(x_i)$ to branch on;

3 Experimental Results

The 32-bit parity problem instances are considered as a challenging problem [4]. To answer the challenge, equality reasoning has been integrated differently in different solvers [5,6,7,8]. EqSatz uses equality reasoning in the search process while Lsat and March_eq use it in their preprocessors.

In Table 1, we present the performance of Dew_Satz on par16* and the challenging par32* instances in comparison with the following state-of-the-art solvers: EqSatz, Satz (ver. Satz215), zChaff (ver. 2004.11.15), March_eq (ver. March_eq_010), Lsat (ver. 1.1). It is important to observe that Dew_Satz can solve the 32-bit parity problem in the range of 411 to 17,564 seconds. It solved the par32-5 and par32-5-c instances without using the preprocessor (with preprocessing, these instances took 27 and 29 hours respectively). The results of Dew_Satz refute the pessimistic view that lookahead-based DPLL must perform poorly on such highly structured problems.

In order to evaluate further the performance of Dew_Satz versus other solvers used above, we extended the empirical study to include some well-known circuit-

Table 1. CPU time (in seconds) comparison. ">24h" shows that the problem cannot be solved in 24 hours.

Instance (#Vars/#Cls)	Satz	Dew_Satz	EqSatz	Lsat	March_eq	zChaff
par16*	12.97	1.26	0.55	0.56	0.17	6.12
par32-1 (3176/10227)	>24h	12,918	242	126	0.22	>24h
par32-2 (3176/10253)	>24h	5,804	69	60	0.27	>24h
par32-3 (3176/10297)	>24h	7,198	2,863	183	2.89	>24h
par32-4 (3176/10313)	>24h	11,005	209	86	1.64	>24h
par32-5 (3176/10325)	>24h	17,564	2,639	418	8.07	>24h
par32-1-c (1315/5254)	>24h	10,990	335	270	2.63	>24h
par32-2-c (1303/5206)	>24h	411	13	16	2.19	>24h
par32-3-c (1325/5294)	>24h	4,474	1,220	374	6.65	>24h
par32-4-c (1333/5326)	>24h	7,090	202	115	0.45	>24h
par32-5-c (1339/5350)	>24h	11,899	2,896	97	6.44	>24h

Table 2. CPU time (in seconds) on realistic benchmark problems

Problem	Dew_Satz	Satz	EqSatz	March_eq	zChaff
barrel6	4.13	271	0.17	0.13	2.95
barrel7	8.62	1,896	0.23	0.25	11
barrel8	72	>5,000	0.36	0.38	44
barrel9	158	>5,000	0.80	0.87	66
longmult10	64	736	385	213	872
longmult11	79	998	480	232	1,625
longmult12	97	1,098	542	167	1,643
longmult13	127	1,246	617	53	2,225
longmult14	154	1,419	706	30	1,456
longmult15	256	1,651	743	23	392
queueinvar12	1.26	0.81	0.67	2.19	0.22
queueinvar14	2.50	1.96	1.17	4.19	0.42
queueinvar16	1.11	1.05	1.06	3.44	0.35
queueinvar18	11	12	1.02	25	1.76
queueinvar20	13	19	1.58	40	3.13
cnf-r3*(8)	10.88	(1) 12,032	2,992	271	11.37
bart*(21)	0.88	0.35	(17) 85,403	(1) 6,838	16
homer*(15)	3,054	(15) 75,000	(15) 75,000	(15) 75,000	(1) 9,245
lisa*(14)	2,955	1,721	5,788	1,211	(3) 30,349
hwb-n20*(3)	177	148	188	46	1,355
hwb-n22*(3)	771	637	716	144	3,700
hwb-n24*(3)	3,457	3,115	4,170	1,115	(3) 15,000
pb-sat*(12)	(2) 13,818	(2) 15,793	(4) 24,478	7,869	(4) 21,099
pb-unsat*(12)	19,547	22,269	(4) 24,293	(1) 19,659	(8) 44,144
philips-org	697	3,845	1974	>5,000	>5,000
philips	295	1,086	2401	726	>5,000

related benchmark problems. All problems used in the study are taken from SATLIB (www.satlib.org), where some of them are used in previous SAT competitions. Some of the problem instances contain more than 600,000 variables. The problems cnf-r3*, bart*, lisa* and pb-sat* are satisfiable, and the others are unsatisfiable. The timebound for this experiment is 5,000 seconds per problem instance. Table 2 shows the runtimes of Dew_Satz, Satz, EqSatz, March_eq and zChaff on these problems. The numbers of instances of some problems are indicated in brackets after the problem names, and the number of instances on which each solver *failed* is also indicated in brackets before the total time. We count 5,000 as the increment in runtime for an unsolved instance. The experimentations were conducted on Intel Pentium 4 PCs with 3 GHz CPU, under Linux.

In general, this extended study further confirms the superior performance of Dew_Satz in comparison with the other four solvers. Where Dew_Satz fails to solve 2 instances in the given timebound (instance pb-sat-40-4-02 needs 6,005 seconds and instance pb-sat-40-4-03 needs 12,958 seconds), Satz, EqSatz, March_eq and zChaff fail on 20, 40, 18 and 21 instances respectively of the 108 given.

The empirical results also show that unit propagation based lookahead in DPLL is still a powerful technique. Simply enhancing it with a straightforward heuristic allows us to solve many more hard problems, as shown by the results above.

Acknowledgments

This work was funded by National ICT Australia (NICTA). National ICT Australia is funded through the Australian Government's *Backing Australia's Ability* initiative, in part through the Australian Research Council.

References

1. Li, C.M., Anbulagan: Heuristics based on unit propagation for satisfiability problems. In: Proceedings of 15th IJCAI, Nagoya, Aichi, Japan (1997) 366–371
2. Anbulagan: Extending unit propagation look-ahead of DPLL procedure. In: Procs of 8th PRICAI, Auckland, New Zealand, Springer, LNAI 3157 (2004) 173–182
3. Bessière, C., Debruyne, R.: Theoretical analysis of singleton arc consistency. In: ECAI-04 Workshop on Modeling and Solving Problems with Constraints, Valencia, Spain (2004) 20–29
4. Selman, B., Kautz, H., McAllester, D.: Ten challenges in propositional reasoning and search. In: Proceedings of 15th IJCAI, Nagoya, Aichi, Japan (1997) 50–54
5. Warners, J.P., van Maaren, H.: A two-phase algorithm for solving a class of hard satisfiability problems. Operations Research Letters **23** (1998) 81–88
6. Li, C.M.: Integrating equivalency reasoning into Davis-Putnam procedure. In: Proceedings of 17th AAAI, USA, AAAI Press (2000) 291–296
7. Ostrowski, R., Grégoire, E., Mazure, B., Sais, L.: Recovering and exploiting structural knowledge from CNF formulas. In: Proceedings of 8th CP. (2002) 185–199
8. Heule, M., van Maaren, H.: Aligning CNF- and equivalence-reasoning. In: Proceedings of 7th SAT, Vancouver, Canada (2004)

Evolving Variable-Ordering Heuristics for Constrained Optimisation

Stuart Bain, John Thornton, and Abdul Sattar

Institute for Integrated and Intelligent Systems,
Griffith University, PMB 50, GCMC 9726, Australia
{s.bain, j.thornton, a.sattar}@griffith.edu.au

Abstract. In this paper we present and evaluate an evolutionary approach for learning new constraint satisfaction algorithms, specifically for MAX-SAT optimisation problems. Our approach offers two significant advantages over existing methods: it allows the evolution of more complex combinations of heuristics, and; it can identify fruitful synergies among heuristics. Using four different classes of MAX-SAT problems, we experimentally demonstrate that algorithms evolved with this method exhibit superior performance in comparison to general purpose methods.

1 Introduction

Algorithms to solve MAX-SAT problems encounter a number of additional challenges to regular satisfiability testing: firstly, unless the optimal cost is known *a priori*, a local search is unable to recognise the optimality of a solution. Secondly, for a complete search to prove optimality, the search space of a MAX-SAT problem must be thoroughly examined, being unable to terminate once a satisfying solution has been found. Additionally, until the current cost bound is exceeded, backtracking search must overlook constraint violations that would have triggered immediate backtracking in satisfiability testing.

To overcome these challenges recent work [1,2] has adopted a two-phase approach, using a greedy local search routine to determine an initial cost bound for a branch and bound procedure, which then determines the globally optimal solution. Each of these works relies on a single ordering heuristic that has been demonstrated to perform well on a generalised range of benchmark instances. However, as good performance on such instances is not necessarily indicative of superior performance on other specific problems [3], how should the algorithm most suited to a specific problem of interest be identified?

Adaptive problem solving methods [4] have been developed to address this and are able to modify their behaviour to suit specific problems. Such methods permit efficient, problem specific algorithms to be developed automatically without the involvement of human problem solving expertise. The contribution of this paper is a method by which new algorithms can be automatically evolved for particular classes of problems. In an empirical study, we show that our evolved algorithms significantly outperform existing approaches on a range of NP-hard MAX-SAT optimisation problems.

2 Existing Adaptive Methods

All of the methods considered here adapt by combining in different ways atomic *measures*, i.e. simple functions that describe the nature of the problem and the state of the search.

The MULTI-TAC system developed by Minton [4] is designed to synthesise algorithms for solving CSPs. Exploration of new algorithms is by way of a beam search, designed to control the number of candidate heuristics that will be examined. As the beam search selects only the best B candidate algorithms for further consideration, MULTI-TAC is susceptible to overlooking *synergies*, i.e. measures that perform poorly individually but well in conjunction with other methods.

The Adaptive Constraint Engine (ACE) of Epstein et al. [5] learns the appropriate importance of individual advisors (measures) for particular problems. ACE is only applicable for use with complete search, as a trace of the expanded search tree is necessary to update advisor weights. Although described as being applicable to over-constrained problems, it does not obviously follow how this type of weight update scheme would apply when every search path eventually derives an inconsistency. There appears to be a practical limitation on the complexity of algorithms that can be learned by ACE, but unlike the beam search method used in MULTI-TAC, the use of feedback to update weights facilitates the identification of synergies between heuristics.

A third approach is the CLASS system developed by Fukunaga [6], which can construct algorithms of arbitrary complexity. Adaptation in CLASS is evolutionary, using a specialised composition operator to generate new algorithms. This operator is solely applicable to algorithms of an *if-then* form and, as the offspring generated with it are always larger and more complex than their parents, term rewriting must be used to reduce the size of generated algorithms.

ACE, MULTI-TAC and CLASS each have different strengths, but clearly the potential exists to overcome a number of their limitations. The foregoing discussion has identified a number of features crucial to the expressiveness and performance of an adaptive system:

1. Ability to represent both complete and local search routines
2. Unrestricted complexity
3. Ability to recognise and exploit synergies
4. Appropriateness for satisfiable and over-constrained problems
5. The ability to learn from failure

Our adaptive system exhibits all of these characteristics and is presented in the next section.

3 Evolving Algorithms

As genetic programming [7] has been developed specifically to address the problem of evolving complex structures, it is surprising that it is yet to be successfully applied to the domain of adapting algorithms. This study sets out to redress this absence from the adaptive constraint algorithm literature, but also to study the importance of more complex, non-linear (multiplicative) combinations of measures that previous works have used in only a limited fashion.

A constraint satisfaction algorithm may be viewed as a procedure that iteratively makes *moves*, i.e. variable-value assignments (in complete search), or reassignments (in local search). At each iteration, procedures of both types rank potential *moves* according to heuristic merit. Such a heuristic is simply a functional expression composed from measures describing the nature of the problem and the state of the search. This representation satisfies criteria 1 & 2 above, being suitable for search procedures of both types and without an *a priori* complexity bound. One method suitable for the adaptation of these functional expressions is genetic programming.

Genetic programming [7] begins with a random population of expressions, which in this case represent search heuristics. Methods analogous to natural selection and biological reproduction are used to breed subsequent populations of heuristics that better solve the target problem. As the probability of incorporating an individual into the next generation is determined probabilistically by its fitness, poorly performing algorithms are not automatically excluded, permitting synergies to be identified (criteria 3). Furthermore, the fitness measure can incorporate a variety of performance data, making genetic programming suitable for both satisfiable or over-constrained problems (criteria 4) and allowing it to distinguish between heuristics, even if they fail to locate a solution (criteria 5).

3.1 Empirical Study

Four different classes of problems were selected from which training instances were drawn. These were hard random MAX-3-SAT problems (*uuf100*) from SATLIB; unsatisfiable *jnh* problems from the DIMACS benchmark set; random MAX-2-SAT problems from Borchers' work[1] [1]; and SAT encoded unsatisfiable quasigroup instances, generated according to [8].

To determine the best algorithm for each particular training instance (listed in Table 1), the evolutionary procedure was run 5 times and for 50 generations for each instance. The initial generation of algorithms all incorporate the MOMS heuristic but are otherwise randomly generated. The fitness measure used was the number of backtracks necessary to determine the optimal solution to the training instance, standardised so that fewer backtracks equates to higher fitness. The composition of each successive generation was as follows, to give a total of $n_p = 50$ algorithms in each generation: the previous $n_c = 3$ best algorithms; $n_b = 36$ new algorithms generated by standard GP crossover; and, $n_m = 11$ algorithms generated by mutation.

The results of the experiments are tabulated in Table 1, both for linear (weighted-sum combinations) and non-linear (multiplicative) combinations of measures. Every evolved algorithm required fewer backtracks than MOMS on its training instance, with algorithms employing linear combinations of heuristics offering mean and median improvements over standard MOMS of 56.2% and 62.7% respectively, but algorithms employing non-linear combinations offering mean and median improvements of 58.4% and 65.3% respectively. There was less distinction in terms of time however, with evolved algorithms offering on average no more than a 34% improvement over MOMS.

On its own though, the ability of an algorithm to perform well on a single training problem is not particularly useful, due to the computational time required for training.

---

[1] For clarity, instances are named as p_*CLAUSESIZE*_#*VARS*_#*CONSTRAINTS*.

Table 1. Comparison of performance of evolved algorithms on training instances, along with the expression of the best performing algorithm for each. Boldface denotes the algorithm requiring the fewest backtracks.

Instance	Cost (GSAT / Optimal)	MOMS BTs	Evolved Linear BTs	Evolved Linear Time %MOMS	With Non-linear BTs	With Non-linear Time %MOMS
uuf100-0420.cnf	(2/2)	11030	8571	123.8%	8580	134.3%
MOMS+Degree-3*(RevJW+Linear)						
uuf100-04.cnf	(2/2)	11085	**8491**	132.0%	8706	116.9%
MOMS+CountSatisfy+10*(ValUsed-10⁻⁴*FwdDegree)						
uuf100-0327.cnf	(3/1)	17950	748	8.64%	**472**	4.3%
MOMS+MOMSLiteral*(2SJW-NumWillDetermine)						
uuf100-0190.cnf	(3/2)	31064	7524	42.5%	**5969**	35.2%
MOMS+2SidedJW*(Linear*MOMSStrict+1)+MOMSStrict						
uuf100-0332.cnf	(3/2)	46709	6015	25.5%	**5378**	23.1%
MOMS+1stOrder+MOMS*(MOMSStrict+NumWillDetermine+RevJW)						
p_2_50_200.cnf	(16/16)	5835	**783**	23.2%	798	21.6%
MOMS+20*(100*FwdDegree+2SidedJW)						
p_2_50_250.cnf	(22/22)	27610	5827	35.5%	**4855**	31.8%
MOMS+(Undetermined+UnitClause)*(JeroslowWang*1stOrder*FwdDegree)						
p_2_100_300.cnf	(15/15)	84062	6619	15.4%	**6521**	14.1%
MOMS+(72*Undetermined²*FwdDegree*Degree)						
jnh310.cnf	(3/3)	4744	3923	89.2%	**3711**	122.4%
MOMS+Degree+(UndetCount*FwdDegree*MOMSStrict*NumConstraints)						
jnh307.cnf	(3/3)	5244	**2668**	68.1%	3177	100.0%
MOMS+FwdDegree-180*Determined						
jnh303.cnf	(3/3)	21554	18102	132.3%	**15830**	103.9%
MOMS+BwdDegree+(BwdDegree*MOMSLiteral*UnitClause*Linear)						
jnh302.cnf	(4/4)	35335	29458	122.7%	**25440**	137.1%
MOMS+MOMSStrict*(UnitClause*UndetCount*MOMSLiteral+1)						
jnh305.cnf	(4/3)	39104	7984	29.5%	**7498**	37.3%
MOMS+CountSatisfy*(MOMSStrict-1stOrder*MOMSLiteral)						
qg3-05.cnf	(5/5)	21935	11817	79.1%	**10998**	71.3%
MOMS+(JeroslowWang*UnitClause+ValUsed)*(MOMSStrict*Linear)						

Table 2. Performance of MOMS and evolved linear & non-linear variants on test sets. Boldface denotes the algorithm requiring fewest mean backtracks.

Class	Num. Instances	MOMS BTs Mean	MOMS BTs Median	Linear BTs Mean	Linear BTs Median	Non-Linear BTs Mean	Non-Linear BTs Median
uuf100	100	1311	295	**1308**	288	1320	289
jnh	34	3592	550	2665	457	**2325**	475
quasigroup	3	2.95E6	311986	238950	132901	**69037**	84530
MAX-2-SAT	6	3.16E6	629613	410180	87362	**100070**	34628

To be truly useful, good performance on a training instance must translate into good performance on a class of similar problems. To demonstrate that evolved algorithms exhibit such performance, the evolved algorithms for each training instance were evaluated on a larger test set of problems of their class.

Performance results for MOMS and the best evolved algorithm in each class are tabulated in Table 2. These results show that evolved algorithms, particularly the non-linear variants, offer significant performance benefits on the larger test sets as well.

4 Conclusions and Future Work

This work has demonstrated a new method for automatically adapting algorithms that exhibits a number of desirable characteristics absent in other work, specifically the ability to discover synergies between heuristics and to explore complex non-linear combinations of heuristics. These two important features are a step toward developing fully automated constraint solving algorithms.

The evolved algorithms were shown to outperform the well-known MOMS heuristic on training instances taken from four different classes of NP-hard optimisation problems. An evaluation of the evolved algorithms on larger test sets of problems showed that on three of the four classes examined, an evolved algorithm substantially outperformed MOMS in terms of backtracks. These results indicate that genetic methods are certainly appropriate for the adaptation of algorithms.

Finally, in evaluating the importance of non-linear algorithms, we found them to have better backtrack performance on 10 of the 14 training instances. Although exhibiting only comparable performance on the *uuf100* test set, non-linear variants achieved superior performance on all other test sets, including both a structured and a smaller random problem set. This suggests that non-linear combinations identify and exploit structure overlooked by a linear approach, and whilst not appropriate for all problem classes, there can be substantial performance gains from non-linear combinations on problem classes that are sufficiently homogenous.

An extended version of this paper is available from the author's homepage at http://stuart.multics.org

References

1. Borchers, B., Furman, J.: A two-phase exact algorithm for MAX-SAT and weighted MAX-SAT problems. Journal of Combinatorial Optimization **2** (1999) 299–306
2. Xing, Z., Zhang, W.: Efficient strategies for (weighted) maximum satisfiability. In: CP '04: Principles and Practice of Constraint Programming. (2004) 690–705
3. Wolpert, D.H., Macready, W.G.: No free lunch theorems for optimization. IEEE Transactions on Evolutionary Computation **1** (1997) 67–82
4. Minton, S.: Automatically configuring constraint satisfaction programs: A case study. Constraints **1** (1996) 7–43
5. Epstein, S.L., Freuder, E.C., Wallace, R., Morozov, A., Samuels, B.: The adaptive constraint engine. In: CP '02 Principles and Practice of Constraint Programming. (2002) 525–540
6. Fukunaga, A.: Automated discovery of composite SAT variable-selection heuristics. In: AAAI'02, Canada (2002) 641–648
7. Koza, J.: Genetic Programming: On the programming of computers by means of natural selection. MIT Press, Cambridge, Massachusetts (1992)
8. Zhang, H., Stickel, M.: Implementing the Davis-Putnam method. Journal of Automated Reasoning **24** (2000) 277–296

Multi-point Constructive Search[*]

J. Christopher Beck

Department of Mechanical & Industrial Engineering,
University of Toronto
jcb@mie.utoronto.ca

Abstract. Multi-Point Constructive Search maintains a small set of "elite solutions" that are used to heuristically guide constructive search through periodically restarting search from an elite solution. Empirical results indicate that for job shop scheduling optimization problems and quasi-group completion problems, multi-point constructive search performs significantly better than chronological backtracking and bounded backtracking with random restart.

1 Introduction

Metaheuristics such as path relinking [5] maintain a small number (e.g., five to ten) of "elite solutions," that are used to guide search into areas that appear promising. This paper introduces the maintenance of multiple solutions to guide constructive tree search. Given a set of elite solutions, we probabilistically choose to start constructive search either from a random elite solution or from an empty solution. If a good solution is found within some bound of the search effort, it is inserted into the elite set, replacing one of the existing solutions.

2 Multi-point Constructive Search

Pseudocode for the basic Multi-Point Constructive Search (MPCS) algorithm is shown in Algorithm 1. The algorithm initializes a set, e, of elite solutions and then enters a while-loop. In each iteration, with probability, p, search is started from an empty solution (line 6) or from a randomly selected elite solution (line 12). The best solution found, s, is inserted into the elite set, in the former case, if it is better than the worst elite solution and, in the latter case, if it is better than the starting elite solution. Each search is limited by a fail-bound and the algorithm has some overall bound on the computational resources. The best elite solution is returned.

Searching from an Elite Solution. Let a reference solution, r, be a set of variable assignments, $\{\langle V_1 = x_1 \rangle, \ldots, \langle V_m = x_m \rangle\}, m \leq n$, where n is the number of variables. At a node in the search, any variable ordering heuristic can be used to choose a variable, V_i, to be assigned. If $x \in dom(V_i)$, where $\langle V_i = x \rangle \in r$, a choice point, $\langle V_i = x \rangle \vee \langle V_i \neq x \rangle$, is made. Otherwise, if $x \notin dom(V_i)$, any value ordering heuristic is used to choose $z \in dom(V_i)$ and a choice point is asserted using value z. An upper

---

[*] This work has received support from ILOG, SA.

Algorithm 1. MPCS: Multi-Point Constructive Search

```
MPCS():
1  initialize elite solution set e
2  while termination criteria unmet do
3      if rand[0, 1) < p then
4          set upper bound on cost function
5          set fail bound, b
6          s := search(∅, b)
7          if s ≠ NIL and s is better than worst(e) then
8              replace worst(e) with s
       else
9          r := randomly chosen element of e
10         set upper bound on cost function
11         set fail bound, b
12         s := search(r, b)
13         if s ≠ NIL s is better than r then
14             replace r with s
15 return best(e)
```

bound is placed on the cost function (line 10), and therefore a value assigned in the reference solution is not necessarily consistent with the current partial assignment. Note that our criterion for assigning a value from a reference solution covers the case where *no* value is assigned (i.e., when r is a partial solution and $m < n$).

Bounding the Cost Function. Before each search (lines 6 and 11), we place an upper bound on the cost function. We experiment with three approaches. *Global bound*: Always set the upper bound on the search cost to the best cost found so far. *Local bound*: When starting from an empty solution, set the upper bound to be equal the cost of the worst elite solution. When starting from an elite solution, set the upper bound to be the cost of the reference solution. *Adaptive*: Use the global bound policy for $|e|$ searches whenever a new global best solution is found then revert to the local bound policy.

Elite Solution Initialization. The elite solutions can be initialized by any search technique. In this paper, we use independent runs of standard chronological backtracking with a randomized heuristic and do not constrain the cost function. The search effort is limited by a maximum number of fails for each run.

Finding a Solution From Scratch. A solution is found from scratch (line 6) using any standard constructive search with a randomized heuristic and a bound on the number of fails. It is possible that no solution is found within the fail bound.

Bounding the Search. The effort spent on each individual search is bounded by a fail bound (lines 5 and 11). We associate a fail bound, initialized to 32, with each elite solution. Whenever search from an elite solution does not find a better solution, the corresponding fail bound is doubled. When an elite solution is replaced, the bound for the new elite solution is set to 32. When searching from an empty solution, we use the mean fail bound of the elite solutions and do not increase any fail bounds if a better solution is not found.

Adaptations for Constraint Satisfaction. To adapt the approach to a satisfaction context, we rate *partial* solutions by the number of unassigned variables. When a dead-end is encountered, the number of variables that have not been assigned are counted. Partial solutions with fewer unassigned variables are assumed to be better. We make no effort to search after a dead-end is encountered to try to determine if any of the currently unassigned variables could be assigned without creating further constraint violations.

3 Empirical Studies

Three variations of MPCS are used, corresponding to the different ways to set the cost bound: multi-point with global bound, *mpgb*; multi-point with local bound, *mplb*; and multi-point with adaptive bound, *mp-adapt*. We set $p = 0.5$ and $|e| = 8$. The effort to initialize the elite solutions is included in the results. For comparison, we use standard chronological backtracking (*chron*) and bounded backtracking with restart (*bbt*) following the same fail-bound sequence used for the multi-point techniques. The *bbt* algorithm is Algorithm 1 with line 12 is replaced by a copy of line 6. The only differences between *bbt* and the MPCS variations is the maintenance and use of the elite solutions. In particular, the same heuristics, propagation, and fail-bound sequence are used across these algorithms. All algorithms are run ten times with aggregate results presented as described below. A time limit of 600 CPU seconds is given for each run: algorithms report whenever they have found a new best solution allowing the creation of normalized run-time graphs. All algorithms are implemented in ILOG Scheduler 6.0 and run on a 2.8GHz Pentium 4 with 512Mb RAM running Fedora Core 2.

The Job Shop Scheduling Problem. An $n \times m$ job shop scheduling problem (JSP) contains n jobs each composed of m completely ordered activities. Each activity, has a pre-defined duration and a resource that it must have unique use of during its duration. There are m resources and each activity in a job requires a different resource. A solution to the JSP is a sequence of activities on each resource such that the *makespan*, the time between the maximum end time of all activities and the minimum start time of all activities, is minimized. We are interested in the optimization version of the problem: given a limited CPU time, return the solution with the smallest makespan found. Ten 20×20 JSPs were generated with randomly selected job routings and the activity durations independently and randomly drawn from $[1, 99]$ [8].

Randomized texture-based heuristics [3] and the standard constraint propagation techniques for scheduling [2] are used. To initialize the elite solutions, $|e|$ independent runs of a randomized algorithm that produces semi-active schedules is used. Each run is limited to 1000 fails. We compare algorithms based on mean relative error (MRE) as shown in Equation (1) where K is a set of problem instances, R is a set of independent runs, $c(a, k, r)$ is the lowest cost found by algorithm a on instance k in run r, and $c^*(k)$ is the lowest cost known for k.

$$MRE(a, K, R) = \frac{1}{|R||K|} \sum_{r \in R} \sum_{k \in K} \frac{c(a, k, r) - c^*(k)}{c^*(k)} \tag{1}$$

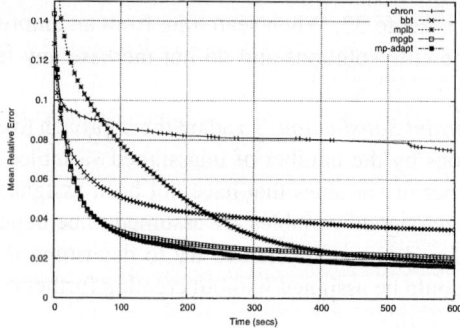

Fig. 1. Mean relative error to the best known solutions for each algorithm over ten independent runs of ten problem instances

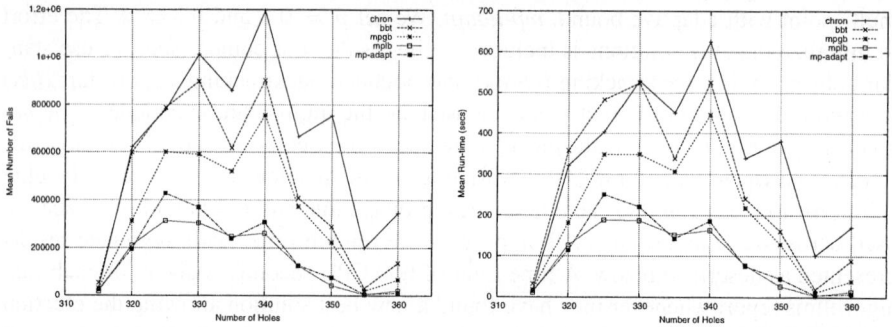

Fig. 2. Mean number of fails (left) and mean run-time (right) for the order-30 problems in each subset. Each point on the graph is the mean of ten independent runs on ten problem instances.

Figure 1 demonstrates that multi-point search is a significant improvement over both *chron* and *bbt*. Statistical analysis[1] is performed for time points $t \in \{100, 200, \ldots, 600\}$. The difference between *bbt* and *mpgb* and between *bbt* and *mp-adapt* is statistically significant at all time points. The *bbt* algorithm performs significantly better than *mplb* at $t = 100$ but significantly worse for $t \geq 300$. Turning to the MPCS variations, *mplb* is significantly worse than *mp-adapt* for $t \leq 400$ and significantly worse than *mpgb* at $t \leq 300$. The *mp-adapt* algorithm is significantly better than *mpgb* at all $t \geq 300$.

The Quasigroup-with-Holes Completion Problem. An $n \times n$ quasigroup-with-holes (QWH) is a partially completed matrix where each row and column is required to be a permutation of the first n integers. A solution requires that all the empty cells ("holes") are consistently filled. The problem is NP-complete and bounded backtracking with randomized restart has been shown to be a strong performer [6]. We generated 100 balanced, order-30 QWH problems (i.e,. $n = 30$) using a generator that guarantees satisfiability [1]. Ten sets with problem instances each are generated with the number of

---

[1] A randomized paired-t test [4] and a significance level of $p \leq 0.005$ were used.

holes, $m = \{315, 320, \ldots, 360\}$. These values were chosen to span the difficulty peak identified in the literature. Each algorithm was run ten times on each problem instance with a limit on each run of 2,000,000 fails.

The same search framework as above was used, implemented in ILOG Solver 6.0 on the same machine. The fail-limit to initialize each elite solution was set to 100 fails. The variable ordering heuristic randomly chooses a variable with minimum domain size while the value ordering is random. All-different constraints with extended propagation [7] are placed on each row and column.

Figure 2 presents the mean number of fails and mean run-time for each subset and algorithm. The MPCS variants *mplb* and *mp-adapt* perform significantly better than all other techniques for $m \geq 325$ for both the mean number of fails and the mean run-time.

4 Conclusion and Future Work

This paper introduces multi-point constructive search. The search technique maintains a small set of *elite* solutions that are used to conduct a series of resource-limited constructive searches. Depending on the outcome, new solutions are inserted into the elite set, replacing existing solutions. Two sets of experiments are conducted and significant performance gains relative to chronological backtracking and bounded backtracking with random restart are observed both on constraint models of optimization problems and satisfaction problems. Experiments are underway to systematically evaluate different parameter settings.

References

1. D. Achlioptas, C.P. Gomes, H.A. Kautz, and B. Selman. Generating satisfiable problem instances. In *Proceedings of the Seventeenth National Conference on Artificial Intelligence*, pages 256–261, 2000.
2. P. Baptiste, C. Le Pape, and W. Nuijten. *Constraint-based Scheduling*. Kluwer Academic Publishers, 2001.
3. T. Carchrae and J.C. Beck. Low knowledge algorithm control. In *Proceedings of the Nineteenth National Conference on Artificial Intelligence (AAAI04)*, pages 49–54, 2004.
4. P. R. Cohen. *Empirical Methods for Artificial Intelligence*. The MIT Press, Cambridge, Mass., 1995.
5. F. Glover, M. Laguna, and R. Marti. Scatter search and path relinking: advances and applications. In G.C. Onwubolu and B.V. Babu, editors, *New Optimization Techniques in Engineering*. Springer, 2004.
6. C.P. Gomes and D. Shmoys. Completing quasigroups or latin squares: A structured graph coloring problem. In *In Proceedings of the Computational Symposium on Graph Coloring and Generalizations*, 2002.
7. J.-C. Régin. A filtering algorithm for constraints of difference in CSPs. In *Proceedings of the Twelfth National Conference on Artificial Intelligence (AAAI-94)*, volume 1, pages 362–367, 1994.
8. J.-P. Watson, L. Barbulescu, L.D. Whitley, and A.E. Howe. Contrasting structured and random permutation flow-shop scheduling problems: search-space topology and algorithm performance. *INFORMS Journal on Computing*, 14(2):98–123, 2002.

Bounds of Graph Characteristics

Nicolas Beldiceanu[1], Thierry Petit[1], and Guillaume Rochart[2]

[1] École des Mines de Nantes, LINA FRE CNRS 2729, FR-44307 Nantes, France
{Nicolas.Beldiceanu, Thierry.Petit}@emn.fr
[2] Bouygues e-lab, 78061 St. Quentin en Yvelines, France
grochart@bouygues.com

Abstract. This article presents a basic scheme for deriving systematically a filtering algorithm from the graph properties based representation of global constraints. This scheme is based on the bounds of the graph characteristics used in the description of a global constraint. The article provides bounds for the most common used graph characteristics.

1 Introduction

Beldiceanu presented in [1] a systematic description of these global constraints in terms of graph properties: among the 224 constraints of the catalog of global constraints, about 200 constraints are described as a conjunction of graph properties where each graph property has a form P *op* V, where P is a graph characteristics, *op* is a comparison operator in $\{\leq, \geq, =, \neq\}$, and V a domain variable[1].

Example 1. Consider the nvalue(N, $\{x_1, ..., x_m\}$) constraint [3], where $N, x_1, ..., x_m$ are domain variables. The nvalue constraint holds iff the number of distinct values assigned to the variables in $\mathcal{X} = \{x_1, ..., x_m\}$ is equal to N. It can been seen as enforcing the following graph property: the number of strongly connected components of the *intersection graph* $G(\mathcal{X}, E)$, where $E = \{x_i \in \mathcal{X}, x_j \in \mathcal{X} : x_i = x_j\}$, is equal to N.

In this context, Dávid Hanák made a preliminary exploitation of this description for designing filtering algorithms, for a particular graph property [4]. In this article we present a systematic approach which aims at providing generic filtering algorithms for the most used graph properties [1]: given a specification of a global constraint C in terms of graph properties, we can derive a filtering algorithm for C.

A global constraint C is represented as an initial digraph $G_i = (\mathcal{X}_i, E_i)$: to each vertex in $\mathcal{X}_i$ corresponds a variable involved in C, while to each arc e in E_i corresponds a binary constraint involving the variables at both extremities of e. To generate G_i from the parameters of C, the set of arcs generators described in [1] is used. When all variables of C are fixed, we remove from G_i all binary constraints which do not hold as well as isolated vertices, i.e., vertices which are not extremity of an arc. This final digraph is denoted by G_f. C is defined by a conjunction of graph properties which

---

[1] A *domain variable* is a variable that ranges over a finite set of integers; $dom(V)$, $min(V)$ and $max(V)$ respectively denote the set of possible values of variable V, the minimum value of V and the maximum value of V.

should be satisfied by G_f. Each graph property has the form P op V; P is a graph characteristics, V is an domain variable and op is one of the comparison operator $\geq, \leq, =, \neq$. Within the global constraint catalog [1], common used graph characteristics are:

- **NARC** and **NVERTEX** denote the number of arcs and vertices: they are respectively used by 95 and 17 global constraints,
- **NCC** and **NSCC** denote the number of connected and strongly connected components; they are used in the description of 19 and 13 global constraints,
- **NSINK** (respectively **NSOURCE**) denotes the number of vertices which don't have any successor (resp. predecessor); they are respectively used by 16 and 15 global constraints; since **NSINK** and **NSOURCE** are similar, the rest of this article considers **NSINK**.

Example 2. Consider the nvalue$(N, \mathcal{X})$ constraint. Parts (A) and (B) of Fig. 1 respectively show the initial digraph G_i generated for the nvalue constraint with $\mathcal{X} = \{x_1, x_2, x_3, x_4\}$ and the digraph G_f associated with the ground solution nvalue$(3, \{5, 8, 1, 5\})$. Each vertex of G_i depicts its corresponding variable. All arcs corresponding to equality constraints that are not satisfied are removed to obtain G_f from G_i. Each vertex of G_f depicts the value assigned to its corresponding variable. The nvalue constraint is defined by the graph property **NSCC** $=$ N. The nvalue$(3, \{5, 8, 1, 5\})$ constraint holds since G_f contains three strongly connected components, which can be interpreted as the fact that N is equal to the number of distinct values taken by the variables x_1, x_2, x_3 and x_4. Part (C) of Fig. 1 will be referenced in Example 3.

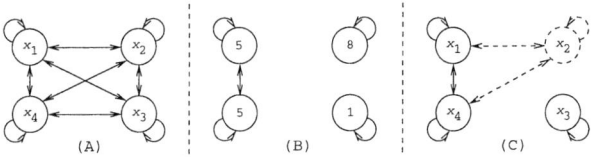

Fig. 1. (A) Initial digraph G_i associated with the nvalue$(N, \{x_1, x_2, x_3, x_4\})$ constraint. (B) Final digraph G_f of the ground solution nvalue$(3, \{5, 8, 1, 5\})$. (C) Intermediate digraph.

2 Filtering from Graph Properties

Given a graph property P op V occurring in the description of a global constraint, this section first shows how to reduce the domain of V in order to enforce P op V. Finally, it discuss the case where several graph properties are used to define a global constraint. We first introduce the notion of *intermediate digraph* derived from the initial digraph G_i, where vertices and arcs can have different status as detailed below. The purpose of this *intermediate digraph* is to reflect the knowledge we currently have about the vertices and the arcs of G_i that may or may not belong to the final digraph G_f. This knowledge comes from two sources:

- Because of the current domain of its variables, a binary constraint associated to an arc of G_i does not hold (or is entailed),
- Because of an external reason, a given arc or vertex of G_i is forced to belong to G_f (or is forced to no belong to G_f).

When a global constraint C is posted the *intermediate digraph* corresponds to G_i, while when all variables of C are fixed the *intermediate digraph* is equal to G_f.

Notation 1. *Let $G_i = (X_i, E_i)$ be the initial digraph of a global constraint C, and $G_f = (X_f, E_f)$ its final digraph. At a given step corresponding to a partial assignment of values to the variables of C, we classify a vertex $v_j \in X_i$ and an arc $e_k \in E_i$:*

- *v_j is a T-vertex (true) iff $v_j \in X_f$; v_j is a F-vertex (false) iff $v_j \notin X_f$; otherwise v_j is a U-vertex (undetermined). X_T, X_F and X_U respectively denote the sets of T-vertices, of F-vertices and of U-vertices.*
- *e_k is a T-arc (true) iff $e_k \in E_f$; e_k is a F-arc (false) iff $e_k \notin E_f$; otherwise e_k is a U-arc (undetermined). E_T, E_F and E_U respectively denote the sets of T-arcs, of F-arcs and of U-arcs.*

The definition of the *intermediate digraph* takes into account the fact that the final graph will not contain any isolated vertex.

Definition 1. *The* intermediate digraph *is the digraph defined from G_i, X_T, X_F, X_U, E_T, E_F, E_U by applying the next rules while they induce some modifications:*

- *Remove all F-arcs,*
- *Any F-vertex which is not the extremity of at least one T-arc is removed; when a vertex is removed, we remove also all its ingoing and outgoing arcs which are turned to F-arcs,*
- *Any U-vertex which is not the extremity of at least one arc is removed,*
- *Any U-vertex which is an extremity of a T-arc is turned to a T-vertex,*
- *If a T-vertex is the extremity of exactly one U-arc e and not the extremity of any T-arc, then e is turned to a T-arc.*

When a vertex or an arc is removed, or when the status of a vertex or of an arc is changed by one of the previous rule the sets X_T, X_F, X_U, E_T, E_F, E_U are updated to reflect this change.

Example 3. Consider again the nvalue$(N, \mathcal{X})$ constraint presented in the introduction, and assume that not all variables of $\mathcal{X} = \{x_1, x_2, x_3, x_4\}$ are fixed: dom(x_1)={5}, dom(x_2)={5}, dom(x_3)={5,8}, dom(x_4)={1}. Furthermore assume that, for an equality constraint ec associated to an arc of the initial digraph G_i of nvalue, entailment is only detected when all variables occurring in ec are fixed. This leads to partition the edges of G_i in the following three sets $E_T = \{(x_1, x_1), (x_1, x_4), (x_3, x_3), (x_4, x_1), (x_4, x_4)\}$, $E_U = \{(x_1, x_2), (x_2, x_1), (x_2, x_2), (x_2, x_4), (x_4, x_2)\}$ and $E_F = \{(x_1, x_2), (x_2, x_3), (x_3, x_1), (x_3, x_2), (x_3, x_4), (x_4, x_3)\}$. The status of the vertices is initially set *undetermined* (i.e. $X_U = \{x_1, x_2, x_3, x_4\}$) and we apply the rules of Definition 1 in order to obtain the *intermediate digraph* depicted by part (C) of Fig. 1. A plain line depicts a T-vertex or a T-arc, while a dashed line indicates a U-vertex or an U-arc. The same style will be used in all other figures of this article in order to depict T-vertices, T-arcs, U-vertices and U-arcs.

Property 1. From the definition of G_f, the global constraint C has no solution if the *intermediate digraph* contains a F-vertex or if it contains a T-vertex which is not the extremity of any arc.

Given a graph property P op V associated to a global constraint C, the *intermediate digraph* will be used for evaluating a lower bound $\underline{P}$ and an upper bound $\overline{P}$ of the graph characteristics P. Section 4 provides the algorithms for computing $\underline{P}$ and $\overline{P}$ for different graph characteristics. It assumes that all U-vertices or arcs of the *intermediate digraph* can be freely turned into T-vertices or T-arcs (resp. F-vertices or F-arcs). According to the comparison operator op, the next table gives the different possible cases for reducing the domain of variable V according to $\underline{P}$ and $\overline{P}$.

$P \leq V$	$min(V) \geq max(\underline{P}, min(V))$
$P \geq V$	$max(V) \leq min(\overline{P}, max(V))$
$P = V$	$min(V) \geq max(\underline{P}, min(V)) \wedge max(V) \leq min(\overline{P}, max(V))$
$P \neq V$	$\underline{P} = \overline{P} \Rightarrow \underline{P} \notin dom(V)$

3 Bounds of Graph Characteristics

This section is devoted to the evaluation of lower and upper bounds of the graph characteristics introduced in Section 2. For this purpose, we will deal with graphs derived from the *intermediate digraph* with different sets of arcs and vertices which are described in the following notations.

Notation 2. *Let Q, R and S be non-empty words over the alphabet $\{T, U\}$.*

- *Given a word W, $w \in W$ denotes a letter of W.*
- *X_Q and E_Q respectively denote $\bigcup_{q \in Q} X_q$ and $\bigcup_{q \in Q} E_q$.*
- *$X_{Q,R}$ (resp. $X_{Q,\neg R}$) denotes $v \in X_Q$ such that there is at least one arc (resp. there is no arc) in E_R where v is an extremity.*
- *$E_{Q,R}$ denotes the set of arcs $(v_1, v_2) \in E_Q$ such that $v_1 \in X_R$ or $v_2 \in X_R$.*
- *$X_{Q,R,S}$ (resp. $X_{Q,R,\neg S}$) denotes $v \in X_{Q,R}$ such that, within the vertices which share an arc with v, there is at least one vertex in X_S (resp. no vertex is in X_S).*
- *$X_{Q,\neg R,\neg S}$ denotes $v \in X_{Q,\neg R}$ such that, within the vertices which share an arc with v, no vertex is in X_S.*

Based on the previous notations, we define four kind of graphs, where $\mathcal{X}$ is a set of vertices and $\mathcal{E}$ a set of arcs:

- $\overrightarrow{G}(\mathcal{X}, \mathcal{E})$ denotes the digraph defined by the vertex set $\mathcal{X}$ and the subset of arcs of $\mathcal{E}$ having their two extremities in $\mathcal{X}$.
- $\overrightarrow{G}(\mathcal{E})$ denotes the digraph defined by the set of arcs $\mathcal{E}$ and the set of vertices which are extremities of arcs in $\mathcal{E}$.
- $\overleftrightarrow{G}(\mathcal{X}, \mathcal{E})$ (resp. $\overleftrightarrow{G}(\mathcal{E})$) denotes the undirected graph derived from $\overrightarrow{G}(\mathcal{X}, \mathcal{E})$ (resp. $\overrightarrow{G}(\mathcal{E})$) by forgetting the orientation of the arcs and by keeping its eventual loops.

Example 4. We illustrate some sets of vertices and arcs previously introduced and some graphs on the *intermediate digraph* depicted by part (C) of Fig. 1:

- $X_{U,T} = \{x_1, x_4\}$, $X_{U,\neg T} = \{x_3\}$,
- $E_{UT} = \{(x_1, x_1), (x_1, x_2), (x_1, x_4), (x_2, x_1), (x_2, x_2), (x_2, x_4), (x_3, x_3), (x_4, x_1), (x_4, x_2), (x_4, x_4)\}$,
- $E_{U,T} = \{(x_1, x_2), (x_2, x_1), (x_2, x_2), (x_2, x_4), (x_4, x_2)\}$,

- $\overrightarrow{G}(X_T, E_T) = \overrightarrow{G}(\{x_1, x_3, x_4\}, \{(x_1, x_1), (x_1, x_4), (x_3, x_3), (x_4, x_1), (x_4, x_1)\})$
- $\overrightarrow{G}(E_U) = \overrightarrow{G}(\{x_1, x_2, x_4\}, \{(x_1, x_2), (x_2, x_1), (x_2, x_4), (x_4, x_2)\})$.

Computing lower and upper bounds of graph characteristics can be seen as computing some graph characteristics on the graphs previously introduced. Some bounds are expressed in terms of graph characteristics that correspond to non-polynomial problems. However in such a case we provide bounds that are sharp. Note that many of the digraphs, which express a global constraint, belong to specific graph classes for which a non-polynomial problem becomes polynomial. Even when the computation is polynomial, we can get better worst-case complexity by exploiting the structure of the *intermediate digraph*.

Bound of graph characteristics	Sharpness	Polynomial
$\mathbf{NARC} \geq \|E_T\| + \|X_{T,\neg T}\| - \mu(\overleftrightarrow{G}(X_{T,\neg T}, E_U))$	yes	yes
$\mathbf{NARC} \leq \|E_{TU}\|$	yes	yes
$\mathbf{NVERTEX} \geq \|X_T\| + h(\overleftrightarrow{G}((X_{T,\neg T,\neg T}, X_{U,\neg T,T}), E_{U,T}))$	yes	**no**
$\mathbf{NVERTEX} \leq \|X_{TU}\|$	yes	yes
$\mathbf{NCC} \geq ncc_T(\overrightarrow{G}(X_{TU}, E_{TU}))$	yes	yes
$\mathbf{NCC} \leq ncc_{T_{ni}} + \mu_l(\overleftrightarrow{G}_{rem})$	yes	yes
$\mathbf{NSCC} \geq nscc_T(\overrightarrow{G}(X_{TU}, E_{TU}))$	yes	yes
$\mathbf{NSCC} \leq nscc(\overrightarrow{G}(X_{TU}, E_T))$	yes	yes
$\mathbf{NSINK} \geq nsink_T(\overrightarrow{G}(X_{TU}, E_{TU}))$	**no**	yes
$\mathbf{NSINK} \leq nsink(\overrightarrow{G}(X_T, E_T)) + \|X_U\|$	**no**	yes

The table provides a lower and an upper bound for the different graph characteristics. Proofs are available in [2]. $\mu(G)$ is the cardinality of a maximum matching of G. $\mu_l(G)$ is the maximum size of a set of edges of G, such that no two edges have a vertex in common, where G eventually contains loops. Given a bipartite graph $G((X,Y), E)$, a *hitting set* is a set of vertices in Y required to cover all vertices of X. $h(G)$ denotes the *cardinality of a minimum hitting set* of G. $nscc(G)$ and $nsink(G)$ respectively denote the number of strongly connected components and the number of sinks of G. $ncc_T(G)$ and $nscc_T(G)$ respectively denote the number of connected components, strongly connected components with at least one T-vertex. $nsink_T(G)$ denotes the number of sinks of G which are T-vertices. $ncc_{T_{ni}}(G)$ denotes the number of connected components formed only by T-arcs and T-vertices which are not isolated vertices.

References

1. N. Beldiceanu, M. Carlsson, and J.-X. Rampon. Global constraint catalog. Technical Report T2005-06, Swedish Institute of Computer Science, 2005.
2. N. Beldiceanu, T. Petit, and G. Rochart. Bounds of graph characteristics. Technical Report 05/2/INFO, École des Mines de Nantes, 2005.
3. C. Bessière, E. Hebrard, B. Hnich, Z. Kızıltan, and T. Walsh. Filtering algorithms for the nvalue constraint. In *CP-AI-OR 2005*, volume 3524 of *LNCS*, pages 79–93. Springer-Verlag, 2005.
4. D. Hanák. Implementing global constraints as structured graphs of elementary constraints. *Scientific Journal Acta Cybernetica*, 2003.

Acquiring Parameters of Implied Global Constraints

Christian Bessiere[1], Rémi Coletta[1], and Thierry Petit[2]

[1] LIRMM (CNRS/University of Montpellier), 161 Rue Ada, 34392 Montpellier, France
{bessiere, coletta}@lirmm.fr
[2] LINA (FRE CNRS 2729), École des Mines de Nantes, 4, Rue Alfred Kastler,
FR-44307 Nantes Cedex 3, France
thierry.petit@cmn.fr

Abstract. This paper presents a technique for *learning* parameterized implied constraints. They can be added to a model to improve the solving process. Experiments on implied Gcc constraints show the interest of our approach.

1 Introduction

Automatic model reformulation is a key issue for researchers [5,4,3]. The objective is to decrease the expertise required to use constraint programming. One way to improve a model consists of adding *implied* constraints. An implied constraint is not mandatory to express the problem but it helps to solve it [7]. In this paper, we assume that we have a model which expresses the problem, but the solving time is not satisfactory. We wish to improve it by automatically adding new implied constraints. Our idea is to use a *learning algorithm* that deduces new *parameterized* constraints from assignments of values to sets of variables. The set of tuples allowed by a parameterized constraint not only depends on its variables and their domains, but also on some extra information provided by *parameters*, which are not necessarily part of the problem variables. For instance, the $\text{NValue}(p, [X_1, \ldots, X_n])$ constraint holds iff p is equal to the number of different values taken by $X_1, \ldots, X_n$. p can be a CSP variable (in its more general definition) or a parameter which leads to different sets of allowed tuples on the X_i's, depending of the values it can take. In our context, a learning algorithm would try, for example, to learn the smallest range of possible values for p s.t. no solution exists outside this range. If the algorithm returns a lower bound $min(p) > 0$, or an upper bound $max(p) < n$, then the learned constraint can be of interest. [1]

2 Learning Parameterized Constraints

The set of tuples allowed by a classical constraint is known once the variables it involves and their domains are set. A parameterized constraint may allow different sets of tuples depending on the possible values for its parameters. Let us first define parameterized constraints in the most general way to let our work be as general as possible.

---

[1] A lot of existing constraints [1] may be used as implied parameterized constraints: AtLeast, AtMost, Change, Common, Count, Gcc, Max, Min, NValue, etc.

Definition 1. *Given a set of parameters $\Delta = \{p_1, ..., p_{|\Delta|}\}$ taking their values in the set of integers $\mathbb{Z}$, a parameterized constraint C is a constraint which expresses a property on the variables it involves (denoted by $var(C)$) depending on the possible values for its set of parameters Δ. Given $s \in \mathbb{Z}^{|\Delta|}$, an assignment of values to the parameters, $C(s)$ refers to the set of allowed tuples of the constraint C when each p_i in Δ takes the ith value in s, noted $s[p_i]$. Given $S \subseteq \mathbb{Z}^{|\Delta|}$, $C(S) = \bigvee_{s \in S} C(s)$.*

Definition 2. *Given a constraint C with parameters Δ and a tuple e on $var(C)$ (or a superset of $var(C)$), S_e contains the combinations s in $\mathbb{Z}^{|\Delta|}$ s.t. $C(s)$ accepts e.*

Our goal is to learn implied constraints on any type of constraint problem: we focus on those parameterized constraints where for any tuple e on $var(C)$, $S_e \neq \emptyset$. The basic idea is to learn the parameters of an implied constraint C by exploiting information provided by solutions and non-solutions of a subproblem (stem from the initial problem by removing variables and constraints). Indeed, if the current model is not good, obviously it should not easily provide instances[2] for the whole problem. By definition, if a learned constraint is valid in a subproblem then it is still valid in the main problem. Variables of the subproblem are then the decision variables involved in the learned implied constraint. W.r.t. optimization problems, in the context of a Branch and Bound algorithm, a way to proceed is to learn new implied constraints at each step of the optimization.[3]

We assume now that the subproblem and the constraint C to learn have been chosen.

Notation 1. $\mathcal{P} = (\mathcal{X}, \mathcal{D}, \mathcal{C})$ *is the problem used to learn an implied constraint.*

Definition 3. *An* implied constraint C *for $\mathcal{P}$ is a constraint s.t. $var(C) \subseteq \mathcal{X}$ and the set $Sol(\mathcal{P})$ of solutions of $\mathcal{P}$ is equal to $Sol((\mathcal{X}, \mathcal{D}, \mathcal{C} \cup \{C\}))$; Namely, for any instance $e \in Sol(\mathcal{P})$, $e[var(C)]$ is allowed by C.*

We consider only constraints for which $C(\mathbb{Z}^{|\Delta|})$ is the universal constraint (i.e., for any tuple e, $S_e \neq \emptyset$). Thus, following Definition 3, $C(\mathbb{Z}^{|\Delta|})$ is an implied constraint for the problem $\mathcal{P}$. The objective of a learning algorithm will be to learn a 'target' set $T \subseteq \mathbb{Z}^{|\Delta|}$, as small as possible, s.t. $C(T)$ is still an implied constraint. Any $s \in \mathbb{Z}^{|\Delta|}$ which is not necessary to accept some solutions of $\mathcal{P}$ can be removed from T.

Notation 2. *Given a problem $\mathcal{P} = (\mathcal{X}, \mathcal{D}, \mathcal{C})$ and a parameterized constraint C, we denote by $required(T)$ the set of elements r of $\mathbb{Z}^{|\Delta|}$ such that $r \in required(T)$ iff $C(\mathbb{Z}^{|\Delta|} \setminus \{r\})$ is not an implied constraint, namely r is compulsory in T if we want $C(T)$ to be an implied constraint in $\mathcal{P}$. $poss(T)$ denotes those r in $\mathbb{Z}^{|\Delta|}$ for which we do not know if they must belong to $required(T)$.*

In other words, $required(T)$ represents those combinations of values for the parameters that are necessary to preserve the set of solutions of $\mathcal{P}$, and $poss(T)$ those for which we have not proved yet that we would not lose solutions without them. The fact that an implied constraint should not remove solutions when we add it to the problem leads to the following property w.r.t. positive instances.

---

[2] Given a problem $\mathcal{P} = (\mathcal{X}, \mathcal{D}, \mathcal{C})$, an *instance* e is an assignment of values to variables in $\mathcal{X}$. It is *positive* if e belongs to $Sol(\mathcal{P})$, otherwise it is *negative*.

[3] We may observe a nice cooperation between the learning and the solving phases: new learned constraints help at each step to solve the problem, and thus to learn the next ones.

Property 1. Let e^+ be a positive instance and $T \subseteq \mathbb{Z}^{|\Delta|}$. If $C(T)$ is an implied constraint for $\mathcal{P}$ then $T \cap S_{e^+} \neq \emptyset$.

Proof. e^+ is a solution of $\mathcal{P}$. At least one $s \in T$ should accept that instance to preserve the set of solutions of $\mathcal{P}$. So, $s \in S_{e^+}$ by Definition 2. □

Corollary 1. *Let e^+ be a positive instance of $\mathcal{P}$ and C a parameterized constraint. If there is a unique $s \in \mathbb{Z}^{|\Delta|}$ such that $e^+[var(C)] \in C(s)$ then $s \in required(T)$.*

Negative instances will help to remove from $poss(T)$ the combinations of parameters that can be removed without losing solutions. When receiving a negative instance e^-, we want to know if it is possible to reduce the target set T in order to reject e^- while preserving $Sol(\mathcal{P})$.

Property 2. Let $\mathcal{P}$ be a problem, C a parameterized constraint, and $S \subset \mathbb{Z}^{|\Delta|}$. If $\mathcal{P}$ augmented with the constraint $C(S)$ has no solution then $C(\mathbb{Z}^{|\Delta|} \setminus S)$ is an implied constraint for $\mathcal{P}$.

Proof. By previous assumption, we know that $C(\mathbb{Z}^{|\Delta|})$ is an implied constraint for $\mathcal{P}$. Since $\mathcal{P} \cup \{C(S)\}$ is inconsistent, we know that $\forall e \in Sol(\mathcal{P}), S_e \cap S = \emptyset$. Thus $Sol(\mathcal{P}+C(\mathbb{Z}^{|\Delta|})) = Sol(\mathcal{P} + C(\mathbb{Z}^{|\Delta|} \setminus S))$. □

Corollary 2. *Let $\mathcal{P}$ be a problem, C a parameterized constraint, $S \subseteq \mathbb{Z}^{|\Delta|}$, and $poss(T)$ a set s.t. $C(poss(T))$ is implied on $\mathcal{P}$. If $\mathcal{P}$ augmented with the constraint $C(S)$ has no solution then $C(poss(T) \setminus S)$ is an implied constraint for $\mathcal{P}$.*

Algorithm 1. Learning Algorithm for Parameterized Constraints

---

Input: $C, \Delta, E = \{e_1, \ldots, e_k\}$ a set of instances for $\mathcal{P}$.
Output: $poss(T)$, s.t. $C(poss(T))$ is an implied constraint for $\mathcal{P}$.
$required(T) \leftarrow \emptyset$; $poss(T) \leftarrow \mathbb{Z}^{|\Delta|}$;
while $(E \neq \emptyset)$ and $(required(T) \neq poss(T))$ do
    Pick $e \in E$;
    if e is positive then
1 | if $|S_e| = 1$ then $required(T) \leftarrow required(T) \cup S_e$; /* Corol. 1*/
    else
      for some $S \subseteq (poss(T) \setminus required(T))$ do
2 | if $Sol(\mathcal{X}, \mathcal{D}, \mathcal{C} \cup C(S)) = \emptyset$ then $poss(T) \leftarrow poss(T) \setminus S$; /* Corol. 2*/
        else put an element of $Sol(\mathcal{X}, \mathcal{D}, \mathcal{C} \cup C(S))$ as positive instance in E

Checking if $\mathcal{P}$ augmented with the constraint $C(S)$ is inconsistent (line 2) is obviously NP-hard. Even if $\mathcal{P}$ in this learning phase is not supposed to be the whole problem we want to reformulate, it is necessary to follow some heuristics to avoid huge numbers of NP-hard calls to a solver. For a parameterized constraint C, different representations of parameters may exist. The more general case studied until now (Algorithm 1) consists of considering that allowed tuples of parameters for C are given in extension as a set T. Corollary 1 may then seem weak. However, in practice, most of parameterized constraints are s.t. any two different combinations of parameters in $\mathbb{Z}^{|\Delta|}$ correspond to disjoint sets of allowed tuples on $var(C)$. We call them *parameter-partitioned* constraints. For instance, NValue$(p, [X_1, \ldots, X_n])$ is parameter-partitioned since a single value of p corresponds to an assignment of the X_i.

Corollary 3. *Let e^+ be a positive instance. If C is a parameter-partitioned constraint, $s_{e^+} \in required(T)$, where s_{e^+} is the only element in S_{e^+}.*

This corollary allows a faster construction of $required(T)$ compared with Algorithm 1. Moreover, existing parameterized constraints are usually defined by sets of possible values for their parameters taken separately, which is less expressive than considering directly any subset of $\mathbb{Z}^{|\Delta|}$. It is possible to exploit this fact. We will note $T[p_i]$ for the values of a parameter we wish to learn. Then, $required(T[p_i]) = \{k_i \in \mathbb{Z} \text{ s.t. } \exists s \in required(T), s[p_i] = k_i\}$, namely the set of values for p_i that are required in $T[p_i]$. Similarly, $poss(T[p_i]) = \{k_i \in \mathbb{Z} \text{ s.t. } \exists s \in poss(T), s[p_i] = k_i\}$. If the possible values for a parameter p_i are a **set of integers**, the learning algorithm uses sets of integers to represent $required(T[p_i])$ and $poss(T[p_i])$. The parameterized constraint will be called with $poss(T[p_1]) \times \ldots \times poss(T[p_{|\Delta|}])$. If the possible values for p_i are a **range of integers**, the learning algorithm uses ranges of the form $[min(poss(T[p_i]))..max(poss(T[p_i]))]$ to represent $poss(T[p_i])$ (resp. $required(T[p_i])$). Properties 1 and 2 can be rewritten to fit these two cases.

Property 3. Let e^+ be a positive instance of $\mathcal{P}$ and C a parameterized constraint s.t. parameters are *sets of integers*. If there is a unique $s \in \mathbb{Z}^{|\Delta|}$ such that $e^+[var(C)] \in C(s)$ then for any $p_i \in \Delta$, $s[p_i] \in required(T[p_i])$.

Property 4. Let $\mathcal{P}$ be a problem, C a parameterized constraint where parameters are a *set of integers*, and $poss(T)$ a set s.t. $C(poss(T))$ is implied on $\mathcal{P}$. Let p be a parameter of C, v a value in $poss(T[p])$, and $S = \{s \in poss(T) \text{ s.t. } s[p] = v\}$. If $\mathcal{P}$ augmented with $C(S)$ has no solution then v can be removed from $poss(T[p])$.

Note that for each negative instance e^-, if the constraint is parameter-partitioned, a heuristic can be used to apply property 4 with $v = s_{e^-}[p]$.

Property 5. Let e^+ be a positive instance of $\mathcal{P}$ and C a parameterized constraint s.t. parameters are *ranges*. If there is a unique $s \in \mathbb{Z}^{|\Delta|}$ such that $e^+[var(C)] \in C(s)$ then for any $p_i \in \Delta$, $min(required(T[p_i])) \leq s[p_i] \leq max(required(T[p_i]))$.

Property 6. Let $\mathcal{P}$ be a problem, C a parameterized constraint where parameters are *ranges*, and $poss(T)$ a set s.t. $C(poss(T))$ is implied on $\mathcal{P}$. Let p be a parameter of C, v a value in $poss(T[p])$, and $S = \{s \in poss(T) \text{ s.t. } s[p] \leq v\}$ (respectively: $S = \{s \in poss(T) \text{ s.t. } s[p] \geq v\}$). If $\mathcal{P}$ augmented with $C(S)$ has no solution then $min(poss(T[p])) > v$ (respectively: $max(poss(T[p_i])) < v$).

3 Experiments

We implemented with Choco [2] a learning algorithm for implied Gcc (global cardinality constraints [6]) where parameters are ranges. On the two intentionally naive models we implemented to evaluate the interest of our algorithm, tables compare the solving time of an initial model with the same model augmented with a learned Gcc.[4]

---
[4] In the tables located at the left the last column indicates the solving time, whereas in the tables located at the right the last column indicates the sum of the learning time and the solving time.

Table 1. Scheduling satisfaction problem with a fixed makespan, precedence constraints, and $m = m_1+m_2$ tasks (requiring one or two resources). $maxi$ is the maximum allowed resource. 15 assignments where used to learn an implied Gcc on a problem relaxed from resource constraints.

<table>
<tr><td colspan="4" align="center">(a) Initial model.</td><td colspan="4" align="center">(b) Augm. Model.</td></tr>
<tr><td>m_1/m_2</td><td>$maxi$</td><td>#nodes</td><td>time (sec.)</td><td>m_1/m_2</td><td>$maxi$</td><td>#nodes</td><td>time (sec.)</td></tr>
<tr><td>4/0</td><td>4</td><td>—</td><td>> 60</td><td>4/0</td><td>4</td><td>47</td><td>0.297 + 0.026</td></tr>
<tr><td>4/0</td><td>3</td><td>42,129</td><td>7.4</td><td>4/0</td><td>3</td><td>47</td><td>0.279 + 0.018</td></tr>
<tr><td>4/0</td><td>2</td><td>85</td><td>0.12</td><td>4/0</td><td>2</td><td>23</td><td>0.265 + 0.015</td></tr>
<tr><td>3/1</td><td>4</td><td>45</td><td>0.030</td><td>3/1</td><td>4</td><td>43</td><td>0.312 + 0.031</td></tr>
<tr><td>3/1</td><td>3</td><td>33</td><td>0.041</td><td>3/1</td><td>3</td><td>30</td><td>0.286 + 0.019</td></tr>
<tr><td>3/1</td><td>2</td><td>7 (no sol)</td><td>0.030</td><td>3/1</td><td>2</td><td>3 (no sol)</td><td>0.279 + 0.013</td></tr>
</table>

Table 2. Optimization problem (allocation). n is the problem size (number of variables), $|E|$ is the number of assignments used to learn implied Gcc's.

<table>
<tr><td colspan="3" align="center">(a) Initial Model.</td><td colspan="4" align="center">(b) Augm. Model.</td></tr>
<tr><td>n</td><td>#nodes</td><td>time (sec.)</td><td>n</td><td>$|E|$</td><td>#nodes</td><td>time (sec.)</td></tr>
<tr><td>10</td><td>110</td><td>0.2</td><td>10</td><td>10</td><td>12</td><td>0.2 + 0.0</td></tr>
<tr><td>15</td><td>2,648</td><td>7.6</td><td>15</td><td>10</td><td>57</td><td>2.6 + 1.1</td></tr>
<tr><td>20</td><td>137,982</td><td>183.2</td><td>15</td><td>20</td><td>50</td><td>3.8 + 1.1</td></tr>
<tr><td></td><td></td><td></td><td>15</td><td>40</td><td>50</td><td>5.9 + 0.9</td></tr>
<tr><td></td><td></td><td></td><td>20</td><td>10</td><td>4,801</td><td>5.7 + 14.9</td></tr>
<tr><td></td><td></td><td></td><td>20</td><td>20</td><td>2,800</td><td>6.8 + 13.0</td></tr>
<tr><td></td><td></td><td></td><td>20</td><td>40</td><td>1,998</td><td>9.1 + 8.4</td></tr>
</table>

References

1. N. Beldiceanu. Global constraints as graph properties on a structured network of elementary constraints of the same type. *Proceedings CP*, pages 52–66, 2000.
2. Choco. A Java library for constraint satisfaction problems, constraint programming and explanation-based constraint solving. *URL: http://sourceforge.net/projects/choco*, 2005.
3. S. Colton and I. Miguel. Constraint generation via automated theory formation. *Proceedings CP*, pages 575–579, 2001.
4. A. M. Frisch, C. Jefferson, B. Martinez Hernandez, and Ian Miguel. The rules of constraint modelling. *Proceedings IJCAI*, to appear, 2005.
5. J.F. Puget. Constraint programming next challenge: Simplicity of use. In *Proceedings CP*, pages 5–8, Toronto, Canada, 2004.
6. J-C. Régin. Generalized arc consistency for global cardinality constraint. *Proceedings AAAI*, pages 209–215, 1996.
7. B. Smith, K. Stergiou, and T. Walsh. Modelling the golomb ruler problem. In J.C. Régin and W. Nuijten, editors, *Proceedings IJCAI'99 workshop on non-binary constraints*, Stockholm, Sweden, 1999.

Integrating Benders Decomposition Within Constraint Programming

Hadrien Cambazard and Narendra Jussien

École des Mines de Nantes, LINA CNRS FRE 2729,
4 rue Alfred Kastler – BP 20722 - F-44307 Nantes Cedex 3, France
{hcambaza, jussien}@emn.fr

1 Introduction

Benders decomposition [1] is a solving strategy based on the separation of the variables of the problem. It is often introduced as a basis for models and techniques using the complementary strengths of constraint programming and optimization techniques. Hybridization schemes have appeared recently and provided interesting computational results [4,5,7,8]. They have been extended [2,3,6] to take into account other kinds of sub-problems and not only the classical linear programming ones. However, decomposition has never been proposed to our knowledge in a generic constraint programming approach. This paper discusses the way a decomposition framework could be embedded in a constraint solver, taking advantage of structures for a non expert user. We explore the possibility of deriving logic Benders cuts using an explanation-based framework for CP and describe Benders decomposition as a nogood recording strategy. We propose a tool implemented at the top of an explained constraint solver that could offer such a systematic decomposition framework.

2 Context

Explanations for Constraint Programming. An explanation records information to justify a decision of the solver as a domain reduction or a contradiction. It is made of a set of constraints C' (a subset of the original constraints) and a set of decisions $dc_1, dc_2, \ldots dc_n$ taken during search. An explanation of the removal of value a from variable v, $expl(v \neq a)$ will be written $C' \wedge dc_1 \wedge dc_2 \wedge \cdots \wedge dc_n \Rightarrow v \neq a$. An explanation is computed for any contradiction during the search and intelligent backtracking algorithms that question a relevant decision appearing in the conflict are then conceivable.

Principles of Benders Decomposition. Benders decomposition can be seen as a form of *learning from mistakes*. It is based on a partition of the variables into two sets: x, y. The strategy can be applied to a problem of the form P :

P : Min $f(y) + cx$	SP : Min cx	DSP : Max $u(a - g(\overline{y}))$
s.t : $g(y) + Ax \geq a$	s.t : $Ax \geq a - g(\overline{y})$	s.t : $uA \leq c$
with : $y \in D, x \geq 0$	with : $x \geq 0$	with : $u \geq 0$

A master problem considers only the y variables. A sub-problem (SP) tries to complete the assignment on x. If it is possible, the problem is solved, but if not, a cut (a constraint rejecting at least the current assignment on y) is produced and added to the master problem: it is called a Benders cut. This cut is the key point of the method, it has the form $z \geq h(y)$ (z represents the objective function $- z = f(y) + cx$) and is inferred by the dual of the sub-problem (DSP). So, even if the cut is derived from a particular $\bar{y}$, it is valid for all y and excludes a large class of assignments. From all of this, it can be noticed that duals variables or multipliers[1] need to be defined to apply the decomposition. However, a generalized scheme has been proposed in 1972 by Goeffrion [2]. Hooker [3] proposed also to enlarge the classical notion of *dual* by introducing an *inference dual* available for all kinds of sub-problems. They suggest a different way of thinking about duality: a Benders decomposition based on *logic*. For a discrete satisfaction problem, the resolution of the dual consists in computing the infeasibility proof and determining under what conditions the proof remains valid: this is exactly what explanations are designed for.

3 A Decomposition Approach in CP

In this paper, we consider problems which can be represented by P :

P : Min obj	MP : Min z	SP^k : Min sz_k
s.t : $Ct(x,y)$	s.t : $Ct^i(x,y)$	s.t : $Ct(x_k, \bar{y})$
with : $x \in D_x, y \in D_y$	$z < \bar{z}$	$x_k \in D_x$
	$y \in D_y$	

$Ct(x,y)$ denotes a set of constraints on variables x, y and obj can be equal to $\{f(x,y), f(y), 0\}$. The problem P will be denoted $\{P_{xy}, P_y, P_0\}$ according to the corresponding objective functions. The decomposition scheme is done among x and y. We suppose that the remaining problem over x can be formulated using n sub-problems exhibiting strong intra-relationships and weak inter-relationships. Ideally, they should be as small and independent as possible to ensure the remaining sub-problem to be easy. So we make the assumption for the sub-problem to offer such an ideal (denoted by P) or approximate structure (denoted P', so we get in the same way $\{P'_{xy}, P'_y, P'_0\}$). Master problem and sub-problems have then the generic form MP and SP (where $Ct^i(x,y)$ is the union of $Ct(x,y)$ and the benders cut gathered at iteration i).

3.1 Benders Cuts as Explanations

The Benders cut is a logic expression over the y variables, generated from the sub-problem solution. The cut must ensure that the algorithm terminates and finds the optimal solution. At iteration k, the added Benders cut must have the following properties:

---
[1] Referring to linear programming duality.

1. It is valid; it does not exclude any feasible solution over the x, y variables of the original problem (according to the current upper bound of z).
2. It must exclude at least the current instantiation $\bar{y}$ of the master that has been proved as sub-optimal or inconsistent

(2) ensures the termination of the algorithm and (1) ensures optimality as the master problem is proved to remain a valid relaxation and to provide a lower bound of P. As the explanation is a subset of the decisions taken by the master, it excludes at least the current assignment. An empty set indicates an infeasible P whereas the complete set excludes only $\bar{y}$. The explanation is proved to be valid as long as constraints compute valid explanations as they perform a valid pruning. Note that the structure of the dual is used through the explanation algorithms embedded within constraints. In fact, the computation of explanations is $lazy^2$. Therefore, such an inference dual provides an arbitrary[3] dual solution but not necessarily the optimal one.

3.2 Decomposition Scheme

One of the key point of Benders decomposition is to be able to derive a master problem that provides a valid lower bound for the original P. We used the following master problems for initial problems P_y, P_0 and P_{xy}:

$$MP_y : \text{Min } f(y) \qquad MP_0 : \text{Min } 0 \qquad MP_{xy} : \text{Min } r(y) = relax(f(x,y))$$
$$\text{s.t } : Ct^i(x,y) \qquad \text{s.t } : Ct^i(x,y) \qquad \text{s.t } : Ct^i(x,y)$$
$$y \in D_y \qquad y \in D_y \qquad y \in D_y$$

One can notice here that MP_y provides a valid lower bound as it is a relaxation of P_y. It is also the case for P_0 as it is a satisfaction problem. However, it is not true in the general case of P_{xy} where a specific master problem must be designed. In fact, a new objective function called $r(y)$ defined on y variables and providing a lower bound has to be defined by the user.

There are some cases where the original function is itself a relaxation (e.g. a coloring problem) but in a generic case, the master problem take the form of a feasibility problem where the cuts added can be seen as $expl(z \geq z^*) \Rightarrow z \geq z^*$.

4 A Benders Decomposition Algorithm for CP

Figure 1 presents our algorithm[4]. It has been implemented as a library of the Java version of the PaLM solver embedded within the choco (see http://choco.sf.net) constraints solver. The standard CP model is only enriched by indicating for each variable the problem to which it belongs (the master or the index of the sub-problem).

---

[2] Not all possible explanations are computed when removing a value for scalability reasons. Only the one corresponding to the solver actual reasoning is kept.
[3] It is also the case for linear duality as any dual solution is a bound for the primal.
[4] Line 8 is used in the case of P_0' and P_y' whereas lines 5, 11, 13, and 14 concerns P_{xy}. The case of P_{xy}' is not yet included.

```
input : an initial solution to the master problem ȳ,
(1)  begin
(2)    repeat
(3)      Cut = ∅
(4)      for each sub-problem spb_k do
(5)        P_xy : update upper bound of spb_k with computeUb(k) using {z̄, sz̄_i, ∀i < k})
(6)        solve spb_k on (ȳ, x_k) to optimality
(7)        add its inconsistency (if spb_k is infeasible)/optimality explanation to Cut
(8)        P'_0, P'_y : spb_{k+1} = ⋃_{i≤k,i>k'} spb_i, with k', the last infeasible sub-problem.
(9)      endfor
(10)     if (Cut ≠ ∅) then
(11)       P_xy : Cut = computeCut(Cut)
(12)       add all explanations ∈ Cut to the master problem
(13)       P_xy : update the upper bound of z with computeUb(0) using {z̄, sz̄_1, ..., sz̄_n})
(14)       P_xy : store (x̄, ȳ) if it is an improving solution
(15)       solve the master problem to optimality
(16)     endif
(17)   until the master problem is infeasible ⋁ Cut = ∅
(18)   P_y, P_0, P'_0, P'_y : the solution (ȳ, x̄) is optimal if Cut = ∅ otherwise, P is infeasible.
(19)   P_xy : the solution (ȳ, x̄) is the optimal solution of P otherwise P is infeasible.
(20) end
```

Fig. 1. A Generic Benders algorithm for P_0, P_y (P'_0, P'_y) and P_{xy}

4.1 Specific Handling for Problems P_0 and P_y

P_0 and P_y are closely related because they both use satisfaction problems as sub-problems. Backjumping algorithms are used to compute explanations (to provide dual informations) on the sub-problems. Moreover, the use of backjumping for the master is possible for P_0 (which is a traditional CSP) and allows the partial avoidance of thrashing on the master problem when adding the cuts. This is a response to Thorsteinsson [5] concerns about possible significant overhead due to redundant computations. Concerning approximated structures: at any iteration k, the next sub-problem $k+1$ considered is chosen according to the rule described line 8. So if one sub-problem is consistent, the next one starts from its solution and consider for branching the variables of both problems. Such a strategy hopes to benefit from the relative independency of sub-problems (it does not imply any overhead compared to solving one single sub-problem) to derive disjoint cuts. There is obviously a compromise between the time spent for solving sub-problems and the accuracy of the retrieved information.

4.2 Specific Handling for Problem P_{xy}

To keep isolated sub-problems, we do not add the objective function as a constraint which could propagate from one sub-problem to another. Instead, we provide a way to compute the bound of one problem according to other known bounds (master and slaves) with an empty explanation. So the propagation is done *at hand* to only incriminate the master problem solution using:

- *computeCut(Explanation[] expls)* (line 11): computes the explanation(s) to be added to the master according to the objective function. A sum would lead to a union among explanations for example;
- *computeUb(int k)* (line 5,13): computes an upper bound on z_k according to $\overline{y}$ and known z_i with $i < k$. In the case $k = 0$ (the master problem) it computes the upper bound of the overall objective function z if every SP_k was feasible.

At each iteration, a lower bound is obtained once the master problem has been solved. The algorithm stops once the lower bound meets the upper bound computed after the slaves. One can notice that the upper bound does not necessarily follow a decreasing trend whereas the lower bound is only growing ensuring the termination of the algorithm as long as variables have finite domains.

5 Conclusion

We have investigated in this paper how to derive logic Benders cuts using an explanation based framework for Constraint Programming. Accuracy of cuts using explanations is nevertheless questionnable. Indeed, remaining sub-problems are not polynomial (compared to a traditional MILP approach for Benders and assuming that LP is polynomial) and explanations constitute a weaker cut as a lazy computation is used. First experimental results using structured random binary problems show that Benders becomes advantageous in case of hard sub-problems compared to a branching using the same structure information within a backjumping algorithm. Moreover, we believe that the presence of subset of variables exhibiting a strong impact over the whole problem could be efficiently used by such an approach. Our next step is to apply the technique on hard academical problems and we are currently investigating how hard latin square instances could be decomposed.

References

1. J. F. Benders. Partitionning procedures for solving mixed-variables programming problems. *Numerische Mathematik*, 4:238–252, 1962.
2. A. M. Geoffrion. Generalized Benders Decomposition. *Journal of Optimization Theory And Practice*, Vol. 10, No. 4, 1972.
3. J.N. Hooker and G. Ottosson. Logic-based benders decomposition. *Mathematical Programming*, 96:33–60, 2003.
4. Vipul Jain and I. E. Grossmann. Algorithms for hybrid milp/cp models for a class of optimization problems. *INFORMS Journal on Computing*, 13:258–276, 2001.
5. Erlendur S. Thorsteinsson. Branch-and-check: A hybrid framework integrating mixed integer programming and constraint logic programming. In *CP'01*, 2001.
6. John N. Hooker A Hybrid Method for Planning and Scheduling. In *CP'04*, pages 305–316, 2004.
7. T. Benoist, E. Gaudin, and B. Rottembourg. Constraint programming contribution to benders decomposition: A case study. In *CP'02*, pages 603–617, 2002.
8. H. Cambazard, P. E. Hladik, A. M. Déplanche, N. Jussien, and Y. Trinquet. Decomposition and learning for a real time task allocation problem. In *CP'04*, pages 153–167, 2004.

Using Boolean Constraint Propagation for Sub-clauses Deduction*

S. Darras[1], G. Dequen[1], L. Devendeville[1], B. Mazure[2], R. Ostrowski[2], and L. Saïs[2]

[1] LaRIA CNRS, Univ. de Picardie, 33 rue Saint Leu, 80039 Amiens Cedex 1, France
{sylvain.darras, gilles.dequen,
laure.devendeville}@u-picardie.fr
[2] CRIL CNRS, Univ. d'Artois, rue Jean Souvraz SP-18, 62307 Lens Cedex, France
{bertrand.mazure, richard.ostrowski,
lakhdar.sais}@cril.univ-artois.fr

Abstract. The Boolean Constraint Propagation (BCP) is a well-known helpful technique implemented in most state-of-the-art efficient satisfiability solvers. We propose in this paper a new use of the BCP to deduce sub-clauses from the associated implication graph. Our aim is to reduce the length of clauses thanks to the subsumption rule. We show how such extension can be grafted to modern SAT solvers and we provide some experimental results of the sub-clauses deduction as a pretreatment process.

1 Introduction

Recent impressive progress in the practical resolution of hard and large SAT instances allows real-world problems to be addressed (e.g. [1,2,3]). Indeed, instances from practical applications contain some structures (e.g. [4,5]) that can be attractive to SAT solvers. Most of modern SAT solver are based on the well-known DPLL procedure [6] where Boolean Constraint Propagation is maintained at each step of the search process. This important part has motivated many works on efficient implementation of BCP (e.g. zchaff [7]) and on extending its practical use.

In this paper, the constraint graph generated by BCP process is used to deduce new resolvents. The set of such possible resolvents can be of exponential size in the worst-case w.r.t. the set of clauses encoded in the constraint graph. We focus on a polynomial time and constant space complexity approach. Then, we show how such an extension can be grafted to modern SAT solvers.

2 Definitions and Preliminaries

A *CNF formula* Σ is a conjunction of *clauses* (the set of clauses is denoted $cla(\Sigma)$), where a clause is a disjunction of *literals*. A literal is a positive or negative propositional variable. The set of variables (resp. literals) occurring in Σ is denoted $var(\Sigma)$ (resp. $lit(\Sigma)$). The negation of a set A of literals (denoted $\bar{A}$) is the set of the corresponding

---
* This work is supported by the Region Picardie under HTSC project.

opposite literals. $A_\vee$ (resp. $A_\wedge$) is denoted as the disjunction (resp. conjunction) of all literals of A.

Let c_1 and c_2 be two clauses of Σ.

i) *subsumption rule*: When $c_1 \subset c_2$ (i.e. c_1 is a sub-clause of c_2), c_1 subsumes c_2.

ii) *resolution rule*: If there exists a literal l s.t. $l \in c_1$ and $\neg l \in c_2$, then a *resolvent* r on l of c_1 and c_2 can be defined as $r = res(l, c_1, c_2) = c_1 \setminus \{l\} \cup c_2 \setminus \{\neg l\}$. A resolvent r is called a subsuming resolvent iff $\exists c \in \Sigma$ s.t. r subsumes c.

Boolean Constraint Propagation consists on setting all unit literals to the value $true$ until encountering an empty clause or until no unit clause remains in the formula.

An *Implication Graph* associated to Σ and a set I of decision literals is a labeled directed acyclic graph $\mathcal{G}_{ig}(\Sigma, I) = (\mathcal{V}, \mathcal{A})$. $\mathcal{V}$ is a set of distinct vertices labeled with the literals of I and the literals forced to $true$ during the BCP process. $\mathcal{A}$ is a set of distinct directed edges $\langle l_i, l_j \rangle$ ($\{l_i, l_j\} \in \mathcal{V}$) such that $l_i = true$ contributes to force $l_j = true$ through the BCP process. The set of edges $\{\forall k \langle l_{i_k}, l_j \rangle\}$ represents the complete implication $\{l_{i_1} \wedge l_{i_2} \wedge \ldots \wedge l_{i_n} \Rightarrow l_j\}$. Each directed edge $\langle l_i, l_j \rangle$ is labeled with the clause of Σ used by the BCP. Thus, each node of the graph corresponds to one variable assignment. The set of literals which force to $true$ a given literal l is named "predecessors" of the labeled vertex l. This set is denoted $pred(l)$. In such a context, each implied literal l from $\mathcal{G}_{ig}$ is labeled with the *decision level* α corresponding to the decision-level where l is assigned.

3 Exploiting BCP for Sub-clauses Deduction

It is well known that BCP can be seen as a restricted form of resolution. At each step a subsuming resolvent is produced between a unit clause and another clause of the formula. Our aim in this paper is to produce such resolvents from $\mathcal{G}_{ig}$. Thus, we start from a given literal of the implication graph, then a new resolvent (internal node) is generated between two clauses corresponding to the implications of such a literal and one of its predecessor from the implication graph. The process is then recursively applied between the current resolvent and an implication of one of its literals. In the following definition, we introduce a sub-inference exploiting such resolution process for sub-clause deduction.

Definition 1. *Let Σ be a formula, $l \in lit(\Sigma)$ and $\mathcal{G}_{ig}(\Sigma, l)$ an implication graph. A clause c is l-sub-inferred from Σ if $\exists c' \in \Sigma$ such that one of the following condition is satisfied : i) $c \in \mathcal{N}$ and $c \subset c'$. ii) $\exists c'' \in \mathcal{N}$ s.t. $c = res(p, c', c'') \subset c'$.*

Proposition 1. *Let Σ be a formula, $l \in lit(\Sigma)$ and $\mathcal{G}_{ig}(\Sigma, l) = (\mathcal{V}, \mathcal{A})$. A sub-inferred clause c can be computed in $O(|cla(\Sigma)| \times (|\mathcal{V}| + |\mathcal{A}|)^2)$.*

Proof. BCP and $\mathcal{G}_{ig} = (\mathcal{V}, \mathcal{A})$ are first processed (in linear time) on $\Sigma \wedge l$ ($|\mathcal{V}| \leq |var(\Sigma)|$). Considering a clause c' from Σ, we try to find any implication clause c represented in $\mathcal{G}_{ig}$ following definition 1. From a vertex s, we first consider the implication $pred(s) \rightarrow s$ from $\mathcal{G}_{ig}$. Let us suppose that there is no way to deduce a clause c that subsumes c' from $\mathcal{G}_{ig}$. The implication clause $pred(s) \rightarrow s$ contains at least one literal p which does not belong to c'. We then substitute $pred(p)$ for p in the implication $pred(s) \rightarrow s$. Following this principle, a subset of

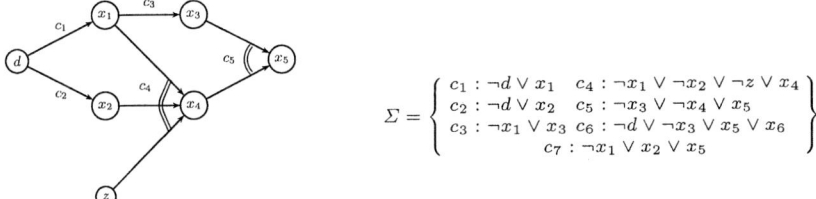

Fig. 1. Formula Σ and it associated BCP setting d to $True$

vertices (possibly all) of $\mathcal{G}_{ig}$ is visited while it exists at least one literal of the current implication which does not belong to c'. This is computed until one or more decision literals (i.e. with no predecessors) which does not belong to c are reached. Thus, the sub-clauses deduction depends on the number of vertices of $\mathcal{G}_{ig}$. If a clause c such that c subsumes c' (as mentioned in definition 1) can be deduced from $\mathcal{G}_{ig}$, the process previously described allows to visit vertices of $\mathcal{G}_{ig}$ until one of the condition of the definition 1 is valid. Consequently, considering one vertex of $\mathcal{G}_{ig}$, only one traversal of $\mathcal{G}_{ig}$ is needed ($O(|\mathcal{V}| + |\mathcal{A}|)$). This has to be computed for all vertices of $\mathcal{G}_{ig}$. As each clause of Σ could be considered, the worst case complexity of this global computation process is $O(|cla(\Sigma)| \times (|\mathcal{V}| + |\mathcal{A}|)^2)$.

Within a practical framework, only a restricted subset of clauses of Σ is considered for each BCP.

Algorithm 1. $GetSubClause(\mathcal{G}_{ig}$:IG, A:set of literals, y:literal, c:clause, α:decision-level)

1: **if** $\exists x_r \in \bar{A} \cup \{y\} | \neg x_r \in c$ **and** $\forall x \in ((\bar{A} \cup \{y\}) - \{x_r\}) \cap \mathcal{V}_\alpha, x \in c$ **then**
2: $\quad \Sigma = (\Sigma - \{c\}) \cup \{c - \{\neg x_r\}\})_{dl > max_{x \notin c, x \in A \cap (\mathcal{V} - \mathcal{V}_\alpha)}(dl_x)}$
3: $\quad$ **if** $pred(x_r) \neq \emptyset$ **then**
4: $\quad\quad GetSubClauseLevel(\mathcal{G}_{ig}, A - \{x_r\} \cup pred(x_r), y, c, \alpha)$
5: $\quad$ **end if**
6: **else**
7: $\quad$ **if** $\forall x \in (\bar{A} \cup \{y\}) \cap \mathcal{V}_\alpha, x \in c$ **then**
8: $\quad\quad \Sigma = (\Sigma - \{c\}) \cup \{(\bar{A} \cap c)_\mathcal{V} \vee y\})_{dl > max_{x \notin c, x \in A \cap \mathcal{V} - \mathcal{V}_\alpha}(dl_x)}$
9: $\quad\quad x = choice(A)$
10: $\quad\quad$ **if** $pred(x) \neq \emptyset$ **then**
11: $\quad\quad\quad GetSubClauseLevel(\mathcal{G}_{ig}, A - \{x\} \cup pred(x), y, c, \alpha)$
12: $\quad\quad$ **end if**
13: $\quad$ **else**
14: $\quad\quad$ Choose $x \in A | x \notin c$ **and** $\neg x \notin c$
15: $\quad\quad$ **if** $pred(x) \neq \emptyset$ **then**
16: $\quad\quad\quad GetSubClauseLevel(\mathcal{G}_{ig}, A - \{x\} \cup pred(x), y, c, \alpha)$
17: $\quad\quad$ **end if**
18: $\quad$ **end if**
19: **end if**

---

4 Inferring Sub-clauses During Search

For a clause c of Σ, the function $GetSubclause$ of algorithm 1 finds according to the definition 1 and if they exists, sub-clauses which directly subsume c (see line 7) and clauses whose resolvents with c subsume c (see line 1). Let us denote $\mathcal{V}_\alpha$ the set of literals assigned at the current decision-level α. Searching for all subsumptions from

Table 1. Preliminary results

Instance	S/U	zchaff nodes	zchaff time	Pretreatment (180s) +zchaff nodes	subs	fixed var.	time	Pretreatment (300s) +zchaff nodes	subs	fixed var.	time
SAT.dat.k90	S	N/A	N/A	N/A	373	2 917	N/A	6 157 239	598	4 419	13 264
abp4-...-403	U	2 843 489	9 751	2 369 440	1 368	359	6 950	1 675 832	1 458	380	4 808
2bitadd_10	U	60 605	40	60 605	0	0	221	60 605	0	0	340
longmult12	U	1 164 158	2 926	1 020 640	48	124	2 736	1 108 196	48	137	3 118
longmult13	U	1 567 022	3 871	1 180 017	49	129	3 220	1 145 954	49	137	2 918
longmult15	U	625 534	675	498 430	37	19	806	384 451	51	170	789
flat200-10	S	14 202	2	14 202	0	0	182	14 202	0	0	303
difp_19_3_wal_rcr	S	2 030 996	2342	1 257 747	330	431	1 999	1 914 713	349	433	6 134
difp_20_3_wal_rcr	S	64380	5	718 328	318	401	541	718 328	318	401	674
i10mul...sat03-353	U	7 806 817	11 808	6 379 809	4 157	59	6 842	6 622 326	4 655	83	8 613
alu4mul...sat03-344	U	4 923 861	14 263	4 703 752	1 005	10	12 942	5 423 715	1 080	10	14 170
7pipe_q0_k	U	1 829 574	453	1 688 006	18 124	52	583	1 785 586	18 125	59	723

the current implication graph $\mathcal{G}_{ig}$ is obtained as follow: $\forall y \in \mathcal{V}_\alpha, \forall c \in \Sigma | y \in c$, $GetSubclause(\mathcal{G}_{ig}, pred(y), y, c, \alpha)$. In algorithm 1, we assume that $y \in \mathcal{V}_\alpha$ and $A \subset \mathcal{V}$ such that $A_\wedge \rightarrow y$.

To illustrate, let us consider formula Σ and the implication graph, obtained from the formula Σ when assigning d to $true$ at decision-level α and assigning z to $true$ at decision-level $\beta < \alpha$ (Fig. 1). To deduce a sub-clause of c_6 and considering implications of x_5 through the implication graph, we will first consider the implication $x_3 \wedge x_4 \rightarrow x_5$. The variable x_3 belongs to the current implication and to the clause c_6. As x_4 does not belong to c_6, any implication containing this literal does not subsume c_6. So we replace x_4 in A by its predecessors x_1, x_2 and z. Following our principle, x_1 and x_2 are not literals of c_6, and d is there common predecessor. We deduce $d \wedge x_3 \wedge z \rightarrow x_5$, and the corresponding clause $\neg d \vee \neg x_3 \vee \neg z \vee x_5$ does not subsume c_6. However, since z has been assigned at a lower decision-level, c_4 can be considered as only composed of $\neg x_1 \vee \neg x_2 \vee x_4$ while z keeps its current value (before backtracking at decision-level β). The deduced clause is then c'_6 : $\neg d \vee \neg x_3 \vee x_5$ (for decision-level greater than β), which subsumes c_6. Following the process on c'_6 upon the current set $A = \{x_3, d\}$, x_3 is chosen (d has no predecessor). Through $\mathcal{G}_{ig}(\Sigma, \{d, z\})$, x_1 and d are successively visited and the implication $d \rightarrow x_5$ is deduced. The corresponding sub-clause : c''_6 : $\neg d \vee x_5$ subsumes c_6. The subsumed literals of c_6 will be restored when backtracking at decision-level β. This level restriction is due to literal z, which does not belong to the clause c_6. Obviously, if c_4 was only composed of literals $\neg x_1 \vee \neg x_2 \vee x_4$, then z would not be a literal of c''_6. Consequently, the corresponding subsumption would have been global (i.e. available for the whole search tree).

5 Experimental Results

Our technique can be applied after each step of BCP, either if it leads to a conflict or not. Comparative results of Table 1 show the impact (on time and number of nodes of zchaff[1]) of a restricted form of our sub-clauses deduction technique, limited to a pretreatment (preprocessing) of the original formula. A time limit of the pretreatment

---
[1] zchaff version 2004.11.15.

has been arbitrarily set to two different values (180 and 300 seconds). After the pretreatment, zchaff is run on the simplified formula. The time limit allowed for solving a given instance has been set to 4 hours. "N/A" means that the solver did not answer before this time limit. Columns named "subs" (resp. "fixed var.") represent the number of subsumptions (resp. variables assigned) found thanks to the pretreatment. Columns "$time$" represent the whole computation time (pretreatment when used + zchaff) to solve the instance. Finally, "S"(resp. "U") means that the instance is Satisfiable (resp. Unsatisfiable). For "Bounded Model Checking" instances ("longmult*" and "abp*"), the number of nodes can decrease by up to 50% in comparison with stand-alone zchaff. However, we note that sub-clauses deduction strongly depends on benchmark type (no subsumption found for "flat*" instances). Let us recall that these preliminary results are only computed at the root of the search-tree. Obviously, this technique can be applied at each node of the search tree. In such a case, sub-clauses deduction can seen as a new form of learning.

6 Conclusion and Future Work

In this paper a new extension of the scope of boolean constraint propagation is presented. Indeed, many new resolvents can be generated using the BCP implication graph leading to a powerful resolution-based technique. We have shown that when a subset of such resolvent (those that achieve a sub-clauses deduction) are considered, we obtain a polynomial time approach that can be grafted to DPLL-like techniques. Clearly, our preliminary experiments are encouraging on some classes of instances. To substantiate our claim on the usefulness of the proposed approach, further experimental validation is needed. Moreover, this work has to be completed by adding dynamic use of sub-clauses deduction at each node of the resolution tree. Considering the computation time of our approach, deduced resolvents will have to be evaluated according to their practical use.

References

1. Kautz, H.A., Selman, B.: Planning as Satisfiability. In: Proc. of ECAI'92, Vienna, Austria (1992) 359–363
2. Marques-Silva, J.P., Sakallah, K.A.: Boolean Satisfiability in Electronic Design Automation. In: In Proc of DAC'00, Los Angeles, USA (2000) 675–680
3. Biere, A., Clarke, E., Raimi, R., Zhu, Y.: Verifying Safety Properties of a PowerPC Microprocessor Using Symbolic Model Checking without BDDs. In: CAV'99. Volume 1633 of Lecture Notes in Computer Science., Trento, Italy (1999) 60–72
4. Williams, R., Gomes, C., Selman, B.: Backdoors To Typical Case Complexity. In: IJCAI'03, Acapulco, Mexico (2003) 1173–1178
5. Li, C.M.: Equivalency reasoning to solve a class of hard sat problems. Information Processing Letters **76** (2000) 75–81
6. Davis, M., Logemann, G., Loveland, D.: A Machine Program for Theorem Proving. Journal of the Association for Computing Machinery **5** (1962) 394–397
7. Zhang, L., Madigan, C.F., Moskewicz, M.W., Malik, S.: Efficient Conflict Driven Learning in a Boolean Satisfiability Solver. In: In Proc. of ICCAD'01, San Jose, CA, USA (2001) 279–285

Extending Systematic Local Search for Job Shop Scheduling Problems

Bistra Dilkina, Lei Duan, and William S. Havens

Intelligent Systems Laboratory, Simon Fraser University,
Burnaby, British Columbia V5A 1S6, Canada
{bnd, lduan, havens}@cs.sfu.ca

1 Introduction

Hybrid search methods synthesize desirable aspects of both constructive and local search methods. Constructive methods are systematic and complete, but exhibit poor performance on large problems because bad decisions made early in the search persist for exponentially long times. In contrast, stochastic local search methods are immune to the tyranny of early mistakes. Local search methods replace systematicity with stochastic techniques for diversifying the search. However, the lack of systematicity makes remembering the history of past states problematic. Typically, hybrid methods introduce a stochastic element into a basically constructive search framework. Lynce [6] uses randomized backtracking in a complete boolean satisfiability solver which incorporates clause (nogood) learning to ensure completeness. Jussein & Lhomme [4] perform a constructive search while keeping conflict sets (nogoods) in a Tabu list and backtrack via a stochastic local search in the space of conflict sets.

Our method, called *Systematic Local Search* (SysLS) [3], follows the opposite approach. We incorporate systematicity within an inherently stochastic search method (like [2]). SysLS searches through a space of complete variable assignments and relaxes the requirement for maintaining feasibility. It preserves full freedom to move heuristically in the search space with maximum heuristic information available. While many local search methods easily get trapped in local optima, SysLS records local optima as nogoods in a search memory. Nogoods force the search away from these maximally consistent but unacceptable solutions. Our method is analogous to other diversification mechanisms in local search (*eg- Tabu search*) but is systematic and inherits the sound resolution rule for nogood learning. In this paper, we extend SysLS for optimization and, in particular, for job shop scheduling problems.

2 Systematic Local Search for Optimization

We begin this section with relevant definitions for the SysLS schema from [3]. A CSP is a tuple (V, D, C) where V is a set of variables with domains D and C is a set of k-ary constraints $(k \leq |V|)$ on k variables in V.

Definition 1. *A nogood is a set of variable assignments* $\lambda_\perp = \{\langle x = a\rangle\}_{x \in X}, X \subseteq V$, *such that no solution to the CSP contains the variable assignments of* $\lambda_\perp$.

Definition 2. *Given a nogood search memory,* Γ, *an assignment* $\langle x = a\rangle$ *is disallowed if and only if* $\exists \lambda_\perp \in \Gamma, \langle x = a\rangle \in \lambda_\perp$ *and* $\forall \langle x' = a'\rangle \in \lambda_\perp \setminus \{\langle x = a\rangle\}$ *is the current assignment of the variable* x'. *Otherwise the assignment is allowed.*

Definition 3. *The* live *domain of a variable* x *is* $\Delta_x = \{a \in D_x | \langle x = a\rangle$ *is allowed*$\}$.

When the live domain of a variable is empty, *nogood resolution* allows the inference of a new nogood from the nogoods disallowing the domain elements. We define a *valuation function* $f_x(a)$ for a variable assignment $\langle x = a\rangle$ which is dependent on the current assignments of the other variables in V. The valuation function is used to guide the search towards feasible solutions. We classify each variable into one of four possible classes within the context of minimizing $f_x(a)$.

1. *MAXIMAL*: A variable x is *maximal* if and only if its current assignment $\langle x = a\rangle$ is such that $\forall b \in \Delta_x, f_x(a) \leq f_x(b)$.
2. *SUBMAXIMAL*: A variable x is *submaximal* if and only if $\exists b \in \Delta_x$ such that $f_x(b) < f_x(a)$.
3. *INF*: A variable x is in an *infeasible* state if its current assignment is $\langle x = a\rangle$ but $a \notin \Delta_x$.
4. *NULL*: Otherwise, x is currently not assigned a value.

In [3], the valuation function $f_x(a)$ for solving CSPs is the number of constraints violated when $\langle x = a\rangle$ given the other current variable assignments (eg- *min-conflicts*). Hence, SysLS perceives the CSP as an optimization problem to minimize the number of violated constraints while inducing new nogoods at every local minima. In this paper, we consider extensions to SysLS for constraint optimization problems (COPs). A solution to a COP is a complete assignment that both satisfies all the constraints and optimizes the objective function, C_{opt}. For most optimization problems, a problem-specific neighbourhood is available for moving in the space of complete feasible assignments. So, here we search in the space of *feasible* variable assignments and concentrate on improving the objective function. Hence, at every local optimum, the constraints are satisfied but the objective value might not be optimal. We wish to record a nogood that captures the subset of variable assignments responsible for the objective value, thus preventing non-solutions w.r.t. optimizing the objective function. Relying on a neighbourhood that preserves feasibility, we can consider the valuation function $f_x(a)$ that guides the search simply as the value of C_{opt} when x is reassigned to a. We can now rewrite the original SysLS algorithm for solving optimization problems.

Figure 1 shows the new search method called $SysLS_{opt}$-NG. The algorithm receives as input of a set of variables V and the objective function C_{opt}. It outputs the first optimal solution or the best solution found. The variable ordering $select(V)$ is based on the classification of variables into the classes described above [1]. It is specified by a precedence order among the classes and then an

---

[1] For the $SysLS_{opt}$-NG instance, we ignore the *NULL* class because we always maintain a complete assignment.

```
Input: variable set V and C_opt
Output: best solution found
1  α ← initial complete assignment;
2  repeat
3      while not all x ∈ α are MAXIMAL do
4          let x = select(V) ;
5          assign(x) ;
6          update the best solution if a better solution is found ;
7      end
8      λ_⊥ = label(C_opt) ;
9      add λ_⊥ to the nogood cache Γ ;
10     simplify Γ (as in [2]) ;
11     if λ_φ ∈ Γ then return the best solution found
12 until stopping criterion;
13 return the best solution found
```

Fig. 1. $SysLS_{opt}$-NG finds an optimal solution for variables V with optimization constraint C_{opt}

order between the variables in each class. $SysLS_{opt}$-NG is parameterized by the variable ordering relation similarly to the original SysLS schema.

Once a variable is chosen, the action taken is specified by $assign(x)$ according to the following state transition rules for variables:

1. If the variable is in the *MAXIMAL* state, do nothing.
2. If the variable is in the *SUBMAXIMAL* state, then we reassign x to one of its maximal values.
3. If the variable is in the *INF* state, we switch the assignment to the maximal allowed domain element. If all elements are disallowed in the current solution, no action is taken until one of its assignments becomes *allowed*.

3   Case Study: The Job Shop Scheduling Problem

We provide a case study of applying $SysLS_{opt}$-NG to *job shop problems* (JSPs). Every JSP has n jobs and m machines. Each job $j \in J$ consists of exactly m operations and each of the m operations is processed on a different machine. The precedence relations between operations of the same job (R_J) are fixed. Each operation has a specified duration. For a complete schedule, no two operations can execute on the same machine at the same time. The objective function (C_{opt}) is to minimize the makespan, *i.e.* the time at which the last operation finishes execution. The JSP is known to be NP-hard.

Below we formulate the JSP as a constraint optimization problem. A variable v is defined as the ordering between two different operations processed on the same machine. For every variable, the domain D contains only two values $D = \{\prec, \succ\}$ specifying the ordering. The subset of $m \times (n-1)$ variables corresponding to the processing sequence on the m machines is denoted V^1. A complete JSP schedule can be represented by a *directed acyclic graph* (DAG) G where the nodes are operations and precedence relations in R_J and V^1 are the arcs between operations whose length is equal to the duration of the source operation. Every operation is scheduled at its earliest start time determined by G and the makespan is equal to the length of the critical path in G. The critical path involves arcs corresponding to some precedence relations in R_J and some variables in V^1. Such a set of variables on the critical path is denoted by V^2 ($V^2 \subseteq V^1$). If the neighbourhood only changes variable assignments in V^2, then the schedule remains feasible as shown in [5]. At a local optimum, $SysLS_{opt}$-NG induces a nogood on the subset of variable assignments responsible for the makespan. Since it is solely determined by the critical path, the nogood contains only the variable assignments in V^2.

Theorem 1. *If any nogood recorded at a local optima represents the assignment of V^2, then nogood resolution is sound with respect to finding the optimal solution. (Proof omitted)*

The parameterized components of the algorithm (Fig 1) are implemented as:

1. **initial solution** - The operations on a machine are ordered by their precedence ordering in their respective jobs.
2. **select(V)** - The precedence between variable classes is $SUBMAXIMAL \prec INF$. The variable ordering within the variable class $SUBMAXIMAL$ is best-improvement. Under class INF, we choose a recency-based diversification scheme. The preference is first given to the oldest variable assignment. Ties are broken by the shorter makespan value. In addition, we never choose an INF variable whose live domain is empty.
3. **stopping criterion** - Stop when either known optimal makespan is reached or the maximum number of iterations has been executed.

4 Experimental Results

The empirical evaluation of $SysLS_{opt}$-NG is on the well-known Lawrence benchmark [2]. We compare our results with two standard heuristic approaches, simulated annealing (**SA**) [5] and Tabu search (**TB**) [1]. We also consider two state-of-the-art specialized approaches: a fast taboo search (**TSF**) [7], and a tabu search using shifting bottleneck procedure (**TSB**) [8]. The maximum number of iterations is set to 20000 similarly to the other authors. All the experiments are run on a PC with an Intel 2.8 GHz processor and 512 MB memory. able 1 shows results in terms of the relative error [3]. Table 2 summarizes the best makespan, the mean relative error (MRE) and the mean run-time over 10 runs ($\bar{t}$) of some very hard instances. The $SysLS_{opt}$-NG performs extremely well on the 40 Lawrence instances where 27 are solved optimally (OPT in Table 1) and the best makespan values are generally within 2% of the optimal. The $SysLS_{opt}$-NG is

---
[2] From OR-Library at http://people.brunel.ac.uk/~mastjjb/jeb/info.html.
[3] $RE = \frac{(\mathcal{L}_{min} - \mathcal{L}_{opt})}{\mathcal{L}_{opt}} \times 100$ ($\mathcal{L}_{min}$ is the best makespan obtained and $\mathcal{L}_{opt}$ is the optimal makespan).

Table 1. Comparison of RE on Lawrence instances

problem	$SysLS$	SA	TB	TSF	TSB
La01-05	0	0.30	0.51	0	0
La06-10	0	0	2.25	0	0
La11-15	0	0	1.43	0	0
La16-20	0.13	0.71	1.19	0	0
La21-25	0.64	1.23	3.29	0.10	0.10
La26-30	0.94	2.01	1.94	0.14	0.46
La31-35	0	0	0	0	0
La36-40	1.15	1.67	3.53	0.26	0.58
OPT	27	23	16	33	33
MRE	0.36	0.74	1.77	0.06	0.14

Table 2. Comparison of best make span on a few hard Lawrence instances

Laxx	$SysLS$	$\bar{t}(sec)$	SA	TB	TSF	TSB
La19	843	11.5	848	860	842	842
La21	1055	308.1	1063	1099	1047	1046
La24	941	224.3	952	989	939	938
La25	979	234.7	992	995	977	979
La27	1255	810.8	1269	1258	1236	1235
La29	1177	872.8	1218	1206	1160	1168
La36	1275	455.8	1293	1302	1268	1268
La37	1411	743.0	1433	1453	1407	1411
La38	1212	634.4	1215	1254	1196	1201
La39	1249	639.5	1248	1269	1233	1240
La40	1240	652.5	1234	1261	1229	1233
MRE	1.14	–	2.13	3.63	0.23	0.52

a hybrid search method that combines desirable properties from systematic and stochastic search methods. The experimental results show that it finds better solutions than the general local search methods and compares favourably to the specialized heuristic approaches. Unlike other approaches which are specially designed for the JSP, the $SysLS_{opt}$-NG is a very general method for solving COPs.

References

1. Faruk Geyik and Ismail Hakki Cedimoglu. The strategies and parameters of tabu search for job-shop scheduling. *Journal of Intelligent Manufacturing*, 15(4):439–448, 2004.
2. M. L. Ginsberg and D. A. McAllester. GSAT and Dynamic Backtracking. In P. Torasso, J. Doyle, and E. Sandewall, editors, *The 4th International Conference on Principles of Knowledge Representation and Reasoning*, pages 226–237. Morgan Kaufmann, 1994.
3. William S. Havens and Bistra N. Dilkina. A Hybrid Schema for Systematic Local Search. In *Canadian Conference on Artifical Intelligence 2004*, 2004.
4. Narendra Jussien and Olivier Lhomme. Local search with constraint propagation and conflict-based heuristics. *Artificial Intelligence*, 139(1):21–45, July 2002.
5. Peter J. M. Van Laarhoven, Emile H. L. Aarts, and Jan Karel Lenstra. Job Shop Scheduling by Simulated Annealing. *Operations Research*, 50(1):113–125, 1992.
6. I. Lynce and J. Marques-Silva. Complete unrestricted backtracking algorithms for satisfiability. In *The 5th International Symposium on the Theory and Applications of Satisfiability Testing*, 2002.
7. Eugeniusz Nowicki and Czeslaw Smutnicki. A Fast Taboo Search Algorithm for the Job Shop Problem. *Management Science*, 42(6):797–813, 1996.
8. Ferdinando Pezzella and Emanuela Merelli. A tabu search method guided by shifting bottleneck for the job shop scheduling problem. *European Journal of Operational Research*, 120:297–310, 2000.

Interactive Reconfiguration in Power Supply Restoration

Tarik Hadzic and Henrik Reif Andersen

Department of Innovation, IT University of Copenhagen
{tarik, hra}@itu.dk

Abstract. Given a configuration of parameters that satisfies a set of constraints, and given external changes that change and fix the value of some parameters making the configuration invalid, the problem of *interactive reconfiguration* is to assist a user to interactively reassign a subset of the parameters to reach a consistent configuration again. In this paper, we present two BDD-based algorithms for solving the problem, one based on a monolithic BDD-representation of the solution space and another using a set of BDDs. We carry out experiments on a set of *power supply restoration* benchmarks and show that the set-of-BDDs algorithm scales much better.

1 Introduction

In this paper we look at the problem of *interactive reconfiguration* where an already existing (and valid) configuration of parameters becomes inconsistent due to change of one or more of the parameters forced upon the configuration for external reasons. For example, in power supply distribution, a fault could cause a power distribution line to be shut down and a new configuration of the distribution network must be found. In this situation, our approach is to change a small subset of the parameters in order to restore consistency. Besides the number of changed parameters, other user-specific criteria are also relevant to consider. Therefore, the user should be given control to interactively reassign this subset of variables, thus effectively exploring the trade-offs between different criteria, for example, finding a configuration of the power distribution network that tries to maximize the number of customers regaining electricity without significantly changing the standard network topology.

2 Theoretical Background

The knowledge about parameters and rules in a configuration problem is captured as a special kind of CSP model:

Definition 1. *A configuration model (CP) C is a triple (X, D, F) where X is a set of variables $\{x_1, \ldots, x_n\}$, $D = D_1 \times \ldots \times D_n$ is the cartesian product of their finite domains $D_1, \ldots, D_n$ and $F = \{f_1, ..., f_m\}$ is a set of propositional formulae over atomic propositions $x_i = v$, where $v \in D_i$, specifying conditions on the values of the variables.*

A *total configuration* is an assignment ρ of values $v_1,\ldots,v_n$ to each of the variables represented as a set of pairs (x_i, v_i) such that $v_i \in D_i$. A *partial configuration* ρ is an assignment to a subset of the variables. A total configuration ρ *is valid* if it satisfies all the formulae, i.e. $\rho \models f_j$ for $j = 1,\ldots,m$, which we also abbreviate as $\rho \models F$. A *partial configuration ρ is valid*, abbreviated as $\rho \models_p F$, if it can be extended to a total valid configuration $\rho' \supseteq \rho$.

Given a configuration model $C = (X, D, F)$ and a partial configuration ρ, *interactive configuration* is the process of assisting a user in interactively reaching a total valid configuration starting from ρ. The interaction satisfies the user-friendly requirement of *completeness of inference* which demands that at every interaction step, for every unassigned variable x, and every selectable value v_x, there is a total configuration satisfying this selection, i.e. $\exists \rho'.(\rho' \supseteq \rho \cup \{(x, v_x)\} \wedge \rho' \models F)$. In previous work [1,2] this functionality was obtained by representing the set of valid configurations $Sol = \{\rho \mid \rho \models F\}$, as a Binary Decision Diagram (BDD) [3] through a proper encoding of the finite domains with Boolean variables. It is called the *monolithic* approach, since Sol is represented as a single BDD. The algorithm facilitating interactive configuration given the already made partial assignment ρ and solution space Sol is denoted as $InCo(Sol, \rho)$ and described in more details in [4,2].

3 Interactive Reconfiguration

For reconfiguration, we model externally forced changes to the current total assignment ρ as a partial assignment ρ_f (f for fixed assignments). The resulting, externally modified configuration is denoted by $\rho[\rho_f] = \{(x_i, v_i) \mid (x_i, v_i) \in \rho_f \text{ or } (x_i \notin \mathrm{dom}(\rho_f) \text{ and } (x_i, v_i) \in \rho)\}$. Given the set of variables R to be unassigned we define $\rho_1 \uparrow R = \{(x_i, v_i) \in \rho_1 \mid x_i \notin R\}$ read as "ρ_1 release R".

Definition 2 (Interactive Reconfiguration). *Given a configuration problem $C(X, D, F)$, a starting valid total configuration $\rho \models F$ and a forced partial as-*

```
InRecoMono(Sol, ρ, ρ_f)                    /* ρ is valid and total */
1:  ρ_1 ← ρ[ρ_f]                           /* ρ_1 is invalid and total */
2:  if Sol^ρ_f is empty then halt          /* no solution: ρ_f ⊭ F */
3:  R ← ShortestPath(Sol^ρ_f, ρ, cost)
4:  ρ_2 ← ρ_1 ↑ R                          /* ρ_2 is valid and partial */
5:  ρ' ← InCo(Sol, ρ_2)                    /* ρ' is valid and total */
6:  return ρ'
```

Fig. 1. The key part of the monolithic algorithm is the $ShortestPath(Sol^{\rho_f}, \rho, cost)$ function (line 3) which computes a release set R given the BDD for the full solution space Sol. We first restrict Sol to Sol^{ρ_f} as BDD operations. We then find the set of variables corresponding to the path of lowest cost (according to the function $cost$) using a depth-first traversal of the BDD. We assign a positive cost to edges representing choices we want to avoid (such as electricity consumers switched off) and zero cost to all other edges (a similar algorithm is described in [5]).

```
InRecoSoB(SSol, ρ, ρ_f)                    /* ρ is valid and total */
1:   ρ_1 ← ρ[ρ_f]                          /* ρ_1 is invalid and total */
2:   R ← PickReleaseSetSoB(SSol, ρ, ρ_f)
3:   ρ_2 ← ρ_1 ↑ R                         /* ρ_2 is valid and partial */
4:   RelSol ← ⋀_{j=1}^m Sol_j^{ρ_2}
5:   ρ' ← InCo(RelSol, ρ_2)                /* ρ' is valid and total */
6:   return ρ'
```

Fig. 2. In a precompilation step, $SSol$ will be computed. We then find (line 2) a release set R in an incremental fashion and compute a single BDD $RelSol$ of the relevant part of the solution space to be used for reconfiguration. The BDD $RelSol$ is found as a conjunction of the BDDs $Sol_j^{\rho_2}$ corresponding to the BDDs Sol_j restricted with the assignment ρ_2.

```
PickReleaseSetSoB(SSol, ρ, ρ_f)
1:   Δ ← dom(ρ_f)
2:   ρ_1 ← ρ[ρ_f]
3:   R ← ∅
4:   while not SoBSAT(SSol, ρ_1 ↑ R) do
5:       if R ∪ Δ = X then
6:           halt  /* all variables tried, no solution: ρ_f ⊭ F */
7:       R ← next(R ∪ Δ) \ Δ
8:   end
9:   return R
```

Fig. 3. In each incremental step, the $next(Y)$ function (line 7) finds from a set of variables Y a next larger set of variables to be tried for a release set. The set is checked for being a release set through the satisfiability check performed with the algorithm $SoBSAT(SSol, \rho)$ (line 4) which determines whether there exists a total $\rho' \supseteq \rho$ fulfilling all the BDDs in $SSol$. The algorithm SoBSAT is implemented as a Propositional Constraint Solver that is based on a BDD representation of individual (propositional) constraints, using the learning and conflict-resolution mechanisms of modern SAT solvers [6,7]. It is implemented on top of the BDD-package Buddy [8].

signment ρ_f such that the updated total configuration $\rho_1 = \rho[\rho_f]$ is invalid. The reconfiguration problem is to find a (small) release set $R \subseteq X \setminus dom(\rho_f)$ such that the partial assignment $\rho_2 = \rho_1 \uparrow R$ is valid if such a set exists or report that it does not exist.

The algorithm in figure 1 presents interactive reconfiguration in the monolithic approach.

Sometimes the monolithic approach is not feasible because the intermediate or resulting BDD for representing the solutions Sol becomes too big. We therefore develop an algorithm based on a *set of BDDs*. There will be a BDD for each of the formulae $f_j \in F$. We denote the j'th BDD by Sol_j and the full set of BDDs by $SSol$. The algorithm in figure 2 illustrates this approach. A key element in the algorithm, is the incremental computation of the release set (line 2) as presented in figure 3.

4 Experimental Evaluation

For experimental evaluation we use a number of instances from the Power Supply Restoration domain [9,10]. They encode the part of the power distribution network that contains local *power sources* each of which supply a number of electric *lines*, some of which are connected to *sinks*: transformer stations that consume electricity from the network and deliver it to final consumers. The instances were created by Stuart Henney, Tine Bak, Rene Jensen and Lars Sonne [11,12] in collaboration with NESA - the Danish power distributor in the Copenhagen area [13]. All the instances are made available for download at [14]. Structural properties of these instances are reported in [4].

Electric lines can become faulty, for example during bad weather conditions, in which case the power source supplying the line is turned off. This affects the entire area supplied from the source, and the problem is in reconfiguring the network by opening and closing lines, to resupply the maximum number of consumers in the affected areas while addressing a number of other domain specific goals (such as minimizing the change of the standard network topology).

For evaluation purposes, three reconfiguration algorithms were developed, a monolithic-BDD algorithm, and two versions of the set-of-BDD algorithms, based on different unassignment heuristics H_1 and H_2 for implementing the *next* function (fig. 3, line 7). In general, heuristic H_1 unassigns lines powered only from the affected power source, while H_2 additionally unassigns lines powered from unaffected neighbouring power sources (more details in [4]). In each simulation,

Table 1. We measured the time needed to calculate a release set R, and to compile a resulting BDD for interactive configuration (fig. 1, fig. 2 - both up to line 4), denoted as t, t_1, t_2 for the monolithic, H_1 and H_2 algorithm respectively. We measured the maximum percentage of defined sinks that can be left powered (S, S_1, S_2) as indication of quality of restoration w.r.t. resupplying the maximum number of customers. We also measured the maximum percentage of unaffected lines (unchanged line directions) denoted as $RDir, RDir_1, RDir_2$, indicating the restoration quality w.r.t. stability of network topology. All the numbers reported are averaged over 100 seed-based pseudo-random simulations (for Complex-P2 and Complex-P3 only 10 simulations) carried at a Pentium-Xeon machine with 4GB RAM and 1MB L2 Cache, running Linux.

Benchmark	Restoration quality						Avg. RT (sec)		
	$S(\%)$	$S_1(\%)$	$S_2(\%)$	$RDir(\%)$	$RDir_1(\%)$	$RDir_2(\%)$	t	t_1	t_2
Std-diagram	98	96.00	96.00	75.54	75.54	75.54	0.17	0.87	1.31
1-6+22-32	100	99.47	99.47	77.33	77.33	77.33	0.50	0.16	0.25
Complex-P2	100	85.19	97.22	84.17	77.31	84.17	3.88	0.14	0.36
Complex-P3	100	90.00	98.42	91.07	91.07	91.07	132.02	0.12	4.44
1-32	-	91.53	99.00	-	91.82	91.82	-	0.10	0.28
Large	-	93.98	98.73	-	94.89	94.89	-	0.27	1.43
Complex-P1	-	79.26	96.94	-	78.96	96.86	-	0.77	15.58
Complex*	-	86.5	91.92	-	85.52	91.67	-	3.11	12.05

we loaded a precalculated valid configuration ρ (representing operational power configuration), and randomly picked a powered line forcing it off. We then ran the reconfiguration algorithms measuring the number of parameters as shown in Table 1.

The numbers in Table 1 indicate that the set-of-BDDs approach scales dramatically better. The biggest instance where the monolithic approach was applicable was the instance Complex-P3 (28 lines and 19 sinks) with response time of 132.02 seconds, compared to the five times bigger instance Complex (146 lines and 119 sinks) that was handled in 42 times shorter time (3.11 seconds). The high percentage of ressupliable sinks and unaffected lines (most quality estimates are above 90%) supports the intuition about the locality of external effects in the real world instances (recovery within the 10% of change in network topology).

Acknowledgments

We would like to thank the anonymous reviewers for their valuable suggestions.

References

1. Hadzic, T., Subbarayan, S., Jensen, R.M., Andersen, H.R., Møller, J., Hulgaard, H.: Fast backtrack-free product configuration using a precompiled solution space representation. In: PETO Conference, DTU-tryk (2004) 131–138
2. Subbarayan, S., Jensen, R.M., Hadzic, T., Andersen, H.R., Hulgaard, H., Møller, J.: Comparing two implementations of a complete and backtrack-free interactive configurator. In: CP'04 CSPIA Workshop. (2004) 97–111
3. Bryant, R.E.: Graph-based algorithms for boolean function manipulation. IEEE Transactions on Computers 8 (1986) 677–691
4. Hadzic, T., Andersen, H.R.: Interactive Reconfiguration in Power Supply Restoration. Technical Report ITU-TR-2004-68, IT University of Copenhagen (2005)
5. Subbarayan, S.: Integrating CSP decomposition techniques and BDDs for compiling configuration problems. In: CP-AI-OR Conference. (May 2005)
6. Goldberg, E., Novikov, Y.: BerkMin: A fast and robust SAT-solver. In: Design, Automation, and Test in Europe (DATE '02). (2002) 142–149
7. Moskewicz, M.W., Madigan, C.F., Zhao, Y., Zhang, L., Malik, S.: Chaff: Engineering an efficient SAT solver. In: Proceedings of the 38th Design Automation Conference (DAC'01). (2001)
8. Lind-Nielsen, J.: BuDDy - A Binary Decision Diagram Package. http://sourceforge.net/projects/buddy (online)
9. Thiébaux, S., Cordier, M.O.: (Supply restoration in power distribution systems – a benchmark for planning under uncertainty)
10. Bertoli, P., Cimatti, A., Slanley, J., Thiébaux, S.: Solving power supply restoration problems with planning via symbolic model checking. In: ECAI'02. (2002)
11. Bak, T., Henney, S.: Power Supply Restoration - a Constraint-based Model for Reconfiguration of 10kv Electrical Distribution Networks. ITU (2004)
12. Sonne, L., Jensen, R.: Power Supply Restoration. Master's thesis, Department of Innovation, IT University of Copenhagen (2005)
13. Nesa. http://www.nesa.dk (online)
14. Power Supply Restoration Benchmarks. http://www.itu.dk/people/tarik/psr (online)

Neighbourhood Clause Weight Redistribution in Local Search for SAT

Abdelraouf Ishtaiwi, John Thornton, Abdul Sattar, and Duc Nghia Pham

Institute for Integrated and Intelligent Systems
{a.ishtaiwi, j.thornton, a.sattar, d.n.pham}@griffith.edu.au

Abstract. In recent years, dynamic local search (DLS) clause weighting algorithms have emerged as the local search state-of-the-art for solving propositional satisfiability problems. This paper introduces a new approach to clause weighting, known as Divide and Distribute Fixed Weights (DDFW), that transfers weights from neighbouring satisfied clauses to unsatisfied clauses in order to break out from local minima. Unlike earlier approaches, DDFW continuously redistributes a fixed quantity of weight between clauses, and so does not require a weight smoothing heuristic to control weight growth. It also exploits inherent problem structure by redistributing weights between neighbouring clauses.

To evaluate our ideas, we compared DDFW with two of the best reactive local search algorithms, AdaptNovelty+ and RSAPS. In both these algorithms, a problem sensitive parameter is automatically adjusted during the search, whereas DDFW uses a fixed default parameter. Our empirical results show that DDFW has consistently better performance over a range of SAT benchmark problems. This gives a strong indication that neighbourhood weight redistribution strategies could be the key to a next generation of structure exploiting, parameter-free local search SAT solvers.

1 Introduction

The propositional satisfiability (SAT) problem is at the core of many computer science and artificial intelligence problems. Hence, finding efficient solutions for SAT has far reaching implications. In this study, we consider propositional formulae in conjunctive normal form (CNF): $\mathcal{F} = \bigwedge_m \bigvee_n l_{mn}$ in which each l_{mn} is a literal (propositional variable or its negation), and each disjunct $\bigvee_n l_{mn}$ is a clause. The problem is to find an assignment that satisfies $\mathcal{F}$. Given that SAT is NP complete, systematic search methods can only solve problems of limited size. On the other hand, relatively simple stochastic local search (SLS) methods have proved successful on a wide range of larger and more challenging problems [1].

Since the development of the Breakout heuristic [2], clause weighting dynamic local search (DLS) algorithms have been intensively investigated, and continually improved [3,4]. However, the performance of these algorithms remained inferior to their non-weighting counterparts [5], until the more recent development of weight smoothing heuristics [6–9]), which currently represent the state-of-the-art for SLS methods on SAT problems. Interestingly, the two best performing DLS algorithms (SAPS [8] and PAWS [9]) have converged on the same underlying weighting strategy: increasing weights on false clauses in a local minimum, then periodically reducing weights according to a problem specific parameter setting. PAWS mainly differs from SAPS in performing additive rather than multiplicative weight updates. A key weakness of these approaches is that their performance depends on problem specific parameter tuning. This issue was partly in the development of a reactive version of SAPS (RSAPS [8]) which used the same adaptive noise mechanism developed in AdaptNovelty+ [10].

The question addressed in the current study is whether there are alternative weighting schemes that can produce further performance gains in the SAT domain. In particular, we are interested in *weight redistribution* schemes, that move around a fixed quantity of weight between clauses. Such an approach offers the advantage of not explicitly reducing weights, thereby avoiding considerable computational overhead, and the need for a problem specific weight reduction parameter. Secondly, we are interested in exploiting structural information contained in the weight distributions between neighbouring clauses. As adding weight to a clause can only immediately affect those clauses with which it shares a variable, it appears promising to connect weighting decisions with the relative level of weight on neighbouring clauses. We combine both weight redistribution and consideration of neighbourhood relationships in the Divide and Distribute Fixed Weights (DDFW) algorithm, which implements weight redistribution between neighbouring clauses.

In the remainder of the paper we introduce DDFW in more detail, and provide an empirical comparison between DDFW, RSAPS and AdaptNovelty+.

2 Divide and Distribute Fixed Weights

DDFW introduces two new ideas into the area of clause weighting algorithms for SAT. Firstly, it evenly distributes a fixed quantity of weight across all clauses at the start of the search, and then escapes local minima by *transferring weight from satisfied to unsatisfied clauses*. The existing state-of-the-art clause weighting algorithms have all divided the weighting process into two distinct steps: i) increasing weights on false clauses in local minima and ii) decreasing or normalising weights on all clauses after a series of increases, so that weight growth does not spiral out of control. DDFW combines this process into a single step of weight transfer, thereby dispensing with the need to decide when to reduce or normalise weight. In this respect, DDFW is similar to the predecessors of SAPS (SDF [7] and ESG [11]), which both adjust *and* normalise the weight distribution in each local minimum. Because these methods adjust weight across all clauses, they are considerably less efficient than SAPS, which normalises weight after visiting a series of local minima.[1] DDFW escapes the inefficiencies of SDF and ESG by only transferring weights between pairs of clauses, rather than normalising weight on all clauses. This transfer involves selecting a single satisfied clause for each currently unsatisfied clause in a local minimum, reducing the weight on the satisfied clause by an integer amount and adding that amount to the weight on the unsatisfied clause. Hence DDFW retains the additive (integer) weighting approach of DLM [6] and PAWS, and

---

[1] Increasing weight on *false* clauses in a local minimum is efficient because only a small proportion of the total clauses will be false at any one time.

combines this with an efficient method of weight redistribution, i.e. one that keeps all weight reasonably normalised without repeatedly adjusting weights on all clauses.

The second and more original idea developed in DDFW, is the exploitation of neighbourhood relationships between clauses when deciding which pairs of clauses will exchange weight. We term clause c_i to be a neighbour of clause c_j, if there exists at least one literal $l_{im} \in c_i$ and a second literal $l_{jn} \in c_j$ such that $l_{im} = l_{jn}$. Furthermore, we term c_i to be a *same sign* neighbour of c_j if the sign of any $l_{im} \in c_i$ is equal to the sign of any $l_{jn} \in c_j$ where $l_{im} = l_{jn}$. From this it follows that each literal $l_{im} \in c_i$ will have a set of same sign neighbouring clauses $C_{l_{im}}$. Now, if c_i is false, this implies all literals $l_{im} \in c_i$ evaluate to false. Hence flipping any l_{im} will cause it to become true in c_i, and also to become true in all the same sign neighbouring clauses of l_{im}, i.e. $C_{l_{im}}$. Therefore, flipping l_{im} will *help* all the clauses in $C_{l_{im}}$, i.e. it will increase the number of true literals, thereby increasing the overall level of satisfaction for those clauses. Conversely, l_{im} has a corresponding set of opposite sign clauses that would be *damaged* when l_{im} is flipped. The DDFW heuristic adds weight to each false clause in a local minimum, by taking weight away from the most weighted same sign neighbour of that clause. However, the weight on a clause is not allowed to fall below $W_{init} - 1$, where W_{init} is the initial weight distributed to each clause at the start of the search. If no neighbouring same sign clause has sufficient weight to give to a false clause, then a non-neighbouring clause with sufficient weight is chosen randomly. Lastly, if the donating clause has a weight greater than W_{init} then it donates a weight of two, otherwise it donates a weight of one. The program logic for DDFW is otherwise based on PAWS, and is shown below:

Algorithm 1. DDFW($\mathcal{F}$, W_{init})

```
1:  randomly instantiate each literal in F;
2:  set the weight w_i for each clause c_i ∈ F to W_init;
3:  while solution is not found and not timeout do
4:      find and return a list L of literals causing the greatest reduction in weighted cost Δw when flipped;
5:      if (Δw < 0) or (Δw = 0 and probability ≤ 15%) then
6:          randomly flip a literal in L;
7:      else
8:          for each false clause c_f do
9:              select a satisfied same sign neighbouring clause c_k with maximum weight w_k;
10:             if w_k < W_init then
11:                 randomly select a clause c_k with weight w_k ≥ W_init;
12:             end if
13:             if w_k > W_init then
14:                 transfer a weight of two from c_k to c_f;
15:             else
16:                 transfer a weight of one from c_k to c_f;
17:             end if
18:         end for
19:     end if
20: end while
```

The intuition behind the DDFW heuristic is that clauses that share same sign literals should form alliances, because a flip that benefits one of these clauses will always benefit some other member(s) of the group. Hence, clauses that are connected in this way will form groups that tend towards keeping each other satisfied. However, these groups are not closed, as each clause will have clauses within its own group that are connected by other literals to other groups. Weight is therefore able to move between groups as necessary, rather than being uniformly smoothed (as in existing methods).[2]

3 Analysis of Results and Conclusions

The results in Table 1 show that overall DDFW dominates AdaptNovelty+ and RSAPS, having the best performance on 11 of the 25 problems, with AdaptNovelty+ having the

Table 1. Comparison of runtimes with best local search performance in bold. The DPLL results are the best of either Satz or zChaff, with dominating DPLL times indicated with a '*'. DDFW was run with a fixed W_{init} value of 8. The problems are taken from the earlier PAWS study [9], where bw_large = blocks world planning, ais = all-interval-series, flat = graph colouring, f and uf = randomly generated hard 3-SAT problems, and the 30v and 50v problems are randomly generated hard binary CSPs, where v = number of variables, d = domain size and c = constraint density. All experiments were performed on a Sun supercomputer with 8 × Sun Fire V880 servers, each with 8 × UltraSPARC-III 900MHz CPU and 8GB memory per node. Problems with a mean flip count of less than one million were tested on 1,000 runs, otherwise tests were over 100 runs, with all runs having a 20 million flip cut-off, except 50v15d40c, which used 50 million.

Problem	DDFW Success	DDFW Mean Time	AdaptNovelty+ Success	AdaptNovelty+ Mean Time	RSAPS Success	RSAPS Mean Time	DPLL Time
bw_large.a	100	**0.00**	100	0.01	100	0.01	0.01
bw_large.b	100	**0.04**	100	0.13	100	0.06	*0.01
bw_large.c	100	**0.49**	61	7.50	84	19.85	0.53
bw_large.d	100	**1.31**	18	19.96	4	109.00	2.01
ais10	100	1.10	100	2.00	100	**0.02**	0.06
logistics.c	100	0.67	100	0.08	100	**0.01**	0.08
flat100-med	100	0.01	100	**0.00**	100	0.00	0.01
flat100-hard	100	**0.03**	100	0.03	100	0.02	*0.01
flat200-med	100	0.11	100	**0.08**	100	0.13	0.12
flat200-hard	100	**0.99**	37	4.32	78	5.04	*0.03
uf100-hard	100	**0.00**	100	0.00	100	0.00	0.01
uf250-med	100	0.02	**100**	**0.00**	100	0.02	1.25
uf250-hard	100	**0.65**	97	1.09	100	0.18	0.32
uf400-med	**100**	**0.06**	100	0.11	100	0.13	57.81
uf400-hard	100	**0.57**	45	12.30	100	4.07	178.92
f800-med	100	0.97	100	**0.25**	16	15.20	timed out
f800-hard	100	**2.81**	72	3.70	8	15.50	timed out
f1600-med	100	3.44	95	**1.88**	0	timed out	timed out
f1600-hard	100	**17.38**	96	18.86	0	timed out	timed out
par16-med	62	36.20	49	53.30	84	52.80	*1.52
par16-hard	48	45.70	21	26.30	71	20.60	*0.57
30v10d80c	100	1.52	100	**0.01**	100	0.15	0.26
30v10d40c	100	2.86	100	**0.02**	100	0.12	0.02
50v15d80c	100	130.00	100	**0.45**	47	60.66	timed out
50v15d40c	56	578.76	98	**169.55**	3	57.70	timed out

---

[2] To the best of our knowledge the only other SAT local search techniques to exploit neighbourhood relationships were [3] and [12]. These approaches used opposite sign relationships to generate new clauses by resolution, and so are not directly related to the work on DDFW. DDFW's weight transfer approach also bears similarities to the operations research subgradient optimisation techniques discussed in [11].

better performance on 8 and RSAPS on 6 of the remaining problems. In addition, DDFW achieved a 95% success rate over the whole problem set, where AdaptNovelty+ and RSAPS achieved 83% and 72% respectively. As versions of AdaptNovelty+ have won the SAT 2004 and 2005 local search competitions, the superior performance of DDFW is a significant achievement. In further tests (not reported here), DDFW was not able to match the performance PAWS or SAPS on the Table 1 problem set, when problem specific parameter tuning was allowed. Nevertheless DDFW showed the best performance on default parameter settings, and, when tuning was allowed, it was significantly better on all bw_large problems and several graph colouring and random 3-SAT problems.

In conclusion, DDFW represents a powerful general purpose SAT solver for problem domains where extensive parameter tuning is not practical. The work on DDFW also represents a first step in the development of a weight redistribution approach to clause weighting, and shows a simple way that neighbourhood structure can be used to guide weight redistribution decisions. In future work we consider it will be promising to extend a DDFW-like approach to handle MAX-SAT problems with hard and soft constraints. Here the natural division between mandatory and optional clause satisfaction can be exploited by redistributing weight from hard to soft clauses, and vice versa, according to whether all hard clauses are currently satisfied.

References

1. Hoos, H., Stulze, T.: Stochastic Local Search. Morgan Kaufmann, Cambridge, Massachusetts (2005)
2. Morris, P.: The Breakout method for escaping from local minima. In: Proceedings of 11th AAAI. (1993) 40–45
3. Cha, B., Iwama, K.: Adding new clauses for faster local search. In: Proceedings of 13th AAAI. (1996) 332–337
4. Frank, J.: Learning short-term clause weights for GSAT. In: Proceedings of 15th IJCAI. (1997) 384–389
5. McAllester, D., Selman, B., Kautz, H.: Evidence for invariants in local search. In: Proceedings of 14th AAAI. (1997) 321–326
6. Wu, Z., Wah, B.: An efficient global-search strategy in discrete Lagrangian methods for solving hard satisfiability problems. In: Proceedings of 17th AAAI. (2000) 310–315
7. Schuurmans, D., Southey, F.: Local search characteristics of incomplete SAT procedures. In: Proceedings of 10th AAAI. (2000) 297–302
8. Hutter, F., Tompkins, D., Hoos, H.: Scaling and Probabilistic Smoothing: Efficient dynamic local search for SAT. In: Proceedings of 8th CP. (2002) 233–248
9. Thornton, J., Pham, D., Bain, S., Ferreira Jr., V.: Additive versus multiplicative clause weighting for SAT. In: Proceedings of 19th AAAI. (2004) 191–196
10. Hoos, H.H.: An adaptive noise mechanism for Walksat. In: Proceedings of 19th AAAI. (2002) 655–660
11. Schuurmans, D., Southey, F., Holte, R.: The exponentiated subgradient algorithm for heuristic boolean programming. In: Proceedings of 17th IJCAI. (2001) 334–341
12. Pullan, W., Zhao, L.: Resolvent clause weighting local search. In: Proceedings of 17th Canadian AI. (2004) 233–247

Computing and Exploiting Tree-Decompositions for Solving Constraint Networks

Philippe Jégou, Samba Ndojh Ndiaye, and Cyril Terrioux

LSIS - UMR CNRS 6168,
Université Paul Cézanne (Aix-Marseille 3),
Avenue Escadrille Normandie-Niemen,
13397 Marseille Cedex 20, France
{philippe.jegou, samba-ndojh.ndiaye, cyril.terrioux}@univ.u-3mrs.fr

Abstract. Methods exploiting tree-decompositions seem to provide the best approach for solving constraint networks w.r.t. the theoretical time complexity. However, they have not shown a real practical interest yet. In this paper, we study several methods for computing a rough optimal tree-decomposition and assess their relevance for solving CSPs.

1 Introduction

The CSP formalism (Constraint Satisfaction Problem) offers a powerful framework for representing and solving efficiently many problems. A CSP instance is defined by a tuple (X, D, C). X is a set $\{x_1, \ldots, x_n\}$ of n variables. Each variable x_i takes its values in a finite domain from D. The variables are subject to the constraints from C which express restrictions between the different possible assignments. Given an instance (X, D, C), the CSP problem, which consists in determining whether a solution (i.e. an assignment of each variable which satisfies each constraint) exists, is NP-complete. In this paper, without loss of generality, we only consider binary constraints (i.e. constraints which involve two variables). So, the structure of a CSP can be represented by the graph (X, C), called the *constraint graph*.

The usual method for solving CSPs is based on backtracking search. This approach, often efficient in practice, has an exponential theoretical time complexity in $O(e.d^n)$ for an instance having n variables and e constraints and whose largest domain has d values. Several works have been developed to improve this theoretical complexity bound thanks to particular features of the instance. The best known bound is given by the "tree-width" w of a CSP. This parameter, related to a tree-decomposition of the constraint graph, leads to a time complexity in $O(n.d^{w+1})$. As $w+1 \leq n$, depending on the instances, we can expect a significant gain w.r.t. enumerative approaches. So several methods have been proposed to reach this bound like *Tree-Clustering* [1] or BTD [2]. Yet, the space complexity, often linear for enumerative methods, is in $O(n.s.d^s)$ with s the size of the largest minimal separators of the graph and so may make such an approach unusable in practice. Hence, most of works based on this approach only present theoretical results. Except [2,3], no practical results have been provided. Moreover, finding an optimal tree-decomposition (i.e. a tree-decomposition with width w) is NP-Hard [4]. So approximate optimal tree-decompositions (with width w^+ s.t. $w \leq w^+ \leq n-1$) are often exploited. Yet, although this choice is first induced by runtime reasons, we will show that it seems sensible in practice. This paper deals with the computation of a suitable tree-decomposition w.r.t. CSP solving.

An algorithmic way to compute a tree-decomposition relies on *triangulated graphs* [5]. As any graph G is not necessarily triangulated, we can triangulate G. A *triangulation* of G consists in adding a set C' of edges to G s.t. $G' = (X, C \cup C')$ is triangulated. The width of G' is equal to the maximal size of cliques minus one in graph G'. The tree-width of G is then equal to the minimal width over all triangulations. Hence, a rough tree-decomposition can be computed by using a non-optimal triangulation. Many algorithms exist for computing such a triangulation. So, in order to make structural methods efficient, this paper studies and compares some of them w.r.t. to CSP solving. This work is performed by using the BTD method [2] (one of few structural methods which have been implemented and used successfully for practical CSP solving).

By lack of place, the ideas we present are not fully developed and explained. A more complete version of this paper can be found in [6].

2 Triangulation Algorithms

This section raises the problem of computing "good" tree-decompositions thanks to "good" triangulations. Several approaches and algorithms have been proposed for triangulations. In any case, they aim to minimize either the number of added edges, or the size of the cliques in the triangulated graph. We can distinguish four classes of approaches. First, computing an **optimal triangulation** is NP-hard. So no polynomial algorithm is known yet and the proposed algorithms have an exponential time complexity. Secondly, we can exploit **approximation algorithms** which approximate the optimum by a constant factor and whose complexity is often polynomial in the tree-width [7]. Unfortunately, implementing these two first approaches do not have much interest from a practical viewpoint (e.g. the latter is time expensive while obtaining results of poor quality). On the other hand, we can exploit **minimal triangulations**. A minimal triangulation computes a set C' s.t. $(X, C \cup C')$ is triangulated and, for every subset $C'' \subset C'$, $(X, C \cup C'')$ is not triangulated. Note that a minimal triangulation is not necessarily optimal. The main interest of this approach is related to the existence of polynomial algorithms (e.g. LEX-M [8] and LB [9] whose time complexity is $O(ne')$ with e' the number of edges in the triangulated graph). Finally, the fourth approach, namely **heuristic triangulations**, generally add some edges to the initial graph until the graph is triangulated. They often achieve this work in polynomial time (between $O(n+e')$ and $O(n(n+e'))$) but they do not provide any minimality warranty. Nonetheless, in practice, they can be easily implemented and their interest seems justified. In effect, these heuristics appear to obtain triangulations reasonably close to the optimum [10]. In the following, we consider two such heuristics: MCS and min-fill. MCS relies on the algorithm of [11] which recognizes the triangulated graphs. Min-fill orders the vertices from 1 to n by choosing as next vertex one which leads to add a minimum of edges when completing the subgraph induced by its unnumbered neighbors.

3 Experimental Study

3.1 Comparison Based on Graphical Criteria

According to the experiments presented in the literature, the two first approaches do not appear very interesting as a first step of a CSP solving method due to a too expensive runtime w.r.t. the weak improvement of the value w^+. Hence, we only assess the interest of the two other approaches by experimenting them on graphs from real-world problems and random structured graphs (partial k-trees).

Table 1 presents empirical results for some graphs of the CALMA archive (real-world frequency assignment problems). We compare four triangulation algorithms, namely n-LEX-M, n-LB, n-min-fill and n-MCS, defined respectively from LEX-M, LB, min-fill and MCS. Precisely, each algorithm n-X fixes the choice of the first vertex and then uses the method X for the remaining vertices. It repeats this process by choosing each vertex as the first vertex. We note that the best results w.r.t. tree-width are performed by n-min-fill and n-LB. However, n-LB offers a more promising trade-off between the runtime and the quality of w^+. These results appear generally better than ones obtained by the MSVS heuristic [12] (based on network flow techniques instead of triangulation). Note that we have observed similar trends on partial k-trees [6].

As an indication, a random choice of the first vertex leads, of course, to worse results. However, these results are often very close to the previous ones. They are obtained in a time divided by n w.r.t. the times provided in table 1. For instance, for CALMA problems, the time does not exceed 2 s.

Table 1. Tree-width obtained after triangulation and triangulation time (in s) for graphs from CALMA archive

Instance	n	e	n-LEX-M		n-LB		n-min-fill		n-MCS	
			w^+	time	w^+	time	w^+	time	w^+	time
CELAR02	100	311	10	0.42	10	0.36	10	0.53	10	0.33
CELAR03	200	721	17	4.71	17	3.71	14	5.78	17	4.32
CELAR06	100	350	11	0.42	11	0.37	11	0.58	11	0.37
CELAR07	200	817	19	4.42	18	3.80	16	6.44	18	4.20
CELAR08	458	1655	20	55.85	19	82.73	16	73.57	19	51.74
CELAR09	340	1130	18	39.96	18	38.89	16	31.43	19	36.36
GRAPH05	100	416	28	1.00	26	0.68	25	1.34	31	0.97
GRAPH06	200	843	58	15.56	53	7.92	54	19.64	58	15.65
GRAPH11	340	1425	106	146.16	90	39.63	91	162.90	104	150.13
GRAPH12	340	1256	99	140.09	85	45.19	85	148.28	96	142.62
GRAPH13	458	1877	146	558.38	120	115.43	126	710.06	131	640.62

Table 2. Runtime (in s) for a value s respectively unlimited and limited to 10. T and M mean that some instances cannot be solved for time reason or for a lack of memory.

Instance	d	t	Time for unlimited s				Time for s limited to 10			
			LEX-M	LB	min-fill	MCS	LEX-M	LB	min-fill	MCS
CELAR02	50	1216	2.72	2.81	2.73	2.80	2.74	2.82	2.72	2.80
CELAR03	30	373	2.22	57.71	M	1.95	2.23	2.60	1.45	1.51
CELAR06	50	1155	3.40	3.52	3.41	3.50	3.43	3.53	3.41	3.48
CELAR07	25	209	12.79	M	13.23	4.66	4.92	4.83	4.86	4.69
CELAR09	25	209	12.47	T	11.82	6.72	4.69	4.88	4.66	4.76

Table 3. Runtime (in s) and value of w^+ for class $(150, 25, 15, t, 5, 15)$ after removing $p\%$ edges (with s limited to 5)

p	t	LEX-M		LB		min-fill		MCS	
		w^+	time	w^+	time	w^+	time	w^+	time
10%	215	18.50	5.53	14.00	3.95	15.97	10.66	14.03	4.06
20%	237	22.00	4.07	14.00	4.37	16.33	6.74	14.00	3.53
30%	257	23.30	82.79	14.00	2.85	17.20	5.49	15.03	3.81
40%	285	24.90	78.22	14.00	1.11	15.33	1.21	15.33	5.88

Here, the quality of a decomposition is only assessed w.r.t. the value of w^+. Nonetheless, from the viewpoint of CSP solving, the most relevant criterion is related to the solving efficiency obtained thanks to the computed tree-decomposition. Of course, this computation must be achieved in reasonable time.

3.2 Comparison Based on CSP Solving Efficiency

In the frame of CSP solving, the quality of a decomposition mostly depends on the practical efficiency we obtain by exploiting it. So we compare LEX-M, LB, min-fill and MCS w.r.t. CSP solving. We consider random CSPs whose graph is one of some CALMA instances (see table 2). Surprisingly, the most interesting decompositions are computed by MCS. Moreover, when we limit the maximal size of separators in the decomposition, the gap between the triangulations significantly decreases. Note that, for efficiency reasons, it is our interest to reduce the value of s, by aggregating the clusters which share a large intersection.

Then, we experiment on partial random structured CSPs (see table 3). For each instance, we randomly produce a random structured CSP [2] and then we remove $p\%$ edges. The least promising method, namely MCS, obtains interesting results. Only LB obtains similar or better results w.r.t. the value of w^+ or the CSP solving. However, on the whole, MCS seems the most robust heuristic since it often provides the best approximation of w^+ while offering a limited value of s and solving efficiently CSP. The value of s seems to be an important criterion for the practical solving efficiency. Indeed, with an unlimited value of s, LB or min-fill cannot success in solving some classes (see table 2). Yet, when s is bounded,

LB and min-fill may obtain results close to ones of MCS. Likewise, bounding the value of s significantly improves the results obtained by TM.

4 Discussion and Conclusion

We have considered several approaches for computing a tree-decomposition by triangulating the constraint graph. First, we have observed that, for solving CSPs, the heuristic triangulations in polynomial time might be sufficient to produce a suitable decomposition. Indeed, the optimal or approximate triangulations turn to be too expensive in time w.r.t. the improvement we can expect for the solving. Besides, the criterion w^+ is not relevant enough for CSP solving. Finally, we have noted that limiting the size s of the largest minimal separator allows us to improve the solving runtime, what contradicts the theory (i.e. the time complexity) which requires to minimize w^+ rather than s.

This study must be carried on. The first way consists in improving the computation of tree-decompositions by computing a decomposition which optimizes the solving instead of minimizing the value w^+. Then, another way relies on the strategies to achieve the best depth-first traversal of the associated cluster tree w.r.t. CSP solving, what corresponds to variable heuristics for enumerative methods. Finally, our study must be extended to Valued CSP.

References

1. R. Dechter and J. Pearl. Tree-Clustering for Constraint Networks. *Artificial Intelligence*, 38:353–366, 1989.
2. P. Jégou and C. Terrioux. Hybrid backtracking bounded by tree-decomposition of constraint networks. *Artificial Intelligence*, 146:43–75, 2003.
3. G. Gottlob, M. Hutle, and F. Wotawa. Combining hypertree, bicomp and hinge decomposition. In *Proceedings of ECAI*, pages 161–165, 2002.
4. S. Arnborg, D. Corneil, and A. Proskurowski. Complexity of finding embeddings in a k-tree. *SIAM Journal of Discrete Mathematics*, 8:277–284, 1987.
5. M.C. Golumbic. *Algorithmic Graph Theory and Perfect Graphs*. Academic Press. New-York, 1980.
6. P. Jégou, S. N. Ndiaye, and C. Terrioux. Computing and exploiting tree-decomposition for (Max-)CSP. Technical Report LSIS.RR.2005.005 (www.lsis.org), 2005.
7. E. Amir. Efficient approximation for triangulation of minimum treewidth. In *Proceedings of UAI*, pages 7–15, 2001.
8. D. Rose, R. Tarjan, and G. Lueker. Algorithmic Aspects of Vertex Elimination on Graphs. *SIAM Journal on computing*, 5:266–283, 1976.
9. A. Berry. A Wide-Range Efficient Algorithm for Minimal Triangulation. In *Proceedings of SODA*, january 1999.
10. U. Kjaerulff. Triangulation of Graphs - Algorithms Giving Small Total State Space. Technical report, Judex R.R. Aalborg., Denmark, 1990.
11. R. Tarjan and M. Yannakakis. Simple linear-time algorithms to test chordality of graphs, test acyclicity of hypergraphs, and selectively reduce acyclic hypergraphs. *SIAM Journal on Computing*, 13 (3):566–579, 1984.
12. A. M. C. A. Koster, H. L. Bodlaender, and C. P. M. van Hoesel. Treewidth: Computational Experiments. Technical Report 01–38, Berlin, Germany, 2001.

Encoding Requests to Web Service Compositions as Constraints

Alexander Lazovik[1,2], Marco Aiello[1], and Rosella Gennari[2]

[1] DIT, Trento U., via Sommarive 14, 38050 Trento, IT
{lazovik, aiellom}@dit.unitn.it
[2] ITC-irst, via Sommarive 18, 38050 Trento, IT
gennari@itc.it

Abstract. Interacting with a web service enabled marketplace in order to achieve a complex task involves sequencing a set of individual service operations, gathering information from the services, and making choices. We propose to encode the problem of issuing requests to a composition of web services as a constraint-based problem.

1 Introduction

Services are autonomous computational entities which live on a network and interact by asynchronous message passing. Services publish standard interfaces to enable their discovery, binding and invocation. The most prominent example is given by the XML-based standards known as web services, and the most interesting open challenge therein is the *service composition* problem, i.e., aggregating services for achieving complex tasks. Here we concentrate on the problem of enabling a user to express complex requests/goals against a pre-compiled composition of services in the form of a business process/domain (in this paper we use these words interchangebly). What we have is a description of a business domain (e.g., an electronic marketplace) and the user's request (e.g., the cheapest travel offer), which is satisfied by invoking the appropriate domain services. We propose to model the domain and request via constraints. Solving such constraints means finding an executable plan to satisfy the user's request in the business domain. Section 2 introduces the example which runs throughout the paper; definitions of the business domain and request language are in Section 3; the constraint encoding is in Section 4; Section 5 concludes the paper — its extended version is [1], e.g., with the encoding algorithms and related work.

2 Organizing a Trip

Let us consider a travel marketplace and the organization of a trip. A generic trip organization can be modeled by a complex business process encompassing several actions and states. Moving from one state to another may involve the discovery of information, the choice of which action to take and even ***nondeterministic actions*** – i.e., their outcome states, hence their effects may be different and not determined until execution. In [2], we showed a business process for organizing a trip with 36 states (http://www.opentravel.org); here we consider a subset of that process. When deciding on a trip, the user may want to book first the hotel of the final destination and then a carrier to reach the hotel location. The figure represents this business process snippet as a state transition system. The first action is the hotel reservation (a_1 leaving state s_1). This may result in the room reservation (state s_2) or in a failure (back to s_1); "which is which" is unknown until execution. Finally, there are two ways to reach s_3, the state in which a carrier for the hotel is booked: i.e., by either flying or taking a train. This means choosing either the reserveTrain action or the reserveFlight one. Given this, a user may also want to have a hotel reserved, prefer flying to taking a train and optionally wish to spend no more than 100 euros.

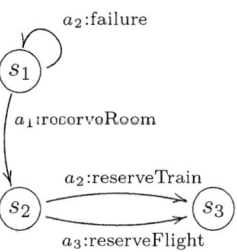

3   Web Service Interactions

Interacting with a web service enabled marketplace to achieve a complex request involves sequencing a set of individual service operations, gathering information from the services and making choices. The complex request of the user is similar to a planning goal, while the business process describing the possible behaviors of the marketplace is similar to a planning domain. Here we propose to model the business domain and the user's request via constraints. The business domain is a state-transition system with one characterizing peculiarity: *nondeterministic actions*. Formally, the domain is a tuple of states, actions, variables, failure states, and a transition function; we refer to [2] for the definition. Here we only note that the transition function maps a state and an action into *a set of states and an individual state*. The rationale is that of all the states an action reaches, one is the action's *normal* outcome, while the others are the action's *failure* states. The **request language** definition is derived from [2]: basic requests are **vital** p, **atomic** p, **vital-maint** p, **atomic-maint** p, with p a proposition. A request g is a basic request or of the form **achieve-all** g, **optional** g **before-then** g, **prefer-to** g. Having an initial state and the user's request g, a *plan* is given by sequences of actions (of the business domain) that leave from the initial state and satisfy the user's request. In Section 4, we obtain a plan by encoding domains and requests as numeric constraints.

Let us reconsider our example of Section 2 and the figure therein: the set of states S is $\{s_1, s_2, s_3\}$, the set of actions $\mathcal{A}$ is $\{\text{bookHotel } a_1, \text{reserveTrain } a_2, \text{reserveFlight } a_3\}$, and the set of variables is $\{price, hotelBooked, trainBooked, flightBooked\}$. The first variable ranges over natural numbers while all the other variables are Boolean. As for the transition function, bookHotel a_1 brings the system nondeterministically into $\langle\{s_1, s_2\}, s_2\rangle$, which means that s_2 is the normal state, whereas s_1 is the failure state. As for the actions' effects on variables, we have: the normal bookHotel action a_1' increases *price* and sets *hotelBooked* to 1 (i.e., true); the failure bookHotel action a_1'' has no effect on the variables; the reserveTrain action a_2 increases *price* and sets *trainBooked* to 1; the reserveFlight action a_3 increases *price* and sets *flightBooked* to 1. The request in Section 2 is now **achieve-all** (**vital** *hotelBooked* = 1; **atomic-maint** *price* < 100; **prefer** (**vital** *flightBooked* = 1 **to vital** *trainBooked* = 1)).

4 Constraint-Based Encoding of the Business Domain

Services offer a set of independently invocable operations. The operations act on a number of variables whose values may depend on a single service invocation or, more generally, on a number of invocations on several independent services. Here, constraints model how the values of a variable spanning across such services may change. Additionally, the user has requests and preferences in achieving complex tasks. We model these via additional constraints on the service domain. In particular there are two types of Boolean variables: ***controlled*** variables, denoted by β_i, and ***non-controlled*** variables, denoted by ξ_i. The rationale is that the constraint system may not choose values for non-controlled variables, and then a solution to the problem is such regardless of their assignments. We also assume that, once executed, a nondeterministic action has always its first execution outcome. The constraints of our encoding have the form $[\forall \xi_i :] \ \overline{c_v} \bowtie \text{value}$ where: *value* is a value from the domain of the variable v; $\overline{c_v}$ is a vector of expressions of the form $\sum \beta_i [\xi_i] a_{i,k}$ (with $\beta_i, \xi_i \in \{0,1\}$), the ξ_i are non-controlled variables, $a_{i,k}$ is the effect of the action a_i for the outcome k, $\bowtie$ is in $\{<,>,\geq,\leq,=\}$, and $[\cdot]$ denotes that the enclosed expression may not occur in the constraint. Formally, a ***service constraint problem*** is a tuple $\mathcal{CP} = \langle \beta, \mathcal{N}, \xi, \mathcal{C} \rangle$, where β is a set of *controlled* Boolean variables, $\mathcal{N}$ is a set of *controlled* variables over $\mathbb{N}$, ξ is a set of *non-controlled* Boolean variables, $\mathcal{C}$ is a set of constraints as above, in which a non-controlled variable is (i) either universally quantified over, (ii) or a value is available and substituted for it. A ***solution*** to a service constraint problem is an assignment to controlled variables such that all the problem constraints are satisfied. The encoding of the service interaction problem is split in the domain encoding (*phase 1*), and the request encoding (*phase 2*).

Phase 1 (domain encoding): given a business domain and an initial state s, the domain-encoding returns a set of constraints c_v as above. In what follows, n represents the number of times a cycle is followed, while a_i represents not only the action but also its effects. The following table briefly illustrates such encoding.

Phase 2 (request encoding): the user's request is added and encoded as follows.

vital $v \bowtie v_0$: if the request is **vital** with respect to v constrained by $\bowtie$ on v_0, the v encoding in the constraint vector c (denoted by c_v) is considered and it is added to the $c_v \bowtie v_0$ constraint set. Also all the ξ_v variables associated with c_v are set to ξ_v^0, that is, the normal execution must be followed.

atomic $v \bowtie v_0$: as above, but all nondeterministic executions are considered, thus all non-controlled variables ξ get universally quantified over.

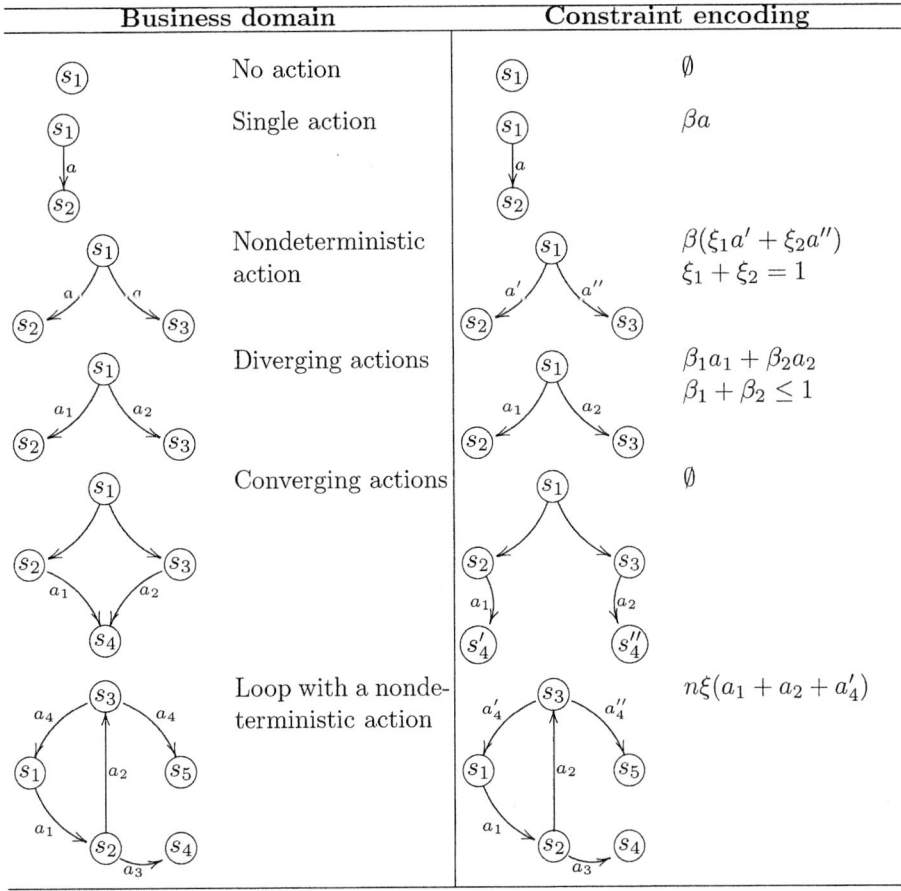

vital-maint $v \bowtie v_0$: all the states visited during execution are considered. One quantifies over the execution steps, repeating the constraints as in the vital case above for each step.

atomic-maint $v \bowtie v_0$: as above, but all nondeterministic executions are considered, so all non-controlled variables ξ get universally quantified over.

achieve-all $g_1 \ldots, g_n$: all sub-requests $g_1, \ldots, g_n$ are recursively executed; all basic requests coming from these are thus considered. If during the execution some choices are made for the same branch point among different sub-requests, then these choices are forced to be always the same by introducing a controlled variable u. E.g., suppose that $u^j, j \in \{1,2\}$, denotes the branch chosen for trying to satisfy the j-th request; $u^j = 0$ expresses that no choices were made; then $u^1 \neq 0 \wedge u^2 \neq 0 \Rightarrow u^1 = u^2$ is added as constraint.

before g_1 **then** g_2: as above, but one tries to satisfy first g_1 then g_2 is.

prefer g_1 **to** g_2: the request variables are instantiated along a certain order. Optional requests are prefer-to request with g_2 equal to true.

The Travel Example Encoded. Let us spell out part of the encoding of the example from Section 2. Its domain and initial state s_1 give the constraint

$\beta_1(\xi_1 na_1^{fail} + \xi_2(a_1^{ok} + \beta_2 a_2 + \beta_3 a_3))$ which represents the paths from state s_1 to s_3 with n being the number of times the cycle is followed. When requests are encoded, for each basic request a new set of variables is introduced. The first subrequest to be parsed is **vital** $hotelBooked = 1$. Only the a_1^{ok} outcome affects the $hotelBooked$ variable, thus the constraint is $\beta_1' \xi_2 a_1^{ok} = 1$ and the non-controlled variables are assigned to normal executions, i.e., $\xi_2 = 1, \xi_1 = 0$. The other **vital** requests are treated similarly. The request of preferring flying to taking the train gives the assignment $\beta_i''' = 1$ and $\beta_i^{iv} = 0$ as first, for all $i \in \{1,..,3\}$. A solution is $\beta_1^{(j)} = 1, \beta_2^{(j)} = 0, \beta_3^{(j)} = 1$, for all $j \in \{1,..,4\}$. This corresponds to booking the hotel (bookHotel) and reserving a flight (reserveFlight), assuming that the total price is less than 100. However, if the flight price is 200, the above is no longer a solution; but the preference constraint allows for an assignment which is a solution, that is, by taking the train (reserveTrain) instead of the plane (if the total cost is less than 100).

5 Concluding Remarks

We propose to model business domains and users' requests via numeric constraints. Pivotal properties of the encoding are its dealing with nondeterministic actions, its being unbounded, its capability of representing the possible executions of domain actions; these are relevant features in a web service enabled marketplaces, and make the encoding a major improvement with respect to [2]. In particular, here we deal with numeric requests without encoding them into Boolean properties. Moreover, we also handle users' preference requests. A number of issues remain open. Most notably, we have not yet assessed the efficiency of the proposed algorithms with respect to the minimality of the encoding. We have not considered the framework in the context of interleaving planning and execution, nor with respect to run-time information gathering. The last is a crucial issue in a web service scenario. However, we have preliminary results in extending the presented work in this direction.

Acknowledgments. R. Gennari is supported by the project grant *Automated Reasoning by Constraint Satisfaction* from the Province of Trento.

References

1. A. Lazovik, M. Aiello, and R. Gennari. Encoding requests to web service compositions as constraints. Technical Report DIT-05-40, Univ. of Trento, 2005. http://www.dit.unitn.it/~aiellom/publications/DIT-05-40.pdf.
2. A. Lazovik, M. Aiello, and M. Papazoglou. Planning and monitoring the execution of web service requests. *Journal on Digital Libraries*, 2005. To appear.

Test Instance Generation for MAX 2SAT
(Extended Abstract)

Mistuo Motoki[*]

School of Information Science,
Japan Advanced Institute of Science and Technology,
1-1, Asahidai, Nomi, Ishikawa, 923-1292, Japan

1 Introduction

Since MAX 2SAT is one of the famous NP-hard optimization problems, many heuristics and (polynomial-time) approximation algorithms have been proposed in the literature [1,4,5,6]. To evaluate the performance of such algorithms, there are two possibilities; theoretical analysis and empirical study.

In theoretical analysis, an approximation ratio of the algorithm is often used as a measure. The approximation ratio is an upper bound on the ratio of an approximated cost to the optimal cost, and hence, this is a worst case measure. It is often difficult to analyze theoretically the performance of heuristics or hybrid algorithms.

On the other hand, empirical study can *estimate* the performance of approximation algorithms from various points of view. There is no difficulty in estimating the performance except generating a number of (random) input instances. Though it is obviously easy to generate test instances without the optimal solutions, we should also know the optimal solution for each test instance. While there exists a number of benchmark instances with the optimal solutions, we still do not have enough number of test instances. Hence, we would like to have a sure way of generating nontrivial test instances systematically, i.e., *instance generator*.

Our ideal goal is to design an algorithm that can randomly generate all possible test instances (i.e., whole 2CNF formulas) with the optimal solution where its running time is polynomial in the length of the output formula.[1] However, if there exists such an algorithm, the recognition of the pair of a test instance and its optimal solution is in NP. On the other hand, the complement problem, i.e., recognizing the pair of a test instance and its suboptimal solution, is also in NP, since random bits used to generate each formula in the algorithm become a witness for both problems. This concludes NP = co-NP and it is unlikely. Therefore we have to relax the problem.

We can consider two relaxations: (i) allow error in the output of the algorithm and (ii) restrict the class of instances generated. The former one gives Monte Carlo algorithms that output a feasible solution instead of the optimal solution with low error

---

[*] This research was partially supported by the Ministry of Education, Science, Sports and Culture, Grant-in-Aid for Young Scientists (B), 1570008.
[1] If we accept exponential time, there exists a trivial algorithm; generate a formula at random, then find the optimal solution by exhaustive search.

probability (for example, [9,10]). In this paper, we focus on the latter approach, i.e., an instance generator randomly outputs a test instance and the optimal solution with probability 1 where the set of instances generated is a strict subset of all possible instances (hereafter, we say such an instance generator is *exact*).

However, this approach creates new difficulties. If the instances generated this way are easy to solve, it is not appropriate to use them for empirical study. Hence, we have to theoretically analyze the hardness of solving the generated instances, for example, solving MAX 2SAT over the formulas generated is NP-hard.

In the literature, Dimitriou proposed an exact instance generator for MAX kSAT [3]. They experimentally showed that by appropriately choosing parameters one can control the hardness of the generated instances leading to an easy-hard-easy pattern. But there is no theoretical guarantee of hardness. Yamamoto also proposed an exact instance generator for MAX 2SAT [10]. To characterize the optimal solutions, this algorithm requires an expander graph, which is hard to randomly generate. Since they use an explicit expander graph construction algorithm, this is not truly a random instance generator.

Unfortunately, for any NP optimization problem U, the decision problem of U over the instances generated by any polynomial-time exact instance generator is in NP $\cap$ co-NP. Hence, it seems difficult to show the computational hardness of instances generated. Moreover, if a solver can efficiently recognize that input instances are generated by a specific instance generator, such instances might be easily solvable. Therefore, we investigate how hard it is to recognize our instances.

We propose an exact instance generator based on the concept of a linear-time algorithm for 2SAT. For the proposed generator, we show that the set of instances generated is NP-complete. From computational point of view, this means that finding an optimal solution for our instances is as hard as searching for a satisfying assignment for satisfiable 3CNF formulas. We also show that it is even NP-hard to approximately recognize our instances.

2 Our Instance Generator

We start with some notations. A *literal* over $X = \{x_1, \ldots, x_n\}$, the set of n Boolean variables, is $x \in X$ or its negation $\bar{x}$. A *k-clause* over X is a disjunction of exactly k literals over X whose underlying variables are distinct. Let *kCNF formula* over X be a collection of k-clauses over X. We allow any clause to appear more than once. A *truth assignment* over X is a map of X to $\{0, 1\}^n$. We use 1 and 0 to denote true and false respectively. A truth assignment t *satisfies* a clause c iff at least one literal in c has a value 1. Otherwise we say t *falsifies* c. MAX 2SAT is a problem to find an assignment that satisfies the maximum number of clauses for given 2CNF formula.

For any 2CNF formula F over X, the *implication graph* of F is a directed (multi) graph $G_F = (V, E)$, where V is the set of all possible literals, i.e., $X \cup \{\bar{x_i} \mid x_i \in X\}$, and $E = \{(v_i \to v_j) \mid v_i, v_j \in V \text{ and } (\bar{v_i} \lor v_j) \in F\}$. Note that if E contains an edge $(v_i \to v_j)$, then the edge $(\bar{v_j} \to \bar{v_i})$ also exists. We say that such an edge is a *complement edge* of the other. For any edge $(v_i \to v_j)$, if one assigns true to v_i, one has to set v_j true to satisfy the original clause $(\bar{v_i} \lor v_j)$; hence the name implication graph. Any 2CNF formula F is unsatisfiable iff G_F has a cycle that contains v and $\bar{v}$ simultaneously [2].

Strictly speaking, if there is one such cycle C, there must be another cycle that consists of all complement edges of the cycle C. Therefore we call such a pair of two cycles as a *contradictory bicycle*. For any truth assignment t over X, let $\mathcal{B}_t$ be the set of 2CNF formulas over X such that any $F \in \mathcal{B}_t$ satisfies the following conditions: (i) F has exactly one clause falsified by t, (ii) G_F has one contradictory bicycle, and (iii) if we remove any clause from F, the remaining formula is satisfiable, i.e., F is a minimal unsatisfiable formula. We also denote by C_t the set of 2-clauses over X satisfied by t.

It is easy to see that we can randomly generate any formula in $\mathcal{B}_t$ for an arbitrary truth assignment t. To illustrate this, w.l.o.g. we assume that $t = 1^n$. Let B be an arbitrary formula of $\mathcal{B}_t$. It is clear that every clause falsified by t consists of two negative literals and B contains exactly one such clause. Such a clause is transformed into edges from a positive literal to a negative literal in the implication graph G_B. Furthermore, each cycle also has exactly one edge from a negative literal to a positive literal. We can divide each cycle into two paths, a path consisting of positive literals only and a path of negative literals only. We remark that there exists at least one common variable as a contradictory variable, in both paths. Also, since any 2-clause is complement-free, the last variable of each path is distinct from the first variable of the other path. Thus, we only need to generate two sequences of variables that have at least one common variable and the first variable of each sequence is distinct from the last variable of the other.

Here, for an arbitrary truth assignment t and a positive number k, we consider a 2CNF formula F that consists of (not necessary distinct) k formulas in $\mathcal{B}_t$ and some clauses in C_t. Obviously, any truth assignment falsifies at least k clauses of F since G_F has k contradictory bicycles. This means that an upper bound of the minimum number of unsatisfiable clauses is k. On the other hand, since there exist exact k formulas of B_t, F has just k clauses falsified by t, i.e., the lower bound is also k. Thus it is clear that t is the optimal solution of F and the minimum number of unsatisfiable clauses in F is k. Let $\mathcal{I}$ be a set of such formulas, i.e., $\mathcal{I} = \{F \mid \exists t \text{ s.t. } F \text{ consists of elements of } \mathcal{B}_t \text{ and } C_t\}$. It is easy to see that we can randomly generate an arbitrary formula in $\mathcal{I}$ and its optimal solution t by appropriate randomized algorithms (see Algorithm 1), e.g., first choose t at random, then construct a formula as a conjunction of some elements of $\mathcal{B}_t$ and C_t. Clearly, the running time of our instance generator is linear in the length of the instance generated. We remark that if the number of additional clauses from C_t is 0, the instance generated has at least two optimal solutions, t and $\bar{t}$, and hence, we add such clauses.

Algorithm 1. An example of generation algorithm

Input: the number of variables n
begin
    Let F be an empty formula;
    Choose $t \in \{0, 1\}^n$ uniformly at random;
    Choose the minimum number of unsatisfiable clauses k (≥ 0);
    for $i = 1$ *to* k **do** Generate a 2CNF formula over X from $\mathcal{B}_t$ at random and add it to F;
    Add r clauses of C_t to F at random (where r is a random nonnegative integer);
    Output: F and t
end

3 The Hardness Results

In this section, we consider the hardness of the instances generated. As described in the introduction, it is not easy to show *computational* hardness of the instances generated. This means that if we can efficiently recognize instances generated, such instances cannot be hard. Therefore, we consider how hard it is to recognize our instances. First, we show the hardness of exact recognition.

Theorem 1. *The set $\mathcal{I}$ of generated instances is* NP-*complete*.

Proof. It is clear that $\mathcal{I}$ is in NP because of the witness, that is, a truth assignment t and a partition into k formulas of $\mathcal{B}_t$ and a subset of C_t for each instance.

Hereafter we show a reduction from 3SAT. Let $F_{3\text{CNF}}$ be an arbitrary 3CNF formula over X with m 3-clauses $c_1, c_2, \ldots, c_m$. For any i, $1 \le i \le m$, we translate the ith 3-clause $c_i = (l_{i,1} \vee l_{i,2} \vee l_{i,3})$ of $F_{3\text{CNF}}$ ($l_{i,*}$ means an arbitrary literal over X) into the 2CNF formula over X and $Y_i = \{y_{i,1}, y_{i,2}\}$, $B_i = (\overline{l_{i,1}} \vee y_{i,1})(\overline{y_{i,1}} \vee l_{i,2})(\overline{l_{i,2}} \vee \overline{y_{i,2}})(y_{i,2} \vee l_{i,3})(\overline{l_{i,3}} \vee \overline{y_{i,1}})(y_{i,1} \vee y_{i,2})(\overline{y_{i,2}} \vee l_{i,1})(\overline{y_{i,2}} \vee l_{i,1})$. We remark that the variables in Y_i appear only in B_i. B_i contains exactly one contradictory bicycle, and thus any truth assignment over $X \cup Y_i$ falsifies at least one clause. Let a 2CNF formula $F_{2\text{CNF}}$ be the conjunction of B_i for all i. Hence $F_{2\text{CNF}}$ has $8m$ clauses over $n + 2m$ variables, $X \cup (\bigcup_i Y_i)$. It is not difficult to show that, in $F_{2\text{CNF}}$, the number of contradictory bicycles is equal to the minimum number of unsatisfiable clauses iff $F_{3\text{CNF}}$ is satisfiable. □

This result directly means that finding an optimal solution of our instances is at least as hard as searching for a satisfying assignment of satisfiable 3CNF formulas. Thus, a polynomial-time algorithm that can obtain an optimal solution for any instance in $\mathcal{I}$ is unlikely. Moreover, in the above discussion we assume that we know the maximum contradictory bicycle packing. It, however, seems hard to obtain the maximum contradictory bicycle packing in general.

Next, we consider the hardness of approximate recognition.

Theorem 2. *For any constant $\varepsilon > 0$, it is* NP-*hard to distinguish any 2CNF formula in $\mathcal{I}$ from the 2CNF formulas in which the ratio of the minimum number of unsatisfiable clauses to the maximum number of contradictory bicycles is $9/8 - \varepsilon$.*

Proof. We consider the same reduction as in the proof of Theorem 1. We have already shown that any satisfiable $F_{3\text{CNF}}$ with m clauses over X is transformed to $F_{2\text{CNF}}$ with $8m$ clauses where the minimum number of unsatisfiable clauses is m.

Now we consider the case $F_{3\text{CNF}}$ is unsatisfiable. For any truth assignment over X that falsifies the ith clause c_i of $F_{3\text{CNF}}$, we can find a truth assignment over Y_i that falsifies exactly two clauses in B_i. We again remark that we can set a truth assignment over Y_i independently of a truth assignment over Y_j since any variable of Y_i does not appear in B_j for any $j \ne i$. Thus, if k clauses of $F_{3\text{CNF}}$ are unsatisfiable, $m + k$ clauses of $F_{2\text{CNF}}$ are unsatisfiable.

Now we focus on 3CNF formulas for which only a fraction $7/8 + \varepsilon$ of the clauses can be satisfied. Such 3CNF formulas are transformed into 2CNF formulas with m contradictory bicycles and $m + (1/8 - \varepsilon)m = (9/8 - \varepsilon)m$ unsatisfiable clauses. Since it is NP-hard to distinguish between such 3CNF formulas and satisfiable 3CNF formulas [7], we conclude the proof. □

Unfortunately, this result does not directly imply hardness of the instances generated for approximation algorithms. However, if there exists an approximation algorithm that approximates any instance of I within a fraction $\frac{8m-9m/8}{8m-m} = 55/56$, such an algorithm can distinguish satisfiable 3CNF formulas from unsatisfiable 3CNF formulas and it is unlikely. We remark that this ratio, $55/56 \approx 0.982$, is still much larger than $21/22 \approx 0.955$ which is the best known inapproximability upper bound for MAX 2SAT [7] (Khot et al. [8] recently improved this ratio to 0.944 under some unproven conjectures).

4 Concluding Remarks

We analyzed that it is hard to recognize instances by the proposed instance generator for MAX 2SAT. On the other hand, the generator is still naïve, that is, our generator is only generating positive instances of NP-complete problem. Hence it may generate a number of easy instances and it is important to eliminate such easy instances.

While we focused on theoretical hardness in this paper, we would like to experimentally check hardness against a number of MAX SAT solvers. Since the proposed instance generator uses many (exposed and hidden) parameters, such as the number of contradictory bicycle, the length of each bicycle, the total number of clauses and so on, we also have to determine an appropriate range of such parameters. We expect that there exists a phase transition phenomenon, and hence, an easy-hard-easy pattern on some parameters. Finally, it is better if we can generate some instances outside of I. Since I is NP-complete, we may apply techniques to generate hard (or negative) instances for other NP-hard problems (e.g., SAT).

References

1. T. Asano and D. P. Williamson. Improved approximation algorithms for MAX SAT. *J. Algorithms*, Vol.42, pp.173–202, 2002.
2. B. Aspvall, M. F. Plass, and R. E. Tarjan. A linear-time algorithm for testing the truth of certain quantified boolean formulas. *Inform. Process. Lett.*, Vol.8, pp.121–123, 1979.
3. T. Dimitriou. A wealth of SAT distributions with planted assignments. In *Proc. of CP 2003*, LNCS 2833, pp.274–287, 2003.
4. U. Feige and M. X. Goemans. Approximating the value of two prover proof systems, with applications to MAX 2SAT and MAX DICUT. In *Proc. of ISTCS 1995*, pp.182–189, 1995
5. M. X. Goemans and D. P. Williamson. .879-approximation algorithms for MAX CUT and MAX 2SAT. In *Proc. of STOC 1994*, pp.422–431, 1994.
6. P. Hansen and B. Jaumard. Algorithms for the maximum satisfiability problem. *Computing*, Vol.44, pp.279–303, 1990.
7. J. Håstad. Some optimal inapproximability results. in *Proc. of STOC 1997*, pp.1–10, 1997.
8. S. Khot, G. Kindler, E. Mossel, and R. O'Donnell. Optimal inapproximability results for Max-Cut and other 2-variable CSPs? in *Proc. of FOCS 2004*, pp.146–154, 2004.
9. M. Motoki. Random instance generation for MAX 3SAT. In *Proc. of COCOON 2001*, LNCS2108, pp.502–508, 2001.
10. M. Yamamoto. On generating instances for MAX2SAT with optimal solutions. Dept. of Math. and Comp. Sciences Research Reports (Series C: Computer Science), C-191, http://www.is.titech.ac.jp/research/research-report/C/C-191.ps.gz, 2004.

Consistency for Quantified Constraint Satisfaction Problems

Peter Nightingale

School of Computer Science, University of St Andrews, Scotland, KY16 9SX
pn@dcs.st-and.ac.uk

Abstract. The generalization of the constraint satisfaction problem with universal quantifiers is a challenging PSPACE-complete problem, which is interesting theoretically and also relevant to solving other PSPACE problems arising in AI, such as reasoning with uncertainty, and multiplayer games. I define two new levels of consistency for QCSP, and give an algorithm to enforce consistency for one of these definitions. The algorithm is embedded in backtracking search, and tested empirically. The aims of this work are to increase the facilities available for modelling and to increase the power of constraint propagation for QCSPs. The work is motivated by examples from adversarial games.

1 Introduction

The finite quantified constraint satisfaction problem (QCSP) is a generalization of the finite constraint satisfaction problem (CSP), in which variables may be universally quantified. QCSP can be used to model problems containing uncertainty, in the form of variables which have a finite domain but whose value is unknown. Therefore a QCSP solver finds solutions suitable for all values of these variables. A QCSP has a quantifier sequence which quantifies (existentially, $\exists$, or universally, $\forall$) each variable in the instance. For each possible value of a universal variable, we find a solution for the later variables in the sequence. Therefore the solution is no longer a sequence of assignments to the variables, but a tree of assignments where the variables are set in quantification order, branching for each value of the universal variables. This is known as a strategy, and can be exponential in size. This generalization increases the computational complexity (under the usual assumption that $P \subsetneq NP \subsetneq PSPACE$): QCSP is PSPACE-complete. QCSP can be used to model problems from areas such as planning with uncertainty and multiplayer games. Intuitively, these problems correspond to the question: Does there exist an action, such that for any eventuality, does there exist a second action, such that for any eventuality, etc, I am successful? Actions are represented with existential variables, and eventualities with universals. Bordeaux and Monfroy [3] and Mamoulis and Stergiou [1] define levels of consistency for various quantified constraints of bounded arity. I introduce a general consistency algorithm for quantified constraints of any arity, based on Bessière and Régin's GAC-Schema [4].

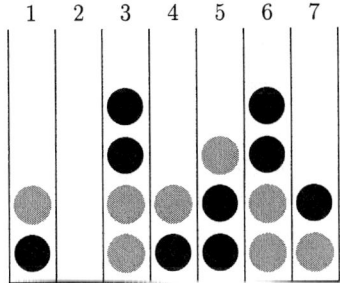

$\exists grey1 \forall black1 \exists grey2 \forall black2 \exists grey3 :$
greywins($grey1, black1, grey2, black2, grey3$)

Fig. 1. Connect-4 endgame

Connect-4. For example consider the Connect-4 endgame in figure 1. The aim of Connect-4 is to make a line of four counters, vertically, horizontally or diagonally. The two players take turns, and can only place a counter at the bottom of a column on the board. It is grey to move, and it can be seen that columns 2 and 4 are the only moves allowing grey to win in 3 moves if black defends perfectly. The five such winning sequences are 2-2-4-4-5, 2-2-5-4-4, 4-4-5-2-2, 4-4-5-2-6 and 4-4-5-6-2. As shown below the figure, this problem can be modelled as a QCSP, with 5 variables representing the column numbers of the 5 moves, with just one 5-ary constraint representing that grey wins (i.e. the constraint is satisfied iff grey wins, thus all the rules of the game are exactly encoded in one constraint). This is similar to a 5-move lookahead constraint, but with the additional restriction that grey must win within the 5 moves. Ideally, the propagation algorithm would restrict all three of the grey move variables. Ignoring the quantification and applying GAC infers nothing. I define two stronger levels of consistency, WQGAC, which infers that $grey1 \in \{2,4\}$, and the stronger SQGAC, which also infers $grey2 \in \{4,5\}$, and $grey3 \in \{2,4,5,6\}$. I give an algorithm for WQGAC in section 3.

2 Defining Quantified Generalized Arc Consistency

A flavour of the definitions of weak and strong quantified generalized arc consistency is given below, based on the full definitions in [8]. $\mathcal{X}_C$ is the variables within the scope of the constraint C. C_S is the set of supporting tuples of the constraint C, with each tuple sorted in quantification order. The domain of variable x_i is D_i.

Definition 1. *Support*

Given some constraint C, a value $a \in D_i$ for a variable $x_i \in \mathcal{X}_C$ has domain support in C iff there exists a tuple $t \in C_S$ such that $t_i = a$ [1] and $\forall x_j \in \mathcal{X}_C : t_j \in D_j$. Similarly, a partial assignment p (which is a set of pairs $\langle x_i, a \rangle$) over C has domain support in C iff there exists a tuple $t \in C_S$ such that for all pairs $\langle x_i, a \rangle$ in p, $t_i = a$ and $\forall x_j \in \mathcal{X}_C : t_j \in D_j$.

---
[1] t_k is used to refer to the element of t corresponding to variable x_k.

Definition 2. *Weak Quantified GAC*

A constraint C is weak quantified GAC (WQGAC) iff for each variable $x \in \mathcal{X}_C$ and value $a \in D_x$, with inner universal variables $x_i, x_j, \ldots$, each partial assignment $p = \{\langle x, a \rangle, \langle x_i, b \rangle | b \in D_i, \langle x_j, c \rangle | c \in D_j, \ldots] \}$ has domain support.

For the example in figure 1, WQGAC is able to prune the following values from $grey1 : 1, 3, 5, 6, 7$, but is unable to prune the other existential variables.

Definition 3. *Strong Quantified GAC*

A constraint C is strong quantified GAC (SQGAC) iff for each variable $x \in \mathcal{X}_C$ and value $a \in D_x$, with inner universal variables $x_i, x_j, \ldots$, each partial assignment $p = \{\langle x, a \rangle, \langle x_i, b \rangle | b \in D_i, \langle x_j, c \rangle | c \in D_j, \ldots \}$ has domain support and *all the supporting tuples can form part of the same strategy*. For any two supporting tuples τ and τ' this is the case iff $\exists \lambda \forall i < \lambda : \tau_i = \tau'_i \wedge \tau_\lambda \neq \tau'_\lambda \wedge \forall (x_\lambda)$ (i.e. the leftmost difference between the tuples must correspond to a universal variable).

For the example in figure 1, an algorithm enforcing SQGAC would be able to prune from all three existential variables, in contrast to WQGAC. An SQGAC algorithm would infer $grey2 \in \{4, 5\}$, and $grey3 \in \{2, 4, 5, 6\}$.

3 A General Algorithm for Enforcing WQGAC

This section describes the proposed WQGAC-Schema algorithm, derived from GAC-Schema[4], a successful framework for GAC. In this section most attention will be given to the differences between WQGAC-Schema and GAC-Schema. On constraints with no universal variables, the behaviour of WQGAC-Schema is identical to GAC-Schema.

The main change to GAC-Schema is to replace the notion of support to match the definition of WQGAC: that a value of some variable must be supported for all sequences of values of inner universal variables. This change does not alter the time complexity. The space complexity increases to $O(nd^n)$. The modified data structure S_C is described below (S and $last_C$ are modified likewise [8]), to be compared with [4].

$S_C(p)$ contains tuples that have been found to satisfy C and which include the partial assignment p. Each tuple supports n partial assignments, so when a tuple is found, it is added to all n relevant sets in S_C. The current support τ for p is included, and is removed when it is invalidated. Domain removals may invalidate other tuples $\lambda \neq \tau$ contained in S_C, but λ may not be removed immediately, so when searching for a new current support for p, $S_C(p)$ may contain invalid tuples.

In all cases the full description of a procedure is given in [8]. To propagate a pruned value (x, a), the procedure is summarized here. For all tuples t in S_C which contain (x, a), t is removed from S_C. If this leaves a partial assignment p unsupported, a new support is sought by calling seekNextSupport(). This procedure is specific to the constraint type.

Predicates. The constraint is defined by an arbitrary expression for which no specific propagation algorithm is known. The user provides a black box function $f_C(\tau)$, which returns *true* iff the tuple τ satisfies the constraint, *false* otherwise. The only change from the GAC-Schema version in [4] is that the variable y and value b have been replaced everywhere with partial assignment p. The basic idea is that supporting tuples are tested in lexicographic order against f_C, skipping forward whenever possible.

Positive Constraints. Here the set of allowed tuples (C_S) is given explicitly. This is slightly altered from the algorithm given by Bessière and Régin [4], with the data structure from Mohr and Masini [7]. The set C_S is sorted by partial assignment, to match the requirements of supporting a value. For each pair $\langle x_i, a \rangle$, the tuples matching $\langle x_i, a \rangle$ are divided into each possible sequence of inner universal assignments. (This does not increase the asymptotic space consumption because each tuple of length n has n references to it.) The seekNextSupport procedure simply returns the next valid tuple in the relevant list.

Negative Constraints. The set of disallowed tuples is given explicitly. Bessière and Régin give an efficient method based on hashing which uses the predicate instantiation and can be used without modification [4].

Testing WQGAC-Schema on a Connect-4 Endgame. To illustrate the strength of WQGAC and the efficiency of WQGAC-Schema, I use the running example (figure 1). The predicate instantiation of WQGAC-Schema is used. To my knowledge, there is no way of representing the quintary constraint with shorter constraints without losing propagation, hence there is no direct comparison to be made. Grey can win in three moves if black defends perfectly, and in two moves if black makes a mistake. There are five winning sequences where black defends perfectly: 2-2-4-4-5, 2-2-5-4-4, 4-4-5-2-2, 4-4-5-2-6 and 4-4-5-6-2. Table 1 shows three consecutive actions on the greywins constraint. (Asserting a value includes calling propagate to exhaustion.) CPU times are given for an implementation in Java, running with the Java 5.0 HotSpot compiler on a Pentium 4 3.06GHz with 1GB of memory. Although some attention was paid to efficiency in the implementation, this was not the main concern and the CPU times could be improved. Only 15.2% of the tuples were tested against the predicate, showing that WQGAC-Schema is effective in jumping over irrelevant tuples.

Testing WQGAC-Schema with Noughts and Crosses. WQGAC-Schema is embedded in a simple backtracking search for QCSP. An experiment based on

Table 1. Connect-4 results

Action	Tuples tested	Total tested %	Values pruned	CPU time
establishWQGAC()	2196		$grey1 : 1, 3, 5, 6, 7$	0.046s
assert $grey1 \neq 2$	207	15.2%	none	0.008s
assert $black1 = 4$	151		$grey2 : 1, 2, 3, 4, 6, 7$ and $grey3 : 1, 3, 4, 5, 7$	0.016s

noughts and crosses (tic-tac-toe) is described in the technical report [8]. First the game is modelled with 9 move variables (with alternating quantification) each with domain size 9, and board state variables for each move. The pure value rule [2] is dynamically applied to universal variables, so that values representing cheating moves are not explored. The question encoded is: can the first player win under any circumstances, to which the answer is no. All constraints are implemented using WQGAC-Schema+predicate. The longest constraints are arity 10, for detecting the winning condition. The search explored 4107 internal nodes in 26.205s, taking on average 6.38ms per node. This is compared to a similar model, with the final 3 moves eliminated and replaced with one large constraint of arity 12. Three constraints of arity 10 are removed. The number of internal nodes is reduced to 3403, explored in 13.782s, on average 4.05ms per node. To an extent, this shows the potential of consolidating a set of constraints into a single high-arity constraint, because better propagation is achieved and the time to reach local consistency at each node is reduced.

4 Conclusion and Acknowledgments

Generalized arc-consistency has been well studied and is very important in CSP. I have defined for QCSP two new levels of consistency based on GAC, and have developed an algorithm for one. This was briefly tested on game problems.

This work is funded by EPSRC, and I would like to thank my supervisor Ian Gent, the anonymous reviewers and Ian Miguel, who made many helpful comments on this paper.

References

1. Nikos Mamoulis and Kostas Stergiou, Algorithms for Quantified Constraint Satisfaction Problems, in *Proc. of the 10th CP*, pages 752-756, 2004.
2. Ian P. Gent, Peter Nightingale and Kostas Stergiou, QCSP-Solve: A Solver for Quantified Constraint Satisfaction Problems, to appear in *Proc. of the 19th IJCAI*, 2005.
3. Lucas Bordeaux and Eric Monfroy, Beyond NP: Arc-Consistency for Quantified Constraints, in *Proc. of the 8th CP*, pages 371-386, 2002.
4. Christian Bessière and Jean-Charles Régin, Arc consistency for general constraint networks: preliminary results, in *Proc. of the 15th IJCAI*, pages 398-404, 1997.
5. Ian Gent and Andrew Rowley, Encoding Connect-4 using Quantified Boolean Formulae, APES Technical Report APES-68-2003, 2003.
6. Alejandro López-Ortiz, Claude-Guy Quimper, John Tromp and Peter van Beek, A Fast and Simple Algorithm for Bounds Consistency of the AllDifferent Constraint, in *Proc. of the 18th IJCAI*, pages 306-319, 2003.
7. Roger Mohr and Gérald Masini, Good Old Discrete Relaxation, in *Proc. of the 8th ECAI*, pages 651-656, 1988.
8. Peter Nightingale, Consistency for Quantified Constraint Satisfaction Problems, CP-Pod Technical Report CPPOD-11-2005, 2005. Available from http://www.dcs.st-and.ac.uk/~cppod/publications/reports/

Alternate Modeling in Sport Scheduling

Laurent Perron

ILOG SA, 9 rue de Verdun, 94253 Gentilly cedex, France
lperron@ilog.fr

Abstract. Sports scheduling is a classical problem in the field of combinatorial optimization. One of the first successful methods to solve a complex instance was implemented using constraint programming. In this article, we explore an alternate and lighter way of modeling the round-robin part of the problem. We show this model can be enriched by additional propagations that complement the all different constraint.

1 Introduction

Until 1996, sports scheduling was done by hand. Under the added pressure of team addition and television network requests, the scheduling itself was given over to computer programs and computer programmers. The set of sports scheduling problems can be roughly divided into two different kinds of problems. The first one minimizes the number of breaks, i.e. sequences of two matches at home or two matches away from home. The second type of problem minimizes the total traveled distance of all teams during the season. These two kinds of problems usually come with additional side constraints: forbidden matches, forbidden sequences in the home/away variables, wishes from television networks and from teams, and fair sub-schedules for different teams (regarding weekdays and weekends in team schedules and regarding television time slots). Please refer to [1] for more details and to [2–6] for resolution techniques.

To solve a particular asian instance involving a double round-robin assignment, we implemented a classical model using a series of variables representing the schedules of each team over the different time periods. Despite our best efforts at that time, we could not find solutions for fourteen teams or more. This was insufficient as the objective was to schedule eighteen or twenty teams. Failure to solve this problem resulted from three factors: (a) lack of propagation among the different constraints of the problem, (b) difficulty in writing an efficient scheduling search strategy and (c) the complexity of the propagation involved just to represent the model.

To overcome these weaknesses, we decided to switch the model to a match model where variables represent matches between teams and their assignment represents the time period in which this match will be played. This model is lighter but still lacks propagation between the global cardinality constraint [7] stating that $n/2$ matches must occur in each time period and the set of all different constraints [8] stating that each team plays all its matches on a different week. This lack of propagation is explored in section 3 and computational results are shown in section 4.

2 Models for Round Robin

The classical team model relies on a matrix of variables, one per team and per time period. The value assigned to this variable corresponds to the opponent of this team in the same time period. Associated with these variables is a parallel matrix of Boolean variables indicating if the match is played at home or away. This is the usual model as found in [5]. In this particular instance, there is a nasty constraint stating that there is a minimum distance d between the two matches between two teams. This constraint is implemented by a set of all different constraints on gliding intervals of length $d+1$. As these two matches must occur in different half-seasons, we can restrict these intervals to those crossing the half of the season. Unfortunately, a translated scheduling is not possible in particular because of additional side constraints and wishes.

Despite our best efforts (Local search, Large Neighborhood Search, randomized strategies, complex heuristics) we were not able to find any feasible solution to the problem for fourteen or more teams. The problem lies in the selection of the variable to assign. The domain of each variable is small and homogeneous, thus killing any attempt based on the size of the domains. We then tried to fill the schedule chronologically, or by alternating teams and time periods. None of this turned out to be robust enough.

Furthermore, propagation is very heavy in the classical model. It involves a lot of all different constraints, many equivalences between simple assignment constraints, a lot of table constraints, and quite a large number of global cardinality constraints. Thus, using this model, every choice point is simply slow.

We then decided to switch to a dual view of the problem using a match representation. In this model, we create $n \times (n-1)$ variables representing all the different matches of the form: team x plays against team y at home. The domain of these variables are all the possibles time periods. We also create a matrix of intermediate home/away binary variables as in the classical model. We added the following constraints on this model: (a) the match variables and the home-away variables are linked together using a custom constraint that simply counts possible home matches and possible away matches for each pair (week, team); (b) for each team and all matches involving this team, an all different constraint states that these matches occur on different days; (c) a global cardinality constraint states that there are $n/2$ matches per week; (d) there is at least one and at most two home matches for every sequence of three home/away variables – this is encoded using a sequence constraint [9]; and (e) the minimum distance constraint is now implemented using a disjunction of minimum differences between the two match variables (a vs. b and b vs. a). This last constraint also implement the fact that each half schedule is full.

This match model is much lighter because it contains only one global cardinality constraint, no gliding all different constraints, no pairing constraint and no huge set of equivalences between constraints.

On the search side, the variables seem to carry more weight than the opponent variables in the previous model. This is linked to the fact that each match variable roughly corresponds to two team variables and two home/away variables. Thus, reducing the domain of a match variable directly reduces the domain of the two opponent variables (directly; both at the same time and not through complex propagation) and the two home/away variables.

Our first experiments demonstrated that the model is lighter. Finding solutions was easier and faster for up to eighteen or twenty teams. The only downside was that there was a high number of fails, even for the small instances. This visible thrashing hinted at a lack of propagation between the different constraints of the model. This will be explored in the next section.

3 Missing Propagation on the Match Model

In this section, we explore the lack of propagation of the round-robin part of the problem. This is encoded as a set of all different constraints (one per team) and a global cardinality constraint (fixing the number of matches per time period).

This is the first propagation rule we implemented: each match belongs to two all different constraints. If we assign a value to this match, this value will be removed from all matches of both all different constraints. If we remove more than the available slack (w.r.t. the global cardinality constraint), then this assignment is not possible and thus we can remove the value from the match.

This constraint can be implemented easily by a careful count of the number of possible matches for a given value in the conflict set (union of the two all different constraints) of a match.

We can go a bit further. For a given match m and a given possible value v for this match, we can examine the residual set of the conflict set of m, i.e. the set of all matches where v is still possible and which are not in the conflict set of m. Then we can compute the maximum number of simultaneous assignments of v that can be made on this residual set while satisfying the all different constraints. If this maximum number is strictly smaller than the number of times that v needs to be assigned minus one (for the assignment of v to m), then we can safely remove v from m.

Unfortunately, in the general case, computing this maximum number of simultaneous assignments is rather intractable. The first propagation rule explores the case when this number is zero. Another tractable case is when the number is one. In that case, this means that the maximum number of simultaneous assignments of the residual set is one, which is equivalent to the case where all matches of the residual sets share a common team.

Both these rules can be implemented using a n^3 propagation rule where n is the number of teams.

4 Experimental Results

To test the propagation properties of all the models described in this article, we implements seven models:

TW1 This is the team model without the pairing constraint
TW2 This is the team model with the pairing constraint
MW1 This is the match model without any additional constraints
MW2 This is the match model with the first propagation rule
MW3 This is the match model with both propagation rules
CM1 This is the combination of TW2 and MW1 with channeling constraints
CM2 This is the combination of TW2 and MW3 with channeling constraints

We run the same exact searches in parallel on all these models. At each step, we records the size of the search space (the sum of the logarithm of the size of the domain of all variables). Then we compare these for the seven models and we store all the search space sizes if at least one of them is different from the others. This denotes a different propagation. Furthermore, we also counted the number of times one model find that the current assignment is unfeasible (failure) when not all of the other models find the same conclusion. Please note that these experiments can be done even if we do not find solutions for the problem.

We present the results in the following table in the following way: for each size and each model, we present in the first line the average size of the search space over all stored datas and in the second line the number of times this model was found inconsistent differently from the other models. Results should be read that way, the lower the figure in the first line, the smaller the search space. This indicates a stronger propagation. The order is reversed for the second line, a greater number of fails indicates again a better propagation that is able to deduce inconsistencies earlier.

Size	TW1	TW2	MW1	MW2	MW3	CM1	CM2
12	210.27	210.27	205.33	204.84	202.70	203.85	201.74
	23	23	39	41	46	46	51
14	292.95	292.95	291.49	291.36	272.58	286.58	268.54
	13	13	14	14	60	28	72
16	364.49	364.49	377.77	376.82	375.55	358.27	357.50
	36	36	10	12	14	47	48
18	441.38	441.38	424.98	424.96	424.58	424.65	424.27
	0	0	11	11	11	11	11
20	633.87	633.87	630.79	630.78	630.35	630.57	630.13
	0	0	0	0	0	0	0

The following points are worth noticing:

- We did not see any differences between TW1 and TW2 (addition of the pairing constraint). This is counter intuitive and should be explored further.
- The second propagation rule propagates much more than the first propagation rule.
- The two models do not have the same propagation and they reinforce each other as seen in the CM2 results. The number of observed failures is much greater than in the other models. This means that we will deduce failure earlier and thus the search space can perform exponantially better.

– It is difficult to compare on the quantitative aspects of these figures. How they translates in the actual solving of the sport scheduling problem falls in the future work section. At this point, we can only compare models and not judge them individually.

5 Conclusion

Sports leagues scheduling problems are and remain challenging. Introducing a dual view of the classical team model provided us with two main achievements.

First, we were able to devise a more meaningful search strategy thanks to a reduction in the number of decision variables. This was instrumental in allowing us to solve problems with up to eighteen or twenty teams while with the original model, we were limited to twelve teams. Second, we were able to create original additional propagation rules that are different from the week-oriented propagations found in the usual model.

As we demonstrated, these new propagation rules can reduce the search space at least as effectively as the best constraints of the original model (symmetric all different/1-factor/pairing). The most interesting aspect is that the new constraints propagate differently than the traditional ones and the combination of the best constraints from both models leads to serious improvements over results obtained with either model.

References

1. Trick, M.: Tutorial on sports scheduling. Tutorial that should have been given at Banff CORS/INFORMS (2004) see http://mat.tepper.cmu.edu/cgi-bin/links/jump.cgi?ID=22.
2. Nemhauser, G.L., Trick, M.A.: Scheduling a major college basketball conference. Operations Research **46** (1998) 1–8
3. Henz, M.: Constraint-based round robin tournament planning. In: ICLP. (1999) 545–557
4. Henz, M.: Scheduling a major college basketball conference—revisited. Operations Research **49** (2001) 163–168
5. Régin, J.C.: Minimization of the number of breaks in sports scheduling problems using constraint programming. Constraint Programming and Large Scale Discrete Optimization, American Mathematical Society Publications, DIMACS **57** (2001) 115–130
6. Henz, M., Muller, T., Thiel, S.: Global constraints for round robin tournament scheduling (2002)
7. Régin, J.C.: Generalized arc consistency for global cardinality constraint. In: AAAI/IAAI, Vol. 1. (1996) 209–215
8. Régin, J.C.: A filtering algorithm for constraints of difference in CSPs. In: AAAI. (1994) 362–367
9. Régin, J.C., Puget, J.F.: A filtering algorithm for global sequencing constraints. In Smolka, G., ed.: Principles and Practice of Constraint Programming - CP97, Third International Conference, Linz, Austria, October 29 - November 1, 1997, Proceedings. Volume 1330 of Lecture Notes in Computer Science., Springer (1997)

Approximations in Distributed Optimization

Adrian Petcu and Boi Faltings

Ecole Polytechnique Fédérale de Lausanne (EPFL), CH-1015 Lausanne, Switzerland
{adrian.petcu, boi.faltings}@epfl.ch

Abstract. We present a parameterized approximation scheme for distributed combinatorial optimization problems based on dynamic programming. The algorithm is a utility propagation method and requires a linear number of messages. For exact computation, the size of the largest message is exponential in the width of the constraint graph. We present a distributed approximation scheme where the size of the largest message can be adapted to the desired approximation ratio, α. The process is similar to a distributed version of the minibucket elimination scheme, performed on a DFS traversal of the problem.

The second part of this paper presents an anytime version of the algorithm, that is suitable for very large, distributed problems, where the propagations may take too long to complete.

Simulation results show that these algorithms are a viable approach to real world, loose optimization problems, possibly of unbounded size.

1 Introduction

Constraint satisfaction and optimization are powerful paradigms that model a large range of tasks like scheduling, planning, optimal process control, etc.

To address distributed optimization, complete algorithms like OptAPO, ADOPT and DPOP have been recently introduced.

In distributed systems, in addition to computational costs, one has to take into account the communication overhead incurred as a consequence of the message exchange. Backtracking algorithms like ADOPT [3] work by trying out many combinations of value assignments, and each one of these state changes requires at least a message. This translates into an exponential amount of single-value messages, which generally entails a big communication overhead that should be avoided.

Centralized/distributed hybrids like OptAPO [2] mitigate the communication explosion by centralizing parts of the problem in some agents, and solving these parts centrally, and then distributing the results. Arguably, this approach suffers from privacy problems, and performance bottlenecks in the centralizing nodes.

Dynamic programming algorithms like *DPOP* [4] generate a linear number of messages. However, in case the problems have high induced width, the messages generated in the high-width areas of the problem get large.

We propose in this paper ADPOP, an approximate version of DPOP, which allows the desired tradeoff between solution quality and computational complexity (see section 3). The second part of this paper (section 4) presents AnyPOP, an anytime version of ADPOP, which provides increasingly accurate solutions while the propagation is still in progress. This makes it suitable for very large, distributed problems, where the propagations may take a long time to complete.

Simulation results on distributed meeting scheduling problems show this approach to be viable for real world, loose, possibly unbounded optimization problems.

2 Definitions and Notation

A discrete *multiagent constraint optimization problem* (MCOP) is a tuple $< \mathcal{X}, \mathcal{D}, \mathcal{R} >$ such that:

$\mathcal{X} = \{X_1, ..., X_m\}$ is the set of *variables*/solving agents; $\mathcal{D} = \{d_1, ..., d_m\}$ is a set of *domains* of the variables, each given as a finite set of possible values. $\mathcal{R} = \{r_1, ..., r_p\}$ is a set of *relations*, where a relation r_i is a function $d_{i1} \times .. \times d_{ik} \to \mathbb{R}$ which denotes how much utility is assigned to each possible combination of values of the involved variables. The goal is to find an assignment $\mathcal{X}^*$ for the variables X_i that maximizes the aggregate overall utility.

3 ADPOP – A Configurable Approximation Method

This is an approximate version of the DPOP algorithm from [4]. DPOP is a distributed version of the bucket elimination scheme from [1], which works on a DFS ordering.

DPOP has 3 phases. First, a DFS traversal of the graph is done using a standard distributed DFS algorithm.

The second phase (*UTIL* propagation) is a bottom-up process, which starts from the leaves and propagates upwards only through tree edges. The agents send *UTIL* messages to their parents. These messages summarize the influence of the sending variable and its whole subtree on the rest of the problem. They are equivalent to the induced constraints computed in the variable elimination steps in the bucket elimination scheme.

When the *UTIL* propagation reaches the root, the top-down solution reconstruction process is initiated.

3.1 Approximations: Dropping Dimensions Through Approximate Projections

The time/space complexity of DPOP's utility propagation is exponential in the induced width (see [4] for the proof). Therefore, in case the problem has high induced width, it is no longer feasible to compute and send exact messages. However, if we renounce exactness, we can impose a limit $maxDims$ on the maximum number of dimensions any message in the system can carry. When the dimensionality of the outgoing message exceeds this limit, the algorithm drops a set S of dimensions to stay below the limit. This is done by applying a maximal/minimal projection on the respective dimensions (retains the upper/lower bounds w.r.t. the respective variables). The set S of dimensions to be dropped can be selected according to a greedy process. The two resulting messages are bundled together and sent to the parent as upper/lower bounds.

This process is similar to Dechter's minibucket elimination scheme (see [1]). However, notice that *ADPOP* is a distributed algorithm, with a well-defined elimination order, given by a DFS traversal of the problem graph. This particular ordering is very well suited for a distributed setting for a number of reasons. First, it can easily be combined with the *most constrained node* heuristic to obtain low-width orderings. Second, it ensures a good degree of parallelism since nodes in disjoint branches can work in parallel. Third, deciding how to combine incoming messages, deciding for which ones to wait and where to send the outgoing ones is made straightforward by the DFS hierarchy.

Furthermore, when the $maxDims$ bound is exceeded, then some dimensions are forcibly removed by approximate projections, as opposed to computing several lower dimensionality messages, as the minibucket scheme does.

Propagating both lower and upper bound messages gives us the ability to determine locally the maximal distance δ from the optimal solution for each value from the domain of the current variable.

This enables several ways of reasoning with bounds. First, let us consider the *UTIL* propagation. If a specified approximation ratio α is given, we can make sure that our future solution will observe this bound by dropping only as many dimensions as allowed by it. Alternatively, if a $maxDims$ bound is specified, then we can drop as many dimensions as needed, and still compute an overall δ that shows how far from the optimum is the solution. In case the obtained δ is not satisfactory, one can repeat the process, with increased $maxDims$, reusing the work that was previously done in the areas where $maxDims$ was not exceeded.

Second, during the value assignment propagation, one can choose the assignments according to two strategies. An *optimistic strategy* that assigns the values with the highest upper bounds gives some chances of finding good solutions by choosing "promising" assignments. On the other hand, a *pessimistic strategy* that chooses the values with the highest lower bounds offers a guarantee on the quality of the chosen solution.

Algorithm Complexity. In all cases, this algorithm produces a linear number of messages. Its complexity lies in the size of the *UTIL* messages.

The worst case is when the exact solution is required ($maxDims = \infty$, or $\alpha = 1$). In this case, the complexity equals the induced width of the graph [4]. If the bound $maxDims$ is imposed and is smaller than the width, no message larger than this is produced, and complexity is exponential in this bound.

In case an approximation ratio is specified, and $maxDims$ is infinite, in the worst case complexity is again exponential in the width of the graph.

4 AnyPOP – An Anytime Algorithm for Large Optimization Problems

In large, distributed constraint networks, it may take a long time until these propagations complete. In the following, we develop a way to decide quickly, *locally*, the value of each variable, based on a *limited* number of *UTIL/VALUE* messages from the neighbors. As time goes by, and the propagation spreads out, and more and more *UTIL/VALUE* messages come from the neighbors, we refine these decisions. As opposed to a local search method, we obtain *guarantees* on the quality of the solution, even before allowing the propagations to complete. There are obvious advantages to this approach: one can quickly start with a reasonably good solution, and refine it as time goes by.

The intuition is simple: the value taken by any node X_i can have an influence on the rest of the problem only through the constraints between X_i and its direct neighbors. *UTIL* messages received by X_i already sum up its influence on the sending subtree. Thus, based on the set of *UTIL* messages X_i already received, and on the valuation structure of the constraints between X_i and its neighbors that did not already send *UTIL* messages, X_i can decide with a certain error bound what is the effect of each one of its values on the rest of the problem.

In some cases, when these error bounds are sufficiently low, X_i can decide on an assignment for itself even before receiving all of its *UTIL/VALUE* messages. In such a case, one can simply start the *VALUE* propagation phase immediately, without waiting for the rest of the *UTIL/VALUE* messages to come.

AnyPOP also exhibits some built-in fault tolerance. If messages are lost, solution quality degrades. However, the algorithm still provides the best solution it can infer based on the information that *was* sent/received successfully.

5 Experimental Evaluation

Our experiments were performed on distributed meeting scheduling problems, where a set of agents try to jointly find the best schedule for a set of meetings. Each agent has a variable for each meeting it is involved in. The values are the possible starting times. All agents must agree on the start time of each meeting, and an agent cannot participate in 2 meetings at the same time. Each agent assigns to each meeting at each particular time a certain utility, and the task is to find the schedule that maximizes the overall utility.

We ran experiments on an especially difficult problem with 70 agents, 140 variables and 204 binary constraints. The induced width is 7, meaning that the biggest message holds over two million values. We ran the algorithm with increasing $maxDims$. Table 1 shows the results in this order: maximal dimensionality, maximal distance δ from the optimum for all *UTIL* messages, the average δ per message, the distance of the approximate solution to the true optimum, the total amount of *UTIL* information transmitted (the sum of the sizes of the individual *UTIL* messages), maximal message size, and the utility of the solutions found.

Table 1. Max. dimensions vs. solution accuracy: problem with 140 vars, 204 constraints, width=7

$maxDims$	Max δ /msg %	Avg δ /msg %	δ /overall %	Total UTIL payload	Max msg size	Utility
1	44.83	13.55	2.90	2104	16	2278
2	36.00	4.54	2.69	10032	128	2283
3	17.14	1.27	2.43	39600	1024	2289
4	13.11	0.57	0.81	130912	8192	2327
5	10.00	0.19	0.43	498200	65536	2336
6	1.36	0.04	0.30	1808904	524288	2339
7	0.00	0.00	0.00	3614064	2097152	2346

The accuracy of the solutions increases with the increase of $maxDims$, culminating with the optimal value for $maxDims = 7$. However, there is also a dramatic increase

Table 2. *AnyPOP* dynamic evolution: problem with 140 vars, 204 constraints, width=7

Snapshot #	Max δ /var %	Avg δ /var %	Utility	δ /overall %	Assig changes
1	94.44	80.77	1555	33.72	0
2	66.07	16.7	1625	30.73	99
3	42.42	3.92	2036	13.21	73
4	13.51	1	2254	3.92	19
5	13.51	0.94	2289	2.43	1

in computation effort and network load. If we compare the first and the last lines of the table, we see that we can achieve a solution which is within 3% of the optimum with 3 orders of magnitude less effort (2k values vs. 3M). Therefore, in some cases it is beneficial to settle for a suboptimal solution obtained with much less effort.

To test simultaneously both *AnyPOP*'s anytime performance and its ability to deal with low resources, we performed another experiment on the same instance, with *maxDims=3*. We took 5 runtime snapshots: the first snapshot was taken *before sending/receiving any message*, and subsequent ones after each node has received another message. The last snapshot is taken after all messages are sent/received. The assignments discovered by each of the snapshots are used to compute the overall utility. We notice a steady progress of the algorithm towards a solution, culminating with the best solution found by *ADPOP* on the same test problem, with the same bound $maxDims = 3$. There is also a steady decrease of the error bounds, and of the assignment changes between snapshots.

6 Conclusions and Future Work

We proposed an approximate algorithm for distributed optimization, allowing for the desired tradeoff between solution quality and computational complexity. We also presented an anytime version of this algorithm, suitable for large distributed problems. Experimental results show that these algorithms are a viable approach to large but loose real world optimization problems.

Future work includes finding heuristics for generating DFS trees with low induced width and "intelligent" selection of the dimensions to be dropped out.

References

1. Rina Dechter. Bucket elimination: A unifying framework for processing hard and soft constraints. *Constraints: An International Journal*, 7(2):51–55, 1997.
2. Roger Mailler and Victor Lesser. Solving distributed constraint optimization problems using cooperative mediation. *Proceedings of Third International Joint Conference on Autonomous Agents and MultiAgent Systems (AAMAS 2004)*, 2004.
3. P. J. Modi, W. M. Shen, and M. Tambe. An asynchronous complete method for distributed constraint optimization. In *Proc. AAMAS*, 2003.
4. Adrian Petcu and Boi Faltings. A scalable method for multiagent constraint optimization. In *Proceedings of the 19th International Joint Conference on Artificial Intelligence, IJCAI-05*, Edinburgh, Scotland, Aug 2005.

Extremal CSPs

Nicolas Prcovic

LSIS - Université Paul Cézanne Aix-Marseille III,
Faculté de St-Jérôme - Avenue Escadrille Normandie-Niemen - 13013 Marseille
nicolas.prcovic@lsis.org

Abstract. We present a new class of binary CSPs called extremal CSPs. The CSPs of this class are inconsistent but would become consistent if any pair of variable assignments among the forbidden ones was allowed. Being inconsistent, they cannot be solved by any local repair method. As they allow a great number of partial (almost complete) solutions, they can be very hard to solve with tree search methods integrating domain filtering. We experiment that balanced extremal CSPs are much harder to solve than random CSPs of same size at the complexity peak.

1 Introduction

Even if the Constraint Satisfaction Problem is NP-complete, it is known that only a small part of the CSP set is hard to solve with the methods used until now. When a problem has a lot of solutions uniformly distributed in the search space, local repair methods are efficient. When a problem is much overconstrained, a tree search associated with a domain filtering technique can allow to prove quickly that the problem has no solution. Only the problems that resist to that two types of solving methods are usually considered as hard.

Characterizations of hardness for CSPs have been found for random CSPs defined by some parameters (number of variables, domain size, graph density and constraint tightness). In this model, the CSPs for which parameters are such that they have probability 0.5 to have a solution are longer to solve than the others on the average. The drawback of this characterization is that it does not give a property that would ensure the hardness of the problem but only a stronger probability to be hard. In addition, some other general properties (e.g., backbone, minimal backdoor and unsatisfiable core size) for explaining problem hardness have been proposed. However, they do not allow a precise description of hard problem's structure. In this paper, we propose a simple yet precise description of CSPs that are necessarily hard to solve with the usual solving techniques.

2 Resistant CSPs

We place ourselves in the context of binary CSPs, where each problem is defined by a triple (X, D, C), where X=$\{x_1, ..., x_n\}$ is the variable set, D=$\{D_1, ..., D_n\}$ is the discrete and finite domain set (where each domain D_i contains the values that can be assigned to variable x_i) and C is the constraint set that explicits the *allowed* variable assignment pairs. We say that a CSP is *consistent* iff it has a solution, that is, a variable assignment set A such that any two variable assignments in A form a pair that belongs to C. A binary CSP can be modeled as a simple vertex-colored graph using what is called its microstructure.

Definition 1. *Microstructure of a CSP*
The microstructure of a CSP is a vertex-colored graph for which each vertex is a variable assignment (with a value of its domain), for which each edge corresponds to an allowed pair of variable assignments and for which each vertex is colored by its variable number.

The microstructure of a CSP with n variables is a n-partite n-colored graph (each part has its own color). The CSP is consistent if its microstructure contains a n-clique (a complete induced subgraph with n vertices).

We consider tree search procedures that filter the domains dynamically by maintaining some kind of local consistency, such as Forward-Checking and MAC. Our idea is to consider the hardest the problems that resist to the best possible value or variable ordering heuristics.

Definition 2. *Minimum search tree (of a procedure)*
Given a tree search procedure, the minimum search tree of an inconsistent CSP is the one that results from a sequence of optimal (dynamic) variable choices that minimizes the total number of nodes in the tree.

In other words, among the set of all the search trees that can be obtained by varying at some points the variable to choose next, the minimum search tree is the one containing the minimum number of nodes. A search tree is a proof of inconsistency. Each node is an elementary step of polynomial time complexity. The search tree depends on the solving procedure that is used.

Definition 3. *CSP resistance*
Given a tree search procedure, a CSP P1 is more resistant than a CSP P2 if the minimum search tree of P1 has more nodes than the one of P2.

Therefore, an (inconsistent) problem is resistant for a procedure if there exists no short proof of its inconsistency, even with the best possible heuristic. If a CSP is resistant then it is also hard in the usual sense (ie, long to solve on the average). Notice that consistent problems are not resistant (even if some may be considered hard in the usual sense) since there exists a short proof of their consistency. We aim at discovering the CSPs that best resist to any tree search procedure.

3 Extremal CSPs

For a given variable set X and domain set D, we are going to define the extremal CSP class, which has the following informal property: any CSP P (with variable set X and domain set D) not in this class is such that there always exists a CSP in this class which is more resistant than P. The general idea is that if we can solve efficiently any CSP of this class then we are also able to solve any CSP outside this class.

Definition 4. *Extremal CSP*
A CSP is extremal if its microstructure is such that it does not contain any n-clique but the addition of any new edge between two vertices of different color would create a n-clique.

In other words, a CSP is extremal[1] if it is inconsistent and if adding any new pair of variable assignments in its constraint set would make this CSP consistent. The extremal CSPs are saturated with partial solutions involving $n - 1$ variable assignments. Therefore, they are potentially hard to solve with any tree search methods because domain filtering techniques maintaining some level of local consistency (arc-consistency, path-consistency or a higher level of consistency) may be totally inoperative. Their relative resistance is explained by the following reasons:

- Adding a new allowed pair of variable assignments to an extremal CSP makes it consistent, so there exists a way of reaching one of its solutions quickly.
- Removing an allowed pair of variable assignments introduces a new possibility for the search procedure to backtrack on a subtree that would have been explored. In others words, a nogood (ie, an implied constraint) is added and the minimum length of the proof of its inconsistency can be shortened.

Each extremal CSP is thus more resistant than a lot of other CSPs: the ones allowing exactly the same pairs of variable assignments plus some other pairs or (exclusive) minus some other pairs. Obviously, the fact that a CSP is extremal does not ensure it is more resistant than any other non extremal CSP of same size. However, any non extremal CSP has at least one extremal CSP of same size which is more resistant. Therefore, *the most resistant CSPs are extremal.*

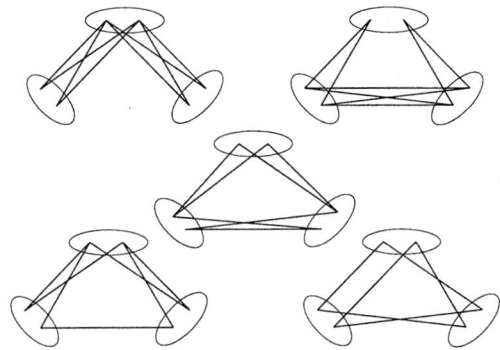

Fig. 1. The only five possible structures of extremal CSPs that have 3 variables and 2 values in their domains. The ellipses surround the vertices of same color. There is no triangle. Adding any edge between two vertices of different color would create a triangle.

---

[1] The *extremal graph theory* is "the study of how the intrinsic structure of graphs ensures certain types of properties (e.g., clique-formation and graph colorings) under appropriate conditions" (Eric W. Weisstein). Hence, microstructures of extremal CSPs are just extremal graphs.

The study of extremal CSPs allows to obtain new means to decide if a CSP is consistent or not.

Proposition 1. *A CSP is inconsistent if and only if its microstructure is a spanning subgraph of the microstructure of an extremal CSP with the same variables and domains.*

Proof. It is obvious that any CSP whose microstruture is a spanning subgraph of the microstructure of an extremal CSP is inconsistent because extremal CSPs are. Now, let G be the microstructure of an inconsistent CSP. By adding iteratively to G one edge that maintains inconsistency, we can always reach an extremal microstructure. G is then a spanning subgraph of the microstructure of an extremal CSP.

We designed a simple procedure for generating extremal CSPs. It consists in starting from a complete n-partite graph (a problem without any constraint) then iterating the following cycle: find a n-clique (a solution) and remove an edge of this n-clique. The procedure halts when the modified microstructure does not contain any more n-clique (the problem is inconsistent). In order to ensure that the problem is extremal, we forbid the removal of an edge of a newly discovered n-clique if it belonged to one of the n-cliques previously found. We thus ensure that adding later any edge would make appear again the n-clique this edge belonged to.

4 Balanced Extremal CSPs

Since not all extremal CSPs are very resistant (they are only more resistant than others), we have to find another property to ensure a strong resistance. According to our definition of resistance, a CSP (extremal or not) can be resistant only if the time spent to solve it is not sensitive to the ordering of the variable selection during the tree search. If it is not the case, there is a high variability in the size of the search tree, then there exists a small search tree generated thanks to a good variable ordering. But if it is not sensitive at all to the variable ordering, this means the problem is totally symmetrical (like the CSP at the bottom right of figure 1). Indeed, only choices between symmetrical alternatives are insignificant because each one leads to an equivalent situation. So in order to generate extremal CSPs that are actually hard, we managed to minimize the variation of degree between their vertices of highest and lowest degree. This is very easy to integrate into our procedure: among all the edges that can be removed from the microstructure, we always select the edge that maintains the lowest variation of degree. The balance between the degrees of the vertices favors the apparition of symmetries but does not guarantee them at all.

In order to verify the hardness of balanced extremal CSPs, after having generated them with our procedure, we solved them thanks to a classical tree search method: a Forward-Checking procedure with the dom/deg^2 dynamic variable ordering heuristic. Table 1 shows results for the first hundred balanced extremal CSPs generated for each parametering (number of variables, domain size). These results are compared with the ones obtained with the same solving procedure on the hardest classical random CSPs of same size from [1], ie random CSPs for which the constraint graph is complete and the constraint tightness is set as to reach the complexity peak.

---

[2] Domain size / degree of the variable in the constraint graph.

Table 1. Comparison of the average number of backtracks (BT) and nodes for different problem sizes between the first 100 balanced extremal CSPs generated by our procedure and 100 instances of the hardest random CSPs. The average values are followed by the intervals of values between brackets.

n	d	balanced extremal CSPs		hardest random CSPs	
		# BT	# nodes	# BT	# nodes
13	8	251 (247-255)	503 (499-507)	11 (0-22)	93 (13-183)
17	6	115 (108-142)	365 (323-512)	10 (0-20)	99 (17-185)
22	5	78 (6-209)	223 (36-575)	7 (0-17)	94 (22-185)
25	4	12821 (5049-30070)	43022 (20948-102431)	6 (5-10)	50 (32-70)

One characteristic of the CSPs we have generated is that their hardness is not an increasing function of the number of variables and domain size. We have conjectured the following cause. As equality between the degrees of the vertices is a necessary but not sufficient condition for symmetry existence, we thought our procedure could have generated very symmetrical CSPs in some cases and no symmetrical CSPs in other cases. For checking this, we have used Nauty [2] to compute the orbits[3] of the microstructures. The more orbits in a graph, the less symmetrical it is. In our experiments, we note that the hardest extremal CSPs (problems for which domain size is 4) are the ones that have some symmetries (90 orbits on the average). Knowing their symmetries can be very useful to accelerate their resolution thanks to various symmetry breaking techniques. However the other extremal CSPs are easier but still much harder than the hardest random CSPs. These CSPs are not symmetrical but have some regularity and a high degree of local consistency that make our variable ordering heuristic and filtering technique inoperative.

5 Conclusion

Aiming at characterizing what a hard CSP is, we have introduced the extremal CSP class. We have shown experimentally that, by generating balanced extremal CSPs (for which microstructure vertices have close degrees), we can build problems that are much harder than random CSPs of same size at the complexity peak. Balanced extremal CSPs have been designed to resist to almost all existing solving techniques: local repair methods, tree search with domain filtering, intelligent backtracking, perfect variable or value ordering, symmetry breaking. So, they constitute a challenge and require elaborating solving techniques that may be totally different from the classical ones.

References

1. Hulubei, T.: The CSP Library. University of New Hampshire. (1999) http://www.cs.unh.edu/ tudor/csp/.
2. McKay, B.D.: Practical graph isomorphism. Congressus Numerantium **30** (1981) 45–87

---

[3] Two vertices of a graph G are in the same orbit iff there exists an automorphism of G (a permutation on the vertex set that leaves G unchanged) that maps one vertex to the other one.

Beyond Finite Domains: The ALL-DIFFERENT and Global Cardinality Constraints

Claude-Guy Quimper[1] and Toby Walsh[2]

[1] School of Computer Science, University of Waterloo, Canada
cquimper@math.uwaterloo.ca
[2] NICTA and UNSW, Sydney, Australia
tw@cse.unsw.edu.au

Abstract. We describe how the propagator for the ALL-DIFFERENT constraint can be generalized to prune variables whose domains are not just simple finite integer domains. We show, for example, how it can be used to propagate set, multiset and tuple variables.

1 Introduction

Constraint programming has restricted itself largely to finding values for variables taken from finite integer domains. However, we might want to consider variables representing sets [11–13], multisets [14], ordered tuples, or other structures. These variable types reduce the space needed to represent possible domain values, improve the efficiency of constraint propagators and inherit all the usual benefits of data abstraction like ease of debugging and code maintenance.

As an example, consider the round robin sports scheduling problem (prob026 in CSPLib). In this problem, we wish to find a schedule satisfying a number of constraints including that a team never plays twice with another team. We therefore would like a propagator which works on an ALL-DIFFERENT constraint posted on variables whose values are pairs of teams. In this paper, we consider how to efficiently and effectively implement the ALL-DIFFERENT constraint on variables whose values are sets, multisets or tuples. Due to space restrictions, we omit proofs. A longer version of the paper is available as a technical report.

2 Propagators for the ALL-DIFFERENT Constraint

Propagating the ALL-DIFFERENT constraint involves removing from the domain of variables those values that cannot be part of a consistent assignment. To design his propagator, Leconte [16] introduced the concept of *Hall set* based on Hall's work [1].

Definition 1. *A* Hall set *is a set H of values such that the number of variables whose domain is contained in H is equal to the cardinality of H. More formally, H is a Hall set if and only if $|H| = |\{x_i \mid dom(x_i) \subseteq H\}|$.*

To enforce domain consistency, it is necessary and sufficient to detect every Hall set H and remove its values from the domains that are not fully contained in H. Régin's propagator [4] uses matching theory to detect Hall sets. Leconte [16], Puget [17], López-Ortiz et al. [9] use simpler ways to detect Hall intervals and achieve weaker consistencies.

3 Beyond Integer Variables

A propagator designed for integer variables can be applied to any type of variable whose domain can be enumerated. For instance, let the following variables be sets whose domains are expressed by a set of required values and a set of allowed values. $\{\} \subseteq S_1, S_2, S_3, S_4 \subseteq \{1,2\}$ and $\{\} \subseteq S_5, S_6 \subseteq \{2,3\}$. Variable domains can be expanded as follows: $S_1, S_2, S_3, S_4 \in \{\{\}, \{1\}, \{2\}, \{1,2\}\}$ and $S_5, S_6 \in \{\{\}, \{2\}, \{3\}, \{2,3\}\}$. By enforcing GAC on the ALL-DIFFERENT constraint, we obtain $S_1, S_2, S_3, S_4 \in \{\{\}, \{1\}, \{2\}, \{1,2\}\}$ and $S_5, S_6 \in \{\{3\}, \{2,3\}\}$. We can now convert the domains back to their initial representation. $\{\} \subseteq S_1, S_2, S_3, S_4 \subseteq \{1,2\}$ and $\{3\} \subseteq S_5, S_6 \subseteq \{2,3\}$.

This technique always works but is not tractable in general since variable domains might have exponential size. For instance, the domain of $\emptyset \subseteq S_i \subseteq [1,n]$ contains 2^n elements. The following important lemma allows us to ignore such variables and focus just on those with "small" domains.

Lemma 1. *Let n be the number of variables and let F be a set of variables whose domains are not contained in any Hall set. Let $x_i \notin F$ be a variable whose domain contains more than $n - |F|$ values. Then $dom(x_i)$ is not contained in any Hall set.*

Lemma 1 helps us to find variables F whose domain cannot be contained in a Hall set. Algorithm 1 prunes the domains of n variables and ensures that domains larger than n do not slow down the propagation.

Algorithm 1. ALL-DIFFERENT propagator for variables with large domains

$F \leftarrow \emptyset$
1 for $x_i \in X$ do if $|dom(x_i)| > |X| - |F|$ then $F \leftarrow F \cup \{x_i\}$
2 Expand domains of variables in $X - F$.
   Propagate the All-Different constraint on variables $X - F$ and find Hall sets H.
   for $x_i \in F$ do $dom(x_i) \leftarrow dom(x_i) - H$
3 Collapse domains of variables in $X - F$.

To apply our new techniques, three conditions must be satisfied by the representation of the variables: computing the size of the domain must be tractable (Line 1), domains must be efficiently enumerable (Line 2) and efficiently computed from an enumeration of values (Line 3). The next sections describe how different representations of domains for set, multiset and tuple variables meet these three conditions.

4 ALL-DIFFERENT on Sets

Several representations of domains have been suggested for set variables. The most common representations use a set of required elements lb and a set of allowed elements ub such that any set S satisfying $lb \subseteq S \subseteq ub$ belongs to the domain [11,12]. The cardinality of dom(S) is $2^{|ub-lb|}$ and can be computed in constant time. Often, to represent more precisely the possible values, a cardinality variable C is added such that $|S| \in$ dom(C). The size of the domain is then given by $\sum_{j \in \text{dom}(C)} \binom{|ub-lb|}{j-|lb|}$ and this can be computed in $O(|\text{dom}(C)|)$ steps.

To increase the expressiveness of the domain representation, Sadler and Gervet [6] suggest adding a lexicographic ordering constraint. We therefore say that $S_1 < S_2$ holds if S_1 comes before S_2 in a lexicographical order. The new domain representation now involves two lexicographic bounds $l \leq S \leq u$. To compute the size of such domains, we consider the binary vector representation where each bit of a vector corresponds to an element in $ub - lb$. The bit is set to 1 if the element belongs to the set and 0 otherwise. Let a and b be the binary vector representation of the lexicographical bounds l and u. Let $a - 1$ be the vector that lexicographically precedes a. Function f computes the number of binary vectors lexicographicaly smaller than or equal to s with k bits set to one. Assuming that $\binom{x}{y} = 0$ for any $y < 0$, the size of domain S is given by the following equations.

$$|\text{dom}(S)| = \sum_{k \in C} (f(b,k) - f(a-1,k)) \quad (1)$$

$$f([s_m, \ldots, s_1], k) = \sum_{i=1}^{m} s_i \binom{i-1}{k - \sum_{j=i+1}^{m} s_j} + \delta(s, k) \quad (2)$$

$$\delta([s_m, \ldots, s_1], k) = \begin{cases} 1 & \text{if } \sum_{i=1}^{m} s_i = k \text{ and } s_0 = 0 \\ 0 & \text{otherwise} \end{cases} \quad (3)$$

Function f can be evaluated in $O(|ub-lb|)$ steps. The size of domain dom(S) therefore requires $O(|ub-lb||\text{dom}(C)|)$ steps to compute.

We can enumerate the sets in dom(S) of cardinality k for each $k \in$ dom(C). Based on the lexicographic bound l, we find the first set of cardinality k. Algorithm T from Knuth [8] provides subsequent sets. Proceeding this way results in a $O(|\text{dom}(C)||ub-lb| + |\text{dom}(S)|)$ algorithm. When there are no lexicographic bounds, the complexity can be reduced to $O(\max(|ub-lb|, |\text{dom}(S)|))$.

5 ALL-DIFFERENT on Tuples

A tuple t is an ordered sequence of n elements that allows multiple occurrences. The most common way to represent the domain of a tuple is simply by associating an integer variable to each of the tuple components. A tuple of size n is therefore represented by n integer variables $x_1, \ldots, x_n$.

To apply an ALL-DIFFERENT constraint to a set of tuples, a common solution is to create an integer variable t for each tuple. If each component x_i

ranges from 0 to c_i exclusively, we add the channeling following constraint $t = \sum_i^n \prod_{j=i+1}^n c_j x_i$.

This technique suffers from either inefficient or ineffective channeling between variable t and the components x_i. Most constraint libraries enforce bound consistency on t. A modification to the domain of x_i does not necessarily affect t. Conversely, even if all tuples encoded in dom(t) have $x_i \neq v$, value v will most often not be removed from dom(x_i). On the other hand, enforcing domain consistency typically requires $O(|\text{dom}(t)|)$ steps which can be time consuming when domains are large.

To address this issue, one can define a tuple variable whose domain is defined by the domain of its components. dom(t) = dom(x_1) $\times \ldots \times$ dom(x_n). The size of such a domain is given by $|\text{dom}(t)| = \prod_{i=1}^n |\text{dom}(x_i)|$ which can be computed in $O(n)$ steps.

As Sadler and Gervet [6] did for sets, we can add lexicographical bounds to tuples $l \leq t \leq u$ in order to better express the values the domain contains.

Let $idx(v, x)$ be the number of values smaller than v in the domain of the integer variable x. Assuming $idx(v, x)$ has a running time complexity of $O(\log(|\text{dom}(x)|))$, the size of the domain can be evaluated in $O(n + \log(|\text{dom}(t)|))$ steps using $|\text{dom}(t)| = 1 + \sum_{i=1}^n \left((idx(u[i], x_i) - idx(l[i], x_i)) \prod_{j=i+1}^n |\text{dom}(x_i)| \right)$

Algorithm M from Knuth [7] enumerates the domain of a tuple variable in lexicographical order. Assuming the domain of all component variables have the same size, this algorithm runs in $O(|dom(t)|)$ steps which is optimal.

6 ALL-DIFFERENT on Multi-sets

Unlike sets, multi-sets allow multiple occurrences of a same element. A multi-set can be represented by a tuple where each component indicates the multiplicity of an element in the multi-set. All algorithms explained in Section 5 can therefore be applied to multi-sets.

7 Indexing Domain Values

Propagators for the ALL-DIFFERENT constraint, like the one proposed by Régin [4], need to store information about the values appearing in the domains of variables. When values are integers, a table T can store information related to value v in entry $T[v]$. Algorithm ?? ensures that no more than n^2 distinct values will be handled by the propagator. When these n^2 values come from a significantly larger set of values, table T becomes very sparse. To allow better direct access, we need to map the n^2 values to an index in the interval $[1, n^2]$. The trie data structure retrieves the value associated to a set, a multi-set, a tuple, or any other sequential data structure of length l in $O(l)$ steps. This technique permits existing propagators to work without a penalty for sparse domain values.

8 Conclusions

We have described how existing propagators for the ALL-DIFFERENT constraint can be generalized to prune variables whose domains are not just simple finite integer domains. In particular, we described how it can be used to propagate set, multi-set and tuple variables. This result can easily be generalized for the global cardinality constraint. Many other global constraints still remain to be generalized to deal with variables which are not just simple integer finite domains, as well as to variables of other types.

References

1. P. Hall. On representatives of subsets. *Journal of the London Mathematical Society*, pages 26–30, 1935.
2. J. Hopcroft and R. Karp. An $n^{5/2}$ algorithm for maximum matchings in bipartite graphs. *SIAM Journal of Computing*, 2:225–231, 1973.
3. ILOG S. A. ILOG Solver 4.2 user's manual, 1998.
4. J.-C. Régin. A filtering algorithm for constraints of difference in CSPs. In *Proc. of the 12th National Conference on Artificial Intelligence*, pp 362–367, 1994.
5. K. Stergiou and T. Walsh. The difference all-difference makes. In *Proc. of the 16th Int. Joint Conference on Artificial Intelligence*, pages 414–419, 1999.
6. A. Sadler and C. Gervet Hybrid Set Domains to Strengthen Constraint Propagation and Reduce Symmetries In *In Proc. of the 10th Int. Conference on Principles and Practice of Constraint Programming*, pp 604–618, 2004.
7. D. Knuth, *Volume 4 of The Art of Computer Programming, Pre-Fascicle 2a: Generating all n-tuples*, http://www-cs-faculty.stanford.edu/~knuth/
8. D. Knuth, *Volume 4 of The Art of Computer Programming, Pre-Fascicle 3a: Generating all combinations*, http://www-cs-faculty.stanford.edu/~knuth/
9. A. López-Ortiz, C.-G. Quimper, J. Tromp, and P. van Beek. A fast and simple algorithm for bounds consistency of the alldifferent constraint. In *Proc. of the 18th Int. Joint Conference on Artificial Intelligence*, pages 245–250, 2003.
10. W. H. Press, B. P. Flannery, S. A. Teukolsky, W. T. Vetterling *Numerical Recipes in C: The Art of Scientific Computing, 2nd Edition* Cambridge Univ. Press, 1992
11. C. Gervet Interval Propagation to Reason about Sets: Definition and Implementation of a Practical Language. CONSTRAINTS journal 1(3) (1997) p. 191-244
12. J.-F. Puget Finite set intervals. In *Proc. of Workshop on Set Constraints*, CP1996.
13. T. Müller and M. Müller. Finite set constraints in Oz. In F. Bry, B. Freitag, and D. Seipel, editors, *13. Workshop Logische Programmierung*, pages 104–115, Technische Universität München, 17–19 September 1997.
14. T. Walsh Consistency and Propagation with Multiset Constraints: A Formal Viewpoint In *Proc. of the 9th International Conference on Principles and Practice of Constraint Programming*, 2003.
15. I.P. Gent and T. Walsh CSPLib: a benchmark library for constraints *Technical report APES-09-1999*, 1999.
16. M. Leconte. A bounds-based reduction scheme for constraints of difference. In *Proceedings of the Constraint-96 International Workshop on Constraint-Based Reasoning*, pp. 19–28, 1996
17. J.-F. Puget. A Fast Algorithm for the Bound Consistency of Alldiff Constraints. In *Proc. of the 15th National Conf. on Artificiel Intelligence*, pp 359–366, 1998

Views and Iterators for Generic Constraint Implementations

Christian Schulte[1] and Guido Tack[2]

[1] IMIT, KTH - Royal Institute of Technology, Sweden
schulte@imit.kth.se
[2] PS Lab, Saarland University, Saarbrücken, Germany
tack@ps.uni-sb.de

Abstract. This paper introduces an architecture for generic constraint implementations based on variable views and range iterators. Views allow, for example, to scale, translate, and negate variables. The paper shows how to make constraint implementations generic and how to reuse a single generic implementation with different views for different constraints. Applications of views exemplify their usefulness and their potential for simplifying constraint implementations. We introduce domain operations compatible with views based on range iterators to access and modify entire variable domains.

1 Introduction

This paper contributes a new architecture based on variable views and range iterators. The architecture comprises an additional level of abstraction to decouple variable implementations from propagators (as constraint implementations). Propagators compute generically with variable views instead of variables. Views support operations like scaling, translation, and negation of variables.

Range iterators support powerful and efficient domain operations on variables and variable views. The operations can access and modify multiple values of a variable domain simultaneously. Range iterators are efficient as they help avoiding temporary data structures. They simplify the construction of propagators by serving as adaptors between variables and propagator datastructures.

The architecture is carefully separated from its implementation. The architecture can be used for arbitrary constraint programming systems and has been fully implemented in Gecode [2].

2 Constraint Programming Systems

This section introduces the model for finite domain constraint programming systems considered in this paper and relates it to existing systems.

We assume that a constraint is implemented by a *propagator*. A propagator maintains a collection of variables and performs constraint propagation by executing operations on these variables. In the following we consider finite domain variables and propagators. A finite domain variable x has an associated *domain* $\text{dom}(x)$ being a subset of some finite subset of the integers.

Propagators do not manipulate variable domains directly but use operations provided by the variable. These operations return information about the domain or update the domain. In addition, they handle failure (the domain becomes empty) and control propagation of other propagators sharing variables.

A *value operation* on a variable involves a single integer as result or argument. We assume that a variable x with $D = \text{dom}(x)$ provides the following value operations: x.getmin() returns $\min D$, x.getmax() returns $\max D$, x.adjmin(n) updates $\text{dom}(x)$ to $\{m \in D \mid m \geq n\}$, x.adjmax(n) updates $\text{dom}(x)$ to $\{m \in D \mid m \leq n\}$, and x.excval(n) updates $\text{dom}(x)$ to $\{m \in D \mid m \neq n\}$.

These operations are typical for finite domain constraint programming systems like Choco [5], ILOG Solver [7,8,3], Eclipse [1], Mozart [6], and Sicstus [4]. Some systems provide additional operations such as for assigning values.

A *domain operation* supports access or update of multiple values of a variable domain simultaneously. In many systems this is provided by supporting an abstract set-datatype for variable domains, as for example in Choco [5], Eclipse [1], Mozart [6], and Sicstus [4]. ILOG Solver [7,8,3] only allows access by iterating over the values of a variable domain.

Range notation $[n \mathrel{..} m]$ is used to refer to the set of integers $\{l \in \mathbb{Z} \mid n \leq l \leq m\}$. A *range sequence* ranges(I) for a finite set of integers $I \subseteq \mathbb{Z}$ is the shortest sequence $s = \langle [n_1 \mathrel{..} m_1], \ldots, [n_k \mathrel{..} m_k] \rangle$ such that I is covered (set(s) $= I$, where set(s) is defined as $\bigcup_{i=1}^{k} [n_i \mathrel{..} m_i]$) and the ranges are ordered by their smallest elements ($n_i \leq n_{i+1}$ for $1 \leq i < k$). The above range sequence is also written as $\langle [n_i \mathrel{..} m_i] \rangle_{i=1}^{k}$. Clearly, a range sequence is unique, none of its ranges is empty, and $m_i + 1 < n_{i+1}$ for $1 \leq i < k$.

3 Variable Views with Value Operations

This section introduces variable views with value operations.

Consider as an example the well-known finite domain constraint model for n-Queens using three alldifferent constraints. To be implemented efficiently, this model requires an alldifferent constraint supporting that the values of $x_i + c_i$ are different, where the x_i are variables and the c_i are integers. Systems with this extension of alldifferent must implement two very similar versions of the same propagator. This is tedious and increases the amount of code that requires maintenance. In the following we make propagators *generic*: the same propagator can be reused for several variants.

To make a propagator generic, all its operations on variables are replaced by operations on variable views. A *variable view* (view for short) implements the same operations as a variable. A view stores a reference to a variable. Invoking an operation on the view executes the appropriate operation on the view's variable. Multiple variants of a propagator can be obtained by instantiating the single generic propagator with multiple different variable views.

For an *offset-view* $v = \text{voffset}(x, c)$ for a variable x and an integer c, performing an operation on v results in performing an operation on $x+c$. The operations on the offset-view are:

$$v.\text{getmin}() := x.\text{getmin}() + c \qquad v.\text{getmax}() := x.\text{getmax}() + c$$
$$v.\text{adjmin}(n) := x.\text{adjmin}(n - c) \qquad v.\text{adjmax}(n) := x.\text{adjmax}(n - c)$$
$$v.\text{excval}(n) := x.\text{excval}(n - c)$$

To obtain both alldifferent propagators, also an *identity-view* is needed. An operation on an identity-view vid(x) for a variable x performs the same operation on x. That is, identity-views turn variables into views to comply with propagators now computing with views. Obtaining the two variants of alldifferent is straightforward: the propagator is made generic with respect to which view it uses. Using the propagator with both an identity-view and an offset-view yields the required propagators.

A *scale-view* $v = \text{vscale}(a, x)$ for a positive integer $a > 0$ and a variable x defines operations such that v behaves as $a \cdot x$:

$$v.\text{getmin}() := a \cdot x.\text{getmin}() \qquad v.\text{getmax}() := a \cdot x.\text{getmax}()$$
$$v.\text{adjmin}(n) := x.\text{adjmin}(\lceil n/a \rceil) \qquad v.\text{adjmax}(n) := x.\text{adjmax}(\lfloor n/a \rfloor)$$
$$v.\text{excval}(n) := \textbf{if } n \bmod a = 0 \textbf{ then } x.\text{excval}(n/a)$$

As an example, consider the implementation of linear equations. With scale-views it is sufficient to implement the simple propagator $\sum_{i=1}^{n} v_i = c$ for views v_i. Then, a general version $\sum_{i=1}^{n} a_i \cdot x_i = c$ (using scale-views) as well as an optimized version $\sum_{i=1}^{n} x_i = c$ (using identity-views) can be obtained.

A *minus-view* $v = \text{vminus}(x)$ for a variable x provides operations such that v behaves as $-x$. Its operations reflect that the smallest possible value for x is the largest possible value for $-x$ and vice versa.

Derived views. It is unnecessarily restrictive to define views in terms of variables. The actual requirement for a view is that its variable provides the same operations. It is straightforward to make views generic themselves: views can be defined in terms of other views. The only exception are identity-views as they serve the very purpose of casting a variable into a view. Views such as offset, scale, and minus are called *derived views*: they are derived from some other view.

With derived views being defined in terms of views, the first step to use a derived view is to turn a variable into a view by an identity-view. For example, a minus-view v for the variable x is obtained by $v = \text{vminus}(\text{vid}(x))$.

The coefficient of a scale-view is restricted to be positive. Allowing arbitrary non-zero constants a in a scale-view $s = \text{vscale}(a, x)$ requires to take the signedness of a into account. This extension is inefficient. A more efficient way is to restrict scale-views to positive coefficients and use an additional minus-view for cases where negative coefficients are required.

Derived views exploit that views do not need to be implemented in terms of variables. This can be taken to the extreme in that a view has no access at all to a variable. A constant-view $v = \text{vcon}(c)$ for an integer c provides operations such that v behaves as a variable x being equal to c. Constant-views allow to obtain optimized variants of more general propagators. For example, $x + y = c$ can the be obtained from $x + y + z = c$ without any overhead.

4 Domain Operations and Range Iterators

A *range iterator* r for a range sequence $s = \langle [n_i \mathrel{..} m_i] \rangle_{i=1}^{k}$ allows to iterate over s: each $[n_i \mathrel{..} m_i]$ can be obtained in sequential order but only one at a time. A range iterator r provides the following operations: $r.\mathrm{done}()$ tests whether all ranges have been iterated, $r.\mathrm{next}()$ moves to the next range, and $r.\mathrm{min}()$ and $r.\mathrm{max}()$ return the minimum and maximum value for the current range. By $\mathrm{set}(r)$ we refer to the set defined by an iterator r (with $\mathrm{set}(r) = \mathrm{set}(s)$).

A range iterator hides its implementation. Iteration can be by position, but it can also be by traversing a list. The latter is particularly interesting if variable domains are implemented as lists of ranges themselves.

Variables are extended with operations to access and modify their domains with range iterators. For a variable x, the operation $x.\mathrm{getdom}()$ returns a range iterator for $\mathrm{ranges}(\mathrm{dom}(x))$. For a range iterator r the operation $x.\mathrm{setdom}(r)$ updates $\mathrm{dom}(x)$ to $\mathrm{set}(r)$ provided that $\mathrm{set}(r) \subseteq \mathrm{dom}(x)$.

With the help of iterators, richer domain operations are effortless. For a variable x and a range iterator r, the operation $x.\mathrm{adjdom}(r)$ replaces $\mathrm{dom}(x)$ by $\mathrm{dom}(x) \cap \mathrm{set}(r)$, whereas $x.\mathrm{excdom}(r)$ replaces $\mathrm{dom}(x)$ by $\mathrm{dom}(x) \setminus \mathrm{set}(r)$.

Global constraints are typically implemented by a propagator computing over some involved data structure, such as for example a variable-value graph for domain-consistent all-distinct [9]. After propagation, the new variable domains must be transferred from the data structure to the variables. This can be achieved by using a range iterator as adaptor. The adaptor operates on the data structure and iterates the range sequence for a particular variable. The iterator then can be passed to the appropriate domain operation.

5 Variable Views with Domain Operations

Domain operations for identity-views and constant-views are straightforward. The domain operations for an identity-view $v = \mathrm{vid}(x)$ use the domain operations on x: $v.\mathrm{getdom}() := x.\mathrm{getdom}()$ and $v.\mathrm{setdom}(r) := x.\mathrm{setdom}(r)$. For a constant-view $v = \mathrm{vcon}(c)$, the operation $v.\mathrm{getdom}()$ returns an iterator for the singleton range sequence $\langle [c \mathrel{..} c] \rangle$. The operation $v.\mathrm{setdom}(r)$ just checks whether the range sequence of r is empty.

Domain operations for an offset-view $\mathrm{voffset}(v, c)$ are provided by an offset-iterator. The operations of an offset-iterator o for a range iterator r and an integer c (created by $\mathrm{ioffset}(r, c)$) are as follows:

$$o.\mathrm{min}() := r.\mathrm{min}() + c \qquad o.\mathrm{max}() := r.\mathrm{max}() + c$$
$$o.\mathrm{done}() := r.\mathrm{done}() \qquad o.\mathrm{next}() := r.\mathrm{next}()$$

The domain operations for an offset view $v = \mathrm{voffset}(v, c)$ are as follows:

$$v.\mathrm{getdom}() := \mathrm{ioffset}(x.\mathrm{getdom}(), c)$$
$$v.\mathrm{setdom}(r) := x.\mathrm{setdom}(\mathrm{ioffset}(r, -c))$$

Providing domain-operations for minus-views and scale-views is similar.

6 Implementation

The presented architecture can be implemented as an orthogonal layer of abstraction for any constraint programming system. The only demand on the implementation language is that it supports *polymorphism* of some kind: propagators operate on different views, domain operations and iterators on different iterators.

C++ features parametric polymorphism through templates. Due to monomorphization, the compiler can perform aggressive optimizations, in particular inlining. Gecode makes heavy use of templates. A thorough inspection of the code generated by several C++ compilers shows that all operations on both views and iterators are inlined entirely. The abstractions thus do not impose a runtime penalty (compared to a system without views and iterators).

Acknowledgements. Christian Schulte is partially funded by the Swedish Research Council (VR) under grant 621-2004-4953. Guido Tack is partially funded by DAAD travel grant D/05/26003. Thanks to Mikael Lagerkvist for helpful comments.

References

1. Pascal Brisset, Hani El Sakkout, Thom Frühwirth, Warwick Harvey, Micha Meier, Stefano Novello, Thierry Le Provost, Joachim Schimpf, and Mark Wallace. ECLiPSe Constraint Library Manual 5.8. User manual, IC Parc, London, UK, February 2005.
2. Gecode: Generic constraint development environment, 2005. Available upon request from the authors, `www.gecode.org`.
3. ILOG S.A. *ILOG Solver 5.0: Reference Manual*. Gentilly, France, August 2000.
4. Intelligent Systems Laboratory. SICStus Prolog user's manual, 3.12.1. Technical report, Swedish Institute of Computer Science, Box 1263, 164 29 Kista, Sweden, April 2005.
5. François Laburthe. CHOCO: implementing a CP kernel. In Nicolas Beldiceanu, Warwick Harvey, Martin Henz, François Laburthe, Eric Monfroy, Tobias Müller, Laurent Perron, and Christian Schulte, editors, *Proceedings of TRICS: Techniques foR Implementing Constraint programming Systems, a post-conference workshop of CP 2000*, number TRA9/00, pages 71–85, 55 Science Drive 2, Singapore 117599, September 2000.
6. Tobias Müller. *Propagator-based Constraint Solving*. Doctoral dissertation, Universität des Saarlandes, Fakultät für Mathematik und Informatik, Fachrichtung Informatik, Im Stadtwald, 66041 Saarbrücken, Germany, 2001.
7. Jean-François Puget. A C++ implementation of CLP. In *Proceedings of the Second Singapore International Conference on Intelligent Systems (SPICIS)*, pages B256–B261, Singapore, November 1994.
8. Jean-François Puget and Michel Leconte. Beyond the glass box: Constraints as objects. In John Lloyd, editor, *Proceedings of the International Symposium on Logic Programming*, pages 513–527, Portland, OR, USA, December 1995. The MIT Press.
9. Jean-Charles Régin. A filtering algorithm for constraints of difference in CSPs. In *Proceedings of the Twelfth National Conference on Artificial Intelligence*, pages 362–367, Seattle, WA, USA, 1994. AAAI Press.

Approximated Consistency for the Automatic Recording Problem

Meinolf Sellmann

Brown University, Department of Computer Science,
115 Waterman Street, P.O. Box 1910, Providence, RI 02912, U.S.A.
sello@cs.brown.edu

In constraint optimization, global constraints play a decisive role. To develop an efficient optimization tool, we need to be able to assess whether we are still able to improve the objective function further. This observation has lead to the development of a special kind of global constraints, so-called optimization constraints [2,5]. Roughly speaking, an optimization constraint expresses our wish to search for improving solutions only while enforcing feasibility for at least one of the constraints of the problem.

Since optimization constraints essentially evolve as a conjunction of a constraint on the objective value and some constraint of the constraint program, for many optimization constraints achieving generalized arc-consistency turns out to be NP-hard. Consequently, weaker notions of consistency have been developed with the aim to get ourselves back into the realm of tractable inference techniques. In [6,7], we introduced the concept of approximated consistency which is a refined and stronger notion of relaxed consistency [1] for optimization constraints. Approximated consistency asks that all assignments are removed from consideration whose commitment would cause a bound with guaranteed accuracy to drop below the given threshold.

We study the automatic recording problem (ARP) that consists in the solution of a knapsack problem where items are associated with time intervals and only items can be selected whose corresponding intervals do not overlap. The combination of a knapsack constraint with non-overlapping time-interval constraints can be identified as a subproblem in many more scheduling problems. For example, satellite scheduling can be viewed as a refinement of the automatic recording problem. Therefore, it is of general interest to study a global constraint that augments the knapsack constraint with time-interval consistency of selected items. This idea gives raise to the Automatic Recording Constraint (ARC), which we want to study in this paper. Obviously, as an augmentation of the knapsack constraint, achieving generalized arc-consistency for the ARC is NP-hard. Consequently, we will develop a filtering algorithm for the constraint that does not guarantee backtrack-free search for the ARP, but that achieves at least approximated consistency with respect to bounds of arbitrary accuracy.

1 ARP Approximation

In the interest of space, we need to omit formal definitions of optimization constraints and approximated consistency. We refer the reader to [1,7,8]. Let us define the Automatic Recording Problem and its corresponding constraint.

Given $n \in \mathbb{N}$, denote with $V = \{1, \ldots, n\}$ the set of *items*, and with $start(i) < end(i) \; \forall \; i \in V$ the corresponding starting and ending times. With $w = (w_i)_{1 \leq i \leq n} \in$

$\mathbb{N}_+^n$ we denote the storage requirements, $K \in \mathbb{N}_+$ denotes the storage capacity, and $p = (p_i)_{1 \leq i \leq n} \in \mathbb{N}^n$ the profit vector. Finally, let us define n binary variables $X_1, \ldots, X_n \in \{0,1\}$. We say that the interval $I_i := [start(i), end(i)]$ corresponds to item $i \in V$, and call two items $i, j \in V$ *overlapping* whose corresponding intervals overlap, i.e. $I_i \cap I_j \neq \emptyset$. We call $p_X := \sum_{i \mid X_i = 1} p_i$ the *user satisfaction (with respect to X)*.

The *Automatic Recording Problem (ARP)* consists in finding an assignment $X = (X_1, \ldots, X_n) \in \{0,1\}^n$ such that (a) The selection X can be stored within the given disc size, i.e. $\sum_i w_i X_i \leq K$. (b) At most one item must be selected at a time, i.e. $I_i \cap I_j = \emptyset \; \forall \, i < j$ s.t. $X_i = 1 = X_j$. (c) X maximizes the user satisfaction, i.e. $p_X \geq p_Y \; \forall \, Y$ respecting (a) and (b). Then, given a lower bound on the objective function $B \in \mathbb{N}$ and domains of the binary variables $X_1, \ldots, X_n$, the Automatic Recording Constraint (ARC) consists in enforcing that a solution to the ARP with $p_X > B$.

In less formal terms, the ARC requires us to find a selection of items such that the total weight limit is not exceeded, no two items overlap in time, and the total objective value is greater than that of the best know feasible solution. Note that enforcing generalized arc-consistency (GAC) on the ARC is NP-hard, which is easy to see by the fact that finding an improving solution would otherwise be possible in a backtrack-free search [3] or by simple reduction to the knapsack constraint [7].

Approximated consistency requires that a lower threshold that is diminished by some fraction of the overall best possible performance is guaranteed to be exceeded. In our pursuit to develop a filtering algorithm for the ARC, let us first study the ARP and see whether we can develop a fast approximation algorithm for the problem. Let $p_{max} := \max\{p_i \mid 1 \leq i \leq n\}$. We develop a pseudo-polynomial algorithm running in $\Theta(n^2 p_{max})$ that will be used later to derive a fully polynomial time approximation scheme (FPTAS) for the ARP.

1.1 A Dynamic Programming Algorithm

The algorithm we develop in the following is similar to the teaching book dynamic programming algorithm for knapsack problems. Setting $\overline{\mathbb{N}} := \mathbb{N} \cup \{\infty\}$ and $\psi := np_{max} + 1$, we compute a matrix $M = (m_{kl}) \in \overline{\mathbb{N}}^{n+1 \times \psi}$, $0 \leq k \leq \psi$, $0 \leq l \leq n$. In m_{kl}, we store the minimal knapsack capacity that is needed to achieve a profit greater or equal k using items lower or equal l only ($m_{kl} = \infty$ iff $\sum_{1 \leq i \leq l} p_i < k$).

We assume that V is ordered with respect to increasing ending times, i.e., $1 \leq i < j \leq n$ implies $e_i \leq e_j$. Further, denote with $last_j \in V \cup \{0\}$ the last non-overlapping node lower than j, i.e., $e_{last_j} < s_j$ and $e_i \geq s_j \; \forall \, last_j < i \leq j$.

We set $last_j := 0$ iff no such node exists, i.e., iff $e_0 \geq s_j$. To simplify the notation, let us assume that $m_{k,0} = \infty$ for all $0 < k \leq \psi$, and $m_{k,0} = 0$ for all $k \leq 0$. Then,

$$m_{kl} = \min\{m_{k,l-1}, m_{k-p_l, last_l} + w_l\}. \quad (1)$$

The above recursion equation yields a dynamic programming algorithm: First, we sort the items with respect to their ending times and determine $last_i$ for all $0 \leq i < n$. Both can be done in time $\Theta(n \log n)$. Then, we build up the matrix column by column, and within each column from top to bottom. Finally, we compute $\max\{k \mid m_{k,n} \leq K\}$. The total running time of this procedure and the memory needed are obviously in $\Theta(|M|) = \Theta(n^2 p_{max})$.

1.2 A Fully Polynomial Time Approximation Scheme

We exploit a core idea from [4] to limit the total number of non-infinity entries per column: According to Equation 1, each column depends solely on the column immediately to the left and the column that belongs to the last predecessor of the currently newly added item. We construct new sparse columns as lists of only non-infinity entries that are ordered with increasing profit. This can be done easily by running through the corresponding lists of columns that determine the entries in the new column. After a new column is created, we "trim" it by eliminating entries whose profit (the corresponding row of the matrix entry) is only slightly better than that of another entry in the column. Formally, we remove an entry if there exists a prior entry m_{kl} in the list if and only if there exists a prior and not previously removed entry m_{jl} such that $j \geq (1-\delta)k$ for some $1 > \delta = \delta(\varepsilon) > 0$. And whenever an entry m_{kl} is removed, its representant entry is set to $m_{jl} := \min\{m_{jl}, m_{kl}\}$. All this can be done in one linear top to bottom pass through the column. Then, after the trimming, successive elements in the list differ by a factor of at least $1/(1-\delta)$. Thus, each sparse column can contain at most $\log_{1/(1-\delta)}(np_{max}) = \frac{\ln(np_{max})}{-\ln(1-\delta)} \leq \frac{\ln(np_{max})}{\delta}$ elements. Note that every new column, before it is trimmed itself, cannot contain more than two times this value. Consequently, the algorithm will only take time $O(\frac{n \ln(np_{max})}{\delta})$.

Now, what error have we introduced by trimming the columns? By induction on the column indices l, it can shown easily that in the lth column, if there existed an entry m_{kl} in the original dynamic program, then there exists an entry m_{jl} in the trimmed version such that $(1-\delta)^l k \leq l \leq k$ and $m_{jl} \leq m_{kl}$. Consequently, the entry $m_{kn} \leq K$ that achieves the optimal profit k has a representant $m_{ln} \leq m_{kl} \leq K$ with $l \geq (1-\delta)^n k$. When setting $\delta = \varepsilon/n$, then it follows $l \geq (1-\frac{\varepsilon}{n})^n k \geq (1-\varepsilon)k$. Consequently, we achieve an FPTAS that runs in time $O(\frac{n^2 \ln(np_{max})}{\varepsilon})$.

2 Approximated Consistency for the ARC

In order to achieve a filtering algorithm for the ARC based on the routine that we developed before, we closely follow the idea of defining a directed acyclic graph over the trimmed dynamic programming matrix. The idea was first introduced in [9] and consequently lead to the filtering algorithms in [7].

We define the weighted, directed, and acyclic graph for the untrimmed matrix as follows: Every non-infinity entry in the matrix defines a node in the graph. In accordance to Equation 1, each node has at most two incoming arcs: one emanating from the column immediately to the left, and another emanating from the column that corresponds to the last predecessor of the item that is newly added in the current column (whereby the column of the last predecessor may be identical to the column immediately to the left). That is, one incoming arc represents the decision not to use the newly added item (we refer to those arcs as zero-arcs), and the other incoming arc represents the decision to add the new item corresponding to the new column (we refer to those arcs as one-arcs). A zero-arc has associated weight 0, a one-arc has the same weight as the item corresponding to the column the target node belongs to. To express that we are only looking for solutions with profit greater B, we add a sink node t and connect it to the graph by directing arcs to t from exactly those nodes in the last column that have profit greater B. With this construction, we ensure a one-to-one correspondence between solutions to the ARP and paths in the graph: A feasible, improving solution corresponds exactly to a path from m_{00} to t that has weight lower or equal K. We call such paths *admissible*. The original numbers in the dynamic programming matrix now correspond to shortest-path distances from $m_{0,0}$ to the individual nodes.

The question that arises is how we can incorporate the idea of trimming a column. Trimming removes nodes from columns so as to make sure that the number of non-infinity entries stays polynomial in every column. We would like to trim, but we must make sure that by removing nodes we do not eliminate arcs from the graph that could actually belong to admissible paths. Otherwise we may end up filtering values from variable domains that could actually lead to improving, feasible solutions with respect to the ARC, i.e. our filtering algorithm could filter incorrectly, which we must prevent.

The algorithm that we propose uses the trimming idea as follows: In the graph, whenever a column entry would be removed by trimming, we keep the respective node and add an arc with weight 0 to the node that represents the node. The trimmed node has no other outgoing arcs, especially none that target outside of the column that it belongs to. This implies that, for new columns that are generated later, the trimmed node is of no relevance, so that we can still keep the column fill-in under control. With this slight modification of the graph, we can ensure that it has polynomial size and that the filtering method achieves ε-consistency for the ARC.

Let us formalize the idea by defining the graph corresponding to the trimmed dynamic program as follows. We define the weighted, directed, and acyclic graph $G(\delta) = (N, A, v)$ (whereby we always only consider nodes m_{qk} which have a non-infinity value in the dynamic program) by setting: $N_R := \{m_{qk} \mid 0 \leq q \leq np_{max}, 0 \leq k \leq n, m_{qk} \ \delta\text{-untrimmed}\}$. $N_T := \{m_{qk} \mid 0 \leq q \leq np_{max}, 0 \leq k \leq n, m_{qk} \ \delta\text{-trimmed}\}$. $N := N_R \cup N_T \cup \{t\}$. $A_0 := \{(m_{q,k-1}, m_{qk}) \mid k \geq 1, m_{q,k-1} \in N_R, m_{qk} \in N_R \cup N_T\}$. $A_1 := \{(m_{q-p_k, last_k}, m_{qk}) \mid k \geq 1, q \geq p_k, m_{q-p_k, last_k} \in N_R, m_{qk} \in N_R \cup N_T\}$. $A_R := \{(m_{pk}, m_{qk}) \mid m_{pk} \in N_T, m_{qk} \in N_R, (1-\delta)p \leq q < p\}$. $A_t := \{(m_{qn}, t) \mid q \geq B, m_{qn} \in N_R\}$. $A := A_0 \cup A_1 \cup A_R \cup A_t$. $v(e) := 0$ for all $e \in A_0 \cup A_R \cup A_t$. $v(m_{q-p_k, last_k}, m_{qk}) := w_k$ for all $(m_{q-p_k, last_k}, m_{qk}) \in A_1$.

Note that, for an admissible path $(m_{00}, \ldots, m_{pn}, t)$ in the graph, the sequence of arcs in A_0 and A_1 (whereby we ignore arcs in A_R and A_t) determines the *corresponding solution* to the ARP when we set all items that belong to skipped columns to 0. That corresponding solution then has the same weight as the path, and according to Section 1.2 for the corresponding solutions profit q it holds: $(1 - \varepsilon)q \leq p \leq q$.

Theorem 1. *Given $1 > \varepsilon > 0$, we set $\delta := \varepsilon/n$.*

1. *If there exists a path $W = (m_{00}, \ldots, m_{pn}, t)$ in $G(0)$ with $p \geq B$ and such that $v(W) \leq K$, then there exists a path $X = (m_{00}, \ldots, m_{qn}, t)$ in $G(\delta)$ such that $q \geq (1-\varepsilon)B$, $v(X) \leq K$, and the corresponding solutions to W and X are identical.*
2. *If there exists a path $X = (m_{00}, \ldots, m_{qn}, t)$ in $G(\delta)$ with $q \geq (1-\varepsilon)B$ and such that $v(X) \leq K$, then there exists a path $W = (m_{00}, \ldots, m_{pn}, t)$ in $G(0)$ such that $p \geq (1-\varepsilon)B$, $v(W) \leq K$, and the corresponding solutions to W and X are identical.*

We exploit this theorem to devise the following filtering algorithm: Thanks to the fact that our graph is directed and acyclic, we can apply linear time shorter path filtering techniques that remove those and only those arcs that cannot be visited by any admissible path. After shorter path filtering, every arc in the pruned graph can be part of a path from m_{00} to t with weight lower or equal K. Since arcs really correspond to decisions to include or exclude and item in our solution, there exists a one-arc (zero-arc) to a node in column i iff item i is included (excluded) in some improving, feasible solution. Consequently, by searching the pruned graph for columns in which no node has incoming one-arcs, we can identify those and only those items that must be excluded in all improving, feasible solutions. The situation is only slightly more complicated when a column has no incoming zero-arcs. In contrast to knapsack approximation, for the ARC there exist arcs that cross several columns. If there still exists such an arc that can be part of an admissible path, then the items that belong to the columns that are bridged can obviously be excluded in some admissible solution. Consequently, if a column has only incoming one-arcs and no arc crosses the column, then and only then it must indeed be included in all feasible improving solutions. Without going into details, we just note that the detection of items that must be included can be performed in time $O(n \log n + |M|)$.

According to Theorem 1 (1), this is a correct filtering algorithm for the ARC, and according to Theorem 1 (2) we are sure to eliminate all assignments that would cause the best optimal solution to drop below $(1 - \varepsilon)B$. Assuming that B is given as a lower bound on the objective, i.e. $B \leq P^*$, we finally have:

Corollary 1. *Approximated consistency for the ARC can be achieved in time* $O(n^2 \ln(np_{max})/\varepsilon)$.

References

1. T. Fahle and M. Sellmann. Cost-Based Filtering for the Constrained Knapsack Problem. *Annals of Operations Research*, 115:73–93, 2002.
2. F. Focacci, A. Lodi, M. Milano. Cost-Based Domain Filtering. *Principles and Practice of Constraint Programming (CP)* Springer LNCS 1713:189–203, 1999.
3. E.C. Freuder. A Sufficient Condition for Backtrack-Free Search. *Journal of the ACM*, 29(1):24–32, 1982.
4. O.H. Ibarra and C.E. Kim. Fast Approximation Algorithms for the Knapsack and Sum of Subset Problems. *Journal of the ACM*, 22(4):463–468, 1975.
5. M. Milano. *Integration of Mathematical Programming and Constraint Programming for Combinatorial Optimization Problems*, Tutorial at CP2000, 2000.
6. M. Sellmann. The Practice of Approximated Consistency for Knapsack Constraints. *Proceedings of the Nineteenth National Conference on Artificial Intelligence (AAAI)*, AAAI Press, pp. 179-184, 2004.
7. M. Sellmann. Approximated Consistency for Knapsack Constraints. *CP*, Springer LNCS 2833: 679–693, 2003.
8. M. Sellmann and T. Fahle. Constraint Programming Based Lagrangian Relaxation for the Automatic Recording Problem. *Annals of Operations Research*, 118:17-33, 2003.
9. M. Trick. A Dynamic Programming Approach for Consistency and Propagation for Knapsack Constraints. *3rd International Workshop on Integration of AI and OR Techniques in Constraint Programming for Combinatorial Optimization Problems (CP-AI-OR)*, pp. 113–124, 2001.

Towards an Optimal CNF Encoding of Boolean Cardinality Constraints

Carsten Sinz

Institute for Formal Models and Verification,
Johannes Kepler University Linz, A-4040 Linz, Austria
carsten.sinz@jku.at

Abstract. We consider the problem of encoding Boolean cardinality constraints in conjunctive normal form (CNF). Boolean cardinality constraints are formulae expressing that at most (resp. at least) k out of n propositional variables are true. We give two novel encodings that improve upon existing results, one which requires only $7n$ clauses and $2n$ auxiliary variables, and another one demanding $\mathcal{O}(n \cdot k)$ clauses, but with the advantage that inconsistencies can be detected in linear time by unit propagation alone. Moreover, we prove a linear lower bound on the number of required clauses for any such encoding.

1 Introduction

Cardinality constraints—expressing numerical bounds on discrete quantities—arise frequently out of the encoding of real-world problems, e.g. in product configuration, radio frequency assignment or in reconstructing images form computer tomographs [1–3]. With considerable progress made over the last years in solving propositional satisfiability (SAT) instances, interest increased in tackling problems that include cardinality constraints using SAT-solvers. This, however, requires an encoding of cardinality constraints in the language of purely propositional logic or, more specifically, in conjunctive normal form (CNF), the predominant input language of modern SAT-solvers.

Boolean cardinality constraints put numerical restrictions on the number of propositional variables that are allowed to be true at the same time. A typical construct like $\leq k\,(x_1, \ldots, x_n)$ expresses that not more than k of the n variables $x_1, \ldots, x_n$ are allowed to be true. The traditional way of converting a constraint like $\leq k\,(x_1, \ldots, x_n)$ to purely propositional logic is by explicitly excluding all possible combinations of $k+1$ variables being simultaneously true, thus obtaining

$$\bigwedge_{\substack{M \subseteq \{1,\ldots,n\} \\ |M|=k+1}} \bigvee_{i \in M} \neg x_i \;,$$

which requires $\binom{n}{k+1}$ clauses of length $k+1$. In the worst case of $k = \lceil n/2 \rceil - 1$ this amounts to $O(2^n/\sqrt{n/2})$ clauses. Better encodings are known [3,4] and will be further improved in this paper. The general idea of these improved encodings is to build a count-and-compare hardware circuit and then translate this circuit to CNF. Besides the constraint's variables $x_1, \ldots, x_n$, additional *encoding variables* $s_1, \ldots, s_m$ will be allowed. Formally, we are looking for an optimal encoding (typically minimizing the number of clauses) according to the following definition.

Definition 1. *A clause set E over the variables $V = \{x_1, \ldots, x_n, s_1, \ldots, s_m\}$ is a clausal encoding of $\leq k \, (x_1, \ldots, x_n)$ if for all assignments $\alpha : \{x_1, \ldots, x_n\} \to \mathbb{B}$ the following holds: there is an extension of α to $\alpha^* : V \to \mathbb{B}$ that is a model of E if and only if α is a model of $\leq k \, (x_1, \ldots, x_n)$, i.e. if and only if at most k of the variables x_i are set to 1 by α.*

2 Encoding Using a Sequential Counter

We now give a CNF encoding for cardinality constraints of the form $\leq k \, (x_1, \ldots, x_n)$ that is based on a sequential counter circuit. The circuit is shown in Fig. 1 and computes partial sums $s_i = \sum_{j=1}^{i} x_j$ for increasing values of i up to the final $i = n$. The values of all s_i's are represented as unary numbers. The overflow bits v_i are set to true if the partial sum s_i is greater than k.

To convert this circuit to CNF, we first build defining equations for the partial sum bits $s_{i,j}$ and the overflow bits v_i. We then simplify these equations, noting that all overflow bits have to be zero. The resulting equations are then converted to CNF, further noting that one direction of the equations can be dropped due to polarity considerations (the basic technique was introduced by Tseitin [5], and later re-invented and extended by different authors, e.g. Jackson and Sheridan [6]). We thus arrive at a set of clauses, call it $\text{LT}_{\text{SEQ}}^{n,k}$, defining the cardinality constraint $\leq k \, (x_1, \ldots, x_n)$ based on the sequential counter (for $k > 0$ and $n > 1$):

$$
\begin{aligned}
&(\neg x_1 \vee s_{1,1}) \\
&(\neg s_{1,j}) \quad \text{for } 1 < j \leq k \\
&\left. \begin{aligned}
&(\neg x_i \vee s_{i,1}) \\
&(\neg s_{i-1,1} \vee s_{i,1}) \\
&\left. \begin{aligned}
&(\neg x_i \vee \neg s_{i-1,j-1} \vee s_{i,j}) \\
&(\neg s_{i-1,j} \vee s_{i,j})
\end{aligned} \right\} \text{for } 1 < j \leq k \\
&(\neg x_i \vee \neg s_{i-1,k})
\end{aligned} \right\} \text{for } 1 < i < n \\
&(\neg x_n \vee \neg s_{n-1,k})
\end{aligned}
$$

$\text{LT}_{\text{SEQ}}^{n,k}$ consists of $2nk + 2n - 3k + 1$ clauses and requires $(n-1) \cdot k$ auxiliary variables for the encoding. Due to its practical importance, we explicitly give the clause set $\text{LT}_{\text{SEQ}}^{n,1}$ (for the case $k = 1$, as a formula):

$$(\neg x_1 \vee s_{1,1}) \wedge (\neg x_n \vee \neg s_{n-1,1}) \wedge \bigwedge_{1 < i < n} \Big((\neg x_i \vee s_{i,1}) \wedge (\neg s_{i-1,1} \vee s_{i,1}) \wedge (\neg x_i \vee \neg s_{i-1,1}) \Big)$$

This clause set consists of $3n - 4$ clauses (and $n - 1$ additional encoding variables) and is thus—with regard to the number of clauses—superior to the naïve encoding for all $n > 5$. The following theorem summarizes our results.[1]

---

[1] Due to space limitations we do not give proofs here. They can be found, however, on the Web at http://www-sr.informatik.uni-tuebingen.de/~sinz/CardConstraints.

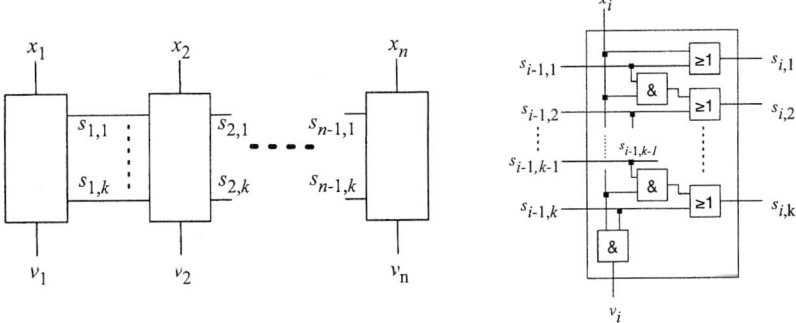

Fig. 1. Left: Circuit for computing $\leq k\,(x_1,\ldots,x_n)$. $s_{i,j}$ denotes the j-th digit of the i-th partial sum s_i in unary representation; variables v_i are overflow bits, indicating that the i-th partial sum is greater than k. **Right:** Sub-circuit for computing a partial sum s_i in unary representation.

Theorem 1. $\mathrm{LT}_{\mathrm{SEQ}}^{n,k}$ *is a clausal encoding of* $\leq k\,(x_1,\ldots,x_n)$ *requiring* $\mathcal{O}(n \cdot k)$ *clauses and* $\mathcal{O}(n \cdot k)$ *auxiliary variables.*

The encoding $\mathrm{LT}_{\mathrm{SEQ}}^{n,k}$ also fulfills the *efficiency condition* given by Bailleux and Boufkhad [3]. If more than k variables are set to true (which violates the cardinality constraint $\leq k\,(x_1,\ldots,x_n)$), this can be detected by unit propagation alone, i.e. by a linear time decision procedure. Moreover, for a partial assignment that sets k of the variables x_i to true, the value of all other x_i's can be derived by unit propagation.

3 Encoding Using a Parallel Counter

The second encoding we present is based on a parallel counter circuit designed by Muller and Preparata [7]. Their counter (shown in Fig. 2) recursively splits the input bits x_i into two halves, and counts the number of inputs that are set to true in each half. The results—represented as binary numbers—are then added using a standard m-bit binary adder. In order to obtain a circuit for cardinality constraints based on this counter, the output bits of the counter are handed on to a subsequent comparator which checks whether or not the counter value is less than k. (The comparator is not shown in Fig. 2.)

Parallel Counter Circuit. The parallel counter consists of $n - \lfloor \log n \rfloor - 1$ full-adders and at most $\lfloor \log n \rfloor$ half-adders, as was shown by Muller and Preparata ('log' denoting the *logarithmus dualis*). The encoding of each half-adder and full-adder is based on the well-known equations for these circuits. We finally obtain three clauses $\{(a \vee \neg b \vee s_{\mathrm{out}}), (\neg a \vee \neg b \vee c_{\mathrm{out}}), (\neg a \vee b \vee s_{\mathrm{out}})\}$ for each half-adder (computing $a \oplus b$) and seven clauses

$(a \vee b \vee \neg c \vee s_{\mathrm{out}})$ $(\neg a \vee b \vee c \vee s_{\mathrm{out}})$ $(\neg a \vee \neg b \vee c_{\mathrm{out}})$
$(a \vee \neg b \vee c \vee s_{\mathrm{out}})$ $(\neg a \vee \neg b \vee \neg c \vee s_{\mathrm{out}})$ $(\neg a \vee \neg c \vee c_{\mathrm{out}})$
  $(\neg b \vee \neg c \vee c_{\mathrm{out}})$

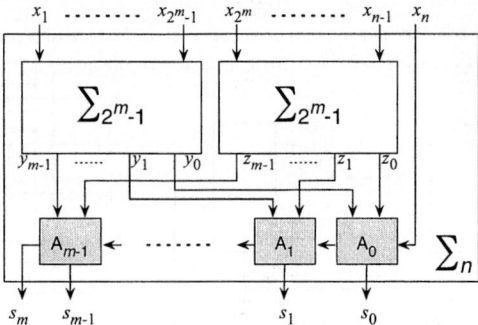

Fig. 2. Parallel counter according to Muller and Preparata [7] for recursively computing the binary number of inputs x_i that are set to true. The sub-circuits A_j are 1-bit-(full-)adders.

for each full-adder (computing $a \oplus b \oplus c$), summing up to at most $7n - 4\lfloor \log n \rfloor - 7$ clauses. Here again, only implications, but not full equivalences, have to be encoded. This is due to the polarity-based simplification technique already used above and the observation that only ones have to be propagated to the outputs, but not zeroes. Auxiliary variables are needed for the sum and carry bits of the half- and full-adders, we therefore need at most $2 \cdot (n-1)$ additional encoding variables.

Comparator Circuit. The comparator circuit has to make sure that the result of the binary counter $(s_m s_{m-1} \ldots s_0)$ is not greater than k. For building this binary comparator we assume that the constraint's limit k is given as an $(m+1)$-bit binary number, say $k = k_m \ldots k_0$. We can then easily give recursive equations to generate the clauses for the $(m+1)$-bit comparator:

$$L(k_0) = \begin{cases} \{\{\neg s_0\}\} & \text{if } k_0 = 0 \\ \emptyset & \text{if } k_0 = 1 \end{cases}$$

$$L(k_i \ldots k_0) = \begin{cases} \{\{\neg s_i\}\} \cup L(k_{i-1} \ldots k_0) & \text{if } k_i = 0 \\ \{\{\neg s_i\}\} \otimes L(k_{i-1} \ldots k_0) & \text{if } k_i = 1 \end{cases}$$

Here $\otimes$ denotes clause distribution, i.e. $A \otimes B = \{x \cup y \mid x \in A, y \in B\}$ for sets of clauses A, B. With this definition, $L(k_m \ldots k_0)$ is the clause set that ensures that the counter's output is less than k. It contains at most $m+1$ clauses. Denoting the combined clause set (parallel counter and comparator) by $\text{LT}^{n,k}_{\text{PAR}}$, we obtain the following theorem (using $m = \lfloor \log n \rfloor$).

Theorem 2. $\text{LT}^{n,k}_{\text{PAR}}$ *is a clausal encoding of* $\leq k (x_1, \ldots, x_n)$ *requiring at most* $7n - 3\lfloor \log n \rfloor - 6$ *clauses and* $2n - 2$ *auxiliary variables.*

4 Comparison, Lower Bound and Conclusion

Criteria for assessing the clausal encodings are (i) the number of clauses required; (ii) the number of additional propositional variables required; and (iii) the time needed to decide the encoding. In our comparison we have included the naïve encoding (mentioned in the introduction) and the encodings of Bailleux&Boufkhad and Warners.

Table 1. Comparison of different encodings for $\leq k\,(x_1,\ldots,x_n)$

Encoding	#clauses	#aux. vars	decided
Naïve	$\binom{n}{k+1}$	0	immediately
Sequential unary counter ($\text{LT}_{\text{SEQ}}^{n,k}$)	$\mathcal{O}(n \cdot k)$	$\mathcal{O}(n \cdot k)$	by unit prop.
Parallel binary counter ($\text{LT}_{\text{PAR}}^{n,k}$)	$7n - 3\lfloor \log n \rfloor - 6$	$2n - 2$	by search
Bailleux & Boufkhad [3]	$\mathcal{O}(n^2)$	$\mathcal{O}(n \cdot \log n)$	by unit prop.
Warners [4]	$8n$	$2n$	by search

With respect to the number of clauses required, our encoding $\text{LT}_{\text{PAR}}^{n,k}$ is the best, as can be seen from Table 1; however, it requires search to check whether the constraint is fulfilled or not. Among the encodings requiring no search is that of Bailleux&Boufkhad and our $\text{LT}_{\text{SEQ}}^{n,k}$ encoding. The latter performs better for small values of k, whereas the former is better for large bounds.

Considering optimality of clausal encodings for $\leq k\,(x_1,\ldots,x_n)$, we have shown elsewhere that for all $n \in \mathbb{N}$ and all k with $0 \leq k < n - 1$, each clausal (CNF) encoding of $\leq k\,(x_1,\ldots,x_n)$ requires at least n clauses. Such a proof touches the realm of Boolean function complexity [8]. It might be an interesting topic for future research to see in how far results from this field are transferrable to the area of minimal clausal encodings. We think that looking for improved lower bounds is worthwhile and still expect much room for improvement here. Moreover, an experimental evaluation of the different encodings should be of great practical value.

References

1. Küchlin, W., Sinz, C.: Proving consistency assertions for automotive product data management. J. Automated Reasoning **24** (2000) 145–163
2. Cabon, B., de Givry, S., Lobjois, L., Schiex, T., Warners, J.P.: Radio link frequency assignment. Constraints **4** (1999) 79–89
3. Bailleux, O., Boufkhad, Y.: Efficient CNF encoding of boolean cardinality constraints. In Rossi, F., ed.: 9th Intl. Conf. on Principles and Practice of Constraint Programming (CP 2003). Volume 2833 of Lecture Notes in Computer Science., Springer (2003) 108–122
4. Warners, J.P.: A linear-time transformation of linear inequalities into conjunctive normal form. Inf. Process. Lett. **68** (1998) 63–69
5. Tseitin, G.S.: On the complexity of derivation in propositional calculus. In Slisenko, A.O., ed.: Studies in Constructive Mathematics and Mathematical Logic. (1970) 115–125
6. Jackson, P., Sheridan, D.: The optimality of a fast CNF conversion and its use with SAT. Technical Report APES-82-2004, APES Research Group (2004) Available from http://www.dcs.st-and.ac.uk/apes/apesreports.html.
7. Muller, D.E., Preparata, F.P.: Bounds to complexities of networks for sorting and for switching. J. ACM **22** (1975) 195–201
8. Wegener, I.: The Complexity of Boolean Functions. Wiley-Teubner (1987)

Approximate Constrained Subgraph Matching

Stéphane Zampelli, Yves Deville, and Pierre Dupont

Université Catholique de Louvain,
Department of Computing Science and Engineering,
2, Place Sainte-Barbe, 1348 Louvain-la-Neuve, Belgium
{sz, yde, pdupont}@info.ucl.ac.be

1 Introduction

Our goal is to build a declarative framework for approximate graph matching where various constraints can be stated upon the pattern graph, enabling approximate constrained subgraph matching, extending models and constraints proposed by Rudolf [1] and Valiente et al. [2]. In the present work, we propose a CSP approach for approximate subgraph matching where the potential approximation is declaratively stated in the pattern graph as mandatory/optional nodes/edges. Forbidden edges, that is edges that may not be included in the matching, can be declared on the pattern graph. We also want to declare properties between pairs of nodes in the pattern graph, such as distance properties, that can be either stated by the user, or automatically inferred by the system. In the former case, such properties can define new approximate patterns. In the latter case, these redundant constraints enhance the pruning.

2 Approximate Subgraph Matching

2.1 Problem Definition

A **subgraph monomorphism** between a pattern graph $G_p = (N_p, E_p)$ and a target graph $G_t = (N_t, E_t)$ is an injective function $f : N_p \to N_t$ respecting $(u,v) \in E_p \Rightarrow (f(u), f(v)) \in E_t$. A constraint model to solve the exact subgraph matching problem has been proposed by several authors [2] [1]. This model focuses on monomorphism and will form our basic monomorphism constraints. The variables $\mathcal{X} = \{x_1, ..., x_n\}$ are the nodes of the pattern graph and their respective domain $D(x_i)$ is the set of target nodes. The assignment must respect two conditions: all variables have a different value and the structure of the pattern must be kept (monomorphism condition). In a CSP framework, the first condition is implemented with the classical *Alldiff*$(x_1, ..., x_n)$ constraint [3] [4]. The second condition is translated into a monomorphism constraint.

A useful extension of subgraph matching is approximate subgraph matching, where the pattern graph and the found subgraph in the target graph may differ with respect to their structure.

Optional Nodes. In our framework, the approximation is *declared* upon the pattern graph. Some *nodes* are declared *optional*, i.e. nodes that may not be in the matching. Specifying optional edges in a monomorphism problem is useless as it is equivalent to omitting the edge in the pattern. The status of the edges depends on the optional state of their endpoints. An edge having an optional node as one of its endpoints is optional. An optional edge is not considered in the matching if one of its endpoints is not part of the matching. Otherwise, the edge must also be a part of the matching.

Forbidden Edges. *Edges* may also be declared as *forbidden* between their two endpoints (u, v), meaning that if u and v are in the domain of f, then (u, v) must not exist in the target graph. A pattern graph with all its complementary edges declared as forbidden induces a subgraph isomorphism instead of a subgraph monomorphism.

A pattern graph with optional nodes and forbidden edges forms an *approximate pattern graph*.

Definition 1. *An **approximate pattern graph** is a tuple (N_p, O_p, E_p, F_p) where (N_p, E_p) is a graph, $O_p \subseteq N_P$ is the set of optional nodes and $F_p \subseteq N_p \times N_p$ is the set of forbidden edges, with $E_p \cap F_p = \emptyset$.*

The corresponding matching is called an *approximate subgraph matching*.

Definition 2. *An **approximate subgraph matching** between an approximate pattern graph $G_p = (N_p, O_p, E_p, F_p)$ and a target graph $G_t = (N_t, E_t)$ is a partial function $f : N_p \to N_t$ such that:*

1. $N_p \setminus O_p \subseteq dom(f)$
2. $\forall\, i, j \in dom(f) : i \neq j \Rightarrow f(i) \neq f(j)$
3. $\forall\, i, j \in dom(f) : (i, j) \in E_p \Rightarrow (f(i), f(j)) \in E_t$
4. $\forall\, i, j \in dom(f) : (i, j) \in F_p \Rightarrow (f(i), f(j)) \notin E_t$

The notation $dom(f)$ represents the domain of f. Elements of $dom(f)$ are called the selected nodes of the matching. This means that $dom(f)$ can be represented by a finite set variable. Its lower bound f_{lb} consists of all selected nodes, and its upper bound f_{glb} consists of selected nodes and nodes that could be selected.

3 Constraints for Approximate Subgraph Matching

Alldiff Constraint. The *Alldiff* constraint must be adapted to variables that may not be assigned. One solution is to create symbolic values $e_1, ..., e_n$ and put e_i in the initial domain of x_i. In a solution, $x_i = e_i$ if x_i is not assigned to any target node. Using these n symbolic values, a global *Alldiff* constraint can still be posted as in the exact case.

Morphism Constraint. The basic morphism condition forcing the matching to respect the pattern structure (see [2]) has been generalized to handle more general morphism conditions as well as optional nodes:

$$MC(x_1, ..., x_n, A, B) \equiv \bigwedge_{i,j} (i,j) \in A \wedge i, j \in dom(f) \Rightarrow (x_i, x_j) \in B$$

The former constraint states that a morphism relation between two pattern nodes x_i and x_j must be forced if and only if they are present in the domain of f. The MC constraint can be rewritten as:

$$\forall\, i \in N_p\ \forall\, a \in N_t : (\ |D(x_i) \cap V_t(a)| = 0$$
$$\wedge\ i \in dom(f)\ ) \Rightarrow a \notin D(x_j) \quad \forall\, j \in V_p(i)\,.$$

The proposed propagator keeps track of relations between all the target nodes and the domain $D(x_i)$ in a structure $S(i,a) = |D(x_i) \cap V_t(a)|$ representing the number of relations between a target node a and $D(x_i)$ (see [2]). The additional condition $i \in dom(f)$ states that only selected nodes should propagate under the morphism condition. The propagation of the morphism constraint of an optional i is computed but performed only when i is in the domain of f. As depicted in Figure 1, all selected nodes propagate in their neighborhood but optional nodes propagate only when they are selected.

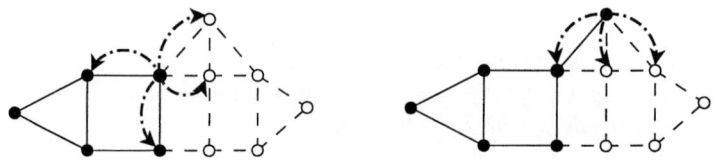

Fig. 1. Pruning method for the approximate morphism condition

Forbidden Edges Constraint. A constraint for the forbidden edges (condition 4 in the matching) can be obtained by parameterizing MC with $\overline{E}_t = \{(a,b) \notin E_t\}$:

$$MC(x_1, ..., x_n, F_p, \overline{E}_t) .$$

The constraints for the approximate subgraph isomorphism problem are then:

$$\text{alldiff}(x_1, ..., x_n) \wedge MC(x_1, ..., x_n, E_p, E_t) \wedge MC(x_1, ..., x_n, F_p, \overline{E}_t) .$$

However a single propagator $MCFA$ handling the last two constraints was implemented, using the relation $|D(x_i) \cap \overline{V}_t(a)| = 0 \Leftrightarrow |D(x_i) \cap V_t(a)| = |D(x_i)|$.

Local Alldiff Constraint. A local alldiff redundant LA^+ constraint checks if there are enough candidate target nodes for x_i neighborhood if x_i is assigned to a target node a. If it not the case, a can be pruned from $D(x_i)$. Note that the x_i neighborhood is restricted to the variables representing selected nodes, noted as $V_p^+(i)$. The LA constraint is expressed as:

$$LA^+(x_i, A, B) \equiv |\cup_{j \in V_p^+(i,A)} D(x_j) \cap V_t(x_i, B)| \geq |V_p^+(i, A)|$$

$$LA^+(x_1, ..., x_n, A, B) \equiv \bigwedge_i LA^+(x_i, A, B) .$$

Constraint LA^+ plays a pruning role. It can be implemented by maintaining the neighborhood variable, with an $O(d)$ time complexity, whenever the domain of x_i is pruned. The structure $R^+(i,a) = |\{ j \in V_p^+(i) \mid a \in D(x_j) \}|$ depends not only on the domain of the neighborhood of x_i but also on the neighborhood variable. Whenever the lower bound of $V_p^+(i)$ changes, the structure $R^+(i, \cdot)$ must be updated in $O(D)$, resulting in a $O(ND^2)$ amortized complexity. Moreover, $R^+(i,a)$ may be incremented from zero to one, resulting in an increment of $CT^+(i,a) = |\cup_{j \in V_p^+(i)} D(x_j) \cap V_t(a)|$, which is not monotone. Nevertheless, when condition $CT^+(i,a) < |V_p^+(i)|$ is fulfilled, a can be safely pruned from x_i, because if there is not enough candidates for a given subgroup of the neighborhood, node i cannot be mapped to node a.

Distance Constraints. Thanks to the parameters A and B, former MC and LA constraints can be used to create redundant constraints such as shortest path constraint MC_{dist}, generalizing other works on shortest path distance [5]. If $dist(a, b)$ denotes the shortest-path distance between node a and b, then the MC_{dist} constraint can be formulated as:

$$MC_{dist}(x_1, ..., x_n, k) \equiv \bigwedge_{i,j} dist(i,j) = k \Rightarrow dist(x_i, x_j) \leq k.$$

Suppose $E_p^k = \{(i,j) \mid dist(i,j) = k\}$ and $E_t^k = \{(a,b) \mid dist(a,b) \leq k\}$. Then MC_{dist} is equivalent to:

$$MC_{dist}(x_1, ..., x_n, k) \equiv MC(x_1, ..., x_n, E_p^k, E_t^k).$$

4 Experiments

Our CSP model for approximate subgraph matching has been implemented inside the CSP framework of Oz/Mozart (www.mozart-oz.org). Parametric propagators were implemented. Various transformations of E_p and E_t were automated to instantiate propagators for the forbidden edges and the distance constraints. We also included facility constraints to declare distance constraints between specific pattern nodes.

Two distinct sets of graphs were selected. The first set comes from [8]. The graphs are characterized by their probability η ($eta = 0.01$ is noted r001 in Table 2) that an edge is present between two distinct node n and n'. Those graphs were used to evaluate vflib algorithm performance [7]. In our experiments, pattern graph size is 20% of the target graph size, target graph size ranges from 20 to 200, and all solutions are searched. The second set contains graphs having different topological structures as explained in [2]. These graphs were generated using the Stanford GraphBase [9] and are the graphs tested in [2], consisting of 406 directed instances and 1225 undirected instances.

Experiments show that CSP approach for subgraph matching solves more problem within a time limit against a C++ specialized checking-based method called vflib described in [7]. The vflib algorithm has been reimplemented in Oz/Mozart. Table 1 shows the percentage of instances solved within a time limit of 5 minutes, for directed and undirected instances. Single specialized propagator $MCFA$ for forbidden edges is more efficient than the version with two propagators. Table 2 supports this asser-

Table 1. Comparison over GraphBase directed and undirected graphs

	All solutions for directed graphs 5 min.				All solutions for undirected graphs 5 min.			
	solved	unsol	total time	mean time	solved	unsol	total time	mean time
vflib C++	63,7%	36,3%	12.01 min.	0.02 min.	48,3%	51,7%	9.31 min.	0.007 min.
ozvflib	59,8%	40,2%	11.52 min.	0.02 min.	39,5%	60,5%	4.43 min.	0.003 min.
CSP	68,7%	31,3%	31.4 min.	0.07 min.	57,7%	42,3%	11.39 min.	0.009 min.

Table 2. Parameterized MC versus $MCFA$

	CSP parameterized MC 5 min.						CSP $MCFA$ 5 min.					
	r001		r005		r01		r001		r005		r01	
	solved	unsol	solved	unsol	solved	unsol	solved	unsol	solved	unsol	solved	unsol
100	100	0	100	0	96	4	100	0	100	0	99	1
200	79	21	62	38	10	90	83	17	80	20	34	66

tion. Preliminary results show that matching with 40% of optional nodes and few (≤ 5) additional distance constraints is tractable.

5 Perspectives

The proposed framework for declarative approximate subgraph matching open various research directions. Better heuristics could be developed when searching for an approximate matching. Our algorithm for exact matching could also be compared with other algorithms dedicated to the largest common subgraph problem. We also intend to apply our approximate matching algorithm for the analysis of biochemical networks. Extensive experiments should highlight the benefits of distance constraints. Finally, as the (approximate) matching is expressed as a combination of (parameterized) constraints, subgraph matching could be integrated in a constraint language handling graph variables, such as CP(Graph) [10] [11].

Acknowledgments

This research is supported by the Walloon Region, project BioMaze (WIST 315432). Thanks also to the EC/FP6 Evergrow project for their computing support.

References

1. Rudolf, M.: Utilizing constraint satisfaction techniques for efficient graph pattern matching. In Ehrig, H., Engels, G., Kreowski, H.J., Rozenberg, G., eds.: TAGT. Volume 1764 of Lecture Notes in Computer Science., Springer (1998) 238–251
2. Larrosa, J., Valiente, G.: Constraint satisfaction algorithms for graph pattern matching. Mathematical. Structures in Comp. Sci. **12**(4) (2002) 403–422
3. Regin, J.C.: A filtering algorithm for constraints of difference in CSPs. In: Proc. 12th Conf. American Assoc. Artificial Intelligence. Volume 1., Amer. Assoc. Artificial Intelligence (1994) 362–367
4. van Hoeve, W.J.: The alldifferent constraint: A survey. CoRR **cs.PL/0105015** (2001)
5. Sorlin, S., Solnon, C.: A global constraint for graph isomorphism problems. In Régin, J.C., Rueher, M., eds.: CPAIOR. Volume 3011 of Lecture Notes in Computer Science., Springer (2004) 287–302
6. Ullmann, J.R.: An algorithm for subgraph isomorphism. J. ACM **23**(1) (1976) 31–42
7. Cordella, L.P., Foggia, P., Sansone, C., Vento, M.: Performance evaluation of the vf graph matching algorithm. In: ICIAP, IEEE Computer Society (1999) 1172–1177
8. Foggia, P., Sansone, C., Vento, M.: A database of graphs for isomorphism and sub-graph isomorphism benchmarcking. CoRR **cs.PL/0105015** (2001)
9. Knuth, D.E.: The Stanford GraphBase. A Platform for Combinatorial Computing. acm, ny (1993)
10. Dooms, G.: Cp(graph): Introducing a graph computation domain in constraint programming (accepted paper). CP2005 (2005)
11. Deville, Y., Dooms, G., Zampelli, S., Dupont, P.: Cp(graph+map) for approximate graph matching. 1st International Workshop on Constraint Programming Beyond Finite Integer Domains, CP2005 (submitted paper) (2005)

Distributed Constraints for Large-Scale Scheduling Problems

Montserrat Abril, Miguel A. Salido, and Federico Barber

DSIC, Universidad Politécnica de Valencia,
Camino de Vera s/n, 46022, Valencia, Spain
{mabril, msalido, fbarber}@dsic.upv.es

Abstract. In this work, we present a distributed model for solving large-scale CSPs. Our technique carries out a partition over the constraint network by a graph partitioning software, such as each subproblem is as independent as possible and, it can be solved in a reasonable time.

The CSP is partitioned into a set of semi-independent subproblems and solved concurrently. The partition is carried out by means of a graph partitioning software called METIS [1]. In this way, the constraint partition is carried out in a preprocessing step in which an agent is committed to study the appropriate number of subproblems. The main idea of our multi-agent model is based on [2] but partitioning the problem in k subproblems as independent as possible, classifying the subproblem in the appropriate order and solving them concurrently. Once the constraints are divided into k blocks by a *preprocessing agent*, a group of *block agents* concurrently manages each block of constraints. Each *block agent* is in charge of solving its own subproblem by means of a search algorithm. This subproblem is composed by its CSP subject to the variable assignment generated by the previous *block agents*. Thus, *block agent* 1 works on its group of constraints. If *block agent* 1 finds a solution to its subproblem, then it sends the consistent partial state to *block agent* 2, and both they work concurrently to solve their specific subproblems; *block agent* 1 tries to find other solution and *block agent* 2 tries to solve its subproblem knowing that its *common variables* have been assigned by *block agent* 1. Thus, *block agent* j, with the variable assignments generated by the previous *block agents*, works concurrently with the previous *block agents*, and tries to find a more complete consistent state using a search algorithm. Finally, the last *block agent* k, working concurrently with *block agents* $1, 2, ...(k-1)$, tries to find a consistent state to find a problem solution.

Our distributed model is being applied to the railway scheduling problem which can be modelled by a CSP which is composed by thousand of variables and thousand of constraints.

References

1. METIS, *http://www-users.cs.umn.edu/ karypis/metis/index.html*.
2. M.A. Salido, A. Giret, and F. Barber, 'Distributing Constraints by Sampling in Non-Binary CSPs', *IJCAI Work. on Distributing Constraint Reasoning*, 79–87, (2003).

Solving Over-Constrained Problems with SAT

Josep Argelich[1] and Felip Manyà[2]

[1] Universitat de Lleida, Jaume II, 69, E-25001 Lleida, Spain
[2] IIIA-CSIC, Campus UAB, 08193 Bellaterra, Spain

We have defined a new formalism, based on Max-SAT, for encoding and solving over-constrained problems. Our formalism is an extension of Boolean CNF formulas in which we deal with blocks of Boolean clauses instead of dealing with individual clauses. Every block, formed by a set of clauses, is declared either as a hard block (i.e., must be satisfied by any solution) or as a soft block (i.e., can be violated by some solution). The idea behind the notion of block is that it encodes a problem constraint (for example, adjacent vertices have different colors); in general, it is not enough a single clause to encode a problem constraint. We call *soft CNF formulas* to this new kind of formulas.

We have implemented two branch and bound solvers, Soft-SAT-S and Soft-SAT-D, for our problem solving approach. Given a soft CNF formula ϕ, our solvers search a truth assignment that satisfies all the hard blocks of ϕ and the maximum number of soft blocks. Both solvers are equipped with lazy data structures and a good performing lower bound. The variable selection heuristic in Soft-SAT-S is static while in Soft-SAT-D is dynamic.

We conducted an experimental investigation for comparing our approach with weighted Max-SAT and Max-CSP. In the instances tested, we observed that Soft-SAT solvers are substantially superior to weighted Max-SAT solvers. On the one hand, our lower bound is of better quality because it takes into account the domain of the variables as in Max-CSP. On the other hand, the distinction between hard and soft blocks allows us to apply more powerful inference techniques; for example, unit clauses in hard blocks can be propagated. With respect to Max-CSP, we observed that Soft-SAT is very competitive as can be seen in the table below; it shows time in seconds. We compared Soft-SAT-S, Soft-SAT-D and the weighted CSP solvers PFC-MPRDAC[1] and Toolbar[2] on sets of 100 graph coloring instances generated with Culberson's generator. Experiments were performed on a 1.6 Ghz AMD64-Opteron with 1 Gbyte RAM.

$\langle n, k, c \rangle$	Soft-SAT-S		Soft-SAT-D		Toolbar		PFC-MPRDAC	
	mean	median	mean	median	mean	median	mean	median
$\langle 15, 15, 8 \rangle$	**56.35**	5.54	325.00	27.19	98.14	19.46	102.81	15.87
$\langle 15, 15, 10 \rangle$	**56.23**	0.03	266.83	0.03	146.65	0.05	105.81	0.13
$\langle 16, 14, 6 \rangle$	153.64	36.53	1068.80	243.54	**110.22**	**29.92**	186.40	64.43
$\langle 16, 14, 8 \rangle$	**88.92**	10.27	464.33	33.93	144.15	23.02	157.84	20.75
$\langle 16, 16, 6 \rangle$	162.34	101.10	1142.79	682.78	**110.50**	**63.65**	199.33	146.87
$\langle 16, 16, 8 \rangle$	**48.63**	12.68	229.35	37.77	105.31	28.12	114.27	29.99

---

[1] http://www.lsi.upc.es/~larrosa
[2] http://carlit.toulouse.inra.fr/cgi-bin/awki.cgi/ToolBarIntro (version July, 2005)

A Constraint Based Agent for TAC–SCM*

David A. Burke** and Kenneth N. Brown

Cork Constraint Computation Centre,
Department of Computer Science, University College Cork, Ireland
d.burke@4c.ucc.ie, k.brown@cs.ucc.ie

The annual international Trading Agent Competition Supply Chain Management (TAC–SCM) game is based around the manufacture and supply of PCs. There are multiple agents in the game, scheduling production, competing for orders from customers and components from suppliers. A key decision to be made each day in the game is what offers should be made to customers. Each day, the agents receive a set of request for quotes (RFQ) from customers, agents respond with offers, and then the customers select the lowest bid.

We have developed an agent to compete in the competition that combines constraint-based optimisation, reasoning with probabilities, and learning of market conditions in an attempt to determine what customer requests to bid on and what prices to bid. Our agent maintains prices that correspond to different probabilities of success in winning contracts, using an online learning approach. By keeping track of the ratio of offers accepted to those made, the prices can be updated iteratively to move closer to their target probability. This range of price/probability pairs is then used as input to a constraint model.

For each request, the model chooses whether or not to bid, and selects a price from the range. These decisions are restricted by capacity and supply constraints. A capacity constraint ensures that we will be able to schedule any new orders we receive with existing orders such that the factory capacity for each day in the current horizon is not exceeded. The agents production ability is also subject to component availability. By ordering components in advance, we know the current amount of components available, and we also know how much of each component will be arriving at each day. This allows us to add a constraint for availability of supplies.

An objective function is specified that maximises our expected profit, where the profit on a request is calculated by subtracting from the selling price the cost of components together with late delivery penalties.

The agent is implemented in Java, using OPL Studio for the constraint-based optimisation. The agent is competing in the competition, which is a real-time simulation of 220 trading days, each day lasting 15 real seconds. Initial results show that the combination of online learning, uncertainty reasoning and constraint-based optimisation is effective and robust, producing a competitive trading agent.

---

* This work is in collaboration with Armagan Tarim, Brahim Hnich and Onur Koyuncu.
** D. Burke is supported by Science Foundation Ireland under Grant No. 03/CE3/I405 as part of the Centre for Telecommunications Value-Chain-Driven Research (CTVR).

Solving the Car-Sequencing Problem as a Non-binary CSP

Mihaela Butaru and Zineb Habbas

Université de Metz, Laboratoire d'Informatique Théorique et Appliquée,
UFR M.I.M., Ile du Saulcy, F-57045 Metz Cedex 1, France
{butaru, zineb.habbas}@univ-metz.fr

Abstract. The car-sequencing problem arises from the manufacture of cars on an assembly line. A number of cars are to be made on a production line; they are not identical because different options are available as variants on the basic model. The different stations which install the various options have been designed to handle at most a certain percentage of the cars passing along the assembly line. Consequently, the cars must be arranged in a sequence so that these capacities are not exceeded. In this paper, the formulation of the car-sequencing problem is presented as a non-binary constraint satisfaction problem (CSP) with constraints of fixed arity 5. A search algorithm based on non-binary forward checking (nFC) is used to solve the problem. For the car-sequencing problem the variables should be assigned consecutively. The choice of value ordering heuristics having a dramatic effect on solution time for this problem, different value ordering heuristics were implemented. Since any possible solution is a permutation of a fixed set of values, a succeed-first strategy for value ordering only postpones the assignment of the difficult classes and a value ordering based on fail-first could be a better choice. These methods are compared on the instances reported in the CSPLib. The results obtained showed the superiority of a strategy of fail-first type against to a succeed-first strategy. In particular, the $MaxUtil$ and $MaxPQ$ heuristics allowed a better exploration of the space of solutions and solved all the instances of problems with 200 variables. It should be underlined the fact that these problems were solved in little time (6 seconds on average) and the longest time is 13 seconds for the instance 90_09, whereas for ILOG Solver the least powerful time exceeds 1 minute. This result can be justified by our encoding. Indeed, we encoded the maximum of constraints (the capacity of each option, the request for each class) inside an explicit 5-ary constraint with very high tightness (close to 0.95). $MaxUtil$ remains the best heuristic because it is surprisingly backtrack-free. Within the future work, the filtering method will be improved. A hybridization between the optimization methods is another way of interesting research. The use of parallelism also seems an interesting direction for solving this type of problem.

Keywords: constraint satisfaction, heuristics, problem solving, scheduling, n-ary CSPs, n-ary Forward Checking.

Dimensioning an Inbound Call Center Using Constraint Programming

Cyril Canon[1,2], Jean-Charles Billaut[2], and Jean-Louis Bouquard[2]

[1] Vitalicom, 643 avenue du grain d'or, 41350 Vineuil, France
ccanon@fr.snt.com
[2] Université François-Rabelais de Tours, Laboratoire d'Informatique,
64 avenue Jean Portalis, 37200 Tours, France
{jean.billaut, jean-louis.bouquard}@univ-tours.fr

One of the critical problems in the call center industries is the staffing problem, since they must face variable demands and because staff costs represent a major part of the costs of these industries. From a modeling point of view, a call center is generally modeled as a $M/M/N$ system, also called the Erlang-C model. In [Koole and Mandelbaum, 2001], the authors present a survey of the state-of-the-art about possible models of a call center.

In this paper, the problem of dimensioning a call center is modeled as a deterministic scheduling problem, where resources represent the employees and jobs correspond to the calls that are received. To each resource are associated tools that correspond to the skills of employees, and a weigth corresponding to the cost of employment. To each job are associated a release date, a processing time, a deadline and a required tool. The objective is to schedule jobs so as to minimize the weighted number of resources needed to perform the jobs.

For solving this problem, we propose exact methods based on Constraint Programming Models. Three different models are presented. The second one is an improvement of the first one, both in terms of constraints definitions and instanciation methods. The last one introduces redundant constraints to speed up the resolution process. An approximated algorithm is also proposed, based on a priority rule and an assignment rule. We also compare our models to a Mixed Integer Linear Program, solved by CPLEX.

Instances are randomly generated with around 45 resources and from 20 to 200 jobs. Feasible solutions are always obtained within two minutes by using these methods. CP models are solved using Eclipse 5.8_77 software with the time limit fixed to two minutes on a PC Pentium III, 1.4 GHz, 512 Mo. CP can solve the problem optimally with up to 80 jobs. For more than 100 jobs, the upper bound given by the heuristic algorithm is never improved within two minutes.

References

Koole and Mandelbaum, 2001. G. Koole and A. Mandelbaum (2002). "Queueing models of call centers: an introduction." Annals of Operations Research. **113**:41-59.

Methods to Learn Abstract Scheduling Models*

Tom Carchrae, J. Christopher Beck, and Eugene C. Freuder

Cork Constraint Computation Center, University College Cork, Ireland
t.carchrae@4c.ucc.ie

For practical reasons, most scheduling problems are an abstraction of the real problem being solved. For example, when you plan your day, you schedule the activities which are *critical*; that is you schedule the activities which are essential to the success of your day. So you may plan what time to leave the house to get to work, when to have meetings, how you share your vehicle with your spouse and so on. On the other hand, you probably do not consider the activities that are easy to arrange like brushing your teeth, going to the shops, making photocopies and other such tasks that can usually be accomplished whenever you have the time available. Scheduling all of these activities at once is often too complicated. Instead, a simpler schedule is produced by considering only the critical activities. However, if a schedule goes wrong, it is often because an activity turned out to be critical but was not scheduled. We typically learn which activities are critical by experience and create an abstract scheduling problem which includes all known critical activities. Instead of scheduling the non-critical activities we estimate their effects in the abstract scheduling problem.

We are interested in automating this abstraction process for scheduling problems. In our approach, given a set of activities A to be scheduled[1], we choose a subset of activities, *critical(A)*, and create a simplified scheduling model which approximates the other activities *non-critical(A)* instead of scheduling them. We then search this abstract model for a good, if not optimal solution. A solution is a partial order schedule for activities in *critical(A)*. This abstract solution is then extended to a solution the entire problem by inserting the remaining activities *non-critical(A)* into the schedule.

While the approach reduces complexity by solving the problem in two stages it does so at a price. There is a risk that the good abstract solution will not produce a good solution to the entire problem. We know that the optimal solution can be found if we schedule everything at once, e.g. *critical(A)=A*, however this has the worst complexity and is impractical in many cases as time does not allow a complete search. Instead, we wish to discover the minimal set of critical activities which still yields good or optimal full solutions in a reasonable amount of time. Our preliminary experiments have shown that by trying many different subsets of critical activities we are able to discover a good set *critical(A)*. Even with all the overhead of exploring different abstract models, we are able to produce better quality solutions than scheduling the entire problem at once. Although our experiments are still underway, we have found that many quick repetitions of this abstract process perform well when the size of *critical(A)* is relatively small.

---

* This work has received support from Science Foundation Ireland under Grant 00/PI.1/C075, Irish Research Council for Science, Engineering, and Technology under Grant SC/2003/82, and ILOG, SA.

[1] We schedule to minimize the makespan (the time required to complete the schedule).

Automated Search for Heuristic Functions[*]

Pavel Cejnar and Roman Barták

Charles University,
Faculty of Mathematics and Physics,
Malostranské náměstí 2/25, Praha 1, Czech Republic
pavel.cejnar@st.cuni.cz

The computer constructed local search heuristic function for a SAT problem can run and solve SAT faster than human designed heuristics.[1] The idea behind this was to start with some predefined primitives chosen in accordance with a human observation and to combine them using genetic programming. This leads to a question whether it is possible to construct an effective heuristic function solely by a computer, a function constructed from very elementary program building blocks not only from predefined higher-level primitives.

We propose an expressive procedural programming language for description of local search heuristic functions and we apply the genetic programming concept to them to get a metaheuristic algorithm with a capability to create potentially very fast local search heuristic.

To have genetic operations fast we keep the representation of individual heuristic functions in the population as simple as possible, e.g. as an ordered list of instructions in a programming language based on the RAM model. However, we've changed the RAM model language to increase the probability of creating a meaningful heuristic function when exchanging random parts of the code. These changes include adding variable types and type checking, using two operand instructions without an accumulator variable or using a full set of conditional relative jumps. To read SAT problem instances on the input we've added special datastructures like a variable for the number of clauses or a list of variables in clauses and we've added special instructions to access these datastructures.

A randomly generated population of heuristics is evolved by means of genetic programming. The Composition genetic operator cuts the code of parents in two random points, exchanges their central parts and fixes jump targets. With a given probability the Mutation genetic operator changes some instruction or its operands. The scoring function evaluates the heuristics on small random SAT instances first to eliminate very poor heuristics and the remaining ones are then scored using larger SAT instances.

We are currently working on an implementation of the proposed framework using a distributed computer system. Depending on the results, it might be possible to further extend the RAM model with specific constructs for description of heuristics but without decreasing its expressive power.

---

[*] Supported by the Czech Science Foundation under the contract 201/04/1102.
[1] Fukunaga, A. S.: Evolving local search heuristics for SAT using genetic programming. GECCO-2004, Part II, volume 3103 of LNCS, 483-494, (2004).

Constraint-Based Inference: A Bridge Between Constraint Processing and Probability Inference

Le Chang and Alan K. Mackworth

University of British Columbia, 2366 Main Mall, Vancouver, B.C. Canada V6T 1Z4
{lechang, mack}@cs.ubc.ca

Constraint-Based Inference (CBI) [1] is an umbrella term for various superficially different problems including probabilistic inference, decision-making under uncertainty, constraint satisfaction, propositional satisfiability, decoding problems, and possibility inference. In this project we explicitly use the semiring concept to generalize various CBI problems into a single formal representation framework with a broader coverage of the problem space, based on the synthesis of existing generalized frameworks from both constraint processing and probability inference communities. Based on our generalized CBI framework, extensive comparative studies of exact and approximate inference approaches are commenced. First, we extend generalized arc consistency to probability inference based on a weaker condition [2]. All the existing arc consistency enforcing algorithms can be generalized and migrated to handle other concrete CBI problems that satisfy this condition. Second, based on our CBI framework we apply junction tree algorithms in probability inferences to solve soft CSPs [1]. We show that the message-passing schemes of junction tree algorithms can be modified to achieve better computational efficiency if the semiring of a CBI problem has additional properties. Third, we study loopy message propagation in probability inference for general CBI problems. We claim in [1] that for CBI problems with a idempotent combination operator, the loopy message propagation is an exact inference approach. Our experimental results also show that the loopy message propagation yields high quality inference approximation for general CBI problems like Max CSPs. Finally, we discuss the possibilities of integrating stochastic approaches into our semiring-based CBI framework. We also discuss context-specific inference with backtracking as a promising inference approach for general CBI problems. In general, we are aiming at studying the most important common characteristics of various CBI problems, borrowing design ideas from other fields based on the analyses and comparison of different inference approaches, and significantly reducing the amount of implementation work targetted previously at the individual problems.

References

1. Chang, L.: Generalized constraint-based inference. Master's thesis, Dept. of Computer Science, Univ. of British Columbia (2005)
2. Chang, L., Mackworth, A.K.: A generalization of generalized arc consistency: From constraint satisfaction to constraint-based inference. In: 5th Workshop on Modelling and Solving Problems with Constraints, Edinburgh (2005) (8pp.).

Scheduling Social Tournaments

Iván Dotú, Álvaro del Val, and Pascal Van Hentenryck

Departamento De Ingeniería Informática,
Universidad Autónoma de Madrid

1 Introduction

Tournament scheduling problems arise in many practical applications and their highly symmetric and combinatorial nature makes them particularly challenging for search algorithms. This research generalizes the modeling and local search approach proposed in [1] in order to schedule some challenging, real-life, social tournaments. The approach also schedules other challenging, social tournaments. Results can be found in the web version of this abstract.

2 The Debating Tournament Problem

The debating tournament problem (DTT) can be seen as a generalization of the social golfer.

The DTP can be modeled like the SGP by relaxing the cardinality constraint, i.e., replacing the value "1" by k in the equations that define the constraints, the violations, and the neighborhood, in order to state not that two golfers cannot play in the same group more than "1" time, but that they cannot play more than k times in the same group, where $k = 2, 3, \ldots$

3 The Judge Assignment Problem

The judge assignment problem, another real-life problem (given to us by W. Harvey) can be viewed as superimposing a judge assignment on top of a debating tournament instance.

The modeling is also similar to the SGP. It receives, as input, a solution to the debating tournament problem. In particular, $x[w, g, p]$ will denote the player scheduled in position p of group g in week w. The decision variables $y[w, g, p]$ associates a decision variable with every week, group, and position, where the set P_r of positions for the judges is included in the set of positions of the debating tournament (i.e., $P_r \subset P$). The goal is to find a schedule σ, where the value $\sigma(y[w, g, p])$ denotes the judge scheduled in position $\langle w, g, p \rangle$.

References

1. Dotú, I., and Van Hentenryck, P. 2004. Scheduling Social Golfers Locally. In *CP-AI-OR'05*

Domain Reduction for the Circuit Constraint

Latife Genc Kaya and John Hooker

Carnegie Mellon University, Pittsburgh, PA 15213, USA

We present an incomplete filtering algorithm for the circuit constraint. The filter removes redundant values by eliminating non-Hamiltonian edges from the associated graph. We prove a necessary condition for an edge to be Hamiltonian, which provides the basis for eliminating edges of a smaller graph defined on a separator of the original graph.

The circuit constraint, $circuit(y_1, \ldots, y_n)$, where $y_j \in \{1, \ldots, n\}$, is true if and only if for each $j \in \{1, \ldots, n\}$, y_j is the successor of j in some permutation of $1 \ldots n$ and $y_j \in D_j$, where D_j is the domain of variable j.

On a graph of vertices $1, \ldots, n$, the circuit constraint can be thought as defining a directed Hamiltonian cycle. Nodes of the graph represent the variables. A directed edge (i, j) exists if and only if j is in the domain of variable i. Moreover, elimination of an edge (i, j) from the graph means elimination of the value j from the domain of variable i. With this representation, the problem of domain reduction for the circuit constraint reduces to identifying and eliminating non-Hamiltonian edges on a digraph.

In this paper, we present a recursive algorithm that eliminates non-Hamiltonian edges from the graph. A much smaller but denser multi-graph is constructed from a vertex separator S of the original graph by adding certain labelled edges to the subgraph induced by the separator. A directed edge (v, w) with *label* C is added if C is a connected component separated by S and (v, c_i) and (c_j, w) are edges of G for some pair of vertices c_i, c_j in C. We prove that edges that appear in no Hamiltonian cycle containing at least one edge of each component label in the constructed graph are non-Hamiltonian in the original graph. The condition that the constructed graph contains such a Hamiltonian cycle is viewed as a constraint. Global cardinality constraint with vertex degree constraints is a relaxation of this constraint. Then by applying a filtering algorithm for the global cardinality constraint together with in and out-vertex degree constraints, non-Hamiltonian edges are identified and eliminated from the graph.

References

1. Hooker, J.: Logic-Based Methods for Optimization: Combining Optimization and Constraint Satisfaction. *John Wiley Sons* (2000).
2. Regin, J.-C.: Generalized Arc Consistency for Global Cardinality Constraint. *AAAI*, (1996).
3. Shufelt J., Berliner, H.: Generating Hamiltonian Circuits Without Backtracking from Errors. *Theoretical Computer Science*, **132(1-2)** (1994) 347-375

Using Constraint Programming for Solving Distance CSP with Uncertainty

Carlos Grandon and Bertrand Neveu

COPRIN project I3S-CNRS/INRIA/CERMICS,
INRIA, 2004 Route des Lucioles BP 93, 06902 Sophia-Antipolis, France
{cgrandon, ncvcu}@sophia.inria.fr

Many problems in chemistry, robotics or molecular biology can be expressed as a Distance CSP (Constraint Satisfaction Problem). Sometimes, the parameters of this kind of problems are determined in an experimental way, and therefore they have an uncertainty degree. A classical approach for solving this class of problems is to solve the CSP without considering the uncertainties, and to obtain a set of solutions without knowing the real solution sub-spaces. A better approach is to apply a branch and prune algorithm to generate a set of disjoint boxes that include all the solution sub-spaces, but without information about independent solution sub-spaces or the different types of boxes.

We propose a new methodology built from the combination of both previous approaches and a *feasibility checker* for tackling uncertainties in a CSP formed by distance constraints. A distance constraint c between two points P_i and P_j in a n-dimensional space can be expressed as $c(P_i, P_j) : \sum_{k=1}^{n}(x_{ik} - x_{jk})^2 = d_{ij}^2$, where x_{ik} is the k-th coordinate of the point P_i, and d_{ij} is the distance value between them. In this class of problems, all fixed values are called *parameters*. When a CSP has parameters with interval values, it is called *CSP with uncertainties*.

In our methodoloty, the main idea consists in solving the CSP without taking into account the uncertainties, by replacing each parameter with interval value by the middle point of the interval, and applying a SSA (solution separation algorithm) to calculate a set of sub-domains. The SSA calculates the equation of the median plane between each pair of solutions. Then, for each solution found, we solve a new CSP built from the original CSP (with uncertainties) and a set of plane inequations. The sub-domain defined by the conjunction of all inequations is equivalent to the sub-space of a Voronoi diagram for the solution. A branch and prune algorithm is then applied for each CSP built. We combine this algorithm with a *feasibility checker* in order to determine when a box is totally included in the solution sub-space. The best results of this methodology are obtained when the following two hypotheses are verified:

- The problem has a finite number of solutions ρ, without taking into account the uncertainties.
- The problem has only connected sets of solutions around each initial solution, when we consider the uncertainties.

The first condition allows the separation of the initial domain into a set of sub-domains containing only one solution found, while the second one, assures the existence of only one solution sub-space in each sub-domain.

Improved Algorithm for Finding (a,b)-Super Solutions

Emmanuel Hebrard and Toby Walsh

NICTA and UNSW, Sydney, Australia
{ehebrard, tw}@cse.unsw.edu.au

Abstract. Super solutions are a mechanism to provide robustness to constraint programs. We introduce a new algorithm that exploits the similarity between a super solution and its repairs in order to do inference during search. It improves on previous methods since it is more space efficient and also faster in practice.

The super model/solution framework [2,3] permits us to formalize a notion of fault tolerance. An (a, b)-super solution is a solution in which, if a small number of variables lose their values, we are guaranteed to be able to repair the solution with only a few changes. We introduce a new algorithm for finding super solutions that solves a *master problem* and a number of *sub-problems* generated during search. This approach is simple and can be implemented using most of the constraint toolkits currently available. We then show how we can do inference while solving a subproblem to reduce the master problem.

The main observation that we make in order to improve the search for a super solution is that there must be at least $n - (a + b)$ variables assigned equally in the master problem and any sub-problem. For a given sub-problem, if the set, or a subset, of variables that need to be assigned the same as in the master problem is known, then we can prune both the master and the subproblem, thus greatly reducing the search space. We introduce two methods to discover these variables. The first method uses classical filtering methods (such as GAC or SAC [1]). The second idea is that, intuitively, a repair must be *close* to the break in the constraint graph. For instance, in a $(1, 1)$-super solution, any "repaired" variable must share a constraint with the "broken" variable. We use the corresponding notion of neighborhood to deduce equalities between master and sub-problems.

References

1. Romuald Debruyne and Christian Bessière. Some practicable filtering techniques for the constraint satisfaction problem. In *IJCAI'97*, pages 412–417, 1997.
2. E. Hebrard, B. Hnich, and T. Walsh. Robust solutions for constraint satisfaction and optimization. In *Proceedings ECAI'04*, 2004.
3. A. Parkes M. Ginsberg and A. Roy. Supermodels and robustness. In *Proceedings AAAI'98*, pages 334–339, 1998.

Local Consistency in Weighted CSPs and Inference in Max-SAT

Federico Heras and Javier Larrosa

Universitat Politecnica de Catalunya,
Barcelona, Spain
{fheras, larrosa}@lsi.upc.edu

Weighted constraint satisfaction problems (WCSP) and Max-SAT are optimization versions of the CSP framework and SAT repectively. They have many practical applications. Most current state-of-the-art complete solvers for WCSP and Max-SAT problems can be described as a basic depth-first branch and bound search that computes a lower bound during the search that can be used together with the cost of the best solution found in order to prune entire search subtrees. Recently, a collection of local consistency properties such as NC*, AC*, DAC*, FDAC* and EDAC* have been proposed for WCSP in order to simplify the problem. In Max-SAT we have recently proposed inference rules to detect unfeasible assignments. Resolution in Max-SAT is an extension of classical resolution for the SAT problem:

$$(x \vee A, u), (\bar{x} \vee B, w) \Rightarrow \begin{cases} (A \vee B, m) \\ (x \vee A, u \ominus m) \\ (\bar{x} \vee B, w \ominus m) \\ (x \vee A \vee \bar{B}, m) \\ (\bar{x} \vee \bar{A} \vee B, m) \end{cases}$$

where A and B are arbitrary disjunctions of literals and $m = \min\{u, w\}$. We use the notation $[P, \ldots, Q] \Rightarrow [R, \ldots, S]$, where $P, Q, \ldots$ are weighted clauses. It means that if there are some weighted clauses matching with $[P, \ldots, Q]$ (left side), they can be replaced by $[R, \ldots, S]$ (right side). We define the neighborhod resolution rule (NRES) as RES restricted to the $A = B$ case. We also present the novel *weighted modus ponens* rule (MP) as:

$$(x \vee y, u), (\bar{x}, w) \Rightarrow \begin{cases} (y, m) \\ (x \vee y, u \ominus m) \\ (\bar{x}, w \ominus m) \\ (\bar{x} \vee \bar{y}, m) \end{cases}$$

where $m = \min\{u, w\}$. It is important to realize that this rule can be obtained by replacing $B = false$ and $y = A$ in the generic resolution rule (RES). Finally, we are studying the relation between the inference rules and the local consistency properties. For example, given an extension of the DPLL algorihtm for Max-SAT if it applies $NRES_0$ rule at each node of the search tree then it enforces the NC* property. If DPLL applies both $NRES_0$ and $NRES_1$ at each node, it enforces AC*. $NRES_k$ denote NRES restricted to $|A| = k$ with $k >= 0$. We present the equivalence of the other local consistency properties for WCSP w.r.t. the new inference rules for Max-SAT.

Modeling Constraint Programs with Software Technology Standards*

Matthias Hoche and Stefan Jähnichen

Fraunhofer FIRST, Kekuléstr.7, 12489 Berlin, Germany
mathoc@first.fhg.de

In [1] Puget argued for a "model-and-run" paradigm for constraint programming. He proposed to develop a standard file format to express CP models. There is no such unified modeling standard available to the CP community, so constraint programs cannot be developed independently from the used CP library and they are hard to maintain.

This research targets platform-independent object-oriented modeling of constraint programs. It will be shown how CP models can be expressed using software technology standards, and further how these standards will enable automated transformation and execution of such models. The work reconsiders results published in [2]. There, we have formally shown how the Unified Modeling Language (UML) and the Object Constraint Language (OCL) can be used to create well formed models of constraint problems called Constraint Network Schemata (CNS). Resting upon this, the author now proposes to see Model Driven Architecture (MDA) as a chance for further research advances.

Although this paper mainly presents ideas for the adaption of MDA techniques, some practical results where achieved already in the domain of surgery planning for hospitals. A first prototypic implementation exists which can solve XML-representations of CNS-models with our finite domain constraint solver firstcs. Therefore, the CNS-model and the input data of a constraint problem are processed from separate XML files to create a Constraint Satisfactory Problem (CSP) in a data-driven way. The CSP is then solved by firstcs and the solution is returned as an XML-file, too.

Such processing simplifies the integration into complex business workflows and helps to increase the acceptance of CP in business applications.

References

1. Jean-Francois Puget. Constraint Programming Next Challenge: Simplicity of Use. In Marc Wallace, editor, *Principles and Practice of Constraint Programming - CP 2004, 10th International Conference, Proceedings,* number 3258, pages 5–8, Toronto, Canada, September/October 2004. Springer-Verlag.
2. Armin Wolf, Henry Müller, and Matthias Hoche. Towards an Object-Oriented Modeling of Constraint Problems. In *W(C)LP,* pages 41–52, 2005.

---

* This work is funded by the EU (EFRE) and the state Berlin, grant no. 10023515.

Solution Equivalent Subquadrangle Reformulations of Constraint Satisfaction Problems

Chris Houghton and David Cohen

Department of Computer Science,
Royal Holloway, University of London, UK

Constraint Satisfaction Problem instances (CSPs) are a natural way to model real life problems such as image processing, scheduling and natural language understanding. In this paper we are concerned with the modeling of problems as CSPs and how this can affect the performance of different solution algorithms. In particular we are interested in modeling in the language of subquadrangles.

A Quadrangle is essentially an 'anything-goes' constraint for some Cartesian product of domains. A Subquadrangle [1] is a constraint all of whose projections to proper subsets of the scope are quadrangles.

Subquadrangles are a very 'natural' way in which to represent constraints. This is because they do not place any restrictions on proper subsets of their scope, thus reducing the number of required constraint checks. This leads us to believe that a subquadrangle aware solver could be particularly efficient.

However, in this paper we shall consider another intriguing use of subquadrangle modeling. Subquadrangles delay the failure of constraint checks until you try and assign a value to the last variable in their scope. This makes them ideal for testing constraint solvers as they are 'backtrack nasty'.

In this paper we present two methods by which we might decompose a given instance into a solution equivalent instance whose constraints are all subquadrangles.

Our first method converts individual constraints into sets of three subquadrangle constraints. This can then be done for each constraint in a CSP in order to convert the entire problem instance. We are able to demonstrate that this new formulation has a high degree of local consistency related to the arity of the original constraints which induce 'backtrack nasty' behavior in search algorithms. Unfortunately, this with this method one of the subquadrangles is always binary.

We also investigate a second method which converts intersecting pairs of constraints. In this method all of the subquadrangles generated are similar in arity to the original constraints.

References

1. R. Rodošek. *Generation and Comparison of Constraint-Based Heuristics Using the Structure of Constraints.* PhD thesis, Imperial College, University of London, July 1997.

Mechanism Design for Preference Aggregation over Coalitions

Eric Hsu and Sheila McIlraith

University of Toronto
{eihsu, sheila}@cs.toronto.edu

Mechanisms are decision functions that map the individual preference orderings of separate parties into a single ordering over the group outcome. Unfortunately, classical impossibility results, readily extended to preferences, show that no mechanism can be "fair" for all scenarios [1]. Further, any positive results typically assume that agents do not form coalitions or other such partnerships.

While coalitions can complicate both theoretical analysis and underlying paradigms of rationality, in a particular setting they can serve to constrain a problem to the point of circumventing traditional impossibility results. *Automated mechanism design (AMD)* [2] attempts to overcome such results by designing specific mechanisms for specific situations on the spot. No perfect mechanism exists that works in every context, but whenever there is information about the players, a fair mechanism can exist for that specific setting.

Our goal is mechanism design for preference aggregation over coalitions. While AMD research has focused on auction and continuous domains, we seek to model preferences in logic and operate over discrete domains. To do so we use a recently-proposed logic for extensive games, based in turn on Alternating Time (*ATL*) temporal logic [3,4]. While such efforts seek to express desirable properties, and *verify* whether a provided mechanism satisfies them, our approach aspires to automatically *generate* satisfying mechanisms. Using a standard CSP solver, we have implemented a preliminary system that does so for an extremely simplified variant of these languages. The general approach is to establish variables representing a blank template game tree, and then instantiate them with the names of players, subject to constraints representing the specified properties. The space of possible trees is combinatorially large, and even tighter control of variable ordering and propagation will be necessary to meet this challenge.

References

1. Pini, M.S., Rossi, F., Venable, K.B., Walsh, T.: Aggregating partially ordered preferences: Impossibility and possibility results. Proc. of 10th Conference on Theoretical Aspects of Rationality and Knowledge (TARK X), Singapore (2005)
2. Conitzer, V.: Complexity of mechanism design. Proc. of 18th Conference on Uncertainty in Artificial Intelligence (UAI '02), Edmonton, Canada (2002) 103–110
3. van Otterloo, S., van der Hoek, W., Wooldridge, M.: Preferences in game logics. Proc. of 3rd International Conference on Autonomous Agents and Multiagent Systems (AAMAS '04), New York, U.S.A. (2004)
4. Alur, R., Henzinger, T.A., Kupferman, O.: Alternating-time temporal logic. Journal of the ACM (2002) 672–713

LP as a Global Search Heuristic Across Different Constrainedness Regions*

Lucian Leahu and Carla Gomes

Dpt. of Computer Science, Cornell University, Ithaca, NY 14853, USA
{lleahu, gomes}@cs.cornell.edu

Recent years have witnessed the emergence of a new area involving hybrid solvers integrating CP- and OR-based methods. The LP relaxation provides bounds on overall solution quality and can be used for pruning in a branch-and-bound approach, especially in domains where we have a combination of linear constraints, well-suited for linear programming (LP) formulations, and discrete constraints, suited for constraint satisfaction problem (CSP) formulations. However, in a *purely combinatorial* setting, so far it has been surprisingly difficult to integrate LP-based and CSP-based techniques.

We study the behavior of heuristics based on the LP relaxation with respect to the underlying constraindness of the problem. Our study focuses on the Latin square (or quasigroup) completion problem as a prototype for highly combinatorial problems. This problem is NP-hard and it exhibits an easy-hard-easy pattern in complexity, measured in the runtime (backtracks) to find a completion [1]. In our previous work [2] we report an interesting phase transition phenomenon in the *solution integrality* of the LP relaxation for this problem.

We find that simple techniques based on the LP relaxation of the problem provide satisfactory guidance for under- and over-constrained instances. In the critically constrained region, the performance of such simple techniques degrades, due to the inherit hardness of the problem. In this setting, we examine a technique that recomputes the LP relaxation every time a variable is set. This leads to a significant increase in performance, suggesting that carefully designed "one step at a time" LP-based heuristics could provide suitable guidance even for the hardest instances. We examine the quality of the guidance provided by the LP relaxation as a function of the structure of the problem, i.e., we characterize the performance of LP heuristics across different constraindness regions in the search space.

References

1. Achlioptas, D., Gomes, C., Kautz, H., Selman, B.: Generating Satisfiable Instances. In: Proceedings of the Seventeenth National Conference on Artificial Intelligence (AAAI-00), New Providence, RI, AAAI Press (2000)
2. Leahu, L., Gomes, C.: Quality of lp-based approximations for highly combinatorial problems. In: International Conference on Principles and Practice of Constraint Programming (CP). (2004)

---

* Research supported by the Intelligent Information Systems Institute, Cornell University (AFOSR grant F49620-01-1-0076).

Consistency for Partially Defined Constraints

Andreï Legtchenko and Arnaud Lallouet

Université d'Orléans — LIFO — BP6759, F-45067 Orléans, France
legtchen|lallouet@lifo.univ-orleans.fr

Partially defined or *Open Constraints* [2] can be used to model the incomplete knowledge of a concept or a relation. In an Open Constraint, some tuples are known to be true, some other are known to be false and some are just *unknown*. We propose to complete its definition by using Machine Learning techniques. The idea of the technique we use for learning comes directly from the classical model of solvers computing a chaotic iteration of reduction operators [1]. We begin by learning the constraint. But instead of learning it by a classifier which takes as input all its variables and answers "yes" if the tuple belongs to the constraint and "no" otherwise, we choose to *learn the support function* $n_{<X=a>}$ of the constraint for each value of its variables' domains. A tuple is part of the constraint if accepted by all support functions for each of its values and rejected as soon as it gets rejected by one. We propose to use as representation for learning an Artificial Neural Network (ANN) with an intermediate hidden layer trained by the classical backpropagation algorithm [4].

When put in a CSP, a constraint should contribute to the domain reduction. We propose to use the learned classifiers also for solving. In order to do this, we take the *natural* extension to intervals [3] of the learned classifiers. Let $N_{<X=a>}$ be the natural interval extension of $n_{<X=a>}$. Then, by using as input the current domain of the variables, we can obtain a range for its output. Since we put a 0.5 threshold after the output neuron, we can reject the value a for X if the maximum of the output range is less than 0.5, which means that all tuples are rejected in the current domain intervals. Otherwise, the value remains in the domain. Our experiments show that the learned consistency is weaker than more classical consistencies but still reduces notably the search space.

We show that our technique not only has good learning performances but also yields a very efficient solver for the learned constraint.

References

1. K.R. Apt. The essence of constraint propagation. *Theoretical Computer Science*, 221(1-2):179–210, 1999.
2. Boi Faltings and Santiago Macho-Gonzalez. Open constraint satisfaction. In Pascal van Hentenryck, editor, *International Conference on Principles and Practice of Constraint Programming*. Springer, 2002.
3. Ramon E. Moore. *Interval Analysis*. Prentice Hall, 1966.
4. D.E. Rumelhart, G.E. Hinton, and R.J. Williams. Learning internal representations by error propagation. *Parallel Distributed Processins*, vol 1:318–362, 1986.

Subnet Generation Problem: A New Network Routing Problem*

Cheuk Fun Bede Leung, Barry Richards, and Olli Kamarainen

IC-Parc, Imperial College London, London SW7 2AZ, UK
cheuk.leung@icparc.ic.ac.uk

We introduce a new type of network routing problem, the subnet generation problem (SGP) which is a special case of the traffic placement problem (TPP). In the TPP, given (1) a network which consists of routers and links, and (2) a set of point-to-point traffic demands to be placed including finding feasible routes, the objective is to minimize the sum of costs of the unplaced demands subject to the Quality-of-Service routing constraints.

The SGP is a TPP with an extra set of constraints that restricts the combinations of demands to be placed. In our SGP, each router has a fixed amount of *information-gain* that is to be transmitted to every other router in the *subnet*. A subnet is defined as any subset of the routers in the network. This means that every router in the subnet will have exactly the same total information-gain. The objective is to find a subnet that maximizes the total information-gain: there must be a demand with a valid path between every pair of routers in the subnet. The reason for creating demands among the routers arises from the fact that every node in a selected group of routers is required to be a client and a server. The figure below shows an example of a subnet and a path solution.

We describe a structure to split the problem into a master problem (select a set of demands to be placed) and a subproblem (compute a feasible set of paths for the demands selected by the master problem). To solve the SGP, we first apply a state-of-art hybrid tree search algorithm[1], designed to solve the TPP. Then, we explore how the subnet structure in the SGP could be used to solve the problem more efficiently. In particular, we focus on balancing search between the master problem and the subproblem to maximize the solution quality within a fixed computational time.

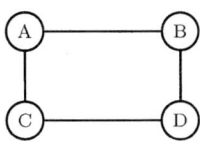

Given network

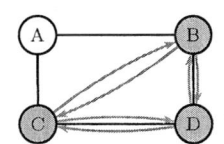
A subnet and created demands

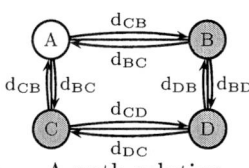
A path solution

---

* I would like to thank Quanshi Xia and Christophe Guettier for their participation.
[1] J. Lever. A Local Search/Constraint Propagation Hybrid for a Network Routing Problem. *International Journal of Artificial Intelligence Tools*, 14(1):43-60, 2005.

Partial Redundant Modeling

Tiziana Ligorio and Susan L. Epstein

The Graduate Center of the City University of New York, USA
tligorio@gc.cuny.edu, susan.epstein@hunter.cuny.edu

Redundant modeling combines different models of the same problem using channeling constraints [1]. Channeling constraints allow different formulations of a problem to interact, propagating the constraints between different formulations. This can result in a significant improvement in performance. Originally, work on redundant modeling assumed that redundant models must fully characterize the problem [1]. Later, Smith argued that only the primal model need fully characterize the problem, while the dual model need only have all the dual variables and channeling constraints between the two models (a *minimal combined model*) [2]. This paper proposes *partial redundant modeling*, an extension of the minimal combined model that encourages more than two models, omits some dual variables and omits all the dual constraints. Partial redundant models originate in problems with a *categorical structure*, where the variables may be subdivided into categories. Often these categories can be identified as groups of variables that fall under n-ary constraints that partition the variables into disjoint sets. Real world problems, such as scheduling and rostering, may also have categorical structure. *Logic puzzles* are a class of problems with a simplified version of categorical structure. A logic puzzle consists of a set of *objects*, a set of *categories* (same-size disjoint subsets of those objects) that must take on different values, and a set of *semantic relations*, which specify the relationships that hold between the categories. In a logic puzzle, each category can be viewed as a subset of CSP variables under an all-diff constraint. Different CSP models can be obtained by selecting the objects in a different category as the domain values, taking all other objects in the other categories to be the variables. We propose to maintain multiple partial redundant models of problems with categorical structure, adding channeling constraints between the n-ary constraints in the redundant partial models. These channeling constraints make certain that value assignments under an n-ary constraint in one partial model are reflected under that n-ary constraint in some other partial model. We call these *categorical channeling constraints*.

References

1. Cheng, B. M. W.,Choi, K. M. F.,Lee, J. H. M.,Wu, J. C. K.: Increasing Constraint Propagation by Redundant Modeling: an Experience Report. In: Constraints Vol. 4. (1999) 167-192.
2. Smith, B. M.: Modeling a Permutation Problem. In: ECAI'2000 Workshop on Modeling and Solving Problems with Constraints, Berlin, Humboldt University (2000).

AND/OR Branch-and-Bound for Solving Mixed Integer Linear Programming Problems

Radu Marinescu and Rina Dechter

University of California, Irvine, CA 92697-3425
{radum, dechter}@ics.uci.edu

Graphical models are a powerful representation framework for automated reasoning tasks. These models use graphs to capture conditional independencies between variables, allowing for a concise representation of the knowledge. Optimization tasks defined within this framework are typically tackled with either *search* or *inference*. Search methods are time exponential in the number of variables and can operate in linear space. Inference algorithms are time and space exponential in the *tree width* of the problem. This potentially higher space complexity makes these methods impractical.

The AND/OR search space for graphical models is a newly introduced framework for search that is sensitive to the independencies in the model, often resulting in exponentially reduced complexities. The AND/OR search is based on a pseudo-tree which expresses independencies between variables, resulting in a search tree exponential in the depth of the pseudo-tree, rather than the number of variables.

The AND/OR Branch-and-Bound algorithm (AOBB) is a new search method that explores the AND/OR search tree for solving optimization tasks in graphical models. In this paper we extend the algorithm for solving combinatorial optimization problems from the class of Mixed Integer Linear Programs (MILP). A MILP instance is a linear program where some of the decision variables are constrained to have only integer values at the optimal solution (we consider only binary integer variables). AOBB can be readily adapted for solving this class of optimization problems by arranging the integer variables into a start pseudo-tree and, then, traversing the corresponding AND/OR search tree. This rather straightforward extension can be further improved. We introduce a *dynamic* version of AOBB which uses a recursive decomposition of the problem, based on hypergraph separators. The hypergraph of a MILP instance has a vertex for each constraint and a hyperedge, which corresponds to a variable, connects all the constraints that contain that variable. A separator translates into a subset of variables that, when instantiated, decompose the problem into independent components. The algorithm traverses an AND/OR search tree based on a pseudo-tree which is recomputed dynamically at each search tree node using the hypergraph separator of the respective subproblem. The search process is guided in both cases by lower-bounding heuristic estimates computed at each node by solving the linear relaxation (i.e. ignoring the integrality restrictions) of the subproblem rooted at that node. Preliminary evaluation of the structural properties of several hard problem instances from the MIPLIB2003 library showed promise that the new AND/OR search schemes can improve significantly over the traditional OR tree search approach. Finally, we mention that more advanced strategies developed in the recent years for integer programming, such as the *branch-and-cut* scheme, can be readily adapted to exploit the AND/OR structural paradigm.

Weak Symmetries in Problem Formulations

Roland Martin and Karsten Weihe

Darmstadt University of Technology,
Algorithmics Group,
64283 Darmstadt, Germany
martin@algo.informatik.tu-darmstadt.de

Unlike symmetries weak symmetries act only on a subset of the variables and/or respect only a subset of the constraints of the problem. Therefore, weak symmetries preserve the state of feasibility only with respect to the subset of variables they act on and only for the constraints they respect. This means if two solutions are symmetric under the weak symmetry they yield different full solutions with potentially different feasibility states.

But weak symmetries cannot be simply broken, since this would result in a loss of solutions that cannot be derived afterwards. Therefore we propose a modelling technique that uses additional variables (*SymVars*) and constraints that enable us to express symmetric states of a solution. The idea is to decompose a problem P in a way such that the variables and constraints respected by the weak symmetry is present in one sub-problem P_1 and the rest in the sub-problem P_2. This way the weak symmetry acts as a common symmetry on P_1. The additional variables and constraints form a new sub-problem P_{sym} that is incorporated and the solving order is to find a solution to P_1, consider a symmetric equivalent by P_{sym} and pass the solution to P_2 which finds a solution for the whole problem. By doing so the symmetry on P_1 can be broken.

Although additional variables are introduced which extends the search space symmetry breaking enables us to reduce the search effort. Whether symmetry breaking does compensate the extension of the search space by the additional variables depends on the problem and the search heuristic. But as soon as a solution for P_1 is found the whole equivalence class of solutions can be considered via P_{sym}.

Weak symmetries occur in various problems. They can be found in real-life problems (especially optimisation problems where the weak symmetry does not respect the objective value) as well as in in classic problem formulations like the magic square problem [1] or extensions of problems like the diagonal latin square [2] or the weighted magic square problem [3].

References

1. Roland Martin, Karsten Weihe *Solving the Magic Square Problem by Using Weak Symmetries* Joint ERCIM/CoLogNet International Workshop on Constraint Solving and Constraint Logic Programming, CSCLP 2005, Uppsala, 2005
2. Warwick Harvey *Symmetric Relaxation Techniques for Constraint Programming* SymNet Workshop on Almost-Symmetry in Search, New Lanark, 2005
3. Roland Martin *Approaches to Symmetry Breaking for Weak Symmetries* SymNet Workshop on Almost-Symmetry in Search, New Lanark, 2005

Towards the Systematic Generation of Channelling Constraints

B. Martínez-Hernández and A.M. Frisch

Artificial Intelligence Group, Dept. of Computer Science, Univ. of York, York, UK

The automatic modelling tool CONJURE [1] generates CSP models from a problem specified in the specification language ESSENCE[1]. Variables in ESSENCE may have domains currently unsupported by solvers. Also, the elements of the domains may be arbitrarily compound, for example, sets of sets, sets of sets of sets. CONJURE uses a set of *refinement rules* to compositionally transform the variables (and constraints) into representations that can be implemented in current solvers. CONJURE can produce multiple alternative (redundant) representations of the same variable that may appear simultaneously in the same model. Currently, CONJURE does not generate the *channelling constraints* [2] that are needed to maintain the consistency between these simultaneous alternatives.

There are several unsolved issues related to channeling constraints and automatic modelling, such as, how to identify the cases where a channelled model performs better than a non-channelled one, and how to implement the channelling constraints efficiently. In this paper however, we focus the automated generation of channelling constraints under the CONJURE framework.

Our work has identified and proved correct, an algorithm to systematically generate the channelling constraints needed in a CONJURE-generated model. We briefly describe this algorithm as follows. Let P be a specification refined by CONJURE into the CSP model P'. Let X be a variable in P that has two representations X_1 and X_2 in P'. Let Y be a new variable with exactly the same domain of X. We can then *re-refine* $X = Y$ (channelling constraint between X and Y) *forcing* the X to refine into X_1 and the Y into X_2. Hence, we produce a correct channelling constraint between X_1 and X_2 providing CONJURE generates correct refinements.

References

1. Frisch, A.M., Jefferson, C., Martínez-Hernández, B., Miguel, I.: The rules of constraint modelling. In: Nineteenth Int. Joint Conf. on Artificial Intelligence. (2005)
2. Cheng, B.M.W., Choi, K.M.F., Lee, J.H.M., Wu, J.C.K.: Increasing constraint propagation by redundant modeling: An experience report. Constraints 4 (1999) 167–192

---

[1] http://www.cs.york.ac.uk/aig/constraints/AutoModel/

AND/OR Search Spaces and the Semantic Width of Constraint Networks

Robert Mateescu and Rina Dechter

School of Information and Computer Science,
University of California, Irvine, CA 92697-3425
{dechter, mateescu}@ics.uci.edu

The primary contribution of this paper consists in using the *AND/OR search* paradigm [1,2] to define the new concept of *semantic width* of a constraint network. The well known parameter *tree-width* is graph based, and cannot capture context sensitive information. This often results in a very loose upper bound on the actual complexity of the problem. A typical example is the compact result of a compilation schemes such as *ordered binary decision diagram* (OBDD), in spite of a large tree-width (and path-width). The semantic width is based on the notion of equivalent constraint networks. The idea is to capture the intrinsic hardness of a problem by the smallest width equivalent network.

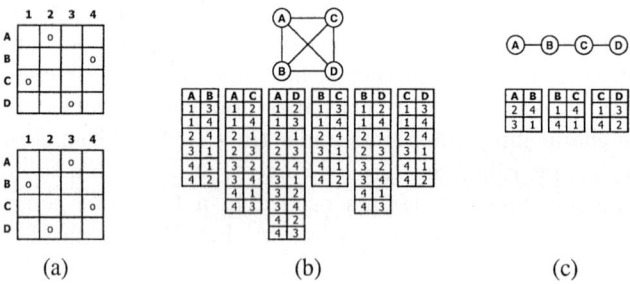

Fig. 1. The 4-queen problem

Example 1. Figure 1a shows the two solutions of the 4-queen problem. The problem is expressed by a complete graph of tree-width 3, given in Figure 1b. Figure 1c shows an equivalent problem, which has tree-width 1. The semantic-width of the 4-queen is 1.

This paper specializes the AND/OR formalism to constraint networks and elaborates the properties of AND/OR search graphs. The semantic width characterizes the size of the *minimal AND/OR graph* and it is clearly hard to compute. Nevertheless, the semantic width can explain why sometimes the minimal AND/OR graph or tree are much smaller than the upper bounds exponential in tree-width or path-width.

References

1. R. Dechter and R. Mateescu. Mixtures of deterministic-probabilistic networks and their AND/OR search space. In *UAI'04*, 2004.
2. R. Dechter and R. Mateescu. The impact of AND/OR search spaces on constraint satisfaction and counting. In *CP'04*, 2004.

Statistical Modelling of CSP Solving Algorithms Performance[*]

Carles Mateu, Ramon Béjar, and Cèsar Fernández

Dpt. d'Informàtica, Universitat de Lleida, Jaume II, 69, E-25001 Lleida, Spain
{ramon, cesar, carlesm}@eup.udl.es

Our goal is to characterize and to be able to predict the search cost, of some of the most important CSP algorithms and heuristics when solving CSP problems by obtaining a statistical model of the algorithm runtime based on inexpensively computed parameters obtained from the CSP problem specification and the associated constraints and nogoods graphs.

Such a model will give us three important items concerning the studied CSP problems. First, the model provides a tool to predict the search cost of a given instance, allowing a portfolio of solvers to decide for the best algorithm before to proceed. Second, the models will give an insight about which are the main features that characterize the complexity of a RBCSP. Finally, another potential benefit of the model is pointing out which features are the algorithms most sensible to, thus helping to guess potential areas of improvement.

This work follows a close related methodology used for SAT problems. In a first step, we define a broad benchmark scenario that covers a full range of cases of random binary CSP (RBSCP) problems. We proceed by solving a large set of instances of each problem, using 3 different algorithms and 3 different variable ordering heuristics for each one. This first analysis gives already a initial insight about what type of algorithms performs better according to the size of the problem. Then we define a set of features to be analyzed in conjunction with the time performance, some directly related to the problem specification parameters and some others related to the structure of the constraints and nogoods graphs. Such a combination of time performance and feature measurements is then analyzed in order to obtain a statistical model based on regression analysis.

So far we have been able to create a model that has a reasonable quality for predicting runtime behaviour of the algorithms analysed. The model created for RBCSP problems includes, as the most significant parameters, the position of the problem respect the phase transition point, the nogood graph minimum degree and an upper bound of the constraint graph tree width (or some related parameter).

Further research is being carried to increase the quality of the model, adding more relevant parameters, especially graph related ones, so the model can be used with a higher degree of confidence. We are also extending this work to model other kinds of more structured problems beyond RBCSP, namely QWH.

---

[*] Research partially supported by projects TIC2003-00950 and TIN2004-07933-C03-03 funded by the *Ministerio de Educación y Ciencia*.

Probabilistic Arc Consistency*

Deepak Mehta and M.R.C. van Dongen

Boole Centre for Research in Informatics/Cork Constraint Computation Centre

The two most popular algorithms for solving Constraint Satisfaction Problems are Forward Checking (FC) [1] and Maintaining Arc Consistency (MAC) [2]. MAC maintains full arc consistency while FC maintains a limited form of arc consistency during search. There is no single champion algorithm: MAC is more efficient on sparse problems which are tightly constrained but FC has an increasing advantage as problems become dense and constraints loose. Ideally a good search algorithm should find the right balance—for any problem—between visiting fewer nodes in the search tree and reducing the work that is required to establish local consistency. In order to do so, we maintain *probabilistic arc consistency* during search. The idea is to assume that a support exists and skip the process of seeking a support if the probability of having some support for a value is at least equal to some, carefully chosen, stipulated threshold.

Arc consistency involves revisions of domains, which require support checks to remove unsupported values. In many revisions, *some* or *all* values find some support. If we can predict the existence of a support then a considerable amount of work can be saved. In order to do so, we propose the notions of a *Probabilistic Support Condition* (PSC) and *Probabilistic Revision Condition* (PRC). If PSC holds then the probability of having some support for a value is at least equal to the threshold and the process of seeking a support is skipped. If PRC holds then for each value the probability of having some support is at least equal to the threshold and the corresponding revision is skipped.

For hard dense problems constraint are generally loose, and on average each value has several supports, in which case the probability of having some support remains high for a while with respect to the number of values removed. This enables PSC and PRC to save checks. For hard sparse problems constraints are generally tight, and on average each value has only a few supports, in which case the probability of having some support drops rapidly with respect to the number of values removed. This forces both PSC and PRC to fail quickly, which in turn forces the algorithm to behave like MAC. Unlike MAC and FC where the strength of constraint propagation is static, maintaining probabilistic arc consistency allows to adjust the strength of constraint propagation dynamically during search and performs well on both dense and sparse problems.

References

1. R.M. Haralick and G.L. Elliott. Increasing tree search efficiency for constraint satisfaction problems. *Artificial Intelligence*, 14(3):263–313, 1980.
2. D. Sabin and E.C. Freuder. Contradicting conventional wisdom in constraint satisfaction. In A.G. Cohn, editor, *Proceedings of the Eleventh European Conference on Artificial Intelligence (ECAI'94)*, pages 125–129. John Wiley and Sons, 1994.

---

* This work has received some support from Science Foundation Ireland under Grant No. 00/PI.1/C075.

GOOSE – A Generic Object-Oriented Search Environment*

Henry Müller and Stefan Jähnichen

Fraunhofer FIRST, Kekuléstr. 7, D-12489 Berlin, Germany
henry.mueller@first.fraunhofer.de

The constraint programming community keeps on creating numerous search algorithms, which differ to a greater or lesser extent. It is an as desirable as difficult task to implement a variety of search algorithms in a unifying framework.

This design proposal states the object-oriented environment GOOSE, which supports development of generic search algorithms. It is inspired by Prosser´s categorisation of backtracking search algorithms [2]. GOOSE is abstract enough to house dissimilar search approaches and separates abstract generic logic from domain details. The research focuses implementation needs and explicitly goes for an efficient object-oriented design, which enforces code reuse and flexibility by adequate use of class inheritance and object composition [1]. GOOSE can be implemented in any modern object-oriented language, and as a proof of concept it is realised within our object-oriented solver firstcs. Up to now the concept handles variants of backtracking search and deals with topics like constraint-based scheduling, static and dynamic variable ordering, justifications and backjumping, optimisation, randomisation and restarting techniques. Multidimensional search structures and control flow organisation are of particular interest. Creating new complete search algorithms is easy: A generic frame algorithm is completed by implementing some domain-specific methods. Plug-and-play like assembly of compatible components easily realises algorithmic variations. The variations are chiefly achieved by using generic decorator or strategy objects [1], which can be exchanged during runtime. First experimental results (job-shop scheduling, 3-SAT, n-queens) indicate a performance loss between 0 % (strong pruning) and 10 % (weak pruning) compared to monolithic equivalents. Future work will cover the introduction of non-systematic generic search algorithms and dynamic adaptive search configuration, e.g. switching dynamically from chronological tree movement to backjumping or from global to local search etc.

Implementing search algorithms according to GOOSE will make them easier to understand and compare, the code will be flexible and reusable.

References

1. E. Gamma, R. Helm, R. Johnson, and J. Vissides. *Design Patterns: Elements of Reusable Object-Oriented Software.* Addison-Wesley, 1994.
2. Patrick Prosser. Hybrid Algorithms For The Constraint Satisfaction Problem. *Computational Intelligence*, 9(3):268, 1993.

---

* This work is funded by the EU (EFRE) and the state Berlin, grant no. 10023515.

Randomization for Multi-agent Constraint Optimization

Quang Huy Nguyen and Boi V. Faltings

Artificial Intelligence Laboratory (LIA),
Swiss Federal Institute of Technology Lausanne (EPFL), Switzerland
{quanghuy.nguyen, boi.faltings}@epfl.ch

In a constraint optimization problem for multiple agents, the agents have conflicting preferences in the final solution and the goal is to find an optimal assignment that maximizes total utilities of all agents. Two major challenges when solving constraint optimization problems for multiple agents are the complexity of finding optimal solution and the incentive compatibility for participating agents. First, computing the optimal solution for large optimization problems are computationally infeasible and it can only be solved approximately by local search algorithms. Second, ensuring honest elicitation among self-interested agents is computationally expensive. It has been shown that the only known mechanism that guarantees truthfulness among agents requires computing optimal solutions, and sub-optimal solutions for such a mechanism will break the incentive compatibility ([2]).

The long-term goal of our research is to solve these two challenges by using randomization in local search algorithms to find near-optimal solutions while ensuring incentive compatibility for bounded-rational agents. Our work is based on the observation that in real-world settings, the potential for manipulation is limited by uncertainty and risk. This uncertainty makes it difficult for a manipulator to predict the consequences of his manipulation and thus makes attempts at manipulating it uninteresting.

In this paper we discuss a general randomization technique, called *random subset optimization*, for escaping from local minima in local search algorithms. In each local choice step, the local search procedure will randomly choose a part of the optimization function, and optimize for this part only. It turns out that this results in a more focussed optimization strategy and is shown to be especially effective in some hard optimization problems. We show that the uncertainty of our randomization algorithms can make the agents' manipulation hard, thus prevent bounded rational agents from manipulating such algorithms. We propose a new hard-to-manipulate local search algorithm using our randomization scheme ([1]). Experiments on randomly generated problems and benchmarks from DIMACS show that our technique is very promising: it outperforms existing local search algorithms both in speed of convergence and solution quality on both decomposable and non-decomposable problems.

References

1. B. Faltings and Q.-H. Nguyen. Multi-agent coordination using local search. In *Proceedings of IJCAI 05*, 2005.
2. Noam Nisan and Amir Ronen. Computationally feasible VCG mechanisms. In *Proceedings of the 2nd ACM conference on Electronic commerce*, pages 242–252. ACM Press, 2000.

Uncertainty in Soft Constraint Problems

Maria Silvia Pini and Francesca Rossi

University of Padova, Italy
mpini@math.unipd.it

Preferences and uncertainty occur in many real-life problems. We are concerned with the coexistence of preference and uncertainty in the same problem. In particular, we consider uncertainty, defined by the theory of possibility [2], that is one non-probabilistic way of dealing with uncertainty, that comes from lack of data or imprecise knowledge.

We propose a method to integrate fuzzy preferences and uncertainty [3], which follows the approach in [2] and allows one to handle uncertainty within a fuzzy optimization engine, which at the same time observing separately the preference and the robustness of complete instantiations. To order the complete instantiations, we define three semantics, which correspond to the attitude to the risk.

We generalize this method in [4] to deal also with other classes of preferences such as probabilistic or weighted constraints [1], and also probabilistic uncertainty. In particular, probabilistic constraints are very useful for modelling real-life scenarios where fuzzy constraints are not the ideal setting, because combining preferences multiplying them is better than taking their minimum value. Weighted constraints are useful to model problems where preferences are penalties (or costs) to be added, and where the best preferences are the smallest ones.

We plan to develop a solver that can handle problems with several classes of soft constraints, together with uncertainty expressed via possibility or probability distributions. The solver will be able to generate solution orderings according the our semantics as well as others that we will define by following different optimistic or pessimistic approaches.

We also plan to develop techniques for reasoning with uncertainty in problems with both positive and negative preferences.

Acknowledgements. This is a joint work with K. Brent Venable (University of Padova, Italy).

References

1. S. Bistarelli, U. Montanari and F. Rossi. Semiring-based Constraint Solving and Optimization. Journal of the ACM, Vol.44, n.2, March 1997.
2. D. Dubois, H. Fargier, H. Prade. Possibility theory in constraint satisfaction problems: handling priority, preference and uncertainty. Applied Intelligence, 6,1996.
3. M.S. Pini, F. Rossi, B. Venable. Possibility theory for reasoning about uncertain soft constraints. Proc. ECSQARU 2005, Springer LNAI 3571 , 2005.
4. M.S. Pini, F. Rossi, B. Venable. Possibilistic and probabilistic uncertainty in soft constraints problems. Proc. of the IJCAI 2005 Multidisciplinary Workshop on Advances in Preference Handling, Edinburgh, July 2005.

Speeding Up Constrained Path Solvers with a Reachability Propagator

Luis Quesada, Peter Van Roy, and Yves Deville

Université catholique de Louvain,
Place Sainte Barbe, 2, B-1348 Louvain-la-Neuve, Belgium
{luque, pvr, yde}@info.ucl.ac.be

We present a propagator which we call *Reachability* that implements a generalized reachability constraint on a directed graph g. Given a source node *source* in g, we can identify three parts in the *Reachability* constraint: (1) the relation between each node of g and the set of nodes that it reaches, (2) the association of each pair of nodes $\langle source, i \rangle$ with its set of cut nodes, and (3) the association of each pair of nodes $\langle source, i \rangle$ with its set of bridges.

Formally, this constraint can be defined as follows:

$$Reachability(g, source, rn, cn, be) \equiv \forall_{i \in N} . \begin{array}{l} rn(i) = Reach(g, i) \wedge \\ cn(i) = CutNodes(g, source, i) \wedge \\ be(i) = Bridges(g, source, i) \end{array} \tag{1}$$

where g is a graph whose set of nodes is a subset of N, *source* is a node of g, $rn(i)$ is the set of nodes that i reaches in g (defined by $Reach(g,i)$), $cn(i)$ is the set of nodes appearing in all paths from source to i in g (defined by $CutNodes(g, source, i)$), and $be(i)$ is the set of edges appearing in all paths from *source* to i in g (defined by $Bridges(g, source, i)$) [1].

Reachability has been implemented using a message passing approach on top of the multi-paradigm programming language Oz [Moz04]. The pruning rules of *Reachability* have been defined using the notion of graph variable [DDD05]. In [QVD05a, QVD05b], we discuss the implementation of *Reachability* in detail and its suitability for finding simple paths with mandatory nodes in directed graphs [2].

References

[DDD05]   G. Dooms, Y. Deville, and P. Dupont. CP(Graph):introducing a graph computation domain in constraint programming. In *CP2005 Proceedings*, 2005.

[Moz04]   Mozart Consortium. The Mozart Programming System, version 1.3.0, 2004. Available at *http://www.mozart-oz.org/*.

[QVD05a]   Luis Quesada, Peter Van Roy, and Yves Deville. Reachability: a constrained path propagator implemented as a multi-agent system. In *CLEI2005 Proceedings*, 2005.

[QVD05b]   Luis Quesada, Peter Van Roy, and Yves Deville. The reachability propagator. Research Report INFO-2005-07, Université catholique de Louvain, Louvain-la-Neuve, Belgium, 2005. Available at *http://www.info.ucl.ac.be/~luque/ SPMN/paper.pdf*.

---

[1] Any node in N is a cut node between i and j if there is no path going from i to j. Similarly, any edge in $N \times N$ is a bridge between i and j if there is no path going from i to j.

[2] The problem of finding a simple path containing a set of mandatory nodes is not trivially reducible to Hamiltonian path.

From Linear Relaxations to Global Constraint Propagation*

Claude-Guy Quimper and Alejandro López-Ortiz

School of Computer Science, University of Waterloo, Canada
{cquimper, alopez-o}@uwaterloo.ca

Recently, many algorithms have been designed to propagate global constraints. Unfortunately, some global constraints, such as the AT-MOST-1 constraint and the EXTENDED-GCC are NP-Hard to propagate. Often, these constraints can easily be written as integer linear programs. Using linear relaxations and other techniques developed by the operation research community, we want to efficiently propagate such constraints.

We model constraints as integer programs that we relax into linear programs. For each value v in a variable domain $\mathrm{dom}(x)$, we create a binary variable x_v. The assignment $x_v = 1$ indicates that $x = v$ while $x_v = 0$ indicates that $x \neq v$. The binary variables are subject to the following linear program.

$$\left. \begin{array}{r} Ax \leq b \\ 0 \leq x_i \leq 1 \end{array} \right\} \mathbf{P}$$

We find a solution to the relaxation using the interior point method. This method always converges to the interior of the solution polytope. Based on this observation, we conclude that if a variable x_i subject to $l \leq x_i \leq u$ is assigned to one of its boundary value l or u, the variable is assigned to this value in any solution. Therefore, if the interior point method assigns variable x_v to 0, we conclude that v does not have a support in $\mathrm{dom}(x)$.

We studied the consistency enforced by our propagator. We proved that if U is a totally unimodular matrix and that **P** has the following form, then GAC is enforced on the equations $Ux \leq b_1$.

$$\left. \begin{array}{r} \begin{bmatrix} U & 0 \\ B & C \end{bmatrix} \begin{bmatrix} x \\ y \end{bmatrix} \leq \begin{bmatrix} b_1 \\ b_2 \end{bmatrix} \\ 0 \leq x_i, y_j \leq 1 \end{array} \right\} \mathbf{P}$$

Some constraints like the CARDINALITY-MATRIX constraint while written in the form $Ax \leq b$ have many totally unimodular sub-matrices of A. For each such sub-matrix, GAC is enforced on the corresponding variables. The resulting consistency is stronger than consistencies enforced by existing propagators.

References

1. O. Guler and Y. Ye *Convergence behavior of interior-point algorithms* Mathematical Programming 60, pages 215–228, 1993.

---

* This is joint work with Emmanuel Hebrard and Toby Walsh.

Encoding HTN Planning as a Dynamic CSP[*]

Pavel Surynek and Roman Barták

Charles University in Prague, Faculty of Mathematics and Physics,
Malostranské náměstí 2/25, 118 00 Praha 1, Czech Republic
pavel.surynek@seznam.cz, roman.bartak@mff.cuni.cz

Constraint satisfaction methodology has proven to be a successful technique for solving variety of combinatorial and optimization problems. Despite this fact, it was exploited very little in the planning domain. In particular hierarchical task network planning (HTN) [2] seems to be suitable for use of constraint programming. The formulation of HTN planning problem involves a lot of structural information which can be used to prune the search space. Encoding of this structural information by means of constraint programming would provide an effective way for such pruning during the search for solution.

This abstract describes a work currently in progress of which the goal is to develop a framework and techniques for solving HTN planning problems using constraint programming methodology. The first step to achieve the goal is to propose a suitable encoding of HTN planning problems into constraints. We encode HTN planning problem for a limited number of steps as a dynamic constraint satisfaction problem [2]. Our encoding translates each construct used in the formulation of HTN problem into a set of variables and constraints. The resulting constraint model is built hierarchically with global tasks (e.g. transport package from location A to location B) on the top of the hierarchy and with primitive actions (e.g. load package into the truck at location A) at the bottom. The dynamicity of our approach consists in construction of this hierarchical model during the search for solution. As the search proceeds and earlier decisions of the search algorithm become fixed, the model is extended with the parts modeling later decisions depending on the previous ones.

Since our encoding relies on the intense combination of constraints via logical conjunctions, it is necessary to use a method for constraints combination that preserves stronger propagation. Such method is for example constructive disjunction [3].

References

1. R. Dechter, A. Dechter: Belief Maintenance in Dynamic Constraint Networks. In Proceedings the 7th National Conference on Artificial Intelligence (AAAI-88), 37-42, 1988.
2. K. Erol, J. Hendler, D. S. Nau: UMCP: A Sound and Complete Procedure for Hierarchical Task Network Planning. In Proceedings of the 2nd International Conference on AI Planning Systems (AIPS-94), 249-254, 1994.
3. J. Würtz, T. Müller: Constructive Disjunction Revised. In Proceedings of the 20th Annual German Conference on Artificial Intelligence (KI-96), 377-386, 1996.

---

[*] This work is supported by the Czech Science Foundation under the contract 201/04/1102.

Specialised Constraints for Stable Matching Problems*

Chris Unsworth and Patrick Prosser

Department of Computing Science, University of Glasgow, Scotland
chrisu/pat@dcs.gla.ac.uk

1 Summary

The stable marriage problem (SM) and the Hospital / Residents problem (HR) are both stable matching problems. They consist of two sets of objects that need to be matched to each other; in SM men to women, and in HR residents to hospitals. Each set of objects expresses a ranked preference for the objects in the other set, in the form of a preference list. The problem is then to find a matching of one set to the other such that the matching is stable. A matching is stable iff it contains no blocking pairs. A blocking pair in a matching M consists of two objects x and y one from each set(x = man and y = woman for SM or x = hospital and y = resident in HR), such that x and y are not matched in M and both x and y would rather be matched to each other than to there assignment in M.

Algorithms have been published for both of these problems and optimal constraint models have been published for the stable marriage problem. So the main question would be why the need for specialised constraint for these problems?

The SM algorithm and the optimal constraint encodings all have a time complexity of $O(n^2)$, but in practice it can take over a minute for the constraint models to find a solution to a problem of size 45 while the SM algorithm can find a solution in less than two hundredths of a second. There have not been any optimal HR constraint models published, but I assume the same performance gap would exist. The advantage of the constraint solutions are their versatility. Many harder variants of the stable matching problems can be solved by adding simple side constraints to the existing models, this is not possible with the matching algorithms. So the motivation behind a specialised constraint is to try and combine the efficiency of the algorithm with the versatility of the constraint models.

In the full version of this paper I discuss issues concerning the creation of specialised constraints to solve these problems. I then go on to present some empirical results that suggest that specialised constraints significantly out perform other constraint encodings, in both time and space requirements.

---

* The author is supported by EPSRC. Software support was given by an ILOG SA's academic grant.

Bounds-Consistent Local Search*

Stefania Verachi and Steven Prestwich

Cork Constraint Computation Centre,
Department of Computer Science,
University College, Cork, Ireland
{s.verachi, s.prestwich}@cs.ucc.ie

With this work we present a hybrid approach to solve large-scale constraint satisfaction and optimization problems. The method proposed can be termed Bounds-Consistent Local Search. It is inspired by the success of a randomized algorithm for the Boolean Satisfiability (SAT) problem called UnitWalk. We have adapted the algorithm UnitWalk to integer programs. The search space is pruned through propagation; particularly we use Bounds-Consistency (BC). In this way we combine Local Search which performs well on large combinatorial optimization problems, and consistency propagation methods used to solve constraint problems. Unit-Walk is a simple algorithm that performs well on different instances of hard SAT problems. It has given best results on industrial problems in SAT competition. It also has been proved it is Probabilistically Approximately Complete (PAC); it means that it succeeds with probability one without restarting for initial assignment. We opted to use bounds-consistency propagation for linear constraints for two reasons. Firstly, because bounds-consistency implies hyper-arc consistency on integer linear inequalities. Hyper-arc consistency is a strong form of consistency, and linear inequalities are an expressive form of constraint that has already been used to model many problems including Multiple Sequence Alignment problem (MSA) from Bioinformatics. Secondly, large domains do not need to be explicitly represented, which saves a lot of memory and reduces runtime overheads. With BC we need only maintain two numbers per integer variable: an upper and a lower bound. BC can be also applied to non-linear constraints such as all-different, which we plan to deal with in future work. The algorithm starts with a random assignment for the variables, and then explores the search space by randomly choosing the variable to be instantiated. It performs bounds propagation before and during search. If domain wipe-out occurs then it restarts the search, using previous successful assignments to guide the selection of domain values. We are improving the algorithm with new heuristics. We have developed a dynamic prioritization heuristic that uses the information gained during the search in order to set up variables' selecting ordering. This prioritization is updated at each new search, and is inspired by an another algorithm called Squeaky Wheel Optimization.

---

* This work has been supported by Science Foundation Ireland under Grant 04/BR/CS0355.

Robust Constraint Solving Using Multiple Heuristics[*]

Alfio Vidotto, Kenneth N. Brown[1], and J. Christopher Beck[2]

[1] Cork Constraint Computation Centre, Dept. of Computer Science, UCC, Cork, Ireland
av1@student.cs.ucc.ie, k.brown@cs.ucc.ie
[2] Department of Mechanical & Industrial Engineering, University of Toronto, Canada
jcb@mie.utoronto.ca

Representing and solving problems in terms of constraints can be difficult to do effectively. A single problem can be modeled in many different ways, either in terms of representation or in terms of the solving process. Different approaches can outperform each other over different problem classes or even for different instances within the same class. It is possible that even the best combination of model and search on average is still too slow across a range of problems, taking orders of magnitude more time on some problems than combinations that are usually poorer. This fact complicates the use of constraints, and makes it very difficult for novice users to produce effective solutions. The modeling and solving process would be easier if we could develop robust algorithms, which perform acceptably across a range of problems.

We present one method of developing a robust algorithm. We combine a single model and a single basic algorithm with a set of variable and value ordering heuristics, in a style similar to [1]. The aim is to exploit the variance among the orderings to get a more robust procedure, which may be slower on some problems, but avoids the significant deterioration on others. During the search, we allocate steadily increasing time slices to each ordering, restarting the search at each point. We demonstrate the performance of the multiple heuristic approach (MH) on a scheduling problem class [2] and on quasi groups with holes (QWH), showing that it is more robust and competitive than the standard recommended heuristic. We also compare to randomized restarts [3], the leading method for QWH and which uses a similar restart policy. We show that MH is poorer in run time and robustness on QWH, but better on the scheduling class.

For the immediate future, we intend to investigate whether MH does perform better on insoluble problems (as indicated by the scheduling results). We will also tune the heuristics and time slices, and attempt to generate them automatically.

References

1. Gomes, C. P.; and Selman, B. 2001. Algorithm portfolios. In *Artificial Intelligence* 126(1-2):43-62.
2. Arkin, E. M.; and Silverberg, E. B. 1987. Scheduling jobs with fixed start and end times. In *Discrete Applied Mathematics*, 18:1-8.
3. Gomes, C. P.; and Shmoys, D. B. 2004. Approximations and Randomization to Boost CSP Techniques. In *Annals of Operation Research*, 130:117-141.

---

[*] Funded by Enterprise Ireland (SC/2003/81), with assistance from Science Foundation Ireland (00/PI.1/C075) and ILOG, SA.

Scheduling with Uncertain Start Dates*

Christine Wei Wu[1], Kenneth N. Brown[1], and J. Christopher Beck[2]

[1] Cork Constraint Computation Center, Dept. of Computer Science, UCC, Ireland
{cww1, k.brown}@cs.ucc.ie
[2] Dept. of Mechanical and Industrial Engineering, University of Toronto, Canada
jcb@mie.utoronto.ca

In manufacturing scheduling, jobs may have uncertain earliest start times, caused by supplier lead-time uncertainty. How should we build initial schedules to be robust to these uncertain release dates? We are attempting to adapt the online decision making methods from [1]: in particular the *expectation* and *consensus* methods, which combine sampling of future scenarios with deterministic optimization.

First, we assume that we have a probability distribution over the release dates, and we use this to select samples, giving them a weight proportional to their probability, which we use when determining the best decision. For expectation, we consider all possible partial schedules of released jobs up to the earliest possible uncertain release date (t_0), for each sample extend each partial schedule, and return the one with the lowest expected makespan. For consensus, we find the optimal decision for each sample, and then choose the one with the highest sum of weights. We consider three possible types of initial decision: (i) partial schedules up to t_0; (ii) independent resource assignments for a single time step; and (iii) a tuple of resource assignments for a single time step. The latter two require re-optimization at each time-step up to t_0.

We have implemented the above in Ilog Scheduler 6.0, and tested them on modified JSP benchmarks [2]. The experiments show that our four adapted methods all provide good results (i.e. weighted relative error not being more than 2%). However, it is also possible to get close to the optimal without reasoning about the uncertain events in advance (e.g. using pure reactive methods). The problems appear to be too easy, and not sensitive to the uncertainties. Future work will investigate why this is the case, to determine the features that do make the problems sensitive to the uncertainty in the release dates.

References

1. R. Bent, P. Van Hentenryck: The Value of Consensus in Online Stochastic Scheduling. Proceedings of the Fourteenth International Conference on Automated Planning and Scheduling (2004).
2. S. Lawrence: Resource constrained project scheduling: an experimental investigation of heuristic scheduling techniques (Supplement), Graduate School of Industrial Administration, Carnegie-Mellon University, Pittsburgh, Pennsylvania (1984).

---

* funded by Enterprise Ireland (SC/2003/81), with support from Science Foundation Ireland (00/PI.1/C075) and ILOG, S.A.

The Role of Redundant Clauses in Solving Satisfiability Problems

Honglei Zeng[1] and Sheila McIlraith[2]

[1] Department of Computer Science, Stanford University, California, USA 94305
hlzeng@cs.stanford.edu
[2] Department of Computer Science, University of Toronto, Toronto, Canada
sheila@cs.toronto.edu

In our work, we investigate the role of redundant clauses in characterizing and solving hard SAT problems. Informally, a redundant clause is one that may be removed from the CNF representation of a SAT instance without altering the satisfying assignments of that instance. Correspondingly, a set of prime clauses is a set of clauses that preserves all the but that contains no redundant clauses. We identify several interesting features of redundant clauses that provide compelling evidence of the correlation between the percentage of redundant clauses and the hardness of instances. We propose a definition of weighted clause-to-variable ratio (WCV), which substantially improves the classic clause-to-variable (m/n) ratio in predicting search cost and explaining the phase transition. WCV is based on a linear combination of the number of prime clauses (NPC) and the number of redundant clauses (NRC). We compare WCV to a number of existing parameters including backbone size and backbone fragility, the constrainedness measure, and the m/n ratio; we posit a variety of advantages to WCV over other measures. We believe that full utilization of redundant knowledge to solve random and real-world SAT problems can significantly improve the performance of SAT solvers, in terms of the scale of the problems that can be dealt with as well as the speed with which these problems are solved.

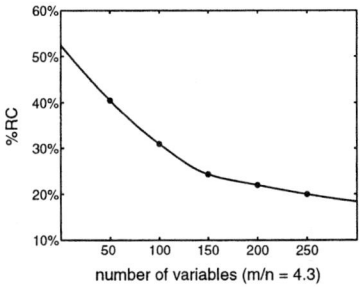
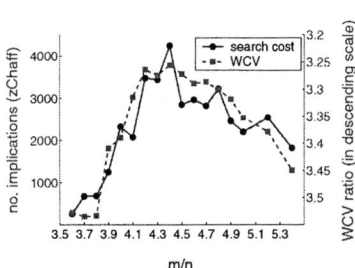

Fig. 1. (a) The percentage of redundant clauses (%RC) decreased as a function of the number of clauses, commencing at 40% and decreasing to 20% when the number of variables reached 250. (b) Correlation between WCV and search cost. n=100.

Applying Decomposition Methods to Crossword Puzzle Problems

Yaling Zheng and Berthe Y. Choueiry

Constraint Systems Laboratory, University of Nebraska-Lincoln
{yzheng, choueiry}@cse.unl.edu

Structural decomposition methods have been proposed for identifying tractable Constraint Satisfaction Problems (CSPs) [1–5]. The basic principle is to decompose a CSP into tree-structured sub-problems. The subproblems are solved independently, then the original CSP is solved in a backtrack-free manner after the tree structure is made arc-consistent, as described in [1]. In [5], we proposed four decomposition methods: HINGE$^+$, CUT, TRAVERSE, and CaT and tested these methods on randomly generated CSPs. We compare these techniques on instances of the fully interlocked Crossword Puzzle Problems (CPPs) [6] taken from a public library [7] and identify special cases of the constraint hypergraphs where some decomposition techniques yield better results than others although in general the opposite holds. Our future work includes: 1) Identifying more such configurations, and building hybrid decompositions techniques that exploit this information; 2) Tailoring existing decomposition methods for fully interlocked CPPs so that every sub-problem, after backtrack search, has few solutions; and 3) Designing a heuristic for applying local search for fully interlocked CPPs. This work is supported by CAREER Award #0133568 from the National Science Foundation.

References

1. Dechter, R., Pearl, J.: Tree Clustering for Constraint Networks. Artificial Intelligence **38** (1989) 353–366
2. Gyssens, M., Jeavons, P.G., Cohen, D.A.: Decomposing Constraint Satisfaction Problems Using Database Techniques. Artificial Intelligence **66** (1994) 57–89
3. Jeavons, P.G., Cohen, D.A., Gyssens, M.: A Structural Decomposition for Hypergraphs. Contemporary Mathematics **178** (1994) 161–177
4. Gottlob, G., Leone, N., Scarcello, F.: A Comparison of Structural CSP Decomposition Methods. Artificial Intelligence **124** (2000) 243–282
5. Zheng, Y., Choueiry, B.Y.: New Structural Decomposition Techniques for Constraint Satisfaction Problems. Recent Advances in Constraints. LNAI Vol. 3419. Springer (2005) 113–127
6. CambonJensen, S.: Design and Implementation of Crossword Compilation Using Sequential Approaches Programs. Master's thesis, IMADA Odense University (1997)
7. CPPLibrary: Crossword Puzzle Grid Library. (http://puzzles.about.com/library) 2005

Asymmetric Distributed Constraints Satisfaction Problems

Roie Zivan and Amnon Meisels*

Dept. of Computer Science, Ben-Gurion University of the Negev, Beer-Sheva, 84-105, Israel
{zivanr, am}@cs.bgu.ac.il

Distributed constraint satisfaction problems (*DisCSPs*) with asymmetric constraints reflect the fact that agents may wish to retain their constraints private. Brito and Meseguer proposed a model for asymmetric constraints which they term *Partially Known Constraints* (PKC). In the PKC model each binary constraint is divided between the two constraining agents. In order to solve the resulting $DisCSP$ with asymmetric constraints, a two phase asynchronous backtracking algorithm was proposed [?]. In the first phase an asynchronous backtracking algorithm is performed, in which only the constraints held by the lower priority agents are examined. When a solution is reached, a second phase is performed in which the consistency of the solution is checked again, according to the constraints held by the higher priority agents in each binary constraint.

The present paper proposes a one phase asynchronous backtracking algorithm which solves $DisCSPs$ with asymmetric constraints. In the proposed *asynchronous backtracking for asymmetric constraints* algorithm (ABT_ASC) agents send their proposed assignments to all their neighbors in the constraints graph. Agents assign their local variables according to the priority order as in ABT but check the constraints also against the assignment of lower priority agents. When an agent detects a conflict between its own assignment and the assignment of an agent with a lower priority than itself, it sends a $Nogood$ to the lower priority agent *but keeps its assignment*. Agents which receive a $Nogood$ from higher priority agents, perform the same operations as if they have produced this $Nogood$ themselves. As in ABT [?], they remove their current assignment from their current-domain, store the eliminating $Nogood$ and reassign their variable.

The ABT_ASC algorithm is evaluated experimentaly on randomly generated $DisCSPs$ and is shown to outperform the 2-phase ABT with respect to two different distributed performance measures. ABT_ASC performs fewer non-concurrent constraints checks by a factor of 6, for the harder problem instances. The load on the network is very similar for both algorithms, counting the total number of messages sent by both algorithms.

---

* Supported by the Lynn and William Frankel center for Computer Sciences.

Full Arc Consistency in WCSP and in Constraint Hierarchies with Finite Domains*

Josef Zlomek and Roman Barták

Faculty of Mathematics and Physics, Charles University,
Malostranské náměstí 2/25, Prague, Czech Republic
zlomek@kti.mff.cuni.cz

Consistency techniques proved to be an efficient method for reducing the search space of CSP and hence they were modified for soft constraint frameworks too. Several algorithms for local consistency in Weighted CSP, where costs are assigned to tuples, were introduced in [2,3]. The strongest form among them is Full Star Directional Arc Consistency (FDAC*). The algorithm for enforcing FDAC* is based on sending costs from one constraint to another in one direction with respect to the fixed order of variables.

We consider the fixed order of variables to be rather limiting so we propose Full Star Arc Consistency (FAC*) which extends the cost sending process by allowing to send the costs in any direction. Because it may not be always possible to send the cost along a directed edge, the proposed extension enables the costs to be sent along other paths. The hope is that by combining more costs we can prune more values from variables' domains. When enforcing FAC*, we choose a variable and move the costs towards the chosen variable. The costs of values of that variable can be used by a value-ordering heuristics during Branch & Bound search.

Constraint hierarchies [1] are another popular soft constraint framework, which provides a very simple way for a user to specify preferences over constraints. It is possible to use the above-mentioned WCSP consistency algorithms for constraint hierarchies too. We show how constraint hierarchies with finite domains using the unsatisfied-count-better comparator [1] can be transformed to WCSP. We believe that constraint hierarchies with other comparators can also be transformed to a generalization of WCSP that still allows to use the algorithms for enforcing FDAC* and FAC*.

References

1. A. Borning, M. Maher, A. Martindale, M. Wilson. *Constraint Hierarchies and Logic Programming.* In Proceedings of 6th International Conference on Logic Programming, pages 149–164, MIT Press, 1989.
2. J. Larrosa, T. Schiex. *In the quest of the best form of local consistency for Weighted CSP.* In Proceedings of IJCAI–03, Acapulco, Mexico, 2003.
3. J. Larrosa, T. Schiex. *Solving Weighted CSP by Maintaining Arc Consistency.* Artificial Intelligence, Volume 159 (1–2), 1–26, November 2004.

---

* Supported by the Czech Science Foundation under the contracts 201/04/1102 and 201/05/H014.

CoJava: A Unified Language for Simulation and Optimization

Alexander Brodsky[1,2] and Hadon Nash[2]

[1] George Mason Unviersity, Virginia, USA
brodsky@gmu.edu
[2] Adaptive Decisions, Inc., Maryland, USA
hnash@adaptivedecisions.com

We have proposed and implemented the language CoJava, which offers both the advantages of simulation-like process modeling in Java, and the capabilities of true decision optimization. We will demonstrate the modeling methodology and implementation techniques, following an optimization application example.

By design, the syntax of CoJava is identical to the programming language Java, extended with special constructs to (1) make a non-deterministic choice of a numeric value, (2) assert a constraint, and (3) designate a program variable as the objective to be optimized.

A CoJava program thus defines a set of nondeterministic execution paths, each being a program run with specific selection of values in the choice statements. The semantics of CoJava interprets a program as an optimal nondeterministic execution path, namely, a path that (1) satisfies the range conditions in the *choice* statements, (2) satisfies the assert-constraint statements, and (3) produces the optimal value in a designated program variable, among all execution paths that satisfy (1) and (2). Thus, to run a CoJava program amounts to first finding an optimal execution path, and then procedurally executing it.

To optimize a process, each real-world device or facility is modeled, tested and debugged in pure Java as a class of objects with private state and public methods which change the state. A process is described as a method of a separate class, which invokes methods of the model objects passing non-deterministic choices for arguments, and which designates an optimization objective.

For model developers, it appears as if the program has simply followed a single execution path which coincidentally produces the optimal objective value. Thus the learning curve for software developers is minimal.

To find an optimal non-deterministic execution path, we have developed a reduction to a standard constraint optimization formulation. Constraint variables represent values in program variables that can be created at any state of a non-deterministic execution. In addition to explicit constraints in assert statements, constraints are constructed to represent transitions from one CoJava program state to the next.

Based on the reduction, we have developed a CoJava constraint compiler. The compiler operates by first translating the Java program into a similar Java program in which the primitive numeric operators and data types are replaced by symbolic constraint operators and data types. This intermediate java program is executed to produce a symbolic decision problem, which is then submitted to an external optimization solver.

Programming with $\mathcal{TOY}(\mathcal{FD})$

Antonio J. Fernández[1], Teresa Hortalá-González[2], and Fernando Sáenz-Pérez[2]

[1] Dpto. Lenguajes y Ciencias de la Computación, Univ. of Málaga, Spain
[2] Dpto. Sist. Inf. y Prog. Univ. Complutense of Madrid, Spain
afdez@lcc.uma.es, {teresa, fernan}@sip.ucm.es

In [1] we presented the language $\mathcal{TOY}(\mathcal{FD})$ that integrates the best features of existing functional and logic languages, as well as finite domain ($\mathcal{FD}$) constraint solving. We believe that $\mathcal{TOY}(\mathcal{FD})$ is more flexible and expressive than the existing approaches of constraint logic programming on finite domain ($CLP(\mathcal{FD})$) as it integrates $\mathcal{FD}$ constraint solving, lazy evaluation, higher order applications of functions and constraints, polymorphism, type checking, composition of functions (and, in particular, constraints), combination of relational and functional notation, and a number of other characteristics. These features allow to write more concise programs, therefore increasing the expressivity level.

From an implementation point of view, $\mathcal{TOY}(\mathcal{FD})$ integrates the higher-order lazy functional logic language $\mathcal{TOY}$ and the efficient $\mathcal{FD}$ constraint solver of SICStus Prolog. From a programming point of view, $\mathcal{TOY}(\mathcal{FD})$ is the first constraint functional logic programming system that provides a wide set of $\mathcal{FD}$ constraints comparable to existing $CLP(\mathcal{FD})$ systems and which is competitive with them. $\mathcal{TOY}(\mathcal{FD})$ supports *relational constraints* including equality, disequality, *arithmetical operators on constraints*, a wide set of well-known *global constraints* (e.g., all_different/1), *membership constraints* (e.g., domain/3), *propositional constraints*, and *enumeration constraints* (e.g., labeling/2, with a number of strategies) with optimization.

$\mathcal{TOY}(\mathcal{FD})$ also provides a glass box approach via a set of predefined functions called *reflection constraints* that allow, at runtime, to recover internal information about the constraint solving process. These functions increase the flexibility of the language as they allow the user to construct specific constraint mechanisms such as new search strategies.

Generally speaking, $\mathcal{TOY}(\mathcal{FD})$ is, from its nature, different to all existing $CLP(\mathcal{FD})$ languages as its operational mechanism is the result of combining the operational methods of logic languages (i.e., unification and resolution) and functional languages (i.e., rewriting). Thus, $\mathcal{TOY}(\mathcal{FD})$ is an alternative to $CLP(\mathcal{FD})$ languages and allows a flexible modelling and quick prototyping at a very high level that cannot be reached by most of the existing constraint systems. $\mathcal{TOY}(\mathcal{FD})$ is freely available in http://toy.sourceforge.net/.

References

1. Fernández, A.J., Hortalá-González, M.T., Sáenz-Pérez, F.: Solving combinatorial problems with a constraint functional logic language. In Wadler, P., Dahl, V., eds.: PADL'2003. Number 2562 in LNCS, New Orleans, Springer (2003) 320–338

Computing *Super*-Schedules

Emmanuel Hebrard, Paul Tyler, and Toby Walsh

NICTA and UNSW, Sydney, Australia
{emmanuel.hebrard, paul.tyler, toby.walsh}@nicta.com.au

RobustScheduler is a graphical tool for computing and visualising robust schedules. It allows to compare optimal schedules (shortest overall duration) with schedules that are *robust*, although not necessarily optimal. Both the optimal and robust schedule are computed and displayed as Gantt charts. Moreover, the consequences of delaying a task on the rest of the schedule can be checked interactively. The robust schedules are more robust than the optimal since a small pertubation (e.g. a machine breaks) gives a proportionally small disturbance to the future, in line with the *Super*-solution/*Super*-model framework ([2,3]).

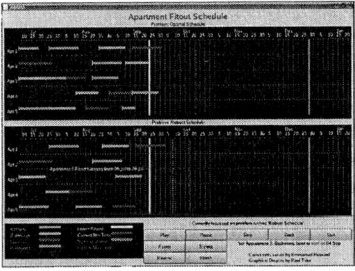

Fig. 1. RobustScheduler screen-shot, above computing the regular optimal schedule, below computing a robust schedule

The underlying constraint solver[1] implements the job-shop scheduling problem using standard constraint programming methods such as shaving [1], specialised variable orderings [5] and specialised constraint propagators. The *Super*-solutions are found using an algorithm introduced in [4].

References

1. J. Carlier and E. Pinson. Adjustment of Heads and Tails for the Job-Shop Problem. *European journal of Operational Research*, 78:146–161, 1994.
2. M. Ginsberg, A. Parkes, and A. Roy. Supermodels and Robustness. In *Proceedings of AAAI-98*, pages 334–339, Madison, WI, 1998.
3. E. Hebrard, B. Hnich, and T. Walsh. Robust Solutions for Constraint Satisfaction and Optimization. In *Proceedings of ECAI-04*, Valencia, Spain, 2004.
4. E. Hebrard, B. Hnich, and T. Walsh. Improved Algorithm for Finding (a,b)-super solutions. In *Proceedings of the Workshop on Constraint Programming for Planning and Scheduling CPPS'05, held along side ICAPS'05*, Monterey, California, 2005.
5. N. Sadeh and M.S. Fox. Variable and Value Ordering Heuristics for the Job-Shop Scheduling Constraint Satisfaction Problem. *Artificial Intelligence*, 86(1):1–41, September 1996.

---

[1] http://www.cse.unsw.edu.au/-ehebrard/codef.htm

Proterv-II: An Integrated Production Planning and Scheduling System*

András Kovács, Péter Egri, Tamás Kis, and József Váncza

Computer and Automation Research Institute,
Hungarian Academy of Sciences,
Kende utca 13-17, 1111 Budapest, Hungary
{akovacs, egri, tamas.kis, vancza}@sztaki.hu

Medium-term production planning and short-term scheduling match future production load and capacities over various horizons and on different levels of detail. Although these two levels of the decision hierarchy are strongly interdependent, traditional systems handle them separately. In the Proterv-II prototype system that was developed for manufacturing industries, the two levels are linked by an automated aggregation procedure that constructs the planning representation from detailed job-shop level data [3].

Projects consist of a number of discrete operations with various resource requirements, interwoven by precedence constraints. Aggregation merges connected components of projects into aggregate activities. The medium-term planner solves a resource-constrained project scheduling problem with variable-intensity activities, subject to strict time windows, but extendible capacities. The objective functions are minimal extra capacity usage and minimal work-in-process. For the solution of the planning problem, an MILP model and a branch-and-cut algorithm with customized cutting planes have been developed [1].

The goal of the short-term scheduler is to unfold the first segments of the medium-term plan into executable detailed schedules. The scheduler computes start times for individual manufacturing operation with respect to resource requirements, precedence relations, sequence-independent setup times, and transportation times. The detailed scheduling problem is solved by constraint-based scheduling techniques. During experiments on large-scale industrial data, Proterv-II generated close-to-optimal production plans that could be unfolded into executable schedules. We are currently improving the performance of the scheduler by novel algorithms adapted to real-life problems [2].

References

1. T. Kis. A branch-and-cut algorithm for scheduling of projects with variable-intensity activities. *Mathematical Programming*, 103(3):515–539, 2005.
2. A. Kovács and J. Váncza. Completable partial solutions in constraint programming and constraint-based scheduling. In *Proc. CP 2004*, pages 332–346, 2004.
3. J. Váncza, T. Kis, and A. Kovács. Aggregation – the key to integrating production planning and scheduling. *CIRP Annals – Manuf. Techn.*, 53(1):377–380, 2004.

---

* This research has been supported by the grants NKFP 2/010/2004 and OTKA T046509.

The Comet Programming Language and System

Laurent Michel[1] and Pascal Van Hentenryck[2]

[1] University of Connecticut, Storrs, CT 06269-3155
[2] Brown University, Box 1910, Providence, RI 02912

COMET is a novel, object-oriented, programming language specifically designed to simplify the implementation of local search algorithms. Comet supports a constraint-based architecture for local search organized around two main components: a declarative component which models the application in terms of constraints and functions, and a search component which specifies the search heuristic and meta-heuristic. Constraints, which are a natural vehicle to express combinatorial optimization problems, are *differentiable objects* in COMET: They maintain a number of properties incrementally and they provide algorithms to evaluate the effect of various operations on these properties. The search component then uses these functionalities to guide the local search using multidimensional, possibly randomized, selectors and first-order control structures such as events, neighbors, and nondeterminism.

As a result, COMET programs often feature models similar to those of constraint programming, although the underlying technology is fundamentally different in nature. In particular, COMET models are high-level, compositional, and modular. It is possible to add new constraints and to modify or remove existing ones, without having to worry about the global effect of these changes. COMET also separates the modeling and search components, allowing programmers to experiment with different search heuristics and meta-heuristics without affecting the problem modeling. COMET has been applied to many applications and is often competitive with tailored algorithms for complex applications.

This system demonstration illustrates COMET on a variety of applications in resource allocation, facility location, and scheduling. It will cover both the sequential and parallel implementations and the COMET environment.

References

1. L. Michel and P. Van Hentenryck. A Constraint-Based Architecture for Local Search. In *OOPSLA02*, pages 101–110, Seattle, November 2002.
2. P. Van Hentenryck and L. Michel. Control Abstractions for Local Search. In *CP'03*, pages 65–80, Cork, Ireland, 2003.
3. P. Van Hentenryck and L. Michel. Nondeterministic Control for Hybrid Search. In *CP-AI-OR'05*, Prague, May 2005.
4. P. Van Hentenryck and Laurent Michel Scheduling Abstractions for Local Search. In *Proceeding of the First International Conference on the Integration of AI and OR Techniques in Constraint Programming for Combinatorial Optimisation Problems (CP-AI-OR-04)*, Nice, France, April 2004.
5. P. Van Hentenryck, L. Michel, and L. Liu. Constraint-Based Combinators for Local Search. In *CP'04*, pages 47–61, Toronto, Canada, October 2004.

Random Stimuli Generation for Functional Hardware Verification as a CP Application

Yehuda Naveh and Roy Emek

IBM Haifa Research Lab, Haifa University Campus, Haifa 31905, Israel
{naveh, emek}@il.ibm.com

Functional verification of modern hardware design consumes roughly 70% of the effort invested in the design cycle. Simulation of randomly generated stimuli is the main means of achieving functional verification. A typical verification effort is centered around a stimuli generator which produces a massive amount of test cases that are simulated on the verified design. Bugs are then identified when the design behaves incorrectly. (in some cases this process is complemented by some amount of formal verification).

In the past few years it became clear across the industry that the most powerful way of generating high-quality stimuli is by utilizing constraint technology. This is because constraints allow for a natural description of hardware systems [1]. Hence, CP is now at the core of all leading verification environments [2].

CSP's arising from stimuli generation are different from other application domains. One striking difference is the existence of variables with huge (e.g. 2^{64}) domains, combined with highly non-linear and non-monotonic constraints. Another is the requirement to produce multiple different solutions, distributed roughly uniformly, for the same CSP. Further, the complexity of the design, and its tendency to change over time, requires a sophisticated modeling capability.

We discuss and demonstrate these and other issues related to stimuli generation, including the modeling and solution of conditional problems [3] and of generative CSPs, both of which abound in this domain. We demonstrate complex stimuli-generation scenarios which are solvable by our special purpose engine, as well as other important scenarios, which are currently not solvable in a reasonable time. The latter impose the challenges of current research.

The constraint engine we demonstrate is being developed at IBM for more than a decade, and is at the core of the stimuli generators used for the functional verification of all of IBM's high-end processors and systems [4,5].

References

1. E. Bin et. al. Using constraint satisfaction formulations and solution techniques for random test program generation. *IBM Systems Journal*, 41:386-402, 2002.
2. www.haifa.il.ibm.com/projects/verification/octopus/index.html; www.synopsys.com/products/vera/vera.html; www.verisity.com/products/specman.html.
3. F. Geller and M. Veksler. Assumption-based pruning in conditional CSP. In CP'05.
4. A. Adir et. al. Genesys-Pro: Innovations in test program generation for functional processor verification. *IEEE Design and Test of Computers*, 21:84-93 (2004).
5. R. Emek et. al. X-Gen: A random test-case generator for systems and SoC. In W. Rosenstiel, editor, *Proceedings of the seventh HLDVT*, pages 145-150 (2002).

A BDD-Based Interactive Configurator for Modular Systems

Erik R. van der Meer

IT University of Copenhagen
ervandermeer@itu.dk

Interactive configuration can be viewed as interactive CSP solving. We see interactive *modular configuration* as interactive *modular CSP* solving, where we define a modular CSP as a labeled rooted directed multigraph, where each vertex is labeled with a CSP, and each edge is labeled with (1) a set of total assignments to the variables of the CSP at the source vertex and (2) a set of equality constraints between the variables in the source and destination CSPs[1].

This allows the modeling of hierarchical systems through the use of edges (to model both *has-a* and *is-a* relationships), and the modeling of unbounded systems through the creation of cycles in the problem graph.

During configuration, the user builds a labeled rooted solution tree which is homomorphic with the problem graph — each solution tree node (object) is associated with a problem graph vertex (class) — and which is isomorphic with the configured system's structure. The nodes are essentially[2] labeled with the sets of full assignments that can still be part of globally consistent solutions.

A new object is *instantiated* when the partial assignment within an object implies a full assignment that is in the assignment set on an outgoing edge from the class. This new object becomes a child of the other object, and is an instance of the class at the destination side of the edge. Configuration starts with the instantiation of the root node from the root vertex.

The user is allowed to assign and unassign variables in arbitrary nodes in arbitrary order. The system removes and adds exactly those values from and to the domains that, although configuration is unbounded, ensure that a finite and fully specified solution tree (configuration) is always reachable without backtracking. It also instantiates and deinstantiates exactly the right objects.

We have developed a research prototype of such an interactive configurator. It is written in ANSI C, and uses the ncurses library for the user interface. While it uses BDDs for knowledge representation, the underlying method should also be applicable to other (compact) finite set representations.

It uses a two-phase approach: an offline compilation phase (which is executed once for a given problem), and an interactive configuration phase with fast user interaction, provided the BDDs remain small.

An important result is that the configuration-time sizes of the BDDs cannot exceed a constant which can be determined at compile time. In particular, they do not grow as a function of the size of the tree[3].

---

[1] The latter can be seen as a way to create shared variables between CSPs.
[2] Not exactly, because we extensively use delayed processing.
[3] The size of the tree is unbounded but always finite.

Author Index

Abril, Montserrat 837
Ågren, Magnus 47
Aiello, Marco 782
Anbulagan 727
Andersen, Henrik Reif 767
Argelich, Josep 838
Artiouchine, Konstantin 62

Bacchus, Fahiem 578
Bain, Stuart 732
Banda, Maria Garcia de la 13
Baptiste, Philippe 62
Barahona, Pedro 373
Barber, Federico 837
Barták, Roman 843, 868, 876
Batnini, Heikel 77
Beck, J. Christopher 737, 842, 871, 872
Béjar, Ramon 861
Beldiceanu, Nicolas 92, 742
Benini, Luca 107
Bent, Russell 122
Bertozzi, Davide 107
Bessiere, Christian 747
Betz, Hariolf 137
Billaut, Jean-Charles 841
Bouquard, Jean-Louis 841
Brito, Ismel 152
Brodsky, Alexander 877
Brown, Kenneth N. 839, 871, 872
Burke, David A. 839
Butaru, Mihaela 840

Cambazard, Hadrien 752
Canon, Cyril 841
Carchrae, Tom 842
Carlsson, Mats 92
Ccjnar, Pavel 843
Chang, Le 844
Cheng, Kenil C.K. 182
Chen, Hubie 167
Chen, Yixin 697
Choueiry, Berthe Y. 874
Cohen, David 17, 851

Coletta, Rémi 747

Dalmau, Víctor 167, 196
Darras, S. 757
Dechter, Rina 857, 860
Dequen, G. 757
Devendeville, L. 757
Deville, Yves 211, 832, 866
Dilkina, Bistra 762
Dongen, M.R.C. van 862
Dooms, Gregoire 211
Dotú, Iván 845
Duan, Lei 762
Dubois, Didier 226
Dupont, Pierre 211, 832

Egri, Péter 880
Emek, Roy 882
Epstein, Susan L. 856

Faltings, Boi 802, 864
Fargier, Hélène 226
Fernández, Antonio J. 878
Fernández, Cèsar 861
Flener, Pierre 47
Fortin, Jérôme 226
Freuder, Eugene C. 445, 842
Frisch, A.M. 859
Frühwirth, Thom 137

Gavaldà, Ricard 196
Geffner, Héctor 1, 682
Geller, Felix 241
Gennari, Rosella 782
Gent, Ian P. 256, 271
Gomes, Carla 853
Grandon, Carlos 847
Guerri, Alessio 107

Habbas, Zineb 840
Hadzic, Tarik 767
Hamadi, Youssef 549
Harvey, Warwick 286
Havens, William S. 762
Hebrard, Emmanuel 848, 879

Hénocque, Laurent   301
Heras, Federico   849
Hoche, Matthias   850
Hooker, John   846
Hooker, J.N.   314
Horrocks, Ian   5
Hortalá-González, Teresa   878
Houghton, Chris   851
Hsu, Eric   852
Hulubei, Tudor   328
Hwang, Joey   343

Ishtaiwi, Abdelraouf   772

Jähnichen, Stefan   850, 863
Jeavons, Peter   17
Jefferson, Christopher   17
Jégou, Philippe   777
Jussien, Narendra   752

Kamarainen, Olli   855
Katriel, Irit   122, 358
Kaya, Latife Genc   846
Kelsey, Tom   256, 271
Kis, Tamás   880
Kleiner, Mathias   301
Kovács, András   880
Krippahl, Ludwig   373
Krokhin, Andrei   388

Lallouet, Arnaud   854
Larose, Benoit   388
Larrosa, Javier   563, 593, 849
Lazovik, Alexander   782
Leahu, Lucian   853
Legtchenko, Andreï   854
Leung, Cheuk Fun Bede   855
Li, Chu Min   403
Li, Hui   415
Ligorio, Tiziana   856
Ligozat, Gérard   534
Linton, Steve A.   256, 271
López-Ortiz, Alejandro   867

Mackworth, Alan K.   844
Maher, Michael   13
Manyà, Felip   403, 838
Marinescu, Radu   857
Marriott, Kim   13

Martínez-Hernández, B.   859
Martin, Roland   858
Mateescu, Robert   860
Mateu, Carles   861
Mazure, B.   757
McDonald, Iain   256
McIlraith, Sheila   852, 873
Mehta, Deepak   862
Meisels, Amnon   32, 875
Meseguer, Pedro   152, 593
Michel, Claude   77
Michel, Laurent   430, 881
Miguel, Ian   256
Milano, Michela   107
Mitchell, David G.   343
Motoki, Mistuo   787
Müller, Henry   863

Nash, Hadon   877
Naveh, Yehuda   882
Ndiaye, Samba Ndojh   777
Neveu, Bertrand   847
Nguyen, Quang Huy   864
Nightingale, Peter   792

O'Callaghan, Barry   445
Ostrowski, R.   757
O'Sullivan, Barry   328, 445

Pearson, Justin   47
Peintner, Bart   607
Perron, Laurent   797
Pesant, Gilles   460
Petcu, Adrian   802
Petit, Thierry   742, 747
Petrie, Karen E.   17
Pham, Duc Nghia   772
Pini, Maria Silvia   865
Planes, Jordi   403
Pollack, Martha E.   607
Prcovic, Nicolas   301, 807
Prestwich, Steven   870
Prosser, Patrick   869
Puget, Jean-François   475, 490

Quesada, Luis   866
Quimper, Claude-Guy   812, 867

Rampon, Jean-Xavier   92
Régin, Jean-Charles   460, 505, 520

Renz, Jochen   534
Richards, Barry   855
Ringwelski, Georg   549
Rochart, Guillaume   742
Rollon, Emma   563
Roney-Dougal, Colva   271
Rossi, Francesca   9, 865
Rueher, Michel   77

Sáenz-Pérez, Fernando   878
Saïs, L.   757
Sakallah, Karem A.   607
Salido, Miguel A.   837
Samulowitz, Horst   578
Sánchez, Martí   593
Sattar, Abdul   732, 772
Schimpf, Joachim   622
Schulte, Christian   817
Sellmann, Meinolf   822
Sheini, Hossein M.   607
Shen, Kish   622
Sinz, Carsten   827
Slaney, John   13, 727
Smith, Barbara M.   17, 256, 637
Somogyi, Zoltan   13
Stergiou, Kostas   652
Stuckey, Peter J.   13
Surynek, Pavel   868

Tack, Guido   817
Terrioux, Cyril   777
Tesson, Pascal   196
Thérien, Denis   196
Thielscher, Michael   667

Thornton, John   732, 772
Truchet, Charlotte   92
Tyler, Paul   879

Unsworth, Chris   869

Val, Álvaro del   845
van der Meer, Erik R.   883
Van Hentenryck, Pascal   122, 358, 430, 845, 881
Van Roy, Peter   866
Váncza, József   880
Veksler, Michael   241
Verachi, Stefania   870
Vidal, Vincent   682
Vidotto, Alfio   871

Wah, Benjamin W.   697
Wallace, Mark   13
Wallace, Richard J.   712
Walsh, Toby   13, 812, 848, 879
Weihe, Karsten   858
Williams, Brian   415
Winterer, Thorsten   286
Wu, Christine Wei   872

Yap, Roland H.C.   182

Zampelli, Stéphane   832
Zeng, Honglei   873
Zheng, Yaling   874
Zieliński, Paweł   226
Zivan, Roie   32, 875
Zlomek, Josef   876